# LAW AMONG NATIONS

# Law
# Among Nations

AN INTRODUCTION TO
## PUBLIC INTERNATIONAL LAW
SIXTH, REVISED EDITION

## Gerhard von Glahn

Professor Emeritus (Political Science), University of Minnesota–Duluth

## MACMILLAN PUBLISHING COMPANY
NEW YORK
### Maxwell Macmillan Canada, Inc.
Toronto

Editor: Bruce Nichols

Production Supervisor: Publication Services, Inc.

Production Manager: Aliza Greenblatt

Cover Designer: Patrice Fodero

This book was set in text by Publication Services, Inc., printed and bound by Book Press.

Macmillan Publishing Company
866 Third Avenue,
New York, New York 10022

Maxwell Macmillan Canada, Inc.
1200 Eglinton Avenue East, Suite 200
Don Mills, Ontario M3C 3N1

Library of Congress Cataloging-in-Publication Data

Von Glahn, Gerhard
    Law among nations : an introduction to public international law /
Gerhard von Glahn. — 6th, rev. ed.
        p.      cm.
    Includes index.
    ISBN 0-02-423175-4
    1. International law.      I. Title.
JX3185.V6      1992
341–dc20                                                    90-25247
                                                            CIP

Printing:    2 3 4 5 6 7 Year: 2 3 4 5 6 7 8

**TO DOROTHY**

# PREFACE TO SIXTH EDITION

The sixth edition has been revised substantially both in internal format and in textual emphasis. Several chapters have been combined because of the interrelationship of their subject contents. Seven Case Studies have been inserted because certain topics were believed to merit more extensive treatment than would have been possible by their inclusion in the chapters to which they related. The amount of anecdotal material, while updated, has not been reduced in scope because the author believes that it helps the student to see the relationships between the law and the subjects affected by the law.

Despite excisions, the length of the text has had to be increased somewhat because of the coverage of events that took place since the writing of the fifth edition, such as the *Nicaragua* v. *United States* case, the continued existence of terrorism, the rise of the Palestinian *intifadah,* and new developments in extradition as well as in chemical warfare methods and controls.

Despite the existence of the United Nations, its recent increased ability to assist in the solution of crises, and the withering away of the phenomenon of the Cold War, armed conflict has not vanished from the world. Since 1945, scores of wars have cost the lives of hundreds of thousands of people. In view of that regrettable record, Part IV, Armed Conflicts, has had to be retained virtually intact from earlier editions. The rules governing land, air, and naval conflicts cannot as yet be shelved. Wherever possible, the word "war" has been replaced with "armed conflict," since many of the new rules of the law relate to hostile actions not generally considered part of traditional war.

Even more than in the past, I have been assisted greatly in preparing this sixth edition by the helpful criticism and suggestions of colleagues and students, both here and abroad. Their advice and their factual contributions are gratefully acknowledged.

G.v.G.

# PREFACE TO FIRST EDITION

Traditional texts in international law have fallen into one of three basic categories: (1) commentaries, heavily weighted with historical background material, (2) casebooks, and (3) combinations of cases and extensive editorial notes.

The writer has long felt a need for a text adapted specifically for the typical undergraduate course in international law: an upper-level offering commonly limited to one semester or two quarters in length. He believes that the bulk of the students enrolled in such a course do not intend to enter law schools, government service, or the employment of an international agency after the completion of undergraduate training. Such students may be assumed to be taking a course in international law because it forms a part of the required curriculum for majors in political science or because of their personal interest in a rather fascinating and timely subject.

If the foregoing assumptions are correct, then available texts, regardless of excellence, do not really satisfy the needs of the student clientele, for those texts are, on the whole, too extensive in their treatment of the subject considering the time available in the typical course. They also require, in the instance of commentaries, a casebook to accompany the text. Such collections are, again, extremely comprehensive in scope and expensive, and they appear to be designed primarily for use in law schools or on the graduate level of instruction.

These considerations led to the writing of a relatively brief text on international law, using the traditional approach to the subject but incorporating in the actual text, whenever called for as illustrative materials, abstracts of classic and modern cases. The volume thus obviates the use of a casebook and stands as a self-contained unit. Admittedly, an obvious disadvantage of this unique feature is that students miss the complete wording of the judges in some of the great classic cases. Nothing would prevent the instructor, on the other hand, from assigning selected cases as outside reading and for practice in briefing. Most of the chapters are followed by lists of suggested readings to make possible the adaptation of the text to a course running for a full academic year.

In view of the notorious inability of undergraduates to read foreign languages with any degree of fluency, the references in both footnotes and suggested readings have been deliberately restricted to sources in the English language. This has meant the sacrifice of a very large number of valuable contributions to international law by foreign scholars but has resulted in references usable by students. The omission of this portion of the scholarly "apparatus" has also kept the volume within manageable limits. Most references have been restricted intentionally to sources likely to be found in the library of a college offering courses in international law; if lacking, they could be added at modest cost. The inclusion of numerous references to legal journals was prompted by the fact that the legal profession has created central reference libraries in many urban centers; such facilities may be available to students by special arrangement.

The inclusion or omission of subject matter is the responsibility of the writer. Dictated by his own experience in teaching international law courses, the selection of topics and the extent of their coverage also reflect his views as to the importance of each of them. Thus, since the text is intended to present a realistic picture of what the law is and not what it ought to be, relatively extensive treatment has been accorded the law of war.

The use of force has not been eliminated from the world scene, and when states or international agencies have recourse to force, the rules of the law designed for such purposes still find application. Despite the eloquence of the writings of many people of goodwill, methods for the peaceful settlement of international disputes have been, and are likely to be, abandoned in favor of war. Neutrality, pronounced dead on many occasions by learned jurists, has shown a perhaps not-too-surprising ability to survive in the practice of nations. And assertions of the present or rapidly approaching existence of a world law must as yet be regarded as utopian.

It may well be that at some future time humans will utilize their reason more fully and bring into being a peaceful world under the rule of law. For the time being, however, realism dictates the regrettable assumption that the scourge of war is with us and will be so for a long time. Hence the rules governing the use of force must be studied by the generations that will be affected most profoundly by recourse to forcible settlements of disputes. Condensation of the law of war and neutrality into a chapter, or total omission of such disagreeable topics, would be an inexcusable and unrealistic approach to the totality of international law.

The title of this volume has been chosen with care: the principles and rules embodied in what is termed *international law* represent not law above nations or supranational law but law *among* nations, *jus inter gentes*. Jurists may smile at such a concept, since to them law must stand above its subjects. This is not true, however, in the case of general international law, which at present is only a weak and developing form of law. It applies to a relatively unorganized community and lacks specialized agencies dedicated to its enforcement. Nevertheless it represents the best that a chaotic community composed of sovereign states has been able to evolve to date. And whenever the often elaborate particular law of such international agencies as the United Nations fails to be applied to relations among states, recourse is had to the general law based on custom and on general lawmaking treaties in order to regulate such relations.

G.v.G.

# CONTENTS

## IV.  TERRITORIAL QUESTIONS

## V.  INTERNATIONAL TRANSACTIONS

## VI.  ARMED CONFLICTS

# ABBREVIATIONS

Certain sources utilized frequently throughout this volume are cited in abbreviated form as follows:

## Books

| | |
|---|---|
| Akehurst | Akehurst, *A Modern Introduction to International Law* (1970). |
| Bishop | Bishop, *International Law: Cases and Materials* (2nd ed. 1962). |
| Brierly | Brierly, *The Law of Nations* (6th ed., by Sir Humphrey Waldock, 1963). |
| Buergenthal & Maier | Buergenthal & Maier, *Public International Law in a Nutshell* (1985). |
| Cheng | Cheng, *General Principles of Law As Applied by International Courts and Tribunals* (1953). |
| Claude | Claude, *Swords into Plowshares: The Problems and Progress of International Organizations* (3rd ed., rev. 1964). |
| Coplin | Coplin, *The Functions of International Law* (1966). |
| Corbett | Corbett, *Law and Society in the Relations of States* (1951). |
| Fenwick | Fenwick, *International Law* (4th ed. 1965). |
| Friedmann | Friedmann, Lissitzyn, Pugh, *Cases and Materials on International Law* (1969). |
| Gould | Gould, *An Introduction to International Law* (1957). |
| Hackworth | Hackworth, *Digest of International Law* (8 vols, 1940–1944). |
| Henkin | Henkin, Pugh, Schachter, Smit, *International Law Cases and Materials* (1980). [Successor to Friedmann] |
| Higgins-Colombos | Colombos, *The International Law of the Sea* (3rd rev. ed. of Higgins and Colombos, same title: 1954). |
| Hudson | Hudson, *Cases and Other Materials on International Law* (1951). |

| | |
|---|---|
| Hyde | Hyde, *International Law Chiefly As Interpreted and Applied by the United States* (3 vols, 2nd ed., 1945). |
| Jacobini | Jacobini, *International Law—A Text* (1968). |
| Jessup | Jessup, *A Modern Law of Nations: An Introduction* (1949). |
| Kaplan-Katzenbach | Kaplan-Katzenbach, *The Political Foundations of International Law* (1961). |
| Land Warfare | US Department of the Army, *The Law of Land Warfare* (FM 27-10, July 1956). |
| Lauterpacht's *Oppenheim* | Oppenheim, *International Law: A Treatise.* Vol. 1, *Peace* (8th ed., by H. Lauterpacht, 1955); Vol. 2, *Disputes, War and Neutrality* (7th ed. by H. Lauterpacht, 1952). |
| Lipsky | Lipsky, ed., *Law and Politics in the World Community* (1953). |
| Mangone | Mangone, *The Elements of International Law* (rev. ed., 1967). |
| Manual | Sørenson, ed., *Manual of Public International Law* (2 vols, 1968). |
| Moffitt | Moffitt, *Modern War and the Laws of War* (1973). |
| Moore | Moore, *A Digest of International Law* (8 vols. 1906). |
| Nussbaum | Nussbaum, *A Concise History of the Law of Nations* (rev. ed., 1954). |
| Pfankuchen | Pfankuchen, *A Documentary Textbook in International Law* (1940). |
| Plischke | Plischke, ed., *Systems of Integrating the International Community* (1964). |
| Reiff | Reiff, *The United States and the Treaty Law of the Sea* (1959). |
| Schwarzenberger | Schwarzenberger, *International Law,* vol. 1 (3rd ed., 1957), vol. 2 (1968). |
| Stark | Stark, *An Introduction to International Law* (9th ed., 1984). |
| Sørenson | Sørenson, ed., *Manual of Public International Law* (2 vols, 1968). |
| Stone | Stone, *Legal Controls of International Conflicts: A Treatise on the Dynamics of Disputes and War* (2nd impr., rev. with Supplement 1953–1958, 1959). |
| Svarlien | Svarlien, *An Introduction to the Law of Nations* (1955) |

| | |
|---|---|
| Tung | Tung, *International Law in an Organizing World* (1968). |
| von Glahn | von Glahn, *The Occupation of Enemy Territory: A Commentary on the Law and Practice of Belligerent Occupation* (1957). |
| Whiteman | Whiteman, *Digest of International Law* (15 vols, 1963–73). |
| Wright | Wright, *Contemporary International Law: A Balance Sheet* (1955). |

## Periodicals, Etc.

| | |
|---|---|
| *AJIL* | *American Journal of International Law* |
| *APSR* | *American Political Science Review* |
| *BYIL* | *British Year Book of International Law* |
| *CSM* | *Christian Science Monitor* |
| *I.C.J. Reports* | International Court of Justice, *Reports of Judgments, Advisory Opinions and Orders* (1947–) |
| *ILM* | *International Legal Materials* |
| *NYT* | *The New York Times.* |
| *P.C.I.J.* | Permanent Court of International Justice, |
| Ser. A. | *Judgments and Orders* (1922–1930) |
| Ser. B. | *Advisory Opinions* (1922–1930) |
| Ser. A/B | *Judgments, Orders, and Advisory Opinions* (1931–1940) |
| *Proceedings* | *Proceedings of the American Society of International Law* |
| *TGS* | *Transactions of the Grotius Society* [London] |
| *Tijdschrift* | *Nederlands Tijdschrift voor International Recht* |
| *Current Policy* | US Dept. of State, Bureau of Public Affairs publication |
| *Gist* | US Dept. of State, Bureau of Public Affairs publication |
| U.S. (in case citations) | *United States Reports* (Supreme Court of the United States). Cases before 1875 are cited by the name of the reporter: |

Dallas (1787–1800)    Howard (1843–1860)
Cranch (1801–1815)    Black (1861–1862)
Wheaton (1816–1827)    Wallace (1863–1874)
Peters (1828–1842)

# LAW AMONG NATIONS

# PART I

# The Law of Nations

# 1

# The Nature and Sources
# of International Law

## A. THE NATURE OF THE LAW

DEFINITION OF INTERNATIONAL LAW    International law is a body of principles, customs, and rules recognized as effectively binding obligations by
sovereign states and such other entities as have been granted international
personality; the law is also increasingly applicable to individuals in their
relations with states. This definition of the subject corresponds closely to
the current opinion of most writers on international law but represents by
no means the only acceptable definition. Few areas of knowledge have been
defined as often and in as many different ways as has international law. As
Jessup pointed out, an old and possibly apocryphal Chinese proverb is said
to counsel, "One should always have in the background of one's mind a
multiplicity of definitions covering the subject at hand in order to prevent
oneself from accepting the most obvious."[1] In the spirit of that advice, the
following additional definitions are offered:

The Law of Nations, or International Law, may be defined as the body of rules
and principles of action which are binding upon civilized states in their relations
with one another.[2]

International law consists in certain rules of conduct which modern civilized
states regard as being binding on them in their relations with one another with
a force comparable in nature and degree to that binding the conscientious person
to obey the law of his country, and which they also regard as being enforceable by
appropriate means in case of infringement.[3]

The Law of Nations is the science of the rights which exist between Nations or
States, and of the obligations corresponding to these rights.[4]

[1]Jessup, 4. (Full references to this and other works cited subsequently by author only may
be found in the list of abbreviations).
[2]Brierly, 1.
[3]Hall, *A Treatise on International Law* (8th ed., Higgins, ed.)(1924), 1.
[4]E. de Vattel, *Le Droit des Gens* (Fenwick, trans.) (1916 [1758]).

3

[International law is] a body of principles, rules, and norms, generally observed by the members of the international society in their international relations or when they are dealing with international organizations or citizens of other states.[5]

On the other hand, the definition given by Abba Eban, then the Israeli ambassador to the United States, on Edward Murrow's television program "Person to Person" on September 20, 1957, corresponds to a widespread popular belief concerning the nature of the law: "International law is the law which the wicked do not obey and which the righteous do not enforce."

It should be realized even at this early point that the scope and, hence, the subjects, of international law are created by states and are determined by those same states. The definition given in the opening paragraph may therefore be changed in the future to accommodate additional categories of subjects. Many modern writers do, in fact, include individuals among the subjects of the law, although they usually are forced to admit that generally, the practice does not yet support their theoretical contention. The variations found currently among definitions of international law can also be explained logically by the fact that the law itself is in a state of transition. (See Chapter 10.)

It should also be kept in mind that international law should not be viewed except in its relationship with political factors, such as the still cherished, though by now impaired, phenomenon of national sovereignty (independence from outside control), which imposes limitations on the law when it conflicts with certain aspects of sovereignty, and the need for what one analyst has described as "housekeeping rules," *i.e.,* the necessary accommodations that make possible interactions between states (recognition of foreign nationality, diplomatic immunity, etc.). Hence, international law should be viewed as a body of rules and regulations that make possible peaceful interactions among the members of the "community of nations." (See also Chapter 4.)

The validity of the accepted rules of international law is not affected, of course, by the absence of universally shared standards and values in a heterogeneous congeries of sovereign states or by the limited scope of that law imposed by the unwillingness of those same states to subordinate their "vital" interests to an international legal order. The obvious danger is that a tendency toward the creation of regional (or particular) law may continue until all legal rules governing the actions of states across the borders of the various systems have disappeared. Such an atomistic division of the law, however, is not anticipated by even the most critical analysts. Within the preceding limits, there is, nonetheless, a community of nations whose international relations are subject to the application of rules that are accepted as binding by those states, out of whose needs the law grew through custom and treaty.

[5]Sheikh, *International Law and National Behavior* (1974), 47.

It is true, however, that although dependence on the legal settlement of many controversies continues among Western states, such legal basis for the resolution of disagreements between the nations of the Communist portion of the world and between certain Asian and African nations, on the one hand, and the Western states, on the other, is, to some extent at least, lacking. A limited degree of regionalism may persist for some time to come.

This conclusion is founded not only on a suspected fear of losing a case but even more on a belief voiced on occasion by African and Asian commentators of standing: that many of the "universal" rules of international law are foreign to their own non-European culture, tradition, or legal system. They assert that such rules and principles are based, in essence, on Western legal thought and political history and are therefore tainted with Christian, imperialistic, capitalistic, and exploitive aspects. They maintain that such rules can, at best, form part of a general customary Western law but not universal international law and, hence, should not be regarded as binding on the new African and Asian states.

The justification of such beliefs is the argument that any system of law, domestic or international, must derive its validity from consensus and that no law will prevail over the mores, customs, and beliefs of a people or a group of peoples. Without such a consensus, the approval of the law will be lacking: the rule may be "on the books" but will remain a dead letter.

The contemporary applicability of the rules of international law may be divided into two related and partially overlapping spheres. Certain rules have been accepted *generally or universally* and represent general law in effect on a worldwide scale, and other rules have been accepted and are applied only within given groups of states (Jessup called these "selective communities"); that is, they represent *particular law,* adopted by some grouping of nations linked by a common philosophy of law as applied to their mutual relations (*regional law*).

## PROBLEMS OF OBEDIENCE TO INTERNATIONAL LAW

In contrast with domestic law, no effective institutional machinery has as yet been developed for the application and enforcement of international law. Existing judicial agencies, including the International Court of Justice, are bypassed frequently, and even those agencies cannot be regarded as true "enforcers" of the law. International law does not possess the equivalent of a hierarchy of tribunals under which a case by appeal can move from lower to higher levels. And there is no effective authority for enforcing decisions or awards handed down by the available courts and tribunals.

This state of affairs raises the question of why nations consistently abide by the rules of international law, with only occasional violations, considering the total number of cases in which the rules are obeyed on a day-to-day basis.

MOTIVATION FOR OBEDIENCE    Much of the discussion of this question of obedience traditionally centered on the unproved assumption that the only real motivation was fear of the use of force by some superior. Because no such superior exists in the international sphere—barring the use of, say, United Nations forces in overwhelming strength or direct unilateral action by one of the superpowers—the assumption cannot be considered valid. Assuredly, fear of "punishment" may on occasion play a part in bringing about a willingness, expressed by word or deed, to abide by the rules of the law, but other and more important causative factors appear to play a part.

Brierly summarized the matter very well: "The ultimate explanation of the binding force of all law is that man, whether he is a single individual or whether he is associated with other men in a state, is constrained, in so far as he is a reasonable being, to believe that order and not chaos is the governing principle of the world in which he has to live."[6]

CONSENT AND OBEDIENCE    It has been asserted by many writers that, inasmuch as consent to rules of international law had been given by states, the latter subsequently felt obliged, or obligated, to honor the rules approved by them in order to achieve thereby specific common aims. Thus the Permanent Court of International Justice stated in the well-known *Lotus* case that

International law governs relations between independent states. The rules of law binding upon states emanate from their own free will as expressed in conventions or by usages generally accepted as expressing principles of law and established in order to regulate the relations between co-existing independent communities or with a view to achievement of common aims.[7]

But the traditional reliance on consent alone does not offer an adequate explanation of the way States act in relation to the law.

The interdependence of States is an undeniable reality and requires a body of law between States as between men and men within a state. There has to be a method/way of regulating conflicting claims, of settling disputes short of force, or anarchy and chaos would prevail.

ENLIGHTENED SELF-INTEREST    Among the nonlegal factors that help maintain the legal norms may be mentioned, as one of primary importance, what could be called enlightened self-interest: the attitude that the risk of losing a decision through the application of the law might well be offset by the advantages accruing to one and all from living in a world society in which quarrels and disputes are settled peacefully under the same set of rules of law. The process of give-and-take applies in the international sphere as it does domestically: those who profit most from living in an order regulated by law can, in the long run, expect to be able to maintain that order only by themselves making concessions, large and small, to make the order accept-

[6]Brierly, 56.
[7]*The S.S. Lotus, P.C.I.J.,* 1927, Series A, No. 10.

able and tolerable to the members profiting least from it. At the same time, both those who profit most from the order and those who profit least have a definite responsibility for seeing to it that the changes and concessions are achieved in an orderly manner and not through eruptions of violence. Such attitudes reflect the basic concept in every code of morality, as well as in every organized community, that the good of the whole may require sacrificing a bit of the good of each part.

NECESSITY    In order to maintain normal relations with other countries, we must be able to predict the behavior of others, and this can be done only in a relatively stable situation. The observance of the known rules of international law thus becomes a requirement for states.

CREDIBILITY    All states attempt to develop some degree of credibility in the eyes of other states, for such credibility is necessary for a successful foreign policy. This credibility is promoted by observing international laws and hurt badly by disregarding them.

HABIT    Habit cannot de discounted as motivating the observance of the law. Routine observance of the rules results from a "habit of law," that is, habitual acceptance of the law by the individual decision makers at the highest levels as well as by the bureaucracies employed in those agencies dealing with international relations.

WORLD OPINION    Some writers and statesmen have claimed that world opinion is important in encouraging states to obey the rules of international law, but this is not only difficult to prove but also requires "world opinion" to be defined in generally satisfactory and meaningful terms. In fact, many modern writers on the law have discounted heavily the factor of world opinion, denying its importance as well as any claim that it could be measured meaningfully.

SOCIAL APPROVAL AND COSTS    In addition, a very real motivation for obedience is encompassed by the desire for social approval, found not only in individuals but also in their grouping called the *state*. There is also the material factor of costs, that is, the relative burdens to a state posed by the alternatives of using force to achieve goals and of using legal processes to redress grievances, and to achieve aims.

DISADVANTAGES OF EXPEDIENCY    There is, finally, the important factor of the disadvantages incurred by resorting to expediency: the usually undeniable advantages in pursuing international policies along established and accepted channels, contrasted with the disadvantages in pursuing headstrong tactics ruthlessly and against the will—and possibly the military strength— of others, with their consequent irritation and lack of future cooperation. Any government contemplating a violation of the law must consider the other states' possible reactions. Equally importantly, law-abiding behavior may have definite advantages for a state: a reputation for principled behavior must be regarded, at least by most states, as an asset and a guarantee of dependability and reliability in the eyes of other states.

## METHODS OF ENFORCING THE LAW

TWO KINDS OF COMPLIANCE    Any discussion of enforcing compliance with international law must include two rather distinct concepts: violation of the rules of law themselves and failure to carry out arbitral awards or judicial decisions. The latter topic is covered later (see Chapter 21); here we shall be concerned primarily with enforcing the law itself.

Compliance might be brought about in a variety of ways, of which the pressure of a presumed "world public opinion" is one of the least effective. Although we often refer to such an opinion whenever a crisis develops or the peace of the world is threatened, the fact is that except on the rarest occasions, the alleged violator of international law pays little attention to world opinion.

A major and as yet unsolved problem centers on the shortness of the world's memory: unless immediate steps (political, economic, military) are taken to force the "delinquent" to observe the rules of law, world opinion will tend to forget soon about the violation of the rules.

DIPLOMATIC PROTESTS    The traditional method of preserving the integrity of the law has been for the injured or offended states to lodge protests against those acts deemed violations of existing law. Such protests are commonly coupled with demands that the wrong done be appropriately righted. Although minor violations of the law may be corrected in consequence of such protests (if only for the sake of expediency and continued good relations), major intentional violations of the law in most instances remain unaffected by lodging diplomatic protests.

OTHER MODES OF LEGAL ENFORCEMENT    If disagreement about claimed violations of international law persist, a variety of devices can be used to secure compliance with the rules of the law: mediation by a third party, reference to a commission of inquiry or conciliation, and so on. (See Chapter 21 concerning the details of these methods for the settlement of disputes.)

Next, or alternatively, reference to an arbitration tribunal or to an international court may be attempted in order to effect compliance with the law. But arbitration will work only if the violator of the law agrees to such a settlement procedure. Adjudication has sometimes been found to be a poor way of securing compliance, in view of the weakness of current international judicial institutions, a weakness caused by the very nature of a decentralized international community.

Finally, compliance with international law may be secured through reference to, and subsequent action by, a universal or regional international agency: the Security Council or the General Assembly of the United Nations (for example, the United States' attempt to have the UN Security Council impose economic sanctions against Iran, from December 1979 to January 1980; The Soviet Union vetoed the proposal in the Security Council), or the various regional agencies, such as the Organization of American States. Such reference initially secures extensive publicity for the alleged failure to comply with the rules of the law and, possibly, public condemnation of the delinquent state, but may, more importantly, lead to the imposition of sanctions against the offending state.

SANCTIONS I    Failing to achieve compliance with international law through the normal methods for the peaceful settlement of disputes can lead to the imposition of sanctions. Sanctions may have several objectives: they may represent an attempt to cause a state to end a offensive (unlawful) practice; they may represent an attempt to punish such an offending state for the offensive practice; or they may represent a combination of these two aims. Political considerations intrude even more than normally at this stage, for only such sanctions are likely to be attempted as will be not only technically feasible but also politically possible and advisable: boycotts, embargoes, reprisals, and pacific blockades, adopted by an individual state, a group of states, or collectively at the behest of a universal or regional agency.[8] Needless to say, the imposition of sanctions will create more difficulties for the state violating international law than they will for the state or states applying the punitive measures.

The threat of sanctions, as punishment for violating the rules of the law, has been shifted from the use of outright force to nonmilitary techniques. Among these are the rupture of diplomatic and possible consular relations; economic sanctions, ranging from selective reductions to total stoppage of trade; travel limitations; financial restrictions on the flow of currencies; and the elimination of transportation (land, sea, air) and mail service and other means of communication to and from the state against which sanctions are established. In addition, the offending state may be suspended or even expelled from membership in an international agency and thus be deprived of the benefits accruing from such membership as well as the ability to vote on policies and decisions. Several agencies of the United Nations may constitutionally revoke aid or membership as an enforcement measure. A member of the United Nations organization itself, once enforcement action has been begun by the Security Council under Article 5 of the charter, may be suspended from membership, and a member that has persistently violated the principles of the charter may be expelled by the General Assembly on recommendation of the Security Council (Article 6 of the charter).

The Security Council itself may use enforcement measures, including sanctions, under Articles 10, 39, 41, 42, 45, and 94(2) of the charter. Thus, concerned over the failure of previous UN measures to end the secession of Southern Rhodesia, the Security Council adopted unanimously, on May 29, 1968, a series of economic sanctions against Rhodesia (See Chapter 19).

Economic sanctions have been shown to be relatively ineffective, particularly in the short run, for they have tended to unify public opinion in the sanctioned state while, concurrently, their application has tended to divide the international community. And once such coercive measures have been

---

[8]Consult Chapter 19 for details of these techniques.

employed, it has become obvious to all parties that previous reliance on criticism and public opinion failed to achieve compliance with the law.

The UN General Assembly (directly or through its Committee on Credentials) has rejected since 1973 the credentials of the South African delegation and has thereby denied it its seats. In the same body, representatives of African countries have demanded since 1974 the expulsion of South Africa from the United Nations, just as there have been repeated demands by a number of Arab governments to oust Israel from its membership in the world organization.[9]

In connection with the foregoing, it should be kept in mind that the United Nations Charter provides (1) that the rights and privileges of membership may be suspended by the General Assembly on the Security Council's recommendation when preventive or enforcement action has been taken against the member (Art. 5); (2) that a member that is a persistent violator of charter principles may be expelled by the General Assembly on the Security Council's recommendation (Art. 6); and (3) that any member two or more years in arrears in its financial contribution may be deprived of its vote by the General Assembly.

In 1969, the Council of Europe was about to suspend Greece from the 18-member organization for denying, without justification of any kind, basic democratic rights to Greek citizens, when Greece resigned (December 11, 1969). After its former military regime had been eliminated, Greece rejoined the Council of Europe (September 14, 1974). The World Meteorological Organization, a United Nations agency, suspended South Africa from membership on April 30, 1975, and the Universal Postal Union decided in early June 1974 to exclude South Africa from its meetings and instead to invite the Organization of African Unity to take part in the UPU's activities.

THE USE OF FORCE    Finally, the ultimate sanction of military force can be employed to secure compliance with international law. In view of current attitudes toward war, a true and legal sanction can now be imposed by the United Nations by means of a collective military effort. Because such a contingency is remote, however, unilateral or multilateral military efforts might conceivably be launched, with or without approval by the Security Council or the General Assembly. The legal standing of such an action would be clouded, to say the least, in view of the rather precise provisions of the UN Charter and the obligations assumed thereunder by the members of the United Nations.

VIOLATIONS OF THE LAWS OF WAR    In regard to the special area of the laws of war, compliance with existing customary or conventional rules may be enforced through the employment of four tools: publicity given by the

---

[9]Concerning South Africa, see *inter alia, NYT,* April 1, 1975, 4; August 20, 1975, 7; September 30, 1975, 12; and similar reports in subsequent years, particularly that on May 24, 1979, A-11. Consult also Alden, Augusti, Brown, and Rode, "The Decredentialization of South Africa," 16 *Harvard Int'l Law Jl.* 576–88 (1975).

offended party to the violations of law claimed; fear of the prosecution of guilty individuals at all levels by the offended party as war criminals (see Chapter 27); reprisals adopted by the offended party; and, possibly, payment of damages or reparations by the state guilty of violations, under the terms of Hague Convention IV of 1899.

Another form of sanction for violations of international law is individual or collective intervention in the internal affairs of a given state by other states or even by an international organization. This subject is discussed elsewhere (see Chapter 8) but can involve some very delicate interpretations of international law if the intervention is to remain lawful as a tool and sanction in the cause of law and not of aggrandizement.

SUMMARY    Common consent appears to be the primary reason for obeying the law: the states of the world have agreed to be bound by generally accepted rules for the conduct of their international relations. Once such agreement had been reached, it became a matter of mutual interest for states to maintain the accepted rules, particularly in view of the reciprocal need for predictable state behavior in the activities covered by the accepted rules.

However—and this has caused much distress to overly optimistic defenders of the law—the principles of international law appear to have been observed by states normally because they do not, as yet, make very stringent demands on those states and do not generally affect what are considered "vital national interests" in the opinions of those states. Therefore, obedience to the law has fallen into line with Jessup's view that "international law reflects and records those accommodations which over centuries states have found it to their interest to make."[10] Self-interest, enlightened or not, appears to have been the basic reason for compliance, and all other factors mentioned must be assigned a secondary or lesser role. Consent to the law and self-limitation in abiding by that consent still represent the essential sanctions of the rules of international law.

It should be noted that violation of the rules of the law by a given state—even if no sanction is attempted—does not render the rule invalid. This principle was stated clearly by the Supreme Court of Hong Kong in the arbitration concerning *The S.S. Prometheus* when it held that

The resistance of a nation to a law to which it has agreed does not derogate from the authority of the law because that resistance cannot, perhaps, be overcome. Such resistance merely makes the resisting nation a breaker of the law to which it has given its adherence, but it leaves the law, to the establishment of which the resisting nation was a party, still subsisting. Could it be successfully contended that because any given person or body of persons possessed for the time being to resist an established municipal law such law had no existence? The answer to such a contention would be that *the law still existed, though it might not for the time being*

[10] Jessup, "International Law in 1953 A.D.," *Proceedings* (1953), 8, 10.

*be possible to enforce obedience to it.* [11](emphasis added) The same conclusion about the validity of a rule of international law holds true, of course, in the sphere of domestic (municipal) legal systems. Violations of, say, a federal law, a Minnesota statute, a city ordinance does not vitiate, does not set aside or nullify the rule in question.

## B. SOURCES OF THE LAW

A common difficulty experienced by both students and judges has been the determination or location of the specific rule of international law that would apply to a given dispute between two countries. If a law code were founded on an international scale, the problem would at most be minimal: a clear-cut listing of all existing rules, exceptions to rules, and variations in national interpretations would enable an inquirer to locate with relative ease the article or paragraph relevant to the case at hand. Unfortunately no such code exists as yet, despite numerous private attempts, often of great value, to compile codes of law on specific subjects within the general sphere and despite the commendable, frequently successful efforts of the International Law Commission of the United Nations.

How, then, are the rules of international law determined or, more to the point at this stage of the coverage of the subject, what are the sources of international law rules and principles? General agreement appears to have been reached, and is contained in Article 38 of the Statute of the International Court of Justice, that there are three major sources of international law, as well as two subsidiary means for determining of the rules of that law. It is in these sources and means that one can verify the existence and the meaning of the rules of law of nations.

### MEANS FOR DETERMINING RULES OF LAW

Article 38 of the Statute directs the Court to apply: (1) international conventions, whether general or particular, establishing rules expressly recognized by the contesting states; (2) international custom, as evidence of a general practice accepted as law; (3) the general principles of law recognized by civilized nations; and (4) subject to the provisions of Article 59, judicial decisions and the teachings of the most highly qualified publicists (writers) of various nations as subsidiary means for the determination of rules of law. We now shall examine the nature and characteristics of these sources.

### International Treaties

In contrast with the commentaries of a hundred years ago, *treaties* are now generally accepted as a major (and by some as *the* major) source of international law. One must beware, however, of taking such a statement too

---

[11] 2 *Hong Kong L.R.* (1904), 207, 225.

literally. Obviously the bulk of the thousands of treaties concluded among nations does not create one single general rule of international law. A commercial treaty between Guatemala and France, a military alliance between the Soviet Union and Bulgaria, or an extradition or consular treaty between the United States and Sri Lanka cannot create any rule of conduct for the community of nations. At best such instruments are declaratory of existing rules.

LAW-MAKING TREATY    There is one type of treaty, however, that can be regarded as a source of international law: the so-called law-making treaty, concluded among a number of countries acting in their joint interest, intended to create a new rule, and adhered to later by other states, either through formal action in accordance with the provisions of the treaty or by tacit acquiescence in and observance of the new rule. A law-making treaty, then, is an instrument through which a substantial number of states declare their understanding of what is a particular rule of law; by which new general rules for the future conduct of the ratifying or adhering states are laid down; by which some existing customary or conventional rule of law is abolished, modified, or codified; or by which some new international agency is created. It is this kind of treaty through which *conventional* international law is created.

In view of the sovereign nature of the modern state, such a treaty is obligatory originally only on those states that signed and ratified it. If the initial number of ratifying states is small, the treaty does not create a new rule of general international law but, at best, only a rule of particular or regional application. As acquiescence in the new rule, formal ratification of it, or adherence to it by additional states increases and as the majority of all states finally accepts the new rule, a new principle or a new interpretation of an old rule becomes a part of general international law. States that specifically refuse to acquiesce in the new rule or that refuse to ratify the treaty or to adhere to it are, of course, not normally bound by the rule, principle, or interpretation in question.

The past 150 years have seen the conclusion of a great number of true law-making treaties. Among the outstanding instruments of this type have been the Declaration of Paris of 1856 (privateering, rights of neutrals in naval war), the Geneva Red Cross Convention of 1864, the Universal Postal Union Convention of 1874, the Hague Conventions of 1899 and 1907, the Covenant of the League of Nations, the Charter of the United Nations, the Geneva Conventions of 1949 (regulation of certain aspects of war, including prisoners of war and belligerent occupation), and the agreements on the Law of the Sea, in Geneva in 1958, the 1961 Vienna Convention on Diplomatic Privileges and Immunities, and others. [12]

[12] Consult also the valuable monographic study by the International Law Commission, "Historical Survey of Development of International Law and Its Codification by International Conferences," 41 *AJIL* (October 1947, Supp.) 29.

CLASSIFICATION OF LAW-MAKING TREATIES    Law-making treaties may be divided into a number of categories on the basis of content and intent. Some of these instruments merely transform into the equivalent of statutory legislation, existing customary law, or legal rules laid down by some judicial agencies. The Final Act of the Congress of Vienna (1815) (Arts. 108, 117, 118) belongs in this grouping, with its codification of rules governing the freedom of navigation on international rivers and the classification of diplomatic representatives.

Other law-making treaties interpret existing customary or conventional rules without necessarily adding new principles to the body of the law. And finally, and most promisingly, a number of law-making treaties have created new principles of law by international agreement, as in the case of the Convention on International Civil Aviation (1944) and the Convention Concerning the International Circulation of Motor Vehicles (1909).

Many law-making treaties combine two or all of these functions: the Hague Conventions on the Laws and Customs of War of 1907, for example.

Even though a law-making treaty may not achieve virtually universal acceptance, it may nevertheless represent a source of international law. In such a case, however, it would be a source of what is called *particular* or, in some instances in which there is a geographic basis for it, *regional international law*, the law binding only the relatively few states involved and thus not establishing a rule of general law. Thus the Latin American states and Spain recognize a right of asylum for political offenders in their respective embassies or legations as well as on their public vessels, though the majority of the world community does not recognize such a right.

RESOLUTIONS AND DECLARATIONS    A special problem has been posed for some time now by the resolutions and declarations adopted by certain inter-American conferences. Because no ratification is required, the resolutions and declarations in question do not correspond to treaties in the orthodox sense. On the other hand, Latin American states have regarded these resolutions as creating binding legal obligations. If such an interpretation can be shown to have been accepted by the participating states through their subsequent actions, then it has to be admitted that in the instances in question, regional law has been created. Thus far there has been little investigation in this field; it must be suspected, however, that in the course of time, a considerable volume of regional (or particular) law has been gathered by this method.

Closely related to the foregoing topic is the question of the legal significance to be attributed to the declarations and resolutions adopted by the General Assembly of the United Nations.

From a traditional point of view, because such declarations and resolutions lack the characteristics of a treaty, they must be denied obligatory force and hence cannot be termed law-making. On the other hand, there appears to be a "theoretical" trend from consent to consensus as a basis for those obligations legally binding states,[13] and *some* of the resolutions and recommendations may be regarded as authoritative evidence of rules of international law.[14]

The nonbinding, non–law-making character of General Assembly (GA) resolutions has been reaffirmed recently by Chamber Three of the Iran–United States Claims Tribunal in its award in *SEDCO, Inc.* v. *National Iranian Oil Co.* (ITL 59-129-3, The Hague, March 27, 1986).[15] The Chamber, discussing standards of compensation, noted that relevant GA resolutions were not binding on states and could not be considered evidence of customary law, although they might reflect such law when there existed virtual unanimity in their adoption. The Chamber held that only one relevant GA resolution, No. 1803,[16] had been approved by a sufficiently broad majority of states to reflect international legal standards of compensation.

General Assembly declarations, if they assert principles observed by the community of nations as legally binding, in fact reformulate legal norms for UN member states and, on occasion, interpret the meaning of such norms, as viewed by the assenting states. The same would be true of General Assembly recommendations under the conditions described.

The view on General Assembly resolutions held by the United States government and believed to be fully in accord with the principles of international law was presented on November 11, 1977, by the U.S. representative to the Sixth (Legal) Committee of the General Assembly:

This Assembly is not a lawmaking body. Its resolutions, in the ordinary course, do not enact, formulate or alter international law, progressively or regressively. In the exceptional cases in which a General Assembly resolution may contribute to the development of international law, it can do so only if the resolution gains virtually universal support, if the Members of the General Assembly share a lawmaking or law-declaring intent—and if the content of that resolution is reflected in general state practices.[17]

Even more to the point, Erik Suy, then legal counsel of the United Nations, wrote:

[13] See the argument favoring this trend in Falk, "On the Quasi-Legislative Competence of the General Assembly," 60 *AJIL* 782 (1966); for a cogent critique of Falk's position, see Onuf, 64 *AJIL* 349 (1970). See also Castañeda, *Legal Effects of United Nations Resolutions* (1970), and Whiteman, vol. 1, 68–70.

[14] Suy, *Innovations in International Law-Making Processes* (1978), reprinted in Schwebel, "The Effect of Resolutions of the U.N. General Assembly on Customary International Law," *Proceedings* (1979), 304–5.

[15] Digested in 80 *AJIL* 969 (1986).

[16] GA Res. 1803, 17 UN GAOR Supp. (No. 17) at 15, UN Doc. A/5217 (1962), reprinted in 57 *AJIL* 710 (1963).

[17] See Bleicher, "The Legal Significance of Re-Citation of General Assembly Resolutions," 63 *AJIL* 444 (1969), and the arbitral award in *Texaco Overseas Petroleum et al.* v. *Libyan Arab Republic* (Jan. 19, 1977), in 17 *ILM* (1978) 1; but also see Buergenthal and Maier, 43.

The General Assembly's authority is limited to the adoption of resolutions. These are mere recommendations having no legally binding force for member states. Solemn declarations adopted either unanimously or by consensus have no different status, although their moral and political impact will be an important factor in guiding national policies. Declarations frequently contain references to existing rules of international law. They do not create, but merely restate and endorse them. Other principles contained in such declarations may appear to be new statements of legal rules. But the mere fact that they are adopted does not confer on them any specific and automatic authority. The most one could say is that overwhelming (or even unanimous) approval is an indication of *opino juris sive necessitatis;* but this does not create law without any concomitant practice, and that practice will not be brought about until states modify their national policies and legislation. It may arise, however, through the mere repetition of principles in subsequent resolutions to which states give their approval. The General Assembly, through its solemn declarations, can therefore give an important impetus to the emergence of new rules, despite the fact that the adoption of declarations per se does not give them the quality of binding norms.[18]

Beyond this point, however, both declarations and resolutions can be held to possess only quasi-legislative authority and normally would require member ratification of a subsequent draft convention based on the initial declaration or resolution. (See Chapter 9 for reference to the Universal Declaration of Human Rights.)

Naturally, if a given resolution, approved by an overwhelming majority of the members of the General Assembly, is then accepted in practice by those members as representing a binding international legal obligation, a new rule of customary international law must be accepted as having come into being. In that instance, only those members that had voted against the resolution in question or that had indicated soon afterward that they would not be bound by the new principle would be exempt from the application of the new legal obligation.

Consensus, then, as expressed in the General Assembly, may represent nothing more than a hopeful exhortation, may turn out to have been the first phase in the creation of a new rule of conventional law, or may be seen as the first phase in the rapid evolution of a new principle of international customary law.

Regrettably, the General Assembly itself does not always acknowledge the limits of its legislative powers and has tended all too often to use phraseology appearing to claim the authority to make new rules of law.[19]

---

[18] Suy, *op. cit. supra* n.14.
[19] For instance, see the wording used in such resolutions as A/RES/2160 (XXI), A/RES/2184 (XXI), A/RES/2189 (XXI), and A/RES/2202 (XXI), all concerned with the question of colonialism.

## International Custom

Custom represents a second source of international law. In contrast with the normal meaning of the term—that is, the description of a habit—a legal custom represents a usage with a definite obligation attached to it. In other words, failing to follow a legal custom entails the possibility of punishment, sanctions, or retaliation; it means, therefore, state responsibility toward other nations.

The presence of customary international law is evident from the existence of an extensive body of detailed rules that comprised the bulk of accepted general international law until shortly after the end of the nineteenth century. Into this sphere of the law fall most of the rules governing such diverse areas as jurisdiction over territory, freedom of the high seas, the privileges and immunities of states, and the rights of aliens.

ORIGIN OF RULES    Some of the rules in question originated through the practices of a few states—practices that were adopted by others because of their usefulness, until at last general acceptance resulted in new rules of law entailing definite legal obligations. In other instances, a custom resulted from the existence of a single nation in some part of the Western world that adopted a given practice toward another in relation to some matter; eventually, other countries accepted that policy or practice without challenge or protest, and when the overwhelming number of states concerned about the subject matter assented, a new rule of law had been created, again as a legal obligation.[20]

In all instances a legal custom has come into being when it can be demonstrated that states act or fail to act in a certain way because a sense of legally binding obligation has developed. Or, as described in Article 38 of the Statute of the International Court of Justice, "international custom is evidence of a general practice accepted as law," with no requirement of universal acceptance.[21]

PROOF OF EXISTENCE OF A TRUE RULE    Obviously, there could be differences about the exact point at which a habitual act (usage) by certain states was transformed into a rule of customary law. In other words, the question is: How often, and by how many different states, does a habitual act have to be performed or be accepted without protest in order to achieve the status of a principle or rule of law entailing a legal obligation?

Observed repeated practice by itself is not sufficient evidence of the existence of a rule of customary law; there must have evolved an obligatory, or binding, aspect to the practice in question. That means that the law has been violated if a given state does not observe the rule in question. All states are bound to carry out the provisions of that rule, or they will be considered delinquent in their observance of the law.

[20]See Maier, "*Ex Gratia* Payments and the Iranian Airline Tragedy," 83 *AJIL* 325 (1989).
[21]This concept was also upheld as valid in *The Paquete Habana; The Lola*, U.S. Supreme Court, 1900, 175 U.S. 677, as well as by Brierly, 61.

The task of determination devolves upon both national and international tribunals, and as yet no rule had been established. At times, little quarreling could ensue because sufficient factual data could be presented to prove the existence of a true rule of customary international law, but at other times, the action in question has been duplicated so seldom that the existence of a rule could be effectively questioned. One of the better illustrations of the evolution of a set of concepts from rudimentary and habitual beginnings to the status of a legal principle was supplied in the decision in the well-known case of *The Scotia*:

## THE SCOTIA

*United States, Supreme Court, 1872*
*14 Wall.(81 U.S.)170*

FACTS    Appeal from Circuit Court, Southern District of New York, in a case of collision between the American sailing vessel *Berkshire* and the British steamer *Scotia*, by which the *Berkshire* was lost.

The owners of the *Berkshire* sued in the District Court to recover their losses, claiming that the collision occurred through the fault of the *Scotia*. The court ruled against the plaintiffs, holding that courts of admiralty were required to take judicial notice of the existence of British orders-in-council promulgating regulations for preventing collisions at sea and of the fact that so many maritime states had accepted those regulations as to create a general rule and usage of the sea. By the regulations in question and in accordance with an Act of Congress in 1864, the *Berkshire* was bound to show only colored lights; as it had failed to do so, no remedy could be obtained for the loss of the vessel. When the case was appealed to the Circuit Court, the decree of the District Court was affirmed.

It appears that the *Berkshire* did not display any colored lights at all but only a white light, at the bow, fastened about four feet above deck level. The *Scotia*, acting in accordance with the regulations mentioned, mistook the white light for the masthead light of a steamer, assuming in consequence that the presumed steamer was some distance away. Subsequently the two vessels collided, the *Scotia* obeying at all times the steering and sailing regulations required under the rules of the sea.

ISSUE*    What was the law prevailing at the place and time of the collision?

DECISION    The law prevailing was the law of the sea, which was violated by the *Berkshire*. Decree of lower court affirmed.

REASONING    (1) In 1863 the British government issued orders-in-council prescribing rules and regulations for the display of lights and for movements of both sailing vessels and steamers. Before the end of 1864, nearly all [34] maritime nations had adopted the same regulations respecting lights.

(2) No single nation can change the law of the sea, which rests on the common consent of civilized communities. It has force because it has been generally accepted as a rule of conduct. But when navigation rules originally laid down by two countries [Great Britain, later the United States] are accepted as obligatory rules by more than 30 of the principal

*Several minor issues have been omitted so as to emphasize the main issue of the case.

maritime nations, those rules have become a part of the law of the sea, a usage has been changed into a legal custom, and the rules in question were the law at the place and at the time the collision occurred. "This is not giving to the statutes of any nation extra-territorial effect. It is not treating them as general maritime laws, but it is recognition of the historical fact that by common consent of mankind, these rules have been acquiesced in as of general obligation. Of that fact we think we may take judicial notice. Foreign municipal law must indeed be proved as facts, but it is not so with the law of nations."

EVIDENCE FOR EXISTENCE OF A RULE    Unlike law-making treaties, which are easily available for study and reference, the evidence for the existence of customary law is scattered and at times extremely difficult to locate. Published diplomatic correspondence often contains clues to the existence of legal custom; instructions to diplomats, consuls, military and naval officers of high rank, and similar documents may point out the accepted customary rules; decisions of domestic courts, referring to habitual practices that have become legal custom, frequently indicate the existence of such custom; and opinions of certain legal officers, especially in Great Britain and the United States, have been found to be of great value in locating rules of customary international law.

WEAKNESSES OF CUSTOMARY LAW    The development and growth of customary international law has clearly shown up some of the inadequacies of this particular source of the law and has led, in more recent times, to the substitution of treaties as the major source of international law. Custom, almost by definition, is a slow process, and in some instances a given usage did not become a general and legally obligatory custom for several hundred years. Some writers have charged, justifiably, that in numerous cases a customary rule, when finally arriving at that exalted position, was outdated and archaic. As a result states, recognizing the inadequacy of a customary rule, fell into the habit of violating it because of that inadequacy.

A second weakness of custom as a source of international law is that as a usage becomes a legal custom, any country objecting to the usage may state its objections from the beginning and refuse to follow the example of others who assent to the practice in question. When the usage changes into a legal custom at a later date, the objecting nation then is not bound by the new rule. On the other hand, it is understood quite generally that when a new state comes into being and is admitted into the community of nations, it is bound by all rules of international law originating in custom. While this attitude may appear unfair in the absence of consent, the assumption of the customary law obligation represents a kind of price of admission to the community of nations; it is similar to the fact that a new member of a club is bound, upon admission, by all existing club rules.(See also Chapter 4.)

REPLACEMENT OF RULES    A new law-making treaty overrides an earlier conflicting rule of customary law (unless the latter represents a rule of *jus cogens*—see "General Principles of Law") and, in fact, has often been drawn up for the specific purpose of achieving the end or modification of a customary rule. When a law-making treaty modifies or replaces a rule of customary international law, the changes in question affect, of course, only the states that are parties to the agreement. In their relations with other states, such parties would still be bound by the rule of customary law.

An important aspect of customary international law hinges on the trend of the past few decades to incorporate customary law into law-making treaties (conventional law). When a provision of such a treaty includes a rule of already existing customary law, the latter is not only binding on states bound by the treaty through ratification or adherence, but remains as customary law binding on all states, even if they are not party to the treaty.[22]

Hence a given rule of international law may be part of conventional law for some states (parties to a treaty) and part of customary international law for all other states. If a party to the treaty in question should no longer be bound by it, it would still be bound by the relevant rule of customary international law found in the law-making treaty.[23]

On the other hand, can a specialized treaty become an obligation for all states as a new legal custom? The answer would appear to be that such would be true for all states not party to the treaty that would formally accept the obligation of the treaty as part of customary international law—provided that the number of concurring and bound states would represent a large majority of all states.

### General Principles of Law

General principles of law form the third source of international law.[24] The meaning of "general principles of law recognized by civilized nations" has been the subject of extensive discussion. Two major opinions prevail: one holds that the phrase embraces such general principles as pervade domestic jurisprudence and can be applied to international legal questions. Such principles might include the concept that both sides in a dispute should have a fair hearing, that no one should sit in judgement on his own case, and so on. The other view asserts that the phrase refers to general principles of law linked to natural law as interpreted during recent centuries in the Western world, that is, the transformation of broad universal principles of a law applicable to all of mankind into specific rules of international law.[25] It must be assumed, however, that from a legal point of view, the law

[22]This principle was upheld by the International Court of Justice in *Nicaragua* v. *United States of America* (see Case History No. 2). See also Lee, "The Law of the Sea Convention and Third States," 77 *AJIL* 541, 553 (1983).

[23]D'Amato, *The Concept of Custom in International Law* (1971), 107–8, and Vierdag, "The Law Governing Treaty Relations between Parties to the Vienna Convention on the Law of Treaties and States Not Party to the Convention," 76 *AJIL* 779, 786 (1982).

[24]Consult Whiteman, vol. 1, 75–90.

[25]One of the most persuasive modern defenses of the view is found in Cheng, 1–26. See also Friedmann, "The Uses of 'General Principles' in the Development of International Law," 57 *AJIL* 279 (1963); and consult Whiteman, vol. 1, 5–8, 21–26, esp. 90–94.

of nature represents at best a vague and ill-defined source of international law.[26] Most modern writers appear to regard general principles of law as a secondary source of international law, infrequently used in practice but possibly helpful on occasion.

When this source of the law was written into the Statute of the Permanent Court of International Justice, the 1920 Committee of Jurists offered several interpretations of the source's meaning. It may well have been their purpose to avoid having an international court not hand down a decision because no "positive applicable rule" existed. The phrase "general principles" did enable a court, however, to go outside the generally accepted rules of international law and resort to principles common to various domestic legal systems.[27] In fact, a number of court decisions and several law-making treaties refer to the general principles concept: the Permanent Court of International Justice, the International Court of Justice,[28] in the 1907 Hague Conventions (in the so-called Martens Clause), and in Articles 67 and 158 of the 1949 Fourth Geneva (Civilians) Convention.[29]

From a theoretical point of view, the acceptance of using general principles in fleshing out the body of international law means repudiating the extreme positivist doctrine that only rules created by means of the formal treaty process or a reliance on general custom are valid.[30]

Thus it appears that, as yet, many international lawyers and diplomats doubt the validity of the claim that "general principles" represent a truly usable source of international law. There has been some dissent from this view, however, in recent decades, notably in the writings of Jessup, Jenks, and particularly Rudolph B. Schlesinger of Cornell University.[31]

## Judicial Decisions

The decisions of courts and tribunals, when applying international law, form at most an indirect and subsidiary source of international law. The decisions

---

[26]See the valuable discussion in Kunz, "Natural-Law Thinking in the Modern Science of International Law," 55 *AJIL* pp. 951–958 (1961). The present writer does not share the belief of some of his colleagues that international law constitutes a science. The law of nations represents an area of state practice, a subject of study, research, and teaching; and to refer to it as a science, except by an unwarranted stretching of the term's meaning, reflects the common modern tendency to reject, or at least to look down on, anything not labeled as scientific or a science.

[27]See Hudson, "On Article 38," 606–20, in his *The Permanent Court of International Justice, 1920–1942* (1943).

[28]*The Chorzów Factory Case* (Claim to Indemnity—Jurisdiction), *P.C.I.J.*, Ser. A, No. 9, 31, and the same case (Claim to Immunity—Merit), P.C.I.J., Ser. A, No. 17, 29; *The Corfu Channel Case, I.C.J., 1949, Reports, 22.*

[29]Roberts, *International Law on Military Occupation and on Resistance* (1980), 19.

[30]On this point, see Brierly, 63; Cheng (2nd ed.), 23; and Lauterpacht's *Oppenheim*, vol. 1, 29. See also Fenwick, 85–88, who viewed General Principles of Law as being General Principles of Right and Wrong.

[31]See Schlesinger, "Research on the General Principles of Law Recognized by Civilized Nations," 51 *AJIL* 734 (1957).

of domestic courts do not even bind their own governments in their international relations; yet a given decision not only reflects the interpretation
of other courts as to the existence or meaning of a rule of international law
but also indicates what that rule is held to mean in the country in question
at the time the decision is drafted. This view was expressed eloquently by
Chief Justice Marshall in the case of *Thirty Hogsheads of Sugar* v. *Boyle:*[32]

The law of nations is the great source from which we derive those rules . . . which are
recognized by all civilized and commercial states throughout Europe and America.
This law is in part unwritten, and in part conventional. To ascertain that which
is unwritten, we resort to the great principles of reason and justice: but, as these
principles will be differently understood by different nations under different circumstances, we consider them as being, in some degree, fixed and rendered stable
by a series of judicial decisions. The decisions of the Courts of every country, so
far as they are founded upon a law common to every country, will be received not
as authority, but with respect. The decisions of the Courts of every country show
how the law of nations, in the given case, is understood in that country, and will
be considered in adopting the rule which is to prevail in this.

As precedents and recorded decisions multiply over the years, a vast and
instructive body of opinion is put on record for inspection and study. The
courts tend to accept those precedents and the opinions laid down by other
courts, domestic and foreign.

On the other hand, the decisions of international tribunals have begun
to play an increasingly important part in determining the existence and
meaning of rules of law. The very nature of an international tribunal such
as the International Court of Justice (a group of carefully chosen, able, and
impartial legal authorities representing many different legal backgrounds
and systems), with its presumed advantage over a national court conceivably
influenced by nationalistic or political considerations, tends to elevate the
decisions and advisory opinions of such a body above mere domestic court
decisions.

It should be kept in mind that the more often a rule involved in a decision
happens to be in line with the basic structure of the regional or general legal
system affected, the more likely will it be accepted, respected, and followed
by the legal persons (states, etc.) in that system. Furthermore, the decisions
of an international tribunal may sometimes be highly effective in changing
the law or abolishing a rule if the latter corresponds no longer to the needs
of the community of nations. Thus the decisions of international courts
and arbitral awards handed down by international tribunals may serve to
interpret a rule, apply a rule, or eliminate an obsolete rule.

## Writings of Publicists

The writings of publicists — that is, the works of text writers and other private commentators — represent a definitely subsidiary source of international

[32] U.S. Supreme Court, 1815, 9 Cranch 191.

law and today are primarily a means for determining varying interpretations of the law.[33] No text writer creates international law, regardless of his professional eminence. At most an outstanding writer may state what the law is in his own time and may speculate on future developments.[34] He thus may discuss as to how the law might be improved on a given point. To the extent that his government may adopt suggestions and utilize them in the development of a usage or incorporate them in a law-making treaty concluded with a number of other states, the writer may be regarded as an indirect source of international law. In past centuries, however, the work of the publicist was of profound importance. The writings of Grotius, Gentilis, de Vattel, and other "greats" in the history of the law played a vital part in the growth of international law, primarily as evidence submitted by authorities to show what the rules were in their time, and not as true sources of new rules.

## Comity

Reports on international events occasionally refer to "rules of comity" (French: *courteoisie*). An example is the practice of a sending state to refrain from publishing the text of a diplomatic note prior to its receipt by the receiving state. Comity represents modes of state behavior that do not involve a binding or legal obligation. If such an obligation existed, the rule in question would be one not of comity but of either customary or conventional law.

A rule may, of course, shift from one sphere to another. For example, the salute expressed through the "dipping" of the flag by one warship to another representing a friendly foreign nation on the high seas formerly represented a rule of customary international law; today the practice is viewed merely as part of international comity. On the other hand, a rule of comity may by treaty become a part of conventional law or may evolve into a component of customary law. The essential determinant in all cases, however, is the existence or the absence of a legally binding obligation.

A violation of a rule of comity can be viewed at most as an unfriendly act, with no claims to reparation attached, in contrast with a violation of a rule of customary or conventional law. In the latter case, at the minimum, an apology or reparation of some sort will be demanded for the international offense incurred.

## Equity

The term *equity* includes such concepts as proportionality, balance, fairness, and impartiality in the endeavor of a court to take account of the particular

---

[33] See the excerpt from the decision of the Supreme Court of the United States in *Hilton* v. *Guyot* (159 U.S. 113), cited in the abstract of the *Paquete Habana* case in Chap. 3.

[34] The most striking modern example of a publicist's influence on the development of new rules of law has been the work of Lemkin who, through his *Axis Rule in Occupied Europe* (1944), contributed materially to the framing of the Convention on Genocide by the United Nations. The term *genocide* was coined by Lemkin.

circumstances of a situation and to avoid inequities that would result from a mere judicial application of a general rule of law.[35]

In the case of *The Diversion of Water from the Meuse (Netherlands v. Belgium)*,[36] Judge Hudson noted that "under Article of the Statute [of the Permanent Court of International Justice], if not independently of that Article, the Court has some freedom to consider principles of equity as part of the international law which it must apply." In the *North Sea Shelf Cases (Federal Republic of Germany v. Denmark, Federal Republic of Germany v. Netherlands)*, the Court asserted that "Whatever the legal reasoning of a court of justice, its decision must by definition be just, and therefore in that sense equitable" and that "equity does not necessarily imply equality."

### SUGGESTED READINGS

#### Nature of the Law in General

Brierly, 1–7, 41–49; Gould, 1–30; Kaplan-Katzenbach, 19–29; Lauterpacht's *Oppenheim*, vol. 1, 15–23.

#### The Sanctions of the Law

Whiteman, vol. 1, 58–66; Renwick, *Economic Sanctions* (1981); Daoudi and Dajani; *Economic Sanctions: Ideals and Experience* (1983).

CASE

*Diggs* v. *Schultz*, U.S. Court of Appeals, D.C. Cir., 1972, 470 F.2d 461, reported in 14 *Harvard Int'l Law Jl.* 395 (1973).

#### Sources of the Law

Brierly, 56–68; Lauterpacht's *Oppenheim*, vol. 1, 24–35; Parry, *Sources and Evidences of International Law* (1965); D'Amato, *The Concept of Custom in International Law* (1971). Consult also Castañeda, *Legal Effects of United Nations Resolutions* (1970); Anand, *International Law and the Developing Countries* (1987); Snyder and Sathirathai (eds.), *Third World Attitudes Toward International Law: An Introduction* (1987).

CASES

*Free Zones of Upper Savoy and the District of Gex Case*, P.C.I.J., 1937, Ser. A/B, No. 70.

*Jurisdictions of the Courts of Danzig, Advisory Opinion*, P.C.I.J., 1928, Ser. B, No. 15.

*New Jersey* v. *Delaware*, U.S. Supreme Court, 1934, 291 U.S. 361.

*United States* v. *The Schooner La Jeune Eugénie, Rabaud and Labatut, Claimants*, U.S. Court of Appeals, 1st Cir., 1822, 2 Mason 409.

[35] See *Cayuga Indians (Great Britain v. United States)* Claims Arbitration Tribunal under the Special Agreement of August 18, 1910, 1926 *Nielsen Rep.* 203, 307.

[36] P.C.I.J. Ser. A/B, No. 70 (1937), 76–78.

# 2

# Development of Law
# Among Nations[1]

## EARLY DEVELOPMENT OF INTERNATIONAL LAW

PRE-GREEK CIVILIZATION    International law as we know it today is a product of Western civilization. Its true existence covers only the past 300 to 500 years, but its roots extend into the distant past. Some have attempted to link the modern law with the customs and usages of pre-Greek civilizations, but it now appears that our present law cannot claim such an impressive genealogy. It is true that even the earliest documents describing relations between states contain evidence of rules and procedures found in modern international law. For instance, a treaty concluded in the very dawn of recorded history, about 3100 B.C., between the rulers of two Mesopotamian communities (Lagash and Umma) provided for the settlement of a boundary dispute through arbitration, with solemn oaths for the observance of the agreement. Any examination of Hebrew, Assyrian, Babylonian, Hindu, and early Chinese records in the fields of warfare and diplomacy reveals many customs and usages that are still part of the practices of modern states.[2]

This should not lead one to assume, however, that the modern law can be traced directly to those early civilizations. In the world of antiquity, our own concept of a community of nations was utterly lacking. The interests of each unit were local, not "international." Although it was true that relations with neighboring countries could not be avoided, the consciousness of a community of mankind—fundamental to the creation of a true system of international law—was absent, except among some of the Greek philosophers.

GREEK CIVILIZATION    Even the Greek civilization, great though its achievements were in many spheres, did not contribute much to the development of modern international law. There were common bonds of race, culture, language, and religion, as well as a distinct feeling of enmity toward all non-Greeks (the "barbarians"), but on the other hand, the well-known pass-

---

[1]See Henkin, 1–10.
[2]See Nussbaum, 1–5; Lauterpacht's *Oppenheim*, vol. 1, 72–74; and the excellent study by Russell, *Theories of International Relations* (1936), chaps. 1–4.

ion of the Greeks for local independence appears to have outweighed the common links among the Greek city-states and their numerous colonies around the shores of the Mediterranean. Relations between the Greek states were based on a feeling of kinship and on convenience, rather than on the concept of a community of states.

DEVELOPMENT OF ROMAN LAW    In contrast with the Greek civilization, ancient Rome contributed immensely to the development of Western law as such and, indirectly, to the subsequent appearance of international law.

Roman legal writers defined two kinds of law in another manner: in philosophical discussions of the law, they characterized as *jus civile* the law that each country created for itself, whereas *jus gentium* referred to a body of law established among all men by reason, based on ideas or ideals of justice and observed by all countries. It thus represented the common basis on which the laws of civilized societies were based.

It was this second interpretation of the *jus gentium* that was preserved among the legal thinkers of the Middle Ages, with increasing emphasis on the existence of a universal law applicable to all states. On the other hand, the medieval period lacked the conditions under which a system akin to modern international law could exist.

Still later, in the seventeenth century, the term *jus gentium* became specialized in its meaning and referred to the principles assumed to prevail in the relations between independent states, was translated as "law of nations" (*droit des gens*) by Vattel in 1758, and became "international law" through its use in that form by the Englishman Jeremy Bentham in 1780. Bentham followed the Latin title of an earlier work by Richard Zouche (1650), who had written about *juris inter gentes,* "law among nations."

The development of modern international law and the derivation of its name were complicated further by the existence of the concept of the law of nature (*jus naturale*), adopted about 150 B.C. by Roman philosophers from Greek Stoic thinkers. The law of nature, later termed *natural law,* was believed to have been naturally implanted in men and to comprehend unchangeable and exact justice, universal in scope and self-evident to any individual exercising his "right reason," or the moral faculty with which he was endowed.

The fall of the Roman Empire was followed by a period of instability, an era in history singularly unfavorable to the observance of a presumed universal law. Contrary to a widespread belief, the medieval period did contain some of the seeds of the future international law as well as of our modern sovereign nations. First and foremost among integrating factors was the Catholic Church. At first, the important element was the existence of a single religion, increasingly centralized administratively and developing a common law (canon law) for its members, irrespective of race, nationality, or location. Ecclesiastical law, as it evolved during the medieval period, influenced many areas regarded today as lying within the sphere of international law: the conclusion of treaties and their observance, authority over territory, the right of conquest with the sanction of the Church, papal activity in arbitration and the general emphasis in canon law on arbitration as a desirable method for settling disputes, and, above all, regulations concerning many facets of warfare. Few chapters in Western intellectual history are more fascinating than the repeated attempts on the part of the Church to eliminate private war and to mitigate the evils of legitimate international conflict.

BEGINNING OF INTERNATIONAL LAW    The germination of the seeds of international law traditionally took place in the sixteenth century, even though the decentralization of the *res publica christiana* of Europe, the true beginning of the law, came somewhat earlier. The rise of Protestantism not only destroyed the traditional unity of Christendom but also made papal arbitration of secular disputes unacceptable to Protestant rulers. The outstanding event of the century was the emergence of the national state, first in England, France, and Spain. A growing number of writers began to debate national and international questions, and a goodly proportion to those questions related directly to the sphere of international law.

The remainder of this chapter will briefly summarize a few of the outstanding writers of this and the succeeding centuries. Limitations of space prevent the inclusion of many authors famous in the history of international law, such as Pierino Belli and Balthasar Ayala on the laws of war; Samuel Rachel on positive law; Martin Huebner and the Abbé Galliani on the laws of neutrality; Christian Wolff, the great teacher of Vattel; and Georg von Martens on the natural rights of states and on certain aspects of positive law.[3]

## WRITERS OF THE LAW

FRANCISCO DE VITORIA (1480–1546)    Vitoria was a well-known Dominican professor of theology at the Spanish University of Salamanca. Two of his works, *De Indis* and *The Law of War Made by the Spaniards on the Barbarians* (1532), relate particularly to international law. Vitoria emphasized the question of what made a war a just one and examined the bases of Spanish authority in the Americas, particularly in regard to relations between Indians and Spaniards.

Starting with the premise that the Indians were the true owners of their lands and goods before the arrival of the Spaniards, Vitoria argued that imperial claims to world domination were invalid; that all men were free under the law of nature; that the pope was neither the civil nor the spiritual

---

[3] Fortunately for the serious student, virtually all the classics in international law are available in the famous *Classics of International Law* (Washington, D.C..U.S. Government Printing Office, v.d.). Summaries of the most important writers are found in Nussbaum and in Lauterpacht's *Oppenheim*, vol. 1, 85–95. Much material on selected writers, such as Vitoria and Grotius, may also be found in standard histories of Western political thought, particularly in the writings of Dunning.

overlord of the world, nor could he claim to be the spiritual lord of nonbelievers; and that war could not be waged against the Indians simply because they refused to acknowledge papal claims to such lordship. And according to Vitoria, the mere discovery of Indian lands by Spain did not confer a valid title, inasmuch as only land without an owner (*res nullius*) could be claimed through discovery.

Certain claims supporting warfare and conquest in the Americas were upheld by Vitoria with a wealth of theological reasoning, and it is in this section of his works that there are so many fascinating speculations. He held that the Spaniards enjoyed certain rights under natural law and the *jus gentium,* including the right to travel and to carry on trade with natives—provided they did not injure the latter. If those rights were denied to visitors, then the latter had been injured, and a resulting war waged against the Indian populations in question represented a just war.

Such speculations naturally led Vitoria to investigate the rules of war themselves. For the first time in Western literature (excluding limited hints in Machiavelli's writings), one encounters here the terms *offensive war* and *defensive war,* and although Vitoria did not spend much time on the subject, he did point out that offensive (aggressive) wars were not to be condemned out of hand, for they might be based on just causes.

Vitoria's discussion of the rules of warfare reflects, almost by necessity, the barbarism and cruelty of his own age; yet the general tone of his remarks is humane and well in advance of the thinking and the practices of his time.

FRANCISCO SUÁREZ (1548–1617)[4]   Another early Spanish writer on the subject of international law was Francisco Suárez, a professor of theology at the university of Coïmbra. In his famous *Treatise on Laws and God as Legislator* (1612), he held that the *jus gentium* was different in kind from natural law, was in fact a body of law applying between independent states rather than one common to all states, and furthermore represented a body of rules voluntarily instituted by men. Although countries were independent, Suárez argued, they were never wholly relieved of some interrelationship among them, were in some measure dependent on one another, and therefore required a body of rules to govern their relations. It is thus with Suárez that one first encounters the modern concept of a society or community of sovereign states, tied together by a body of law applying to their mutual relations.

HUIGH CORNETS DE GROOT (1583–1645)   Better known as Hugo Grotius, de Groot is generally accepted as the father of international law.[5] His interest in the subject developed through an unusual and important case. During the war against Spain, a fleet of the Dutch East India Company captured

---

[4]Nussbaum, 80–91.

[5]See *id.*, 102–14, and Lauterpacht's *Oppenheim*, vol. 1, 91–94. The two major works of Grotius are available in English: *The Law of War and Peace*, Kelsey *et al.*, trans. (1925); and *The Freedom of the Seas*, Magoffin, trans. (1916).

a Portuguese vessel in 1601. The ship was brought, with its cargo, to Holland and sold as a prize of war, Portugal then being under Spanish domination. Oddly enough, some stockholders in the company objected to the highly profitable transaction, claiming that Christians should not wage war, certainly not on one another. The company retained Grotius, requesting an opinion on the objections raised, and the young lawyer fulfilled his assignment by writing an essay, *De Jure Praedae Commentarius* (Commentary on the Law of Prize and Booty), in 1604–1605. Most of this work remained in manuscript form and was discovered only in 1864; the twelfth chapter, however, was revised and published in 1609 under the title *Mare Liberum* (The Freedom of the Seas), an illuminating study of the doctrine of the freedom of the seas.[6]

Grotius wrote his greatest work, *De Jure Belli ac Pacis Libri Tres* (Three Books on the Law of War and Peace), the first systematic treatment of positive international law, in 1625, in France. Despite its title, the work dealt only incidentally with the law of peace, and most of it was concentrated, as in the case of most of his predecessors, on war. Nevertheless the portions of the book dealing with peace (Bk. II, chaps. 1–19)—filled with elaborate rules of national conduct based on the Scriptures, ancient history, and the classics—represented a unique contribution to the law and, in addition, a decided innovation in the works on the subject.

With respect to the laws of warfare, Grotius leaned heavily toward the Scholastic writers, with frequent citations, particularly from the works of Vitoria. In discussing the nature of the traditional *jus gentium*, however, Grotius went to considerable lengths to explain that it represented, in his opinion, law both human (that is, not divine in origin) and volitional, a body of rules deliberately created by human beings to serve human needs.

It was Grotius's distinction between a natural law of nations, as developed by him, and the customary or voluntary law, expounded by Zouche, that was the direct cause of the rise of three separate schools of legal philosophy in the seventeenth and eighteenth centuries: the Naturalists, the Positivists, and the Grotians. The Naturalists, led by Samuel Pufendorf, denied that any positive law of nations originated from custom or treaties; they maintained, with Thomas Hobbes, that international law was merely a part of the law of nature.

The Positivists, in turn, opposed the followers of Pufendorf in believing that a positive law of nations had its true origin in custom and treaties, hence in the consent of states, and that this law was far more important

---

[6]The complete work was made available in English for the first time in 1950 as the final number of the *Classics of International Law* (2 vols., London). The *Commentary* is characterized by an unusual emphasis on the rights of the individual under natural law, an emphasis said to be unequaled again in the literature of international law until very recently. A good summary may be found in *Current History*, October 1951, 225–26.

than any natural law of nations. Some of the writers of this school went so far as to deny the very existence of a law of nature. The leading positivist was the famous Dutch jurist Cornelius van Bynkershoek.

The Grotians held to a middle position in the controversy, asserting that Grotius himself had drawn tenable distinctions between natural and voluntary law. But they differed from the founder in insisting that both kinds of law were equally important.

Virtually all forerunners of Grotius had limited their learned discussions of war, both just and unjust, to the beginning of a conflict. Thus Grotius opened a vast new area for speculation and debate when he included in his work a detailed discussion of the conduct of military operations and their legal consequences and considerations. With insight, tolerance, and an eloquent use of examples borrowed from the past, he urged moderation in warfare and discussed the status and fate of hostages, the destruction of property, the problem of the defeated peoples' religious beliefs, and a host of other questions ignored or evaded by his predecessors. He did not believe that this particular portion of the *Law of War and Peace* represented a collection of legally binding principles; rather, he saw his discussion of the conduct of hostilities as a form of personal advice to statesmen and military commanders. It is a tribute to the essential goodness of human nature that even his early readers and critics regarded this section of the work as one of the most admirable contributions made by Grotius.

The writings of Grotius also contributed much new and original thought on a great number of specific topics, particularly those of neutrality, freedom of the seas, treaties, and diplomatic practice. Neutrality did exist in fact, though much hampered, in his own time, but his was the first analysis of the legal status, rights, privileges, and duties of a neutral state. Considering the time in which his contribution was composed, it is not strange that belligerents received far more favorable treatment at his hands than did neutral nations. In regard to the high seas, Grotius was the first writer to proclaim the concept of the freedom of the world's oceans and to attack with energy and learning the monopolistic claims of his own era to navigation and fishing privileges.

Treaties appeared in his books as distinct from normal contracts and, furthermore, as binding, in general, on the successors of a ruler who had been an original party to the agreement in question. Grotius, as could be expected, upheld good faith and the sanctity of international pacts but apparently could not bring himself to deny the old claim that a treaty was null and void when the conditions prevailing at the time of its conclusion had changed substantially. So he compromised, accepted the voidance of a treaty specifically made in contemplation of a continuation of existing conditions, and finally went so far as to admit that if a state found further observance of an agreement "too grave and unbearable," it would be freed of its obligation.

One rather novel aspect of the concept of lawful or just war of Grotius is the question of war as a punitive measure. Earlier writers had maintained that only "superiors" were entitled to inflict punishment. Grotius, on the other hand, believed that equals could also inflict penalties or sanctions. He regarded war as a punitive action aimed against state crimes, analogous to the domestic punishment of crimes committed by individuals (see *Law of War and Peace,* Bk. II, chap 20). Sovereigns were thus held to be able lawfully to exact punishment, not only for injuries sustained by them or their subjects, but also in respect to acts that constituted, with regard to any person whatsoever, a violation of the law of nature or international law. This right of punishment originated in the law of nature, according to Grotius. The modern reader will find in the relevant pages of Grotius strong echoes of the demands voiced during World War II for the punishment of war criminals. In fact, the following chapter (Bk. II, chap. 21) contains a striking passage to the effect that subjects made themselves responsible for crime of their sovereign if they consented to it or acted illegally under his persuasion or command. Thus Grotius would have denied that one could escape just punishment for war crimes by pleading the defense of "superior orders."

SAMUEL PUFENDORF (1632–1694)    Pufendorf was the world's first professor of international law. However, scholars still disagree, in a surprisingly voluminous literature, as to whether he contributed much or little to the growth of the law, beyond being the founder of the so-called naturalist school of legal philosophy.

Pufendorf developed a new system of jurisprudence of his own, which he eventually published in 1660 under the title *Two Books on the Elements of Universal Jurisprudence.* The work attracted considerable attention, and in consequence of his new fame, Pufendorf was appointed to a newly created professorship of natural and international law at the University of Heidelberg. In 1670 he went to Sweden to teach at the University of Lund; there he wrote and published a second major work, *Eight Books on the Law of Nature and of Nations* (1672).[7] The rest of his life was devoted to historical studies, first at Stockholm and later at Berlin.

The *Elements* summarized Pufendorf's essential contributions to international law. As did the majority of thinkers of his age, Pufendorf implicitly believed in the existence of a state of nature antedating the historical state and held that in this prepolitical situation a law of nature was binding on all men. Only this law, rather than the consent of states, could establish legally binding principles and hence had to be regarded as the sole source of international law. His concept of the law of nature embraced those standards of behavior that experience and reason (the latter growing out of both experience and instruction) showed men, as they grew in knowledge, to be

---

[7] Both works are available in English; the *Elements,* Moore, trans. (1927); the *Eight Books,* C.H. and W.A. Oldfather, trans. (1931).

essential for their own good and for the good of human society of which they formed a part in accordance with the design of nature.

CORNELIUS VAN BYNKERSHOEK (1673–1743)    A celebrated Dutch jurist and member (and, from 1724 to his death, president) of the Supreme Court of Holland, Zeeland, and West Friesland, Bynkershoek was the leading exponent of the positivist school. Although he never wrote a comprehensive treatise on the law of nations, he dealt with specific parts of the subject in a number of well-known works, notably the early *Dominion of the Seas* (1702), *Jurisdiction over Ambassadors* (1721), and his major work, *Questions of Public Law* (1737).[8]

Most of Bynkershoek's contributions to the development of the law were in the rules governing neutrality, with emphasis on a neutral duty to abstain from showing any preference to a belligerent, on blockade, on prize law, and on the subject of treaties in general. One famous tenet of the Dutch jurist has become beloved by all historians of international law: he held that control of territorial waters off a national coast extended only as far as cannon could carry. This principle, almost universally accepted shortly after its formulation, became the basis of the three-mile limit of territorial waters when the range of coastal artillery remained fixed, for an appreciable period of time during the late eighteenth century, at about three nautical miles. (One such mile equals approximately 1.15 common or statute miles.)

EMMERICH DE VATTEL (1714–1767)    A leading early proponent of the Grotian school of legal philosophy, Vattel was a native of Switzerland. During most of his adult life he served in a diplomatic capacity, later as a privy councilor in charge of foreign affairs, under the Elector of Saxony. His major work, *International Law: Or, Principles of Natural Law Applied to the Conduct and Affairs of Nations and of Sovereigns* (1758), designed as a practical manual for statesmen, became the standard European reference work in international law and is cited on rare occasions even today.[9] Despite vital contributions of Grotius, no single writer has exercised as much direct and lasting influence on those conducting international affairs in the legal sphere, at least until very modern times, as did Vattel.

Vattel's writings, almost forgotten now except in France, have been criticized severely by modern legal historians. Most of the adverse comments center on his deliberate diminishment of the importance attributed to natural law, compared with that accorded to voluntary law, while at the same time lacking any convincing explanation of the pertinent question, Why should states feel obliged to observe a voluntary law of nations? This failure to supply an adequate basis for obedience trapped Vattel into unfortunate contradictions and exceptions to dogmatic statements.[10]

[8]English versions of the three works are available: the *Dominion*, Magoffin, trans. (1923); the *Jurisdiction over Ambassadors*, Laing, trans. (1939); the *Questions*, Frank, trans. (1930).
[9]The work was translated into English by Fenwick (1916).
[10]Corbett, 29–32, supplied some illuminating examples of such "flaws" in Vattel's reasoning.

Nevertheless, despite theoretical weaknesses, Vattel's work went through edition after edition and was a best-seller among legal commentaries for many decades. It was a particular favorite in the United States and as late as 1887 was cited in decisions of the Supreme Court of the United States.

## PROGRESS OF INTERNATIONAL LAW SINCE 1800

International law has progressed far since the days of the classical writers. As Oppenheim pointed out,[11] three factors proved to be of particular importance: the willingness of most states, after the Congress of Vienna, to submit to the rules of the law; the conclusion of numerous law-making treaties during the past 150 years; and the rise of the positivist school to a position of predominance in legal thought.[12] By the end of the nineteenth century, most authorities on international law conceded only the will of nations to be the source of the law, a view typical of a period in which the absolute sovereignty of states was affirmed with conviction by virtually every statesman and publicist.

The growth of positivist thought had taken place concurrently with the decline of natural law doctrines. As nationalism prompted state after state to engage in power politics of the crassest sort, the concept of an international law based primarily on moral foundations, on principle, retreated and in its place was substituted the criterion of effectiveness, of "is" over "ought." Many positivists did not deny the existence of an order superior to man-made law but denied emphatically that such an order bore any kind of relationship to legal rules prevailing in relations among states.

Since the end of World War I, a change in outlook has been in evidence, and the trend of juristic thinking has veered away to some extent from a rigid adherence to the traditional positivist philosophy. Many leading publicists admit today that when no rule based on actual state practice exists, reference can and should be made to principles of justice and general principles of law.

It can scarcely be doubted that moral principles and ethics play only a relatively minor part in the bulk of modern international relations and that such parts of international law as are observed in the regular practices rest essentially on custom and treaties. Hence the basic element of positivism, the exclusion of everything not directly traceable to explicit or implied agreements among states, appears to have considerable validity, provided that it is related to actual observance and not expanded into an all-inclusive and static system.

When viewed from this position, international law can be analyzed and explained in realistic terms and can be shown to grow and expand in scope

---

[11]Lauterpacht's *Oppenheim,* vol. 1, 106–7.

[12] See the valuable study by Humphrey, "On the Foundations of International Law," 39 *AJIL* 231 (1945); Ago, "Positive Law and International Law," 51 *AJIL* 691 (1957); Gould, 69 86; as well as Whiteman, vol. 1, 9–19.

even in this age of power politics. At the same time, a modified positivist approach along the preceding lines may show the weakness of approaches such as that taken by the neopositivist school founded by Hans Kelsen. The latter tried to separate completely the world of actuality and a world of legal norms. Such a divorce of principles supposedly establishing the conduct of states from the political aspirations and political methods utilized in their individualistic struggle for survival and power must be condemned as an extremely unrealistic and scarcely fruitful enterprise, except when viewed as a contribution to pure legal philosophy. [13]

The approach adopted in this volume reflects a modified positivist point of view, emphasizing the rules of law accepted in the actual conduct of international relations and based on customs and treaties as the law's basic sources. It must not be forgotten, however, that just as the theories underlying the nature of the law change, so do the principles and rules that comprise that law. International law is, and has been for some decades, in a state of transition.

It should be noted that the keystone of Soviet legal thought has been the doctrine of national sovereignty, with particular emphasis on nonintervention in the internal affairs of other states, in this case, of course, in the affairs of the Soviet Union. This emphasis may strike Western observers as incongruous, in view of the Soviet Union's actual foreign policies, but it is typical of a society claiming to be revolutionary. Nonintervention would obviously be based on a double standard as long as the missionary zeal for world improvement dominated the Soviet outlook on foreign affairs. Mutuality would then depend entirely on the revolutionary society's current foreign policy, which, at all times, would insist that no intervention should be applied to it.

After World War II, Soviet writers tended to emphasize a tripartite division in international law: one body of rules was said to apply to relations between "socialist" (Communist) states; another body of rules was held to apply between non-Communist ("bourgeois") states; and a third group of principles and rules was held to govern relationships between socialist and bourgeois nations. The last of these groupings was the one that appeared to be heavily influenced by the twin concepts of consent and absolute sovereignty. [14] In the late 1950's, Professor G. I. Tunkin, head of the Department of International Law at the Moscow State University and probably the foremost exponent of the relevant Soviet legal opinion, differed sharply with the views of the Soviet legal scholars who believed in the concurrent existence of three sets of rules of international law. Tunkin furthermore anticipated that peaceful coexistence between socialist and nonsocialist states would lead to an

---

[13] See Kelsen, *General Theory of Law and State* (1945), and his *Principles of International Law* (1952), especially the latter work on 403–47 (a second edition, revised and edited by Tucker, appeared in 1966).

[14] Kulski, "The Soviet Interpretation of International Law," 49 *AJIL* 518, 518–23 (1955).

effort to agree on certain specific rules of conduct for states (lawmaking treaties, continued development of customary law, the UN General Assembly's resolutions, decisions of international judicial agencies, and so on). In connection with the foregoing, Tunkin stressed the absolute acceptance of the existence of state sovereignty.[15]

The key concept developed in the 1960's by Soviet legal experts is a sort of "natural law" based on the Marxist-Leninist "laws" of societal development. According to this new interpretation, those laws govern the base, which, in turn, plays a determinative role in forming the elements of the superstructure. The "laws" thus represent the basis on which international legal norms are created and establish the boundaries within which the formation of such norms takes place. International legal norms (principles) contradicting or violating the "laws of societal development" will, so the theory asserts, yield to the force of those laws.[16]

Contrary to popular belief, the Soviet Union has observed routinely most of the rules of customary international law as well as the non-political (technical) agreements concluded with other states and public international organizations. Russian acceptance and observance of international law find their obvious basis in expediency dictated by the need for coexistence with non-Communist states as well as by the obvious fact that selected interests of Communist and non-Communist states do coincide. On the other hand, international law has also been utilized extensively and frequently for the promotion of the political and ideological aims of the Soviet state. Propaganda campaigns in Third World nations as well as in Latin America have centered repeatedly on slogans based on ideas culled from the principles of international law, primarily on component parts of sovereignty, such as self-determination, nonintervention, and equality.

## SUGGESTED READINGS

### Development of the Law, General

Gould, 31–100; Paul Guggenheim, "What Is Positive International Law?" in Lipsky, 15–30; Kaplan-Katzenbach, 56–80; and Cornelius F. Murphy, Jr., "The Grotian

[15]For an abstract of other aspects of Tunkin's teachings, see Slywotzsky's review of Tunkin's major work in 16 *Harvard Int'l Law Jl.* 767–72 (1975); or, preferably, consult the book itself: Tunkin, *Theory of International Law*, Butler, trans. (1974). See also Hazard, "Soviet Socialism as a Public Order System," 53 *Proceedings* (1959), 30, 33–34, But see Quigley, "*Perestroika* and International Law", 82 *AJIL* 788–97 (1988), and Mullerson, "Sources of International Law: New Tendencies in Soviet Thinking," 83 *AJIL* 494 (1989).

[16]See the lucid and authoritative analysis in Ramundo, *Peaceful Coexistence: International Law in the Building of Communism* (1967); as well as the brief but heavily documented study by Quigley, "The New Soviet Approach to International Law," 7 *Harvard Int'l Law Club Jl.* 1 (Winter 1965); and consult Whiteman, vol. 1, 29–32.

Vision of World Order," 76 *AJIL* 477 (1982); and especially Lauterpacht, *The Development of Int. Law by the Int. Court* (1982); Whiteman, vol. 1, 131–220.

## Soviet Attitudes

Greg Russell, "Soviet International Law and Ideology," 2 *Global Perspectives* (Spring, 1984), 7–29. See also the list of suggested readings in Henkin at 33–34.

# 3

# Relationship Between International Law and Municipal Law

International law is basically a system of law applicable to states and relations between states, with its rules, whether customary or conventional, relating to all or most of the more than 150 members of the community of nations. Inasmuch as that community lacks a central authority, the rules of international law can be "put into effect," that is, can be applied and enforced, only through the governments of the individual states—members of the community. Each of the latter, however, possesses its own constitution (or its equivalent) and its own distinct domestic system of executive, legislative, and judicial powers.

It is therefore necessary to analyze the relationship between international law and the domestic (municipal) legal systems of states. This means a threefold investigation of relations between customary international law and municipal law, of treaty-law or conventional international law, and of conflicts arising between provisions of international law and the constitutions and organs (both function and authority) of domestic governments.

## CUSTOMARY INTERNATIONAL LAW AND MUNICIPAL LAW

The primary question arising concerning the relations between customary international law and municipal law is the degree to which rules of international law have been incorporated/absorbed into municipal law so that they have become part of the "law of the land," with little conflict to be expected in the application or enforcement of the international law norm.

Anglo-American legal opinion has long accepted that customary international law was part of the "law of the land" and was enforced, accordingly, by domestic authorities (doctrine of incorporation). For Great Britain, this position was laid down in a now-classic case:

37

## WEST RAND CENTRAL GOLD MINING CO., LTD.,
## v. THE KING

*Great Britain, King's Bench Div.,*
*1905 (1905) 2 K.B.*
*391*

FACTS    The company was a British concern operating a gold mine in the Transvaal, South Africa. In October 1899, a quantity of gold valued at £3,804 was seized from the company by officials of and by order of the South African Republic. The company claimed that under the laws of the Republic, the government had to return to the owners either the seized gold or its value. Neither action was taken, however, as the South African Republic was conquered in the war that started in October 1899 and became a part of the British Empire under the terms of a proclamation dated September 1, 1900. The company sought to recover the gold or its value from the British government by a petition of right, arguing that the government had succeeded to all duties, rights, property, and obligations of the defunct South African Republic by virtue of the conquest and annexation of that republic.

ISSUES    (1) Whether under international law the sovereign of a conquering state is liable for the obligations of a conquered state;

(2) Whether international law forms part of the law of Great Britain;

(3) Whether the rights and obligations which were binding on the conquered state had to be protected and could be enforced by the domestic courts of the conquering state.

DECISION    Judgment for the Crown.

As to issue (1): The sovereign of a conquering state is free to decide which obligations of a conquered state are to be accepted as a liability of the conquering state.

As to issue (2): Only such parts of international law as have either been accepted by Great Britain or as have been so widely accepted that it could not be supposed that any civilized state would repudiate them, form a part of the law of England.

As to issue (3): Domestic courts of a conquering state cannot exercise jurisdiction over matters that fall properly under the jurisdiction of the government and that are determinable by treaty or by act of state; rights claimed under such matters cannot be enforced by domestic courts of the conquering state.

REASONING    (1) Passages from various writers on international law were cited in support of issue 1, but in many instances their pronouncements must be regarded as their views as to what ought to be, from an ethical standpoint, rather than the statement of a rule or practice so universally approved as to constitute law among independent nations.

The proposition that a conquering state should assume, under international law, the obligations of a conquered country cannot be sustained. When making peace, the sovereign of the conquering state is entirely free to state to what extent he is willing to adopt as his own the obligations in question. If the conquering state, by proclamation or otherwise, has promised something that is not consistent with the repudiation of some particular obligations, then good faith should prevent repudiation. But silence by the conquering state cannot be accepted as confirmation and adoption of all liabilities of the conquered state.

(2) It is true that whatever has received the common consent of civilized

nations must have received the consent of Great Britain, and that to which the latter had assented along with other nations in general could properly be called international law. As such it will be acknowledged and applied by British courts when legitimate occasion arises for those courts to decide questions to which doctrines of international law are relevant. But any doctrine so invoked must be one really accepted as binding between nations, and the international law sought to be applied must, like anything else, be proved by satisfactory evidence. The latter must show either that the particular proposition put forward has been recognized and acted on by England or that it is of such a nature and has been so widely and generally accepted that it can hardly be supposed that any civilized state would repudiate it. The mere opinions of jurists, however eminent or learned, that it ought to be so recognized, are not in themselves sufficient. They must have received the express sanction of international agreement or have gradually grown to be a part of international law by their frequent practical recognition in dealings among various nations.

"The expression 'the law of nations forms a part of the law of England,' ought not to be construed so as to include as part of the law of England opinions of textwriters upon a question as to which there is no evidence that Great Britain has ever assented, and *a fortiori* if they are contrary to the principles of her laws as declared by her Courts."

(3) The obligations of conquering states with regard to private property, particularly land as to which the title was perfected before conquest, are entirely different from obligations arising out of personal contracts. Cession of territory does not mean the confiscation of private property of individuals. The question of the adoption by the conquering state of contractual obligations of the conquered state toward individuals is an entirely different matter.

More recently, Lord Atkin stated in connection with *Chung Chi Cheung* v. *The King* (see Chapter 17) that

the Courts acknowledge the existence of a body of rules which nations accept among themselves. On any judicial issue they seek to ascertain what the relevant rule is, and, having found it, they will treat it as incorporated into the domestic law, so far as it is not inconsistent with rules enacted by statutes or finally declared by their tribunals.

The traditional theory of the absorption of international law in the domestic law of a state, illustrated by the *West Rand Central* Case, has been supplanted by the more up-to-date British theory of transformation, as expressed by Lord Denning in *Trendtex Trading Corporation, Ltd.* v. *Central Bank of Nigeria*[1] in 1977:

Seeing that the rules of international law have changed—and do change—and that the courts have given effect to the changes without any Act of Parliament, it follows

---

[1]U.K., Court of Appeal, Civil Division, Jan. 13, 1977 [1977], *All E.R.* 881, reported in 72 *AJIL* 417, 418 (1978).

to my mind inexorably that the rules of international law, as existing from time to time, do form part of our English law. It follows, too, that a decision of this court, as to what was the ruling of international law 50 or 60 years ago, is not binding on this court today. International law knows no rule of *stare decisis*. If this court today is satisfied that the rule of international law on a subject has changed from what it was 50 or 60 years ago, it can give effect to that change, and apply the change in our English law, without waiting for the House of Lords to do it.

The reader will have noted that the opinions handed down in the preceding cases refer to rules of *customary* international law that have either been accepted generally or been agreed to specifically by the country in question. Treaties that affect private property rights or that require in their implementation a change or modification of common law or statute must be agreed to through the medium of an enabling act passed by a legislative body such as Parliament. If enabling legislation were not required, it would be possible for the Crown to legislate for the people of England without obtaining the consent of the government's legislative branch. At the same time, English courts have held repeatedly that international law is part of the common law and that the latter must always yield to statutory law. Thus the courts are generally bound by an Act of Parliament, even though that act may conflict with a rule of international law.

The binding force of statutory enactments, as far as British courts are concerned, has been laid down most forcefully in a very well known case:

### MORTENSEN v. PETERS

*Great Britain, High Court of Justiciary of Scotland,*
*1906*
*(1906) 8 S.C., 5th Series, 99, 14 Scot. L.T. 227*

FACTS    Appeal from decision of a sheriff who had imposed a fine of £50, with the alternative of 15 days in prison.

Mortensen, a Danish citizen resident in England and master of a trawler registered in Norway, had been charged with violating the Sea Fisheries Act and Herring Fisheries (Scotland) Act by "otter trawling" in the Moray Firth at a distance of more than three marine miles from the nearest land. The statutes in question, and a by-law enacted by the Fishery Board in 1892, forbade the fishing method in question in the Moray Firth, that body of water having a mouth of approximately 75 miles across from point to point.[2] Mortensen appealed, arguing that the statutes and by-law applied only to British subjects or to persons within British territory and that the place in question—that is, the location where the alleged violation of law had

---

[2] Normally the territorial sea of Great Britain, at that time, extended three marine miles from the low-tide mark; hence a body of water fronting on the ocean and having a width at the mouth of 75 miles included a goodly portion of waters termed *high seas*, not subject to the jurisdiction of the coastal state. See Chapter 15 for a detailed discussion of the subject of territorial waters.

taken place—was outside British territory under international law and hence not subject to the statutes and by-law.

Peters, the Procurator-Fiscal of the Court, argued in reply that the terms of the statutes and by-law were universal and that even if international law were applied, the offense had been committed in British waters and that even if the Moray Firth were not part of British territory for all purposes, the British government was fully entitled to undertake protective measures as regards fishing in those waters.[3]

ISSUES    (1) Whether a British statute applied not only to British subjects but also to all other persons within British territory;

(2) Whether the waters of the Moray Firth outside the three-mile limit were British territorial waters and hence subject to British jurisdiction;

(3) Whether domestic courts were bound by a statute contravening a rule of international law.

DECISION    The court ruled unanimously in the affirmative on all three issues and upheld Mortensen's conviction.

REASONING    (1) The wording of the legislation in question—that is, the use of such expressions as "it shall not be lawful," "every person who . . . ," and so on—clearly indicated that the legislature intended, for this purpose, to have the statutes apply against all persons, regardless of nationality. The purpose of the legislation would have been defeated if only British fishermen had been controlled and all others would have been free to use any method of fishing in the area.

(2) There were many instances on record in which a given nation legislated for waters beyond a three-mile limit and land embraced by that nation and in which the validity of such legislation had been upheld by the courts.

(3) "There is no such thing as a standard of international law extraneous to the domestic law of a kingdom, to which appeal may be made. International law, so far as this Court is concerned, is the body of doctrine regarding the international rights and duties of States which has been adopted and made part of the law of Scotland. . . . It may probably be conceded that there is always a certain presumption against the Legislature of a country asserting or assuming the existence of a territorial jurisdiction going clearly beyond limits established by the common consent of nations—that is to say, by international law. Such assertion or assumption is of course not impossible. . . . A Legislature may quite conceivably, by oversight or even design, exceed what an international tribunal (if such existed) might hold to be its international rights. Still, there is always a presumption against its intending to do so. . . . In this Court we have nothing to do with the question of whether the Legislature has or has not done what foreign powers may consider a usurpation in a question with them. Neither are we a tribunal sitting to decide whether an Act of the Legislature is *ultra vires* [in excess of authority conferred by law and hence invalid] as in contravention of generally acknowledged principles of international law. For us an Act of Parliament duly passed by Lords and Commons and assented to by the King, is supreme, and we are bound to give effect to its terms."

---

[3] The Norwegian registration of Mortensen's vessel by its British owners represented a common subterfuge adopted at that time by British operators of fishing vessels, apparently in order to avoid compliance with the protective legislation which, it was believed, did not apply to ships flying a foreign flag and plying their trade beyond the three-mile limit.

POSTSCRIPT    Following the decision in *Mortensen* v. *Peters,* several foreign masters of trawlers registed in Norway were arrested and convicted in Scotland for the same offense in the same place. They were released, however, following a series of protests by the Norwegian government. Norway then issued a warning to all trawlers registered under its flag that no further diplomatic protection would be extended if charges of illegal fishing in the Moray Firth were lodged against them, and it also amended its own regulations so as to make it more difficult to register foreign vessels in Norway.

The British Foreign Office in turn admitted through Mr. Walter Runciman in the House of Commons in 1907 that the Fisheries Acts as interpreted in the Mortensen case were "in conflict with international law." Subsequently Parliament enacted a statute prohibiting the landing and selling in Great Britain of any fish caught by prohibited methods in the prohibited areas in question.

It appears necessary at this point to consider for the last time the theory of international law. The generally accepted view that a given state's expressed willingness to be bound by a rule of the law corresponds to consent is still valid today, despite the logical consequence that if a state changed its mind, it could "undo" its consent and might claim to be longer bound by the rule in question. This would, of course, dissolve the concept of general international law—the law would disappear in chaotic dissolution. But it is well known that states have been held obligated by rules to which they had not consented expressly or by implication. This demonstrates the contention made here, that what gives a rule its binding force in relation to a particular state is not only the possible consent of that state but also the fact that an international consensus of states views the rule as a part of a system of international legal rules and principles. This consensus, or *common consent,* of the group—the express or tacit approval of most of the community's members—is what binds a particular state, especially in the instance of customary law. No member of the group has a right to change unilaterally the provisions of that consensus, for the rules created by common consent can be changed only by common consent. The Permanent Court of International Justice expressed this view in its judgment in the case of the *S.S. Lotus:*[4]

International law governs relations between independent States. The rules of law binding upon States therefore emanate from their own free will as expressed in conventions or by usages generally accepted as expressing principles of law and established in order to regulate the relations between these co-existing independent communities. . . .

Although customary international law is "the law of the land" and as such is binding on all states, it should be kept in mind that if a given government violates a rule of that law by an executive or legislative act,

[4]*P.C.I.J.,* 1927, *The SS Lotus (France* v. *Turkey),* Ser. A, No. 110, 4.

the latter domestically has priority over the rule of customary law but internationally the state in question has committed a delict.

In the United States, for instance, the Constitution does not prohibit the president or Congress from violating international customary law. Hence, American courts will uphold acts of the political branches in violation of customary law as long as such acts are within the constitutional authority of the branch in question.[5] In the *Paquete Habana* case,[6] the Supreme Court had noted that "this rule of [customary] international law is one which prize courts, administering the law of nations, are bound to take judicial note of, and to give effect to, *in the absence of any treaty or other public act of their own government in relation to the matter*." (Emphasis added.) It also quoted with approval what has become a famous passage from *Hilton* v. *Guyot*[7]: "International law is part of our law, and must be ascertained and administered by the courts of justice of appropriate jurisdiction. . . . For this purpose, where there is no treaty and no controlling executive or legislative act or judicial decision, resort must be had to the customs and usages of civilized nations."

Similarly, Chief Justice Marshall had asserted in the case of *The Nereide*[8] that the Supreme Court was bound by international law which was part of the law of the land until a contrary act had been passed by Congress. In the case of *Murray* v. *The Charming Betsey,*[9] the same court held that an interpretation of a congressional act should not be such as to violate international law if any other possible interpretation remained.

On the other hand, the Supreme Court repeatedly ruled in favor of the (domestic) priority of legislative acts that violated a rule of customary international law.

## TREATIES AND DOMESTIC LAW

The subject of treaties and domestic law relates only to law-making treaties. A state is bound by such a treaty by ratification of, or accession to, such an agreement. If this consent or approval does not take place, the state in question will not be bound by the treaty except to the extent that general customary law is embodied in provisions of the treaty; such customary law provisions will bind the state even if no ratification takes place. Also binding on a state would be the rules found in an unratified law-making treaty when

---

[5] See Henkin, *Foreign Affairs and the Constitution* (1972), 221–22. See also the interesting papers on "May the President Violate Customary International Law?" in 80 *AJIL* 913 (1986) and *id.*, 81, 377 (1987), and Paust's dissenting "The President *Is* Bound by International Law." *id.*

[6] *The Paquete Habana; The Lola,* U.S. Supreme Court 1900, 175 U.S. 677; see also the Case Abstract below.

[7] U.S. Supreme Court 1895, 159 U.S. 113.

[8] *The Nereide,* U.S. Supreme Court 1815, 9 Cranch 388.

[9] *Murray* v. *The Charming Betsey,* U.S. Supreme Court 1804, 2 Cranch 64.

such rules were transferred from a treaty of this nature to which the state in question had consented by ratification or accession. For instance, the United States has to date failed to ratify the two 1966 UN Human Rights Covenants as well as the 1982 UN Law of the Sea Convention. None of the three agreements is binding on the United States, except for rules of general customary law found in the Law of the Sea Convention and for the substance of several 1958 law-making conventions dealing with the law of the sea, ratified by the United States, and now found in the 1982 convention, which is intended to replace the earlier agreements for states ratifying the newer instrument.

Just as in the case of rules of customary law, so rules created through law-making conventions (treaties) can be rendered inoperative within a state (*i.e.,* domestically) by executive or legislative acts of a given government. In such a case, an international delict is created, but the domestic courts of the country in question will accord priority to the governmental act over the international rule. A current example is supplied by the refusal of Israel to honor in full the provisions of the Fourth Geneva Convention Relative to the Protection of Civilian Persons in Time of War, of 1949. (See Chapter 23.) That treaty details the rights and duties of a belligerent occupant (Israel in the West Bank, the Gaza Strip, and East Jerusalem). Israel has stated repeatedly that it would honor the humanitarian provisions of the treaty, whereas the *entire* instrument is generally regarded as a key component of international humanitarian law. The Israeli government did not adopt (incorporate) the Fourth Geneva Convention in its domestic law, despite the fact that it had signed and ratified the treaty. Numerous acts of the Israeli military authorities in the occupied territories represent, in the view of outside experts or governments, violations of the Fourth Geneva Convention and as such are international delicts, but from the domestic (Israeli) point of view the Military Orders and their execution superseded (assumed priority over) the treaty obligations involved. On the other hand, a signed and ratified (or acceded to) treaty represents a binding obligation on a state, even if the agreement is not a law-making treaty. If the treaty cannot become effective without domestic implementing legislation[10] and the latter is absent, the obligation imposed by the treaty still remains *vis à vis* other parties to the instrument.

Keeping the above in mind, it is generally true, as far as the United States is concerned, that customary and conventional rules of international law override earlier legislation, *provided* that the rules do not violate express prohibitions contained in the Constitution of the United States or, in the case of conventional rules, require implementation through legislation that has not yet been forthcoming. It has to be assumed, of course, that a

---

[10]Such as the Convention on the Prevention and Punishment of the Crime of Genocide, as far as the United States was concerned—see Chapter 13.

treaty, properly signed and ratified, is in accordance with the Constitution; otherwise bad faith would have been manifested in the act of ratification.

The separate members of a federal state are automatically bound by the principles of international law, customary or conventional, to which their federal government has assented or by which it is obligated. Existing constitutional or statutory provisions of such member states contravening the principles binding the federal authorities are null and void in regard to domestic effect. These concepts have been illustrated in the American case of *Missouri* v. *Holland:*

### STATE OF MISSOURI v. HOLLAND, U.S. GAME WARDEN
*Supreme Court of the United States, 1920*
*252 U.S. 416*

FACTS    Bill in equity brought by the state of Missouri to prevent a game warden of the United States from attempting to enforce the Migratory Bird Treaty Act of July 3, 1918, and the regulations made under that act by the Secretary of Agriculture.

Congress had passed an act that sought to regulate the hunting of migratory birds by providing closed seasons and other forms of protection. That act had been held by a U.S. District Court to contravene the provisions of the Constitution as an invasion of the reserved powers of the states (*United States* v. *Shauver,* 214 F. 154; *United States* v. *McCullagh,* 221 F. 288).

On December 8, 1916, the President proclaimed a treaty between the United States and Great Britain that recited the value of migratory birds, described their annual migrations through parts of Canada and the United States, and provided for specific closed seasons and other forms of protection for migratory birds. Both countries agreed that they would make, or submit to their lawmaking bodies, proposals to carry out the provisions of the treaty. In implementation of the agreement, Congress passed the Migratory Bird Treaty Act of 1918, authorizing, among other provisions, the Secretary of Agriculture to issue regulations compatible with the terms of the treaty. These regulations were issued in July and October of 1918. When Holland, a United States game warden, attempted to enforce the federal regulations, the state of Missouri brought a bill in equity to prevent such enforcement.

ISSUE    Whether the treaty and statute were void as an interference with the rights reserved to the states under the Constitution.

DECISION    The court upheld both the treaty and the statute.

REASONING    (1) By Article 2, section 2 of the Constitution, the power to make treaties is delegated specifically to the federal government.

(2) By Article 6 of the Constitution, treaties made under the authority of the United States, along with the Constitution and laws of the United States made in pursuance thereof, are declared to be the supreme law of the land.

(3) If the treaty is valid, then the statute implementing the treaty is valid also.

(4) The treaty in question does not contravene any prohibitive words to be found in the Constitution.

(5) Wild birds are not in the possession of anyone, but possession is the beginning of ownership. Migratory birds travel from state to state; hence the whole foundation of any states' rights is the relatively momentary presence of birds in their boundaries.

(6) Valid treaties are binding within the territorial limits of the states as they are elsewhere throughout the United States. Although the bulk of private relations usually fall under the control of the states, a treaty may override the power of the latter.

(7) A national interest of the first magnitude is involved. The states cannot be relied on to protect that interest; hence the federal government has the right to act, in the absence of prohibitory wording in the Constitution.

The decision in the *Missouri* case resulted in a dread among the opponents of a strong and centralized national government that the treaty power might be utilized to circumvent the provisions of the U.S. Constitution. In consequence, those opponents attempted, without success, to bring about passage of the so-called Bricker Amendment. That proposal would have permitted treaties to become effective in the domestic sphere only through legislation that would have been valid under the Constitution in the absence of the treaty in question.[11]

On the other hand, if statutory legislation is enacted subsequent to assent to customary or conventional international law, and conflicts with the latter, then American courts are bound by the later (federal) legislation. In doubtful cases there is a strong presumption that Congress did not intend to override international law: " . . . the laws of the United States ought not, if it be avoidable, so be construed as to infract the common principles and usages of nations. . . . "[12] and " . . . An Act of Congress ought never to be construed to violate the law of nations, if any other possible construction remains, and, consequently, can never be construed to violate neutral rights, or to affect neutral commerce further than is warranted by the law of nations as understood in this country."[13]

It thus can be asserted that in actual American practice, a treaty would not be considered either abrogated or modified by subsequent legislation unless Congress *clearly* indicated such an intention in the statute itself.[14] When Congress has, on occasion, decided that the United States should violate a treaty or a rule of international law by deliberately enacting legislation in conflict with such obligations, the courts have applied that legislation,[15] provided it fell within the constitutional powers of Congress, in view of the fact that the Constitution does not forbid Congress to disregard

[11]See Bischop, 104–5.
[12]*Talbot* v. *Seeman,* 1801, 1 Cranch 1.
[13]*Murray* v. *The Charming Betsey,* 1804, 2 Cranch 64.
[14]See *Cook* v. *United States,* 1939, 288 U.S. 102, for a detailed analysis of this matter by the Supreme Court; see also *McCullough* v. *Sociedad de Marineros,* 1963, 372 U.S. 10, 21–22, and *Restatement (Third), supra* Chap. 1, n. 28, at §§ 114, 115.
[15]*Whitney* v. *Robertson,* 1888, 124 U.S. 190; *Chinese Exclusion Case,* 1889, 130 U.S. 581.

or to violate international law. On the other hand, such legislation would cause the U.S. government to be responsible to other states for violating the treaty or international law. [16]

It must also be assumed that a widely recognized rule of customary international law provides that a rule of municipal law adopted subsequent to a treaty and that conflicts with the provisions of the earlier treaty cannot alter the provisions of the treaty in international law. Article 27 of the 1969 Vienna Convention on the Law of Treaties states that a "party may not invoke the provisions of its internal law as justification for its failure to perform a treaty." Even before 1969, the customary law rule had received judicial support in a surprising number of municipal court decisions. Thus, in *Librairie Hachette S.A.* v. *Société Cooperative,* the Swiss Civil Court of Geneva held that the Swiss federal law on cartels of 1962 was superseded by the Franco-Swiss Convention on Jurisdiction and Execution of Judgments of 1869. More recently the Supreme Court of Belgium, in the important decision in *État Belge* v. *S.A. "Fromagerie Franco-Suisse le Ski,"*[17] held that a treaty does not void the conflicting internal law of a party to that treaty but suspends operation of that law as to any areas of conflict with the treaty; that is, when a domestic law conflicts with a rule of international treaty law that has direct effect within the domestic (municipal) legal order, the treaty prevails, because of the "very nature of international treaty law." The rule has even been recognized in some national constitutions, such as those of France and the Netherlands. [18]

But, when a state has failed to adopt by treaty, legislation, or other public act a policy contrary to a rule of international law previously assented to by that state, then the courts under the latter's jurisdiction are bound to accept, or at least to take judicial notice of, that rule. This principle has been elucidated most clearly by the Supreme Court of the United States in a classic decision:

## THE PAQUETE HABANA; THE LOLA
### Supreme Court of the United States, 1900
### 175 U.S. 677

FACTS    Two appeals from decrees at the U.S. District Court, Southern District of Florida, condemning two fishing vessels and their cargoes as prizes of war.

Each vessel, operating out of Havana, was regularly engaged in Cuban coastal waters, sailed under the Spanish flag, and was owned by a Spanish sub-

---

[16]See *Letter* of the Secretary of the Treasury, April 7, 1986, concerning tax reform legislation that overrides Bilateral Tax Treaties, 25 *ILM* (1986), 760.

[17]2 *Common Market Rep. (CCH)* (1971), par. 8141; this is not true in the United States: a subsequent federal law prevails over a treaty, as far as U.S. courts are concerned.

[18]France, Article 26 of the constitution of 1946, as modified by Article 5 of the constitution of 1958; and Article 66 of the Netherlands constitution.

ject of Cuban birth, living in Havana. The cargo, when the vessels were seized, consisted of fresh fish. Apparently neither captain had any knowledge, until the vessels were captured, that a state of war existed between Spain and the United States or that a blockade of Spanish ports had been proclaimed by the United States.

Both vessels were brought to Key West and condemned in the U.S. District Court, with a decree of sale of both vessels and cargoes.

ISSUE    Whether unarmed coastal fishing vessels of one belligerent are subject to capture by vessels of another belligerent.

DECISION    (1) Unarmed coastal fishing vessels are exempt from seizure by a belligerent.

(2) Decree of District Court reversed, proceeds of the sale of vessels and cargoes to be restored to the claimants, with damages and costs.

REASONING    (1) By an ancient usage among civilized nations, beginning centuries ago and "gradually ripening into a rule of international law," coastal fishing vessels pursuing their vocation have been recognized as exempt, with their cargoes and crews, from capture. This usage can be traced by means of documents back as far as A.D. 1403 in England. Subsequent evidence indicates that France and other countries followed the same usage. Eminent writers on international law have indicated through the past few centuries that the usage became general in scope.

(2) The United States recognized the immunity of coastal fishing vessels as far back as the Mexican War of 1846.

(3) In most recent times, numerous states issued specific orders to naval commanders concerning fishing vessels, recognizing their exemption from seizure unless military operations should make it necessary.

(4) "International law is part of our law, and must be ascertained and administered by courts of justice of appropriate jurisdiction, as often as questions of right depending upon it are duly presented for their determination. For this purpose, where there is no treaty and no controlling executive or legislative act or judicial decision, resort must be had to the customs and usages of civilized nations; and, as evidence of these, to the works of jurists and commentators, who by years of labor, research, and experience, have made themselves peculiarly well acquainted with the subjects of which they treat. Such works are resorted to by judicial tribunals, not for the speculations of their authors concerning what the law ought to be, but for trustworthy evidence of what the law really is. . . . " [*Hilton* v. *Guyot,* 159 U.S. 113].

(5) " . . . at the present day, by the general consent of the civilized nations of the world, and independently of any express treaty or other public act, it is an established rule of international law, founded on considerations of humanity to a poor and industrious order of men, and of the mutual convenience of belligerent States, that coast fishing vessels, with their implements and supplies, cargoes and crews, unarmed and honestly pursuing their peaceful calling of catching and bringing in fresh fish, are exempt from capture as prize of war."

(6) "This rule of international law is one which prize courts, administering the law of nations, are bound to take judicial notice of, and to give effect to, in the absence of any treaty or other public act of their own government in relation to the matter."

It should be noted that the rule discussed in the preceding decision is no longer observed by leading maritime powers in time of war, even though it was affirmed as late as 1907 in Hague Convention No. XI. The establishment of tight blockades of enemy coasts during both world wars with the avowed intention of cutting off all food supplies from the enemy state, together with repeated clear evidence that ostensible fishing vessels have acted as the eyes and ears of their naval forces, led to the issue of administrative regulations by virtually all naval powers that had the "public act" character required to set aside the effective application of the rule laid down in the case of *The Paquete Habana*.

In summary, using the United States as a typical example: Should Congress enact legislation inconsistent with prior treaty obligations, a U.S. court will apply and enforce that legislation. Similarly, when a question of sovereign immunity arises, the court will be free to decide the issue under the rules of international law as long as the President or the Congress have not issued contrary directives.

The general concept of the "incorporation" of international law into the "law of the land," found originally only in the Anglo-Saxon countries, has spread in modern times into many other parts of the world. Courts of numerous countries (Belgium, France, and Switzerland, to name but a few) have sustained the doctrine.

The "assent" of states, which has been mentioned repeatedly, should not be overestimated in connection with the doctrine of incorporation. The practice of states indicates clearly that express assent, particularly in the form of legislation or executive acknowledgment, is often lacking. Customarily accepted rules and principles of international law, as distinct from conventional law arising out of specific law-making treaties, must be regarded as part of the "law of the land" and do not require express assent in order to become such a part. Interestingly, the constitution of the Netherlands provides specifically for an absolute supremacy of treaties over domestic law but does not apply this principle to the rules of customary international law.

## SUGGESTED READINGS

### The International/Municipal Relationship in General

Whiteman, vol. 1, 103–16; Falk, *The Role of Domestic Courts in the International Legal Order* (1964); Bishop, 71–75; Deener, "International Law Provisions in Post-World War II Constitutions," 36 *Cornell L. Q.* (1951), 505; Lauterpacht's *Oppenheim,* vol. 1, 35–47; O'Connell, "The Relationship Between International Law and Municipal Law," 48 *Georgetown L. Jl.* (1960), 431; Charney, "The Power of the Executive Branch of the United States Government to Violate Customary International Law," 80 *AJIL* 913 (1986); Henkin, "The President and International Law," *id.,* 930; Glennon, "Raising *The Paquete Habana*: Is Violation of Customary International

Law by the Executive Unconstitutional?," 80 *NW. U. L. Rev.* 322 (1985); Kirgis, "Federal Statutes, Executive Orders and 'Self-Executing Custom'," 81 *AJIL* 371 (1987).

CASES

*The Scotia,* 1871, 14 Wallace 170.

*Certain German Interests in Polish Upper Silesia, P.C.I.J.,* 1926, Ser. A. No. 7.

*Exchange of Greek and Turkish Populations,* Advisory Opinion, *P.C.I.J.,* 1925, Ser. B, No. 10.

*The Greco-Bulgarian "Communities,"* Advisory Opinion, *P.C.I.J.,* 1930, Ser. B, No. 17.

*Treatment of Polish Nationals in Danzig,* Advisory Opinion, *P.C.I.J.,* 1932, Ser. B, No. 44.

*In re Aircrash in Bali, Indonesia on April 22, 1974,* U.S. Court of Appeals, 9th Cir., Aug. 24, 1982, 684 F. 2d 1301, reported in 77 *AJIL* 153 (1983).

# PART II

## Subjects of International Law

# 4

# The Community of Nations

The existence and application of a system of law relating to all civilized states presupposes a system of common values and attitudes, a sense of community, or, in other words, that vague concept called the *community*, or *family*, of nations. This idea had been implanted firmly in the European tradition by the time international law assumed its modern form, even though no formal machinery existed then through which the community could operate in the legal or political sphere.

## REALITY OF THE COMMUNITY CONCEPT

The concept of a community of mankind is one of the oldest heritages in Western civilizations. Its origins can be traced back to the Stoic philosophers of antiquity and to such conceptions as the brotherhood of man, the social nature of man, and man's membership in a worldwide community ruled by right reason (natural law). Such beliefs, transmitted through the centuries by philosophers such as Cicero and Seneca, by Roman jurists, and by the Christian Church, received new vigor during the Renaissance when legal theorists faced the problem of a politically divided Europe.

Renaissance thought, well expressed by Suárez and other scholars, held that man's nature, need, and desire for mutual help could not be fulfilled in individual states but involved humanity as a whole in one great society. And that society, just like its component political parts, needed a body of law to regulate and order the relations between those parts. This conception of a world society ruled by a universal and obligatory law has dominated the thinking of most subsequent writers in the field.

On the other hand, there has developed a general assumption that there did exist a worldwide community composed of states and that these units possessed both rights and moral obligations. Indeed, such a community does exist, for the simple reason that people talk, write, and, within limits, behave as if there were such a community. It would, of course, be wrong to assume that this essentially hypothetical community has the coherence and unity of communities of a more limited scope, such as the state and lesser associations of people. As writers have pointed out on numerous occasions, the community of states fails to achieve normal standards of coherence because

53

equality among its members is not achieved except "before the law" and, more importantly, because the basic principle that the good of the whole is more weighty, more vital, than the good of any part is not accepted by the community of states—at least not yet.

## DEVELOPMENT OF THE COMMUNITY

A state may exist for a long time, functioning as an operative political community, without being a "state" in the legal sense. Transformation into the legal personality known as a state comes about only through the admission of the entity in question as a recognized member of the community of nations. Numerous communities possessing territory, citizens, a government, and all other appurtenances commonly associated with the concept of a state were not "persons" in international law until admitted to the community.

BEGINNING OF THE COMMUNITY OF NATIONS    The end of the Thirty Years' War (1648) is generally held to mark the true beginning of the community of nations itself: the European states participating in the peace settlements at Münster and Osnabrück may be said to have constituted the charter members of a community that remained limited in the number of its members, even though occasional accessions were recorded. But until 1856 only Christian nations could join the group of states subject to the rules of international law. And from a geographic point of view, legal writers were concerned until the beginning of the nineteenth century about the *droit des gens de l'Europe* (the law of the nations of Europe), referring to all other states as *pays hors chrétienté* (countries outside Christianity). By the terms of Article 7 of the Treaty of Paris, the Ottoman Empire was admitted "to participate in the public law and system of Europe." Soon the various Balkan states followed suit, and by the end of the nineteenth century such non-European and non-Christian countries as Persia, Siam, China, and Japan had been admitted to the community. The current century witnessed a great expansion in the membership of the community, until today there are more than 150 states, and as yet there is in sight no closing of the gates.

LEGAL STATUS OF THE COMMUNITY    The legal status of the community has been the subject of much dispute among jurists. Beginning originally as a concept primarily moral in nature, the community achieved increasingly positive status. Newly admitted members were, and still are, bound at once and without choice by all generally accepted rules of customary international law; they were expected to adhere, in general, at their early convenience to the major law-making treaties in force. Their position was stated clearly by Secretary of State Daniel Webster as early as 1842:

Every nation, on being received, at her own request, into the circles of civilized governments, must understand that she not only attains rights of sovereignty and the dignity of national character, but that she binds herself also to the strict and faithful observance of all those principles, laws, and usages which have obtained currency among civilized states, and which have for their object the mitigation of the miseries of war.[1]

PROBLEMS POSED BY INTERNATIONAL ORGANIZATIONS    Several problems were posed for the community of nations by the creation first of the League of Nations and later of the United Nations. The basic concept of the League was a universal body, even though its initial membership was limited in number and though specific provision for withdrawal from the organization was inserted in its Covenant. Even though numerous countries were neither original nor subsequent members of the League, the admission of countries hitherto not regarded as full or qualified members of the family of nations was generally accepted by all other countries as evidence of admission into that family. The United Nations, has a current membership of 157 states and includes all of the major powers. (A number of states, such as Switzerland, Liechtenstein, Monaco, and Western Samoa, not members of the United Nations, must be regarded as full or limited members of the family of nations). On the other hand, two formal members of the United Nations, the Ukrainian and the Byelorussian republics, are not generally acknowledged to be independent states in the legal sense or in practice. They were admitted, even though they are merely components of the Soviet Union, in deference to power politics at the San Francisco Conference in 1945. On the other hand, both have been allowed to accede to such law-making conventions as the 1963 Vienna Convention on Consular Relations. But membership in a comprehensive international organization is not necessarily equal to membership in the family of nations, nor is the reverse true.

## MEMBERS OF THE COMMUNITY OF NATIONS

Who are the members of the community of nations? States, by definition, alone are eligible for such membership. Although certain international agencies, such as the European Coal and Steel Community and the United Nations, possess juridical personality through the treaties creating them, they are not "persons" in the meaning of being members of the family of nations.

### Fully Sovereign and Independent States

In order to be a legal person, a state must own to certain characteristics. It must, first of all, occupy a fixed *territory* over which it exercises exclusive jurisdiction. Within this territory, there must be *stability* of organization and administration, and the entity must be able to fulfill its international duties and obligations.

*Population* represents an obvious second characteristic of a state, for without it no government would be possible. An uninhabited island or Robinson

[1]Moor, vol. 1, 10.

Crusoe's island would represent territory but could not be a state without the presence of a population.

*Operation of a government* is a third characteristic of a state, for without it there could be no assurance of internal stability and the ability to fulfill international obligations.

A recent example of the absence of stability and of the absence of a really functioning government has been supplied by Lebanon. After more than 15 years of civil war, the legal government was still unable, at the time of writing, to operate along normal lines. Authority, such as it was, had been exercised by rival Christian and Moslem factions, the latter being supported by a 45,000-man Syrian "peacekeeping force." On October 3, 1990, the rebel Christian general Michel Aoun capitulated after heavy Syrian attacks and found refuge, with his family, in the French embassy in Beirut. Following a peace accord signed by the leaders of the main Shiite (Moslem) militias, greater control of portions of the country was made possible for the Lebanese army. By November 20, Moslem militia units began to evacuate Beirut. But the government of Lebanon did not enjoy true authority and some of its leading figures admitted that true independence and normal governmental authority were still in the future.[2]

Historically, Africa has been noted in recent decades for the frequency of governmental coups, attempted or successful. Between 1956 and 1986, for example, the continent witnessed 56 successful coups, with Nigeria leading all other African states with six coups since independence in 1960.

The presence of all three factors would not, however, necessarily guarantee the existence of a state in the legal sense. Puerto Rico, for instance, has territory, a government, and a population; yet it is not a state in the international-law meaning of the term, is not "person" subject to that law. It lacks the final and decisive requirement to be met by a state: *independence*. Unless a group of people possessing territory and governmental institutions also possesses independence—that is, the ability to regulate its internal affairs without outside interference or control—that group cannot properly claim to be a state. This necessary ingredient, independence, must be as absolute as the modern legal order of the world permits it to be: there must not be even nominal subordination to an outside governmental authority. And a state must possess the ability to enter into relations with other states.

Statehood, furthermore, means the possession of certain other characteristics. The state must be able to assume responsibility for actions taken by any of its members acting as agents or in some other official capacity.

In short, if a given entity has a territory, a population, a government operating effectively within the territory, independence from outside control, and specific international capacities, then it is a state in the true legal

---

[2]See *Time,* May 1, 1989, 46–47 and Oct. 29, 1990, 51; *CSM,* Oct. 19, 1988, 7, Feb. 1, 1989, 3, and May 11, 1989, 19. Also see AP Dispatches since May, 1990, particularly those of Oct. 14 and Nov. 6, 1990.

sense of the term. Once admitted, such a state is a full-fledged member of the family, or community, of states. Thus the United States, the United Kingdom, France, the Soviet Union, Denmark, Turkey, and scores of other countries are full members of the community. They are true international legal persons and represent in every way what are called *subjects of international law.*

## Unions of Sovereign States

In addition to these individual independent states, historical development has caused the appearance of what are commonly termed *composite international persons.* Such an entity comes into being when two independent states are linked in such a manner that they act internationally as a single unit. Two varieties of such composite units exist today: real unions and federal states. On the other hand, so-called personal unions and confederations are not international persons, except in regard to their individual components.

PERSONAL UNIONS    A personal union exists when two sovereign states are joined by possessing the same monarch. Examples are the union of Great Britain and Hanover from 1714 to 1837, that of the Netherlands and Luxembourg from 1815 to 1890, that of Belgium and the Congo Free State from 1885 to 1908, and, since 1931, each of the 49 members of the British Commonwealth of Nations in its relation to Great Britain (union through Queen Elizabeth II at the present time; she is, concurrently, queen of Canada and queen of England). It should be noted that several members of the Commonwealth no longer accept the British sovereign as their head of state but, instead, regard that sovereign as the symbol of a voluntary association (India, Pakistan, Malaysia, and others). These entities are, of course, not components of any personal union. On the other hand, the Commonwealth as such was granted observer status by the UN General Assembly in October 1976, thus joining such other observers as those of EEC (the European Economic Community) and the Palestine Liberation Organization.

In the case of personal unions, each state in question remains a separate and distinct person under international law. Theoretically the members of the union could even wage war against one another, unlikely as such a possibility would be. If, as has happened, the members of the union are represented in a given foreign capital by the same individual, that agent is the envoy of both states at the same time but not of the union itself.

CONFEDERATION    Confederations are encountered when a number of independent states are linked by treaty in a union with central governmental organs of its own, invested with specified powers over the member states but not over the citizens of those states. Such a confederation normally is not an international person: each of its member states remains a separate subject of international law. It may conclude treaties with other countries (provided such agreements do not prejudice the interests of the confederation as a whole), maintain its own diplomatic representation abroad, and act in virtually all respects as an independent nation. History has demonstrated repeatedly that this form of organization has not been very satisfactory, and in every modern instance a different structural form has replaced the original confederation—usually the federal form. The most prominent recent confederations have included that of the Netherlands from 1580 to 1795; the United States from 1778 to 1787; the German Confederation from 1815 to 1866; Switzerland from 1291 to 1798 and again from 1815 to 1848; the short-lived Confederation of the Rhine from 1806 to 1813; the United Arab Emirates, the Confederation of Senegambia (Senegal and The Gambia), 1982, dissolved in August 1989;[3] and the unusual parliamentary Arab Maghreb Union of 1989 (Algeria, Libya, Mauritania, Morocco, and Tunisia).[4] One of the briefest of all was the Republic of Central America, embracing El Salvador, Nicaragua, and Honduras from 1895 to 1898.

REAL UNIONS    A real union, on the other hand, comes into existence when two independent states are linked by treaty under the same ruler or government and henceforth act internationally as a single unit.[5] A real union therefore is not a single state but a union of two separate states acting as a single composite international person. Normally, under the treaty or constitution linking the components, they cannot wage war against each other or separately against a foreign state; they might conclude separate treaties of commerce or extradition, to cite two examples, but it would always be the union that would conclude the agreement on behalf of the individual members, because the latter no longer has the status of international persons. Modern history has seen several real unions: Austria-Hungary between 1867 and 1918, Denmark and Iceland from 1918 to 1944, Italy and Albania from 1939 to 1945,[6] the Swedish-Norwegian union from 1814 to 1905, and the creation of Tanzania by Tanganyika and Zanzibar in 1964. The members of a real union represent, without question, potential individual international persons and normally achieve that status as soon as the real union is dissolved. On December 1, 1989, (Marxist) South Yemen and (pro-Western) North Yemen announced agreement to merge into a single state, to be governed under a 136-article unity constitution. The merger, following legislative approval in both countries, took place on May 22, 1990. The new entity was styled the Yemeni Republic.

FEDERAL STATES    A federal state is a permanent union of several previously independent states, with governmental organs of its own and power over its member states as well as over the citizens of the latter. A federal state

---

[3]See 168 *National Geographic* (1985), 226–27; *CSM,* May 5, 1988, 7–8; and Miller, "Gambia Weathers Senegal Split," *CSM,* July 19, 1990, 8.
[4]*CSM,* June 13, 1989, 6. The 1989 agreement followed the 1986 Moroccan denunciation of a 1984 Libya-Morocco Union of States Treaty: 26 *ILM* 597 (1987), *CSM,* Sept. 7, 1984, 13.
[5]See Whiteman, vol. 1, 476–544.
[6]*Id.,* 366–68, 374–80.

is a real state, from the point of view of international law, primarily by virtue of the extensive authority exercised by the central government over the citizens of the separate member states. It is the federal state that alone is competent to declare war, make peace, and conclude international political or military agreements; none of the member states can participate in any of these activities, and none of them can be considered an international person in the meaning of that term. Domestic constitutional provisions may, on occasion, permit limited international activity to members of a federal state, as was the case under the German constitution of 1871 and now is true in the instances of Canada,[7] West- and now reunited Germany, Switzerland, and, theoretically, the USSR. Such privileges in the international sphere must, however, be regarded as abnormal. By all standards applied to international persons, members of a federal union are not persons under international law. It should be noted, too, that in all the instances cited above, the "international" powers of the units in question are severely limited in scope, extending normally only to cultural and educational questions.

Most federal states provide, in relevant constitutional documents, for complete and exclusive assumption of foreign relations by the federal central authority. This is particularly true in the case of the United States and those federal states whose constitutions were modeled on the American pattern. The most striking exceptions to the general rule are the already-mentioned Soviet republics of the Ukraine and Byelorussia. Neither entity can claim to be a state in the true sense, even though both enjoy the status of voting members in the United Nations, "participated" in the making of the satellite and Italian peace treaties in 1947, and formally acceded to a number of law-making treaties such as the Vienna Convention on Consular Relations.

Leaving aside the category of qualified full members of the community, full sovereignty is generally held to be a necessary condition of statehood and international personality. For example, Count 30 of the indictment charging the defendants before the Tokyo War Crimes Tribunal with waging aggressive war against the Commonwealth of the Philippines was set aside by the tribunal, which pointed out that from a legal point of view the Philippines had to be regarded as a part of the United States prior to its achievement of independence and that the aggressive war in question had been waged against the United States, not against a nonsovereign entity styled the Commonwealth of the Philippines.

### Qualified Full Members

In addition to fully independent and sovereign states, the community of nations includes a number of categories of states that have been termed qualified full members: neutralized states and states admitted to the community under conditions.

[7] See Fitzgerald, "Educational and Cultural Agreements and Ententes: France, Canada, and Quebec—Birth of a New Treaty-making Technique for Federal States?" 60 *AJIL* 529 (1966).

NEUTRALIZED STATES    A neutralized state differs from a neutral state in that the status of permanent neutrality (except for the obvious right of self-defense in the case of direct attack) is imposed on the neutralized state by a group of outside powers, whereas a neutral state voluntarily adopts its status at the outset of a conflict between other countries or even in peacetime, such as was done by Malta on May 15, 1981.[8] A neutralized state normally is also forced to agree not to enter into an alliance requiring its participation in any future conflict. The powers requiring its neutrality in turn obligate themselves to respect that status. The number of neutralized states has never been very large: Switzerland (since 1815); Belgium (1831 and 1839); Luxembourg (1867); the Ionian Islands (1836–1864); the Congo (1885); and, the latest, Laos (1962 to date). Both world wars saw violations of many guarantees extended to neutralized states, and it is doubtful whether any members of the community of nations can be regarded as remaining in this category except for Laos and Switzerland.

An interesting sidelight cast on the neutralized status of Switzerland was its admission into the League of Nations without being required to accept the obligations imposed on other members by Article 16 of the Covenant: in 1920 the League of Nations "recognized" the permanent neutrality of Switzerland. On the demise of the League, Switzerland decided not to become a member of the United Nations but does "participate" in the operation of the International Court of Justice. On March 16, 1986, Swiss voters rejected by a 3–1 margin a government-sponsored proposal to join the United Nations.

The neutralization of the small South Asian kingdom of Laos was accomplished by a fourteen-nation conference held in Geneva in July 1962. The final Declaration and Protocol, both dated July 23, 1962, marked the emergence of a neutralized state in an obvious attempt to prevent a further degeneration of an already explosive military and political situation in South Asia.[9]

Numerous writers have maintained that a neutralized state is not an international person equal in standing to fully sovereign states, because the right to go to war has been asserted traditionally as one of the characteristics of an independent state and because a neutralized state has been deprived of the free exercise of this right, except in direct self-defense. The present writer does not share this attitude and feels that a neutralized state is as sovereign as other states are. But because of the widespread belief that something of vital importance has been taken away through neutralization, this group of states usually is placed in the category of qualified full members of the community of nations. Two European states, Sweden and Finland, have voluntarily adopted permanent neutrality.

[8]See documentation in 21 *ILM* 396 (1982).
[9]On neutralized entities in general, consult Black *et al., Neutralization and World Politics* (1968); as well as Whiteman, vol. 1, 342–45; on Switzerland, see vol. 1, 345; on Austria, 348–55; on Laos, 355–57.

STATES ADMITTED UNDER CONDITIONS    A second grouping commonly encountered in this category comprises countries that were admitted into the community of nations under specific conditions, that is, under a formal engagement to adhere to certain rules or to fulfill certain promises imposed by the other members as a kind of price of admission. The theory behind this arrangement was that admission under conditions represented in no way a reflection of the sovereignty of the country in question, because the obligations assumed were embodied in the texts of formal treaties, entered into freely. Those conditions varied, of course, from case to case. When Montenegro was admitted into the community in 1878, special obligations regarding religious and racial toleration, maintenance of fortifications, and freedom of transit across the country were imposed by the Congress of Berlin. When the new states of Poland, Czechoslovakia, and Yugoslavia were admitted in 1919, special conditions concerning the treatment of various minority groups were imposed.

One of the most recent examples (admission under conditions but not of neutralization) was supplied by Austria after World War II. A treaty signed at Vienna on May 15, 1955, by the Soviet Union, the United States, the United Kingdom, and France on the one hand, and Austria on the other, reestablished an independent Austrian state.[10] The document contained a long list of conditions imposed by the four powers, including, among other matters, a prohibition on political or economic union with Germany, the granting of equal human rights, a prohibition of selected categories of weapons, and denial of the rights to use aircraft of Germany or Japanese design or assembly.

DIVIDED STATES    A peculiar phenomenon in the post-1945 world, reflecting a bipolar orientation of world politics, was the emergence of several states divided into two entities, each equipped with an operative government: Germany (Federal Republic and Democratic Republic), Korea (North and South), China (Republic of China and People's Republic), Vietnam (North and South), and Cyprus.

The legal status of the pre-1990 German subdivisions, particularly during the Allied occupations, represented one of the more complicated aspects of the international scene since 1945. In time, however, the two major units, the Federal Republic and the Democratic Republic, functioned as independent states, each ultimately recognized by over 100 nations.

A treaty designed to normalize relations between the two Germanys was ratified in June 1973. Both states became members of the United Nations in September of that year and on June 20, 1974, East and West Germany opened formal diplomatic relations with one another.

1990 witnessed a multitude of steps deemed necessary to reunite both Germanys. The Berlin Wall and other installations along their common

[10]Full text in 49 *AJIL* Supp., 162 (1955). Consult also Clute, *The International Legal Status of Austria 1938–1955* (1962).

border were opened and then removed; the West German currency became the common monetary unit for both; in July, the Federal Republic pledged to reduce the military forces of a united country to a maximum of 370,000 troops. In the same month, a West German–Soviet Union agreement approved membership of a unified Germany in NATO, withdrawal of Soviet troops from East Germany within three to four years, and renunciation by Germany of nuclear, chemical, and biological weapons.

On August 31, the two Germanys signed a treaty of almost 1,000 pages detailing the mechanics of reunification. Then (September 12) the foreign ministers of the Soviet Union, Great Britain, France, the two Germanys, and the US Secretary of State signed the "Treaty on the Final Settlement with Respect to Germany," including a German renunciation of war and a pledge to recognize Poland's 1945 western borders. The agreement also was to end the Allies' occupation rights on ratification in 1991.

The September 12th treaty removed the last obstacle to a unification of the two Germanys on October 3, 1990. A part of its implementation was represented by the withdrawal of East Germany from the Warsaw Pact military system on September 24, 1990.[11]

The history of the two Chinas followed a somewhat different course. After the flight of the Nationalist government to Taiwan, the United States continued to recognize that government as the lawful and only government of China and denied recognition to the People's Republic of China (see also Chapter 5). However, at the end of a visit by President Richard Nixon to mainland China, a joint communiqué was issued by the governments of the People's Republic and the United States (Shanghai, February 27, 1972), pledging a commitment by both to normalize their relations; this communiqué was reaffirmed by a second joint statement on February 22, 1973.[12]

Rapprochement was, however, not followed at once by formal recognition of the People's Republic by the United States. Instead, each country established (1973) a liaison mission at the ambassadorial level in the capital of the other. Finally, after prolonged secret negotiations, it was announced on December 15, 1978, that the countries in question had agreed to recognize each other as of January 1, 1979, and also to establish diplomatic relations. The United States, for its part, recognized the government of the People's Republic as the sole legal government of China. It was also agreed that on

---

[11] The literature on post-1945 Germany is enormous. For the pre-independence period of the western part, see von Glahn, 273–90; for later developments, consult Whiteman, vol. 1, 325–32, vol. 2, 787–99, 911-16, 969–83; from the copious press accounts of the events in 1990, see, *inter alia, Time,* July 20, 1990, 25; *NYT,* Sept. 1, 1990, 3; *CSM,* Sept. 4, 1990, 5; *id.,* Sept. 13, 1990, 3; and AP Dispatch, Sept. 13, 1990. See also Treaty Establishing a Monetary, Economic and Social Union, Bonn, May 18, 1990, in 29 *ILM* 1108 (1990), and Treaty on the Final Settlement with Respect to Germany, Moscow, Sept. 12, 1990, in *id.* 1186.

[12] Texts of communiqués in 11 *ILM* 443 (1972); and 12 *ILM* 431 (1973), respectively.

the same date, the United States would notify the government on Taiwan that it was withdrawing its recognition and that the Mutual Defense Treaty of 1954 between the Republic of China and the United States would be terminated in accordance with the provisions of that treaty, that is, at the end of 1979. Furthermore the United States would withdraw its remaining military personnel from Taiwan within four months. Formal diplomatic relations (exchange of ambassadors and establishment of embassies) commenced on March 1, 1979 (see also Chapter 5).

From a factual point of view, the Republic of China continued to exist as an independent entity, even though it is recognized by only 23 members of the family of nations. The United States government had taken pains to assure the authorities on Taiwan that nongovernmental relations between them and the United States would continue, through a corporation created in the United States for that purpose, and that shipment of "defensive" military supplies would be continued from the United States to Taiwan.

The People's Republic replaced the Republic of China as the representative of "China" in the United Nations on October 25, 1971, by action of the General Assembly. The United States had supported the admission of the People's Republic but had opposed an expulsion of the Republic of China. This "two Chinas" concept of membership had been rejected emphatically, however, by both Chinese governments before the General Assembly action took place.

The government of the Republic of Korea (South) had been accepted by the bulk of the then membership of the United Nations as the only lawful government of all of Korea, and by 1968 had been recognized by over 70 states. The People's Republic of Korea (North), on the other hand, had been recognized only by members of the socialist bloc. On October 12, 1972, both Korean governments began political conferences at Panmunjom, with the object of improving their mutual relations and seeking a reunification of their country. Both series of meetings soon lapsed, owing to increasing intransigence on the part of both sides. In May 1973, the People's Republic was admitted to membership in the World Health Organization, within weeks received observer status at the Geneva headquarters of the United Nations, and in June 1973, obtained observer status (enjoyed already for a long time by South Korea), at the UN New York headquarters.

By the end of July 1973, restarted discussions between the two Koreas had been abandoned again, but both governments vigorously denounced and opposed a "German solution" to their problems—each preferring to adhere to the concept of an eventual unification solution. Following the attainment of observer status by the People's Republic, both Korean governments resumed intermittent political discussions with no tangible results. In 1990, however, the two Koreas signed an agreement (July 26) setting up meetings between the prime ministers of the two entities. The 19-point document called for a meeting in Seoul on September 4–7 and another in Pyongyang on October 16–19. Predictably, the first meeting represented a mere exchange of points of view, with no detailed discussion of issues and problems. On September 13, both Koreas were reported to be in agreement that they would discuss another Northern demand: that the two states join the United Nations as a single member. The second round of talks (Oct. 17–19, 1990) also ended without formal agreement.

From a legal point of view, the July agreement signed by North Korea represented a tacit recognition of the legitimacy of the South Korean government. It should be noted that the Korean War (1950–53) ended without a peace treaty and that the two states are technically still at war. [13]

The Republic of Vietnam (South) and the Democratic Republic of Vietnam (North) both emerged in 1954 as independent states, despite the provisions of the 1954 Geneva Agreements. Each division had an operative government and the normal attributes of sovereignty, and each enjoyed recognition by many countries. For a time, each had to be regarded as a full member of the family of nations. However, after the United States had ended its war with North Vietnam and had withdrawn from the South, the latter's government soon fell victim to attack from the North, and on July 3, 1976, the two parts of Vietnam were officially reunited. The capital of the North, Hanoi, became the capital of the new Socialist Republic of Vietnam. The United States government had used its veto repeatedly to bar UN membership for the two Vietnams, but after Vietnam had been reunited, the new entity was formally admitted to the United Nations on September 21, 1977.

A coup in 1974, led by Greek army officers and aimed at a union of the island with Greece, led five days later to a Turkish invasion of the northeastern part of Cyprus. Soon about 38 percent of the island was in Turkish hands, which meant that the 18 percent Turkish ethnic element of the population was cut off from the central government. Protection was provided by (currently) 20,000 Turkish troops. Over the years, many ethnic Greek Cypriots fled or were forced to leave the northern sector, and allegedly some 50,000 Turkish citizens were brought from the mainland to alter the demographic character of northeastern Cyprus. Gradually political institutions developed in what was called the "Turkish Federated State of Cyprus," and on November 15, 1983, the Turkish-Cypriot legislative body unilaterally proclaimed independence of the "Turkish Republic of Northern Cyprus." The entity was recognized promptly by Turkey, but no other state has followed suit.

The Turkish and Turkish-Cypriot actions violated a number of UN resolutions adopted beginning in 1974, notably the General Assembly resolution of May 13, 1983 calling for the withdrawal of Turkish forces from the island. On November 18, 1983, the Security Council passed a resolution deploring the "purported secession," declaring the self-proclaimed repub-

[13]See Whiteman, vol. 1, 320–25; *U.S. News & World Report,* Aug. 20, 1990, 41; *Time,* Sept. 17, 1990, 60; Jones, "Thaw Begins in Korean Cold War," *CSM,* Sept. 4, 1990, 3 and Oct. 31, 1990, 5; AP Dispatches, July 26 and 27, 1990.

lic to be legally invalid, calling for the withdrawal of the declaration of independence, and asking all states not to recognize the new entity.

After lengthy secret and indirect negotiations through UN Secretary-General Pérez de Cuéllar, a draft agreement to settle the dispute between the two communities was worked out in late 1984. The scheme provided for reunification in a federal republic of Cyprus, with a Greek president, a Turkish vice-president, and two legislative houses: in the Assembly the Greeks would have 70 percent and the Turks 30 percent of the seats, while in the Senate the seats would be divided on a 50-50 basis. The Turkish sector was to return 8 percent of Cyprus' land area to the Greek community, after which the northern unit would comprise 29 percent of the island's total land area. But four key elements of a lasting settlement remained to be negotiated: (1) the line of demarcation between the Turkish portion and the Greek-Cypriot portion (that is, what sections would be returned to the latter); (2) definition of such rights as to move, to own land, and to settle on the island; (3) withdrawal of the Turkish troops from Cyprus; and (4) the nature of international guarantees, if any, to protect whatever settlement would be achieved. When the heads of the two entities met in January 1985 at the United Nations in New York, it developed that the leader of the Turkish Cypriots was ready to sign the preliminary agreement of 1984 while the President of Cyprus maintained that the meeting had been called to negotiate the four points mentioned above, for those questions had to be settled before any agreement could be signed. At that point the talks collapsed.[14]

## The City of the Vatican

The listing of members of the community of nations would be incomplete if the State of the City of the Vatican were not included.[15] Most of the questions that had plagued relations between the Holy See and Italy since the extinction of the Papal States in 1870 were resolved by the Lateran Treaty of 1929. That agreement recognized the State of the City of the Vatican as a sovereign and independent state occupying 108.7 acres in Rome. The independence of the Vatican was again upheld in July 1987 when the Italian Court of Cassation voided arrest warrants against Archbishop Paul Marcinkus, head of the Vatican Bank, and two other senior Vatican bank officials, all charged with being accessories to fraudulent bankruptcy in the Italian Banco Ambrosiano scandal. The Court ruled that the 1929 Lateran Treaty protected "central bodies" of the Church from "every interference" by the Italian government.

Most unusual, however, was the unilateral declaration issued by the Vatican, stating that the country wished to remain aloof from the worldly riv-

[14] See AP Dispatch, Nov. 19, 1983. On May 11, 1984, the Security Council again passed a resolution condemning the Turkish Cypriots for their secession and urged them to repeal their declaration of independence.

[15] See Lauterpacht's *Oppenheim,* vol. 1, 250–55, and Whiteman, vol. 1, 587–93.

alries of other states, except when parties to a dispute called unanimously on the Vatican to assist in arriving at a peaceful solution. That declaration, laid down in the 1929 Lateran Treaty with Italy, is the reason for the unique position occupied by the City of the Vatican in the community of nations. It is true that as the ideological conflict between communism and the free world deepened in intensity and extent, the Vatican state took an active part in that struggle. But in regard to the "normal" rivalries of states for territory, power, and military advantages, the Vatican has observed its self-imposed abstention.

There cannot be any doubt that the Lateran Treaty and the subsequent recognition extended to the Vatican State by many countries admitted a new member into the community of nations. Today over 100 states maintain diplomatic relations with the Vatican, proof of its wide acceptance.

The Vatican State has worldwide interests and carries on many activities on a global basis; it is a member of at least one major international organization (the Universal Postal Union) and maintains a small accredited observer mission (with a staff of fourteen) at the United Nations in New York. All in all, the state represents a special type of member of the community of nations and is, therefore, normally listed separately from the other categories of full and qualified members.

A second special subject of international law, yet not really a member of the community of nations, is the Sovereign Military Order of the Knights of Malta. Founded in the days of the Crusades as the Order of St. John, it was engaged in the care of the wounded and the sick. Its original seat was in Acre; then it was moved in 1291 to Cyprus and, in 1310, to the island of Rhodes. In 1522 the Turks drove the Order from that location, and in 1530 Malta became the seat of the organization, leading to its present name. After Malta had been occupied by French forces in 1798 and had been annexed in 1800 by Great Britain, the Order had no state territory of its own and moved to Rome, where, today, its headquarters occupy about one large city block. The Knights of Malta, with a membership of about 8,000, operate hospitals and other medical facilities in many parts of the world. The Order maintains diplomatic relations with the City of the Vatican and with some 25 countries, mostly located in Latin America. It also concluded postal agreements with 10 countries and has been recognized as a (landless) sovereign nation by some 40 countries. In view of its special status, the Order can be classified as a nonstate subject of international law, although of a somewhat peculiar nature.

DWARF STATES    Three small countries in Europe are commonly joined in the category of dwarf states: Liechtenstein (62 sq. miles), San Marino (24 sq. miles surrounded by Italy), and Monaco (0.73 sq. mile). They represent curious legacies of the past, anachronistic survivals from conditions prevailing in the seventeenth century, strangely out of place in a world of superpowers, nuclear weapons, and space satellites. Until recently none of the little countries could be said to participate to any real extent in the international relations of the world, but in the past decade or so, Liechtenstein, Monaco, and to some extent San Marino have emerged from their relative seclusion, have sent capable and active delegates to a number of international conferences, and have signed and ratified a surprisingly large number of conventions, thus demonstrating their right to be called, at the very least, limited members of the community of nations.

The existence of extremely small and thinly populated political entities, such as the Maldive Islands (115 sq. miles, 179,000 people), Dominica (290 sq. miles, 74,000 people), Kiribati (266 sq. miles, 63,000 people), Tuvalu (10 sq. miles, 8,600 people) and Nauru (8 sq. miles, 8,000 people) poses few political problems as yet, but it has complicated the membership problem of the United Nations. The issue of these "ministates," more of which are expected to come into being, led to a warning, in 1967, by the UN Secretary-General that a line would have to be drawn somewhere before most of these entities attempted to join the United Nations.[16] But nothing has been done thus far about the matter. Western Samoa elected not to join the organization but created an arrangement under which the former colonial power, New Zealand, was to represent Samoan interests in the United Nations, leaving Western Samoa free to join its specialized agencies whenever membership might appear desirable. However, the prospect of many additional small member states in the United Nations persists. The obvious solution—barring ministates—has been deemed politically undesirable. Hence hopes have been expressed by various UN delegations that small political units in the Caribbean and elsewhere would be granted self-government in the form of groupings under an arrangement (with the present colonial or protecting power) that would permit them to opt for group independence at a later date.

CONDOMINIUMS    A territory jointly governed by two or more states is called a *condominium*. Modern history has produced a surprisingly large number of such entities,[17] two of which are still in existence today. The best known of all was the Anglo-Egyptian Sudan, under the joint control of Egypt and Great Britain between 1889 and 1956, in which latter year the Sudan emerged as an independent state. The international Régime of the Tangier Zone was abolished by treaty on October 29, 1956, and the zone was integrated into Morocco.

[16]*NYT* Dec. 24, 1967, 22; May 29, 1966, 53; and April 13, 1969, 27.
[17]Schleswig-Holstein (Prussia and Austria, 1864–1866); Samoa (Great Britain–USA–Germany, 1889–1900); the New Hebrides (Great Britain–France, 1906–1980); the Anglo-Egyptian Sudan (Great Britain–Egypt, 1889–1956); Tangier (Great Britain–France–Spain–Portugal–Belgium–The Netherlands–Italy, 1923–1956); Albania (International Commission, 1913–1914); the Saar (International Commission under the League of Nations, 1919–1934); Leticia (International Commission under the League, 1933–1934); Memel (Allied Conference of Ambassadors, 1919–1923); the Île des Faisans (France–Spain, 1856 to date), and a few others.

In the Southwest Pacific, the island group of the New Hebrides had been under joint Anglo-French administration since 1887. Under the Condominium Treaty of 1906, the native population was placed under two resident commissioners, one British, the other French. The condominium became independent, as scheduled, under the name of Vanuatu, on July 30, 1980 (5,700 sq. miles, est. population: 136,000).

Europe contains two condominiums. The Île des Faisans (Isle of Pheasants) is located near the mouth of the Bidassoa River, which forms the common frontier between Spain and France for a distance of seven miles to the Bay of Biscay. Under treaties concluded in 1856 and 1901, the two countries police the island in turn for periods of six months, and individuals committing offenses in the condominium are subject to their respective national authorities.

Andorra, located between France and Spain, has been a political entity since A.D. 1278 but must be listed among condominiums because technically it is ruled by two coprinces: the head of state of France and the Spanish prince-bishop of Urgel and Andorra. Actual government is, for the most part, in the hands of a general council, elected by the citizens of the condominium.

Condominiums are not members of the community of nations: they play no active part in international relations, have no governments of their own, and do not possess any vestige of national sovereignty.

MANDATES    Article 22 of the Covenant of the League of Nations established a system of "mandates" whereby a form of international supervision was created for certain colonies and territories formerly under German or Turkish sovereignty. The areas in question had been detached from their legal owners after the defeat of the Central Powers in World War I, but this action had not been followed by annexation in view of wartime promises to refrain from seeking territorial aggrandizement or to grant full independence to certain Turkish territories. The concept underlying the mandate system was that the well-being and development of the areas in question constituted a trust of civilized nations and that these territories should be placed under the tutelage of advanced states, subject to the supervision of the League of Nations, on whose behalf they were to be administered. [18]

Because the areas under mandate had arrived at varying stages of development, three separate groupings were devised. The A mandates consisted of former subdivisions of the Ottoman Empire, all deemed to have reached a stage of development at which independence could soon be granted. These areas were provisionally recognized as states, subject to a temporary system of administrative control and assistance by a mandatory power having limited authority within its assigned territory. All of the Class A mandates have achieved independence by now.

[18]On the mandate system as a whole, see Whiteman, vol. 1, 598–731.

The Class B mandates consisted of all but one of the former German colonies in Africa. Unlike the Class A mandates, the territories in this second group did not have any degree of international personality. They were administered separately from the neighboring colonies of the mandatory power, subject to restrictions and regulations embodied in the terms of the mandate instrument. All former Class B mandates are now independent or have been joined to other African entities.

The third group, styled Class C mandates, comprised the former German South-West Africa and all former German colonies in the Pacific. These territories, because of the smallness of their populations, their remoteness from the centers of civilization, or their relative backwardness, were administered under the laws of the mandatory power as integral portions of its own territories, subject to protective safeguards for the indigenous population, again embodied in the terms of the mandate agreement. All but a portion of one of the former Class C mandates have achieved independence: the Republic of Palau being the exception.

TRUST TERRITORIES    Ten then non-independent Class B and Class C mandates, with the exception of South-West Africa, were placed under the trusteeship system of the United Nations in 1946–1947 through bilateral agreements concluded between that organization and the former mandatory powers. The United States was substituted for Japan as trustee for the former German colonies in the Pacific north of the equator. In addition, the former Italian colony of Somaliland was transformed into a trust territory, and Italy, though not a member of the United Nations, was appointed its trustee.

SOUTH-WEST AFRICA (NAMIBIA)    The League of Nations had placed the former German colony of South-West Africa as a Class C mandate under the legal supervision of South Africa, to be administered under the laws of the mandatory state "as integral portions thereof subject to . . . safeguards . . . in the interests of the indigenous population" (League of Nations Covenant, Art. 22, par. 6). After the dissolution of the League in 1946, South Africa claimed that that act had also ended the mandate, refused to continue the submission of the required annual report, and made it clear that South Africa was contemplating the annexation of South-West Africa. It also refused to enter into a trusteeship agreement with the United Nations. It appears reasonable to assume that the refusal was based on a desire to set aside such protective safeguards as could be required of a trustee so that South Africa's racist policies (*apartheid*) could be applied in the territory.

For subsequent developments to the achievement of independence by Namibia (South-West Africa), see the Case Study at the end of this Chapter.

TRUST TERRITORIES    Trust territories under the United Nations never had any international personality. The trustee represented the trust territory for any possible international relations and at the same time assumed any possible international duties and obligations on behalf of the territory.

Under the provisions of Articles 82 and 83 of the United Nations Charter, specific parts or all of a given trust territory could be designated as a strategic area. If this was done in any trusteeship agreement, supervision of the administration of the affected area was transferred from the Trusteeship Council to the Security Council. Only one trustee took advantage of this arrangement: the trust territory administered by the United States was classified as a strategic trust territory. The basic difference between the two types was that in a strategic trust area, the administering state could close off certain areas for security reasons and could construct military bases. [19] However, if one of the permanent members of the Security Council should administer a trust territory, the latter became a strategic area or trust territory and, as such, fell under the authority of the Security Council, in accordance with Art. 83, par. 1, of the U.N. Charter. That paragraph provides that "[a]ll functions of the United Nations relating to strategic areas, including the approval of the terms of the trusteeship agreements and of their alteration or amendment, shall be exercised by the Security Council." It should be noted that the Security Council had left the routine supervision of the American trust territory to the Trusteeship Council; the authority to make major decisions, such as on termination, does appear to have been reserved by lack of specific delegation. [20]

Excluding South-West Africa (Namibia), one U.N. trust territory remained: the U.S. Trust Territory of the Pacific Islands, east of the Philippines. It was composed of 2,141 islands and atolls, with some 150,000 inhabitants on 100 of the islands. The islands were later grouped in four districts: the Northern Mariana Islands, the Marshall Islands, Micronesia, and Palau.

Beginning in about 1969, discussions among the islanders and between them and the U.S. government started the process leading to eventual termination of the strategic trust system. In 1975, a "Covenant" was signed between a U.S. negotiator and the chairman of the Northern Mariana Political Status Commission, which provided for self-government under a locally adopted constitution, with U.S. responsibility for defense and foreign affairs. The Covenant was then ratified in June 1975 by a plebiscite of the islanders and approved by the U.S. Congress in March 1976. After a constitution had been drawn up and approved in the islands, President Carter proclaimed acceptance of the instrument. A similar process was followed in the case of a second grouping, the Federated States of Micronesia, and also of the Republic of the Marshall Islands. Only the Republic of Palau lagged behind in this process, for it proved to be temporarily impossible to secure

[19]See Trusteeship Agreement for the Former Japanese Mandated Islands, approved by U.N. Security Council April 2, 1947, United States July 18, 1947, 61 Stat. 3301, TIAS No. 1665, 8 UNTS 189.
[20]See the important heavily documented argument to this effect in Clark, "Letter to the Editor in Chief," 81 *AJIL* 927 (1987).

a required majority in the plebiscite on the Covenant involved. The major cause of the repeated failure was the inclusion of provisions permitting the United States to store nuclear weapons on the main island of the group.

In May 1986 the UN Trusteeship Council concluded that the United States had satisfactorily discharged its obligations under the Strategic Trust Agreement and that the trusteeship system in the Northern Marianas, Micronesia, and Marshall Islands was to end. In consequence, President Reagan proclaimed (Nov. 3, 1986) that the three Covenants mentioned above were in effect, but that the United States would continue to act as the Administrative Authority in the Republic of Palau under the Trusteeship Agreement until the process of ratification by plebiscite had been completed. The terminology used to designate the three new entities was interesting: the Commonwealth of the Northern Mariana Islands, in political union with and under the sovereignty of the United States, was the formula adopted. Foreign affairs and defense were reserved for the United States in all three cases.

It should be noted that the government of the United States had failed, in the case of the three island groups, to receive (or ask for) the approval of the UN Security Council. A number of writers have held that such approval was required by Article 83 of the UN Charter (see above). Despite the American failure to have termination of the trusteeship for the three island group, the new entities appear to function as planned. In any case, the Republic of Palau remains, at the time of writing, the last remnant of the strategic trusteeship system.[21]

ASSOCIATED STATES    Before leaving the "state" section on the subjects of international law, a new category in that group should be mentioned: associated states. This modern terms refers to an entity which has delegated certain governmental functions (primarily foreign affairs and or defense) to a "principal state" while retaining, in contrast to the now vanished Protectorate, its *international* status: it is still regarded as a member state by the other components of the family of nations.[22] In the Pacific area just discussed, the Federated States of Micronesia, the Commonwealth of the Northern Marianas, and the Republic of the Marshall Islands appear to fall within the category of Associated States.

REBEL MOVEMENTS    Liberation and rebel movements have figured repeatedly in various delegations' attempts to be seated at international gatherings restricted to members of the community of nations. A typical instance took place at the beginning of the 1974 Conference on the Rules of War,

[21]For the covenants, see the texts in 14 *ILM* 344–78 (1975); also see "Trust Territories," in 81 *AJIL* 405–8 (1987), and "Diplomatic Relations" in 84 *AJIL* 237 (1990); Novak, "Micronesia Wrestles with Red Tape on Road to Real Independence," *CSM*, Feb. 4, 1987, 32, and Kluge, "Palau isn't sure whether 'Paradise' is there—or here," 17 *Smithsonian*, Sept. 1986, 44–54.
[22]Hannum and Lillich, "The Concept of Autonomy in International Law," 74 *AJIL* 858, 859 at n. 13 (1980).

convened by Switzerland in Geneva. A delegation from the then rebel-controlled portion of Portuguese Guinea (now Guinea-Bissau) was seated, but representatives of liberation movements, including the Vietcong Provisional Government in South Vietnam, had to be content with observer status — which, nevertheless, represented recognition of their existence.

The same year, 1974, witnessed a remarkable rise in status of the Palestine Liberation Organization (PLO) when the UN General Assembly voted 105 to 4 (with 20 abstentions) to invite the PLO as the representative of the Palestinian people to participate in the deliberations of the Assembly on the question of Palestine. The General Assembly also granted the PLO observer status at the United Nations and in 1975 at the UN Food and Agriculture Organization's governing conference in Rome. In January 1976, the Security Council opened its debate on Middle Eastern questions by voting to permit the PLO to participate in the discussions with the rights of a UN member. Inasmuch as the issue was termed a procedural question, the lone opposing vote of the United States could not prevent the temporary seating of the PLO. Later in 1976, the PLO was accepted as a new member of the developing nations Group 77 at the UN Conference on Trade and Development held in Manila and was accorded observer status by the International Labor Organization. On September 6, 1976, the PLO was granted full voting membership in the Arab League. All these activities enhanced greatly the status of a liberation movement, even though many analysts and not a few governments harbored serious doubts as to whether the PLO should really be regarded as the true representative of the Palestinians and whether the traditional status of rebels should be altered as was done in the case of the PLO. More recently (December 1988), the General Assembly changed the name of the observer delegation from "PLO" to "Palestine," and a month later the Security Council, by an 11–1 vote, granted the mission a status almost equal to that of a regular UN Member by permitting it to address the Council directly. Up to that time, this could be done only through the sponsorship of a UN Member. (See also Chapter 5 concerning Austrian and Indian "recognition" of the PLO and Chapter 16, Case History No. 7A concerning the United States attempt to close down the PLO observer mission at the United Nations.)

INTERNATIONAL ORGANIZATIONS    Public international organizations — that is to say, agencies established for state purposes by states — do have in some instances a definite international personality, with powers of negotiation, of concluding binding international agreements, of appearing as plaintiffs or defendants before international tribunals, and, recently, of being able to claim immunity from legal process for defined categories of their officials in the same manner as for accredited representatives of members of the community of nations. A number of these organizations must be regarded as international persons, notably the United Nations (see Chapter 7).

The legal character of the League of Nations was the subject of much scholarly disagreement. Most jurists held that it did possess a minimum of corporate capacity: it supervised the administration of mandated territories; it concluded certain agreements with its host state, Switzerland; it administered its own properties; and it concluded contracts as a corporate body. But beyond these minimal aspects of international personality, the League's proponents could not show convincing evidence that the organization was much more than an international agency with limited objectives.

The position of the United Nations has been wholly different since its inception: it possesses a definite international personality, even though it is not a state. It should not be included in the membership of the community of nations, but as an international legal person, it falls under the definition of international law given in Chapter 1.

By deliberate intention, identified as an effort to avoid real or fancied defects in the League Covenant, numerous articles in the UN Charter (Arts. 24, 26, 41, 42, and 104) specifically outline both the legal powers and the responsibilities of the United Nations and, incidentally, spell out its status as an international legal person.

The European Community (EC), founded in 1967, unites three earlier entities: the European Economic Community (or Common Market), the European Coal and Steel Community, and the European Atomic Energy Commission. The European Community (EC) is authorized to conclude binding agreements with both nonmember countries and international organizations. The European Economic Community is capable of making regulations binding its member states as well as industrial concerns operating within its functional sphere. The EC, the Economic Community, and the Coal and Steel Community all have the status of international legal persons, but all three are limited in their international capacities.

The powers conferred on some of these organizations can no longer be said to be merely powers or rights of the separate member states, and thus it was only logical to grant legal status as subjects of international law to the agencies exercising those powers.

✿ STATUS OF TRIBES    Tribes in North America and elsewhere were at one time held by a few writers to be equivalent to international persons. States, on the other hand, usually denied such status to tribes, and agreements made with them were subsequently often (and quite unfairly) denied the character of binding treaties, regardless of the nomenclature applied to the original agreement at the time of its conclusion. Tribes do not constitute members of the community of nations.[23]

[23] In an effort to promote the interests and welfare of tribes and certain indigenous peoples, the International Labour Organisation adopted in June 1989 its Convention No. 169: Convention concerning Indigenous and Tribal Peoples in Independent Countries. The text of the instrument to be ratified by the member states of the agency is reproduced, with a Background/Content Summary, in 28 *ILM* 1382 (1989).

## SUGGESTED READINGS

### Special Problems

Sereni, "The Status of Croatia Under International Law," 35 *APSR* 1144 (1941); Eagleton, "The Case of Hyderabad Before the Security Council," 44 AJIL 277 (1950); Clough, "Taiwan's International Status," 141–59 in Hungdah, ed., *Occasional Papers/Reprints Series in Contemporary Asian Studies* [School of Law, Univ. of Maryland], (1981); Gambia-Senegal: *Agreement and Protocols Concerning the Establishment of a Senegambian Confederation* (Dakar, Dec. 17, 1981), 22 *ILM* 260 (1983).

Hendry and Wood, *The Legal Status of Berlin* (1987); Haas, "Independence Movements in the South Pacific," 11 *Pacific Viewpoint* 97–119 (1970); MacDonald, "Secession in the Defence of Identity—The Making of Tuvalu," 16 *id.* 26–44 (1975); Necatigil, *The Cyprus Question and the Turkish Position* (1989); Crawford, *The Creation of States in International Law* (1989); van Praag, *The Status of Tibet: History, Rights, and Prospects in International Law* (1987).

### Ministates

Elmer Plischke, *Microstates in World Affairs: Policy Problems and Options* (1977).

### The Trusteeship System

Whiteman, vol. 1, 731–911, and vol. 13, 679–99; Armstrong & Hills, "The Negotiations for the Future Political Status of Micronesia (1980–1984)," 78 *AJIL* 484 (1984); Armstrong, "The Emergence of the Micronesians into the International Community," 5 *Brooklyn J. Int'l L.* 207 (1979).

### The Community in General

CASES

*The Helena,* Great Britain, High Court of Admiralty, 1801, 4 Ch.Rob.3.

*Principality of Monaco* v. *Mississippi,* U.S. Supreme Court, 1933, 291 U.S. 643 and 292 U.S. 313.

*The Indonesia Case,* Security Council of the U.N., July 31–August 1, 1947, in 3 *United Nations Bulletin* 215 (1947).

*Nationality Decrees Issued in Tunis and Morocco,* Advisory Opinion, P.C.I.J., 1923, Ser. B, No. 4.

*Diggs* v. *Dent,* U.S. District Court, Dist. of Columbia, 1975, in 14 *ILM* 797 (1975).

*Diggs* v. *Schultz,* U.S. Court of Appeals, Dist of Columbia, 1972 470 F.2d 461, reported in 67 *AJIL* 547 (1973).

### Associated States

CASES

*Morgan Guaranty Trust Co.* v. *Republic of Palau,* 639 F. Supp. 706, U.S. Dist.Ct., S.D.N.Y., July 10, 1986, reported in 81 *AJIL* 220 (1987).

*Bank of Hawaii* v. *Balos,* 701 F. Supp. 744, U.S. Dist. Ct., D. Haw, Dec. 12, 1988, reported in 83 *AJIL* 583 (1989).

# Case Study No. 1

# Namibia

During the twentieth century, a multitude of colonial territories changed into independent and self-governing entities. This phenomenon was duplicated in the sometimes very intricate process of achieving independence by trusteeship territories. That development was illustrated strikingly by the example of Namibia (South-West Africa), which included questions of international law, of title to territory, of international diplomacy, of nationalism, and of self-determination.

In 1946, over strong South African objections, the UN General Assembly sought to extend the new trusteeship system to South-West Africa. The South African authorities continued to administer the territory as they had done in the past under the League of Nations mandate. But they also began, gradually, to introduce their own racial policies (*apartheid*) into the territory.

In 1949 the General Assembly requested the International Court of Justice (hereafter ICJ) to render an advisory opinion on the legal status of South-West Africa. The Court held unanimously that the extinction of the League had not affected the administration of the territory. It also held that the General Assembly and the ICJ had to be judged to have assumed the functions of the League and its judicial organ in regard to the mandates, and that, furthermore, South Africa lacked the authority to change by itself the legal status of South-West Africa. On the other hand, the Court held, by a 8–2 vote, that South Africa was not obliged to place the territory under the UN Trusteeship Council.[1]

A 1959 resolution of the General Assembly's Fourth Committee, approved by the parent body, had recommended that individual members initiate legal action against South Africa. This suggestion was carried out by Ethiopia and Liberia, who claimed that, notwithstanding the continuation of the mandate and South Africa's continuing obligations under the League Covenant and Article 22 of the mandate, South Africa had violated its obligations

---

[1]*International Status of South-West Africa* (Advisory Opinion), *I.C.J. Reports, 1950*, 128, digested in 44 *AJIL* 757 (1950). A subsequent Advisory Opinion on the *Admissibility of Hearings of Petitioners by the Committee on South-West Africa, I.C.J. Reports, 1956*, 23, digested in 50 *AJIL* 954 (1956), declared that the UN Committee on South-West Africa (created by the General Assembly in November 1953) could grant oral hearings to petitioners on matters relating to the territory in question.

(no submission of required annual reports, introduction of *apartheid*). In December 1962, the ICJ ruled that it possessed jurisdiction.[2]

The International Court of Justice handed down its second judgment, on the merits as distinguished from the admissibility of the claims, on July 18, 1966.[3] It rejected the claims of the applicants by holding that they could not raise the issue because they lacked a substantial legal right or interest in the claims. It held that the Mandatory Power was responsible for its conduct only to relevant international authorities. Hence, the Court ruled (by the President's casting vote, the rest being divided equally) that it was unnecessary to give a ruling on the merits of the cases, even though the Court had had to consider the substance of the dispute in order to decide on the validity of the claims.

The 1966 judgment dismissing the claims of the applicant states produced much criticism, including a 129-page dissent by the United States judge Philip C. Jessup. He pointed out the extraordinary change in the court's views: in three previous advisory opinions and in its judgment of 1962, the court had never deviated from its conclusion that the mandate survived the dissolution of the League of Nations and that South-West Africa was still a territory subject to the mandate. By its 1966 judgment, however, the court had, in effect, decided that the applicants had no standing to ask the court even for a declaration that the territory was still subject to the mandate.[4]

In the same year, the Southwest Africa People's Organization (SWAPO), seeking an independent South-West Africa to be called Namibia, started a guerrilla war of independence against South Africa—a conflict to last until 1989.

Adjudication having failed, the 36 African members of the United Nations proceeded to embrace political action through termination of the mandate over South-West Africa and transfer of legal control to the General Assembly as the relevant organ of the United Nations. On October 27, 1966, the General Assembly, by its Resolution 2145 (XXI), ended the mandate and asserted that henceforth South-West Africa constituted a direct responsibility of the United Nations.[5]

On May 19, 1967, the General Assembly decided, by a vote of eighty-five to two, with thirty abstentions, to create an eleven-member council (UN Council for Namibia) to assume control over the territory from South Africa.[6]

[2] *South-West Africa Cases (Ethiopia v. South Africa; Liberia v. South Africa), Preliminary Objections. I.C.J. Reports, 1962*, 6, digested in 57 *AJIL* 640 (1963).
[3] *South-West Africa Cases (Ethiopia v. South Africa; Liberia v. South Africa), Second Phase. I.C.J. Reports, 1966*, 6; digested and excerpted in 61 *AJIL* 116 (1967). Consult also the searching analysis by Katz, *The Relevance of International Adjudication* (1968), 69–103.
[4] See the excellent analysis by Kahn, "South Africa II: South West," *The New Yorker,* Feb. 3, 1968, 32–74, *passim.*
[5] Text of G.A. Res. 2145, 21 GAOR, Supp. 16 (A/6316) in 61 *AJIL* 649 (1967).
[6] Resolution 2248 (S-V); consult also the detailed study by Dugard, "The Revocation of the Mandate for South West Africa," 62 *AJIL* 78 (1968), and Whiteman, vol. 13, 756–68.

By the fall of 1967, no United Nations control over South-West Africa had been achieved. The international status of the territory was reasserted, however, by the General Assembly in a resolution condemning illegal application of the "Terrorism Act" to South-West Africa (December 16, 1967)[7] On the same day, the General Assembly adopted Resolution 2325 (XXII), confirming its earlier decisions on the termination of the mandate and assumption of control by the United Nations, calling on the government of South Africa to withdraw militarily and administratively from the former mandate and urging all member states to take effective economic measures against South Africa to bring about such withdrawal.

The Security Council entered into the South-West Africa dispute by its Resolution 245 (January 25, 1968). Noting the pertinent General Assembly resolutions and condemning the refusal of South Africa to comply with Assembly Resolution 2324 (XXII) relative to the trial of certain indigenous inhabitants of the territory, the Security Council invited all member states to "exert their influence" to induce South African compliance.[8]

Elsewhere, but related to the South-West African developments, a new government in Portugal granted independence to Angola (1974) and a civil war started almost immediately between the Marxist MPLA government of the former colony, the Front for the National Liberation of Angola (FNLA), and the Union for the Total Independence of Angola (UNITA). The UNITA group had fought the Portuguese in colonial days and now opposed the new government of Angola. The latter received assistance in the form of troops from Cuba, advisers from North Korea, and matériel from the Soviet Union. South Africa sent matériel to UNITA, and the United States supplied the latter with weapons and other supplies.

On July 29, 1970, the Security Council requested (Res. 284) an advisory opinion by the International Court of Justice regarding the legal consequences for states of the continued presence of South Africa in Namibia (since termination of the mandate, the United Nations has referred to South-West Africa as the "International Territory of Namibia") despite Security Council Resolution 276 (1970). The court's advisory opinion was delivered on June 21, 1971. It held that, South Africa's continued presence in Namibia being illegal, it was obligated to withdraw its occupation of the territory immediately; that member states of the United Nations were obligated to recognize South Africa's illegal presence and to refrain from any dealings with South Africa implying recognition or support of the latter's presence and administration in Namibia; and that nonmembers of the United Nations should

---

[7]G.A. Resolution 2324 (XXII), text in 62 *AJIL* 488 (1968). See also the statement by U.S. Ambassador Goldberg, *id.*, 488–93, as well as Dugard, "South West Africa and the 'Terrorist Trial', " 64 *AJIL* 19 (1970).
[8]Text in 62 *AJIL* 759–60; see also Security Council Res. 246 (March 14, 1968), text in *id.*, 764–65, and its Res. 309 (1972) in 11 *ILM* 436 (1972).

give assistance to all action taken by the United Nations with regard to Namibia.[9]

In view of the wording and content of the Advisory Opinion of June 21, 1971, the Mandate of South Africa for South-West Africa was revoked lawfully by the General Assembly; hence the presence of South Africa in the territory had been illegal since October 27, 1966.

In 1977 the then Western members of the Security Council (the United Kingdom, Canada, France, the United States, and the Federal Republic of Germany—collectively termed the Western Contact Group) began an intensive effort to bring about an acceptable peaceful transition from the then current status of Namibia to independence. Those efforts led (September 1978) the Security Council to adopt its Resolution 435 (1978), which called for a cease-fire in the continuing guerrilla war between SWAPO and South Africa, for U.N.-sponsored elections, and for a "Transition Assistance Group" in Namibia. South Africa did hold elections under its own auspices, after which some governmental functions were transferred to an interim white administration and a collection of white and black "entities of limited legitimacy."[10] The elections were ignored by SWAPO and the outside world; the new interim government was condemned by the Security Council in a resolution also calling for new sanctions against South Africa (June 20, 1985).

Details of the future policies to apply to Namibia in accordance with Resolution 435 were then developed in the course of numerous consultations among South Africa, SWAPO, the Western Contact Group, and the so-called "front-line states" (Angola, Botswana, Mozambique, Tanzania, Zambia, and eventually Zimbabwe).

Military considerations must be considered to have complicated the search for an acceptable solution to the Namibian problem. The United Nations had planned sending 7,500 troops of the United Nations Transitional Assistance Group (UNTAG) to the territory in order to replace South African forces and to supervise elections under United Nations' auspices. Instead, South Africa maintained a military presence in Namibia and asserted repeatedly that its troops would be pulled out only when a Cuban contingent estimated at 50,000 men had been removed from neighboring Angola. It was this linkage of Cuban withdrawal to a South African pullback that prevented further meaningful steps to a Namibian solution. Angola, in turn, asserted that it needed the Cuban contingents in order to protect itself against the UNITA guerrillas allegedly backed by South Africa. Military confrontation was at times replaced by South African incursions deep into Angola, notably in December 1983. The UN Security Council, which had

---

[9]*Legal Consequences for States of the Continued Presence of South Africa in Namibia (South West Africa) Notwithstanding Security Council Resolution 276 (1970)*, (Advisory Opinion of June 21, 1971), *ICJ Reports*, 1971, 16, in 66 *AJIL* 145 (1972).

[10]Text of Res. 435 in 28 *ILM* 950 (1989). See also Rotberg, "Namibia is no Afghanistan," *CSM*, April 28, 1988, 13.

passed numerous resolutions since 1977 on the Namibian problem, adopted still another one on January 6, 1984, calling for South African withdrawal from Angola; in response, the South African foreign minister stated that his country would repel actual or threatened attacks on Namibia from any source, regardless of world opinion. South Africa then began to pull back its forces from their deepest points of penetration in Angola and an informal armistice came into being. In the middle of February 1984, the United States met with South Africa and Angola and committed itself to participating in the supervision of a formal cease-fire. The United States supplied a small staff of seven for a liaison office in Windhoeck, and a joint commission of Angolans and South Africans began to monitor the troop disengagement. The commission eventually moved fifty miles into Angola. South Africa had agreed to end all military activities in Angola while the latter had agreed to keep Cuban and SWAPO units north of a specified line of demarcation. By June 15, 1984, however, the South African pullback stopped because of alleged failure on the part of Angola to keep SWAPO forces out of the Angolan zone being vacated by the South Africans. In June, too, South Africa proffered a new plan: it would cede control over Namibia to France, West Germany, the United Kingdom, Canada, and the United States, singly or collectively, thereby circumventing all UN plans for the independence of Namibia. When that scheme was rejected immediately, South Africa promptly came up with another plan: that the SWAPO would assume control over the territory but that key positions in that interim government would be reserved for representatives of six South Africa-supported "internal" parties. In July, 1984, South Africa and SWAPO representatives held unsuccessful talks about ending the conflict along the Angolan-Namibian border. In October, the President of Angola stated that he had agreed to work with the United States Government for Namibia's independence but warned that South African withdrawal from Angola and independence for Namibia had to precede arrangements for the departure of Cuban troops from Angola. Then, on October 31, 1984, representatives of the United States and South Africa met in the Cape Verde Islands and discussed the Namibian problem, considering the statements of the Angolan President as well as details of a proposed Angolan peace plan, transmitted to South Africa via the United States. That plan included, *inter alia,* a three-year phased Cuban withdrawal from Angola.[11] In February 1985, the United States announced the closing of its liaison office. And after several meetings in the Congo between U.S. and Angolan delegations, Cuban representatives for the first time took part in the negotiations as members of the Angolan group.

Angola, South Africa, and Cuba, with the United States acting as mediator, then started, after numerous preliminary talks, discussion on the withdrawal of all foreign troops from both Angola and Namibia (June 24, 1988).

[11]See *CSM,* Nov. 27, 1984, 13, 15 (Angola's peace plan).

The forces in question comprised between 45,000 and 50,000 Cubans in Angola and 20,000 to 25,000 South African and auxiliary troops in Namibia and southern Angola. A tentative accord was reached on July 13, linking the withdrawal of the Cuban troops to the implementation of the 1978 Security Council resolution (Res.435-1978, Sept. 29, 1978) calling for independence for Namibia. [12] South Africa agreed to November 1, 1988 as the date for that independence, provided agreement would be reached on the withdrawal of the Cuban troops from Angola.

On August 8, 1988, South Africa, Angola, and Cuba announced that with mediation by the United States they had agreed on an immediate cease-fire in Angola and in Namibia, asserting that "a *de facto* cessation of hostilities is now in effect."[13]

All parties also agreed on November 1, 1988, as the date for implementation of Resolution 435, withdrawal of South African forces from Angola, and the establishment of a Joint Military Monitoring Commission along the Angola-Namibia border. SWAPO, in turn, announced the stoppage of all combat operations on September 1, 1988, if South Africa would observe a cease-fire. [14]

One can only speculate about the reasons South Africa "capitulated" in 1988 and not earlier, say in 1968. Several or all of the following factors may have led to a change in policy:

(a) Increasing political pressure brought to bear by the Western Contact Group, especially by the United States;
(b) The relatively mild but increasingly real effects of U.S. sanctions on the South African economy;
(c) Continuing condemnation of both *apartheid* and the control over Namibia by the UN General Assembly as well as by neighboring African states;
(d) The continuing sizable costs of South Africa's military campaigns in Angola and Namibia.

In November 1988, in Geneva, the three parties agreed on a timetable for, among other things, the "phased and total" withdrawal of the Cuban troops. In December, the parties approved the "Brazzaville Protocol" proposing April 1, 1989, as the new date for implementing Resolution 435 and establishing December 22 as the date for the formal signing of a tripartite agreement between Angola, Cuba, and South Africa. [15] Angola then signed a separate agreement covering the withdrawal of the Cuban forces: by April 1, 1989, not more than 47,000 Cuban troops would remain; half of the remainder were to be withdrawn by November 1, 1989, and the rest by July 1, 1991. By August 1, 1989, all Cuban troops had to be stationed

[12] Text in the valuable U.S. Dept. of State, *Southwestern Africa Regional Brief* (Dec. 1988) 5.
[13] *NYT,* August 9, 1988, at 1 and 4.
[14] *Id., loc.cit.*
[15] Text in 28 *ILM* 951 (1989).

north of the 15th Parallel. The first phase of this scheme was carried out by January 20, 1989, by which time 3,000 troops had left Angola by sea or air.

April 1, 1989 was also the date on which Resolution 435 became operative, and by then the first units of the Transitional Assistance Group (UNTAG) had moved into Namibia. UNTAG's basic functions were to maintain order and to supervise elections to be held for a representative assembly. U.N. Secretary-General Javier Perez de Cuellar had planned on sending a contingent of ultimately 7,000 troops, but was limited to a total of some 6,150 peacekeepers, including 4,650 soldiers, 500 police supervisors, and a minimum of 1,000 civilian election monitors. About 1,200 of the armed UNTAG contingent were in place when the transition period began on April 1, 1989.[16] Among the countries scheduled to supply military units were Australia, Finland, Malaysia, and Kenya.

Once "free and fair" elections had taken place on November 1, 1989, full independence was scheduled when the elected assembly adopted a new constitution for Namibia. The withdrawal of the Cuban troops from Angola was to be verified by a Security Council–approved U.N. Angola Verification Mission (UNAVEM) of 70 members, deployed at Angolan ports and airports.

It should also be mentioned that none of the agreements mentioned or Security Council Resolution 435 required immediate or even early withdrawal of South African forces from Namibia. Such withdrawal was thought to be in stages related to the removal of Cuban troops from Angola. In fact, however, by July 1989, the South African forces in Namibia had been reduced from 15,000 to 1,500 men confined to a few designated bases. The last units withdrew to their own country on November 23/24, 1989.

It will have been noted that the United States was not a party to the 1988 Tripartite Agreement, but after its role as mediator was expected to play an important part in the future of Namibia as a member of the Security Council and as an observer in the Joint Monitoring Commission mentioned earlier. On the other hand, UNITA also was not a party to the Tripartite Agreement, and its estimated 50,000 guerrillas were free to continue their civil war with the Angolan government until the latter would agree to negotiate arrangements for sharing power.

Returning to Namibia: On March 31, 1989, the United Nations' special representative (a former Finnish diplomat) arrived in Namibia to advise South Africa's interim administrator-general on carrying out the plans for Namibian independence. On April 1, an official cease-fire between SWAPO and South Africa took effect and SWAPO became a legal political party. However, less than 24 hours later a SWAPO force from Angola invaded Namibia and relatively heavy fighting developed between the invaders and South African security forces. During a six-day period, 263 guerrillas and

[16]See 28 ILM 986 (1989).

27 members of the security forces were reported to have been killed. The incursion caused a suspension of the demobilization of the territorial forces (South African-led Namibian security forces) scheduled for completion by the middle of May. Finally the leaders of SWAPO ordered its guerrillas to cease fighting and to withdraw to their bases in Angola (April 8, 1989), and one day later South Africa agreed to safe passage for the SWAPO units. According to plan, the nearly 2,000 guerrillas in question were to be sent to camps in northern Namibia under UNTAG control. After being disarmed, they were to be ordered back to Angola north of the sixteenth Parallel. In fact, however, most of the SWAPO soldiers slipped into Angola at night.

On May 13, *apartheid* was abolished officially in Namibia, although the central pension system and many local services remained segregated until their abolishment could be made a reality.

In view of the fact that the pre-independence Namibian bureaucracy was predominantly South African, the United Nations had established in 1976 the United Nations Institute for Namibia (UNIN) in Lusaka, Zambia. The Institute was intended to train students (about 300 in September 1989) during two- to three-year courses in social services, teaching, law, management, and administration. The graduates were expected to form the nucleus of a Namibian bureaucracy after independence. By the fall of 1989, some 1,500 Namibians had graduated from UNIN: some 200 were reported to have gone on to do graduate work in the West, others to be temporarily employed by various African governments or were said to be acting as SWAPO diplomatic representatives. The bulk of the graduates, however, stayed in refugee camps in Angola and Zambia, pending a return to Namibia.[17] The funding of UNIN was reported to be sufficient until 1991, when the new Namibian government was to decide whether or not to continue the Institute in Namibia.

Another significant step taken in the rebuilding of the former South-West Africa was the first (June 1989) airlifting of refugees to their home country from Angola and Zambia. The total cost of bringing back refugees was then estimated at $39 million. And in September, hundreds of detainees returned to Namibia from former SWAPO prison camps in Angola.

Also in September, the UN Secretary-General, under pressure from numerous African states, agreed to increase UNTAG's civilian police contingent by 500 to a total of 1,500 officers.

As the time of the elections approached, observers began to forecast a victory for SWAPO, especially because of that group's close identification with the dominant Ovambo tribe. The latter accounted for about 60 percent of the 1.4 million total population.

[17] See the detailed coverage of UNIN in Swenarski, "Future Leaders Learn Next-Door," *CSM*, Sept. 7, 1989, 12–13.

On the first election day (November 7, 1989), 10 political groups composed of more than 40 political parties began to compete for the two-thirds majority in a 72-seat Constituent Assembly that was to write Namibia's constitution. That majority was to be elected on the basis of proportional representation from the seven parties winning the most votes. The major opponent of SWAPO was the Democratic Turnhalle Alliance, favoring private enterprise and a capitalistic economy; it had been part of the transitional government. The election saw a very high degree of voter participation: 97 percent of the 701,483 registered voters cast ballots. SWAPO gained 41 of the 72 Assembly seats, with 57.3 percent of votes cast (95 percent in Ovamboland). The Turnhalle Alliance won 21 seats, the rest of the latter being scattered among minor groups. SWAPO therefore had to make accommodations with others to gain the 48 Assembly seats required for approval of the constitution.

By the end of 1989, the Constituent Assembly had agreed in principle on a democratic Western-style constitution. The final draft was cleared well in advance of the target date for independence, April 1, 1990. Actual independence came on March 21, 1990, with the new President being sworn in the next day by the UN Secretary-General. On April 23, 1990, Namibia became a member of the United Nations, and on September 11 the General Assembly decided to dissolve the Council for Namibia. That body had "administered" the territory before independence.

One other, somewhat complicated problem should be mentioned: the fate of Walvis Bay. The area in question (800 square miles), inhabited by some 25,000 people, contains the only deep-water port in South-West Africa. It had been a British colonial possession since 1878 and later became a part of the Cape Colony. The latter in turn became the Cape Province of South Africa. In 1922 the enclave was transferred to the administration of the authorities ruling South West Africa, as if part of the mandate. Then, in June 1977, South Africa proposed to retain the enclave, regardless of the mandate's future. It announced, over strong protests by SWAPO and others, that as of September 1, 1977, the Walvis Bay area would cease to be administered by South-West African authorities and would revert to the administration of the Cape Province.

South Africa's case rested primarily on the undisputed fact that the British ownership of the Walvis Bay enclave had preceded the establishment of German colonial rule over the rest of South-West Africa: never having been a part of the German colony, it had never been a part of the mandate. On the other hand, Namibia's constitution lays claim to the enclave.

The Western countries involved in promoting Namibian independence in the 1970's had agreed to leave the status of Walvis Bay to post-independence negotiations between Namibia and South Africa. At the time of this writing, such negotiations appear to be close to reality.

## CASE STUDY NO. 1: SUGGESTED READINGS

A complete collection of documents covering developments on Namibia's road to independence and in achieving peace in the region for the period July 20, 1988– May 19, 1989, is found in 28 *ILM* 944 (1989); One of the best concise accounts of the coming of Namibian independence is US Dept. of State, Bureau of Public Affairs, *Southwestern Africa Regional Brief: Namibia: A Nation is Born* (March 1990).

See also Berat, *Walvis Bay* (Decolonization and International Law), 1990; Battersby, "Democracy Takes Root in Namibia," *CSM,* Sept. 12, 1990, 6; his "Namibia's Combatants Seek New Role in Society," *CSM,* Sept. 17, 1990, 6; and his "South Africa, Namibia Try for Walvis Bay Settlement," *CSM,* Sept. 21, 1990, 4.

# 5

# Recognition of States and Governments

## RECOGNITION IN GENERAL

The term *recognition* means "a formal acknowledgment or declaration by the government of an existing state that it intends to attach certain customary legal consequences to an existing set of facts, which, in its view, justify it (and other states) in doing so."[1] Normally recognition has a more specialized meaning in international law, relating to the acknowledgment of the existence of a new state or a new government in an existing foreign state, coupled with an expression of willingness by the recognizing state to enter into relations with the recognized entity or government. Recognition is also used with reference to belligerent communities or insurgents, in connection with the validity of title to territory (for example, recognition of conquest) and, lastly, with reference to the commission of acts by governments (see Chapter 7, under "State Immunity").

Despite much reasoned argument to the effect that the recognition of new states (and new governments) is a legal matter, the majority of writers as well as the practice of states agree that it is, rather, *a political act with legal consequences*.[2] This is demonstrated convincingly by the dependence of national courts on executive recognition policy. On the other hand, definite and important legal effects sometimes also tinged with moral overtones, result from the political act.

The basically political character of the act of recognition was demonstrated convincingly in 1988, after the Palestine National Council, the "legislature" of the Palestine Liberation Organization (PLO), declared on November 15, 1988, the independence of the "State of Palestine." That entity was devoid of a defined territorial jurisdiction and an identified and functioning government.[3] Its alleged population lived in part under Israeli occupation and

---

[1] Kaplan-Katzenbach, 109.
[2] See Whiteman, vol. 2, 5–13, 21, 24–26.
[3] This should be accepted as correct, despite a TV-news report on April 2, 1989, to the effect that the Palestine National Council had named Yasser Arafat president of the Palestinian State, to hold office until free elections could be held in the territories currently occupied by Israel.

in part in various Arab states (often in refugee camps). It therefore lacked an authority exercising effective control of that population. Nevertheless the State of Palestine was "recognized" within two days by 23, and by January 7, 1989, by about 70 governments. In some instances, recognition fell short of the traditional format: on November 18, 1988, the Soviet Union announced that it [r]ecognizes the proclamation of the Palestinian State," a formula also utilized by Czechoslovakia. On the other hand, the PLO opened (January 1, 1989) the "Embassy of Palestine" in Riyadh in a building donated by the king of Saudi Arabia, and a number of states had upgraded PLO missions to embassy status (Jordan, Iraq, Algeria, Bahrain, and the United Arab Emirates); China and Qatar announced that they would follow suit.

In summary, the basic function of recognition ought to be acknowledgment as fact something that has been uncertain up to then, namely, some community's possession of statehood. When such recognition is granted, it indicates the willingness of the recognizing state to accept the consequences of its act and to enter into normal relations with the recognized state. A duty to recognize new states cannot be demonstrated convincingly, despite many ingenious attempts to do so.

## FORMS OF RECOGNITION

Recognition of a state or government is said to be *express*, or *explicit*, when a formal statement is issued by a recognizing state. It is *implied*, or *tacit*, when a state enters into official relation with a new state or government by sending a diplomatic representative to it, acknowledges or salutes its flag, communicates officially with its chief of state, concludes an agreement with it, or otherwise, by deed, takes note of its existence as a state. However, in all such instances, there must be a clear indication of intent to recognize the state or new government, otherwise the implied recognition will be deemed to have been lacking. This would be true, for instance, if only technical contacts by lower-level government personnel were involved.

Thus the United States, though it had not recognized the *government* of the People's Republic of China, dealt directly with that government from 1955 through the arrangement of over one hundred "ambassadorial talks," originally held in Geneva, from 1958 to 1968 and in 1970 in Warsaw and in 1972 in Paris.[4] Participants were the Chinese and American ambassadors accredited to Poland, later those accredited to France. The U.S. government had indicated repeatedly that no intent to recognize the People's Republic of China should be construed from the fact that talks were under way. Then on February 22, 1973, the United States and China announced the forthcoming establishment of official government liaison offices in Washing-

[4]Consult Kenneth T. Young, "American Dealings with Peking," 45 *Foreign Affairs* 77–87 (1966), and his *Diplomacy and Power in Washington–Peking Dealings: 1953–1967* (1967); as well as the documentary material in Whiteman, vol. 2, 551–55.

ton and Peking in order to hasten normalization of relations between the two countries, and in late May 1973, those offices came into being. Official recognition took place on January 1, 1979.

Other examples of *relations officieuses* in the absence of formal recognition abound in modern international relations: the United States successfully mediated the settlement of the Angola–South Africa conflict (see Chapter 4) despite the fact that the U.S. had not recognized the Angolan government since Angola's independence, followed by an official visit by the U.S. Assistant Secretary of State for African Affairs to discuss future bilateral relations (June 1989). Again, the Holy See (the Vatican) occasionally deals with the State of Israel despite the failure to "recognize" the latter.[5] Such dealings take place through a mission headed by an Apostolic Delegate lacking diplomatic (ambassadorial) status.

Explicit recognition, on the other hand, was exemplified by the announcement on the same day (January 10, 1984) by the United States and the Vatican that they had reestablished formal diplomatic relations after a lapse of 117 years. From 1797 to 1867, the United States stationed a consul, a *chargé d'affaires*, or a "minister resident" at the papal state. The U.S. Legation remained closed from 1867, but in 1939 a personal representative was appointed by President Franklin Roosevelt. After President Harry Truman failed to gain Senate approval for his ambassadorial nominee, there was no regular contact with the Vatican until President Richard Nixon recreated the post of personal representative—a position devoid of diplomatic status. Following Senate approval (March 7, 1984), the United States sent an ambassador to the Vatican and the latter was represented in Washington by an Apostolic Pro Nuncio (if the papal envoy were a cardinal instead of an archbishop, his title would be Nuncio). In 1982, Great Britain, Denmark, Norway, and Sweden all restored full diplomatic relations with the Vatican after a 400-year hiatus; at the time of writing, 107 states recognized the Vatican State.

## RECOGNITION OF STATES

A state comes into existence when the community involved acquires the basic characteristics associated with the concept of a state: a defined territory, an operating and effective government, and independence from outside control. Because all these aspects of statehood involve ascertainable facts, the dating of the beginning of a new state is merely a question of fact and not law. The new state exists, regardless of whether it has been recognized by other states, when it has met the factual requirements of statehood.

The establishment of the new state of Israel on May 14, 1948, was followed within a few hours on May 15 by a statement from President Truman that read:

[5]See G. Iran, "The Vatican and the State of Israel," 19 *The Link*, August/Sept. 1986, 4, 13–14.

This government has been informed that a Jewish state has been proclaimed in Palestine, and recognition has been requested by the provisional government thereof. The United States Government recognizes the provisional government as the *de facto* authority of the new state of Israel.

That statement represented *explicit* recognition both of the new state and of its government. To have recognized the state alone would have represented a manifest absurdity (*de jure* recognition followed on January 31, 1949). On the other hand, the U.S. action could well be regarded as a case of *premature* recognition because the characteristics listed above could not have been verified or did not exist at the time of the presidential statement.

The reasons for the decision to recognize a new state vary, of course, from case to case. Commercial considerations may play a part; other factors of importance may include the number of states that have already extended recognition, domestic political repercussions, the possibility of enlisting the new state as a military ally, humanitarian motives, and so on.

NONRECOGNITION OF STATEHOOD    Most writers agree that nonrecognition of an existing state represents a rather ineffectual political measure. The disadvantages resulting from nonrecognition are numerous, including the fact that the legitimate interests of one's citizens cannot be protected adequately in the unrecognized state. The latter cannot have access to the courts of the state refusing recognition, but on the other hand, it is also immune from suit in those same courts.

There is, of course, no requirement to recognize a new state. The U.S. State Department outlined the factors in recognizing statehood when it supplied to the press on November 1, 1976, a statement of the criteria applied by the United States in deciding whether or not to recognize a new state:

In the view of the United States, international law does not require a state to recognize another entity as a state; it is a matter for the judgment of each state whether an entity merits recognition as a state. In reaching this judgment, the United States has traditionally looked to the establishment of certain facts. These facts include effective control over a clearly-defined territory and population; an organized governmental administration of that territory; and a capacity to act effectively to conduct foreign relations *and to fulfill international obligations*. The United States has also taken into account whether the entity in question has attracted the recognition of the international community of states. (Italics added. See "Subjective Test" for comment on the italicized portion.)[6]

Thus far there appear to have been several instances of what could be termed *collective nonrecognition*, that of Manchukuo and that of Transkei and other Bantustans. On February 24, 1933, the Assembly of the League of Nations adopted a resolution stating that its members would not recognize

[6]71 *AJIL* 337 (1977).

the new state of Manchukuo either *de facto* or *de jure*. The League then created an Advisory Committee to counsel members on any measures to be taken by them as a result of the joint decision not to recognize the new state.[7] On October 26, 1977, Transkei declared its independence from South Africa, and on the same day, the UN General Assembly passed by a vote of 134 to 0 (with the United States as the only abstaining member) a resolution declaring the independence invalid and denying recognition to the new entity.[8]

COLLECTIVE RECOGNITION    It has often been asserted that a state may be formally recognized through the collective action of a number of other states. Virtually every instance cited, however, could be shown to represent individual recognition of a new state, granted either simultaneously or within a very short interval of time by several other states. The frequently mentioned case of the recognition of Estonia by the League of Nations represents an excellent illustration of the fact that admission into an international organization does not mean collective recognition by the organization's members.

The establishment of the United Nations was followed by similar claims of collective recognition, but no change in the situation can be shown to have taken place. Admission of a state into the United Nations does not mean that the other members of the organization have to grant the new member access to their courts, exchange diplomatic representatives with it, or in any other manner deal with the new member as a recognized state outside the United Nations. The latter "does not possess any authority to recognize either a new State or a new government of an existing State."[9]

DEFACTO RECOGNITION    At times an effort has been made to compromise between the desirability of admitting that a community is in fact a state and continuing doubts as to whether a community, under prevailing conditions, is "legally" a state. The resolution of the conflict between these ideas often takes the form of *de facto* recognition, as opposed to acceptance of *de jure* statehood. In other words, a provisional recognition takes place.

From a logical as well as a practical point of view, *de facto* recognition is objectionable. The community in question either is or is not a state. Hence, many writers condemn what has been termed "the bastard institution of so-called '*de facto*' recognition, according to which the [states] can deal with a

---

[7]See Hackworth, vol. 1, 333–38 (1940). Eventually Manchukuo was recognized by Japan, Germany, Italy, Hungary, Poland, the Soviet Union, Thailand, the Vatican, and a few other states.

[8]"Resolution on the So-Called Independent Transkei and Other Bantustans," G.A. Res. 31/6, 31 U.N. GAOR, Supp. (No. 39) 10, U.N. Doc. A/31/39 (1977). See *NYT*, October 27, 1977, 1, 9; as well as Witkin, "Transkei: An Analysis of the Practice of Recognition — Political or Legal?" 18 *Harvard Int'l Law Jl.* 605 (1977). Transkei's subsequent five fellow "nonstate" Bantustans (Bophuthatswana, 1977, Venda, 1979, Ciskei, 1982, and others) have likewise failed to win recognition except by each other, South Africa, and Zimbabwe.

[9]Secretary-General Trygve Lie, March 8, 1950. See also Aufricht, "Principles and Practices of Recognition by International Organizations," 43 *AJIL* 679 (1949), and Whiteman, vol. 2, 563–67.

perfectly independent community as a state while refusing to it the rights of a State."[10]

The expressions "recognition of a *de facto* state," "recognition of a *de facto* government," and so on are preferred. As Whiteman pointed out, "In prevailing practice, when the United States extends recognition, it is recognition *per se,* not *'de facto'* recognition."[11]

In particular, recognition of a belligerent community would be more acceptable than *de facto* recognition of a rebel community (or authority). In fact, it would be a recognition of a *de facto* community or authority.

BELLIGERENT COMMUNITIES AND INSURGENTS    Certain communities, seeking to achieve independence from a parent country or to secure control of the entire state for a rebel government, lack statehood and yet occupy, after the initiation of hostilities, territory extensive enough to remove the conflict from the characteristics of a purely local uprising. Frequently the hostile actions in question impinge on the interests of other countries, and it becomes desirable to have the laws of war apply to the situation described.

When this point is reached in the development of a rebellion, other states may grant to the community a limited measure of international personality by recognizing a status of belligerency and by terming the group a belligerent community.[12] Obviously the rebellious community cannot obtain its limited standing by its own desire or proclamation. Recognition of a status of belligerency by other states is necessary for the legal creation of that status. Such recognition takes place frequently through express proclamation to the effect that a given community is recognized as a belligerent community. Regardless of the method adopted, however, the fact that belligerency has been acknowledged requires treatment (by the other countries in question) of the community as a state engaged in war and, on the other hand, imposes on that community responsibility for all violations of the laws of war and for the treatment of foreign property and alien persons. Normally the warships of the belligerent community are treated as belligerent warships and are granted the right of visit and search.

Among recent examples of this special kind of recognition was the announcement by the governments of France and Mexico (August 28, 1981) that they officially recognized a coalition of Salvadoran left-wing groups as "a representative political force" with which to deal in attempts to end the civil war in El Salvador. "A spokesman for the Mexican Foreign Ministry said the statement was a *political recognition* of the opposition groups but does not imply a break with the government of El Salvador."[13] (Emphasis added)

[10]Baty, "Abuse of Terms: 'Recognition'; 'War'," 30 *AJIL* 377, 378 (1936).
[11]Whiteman, vol. 2, 3–4; see also Cochran, "De Facto and De Jure Recognition: Is There a Difference?" 62 *AJIL* 457 (1968).
[12]See Whiteman, vol. 1, 930-46, for examples.
[13]*International Herald Tribune* (Paris), August 29/30, 1981, at 1.

The latest resort, at the time of writing, to this kind of government action was reported in the press on April 7, 1989, when administration sources revealed that the President of the United States had selected a special envoy to the Afghan rebels fighting the Soviet-supported government in Kabul. It was emphasized at the time that this step fell short of formal recognition of the Afghan government-in-exile. The appointment was said to carry the rank of ambassador, but the person chosen was to be based in Washington and was to travel frequently to the region. The United States had closed its embassy in Kabul soon after the Russian military withdrawal, but formal diplomatic ties with the Kabul government had not been severed.

On the other hand, the United States, fearing a Khmer Rouge victory, ended recognition of rebels fighting the Cambodian government backed by Vietnam (July 18, 1990). Instead, the United States opened talks with Vietnam.

A belligerent community lacks the right to send or receive diplomatic agents, to join international organizations, and to benefit from multilateral conventions concerned with peacetime international relations and activities of states.

The recognition of belligerent communities posed, in the past, many of the more perplexing problems connected with recognition. Traditionally, certain conditions had to have been satisfied if recognition was to be extended to a rebel group or territory: (1) a government and military organization had to have been established and be operative in the rebel-controlled area; (2) the rebellion had to have reached a stage beyond mere local revolt— that is, a condition of warfare equivalent to conflicts between states had to have developed; (3) the rebel government had to in fact control a reasonable portion of the territory of the parent state (domestic revolt) or overseas territory (colonial revolt).

The degree to which these conditions have been met is determined by out-side states. If the conditions have been satisfied, then the recognition of the rebels as a belligerent community is lawful. When recognition takes place, then the rules of international law regarding warfare and neutrality come into force, and furthermore, the parent state is freed from all international responsibility for the acts of the rebels from the inception of the revolt. This last statement holds true, however, *only* if the parent government has made some attempt, implied in the second condition above, to assert its authority over the rebels. One of the most recent instances of the recognition of a belligerent community occurred in June 1979, during the then 19-month-old civil war in Nicaragua. The so-called Andean Group (Bolivia, Colombia, Ecuador, Peru, and Venezuela) declared that "a state of belligerency" existed in Nicaragua and that the forces of the Sandinista National Liberation Front (FSLN) represented a "legitimate army." That declaration then permitted the members of the Andean Group to supply the rebels with weapons and other supplies without violating the numerous Latin American (and general international law) prohibitions against illegitimate intervention in the domestic affairs of a country. Just before the Andean Group's action, the rebels had announced the formation of the "Provisional Junta of the Government for National Reconstruction."

Earlier well-known examples of the recognition problem discussed here occurred when Great Britain, within only 30 days after the outbreak of the Civil War in the United States, recognized the Confederate States as belligerents, and when the United States failed to recognize the belligerent status of the rebels in Cuba as late as December 7, 1896.[14]

If the lawful government recognizes the rebels as a belligerent community, a foreign state is free to grant or withhold the same recognition. If the foreign state withholds recognition, then it has to refrain from assisting the rebel group but is free to grant or withhold aid to the lawful government. In fact, unless the foreign state wishes to enter the conflict, it will withhold, after its recognition of belligerency, all aid to both sides in the conflict under way.

If the lawful government does not recognize the rebels as a belligerent community, a foreign state also is free to grant or withhold such recognition. If it fails to recognize a state of belligerency, the foreign state must abstain from all assistance to the rebels but is free to assist the lawful government.[15]

Recognition of belligerency is not synonymous with recognition as a state, as the belligerent community is still legally an integral part of the state against whose government it is conducting hostilities. Statehood in the legal sense can be acquired by the community only if and when it succeeds in its enterprise, either by achieving independence or replacing the lawful government of its state by its own chosen representatives. Until such success is recorded, the belligerent community possesses only limited, temporary aspects of an international personality.

In contrast, a rebellion that has not yet achieved the standing of a belligerent community is said to be a state of *insurgency,* a condition described as intermediate between internal tranquillity and civil war. Recognition of insurgency is to be viewed primarily as a domestic matter by other states, because it normally entails issuing a proclamation calling public attention to the existence of an insurgent group in a foreign country and cautioning the public to exercise due caution regarding travel, business relations, and other dealings with and in the area in question. Such a proclamation of a state of insurgency does not correspond to the recognition of a belligerent community and does not create rights under international law for the rebellious group involved.

An insurgent group represents a transitory phase in an unstable political situation: either the rebels are quickly subdued by the lawful government

---

[14] See the analysis by the Supreme Court in the case of *The Three Friends,* 166 U.S. 1, 57, 63 (1896).

[15] See Lauterpacht, *Recognition in International Law* 124, (1947).

of their country or they develop their activities to the point that they gain stature as a belligerent community, with rights and obligations accruing from recognition of this status by foreign countries.[16]

PREMATURE RECOGNITION    Recognition of a belligerent community should be viewed as premature and illegal if the conditions listed above have not yet been met by the community at the time of its recognition. France's recognition of the United States in 1778 was undoubtedly premature and was soon followed by an expected declaration of war by Great Britain against France. Recent decades have repeatedly seen instances of this kind, such as when India recognized the Bangladesh rebels as the legal government (of the state of East Pakistan) on December 6, 1971, whereas East Pakistan first declared its independence on March 25, 1972. Other recent examples of premature recognition include that of Biafra (Nigerian Civil War) by Tanzania, Gabon, the Ivory Coast, and Zambia in 1968 and by Haiti in 1969, as well as the granting of embassy status to the National Liberation Front (South Vietnam) mission in Peking by the People's Republic of China in December 1967.

On March 13, 1980, the chancellor of Austria, Bruno Kreisky, confirmed that his government had become the first Western European state to grant "full diplomatic recognition" to the Palestine Liberation Organization. Kreisky stated that acceptance of the PLO delegate to the United Nations organization in Vienna as the Palestinian representative to Austria constituted "a new form of diplomatic recognition." It meant, he added, recognition "of a people without a state and without territory of its own." The Indian government extended full diplomatic recognition to the PLO on March 26, 1980, and announced that the PLO representative office in New Delhi, established in 1976, would henceforth be officially considered an embassy-level mission. And in October 1981 the Soviet Union awarded the PLO's Moscow office "official diplomatic status."

Some writers would place the above examples into the category of a *de jure* recognition of statehood; the present writer, however, believes that despite the use of diplomatic nomenclature, all of the acts listed should be categorized as *relations officieuses* (official relations) in an absence of recognition.

RETROACTIVE EFFECTS OF RECOGNITION    It has been generally accepted that the recognition of a new state or a new government has retroactive effects to the moment of initial existence. This means that the state extending recognition accepts as valid all official acts of the new state's government, *from its inception*. The recognizing state has a right to set a date as the official commencement of the life of the recognized state, and henceforth all acts of the latter that took place between the specified moment of birth and the date of recognition are held to be as valid as if recognition had been accorded at the time the new state came into being.

---

[16]See *Republiek Maluku Selatan* v. *De Rechtspersson Nieuw-Guinea,* Netherlands, High Court of Justice for New Guinea, 1952, reported in 49 *AJIL* 511 (1954).

## THE RECOGNITION OF GOVERNMENTS

Recognition of a government is a political act differing from the recognition of a state only in the nature of the entity being recognized. A government is merely an operative agency of a state, but it is that part of a state which undertakes the actions that, attributable to the state, are subject to regulation by the application of the principles and rules of international law.

Logically the recognition of a *new* state automatically means recognition of the government of that state, for no one can envision recognition of the whole unit without including its operating agency, its government. It would, of course, be possible to recognize a provisional government as a *de facto* government while extending recognition to the state on a *de jure* basis, as was done in the American recognition of the state of Israel, but this would still represent a concurrent recognition of both entities. [17]

The real problems in the recognition of governments tend to appear when a government's form changes, either because of a change in type or through an unconstitutional or otherwise irregular transfer of authority from one group to another group within the state in question. What is involved is the authority of a new group or a new person to act as the governing agency of a state and to represent it (to act as its agent) in its international relations.

It must be remembered that changes in the form of a *government* or in its personnel do not affect the continuing existence of the *state* involved.

In any event, even thorough transformations of a state's constitution do not necessarily affect the latter's continuity of legal personality. The classic example commonly cited is that of France between 1791 and 1875, during which time a succession of constitutional changes produced, after the monarchy, a republic, an empire, a return to monarchy, again an empire, and finally the Third Republic. But during these changes in its government's form, France remained the "State of France," the identical international legal person, with the same rights and immunities and with the same unchanged international obligations. These concepts were illustrated in the case of *The Sapphire:*

### THE SAPPHIRE

*United States, Supreme Court, 1871*
*11 Wallace 164*

FACTS    The private American ship *Sapphire* and the French naval transport *Euryale* collided in the harbor of San Francisco on December 22, 1867. The *Euryale* suffered heavy damage. Two days later, a libel was filed in the District Court, in the name of Napoleon III, Emperor of the French, as owner of the

---

[17] Following the Israeli elections of October 24, 1948, and January 25, 1949, the U.S. government extended *de jure* recognition to the government of Israel on January 31, 1949; see Myers, "Recognition of States," in "Contemporary Practice of the U.S. Relating to International Law," 55 *AJIL* 697, 703 (1961).

*Euryale,* against the *Sapphire.* The owners of the American ship filed an answer, alleging that the damage had been caused through the fault of the French vessel. The District Court decided in favor of the libelant (Napoleon III) and awarded him $15,000, representing the total amount claimed. The owners of the *Sapphire* appealed to the Circuit Court, which, however, upheld the verdict of the lower court. They then appealed to the Supreme Court of the United States in July 1869. In the summer of 1870, Napoleon III was deposed as emperor. The case came to be argued on February 16, 1871.

QUESTIONS    (1) Did the emperor have a right to bring a suit in United States courts?

(2) If such a suit had been brought rightly, had it not become abated by the deposition of the emperor Napoleon, or, in other words, did the French state, because of the change in its form of government, lose the identity that had permitted it to sue in a foreign court?

DECISION    The Supreme Court believed that the officers of the *Euryale* had also been at fault and that, both parties being at fault, the damages should be equally divided between them. It therefore reversed the decree of the Circuit Court and remitted the cause to that court with directions to enter a decree in conformity with the opinion of the Supreme Court.

REASONING    In regard to question (1): There was no question in the minds of the court as to the right of a recognized friendly foreign sovereign to sue in United States courts. "A foreign sovereign as well as any other foreign person, who has a demand of a civil nature against any person here, may prosecute it in our courts. To deny him this privilege would manifest a want of comity and friendly feeling."

As regarded question (2): The suit brought originally in the name of Napoleon III had not become abated by the emperor's deposition. "The reigning sovereign represents the national sovereignty, and that sovereignty is continuous and perpetual, residing in the proper successors of the sovereign for the time being. Napoleon was the owner of the *Euryale,* not as an individual, but as sovereign of France. . . . On his deposition the sovereignty does not change, but merely the person or persons in whom it resides. The foreign state is the true and real owner of its public vessels of war. The reigning emperor, or National Assembly, or other actual person or party in power, is but the agent and representative of the national sovereignty. A change in such representative works no change in the national sovereignty of its rights. The next successor recognized by our government is competent to carry on a suit already commenced and receive the fruits of it. . . . The vessel has always belonged and still belongs to the French nation."

Similarly, the complete changes brought about in the Russian government through the two revolutions of 1917 did not affect the legal personality of the State of Russia, and even though the final government emerging from the internal upheavals of the nation was not recognized by other countries for a number of years, the State of Russia continued to exist as a member of the community of nations and as a legal person under international law.

## Principles of the Recognition of Governments

The normal transfer of power from one group or one individual to another in accordance with the constitutional provisions in force in a given country does not require the recognition of the new government by outside states. Strictly speaking, there is no "new" government at all, in view of the presumed direct and automatic transfer of authority involved. A political party in charge of a country's government may be replaced by another party as a result of an election; yet from an international legal point of view, the same government continues to function.

Even when minor constitutional irregularities have occurred in the transfer of authority, other states frequently find it convenient to overlook such infractions of domestic law and to view the government in question as a direct and continuing successor of the preceding one. This is particularly true when all available information indicates that stability is assured in the country in question and that the nation's international obligations will continue to be honored as in the past.

The question of recognizing a new government arises, on the other hand, when serious violations of a constitution are recorded or when the basic form of government in a country is changed. The "outsiders" then have to pass individual judgment on the new government's competence to represent its state in its foreign relations. This judgment is obviously important, for a state can be held legally responsible only for the actions of its government recognized as such by other states.

OBJECTIVE TESTS    Traditionally a government's judgment as to the competence of another, new, government is based on the answers to certain objective questions or tests. If (1) the new government exercises *de facto* control over its country's administrative machinery; if (2) there is no resistance to the new government's authority; and if (3) the latter appears to have the backing of a substantial segment of public opinion in its country—then it can be said that the so-called objective tests of its competence to act as the state's representative have been met and that recognition should be extended, provided that political objections to recognition do not bar the latter.

No rule of the law has ever ascribed anything like a sacred character to the constitution of any country. No rule of the law can be held to deprive a people of its right to change its form of government, whether by ballot or by bullet, nor does any existing rule maintain that such a change must be the handiwork of a majority in any nation.

Between roughly 1913 and 1929, the United States government insisted that in order to be recognized *de facto* or *de jure,* a new government had to come into office by legal and constitutional means. This so-called Wilson Doctrine was applied to new governments in Mexico, El Salvador, Costa Rica, and Nicaragua. It denied to the peoples of those states the right to select their own governments by whatever means they chose. It meant that the U.S. government claimed the right to determine the legality of a foreign government, and assuredly this meant U.S. concern with a purely internal and sovereign sphere of another state. Commendably, the doctrine was abandoned when the Hoover administration came into office.

In the absence of special political considerations, a new government was normally recognized promptly by other governments, once the objective tests relating to its *de facto* authority had been satisfactorily met. Examples abound in modern history: the establishment of a republic in France in 1870, the republican government of Brazil following the overthrow of the empire in 1889, the Vargas government in Brazil in 1930, and the government of Fidel Castro in Cuba in more recent years. The list of illustrations could be extended almost indefinitely; it would also include the Hitler government of Germany in 1933, which was recognized at once despite its revolutionary character and the highly dubious methods, from a constitutional point of view, through which it came to power.

SUBJECTIVE TEST   The second half of the nineteenth century, however, saw the emergence of a second, subjective test, applied by some states to a new government. This second test centered on the determination of willingness (or better, capacity as well as willingness) to discharge existing international obligations and to behave in accordance with the principles of international law. [18]

It might seem that such a test would be superfluous, for any government judged to represent its state might be expected to assume the legal obligations of that same state. But if a given new government came into power by unconstitutional, possibly even violent means, could this not indicate that it would perhaps adopt a rather cavalier attitude toward its international obligations, just as it had admittedly done toward its domestic constitution and laws?

Such considerations led to the application of the second test. It had to have, of necessity, a subjective character, for it had to do with the expected future behavior of a government and could not be exposed to the same factual investigation possible in the application of the traditional objective tests.

The emergence of ideologies regarded, rightly or wrongly, as inimical or subversive by many governments served to center additional attention on the subjective test for recognition. No doubt political motives played a part then, for if a given regime had indicated its subversive ambitions before the seizure of power, it would appear logical that it would not subsequently honor any of its obligations that conflicted with those aims or impeded their achievement.

It is in this context that we find the reason for the refusal of monarchical governments to recognize the French revolutionary governments between

---

[18]See Whiteman, vol. 2, 71, 73, 119-33.

1789 and 1793, for the widespread hesitation to recognize the Russian government that emerged from the November 1917 revolution, and for the United States' prolonged refusal to recognize the Communist government of China.

In all instances cited, the new governments succeeded within a relatively short time in assuming virtually complete domestic authority, thereby satisfying the requirements laid down in the objective tests demanded for recognition. In the latter two instances, however, application of the second test was cited repeatedly as the basis for nonrecognition.

POLITICAL AND ECONOMIC FACTORS    Both political and economic motives enter into the recognition picture when there is a question of concessions or debts granted or incurred by a previous government. In Latin America, particularly, governments began to demand a formal pledge to honor past obligations as the price of recognizing a new government. Unfortunately, such pledges were often given very freely, for the new governments were anxious to be recognized. When they in turn were overthrown at a later date, the successor government often refused to honor such pledges, regarding them as mere personal promises of an extinct regime. When major nations such as the United States then failed to recognize the latest and "uncooperative" government, such denial of recognition, it is said, was the direct cause of still another revolution, with the newest leaders willing to make the required pledge as the price of recognition. The power to grant or to withhold recognition thus came to represent an effective method of intervening in a country's internal affairs, without violating, technically, the duty of nonintervention.

COLLECTIVE RECOGNITION    Recognition of a new government represents, generally, an individual political act by the recognizing government, just as in the case of recognizing new states. Collective recognition of a new government has been a rare event. The writer recalls only one such instance in recent history: the five members of the Association of Southeast Asian Nations (Thailand, Malaysia, Indonesia, Singapore, and the Philippines) jointly recognized the new government of Cambodia on April 18, 1975, within 36 hours after the surrender of the Cambodian capital of Phnom Penh to Communist forces.

On the other hand, it is possible for an international organization to recommend to its member states that a given government be recognized by them, individually, as the *de facto* or *de jure* government of a state. This was done, for instance, through a resolution dated December 12, 1948, by which the General Assembly of the United Nations declared the government of the Republic of Korea to be the only lawful government in Korea.[19]

## The Consequences of Recognition

In general, the recognition of a new government means that the recognizing government acknowledges the stability of the recognized new government

[19]See Dugard, *Recognition and the United Nations* (1987), especially at 45–51.

as well as its willingness to honor its obligations; that the recognizing government acknowledges its willingness to enter into normal international relations, including the exchange of diplomatic agents, with the recognized government; and that the recognizing state henceforth will hold the recognized government responsible for its international obligations as well as all official acts affecting them. As in the case of the recognition of states, the recognition of a new *de jure* government has retroactive effects, dating back to the inception of the new government. Retroactivity of recognition thus validates acts of a *de facto* government that has subsequently become the new *de jure* government, but it does not invalidate legal acts of the previous *de jure* government.[20] This principle was expressed extremely well when in the well-known case of *Underhill* v. *Hernandez* (168 U.S. 250 [1897]), the court held that if the party seeking to dislodge the existing government succeeds, and if the independence of the government it has set up is recognized, then the acts of such government, from the commencement of its existence, are regarded as those of an independent nation.

Once recognition has been extended to a new government, the latter has access to the courts of the recognizing state:

### REPUBLIC OF CHINA v. MERCHANTS' FIRE ASSURANCE CORPORATION OF NEW YORK

*United States, Court of Appeals,*
*Ninth Cir., 1929, 30 F. {2d} 278*

FACTS   The Republic of China had insured certain of its public buildings with the defendant company, among them the building of the Chinese Government Telephone Administration in Wuchang. Fire damaged this particular structure. After the loss occurred, Wuchang was captured by the troops of the "National Government" from the lawful government of the Republic of China. Soon afterward, the National Government, by then controlling 15 of the 18 provinces of China, demanded payment for the loss from the insurance company. When the latter refused payment, the National Government filed suit against the company in the [then] United States Court for China.

The insurance company claimed that the plaintiff was not the Republic of China but merely a revolutionary organization, not recognized as the government of the Republic of China, hence without any legal capacity to sue in United States courts. The company was sustained and the case was dismissed. The National Government appealed this dismissal.

ISSUE   Under what conditions, and when, may an unrecognized government originating through unconstitutional or revolutionary acts sue in the courts of a foreign state?

DECISION   The National Government

---

[20]See the classic case of *Oetjen* v. *Central Leather Co.*, U.S. Supreme Court 1918, 246 U.S. 297, and the clear exposition of the issue in *Short* v. *Islamic Republic of Iran*. AWD 312-11135-3, Iran–United States Claims Tribunal, The Hague, July 14, 1987, reported in 82 *AJIL* 140 (1988).

won its appeal. In view of events that had taken place since the dismissal of the suit in the lower court, the Circuit Court reversed that decision.

REASONING    1. The courts of a state cannot recognize the existence of a government that originated in revolution until it has first been recognized by the political department of the government under which such courts function. By this standard, the National Government, unrecognized at the time it sought access to the United States Court for China, had no legal capacity to sue in that court.

2. However, on July 25, 1928, a commercial treaty was concluded between the American minister to China and the minister of finance of the National Government of the Republic of China. This treaty, although not yet given consent for ratification by the Senate of the United States, constituted recognition by the Executive Department of the United States of both the National Government and of its accredited representatives. In addition, a telegram from the U.S. Secretary of State to the Circuit Court stated that the minister of the National Government had been officially received by the president of the United States.

These actions, the court held, conclusively settled the question of the United States' recognition of the National Government: implicit recognition had taken place through entering into negotiations, sending a diplomatic agent, and receiving a diplomatic agent in formal audience.

Hence the changes that had taken place had to be recognized by the court, and the recognition extended to the National Government validated the suit already begun by it in the United States courts.

Following recognition, the new government acquires title to its predecessor's assets located in the territory of the recognizing state, including bank deposits, investments, embassy or legation buildings, the contents of consular offices, and so on. It also falls heir to all claims previously asserted by its predecessor government.[21]

## Provisional Recognition

On occasion it has been difficult to apply, at once, objective and subjective tests to a new revolutionary government. Under such circumstances, it has been the frequent practice of states to grant what is called provisional or *de facto* recognition to the new government. This means that the foreign states in question indicate their willingness to deal with the new government purely on the basis and to the extent of its control of its country's administration. In the event of a civil war, however, in which two "governments," one "rebel" and the other *de jure,* contend for control of their country, another state may feel compelled, for a variety of reasons, to grant *de facto* recognition to the "rebel" government. Then each of the two parties would be recognized, if certain conditions prevailed, but each of the two governments would be recognized *only* with reference to the territory it actually controlled. It should be added that in such a case, only the representatives of the *de jure* government would enjoy normal diplomatic

[21]Whiteman, vol. 2, 665–746.

immunities and privileges; representatives of the rebel *de facto* government would be regarded as "agents," having a rather cloudy legal status.

The danger of such *de facto* recognition is that the legitimate government, the *de jure* sovereign, might well take umbrage at the provisional recognition of the rebel group as a government. Should that legitimate government emerge as the victor in the war, the provisional recognition extended to its opponents by outsiders could result in logical hostility, for by any standard the recognition granted would have been premature and inimical to the sovereign status of the lawful government.

The Spanish Civil War, caused by the rising of a faction headed by General Francisco Franco, supplied a variety of interesting situations showing the working of provisional recognition. When Clement Atlee asked Prime Minister Neville Chamberlain in the House of Commons on November 4, 1937, what the significance was of the provisional recognition extended by Great Britain to the Franco regime, the Prime Minister replied, in part, that

the protection of British nationals and British commercial interests throughout the whole of Spain including those large areas . . . of which General Franco's forces are now in effective occupation [made it] increasingly evident that the numerous questions affecting British interests in these areas cannot be satisfactorily dealt with by means of the occasional contacts which have hitherto existed . . . His Majesty's Government have entered upon negotiations for the appointment of agents by them and by General Franco respectively for the discussion of questions affecting British nationals and commercial interests, but these agents will not be given any diplomatic status.[22]

As has been indicated earlier, it is quite possible for a given state to have dealings (*relations officieuses*) with an unrecognized government without proceeding to recognition, provided the absence of intent to recognize is made clear. Thus the United States maintained agents in several Latin American republics before recognizing the latter as states independent from Spain, a course of action also pursued by Great Britain at the time. During the American Civil War, Great Britain sent a number of official agents to the Confederate States, yet did not recognize the latter as an independent entity. Many other governments have acted similarly in modern history.

Such relations with unrecognized states or governments create problems for the courts of a state maintaining the unofficial contacts in question.[23]

The proper manner of handling the knotty problem of recognition in the event of a civil war was represented, in this writer's opinion, in the decision in the *Campuzano* case:

[22]Cited by Briggs, "Relations Officieuses and Intent to Recognize: British Recognition of Franco," 34 *AJIL* 47–48 (1940); see also 1 Hackworth, 327–28.
[23]A classic modern case, cause of the inquiry mentioned above is *Government of the Republic of Spain* v. *S. S. Arantzazu Mendi and Others*. Great Britain, House of Lords, February 23, 1939, 55 *The Times Law Reports* (1939), 454; see also Briggs, "De Facto and De Jure Recognition: The Arantzazu Mendi," 33 *AJIL* 689 (1939); his article reported in detail the arguments advanced by both sides at all three levels of judicial consideration.

## THE SPANISH (REPUBLICAN) GOVERNMENT
### v. FELIPE CAMPUZANO
*Norway, Supreme Court, November 2, 1938*

FACTS    At the time of the outbreak of the Spanish Civil War in 1936, the Spanish minister in Oslo was absent on vacation and the affairs of the legation were in the hands of the secretary of the legation, Felipe Campuzano, as chargé d'affaires. On August 13, 1936, Mr. Campuzano notified the Norwegian Ministry of Foreign Affairs that he had resigned and was no longer a representative of the Spanish Republic, and when the Spanish minister returned, he, too, sent a similar declaration to the ministry. He left Norway a few weeks later to join General Franco's Nationalist regime.

For several months, neither Spanish government had a representative in Norway. On December 10, the Norwegian Ministry of Foreign Affairs was notified by the Republican government of Spain that Dr. Joaquin Pastor had been appointed secretary of the legation and chargé d'affaires in Oslo; he arrived at his post at the end of 1936.

During the interval mentioned, the Spanish legation had to be moved from its former accommodations, and Mr. Campuzano assumed responsibility for this action. He directed that portions of the movables be stored by the moving company but that others, including the legation archives, be brought to his house. When Dr. Pastor arrived in Oslo, he claimed possession of all contents of the former legation, but Campuzano refused to surrender the archives and certain other articles in his possession, arguing that he held them on behalf of the Nationalist government as the true government of Spain.

Dr. Pastor, on behalf of the Spanish Republic, sued in a Norwegian court for possession of all legation property. The case ultimately came before the Norwegian Supreme Court by appeal.

ISSUES    (1) The Spanish Republican government, claiming to be the only Spanish government recognized by Norway, asserted legal ownership of all property belonging to "Spain" or the "Spanish State." Should all such property be turned over to its representative, Dr. Pastor?

(2) Felipe Campuzano argued that the Nationalist government, as the lawful government of Spain, was immune from suit in Norwegian courts as a foreign sovereign state. Should this argument be denied, the articles in his custody belonged to "Spain." "Spain," so ran his contention, was represented by General Franco's government, which, in turn, was represented by Campuzano in Norway. Hence he should be permitted to retain possession of the articles he removed from the legation premises.

DECISION    For Dr. Pastor, against Campuzano; all articles removed from the legation building were ordered to be returned under the control of Dr. Pastor.

REASONING    (1) The government of Norway recognized the Spanish Republican government as the only government of Spain or of the Spanish state.

(2) The properties in question belonged to the Spanish state.

(3) As long as the Republican government was the only Spanish government recognized by Norway, it was entitled, through its accredited representative in Norway (Pastor), to possession of all Spanish public property located in Norway.[24]

[24] See also Leich, "Recognition of Governments" (Noriega Government in Panama), 82 *AJIL* 566 (1988).

On March 12, 1966, the French government evicted the staff of the Chinese Nationalist embassy from the embassy building, having recognized the government of the People's Republic of China in 1964. The French government properly considered the embassy premises to be the property of the representatives of that government of China that had received recognition by France.

DERECOGNITION     Derecognition means, in international law, the withdrawal of recognition by one government from another government, a withdrawal normally and logically accompanied by the recognition of a different government of the state in question. It is important to note that just as in the case of the recognition of a successful rebel government, the lawful acts of a recognized government undertaken before the latter's derecognition retain their validity. Recognition of a new government does not operate retroactively to deprive the lawful acts of its predecessor of their legal effect. On the other hand, the newly recognized government is retroactively responsible for all of its acts before recognition took effect.

The most publicized modern example of derecognition achieved its legal effects when on January 1, 1979, the United States "recognized" the People's Republic of China (PRC) as the sole and legitimate government of China and simultaneously withdrew its recognition from the Republic of China (ROC) on Taiwan. At the same time the United States "acknowledged" China's position that there was but one China and that Taiwan was part of China. The announcement of these steps represented the end product of a series of diplomatic moves started under President Nixon. The United States had already agreed in 1974 in the so-called Shanghai Communiqué that certain conditions would have to be satisfied before there could be diplomatic relations with the PRC: the United States would end all diplomatic and official relations with the ROC, withdraw all U.S. military units from Taiwan, and end the Mutual Defense Treaty of 1954 with the Republic of China. Those conditions were met (the treaty lapsing on January 1, 1980) before the ROC was derecognized.

After the U.S.–PRC recognition was announced, Congress created, under the Taiwan Relations Act, the "American Institute in Taiwan" (a "private and nonprofit corporation") to serve as the United States' nongovernmental link with Taiwan. The Institute was staffed with "retired" or "on leave" personnel of the U.S. Department of State. In turn, the ROC maintained the "Coordinating Council for North American Affairs" in Washington, headed by a former ROC ambassador.

Worldwide recognition of the Republic of China as a state declined dramatically in recent decades. Currently, only 23 countries still recognize the ROC, with 20 embassies, one consulate general (Nauru) and one honorary consul-general (United Arab Emirates) on Taiwan. The ROC was also derecognized and thus forced to withdraw from a number of international organizations, such as the International Monetary Fund, the World Bank, the International Development Association, and the International Finance Corporation.

## Consequences of Nonrecognition: Position of a Nonrecognized Government in National Courts

Nonrecognition is, in some respects, a strange concept. It often assumes that through what sometimes is an act of moral disapproval, one nation may be able to let loose such disruptive forces in another that the government of the latter cannot long survive. Or sometimes it assumes that the status conveyed through recognition might place a government so honored in a position of such strength that it will last for a long time. In most instances, history does not bear out the alleged truth of either assumption. Nevertheless the failure of a government to be recognized by foreign governments produces definite legal consequences, well established through numerous court decisions. Those consequences represent one of the most interesting areas in international law.

NONRECOGNIZED *DE FACTO* GOVERNMENT    It has been established that a nonrecognized government does not have a right of access to the courts of such other states as deny it recognition; that is, an unrecognized government cannot sue in such courts (but see below re Taiwan and also the United States). In one of the classic cases dealing with this principle, *R.S.F. Soviet Republic* v. *Cibrario,*[25] the court pointed out that it could not find any precedents for the concept that an unrecognized government could seek relief in United States courts and then proceeded to cite with approval the following British decision:

### A. M. LUTHER v. JAMES SAGOR & CO.
*Great Britain, Court of Appeal, 1921*
*3 K.B. 532, 37 The Times Law Reports, 777–784*

FACTS    The plaintiffs were a company incorporated in 1898 in the empire of Russia. Their head office was at Reval, where they had a factory for the manufacture of veneers and plywood. They had another factory at Staraja Russa, where, in 1919, a large stock of boards marked with the name "Venesta" or "V.L.," the trademark of Venesta, Ltd., a British company, was stored.

In January 1919, Russian authorities, acting under a decree of confiscation of June 20, 1918, took over the plaintiffs' factory at Staraja Russa.

On August 14, 1920, L. B. Krassin, a representative of the Russian Commercial Delegation in London, made a contract with James Sagor & Co., selling to this British firm a quantity of plywood including the wood seized at Staraja Russa. When James Sagor & Co. imported the wood into England, the plaintiffs claimed the goods seized in 1918 as their property and asked for an injunction restraining the defendants from selling the wood in question. The defendants, in turn, claimed that the seizure of the wood and its subsequent sale to them were acts of state of the Soviet government and conferred a clear title to the purchasers.

[25]United States (Court) of Appeals of New York, 1923, 235 N.Y. 255, 139 N.E. 259.

When the injunction asked for was granted to the plaintiffs, the defendants appealed.

ISSUE     Had the Russian government been recognized by the British government so that its decrees and official acts would be recognized by British courts?

DECISION     The appeal was allowed, and the decision of the lower court was reversed. Great Britain had recognized the Soviet government as the *de facto* government of Russia; hence the acts of that government had to be accepted as valid acts of state by British courts.

REASONING     (1) The Secretary of State for Foreign Affairs, in a letter dated July 28, 1920, had stated that L. B. Krassin was the authorized representative of the Soviet government, had been received by the British government for the purpose of carrying out certain negotiations, and was to be exempt from process in all British courts. This letter had not been accepted in the lower court as sufficient proof of recognition.

(2) A second letter from the Secretary of State, dated October 5, 1920, stated that "His Majesty's Government assent to the claim of the Delegation to represent in this country a State Government of Russia." This letter, too, had been termed insufficient proof of recognition in the lower court.

(3) Still another letter from the Secretary of State, dated November 27, 1920, had reaffirmed the contents of the earlier communications; it carried the additional comment that "I am to add that His Majesty's Government have never officially recognized the Soviet Government in any way." The lower court had held that this letter supplied proof of nonrecognition.

(4) On March 16, 1921, a trade agreement was concluded between the British government and the government of the Russian Socialist Federated Soviet Republic. This fact came to light only after the decision had been handed down in the lower court. In consequence, an inquiry was made by the appellant's solicitors to the Under-Secretary of State for Foreign Affairs concerning the status of the Soviet government, and the reply, dated April 20, 1921, said, "I am to inform you that His Majesty's Government recognizes the Soviet Government as the *de facto* Government of Russia." This statement changed the entire aspect of the case, and the appeal was sustained. An act of state of a recognized foreign government, going back to the latter's inception, could not be questioned in a British court.

[NOTE:     The French government protested, in a note dated May 25, 1921, against British recognition of the Soviet government as revealed in the above decision. The British government, replying in a note of June 14, 1921, rejected the French complaint.]

Despite the normal inability to gain access to the courts of a nonrecognizing government, exceptions have been carved out by courts. Thus an important 1988 decision by the U.S. Circuit Court of Appeals held (1) that a foreign state *may* have standing to sue in U.S. courts even if the United States does not recognize its government or have diplomatic relations with it; and (2) that an unrecognized government *will* have standing to sue if the executive branch of the U.S. government has indicated its willingness to permit the plaintiff government to litigate its claims in U.S. courts.[26]

In the interesting case of *Transportes Aereos de Angola* v. *Ronair, Inc.,*[27] a successful attempt by a corporation to sue in the United States when its own government (People's Republic of Angola) had not been recognized by the United States government, the court pointed out that when diplomatic relations had been severed with a government previously recognized by the United States, the privilege of resorting to American courts had not likewise been withdrawn but, more importantly, that separate juridical entities, which were not alter egos of the governments under which they were organized, may maintain suit in United States courts, even though their parent governments would be unable to do so. (See *Amtorg Trading Corporation* v. *United States,* 71 F.2d 524, [CCPA 1934]; *Banco Para el Comercio* v. *First National City Bank,* 658 F.2d 913, [C.A. 2, 1981].) In the Angolan case, even though the company was wholly owned by the Angolan government, the court believed that it could well be a "discrete and independent entity." The court stated:

In those cases in which an instrumentality of an unrecognized government or the government itself has been precluded from adjudicating a legal claim in the United States, the executive branch ordinarily steadfastly opposed the foreign party's standing to sue, thus leaving the court with no recourse but to give effect to the critical issue of non-recognition. In this case, however, not only did the Department of Commerce, in consultation with the Department of State, place its imprimatur on TAAG's ( the Angolan corporation) commercial dealings with Ronair by issuing a license to export the Boeing aircraft to Angola, but the State Department itself has unequivocally stated that allowing TAAG access to this Court would be consistent with the foreign policy interests of the United States.

An exception to the general rule of denying a nonrecognized government access to the courts was forced on the United States government by the derecognition of the Republic of China. The Taiwan Relations Act (TRA) of 1979,[28] caused the United States to treat Taiwan as a state and its governing authorities as a government, despite the formal derecognition of both by the United States. Thus the Act provided:

[26]*National Petrochemical Co. of Iran* v. *The M/T Stolt Sheaf.* 860 F.2d 551. U.S. Court of Appeals, 2d Cir., Oct. 31, 1988, reported by J.M. Marcus in 83 *AJIL* (1989) 368; see also *Upright* v. *Mercury Business Machines Co.,* United States, 12 App. Div. 2d 36, 213 N.Y. S.2d 417 (1961); *Iran Handicraft and Carpet Export Center* v. *Marjan International Corporation,* 655 F.Supp. 1275. U.S. Dist. Court S.D.N.Y., March 17, 1987, reported in 81 *AJIL* 954 (1987); and *Ministry of Defense of the Islamic Republic of Iran* v. *Gould, Inc.,* No. CV 87-03673-RG. U.S. Dist. Court, C.D. Cal., Jan. 14, 1988, reported in 82 *AJIL* 591 (1988).
[27]*Transportes Aereos de Angola* v. *Ronair, Inc. and Jet Traders Investment Corporation.* U.S. Dist. Court, Dist. of Delaware, August 18, 1982, in 21 *ILM* 1081 (1982).
[28]U.S. Public Law 96-8-April 10, 1979, *United States Statutes at Large,* vol. 93, 14.

Sec. 4 (a) . . .

The absence of diplomatic relations or recognition shall not affect the application of the laws of the United States to Taiwan as they applied prior to January 1, 1979. . . .

Sec. 4 (b) . . .

(1) Whenever the laws of the United States refer or relate to foreign countries, nations, states, governments, or similar entities, such terms shall include and such laws shall apply with respect to Taiwan.

(7) The capacity of Taiwan to sue and be sued in the courts of the United States, in accordance with the laws of the United States, shall not be abrogated, infringed, modified, denied, or otherwise affected in any way by the absence of diplomatic relations or recognition.

A common practice in the event of nonrecognition of a new foreign government is the freezing, by the nonrecognizing state, of all assets of the new foreign government found in the territory of the state denying recognition. Examples abound in recent history, such as the actions of the United States in freezing the governmental assets of Cambodia and South Vietnam (1975), North Vietnam, North Korea, Cuba, Rhodesia, and the People's Republic of China (1950–1979).

NONRECOGNIZED *DE JURE* GOVERNMENT    The view that an unrecognized government does not have access to the courts of nonrecognizing states is not shared by all writers in international law. Thus the problem of the ships of the Baltic states annexed by the Soviet Union brought forth a strong dissent by Herbert W. Briggs in regard to the nonaccess theory.[29] The occasion for his comments was the study of a rather perplexing question in the sphere of recognition: the status of the three republics of Estonia, Latvia, and Lithuania, annexed by the Soviet Union in 1940.

After annexation, the three new Soviet republics were remade into the pattern of the Soviet Union, including the nationalization of all means of transportation. The formerly private shipping lines owned by Estonian, Latvian, and Lithuanian individuals or companies were transferred to various governmental agencies of the Soviet Union.

A number of vessels flying the flag of one of the three states happened to be outside their national territorial waters at the time of annexation, and the captains in question refused to return them into the jurisdiction of the Soviet Union or its satellites. Subsequently the Soviet Union attempted to gain possession of individual ships or, in some instances, of insurance payable for the loss of the Baltic ships sunk during World War II, by having recourse to national courts in several countries. These attempts were rebuffed, as a number of states, including the United States, refused to recognize the

[29]Briggs, "Non-Recognition in the Courts: The Ships of the Baltic Republics," 37 *AJIL* 585, 595–96 (1943).

Soviet government as the *de jure* government of the Baltic states.[30] (See also the relevant discussion of the *Baltic Ship Cases* in Chapter 7.)

It has been reported that when the Soviet Union reoccupied Estonia in 1944, hundreds of Estonians fled on fishing boats and other small vessels to Sweden. The Swedish government interned all such vessels and regarded the refugees as Soviet citizens. The Soviet government brought pressure to bear on Sweden and the latter eventually permitted Soviet tugs to remove the Estonian craft as "stolen Soviet state property."

In accordance with its policy of recognizing the continued presence of the Baltic states, the United States permitted the continued presence of legations or consulates of the three nations, financed in part through Baltic assets that the United States had frozen after the Soviet absorption. The three Baltic republics still maintained consulates in Washington, D.C., and even issued, on demand, passports to persons entitled to such. A State Department desk maintained regular contact with the consulates, which were under the European bureau, not the Soviet Union one. The United States insisted that the treaties concluded with the Baltic states were still in effect. And each year the President of the United States, in accordance with a resolution of Congress, proclaimed Captive Nations Week to remind the public of the three countries that had fallen under Soviet rule.

It should be noted that when the U.S. Secretary of State and the Soviet Foreign Minister met in Namibia in March, 1990, the United States had seemingly abandoned its policy of not recognizing the annexation of the three Baltic states: the two diplomats were reliably reported to have agreed that the three states should negotiate their independence in accordance with new Soviet legislation requiring, among other conditions, a five-year transition period.

IMMUNITY OF DE FACTO GOVERNMENT    An unrecognized government enjoys immunity in the courts of foreign states. Although this condition may appear paradoxical to some, it is based on logic: you cannot sue something whose existence you deny!

In a classic case, *Wulfsohn* v. *Russian Socialist Federated Soviet Republic,*[31] the court pointed out that, even by admission of the plaintiff, the RSF Soviet Republic was the existing *de facto* government of Russia, in control of the political and military power within its national territory, regardless of whether this government had been recognized by the government of the United States. The fact of existence of this Russian government meant that in

---

[30]See, among others, *Latvian State Cargo and Passenger SS Line* v. *McGrath,* U.S. Court of Appeals, Dist. of Col., Feb. 23, 1951, 188 F. [2d] 1000, reported in 45 *AJIL* 796 (1951). See also *In re Estate of Kasendorf,* Supreme Court of Oregon, 1960, 353 Pac. 2d 531, reported in 55 *AJIL* 494 (1961), on treaties; and *In re Estate of Bielinis,* Surrogate's Court, New York County, N.Y., 1967, 284 N.Y. S. 2d 819, reported in 62 *AJIL* 499 (1968), as well as Roosaare, "Consular Relations Between the United States and the Baltic States," *Baltic Review,* June 1964, 11–36, on U.S. relationships with the defunct Baltic republics.

[31]United States Court of Appeals of New York, 1923, 234 N.Y. 372.

its territory, its jurisdiction was absolute and exclusive. Without its consent, such a government could not be brought before a foreign court. Judicial determination was prevented when an act was undertaken by a sovereign in his sovereign character, and only negotiation at the diplomatic level, or reprisals, or war, could be cited as methods of securing redress for injuries suffered as the result of such an act. Hence, once it was established as fact that an unrecognized government was actually in control in its national territory, it was immune from suit in other countries unless it waived such immunity.

RIGHT OF ACCESS TO COURTS OF A RECOGNIZED REPRESENTATIVE    Finally, the representative of a nonexisting government may undertake legal action in the courts of such other states as recognize him as the representative of that state. This apparent paradox results from the doctrine that the existence of a state as a legal person continues unimpaired despite *de facto* changes in forms of government or executive personnel.

One of the governing cases on this point is the well-known *Lehigh Valley Railroad Company* v. *State of Russia.*[32] Originally the state of Russia had sued the Lehigh Valley Railroad Company in the U.S. District Court for breach of contract of carriage, arising out of the Black Tom explosion and fire on July 30, 1916, which had caused the loss of a large shipment of explosives and ammunition being sent to Russia. At the time of loss, the goods in question had been the property of the State of Russia.

Following the overthrow of the imperial government, Boris Bakhemeteff was recognized on July 5, 1917, by the United States Department of State as the accredited representative of the successor government of Russia (the Provisional Russian Government). He continued to act as its representative until July 30, 1922, when he retired. Thereafter the Department of State recognized Mr. Ughet, the financial attaché of the Russian embassy, as the custodian of all property of the Russian state for which Bakhemeteff had been responsible.

The United States government had not recognized the Soviet government that had succeeded to power in Russia in November 1917; therefore the Provisional Government had been the last Russian government recognized by the United States.

Bakhemeteff had started the suit against the Lehigh Valley Railroad Company on July 23, 1918. Although by this time the government he represented had already ceased to exercise any authority in Russia, the United States recognized him as the representative of the State of Russia and as the custodian of all property and interests of that state in the United States.

The court held that the State of Russia survived; that Ughet, recognized by the Department of State as successor-custodian to the retired Bakhemeteff, could lawfully continue suits on behalf of the State of Russia, started by his predecessor; and that

[32]U.S. Court of Appeals, 2nd Cir., 1927, 21 F. [2d] 396.

... the suit did not abate by the change in the form of government in Russia; the state is perpetual, and survives the form of its government. . . . The recognized government may carry on the suit, at least until the new government becomes accredited here by recognition.

## Recognition of "Absentee Governments"

Acts of territorial aggrandizement by states have frequently led to the establishment of governments-in-exile, or "absentee governments."[33] In most instances these bodies continued to be recognized by other states for varying periods of time as their nations' *de jure* governments. Such practice affirmed effectively the continued existence of a state even though its territory was physically under the control of another state. Among more recent examples may be cited the absentee governments of Ethiopia, Poland, Czechoslovakia, Norway, the Netherlands, Belgium, Yugoslavia, Greece, and Luxembourg, all during World War II. In each instance, the continued recognition of the absentee government represented a repudiation of the new *de facto* administration instituted by an aggressor state. As long as an absentee government continued to be recognized as representing its country, it could speak in virtually all respects in the name of that country. However, as soon as recognition was withdrawn by hitherto recognizing states, the personnel of the absentee government was deprived of all legal standing and could no longer claim to represent its country legally. Both of these principles were illustrated in the well-known case of

### HAILE SELASSIE v. CABLE AND WIRELESS, LTD. NO. 2

*Great Britain, Court of Appeal, 1939*
*{1939} Ch. 182*

FACTS    Haile Selassie, as emperor of Ethiopa, had entered into a contract with the defendant company for the construction of certain public service installations. Breach of contract was charged, and the emperor attempted to recover certain sums of money already paid to the defendants. Before the emperor's suit, Italy had invaded Ethiopia, and the imperial government had evacuated the country and had assumed the status of a government-in-exile, continuing to be recognized by Great Britain as the *de jure* government of Ethiopia.

When the emperor sought a writ in a British court, asking for an accounting of the contractual agreement in question and for payment of the sums claimed, the Italian government also filed a claim, as the *de facto* government (recognized as such by Great Britain).

The court of first instance ruled on January 4, 1937, in favor of Haile Selassie, holding that as head of the recognized *de jure* government of Ethiopia, he possessed the right to sue for and to recover moneys due to the state in question. The defendant company appealed this verdict.

[33] See Whiteman, vol. 1, 921–30; vol. 2, 467–86; vol. 6, 66–76; consult also Oppenheimer's still valuable brief study, "Governments and Authorities in Exile," 36 *AJIL* 568 (1942); and Brown, "Sovereignty in Exile," 35 *AJIL* 666 (1941).

While the appeal was pending in the Court of Appeal, the prime minister announced in the House of Commons on November 3, 1938, that the British government intended to recognize the *de facto* sovereign of Ethiopia as the *de jure* sovereign of that country. The hearing of the appeal was suspended until such recognition should have been granted.

A little later, a certificate dated November 30, 1938, and signed by the Secretary of State for Foreign Affairs was forwarded to the court. The document stated that the recognition of the *de facto* sovereign as the *de jure* sovereign of Ethiopia had been effected officially.

ISSUE    Who was entitled to sue in the British courts on behalf of the state of Ethiopia on the resumption of the hearing of the appeal?

DECISION    The Court of Appeal ruled in favor of the defendants, holding that Haile Selassie's claim had to be dismissed by virtue of his failure to be the recognized government of Ethiopia.

REASONING    The effect of the certificate supplied by the Secretary of State for Foreign Affairs was that

(1) The *de facto* sovereign of Ethiopia, now recognized as the *de jure* sovereign, was entitled by succession to the public property, including claims, of the state of Ethiopia; hence plaintiff's claim to such property and claims was no longer in existence;

(2) The right of succession dated back to the date of the *de facto* recognition of the king of Italy as sovereign of Ethiopia, that is, to the second half of December 1936;

(3) Because *de facto* recognition took place before the issue of the writ in the lower court (January 4, 1937), the plaintiff's claim failed and had to be dismissed.

Following the expulsion of Italian forces from Ethiopia, Haile Selassie resumed his position as emperor of that country and was recognized by Great Britain as the *de jure* and *de facto* government of the country.

It may be of interest to note that Mexico continued to be host to an embassy (the only one left in the world) of the Spanish Republic overthrown by the Nationalist rebels in 1939 until diplomatic relations between Mexico and the kingdom of Spain were resumed in 1978, and as late as December 1981, a remnant of the World War II Polish government-in-exile was found in London. It was then allegedly recognized by no one except the Vatican.

TREATY RELATIONS (UNRECOGNIZED AND ABSENTEE GOVERNMENTS)    The lack of formal recognition between two governments is no longer considered, in many quarters, a barrier to what could be termed formal relations, including the conclusion of bilateral treaties between those governments (again, always provided that the intent not to recognize is present and clear). A rather remarkable instance was the conclusion, in June 1970, of a trade agreement between Greece and Albania: the Greek government had not recognized the government of Albania, and the latter was still technically at war with Greece, dating back to the days of World War II. Again, absentee governments are at liberty to conclude binding treaties with one another or with other governments (although normally, in the latter case, only with such governments as recognize the absentee government).

## SUGGESTED READINGS

### Recognition of States, General

Brierly, 140–50; Briggs, 105–17; Gould, 213–40; Hyde, vol. 1, 148–204; Lauterpacht's *Oppenheim*, vol. 1, 125–33; see the extensive collection of materials in Whiteman, vol. 2, 133–242; James Crawford, *The Creation of States in International Law* (1979); and Dugard, *Recognition and the United Nations* (1987).

CASES

*The Annette*, Great Britain, Probate, Divorce, and Admiralty Division, 1919, Probate 105.

*The Gagara*, Great Britain, Court of Appeal, 1919, Probate 95.

*Kennett et al.* v. *Chambers*, U.S. Supreme Court 1852, 14 How. (55 U.S.) 38.

### Recognition of Governments in General

Lauterpacht's *Oppenheim*, vol. 1, 133–52; Galloway, *Recognizing Foreign Governments: The Practice of the United States* (1978); Jessup, "The Spanish Rebellion and International Law," 15 *Foreign Affairs* 260–79 (1937); Houghton, "Policy of the United States and Other Nations with Respect to the Recognition of the Russian Soviet Government, 1917–1929," *International Conciliation*, No. 247 (February 1929), 83–108; Lubman, "The Unrecognized Government in American Courts: *Upright* v. *Mercury Business Machines*," 62 *Columbia Law Review* 275 (1962); Whiteman, vol. 2, 72–119, 242–467; Peterson, "Recognition of Governments Should Not Be Abolished," 77 *AJIL* 31, esp. 37 (1983); and his letter to the editors-in-chief, *id.*, 615.

CASES

*State of the Netherlands* v. *Federal Reserve Bank of New York*, U.S. Court of Appeals, 2nd Cir., 1953, 201 F.(2d) 455, abstracted in 47 *AJIL* 496–500 (1953).

*Dougherty* v. *Equitable Life Assurance Society*, U.S. Court of Appeals of New York, 1934, 266 N.Y. 71.

*Guaranty Trust Co.* v. *United States*, U.S. Supreme Court 1938, 304 U.S. 126.

*The Rogdai*, U.S. Dist. Court, N.D. of Calif., 1920, 278 Fed. 294.

*The Tinoco Claims Arbitration* (Great Britain–Costa Rica), 1923; see 18 *AJIL* 147 (1924).

*United States* v. *Pink, Superintendent of Insurance (N.Y.)*, U.S. Supreme Court 1942, 315 U.S. 203.

*Kunstsammlungen zu Weimar and Grand Duchess of Saxony-Weimar* v. *Elicofon*, U.S. Court of Appeals, 2nd Cir., 1973, 478 F.2d 231, reported in 15 *Harvard Int'l Law Jl.* 180 (1974); see also relevant documents in 11 *ILM* 1259 (1972); 12 *ILM* 1163 (1973); 20 *ILM* 1122 (1981); and the final decision in the case, 21 *ILM* 773 (1982).

*Republic of Vietnam* v. *Pfizer, Inc.*, U.S. Court of Appeals, 8th Cir., June 15, 1977, reported in 72 *AJIL* 152 (1978).

*National Petrochemical Co. of Iran* v. *The M/T Stolt Sheaf*, U.S. Court of Appeals, 2nd Cir., Oct. 31, 1988, 860 F.2d 551, reported in 83 *AJIL* 368 (1989).

## The China Problem

For the early years of the nonrecognition of China, see Newman, *Recognition of Communist China?* (1961), particularly 242–61 for a discussion of U.S. precedents and their legal implications. For more recent developments prior to recognition in 1979, see the documents in Whiteman, vol. 2, 90–110; and particularly, Li, *De-Recognizing Taiwan: The Legal Problems* (1977). For an overall study concerning Taiwan, see Chiu, ed., *China and the Taiwan Issue* (1979).

CASE

*Bank of China* v. *Wells Fargo Bank & Union Trust Co.,* U.S. Dist. Court, N.D. of Calif., March 17, 1952, reported in 47 *AJIL* 148 (1953).

## The Baltic States

CASE

*Latvian State Cargo and Passenger SS Line* v. *Clark,* U.S. Dist. Court, Dist. of Columbia, November 4, 1948, reported in 43 *AJIL* 380 (1949).

## Recognition of Belligerency in General

Chen, *The International Law of Recognition* (1951), 303–407; Hackworth, vol. 7, 166–73; Lauterpacht, *Recognition in International Law,* 175–238; Whiteman, vol. 2, 486–523; and see *Time,* August 16, 1982, 34, concerning the recognition of the Saharan Arab Democratic Republic (a.k.a. the Polisario guerrillas) by the Organization of African Unity as its fifty-first member.

CASES

*United States* v. *Three Friends,* U.S. Supreme Court 1897, 166 U.S. 1.
*Boguslawski* v. *Gdynia-Ameryka Linie Zeglugowe Spolka Akcynja,* Great Britain, Court of Appeal, June 15, 1950, reported in 45 *AJIL* 202 (1951); appeal, House of Lords, July 11, 1952, reported 47 *AJIL* 155 (1953).

# 6

# State Succession

The subject of State Succession has been disparaged by some writers as possessing at most tangential relevance to the contemporary international scene. The present writer believes, however, that state succession should continue to be included in any survey of international law because it may reappear as the result of future events, such as a possible disintegration of the Soviet Union or of the Yugoslavian state.

The rather vague term "state succession" is used generally to describe the legal consequences resulting from a change in sovereignty over territory.[1] Such changes have been recorded throughout much of history, but have occurred most frequently during the decades following World War II through the attainment of independence by former colonies and protectorates. It is troublesome, however, that there does not yet exist a generally accepted body of legal norms governing the various known varieties of changes in sovereignty. After more than a decade of preparatory work by the International Law Commission, two UN-sponsored conferences did result in two conventions: the Convention on Succession of States in Respect of Treaties (Vienna, August 23, 1978), and the Convention on Succession of States in Respect of State Property, Archives and Debts (Vienna, April 8, 1983).[2] But neither instrument was in force at the time of writing, having failed to secure the required number of ratifications or accessions.

State succession may occur in a number of ways, usually divided by writers into three categories: (1) The achievement of independence by a territory "previously under the sovereignty, suzerainty, protectorate, mandate, trusteeship, or other form of legal control"[3] of another state or that was in a federal or a real union (see Chapter 4) with other legal persons, and also including secession from a state; (2) the loss of the status of a state through annexation, merger, or the imposition of protectorate status by another legal person; and (3) the change in sovereignty over an area from one state to another state through cession or annexation (See Chapter 14).

---

[1] The standard work on the subject is still the monumental work by O'Connell, *State Succession in Municipal Law and International Law*, 2 vols. (1967).
[2] Text of the 1978 convention is in 72 *AJIL* 978 (1978) and 17 *ILM* 1488 (1978); text of the 1983 convention in 22 *ILM* 306 (1983).
[3] Friedmann, 431.

In cases of the first category, rights and obligations under treaties have normally been decided by so-called devolution agreements between the predecessor state and the newly independent entity concerning the extent to which the latter would assume rights and duties originally created by treaties for the predecessor state.[4] In cases of the second category, domestic legislation of the successor state or premerger agreements between the prospective parties decide the status of both rights and obligations of each entity. In cases of the third category, the successor state alone decides the fate of both rights and obligations of the extinct predecessor entity.

In all three categories, however, rules of international law enter into the picture, regulating the rights and obligations of predecessor and successor in relation to outside states, to third parties.

Before entering into details, it should be emphasized that the international personality of a state normally remains unaffected by increases or losses in territory, with corresponding gains or reductions in population, unless the changes in question are so profound as to change the state's central organization (basic structure) or involve a loss to the state of the "core area" in which its government center is located.

A good example of dramatic growth in size and population is the development of the United States of America from its beginnings in the eighteenth century to its present extent. Despite an enormous expansion in area and population, the international legal personality of the United States has remained unchanged since 1783. Relevant increases in the area of other nations, such as Romania after 1918 or the Soviet Union after 1938, did not affect their legal personality in any manner.

What about a shrinkage in the territory of a given state? The standard examples usually cited show that despite often drastic losses, the states remained unaffected in regard to their legal personality: Poland (partitions of 1772 and 1793) remained unchanged from a legal point of view until 1795; Turkey, despite losses in 1856, in 1878, in 1911–1913, and as a result of World War I, remained legally unaffected; and if the Confederacy had succeeded in its secession plans, the legal identity of the United States would have remained unchanged.

### Partial Extinction

Some writers in international law held that when a previously independent state changed to the status of a protectorate, its legal personality could be characterized as having suffered a "partial" extinction. The present writer does not share this view and believes that the correct description of such a change would be that the capacity of the protectorate's legal personality to act has been placed in a state of suspension, capable of reanimation and full operation on the termination of its protectorate status.

In other words, the legal personality of, for instance, Morocco was unable to function in the international sphere from the legal inception of the

[4]Friedmann, 433–39; Henkin, 675.

French protectorate in 1912 until Moroccan sovereignty was restored by the Joint Declaration of March 2, 1956 and subsequent agreements ending the protectorate status of the Spanish portions.

## STATE SUCCESSION

Hugo Grotius developed the basic theory of state succession as a corollary of the principle in Roman civil law under which an heir succeeded to the assets, the rights, and also the obligations of a deceased individual, becoming, as it were, at least in the law, the latter's substitute.

The nature of states as sovereign entities having a legal personality precludes, of course, a strict application of the Roman rule to international law. Many modern writers question the existence of true succession, even though most treatises still hold to the traditional terminology. Generally, two varieties of state succession are recognized: (1) universal succession and (2) partial succession.

### Universal Succession

Universal succession is said to occur when one state absorbs, or takes over completely, the international personality of another state. This event may be caused by forcible annexation or by the absorption of the extinct state into a federal structure. On the other hand, if a given state is somehow divided into a number of separate states, there is also universal succession, involving this time as many successor states as there are new entities created.

EXTINCTION BY VOLUNTARY ACT    How may a state become extinct? On occasion the international personality of a state has been ended by a voluntary act. One instance would be the breakup of a federation into separate states, as in the case of the Republic of Colombia when it separated in 1828–1830 into three separate states (Ecuador, Venezuela, and New Granada). One of these, New Granada, reverted to the name of Colombia at a later date and possibly retained the legal personality of Colombia even after 1830.

MERGER    Again, extinction may come about through merger with another state: the cases of Texas (union with the United States) and Syria (temporary merger with Egypt in the United Arab Republic) come to mind. In the latter example, incidentally, both states lost their individual personalities, and a new state came temporarily into being.

EXTINCTION BY FORCIBLE MEANS    Forcible annexation of conquest has been a common method for the extinction of hitherto independent states. World history is filled with examples: the Transvaal in 1901 and Korea in 1910 are favorite illustrations. Later annexations have posed problems in view of the existence of the League of Nations and subsequently of the United Nations, both of which "prohibited" conquest.

There has been considerable disagreement on the absorption of the three Baltic republics of Estonia, Latvia, and Lithuania into the Soviet Union in 1940. Because numerous states have refused to accept the Russian acts of state relating to the three republics, it appears that some vestige of international personality has remained in each of them. (See "Nonrecognized *De Jure* Government" in Chapter 5.)

RIGHTS AND OBLIGATIONS OF A TOTALLY EXTINCT STATE     When a state's international personality is extinguished, its international rights and possibly also the obligations also come to an end. (See Chapter 3: *West Rand Central Gold Mining Co., Ltd.* v. *The King*.) All treaties and other agreements concluded by the defunct state with other countries automatically become null and void, with two possible exceptions: (1) If the defunct state was a party to a multilateral treaty *not* hinging on its being a party, that agreement would still be in effect for the other parties to the treaty; and (2) If an agreement did create a territorial servitude on the territory of the defunct state, it would be considered to be still in effect and to bind the successor state. The rights of the defunct state cease to be enforceable in its name, and its obligations can no longer be brought against it as a legal person. If there is a successor state, then the rights of the extinct entity devolve upon it, and the obligations of the entity *may* be assumed, if at all, by the successor state.

In the case of a totally extinct state, its obligations become extinct, and the successor state becomes liable for such state debts as were passed to it by the extinct entity. This statement accords with Article 34 of the 1983 Vienna Convention, *but* state practice since ancient times has often followed a different formula. The rights of the extinct state devolve upon the successor, but the obligations of the extinct state *may* be assumed by the successor state, as briefly discussed below.

RIGHTS AND OBLIGATIONS OF THE SUCCESSOR STATE     Under the more normal instance of the absorption of one state by another, the question arises as to the extent to which the successor state acquires both the rights and the obligations of the defunct state. If third states have any claims against the latter, the settlement of such obligations is up to the successor state. The citizens of the defunct state have no right of appeal under international law against any actions taken by the annexing state, for their former country has lost its international personality and is no longer a subject of international law. Any claims by or against such citizens involving their former government now become domestic questions of the annexing state.

The new sovereign also decides to what extent it will be bound by the extinct state's obligations toward its citizens: any rights possessed by such individuals under the laws of the extinct state will avail them nothing, for normally those laws have been set aside and do not exist anymore.

The extinction of the personality of a state results traditionally in an abrogation of all political and military treaties previously concluded between the now extinct entity and other states. This is true, of course, only in the case of total extinction; if succession involves only a portion of the original owner's territory, the latter is still bound by treaties with other countries because such a state's legal personality continues alive; only those provisions of treaties relating to lost parts of the territory no longer bind the former sovereign.

Despite the absence of applicable rules of law, successor states have generally been willing to assume contractual obligations of the extinct state with respect to third states or the citizens of such states. This has been true in the case of contracts involving concessions such as mining rights and transportation facilities.

On the other hand, no common practice can be discovered in relation to the debts contracted by the predecessor state. Debts owed to the citizens of the latter become domestic questions of the annexing state. In the case of partial succession of the sort described in the next section, the instrument transferring the areas in question may regulate such questions. Debts owed to third states or their citizens may or may not be honored by the successor state. The government of the United States took over the debts of its member states in 1790, but it refused in 1845 to assume the obligations of the Republic of Texas, although arrangements were made to pay the sum in question out of the proceeds of the sale of public land in Texas.

## Partial Succession

Partial succession occurs when a state assumes sovereignty over portions of territory formerly belonging to another state; when a new international personality is created by the secession of a territory from an existing state; or when a member state of a federation or a confederation obtains independence. Partial succession poses many complicated problems centering on the distribution or division of the rights and obligations somehow attached to the territory involved in the succession.

EFFECTS ON PUBLIC AND PRIVATE PROPERTY RIGHTS    Normally there are only two parties involved in such questions, and, fortunately, experience has taught most states to specify how they are to be settled between them. Such matters are usually incorporated in the instrument transferring title to the territory. On occasion, however, third parties are involved in partial succession, usually because of their or their citizens' claims relating to the transferred territory.

Unless otherwise agreed on by the states concerned or by some appropriate international organization, the passing of state property of the predecessor to the successor state or states takes place without compensation. This principle applies to both partial or total extinction of the predecessor state. The property of third states, or the rights and interests of third states, recognized as such under the laws of the predecessor state, are not affected by state succession.

Under partial succession, the public property of the ex-titleholder in the transferred territory passes to the successor state.

Private property rights in territory ceded by one state to another or annexed by another are not formally affected by the change. Titles to land, provided they were complete and perfect at the time of change, are usually protected by the successor state, unless the latter is of the socialist variety and supports the nationalization of all land.

DOMESTIC AND FOREIGN DEBTS   Debts of the transferred area may or may not be assumed by the new sovereign; writers have commonly asserted that at least such debts as have been closely associated with the development of the transferred territory ought to be assumed by the successor state. But most successor states have in practice been reluctant to assume such obligations.

On occasion, however, the successor state has assumed domestic and/or foreign debts. Again, when it has been shown that a particular debt had been incurred solely for the benefit of the transferred area, a few successor states have actually assumed the debt.

An unusual feature of the 1919 peace settlement with Germany was the acquisition of all German governmental property in the ceded areas by the successor states and payment for such property by the successor states to the Allied Reparations Commission (except for territories ceded to Poland). The successor states (except for France) also assumed portions of the German debt, both national and state, proportionate to the area in each transfer in question.

When part of a state is transferred to another state, the passing of the state debt from predecessor to successor normally is settled by agreement between the parties. Article 37(2) of the 1983 Vienna Convention provides that in the absence of such an agreement, the predecessor's state debt is to pass to the successor state "in an equitable proportion."

On the other hand, when the successor is a newly independent state (say, an ex-protectorate or an ex-colony), no state debt of the predecessor state normally passes to the new entity unless an agreement between the parties provides otherwise in view of the link between the predecessor's state debt and its activities in the newly independent area. When two or more states unite to form one successor state, the state debt of the two or more predecessors passes on to the new entity. When part or parts of a state's territory separate from that legal person and form a state, the state debt of the predecessor state passes to the successor state on a proportional basis, unless the parties agree otherwise. And finally, when a state dissolves and ceases to exist and the parts of the predecessor state's territory form two or more successor states, the state debt of the dissolved unit passes, normally, in equitable proportions to the successor states.

Insofar as state succession affects the debt obligations of successor governments, there is as yet no generally accepted rule, at least not until the 1983 Vienna Treaty (see below) is in effect. Most writers hold that a successor state is indeed liable for the obligations of the predecessor, regardless of whether there have been revolutionary or ideological changes.

Unless otherwise decided between the parties (states) involved, debts owed to the predecessor state by virtue of its sovereignty over or its activities in the territory to which title is being passed become debts owed to the successor state.

EFFECTS ON TREATIES    One other aspect of state succession merits brief examination, in view of the number of controversies it has caused in international relations. If one party to an international agreement changes its form of government or expands or contracts its geographical boundaries, the provisions of the treaty in question are usually not affected by such changes, even if the expansion of territory involves the inclusion of other former states in the one that is a party to the agreement. Unless the changes suggested the desirability of new treaties, the prior agreements have generally been regarded as remaining in full force and effect.

The many and complicated questions about state succession with respect to treaties raised by the emergence of new countries after World War II led to the drafting of the 1978 Vienna Convention.

The comprehensive coverage of this treaty answers almost all questions imaginable; yet by its very breadth it exceeds the limits of discussion possible in a general text. But one aspect of the subject should be kept in mind: the new instrument covers in detail the absence of applicability of past treaties concluded by the original sovereign, not only with respect to former colonial territories, but also with respect to seceding territories (unless, of course, the newly independent colony or newly seceded territory agrees specifically to be bound by the treaties in question).[5]

Generally, in the case of the extinction of a state (universal succession), all political treaties (including alliances), treaties of extradition, commerce, and navigation (except in the case of servitudes created by a treaty) are automatically abrogated. This also is true for portions of a state detached from it in partial succession and also for newly independent states in regard to treaties concluded by the previous sovereign.

Some of the specific rules governing state succession in respect of treaties can be summarized as follows:

SUCCESSION IN PARTIAL EXTINCTION    When part of the territory of a predecessor state becomes part of a successor state, treaties of the former cease to be in effect in respect of the transferred part, and treaties of the successor state are in effect for the transferred part from the date of succession. This is called by some writers the "moving frontiers" rule.

NEWLY INDEPENDENT STATES    A newly independent state is not bound to maintain in force treaties applicable to the predecessor state. The newly independent entity may signify its status as a party to a multilateral treaty of the predecessor state by notification in writing of succession/accession. This would not be true, however, if it were established that application of the given multilateral agreement to the newly independent state would be incompatible with the object or purpose of the treaty or would radically change the conditions for the operation of the treaty. If the latter requires the consent of its various parties, the newly independent state must obtain such consent before becoming a party to the treaty.

[5]Consult Keith, "Succession to Bilateral Treaties by Seceding States," 61 *AJIL* 521 (1967); Dumbauld, "Independence under International Law," 70 *AJIL* 425 (1976).

Normally the successor state concludes a so-called devolution agreement with the predecessor state concerning which treaties applicable to the latter shall also apply to the successor state, the newly independent entity. On the other hand, a number of newly independent states recently chose to start their international life with "a clean slate" as far as the predecessor treaties were concerned, *i.e.,* they were unwilling to be bound by any of the agreements in question.

BILATERAL TREATIES    A bilateral treaty between another state party and the predecessor state relating to the newly independent state remains in effect after succession only if the new state and the other state party expressly agree to that effect or if their conduct indicates that they have so agreed.

MERGER OF STATES    If two or more states unite and form one successor state, any treaty in force at the time of succession in respect to any of the merged entities continues in force in respect to the successor state unless the latter and the other state party or parties otherwise agree or if it appears from the treaty in question that its application to the successor state (merged entity) would be incompatible with the object or purpose of the treaty. It should be noted that any treaty continuing in force as to the merged successor state applies only in respect of the part of the territory of the successor state in respect of which the treaty was in force at the date of succession, unless, in the case of a multilateral treaty, the successor state notifies the other parties to that agreement that the latter shall apply to all of its territory or if in the case of a bilateral treaty the successor state and the predecessor state otherwise agree.

REMAINDER OF A STATE AFTER PARTIAL SUCCESSION    When, after separation of any part of the territory of a state, the predecessor state continues to exist, any treaty that at the date of succession was in force in respect of the predecessor state will continue in force in respect of the latter's remaining territory unless the states concerned otherwise agree or it is established that the treaty related only to the territory separated from the predecessor state or if it appears from the treaty that its continued applicability in respect to the predecessor state would be incompatible with the object and purpose of the agreement.

STATE SUCCESSION AND SERVITUDES    If a servitude (see Chapter 14) exists in respect of a particular territory, state succession does not as such affect obligations relating to the use of that territory or to restrictions on its use, established by a treaty for the benefit of any territory of a foreign state, a group of states, or all states, and considered as attaching to the territory in question. State succession also does not, as such, affect any rights established by treaty for the benefit of any territory and relating to the use, or to restrictions on the use, of any territory of a foreign state, a group of states, or all states, and considered as attaching to the territory in question.

TOTAL EXTINCTION    If a state becomes totally extinct (usually through conquest), its treaty rights and obligations are extinguished. This statement is subject to two exceptions: if the extinct state's rights included a servitude, that treaty right would be inherited, so to speak, by the successor state. And if the extinction of the state in question were not recognized by other states (*e.g.,* the exile governments of Europe during World War II or the three Baltic states since 1940), then those states not recognizing the extinction in question would continue to have the same treaty relations with the "extinct" entity that they had before state succession took place.

## SUGGESTED READINGS

### Loss of Personality, General

Lauterpacht's *Oppenheim,* vol. 1, 153–69; Moore, vol. 1, 385–414; Skubiszewski, "Poland's Western Frontier and the 1970 Treaties," 67 *AJIL* 23, esp. 24–28 (1973).

CASES

*German Settlers in Poland, P.C.I.J.,* 1923, Ser. B, No. 6.

*D.D. Cement Co.* v. *Commissioner of Income Tax,* India, Pepsu High Court, June 7, 1954, *All India Rep.* 1955 Pepsu 3, reported in 49 *AJIL* 572 (1955).

*United States* v. *Prioleau,* Great Britain, High Court of Chancery, 1865, 71 *Eng. Rep.* 580 (1865).

*United States ex rel. Schwarzkopf* v. *Uhl,* U.S. Court of Appeals, 2nd Cir., 1943, 137 F. (2d) 898.

*Molefi* v. *Principal Legal Adviser et al.,* Lesotho, High Court, 1969, reproduced in 8 *ILM* 581 (1969); see also the Privy Council (United Kingdom) Judgment on appeal (Privy Council Appeal No. 27 of 1969), 9 *ILM* 879 (1970).

# 7

# Rights of International Legal Persons

## THE RIGHTS OF STATES

TRADITIONAL THEORIES    Until shortly before the end of the nineteenth century, almost all jurists agreed that the states belonging to the community of nations enjoyed the possession of so-called fundamental rights, including the right of equality, existence, external independence, self-defense, territorial supremacy (sovereignty), intercourse, and respect.

These asserted rights were stated to be basic and absolute and were held to be essential to any community claiming to be a state. Their basis was found in the doctrine of natural law, and a key version of the theory maintained that the rights in question represented legal principles on which all positive international law was built and which could be deduced from the nature of that law. That version ignored the obvious fact that legal principles could only be created by a legal order and could not be presupposed by it.

Still another school of thought held that the fundamental rights in question could be deduced from the personality of the state. Such a view presupposed, however, that the state existed as a personality, as a subject of rights, before it ever entered the community of nations and that it claimed retention of those rights on its voluntary entrance into that community. This theory closely approached the old concept of the social contract. Such a contract has never taken place, of course, and must be regarded as a fiction. As such it is a most convenient one by which to assert that the members of the community are bound by common duties and enjoy common rights. The fictional aspect of this theory is shown clearly by the fact that when a new state enters a legal order, it is bound by customary international law without any explicit act of acceptance. The law applies to it as soon as it is recognized as a state by the community's other members.

RECENT ATTEMPTS TO DEFINE THE RIGHTS AND DUTIES OF STATES    Until recently it has been only within the regional inter-American community that repeated efforts have been made to proclaim a general and definitive declaration of the rights of states. Starting with the Declaration of the Rights and Duties of Nations of the American Institute of International Law in 1916, a project called Fundamental Rights and Duties of American Republics was prepared for the meeting of the International Commission of Jurists at Rio de Janeiro in 1927. This project resulted in a draft treaty at the Havana Conference of 1928, but the draft was not accepted because of the United States' strong opposition to the absolute form of the nonintervention duty outlined in the draft.

Official action concerned with the rights and duties of states was then taken at the Montevideo Conference of 1933 through the adoption of a convention on the subject, followed by a reiteration of most of the principles involved at the Buenos Aires Conference of 1936 and at the Lima Conference of 1938.

The most ambitious modern attempt to define the rights and duties of states resulted, however, from Resolution 178 (II) of the General Assembly of the United Nations, adopted on November 21, 1947, asking the International Law Commission to prepare a draft declaration of such rights and duties. This draft, delineating four rights (independence, territorial jurisdiction, equality in law, and self-defense) and 10 duties, has been criticized on many counts, both during its formulation and afterward. Thus far no further progress on the project has been reported.

It should be mentioned that the General Assembly passed, on December 12, 1974, a rather controversial resolution (3281-XXIX) entitled Charter of Economic Rights and Duties of States, by a vote of 120 in favor to 6 against, with 10 abstentions.[1] As a resolution and with certain key countries opposing its adoption, the resolution has had no binding effect; yet it has been referred to frequently by Third World countries in the United Nations.

## RIGHT OF EXISTENCE

The so-called right of existence has been held to be the fundamental condition for all other rights claimed by a state, for obviously an inability to continue its existence would lead to the extinction of the legal personality of any member of the community of nations. Governments have frequently insisted on this right but have styled it variously as the "right of self-defense" and the "right of self-preservation," depending on the issues confronting them at the time. In regard to existence in the narrow meaning of the term, no such right can exist, for obviously existence represents an essential inherent characteristic of a state rather than a right.

RIGHT TO A CONTINUED EXISTENCE  What is involved from a practical point of view in this "right" is a right to a *continued* existence, that is, the preservation of a state's corporate integrity through self-defense or some other mechanism. This concept raises at once a number of interesting questions. Initially, it can be said that states have a duty to respect the existence of all other states; yet if this rule were to be inflexible and were to be regarded as

[1] Text in 14 *ILM* 251 (1975).

an absolute right, then all states would have the duty to admit and endure every violation committed in self-preservation. But no state is obliged to do this and, instead, can defend itself and may do so lawfully in any case of true necessity. This matter of necessity, however, cannot be left to the determination of each individual state, in view of the well-known fact that states have committed aggression against other states under the plea and guise of necessary self-defense.

## RIGHTS OF INDEPENDENCE AND OF TERRITORIAL SUPREMACY

DOMESTIC INDEPENDENCE    Oppenheim correctly held that the independence of a state as well as its territorial and personal supremacy (supreme authority in its territory and over its citizens) was not a right at all but was a recognized and protected quality or characteristic of states as international persons.[2] Independence means that a state is free to manage its affairs without interference (domestic independence); that is, that it can organize its government as it sees fit, adopt a constitution to suit its own needs, lay down rules and regulations for the property rights as well as the personal rights of its citizens and subjects, determine under what specific conditions foreigners will enter its territory, and so on. In other words, an independent state is "absolute master" in its own house, subject only to such limitations as are imposed on it, either by the rules of general international law or by such treaty arrangements as it has made with other states. In essence, therefore, domestic independence means freedom from interference on the part of other states.[3]

EXTERNAL INDEPENDENCE    A second aspect of independence relates to the right of a state to conduct its foreign relations to the best of its ability in such manner as it desires, again without supervisory control by other states (external independence). The absence of such control is necessary if a given state is to act as a free agent and is to be able to fulfill such international obligations as it assumes in dealing with other states. This external independence is regarded as a basic test for the admission of new members into the community of nations, because those states lacking this quality cannot qualify for admission. Yet this external independence, again, rests on a duty of other states to refrain from interference and hence essentially belongs among the states' duties rather than rights.

One of the most important aspects of this asserted "right" is the respect of each sovereign state for the independence of every other sovereign state. It is

---

[2]Lauterpacht's *Oppenheim,* vol. 1, 286; for further details on the subject in general, consult this source at 286–97, and Whiteman, vol. 5, 88–124. See also T. McCoy, "U.S. Embrace Restricts Honduran Sovereignty," *CSM,* Aug. 3, 1989, 19.

[3]See also *Attorney-General of New Zealand* v. *Ortiz* [1982] 3 W.L.R. 570, United Kingdom, Court of Appeal, May 21, 1982, reported in 77 *AJIL* 631 (1983).

in consequence of this respect that the courts of one country will not sit in judgment on the acts of the government of another state, committed within the latter's own territorial jurisdiction. Without such recognition of official actions (the *act-of-state doctrine*) by outside judicial agencies, the right of independence would mean very little. Thus the U.S. Supreme Court was correct when it upheld (October 10, 1984) rulings of two federal courts of appeals barring 14 former hostages and four family members from suing the government of Iran for the sum of $65 million in damages in consequence of the Iranian seizure of the U.S. embassy in Tehran. The courts of appeals had held correctly that U.S. embassies abroad did not constitute U.S. territory and therefore the Iranian acts in question had taken place on foreign soil.

The right to independence also logically involves a frequently voiced claim to a right of self-determination. The latter term appears to imply the right of any people to choose its own political institutions (including, of course, its own government). Numerous legal writers and political leaders supported this idea that "national" or "ethnic" groups possessed a right to "self-determination." The concept itself made its appearance shortly before the settlements at the Versailles Peace Conference after World War I. President Wilson supported the idea but, it appears, with some ambivalence, since he did not favor self-determination within the borders of what was then Russia proper. After World War II, the principle of self-determination emerged even more clearly and soon took the form of an assertion that a *legal right* of self-determination existed. The Charter of the United Nations [Arts. 1(2); 73; 76(b)] and resolutions passed by the General Assembly affirmed the existence of such a right, an influential factor in the wave of decolonization in the ensuing decades. But at the same time a rejection of the "right" of self-determination took place not only in Eastern Europe, but also in places like Kashmir and Nigeria.

Not all legal writers, however, became enamored of the new right, and some even doubted its very existence.[4] A few pointed out that in some respects promotion of a right of self-determination for some foreign group really violated the prohibition on intervention found in the Charter of the United Nations [Art. 2(4)]. The Charter, in which equal rights and self-determination are mentioned prominently (Article 1), also speaks in Article 2(4) of the (virtually sacred) territorial integrity of the members. This seems to be a contradiction, for the preservation of territorial integrity seems to conflict with a secession movement sanctioned, on the surface at least, by the principle of self-determination. In practice, the members of the United Nations appear to have, in general, supported self-determination for colonial peoples only, as shown by their repeated failures to accord recognition to secessionist rebel groups, even though both Human Rights Covenants of 1966 (see Chapter 9) mention self-determination without any qualification

---

[4]See Franck, "Legitimacy in the International System," 82 *AJIL* 705, 746 (1988), and Henkin, 211–13.

(Article 1 in each instrument). The true interpretation, however, was laid down much earlier in the 1960 "Declaration on the Granting of Independence to Colonial Countries and Peoples," in which the General Assembly endorsed the idea that "any attempt aimed at the partial or total disruption of the national unity and the territorial integrity of a country is incompatible with the purposes and principles of the Charter of the United Nations."[5]

RESERVED SPHERE OF DOMESTIC QUESTIONS    The problem that has not yet been resolved satisfactorily is this: Where is the line that separates purely domestic questions from the sphere of action subject to the authority of general international law? Normally every government will insist that certain activities are completely under its jurisdiction and are not subject to any outside authority. Examples of such "domestic questions" abound in the history of international relations: it is generally accepted that regulation of immigration represents a sphere subject to exclusive national control and that large but unspecified areas, particularly when deemed to relate to "vital national interests" such as defense, are wholly exempt from regulation except with the specific consent of the state in question.

The Charter of the United Nations also contains, in Article 2(7), a recognition of the concept of a reserved sphere of domestic questions, exempt from interference even by a global political organization.

## RIGHT OF EQUALITY

MEANING OF EQUALITY IN FACT; EQUALITY IN LAW    One of the oldest "rights" claimed for states has been the right of equality. This principle has been asserted since the days of Hugo Grotius by an impressive array of jurists and has been affirmed in countless governmental proclamations, particularly among the American republics. It is obvious that in most aspects, the states of the world are not at all equal, differing as they do in area, population, resources, access to oceans, armament, and, in general, in all the factors in the concepts of national power and power politics. What is involved in the "right" to equality is, rather, an equality in law, or an equality before the law, of all members of the community of nations.

The Permanent Court of International Justice, in 1935, distinguished between equality in fact and equality in law in its opinion on the *Minority Schools in Albania:*

It is perhaps not easy to define the distinction between the notions of equality in fact and equality in law; nevertheless, it may be said that the former notion excludes the idea of merely formal equality. . . . Equality in law precludes discrimination of any kind; whereas equality in fact may involve the necessity of different treat-

[5]General Assembly Res. 1564, U.N. Doc. A/4684 (1960) 66; see also Nanda, "Self-Determination in International Law," 66 *AJIL* 321 (1972).

ment in order to attain a result which establishes an equilibrium between different situations.[6]

Ironically enough, Article 2 of the Charter of the United Nations contains, among other principles, the notion of the "sovereign equality of its Members"; yet this concept is violated in Article 23 of the same instrument, in which five major powers are granted permanent seats on the Security Council, and the other 10 members of the body are elected for two-year terms. The 10 nonpermanent members of the Security Council suffer a further diminution of their "sovereign equality" through the provisions of Article 27, which spells out the voting procedure in the Security Council, including the veto power of the permanent members. On the other hand, Article 23 may be taken to represent a realistic appraisal of the role traditionally played in international relations by the great powers.

MEANING OF EQUALITY IN LAW    What, then, is meant by equality in law? It means that a state has one vote (unless it has agreed to the contrary) whenever a question has to be settled by consent among states. It means that legally the vote of the smallest state carries as much weight as does the vote of the largest and most powerful member of the community of nations. It means that no state may claim jurisdiction over another state and that hence no state normally can be sued in the courts of another state or can be subjected to the taxing power of the latter without its own consent. And it means that for a variety of reasons, each state accepts the validity of official acts of another state, insofar at least as those acts take effect in the territory of the latter.

There is still one other aspect of equality, the part that the doctrine plays in the adoption and applicability of new rules of international law. No state is bound by a new rule of law unless it explicitly or implicitly assents to that rule. This doctrine was expounded by U.S. Chief Justice John Marshall in the case of *The Antelope,* in which he held that the slave trade, then lawful under international law, could not be declared to be piracy by one state in order to limit the rights of other states:

No principle of general law is more universally acknowledged, than the perfect equality of nations. Russia and Geneva have equal rights. It results from this equality, that no one can rightfully impose a rule on another. Each legislates for itself, but its legislation can operate on itself alone. . . . As no nation can prescribe a rule for others, none can make a law of nations.[7]

No serious controversy has centered on this concept, according to which no state would be bound by new rules to which it had not agreed. But what

[6]*Minority Schools in Albania,* Advisory Opinion, P.C.I.J., 1935, Ser. A/B, No. 64.
[7]United States, Supreme Court, 1825, 10 Wheaton 66; see also *Le Louis,* 1817, 2 Dodson 210, and *The Scotia,* 1871, 14 Wallace 170, for similar statements in Supreme Court decisions.

about the right of any state, great or small, to participate on an equal basis in formulating new rules of law? What would happen if a small state, of no military strength or economic importance, were to set itself against the will of the rest of the states? Would there be any need at all for consulting such a state when new rules were drawn up? It has been pointed out that the Great Powers refused to accept the equality of states in this matter and proceeded to draw up rules among themselves that often assumed, at the very least, the character of particular international law: the Congress of Vienna (1815), the Congress of Paris (1856), the Congresses of Berlin (1878 and 1885), the Algeciras Conference of 1906, and so on.

The dramatic change occurred during the two Hague Peace Conferences of 1899 and 1907, when the attendance by delegations from many of the small nations and a strict observance of the principle of equality in voting procedures forced the Great Powers to pay attention to the views of the smaller states. States signed or failed to sign conventions, ratified agreements with reservations, and even failed to ratify conventions signed by their own delegations—all on a basis of absolute legal equality. The results of such procedures were conspicuously displayed in the defeat of a project to create the Judicial Arbitration Court, a plan generally favored by all the Great Powers but defeated by the vigorous opposition of the smaller states to a court not constituted on a basis of complete equality of all independent states.

The Charter of the United Nations, partially restoring *inequality* among the members, indicates the direction of recent thought on the question of equality in law.

First, unanimity has been abandoned in all organs of the United Nations, whereas it was still the rule in the Council and Assembly (in the latter under certain conditions) of the League of Nations. Qualified majorities may be required under specific circumstances, but unanimity, formerly assumed to be an essential element in state equality, has been forsaken. On the other hand, equality of representation has been preserved in the General Assembly as well as in the Economic and Social Council; it has been abandoned in the Security Council. Only the Security Council can make its decisions binding on the member states of the United Nations; in all other true organs of the organization, decisions represent recommendations rather than binding obligations.

## RIGHT OF SELF-DEFENSE

DETERMINATION OF WHAT SELF-DEFENSE CONSTITUTES    There can be no doubt that every legal system in the world recognizes and supports a right of self-defense.[8] What is in question are the conditions under which such

[8] See Whiteman, vol. 5, 966–1048.

a right might be invoked and the means that are to be employed in its exercise. Many writers have asserted that the use of force by a given state can be justified, even though no armed attack on it has taken place as yet in the course of a dispute with another state.

LIMITATION ON THE RIGHT OF SELF-DEFENSE    On the other hand, there is a fairly recently developed and commonly accepted limitation on the right of self-defense: force used to defend a state must be reasonably proportionate to the danger that is to be averted. And at the same time an increasingly widespread attitude holds that the question of whether the defensive actions taken by a given state are really necessary or whether they should be regarded as excessive can be determined by independent outside judges, such as by an international court, an arbitration tribunal, or even an international political body (say, the Security Council) acting as a judicial agency.[9] It is obvious that any such determinations would assume an *ex post facto* character in view of the time element involved. Immediate danger of extinction through armed attack or successful fifth-column activities does not permit recourse to judicial investigations of means to be employed to repel the danger before the desired steps are taken.

Illustrating the desire to submit the question of "lawful" self-defense to outside determination was the rather categorical statement by the International Military Tribunal at Nuremberg that

whether action taken under the claim of self-defense was in fact aggressive or defensive must ultimately be subject to investigation and adjudication if international law is ever to be enforced.[10]

UN CHARTER PROVISIONS RELATING TO SELF-DEFENSE    The Charter of the United Nations deals in two key positions with the problem of self-defense. Article 2(4) states that

all members shall refrain in their international relations from the threat or use of force against the territorial integrity or political independence of any State, or in any other manner inconsistent with the purposes of the United Nations.

The main provisions of Article 51 read:

Nothing in the present Charter shall impair the inherent right of individual or collective self-defense if an armed attack occurs against a Member of the United Nations, until the Security Council has taken the measures necessary to maintain international peace and security.

[9] Consult Lauterpacht's *Oppenheim*, vol. 1, 297–304, esp. 299, on self-preservation; and see Stone, 243–53, on the subject.
[10] *Trial of the Major War Criminals before the International Military Tribunal, Nuremberg, 14 November 1945–1 October 1946,* Nuremberg, 1947–1949 (42 vols.), vol. 1, 208.

If the veto is used to prevent the Security Council from taking the measures in question, the power to exercise judgment and control may be assumed by the General Assembly under the "Uniting for Peace" Resolution of 1950. [11]

Under general international law a state has always been the sole judge of whether a degree of emergency exists that justifies the employment of force in self-defense. Article 51, at least in theory, imposes a limitation: a state acting on the basis of self-judgment does so at its own peril, and its actions are, again in theory, subject to scrutiny by the Security Council.

It is not surprising, therefore, that what the provisions of the Charter imply with respect to the right of self-defense has been the subject of considerable controversy. Many writers have asserted that the use of *inherent* in Article 51 clearly establishes a right of states to use force in self-defense and that Article 51 does not imply an impairment of that right until the Security Council (or the General Assembly) has acted. Such a view, shared by the present writer, holds therefore that the right of self-defense is not at all based on the Charter but is a normal right of states under international law. What Article 51 does, in this view, is to limit the exercise of the right in question. Support for the inherent right of self-defense is found in the statement of Committee I at the San Francisco Conference, which declared unequivocally (in the preparatory stages) that "the use of arms in legitimate self-defense remains admitted and unimpaired." Brierly pointed out that there is no indication that the inclusion of armed attack in Article 51 was intended to prevent the use of force in meeting unlawful forceful acts not in the nature of an armed attack. For instance, heavy and continuing troop concentrations along a border might lead to the "anticipatory" or "preventive" use of force to meet the threat of attack before the latter actually materialized. [12] This concept, shared by the present writer, would justify the "preventive attack" by Israel on its Egyptian and Arab neighbors in the case of the Six-Day War of 1967. On the other hand, certain other anticipatory attacks have been characterized as self-defense when the factual basis for such a judgment was not as clear, such as Israel's invasion of Lebanon, as described by Abraham D. Sofaer, Legal Advisor to the U.S. Department of State. [13]

Logic and practice have combined to clarify the apparent restriction of Article 51 to cases of attack "against a Member of the United Nations." The

---

[11] General Assembly, 1950; text in 9 *UN Bulletin* 508.

[12] See Stone, 244, n. 8, and the opposing arguments quoted in Whiteman, vol. 5, 868–71. State practices does not affirm either view of self-defense: see Higgins, *The Development of International Law through the Political Organs of the United Nations* (1963), 200–203. The United Kingdom has supported the right in question, whereas the provisions of the North Atlantic Treaty fail to do so.

[13] Saikowski in *CSM*, April 4, 1986, 16. See also the excellent analysis of the entire question in Schachter, "Self-Defense and the Rule of Law," 83 *AJIL* 259 (1989), as well as Baker, "Terrorism and the Inherent Right of Self-Defense (A Call to Amend Article 51 of the United Nations Charter)," 10 *Houston J. Int'l. Law* 25 (1987).

wording can be taken to mean that collective self-defense cannot be applied through the use of armed force if aggression has been committed against a nonmember state. The events of 1950, however, showed that the invasion of South Korea, a nonmember, resulted in the utilization of collective defense efforts by the United Nations.

General agreement on the subject of defense against armed attack can be said to exist only on two counts: resort to force in self-defense is lawful in the event of instant and overwhelming necessity, and acts taken in self-defense must be limited to defense itself and must not be transformed into reprisals or "punitive sanctions" (see also Chapter 23 under "United Nations").

One of the problems of self-defense is the status of the law governing the use of force to defend nationals abroad. This troublesome point arose again in the *Case Concerning United States Diplomatic and Consular Staff in Tehran (U.S.A. v. Iran)* in 1980 (see Chapter 19 for details). The point at issue was the abortive attempt by the United States to rescue the American hostages held in Tehran. Although the International Court of Justice did not deal directly with that attempt, it has been pointed out that certain portions of the judgment in this case hinted at the idea that "armed attacks" under Article 51 of the UN Charter might cover matters other than a major military assault on a country. At two points in the judgment, the court referred to an "armed attack" in regard to the takeover of the U.S. embassy, and the United States asserted to the Security Council that the mission had been carried out "in exercise of its inherent right of self-defense with the aim of extricating American nationals who have been and remain the victims of the Iranian armed attack on our Embassy."[14] More recently occurred the United States' attack on Panama (December 19, 1989). The official White House spokesman asserted that the invasion was legally justified by the necessity to protect American lives, to uphold American rights under the Panama Canal treaty, and to apprehend [for trial in the United States] Panama's leader, General Manuel Noriega, as a trafficker in drugs. A few days later, the U.S. Ambassador to the United Nations (Pickering) stated, "We acted in Panama for legitimate reasons of self-defense and to protect the integrity of the Canal treaties." Almost all United Nations members rejected the American argument that the United States acted in self-defense to protect the 35,000 U.S. citizens in Panama (see Chapter 12).

Nothing is said in Article 51 concerning unfriendly actions aimed at one state by another state but lacking any aspects of an armed attack. Failing an application of Article 2(4) under given circumstances, a virtually unlimited right of self-defense by means short of the threat or use of force seems to be indicated.

COLLECTIVE SELF-DEFENSE    The employment of the term *collective self-defense* is somewhat misleading, for what is actually meant is defense against attack,

---

[14]See Stein, "Contempt, Crisis, and the Court: The World Court and the Hostage Attempt," 76 *AJIL* 499, 500 n. 7 and 8 (1982); Ronzitti, *Rescuing Nationals Abroad through Military Coercion and Intervention on Grounds of Humanity* (1985).

by one state or a group of states, of another state.[15] The concept does not refer to an action in the name or under the authority of the United Nations as an organization. It is, in other words, *not* synonymous with *collective security*. It means, rather, an independent exercise of armed force by states on behalf of another state under the specific conditions outlined in Article 51 of the Charter. It does not in any manner correspond to the punishment of an aggressor or to a police or enforcement action by the United Nations, but merely to the assistance given to repel an illegal armed attack on a state.

## RIGHTS OF INTERNATIONAL ORGANIZATIONS

Among the subjects of international law are included not only independent states but also certain international legal persons, that is, international organizations. Whatever may have been the legal status of such agencies before World War II, there can be no question that since 1945 a number of organizations, created by states through international conventions, have enjoyed the position of subjects of the law. The attributes of their international personality, however, are limited by the treaty creating each of these international agencies. It is this treaty alone that shapes their constitution and delegates authority to them. They therefore are not original subjects, such as states, of international law but are what should be termed *derived,* or *derivative,* subjects of that law.

The primary document certifying this relatively new development in international law is the Advisory Opinion of the International Court of Justice on *Reparations for Injuries Suffered in the Service of the United Nations.*[16] The court stated that "Fifty States, representing the vast majority of the members of the international community, had the power, in conformity with international law, to bring into being an entity possessing objective international personality, and not personality recognized by them alone, together with capacity to bring international claims."[17]

Because states, both in their corporate capacity and in the person of the chief of state, have certain privileges, the question arises as to the possession of similar privileges by international organizations that have achieved international legal personality.

HISTORY OF PRIVILEGES    The history of the privileges enjoyed by international organizations shows that three approaches were adopted successively by the community of nations. Initially, rather far-reaching privileges, designed to ensure an organization's complete independence, were granted.

---

[15]See Whiteman, vol. 5, 1049–1175.
[16]International Court of Justice, 1949, *I.C.J. Reports, 1949,* 174.
[17]*Id.,* 174, 178, 179, 185; the opinion was reprinted in 43 *AJIL* 590 (1949); see also Wright, "Responsibility for Injuries to United Nations Officials," 43 *AJIL* 95 (1949), and his "The Jural Personality of the United Nations," *id.,* 509. The most comprehensive analysis available of the legal status of the United Nations is Weinberg, *The International Status of the United Nations* (1961).

This practice was followed, between 1919 and the end of World War II, by the extension of diplomatic immunity to the essentially nondiplomatic functionaries of international agencies. And since 1945, the granting of privileges and immunities, as phrased typically in Article 105 of the UN Charter, has covered everything "necessary for the fulfillment of its purposes." A reversion to the older style of diplomatic privileges should be observed, however, in the United Nations General Convention.[18]

It should be kept in mind that the privileges and immunities of international organizations are a matter wholly separate and different from the privileges and immunities of officials or agents of those same organizations. What matters here, however, is the status of the organizations themselves, with reference to immunity from suit, process, execution, and so on.

LEGAL PERSONALITY OF THE UNITED NATIONS    In regard to the United Nations, Article 105 of the Charter states that the organization shall enjoy such immunities as are necessary for the fulfillment of its purposes. It should be noted that there is no comparison with state immunities; instead, a standard appropriate to its needs has been created. The report of the drafting committee in 1945 mentioned immunity from suit as an example of necessary privileges under Article 105 and made it clear that that article was to be regarded as self-executing. Other provisions of the Charter supply additional evidence that the United Nations is a legal person, by stating its jural powers as well as responsibilities (Arts. 24, 26, 41, and 42), by authorizing it to conclude binding agreements with its members and with specialized international agencies (Arts. 43 and 63), and by stating explicitly that "The Organization shall enjoy in the territory of each of its Members such legal capacity as may be necessary for the exercise of its functions and the fulfillment of its purposes" (Art. 104).

UN CHARTER AND DOMESTIC LEGISLATION    One of the important aspects connected with the legal status of the United Nations, as well as with the subject of treaties (discussed subsequently), is whether the Charter, as a multipartite treaty, might be taken to supersede conflicting domestic legislation of member states. This issue came into prominence in the well-known case of *Sei Fujii* v. *State of California*.[19] Fujii had sued in an attempt to have the

---

[18]The full text of the convention, as approved by the General Assembly on Feb. 13, 1946, is found in 43 *AJIL* Supp. 1 (1949). Concerning immunity, see Article 4, sec. 11, par. f and g; Article 5, sec. 18, par. e and f; and sec. 19 of the convention. The same wording is also found in the constitution of the Food and Agriculture Organization (Art. 15, par. 2, and Art. 7, par. 4) and in Article 19 of the Statute of the International Court of Justice. On the other hand, the style found in Article 105 of the Charter is duplicated in the constitution of the ITO (Art. 74) and of the World Health Organization (Art. 67). Consult also the "Headquarters" *Agreement between the United States and the United Nations* of June 26, 1947 and the *Interim Agreement* of Dec. 18, 1947 between the same parties; both documents reprinted in 43 *AJIL* 8 (Jan. 1949 Supp.).

[19]242 Pac. [2d] 617, 1952, reprinted in full in 46 *AJIL* 559 (1952); see also 44 *AJIL* 543, 590 (1950); and 46 *AJIL* 682 (1952) for notes by Hudson and Fairman.

California Alien Land Law set aside as violating the Charter of the United Nations. The law prohibited ownership of land by an alien who was ineligible for citizenship—unless some contrary treaty right existed. The California Supreme Court, in holding that the law was indeed invalid and basing its decision on a violation of the Fourteenth Amendment to the Constitution of the United States, said in part:

The humane and enlightened objectives of the United Nations Charter are, of course, entitled to respectful consideration by the courts and Legislatures of every member nation, since that document expresses the universal desire of thinking men for peace and for equality of rights and opportunities. The Charter represents a moral commitment of foremost importance, and we must not permit the spirit of our pledge to be compromised or disparaged in either our domestic or foreign affairs. We are satisfied, however, that the Charter provisions relied on by plaintiff [U.N. Charter, Preamble and Arts. 1, 55, 56] were not intended to supersede existing domestic legislation, and we cannot hold that they operate to invalidate the alien land law.[20]

The California court did not deny that the UN Charter was a treaty and that the United States Constitution provided (Art. VI) that treaties made under the authority of the United States are part of the supreme law of the land. A treaty, however, did not automatically supersede local laws that were inconsistent with it unless the treaty provisions were self-executing. In other words, when the terms of the treaty imputed the existence of a contract, when either party engaged to perform a particular act, then the treaty related to the political and not to the judicial department. The legislative branch then had to execute the contract before the treaty could become a rule for the courts. And in the case at hand, there had been no such execution by the legislative branch. On the other hand, when an international agreement to which the United States is a party indicates an intention that its provisions are to be effective under the domestic law of the parties at the time the agreement enters into force, it will normally be held by the (U.S.) courts to be self-executing under the laws of the United States. Its provisions will be law within the country. The decision as to whether a given agreement is self-executing must be made either by the courts or by the Executive Branch (see Chapter 13 under the ratification of the Genocide Convention).

AGENCIES HAVING LIMITED LEGAL PERSONALITY    Certain international organizations possess what may be termed *limited international personality.* Thus the European Coal and Steel Community (ECSC) and the European Economic Community (EEC) have the right, under their basic instruments, to conclude agreements with states and to deal with the representatives of

[20]See 26 *Department of State Bulletin,* May 12, 1952, 744. Although the California Supreme Court split 4 to 3 on the constitutional issues in the case, all seven justices agreed that the human rights provision of the United Nations Charter did not operate by itself to invalidate the Alien Land Law.

such states. Many countries, including the United States, have concluded treaties with the ECSC and EURATOM, and several states maintain a diplomatic mission accredited to these agencies. The privileges and immunities of public international organizations in the United States are governed by the International Organizations Immunities Act of 1945. Thus, for example, the International Bank for Reconstruction and Development (World Bank), having been designated by the president under the Act, enjoys immunity from suit and every form of judicial process unless such immunity is waived by the Bank for any proceedings or by the terms of a contract.

INTERNATIONAL PUBLIC CORPORATIONS    Quite different in status, in regard to international personality, are certain other international organizations that may be termed *international public corporations.* Such entities as the International Monetary Fund and the World Bank do not have the status of persons under international law and hence are not subjects of that law. The entities in this category represent what are currently referred to as *supranational corporations.* Thus far, at least, it has not appeared necessary to the community of nations to give such technical agencies the privileges and immunities pertaining to persons under international law.

## IMMUNITIES OF STATES

Independence from outside control represents not only an alleged right of each sovereign state but also an essential characteristic of each such entity. Over time, each independent state consented to waive the exercise of a portion of its presumably exclusive territorial jurisdiction when the government of another independent state intruded, under certain conditions and in time of peace, into that jurisdiction. In other words, initially by comity or courtesy and later on the basis of customary international law, the foreign sovereign enjoyed immunity from suit and other aspects of territorial jurisdiction.

According to the classical, or absolute, theory of sovereign immunity, a foreign sovereign could not, without his consent, be made a defendant in the courts of another sovereign. But according to a newer and restrictive theory of sovereign immunity, such exemption has been recognized only with respect to sovereign or public acts of a state and not necessarily with respect to its so-called private acts.

Long ago, the principle of sovereign immunity embraced both the government of a foreign sovereign (state immunity) and the individual head of the state in question (personal immunity). Today the two forms of immunity are distinct and must be discussed separately.

### Personal Immunity of a Foreign Sovereign

THEORY OF ABSOLUTE IMMUNITY    Little has changed in the theory of the personal immunity of a foreign sovereign or head of state, an immunity based on old and recognized customary rules of international law. Regardless of whether an individual is constitutionally the actual head of a state or only its nominal head, he or she enjoys complete immunity from suit or judicial process in the territory of another state. This principle applies equally to crowned heads of state and elected heads of state, as well as to their immediate families. In the United States, the Supreme Court has mandated that the courts of this country are bound by suggestions of immunity which are submitted to the courts by the executive branch.[21] And whatever the sovereign may do in the territory of another state, he or she is immune from all prosecution, civil or criminal.

Examples of this immunity abound in the literature of international law, and some of the questions raised by personal immunity are fascinating indeed, even though the problems of state immunity are far more important today. The leading case, cited in virtually every collection, is *Mighell* v. *Sultan of Johore*, decided in 1894:

### MIGHELL v. SULTAN OF JOHORE
### COURT OF APPEAL
*Great Britain, Queen's Bench Division*
*(1894) 1 Q.B. 149*

FACTS    The Sultan of Johore, visiting in England, used the pseudonym of Albert Baker. He became acquainted with the plaintiff and promised to marry her. When he failed to keep that promise, she sued him for breach of promise, and he in turn pleaded that English courts had no jurisdiction since he was an independent sovereign ruler who had not waived his privilege of immunity. The Court of First Instance upheld the Sultan and the case came to the Court of Appeal at the request of the plaintiff.

The Court inquired at the Colonial Office as to the legal status of the Sultan of Johore and received a reply stating that the Sultan was an independent sovereign ruler.

ISSUES    (1) Whether the letter sent on behalf of the Secretary of State for Colonies was sufficient proof of the status of the Sultan of Johore.

(2) Whether the Sultan was immune from the jurisdiction of British courts.

DECISION    Judgment for the defendant; appeal dismissed.

As to Issue No. 1: Certification by a Minister of the Crown as to the status of the Sultan of Johore was sufficient and decisive, insofar as British courts were concerned.

As to Issue No. 2: In view of the facts brought out in the letter from the Colonial Office, the Sultan of Johore had to be regarded in British courts as an independent sovereign ruler and hence as immune from the jurisdiction of those courts.

REASONING    (1) Certification of the status of a foreign sovereign by means of an official communication from an advisor of the British sovereign binds English courts and is to be accepted as conclusive as far as those courts are concerned. [A similar situation would prevail if an American court were to inquire about such a matter of the Department of State; the court would

---

[21]*Ex parte Republic of Peru (The Ucayali)*, 1943, 318 U.S. 578, 589.

accept the "certificate" of the Department as conclusive.]

(2) The relationship existing between
Great Britain and the Sultanate of
Johore was based on a treaty of protection by which the Sultan was to
enjoy the protection of Great Britain,
engaging, on his part, not to enter into
treaties with any foreign states. In the
opinion of the Court, "the agreement
by the Sultan not to enter into treaties
with another Power does not seem . . .

to be an abnegation of his right to enter into such treaties, but only a condition upon which the protection stipulated for is to be given. If the Sultan
disregards it, the consequences may be
the loss of that protection, or possibly other difficulties with this country;
but I do not think that there is anything in the treaty which qualifies or
disproves the statement in the letter that
the Sultan of Johore is an independent
sovereign."

Similarly, the Gaekwar of Baroda, named as correspondent in the divorce
suit of *Statham* v. *Statham and the Gaekwar of Baroda,*[22] was declared by a
British court to be immune from suit because of his position as sovereign
of an independent state in India.

Foreign sovereigns or heads of state not only enjoy personal immunity
from suit, but also cannot be named as a party defendant to a suit brought
against them in their official capacity as the representative of their state. This
was brought out in the well-known case of *De Haber* v. *Queen of Portugal,*[23]
in which a British court dismissed on grounds of immunity a suit for money
allegedly wrongfully paid to the government of Portugal.

On the other hand, if a former head of state is involved in a case in
another country, especially if the successor government of his or her own
state waives any claim to immunity (or should seek to prosecute him or
her), then no immunity exists for the former head of state.[24]

If the foreign sovereign submits to the jurisdiction of a court and later
is cited as defendant in an appeal from an earlier decision, it may be held
that any claim of immunity put forth against the second action should
be denied. This point of view was stated elaborately in *Sultan of Johore* v.
*Abubakar Tunku Aris Bendahar.*[25] The sultan of Johore had brought a suit in
a Japanese court in Singapore (during the Japanese occupation of Malaya in

[22]Great Britain, Probate Court, 1912, [1912] 12.

[23]Great Britain, Court of Queen's Bench, 1851, 17 Q.B. 196. See also the U.S. government's
"suggestion" of immunity in *Estate of Silme G. Domingo et al.* v. *Ferdinand E. Marcos et al.*
(Civil Action No. C82 1055V), U.S. Dist. Court, W.D. Wash., 1982, reported in 77 *AJIL*
305 (1983).

[24]See *Republic of the Philippines* v. *Marcos,* 806 F.2d 344, U.S. Court of Appeals, 2d Cir.,
Nov. 26, 1986, reported in 81 *AJIL* 417 (1987) and *In Re Doe,* 860 F.2d 40. U.S. Court
of Appeals, 2d Cir., Oct. 19, 1988 [also *re* Ferdinand—and Imelda—Marcos], reported by
Born and Callcott in 83 *AJIL* 371 (1989).

[25]British Commonwealth of Nations, Privy Council, Apr. 22, 1952, reported in 47 *AJIL*
153 (1953).

World War II) against his son and the Japanese Custodian of Alien Property to obtain title to two lots in Singapore. The sultan won his case, but after the defeat of Japan, his son started a suit in the new Supreme Court of the Colony of Singapore to set aside the verdict of the Japanese occupation court. The sultan promptly claimed personal sovereign immunity and, when this claim was denied, appealed to the Privy Council.

Although the sultan and the British government were in agreement about his status as an independent sovereign, the denial of his claim to immunity was upheld for the reason that the proceedings before the Supreme Court of Singapore represented an appeal from the judgment in a case brought by the sovereign, who by that initial act had waived his normal immunity. The Privy Council commented that there had not been established (in England) any absolute rule exempting a foreign sovereign from any and all jurisdiction of British courts.

It might be added that a change appears to have been under way for some 40 years or so in connection with the traditional rule that a state or its sovereign loses the right to immunity in the event of counterclaims brought against it (or him, in the case of a head of state) by the defendants in a case originally brought to the courts of another country.[26] Such counterclaims have generally been barred by national courts because it appears settled that sovereign immunity is not waived by commencement of an action in a foreign court.[27] In 1955, however, the decision of the U.S. Supreme Court in *National City Bank* v. *Republic of China*[28] and other cases indicated that if the counterclaims by the defendants arise out of the same action and the same matter as the original claim, domestic courts may deny immunity with respect to such counterclaims to the foreign state or sovereign.[29]

## State Immunity

The question of state immunity is a far more complicated and also more important subject than the somewhat archaic personal immunity of heads of state. As was pointed out earlier, the traditional absolute theory of immunity exempted a state in every way from the jurisdiction of other countries: its government could not be sued abroad without its consent; its public property could not be attached; its public vessels could not be arrested, boarded, or

---

[26]See Robert B. Looper, "Counterclaims Against a Foreign Sovereign Plaintiff," 50 *AJIL* 647–53 (1956); and *Republic of China* v. *Pang-Tsu Mow,* U.S. Court of Appeals, Dist. of Col., 1952, 201 F.2d 195.

[27]See *Kingdom of Roumania* v. *Guaranty Trust Co.,* 1918, U.S. Court of Appeals, 2nd Cir., 250 F. 341; and *Republic of Haiti* v. *Plesch et al.,* 73 New York Supreme Court, Special Term, 1947, 73 N.Y.S. [2d] 645.

[28]U.S., Supreme Court, 1955, 348 U.S. 356.

[29]See *Banco Nacional de Cuba* v. *Chemical Bank New York Trust Co.,* U.S. District Court, S.D.N.Y., Oct. 16, 1984, in 79 *AJIL* 459 (1985).

sued; nor could any property or real estate owned by the state be taxed or attached in whatever country it might be located.

GOVERNMENTAL PROPERTY ABROAD    It regard to governmental property abroad, only the title to such property could be questioned in the courts of another country; once sovereign claim to title was established, absolute immunity prevailed.[30]

One of the classic cases illustrating the traditional theory of state immunity was that of the *Schooner Exchange:*

## THE SCHOONER EXCHANGE v. MACFADDON
### United States, Supreme Court, 1812
### 7 Cranch 116 (1812)

FACTS    The defendants, MacFaddon and Greetham, alleged that they were the sole owners of the *Exchange* when it sailed from Baltimore for San Sebastian, Spain, on October 27, 1809; that the schooner was seized on December 30, 1810, by persons acting under the decrees and orders of Napoleon, Emperor of France, in violation of international law; that the vessel, renamed the *Balaou,* was in Philadelphia in possession of a certain Dennis Begon, although no sentence of decree of condemnation had been pronounced against the ship by any court of competent jurisdiction; that they asked that the courts restore the vessel to their ownership. The U.S. District Attorney had appeared in the District Court and argued that because peace existed between France and the United States, public vessels of France could freely enter and leave the ports of the United States, and that the former *Exchange* was now a public vessel of France, hence immune from American jurisdiction. The District Court dismissed the suit of MacFaddon and Greetham, a decision that was reversed by the Circuit Court, and so the case came, by appeal, before the Supreme Court of the United States.

ISSUE    Could an American citizen assert in an American court title to an armed public vessel of a foreign country, found within the waters of the United States?

DECISION    Sentence of Circuit Court reversed and decision of District Court affirmed: the suit was dismissed for want of jurisdiction.

REASONING    (1) The jurisdiction of a state within its own territory is necessarily exclusive and absolute. It is not subject to any limitation not imposed by the state on itself. All exceptions to this complete and absolute jurisdiction must be traced to the consent of the nation itself. But the perfect equality and absolute independence of sovereigns have given rise to a class of cases in which ev-

[30]See *French Republic* v. *Board of Supervisors of Jefferson County,* U.S. Court of Appeals of Kentucky, 1923, 200 Ky. 18, 252 S.W. 124; *Brownell* v. *City and County of San Francisco,* U.S., California Court of Appeals, 1st Dist., Div. 1, 1954, 126 Cal. App. [2d] 102, 271 P. 2d 974; and the valuable pioneer study by Bishop, "Immunity from Taxation of Foreign State-owned Property," 46 *AJIL* 239 (1952).

ery sovereign is understood to waive the exercise of parts of that complete exclusive territorial jurisdiction, and one of these applies to warships entering the ports of a friendly power. If a sovereign permits his ports to remain open to the public ships of friendly foreign states, the conclusion is that such ships enter by his assent. And "it seems, then, to the court, to be a principle of public law, that national ships of war, entering the port of a friendly power open for their reception, are to be considered as exempted by the consent of that power from its jurisdiction."

The courts are not competent to enforce their decisions in cases of this description.

(2) The *Exchange* [captured by the French navy in pursuit of its blockade of England] had been transformed in the port of Bayonne by order of the French government into a public armed vessel of France. The vessel must be presumed to have entered American waters and the port of Philadelphia under the implied promise that while behaving in a friendly manner, it would be exempted from the jurisdiction of the United States.

ACT-OF-STATE DOCTRINE    International law is said to require each state to respect the validity of the public acts of other states, in the sense that its courts will not pass judgment on the legality or the constitutionality of a foreign sovereign's acts under his own laws. One of the classic statements of this so-called act-of-state doctrine is found in the dictum of Chief Justice Fuller in *Underhill* v. *Hernandez:*

Every sovereign state is bound to respect the independence of every other sovereign state, and the courts of one country will not sit in judgment on the acts of the government of another done within its own territory.[31]

The act-of-state doctrine, which represented the basic principle underlying the *Exchange* case, could also be phrased to read that "international law requires each State to respect the validity of foreign State acts, in the sense of refusing to permit its courts to sit in judgment on the legality or constitutionality of the foreign act under foreign law."[32]

Similarly, a number of other decisions of the Supreme Court appeared to indicate that the act-of-state doctrine formed a principle of international law. In fact, however, the practice of many states indicated that they did not regard such an interpretation as correct. The U.S. Supreme Court joined this point of view in 1964, when in *Banco Nacional de Cuba* v. *Sabbatino* (376 U.S. 398, 421) it held that the act-of-state doctrine was not a rule of international law and that its application was not required by that law.

In the *Sabbatino* case, the court stated that instead of laying down or

[31]U.S. Supreme Court, 1897, 168 U.S. 250. See also the monographic treatment in Zander, "The Act of State Doctrine," 53 *AJIL* 826 (1959).
[32]Briggs, 404.

reaffirming an inflexible and all-inclusive rule, the judicial branch would not examine the validity of an act of expropriation within its own territory by a foreign sovereign government (existing and recognized by the United States at the time of suit) in the absence of a treaty or other controlling legal principles, even if the allegation was made that the expropriation violated customary international law.[33]

As a direct consequence of the *Sabbatino* case, Congress incorporated in 1964 a new paragraph into the Foreign Assistance Act of 1961. Amended in 1965, the paragraph (620[a]2) provided that no courts in the United States were to decline on the ground of the federal act-of-state doctrine to determine the merits implementing the principles of international law in a case in which a claim to property was asserted, based on confiscation after January 1, 1959, by an act in violation of the principles of international law. The Department of State strongly objected to this so-called Sabbatino or second Hickenlooper amendment.[34] The latter, however, did not affect the determination of a foreign government's immunity from suit in United States courts.[35]

The most recent U.S. Supreme Court review of an act-of-state case of importance came in 1990, in the case of *W. S. Kirkpatrick & Co. et al.* v. *Environmental Tectonic Corp., International* on January 17, 1990.[36]

The Court held that the act of state doctrine only precluded examination of the validity or legality of foreign governmental acts performed in that government's territory. Other considerations, such as motivation, played no part in the application of the doctrine.

SEIZURE OF GOVERNMENT PROPERTY    Another aspect of immunity pertains to the seizure of the property of a foreign state. In a classic case in this sphere, the court ruled that a foreign sovereign cannot be deprived of his property by the domestic tribunals of another state:

[33]U.S. District Court, S.D.N.Y., 1961, 193 F. Supp. 375, digested in 55 *AJIL* 741 (1961); affirmed on appeal, Court of Appeals, 2d Cir., 1962, 307 F.2d 834, reprinted in 56 *AJIL* 1085 (1962); reversed and remanded, Supreme Court, 1964, 376 U.S. 398, abstracted at length in 59 *AJIL* 799 (1964) (including Justice White's lengthy dissent); U.S. Dist. Court, S.D.N.Y., 1965, on remand, 243 F. Supp. 957, and Memorandum Opinion, Nov. 15, 1965, 272 F. Supp. 836, digested in Whiteman, vol. 6, 31–36 and reproduced at length in 60 *AJIL* 107 (1966); decision affirmed on appeal, Court of Appeals, 2d Cir., 1967, 383 F. 2d 166; *certiorari* denied, 1968, 390 U.S. 956; rehearing denied, 1968, 390 U.S. 1037. The complicated series of decisions is analyzed carefully, with supporting documents, in Whiteman, vol. 6, 20–36.
[34]See Whiteman, vol. 6, 27–31, for details. The formal reference to the "Hickenlooper" amendment is Section 620(e)(2) of the Foreign Assistance Act of 1961, as Amended [22 U.S.C. 2370(e)(2)]; the section in question is reprinted in 57 *AJIL* 749 (1967). Consult also Lowenfeld, "The Sabbatino Amendment—International Law Meets Civil Procedure," 59 *AJIL* 899 (1965).
[35]*American Hawaiian Ventures* v. *M V J. Latuharhary,* U.S. District Court, N.J., 1966, 257 F. Supp. 622, reported by Matthews in 8 *Harvard Int'l. L. Jl.* 357 (1967).
[36]Text, with Ristau's "Introductory Note," in 29 *ILM* 182 (1990).

## VAVASSEUR v. KRUPP
### Great Britain, Court of Appeal
### 1878, 9 Ch. Div. 351.

FACTS    Josiah Vavasseur had brought an action against Friedrich Krupp, of Essen, Germany, Alfred Longsden, his agent in England, and Ahrens & Co., described as agents of the government of Japan, claiming an injunction and damages for infringement of his patent for making shells and other projectiles. The shells in question had been brought to England in order to be placed aboard three warships being built there to the order of the Japanese government.

On January 18, 1878, an injunction was granted by a British court, restraining the defendants and the owners of the wharf where the shells were stored from selling or delivering the shells to the Japanese government or any of its agents.

On May 11, 1878, an application was made to the British court on behalf of the Emperor of Japan and his envoy extraordinary [to Great Britain] that, notwithstanding the injunction granted, the emperor and his agents be permitted to remove the shells and proposing that, if and insofar as it might be necessary, the emperor and his envoy be added to the list of defendants in this suit. The emperor submitted to the jurisdiction of the British court and deposited £100 as security for costs, and his name was added to the list of defendants. A motion then was made to dissolve the injunction. The Master of the Rolls granted permission to remove the shells from the wharf. This decision was appealed.

ISSUE    Could British courts deprive a foreign sovereign of his public property or deny him the right to remove such property from British jurisdiction?

DECISION    Appeal against the order of the Master of the Rolls dismissed, injunction dissolved. English courts may not deprive a foreign sovereign of his public property.

REASONING    (1) The shells were bought by the emperor of Japan for the purposes of his government. They were the lawful property of the emperor, transported to England on their way to Japan. Even if the patent of Vavasseur had been infringed, this was not a question to be considered. The shells themselves were not affected by any alleged violation of the patent laws.

(2) Vavasseur's claim that the emperor of Japan, by having himself added to the list of defendants, submitted to the jurisdiction of the British courts is irrelevant. The emperor submitted to British jurisdiction for the single purpose of having the injunction dissolved and clearly never intended to waive immunity and have his public property submitted to the jurisdiction of a foreign court.

(3) If Vavasseur had any claims against F. Krupp in Essen, those claims should be prosecuted against F. Krupp. The emperor of Japan, having lawfully acquired public property in Germany, was in no way connected with the alleged violation of patent rights.[37]

---

[37] A similar interpretation may be found in *Ex Parte Republic of Peru (The Ucayali)*, U.S. Supreme Court, 1943, 318 U.S. 578. Consult also *Banque de France v. Equitable Trust Company*, U.S. Dist. Court, S.D.N.Y., 1929, 33 F.2d 202.

In general, the rule is that both the personal and the real property of a foreign sovereign located in another state is immune from suit and seizure. On the other hand, jurisdiction over such foreign state-owned property may be assumed by the local courts of another country when the foreign state has consented to the exercise of such jurisdiction. That consent may be either explicit or implicit. The latter instance would be the case if the foreign state voluntarily appeared in court to seek a remedy for the dispute at hand, in which event the defendant may well file a counterclaim: with that filing, the foreign state's immunity disappears. But the counterclaim must arise out of the *original* action and cannot relate to some other matter of any kind. Immunity from suit also is implicitly waived when a state enters into an agreement to arbitrate a dispute.[38]

NEED FOR RESTRICTING STATE IMMUNITY    Although for decade after decade the immunity of foreign governments was affirmed by the courts of major countries, the passage of time brought new problems connected with state immunity. The fact that extensive commercial activities of modern governments began to be carried on beyond their borders through government-owned corporations resulted in more and more pleas of sovereign immunity when such corporations, or, in some instances, the vessels operated by them, were sued in foreign courts.

Consequently there arose in the twentieth century a steadily increasing need for clarification of the status of such enterprises, for a distinction between public and private activities of sovereigns, together with a growing conviction that the private activities of a foreign sovereign ought not to give rise to state immunity in foreign courts.

It is very important to draw a distinction between the sovereign acts discussed. They may be public acts that confer immunity abroad on the state or private acts that would not enjoy such immunity. There are two tests applicable to the determination of state immunity: the "nature of the act" and the "purpose of the act." The latter has been adopted by France and several other countries and is a more precise way to determine state immunity. The "nature of the act" test can merely spell out whether or not a given sovereign act is commercial in nature. If the act is commercial, then under modern usage the state in question lacks immunity for it in foreign courts. The more accurate "purpose" test reflects the fact that sovereign acts may indeed be commercial but reflect state purposes. In that case the acts in question would enjoy the protection of *jus imperii* (the law of sovereignty) and the state would enjoy immunity abroad. To illustrate: if a state imports quantities of woolen materials for sale in its territory, that act would lack

---

[38] See *In re Maritime International Nominees Establishment v. Republic of Guinea.* U.S. Dist. Court, D.C., Jan. 12, 1981, 505 F. Supp. 141, reported in 75 *AJIL* 963 (1981), the brief for the U.S. Court of Appeals, Oct. 22, 1981, reprinted in 20 *ILM* 1436 (1981); *In the Matter of the Arbitration between Maritime International Nominees Establishment* v. *The Republic of Guinea, Appellant, United States of America, Intervenor,* U.S. Court of Appeals, D.C., Nov. 12, 1982, in 21 *ILM* 1355 (1982).

protection under the *jus imperii,* it would be a private commercial act under *jure gestionis,* and the state would not be immune for it abroad. But if the state imported the textiles in question for conversion into army uniforms, this would be a sovereign public act and fall under the protection of the *jus imperii;* the state would enjoy immunity for the act in foreign courts.

Curtailment of the traditional automatic immunity of foreign sovereigns proceeded rather slowly until 1924, when many countries began to recognize the government of the Soviet Union, and the process of restricting state immunity was hastened, in part, because the Soviet Union had adopted state-conducted monopolies in foreign trade and shipping.

ATTEMPTS TO RESTRICT STATE IMMUNITY   Even before 1924, state immunity, though upheld generally, had been questioned in cases involving governmental ownership and operation of merchant vessels. In one of the earliest relevant cases, a British court of appeals reversed the judgment of the High Court of Admiralty in the case of the *Parlement Belge* (1880, L.R.S.P.D. 197) and decided that the vessel, owned and operated by the Belgian government as a mail packet as well as for general commercial purposes, was immune from suit *in rem* in a case for damages resulting from a collision. The *Parlement Belge* decision caused a lot of trouble after World War I, when an increasing number of states began to engage in ordinary commercial transactions by means of public commercial vessels and claimed for these the same immunities traditionally attached to true public vessels such as warships.[39]

For its part, the United States concluded 14 treaties in the decade following 1948, including a requirement for each party to waive sovereign immunity for all state-controlled enterprises involved in shipping, industrial, or other commercial activities in the other party's territory. It was later reported that this American practice was suspended after 1958 because it was feared that otherwise the United States would be unable to invoke its own sovereign immunity if sued in foreign courts.[40]

Other governments proceeded to attempt to differentiate between sovereign activities (*acta jure imperii*) of a state, such as matters connected with its armed forces or, say, the nationalization of foreign-owned enterprises, and nonsovereign activities of a state (*acta jure gestionis*), such as engaging in private commercial transactions, in an effort to develop an acceptable basis for a denial of sovereign immunity. In recent decades, almost every major country has denied governmental immunity to corporations wholly or partly owned by a foreign state,[41] and in some cases, governments have vo-

---

[39]Thus see the well-known American cases of *Berizzi Brothers Co.* v. *SS Pesaro,* U.S. Supreme Court, 1926, 271 U.S. 562; *The Maipo* (D.C.) 252 F. 627, and 259 F. 367, as well as the British cases of *The Gagara,* L.R. [1919] P.D. 95, *The Porto Alexandre,* L.R. [1920] P.D. 30, and *The Jupiter,* L.R. [1924] P.D. 236.

[40]See Friedmann, 656, for an illustrative excerpt from one of the treaties in question.

[41]See *The Uxmal,* U.S. Dist. Court, Mass., 1941, 40 F. Supp. 258, and *Mirabella* v. *Banco Industrial de la Republica Argentina,* United States, Superior Court, New York County, N.Y., 1963, 237 N.Y.S. 2d 499.

luntarily disclaimed immunity status for government corporations engaged in commercial activities:[42]

March 17, 1978

Dear Mr. Ambassador:

I wish to inform you that Hungarian state enterprises, including those which conduct foreign trade, are legal persons carrying out independent economic activities as provided for in the Civil Code of the Hungarian People's Republic and in accordance with the provisions of Law No. VI of 1977 on State Enterprises. On the basis of Section 31, paragraph [4] of the Civil Code, and of Section 27, paragraph [3] of the Law on State Enterprises, they themselves are responsible with their assets for their obligations. Accordingly, they shall not claim or enjoy immunities from suit or execution of judgment or other liability with respect to commercial transactions; they also shall not claim or enjoy immunities from taxation except as may result from other bilateral agreements.

Sincerely,

Jozsef Biro
Minister for Foreign Trade

His Excellency
    Philip M. Kaiser
        Ambassador of the United States
            of America to the Hungarian
                People's Republic
                    Budapest

THEORY OF RESTRICTED STATE IMMUNITY (TATE LETTER)    A significant change in American policy with respect to state immunity occurred in 1952 when the then Acting Legal Adviser to the Department of State, Jack B. Tate, wrote a letter to the Acting Attorney General, outlining acceptance of the restrictive theory of immunity by the United States government.[43] Tate pointed out that the expansion in adoption of the restrictive theory by more and more countries, justified the restrictions involved, and in effect laid down the view of the Department of State that henceforth "private activities of foreign sovereigns would be denied immunity in American courts."

The policies subsequently followed by the United States were outlined clearly in *Victory Transport Inc.* v. *Comisaria General de Abastecimientos y Trans-*

---

[42] 17 *ILM* 1483 (1978). If, on the other hand, the corporation exists as an integral part of the government itself, then a claim of immunity might have been allowed until fairly recently: *Mason* v. *Intercolonial Railway of Canada,* United States, 1908, 197 Mass. 349, 83 N.E. 876; *Dunlop* v. *Banco Central del Ecuador,* United States, Superior Ct., New York County., N.Y., 1943, 41 N.Y.S. 2d 650; and *Baccus S.R.I.* v. *Servicio Nacional del Trigo,* Great Britain, 1957, 1 Q.B. 438 (C.A.).

[43] Text in 26 *Department of State Bulletin* (June 23, 1952) 984 and also in Whiteman, vol. 6, 569–71. For a detailed analysis of the letter, consult Bishop, "New United States Policy Limiting Sovereign Immunity," 47 *AJIL* 93 (1953).

*portes* (1964).[44] Claims of sovereign immunity were presented to a court by either of two procedures. The foreign sovereign requested that its claim to immunity be recognized by the Department of State, which normally presented its suggestion to the court through the Attorney General or some other law officer acting under his direction. Alternatively, the accredited representative of the foreign sovereign could present the claim of sovereign immunity directly to the court in question. If the Department of State did not find it expedient to respond to a request for immunity, the court had to decide for itself whether it was the established policy of the Department of State to recognize claims of immunity of the type in the case at hand.

The Tate letter outlined the department's policy of declining immunity to friendly foreign governments in suits arising from private or commercial activities. But that same letter offered no guidelines or criteria for distinguishing between a sovereign's private and public acts. Hence the absence of a suggestion on immunity by the Department of State left it to the court to determine whether a given sovereign was indeed entitled to immunity.

In the *Victory Transport* case, the court held that

since the State Department's failure or refusal to suggest immunity is significant, we are disposed to deny a claim of sovereign immunity that has not been "recognized and allowed" by the State Department unless it is plain that the activity in question falls within one of the categories of strictly political or public acts about which sovereigns have traditionally been quite sensitive. Such acts are generally limited to the following categories:

(1) internal administrative acts, such as expulsion of an alien.
(2) legislative acts, such as nationalization.
(3) acts concerning the armed forces.
(4) acts concerning diplomatic activity.
(5) public loans.

We do not think that the restrictive theory adopted by the State Department requires sacrificing the interests of private litigants to international comity in other than these limited categories.

Thus there existed a major flaw in the American determination of state immunity following the Tate letter: an inconsistency of practice caused by the courts' reliance on State Department certification. The Department would suggest immunity in one case and fail to make a suggestion in the next one, leaving the courts to determine immunity without any guideline from the Department. The inconsistency in question can be observed by a comparison of key decisions on state immunity after Tate, such as the *Victory Transport* case[45] with *Isbrandtsen Tankers Incorporated* v. *President of India,* 1971.[46]

[44]U.S. Court of Appeals, 2d Cir., 1964, 336 F.2d 354, 358–360, 362. *Certiorari* denied 381 U.S. 394 (1965); key portions of decision may be found in Whiteman, vol. 6, 578–80.
[45]Whiteman, *loc. cit.,* n. 44.
[46]U.S. Court of Appeals, 2d Cir., 1971, 446 F.2d 1198, reported in 66 *AJIL* 396 (1972), *certiorari* denied 98 U.S. 452 (1971). See also the *Note* by Benjamin, 13 *Harvard Int'l. L. J.* 527 (1972).

The operation of the doctrine laid down in the Tate letter was illustrated in the case of *Chemical Natural Resources, Inc.* v. *Republic of Venezuela:*

### CHEMICAL NATURAL RESOURCES, INC. v. REPUBLIC OF VENEZUELA

United States, Supreme Court of Pennsylvania,
1966, 420 Pa. 134; 215 At. 2d 864; certiorari denied,
87 Sup. Court 50 (1966)

FACTS    Chemical Natural Resources, Inc. (hereinafter cited as Chemical), a U.S. corporation, sued Venezuela. The plaintiffs had contracted with the Venezuelan government for the construction of power generation facilities, the power to be bought by the Venezuelan government; the latter canceled the contract and expropriated all installations involved. Efforts to obtain redress in Venezuelan courts failed.

In the fall of 1963, a ship, the *SS Ciudad de Valencia,* operated by the Venezuelan government through a wholly owned company and engaged in commerce, arrived in Philadelphia. Chemical attempted, through a writ, to seize the vessel as part payment for damages claimed. The ship was seized.

Venezuela challenged the jurisdiction of the (Pa.) Court of Common Pleas, claiming that the vessel was not government property and that U.S. courts could not exercise jurisdiction. Venezuela also secured the intervention of the U.S. Department of State, which filed a "Suggestion of Immunity." The lower court denied that Venezuela was entitled to immunity. Venezuela then filed an appeal with the Pennsylvania Supreme Court.

MAIN ISSUE    Did Venezuela enjoy sovereign immunity, despite the doctrine laid down in the Tate letter of 1952?

DECISION    Appeal of Venezuela quashed, but a writ of prohibition issued, dissolving attachment of the vessel.

REASONING    The court pointed out that the established rule of law was that foreign sovereigns "duly recognized by the State Department, and their property" were not amenable without their consent to suit in the courts of the United States, and that "a determination of Sovereign Immunity by the Executive branch . . . is . . . conclusive." The court also held that the Tate letter meant that the Department of State had abandoned the principle of *absolute* governmental immunity, but it appeared that the department "has silently abandoned the 'revised and restricted policy' set forth in the Tate Letter and has substituted a case-by-case foreign Sovereign Immunity policy, that is, the State Department will recognize and suggest, or fail to recognize or grant or suggest Sovereign Immunity *in each case* presented to it, depending (a) upon the foreign and diplomatic relations which our country has at that particular time with the other Country, and (b) the best interests of our Country at that particular time."

Much of the foregoing discussion may have implied that the absolute immunity theory has been discarded in favor of the doctrine of restricted sovereign immunity. Nothing could be further from the truth, however, for only a limited number of countries have as yet developed a substantial foundation of judicial decisions favoring the restrictive theory, and although several states may point to judicial dicta leaning in the direction of the restrictive theory, most of the nations of the world still assert the validity of the older doctrine.[47] But some of these appear to be modifying their stand regarding total immunity from suit without consent, at least in recent years. Thus Argentina, Uruguay, and Venezuela now allow a few exceptions to the strict application of the rule, and Chile makes state immunity entirely dependent on reciprocity.

One of the more unusual minor instances of a dispute involving state immunity took place in Canada. Wallace Edwards, a Toronto businessman, had tried unsuccessfully to collect the sum of $25,000, plus $10,000 in interest, from the government of the Soviet Union. The claim represented the balance of a printing bill for work done in 1967 for the Soviet pavilion at Montreal's Expo '67. The Canadian Department of External Affairs informed Edwards that the Soviet government enjoyed immunity, and other Canadian authorities discouraged or blocked Edwards's attempts to impound the ice skates of a Russian hockey team and, later, to have a local court order the seizure of a Russian airliner. But in 1980, the creditor persuaded the Toronto sheriff to impound a Soviet freighter once it had docked, and Edwards also attempted to freeze the bank accounts of the Soviet embassy in Ottawa. The Soviet government finally agreed to pay the balance of the bill due as well as the interest demanded, plus a case of Russian vodka and a pound of Russian caviar.[48]

The United States, despite an occasionally uneven record in applying the theory of restricted state immunity, adhered to the basic principle originally laid down in the Tate letter until 1977.[49]

---

[47] See, on the other hand, the impressive support of the restrictive theory represented in the decisions in a number of cases brought against the Republic of Nigeria and the Central Bank of Nigeria, in 16 *ILM* (1977): *Trendtex Trading Corporation* v. *Central Bank of Nigeria,* United Kingdom, Court of Appeal, 1975, 471; *Nonresident Petitioner* v. *Central Bank of Nigeria,* Federal Republic of Germany, District Court, Frankfurt, Dec. 2, 1975, 501; and *National American Corporation* v. *Federal Republic of Nigeria and Central Bank of Nigeria,* U.S. Dist. Court, S.D.N.Y., Oct. 13, 1976 and Feb. 8, 1977, 420 F. Supp. 954 (1976) and 425 F. Supp. 1365 (1977), 505–19.

[48] *Time,* Nov. 3, 1980, 54; *Newsweek,* Nov. 3, 1980, 59. On July 15, 1982, the "Act to Provide for State Immunity in Canadian Courts" came into force; Article 5 ruled that immunity could not be claimed in any proceedings that related to any commercial activity of a foreign state. Text of the Act is found in 21 *ILM* 798 (1982).

[49] See *Alfred Dunhill of London, Inc.* v. *Republic of Cuba.* U.S. Supreme Court, 96 S.Ct. 1854, May 24, 1976, reported in 70 *AJIL* 828 (1976), and in full, in 15 *ILM* 35 (1976), *Petrol Shipping Corporation,* U.S. Court of Appeals, 2d Cir., April 21, 1966, 360 F.2d 103, reported in 60 *AJIL* 859 (1966); *Aerotrade* v. *Republic of Haiti,* U.S. Dist. Court, S.D.N.Y., May 24, 1974, reported in 16 *Harvard Int'l. Law Jl.* 168 (1975), and in full in 13 *ILM* 969 (1974). See also *The Philippine Admiral* v. *Wallem Shipping* (Hong Kong), United Kingdom, Judicial Committee of the Privy Council, Nov. 5, 1975, reported in 70 *AJIL* 364 (1976), and in 15 *ILM* 133 (1976). This last case has been cited, with approval, in several subsequent decisions dealing with the restriction of sovereign immunity. See also the instructive as well as entertaining account by Charles N. Brower, "Litigation of Sovereign Immunity before a State Administrative Body and the Department of State: The Japanese Uranium Tax Case," 71 *AJIL* 438 (1977).

THE UNITED STATES' NEW SOVEREIGN IMMUNITY POLICY    After four years
of work by the Departments of State and Justice, a new law, the Foreign
Sovereign Immunities Act of 1976, was passed by Congress, was signed by
President Gerald Ford, and became effective on January 19, 1977.[50]

The act has four objectives: it vests sovereign immunity decisions exclusively in the courts, eliminating thereby a political institution, the Department of State, from relevant decisions concerning the law; it codifies the
restrictive theory of sovereign immunity by limiting the latter to public
acts and excluding all commercial or private acts; it lays down detailed
methods for beginning a lawsuit against a foreign state through service of
process and obtaining personal jurisdiction over foreign government defendants; and, finally, it gives U.S. citizens the remedy of execution to satisfy
a final judgment against a foreign state.[51]

Two of these points are of special interest. In one instance, the policy
intends that execution against a foreign sovereign should be limited to such
assets as were being used for the commercial acts that prompted the claim in
the first place—and such assets should not be available for the satisfaction of
a claim to a greater extent that would be all commercial assets of American
firms operating in a foreign state for the satisfaction of a judgment against
one American company. In the second case, the concept of serving process
on a foreign sovereign by means of the mails, although eliminating some
aspects of the currently illegal personal service by a marshal or other court
officer, would appear to be of dubious legality under both customary and
conventional law. (See Vienna Convention on Diplomatic Relations, 1961,
Art. 29.)

But the shift of the responsibility of determining the presence or absence
of sovereign immunity to the courts represents a rather startling change in
policy. Until adoption of the new policy, the holding of the court in *Chemical
Natural Resources, Inc.* v. *Republic of Venezuela* prevailed: determination of
immunity was a function of the Executive Branch, and a case-by-case grant
or denial of immunity was U.S. policy.

The new statutory immunity policy of the United States was delineated
well by Fisher, J., as "The central goals of the Immunities Act are to codify
the 'restrictive theory' of sovereign immunity recognized under international

<hr/>

[50]Text of act in 71 *AJIL* 595 (1977) and in 15 *ILM* 1388 (1976). A section by section
analysis and explanation of the act is found in 15 *ILM* 88 (1976). See also Jeffrey N.
Martin, "Sovereign Immunity—Limits of Judicial Control," 18 *Harvard Int'l. L. J.* 429
(1977). The act was amended twice in November 1988; see texts in 28 *ILM* 396 (1989).
[51]Consult also the following concerning the 1976 act: *Report of Committee of the Whole House
on the State of the Union,* on "Jurisdiction of United States Courts on Suits against Foreign
States," Sept. 9, 1976, reproduced in 15 *ILM* 1398 (1976); Atkeson, Perkins, and Wyatt,
"H.R. 11315—The Revised State–Justice Bill on Foreign Sovereign Immunity: Time for
Action," 70 *AJIL* 298 (1976); Delaume, "Public Debt and Sovereign Immunity: The Foreign
Sovereign Immunity Act of 1976," 71 *AJIL* 399 (1977); and Brower, Bistline, and Loomis,
"The Foreign Sovereign Immunities Act of 1976 in Practice," 73 *AJIL* 200 (1979).

law as the statutory law of this country and to provide that the validity of claims of sovereign immunity interposed in suits against foreign states shall be determined by the United States courts rather than by the State Department."[52] One of the statutory waivers set out in the Immunities Act states that "A foreign state shall not be immune from the jurisdiction of courts of the United States or of the States in any case ... in which the action is based upon a commercial activity carried on in the United States by the foreign state" [28 U.S.C. § 1605 (a)(2)]. It should be mentioned that the commercial activity exception to sovereign immunity was delineated clearly for the United States as related to the Foreign Sovereign Immunities Act of 1976 in two key decisions in 1989. The exception applies only to transactions that cause *direct, substantial,* and *foreseeable* effects in the United States.[53]

The adoption of the new statutory policy concerning sovereign immunity led to court decisions quite different from those handed down before 1977.[54]

It should be emphasized that in order to claim immunity under the restrictive theory, the enterprise in question, whether it be a business or a vessel, must be in the possession and also in the service of the government making the claim. This principle was illustrated in the case of

*REPUBLIC OF MEXICO* v. *HOFFMAN*
*(THE BAJA CALIFORNIA)*
Supreme Court of the United States, 1945
*324 U.S. 30, 65 S.Ct. 530.*

FACTS    Hoffman sued the *Baja California* in the U.S. District Court, Southern District of California, for damages allegedly caused when the Mexican ves- sel allowed her tow to collide with Hoffman's vessel, the *Lottie Carson.* The Mexican ambassador filed a suggestion with the Court that the vessel was owned by

[52]*Behring International* v. *Imperial Iranian Air Force.* U.S. Dist. Court, N.J., Civil Action No. 79–675, July 24, 1979 and Aug. 13, 1979, in 18 *ILM* 1369, 1376 (1979).

[53]*America West Airlines, Inc.* v. *GPA Group Ltd.*, 877 F.2d 793, U.S. Court of Appeals, 9th Cir., June 12, 1989, and *Rush-Presbyterian-St. Luke's Medical Center* v. *Hellenic Republic*, 877 F.2d 574, U.S. Court of Appeals, 7th Cir., June 14, 1989. Both cases reported in 84 *AJIL* 262 (1990). See also *Transamerica Steamship Corp.* v. *Somali Democratic Republic*, 767 F.2d 998, U.S. Court of Appeals, D.C. Cir., July 12, 1985, in 80 *AJIL* 357 (1985); *Martin* v. *Republic of South Africa*, 836 F.2d 91, U.S. Court of Appeals, 2d Cir., Dec. 29, 1987, in 28 *ILM* 583 (1988).

[54]*Carey and New England Petroleum Corporation* v. *National Oil Corporation* and *Libyan Arab Republic*, U.S. Dist. Court, S.D.N.Y., June 16, 1978, in 17 *ILM* 1180 (1978); *Reading and Bates* v. *National Iranian Oil Company*, U.S. Dist. Court, S.D.N.Y., Sept. 27, 1979, *id.*, 18, 1398 (1979); *Texas Trading and Milling Corp.* v. *Federal Republic of Nigeria and Central Bank of Nigeria*, U.S. Court of Appeals, 2d Cir., 1981, 647 F.2d 300, reported in 75 *AJIL* 968 (1981), *certiorari* denied 102 S.C. 1012; *Letelier* v. *Republic of Chile*, in 19 *ILM* 409 (1980). reversed, U.S. Court of Appeals, 2d Cir., Nov. 20, 1984, 748 F.2d 790, reported in 79 *AJIL* 447 (1984).

and in the possession of the Mexican government, making it immune from suit. The U.S. Department of State did not suggest immunity to the Court. The District Court found that the *Baja California* was operated by a private Mexican company to which its owner, the Mexican government, had delivered it under a contract for five years. The vessel was operated at the company's expense as a freighter between Mexican ports and also between Mexican and foreign ports. The company had agreed to pay the Mexican government 50 percent of its net profits and to assume all net losses, if any. The District Court denied immunity and ruled in favor of Hoffman's claim. The Court of Appeals affirmed that decision. Mexico appealed to the Supreme Court.

ISSUE    Does a vessel's immunity require that it be in the possession and service of the government making the claim?

DECISION    The Supreme Court affirmed the decisions of the two lower courts, denied immunity to the *Baja California,* and awarded damages to Hoffman.

REASONING    In the case of *The Navemar* [303 U.S. 68, 58 S. Ct. 432], it was decisive that that vessel when seized by judicial process was not in the possession and service of the foreign government seeking immunity. Here both lower courts found that the Republic of Mexico was the owner of the *Baja California,* but while the State Department certified that it recognized that ownership, it did not certify that it allowed the immunity or recognized the ownership without possession by the Mexican government. It appeared that the Department had never allowed a claim of immunity without possession by the claimant. Hence the Supreme Court would not act contrary to what was established policy.

One of the problems encountered repeatedly in the sphere of international finance has been a default on securities floated abroad by governments, their subdivisions, or their state-owned enterprises. This phenomenon reached global proportions during the Great Depression and emerged again after 1970. The bilked bondholders quite commonly were frustrated in their search for justice by invocation of the plea of sovereign immunity. A recent case, *Jackson* v. *The People's Republic of China,* [55] helped significantly in clearing up an important aspect of the Foreign Sovereign Immunities Act.

Jackson and eight other bondholders filed a class action suit against the People's Republic of China (PRC) to receive payment on certain railway bonds issued in 1911 by the Imperial Government of China. The bondholders were entitled to both the principal amount and interest at the rate of 5 percent. The Imperial Government was replaced by the Republic of China in 1912, and the latter paid the interest due until December 15, 1930, with two partial payments made in 1937–38. In 1947 the Republic announced that payments would be resumed once economic conditions made this feasible.

[55] U.S. Dist. Court, N.D. Ala., 1982, 550 F. Supp. 869, and the text of a Chinese *aide-mémoire* of Feb. 2, 1983, in 22 *ILM* 75 (1983); the "Statement of Interest of the U.S." of Aug. 18, 1983, in *id.,* 1077 (1987). See also the valuable background report by Oka, "1911 Chinese Bonds Draw Heated Diplomatic Interest," *CSM,* Mar. 11, 1983, 10.

In 1949 the government of the Republic, having been defeated on the mainland, retreated to Taiwan. Since then, no payments on the bonds have been made. When the Jackson suit was filed, service was made on the PRC through the Department of State, but the Chinese authorities failed to reply. The District Court ruled in favor of the plaintiffs, holding that a foreign state was not immune from suits based on commercial activities (in this instance China, the predecessor government, authorizing sale of the bonds in 1911) and that the People's Republic was liable for the debts of the former Imperial Government. The Court entered a default judgment, awarding damages of $41.3 million plus interest.

In August 1983, the People's Republic (at the suggestion of the U.S. Department of State) made a special appearance and obtained an order under the Federal Rules of Procedure, setting aside the judgment of the District Court. At the request of the People's Republic, the U.S. District Court, having been presented with a "statement of interest" by the Department, dismissed the complaint for want of subject jurisdiction and held that the Foreign Sovereign Immunities Act of 1976 could not be applied retroactively to events on which the plaintiffs' cause was based. The Court based its decision on the fact that the Act provided for a 90-day grace period and also on the precise wording of the "jurisdictional section" of the Act (the district courts "shall have" jurisdiction, etc.): *Jackson* v. *People's Republic*.[56] Jackson thereupon filed notice of appeal. The Court of Appeals affirmed the 1984 decision of the District Court.[57] The Supreme Court denied *certiorari* (107 S.C. 1371 1987).

It should be mentioned in connection with the foregoing case that the government of the People's Republic distinguishes between itself, as a sovereign legal person or entity, and a number of state corporations owned by but not legally part of the government of the People's Republic. Those corporations, when engaged in foreign commercial operations, lack immunity in both foreign and Chinese courts. On the other hand the railway bond controversy developed, in part, because the securities represented the activities of a predecessor government that had not made this distinction.

One of the unusual and unexplained aspects of the railway bond case was the delay by the plaintiffs in filing their claim—40 years after the cessation of interest payments and 18 years after the bonds were scheduled to mature. Several commentators agreed that the claim should have been filed in 1966, as in that year the U.S. government requested that all of its citizens holding property claims against mainland China register those claims with the United States. But the plaintiffs in the railway bond case did not file any claim at that time.

[56]596 F. Supp. 386. U.S. Dist. Court, N.D. Ala., E.D., Oct. 26, 1984, reported in 79 *AJIL* 456 (1985).
[57]*Jackson* v. *People's Republic of China*. 794 F.2d 1490. U.S. Court of Appeals, 11th Cir., July 25, 1986, reported in 81 *AJIL* 214 (1987), the analytical decision in 25 *ILM* 1466 (1986).

Revised practices connected with claims of sovereign immunity have not been limited to the United States. After lengthy discussions, the Council of Europe drew up the European Convention on State Immunity and Additional Protocol, which was signed on May 16, 1972, by the Federal Republic of Germany, Luxembourg, the Netherlands, Switzerland, and the United Kingdom. That instrument entered into force on June 11, 1976. Subsequently, the British government drafted its (United Kingdom) State Immunity Act of 1978, which came into force on November 22, 1978, and covered much the same territory as did the U.S. legislation. Unfortunately, some of the wording of the 1978 Act had been composed rather carelessly, and in one case the court had to sanction the garnisheeing of the bank accounts of a foreign embassy, even though the court admitted that the practice in question violated international law. The court had to follow the wording of the statute despite its flaw; hence the Republic of Colombia lost the case.[58] In effect it brought the European Convention into force for the United Kingdom.

IMMUNITY AFTER SEVERANCE OF DIPLOMATIC RELATIONS    The political nature of recognition implies continued enjoyment of immunity after a severance of diplomatic relations between two states. Thus the United States courts have sustained, at least since 1962, Cuban sovereign immunity despite the severance of diplomatic relations.[59]

STATUS OF NONRECOGNIZED FOREIGN GOVERNMENTS    Nonrecognition of a foreign government normally results in its inability to assert immunity for its vessels in foreign ports or waters. On the other hand, the Soviet Union's seizure, in 1940, of the three Baltic republics of Estonia, Latvia, and Lithuania, followed by the absorption of the three states into the Soviet Union, was not recognized as lawful by a considerable number of foreign states, including notably the United States, Great Britain, and Eire. These and other governments have refused to recognize the transfers of sovereignty involved in the absorption of the three Baltic republics.

At the time of the Soviet takeover, a number of vessels belonging to private owners, particularly in Estonia and Latvia, happened to be on the high seas. Several of the ships in question came into ports of the Republic of Eire and at once became the objects of suits. The Soviet Union asserted that the vessels were state property, that as such they were immune from the jurisdiction of Irish courts without the consent of their sovereign owner, and that this immunity existed whether the ships were used for public purposes

---

[58] *ALCOM Limited* v. *Colombia et al.*, United Kingdom, Supreme Court of Judicature, Court of Appeal (Civil Division), October 24, 1983, reproduced in full in 22 *ILM* 1307 (1983); reversed by House of Lords in *Alcom Ltd.* v. *Republic of Colombia*, [1984] 2 All E.R. 6. House of Lords, April 12, 1984, and reported in 79 *AJIL* 143 (1985).

[59] See *Rich* v. *Naviera Vacuba, S.A. and Republic of Cuba; Mayan Lines* v. *Republic of Cuba and the M/V Bahia de Nipe; United Fruit Sugar Co.* v. *5,000 Tons of Sugar; Navarro and Others* v. *the M/V Bahia de Nipe*, U.S. Court of Appeals, 4th Cir., Sept. 7, 1961, 295 F.2d 24, reported in 56 *AJIL* 526, 550–52 (1962).

or for commerce and whether or not they were in the possession of the sovereign.

The plaintiffs in the cases—that is, the accredited representatives of the "defunct" Baltic governments—sought to act as trustees in order to prevent acquisition of control over the vessels by agencies of the Soviet Union. These so-called Baltic Ship Cases, reinforced by corresponding decisions in a number of other countries, including the United States,[60] helped establish the doctrine that nonrecognition of an alleged successor state or government results in a failure to create immunity claimed for vessels of that state or government.

The UN International Law Commission has worked since 1978 on the subject of the jurisdictional immunities of states and their property. In February 1988, a draft convention on this topic was transmitted by the UN Secretary-General to the member states for comments.[61]

**PRIVILEGE TO BRING SUIT**    No discussion of state immunity can be concluded without mentioning the privilege of foreign sovereigns to bring suit in the courts of a friendly state. General agreement prevails concerning the duty of such a sovereign (state) to adhere to the procedures established for and in the courts of the state in which the suit is being brought. By implication, the privilege to sue is accompanied by the consent to submit to the jurisdiction of the court in question with reference to any counterclaims arising out of the same suit.

A number of the principles governing the right of a foreign sovereign to sue in the courts of another state were illustrated in the reasoning of the British High Court of Chancery in the old case of

### EMPEROR OF AUSTRIA AND KING OF HUNGARY v. DAY AND KOSSUTH

*Great Britain, High Court of Chancery, 1861*
*3 De Gex, Fisher & Jones 217*

FACTS    This was an appeal from a decision of a lower court, ordering Day and Kossuth to refrain from issuing monetary notes purporting to be notes of the Hungarian state and ordering them to deliver to the plaintiff the notes already produced as well as the printing plates utilized in such production.

The plaintiff was the King of Hungary. In that capacity he possessed the exclusive right of authorizing the issue of notes to be circulated in Hungary as money, as well as the exclusive right of authorizing the affixing of the royal coat of arms of Hungary to any document intended to be circulated in Hungary. Al-

[60]See *Zarine* v. *Owners, etc., SS Ramava; McEvoy & Ors.* v. *Owners, etc., SS Otto; McEvoy and Veldi* v. *Owners, etc., SS Piret and SS Mall*, Eire High Court, April 29, 30, and May 1 and 16, 1941, 75 *Irish Law Times Reports* 153, in 36 *AJIL* 490 (1942), and the American case of *Latvian State Cargo & Passenger SS Line* v. *McGrath*, U.S. Court of Appeals, D.C. Cir., 1951, 188 F.2d 1000.
[61]See 26 *ILM* 625 (1987) and McCaffrey, "The Thirty-Eighth Session of the International Law Commission," 81 *AJIL* 668, 668–76 (1987).

most all the money circulating in his kingdom had been issued by the National Bank of Austria under the authority of the plaintiff acting as king of Hungary and emperor of Austria.

Day and Sons, a printing company in England, had been employed by Kossuth to prepare plates for the printing of notes purporting to be notes of the state or nation of Hungary, of various denominations, intended to be circulated as money in Hungary. After the plates had been prepared, Day and Sons began printing notes from the plates. The total face value of the notes prepared exceeded 100 million florins.

The plaintiff charged that if these notes were sent to Hungary, they would infringe on his exclusive right and would be used to promote revolution and disorders; that they had never been authorized by him; that he had never permitted the use of the royal arms on the notes; and that Day and Sons knew of the lack of authority on the part of Kossuth to issue the notes and knew for what purposes they were to be used. The plaintiff requested that all the plates and all the notes in question be delivered to him and that an injunction be issued restraining Day and Sons from printing or delivering any such notes to Kossuth.

The lower court upheld the claims of the plaintiff; Day and Kossuth appealed.

ISSUES    (1) Can a recognized foreign sovereign sue in English courts, and under what conditions?

(2) Does the infringement of the prerogatives of a foreign sovereign constitute a ground of suit in an English court?

(3) Can a foreign sovereign sue in an English court on behalf of his subjects?

DECISION    A recognized foreign sovereignty may, under certain conditions, sue in an English court; an English court cannot interfere with or deal with the prerogatives of a foreign sovereign; a foreign sovereign can bring a suit in an English court on behalf of his subjects. Decree of lower court affirmed, except for a modification excluding the lower court's prohibition against the use of the Hungarian coat of arms by Kossuth.

REASONING    Re issue (1): The Lord Chancellor held that a foreign sovereign, recognized by the British government, could sue in an English court, provided that his suit did not involve the maintenance of his political power or involve an alleged wrong sanctioned or approved by the government of England. He therefore could sue if a wrong had been done to him by an English subject not authorized to do so by the government of England, with respect to property belonging to the foreign sovereign in his individual or corporate capacity.

However, in regard to Kossuth's use of the royal coat of arms of Hungary, no prohibition on such use could be sustained, because the coat of arms in question was a "property" of which any Hungarian subject could make use.

Re issue (2): The plaintiff had argued that the sovereign prerogative to coin or issue money was acknowledged by all nations and by international law, and that because international law was a part of the law of England, the English courts should interfere in favor of protecting that sovereign prerogative. The court felt, however, that the domestic courts of a state should not interfere, favorably or unfavorably, with the prerogatives of foreign sovereigns.

Re issue (3): The court held that the injury claimed by the plaintiff affected the private rights, not the political rights, of the subjects of the plaintiff; that is, if the notes were sent to Hungary, the value of the Bank of Austria notes would be affected adversely and thereby an adverse effect would be created relative to the rights of all property owners in Hungary. This claim was upheld by the court, which believed that the plaintiff could sue on behalf of his Hungarian subjects, representing their collective interest in the English court.

The right of access to foreign courts, however, does not permit a state to bring suit for the enforcement of its own revenue or penal laws by the foreign court, at least not in the absence of some form of reciprocal agreement to enforce such laws of another jurisdiction. The classic instance illustrating this point is the well-known case of

### H.M. THE QUEEN OF HOLLAND (MARRIED WOMAN) v. DRUKKER

*Great Britain, Chancery Division, 1928,*
*L.R. {1928} 1 Ch. Div. 877*

FACTS    The plaintiff (the queen of the Netherlands) sued in this action as a married woman, alleging that she was a creditor of the estate of David Visser, a Dutch subject, who had died in Amsterdam on December 27, 1926. The defendants were Moritz Drukker and others. Mr. Drukker was the executor of Visser's will; the other defendants were the heirs to Visser's estate in England, amounting (after all British dues and fees) to £1,150 in value.

The plaintiff alleged that under Dutch law the estate of Visser owed to the Dutch government certain "succession" duties, which, under the same law, enjoyed priority over all other debts not secured by mortgages or pledges. Under the Dutch laws, the administrator of the estate was obliged to give the Dutch government a comprehensive statement of the nature and value of the estate and was to pay the dues (duties, taxes) owed by the estate.

The plaintiff asked the British Court of Chancery to assume control over Visser's estate in England and to see to it that the "succession" duties claimed were paid to the Dutch government.

ISSUE    May a foreign sovereign sue in the domestic courts of a friendly state to obtain enforcement of that sovereign's fiscal legislation?

DECISION    Domestic courts will not enforce the fiscal legislation of a foreign sovereign; action dismissed.

REASONING    (1) For over 200 years, English courts have refused to take judicial notice of the revenue laws of foreign states and have refused to collect the taxes of foreign states for the benefit of the sovereigns of those states.

(2) A foreign state cannot, therefore, sue in English courts to recover taxes allegedly to be paid under the revenue laws of that state.

(3) Because the foreign sovereign (the queen of Netherlands) has submitted to the jurisdiction of the English Court of Chancery in bringing this suit in the court, and because the sovereign has lost the suit by the dismissal ordered, the foreign sovereign is ordered to pay the costs of the action.

In the United States, where federal courts will not examine the validity of foreign expropriations of property located in the countries concerned, the same courts will not permit a foreign government to take property located in the United States without payment of compensation. "Our courts will not give 'extra-territorial effect' to a confiscatory decree of a foreign state, even where directed against its own nations."[62]

## IMMUNITIES OF INTERNATIONAL ORGANIZATIONS

IMMUNITIES ACT    The General Convention on the Privileges and Immunities of the United Nations (February 13, 1946, 1 U.N.T.S. 15) left no doubt as to the need for an immunity from suit as well as from every other form of legal process without an explicit waiver.[63] On that occasion, in contrast with the initial drafting of the UN Charter, an analogy of the corresponding immunity enjoyed by states was included. It is significant that in the International Organizations Immunities Act [59 Stat. 669] (which, together with the UN Charter, governed United Nations immunities in the United States before the latter acceded to the General Convention: accession deposited and effective on April 29, 1970), it was stipulated that United Nations immunity could be waived only expressly by contract or for the purpose of any proceeding. Prior to American accession to the General Convention, the Immunities Act had been invoked only rarely by the United Nations.

IMMUNITIES ENJOYED BY THE UNITED NATIONS    United Nations immunity under the provisions of the United Nations General Convention is practically complete. It includes immunity for United Nations assets, wherever located, from any legal process; immunity of all United Nations premises from search, requisition, expropriation, confiscation, and any other sort of interference; immunity of archives; complete freedom from all financial controls, moratoriums, or other monetary regulations; freedom to hold funds in any desired currency or metal; freedom to transfer funds; an absolute exemption of all assets and revenue from all direct taxes; exemption from all customs duties as well as from any foreign trade prohibitions on goods needed for the official use of the organization; a guarantee of most-favored diplomatic treatment in regard to rates, priorities, and so on, connected with all media of communications; exemption from all forms of censorship; the right to use codes; and the privilege of transporting correspondence by courier or otherwise under the full complement of customary diplomatic immunities.

The status of the United Nations headquarters in the United States, on the other hand, depending on the "housekeeping" agreement of June 26, 1947 between the United Nations and its host, presents some rather interesting

[62]*Maltina Corp.* v. *Cawy Bottling Co.,* U.S. Court of Appeals, 5th Cir., 462 F.2d 1021, *certiorari* denied, 409 U.S. 1060 (1972), cited in *Tran Qui Than* v. *Blumenthal,* U.S. Dist. Court, N.D.Cal., Apr. 27, 1979, reprinted in 18 *ILM* 219 (1980).
[63]Text of the convention in 43 *AJIL* 1 (1949 Supp.).

deviations from the virtually absolute immunity provided for in the General Convention.[64]

UN ZONE    The United Nations zone in New York City is definitely within the United States, with no attempt made to create or uphold any fictitious extraterritoriality. United States civil and criminal laws (federal, state, and local) apply in the zone, which is merely granted "inviolability." Inviolability means that although the zone is United States territory, United States officials (federal, state, or local) may enter the zone only with the consent of the Secretary-General; the latter must also grant specific approval if any service of legal process is contemplated by American authorities.[65] Within the area in question, the United Nations may operate its own radio station, airport, and postal service. An arbitration tribunal of three members is to settle all disputes between the host sovereign and the United Nations concerning the interpretation of the agreement.

UNITED STATES—UNITED NATIONS RELATIONSHIP WITH RESPECT TO IMMUNI-TIES    Because the relations between the United Nations and the United States, in regard to immunities, are governed not only by treaty but also by elaborate domestic legislation, it does not appear likely that any restrictive theory of state immunity developed by the United States government will affect the operations or legal status of the United Nations.

The wording of Article 105 of the Charter appears to indicate clearly that the organization's immunities are not to be based conditionally on reciprocity, but should be viewed as the unconditional grant by the member states of certain privileges and immunities.

OTHER INTERNATIONAL ORGANIZATIONS    Public international agencies possessing international legal personality enjoy immunity from suit for all non-commercial activity of such agencies.[66]

# RIGHT OF INTERVENTION

One of the key duties or obligations of states, founded on both customary and conventional international law, is the prohibition on intervention in the affairs of any other state in the community of nations. (See Chapter 8 on the subject of unlawful intervention.) However, not all forms of intervention are prohibited. Some varieties of the act have been approved by writers and by

[64]See text of agreement and related documents in 43 *AJIL* 8 (1949 Supp.); and consult Chapter 20 and also Whiteman, vol. 13, 32–188.
[65]See *People* v. *Weiner,* 85 Misc. 2d 161, 378 N.Y.S. 2d 966 (Crim. Ct. of City of N.Y., 1978), reported in 18 *Harvard Int'l. L Jl.* 198 (1977).
[66]See *Broadbent et al.* v. *Organization of American States et. al.,* U.S. Court of Appeals, D.C. Cir., Jan. 8, 1980, No. 78–146, in 19 *ILM* 208 (1980), for a careful exposition of the matter. See also Mark Gordon's documented analysis of the case in 21 *Harvard Int'l. L. Jl.* 552 (1980); *Standard Chartered Bank* v. *International Tin Council,* U.K., High Court of Justice (Queen's Bench Division), Apr. 17,1986, in 25 *ILM* 650 (1986), a case involving jurisdictional immunity and contracts with international organizations.

governments: they form a part of customary international law. Their support as true rights of states has been based on humanitarian considerations, but more often logic has dictated the correctness of a particular employment of intervention, despite the overall legal prohibition. Other lawful interventions may be based on bilateral treaties between two countries, granting the right to intervene to one against the other under certain conditions.

It should be remembered, however, that on occasion arguments advanced in defense of a particular intervention have been difficult or impossible to justify on the basis of facts; they represented a mere facade to hide the true purposes of an illegal intervention.

The following list comprises most legal forms of intervention, together with some illustrative examples.

1.  The right to a legal intervention may have been granted by treaty to a state *vis-à-vis* another. An example of this variety was a treaty concluded between the two countries in 1921 that granted to the Soviet Union a discretionary right of military intervention in Iran if certain Russian interests in Iran were viewed by the Soviet government as "menaced." The Iranian government announced on November 5, 1979 its unilateral abrogation of the two articles in the 1921 treaty granting the Soviet Union a right of intervention.[67]

    On the other hand, the Treaty of Friendship, Goodneighborliness and Cooperation, signed by the Soviet Union and Afghanistan on December 5, 1978, provided in Article 4 that the two parties "take by agreement appropriate measures to ensure the security, independence, and territorial integrity of the two countries." This portion of the treaty could be interpreted to justify the Soviet invasion of Afghanistan on December 27, 1979, provided a *legitimate* request to do so had been issued by the Afghan authorities. (See also below under item 5.)

2.  If a given state has been restricted by treaty either in its territorial supremacy or in its external independence and violates the restrictions imposed, the other party or parties to the agreement will possess a lawful right of intervention.

3.  If a state "seriously" violates generally accepted rules of customary or conventional law, other states will have a right to intervene. Thus, if a belligerent proceeded to violate the rights of neutral states during a conflict, the neutrals would have rights of intervention against the violating belligerent state.

4.  Again, if the citizens of a state are mistreated in another state, the former, it has been asserted, possesses a lawful right to intervene on behalf of its citizens after all available peaceful remedies have been exhausted. Despite much opposing argument by certain writers, the practice of states still supports this right.

[67] See W. Michael Reisman, "Termination of the USSR's Treaty Right of Intervention in Iran," 74 *AJIL* 144 (1980).

The most frequently cited instances are the interventions in Nicaraguan internal affairs by the United States, beginning 1909, on grounds of protecting American private interests and citizens in that republic, and the collective intervention in China in 1900 through the joint military and naval expedition sent there by Germany, France, Great Britain, Italy, Austria-Hungary, Russia, Japan, and the United States. More recently, military intervention in Grenada (October 25, 1983) by the United States, members of the Organization of Eastern Caribbean States (OECS), and two other Caribbean states was justified by the United States primarily by a need to protect some 1,000 American citizens on the island following a period of political upheaval and the absence of a truly functioning government (see below).

5. Lawful intervention (intervention by right) occurs in the case of collective action undertaken by an international organ on behalf of the community of nations or for the enforcement of the principles and rules of international law.[68] This has been claimed to apply to both preventive and remedial action undertaken on behalf of or by the agencies of such bodies as the United Nations. It must be emphasized that military intervention at the behest of the United Nations or a regional defense organization (under the UN Charter) must be viewed as lawful, indeed as intervention by right. In the instance of the Grenada episode of 1983, the determination of legality hinges in part on whether the OECS could be regarded as having transformed itself, temporarily, into such a regional organization under the UN Charter.

In regard to the invasion of Grenada in 1983, the United States stated that it had received an urgent appeal from the OECS, an organization created by treaty in 1981.[69] The group met (without Grenada) on October 21 and decided that the collapse of the Grenadan government posed a threat to the region's security and stability. Therefore, the OECS members resolved to take appropriate measures to meet that threat, under Articles 3 and 8 of the OECS Treaty, and they also sought the assistance of friendly foreign states to participate in a collective security force. As a result, four OECS member states were joined by Barbados, Jamaica, and the United States in mounting the invasion of Grenada. It must be pointed out that the United States is a member of the Organization of American States (OAS) and that Article 15 of the OAS Charter of 1948 reads: "No state or group of states has the right to intervene, directly or indirectly, in the internal or external affairs of another state," whether by armed force or otherwise; and Article 17 of the same charter reads

---

[68] See Lauterpacht's *Oppenheim*, vol. 1, 320, and Quincy Wright, "The Legality of Intervention under the United Nations Charter," *Proceedings* 79 88 (1957).
[69] The members were Antigua, Dominica, Grenada, Montserrat, St. Kitts/Nevis, Saint Lucia, Saint Vincent, and the Grenadines. The text of the 1981 OECS Treaty is to be found in 20 *ILM* 1166 (1981).

in part: "The territory of a state is inviolable; it may not be the object, even temporarily, of military occupation or other measures of force taken by another state . . . on any grounds whatever." The U.S. Department of State maintained, however, that the collective action against Grenada was "consistent with the OAS Charter. The Charter specifically allows OAS members to take collective action pursuant to regional security treaties in response to threats to peace and security. The Rio Treaty is one such treaty. The OECS states are not parties to the Rio Treaty, and the OECS Treaty is their regional security arrangement. . . . Article 8 of the OECS Treaty authorizes the OECS to coordinate the efforts of member states for collective defense."[70] It should be remembered that the OAS was not consulted and that most of its members disapproved of the invasion, referring to it as a violation of international law and the principle of nonintervention. Some legal commentators pointed out, on the other hand, that Articles 22 and 28 of the OAS Charter, as well as Article 52 of the United Nations Charter, could be utilized to justify the invasion of Grenada. This, they asserted, was particularly true in view of Grenada's military buildup and a serious collapse of law and order on the island, including the execution of several members of the previous government and other citizens, that might eventually have resulted in the taking of American hostages.[71] Other factors cited subsequently in support of the legality of the invasion were the presence of some 125 Cuban troops, about 675 Cuban construction workers with militia training, and some Soviet advisors and the discovery of five Grenadan agreements with the Soviet Union, Cuba, and North Korea for military supplies and equipment.

It is interesting to note that a few days after Grenada's Governor General was recognized by the United States and the OECS members involved as the country's constitutional authority, he expelled all Soviet, Cuban, and Libyan diplomats. By Christmas 1983, all U.S. combat forces had been withdrawn from Grenada. By November 1984, only 250 U.S. military police and support troops remained to train Grenadan security forces, plus the 396-man Caribbean Peacekeeping Force, consisting mostly of members of several constabularies. Withdrawal of all foreign units was completed by the end of September 1985.

6. Intervention is lawful when it takes place at the genuine and explicit invitation of the lawful government of a state. An example of this kind of intervention was supplied by the landing of American Marines in Lebanon in 1958[72] and the sending of requested British troops to Jordan,

---

[70]U.S. Department of State Memorandum, "Legal Authority for U.S. Action in Grenada," Oct. 26, 1983, 1.

[71]*Id.*, 2; and *CSM,* Oct. 27, 1983, 1, 24.

[72]See Quincy Wright, "United States Intervention in the Lebanon," 53 *AJIL* 112 (1959); consult Whiteman, vol. 5, 519–22, 845–48. Eventually about 6,000 Marines and 8,000 Army personnel had been sent to Lebanon.

following charges of United Arab Republic intervention in the internal affairs of Jordan. On January 25, 1964, British forces went into action in Tanganyika, Uganda, and Kenya, in each instance at the request of the respective government, in order to put down mutinies by African troops. Among recent instances of (military) intervention by invitation were the presence (and participation in civil war operations) of French forces in Chad, first by logistic support in 1977 and then by the sending of combat troops in 1978, together with units from Zaire (both withdrawn in March 1979; Chapter 14); and the presence of Cuban troops in Angola, Mozambique, and Ethiopia. In August 1981, a detachment of 1,500 Senegalese troops moved into The Gambia and quickly defeated leftist Gambian rebels who had attempted to overthrow the legitimate government. The Senegalese came at the request of the lawful government and in accordance with a mutual defense pact between Senegal and The Gambia. Other examples of intervention by invitation include the invited Indian force of 100,000 men in Sri Lanka (July 1987 to March 24, 1990); the brief Indian intervention in the Maldives to foil a coup (1988–1989); but *not* the alleged invasion of Afghanistan by 100,000 Soviet troops (December 24, 1979 until their withdrawal in 1988–1989).

In August 1983, the French government sent 3,500 paratroopers, 800 vehicles, and later 40 Jaguar fighter bombers into Chad (northern Africa) after Libyan troops had been sent there by invitation to support rebels fighting the Chad government. The French forces established a defense line roughly through the middle of Chad, and when they extended that line northward in January 1984, Libya received a formal request from the rebel leadership to intervene in Chad on behalf of the "Transitional Government of National Unity." On April 30, 1984, Libya's leader, Colonel Moammar Gadhafi, acknowledged for the first time the presence of Libyan forces in Chad. On September 17, 1984, France and Libya announced the impending phased withdrawal of their forces from Chad, but when, after French withdrawal, some 800–1,000 Libyan soldiers were still found in Chad, the French government sent its jets back over Chadian territory. After notable military victories by Chadian troops, including the seizure and subsequent loss of the disputed Aozou Strip, the two protagonists agreed in September 1987 to a ceasefire and a peaceful settlement of their territorial dispute. In September 1988, Libya announced the upcoming release of all Chadian prisoners of war, and in the next month, both countries decided to restore normal diplomatic relations.[73]

Most important of all recent examples of this kind of intervention was the involvement of the United States and other states in the Vietnamese

[73]See *CSM*, Sept. 18, 1984, 9; Sept. 19, 1984, 9, 12; Nov. 20, 1984, 1; see also Chapter 23 under "One-Party Peacekeeping Forces" for the OAU Force in Chad at an earlier date.

conflict. The present writer believes that the United States intervention in that conflict constituted a lawful intervention.[74] Under generally accepted rules of international law, outside assistance cannot be requested by a government faced by a purely domestic civil war in which the outcome is in doubt, for such a government cannot truly speak for its country. But if a civil war is aided and promoted from the outside, by agencies of another state—if, in other words, there has been subversive intervention—then the target government has a legal right to ask for assistance in its struggle to survive. This appears to have been the situation in South Vietnam after the initial phases of the civil war, which began as a domestic uprising against the government in Saigon in 1957. Infiltration from North Vietnam appears to have started in early 1958, even though North Vietnamese *military units* did not penetrate the demilitarized zone until after the Gulf of Tonkin episodes in early August 1964.

Under traditional international law, the American intervention would thus have qualified as legitimate assistance rendered to a friendly, recognized government at the latter's request, whereas the North Vietnamese activities, amounting to aid to rebels, would have constituted an unlawful use of force unless North Vietnam then went to war against South Vietnam.

Under the conditions described—that is, a civil war supported, on the rebel side, from the outside—third parties may assist the incumbent government, regardless of a possible diminution of the control exercised by it over its national territory. In the case of South Vietnam, six countries sent combat forces: the United States, South Korea, Thailand, Australia, New Zealand, and the Philippines. Many others provided medical and nonmilitary assistance.

7. Humanitarian intervention was claimed by such writers as Grotius, Vattel, and Westlake to be legally valid when a state treated its people "in such a way as to deny their fundamental human rights and to shock the conscience of mankind."[75] Such interference in the affairs of others is defended by the argument that if certain practices or actions, revolting when judged by generally accepted standards of morality and decency, continue to take place in a given state despite protests and objections by its neighbors, then humanitarian considerations outweigh the prohibition of intervention and justify a decision to interfere.

---

[74]This endorsement of the legality of U.S. intervention has been shared by other writers as well as by the Department of State: see, *inter alia,* John N. Moore, "The Lawfulness of Military Assistance to the Republic of Viet-nam," 61 *AJIL* 1 (1967); Leonard C. Meeker (Legal Adviser of the Department of State), "The Legality of United States Participation in the Defense of Viet-nam [Legal Memorandum submitted to the Senate Committee on Foreign Relations, Mar. 4, 1966]," 60 *AJIL* 565 (1966); Hulland and Novogrod, *Law and Vietnam* (1968). For other materials representing many differing points of view, see "Suggested Readings."

[75]Lauterpacht's *Oppenheim,* vol. 1, 312.

Humanitarian intervention has been carried out by individual countries (Russia in Turkey on behalf of Bulgarian nationalists in 1877; the United States in Cuba in 1898) or on a collective basis (the Great Powers in Turkey on behalf of Greece in 1827; France in Syria in 1860, on the basis of an agreement among the major powers; the European Great Powers plus Japan in China in 1900, during the Boxer Rebellion).

The most recent instances of an intervention claimed to be humanitarian in nature were the aborted U.S. attempt (April 24, 1980) to rescue the 53 American hostages held then in Tehran (President Carter characterized the enterprise as "a humanitarian mission . . . not directed against Iran . . . not directed against the people of Iran")[76], the Grenada operation discussed earlier; and the U.S. occupation of Panama (1989), during which President Bush claimed the protection of American residents (35,000) to have been the major purpose of the invasion;[77] and the evacuation by U.S. Marines of foreigners from Monrovia, the wartorn capital of Liberia, on August 19, 1990. Among the some 800 people flown by helicopters to Freetown, Sierra Leone, were not only American citizens but about 670 nationals of Lebanon, as well as some Germans, French, Chinese, Indians, and a Ghanain priest.

8. The "abatement" of an international nuisance—frequently characterized by the addition of the adjective *intolerable*—has been claimed on occasion to be a variety of a legal right of intervention. It could be argued that this was one of the reasons cited in the United States in 1898 in partial justification of armed action in Cuba. The argument was actually utilized by Japan in 1932 in defense of the invasion and conquest of Manchuria. It was also brought forward, in conjunction with the concept of *debellatio* (see Chapter 22), in 1939, in defense of Russian interference in the form of invasion followed by annexation when the Polish state had crumbled under German attack. And still another example—American—may be found in the dispatch of military forces into Mexico in 1916–1917, following civil disturbances in northern Mexico, the Villa raid (Columbus, New Mexico), and the inability of the Mexican government to restore order along the United States border.

The abatement theory holds that when conditions in the territory of a neighboring state border on anarchy, with the concurrent inability of the constituted authorities to restore order and to prevent a spilling over of the disturbance into one's own territory, then one has a duty to intervene—quite likely by armed force—to restore order along one's frontiers and to end the chaos next door. If no selfish aims are involved in the intervention in question, if no territorial aggrandizement or other gain is contemplated or realized, then it is difficult, in many instances,

[76]*NYT,* Apr. 26–28, 1980, *passim; Current Policy No. 170* (Apr. 1980).
[77]See "Protection of Nationals," 84 *AJIL* 545 (1990).

to deny a right, based on self-defense or self-preservation, to violate the ban on intervention for the sake of abating the nuisance at one's doorstep.

If a moral consensus can be shown to exist, if the "conscience of mankind" is outraged by a repetition of repulsive practices within a state, then conceivably there may be a moral justification for intervention by other states. The question remaining would, of course, be the old one: Does the end justify the means? In this instance, justification might be admitted in favor of interference, provided an absence of selfish aims could be demonstrated.[78] Humanitarian intervention has been traditionally a part of customary international law, and almost all writers as well as governments believed that the coming of the League of Nations had not affected this type of intervention. However, Article 2 (4) of the Charter of the United Nations appears to prohibit humanitarian intervention, particularly if it involves the threat or use of force. Today there is a sharp difference of opinion among both scholars and governments. A growing number in each category appears to believe that humanitarian intervention is again justified in view of the commission of official atrocities, including what must be termed genocide in several cases (in Cambodia, in particular), coupled with the manifest inability of the United Nations to intervene by force once it has been determined that there has been an action involving atrocious behavior by a government, especially if that action is deemed to represent a threat to or a breach of the peace (Pakistan in East Pakistan before the independence of Bangladesh).

In late November 1964, rebel forces in the ex-Belgian eastern Congo had captured or isolated hundreds of white residents, increasing numbers of whom were killed. The United States government agreed, for humanitarian reasons, to supply air transport for Belgian paratroopers and for the evacuation of white refugees. Within four days, this operation had been completed, and two days later all paratroopers had been removed from the Congo. This intervention resulted in widespread strong criticism from African members of the United Nations, and an unsuccessful attempt was made by 18 of them to have the Security Council condemn the rescue operation as illegal, whereas most writers and a number of governments praised it as one of the clearest modern instances of true humanitarian intervention.[79] The same claim can be made for the May

---

[78]See, inter alia, Lillich, ed., *Humanitarian Intervention and the United Nations* (1973), and especially the study by Franck and Rodley, "After Bangladesh: The Law of Humanitarian Intervention by Military Force," 67 *AJIL* 275 (1973). Concerning the 1979 Vietnamese intervention in Cambodia (1978–1990), which resulted in the fall of the Pol Pot government and its replacement by a Vietnamese-supported government, see the letters to *NYT* by Rubin, Mar. 20, 1979, A-18, and Rostow, Apr. 10, 1979, A-18, on the question of humanitarian intervention by Vietnam.

[79]See also 59 *AJIL* 614 (1964).

1978 rescue operations in Zaire by French and Belgian forces, transported in U.S. Air Force aircraft.[80]

9. Self-defense, under certain conditions, has been held by many writers to constitute a legal right of intervention, although it appears at times to be identical with the abatement right. Thus it has been argued by a few writers that the *initial* stages of the 1982 Israeli invasion of Lebanon represented an act of lawful intervention, on the basis of objectives voiced then by the invaders: driving PLO concentrations from Lebanese border regions into the interior in order to rid Israel of continuing attacks across its borders. The present writer fails to discern a difference from the abatement theory. On the other hand, self-defense appears to grant a legal right of intervention under certain conditions.[81]

## SUGGESTED READINGS

### Immunities of States

Briggs, 442–51; Delson, "The Act of State Doctrine—Judicial Defense or Abstention?" 66 *AJIL* 82 (1972); Jacobs, King, and S. Rodriguez III, "The Act of State Doctrine: A History of Judicial Limitations and Expectations," 18 *Harvard Int'l. L. Jl.* 677 (1977); Higgins, "The Death Throes of Absolute Immunity: The Government of Uganda before the English Courts," 73 *AJIL* 465 (1979); Singer, "The Act of State Doctrine of the United Kingdom: An Analysis, with Comparisons to United States Practice," 75 *AJIL* 283 (1981); Crawford, "Execution of Judgments and Foreign Sovereign Immunity," 75 *AJIL* 820 (1981); International Law Association, *Draft Articles for a Convention on State Immunity,* 22 *ILM* 287 (1983); and Organization of American States, *Inter-American Draft Convention on Jurisdictional Immunity of States,* 22 *ILM* 292 (1983). See also Delaume, "Economic Development and Sovereign Immunity," 79 *AJIL* 319 (1985), and Schreuer, *State Immunity: Some Recent Developments* (1988).

### The Sabbatino Case

See list of references in Whiteman, vol. 6, 36, as well as Mooney, *Foreign Seizures: Sabbatino and the Act of State Doctrine* (1967); Falk, "The Complexity of Sabbatino," 58 *AJIL* 935 (1964); Halberstam, "Sabbatino Resurrected: The Act of State Doctrine in the Revised Restatement of U.S. Foreign Relations Law," 79 *AJIL* 68 (1985).

### The Banco Nacional de Cuba Case

This now-famous case has been three times in the Second Circuit Court of Appeals and twice in the Supreme Court: see *Banco Nacional de Cuba* v. *First National City*

---

[80]*NYT,* May 20, 1978, 3, and 72 *AJIL* 917 (1978).
[81]The classic and interesting example for this category is found in *The Caroline Case (Great Britain* v. *United States),* 1837, found in Moore, vol. 2, 412; Cheng, 84–87; and Jennings, "The Caroline and McLeod Cases," 32 *AJIL* 82 (1938).

*Bank,* U.S. Court of Appeals, 2d Cir., May 11, 1973, reported in 12 *ILM* 636 (1973). The earlier history of the litigation is *First National City Bank* v. *Banco Nacional de Cuba,* 40 U.S.L.W. 4652 (U.S., June 7, 1972), *rev'g* 442 F.2d 530 (2d Cir. 1972); 400 U.S. 1019 (1971), *vacating* 431 F.2d 394 (2d Cir. 1970), *rev'g* 270 F. Supp. 1004 (S.D.N.Y. 1967). The relevant decisions, rulings, briefs, and other related materials may be found in 6 *ILM* 898 (1967); 9 *ILM* 1125 (1970); 10 *ILM* 56, 509, 1191 (1971); 11 *ILM* 27, 348, 811 (1972). The key decisions were also reported in 65 *AJIL* 195, 391, 812 (1971), and 65 *AJIL* 856 (1972).

OTHER CASES

*Sullivan* v. *State of Sao Paulo; Sullivan* v. *State of Rio Grande do Sul,* U.S. Court of Appeals, 2d Cir., 1941, 122 Fed. Rep. (2d Ser.) 355, reported in 36 *AJIL* 131 (1942).

*Republic of Iraq* v. *First National City Bank, Administrator,* U.S. Dist. Court, S.D.N.Y., 1965, 241 F. Supp. 567; affirmed, Court of Appeals, 2d Cir., 1965, 353 F.2d 47; *certiorari* denied, Supreme Court, 1966, 382 U.S. 1027. Consult also the relevant *Note* by Mark T. Horlings, 7 *Harvard Int'l. L. Club J.* (1966), 316; and see Whiteman, vol. 6, 36–41 on this case, as well as *id.,* 54–66, on acts of state affecting property rights in the forum state.

*Industria Azucarera Nacional, S.A. et. al.* v. *Empresa Navegacion Mambisa,* U.S. District Court, Dist. of the Canal Zone, Nov. 1, 1973, reported, with *Note* by Sandler and all relevant documents, in 13 *ILM* 120 (1974).

*Occidental Petroleum Corp.* v. *Buttes Gas & Oil Co.,* U.S. District Court, Central Division, Cal., Mar. 17, 1971, reported in 65 *AJIL* 815 (1971).

*Buttes Gas and Oil Co.* v. *Hammer,* United Kingdom, House of Lords, Oct. 29 1981 [1981] in 3 W.L.R. 787, in 21 *ILM* 92 (1982); also in 76 *AJIL* 399 (1982).

*Quereshi* v. *Union of Soviet Socialist Republics,* Pakistan, Supreme Court, July 8, 1981, P.L.D. 1981 Supreme Court 377, in 20 *ILM* 1060 (1981).

*Hunt* v. *Mobil Oil,* U.S. Court of Appeals, 2d Cir., Jan. 12, 1977, 550 Federal Reporter, 2d Ser. 68 (1977), reported in 16 *ILM* 803 (1977).

*Yessenin-Volpin* v. *Novosti Press Agency, et al.* U.S. Dist. Court, S.D.N.Y., Jan 23, 1978, 443 F. Supp. 849–57 (1978), reported in 17 *ILM* 720 (1978).

*East Europe Domestic International Sales Corporation* v. *Terra,* U.S. Dist. Court, S.D.N.Y., Mar. 13, 1979, in 18 *ILM* 977 (1979).

*Libya* v. *Libyan American Oil Co.* (LIAMCO); (1) Award of the Arbitral Tribunal, Apr. 12, 1977, in 20 *ILM* 1 (1981); (2) Decision of the Swiss Federal Supreme Court of June 20, 1980, 20 *ILM* 151 (1981); (3) *Libyan American Oil Co.* v. *Socialist People's Libyan Arab Jamahirya,* on appeal from the U.S. Dist. Court, D.C., Excerpts from the *amicus curiae* brief submitted by the United States to the U.S. Court of Appeals, D.C. Cir., June 16, 1980, and Nov. 7, 1980, 20 *ILM* 161 (1981).

*International Association of Machinists and Aerospace Workers* v. *Organization of Petroleum Exporting Countries* (OPEC), U.S. Court of Appeals, 9th Cir., 1981, 649 F.2d 1354, in 76 *AJIL* 160 (1982).

*Callejo* v. *Bancomer, S.A.* 764 F.2d 1101. U.S. Court of Appeals, 5th Cir., July 8, 1985, reported in 80 *AJIL* 170 (1986).

*Verlinden B.V.* v. *Central Bank of Nigeria,* U.S. Supreme Court, May 23, 1983, 461 U.S. 480, 103 S. Ct. 1962 (1983), and see analysis in 79 *AJIL* 779 (1985).

*Sonatrach* v. *Migeon,* France, Court of Cassation, 1st Civil Chamber, Oct. 1, 1985, in 26 *ILM* 998 (1987).

*Braka* v. *Bancomer, S.N.C.,* U.S. Court of Appeals, 2d Cir., 762 F. 2d 222, with Kahale's *Note,* in 24 *ILM* 1046 (1985).

*Callejo* v. *Bancomer,* U.S. Court of Appeals, 5th Cir., No. 84–1270, July 8, 1985, in 24 *ILM* 1050 (1985).

Radicati di Brozolo's Case Note on two interesting Italian cases: *Benamar* v. *Embassy of the Democratic and Popular Republic of Algeria,* Corte di Cassazione, May 4, 1989, and *Socialist People's Libyan Arab Jamahiriya* v. *Rossiter S.R.L.72,* Corte di Cassazione, May 25, 1989, in 84 *AJIL* 573 (1990).

# 8

# Duties of States

It was pointed out earlier that many of the alleged rights of states either reflect their characteristics or, in certain instances, represent their duties or obligations. Whether or not one admits the existence of a moral code prevailing in the relations among nations, the fact remains that practicing diplomats, Machiavellian or otherwise, have agreed that some sort of code does exist. Thus states concluding treaties among themselves expect that the agreements will be observed; whoever breaches the treaty will either deny that fact or defend it by elaborate arguments designed to show that the act was morally or legally just. It therefore becomes necessary now to investigate what may be properly included among the duties of states in their mutual relations.

The most modern, though incomplete, listing of the asserted duties of states may be found in the Draft Convention on the Rights and Duties of States, prepared in 1949 by the International Law Commission in conformity with a resolution of the United Nations General Assembly.[1] The following discussion deals with all the duties mentioned by the commission, as well as with several additional obligations generally recognized as binding by the members of the community of nations.

## UNLAWFUL INTERVENTION

One of the oldest duties of states, enshrined in both customary international law and numerous multilateral conventions, is the basic obligation of a state to abstain from intervention in the internal and external affairs of any other state.[2] The inclusion of "and external" represents, however, a very recent addition to an old principle. History indicates that states generally do not regard interference with the foreign affairs (read "policies") of another state as being unlawful or even reprehensible. In fact, many external policies of states appear to be directed at blocking the success of another state's external policies, and no one appears to regard such a conflict as unlawful in nature.

[1] Text in 44 *AJIL* 15 (1950 Supp.).
[2] See the heavily documented Damrosch, "Politics across Borders: Nonintervention and Non-forcible Influence over Domestic Affairs," 83 *AJIL* 1 (1989), and the valuable study by Sadurska, "Threats of Force," 82 *AJIL* 239 (1988).

DEFINITION OF INTERVENTION   Few terms in international law have led to more acrimonious arguments than has the prohibition of intervention. Not only is there a general lack of agreement on its definition, but many writers as well as diplomats have attempted to demonstrate that under specific conditions there existed not merely a right but a duty by one state to intervene in the affairs of another state.

The majority of commentators agree that intervention under present-day international law means *dictatorial* interference by one state in the affairs of another state for the purpose of either maintaining or changing the existing order of things,[3] rather than mere interference per se. Such intervention concerns the independence, territory, or supremacy of the state involved.

There cannot be any doubt that such intervention is prohibited by international law, for that law has been created, at least in part, to protect the international personality of the states of the world.[4] However, there are exceptions to this principle, as has been shown in the previous chapter, for some interventions take place by right and are thus lawful.

## ARMED INTERVENTION

INTERVENTION BY INVITATION   In the case of "invitational intervention," as in the case of other forms of intervention, the particular circumstances of a given instance determine whether the intervention has any legal standing at all. Thus the invasion of Austria by German armed forces in 1938 did take place at the request of an Austrian government, to be sure, but it was highly dubious whether the government in question could be regarded at the time as the lawful government of the Republic of Austria.

Comparable in many respects to the Austrian situation, the military intervention by the Soviet Union in Hungary in 1956 represented, in American eyes, an illegal intervention because the Kadar government, which had asked for Soviet assistance under the terms of the Warsaw Pact, represented not a legitimate government in Hungary but a puppet regime established by the very state whose military aid and intervention were requested.[5]

On the other hand, the invasion of Czechoslovakia by Soviet and other Warsaw Pact forces in August 1968 was wholly illegal, even though initially justified by the Soviet Union as an invitational intervention. Subsequently no evidence whatever of any invitation could be produced by the Soviet government. The so-called Brezhnev Doctrine, asserting the Soviet Union's

---

[3]See Lauterpacht's *Oppenheim*, vol. 1, 305; Brierly, 402; Whiteman, vol. 5, 452–53; Fenwick, "Intervention: Individual and Collective," 39 *AJIL* 645 (1945).
[4]The General Assembly, its Sixth Committee, and a 31-member Special Committee worked at length drafting an acceptable code of legal principles governing friendly relations among states: see Whiteman, vol. 5, 24–33; and the "Declaration on the Inadmissibility of Intervention in the Domestic Affairs of States and the Protection of Their Independence and Sovereignty," adopted by the Assembly on Dec. 19, 1966 (UN Doc. GA 2225-XXI-1966).
[5]See Whiteman, vol. 5, 667–702.

right to intervene in any socialist country if the existence of socialism was threatened in any manner, reflected power politics on a hegemonial basis, not a legal right. The wording of the long-famous doctrine bears repetition:

"The CPSU [Communist Party Soviet Union] has always advocated that each socialist country determines the concrete forms of its development . . . but if there is . . . deviation from . . . the common natural laws of socialist construction, . . . a threat to the security of the socialist commonwealth as a whole—this is no longer merely a problem for that country's people, but a common problem—the concern of all socialist countries.[6]

Similarly, the Soviet Union's illegal invasion of Afghanistan, on December 27, 1979, was allegedly at the invitation of the Afghans' Marxist government. That government had been engaged in an increasingly unsuccessful war against Muslim rebel groups in the mountainous areas of Afghanistan, and it appeared that the Soviet Union wanted to "clean up a mess," as one correspondent put it. However, the alleged sender of the invitation, President Hafizullah Amin, and some members of his family were promptly executed by the invaders in a coup engineered by the latter. Ultimately well over 100,000 Russian combat troops were in Afghanistan. A new ("postinvitation") government was installed, headed by another Marxist, Babrak Karmal, brought back from exile by the Soviet Union. Though the Brezhnev Doctrine was not invoked officially by the Soviet Union in this instance, the claimed principle of the doctrine appears to have played a major part in Russian decision making in the Afghan situation.[7]

A more recent example of illegal intervention in response to a fictitious invitation took place on August 1, 1990. The Revolutionary Command Council of Iraq, headed by Saddam Hussein, announced that the government of neighboring Kuwait had been overthrown. It claimed that in response to "the request form the interim government of Kuwait," Iraq had decided to cooperate with the latter and stated that Iraqi troops had crossed the border of Kuwait. The claimed purpose of that move was to defend the revolution and the people of Kuwait. On August 4, Baghdad TV declared that the new

---

[6]In *Pravda* and *Izvestia*, Nov. 13, 1968, at 1–2; in *Current Digest of the Soviet Press*, XX, 39, at 4.

[7]On the invasion of Czechoslovakia, see *NYT*, Aug. 21–30, 1968, *passim*, and see *id.*, May 8, 1976, at 5 for a reaffirmation of the Brezhnev Doctrine. On the conflict in Afghanistan, consult *id.*, Dec. 27, 1979–Jan. 31, 1980, *passim*. See also the following reports of the U.S. Dept. of State, Bureau of Public Affairs: *Current Policy* No. 123 (Jan. 4, 1980), No. 124 (Jan. 6, 1980), No. 128 (Jan. 15, 1980), as well as *Special Reports* No. 79 (Feb. 1981), No. 91 (Dec. 1981), and No. 112 (Dec. 1983). See especially the summary of a *Memorandum* by the legal adviser of the Dept. of State (Dec. 29, 1979) in 74 *AJIL* 418 (1980) on the illegality of the Soviet invasion, as well as General Assembly Resolution A/37/37 (Nov. 1982), reprinted in Dept. of State *Current Policy* No. 441 (Nov. 1982), calling for immediate withdrawal of the "foreign troops" from Afghanistan. Also study Dept. of State *Current Policy* No. 636 (Nov. 14, 1984), *Special Report* No. 118 (Dec. 1984), and *Gist* (Dec. 1984).

Kuwait leadership was composed of Kuwaiti army officers. A few days later, the new governement was dissolved and Kuwait was "annexed" by Iraq and declared to be a province of the latter state.

Most other forms of military intervention would have to be considered unlawful (Anglo-French intervention in Egypt, 1956; French intervention in the Central African Empire, 1979), despite occasional laudable intentions.[8] Despite this interpretation, many military interventions have taken place, particularly in recent decades. Thus in 1971, 16,000 South Vietnamese troops, supported by American aircraft and artillery, invaded Laos, in the hope of forcing their common enemies to make a stand. It was this Laotian incident that made the term incursion famous as a euphemism for invasion.[9] The latter word is no longer fashionable, being tinged with a faint aura of illegality. Recent examples culled from a much longer list include South African forces attacking guerrilla units in neighboring Mozambique in January and February 1981; South African forces invading Lesotho's capital (Maseru) on December 9, 1982, killing at least 37 people. On a much more massive scale, South Africa repeatedly invaded Angola in recent years, asserting an illegal granting of sanctuary to SWAPO units which, in turn, invaded Namibia (see Chapter 4).

Recent instances of military intervention by invitation include the minor French operation in the Comoros Islands and the massive Indian incursion into Sri Lanka.

On December 15, French troops landed on the Comoros Islands at the request of the local government. Their purpose was to evict a group of mercenaries who had controlled the country after the assassination of its president.

In the instance of Sri Lanka, fighting broke out in July 1983 between the Sinhalese majority and the Tamil minority over Tamil demands for a separate homeland. On July 29, 1987, the Prime Minister of India sent troops (ultimately numbering 100,000) under the terms of an agreement reached earlier with the Sri Lankan government to end the growing guerrilla warfare and to enable the Tamil minority to reach a political settlement with the island's government. In September 1987, certain Tamil rebel groups refused to disarm, and some Sinhalese factions openly questioned the validity of the agreement with India. The uprising ended, however, in December 1989, after most of the rebel leadership had been killed by Sri Lankan forces. The new Indian government then promised that its remaining 50,000 troops

[8]Consult Whiteman, vol. 5, 629–58; and also *Time*, Oct. 8, 1979, 62–64. See also Chapter 23.
[9]See Newman, *Strictly Speaking* (1974), 63–64; and Rawson, *A Dictionary of Euphemisms and Other Doubletalk* (1981), 143. Incursion is quite often used to denote an invasion intended to prevent an attack, that is, as a synonym for "preventive strike," such as Israel's 1981 attack on Iraq's nuclear installation. During the 1983 invasion of Grenada, one U.S. military spokesman, apparently trying not to use "invasion," referred to the initial phase of the invasion as a "predawn vertical insertion."

would be brought home by March 31, 1990. In fact, the last Indian troops withdrew from the island on March 24, 1990. (See also Chapter 20 *sub* India Peacekeeping Force.)

Most recently, the government of the African state of Rwanda requested military aid from France and Belgium against invading Rwanda refugees from Uganda (September 4, 1990). In response to the genuine invitation, 500 Belgian paratroopers arrived the next day in the former Belgian colony and assumed control of the capital's airport and surrounding roads. French military units were then deployed in defensive positions around the French embassy. Both the German and the French governments then proceeded to evacuate most of their nationals from Rwanda.

COLLECTIVE INTERVENTION    Another variety of intervention has been defended on a number of occasions: collective intervention, sometimes referred to as *universal sanction*. The classic example of this variation took place in 1863 when joint intervention in Japanese affairs was agreed on by the governments of Great Britain, the Netherlands, France, Russia, and the United States in order to compel Japan to desist from attacking foreign vessels, particularly in the Strait of Shimonoseki.

On other occasions, Greece requested UN intervention in 1947 when armed bands allegedly invaded Greece (from Albania, Bulgaria, and Yugoslavia),[10] and Guatemala, in 1954, requested UN action to halt aggressive attacks launched from Honduras and Nicaragua with covert United States support.[11]

No matter how moral or desirable or plausible some of the foregoing justifications of intervention have appeared in specific instances, the fact remains that intervention per se is an act violating rights that should be inviolable and represents a hostile act.

The past few years have witnessed other instances of armed intervention, surrounded in a number of cases by a multitude of contributory and confusing issues. On April 17, 1961, came the ill-fated attempt of the United States to overthrow the Castro government in Cuba, by helping form a liberation force composed of about 1,500 Cuban exiles trained and equipped with the benevolent support of the United States. The attempt to establish a beachhead in the Bay of Pigs failed, in part because of a leakage of information concerning the landing plans and in part because of a denial of air and naval cover by the United States. A contributing factor to the disastrous results of the enterprise was that an expected massive uprising of the Cuban civilian population did not materialize. But without doubt, and by official admission, the government of the United States had attempted to intervene in Cuban affairs through the utilization of a "friendly" armed force. The

---

[10]Text of Greek note in *World Report,* Aug. 12, 1947, 37–38; also consult Whiteman, vol. 5, 281–91, 383–84, 433–42.

[11]See the analysis by Travis, "Collective Intervention by the Organization of American States," *Proceedings* 100–110 (1957); and Whiteman, vol. 5, 426–28, 802–8. On collective intervention in general, consult *id.,* 544–64.

fact that this force consisted of Cuban rather than of United States citizens had nothing to do with its illegality.

The locale of the 1961 American intervention in the Western Hemisphere emphasized the illegal nature of the enterprise, in view of the existence of numerous regional arrangements prohibiting such intervention in the Americas. The Charter of the Organization of American States, the Saavedra Lamas Anti-War Treaty of 1933, the Montevideo Convention of 1933 on the Rights and Duties of States, the Buenos Aires Protocol on Non-Intervention of 1936, the Buenos Aires Convention of 1936 on the Fulfillment of the Existing Treaties Between the American States, the Act of Chapultepec of 1945, and the Declaration on Intervention of the Caracas Conference of 1954—all these instruments, to which the United States is a party, condemn and prohibit the action that the United States promoted against Cuba in 1961. Yet, and here political considerations both domestic and foreign intruded, large numbers of American citizens were bitterly disappointed at the failure of the United States to support the Cuban invasion by sending along its own armed forces in order to crush the Cuban Castro government.

The duty to abstain from armed intervention clearly means also that no state may permit the use of its territory for the staging of hostile expeditions against another state (for example, the 1961 Bay of Pigs episode). Thus the United States acted correctly in arresting, on January 2, 1967, a group of 73 armed men on a Florida key. The individuals in question were preparing to invade Haiti in an effort to overthrow the incumbent government with the expected help of indigenous malcontents. A year later, the leaders of the group were sentenced to prison by a U.S. District Court.[12] In 1981, a small expedition was captured near New Orleans before it could board a vessel for an invasion of the island republic of Dominica, and another small group, consisting mostly of Canadian or naturalized U.S. citizens, was rescued from its sinking ship by the U.S. Coast Guard in January 1982 and then was arrested when it was discovered that the group had been attempting to invade Haiti. In July 1986, 14 men were arrested in New Orleans and charged with plotting to overthrow the government of Suriname (formerly Dutch Guiana). The conspirators were unlucky when they tried to recruit another person who, it turned out, was a special agent of the FBI. It was the third time in five years that a New Orleans–based plot to overthrow a foreign government had been foiled.

The most publicized recent instance of a country's failure to prevent the use of national territory as a base for attacking a neighboring state was the tolerated use of Honduran territory by the U.S.-supported Contras, rebels against the legal government of Nicaragua.[13] The latter had instituted pro-

---

[12]See also the case of *Bush* v. *United States*, U.S. Court of Appeals, 5th Cir., 1968, 389 F. 2d 485, reported in 62 *AJIL* 977 (1968).

[13]See, *e.g.*, "United States: Legislation Relating to Nicaragua," 26 *ILM* 433 (1987); "The Good Friday Accords," 83 *AJIL* 544 (1989).

ceedings against Honduras in the International Court of Justice on July 28, 1986. The Court's decision on jurisdiction was handed down on December 20, 1988.[14] The Court affirmed its jurisdiction as based on the Pact of Bogotá (American Treaty on Pacific Settlement, April 30, 1948, 30 UNTS 55), despite disagreement among the justices on this point. The Court's decision on the *Merits* of the case was still pending at the time of this writing.

Nicaragua had also instituted proceedings against Costa Rica on July 28, 1986, charging the latter country with unlawful border and transborder armed actions.[15]

On the other hand, Cuba violated its obligations when it not only set up training schools for leaders of subversive movements in Latin America but permitted such individuals as well as members of the Cuban armed forces to depart from Cuba for their respective target states. In one instance, in May 1967, such a group, including four Cuban army officers, was captured or killed while landing in Venezuela (for example, the exploits, until his capture and execution, of Ernesto "Ché" Guevara in Bolivia in 1967–1968).

By definition, so-called national wars of liberation are likely to involve outside armed intervention, preceded by and accompanied by outside propaganda. Such wars must be regarded as illegal intervention (see Chapter 23 concerning such conflicts).

A "textbook illustration" of a combination of unlawful state practices in the sphere of intervention has been provided in the decision of the International Court of Justice in the *Case Concerning Military and Paramilitary Activities in and against Nicaragua (Nicaragua v. United States of America), Merits, Judgment, ICJ Reports, 1986,* 14.[16] See Case History No. 2, "*Nicaragua v. United States,*" at the end of this chapter. The coverage of the case in question had to be more extensive than the treatment accorded the abstracted cases for two reasons: the extraordinary complexity of the decision on Merits and the procedural questions raised by the absence of the respondents, etc.

## UNARMED INTERVENTION

Thus far this discussion of intervention has centered on the traditional interference in the internal affairs of another state by means of armed force. Obviously this is not the only form of intervention possible.

[14] *Border and Transborder Armed Actions (Nicaragua v. Honduras), Jurisdiction and Admissibility.* 1988 *ICJ Rep.* 69, in 28 *ILM* 335 (1989), digested in 83 *AJIL* 353 (1989).
[15] Both applications in 25 *ILM* 1290 (1986).
[16] Text in 25 *ILM* 1023 (1986). Consult also Highet, "Evidence, the Court, and the Nicaragua Case," 81 *AJIL* 1 (1987) and "Appraisals of the ICJ's Decision: *Nicaragua v. United States (Merits),*" *id.,* 77 (Introduction by H. G. Maier).

## Subversive Intervention by States

One of the most difficult problems in this sphere is that dealing with what Wright termed "subversive intervention."[17] In a world torn between a variety of rival ideologies, with authoritarian and sometimes totalitarian regimes in control of several states and with conditions quite out of consonance with elementary concepts of human dignity prevailing in a number of areas, the writer on international law questions is faced with an enormous dilemma.

LEGAL OBLIGATIONS TO ABSTAIN FROM INTERVENTION    On the one hand, there is an undoubted legal obligation, reiterated in the Charter of the United Nations, to abstain from intervention and to respect the territorial integrity and political independence of all other states. At the same time, there is an equally legal obligation, enshrined in the same Charter, for the members of the United Nations to seek the realization of principles of respect for human rights and the self-determination of peoples. To be sure, the relative standing in law of these two sets of obligations—a phrase unorthodox enough to horrify a lawyer, who cannot conceive that one legal obligation should prevail over another equally legal one—is not quite the same. That is, the duty to abstain from intervention is firmly grounded in rules of customary law as well as in numerous multilateral treaties, whereas many of the obligations relating to human rights and self-determination lack as yet an acceptance by the members of the community of nations. Thus far at least, no state has a right to proceed by some measure of intervention to force compliance by another state in regard to human rights, and so on.

On the other hand, it has been generally recognized that there is an obligation or duty to abstain from subversive intervention—that is, from engaging in propaganda, official statements, or legislative action of any kind—with the intention of promoting rebellion, sedition, or treason against the government of another state. Thus Libya's leader, Colonel Moammar Gadhafi, violated the rule when, during a 14-year period of squabbling with Morocco, he organized a radio campaign inciting the Moroccan people to overthrow their king. The latter, amusingly enough, responded with a single radio program directed toward Libya and consisting for all of 24 hours entirely of the sounds of "yapping dogs."

The General Assembly of the United Nations unanimously adopted a resolution on November 3, 1947, condemning all forms of seditious propaganda, limited, however, to propaganda likely to provoke threats to peace or an act of aggression. On December 1, 1949, the Assembly urged all states to refrain from, among other things, any threats or acts aimed at fomenting civil war or subverting the will of the people in any other state, a request that was reiterated in tones of greater concern on November 17, 1950.

The United States and the Soviet Union have been foremost in condemning subversive intervention. The former has generally been highly critical of

[17]Wright, "Subversive Intervention," 54 *AJIL* 521 (1960), a pioneer investigation of this subject from a legal point of view, frequently cited by subsequent writers.

the subversive activities promoted by the Communist bloc states, labeling such efforts "indirect aggression." Several of its spokesmen have pointed out the comparatively greater danger of such disguised indirect aggression when compared with the menace of an open expedition against a given state. [18] But the official U.S. condemnation of "leftist" intervention in Latin America ignored, for obvious reasons, the equally illegal support on the part of the United States of the estimated 15,000 guerrillas opposing the Sandinista government of Nicaragua (1981–1984).

The Soviet Union and its friends, on the other hand, continuously criticized every form of aid by non-Communist countries as a manifestation of imperialist intervention and attacked with vigor such American public media of information as Radio Liberty, Radio Free Europe, and Radio Martí as illegal and subversive capitalist enterprises. The stations were in part covertly funded by the Central Intelligence Agency until 1971, when the U.S. Congress became responsible for their financial support. They broadcast news and analysis unavailable through the state-controlled news agencies in Eastern Europe. Similar attacks have been voiced over the years against the global operations of the Voice of America (VOA) system, also operated by the United States government. Verbal and written criticism has been supplemented—often quite successfully—by "jamming" the Western broadcasts (see also Chapter 18 under Radio Communications). [19]

**PROBLEMS OF SUBVERSIVE INTERVENTION**    Just what is meant by *subversive intervention?* Unlike *warmongering*, it consists of communications and activities undertaken by one state that are calculated to overthrow (or at least undermine in effectiveness) the existing domestic political (and, frequently, also economic) order of another state. By all criteria applicable, such an enterprise is a violation of international law—yet both great and small powers have practiced subversive intervention up to now. The trouble is that although the jurisdiction of any state is territorial and limited to its own domain, many states have interests abroad or follow a foreign policy that involves other states, often to a close extent. When such a foreign policy or such interests appear to demand that a more friendly, a more amenable, a more radical, or a more conservative government is needed in another state to serve better the interests of the first one, then the temptation is indeed great to attempt to subvert the other state in such a manner that

---

[18]See, *e.g.,* "The Case against Castro," *U.S. News & World Report,* Dec. 21, 1981, 24–25; U.S. Department of State, *Special Reports:* No. 80, *Communist Interference in El Salvador* (Feb. 23, 1980); No. 88, *Soviet 'Active Measures'—Forgery, Disinformation, Political Operations* (Oct. 1981); No. 90, *Cuba's Renewed Support for Violence in Latin America* (Dec. 14, 1981); No. 101, *Soviet Active Measures* (July 1982), and its sequel, No. 110, *Soviet Active Measures* (Sept. 1983).

[19]See the following on the entire topic: the Annual Report of the U.S. Commission on Public Diplomacy; Murti, *The International Law of Propaganda* (1989); von Glahn, "The Case for Legal Control of 'Liberation' Propaganda; " 31 *Law and Contemporary Problems* (Duke University) 554–88 (Summer 1966); and "The War of Words," 99 *U.S. News & World Report,* Oct. 7, 1985, 34–39, at 42.

the desired results are achieved. The problem of coping with such subversive intervention is complicated by considerations of freedom of opinions that may prevail in a given country and by the technical problems of stopping propaganda across national frontiers. As President Gerald Ford of the United States phrased it in his press conference of September 16, 1974, "Our Government, like other governments, does take certain actions in the intelligence field to help implement foreign policy and protect national security. I am informed reliably that Communist nations spend vastly more money than we do for the same kind of purposes." The actions that Ford referred to were the activities, costing around $8 million, of the U.S. government between 1970 and 1973 in an effort to undermine, economically and politically, the government of President Salvador Allende Gossens of Chile.[20]

At the same time, although subversive intervention against a given government must be regarded as unlawful, it must be emphasized that aid or assistance to a government may also be viewed as meddling and, on occasion, as intervention. In other words, broadcasts, films, periodicals, program tapes for provincial stations, and so on, shipped, transmitted, or otherwise supplied by the Soviet Union and other socialist countries to Chile before the military coup of 1973, could be regarded as intervention in Chilean affairs when seen from the point of view of the Chilean opponents of President Allende and of foreign (read: U.S.) investors.

On the other hand, certain kinds of "assistance" must be characterized as intervention. A case in point occurred in Italy in 1947–1948. Left-wing influence was rising in that country, and the United States decided to grant open assistance in the form of economic and military aid to the Italian government. But the United States also opted in favor of aiding more moderate political parties, and large-scale financial assistance was given covertly in the form of campaign funds for anti-Communist politicians and parties. The strategy paid off at election time, but must be grouped under impermissible intervention.

Inasmuch as two wrongs do not make a right, subversive intervention of the "dictatorial" type represents a violation of international law—in the strictest sense even when it takes a form such as blocking needed foreign loans to a target state.

### Subversive Intervention by Private Groups

All discussion thus far has dealt with those actions of governments promoting some form of subversive intervention. When similar acts are undertaken by private individuals or groups, governments have usually refused to accept

[20]*NYT*, Sept. 8, 1974, 1, 26; Sept. 15, 1974, 1, 19, E.-23; Dec. 5, 1975, 1, 10. See also *Covert Action in Chile* (Staff Report of the Select Committee to Study Governmental Operations with Respect to Intelligence Activities, U.S. Senate, 94th Congress, 1st Session) (Washington, D.C., 1975), as well as the summary of a *Memorandum* dated Oct. 25, 1974, by the Acting Legal Adviser of the Department of State, in 69 *AJIL* 382 (1975).

responsibility for such acts. Obviously a state adversely affected by propaganda emanating from private sources in a neighboring country will not only protest the act but will attempt to prevent the subversive propaganda from reaching its own citizens by censorship, jamming of broadcasts and telecasts, and so on. In all fairness, no matter what its nature, such defensive measures appear to be the right of any government and cannot be termed illegal.

LIBEL AND SLANDER AGAINST FOREIGN GOVERNMENTS    One aspect of this problem pertains to libel and slander against foreign governments. If private individuals utter libelous statements, no responsibility devolves on their government. There are, however, a few democratic states that apparently are willing to prosecute their own citizens for libeling foreign governments or the heads of the same, provided that there is reciprocity in this matter, that is, if the libeled state provides for similar punishment of its own citizens for equivalent acts.

If, on the other hand, a public official engages in such pursuits, it appears to be a duty of his government to restrain him, to rebuke him, or even to punish him, if friendly relations with the government allegedly slandered or libeled are to be preserved. On the other hand, allegedly slanderous remarks issuing from local or state officials not directly linked to a national government do not give rise to any national responsibility, unless, of course, political considerations demand the tender of an apology to the offended government or head of state.

Similarly, private broadcasts and telecasts attacking or libeling foreign governments must not be regarded as creating state responsibility, unless the offensive statements have emanated from a government-owned or controlled station or system. In the latter case, such as statements made through a station operated as part of the Voice of America network, government responsibility would have been created.

Private intervention may also take the form of aid to rebels in another country. This action may involve funding foreign rebel movements or the actual shipment of weapons, ammunition, and other forms of military assistance. A prime example has been the continuing extensive aid of both kinds by private American sources to the illegal Irish Republican Army (IRA) in Northern Ireland.

## OTHER DUTIES OF STATES

A second duty of states, generally accepted in theory but all too often violated in practice, is the obligation to refrain from fomenting civil strife in the territory of another state and to prevent the organization within its own territory of activities calculated to produce such civil strife. This duty has already been discussed in connection with the duty of nonintervention, even though the Draft Convention on the Rights and Duties of States, of the International Law Commission, lists it as a separate item. It represents a major problem in modern international relations, with frequent unrepentant violations of the duty in question.

A third duty that every state has is to make certain that the conditions prevailing in its territory do not menace international peace. This duty, developed by the International Law Commission from a portion of the Panamanian draft of the convention just mentioned, needs little comment. It appears to be a corollary to the concept of national sovereignty, with each state presumably having exclusive authority in its territory, that such authority should be wielded in an effective manner to prevent any danger to neighboring states. It a state fails to maintain a degree of control sufficient to prevent such danger to its neighbors, then it is obligated to assume responsibility for the consequences of its failure as a sovereign government.

A fourth duty, technically applicable only to the members of the United Nations under Article 2(3) of the UN Charter, is an obligation to settle international disputes by peaceful means. Because the Charter as a treaty is not binding on nonmembers of the organization, countries that do not belong to the United Nations appear to be entitled in law to adopt forcible measures to settle disputes among themselves, either *ab initio* or after a failure of peaceful methods. On the other hand, the record since 1945 shows that members of the United Nations, too, have resorted to force outside the permissible condition of self-defense.

Corollary to the fourth duty is an asserted fifth one, a duty to abstain from resort to war as an instrument of national policy and to refrain from the threat of the use of force against another state. This alleged duty depends obviously on the interpretation adopted of the status of war under current international law. Support of this fifth duty negates one of the traditional characteristics or rights of a sovereign state, the right to go to war when other methods of obtaining justice, satisfying claims on another state, or achieving presumably essential or vital national goals have failed. In view of the debatable nature of this fifth duty of states, its validity will be considered in Chapter 20.

A sixth duty, again applicable to all members of the United Nations, is to refrain from giving assistance to any state against which the United Nations is taking preventive or enforcement action. This duty is merely a restatement of Article 2(5) of the UN Charter. An interesting aspect of this obligation is its nonapplicability to states that are not members of the United Nations. If, for instance, that organization had approved a military enforcement action against one of its members, a nonmember would still be free to come to the assistance of that member.

A seventh duty, apparently under Article 2(4) of the UN Charter and binding only on the member states of the United Nations, is to abstain from recognizing any territorial acquisitions made by a state acting in violation of the Charter's provisions. This appears to be a restatement of the old Stimson Doctrine. Unfortunately this duty has not always been observed by the members of the organization. Instances such as Indian aggression against

Hyderabad and in 1961 against Portuguese enclaves in India, Chinese acquisitions of Burmese and Indian territories and Tibet, and India's seizure
of portions of Kashmir come to mind.[21]

Again, there is an eighth duty for all states to carry out in good faith
the obligations arising out of treaties and other sources of international law,
and no state may invoke provisions in its constitution or laws as an excuse
for failure to carry out this duty. As will be discussed later (Chapter 17),
one of the oldest principles of international law is the doctrine of *pacta sunt
servanda* (treaties must be observed), even though there are differences of
opinion as to the absolute nature of the rule and the possible conditions
under which it can be set aside lawfully. The duty of honoring obligations
in good faith is an essential and basic condition for a legal order, and there
can be no doubt as to its existence.

The ninth duty of every state, frequently asserted, is that of conducting its
relations with other countries in accordance with international law. This,
like the preceding duty, is a basic condition for the existence of a legal
order. Although compliance in every case cannot be expected, the duty is
undeniable and is a binding obligation or duty of states.

A tenth duty, of quite modern origin, is an obligation by a state to see to
it that no acts are performed in its jurisdiction that in some manner pollute
the waters or the air of a neighboring state or the high seas. As yet there are
few general treaty laws regarding this subject, and even fewer for pollution
by private persons.[22]

In 1909, a treaty between the United States and Great Britain, dealing
with Canadian-American boundary waters, provided that neither country
in question would permit the pollution of such waters to the injury of the
health or property of the other. In 1928, this agreement led to the submission to an International Joint Commission of a claim by the United
States that damage was caused to the state of Washington by the fumes
originating from a smelter located in British Columbia. When the United
States refused to accept the decision of the commission, the dispute was
referred to arbitration under a 1935 treaty. The United States was then
awarded the arbitral decision in March 1941.[23] It is interesting to note that

[21]See Wright, "The Goa Incident," 56 *AJIL* 617 (1962), as well as Whiteman, vol. 2,
1140–45; Eagleton, "The Case of Hyderabad before the Security Council," 44 *AJIL* 277
(1950); the pre-UN analysis by Garner, "Non-Recognition of Illegal Territorial Annexation
and Claims to Sovereignty," 30 *AJIL* 679 (1936); and Briggs, "Non-Recognition of Title by
Conquest and Limitations of the Doctrine," *Proceedings* 72–89 (1940).
[22]See the cogent analysis in Handl, "State Liability for Accidental Transnational Environmental Damage by Private Persons," 74 *AJIL* 525 (1980), and the ensuing correspondence,
75 *AJIL* 645 (1981).
[23]See Hackworth, vol. 2, 344–46; the award of the tribunal in the *Trail Smelter Arbitration*
(*U.S.–Canada*) of Mar. 11, 1941 was reprinted in full in 35 *AJIL* 684 (1941). Consult also
Lester, "River Pollution in International Law," 51 *AJIL* 828 (1963); and Whiteman, vol. 6,
253–68, 276.

the arbitration tribunal asserted that under the principles of international law, no state had the right to use or to permit the use of its territory in such a manner as to cause injury by fumes in or to the territory of another state or the property of persons therein and also that the Dominion of Canada was responsible in international law for the emissions from the Trail Smelter.

Continuing problems with transboundary air pollution led to the drafting of the "Convention on Long-Range Transboundary Air Pollution (November 13, 1979).[24] This convention was adopted by acclamation by the High-Level Meeting within the Framework of the Economic Commission for Europe on the Protection of the Environment (Geneva). Also adopted was a resolution on long-range transboundary air pollution as well as a declaration on low-level and nonwaste technology and waste reutilization and recycling.

Related to the question of state responsibility for "nuisance damage" caused by smoke, fumes, and water pollution is the problem of responsibility for the fallout and other by-products of testing nuclear devices or from operating nuclear reactors on land or in vessels, particularly in the event of reactor failure or malfunction.

The resumption of nuclear testing by the Soviet Union and the United States in 1962, together with the growing problem of how to dispose of dangerous radioactive waste materials, pointed up the relevance of including Article 25 in the 1958 Convention on the High Seas. The article provided that each state should take measures to prevent pollution of the seas from the dumping of radioactive waste, taking into account any standards and regulations that might be formulated by competent international organizations.

The treaty also called for cooperation by all states with the relevant international agency in taking measures to prevent pollution of the seas or the airspace above resulting from any activities with radioactive materials or other harmful agents.

The question of nuclear tests was partially settled outside the framework of any international organization. After 425 announced test blasts, the United States, Great Britain, and the Soviet Union succeeded, in 10 days of negotiation, in producing the Partial Nuclear Test Ban Treaty (Moscow Treaty) of 1963. The instrument, signed on August 3, 1963, and in force on October 10, 1963, represented an agreement among the three powers to "prohibit, to prevent, and not to carry out any nuclear weapons test explosions or any other nuclear explosion" in the atmosphere, in outer space, or under water. Underground testing was excluded deliberately because of Russian insistence that adequate inspection of such tests would open the way to espionage.

The three parties also agreed in the treaty to refrain "from causing, encouraging or in any way participating in the carrying out of any nuclear weapons test whatever." This provision was quite obviously aimed at France and the People's Republic of China.

[24]Text reprinted in 18 *ILM* 1442 (1979); see also Rosencranz, "The ECE Convention of 1979 on Long-Range Transboundary Air Pollution," 75 *AJIL* 975 (1981).

The treaty, to be of indefinite duration, permitted unilateral denunciation by any signatory on three months' advance notice at any time that "extraordinary events . . . have jeopardized the supreme interests of its country." It also invited other nations to become signatories, and in a matter of weeks over 100 additional states had thus adhered to the agreement.[25]

The omission of underground testing in the 1963 agreement was rectified in part when the United States and the Soviet Union concluded a treaty on the Limitation of Underground Nuclear Weapon Tests, signed in Moscow on July 3, 1974, and entering into force on the day of exchange of ratifications.[26] This treaty, in turn, was followed by the American-Soviet Treaty on Underground Nuclear Explosions for Peaceful Purposes (Moscow and Washington, May 28, 1976).[27] These last two agreements were supplemented by an agreement, initially of five years' duration, on ceilings for underground nuclear tests. The instrument, signed by the United States and the Soviet Union on May 28, 1976, provides, among other things, for obligatory on-site inspection if any test explosion exceeds 150 kilotons, with optional (both sides approving) observers permitted at any explosions between 100 and 150 kilotons.[28] Testing continued, and by 1989 the United States had recorded 932 test explosions as against 638 for the Soviet Union. The latter had resumed underground testing on February 28, 1987, after a 19-month moratorium, following repeated unsuccessful calls for the United States to follow suit.[29] French underground tests at the Mururoa site continued; however, France announced on June 6, 1989, a cutback in the program because of its high costs.

Returning to air (and now also to water) pollution: the Soviet nuclear plant accident at Chernobyl, which caused widespread atmospheric and river pollution, was followed by the International Atomic Energy Agency (IAEA) with the development through a conference of experts (1986) of a comprehensive "Convention on Early Notification of a Nuclear Accident" signed by 54 countries. That instrument entered into force October 27, 1986. At the same time, a "Convention on Assistance in the Case of a Nuclear Accident or Radiological Emergency" had been drawn up; this entered into force on February 26, 1987. Both instruments were ratified by the Soviet Union on December 23, 1986.[30]

[25]See also McBride, *The Test Ban Treaty* (1967). The text of the agreement may be found in 57 *AJIL* 1026 (1963). At the time of this writing, France and the People's Republic of China are the only major countries that have not signed or ratified the agreement or adhered to it. Both have continued occasional atmospheric tests. France announced on May 29, 1981, the cessation of its nuclear atmospheric tests.
[26]Text, with protocol, in *NYT,* July 4, 1964, 2; and in 68 *AJIL* 805 (1974).
[27]Text in 15 *ILM* 891 (1976).
[28]*NYT,* May 29, 1976, 1, 5 (text of treaty on 4).
[29]See "The First Step: Halt Nuclear Weapons Testing," 18 *The Defense Monitor,* No. 1 (1989), at 1; "U.S. Nuclear Testing Policy," *Gist,* (May 1986) 1–2.
[30]Texts and related documents in 25 *ILM* 1370 (1986). See also Cameron and Hancher, eds., *Nuclear Energy after Chernobyl* (1988); Adede, *The IAEA Notification and Assistance Conventions in Case of a Nuclear Accident* (1987); Sands, ed., *Chernobyl: Law and Communication* (1988).

Among other dangers resulting from a virtually unhampered global industrial development—and appreciated only recently—has been the destruction wrought in the ozone-enriched air shielding the earth from the radiation of the sun. After the basic fact was established that man-made compounds called chlorofluorocarbons (CFCs), used primarily in aerosols, fire suppression, and coolants, damaged the ozone layer, legal measures to halt the process began to appear. A UN conference drafted the "Vienna Convention for the Protection of the Ozone Layer" of March 22, 1985.[31]

By 1990 little in the way of positive efforts to deal with the ozone problem had been recorded. On the other hand, governments increasingly began to realize need for the enormous practical and financial efforts necessary to diminish or solve that problem. After December 1988 the ozone layer was the topic of international conferences called by the European Council of Environmental Ministers, the Council of the European Communities, the UN General Assembly, and the Governing Council of the UN Environmental Program.[32] The general conclusion appears to have been that widespread realization of the danger from serious depletion of the ozone layer would lead to the global ratification of the Vienna Convention. That step, in turn, would lead to the assumption of a global duty for every member of the family of nations.

A more positive step was taken through the conclusion of an agreememt by 61 nations at London on June 29, 1990. Among other provisions, the instrument provided for the phasing out of fluorocarbons by the year 2000 and for rapid development of acceptable substitutes. China and India announced that they would join the agreement after the industrial nations promised the necessary technology. That group agreed to create a $240 million fund to defray expenses of Third World states in phasing out fluorocarbons.

One indication of the extent of the financial aspects involved in protecting the ozone layer was supplied by the DuPont Company in the United States, which agreed to abandon its $750-million-a-year market for chlorofluorocarbons.

Another global problem rising rapidly in both cost and complexity has been the moving and disposing of regular as well as of hazardous wastes. Caused primarily by the industrial nations, the accumulation of wastes has demanded increasing attention, particularly in its transborder aspects.

In order to reduce the dangers involved in the international movement of wastes, the Council of the Organization for Economic Cooperation and Developement handed down a "Decision" on May 27, 1988, followed by

[31] Text and related documents of the Convention in 26 *ILM* 1516 (1987); entered in force on Sept. 22, 1988. See also *NYT,* Aug. 2, 1988, at 8; *CSM,* Sept. 23, 1988, at 12; the *Protocol* appeared in 26 *ILM* 1541 (1987). Concerning expected replacement production problems; *id.,* April 17, 1990, 10–11; and esp. *U.S. News & World Report,* Feb. 19, 1990, 45–46.
[32] See 28 *ILM* 1306, 1326 (1989) for the texts agreed on at such meetings. See also Brice in *CSM,* July 2, 1990, 3, and Wallace, *id.,* Nov. 9, 1990, 3.

the adoption of a "Decision-Recommendation" (July 8, 1988) relating to information to the public on the subject of the May 27 "Decision."[33]

A two-part UN conference on hazardous waste attempted to draft a "Global Convention on the Control of Transboundary Movements of Hazardous Wastes." However, in contrast to the participating developing nations, developed countries, particularly the United States, resisted attempts to limit the trade in toxic wastes. Several countries have acted positively to discourage the flow of hazardous shipments, such as Togo banning the import, sale, transport, or storage of radioactive wastes; the Ivory Coast imposing penalties on persons importing wastes; and Nigeria passing a Harmful Waste Decree with life imprisonment for convicted violators. The Council of Ministers of the Organization of African Unity passed a 1988 resolution aimed at the importation of harmful wastes.[34]

Still another pollution area of great concern to coastal states has been the spillage of oil along certain coasts or on the high seas. The prevention of this problem has by now become a recognized international duty of states. Modern oil tanker wrecks such as that of the *Torrey Canyon* (1967, off England; spillage 37.0 million gallons), *Sea Star* (1972, off Oman, 34.0), *Amoco Cadiz* (1978, off France, 68.7), *Atlantic Empress* and *Aegean Captain* (1979, off Trinidad and Tobago, final total 90.4), *Independenta* (1979, off Turkey, 28.9), *Castille de Bellver* (1983, off Cape Town, 78.5), and the *Exxon Valdez* (1989, off Alaska, 11.0—essentially a domestic American disaster) all caused heavy property losses and indicated the need for further international regulation of marine oil pollution.

Such agreements as the 1954 Convention for the Prevention of the Pollution of the Seas by Oil, even as amended in 1962, do not appear to go far enough to ensure adequate protection against oil spills.[35]

It should be kept in mind that only 10 percent of ocean pollution is caused by ships at sea (through wrecks, hull damage, or discharge of wastes); the pollution of the high seas as well as the continental shelves and territorial seas remains significant in the total pollution picture. Major accidents have continued to cause ocean pollution. But attempts to clean up the oceans have begun or are at least in the planning stages under the auspices of the UN Environment Program. A major agreement, the Protocol for the Protection of the Mediterranean Sea against Pollution from Land-based Sources (Athens, May 16, 1980)[36] came into force in August 1983 after the necessary 6 states

---

[33]Texts and related documents are reprinted in 28 *ILM* 257 (1989).

[34]See 28 *ILM* 391, 567 (1989); *CSM*, Nov. 7, 1988, at 8, and Mar. 30, 1989, at 6, Jan. 9, 1990, at 5, and especially Langan's article, Aug. 15, 1989, at 9.

[35]See the "Suggested Readings" at the end of this chapter for materials on the subject. See *Time,* Apr. 30, 1984, at 45, concerning the *Amoco Cadiz,* as well as the Associated Press (hereafter AP) report in major newspapers on Jan. 11, 1988 about the award of U.S. $85.2 million by a U.S. District Court to France and some 90 other plaintiffs for damages from the spill of over 68 million gallons of oil.

[36]Text in 19 *ILM* 869 (1980).

out of 16 signatories had ratified it. Once ratification is complete, funding will be sought to clean up one of the world's most polluted seas by the end of the century. The Third Conference on the Law of the Sea was concerned with pollution questions during most of its sessions between 1973 and 1982, and the resulting convention (UNCLOS III) in its Articles 192 through 233 covers definitions, controls, monitoring, and antipollution enforcement — all to be under the proposed International Sea-Bed Authority.[37] When that Authority functions as planned, the world may be able to boast for the first time of global control over ocean pollution.

As in the case of oil spills from tankers (ocean pollution), so a new duty of states appears to have surfaced in the wake of the 1986 Swiss chemical spill in the Rhine River: a duty to prevent chemical (especially toxic) industrial spills into coastal waters and inland rivers.[38] Many rivers are now heavily polluted, and this condition is caused by, and also affects, several states. The best-known current example is the River Elbe, with Germany and Czechoslovakia sharing the guilt and the consequences.

Another obligation or duty of states is that of preventing the counterfeiting, within their jurisdiction, of the coins, currencies, postage stamps, and securities of another state.[39] Even when given states have not adhered to international conventions prohibiting such practices, they tend to regard it as their obligation to prevent counterfeiting by passing appropriate domestic legislation. However, just as in the case of practically all other state duties, the advent of a state of war cancels the duty in question insofar as it applies to enemy states. In World War II, Germany counterfeited British £5 notes, whereas Great Britain counterfeited German postage stamps in order to expedite the mailing of propaganda postcards addressed to random samplings of German citizens in cities bombed by the Royal Air Force. Excellent imitations of German official mailbags filled with such stamped and addressed cards were dropped from planes in the hope that German citizens, believing the bags to have been lost from mail trucks during the confusion of a bombing attack, would turn them in to the nearest post office for dispatch to the addresses.

Many writers, as well as the International Law Commission, have asserted that there exists a twelfth duty requiring *each* state to treat all persons in its jurisdiction with respect for their human rights and fundamental freedoms, without distinction as to race, sex, language, or religion. This duty cannot, however, be admitted as yet to exist on a general basis, no matter

[37] See Boyle, "Marine Pollution under the Law of the Sea Convention," 79 *AJIL* 347 (1985).
[38] See *CSM,* Nov. 13, 1986, at 11/12; Nov. 14 at 2; Nov. 20 at 15; Nov. 19, Nov. 21, Nov. 24, all at 2; Dec. 5, 1986, at 21; and *Time* Nov. 24, 1986, at 36–37.
[39] See Whiteman, vol. 6, 268–75; Hackworth, vol. 2, 350–54; and the two classic cases of *Emperor of Austria and King of Hungary* v. *Day and Kossuth,* 1861, abstracted in Chapter 7, and *United States* v. *Arjona,* U.S. Supreme Court, 1887, 120 U.S. 479. There have been in force since 1931 The International Convention and Protocol for the Suppression of Counterfeiting Currency (Geneva, 1929); the United States is not a party.

how admirable it may be from a moral point of view. The undoubted drastic degree of intervention in essentially domestic affairs of states in the application of this duty gives rise to this doubt as to the existence of the duty itself. It may well be that at some future time it may be accepted by the majority of the members of the community of nations and may be implemented by appropriate domestic legislation. But even granting such internal compliance with the duty, the question of enforcing it will have to be resolved before it can be maintained that this asserted duty is in effect and consequential in nature. (See also Chapter 10.)

## SUGGESTED READINGS

### Duties of States

Whiteman, vol. 5, 321–32; Vincent, *Nonintervention and International Order* (1974); Lillich, ed., *Humanitarian Intervention and the United Nations* (1973); Teson, *Humanitarian Intervention: An Inquiry into Law and Morality* (1988); Ronzitti, *Rescuing Nationals Abroad through Military Coercion and Intervention on Grounds of Humanity* (1985); Reisman and Silk, "Which Law Applies to the Afghan Conflict?" 82 *AJIL* 459 (1988).

### The Conflict in Vietnam

Consult, *inter alia,* Shaplen, *The Lost Revolution* (1965); the most valuable collection by Falk, ed., *The Vietnam War and International Law* (vol. 1, 1968; vol. 2, 1969; vol. 3, 1972; vol. 4, 1976); J. N. Moore, *Law and the Indo-China War* (1972); Hull and Novogrod, *Law and Vietnam* (1968); Wright, "Legal Aspects of the Viet-Nam Situation," 60 *AJIL* 750 (1966); J. N. Moore, "The Lawfulness of Military Assistance to the Republic of Viet-Nam," 61 *AJIL* 1 (1967).

### Intervention in Cambodia (1970–1973)

Statement of John R. Stevenson, Legal Adviser, U.S. Dept. of State, May 28, 1970, in 64 *AJIL* 933 (1970); Falk, "The Cambodian Operation and International Law," 65 *AJIL* 1 (1971); J. N. Moore, "Legal Dimensions of the Decision to Intercede in Cambodia," 65 *AJIL* 38 (1971).

### Intervention in Civil Strife

Whiteman, vol. 5, 250–57, 276–81, 522–34; Rosenau, ed., *International Aspects of Civil Strife* (1964); Miller, *World Order and Local Disorder: The United Nations and Internal Conflicts* (1967).

### Intervention in the Dominican Republic

Carey, ed., *The Dominican Republic Crisis of 1965* (1967); Draper, *The Dominican Revolt: A Case Study in American Policy* (1968); Lowenthal, *The Dominican Intervention*

(1972); Slater, *Intervention and Negotiation: The United States and the Dominican Revolution* (1970); Gleijeses, *The Dominican Crisis: The 1965 Constitutionalist Revolt and American Intervention* (1979).

CASE

*Flota Mercante Dominicana, C. por A.,* v. *American Manufacturers Mutual Insurance,* U.S. Dist. Court, S.D.N.Y., 1967, 272 F. Supp. 540, reported in 62 *AJIL* 501 (1968).

Subversive Intervention

Havighurst, ed., *International Control of Propaganda* (1967); Lisann, *Broadcasting to the Soviet Union: International Politics and Radio* (1975); Whiteman, vol. 5, 257–75, 455–59, 837–43.

Environmental Pollution (Land, Sea, Air)

(a) General:
Kelson, "State Responsibility and the Abnormally Dangerous Activity," 13 *Harvard Int'l. L. Jl.* 197 (1972); UN Conference on the Human Environment (Stockholm, 1972), Final Document (June 16, 1972) in 11 *ILM* 1416 (1972); Schachter and Serwer, "Marine Pollution Problems and Remedies," 65 *AJIL* 84 (1971); Kirgis, "Technological Challenge to the Shared Environment: United States Practice," 66 *AJIL* 290 (1972); United Nations, *Protocol to the 1979 Convention on Long-Range Transboundary Air Pollution, on Financing the Monitoring and Evaluation of Air Pollution in Europe* (Geneva, Sept. 28, 1984), in 24 *ILM* 483 (1985); Flinterman, Kwiatkowska, and Lammers, eds., *Transboundary Air Pollution: International Legal Aspects of the Co-operation of States* (1986); Springer, *The International Law of Pollution* (1983); Smith, *State Responsibility and the Marine Environment* (1988).
(b) Pollution of Water:
*Final Act of the Conference on the Protection of the Mediterranean Sea* (UN Environment Programme, Barcelona, Feb. 16, 1976, with the resulting Convention in effect on Feb. 12, 1978), in 15 *ILM* 285 (1976); M'Gonigle and Zacher, *Pollution, Politics, and International Law* (1979); Van Lier, *Acid Rain and International Law* (1981); SEDCO-United States, "Agreement Concerning Settlement of Claims Arising from the 1979 Oil Well Blowout and Oil Spill in the Gulf of Mexico," Mar. 1, 1983, in 22 *ILM* 580 (1983); Lammers, *Pollution of International Watercourses: A Search for Substantive Rules and Principles of Law* (1984).

CASE

*Nuclear Tests Case (Australia* v. *France), Reports, 1973,* 99. International Court of Justice, *Order of June 22, 1973, Concerning Interim Measures of Protection,* 12 *ILM* 749 (1973); digested in 67 *AJIL* 778 (1973). See also *NYT,* May 18, 1973, at 10, June 23, 1973, at 3, and Nov. 4, 1973, at 14; *Judgment of December 20, 1974, ICJ Reports, 1974,* holding that the dispute had disappeared, hence no jurisdiction could be exercised, excerpted by Evans in 69 *AJIL* 668 (1975).

# Case Study No. 2

# Nicaragua v. United States of America

The basic concept of the rights of a state, as outlined in Chapter 7, means that corresponding duties devolve on other states not to impair, violate, or even deny those rights. In other words, it is the duty of a state not to interfere with the rights to independence, equality, territory, and so on. If unlawful interference does take place, the target or victim state has a valid claim before a court asking for an order to end the delict and, if such is appropriate, to collect damages from the party guilty of the unlawful acts.

This principle was well illustrated by the case of *Nicaragua* v. *United States of America*. As will be seen, the International Court of Justice drew up in its verdict an impressive list of unlawful acts by the United States in violation of the rights of Nicaragua. While some legal writers have disagreed with the Court's approach to the question of customary law and its nature (the rights in question having been based on that law), no one could deny that the U.S. actions violated Nicaraguan sovereign rights and constituted an almost classic case of unlawful intervention.

The history of relations between the United States and the Republic of Nicaragua has been marked since 1854 by many instances of U.S. intervention in Nicaraguan affairs, although not all such actions could be blamed on the United States.

In 1854, U.S. sailors and marines destroyed the port and city of Greytown in reprisal for affronts to the American Minister to Central America. In 1857, American forces landed in Nicaragua to foil efforts of William Walker, an American adventurer, to take over the country. In 1894, during revolutionary battles in Nicaragua, troops were landed to protect American lives and property, followed by further military intervention in 1898 and 1899. In 1909, a threat of British military intervention to collect unpaid debts caused the United States to help the Conservative Party in Nicaragua to overthrow the Liberal José Santos Zelaya. This was followed by a period of U.S. military and financial control. While the so-called Knox-Castrillo Convention of June 6, 1911 had authorized both U.S. intervention and a customs receivership to refund Nicaragua's national debt, it had been rejected by the United States. In the following year, aid by U.S. marines kept the Conservative President Adolfo Díaz in office. But in 1912, a Nicaraguan revolt caused marines to be landed on August 14, 1912, and as disorders spread, U.S. troops assisted in the defeat of the forces of the Liberal party. A small marine detachment remained in Nicaragua until 1925 to assist in quelling further uprisings and to supervise elections. A new civil war erupted in 1926, and U.S. military forces returned to Nicaragua. In 1927, Henry L. Stimson negotiated a settlement between the warring factions, and the Liberal José Moncado was elected to the presidency (November 4, 1928) in an election supervised by the United States. The American "Good Neighbor" policy caused the withdrawal of U.S. forces in 1933 and a renunciation of intervention. Unfortunately for Nicaragua, or so it has been claimed, the policy helped U.S.-trained military men to establish long-term dictatorships. In Nicaragua's case, Anastasio (Tacho) Somoza ruled from 1936 to 1956. Even after Somoza's assassination, his family continued to rule the country as its private domain.

Back in 1927, Augusto Sandino started a rebel movement against U.S. marines, and when the latter withdrew in 1933, they left behind a newly formed Nicaraguan army, the National Guard (*Guardia Nacional*) under the leadership of Somoza. Sandino was killed in 1933, but his movement continued and gained increasing support in the country. In 1961 it organized itself as the Sandinista National Liberation Front and ultimately succeeded in July 1979 in overthrowing the Somoza regime. Many political leaders fled to Miami or to neighboring countries, while elements of the National Guard retreated to the border regions of Honduras and Costa Rica. The Carter administration began a program of economic aid to Nicaragua despite the increasingly left-wing orientation of that country's government.

The bulk of the opponents of the Sandinistas, officially termed the Nicaraguan Democratic Force and popularly known as the Contras, was being trained with U.S. financial and matériel support in Honduras by CIA personnel and, it has been charged, by Argentine military officers. After initial training, the Contras pushed into the border regions of Nicaragua.

The American government began to charge the Sandinistas with supporting aggression and terrorism against El Salvador, Honduras, Costa Rica, and Guatemala. It suspended aid to Nicaragua in an avowed effort to assist in stopping an alleged flow of military supplies to the rebel movement in El Salvador's civil war. Such equipment and ammunition were said to come from the Soviet Union and Cuba, and then be moved from Nicaragua into El Salvador.

On September 8, 1983, the CIA allegedly directed an attack on the oil storage and pipeline facilities at the Nicaraguan port of Puerto Sandino. In October, the CIA was accused of directing an attack on the Nicaraguan oil port of Corinto. The latter enterprise reportedly destroyed 3.2 million gallons of fuel, injured more than 100, and forced the evacuation of 22,000 Corinto residents. It was carried out by mercenaries who reached the port by speedboats from an off-shore mother ship from which CIA agents directed operations. The CIA-supported Contras (Nicaraguan Democratic Force, or NDF) admitted both attacks, and on March 30, 1984, the CIA itself agreed that "unilaterally controlled Latino assets" carried out both raids.[1]

The covert American backing of the anti-Sandinista Contras assumed an even more dramatic form when, in March 1984, the CIA directly supported the mining of the Nicaraguan ports of Corinto and Puerto Sandino. The motive for these operations was the interdiction of claimed arms and ammunition shipments from Nicaragua to the Salvadorean rebels. A total of seven Nicaraguan vessels and six ships registered in other countries were damaged by the mines. There was no warning that mines had been laid, although such is required under international law (see Chapter 25), and no one in the United

[1]See AP dispatches to major newspapers March 31 and April 18, 1984.

States appeared to have considered that the laying of mines represented the institution of a hostile blockade, that is, of an act of war. The Contras immediately claimed responsibility for the mining.

Nicaragua introduced a resolution in the Security Council on March 30, 1984, denouncing the United States for the "escalation of military aggression brought against Nicaragua" and calling for an immediate end to the mining operations. When the resolution came to a vote April 7, the United Kingdom abstained, 13 members supported the resolution, and the United States cast a veto, thus killing Nicaragua's resolution.

The United States then warned France not to remove the mines (April 7) and the U.S. Senate voted $21 million in aid to the Contras. On April 8, U.S. newspapers reported that the CIA had directed the mining of the ports, and on the next day, Nicaragua accepted a French offer to remove the mines.

The covert aid given to the Contras violated beyond question a number of treaties to which the United States was a party, including the UN Charter, Article 2(4), which reads: "All members shall refrain in their international relations from the threat or use of force against the territorial integrity or political independence of any state." On the other hand, the U.S. administration relied on the provision of the Charter on the right of collective self-defense. One issue raised in the ensuing Congressional debate was whether or not the Reagan administration had violated the Neutrality Act of 1794 by aiding a rebellion against Nicaragua's leftist government. That venerable legislation forbids U.S. citizens from supporting or taking part in a military action against a foreign country with which the United States is not at war.

It may be of interest to recall that during the Greek "emergency" in 1947, the United States had viewed major assistance to rebels in Greece by Albania, Bulgaria, and Yugoslavia as an "armed attack."[2]

Following disclosure of the various activities carried on by the CIA against Nicaragua, Congress (October 1984) voted to cut off all CIA aid to the Contras, at least until February 28, 1985.

Returning to the legal aspects of the dispute: Following the U.S. veto in the Security Council, Nicaragua was expected to file a complaint with the International Court of Justice (ICJ). The United States announced on April 6, 1984 that it would not accept the jurisdiction of the Court in any Central American disputes for the next two years.

When the United States first accepted the Court's compulsory jurisdiction in 1946, it added two reservations: the Connally Amendment, giving the U.S. government the right to exclude all disputes it declared to be within its domestic jurisdiction (see Chapter 18), and the so-called Vandenberg Amendment, excluding from the jurisdiction of the Court these disputes affecting states involved in multilateral agreements. The American action of April 6, 1984 appeared to have added a third exception for two years: disputes in Central America. At that time, only 47 out of 159 UN members had accepted the compulsory jurisdiction of the ICJ, and all but 7 of them had deposited reservations that allowed them to ignore the Court.

What is technically known as the "contentious jurisdiction" of the ICJ applies only to disputes between states that have accepted such jurisdiction. The governing principle is laid down in Article 36 of the Court's Statute, in which

---

[2] See Tucker, "The Interpretation of War under Present International Law," 4 *Int'l L. Q.* 11, 31 (1951).

three basic kinds of submission to jurisdiction are listed: the disputants may accept jurisdiction *ad hoc* for settlement of an already existing dispute [Art. 36(1)]; they may adhere to a treaty in which acceptance of ICJ jurisdiction is pledged directly or indirectly [*id.*]; or they may adhere to the "Optional Clause" under which states (parties to the Statute) may declare *unilaterally* that they accept the jurisdiction of the ICJ relative to any other state accepting the same obligatory jurisdiction in all legal disputes [Art. 36(2)]. The Connally Reservation of the United States included, as mentioned already, several reservations, one of which excluded from the Court's jurisdiction "disputes with regard to matters which are essentially within the domestic jurisdiction of the United States of America as determined by the United States of America." It should be noted, however, that the Connally Amendment related to Article 36(2) of the Statute. If the United States were to be sued by a party with which the United States had a treaty conferring mandatory jurisdiction on the ICJ, then Article 36(1) would apply!

Furthermore, when the United States accepted compulsory ICJ jurisdiction under Article 36(2), it agreed that the amendment/reservation was to remain in force for five years and thereafter until the expiration of six months "after notice may be given to terminate this declaration." Then, in 1984, the United States sought to amend the declaration by asserting an immediate denial of jurisdiction for "Central American disputes arising out of or related to events in Central America" for a period of two years. This effort to modify the 1946 Declaration was rejected by the ICJ in *Military and Paramilitary Activities in and against*

*Nicaragua (Nicaragua v. United States of America), Jurisdiction and Admissibility.*[3]

Although the American attempt to modify its 1946 Declaration surprised many, it did not represent something new. A number of countries had supplied precedents. In the 1950s, Australia, Great Britain, and India refused to accept the Court's jurisdiction in specific disputes. Canada, expecting a U.S. suit concerning marine pollution, informed the Court that it would not accept any ruling on the matter. And France (1973) rejected the jurisdiction of the Court when New Zealand and Australia charged France with violating international law through nuclear tests carried out in the Pacific.

Ignoring the American "modification" attempt, Nicaragua filed its petition with the ICJ on April 9, 1984, charging the United States with "training, supplying and directing military and paramilitary actions against the people and Government of Nicaragua" with the intent to "overthrow or destabilize the Government of Nicaragua," as well as with the mining of ports with the help of the CIA. On April 26, in its opening statement at preliminary hearings before the ICJ, Nicaragua asked the Court to declare that the United States had violated international law and requested the payment of reparations for damages caused by the American actions.

The American agents argued that the ICJ lacked jurisdiction because Nicaragua had not formally accepted the Court's compulsory jurisdiction. They also asserted that the ICJ was not "institutionally designed" to solve "the regional conflict that is tragically engulfing Central America."

On May 10, 1984, the Court rejected the request of the United States that

---

[3] 1984 *ICJ Rep.* 392, 398 (*Judgment of November 26, 1984*); see the excellent summary in 79 *AJIL* 442 (1985).

the case be stricken from the docket for lack of jurisdiction. Instead, the Court unanimously called on both parties to observe certain "provisional measures" (commonly termed interim measures): the United States should immediately halt any actions to blockade or mine Nicaragua's ports, and by a vote of 14 to 1, the United States dissenting, ordered that "the right to sovereignty and to political independence possessed by the Republic of Nicaragua" should be fully respected and not placed in jeopardy by military or paramilitary activities.[4]

The United States ignored the Court's orders. Despite its April 1984 refusal to recognize the Court's jurisdiction over Central American questions, the United States had continued to participate in the hearings relating to the Nicaraguan case. This situation changed after the Court ruled that Nicaragua's case was admissible and that the Court possessed jurisdiction (see below).

Proceedings (oral arguments) in *Nicaragua* v. *United States (Jurisdiction and Admissibility)* began on September 12, 1984. Nicaragua charged that the United States had ignored the Court's order to end assistance to the Contras and was waging armed attacks to overthrow the Nicaraguan government. At the end of its presentation, Nicaragua asserted that it was entitled to $375 million in compensation for damages caused by the Contras. The Department of State, for its part in the "arguments," released on September 13 a 131-page report to prove that Nicaragua was responsible for the disturbances in Central America.

Inasmuch as the United States had disputed the jurisdiction of the Court, Nicaragua offered two reasons for upholding that jurisdiction: the compulsory jurisdiction under Article 36(2) in the Court's Statute, and a compromissory clause — Article 24(2) — in the Treaty of Friendship, Commerce and Navigation (FCN) between the United States and Nicaragua, of January 21, 1956.[5]

The Court handed down its opinion on jurisdiction and admissibility on November 26, 1984.[6]

It upheld its jurisdiction under the compromissory clause of the FCN at every stage of the case, denied the U.S. view about jurisdiction that had asserted that the FCN treaty applied solely to commercial relations, and upheld the Nicaraguan claim that the U.S. support of the Contras violated the provisions of the compromissory clause. The Court also held that Nicaragua's application was admissible, contrary to the argument advanced by the United States.[7]

---

[4] *Military and Paramilitary Activities in and against Nicaragua (Nicaragua* v. *United States of America). Provisional Measures,* 1984 *ICJ Rep.* 169 (Order of May 10).

[5] A compromissory clause is found in many treaties: The parties agree to submit disputes to the ICJ or another named body for third-party settlement. See also Charney, "Compromissory Clause and the Jurisdiction of the International Court of Justice," 81 *AJIL* 855 (1987).

[6] *Case Concerning Military and Paramilitary Activities in and against Nicaragua (Nicaragua* v. *United States of America), Jurisdiction and Admissibility,* 1984 *ICJ Rep.* 392 (Judgment of November 26), reproduced in 24 *ILM* 59 (1985), including all separate opinions and the dissenting opinion of the U.S. judge. An almost complete documentation of *Nicaragua* v. *United States* through January 1985 is found in *id.,* at 38, 246. See also Sitomer, "U.S. Case Will Test Its Credibility," *CSM,* December 14, 1984, 26–27, and *Time,* December 10, 1984, 42–43.

[7] See J. N. Moore, "The Secret War in Central America and the Future of World Order," 80 *AJIL* 43 (1986); for views supporting the Court's jurisdiction, see Briggs, "*Nicaragua* v. *United States,* 79 *AJIL* 373 (1985), and Rowles, " 'Secret Wars,' Self-Defense and the Charter — A Reply to Professor Moore," 80 *AJIL* 568 (1986). See also Franck, "Icy Day at the ICJ," 79 *AJIL* 379 (1985).

Despite the April 1984 refusal to recognize the Court's jurisdiction in Central American questions, the United States had continued to participate in the hearings relating to the Nicaraguan case. But on January 18, 1985, the United States announced that it would not participate further in the case and would reconsider its 1946 acceptance of the compulsory jurisdiction of the Court: " . . . the United States is constrained to conclude that the judgment of the Court was clearly and manifestly erroneous as to both fact and law. . . . Accordingly, it is my duty to inform you that the United States intends not to participate in any further proceedings in connection with this case."[8] This statement was supported by the official "Observations on the ICJ's November 26, 1984, Judgment on Jurisdiction in the Case of *Nicaragua* v. *United States of America.*"[9]

Ultimately the United States deposited with the Registrar of the Court (October 7, 1985) a formal notice of the cancellation of the U.S. Declaration of August 26, 1946. In other words, the United States would no longer accept the compulsory jurisdiction of the Court in international disputes. The United States henceforth would participate only in routine commercial and boundary cases and not in any disputes judged by the United States to be political in nature.

It was and is, of course, impossible to predict the effect of the American action on the Court. One may hazard the guess that the United States will bring disputes before the court if two conditions are met: the United States judges the dispute to be nonpolitical and expects to win a favorable verdict from Court. The first condition would remove most major international disputes the from the jurisdiction of the Court: most of such disagreements involve political factors. The second condition poses the same problem that is said to have plagued the early years of the International Court: the ever-increasing number of Third World countries were then said to eschew litigation for fear of losing prestige if the Court ruled against them.

The present writer believes that the cancellation of the American acceptance of compulsory jurisdiction will have little effect on the International Court. The number of states still bound by the "Optional Clause" by now is small; the American action simply increased by one the total of those not bound to accept the jurisdiction of the Court.

In 1985, the United States imposed a trade embargo on Nicaragua and gave $27 million in "humanitarian aid" to the Contras. In 1986, the donation was increased to $100 million.

Nicaragua filed two applications with the International Court (July 28, 1986) against Costa Rica and Honduras.[10] The applications charged the two countries with "border and transborder" armed actions against Nicaragua in violation of customary international law, the UN Charter, the Oas Charter, and the American Treaty for the Peaceful Settlement of Disputes (Pact of Bogotá). Article 31 of the last-named instrument was cited specifically in both applications because all three parties had agreed in that Article to accept the compulsory jurisdiction of the Court.

The proceedings against Costa Rica were dismissed by the Court on August

[8] Excerpt from Note of D. R. Robinson (Legal Adviser) to the Registrar of the Court, Jan. 18, 1985, in 24 *ILM* 246 (1985).
[9] 24 *ILM* 249 (1985). See also Highet, "Litigation Implications of the U.S. Withdrawal from the *Nicaragua* Case," 79 *AJIL* 992 (1985). The question of nonappearance before the ICJ is discussed in Chapter 18.
[10] Texts in 25 *ILM* 1290 (1986).

19, 1987, seven days after Nicaragua notified the Registrar that it had discontinued the judicial proceedings instituted against Costa Rica. The latter thereupon stated that it would not object to the discontinuance.

The proceedings against Honduras remained pending as of December 1990. The Court had ruled on December 20, 1988 that it had jurisdiction to entertain the dispute. Nicaragua filed its pleading on Merits, but on December 14, 1989 the Court issued an order extending the time limit for the filing of the Honduras Counter-Memorial to a date to be established after June 11, 1990.

Both Nicaraguan complaints had been filed before the foreign ministers of five Central American states had adopted a regional peace plan in 1987 (see below).

Returning to the main issue: on June 27, 1986, the International Court of Justice handed down its decision on the Merits in *Nicaragua* v. *United States*.[11] Both the length and the complexity of the issues found in the Judgment on Merits preclude the inclusion of an abstract as was done in other parts of this volume. For example, the Court embarked on a fascinating (and subject of much critical comment) investigation of the nature of rules of international customary law. Limitations of space prevent a detailed discussion of such judicial excursions. Fortunately, however, the justices drew up a 16-part summary (the "operational part") in the Judgment itself. The 16 points, plus the voting of the 15 judges, follow:

1. The Court decided that in adjudicating the dispute in question, it was required to apply the "multilateral treaty reservation" found in Article 36(2) of the Court's Statute (11 votes to 4).

2. The Court rejected the justification of collective self-defense brought forward by the United States (12 votes to 3).

3. The Court decided that the United States, by training, arming, equipping, and supplying the Contras, acted in breach of its obligation under customary international law not to intervene in the affairs of another state (12 votes to 3).

4. The Court decided that the United States, by attacks on Nicaraguan territory in 1983–1984, acted in breach of its obligation under customary international law not to use force against another state (12 votes to 3).

5. The Court decided that the United States, by directing or authorizing overflights of Nicaraguan territory, acted in breach of its obligation under customary international law not to violate the sovereignty of another state (12 votes to 3);

6. The Court decided that, by laying mines in the internal or territorial waters of Nicaragua during the first months of 1984, the United States acted in breach of its obligations under customary international law not to use force against another state, not to intervene in its affairs, not to violate its sovereignty, and not to interrupt peaceful maritime commerce (12 votes to 3).

7. The Court decided that, by the acts referred to in part 6 above, the United States acted in breach of its obligations under Article 19 of the Treaty of Friendship, Commerce, and Navigation (FCN) of 1956 (14 votes to 1).

[11] *Military and Paramilitary Activities in and against Nicaragua (Nicaragua* v. *United States of America), Merits.* 1986 *ICJ Rep.* 14, June 27, 1986. Text, including all separate or dissenting opinions, in 25 *ILM* 1023 (1986); the 16-part "operative part" of the Judgment is found *id.,* 1089. For commentaries on the Judgment, see the Suggested Readings at the end of this Case History.

8. The Court decided that the United States, by failing to make known the existence and location of the mines laid by it, acted in breach of its obligation under customary international law (14 votes to 1).

9. The Court found that the United States, by producing in 1983 a manual entitled *Operaciones Sicológicas en Guerra de Guerrilla* and disseminating it to Contra forces, encouraged the commission by them of acts contrary to general principles of humanitarian law. But the Court did not find a basis for concluding that any such acts that may have been committed were imputable to the United States as acts of the United States (14 votes to 1).[12]

10. The Court decided that the United States, by the attacks on Nicaraguan territory referred to in part 4 above and by declaring a general embargo on trade with Nicaragua on May 1, 1985, committed acts calculated to deprive the FCN Treaty of 1956 of its object and purpose (12 votes to 3).

11. The Court decided that the United States, by the attacks on Nicaraguan territory referred to in part 4 above and by declaring a general embargo on trade with Nicaragua on May 1, 1985, acted in breach of its obligations under Article 19 of the FCN Treaty of 1956 (12 votes to 3).

12. The Court decided that the United States was under an obligation to immediately cease and refrain from all such acts as might constitute breaches of the foregoing legal obligations (12 votes to 3).

13. The Court decided that the United States was under an obligation to make reparation to Nicaragua for all injury caused to Nicaragua by the breaches of obligations under customary international law enumerated above (12 votes to 3).

14. The Court decided that the United States was under an obligation to Nicaragua for all injury caused to Nicaragua by the breaches of the FCN Treaty of 1956 (14 votes to 1).

15. The Court decided that the form and amount of such reparation, failing agreement between the Parties, would be settled by the Court, and reserved for this purpose the subsequent procedure in the case (14 votes to 1).

16. The Court recalled to both Parties their obligation to seek a solution to their disputes by peaceful means in accordance with international law (Unanimous).

The absence of action by the United States following the Merits Judgment indicated clearly that the United States was still unwilling to accept the jurisdiction of the Court in what was regarded as a political and non-justiciable dispute.

The ending of the military phases of the U.S.–Nicaragua dispute was stymied by the problem of what to do about the 10,000–12,000 Contras. In the Fall of 1987, a cease-fire with the Contras had come into effect, and in January 1988, direct talks had begun between the Sandinista administration and leading elements among the Contras. In April 1989, the United States had allocated $49.75 million in nonmilitary aid to the Contras based on camps in Honduras. On August 7, 1989, the presidents of Nicaragua, Honduras, Costa Rica,

---

[12] The manual, produced by the CIA, advocated the "neutralization" of government leaders by the "selective use of violence," and recommended the hiring of professional criminals to carry out "selective jobs." The manual was recalled soon after its existence became known.

Guatemala, and El Salvador agreed on a plan to disband the Contras by December 8, 1989. The Contras, however, objected to the scheme; this plan, the so-called Tela (Honduras) Declaration, did not envisage the use of military force but rather of voluntary cooperation. It involved persuading the Contras and their families either to return to Nicaragua or to be resettled in other Latin American countries. A UN-appointed Commission was to supervise demobilization and voluntary repatriation.

On August 25, 1989, the Secretary-General of the Organization of American States (OAS) and the UN Secretary-General agreed that the work of the "International Support and Verification Commission" would begin on September 6, 1989.

Honduras, having cultivated for years the fiction that it was not helping the Contras by permitting them bases on its territory, was caught in the dilemma of its dependence for aid from the United States and its obligation to honor the Tela Declaration. According to that agreement, all Contra bases on Honduran soil were to be gone by November 7, 1989. And Honduras lacked the military strength to honor that obligation if voluntary cooperation failed—as it did, not unexpectedly.

Execution of these fine schemes came to a temporary halt when Nicaraguan President Ortega announced the end of the 19-month cease-fire with the Contras (November 1, 1989). He justified his action by referring to a spate of minor military attacks on the part of the Contras, in violation of the cease-fire, attacks which Ortega blamed on the United States. On November 8, however, Nicaragua floated a new plan: continued use of the Verification Committee, withdrawal of Nicaraguan forces from routes used by Contras to travel from Honduras into Nicaragua, and reinstatement of the cease-fire on November 30, 1989. On the other hand, Nicaragua would stop all arms imports until April 25, 1990, if its plan were approved, and would restore the civil rights of all returning Contras.

When fighting resumed near the Honduran border, the United States reimposed its trade embargo against Nicaragua.

On November 5, 1988, Honduras announced that unarmed Contras could find refuge in Honduras in order to escape the ongoing Nicaraguan offensive. Ten days later, Nicaragua made the first of several peace offers: initially, it would restore the cease-fire in exchange for the return of the estimated 5,000 Contras to their Honduran bases. Then, to the surprise of the United States and the Organization of American States, Nicaragua produced a new cease-fire proposal that omitted the past demand for the withdrawal of all Contras from Nicaragua and substituted a requirement of a pull-out of only 2,000 Contras. That offer did not produce any results.

The resumption of the regional peace talks by the five presidents (December 1989 in San José, Costa Rica) was highlighted by a unanimous declaration of the presidents in which they condemned guerrillas (both the Contras and El Salvador's Farabundo Marti National Liberation Front (FLM). The five leaders also asked that "nations with interests in the region" should be more directly involved in the peace negotiations. The states in question were said to be the United States, the Soviet Union, and Cuba. Finally, the five presidents requested United Nations participation in the attempt to demobilize guerrilla forces.

That subject was in the forefront of discussion when the United States promised to allocate funding, up to $3 million to assist in the relocation of the Contras to their own country, provided democratic conditions existed there (December 12, 1989). On the same day, the United States explained to the Contra leadership that U.S. assistance to the Contras ended after Nicaragua's elections (February 15, 1990). Furthermore, the only aid planned for the Contras after that date would be funds to finance the return of Contras from their Honduran camps.

The United States had decided on a $9 million package in support of the anti-Sandinista parties in the coming Nicaraguan election. Of the total, $8 million was intended for the use of the National Endowment for Democracy to cover such expenses as voter registration, poll monitoring, and so on, as well as paying up to 50 percent tax on foreign contributions required by law in Nicaragua. The remaining $1 million was intended for the expenses of three poll-watching groups. None of the funds could be used for direct campaign expenses. Many legal scholars, including the present writer, believe that the funding of elections in foreign countries by an outside government represents an unlawful intervention (interference) in foreign domestic affairs. In the Nicaraguan instance, however, the American funding did not cover campaign expenses but the actual mechanism of an election, so it was within the scope of the relevant Nicaraguan legislation, and it took place with the apparent agreement of the incumbent government. Hence the United States funding of the Nicaraguan election appears to have been lawful from the point of view of international law.

The election took place on February 25, 1990 after intense campaign efforts by the Sandinista Front and the opposing National Opposition Front (UNO).[13] More than 7,000 foreign observers watched the proceedings—2,500 of these were 'official,' and 669 were on teams from the United Nations, the Organization of American States, and a delegation led by former U.S. President Jimmy Carter. A 239-member team represented the United Nations. To the surprise of many, President Daniel Ortega lost the election to Violeta Barrios de Chamorro. The latter gained 54 percent of the vote to 41 percent for the Sandinista Front.

In the wake of UNO's victory, Cuba announced an end to military cooperation with Nicaragua (March 9), and the United States lifted the five-year-old trade embargo against Nicaragua (March 13), with President Bush proposing a $300 million aid package for the new administration in Managua.

In the meantime, American aid for the Contras had ended. The latter agreed on March 24 to begin disbanding their troops by April 20. The 12,000 troops in Honduras were to be demobilized there, and the 9,000 troops inside Nicaragua were to move into security zones supervised by a UN peacekeeping force and Cardinal Obando y Bravo.

On April 19, 1990, a formal truce was arranged between the Contras, the Sandinista government, and the incoming UNO government. The agreement provided for a cease-fire effective that day, withdrawal of Sandinista forces at least 12 miles from the borders of five security zones, and the immediate move of all Contras in Nicaragua to those zones. Beginning April 25, disarmament of Contras was to begin, with total disarmament and demobilization scheduled to be completed by June 10. Soon American television viewers were treated to scenes in the security zones where Contras surrendered weapons to UN troopers, who immediately destroyed those weapons.

[13] See Ridenour, "A Matter of Sandinista Shenanigans," and Marker, "A Catalog of Constant U.S. Interference," *CSM*, Feb. 14, 1990, 19.

## SUGGESTED READINGS

### *Nicaragua* v. *United States, Merits*

See the appraisals by a number of legal scholars in 81 *AJIL* 78, 129 (1987); Highet, "Evidence, the Court, and the Nicaragua Case," 81 *AJIL* 1 (1987); Scott & Carr, "The ICJ and Compulsory Jurisdiction: The Case for Closing the Clause," *id.,* 57; UN Security Council, "Excerpts from Verbatim Records Discussing the ICJ Judgment in Nicaragua *v.* United States (July 29–31, 1986)," in 25 *ILM* 1337 (1986); Meron, "Nicaragua and International Law: The 'Academic' and the 'Real,' " 79 *AJIL* 657 (1985). See also Leigh's convenient summary of the Judgment in 81 *AJIL* 201 (1987); Reisman, "Has the International Court Exceeded Its Jurisdiction?" 80 *AJIL* 128 (1986), and his "Respecting One's Own Jurisprudence: A Plea to the International Court of Justice," 83 *AJIL* 312 (1989); McWhinney, *The International Court of Justice and the Western Tradition of International Law* (1987), 99–136; D'Amato, "Trashing Customary International Law," 81 *AJIL* 101 (1987); Franck, "Some Observations on the ICJ's Procedural and Substantive Innovations," *id.,* 116.

# PART III

# The Law and the Individual

# 9

# Jurisdiction over Persons

The Rights of Independence and of Territorial Supremacy, covered briefly in Chapter 7, include internal as well as external freedom from outside interference. The former involves, *inter alia,* supreme authority over all persons or property located in the territory of a state. As a result of this Right, the state decides who are its citizens (by birth or some other principle), the permission to allow aliens to enter its territory, and the conditions under which they reside or work in the state, regulate the property rights of its citizens, etc. The same Right also refers to the external independence of states. This means an assertion of supreme authority to determine its relations with other states and, in consequence, responsibility to others for its lawful obligations toward other states. The Right also includes a number of rules concerning the control (authority) of a state over its citizen when they journey beyond the territorial boundary of that state.

Both aspects of the Right of Territorial Supremacy are usually referred to as the Right or Principle of Territoriality. This principle should be kept in mind when reading Chapter 12 (Extradition) inasmuch as the principle in question is the underlying factor or basis for Extradition or for the success or failure of the latter's operation.

Territorial Supremacy is not absolute and never has been so. The principle, or Right, is subject to limitation imposed by rules of international law. These limitations are covered here and in Chapters 11–13.

## NATIONALITY OF INDIVIDUALS

MEANING OF NATIONAL; NATIONALITY    Each state is composed of a multitude of persons and, as part of its sovereign powers, exercises jurisdiction over those persons. Its primary concern is with those individuals who are its citizens, its true members. Legal writers as well as legislators in many countries employ two terms in this connection, and it should be kept in mind that the two may not always be synonymous: *nationals* and *citizens.* *National,* in popular usage, has a broader meaning than *citizen* does: before the Philippines became independent, the inhabitants of the archipelago were nationals of the United States but not citizens thereof. When the Philippines became independent, all Filipinos not naturalized in other countries (hence including all born in the islands but residing as nationals in the United States) became citizens of the Republic of the Philippines and lost their status as nationals of the United States. On the other hand, a citizen of any country is, at the same time, a national of that country.

Because domestic laws of states relating to citizenship vary greatly, the following discussion uses the terms *national* and *nationality* as referring more adequately to an international law approach. The relationship between state and citizen represents a link through which an individual normally can and does enjoy the protection and benefits of international law. If an individual lacks a nationality tie to a state, he is without protection if a wrong is done to him by any government, for without this tie no state would be willing to protect or take up his cause against the government that had committed the wrong.

In the United States, *national* means a person owing permanent allegiance to a state, and "national of the United States" means either a citizen of this country or a person who, though not a citizen of the United States, owes such permanent allegiance to the United States.

Today most of the 15,000 Samoans in American Samoa are U.S. "nationals," not U.S. citizens. They are, for instance, not permitted to vote in presidential elections. The present writer has used citizen and national interchangeably here.

Nationality, then, is the bond that unites individuals with a given state, that identifies them as members of that entity, that enables them to claim its protection, and that also subjects them to the performance of such duties as their state may impose on them.

RIGHT OF THE STATE TO CONFER NATIONALITY    Each state is free to decide who shall be its nationals, under what conditions nationality shall be conferred, and who—and in what manner—shall be deprived of such status.[1] The prevailing principle was stated in somewhat general terms in *Tomasicchio* v. *Acheson*.[2]

Citizenship depends, however, entirely on municipal law and is not regulated by international law. Acquisition of citizenship of the United States is governed solely by the Constitution and by Acts of Congress.

INTERNATIONAL LAW AND NATIONALITY    Contrary to popular belief, there exist only a few rules of customary law, of multilateral treaties, and of "general principles" dealing with the subject of nationality. Despite attempts to draft comprehensive global law-making treaties on the subject, none has as yet met with success.

[1]See "The Law of the Union of Soviet Socialist Republics on Citizenship of the U.S.S.R." (effective July 1, 1979), in 20 *ILM* 1207 (1981).
[2]U.S. Dist. Court, D.C., 1951, 98 F. Supp. 166.

LIMITATION ON RIGHT OF THE STATE TO CONFER NATIONALITY    Despite the
acknowledged fact that most of the details of nationality are governed by
domestic law, a limited number of rules of international law (some general,
some particular in scope) apply in this sphere and do regulate certain aspects
of nationality. Thus the Permanent Court of International Justice held in
the case of the *Nationality Decrees Issued in Tunis and Morocco*[3] that the discretion relating to nationality that normally represents an exclusive prerogative
of each state may under certain conditions be restricted by some form of
international obligation and that in such cases jurisdiction, which in principle belongs solely to the state, would be limited by rules of international
law.

MODES OF ACQUIRING NATIONALITY    Nationality may be acquired through
either of two modes: by birth or by naturalization. Most of the population
of almost all states acquires its nationality by the former method, but tens
of thousands of persons, as well as individuals singly, have received a new
nationality by the second method.

LAW OF THE SOIL (JUS SOLI)    By general agreement, *i.e.,* customary international law, any individual born on the soil of a given state of parents who
are nationals of that state is regarded as a national of the state in question. (This has not always been true, however, as will be discussed later.)
Beyond this point, the United States and most Latin American states follow the law of the soil (*jus soli*), according to which mere birth on the
soil of a state is sufficient to create the bond of nationality, irrespective to
the parents' allegiance. There are exceptions to this rule, based on comity
or courtesy rather than on international law: children of foreign heads of
state, foreign diplomats,[4] and, in a few cases, foreign consular officials are
not claimed as its nationals by the state on whose soil they happen to be
born.

One other condition serves to void the usual application of the *jus soli*
in the United States: a child born in a portion of the United States then
under the occupation of enemy military forces does not acquire American
nationality under the *jus soli*.[5] This position is quite logical, because during
such occupation the authority of the legitimate sovereign is suspended and
the enemy occupation forces exercise temporary control over the territory in
question. A child born there would, therefore, not be a person "born in the
United States and subject to the jurisdiction thereof."

The concept of *jus soli* was illustrated in the classic case of

---

[3] Advisory Opinion, *P.C.I.J.,* 1924, Ser. B, No. 4.
[4] See *In re Thenault,* U.S. District Court, D.C., 1942, 47 F. Supp. 952. In the United
States, children born on U.S. territory to foreign diplomats *not* accredited to the American
government would normally be regarded as U.S. citizens. See Department of State MS. File
130, Dec. 14, 1937, concerning Marie de Hedry, reprinted in Whitaker, *Politics and Power*
316–77. (1964)
[5] See *Inglis* v. *Sailor's Snug Harbour,* U.S. Supreme Court, 1830, 3 Peters 99.

## UNITED STATES v. WONG KIM ARK
### United States, Supreme Court, 1898, 169 U.S. 649

FACTS   Wong Kim Ark was born in San Francisco in 1873 of Chinese parents who were subjects of the emperor of China but were permanently domiciled in the United States. Because they were Chinese, the parents were then not eligible for United States citizenship by naturalization. Wong Kim Ark went to China in 1894 and on his return to the United States in 1895 was refused admission to this country by the collector of customs, on the ground that he was a Chinese laborer, not a citizen, and not within any of the privileged classes named in the Chinese Exclusion Act then in force.

Wong Kim Ark sued for a writ of habeas corpus, claiming American nationality on the ground of birth. The case eventually came by appeal before the Supreme Court.

ISSUE   Would a child born in the United States of alien parents ineligible for citizenship become at birth a national (citizen) of the United States by virtue of the first clause of the Fourteenth Amendment of the Constitution: "All persons born or naturalized in the United States, and subject to the jurisdiction thereof, are citizens of the United States and of the State wherein they reside."

DECISION   The court decided in favor of Wong Kim Ark: under the Fourteenth Amendment, his birth on United States soil conferred citizenship on him at birth.

REASONING   (1) "It is the inherent right of every independent nation to determine for itself, and according to its own Constitution and laws, what classes of persons shall be entitled to its citizenship."

(2) "The Fourteenth Amendment affirms the rule of citizenship by birth within the territory, in allegiance and under the protection of the country, including all children here born of resident aliens, with the exceptions or qualifications (as old as the rule itself) of children of foreign sovereigns or their ministers, or born on foreign public ships, or of enemies within and during a hostile occupation of our territory, and with the single additional exception of children of members of the Indian tribes owing direct allegiance to their several tribes. The amendment, in clear words and in manifest intent, includes the children born within the territory of the United States of all other persons, of whatever race or color, domiciled within the United States."

LAW OF THE BLOOD (JUS SANGUINIS)   Most Euorpean states, on the other hand, adhere primarily to the civil law principle of the law of the blood (*jus sanguinis*), according to which a child's nationality follows that of the parents, regardless of the place of its birth. Thus a child born to French parents in the United States would be a French national under the *jus sanguinis* as well as an American national under the *jus soli*. In the United States that individual would be an American citizen, in France a French citizen, and in Ghana, a citizen of both France and the United States (dual nationality).

COMPLICATIONS OF DETERMINING CITIZENSHIP   To complicate matters, most states do not follow either of these principles slavishly but accept both, with varying emphasis on one or the other, tailored usually to specific residence requirements.

Children born aboard vessels registered in the United States are not nationals of this country under *jus soli*. In the classic case of *Lam Mow* v. *Nagle*,[6] Lam Mow was refused admission to the United States in 1927 as an alien. He had been born on the high seas aboard a merchant vessel registered in the United States. His parents, domiciled in the United States but nationals of China, were returning to this country from a visit to China. The plaintiff contended that birth aboard an American ship constituted birth in the United States. The Circuit Court ruled, however, that the words of the United States Constitution (Art. 14, sec. 1) applied only to the land areas and territorial waters of the United States: areas possessing both a fixed location and recognized boundaries. Because vessels lack the element of fixed location, the court held that persons born aboard American vessels on the high seas followed the nationality of their parents. Hence Lam Mow was declared to be a Chinese national, and so his application for admission was denied.[7]

Countless controversies concerning the nationality of individuals have arisen over the years because each state stresses one of the two modes of acquiring nationality. Generally, when two states have a claim on a person's allegiance on the basis of birth, the state asserting its primary preference as to principle *and* exercising actual control over the person of the individual is acknowledged by the other claimant to be the sovereign of the person in question.

DOCTRINE OF EFFECTIVE LINK    Arising out of the practice of *jus soli* and *jus sanguinis*, a new concept of importance in the field of nationality has come into being: the Doctrine of Effective Link. Its best-known exposition is to be found in the decision of the International Court of Justice in *The Nottebohm Case (Liechtenstein v. Guatemala)*.[8] The Court held that there must exist a specific link effective in nature, a genuine connection between a state and its citizen. While the doctrine has been criticized strongly, it appears to be generally accepted today.

NATURALIZATION    A second mode of acquiring nationality is through naturalization, that is, through a (generally) voluntary act by which the

[6]U.S. Court of Appeals, 9th Cir., 1928, 24 F.2d 316.

[7]Aircraft registered in the United States, by analogy, would not be considered to be U.S. territory for purposes of conferring citizenship by birth. On the other hand, it is interesting to note that in *Ching Lan Foo* v. *Brownell* (U.S. District Court, D.C., 1957, 148 F. Supp. 420), the court ruled that American ships on the high seas should be considered to be part of United States territory for purposes of an alien being "physically present in the United States" in the meaning of the Immigration and Nationality Act of 1952.

[8]*The Nottebohm Case (Liechtenstein v. Guatemala)*, International Court of Justice 1953, *Preliminary Objection* (Nov. 18, 1953) *ICJ Rep.* 111 (1953), in 48 *AJIL* 327 (1954); *Judgment (Merits)*, (Apr. 6, 1955), *ICJ Rep.* 1955, 4, in 49 *AJIL* 396 (1955); see also Kunz, "The Nottebohm Judgment (Second Phase)," 54 *AJIL* 536 (1960).

national of one state becomes the citizen of another. Although normally involving an individual, naturalization may also apply to whole groups through an executive or legislative act. It is in such collective naturalization that the voluntary aspect of individual naturalization may be absent.

Each state possesses, under international law, a sovereign right to decide what aliens to admit, to whom to grant citizenship, and under what conditions. This right might appear to conflict with the pledge, contained in the 1948 UN Universal Declaration of Human Rights, to treat individuals without discrimination (in terms of race, color, sex, language, religion, opinions held, and so on). In practice, however, the sovereign right over admission still prevails over that pledge. Thus several states discriminate in varying degrees against persons of Asian or African ancestry; a number of states have established educational qualifications for entry; physical and mental defects are grounds of inadmissibility under the laws of many members of the community of nations; individuals with criminal records frequently are denied permission to cross borders; and in many states, political opinions or membership in specified political groupings are causes for nonadmission. Some countries exclude aliens whose occupations are not needed. And there still are 33 grounds for excluding aliens from the United States. In other words, regulations governing admission (and, it must be emphasized, governing the granting of citizenship to aliens) are deemed to be purely domestic in nature and therefore not subject to the application of international law. And an alien once admitted still may have problems, for states still maintain strict and detailed deportation laws. It was estimated that once there were 700 grounds for deporting aliens from the United States or for causing loss of citizenship to naturalized citizens; but this situation has changed in recent decades.

COLLECTIVE NATURALIZATION    Collective naturalization, also often purely internal in nature,[9] may on occasion bear an indirect relationship to international law when it is based either on treaty provisions (cession of territory, followed by collective naturalization of the inhabitants by the acquiring state), or on conquest followed by annexation of the conquered territory.

## Dual Nationality

It was noted earlier that individuals sometimes hold two nationalities concurrently. Thus a number of Japanese-descent American nationals present in Japan at the outbreak of war in 1941 were forced to enter the Japanese armed forces. According to American laws, the individuals were nationals

---

[9]Such as the actions of the United States in the collective naturalization of the inhabitants of Hawaii, Puerto Rico, Alaska, the Virgin Islands, and certain Indians living in the United States as members of tribes (1924).

of the United States under *jus soli;* but under the prevailing Japanese laws, they were Japanese citizens under *jus sanguinis*.[10]

DOCTRINE OF INDELIBLE ALLEGIANCE    Another and formerly common basis for an individual's possession of dual nationality is the unwillingness of a state to grant to its nationals the right to expatriate themselves by being naturalized in another state. Such an attitude is founded in the "doctrine of indelible allegiance," originally formulated in Great Britain but abandoned later by that state. Under this theory, an individual cannot lose his nationality without the prior consent of his sovereign. Such consent was usually denied until well past the middle of the last century.

A few states have insisted, down to recent years, that recognition of naturalization should hinge on explicit approval by the recognizing state of each individual's naturalization abroad. Such a recalcitrant attitude by states has, understandably, led to countless disputes because of such a fairly strict adherence to the doctrine of indelible allegiance. Most commonly affected have been former citizens of France, Egypt, Greece, Iran, Poland, Rumania, Syria, and Turkey. Czechoslovakia, it has been reported, did not recognize American-born children of Czech parents as U.S. citizens as late as 1965.

The problem of dual nationality itself, irksome as it is to both the states and the individuals concerned, has not yet been settled by means of a general international convention.[11] The Convention on Certain Questions Relating to Conflict of Nationality Laws, signed at The Hague in 1930, was a modest beginning. This instrument, to which the United States did not become a party, stated that a person having two or more nationalities could be regarded as its national by each of the states whose nationality he possessed (Art. 3); that a state could not afford diplomatic protection to one of its nationals against a state whose nationality such a person also possessed (Art. 4); that in a third state a person having dual nationality should be treated as if he had only one (Art. 5); and that a person possessing two nationalities acquired involuntarily was entitled to renounce one of them but only with the permission of the state whose nationality he desired to surrender (Art. 6). In general, states today follow in practice almost all of those provisions, despite the absence of general conventional rules.[12]

---

[10]See *Kiyokuro Okimura v. Acheson,* U.S. Dist. Court, Hawaii, 1951, 99 F. Supp. 587, digested in 46 *AJIL* 157 (1952), together with numerous relevant citations. Consult also Nissim Bar-Yaacov, *Dual Nationality* (1961), which includes many case citations and an excellent bibliography.

[11]See *Esphahanian* v. *Bank Tejarat,* The Hague, Iranian–United States Claims Tribunal, AWD 31-157-2, Mar. 29, 1983, reported in 77 *AJIL* 646 (1983).

[12]See *Tomasicchio* v.*Acheson,* U.S. District Court D.C., June 18, 1951, 98 F. Supp. 166, reported in 46 *AJIL* 155 (1952); Rode, "Dual Nationals and the Doctrine of Dominant Nationality," 53 *AJIL* 139 (1959), as well as the report on the British case of *Oppenheimer* v. *Cattermole,* 1971, *et seq.,* before the Appellate Committee of the House of Lords (1975), in 16 *Harvard Int'l L. Jl.* 749 (1975).

## Special Status of Women and Children

One of the most interesting aspects of nationality was the special status for women and children created by certain laws of the United States. Traditionally, both English and American law did not deprive a female citizen of her nationality when she married an alien. In the course of time, however, this old common-law principle underwent considerable changes.

In 1855, an act of Congress conferred United States citizenship on any alien woman who married an American citizen. Then, in 1907, another act provided that "any American woman who marries a foreigner shall take the nationality of her husband" and went on to state that such a woman would resume her American citizenship when the marriage in question terminated; resumption of citizenship would then take place either by continuing residence in the United States or by registration at any American consulate. Great Britain had enacted similar legislation, and by 1908 all major countries in Europe and the Americas had created a uniform rule on this subject, because European and Latin American states had long followed policies virtually identical with those found in the 1907 law.

The new United States regulations soon produced some rather ridiculous situations, such as when an American woman married an engineer of British nationality and promptly lost her United States citizenship, even though the couple resided in Portland, Oregon.

CABLE ACT    At last the Cable Act of September 22, 1922 (42 *Statutes at Large* 1021), brought some order into the United States nationality picture while marking, at the same time, a break in American policy with the rules generally observed elsewhere. The act, adopted in order to make married women independent, provided that an alien woman would not acquire United States nationality by marriage to an American citizen or through the naturalization of her husband but had to be naturalized personally in accordance with prevailing regulations. Furthermore the Cable Act reversed the act of 1907 and stated that a woman citizen of the United States would not lose her nationality by marriage to an alien unless she formally renounced her citizenship or married an alien ineligible for United States citizenship. Finally, the Cable Act provided for speedy renaturalization for women who had lost their citizenship under the 1907 law, unless the alien husbands were ineligible for citizenship. A 1936 law reinstated the 1907 method for regaining citizenship for women whose marriages had terminated, and then a 1940 amendment provided that even if the marriage had not terminated, a native-born women who had married an alien between 1907 and 1922 resumed her citizenship if she had lived in the United States continuously from the date of marriage.

CONVENTION ON THE NATIONALITY OF WOMEN    The emancipation of women and the grant of female suffrage in more and more countries led to a demand abroad that the old principle of "family unity," as applied to nationality, be brought up to date in accordance with the new United States rules. Thus a League of Nations Committee of Experts prepared a draft convention on the status of married women as early as 1926, and at the Conference of American States in Montevideo (1933), the Convention on the Nationality of Women was adopted that prohibited distinctions based on sex as regarded nationality. The 1933 instrument was ratified, however, only by the United States and a limited number of the Latin American states, so that at present it is only of "partial regional" application.[13]

STATUS OF CHILDREN    Other complicated questions have arisen with respect to the nationality of children, particularly illegitimate offspring and foundlings. A number of international conventions have been developed to deal with such questions, but limited ratification has caused the problems to continue.

One question appears to be of interest in this connection: the status of children removed from the country of their birth by their parents when those parents subsequently became citizens of another state.

Under United States legislation, a native-born U.S. citizen taken abroad by his parents while under the age of 21 years loses his American nationality through the parents' foreign naturalization unless the citizen in question returns to the United States to establish a permanent residence before his twenty-fifth birthday.[14] Most countries now hold that minor children follow the nationality of their parents, and when the latter changes through naturalization, the nationality of the minor child changes accordingly.

States have declined, on occasion, to permit minor children, nationals under *jus soli,* to accompany departing parents abroad when it appeared likely that such departure would jeopardize the children's retention of nationality.

## Loss of Nationality

The questions of denaturalization and expatriation are closely connected with both naturalization and dual nationality. Each country establishes its own rules and determines the acts or omissions that would cause loss of its nationality to native-born citizens, naturalized citizens, or both.[15]

CAUSES OF LOSS OF NATIONALITY    The acts that cause expatriation or denaturalization vary from country to country, and no complete list can be drawn up. They include, among others, voting in foreign elections, service in the armed forces of another country (especially when an oath of allegiance forms a prerequisite for such service), acceptance of an office abroad that is reserved under the relevant laws for citizens of the foreign state in question,

[13]See the case of *U.S.A. ex rel. Florence Strunsky Mergé* v. *Italian Republic,* Italo-American Conciliation Commission, 1955, digested in 50 *AJIL* 154 (1956).

[14]Immigration and Nationality Act of 1952, sec. 349(a), par. 1. See also the famous decision in *Marie Elizabeth Elg* v. *Frances Perkins, Secretary of Labor et al.,* U.S. Supreme Court, 1939, 307 U.S. 325, in 33 *AJIL* 773 (1939).

[15]The following cases are useful for illustrative purposes: *Terada* v. *Dulles,* U.S District Court, Hawaii, 1945, 121 F. Supp. 6, reported in 48 *AJIL* 663 (1954); *Trop* v. *Dulles,* U.S. Supreme Court, 1958, 356 U.S. 86; and *Mitsugi Nishikawa* v. *Dulles,* U.S. Supreme Court, 1958, 356 U.S. 129.

desertion in time of war, "disloyalty," treason, and formal renunciation of nationality either through naturalization abroad or through an official declaration filed with an embassy, legation, or consul of one's country. [16]

In the United States, expatriation, that is, a formal renunciation of citizenship, raises no further legal questions: the individual in question has lost his former citizenship. In the interesting case of *Davis* v. *District Director of Immigration, etc.* (481 F. Supp. 1178, D.D.C., 1979), a former citizen of the United States formally renounced his nationality in order to become a "world citizen," and was denied entrance as an immigrant without a visa. In many such cases decided by American courts, "intent" plays a major role: the government must prove that the individual in question intended to renounce his American citizenship by whatever act had been involved in the case.

In the instance of naturalized citizens, many recent cases indicate that if the defendant procured his U.S. citizenship illegally, such as by fraud or by omitting relevant information at the time he or she applied for such citizenship, the latter would be lifted and the individual would be subject to deportation. Illegal procurement of citizenship was abolished as a ground for denaturalization in 1952, but was reintroduced in 1961. It should be mentioned that many of the defendants in recent denaturalization cases had also been accused of war crimes committed during World War II. [17]

## Statelessness

Statelessness—that is, the lack of nationality—used to occur only rarely before World War I: the relatively few recorded instances usually pertained to the accidental loss of nationality without the corresponding acquisition of a new one, frequently in connection with illegitimate children. The problem cannot be discussed, however, before terms have been clarified. "Stateless persons"—that is, "*de facto* stateless" individuals—are persons who have a nationality that does not give them protection outside their own country.

[16] See Boudin, "Involuntary Loss of American Nationality," 73 *Harvard L. Rev.* 1510 (1960); cf. the landmark decision in *Schneider* v. *Rusk,* 377 U.S. 163 (1964), concerning congressional power and naturalized citizens. See also other cases listed under "Suggested Readings."

[17] Such as in *United States* v. *Fedorenko,* U.S. Court of Appeals, 5th Cir., 1979, 597 F.2d 946, reported in 74 *AJIL* 186 (1980), affirmed in *Fedorenko* v. *United States,* U.S. Supreme Court, 101 S. Ct. 737, January 21, 1981, reported in 75 *AJIL* 669 (1981). Fedorenko was deported to the Soviet Union on December 19, 1984. He had been charged with lying to immigration officials on entering the United States in 1949, about his job as a Nazi death-camp guard. Most prominent in this category of cases was the Rumanian Orthodox Archbishop Valerian Trifa, also accused of war crimes. He voluntarily gave up his American citizenship before it was taken from him (in August 1980) but remained in the United States until he was deported to Portugal in October 1984. Trifa had requested to be sent to Switzerland, but that government refused to take him; the United States then asked West Germany to admit him, inasmuch as he had left Rumania under German SS protection during World War II, but the Federal Republic refused because he was not a German citizen. See also Chapter 27 on loss of citizenship.

This category embraces most of the individuals commonly referred to as refugees.

In Africa, for example, true refugees are defined as people who are outside their country of origin because of persecution (Geneva Convention definition) or who have fled general conditions of violence (Organization of African Unity Convention definition).[18] On the other hand, a true stateless person—that is, "stateless *de jure*"—is quite rare, being an individual who has been stripped of nationality by his own former government; however, such action took place on a massive scale during the post–1917 Russian civil wars, during the Nazi regime in Germany, and on a smaller scale, normally limited to individuals, in the Soviet Union and the German Democratic Republic.[19]

SCOPE OF THE PROBLEM    The scale of the problem of *de facto* statelessness, of refugees, has been, and still is, staggering both in numbers and in terms of human misery. Some 2 million persons fled Russia during the post-revolutionary years. After the end of World War II in Europe, some 8 million displaced persons had to be helped; most of these were eventually repatriated or resettled. At the end of 1989, to cite only a few examples, about 4 million refugees lived in various African countries; more than 1.5 million Palestinians existed as refugees in the Middle East; well over 4 million Afghan refugees were still in Pakistan and Iran, despite the Russian withdrawal from their homeland; and almost 300,000 ethnic Turks expelled by Bulgaria had fled to Turkey. The total number of "international" (as contrasted with "internal") refugees in 1989 totaled over 14.36 million. None of the 1989 totals included resettled refugees. Of the more than 2 million refugees who escaped following the fall of Indochina (spring 1975) from Cambodia, Laos, and Vietnam, over 1.5 million had been resettled by the end of 1989, including large numbers in the United States. Repatriation of refugees would appear to be a simple solution if the actual problems involved were ignored. The example of the British colony of Hong Kong serves to illustrate some of the difficulties to be encountered.

In December 1989 the Hong Kong authorities forcibly repatriated a small number (51) of Vietnamese boat people who, together with some 54,000 of this group, had been living in camps in the colony. Outside protests stopped further attempts to utilize forcible deportation. The Hong Kong authorities then began (March 1990) a program of voluntary repatriation of boat people. Relatively few (4,470) of the latter chose to accept the scheme.

On September 22 the UN High Commissioner for Refugees, the British government, Hong Kong, and Vietnam concluded an agreement to identify

[18]*Gist* (August 1989), 1.

[19]Such as the case of *Époux Gunquène c. Mlle Falk et Autres,* France, Court of Cassation, 1950, reported in 45 *AJIL* 799 (1951); the Russian examples of Mstislav Rostropovich and his wife and of Major General Pyotr Grigorenko, widely reported in March 1978 through the Associated Press, and the continuing expulsion of critics from the GDR, such as those reported in *NYT*, Sept. 24, 1977, 1, 5.

boat people who had not volunteered to go home but who might not object to do so soon. About 9,000 of the boat people in Hong Kong had been classified as "refugees", and it had been decided to settle those individuals in Western countries. The remaining 45,000 boat people were to be screened as to their status: they would be classified as *refugees* (for future homes in the West) if they faced political persecution on returning home, or as *economic migrants* facing repatriation. Mandatory return to Vietnam was expected to be adopted if sufficient numbers of boat people refused an offer of voluntary repatriation. On October 4, 1990, the Vietnamese government was reported to have agreed to the principle of forced repatriation of boat people from Hong Kong.

PROBLEMS OF STATELESS PERSONS    The day-to-day difficulties encountered by a stateless person may assume almost incredible complexity, whether they relate to such matters as identity documents, travel permits, work cards, marriage licenses, and other kinds of papers normally issued to citizens in the twentieth century, or whether they are connected with such mundane questions related to survival as ability to speak the local language or to learn the work skills with which to earn a living. Attempts to alleviate some of these problems have sometimes been successful, but, more often than not, they have failed.

INTERNATIONAL RELIEF ACTIONS    Most international attempts to relieve the distress of refugees and other stateless persons have been based on some international agreement. In 1921 the League of Nations created the Office of High Commissioner for Refugees, mostly concerned with the human flotsam of the Russian Revolution. During and after World War II, the United Nations Relief and Rehabilitation Administration (UNRRA, 1943–1947) carried on global and massive relief activities. It was succeeded by the UN International Refugee Organization (IRO), active in many countries between 1947 and 1952. In the latter year, the Office of the UN High Commissioner for Refugees (UNHCR) began its continuing efforts to find what are still hoped to be final or permanent solutions for the refugee–stateless-person problem. At the time of this writing, the High Commissioner, despite a half-billion dollar budget and a staff of 1,500, must rely on additional voluntary contributions for the protection and eventual resettlement of some 10 million refugees. A special agency of the United Nations, the UN Relief and Works Agency (UNWRA) has operated since 1950 in the Middle East to minister to the needs of refugees from the Israel-Arab conflicts of 1948–1949, 1956, 1967, and 1973 (UNWRA listed 1,706,486 registered Palestine refugees as late as 1978). More recently came the failure of a 92-member UN conference held in Geneva in January–February 1977 in order to conclude a treaty under which refugees would be protected from being returned to the state from which they had fled. A second conference (38 participating states), called by the High Commissioner, met in December 1978 in Geneva. Its specific subject had been consultation about the flow of refugees from Vietnam, but no reportable accomplishments were recorded.

In June 1979, the U.S. government announced that it would double the intake of Indochinese refugees to 14,000 monthly, and in the same month, Vietnam signed an agreement with the UN High Commissioner for Refugees to allow an "orderly departure" of emigrants and accepting assistance from the United Nations agency in the granting of exit visas for "family or humanitarian reasons." These steps did not halt the Indochinese exodus, and a conference on Indochinese refugees, called by the UN Secretary-General, met in July 1979. The tangible results of this meeting in Geneva consisted in the agreement by a number of South Asian countries to take in 260,000 refugees and a multinational pledge of about $190 million for the relief program.

In October 1981 the Office of the UN High Commissioner for Refugees was awarded the Nobel Peace Prize for its work with the millions of homeless scattered around the world.

In order to call attention to the staggering dimensions of the African refugee problem, the first International Conference on African Refugees Assistance (ICARA) was held in 1981 in Geneva under United Nations auspices. About $600 million (short of the expectations nourished by the African states) was pledged by various countries. ICARA II met in Geneva in July 1984 in order to resolve these problems, and the solutions were to be implemented by various UN agencies, in addition to the Office of the High Commissioner. It was also hoped that at least $800 million would be pledged by the participants. On February 7, 1985, the Office of the UN High Commissioner for Refugees launched the first of several appeals for funds to assist refugees in four African countries: Sudan, Ethiopia, Somalia, and the Central African Republic.

The U.S. Refugee Act of 1980, based in part on the 1951 Convention (see below), canceled the former American ideological and geographic restrictions in favor of the much broader UN definition of a refugee based on the latter's fear of persecution. The law says that that fear must be "on account of" any of five objective factors: race, religion, nationality, membership in a particular social group, or political opinion. The law also created a ceiling of 231,700 refugees to be admitted to the United States in the fiscal year 1980, but permitted the President to admit additional refugees. That authority was invoked, for example, in April 1980 in reference to the influx of Cuban refugees. (See Chapter 12 under "Diplomatic Asylum.")

TREATY STEPS TAKEN IN CONNECTION WITH STATELESSNESS    One of the earliest instruments intended to alleviate the plight of stateless person (disregarding the various agreements outlined above) was the Special Protocol Concerning Statelessness, signed in The Hague on April 12, 1930.[20] The

---

[20]Text in 13 *ILM* 1 (1974).

agreement had been signed by 20 governments, and accessions had been deposited by four others when it was announced that the protocol had at last entered into force on October 11, 1973. The People's Republic of China then informed the United Nations Secretariat that it would not recognize the ratification by the Republic of China (1935), and consequently the Secretary-General deemed the Chinese ratification as withdrawn and the protocol as not in force.[21]

The situation of some stateless persons was improved by the entering into force of the 1951 Geneva Convention on the Status of Refugees, which was ratified or acceded to by 54 countries. The United States is a party to the instrument through the 1967 UN Protocol Relating to the Status of Refugees (in force October 4, 1967). The 1951 convention contains, among other matters, a core of basic rights of stateless persons. In addition, the 1954 UN Conference on the Status of Stateless Persons drew up the Convention Relating to the Status of Stateless Persons, but that agreement, originally signed by 22 states, has not yet come into force.[22] Again, the Convention on the Reduction of Statelessness, adopted in August 1961 by the UN Conference on the Elimination or Reduction of Future Statelessness, entered into force on December 13, 1975.[23] But that instrument, by which it was attempted to introduce some order into the world's mass of conflicting nationality laws, has received to date only eight ratifications. From a global point of view, its practical effects should be viewed as slight at best. Similarly, the Organization of African Unity Convention of Refugee Problems in Africa of September 10, 1969, suffered from minimal endorsement by member states: when the convention entered into force automatically on November 27, 1973, through ratification by Algeria, the instrument had been ratified by only 14 of the OAU's 42 member states. The convention expanded the definition of the African refugee and contained specific regulations concerning nondiscrimination, voluntary repatriation, and the issue of travel documents.

It is easy to see why no really effective instrument has been adopted by the members of the community of nations: it would require far-reaching intervention in and regulation of what virtually every state still normally regards as representing matters of exclusively national jurisdiction and determination.

One of the most interesting cases involving statelessness was decided in 1947:

---

[21]*id.,* 790.

[22]Text in 63 *AJIL* 389 (1969 Supp); text of the protocol, *id.,* 385; see also letter from Secretary of State Dean Rusk to the president, *id.,* 123–28. Two cases relevant to both instruments are *Ming* v. *Marks,* U.S. District Court, S.D.N.Y., 367 F. Supp. 673, reported 68 *AJIL* 534 (1974), and *Cheng* v. *Immigration and Naturalization Service,* U.S. Court of Appeals, 3rd Cir., 1975, 521 F.2d 1351, reported 70 *AJIL* 578 (1976).

[23]Text in 8 *ILM* 1288 (1969).

## U.S. EX REL. STEINVORTH v. WATKINS
### United States, Court of Appeals, 2nd Circuit, 1947
### 159 F. (2d) 50

FACTS    Steinvorth was born in Costa Rica of German parents who took him to Germany in 1901. During World War I he served in the German army and then returned to Costa Rica as a permanent resident in 1920. In 1941 he chose Costa Rican citizenship after the German consul there had informed him that this act would cancel his German citizenship.

On September 23, 1944, the president of Costa Rica caused a resolution to be published that stated that Steinvorth had lost his Costa Rican citizenship. The next day Steinvorth was arrested by Costa Rican authorities and taken to the United States by American officials, in cooperation with the Costa Rican authorities. In the United States, he was interned as an enemy alien. He petitioned for habeas corpus, but this petition was denied by the District Court, Southern District of New York. He then appealed to the Circuit Court.

ISSUE    Was Steinvorth an enemy alien, a status that would have made his internment lawful?

DECISION    The order of the District Court was reversed, and the appellant was discharged from custody and internment, because he was not an enemy alien but a stateless person.

REASONING    Under German law, Steinvorth terminated his German citizenship by opting for Costa Rican citizenship in 1941. The 1944 cancellation of his Costa Rican nationality could not be judged by an American court. It was an act of state done in a foreign jurisdiction, and an American court had to accept it as canceling Steinvorth's citizenship in Costa Rica.

But the termination of his Costa Rican citizenship did not restore his German nationality: that could have been done only by Germany itself, and there was no evidence submitted that anything that had happened since September 23, 1944, had made him a German citizen again. After that date, Steinvorth was a stateless person. The government of the United States could hold Steinvorth only if he were a native, a citizen, or a subject of a hostile country. Because he was none of these but was a stateless person, he had to be released.

## NATIONALITY OF BUSINESS ENTERPRISES

CORPORATIONS    Corporations enjoy the status of legal or juristic persons and therefore can be said to be endowed with nationality similar to the manner in which a natural (human) person possesses nationality.

The traditional Anglo-American determinant of a corporation's nationality was domicile or, more specifically, the place of incorporation. In the case of unincorporated associations, nationality was determined on the basis of the state in which they were constituted or in which their governing body normally met or was located.

Among most European states, on the other hand, for a long time the concept was preferred that a corporation's nationality was determined either by the location of its home office (*siège social*) or—a minority view—by the place in which the principal business operations were carried on.

PARTNERSHIPS    In the case of business enterprises without legal personality, such as partnerships, no nationality as such can be assigned to the firm. The interests involved are those of the partners, and the nationality of the latter determines which state is entitled to represent the firm's interests. It does not matter, for purposes of determining the "nationality" in question, where the operating establishment of the partnership is located: the nationality of the partners is the decisive factor.

TESTS OF DOMICILE AND OF CONTROL    The events of World War I, particularly the development of economic warfare, led to a change in the definition of nationality, away from the test of domicile and in the direction of the test of control. In other words, regardless of the nominal seat of headquarters or the place of incorporation, a company began to be viewed as invested with the status of an enemy national if the persons in control of the enterprise resided in an enemy country or were found to be acting under the control or instructions of enemy nations (shareholders, silent partners, directors, and so on).[24]

On the whole, the "control test" appears to be a more precise device through which the national character of a business enterprise may be determined. Nevertheless the older test of domicile is still utilized side by side with the newer test. Such concurrent use is not as capricious as it might first appear: the availability of two devices or tests enables states to employ whichever appears most suitable at a given time when the question arises of protecting a business enterprise located in a foreign jurisdiction. Also, in time of war, either test may be applied to determine the enemy or neutral or friendly character of a given firm and may, it must be admitted, result in some rather dubious but highly profitable seizures of alleged enemy firms.

It should be mentioned that there are as yet few generally accepted rules in general international law as to the diplomatic protection of corporate entities. The nationality of the corporation does not appear, by itself, sufficient to generate a claim to protection abroad. State practice indicates that states normally will not afford diplomatic protection to corporations that are their own nationals, if a majority of the stockholders are citizens of another state. On the other hand, states are normally willing to grant such protection on behalf of those stockholders who are their own nationals, even if the corporation is in fact a foreign national. (See also Chapter 11.)

[24]See the classic but disputed case of *Daimler Co., Ltd.* v. *Continental Tyre & Rubber Co., Ltd.,* Great Britain, House of Lords, 1916, [1916] 2 A.C. 307. For American cases, consult *Clark* v. *Uebersee Finanz-Korporation, A.G.,* U.S. Supreme Court, 1947, 332 U.S. 480, as well as *Uebersee Finanz-Korporation, A.G.* v. *McGrath,* U.S. Supreme Court, 1952, 343 U.S. 205. The famous and controversial *Interhandel* case involving a Swiss company assertedly controlled by German interests and in turn controlling the General Aniline and Film Corporation complex in the United States is so complicated that its discussion is beyond the scope of a general text; the interested reader is referred to the sources listed in the relevant section of the "Suggested Readings."

# JURISDICTION OVER NATIONALS ABROAD

**RIGHT OF JURISDICTION**    Assertion of the continuing bond between a state and each of its nationals occurs most frequently in connection with the commission of crimes or other offenses by those nationals beyond the territorial jurisdiction of their state. Some countries assert a right to punish their nationals for offenses committed, regardless of the location of the offense. Other states, notably Great Britain and the United States, have traditionally restricted their criminal jurisdiction to acts committed within their territory. But even in the latter countries, there has been a significant change in attitude during recent decades.

In the classic decision upholding the traditional Anglo-American view, *American Banana Co.* v. *United Fruit Co.*,[25] the Supreme Court of the United States refused to enforce the provisions of the Sherman Anti-Trust Act against the United Fruit Company for activities undertaken in Panama and Costa Rica (where such acts did not violate local law), saying in part that "a conspiracy to do acts in another jurisdiction does not draw to itself those acts and make them unlawful, if they are permitted by the local law." The Court thus ruled that violations of American law committed abroad by United States nationals did not constitute grounds for trial in the United States if the acts in question did not violate the laws of the foreign state in which the acts had taken place. If, on the other hand, a crime was committed abroad by one national against another national and the culprit returned home, then his government could try him for the crime. Again, if a national commits an offense abroad that has its effects in his own state, he may be tried for the offense when he returns to his country. A corporation may be tried at once in the United States.[26]

Current United States statutes provide that U.S. nationals abroad can be prosecuted in this country for contempt of court (such as failure to attend a trial in a criminal action when officially summoned),[27] treason committed in the United States or elsewhere, unauthorized attempts by any citizen, "wherever he may be," to influence a foreign government in its relations with the United States. The U.S. government also imposes its income tax on citizens wherever resident and, in time of a military draft, obligates all male citizens of the proper age to register.

---

[25]U.S. Supreme Court, 1909, 213 U.S. 347; but see the later Haight, "International Law and Extraterritorial Application of the Antitrust Laws," 63 *Yale L. Jl.* 639 (1954); and two U.S. Supreme Court cases: *United States* v. *Sisal Sales Corp.*, 1927, 274 U.S. 268, and *Steele* v. *Bulova Watch Co.*, 1952, 344 U.S. 280. Consult Swigert's heavily annotated Note, "Extraterritorial Jurisdiction—Criminal Law," 13 *Harvard Int'l L. Jl.* 346 (1972).

[26]*Sachs* v. *Government of the Canal Zone*, U.S. Court of Appeals, 5th Cir. 1949, 176 F.2d 292, involving a United States citizen who composed libelous articles in Panama for publication and circulation in the Canal Zone. See also *United States* v. *Aluminum Co. of America*, U.S. Court of Appeals, 2nd Cir., 1945, 148 F.2d 416. Consult Whiteman, vol. 6, 118–60, citing numerous relevant cases.

[27]*Blackmer* v. *United States*, U.S. Supreme Court, 1932, 284 U.S. 421, 52 S. Ct. 252.

British laws provide for punishment not only for treason, but also bigamy, perjury, homicide, and other crimes committed abroad by a British subject. India's criminal laws apply to Indian nationals everywhere, regardless of the magnitude of the offense. In France, a citizen can be prosecuted for any crime and many misdemeanors committed abroad. In West Germany, criminal laws apply to citizens wherever offenses have taken place, even to persons who became German citizens after the criminal act had been committed.

A somewhat different kind of claimed extraterritorial jurisdiction has surfaced lately in connection with efforts to combat domestic terrorism: under Israel's "Offenses Committed Abroad Statute," Palestinian-Americans visiting the occupied West Bank have been arrested, tried, and convicted because of their association with Palestinian organizations in the United States. The groups in question are "'illegal" in Israel, but were legal in the United States. The legal status of such extraterritorial jurisdiction claims has not yet been determined.

**EXTRATERRITORIAL JURISDICTION (CONFLICT OF JURISDICTION)**    The subject of extraterritorial jurisdiction received a surprising amount of attention in 1981 and 1982. Following the establishment of martial law by the Polish government on December 13, 1981, the President of the United States announced on December 29 a series of economic sanctions against both Poland and the Soviet Union. These steps included the suspension of export or reexport licenses to the Soviet Union of equipment and technology for the transmission and refining of petroleum and gas, regardless of preexisting contractual obligations and including goods of U.S. origin already in foreign hands. On June 22, 1982 (effective date), the sanctions were expanded by amendment of sections of the Export Administration Regulations.[28] The new sanctions meant that persons in a third country could not reexport machinery (or its components) for the exploration, production, transmission, or refinement of oil and natural gas, if it was of U.S. origin, without permission of the U.S. government. Moreover, any person subject to the jurisdiction of the United States[29] was required to obtain prior written authorization by the Office of Export Administration, for the export or reexport to the Soviet Union of non-U.S. goods and technical data related to oil and gas exploration, production, transmission, and refinement. Finally, no person in the United States or *in a foreign country* (emphasis added) could

---

[28]See *Current Policy No. 697*, "Economic and Political Aspects of Extraterritoriality" (May 1985); *Gist, "Controlling Transfer of Technology"* (Feb. 1984) and "Controlling Transfer of Strategic Technology," (Apr. 1985); and 18 *ILM* 1508 (1979); 21 *ILM* 164 (1982); and *id.*, 855, 864.

[29]Defined as (i) any person wherever located who was a citizen or resident of the United States; (ii) any person actually within the United States; (iii) any corporation organized under the laws of the United States; or (iv) any partnership, association, corporation or other organization, wherever organized or doing business, that was owned or controlled by persons specified in paragraphs (i), (ii), or (iii).

export or reexport to the Soviet Union foreign products directly derived from U.S. technical data relating to machinery and the like utilized for the exploration, production, transmission, or refinement of petroleum or natural gas or commodities produced in plants, based on such U.S. technical data.

The European Community as a group and other countries individually (such as the United Kingdom) protested immediately against the U.S. amendments of June 22, 1982. They asserted that the measures violated international law because of their extraterritorial aspects. They sought to regulate companies not of U.S. nationality as to their conduct outside the United States, particularly the handling of property and technical data of those companies not within the United States. The U.S. amendments also sought to impose the restrictions of U.S. law, by threatening discriminatory sanctions in trade that was inconsistent with normal commercial practice established between the United States and other countries. The U.S. amendments thus contradicted the two generally accepted bases of jurisdiction in international law: the territoriality and the nationality principles. The *territoriality principle* (the notion that a state should restrict its rule making in principle to persons and goods within its territory) is a fundamental rule of international law, particularly as it concerns the regulation of social and economic activities by a state. The *nationality principle* (the prescription of rules for nationals, wherever they are) could not become the basis for an extension of U.S. jurisdiction under the amendments, that is, over companies incorporated in other states on the basis of some corporate link (parent company–subsidiary) or companies incorporated in other states because they had a tie to a company incorporated in the United States or other U.S.-controlled company through royalty payments, a licensing agreement, payment of some other compensation, or because they bought certain goods originating in the United States. The International Court of Justice, in the *Barcelona Traction* case[30] declared that there were two generally accepted criteria: the place of incorporation and the location of the registered office of the company in question. And finally, the U.S. amendments appeared to imply that technological links to U.S. companies or the possession of U.S.-origin goods should be considered as unalterably American, even though their patents might well have been registered also in other countries. As the European Communities, in their *Comments on the U.S. Regulations Concerning Trade with the U.S.S.R..*[31] pointed out, goods and technology did not have any nationality, and there were no known rules of international law for using goods or technology situated abroad as a basis for establishing jurisdiction over the persons controlling them.

---

[30]*Case Concerning the Barcelona Traction, Light and Power Company, Ltd. (Belgium v. Spain)*, 3 *I.C.J. Reports* (1970). 43
[31]21 *ILM* 891 (1982). See also the address of the Legal Adviser of the Department of State (June 30, 1982) in 76 *AJIL* 839 (1982).

The United Kingdom issued an Order on June 30, 1982, forbidding British companies to comply with the American regulations because the latter were regarded as damaging to the trading interests of the United Kingdom. There were also a number of court cases relating to the problem of expanding territorial jurisdiction, including *Dresser Industries, Inc.* v. *Baldrige* and *Compagnie Européene des Petroles S.A.* v. *Sensor Nederland B.V.*[32] The American sanctions on oil and gas equipment were finally lifted on November 13, 1982.

Typical of foreign reluctance to accept United States insistence on extraterritorial jurisdiction was the decision of the (United Kingdom) High Court of Justice (Queen's Bench Division, Commercial Court) in *Libyan Arab Foreign Bank* v. *Bankers Trust Co.,* of September 2, 1987.[33] The case centered on control of Libyan bank deposits in the London branch of the Bankers Trust Co. after the U.S. President had "frozen" all Libyan assets "in the United States." The Court affirmed the general rule that the law of the place where an account was kept governed: in this case, English law, not American regulations, applied to the London bank account.

TAXATION    A state may lawfully tax its nationals for income earned abroad. In order to avoid the double taxation of an individual or corporation, the United States and other governments have recently concluded numerous agreements.

TREASONABLE ACTS    Beginning with World War II, a new and fascinating sphere of jurisdiction over nationals has received much publicity: the right of a state to punish "treasonable" acts committed outside its territorial jurisdiction, either by its own nationals or by such aliens as can be held to owe allegiance to the state in question either because of the protection given to them as residents of that state or because they travel abroad under its passports.

The best-known United States case in this special category is *Chandler* v. *United States.*[34] Chandler, indicted for treason to the United States committed while residing in Germany, asserted that the constitutional definition of treason did not cover adherence to an enemy by one residing in enemy territory. This interpretation was denied by the District Court, which said, in part:

---

[32]*Dresser Industries, Inc.* v. *Baldrige,* U.S. District Court (D.C.), Sept. 13, 1982, 549 F. Supp. 108, reported in 77 *AJIL* 626 (1983); *Compagnie Européene des Petroles S.A.* v. *Sensor Nederland B.V.,* The Netherlands, District Court at The Hague, Sept. 17, 1982, in 12 *ILM* 66 (1983). See also Lange & Born, *The Extraterritorial Application of National Laws* (1987);

[33]26 *ILM* 1600 (1987). See also Canada, "Foreign Extraterritorial Measures Act" (entered into force on Feb. 14, 1985), in 24 *ILM* 794 (1985).

[34]*United States* v. *Chandler,* U.S. District Ct. Mass., 1947, 72 F. Supp. 230, reported in 42 *AJIL* 223 (1948); *Chandler* v. *United States,* U.S. Court of Appeals, 1st Cir., 1948, 171 F.2d 921, digested in 43 *AJIL* 804 (1949); *certiorari* denied by Supreme Court in 1949: 336 U.S. 918.

Treasonable acts endanger the sovereignty of the United States. It has never been doubted that Congress has the power to punish an act committed beyond the territorial jurisdiction of the United States which is directly injurious to the Government of the United States.... An alien domiciled in a foreign country as the defendant Chandler admittedly was during the period alleged in the indictment was bound to obey all the laws of the German Reich as long as he remained in it, not immediately relating to citizenship, during his sojourn in it. All strangers are under the protection of a sovereign state while they are within its territory, and owe a local temporary allegiance in return for that protection....

At the same time a citizen of the United States owes to his government full, complete, and true allegiance. He may renounce and abandon it at any time. This is a natural and inherent right. When he goes abroad on a visit or for travel, he must, while abroad, obey the laws of the foreign country, where he is temporarily. In this sense and to this extent only he owes a sort of allegiance to such government, but to no extent and in no sense does this impair or qualify his allegiance or obligation to his own country or to his own government.

This statement, particularly the portions dealing with a limited allegiance owed to a foreign host government, may be taken to represent the generally accepted view. A citizen of state X, traveling in state Y, must obey the traffic and sanitation regulations imposed by local law: to that extent, as an example, he owes a limited and temporary allegiance to state Y. But in allegiance that person is, and must remain until renouncing it, a citizen and subject of state X.

In another celebrated case, *Gillars* v. *United States*,[35] the Court of Appeals, in affirming the conviction of a U.S. national for treason (voluntary broadcasting in Germany on behalf of the German government during World War II), emphatically insisted that

obedience to the law of the country of domicile or residence — local allegiance — is permissible but this kind of allegiance does not call for adherence to the enemy and the giving of aid and comfort to it with disloyal intent.

The court rejected the defendant's argument that her duties to the United States had ceased before the start of her broadcasts in Germany because an American consular officer had revoked her United States passport. Said the court: "The revocation of a passport...does not cause a loss of citizenship or dissolve the obligation of allegiance arising from citizenship."

The case now viewed as governing in the case of treason committed by aliens regarded as owing allegiance to a host state or traveling, in some manner, on its passports is that of "Lord Haw Haw" or, more properly, William Joyce.[36]

[35] U.S. Court of Appeals, 1950, 182 F.2d 962, digested in 45 *AJIL* 372 (1951).

[36] *Rex* v. *Joyce*, Great Britain, Court of Criminal Appeal, 1945, 62 *Times Law Reports*, 57. (Text, in 40 *AJIL* [1946], 210, represents also a good example of historical research.) Dismissal of Joyce's appeal had brought the case to the House of Lords.

## JOYCE v. DIRECTOR OF PUBLIC PROSECUTIONS
*Great Britain, House of Lords, 1946*
*62 Times Law Reports 208*

FACTS   Joyce was born in the United States in 1906. When he was about three years old, he was taken to Ireland, where he stayed until 1921, when he went to England. He remained in England until 1939. "He was, therefore, brought up, educated, and settled within the King's dominions." On July 4, 1933, he applied for a British passport, describing himself as a British subject by birth, claiming to have been born in Galway. The passport was requested for the purpose of holiday touring on the Continent. Joyce received the passport, valid for a period of five years. On September 26, 1938, he applied for a renewal of the passport for one year, declaring himself to be a British subject by birth.

On August 24, 1939, he applied once more for a one-year renewal of the passport, again describing himself as a British subject by birth. He then left for Germany. When he was arrested later in that country, he possessed a document showing that he had been hired by the German Radio Corporation of Berlin–Charlottenburg, as of September 18, 1939, as an announcer of English news. In this document, his "work book," Joyce's nationality was given as "Great Britain." Up to August 24, 1939, at least, Joyce owed allegiance as an alien resident, living in England under the protection of the British Crown, to the British government.

Between the beginning of his employment in Germany and until at least July 2, 1940, Joyce broadcast propaganda on behalf of the enemies of Great Britain under the name of "Lord Haw-Haw."

He was found in Germany at the end of World War II, arrested, and brought to trial in London on charges of treason. The court of first instance found him guilty, and from that verdict an appeal was taken to the Court of Criminal Appeal. On affirmation of the original verdict, the case was brought by appeal to the House of Lords.

ISSUES   [Major issues only are listed.] (1) Could a British court assume jurisdiction to try an alien for an offense against British law committed in a foreign country?

(2) Did Joyce owe any allegiance to Great Britain between September 18, 1939, and July 2, 1940?

(3) Because the renewal of Joyce's passport did not give him any British protection and he had no intention of availing himself of such, did he still owe any allegiance to Great Britain during the period spent in Germany?

DECISION   Verdict of lower court upheld. All three (major) issues answered in the affirmative.

REASONING   (1) Allegiance was owed to the Crown by such aliens as resided within the king's realm. All who were brought within the king's protection were *ad fidem regis;* they owed him allegiance from the day they came into his realm. Now, treason was the betrayal of a trust. Joyce, having long resided in British jurisdiction and owing because of this stay allegiance to the Crown, applied for and received a passport and then proceeded to adhere to the king's enemies.

(2) A passport served as a means of identification. The possession of a British passport by one who was not a British subject gave him rights and im-

posed on the sovereign obligations that would otherwise not have been given or imposed. Joyce maintained by his own act of obtaining the passport the bond that bound him to Great Britain when he resided there. As one owing allegiance to the king, he sought and obtained the protection of the king for himself while abroad. In other words, he extended the duty of allegiance beyond the moment he left English territory. As long as Joyce held the passport, he was, within the meaning of a statute of A.D. 1351, a person who, if he adhered to the king's enemies in the realm or elsewhere, committed an act of treason.

(3) Because of the foregoing conclusion, a British court possessed jurisdiction to try Joyce.

(4) Because the appellant had admittedly adhered to the king's enemies outside the realm, he had been rightly convicted. NOTE: William Joyce was subsequently executed by hanging.

## JURISDICTION OVER ARMED FORCES ABROAD

The jurisdiction of a state normally extends to its armed forces stationed beyond its territory. This authority is not as completely exclusive as might appear at first thought. Even though such armed forces enter a given state with the tacit or express permission of the territorial sovereign, they may not always be immune from the latter's jurisdiction, despite the statement of the court in the *Schwartzfiger* case[37] that "exemption from the local jurisdiction is recognized by all civilized nations; and is not considered a diminution of their sovereignty or independence."

The obvious remedy to be adopted, if a multitude of irritating controversies is to be avoided, is to conclude a special agreement with the host state, in which the latter stipulates precisely to what extent it is willing to waive any claims to jurisdiction over allied or friendly troops crossing its territory or stationed therein.

Until World War II, agreements along the lines mentioned continued to reserve far-reaching authority over visiting military forces to the host state. Thus Article IV of the Anglo-American agreement of March 27, 1941 (modified in 1950), governing the status of United States military personnel in British islands off the American coasts, reserved British authority over all nonmilitary offenses committed by such personnel outside air and naval bases. A complete waiver of jurisdiction did not occur until after the United States entered the war.

STATUS OF FORCES AGREEMENTS    Since World War II, the lessons learned during that conflict have resulted in the conclusion of so-called Status of Forces Agreements, through which the position of friendly armed forces has been regularized. At the time of this writing, the United States had left in force over 20 such agreements, of which several did not concern land-based contingents.

Thus, for example, the Status of Forces Agreement (NATO) of June 10, 1951 (in effect as of August 23, 1953), provided in Article VII for concur-

[37] Panama, Supreme Court, 1925: see Hackworth, vol. 2, 405; and 21 *AJIL* 182 (1927).

rent jurisdiction by both the sending and "receiving" states over members of the visiting military armed forces, over civilian component personnel, and over the dependents of both those categories.[38] The U.S. Congress, concerned about the fairness of trials of the groups mentioned in foreign courts, then passed legislation requiring the presence of an American observer at all foreign trials of its military personnel and the related groups mentioned. The avowed purpose was to ensure that the American constitutional rights of defendants from the three groups were safeguarded.

The Soviet Union has concluded similar agreements with the Eastern European countries in which Russian military units have been stationed.

Security treaties concluded by the United States with Japan and a number of other countries have authorized the making of administrative agreements for the disposition and immunities of United States armed forces stationed in the countries involved.[39] The operation of those postwar arrangements was illustrated in the much publicized case of *Wilson* v. *Girard.*[40]

One of the more unusual trials conducted in the United States (under the 1944 Friendly Foreign Forces Act) took place in October 1976. Not only was it the first trial conducted in the United States under that Act, but it was also the first trial since the American Revolution conducted under the laws of the British Commonwealth. The eight-day-long trial centered on a charge of rape against an Australian sailor who was in Baltimore, Maryland, in connection with the Tall Ships Bicentennial celebration in 1976. The Australian navy spent more than $100,000 flying in judges, lawyers, and other court personnel for the trial, which was held in the Washington Navy Yard. The verdict was in favor of the defendant, Kevin Clarke.[41]

Just as in the case of states, the United Nations has to make formal arrangements for the stationing of its Peace-Keeping Forces in various countries. This is normally done through an exchange of letters that takes the place of a treaty.[42] See Chapter 20 concerning UN Forces, past and present.

---

[38]Text in 48 *AJIL* 83 (1954 Supp.). Consult also Rouse and Baldwin, "The Exercise of Criminal Jurisdiction under the NATO Status of Forces Agreements," 51 *AJIL* 29 (1957), which examines many of the difficulties encountered with such concurrent jurisdiction, as well as Baxter, "Jurisdiction over Visiting Forces and the Development of International Law," *Proceedings* (1958), 174–80, with discussion of that paper, *id.,* 181. At the end of March 1989, United States forces abroad numbered 2,115,773.

[39]Consult the Note "Criminal Jurisdiction over American Armed Forces Abroad," 70 *Harvard L. R.* 1043 (1957), and see *United States* v. *Ekenstam et al.,* U.S. Court of Military Appeals, June 22, 1956, 7 U.S.M.C.A. 168, 21 C.M.R., digested in 50 *AJIL* 961 (1956). The American-Japanese Security Treaty of 1951 was replaced by a new Treaty of Mutual Cooperation and Security, signed on January 19, 1960, which also regulated the status of American armed forces in Japan: text in 38 *Current History* 293 (1960). See also *United States ex rel. Stone* v. *Robinson,* U.S. Dist. Court, W. D. Penna., Jan. 23, 1970, as amended Jan. 30, 1970, 309 F. Supp. 1261, reported in 64 *AJIL* 955 (1970).

[40]U.S. Supreme Court, 1957, 35 U.S. 324, in Friedmann, 525–28.

[41]AP dispatch, Oct. 14, 1976.

[42]See, *e.g.,* the agreement of Mar. 31, 1964, on the stationing of a UN Force in Cyprus in Henkin, 460–61.

# JURISDICTION OVER ALIEN PERSONS[43]

RIGHTS OF EXCLUSION AND DEPORTATION    The exercise of territorial jurisdiction over aliens represents one of the logical consequences of the possession of sovereignty or independence by states. Each country is free to exclude or to admit aliens; the determination of the principles to be applied in this connection is of purely domestic concern.

Concurrent with the right of exclusion goes an equally unfettered right of each state to expel not only any alien who has illegally gained entry into its territory but also any alien whose conduct, after legal entry, is deemed prejudicial to public order and security. Deportation of such unwanted aliens normally is made to their home state. The latter may refuse admission to such deportees. The usual reasons for such rejection center on the stateless character of some of the individuals in question or, even more commonly, on their criminal record.[44]

Because deportation is not a criminal proceeding—at least, not in the United States—the *ex post facto* doctrine is not applicable. Congress has an unquestioned right to legislate retroactively in order to provide legal standing for the expulsion of aliens for the commission of offenses that did not render them subject to deportation when the offenses were committed.[45]

RIGHT OF TRIAL AND PUNISHMENT    Aliens legally admitted to the territorial jurisdiction of a state may, of course, be punished for any offenses they commit on the territory of the host state or on ships or aircraft registered in that state. They may be tried and punished for having, anywhere, counterfeited its currency, postage stamps, or official documents. Any state may try and punish an alien in its territory for a crime, wherever it may have been committed, constituting piracy under the law of nations. A state may prosecute and punish aliens within its territory for a crime, regardless of its location, against its independence or security. This right is regarded as part of a nation's right of self-defense.

The United States' attitude, affirming the right of American courts to try aliens for crimes committed beyond American territorial jurisdiction, is illustrated clearly in

### UNITED STATES v. RODRIGUEZ
### U.S. District Court, S.D. Cal., 1960, 182 F. Supp. 479

FACTS    Rodriguez, a citizen of Portugal, was charged with making a false statement in an immigration application and obtaining an immigrant visa based on false claim. He represented that he was the husband of Kathleen Walker, an

---

[43] See the materials in Whiteman, vol. 8, 348–79, 427–539, 573–622, 634–60.

[44] *Caranica* v. *Nagle*, U.S. Court of Appeals, 9th Cir., 1928, 28 F. (2d) 955; but see *Narenji* v. *Civiletti*, U.S. Court of Appeals, D.C. Cir., (1979), 617 F.2d 745, analyzed by Kraiem in *Note* (Iranian Students in U.S.), 21 *Harvard Int'l. L. Jl.* 467 (1980).

[45] See *Lehmann* v. *United States ex rel. Carson*, U.S. Supreme Court, 1957, 353 U.S. 685; *Mulcahey* vs. *Catalanotte*, U.S. Supreme Court, 1957, 353 U.S. 692.

American citizen, and claimed that by reason of that marriage, he was a non-quota immigrant. The government asserted that the marriage was a sham entered into in Mexico without intention of consummation and for the sole purpose of enabling the defendant to obtain a nonquota visa, to which he was not entitled. Defendant had moved to dismiss the indictment.

ISSUE     Could an alien be tried in a United States court for an offense committed abroad?

DECISION     Motions to dismiss the indictment denied; Rodriguez was found guilty of the crime charged.

REASONING     The United States government, under what is termed the *protective principle of jurisdiction,* may acquire jurisdiction over a crime by reference to the national interest injured by the of-fense. In certain cases, in which the laws of the United States are violated and in which the crime constitutes an offense directed at the government in its capacity as sovereign, the government has the power to punish those who have broken its laws, should those persons later be found in the United States.

Entry by an alien into the United States secured by means of false statements or documents is an attack directly on the sovereignty of the United States. The crimes with which the defendant was charged fit in that category of crimes that the law of nations recognizes as offenses against sovereignty and within the express power of Congress to fashion penal legislation concerning offenses "against the Law of Nations," Article I, section 8, clause 10. Also, Congress was expressly authorized in Article III, section 2, clause 3, to provide for the place of trial when the crime has not been "committed within any State."

A growing number of states are viewing favorably a concept under which crimes committed by aliens abroad would fall within the jurisdiction of any state arresting the offender, provided that an offer of extradition had been made to the state in whose territory the crime had been committed and that this offer had not been acted on.

LEGAL POSITION OF THE ALIEN     The alien's legal position within the territorial jurisdiction of a state depends primarily on the judgment of the host government, which decides what rights, other than protection of life and property, shall be conceded to him. Most states have been willing, in recent decades, to grant to the alien civil rights substantially the same as those enjoyed by the nationals of those states, while denying to aliens the political rights and privileges enjoyed by those nationals. Thus aliens normally have the right to hold, inherit, and transfer real estate; the right to make contracts; the right to practice professions and licensed occupations (subject to certain restrictions in various states);[46] the right of religious worship (vi-

---

[46] See *Ambach v. Norwick,* U.S. Supreme Court, April 17, 1979, 99 S. Ct. 1589, reported in 73 *AJIL* 683 (1979), upholding a state law forbidding public school teaching by aliens. See also Chapter 11 under "Status of Aliens."

olated on occasion, however, in a number of states); and most of the normal civil rights in existence in a given country.

Ownership of real estate, a subject of many contentious arguments between states, is frequently restricted on a geographical basis: no alien ownership is permitted within a given distance measured from a frontier. In certain countries, aliens are banned from owning or operating specific types of industrial enterprises subject to grants of concessions by the national government, grants that by law are available only to citizens of the state in question. Ownership of media of mass communication is frequently forbidden to aliens. In the United States, certain activities are barred to aliens, such as holding public office[47] or being employed as public officers or employees declared by law to be peace officers.[48]

One of the more controversial aspects of territorial jurisdiction over aliens is their induction into the host state's armed forces or labor services. For obvious security reasons, only friendly aliens—that is, neutral citizens or "enemy citizens" opposed ideologically or in some other manner to a hostile government—are conscripted in time of war. Many, but certainly not all, countries, such as the United States, reward military service by citizenship, often through a greatly accelerated procedure of naturalization. Refusal to serve may cost the alien the chance to be naturalized at a later date and frequently leads to deportation at the earliest possible occasion. In a most interesting decision in the case of *McGrath* v. *Kristensen*,[49] the Supreme Court of the United States held that Kristensen, a Danish national who had come to the United States in August 1939 and had been unable to leave as planned because of the outbreak of war, was "not residing in the United States" for purposes of liability for military service. His filing a claim for relief from the application of the Selective Service Act did not, therefore, make Kristensen ineligible for citizenship.

An interesting situation has existed for some time in South Africa. Under the South African Amendment Act No. 43 of 1984, white residents who had been granted the status of permanent residents could be conscripted into the country's armed forces. This was made possible by the legalization of *compulsory* and *automatic* conferment of South African citizenship for certain categories and age groups of the permanent residents. Should such an alien declare his unwillingness to become a South African citizen (in order to avoid military service), the alien *ipso facto* lost his permanent resident status.

---

[47]*Sugarman* v. *Dougall*, U.S. Supreme Court, 1973, 413 U.S. 634, reported in 68 *AJIL* 335 (1974).

[48]*Cabell* v. *Chavez-Salido*, U.S. Supreme Court, 1982, 102 S. Ct. 735, reported 76 *AJIL* 616 (1982).

[49]U.S. Supreme Court, 1950, 340 U.S. 162; see also Whiteman, vol. 8, 540–73; Fitzhugh and Hyde, "The Drafting of Neutral Aliens by the United States," 36 *AJIL* 369 (1942); Houck, "Neutral Aliens Who Sought Relief from Military Service Barred from Becoming U.S. Citizens," 52 *Michigan L. Rev.* 265 (1953).

# JURISDICTION OVER ALIEN
# CORPORATIONS

A state may permit alien corporations to do business within its territorial jurisdiction, but such discretionary permission entails adherence by the enterprises concerned to all regulations issued for them by the state in question.

Even though a given enterprise may be incorporated under the laws of the state in which it operates, it may be classified and treated as an alien corporation if the test of control is applied by the state granting the charter (directly or through one of its political subdivisions).

The fact of alien ownership does not serve to protect an enterprise against nationalization, nor does such ownership—whether complete or partial, public or private—guarantee prompt, effective, and equitable compensation in the event of nationalization. In every respect (except certain foreign-government–owned enterprises of a special nature), alien holdings are on a basis of equality of treatment with the holdings of nationals of the expropriating state. (See also Chapter 11.)

MULTINATIONAL CORPORATIONS    One of the intriguing modern aspects of the relationships between a given state and alien corporations pertains to the so-called multinational corporations. These vast enterprises, with a multitude of branches and/or subsidiaries located in many countries, have been increasingly attacked, and in many instances condemned out of hand, because they have been deemed to take out all profits and to leave nothing, or to give nothing, to their various host states. There have been provable instances that these assumptions were at least partly correct and that the independence of smaller and weaker countries would be impaired seriously unless rigid controls could be established over the alien enterprises. It was feared, also, that such controls would represent impossible undertakings if attempted by the weak countries in question. During the last 20 years, beginning around 1970, such fears have abated somewhat. National investigation of multinational enterprises—of their policies, activities, and diversion of profits—began in many countries, supplemented by research and then the drafting of intergovernmental guidelines and agreements by international organizations. Thus the Organization of Economic Cooperation and Development agreed in 1976 on a (voluntary) code of conduct for multinational cooperations. The 24-member organization adopted the "code" officially in Paris on June 21, 1977.[50] In the United Nations, the chief emphasis on multinational corporation problems has centered in the Commission of Transnational Corporations and the related Centre of

---

[50] Key excerpts from the code were reproduced in *NYT*, May 27, 1976, 6; see also 15 *ILM* 961 (1976); and 18 *ILM* 986, 1171 (1979).

Transnational Corporations. The commission, at latest report, was still completing a draft code on transnational (multinational) corporations.[51]

Host states, on an individual or a regional basis, have also begun to impose a growing variety of restraints (such as the Andean Group Investment Code, 1970–1971) on the operations of alien enterprises, particularly those of a multinational character; the home countries of certain multinationals have also begun to introduce (relatively mild) restraining legislation. By 1984 it could be asserted that although abuses could still be found in the operations of multinational corporations, the entire climate in which they had been operating had begun to change on a global basis.[52]

INTERGOVERNMENTAL COMPANIES    A new variety of international corporation, public in its purposes but either private or private/public in its (legal) corporate form, has come into being since the end of World War II. Examples of this new type are, *e,g.*, the European Company for the Chemical Processing of Irradiated Fuels (Eurochemie), the International Moselle Company, the Scandinavian Airlines System (SAS), Air Afrique (formed by 11 ex-French colonies), and the International Telecommunication Satellite Organization (INTELSAT).[53]

## SUGGESTED READINGS

### Nationality

Whiteman, vol. 8, 1–22, 64–101, 105–13, 119–87; Goodwin-Gill, *International Law and the Movement of Persons between States* (1978); Plender, ed., *International Migratory Law* (1988); Hannum, *The Right to Leave and Return in International Law and Practice* (1987), and his *Basic Documents on International Migratory Law* (1988); Seidl-Hohenfeldern, *Corporations in and under International Law* (1987).

CASES

(1) General:
*Kaplan* v. *Tod,* U.S. Supreme Court, 1925, 267, U.S. 228.

---

[51]See the relevant documents, dating to 1976, 15 *ILM* 779 (1976); and also Rubin, "Reflections Concerning the United Nations Commission on Transnational Corporations," 70 *AJIL* 73 (1976). A late version of the Code is found in 22 *ILM* 192 (1983), together with the commission's relevant information paper, *id.,* 177.

[52]See, *inter alia,* Rubin, "Developments in the Law and Institutions of International Economic Relations," 68 *AJIL* 475 (1974); the various papers under the heading "Operating in More Than One Jurisdiction: The Captain's Paradise?" *Proceedings* (1974), 250–65; Simmonds, ed., *Legal Problems of Multinational Corporations* (1977); Modelski, ed., *Transnational Corporations and World Order* (1979), particularly chaps. 16–21, dealing with the regulation of multinational corporations; Vagts, "The United States and Its Multinationals: Protection and Control," 20 *Harvard Int'l L. Jl.* 235 (1979); and key excerpts from a letter dated September 18, 1979, to Senator Edward M. Kennedy from U.S. Assistant Attorney General John H. Shenefield, reproduced in 74 *AJIL* 179 (1980).

[53]On all these, and others, see Henkin, 232–34.

*Schmidt* v. *United States*, U.S. Court of Appeals, 2d Cir., 1949, 177 F.2d 450, reported in 44 *AJIL* 414 (1950).

*Stoeck* v. *Public Trustee*, Great Britain, Chancery Division, 1921, [1921] 2 Ch. 67.

*United States* v. *Best*, U.S. Dist. Court Mass., 1948, 76 F. Supp. 138 and 857; and also *Best* v. *United States*, U.S. Court of Appeals, 1st Cir., 1950, 184 F.2d 131.

*Choolokian* v. *Mission of Immaculate Virgin*, N.Y. Supreme Court, Sp. Term, N.Y. County, Dec. 30, 1947, reported in 42 *AJIL* 507 (1948).

*Ramos-Hernandez* v. *Immigration & Naturalization Service*, U.S. Court of Appeals, 9th Cir., 1977, 566 F.2d 638, reported in 72 *AJIL* 673–74 (1978).

*The Case of Leonid Rigerman, NYT,* Dec. 20, 1970, 3; Feb. 14, 1971, 8; 65 *AJIL* 393 (1971).

*United States ex rel. Schwartzkopf* v. *Uhl*, U.S. Court of Appeals, 2d Cir., 1943, 137 F.2d 898.

(2) Dual Nationality:

*The Canevaro Case,* Tribunal of the Permanent Court of Arbitration, 1912, in James B. Scott, *Hague Court Reports,* 1916, 284.

*Kawakita* v. *United States,* U.S. Supreme Court, 1952, 343 U.S. 717.

(3) Loss of Citizenship:

*Perez* v. *Brownell,* U.S. Supreme Court, 1958, 356 U.S. 44, reported in 52 *AJIL* 767 (1958).

*Trop* v. *Dulles,* U.S. Supreme Court, 1958, 356 U.S. 86, reported in 52 *AJIL* 777 (1958).

*Kennedy, Attorney General,* v. *Mendoza-Martinez; Rusk, Secretary of State,* v. *Cort,* U.S. Supreme Court, 1963, 372 U.S. 144, reported in 57 *AJIL* 666 (1963).

*Afroyim* v. *Rusk,* U.S. Supreme Court, 1967, 387 U.S. 253, reported in 62 *AJIL* 189 (1968).

## The Nottebohm Case

The commentary on the *Nottebohm* case is extensive: see the literature cited in Kunz, "The Nottebohm Judgment (Second Phase)," 54 *AJIL* 536 (1960). Consult also the digests of the decision of Nov. 18, 1953, by the Court on the Preliminary Objection, *ICJ Reports, 1953,* 111 in 48 *AJIL* 327 (1954); and of the 1955 judgment in *The Nottebohm Case (Liechtenstein* v. *Guatemala),* International Court of Justice, April 6, 1955, *ICJ Reports, 1955,* 4, in 49 *AJIL* 396 (1955).

## Jurisdiction over Nationals Abroad

Lowe, *Extraterritorial Jurisdiction* (1985); Lange and Born, eds., *The Extraterritorial Application of National Laws* (1987).

CASES

*Rex* v. *Neumann,* Union of South Africa, Special Criminal Court, Transvaal, 1946, reported in 44 *AJIL* 423 (1950).

*United States* v. *Laub,* U.S. Supreme Court, 1967, 385 U.S. 475, reported in 61 *AJIL* 808 (1967); see also the Note by McDonell, 8 *Harvard Int'l. L.Jl.,* 177 (1967).

## Stateless Persons and Refugees

Holborn, *Refugees: A Problem of Our Time (The Work of the United Nations High Commissioner for Refugees 1951–1972),* 2 vols. (1975); Weis, *Nationality and Statelessness in International Law* (2d ed., 1979); Nanda, "World Refugee Assistance: The Role of International Law and Institutions," 9 *Hofstra L. Rev.* 449 (Winter 1981); Goodwin-Gill, *The Refugee in International Law* (1985); Gorman, *Coping with Africa's Refugee Burden: A Time for Solution* (1987); Martin, *The New Asylum Seekers: Refugee Law in the 1980's* (1988); On U.S. refugee policies, see *Current Policy,* Nos. 738 (Sept. 1985); *851* (July 1986); *872* (Oct. 1986); *945* (April 1987); *981* (July 1987); *1004* (Oct. 1987); *1036* (Feb. 1988); *1052* (March 1988); *1184* (June 1989). Also see *NYT,* June 28, 1986, 9; Barnett, "Refugee Bananza for Soviet Jews and Christians," *CSM,* Aug. 28, 1989, at 19; Horst, "Refugees: A Fact of Life," *id.,* June 10, 1987, 18–19; *id.,* Sept. 25, 1986, 1, 32; and *id.,* June 16, 1987, at 16. See also the texts of U.S. 1986 legislation concerning immigration (introd. by A. H. Leibowitz) in 26 *ILM* 479 (1987), and *Time,* April 28, 1986, at 34. On deportation policies, see *CSM,* March 2, 1988, at 3.

CASES

*Coriolan* v. *Immigration and Naturalization Service,* U.S. Court of Appeals, 5th Cir., 1977, 559 F.2d 993, reported in 72 *AJIL* 924 (1978).
*Haitian Refugee Center, Inc.* v. *Gracey,* U.S. Dist. Court, D.D.C., 600 F. Supp. 1396, Jan. 10, 1985, reported in 79 *AJIL* 744 (1985).

## Position of Aliens

Union of Soviet Socialist Republics, "Law on the Legal Status of Foreign Citizens in the U.S.S.R." (June 24, 1981, entered into force on Jan. 1, 1982) in 20 *ILM* 1211 (1981); Council of Europe, *Human Rights of Aliens in Europe* (1985).

CASES

*United States* v. *Rocha,* U.S. Court of Appeals, 2d Cir., 1961, 228 F.2d 545, *certiorari denied,* 1961, 366 U.S. 942.
*United States* v. *Pizzarusso,* U.S. Court of Appeals, 2d Cir., 1968, reported in 62 *AJIL* 975 (1968).
*Abourezk* v. *Reagan,* U.S. Court of Appeals, D.C. Cir., March 11, 1986, in 25 *ILM* 319 (1986), affirmed by Supreme Court in a 3–3 deadlock on Oct. 19, 1987.

## Authority over Armed Forces Abroad

Whiteman, vol. 6, 379–427; F. Kalshoven, "Criminal Jurisdiction over Military Persons in the Territory of a Friendly Foreign Power," 5 *Tijdschrift* 165 (1958). On U.S. foreign military bases and troops abroad, see 15 *Defense Monitor,* No. 4 (1986); *U.S. News & World Report,* Oct. 20, 1986, 16–18, and June 29, 1987, 28; *CSM* March 17, 1987, 2 and 9, March 30, 1987, at 12, April 27, 1987, at 4, Sept. 30, 1988, at 2, Nov. 23, 1988, at 2; *Time,* Oct. 10, 1988, at 60.

CASES

*Reid* v. *Covert; Kinsella* v. *Krueger (On Rehearing),* U.S. Supreme Court, 1957, 354 U.S. 1, excerpted at length in 51 *AJIL* 783 (1957).

*United States* v. *Keaton,* U.S. Court of Military Appeals, 1969, reported in 64 *AJIL* 431 (1970).

*Williams* v. *Rogers,* U.S. Court of Appeals, 8th Cir., 1971, 449 F. 2d 513, reported 66 *AJIL* 402 (1972).

*Public Prosecutor* v. *Starks and Eaton,* Republic of China, Taiwan High Court, Taichung Branch, 1971, reported in 70 *AJIL* 145 (1976).

*Holmes* v. *Laird,* U.S. Court of Appeals, D.C., 1972, 459 F.2d 1211, reported in 67 *AJIL* 153 (1973); decision reproduced in full in 11 *ILM* 584 (1972).

*Christopher Collins et al.* v. *Caspar Weinberger, Secretary of Defense, et al.,* U.S. Court of Appeals, D.C., No. 82–1857, May 17, 1983, in 22 *ILM* 799 (1983).

## The Interhandel Case

Briggs, "Towards the Rule of Law?" 51 *AJIL* 517 (1957) and the reply by Jacoby, "Towards the Rule of Law?" 52 *AJIL* 107 (1958); Mason, "The General Aniline and Film Co. Case," *Proceedings* (1958), 114–25, and the commentaries thereon, at 125–32; Briggs, "Interhandel: The Court's Judgment of March 21, 1959, on the Preliminary Objections of the United States," 53 *AJIL* 547 (1959); *Interhandel Case (Switzerland* v. *U.S.A.)* (Request by the Swiss Government for the Indication of Interim Measures of Relief), *Order of the International Court of Justice, October 24, 1957,* in *ICJ Reports, 1957,* digested in 52 *AJIL* 320 (1958), and the text of the Judgment itself, *ICJ Reports 1959,* 6, or an excellent digest by Bishop in 53 *AJIL* 671 (1959). Consult also Simmonds, "The Interhandel Case," 10 *Int'l. and Comp. L. Quarterly* 495 (1961). For various stages in the lengthy litigation, consult 46 *AJIL* 554 (1952); 51 *AJIL* 818 (1957); 53 *AJIL* 177, 671 (1959); 59 *AJIL* 97 (1965); 61 *AJIL* 615 (1967); and *Newsweek,* March 22, 1965, 71.

## Multinational Corporations

Kumar and McLeod, eds., *Multinationals from Developing Countries* (1981); Feld, *Multinational Corporations and U.N. Politics: The Quest for Codes of Conduct* (1980); Akinsanya, *Multinationals in a Changing Environment* (1984); Rubin, "Transnational Corporations and International Law: An Uncertain Partnership," 4 *Chinese Yrbk. of Int'l. Law* (1985) 39; Kline, *International Codes and Multinational Business* (1985); Acquaah, *International Regulation of Transnational Corporations: The New Reality* (1986).

# 10

# Individuals Under the Law

### THE INDIVIDUAL: FROM OBJECT TO OBJECT

Before the twentieth century, the virtually universal belief prevailed that the treatment of its citizenry by a state fell outside the province of international law, inasmuch as the individual, alone or collectively, was merely an object and not a subject of the law of nations.

Since World War I, however, the community of nations has become increasingly aware of the need to safeguard the minimal rights of the individual. In consequence, human rights have become a matter of vital and, at times, acrimonious concern to the traditional subjects of international law, and the individual has begun to emerge, to some extent at least, as a subject of that law.

#### Restrictions on the Jurisdiction of States over Their Nationals

Early concern about what are today called human rights was limited to a guarantee of certain religious rights to minority groups within the populations of given states. The broader concerns with the rights of human beings to life, liberty, and also equality before the law were mostly unformulated politically and legally until the last decades of the nineteenth century, being bound up with the emergence of democratic forms of government.

The numerous changes in territorial ownership occurring after World War I pointed up the need for an expansion of the rights guaranteed to minorities, particularly because of the growth of nationalistic sentiments and the very real danger of suppression and oppression faced by racial, ethnic, linguistic, and religious minorities. In consequence, the Principal Allied and Associated Powers concluded a number of treaties with such countries as Czechoslovakia, Austria, Greece, Bulgaria, Hungary, Poland, Turkey, Rumania, and Yugoslavia, in which those states promised just and equal treatment of their minority groups.

Sometime later, similar guarantees were given by Albania, Estonia, Iraq, Latvia, and Lithuania, as conditions of their admission to the League of Nations. Unlike the earlier guarantees, however, these subsequent grants of rights to minorities took the form of unilateral declarations by the countries in question. In turn, a legal obligation was created for those declarations by various resolutions adopted by the Council of the League.

MINORITIES CLAUSES   In order to ensure observance of the various rights guaranteed to minorities, the affected sovereign states acknowledged the "minorities clauses" to constitute "fundamental laws" and agreed that the clauses were "placed under the guarantee of the League of Nations" and would not be altered without the consent of a majority of the League's Council. The League, in turn, worked out a definitive procedure to be adopted in dealing with any questions arising under the clauses in question.

All this looked fine on paper, but trouble appeared as soon as implementation became the issue. Regardless of the motives that had inspired acquiescence in the guarantees extended to minorities, the governments in question all too soon shared a growing conviction that the guarantees represented intolerable intrusions into the domestic jurisdictions of sovereign states. The Permanent Court of International Justice had to point out again and again that mere laws were not enough, that the prohibitions laid down in the minorities clauses had to operate in fact, and that a law supposedly general in its effects but actually discriminating against minorities and their members constituted a violation of obligations. [1]

During World War II the necessity of promoting and preserving human freedoms and rights was affirmed in such statements as the Atlantic Charter (August 14, 1941), the Declaration by the (wartime) United Nations (January 1, 1942), and the Tehran Declaration (December 1, 1943). In the Nuremberg war crimes trials, there was an assumption implicit in the proceedings that the international community could apply international law directly to individuals. [2] But after the war, no provisions for the protection of minorities were included in the various peace treaties except, on a limited basis, in the Italian Treaty (Annex N, par. 1) and in the Austrian State Treaty (Art. 7). On the other hand, such treaties, with the exception of the one concluded in 1951 with Japan, provided for the granting of human rights and freedoms to individuals by Bulgaria, Finland, Hungary, Italy, and Rumania, and these requirements were also incorporated in the 1955 Austrian instrument.

## UN Emphasis on Human Rights

UN CHARTER   The interest in the subject of human rights, arising sporadically in the United Nations beginning with the founding Conference of San Francisco in 1945, has been characteristic of a modern disposition to enlarge the concept of what is legitimately of international interest or concern. [3] The Charter of the United Nations asserts in the sweeping terms

[1] See Advisory Opinion relating to *German Settlers in Poland,* Ser. B, No. 6; Advisory Opinion on the *Treatment of Polish Nationals in Danzig,* Ser. A/B, No. 44; Advisory Opinion on *Minority Schools in Albania,* Ser. A/B, No. 64.
[2] Jessup, *A Modern Law of Nations* (1946), 161–62; Wright, *Contemporary International Law: A Balance Sheet* (1945), 19–23.
[3] Consult the suggestive and valuable Luard, ed., *The International Protection of Human Rights* (1967).

of its Preamble that the members are "determined . . . to reaffirm faith in fundamental human rights, in the dignity and worth of the human person, in the equal rights of men and women." "Article 1 of the Charter lists, among the purposes of the organization, the "promoting and encouraging [of] respect for human rights and for fundamental freedoms for all without distinction as to race, sex, language, or religion." Article 13 assigns to the General Assembly the task of initiating and making recommendations directed to the accomplishment of these purposes. Article 55(c) commits the United Nations to promote "universal respect for, and observance of, human rights and fundamental freedoms." Article 62 directs the Economic and Social Council to make recommendations in pursuance of Article 55(c), and Article 68 sets up a commission for the "promotion of human rights."

This multitude of provisions did not spell out, however, any bill of human rights, beyond mentioning discrimination, nor did it command the members to enact and enforce appropriate domestic legislation. In fact, no sanctions or enforcement machinery were set up. Only Article 56 represented a pledge by all member states to take joint and separate action to achieve the purposes outlined in Article 55.

It should be remembered also that Article 2 (7) of the UN Charter denied authority to the United Nations "to intervene in matters which are essentially within the domestic jurisdiction of any state." This *explicit* prohibition appeared to limit the rights of the organization to deal with alleged violations of human rights beyond discussion in the General Assembly and recommendations with regard to such violations. Furthermore, it appeared that if any member state heeded such recommendations and acted on them against a state accused of violating human rights, a charge of illegal intervention in the internal affairs of a sovereign state could be lodged. The General Assembly did engage in such discussions on numerous occasions. It should be noted, however, that the denial of human rights does not in every single instance represent a threat to international peace, contrary to what the United Nations tends to assume in cases selected arbitrarily by itself. Were all countries to go along with the UN thesis, wholesale intervention in domestic affairs of countries would be justified on the basis of a somewhat untenable presumption.

In order to achieve positive protection of human rights, the Economic and Social Council (hereafter abbreviated as ECOSOC) proceeded as early as 1946 to produce multilateral conventions through the Commission on Human Rights as a drafting body. The obvious by-product of such an endeavor, if successful, would be the shift of the individual into the position of a partial subject of international law.

Ultimately, on December 10, 1948, the General Assembly approved the Universal Declaration of Human Rights, with no opposition, but with eight abstentions (the Soviet bloc, Yugoslavia, Saudi Arabia, and South

Africa).[4] This document of 30 articles, containing a detailed list of personal, civil, political, and social rights "as a common standard of achievement for all peoples and all nations," nevertheless had to be judged to be vague and even ambiguous in parts. Being merely a declaration, it possessed no legally binding force, being comparable in this respect to the hortatory clauses found in some of the older state constitutions in the United States. Legal obligations can be created only through the ratification by member states of some convention on human rights, not by a voting consensus of the General Assembly. Furthermore, Article 22 of the declaration recognized that the realization of the rights in question had to be in accordance with the organization and resources of each state.

On the other hand, the Declaration had to be considered an expository interpretation of the Charter's very general human rights provisions, and those provisions represented, at least in theory, binding obligations on all member states. The Declaration has also served as a convenient standard by which many jurists and even national courts have evaluated compliance with the broad human rights provisions of the UN Charter. The Declaration should, therefore, be viewed as marking a definite advance toward the realization of human rights, on a global basis and as somewhat distinct from other declarations adopted by the General Assembly.

A number of jurists have argued that the Declaration has acquired the status of customary international law. The present writer disagrees with that view, but supports the more limited concept that *some* of the rights listed in the Declaration (such as freedom from torture, slavery, murder, etc.) are parts of customary international law. There also is a growing belief in legal circles that government policies of discrimination related to rights catalogued in the Declaration represent violations of the UN Charter.

The next step was the creation of draft treaties (styled Human Rights Covenants) for eventual ratification by the members. It is interesting, however, that a number of states proceeded at once to include selected portions of the Universal Declaration into their domestic law and that certain international agreements incorporated all of the rights cited in the declaration.

The Commission of Human Rights proposed at first a single instrument, covering all aspects of such rights, but such an omnibus covenant encountered sufficient opposition in the General Assembly so that several instruments were produced subsequently: the International Covenant on Civil and Political Rights; the International Covenant on Economic, Social and Cultural Rights; and the Optional Protocol to the Covenant on Civil and Political Rights. Although the initial drafts were completed in 1954, bitter disagreements about the contents and enforcement provisions in both the General Assembly and its Third Committee resulted in delay and in

[4]Text in *Yearbook of the United Nations, 1948–1949,* 535–37, and in many other readily available sources. The Communist states later accepted the Declaration in the Final Act of the Helsinki Conference of 1975.

considerable redrafting. Finally, the instruments were adopted by the General Assembly (December 16, 1966): the Covenants 106–0, the Protocol 66–2. They represent the achievement of the "international bill of rights" contemplated by the Assembly when it adopted the Universal Declaration in 1948.[5]

COVENANT OF CIVIL AND POLITICAL RIGHTS    The Covenant on Civil and Political Rights guarantees freedom of religious expression, peaceful assemblage, and movement. It prohibits inhuman treatment as well as arbitrary arrest or detention, asserts a right to life and to a fair trial, and provides for the protection of all varieties of minorities. Under the provisions of the Optional Protocol, individuals and groups are granted the right to appeal to the 32-member UN Commission on Human Rights. Both the covenant and the Optional Protocol entered into force on March 23, 1976; by February 1984, 73 countries had ratified or acceded to the Covenant. The United States signed (but did not ratify) the Covenant on October 5, 1977. On the other hand, only 28 parties had ratified or acceded to the Optional Protocol by February 1984.

COVENANT ON ECONOMIC, SOCIAL, AND CULTURAL RIGHTS    The Covenant on Economic, Social, and Cultural Rights embraces the right to work, education, medical care, and related economic and social benefits. It entered into force on January 3, 1976; by February 1984, 75 countries had ratified or acceded to the Covenant. The signature of the United States (but not its ratification) was added on October 5, 1977.[6]

Both covenants became the object of bitter (and at times misinformed) criticism. Several presidents failed to transmit the two instruments to the U.S. Senate mostly because of honest doubts about certain provisions in both covenants that were felt to be in violation of the Constitution or the laws of the United States. A considerable body of public opinion arguably agreed with the view that: "We believe that under present conditions 'economic and social rights' are really more in the nature of aspirations and goals than 'rights.' This semantic distinction is highly important. It does not make sense to proclaim that a particular level of economic and social entitlements are rights if most governments are not able to provide them. In contrast, any government can guarantee political and civil rights to its citizens."[7]

Finally President Carter sent both covenants to the Senate for advice and consent to ratification (February 23, 1978), but he indicated in his transmittal precisely what reservations, understandings, and declarations

[5] Texts of the three instruments reprinted in 61 *AJIL* 861 (1967); see also Henkin, ed., *The International Bill of Rights: The Covenant on Civil and Political Rights* (1981).
[6] See Alston, "U.S. Ratification of the Covenant on Economic, Social and Cultural Rights: The Need for an Entirely New Strategy," 84 *AJIL* 365 (1990).
[7] Dobriansky (Deputy Asst. Secretary for Human Rights and Humanitarian Affairs), "U.S. Human Rights Policy: An Overview," *Current Policy No. 1091*, (Sept. 1988), 2–3.

were being forwarded to the Senate.[8] Those reservations pertained mostly to conflicts between a provision in a covenant and relevant provisions in the U.S. Constitution or legislation. At the time of writing, the Senate has taken no action on either covenant beyond holding preliminary hearings in November 1979. It should be noted that neither instrument contains provisions for effective enforcement in the event of its violation.

When the Soviet Union ratified both covenants on September 27, 1973, it did not ratify the Optional Protocol, and semiofficial Soviet sources asserted that the Covenant on Civil and Political Rights justified its curbs on emigration.

Implementation of the Covenant on Civil and Political Rights was entrusted to the Human Rights Committee (HRC). Because both state-to-state complaints and individual communications are optional, the main portion of the committee's work has centered on the reports submitted to it by states. To the writer's knowledge, the committee has made only one decision on an individual communication (*Communication No. R.1/5, of Valentini de Bazzano: Violation of the Covenant in Uruguay*), on August 15, 1979.[9]

Other draft instruments in the sphere of human rights adopted by the General Assembly also tended to transform the individual into a partial subject of international law. Thus the International Convention on the Elimination of All Forms of Racial Discrimination, adopted unanimously in 1965, represented a detailed prohibition of 19 objectionable discriminatory practices, with nine articles devoted to implementation. That instrument entered into force on January 4, 1969, though not for the United States.[10]

In its 1967 session, the General Assembly, besides urging speedy ratification of the Anti-Radical Discrimination Treaty, also adopted the Declaration on the Elimination of Discrimination against Women and the Declaration on Territorial Asylum. And in 1981 the Assembly adopted the Declaration on the Elimination of All Forms of Intolerance and of Discrimination Based on Religion or Belief.[11]

---

[8]See details in 72 *AJIL* 620, 623 (1978). Concerning the problems posed by the two covenants for the United States in its internal and foreign policies, consult, *inter alia,* Van Dyke, *Human Rights, the United States, and World Community* (1970); Ferguson, "The United Nations Human Rights Covenants: Problems of Ratification and Implementation," *Proceedings* (1968), 83; statements by Deputy Secretary of State Warren Christopher and Assistant Secretary of Human Rights and Humanitarian Affairs Patricia N. Derian before the Senate Committee on Foreign Relations, Nov. 14, 1979, reproduced in *Current Policy, No. 112* (Dec. 1979); and a letter from a U.S. Assistant Legal Adviser (Apr. 16, 1980), reproduced in part in 74 *AJIL* 661 (1980).

[9]Text of decision in 19 *ILM* 133 (1980).

[10]Text in 5 *ILM* 350 (1966). The treaty had been signed on behalf of the United States on Sept. 28, 1966. President Carter sent it to the Senate on Feb. 28, 1978; see 72 *AJIL* 620 (1978), concerning the various reservations and understanding accompanying the letter of transmittal. At the time of this writing, no Senate action on the treaty had taken place. Consult also the monograph by Nathanson and Schwelb, *The United States and the United Nations Treaty on Racial Discrimination* (1975).

[11]The Convention entered into force in 1981, but not yet for the United States; the 1981 Declaration (Resolution 36/55, consisting of eight Articles) is found in 21 *ILM* 205 (1982).

Twelve years after the inception of the project, the General Assembly at last adopted the comprehensive Convention on the Elimination of All Forms of Discrimination against Women (Res. 34/180, December 18, 1979, with 130 in favor, none against, 10 abstentions), which entered into force on September 3, 1981, though the United States is not a party to the treaty.[12]

Related instruments recently under consideration by the Third Committee of the General Assembly include a draft declaration and draft convention on the Elimination of All Forms of Religious Intolerance, and the Convention on the Non-Applicability of Statutory Limitations on War Crimes and Crimes Against Humanity (see Chapter 27).

Many years ago the United Nations established the Human Rights Commission under the ECOSOC, designed to develop the United Nations' human rights programs, as laid down in the Charter and in the Universal Declaration. Composed of 43 members, elected from as many member states, the commission meets annually for five weeks. It has been criticized severely over the years for confining its investigations to South Africa, Chile, and the Israeli-occupied Arab territories at a time when wholesale violations of human rights have been taking place in dozens of other countries, such as Burundi, Uganda, the Soviet Union, South Korea, Cambodia, Bolivia, Argentina, and Uruguay. Commission subgroups, to be sure, have reviewed complaints about countries that showed a consistent pattern of "gross violations."[13] But although the subgroups reported to the commission, no action in the form of an inquiry was taken, except on the perennial three cases mentioned above.

The most recent expansion by the United Nations of the scope of human rights came with the adoption by the General Assembly of the UN Convention on the Rights of the Child (November 28, 1989).[14] That instrument entered into force on September 2, 1990, and by September 27 a total of 45 states had ratified the convention. The latter figure, however, included only five Western countries (France, the Vatican State, Portugal, Sweden, and the Soviet Union). The United States was not among the more than 100 countries to sign the treaty. That decision apparently was based on two major U.S. objections: the convention prohibited the death penalty for persons under the age of 18, and it did not define a fetus as a child and thus protected by the treaty.

The major weakness of virtually all recent UN instruments dealing with human (and therefore individual) rights lies in their implementation. Most governments view with mixed feelings the growth of the doctrine that under

[12] Text of 1979 convention in 19 *ILM* 34 (1980).
[13] See Statement by Ambassador Jeane J. Kirkpatrick, *Double Standards in Human Rights, Current Policy No. 353* (Nov. 24, 1981).
[14] Text of the convention was reprinted in 28 *ILM* 1448 (1988), with corrections to the text in *id* 1340 (1990). A list of ratifying countries as of Sept. 27, 1990, appeared in *id* 1339 (1990). See also *Current Policy No. 1237* (Defining the Rights of Children) (Dec. 1989).

certain explicit conditions, individuals may be, and should be, considered subjects of international law. Some countries, such as the Soviet Union, even insisted that no individual may claim UN protection against his own state: it is asserted that United Nations jurisdiction in the sphere of human rights is limited to preventing danger to peace and that this means discrimination against an entire racial group, such as in the instance of South Africa's *apartheid*. [15] Ratification of a human rights covenant is viewed by many states as somewhat dangerous, even without the presence of effective implementation provisions. If the latter were to be provided, then reluctance might easily change to unwillingness to participate in any effort to promote human rights. Nevertheless, the principal objective of such rights covenants is the creation of domestic laws conforming to an international standard. This objective represents the essence of any attempt to protect the individual through the means of international law. On the other hand, some believe that the continued production of nonimplemented conventions on human rights has harmed the United Nations as well as the ECOSOC.

Nevertheless, if and when human rights covenants, together with implementing provisions or protocols, have come into force through governmental ratification or adherence, the individual will have become, under specified conditions, a subject of international law, enjoying qualified but real rights under that law. [16]

REGIONAL AGENCIES: EUROPE    Before leaving this subject, brief attention must be paid to regional efforts in the sphere of human rights and freedoms. Perhaps more important, in the short run, than the activities of the United Nations has been a relatively early European attempt to protect human rights: in 1953 there entered into force the European Convention for the Protection of Human Rights and Fundamental Freedoms, signed in Rome in 1950. [17] Fifteen states have now been obligated through their ratifications to submit designed types of human rights disputes among themselves to

[15] On February 10, 1989, however, the Presidium of the USSR Supreme Soviet adopted a Decree under which the Soviet Union recognized the binding jurisdiction of the International Court of Justice in respect of the following international agreements: 1948 Convention on the Prevention and Punishment of the Crime of Genocide, 1949 Convention for the Suppression of the Traffic in Persons and of the Exploitation of the Prostitution of Others, 1952 Convention on the Political Rights of Women, 1965 International Convention on the Elimination of All Forms of Racial Discrimination, 1979 Convention on the Elimination of All Forms of Discrimination against Women, and 1984 Convention against Torture and Other Cruel, Inhuman or Degrading Treatment or Punishment. See 83 *AJIL* 457 (1989) for letter of transmittal to the UN Secretary-General.

[16] See 1 *The International Lawyer* 589 (July 1967), for texts of other UN Human Rights Conventions: on slavery (1956), on forced labor (1957), and on the political rights of women (1953); consult Carey, "The U.N.'s Double Standard on Human Rights Complaints," 60 *AJIL* 792 (1966).

[17] Text in 45 *AJIL* 24 (1951 Supp.); see also discussion of the convention in *Manual*, 503–5; Weil, "The Evolution of the European Convention on Human Rights," 57 *AJIL* 804 (1963).

binding decisions of an international agency. And 10 of the states concerned have gone farther and have granted to private associations as well as to individuals the right to file complaints.

Initially, complaints are received and investigated by the European Commission on Human Rights, consisting of one member from each of the ratifying states. If a complaint is found admissible, a subcommission hears the complaint, with a view to negotiating a friendly solution. To be sure, only a tiny fraction of all complaints have thus far been found admissible: a majority have had to be rejected because the state in question had not been among those permitting the filing of complaints by individuals or because local remedies had not been exhausted by the complainants, among other reasons.

If the subcommission fails to achieve a satisfactory settlement, the full commission normally reviews the complaint for a finding of facts and an opinion on the merits, both of which are then sent to the Committee of Ministers of the Council of Europe, which is empowered to hand down a binding decision by a two-thirds vote. For those states that have ratified an optional protocol conferring jurisdiction on the European Court of Human Rights, a binding decision will be issued by that court, which consists of 18 judges elected by the Assembly of the Council of Europe, one from each member state of the council. Noncompliance with a decision of the court entails at most adverse publicity, because no enforcement machinery was provided in the basic convention or in the optional protocol. In the event of a refusal to carry out a human rights decision handed down by the Committee of Ministers, enforcement measures appear to be limited to publicity and possibly to expulsion from the Council of Europe under the provisions of Article 8 of its statute.

In 1927 the European Court held in the Simmenthal case [1978, ECR 629] that the national courts of member states of the Community had to apply Community law and had to refuse to apply any national law in conflict with Community law.

An interesting procedural development came when a state rather than an individual brought an application to the Commission. Only one case, relating to Northern Ireland,[18] has been brought by a state and referred to the Court by the European Commission of Human Rights: the case brought in 1982 against Turkey by applications by France, Norway, Denmark, Sweden, and the Netherlands[19] resulted in the first "friendly settlement" reached by the Commission in an interstate litigation; other cases were handled by the Committee of Ministers.

The Convention on Human Rights has been, thus far, more effective than many jurists had anticipated, even though only 2 percent of all complaints have been found admissible. Several relatively significant cases were rendered

---

[18] *Lawless Case* (Merits), European Court of Human Rights, 1961, in 56 *AJIL* 187 (1961).
[19] *Report of the Commission* in 25 *ILM* 308 (1986).

innocuous when the states involved quickly changed the relevant legislation in anticipation of an unfavorable decision by the court. Individuals have also benefited by being given comprehensive procedural protection before the court in such matters as the right to counsel and private hearings.

The Soviet Union and its allies in the Warsaw Pact had pressed since 1954 for a European Conference on Security and Cooperation, initially intended to be limited to European states. Eventually it was agreed that the United States and Canada, in view of their NATO commitments, should also participate. Multilateral preparatory talks began in November 1972, and the working phase of the conference began in September 1973. It ended on July 19, 1975, when it was announced that a final document would be signed by the representatives of the 35 participating states at a meeting in Helsinki (July 30–August 1, 1975). That instrument, the "Final Act" of the conference, was termed the Declaration of Principles Guiding Relations between Participating States.[20] Contrary to journalistic reports at the time, the document signed was merely a political statement of intent; it was not a treaty, nor could it be regarded as a legally binding agreement in international law terminology. Section VIII ("Basket Three") of the declaration deals with human rights, including freedom of thought, conscience, religion or belief, citing the UN Charter, the Universal Declaration, and the two UN covenants.

In summary, the Final Act called on the 35 signatory states to respect the human rights and individual freedoms mentioned above; respect the inviolability of existing borders; refrain from the threat or use of force against any state; refrain from any intervention, direct or indirect, in the internal or external affairs of other states; grant exit visas to permit the reunification of families; support confidence-building measures such as advance notification of military maneuvers and exchange of observers for maneuvers; and facilitate a freer exchange of people, publications, and information.[21]

It was also decided that at least one follow-up conference should be held at Belgrade in 1977. That session ended on March 8, 1978, with a "Concluding Document"[22] that made no mention of "Basket Three."

The 1980 Madrid Conference opened on schedule on November 11, after nine weeks of preliminary talks, during which it proved to be impossible to agree even on an agenda for the conference. With misgivings, the Spanish prime minister opened the first plenary session, remarking that "sometimes it seems we are engaged in a dialogue of the deaf." His pessimism was well founded: instead of lasting for a few months as planned, the Madrid meeting continued for 32 months, well into 1983, a victim of the breakdown of

---

[20]Text in 70 *AJIL* 417 (1976). It is of interest to note that among the 35 signatories were the Holy See, Liechtenstein, Monaco, and San Marino.
[21]See, *inter alia,* Russell, "The Helsinki Declaration: Brobdingnag or Lilliput?" 70 *AJIL* 242 (1976); Buergenthal, ed., *Human Rights, International Law and the Helsinki Accord* (1977).
[22]Text in 17 *ILM* 414 (1978); see also a collection of related documents, *id.,* 1206.

East-West détente and also of a "consent rule" requiring all 35 participants to agree to all decisions. (By February 1982, the Spanish foreign minister referred to the conference as "an international meeting with Franz Kafka in the chair.") Disagreements about human rights as well as over the Soviet invasion of Afghanistan blocked progress on countless occasions, and at the very end, Malta held out stubbornly for its demand for a follow-up conference on security in the Mediterranean, leading to several proposals to expel the Republic of Malta (which eventually withdrew its demand and voted for the conference's final agreement). Despite minor compromises achieved during the long meeting, the results had to be viewed as extremely disappointing.[23]

Next, a conference held at Vienna (November 1986–January 17, 1989) resulted in the adoption of a human rights and security agreement by a consensus of the 35 original signers of the Helsinki Accords. Only Romania refused to commit itself to a pledge to grant greater religious freedom and emigration rights.[24]

The writer has been criticized about the amount of space given to the Madrid Conference and the early history of the Helsinki Accords. The reason for the anecdotal digression was a desire to show some of the difficulties encountered in developing humanitarian (or human rights) law.

The "Helsinki Process" was implemented strikingly by three conferences held in 1990: the Bonn Conference on Economic Cooperation in Europe (April), the Copenhagen meeting of the Conference on the Human Dimension (June),[25] and the November meeting of the Conference for Security and Cooperation in Europe (CSCE) in Paris.

Whereas the Bonn conference was directed exclusively at economic questions, the Copenhagen meeting, attended by 35 participating states and one observer (Albania), centered on fundamental freedoms and every conceivable variety of human rights, including the rights of the child (see below).

The Paris conference of CSCE, attended by representatives of 34 states (including the Soviet Union, the United States, and Canada), resulted in two major agreements:

1. A major weapons reduction treaty, reducing dramatically the conventional arms arsenals of European states, together with a secondary agree-

---

[23]See 22 *ILM* 1395 (1983), and the excellent summary (to Oct. 1986) by the Office of the Historian, Department of State, "The Conference on Security and Cooperation in Europe," Department of State Publication No. 9511 (Oct. 1986).

[24]The documents for the earlier Madred meeting are to be found in 22 *ILM* 1395 (1983); those from the Vienna meeting, in 28 *ILM* 527 (1989); see also the AP dispatches to major metropolitan newspapers on Jan. 16, 1989. The interesting *Current Policy Nos. 813* (Apr. 1956), *914* (Feb. 1987), and *920* (Mar. 1987), relating to East-West diplomacy and to the Soviet Union, are unfortunately somewhat dated today.

[25]Texts of final documents see 29 *ILM* 1054 (1990) for Bonn, and 29 ILM 1305 (1990) for Copenhagen.

ment signed by the 22 states members of NATO and the Warsaw Pact, disclaiming any future aggression against each other.
2. The so-called Charter of Paris, in which the 34 leaders present declared the end of the Cold War and promised that all future relations between them would be based on respect and cooperation. In addition, the Charter contained provisions for regular meetings of heads of state, foreign ministers, and senior foreign office personnel. It also called for the opening of a small CSCE administrative secretariat in Prague, for an office in Warsaw to monitor elections, and for a conflict prevention center, to be located temporarily in Vienna. Mentioned favorably but not detailed in the Charter was also the concept of a CSCE parliamentary assembly.

REGIONAL AGENCIES: LATIN AMERICA    The Eighth Conference of American States, meeting in Lima in 1938, approved a resolution (XXXVI) condemning the persecution of individuals or groups for racial or religious motives, at the same time denying (Resolution XXVII) the right of any racial or religious group to claim the status of a minority. By the spring of 1948, however, concern about human rights and their protection led to the adoption, at the Ninth Conference of American States, of Resolution XXX, the American Declaration of the Rights and Duties of Man.[26] This document contains no enforcement provisions, but lists in great detail the rights in question. Articles 29 to 38, however, cover duties that in a number of instances really represent additional rights rather than duties per se.

In 1959, the Fifth Meeting of Consultation of Ministers of Foreign Affairs, in Santiago, Chile, created the Inter-American Commission on Human Rights to promote respect for human rights. The commission has been composed of seven members, elected, as individuals, by the OAS Council.[27] Its functions were expanded in November 1965, at the Second Special Inter-American Conference at Rio de Janeiro, through Resolution XXII. But this enlargement was limited to setting up an information and reporting service for the commission; no true enforcement machinery was created.[28]

In view of the continuing widespread violations of human rights in Latin American countries, such as Argentina, Brazil, Chile, El Salvador, Guatemala, Haiti, Nicaragua, Paraguay, Peru, and Uruguay, the Commission on Human Rights has had to answer many complaints by means of careful investigation.[29] It has to be noted, however, that the OAS accepted a number of the reports in question by means of greatly toned-down res-

[26]Text in 43 *AJIL* 133 (1949 Supp.).

[27]See Pan American Union, *Doc. 89* (English), Rev. 2, Oct. 12, 1959, 10. Consult also Thomas Buergenthal, "The Revised OAS Charter and the Protection of Human Rights," 69 *AJIL* 828 (1975).

[28]See Fox, "Inter-American Commission on Human Rights Finds United States in Violation," 82 *AJIL* 601 (1988).

[29]See, for instance, the excerpts from its "Report on the Status of Human Rights in Chile (1974)," 14 *ILM* 115 (1975).

olutions so as to avoid embarrassment to the countries criticized. In the instance of one report on Chile, it has been claimed that at one point in the OAS proceedings, Chile expressed a willingness to vote in favor of its own condemnation for government-sanctioned violations of human rights, in view of the innocuous resolution of censure—but then reconsidered in view of the likely unfavorable publicity.

On the other hand, the Commission did meet (April 21, 1980) with the president of Colombia and subsequently assisted in solving the crisis of the diplomatic hostages held in the Dominican embassy in Bogotá.

In November 1969, in San José, Costa Rica, the OAS adopted a comprehensive American Convention on Human Rights, complete with provisions for the Inter-American Court of Human Rights.[30] Modeled closely on the European human rights convention model, the inter-American instrument appeared to be very promising at the time of its creation, but the subsequent record on the protection of human rights by many Latin American countries has been deplorable. The court handed down its first decision on November 13, 1982: *Government of Costa Rica (In the Matter of Viviana Gallardo et al.).*[31] The court refused to admit the application of Costa Rica and referred the matter to the Inter-American Commission. In September 1982, the court handed down two Advisory Opinions, relating to two articles in the American Convention on Human Rights.[32] By May 10, 1990, a total of 11 State Parties to the Convention had ratified (recognized as binding) the jurisdiction of the Inter-American Court on all matters relating to the interpretation or application of the Convention.

REGIONAL AGENCIES: AFRICA   In June 1981, the Eighteenth Assembly of Heads of State and Government of the Organization of African Unity adopted (in Banjul, The Gambia) the Banjul Charter on Human and Peoples' Rights, the first human rights convention on the African continent.[33] This instrument, not yet in effect at the time of writing, provided, among other things, for an African Commission on Human and Peoples' Rights.

---

[30]Text in 65 *AJIL* 679 (1971), and 9 *ILM* 673 (1970). The convention entered into force on July 18, 1978. It had been signed on behalf of the United States on June 1, 1977. On Feb. 23, 1978, President Carter transmitted the convention to the Senate for advice and consent to ratification. At this time, there has been no Senate action. See the analysis of the convention in the "Report of the Delegation to the Inter-American Specialized Conference on Human Rights (Apr. 22, 1970)," in 9 *ILM* 710 (1970); the Statute of the Court in 19 *ILM* 634 (1980).

[31]20 *ILM* 1424 (1981).

[32]22 *ILM* 37 (1983); Since 1982, the major case handled by the Court has been the *Velásquez Rodríguez Case* (the title of the case actually covers three separate cases), *Judgment* of July 29, 1989, in 28 *ILM* 291 (1989), including Introductory Note by Buergenthal; see also *CSM*, Jan. 29, 1988, 9–10, and Aug. 1, 1988, 2. Of interest also is an Advisory Opinion of the Court, *Advisory Opinion OC 5/85*, of Nov. 13, 1985, concerning Costa Rican law for the practice of journalism, in 25 *ILM* 123 (1986).

[33]Text in 21 *ILM* 58 (1982).

THE UNITED STATES AND HUMAN RIGHTS   In 1976, the U.S. Congress enacted, over strong administration objections, a law requiring annual reports to the House Foreign Affairs Committee and the Senate Foreign Relations Committee from the Department of State on the observance of human rights in all countries receiving U.S. aid or purchasing arms from the United States. Those reports proved to be extremely discouraging to any proponent of the observance of human rights, particularly when it was realized that certain countries frequently accused of human rights violations were missing from the compilations because they were not recipients of U.S. aid.

President Carter and the U.S. Department of State had frequently spoken out publicly against human rights violations in various foreign countries, drawing in return repeated charges of intervention in the internal affairs of those states.[34] From a practical point of view, U.S. verbal condemnation produced no major effects at all. Hence more active steps were taken. An amendment to Public Law 480 (1977) required that future recipients of food aid (some 28 countries) had to sign a new human rights clause in the Food for Peace contracts, or no such aid would be forthcoming. The first two states to agree to this link between economic aid and human rights were Indonesia and Guinea (December 1977). The Carter administration also began to reduce economic assistance to certain countries accused of gross violations of human rights. However, after a 1975 congressional amendment had required justification of military assistance to countries whose observance of human rights had been challenged, several (Argentina, Brazil, Chile, El Salvador, Guatemala, and Uruguay) denounced this link (and the congressional committee reports on human rights observances) as illegal interference in domestic matters and rejected all further U.S. military assistance.

## Summary

It must be emphasized that the problem of the status of the individual centers on the question of whether or not there is a legal right of international representation regarding the treatment of an individual. If such a right does not generally exist—and this appears to be true—then domestic jurisdiction can be invoked by a state in rejecting suggestions or even reprimands from the outside. Once such a right has been acknowledged, the individual's status has been changed at last.

But most individuals lack the ability to assert their rights before an international tribunal. As long as this situation prevails, general international law probably cannot grant real rights to individuals. Only their state can take

---

[34]NYT, Feb. 1, 1977, 1, 6; Feb. 6, 1977, E-1; Feb. 13, 1977, E-3; Mar. 22, 1977, 1, 14; May 18, 1977, A-14; July 18, 1977, 11 (French reaction); Oct. 26, 1977, A-3; and so on; See also Vogelsang, "What Price Principle? U.S. Policy on Human Rights," 56 *Foreign Affairs* 820 (1978); Cohen, "Conditioning U.S. Security Assistance on Human Rights Practices," 76 *AJIL* 246 (1982). See also U.S. Department of State, "Plight of Iranian Bahàis," *Gist*, (October 1984), and "Human Rights in Afghanistan," *Gist* (December 1984).

up their cause by bringing a suit or filing a protest or claim with another state. This means that as yet it is the state that possesses an international legal right, not the individual.

## SUGGESTED READINGS

### Individuals under the Law: General

Whiteman, vol. 1, 50–58; Lauterpacht, *An International Bill of the Rights of Man* (1945); Brownlie, ed., *Basic Documents on Human Rights* (1971); Henkin, *The Rights of Man Today* (1978); Franck, *Human Rights in Third World Perspective* (1982); Vasek, ed., *The International Dimensions of Human Rights,* 2 vols. (1982); Meron, ed., *Human Rights in International Law* 2 vols., (1983).

### Human Rights Law-Making

Meron, *Human Rights and Humanitarian Norms as Customary Law* (1989), and his *Human Rights Law-Making in the United Nations: A Critique of Instruments and Process* (1986); Bloed, ed., *From Helsinki to Vienna: Basic Documents of the Helsinki Process* 1990; Manin, "The Helsinki Final Act and Human Rights," 4 *Chinese Yrbk Int'l Law* 175 (1984); Lillich, "The Paris Minimum Standard of Human Rights Norms in a State of Emergency," 79 *AJIL* 1072 (1985); Meron, "The Meaning and Reach of the International Convention on the Elimination of All Forms of Racial Discrimination," *id.,* 283; Whiteman, vol. 13, 660-79; MacChesney, "Should the United States Ratify the Covenants? A Question of Merits, Not of Constitutional Law," 62 *AJIL* 912 (1968); Garibaldi, "General Limitations on Human Rights: The Principle of Legality," 17 *Harvard Int'l. L. Jl.,* 503 (1976).

### The Americas

Buergenthal, Norris, and Shelton, *Protecting Human Rights in the Americas: Selected Problems* (1982); Nydell, "A Court for the Americas: Hopes and Illusions," 1 *Global Perspectives* 35 (Spring 1983); Buergenthal, "The Advisory Practice of the American Human Rights Court," 79 *AJIL* 1 (1985), and (with Norris) *Human Rights: The Inter-American System* (1982), as well as his "The Inter-American Court of Human Rights," 76 *AJIL* 231 (1982).

CASE

*Velásquez Rodríguez Case,* Inter-American Court of Human Rights, No. 4, July 29, 1988, in 28 *ILM* 291 (1989) and 83 *AJIL* 361 (1989).

### Africa

International Commission of Jurists (Geneva), *Uganda and Human Rights {Reports to the UN Commission on Human Rights}* (1977); Ullman, "Human Rights and Economic Power: The United States versus Idi Amin," 56 *Foreign Affairs* 529 (1978); Hamalengwa, Flinterman, and Bankwa, *The International Law of Human Rights in Africa* (1987).

## Europe

Castberg, *The European Convention on Human Rights* [First English-language edition of 1971 Norwegian edition] (1974); Murphy, "Objections to Western Conceptions of Human Rights," *Hofstra L. R.* 433 (1981).

CASES: EUROPEAN COURT OF HUMAN RIGHTS

*The Lawless Case,* European Court of Human Rights, 1960 (*Preliminary Objections and Questions of Procedure*), excerpted in 56 *AJIL* 171 (1962).

*Case Relating to Certain Aspects of the Laws on the Use of Languages in Education in Belgium (Preliminary Objection),* European Court of Human Rights, 1967, reported in 61 *AJIL* 1075 (1967); *Judgment* (July 23, 1968) excerpted in 8 *ILM* 825 (1969).

*The Neumeister Case,* European Court of Human Rights, 1968: *Judgment* excerpted in 8 *ILM* 547 (1969).

*The "Sunday Times" Case,* European Court of Human Rights, 1979, in 18 *ILM* 931 (1979); see also Wagner, "Human Rights: Government Interference with the Press — the *Sunday Times Case,*" 21 *Harvard Int'l. L. Jl.* 260 (1980).

*The Ringeisen Case,* European Court of Human Rights, 1972: *Judgment* in 11 *ILM* 1062 (1972); *Interpretation of the Judgment,* June 23, 1973, in 12 *ILM* 735 (1973).

*König* v. *Federal Republic of Germany,* European Court of Human Rights, 1978: *Judgment* (June 28, 1978) in 17 *ILM* 1151 (1978).

*The Marckx Case,* European Court of Human Rights, 1979: *Judgment* in 19 *ILM* 109 (1980).

*Case of Foti and Others,* European Court of Human Rights, 1982: *Judgment* in 22 *ILM* 380 (1983).

CASE: COUNCIL OF EUROPE.

*The Greek Case,* Council of Europe: Consultative Assembly Resolution (Jan. 31, 1968) in 7 *ILM* 706 (1968); Consultative Assembly Recommendation (Jan. 30, 1969) in 8 *ILM* 890 (1969); Committee of Ministers Resolution (Apr. 15, 1970) in 9 *ILM* 781 (1970). See also Buergenthal, "Proceedings against Greece under the European Convention of Human Rights," 62 *AJIL* 441 (1968), and also *Denmark/Norway/Sweden/The Netherlands* v. *Greece,* European Commission of Human Rights, Jan. 24, 1968, digested in 62 *AJIL* 988 (1968). Greece withdrew from the Council of Europe following the initiation of the above proceedings.

# 11

# Responsibility for Injuries to Aliens

## INTRODUCTION

Few areas in the international law of peace have evoked more numerous and more controversial questions than have the relations between a state and the aliens residing in its territory. In its broader aspects this sphere of the law applies to not only foreign citizens living in a given state but also to contractual agreements concluded between a state and the citizens of foreign countries, as well as the property of aliens located in a given country.

Each state is the sole judge of the extent to which aliens enjoy civil privileges within its jurisdiction. But beyond those permissive grants, each alien, as a human being, may be said to be endowed with certain rights, both as to person and to property, that are his by virtue of his being. It is primarily in connection with those basic rights that a responsibility by the host state arises. It is in this sphere that claims originate and, under certain conditions, may be advanced against the host state by the government to which the alien owes allegiance.[1]

CONCEPT OF IMPUTABILITY  Traditional theory and practice insisted that only a state could incur direct or indirect international responsibility in this sphere. The actual author or authors of the act or omission responsible for the injury suffered by an alien were not involved in any international claim because only the state could be charged with a duty or responsibility to make reparation for such injury. The technical name for this concept is *imputability*, which means the legal attribution of a particular act by a person or group of persons to a state or some other international person, whereby the act in question is henceforth considered the latter's own act and hence responsibility. This concept was basic to the entire notion of state responsibility in international law, because many acts creating such responsibility were undertaken by natural persons or groups of such persons.

[1]General note: See Hackworth, vol. 5, 471–851; Moore, vol. 6, 605–1037; Hyde, vol. 2, 871–1012; Jessup, 94–122; and Whiteman, vol. 8, 697–1291.

251

In recent decades, it has become increasingly apparent that only tradition has prevented a combination of state responsibility and the responsibility of the organs or individuals directly for the act or omission in question (attributable liability).

The United Nations' International Law Commission, after devoting portions of several sessions to the question, provisionally adopted thirty-two of its Draft Articles on State Responsibility (hereafter "Articles"), at the end of its thirty-first session in 1979.[2] Those articles clearly laid down the concept of imputability for state organs (Art. 5: "For the purposes of the present articles, conduct of any State organ having that status under the internal law of that State shall be considered as an act of the State concerned under international law, provided that organ was acting in that capacity in the case in question") as well as for certain other agencies and organs of subordinary units of a state, under specified conditions (see "Responsibility for the Acts of Officials"). Although the commission's provisional articles have not been approved officially by the members of the United Nations, the practice of states has indicated clearly, for many years, that imputability is an accepted principle in international law. On the other hand, new "third-world" States have generally voiced strong criticisms against the rules governing state responsibility for injuries to (resident) aliens.[3]

STATUS OF ALIENS     Under normal conditions aliens traveling through or residing in a given state enjoy no special privileges because of their alien status. They cannot claim any substantive rights greater than those of the citizens of their host state and, indeed, lack any special political or civil rights reserved for the latter by their own state.[4]

In like manner, aliens normally must use the same courts and the same legal procedures utilized by the local citizens in seeking redress for injuries or wrongs suffered by them. The laws of the host state protect aliens to the same degree that they protect the local citizens, subject to any existing legal limitations on the aliens' property and contract rights. Thus, if a given state should prohibit the ownership by aliens of uranium mines, a citizen of a foreign country, residing in the state in question, could not find judicial relief in the courts of the host state if he tried to acquire ownership of such a mine and was blocked in such endeavors.

Similarly, aliens do not enjoy a privileged status with reference to taxes. If, however, some form of discriminatory tax is imposed, the state is responsible, and an international claim may be lodged against it. In the past, such

[2] Text in 18 *ILM* 1568 (1979).
[3] See the most frequently cited example, Roy, "Is the Law of Responsibility of States a Part of Universal International Law?" 55 *AJIL* 866 (1961), reprinted in part in Henkin, 690–91.
[4] See Chapter 10 concerning jurisdiction over aliens, and also the important and still timely monographic treatment by McDougal, Lasswell, and Chen, "The Protection of Aliens from Discrimination and World Public Order: Responsibility of States Conjoined with Human Rights," 70 *AJIL* 432 (1976).

discrimination was excluded through specific provisions found in commercial and other treaties, but now it can be asserted that a rule of customary international law protects aliens against discriminatory taxation, even though they are not protected against possible double taxation, by their host state and their own government, in the absence of contrary agreements.[5]

Many states reserve certain occupations or professions for their own citizens. Such restrictions may originate for numerous reasons: certain occupations require security considerations and hence, it is felt, ought to be staffed with loyal nationals; in some professions, national standards are deemed to require training in the schools or colleges of the particular state in question, and so on. As long as reasonable objectives or logical purposes are behind the restrictions and as long as the latter apply only to individuals desiring to enter the occupations in the future, no objections can be raised by other states.[6] On the other hand, there are treaties that specifically forbid such limitations, and a violation of such an agreement could create state responsibility.

What if an alien is exposed to an openly oppressive or discriminatory law or encounters a clearly unfair administration of a law? Or, again, what if the alien, seeking justice in the courts of the host state, should be denied justice? Or what if an alien being prosecuted for a violation of local law is singled out for disproportional punishment?

DENIAL OF JUSTICE    In all these instances, there is said to have been a denial of justice, and such a denial may justify a claim by the alien's own state, in his or her name and behalf, to secure justice for the alien in question. Such a claim would, if advanced properly, rest on a right of the alien's state and would involve the application of principles of international law.

*Denial of justice,* or, more correctly, denial of procedural justice, a much disputed term, refers to any failure on the part of the authorities of the host state to provide adaquate means of redress to the alien when his or her substantive rights have suffered or, if the alien has violated the laws of the host state, to observe due process of law in the prosecution and punishment of the alien offender. A broad interpretation of the term would expand its meaning to include such matters as denial of access to the local courts, inefficiency in the performance of police and judicial processes, or an obviously unfair treatment or judicial decision. But a word of caution is necessary: the real question in a "denial of justice" has usually been whether or not a state was responsible internationally for some particular act or

---

[5] A representative case illustrating the problem at hand is *Burnet* v. *Brooks*, U.S. Supreme Court, 1933, 288 U.S. 378.

[6] See Travers, "The Constitutional Status of State and Federal Governmental Discrimination Against Resident Aliens," 16 *Harvard Int'l L. Jl.* 113 (1975); as well as *Espinoza* v. *Farah Manufacturing Co.*, U.S. Supreme Court, 1973, 94 S. Ct., 334, reported in 68 *AJIL* 332 (1974); *In re Griffiths*, U.S. Supreme Court, 93 S. Ct. 2851, reported *id.*, 334–35; and *Sugarman* v. *Dougall*, U.S. Supreme Court, 1973, 413 U.S. 634, reported *id.*, 335.

some specific omission of an act, which under international law (1) was wrongful, (2) was attributable, and (3) caused an injury to an alien; it has not been whether such act or omission could be called denial of justice. In the absence of agreement among authorities on the meaning of term, there must be specific reference to its special circumstances in each case before it can be claimed that responsibility has arisen because of a denial of justice.

MINIMUM STANDARD OF JUSTICE   Now standards of justice and the treatment of citizens vary considerably from country to country. Many governments, proceeding from the assumption that an alien entered their jurisdiction voluntarily, have asserted that no special favors should be granted to him, even if their treatment of their own citizens falls below the standards prevailing in the alien's own country. This attitude, more prevalent than might be supposed, raises the question of the so-called minimum standard of justice. Is there a minimum standard below which no civilized state would or should go?

The United States, Great Britain, and other countries have insisted for many decades that there is indeed such a minimum standard, a view shared by a number of international arbitration tribunals.[7] As Elihu Root, the distinguished American jurist, once stated,

If any country's system of law and administration does not conform to that standard, although the people of the country may be content and compelled to live under it, no other country can be compelled to accept it as furnishing a satisfactory measure of treatment to its citizens.[8]

Without a governing general international treaty, the rights of aliens may be assumed to be based on customary law, as was pointed out in *Hines* v. *Davidowitz et al.* (U.S. Supreme Court, 1941, 312 U.S. 52):

Apart from treaty obligations, there has grown up in the field of international relations a body of customs defining with more or less certainty the duties owing by all nations to alien residents—duties which our State Department has often successfully insisted foreign nations must recognize as to our nationals abroad. In general, both treaties and international practices have been aimed at preventing injurious discrimination against aliens.

The nature of the claimed minimum standard is also disputed. This writer believes that the closest approach to a definition of a minimum standard of justice has thus far been achieved in the adoption, on December 10, 1948, of the Universal Declaration of Human Rights by the General Assembly of the United Nations. Significantly, the states of Latin America, opposed

---

[7]See Foreign Claims Settlement Commission (U.S.), Decision No. W-16119, *In the Matter of the Claim of Hugo Schlessinger and Eugene Schlessinger* (December 7, 1966), excerpted in 61 *AJIL* 823 (1967).
[8]Presidential Address, *Proceedings* (1910), 20–21.

traditionally to the concept of a minimum standard and upholding the idea of equality of treatment as late as the Montevideo Conference of 1933 (Convention on the Rights and Duties of States, Article 9), approved in 1948 at the Ninth International Conference of American States at Bogotá the American Declaration of the Rights and Duties of Man closely related to the United Nations instrument.[9]

Assuming—in order to justify many instances in which state responsibility is created—that there is a minimum standard of justice, ill-defined though it as yet may be, then we have to examine the precise conditions under which a state becomes responsible for what befalls an alien within its jurisdiction.

First, because every state is responsible for preserving law and order in all territories under its control, any state is, indirectly, responsible when any violence or violation of the law takes place. But obviously no government can be expected to prevent all violence (though all would wish for such an ability), and therefore the responsibility of a state ceases when it makes available to the injured party the necessary facilities or means of redress for the wrongs suffered. In other words, a state is not responsible for, say, an attack on an alien by some individual, but it would be held responsible if it failed to provide the alien with proper means of redress.

The practice of states and the decisions of national and international courts have demonstrated that as soon as a state espouses a claim by one of its nationals, the whole character of the claim changes: it is henceforth a claim by a state against a state.

Now, to exercise diplomatic protection (which is involved, of course, in the concept of asserting a national's claim as a claim of the state) represents without question a discretionary right of a state. The latter may refuse to exercise this right for political reasons, even if its nationals have suffered injury through a violation of international law. And, as will be seen in connection with the Calvo Clause, the state may exercise its right even if the injured nationals refuse to make a claim. Damages, if they are part of the settlement of a claim, are paid by a state to a state. The claimant state, in effect, claims for a wrong, for an injury, done to it as a state in the person of its citizens.

RULES OF LOCAL REMEDIES    It may not be amiss to mention at this point an aspect of state responsibility applicable to any injury to aliens, regardless of the source of that injury: the rule of local remedies.

It is a rule of customary international law that the international responsibility of a state for an injury to an alien may not be invoked (say, in the form of an international claim) so long as local remedies, available to the injured alien under the laws of the host state and providing adequate means of redress, have not been exhausted.

[9]Text in 43 *AJIL* 133 (1949 Supp.).

The injured alien must have resort to local remedies which, normally, are represented by the courts of the host state, if only to determine whether the alleged injury has occurred, whether a denial of justice has taken place, whether a violation of international law is evident, or whether any degree of state responsibility has already been created. Until such resort to local remedies has taken place, no international claim should be lodged against the host state, unless there is a question as to whether local remedies were available to the alien, provided adequate means of redress, or had been exhausted *ab initio*.[10]

The rule of the exhaustion of local remedies appears to be of lesser significance in recent decades than had been the case during the first four decades of this century. A major reason, according to specialists,[11] has been the increasing utilization of lump-sum agreements to settle the vexatious problem of nationalization claims. And the so-called Algiers Accords, which authorized the creation of the Iran–United States Claims Tribunal, are said to have waived by implication the rule about local remedies (none such were available in Iran to foreign interests at the time the claims originated) and the Tribunal did not have to enter into that question.

## MIXED CLAIMS COMMISSIONS

Any discussion of the treatment of aliens must be preceded by an explanation of one of the major means to settle claims for injuries of those aliens, the Mixed Claims Commissions. The United States originated the practice of establishing mixed claims commissions through the Jay Treaty with Great Britain. Many other such commissions have been created since then, such as the one between the U.S. and Germany about World War I claims and the one between the U.S. and Italy after World War II. The latest, and one of the most important, certainly, in terms of number of claims and amount of money involved, was the already mentioned Iran–United States

[10]See "Articles," n. 2, no. 22; Mummery, "The Content of the Duty to Exhaust Local Judicial Remedies," 58 *AJIL* 389 (1964); Lillich, "The Effectiveness of the Local Remedies Rule Today," *Proceedings* 101 (1964). See also Cheng, 177–83; Hackworth, vol. 5, 501–26; Dawson and Head, *International Law, National Tribunals, and the Rights of Aliens* (1977). Consult also *The Ambatielos Case* (*Greece* v. *United Kingdom*), International Court of Justice, 1952–1953, *I.C.J. Reports, 1952*, 28, and *I.C.J. Reports, 1953*, 10. See also the relevant arbitration decision of March 6, 1956, in 50 *AJIL* 674 (1956); and *The Panevezys-Saldutiskis Railway Case* (*Estonia* v. *Lithuania*). Permanent Court of International Justice, *P.C.I.J., 1939*, Ser. A/B, No. 76, and its coverage by Hudson, 34 *AJIL* 1 (1940).
[11]Such as Trindade, *The Application of the Rule of Exhaustion of Local Remedies in International Law* 127, (1983). But see the recent *Case of Elettronica Sicula S.p.A. (ELSI)* (*United States* v. *Italy*), Int. Court of Justice, July 20, 1989, [1989] *ICJ Rep.* 15, in 28 *ILM* 1109 (1989); digested in 84 *AJIL* 249 (1990), in which the Court's panel held that the plaintiff had sufficiently exhausted all local remedies for the claim to be admissible. Also see Ennis, "Exhaustion of Local Remedies and External Measures," 84 *AJIL* 887 (1990).

Claims Tribunal. Many of the claims discussed in the following pages were handled through U.S.–Mexican Commissions, because at one time a very large number of claims were lodged by the United States against Mexico as a result of disturbed political—and military—conditions in that country.

The concept of lump-sum payments, mentioned earlier, is related to claims commissions; in this case, to national commissions. In many recent instances, states with claims against another state for injuries (physical, monetary, etc.) to citizens of the claiming state, have at length achieved agreements as to payment to the aggrieved state of a lump-sum settlement in satisfaction of all claims against the state guilty of the delict in question. The claimant state then creates its own *national* claims commission to which it turns over the funds collected, and the national commission examines the claims of its citizens and decides who will be paid how much from the lump sum collected, in satisfaction of all claims.

It should be noted that just as there is no rule of international law requiring a state to espouse a claim of an injured citizen, so no rule of the law governs the pursuit of an espoused claim or the manner in which the claimant state disposes of any financial settlement reached. Normally a state would pay all of the sums in question to the claimant citizen, with perhaps a small deduction for collecting expenses, but in the absence of a rule in the law, a state *could* actually retain all funds received from the delinquent state.[12]

## RESPONSIBILITY FOR THE ACTS OF OFFICIALS

RESPONSIBILITY DETERMINED BY STATUS OF OFFICIALS    States are responsible for the acts of public officials affecting alien persons or property, but although these officials in a general way are the agents of the state, they are not equally related to that same state. Obviously, heads of state and national legislatures are directly connected with the state, and their acts become a direct responsibility of the state. This is also true, but on a less immediate basis, for the major administrative officials and the courts of a state. Because their relationship to the state is slightly more remote than is that, say, of a president, the state may at its discretion disavow the acts of administrators and, still responsible for these acts to another country, rid itself of the charge of international wrongdoing.

When the lower echelons of public officials are concerned in an act or omission affecting an alien, then their relative remoteness from the authority of the state creates, usually and at most, an indirect responsibility of the state. True responsibility arises only if the state fails to punish the offending lower official, sheriff, police officer, or whatever.

[12]Concerning the Iran–United States Tribunal, see 77 *AJIL* 642 (1983); consult especially *Sperry Corporation* v. *United States*, 853, F.2d 904, U.S. Court of Appeals, Fed. Cir., August 10, 1988, in 83 *AJIL* 86 (1989).

Regardless of the status of a public official, full and complete state responsibility may, however, be created under certain conditions. Thus, if an official at any level commits an unauthorized act against an alien and his government subsequently approves the action and ratifies or endorses it, then the act not only creates full state responsibility but the official concerned also is absolved of all liability.

If, on the other hand, the injury done to the alien was caused during the proper exercise of authority by law-enforcement agencies or agents, no state responsibility is created.[13]

LACK OF DUE DILIGENCE    Examples of how state responsibility for injuries suffered by aliens is created abound in the law literature. The following examples, several of which are classic cases, shown how "denial of justice" is established on the basis of the facts in a given incident.

### UNITED STATES (LAURA M. B. JANES CLAIM) v. UNITED MEXICAN STATES

*United States–Mexico, General Claims Commission, 1926*
*(Opinions of Commissioners, 1927, 108)*

FACTS    Byron E. Janes, American superintendent of the El Tigre Mine at El Tigre, Sonora, Mexico, was shot to death at that location on July 10, 1918, by Pedro Carbajal, a discharged employee of the El Tigre Mining Co. The killing occurred in view of many persons living near the company's office. The local police chief was informed of Janes's death within five minutes and came at once. However, he delayed the assembling of his men, and then a further delay was caused by his insistence on a mounted posse. An hour after the shooting, the posse left in pursuit of the murderer, who had hurried away on foot.

No trace of Carbajal was found, even though he stayed at a ranch some six miles from El Tigre for a week and, so it was rumored, visited the village twice during that period. Later it was reported that the fugitive was at a mescal plant seventy-five miles south of El Tigre. When the Mexican civilian and military authorities were informed of this news, no steps were taken to capture Carbajal until the mining company offered a reward. Then a small military detachment was dispatched to the mescal plant, but Carbajal had left again before the soldiers arrived. No further steps were taken by the Mexican authorities, beyond the circulation among the judges of first instance in the state of Sonora of a request for the arrest of the fugitive killer.

Mrs. Laura Janes, on her own behalf and that of her children, lodged a claim against Mexico with the U.S. Department of State, charging lack of diligence by the Sonora authorities in apprehending, trying and punishing Pedro Carbajal. The department agreed to press a claim against Mexico on Mrs. Janes's behalf.

ISSUE    Were the authorities of Sonora guilty of a lack of due diligence in the Janes case, and did they thereby give rise

[13] See *In the Matter of the Death of James Pugh (Great Britain v. Panama)*, Arbitral Decision of July 6, 1933, reproduced in 36 *AJIL* 708 (1942).

to an American claim against the United Mexican States?

DECISION    The General Claims Commission decided that there had been a proven case of lack of due diligence and awarded the United States, on behalf of Mrs. Janes and her children, the sum of $12,000.

REASONING    The Mexican government was liable for not having measured up to its duty of diligently pursuing and properly punishing the offender (in both cases through the authorities of the state of Sonora). The damage caused by the culprit was the damage caused to Janes's relatives by his death; the damage caused by the government's negligence was the damage resulting from the nonpunishment of the murderer. If the government had not failed in its duty, Janes's family "would have been spared indignant neglect and would have had an opportunity of subjecting the murderer to a civil suit."

The commission admitted that the measure of the damage caused by the delinquency of the government was more difficult than the measure of the damage caused by the killing itself. Taking into account the grief suffered by Janes's death and the additional suffering caused by the apparent neglect of its duty on the part of the Mexican government, the commission settled on the sum of $12,000 as satisfaction for the damage caused by the nonapprehension and nonpunishment of the murderer.

EXERCISE OF DUE DILIGENCE    In contrast with the Janes claim, in which lack of due diligence resulted in an assumption of responsibility by a state, the following case shows what happens when reasonable diligence is exercised:

## UNITED STATES (L. F. H. NEER CLAIM) v. UNITED MEXICAN STATES

*United States–Mexico, General Claims Commission, 1926*
*(Opinions of Commissioners, 1927, 71)*

FACTS    Paul Neer, an American Citizen, was superintendent of a mine near Guanacevi, State of Durango, Mexico. On November 16, 1924, about 8 P.M., when he and his wife were riding from the village to their nearby home, they were stopped by a group of armed men who, after exchanging a few words with Neer, engaged in a gunfight with him. The American was killed.

Mrs. Neer summoned help, and the village authorities went to the scene of the killing on the night it took place; on the following morning the local judge examined some witnesses, including Mrs. Neer. Several days passed during which a number of suspects were arrested but released subsequently because of lack of evidence. Mrs. Neer was unable to supply a detailed description of the members of the group which had been involved in the affair.

Mrs. Neer filed a claim for $100,000, on behalf of herself and her daughter, with the U.S. Department of State against Mexico, charging that the Mexican authorities showed an unwarrantable lack of intelligent investigation in prosecuting the culprits involved in the death of her husband. The claim was placed before the United States–Mexico General Claims Commission.

ISSUE    Had there taken place a lack of due diligence on the part of the Durango authorities and was the lack of diligence of such a nature as to create state responsibility for Mexico?

DECISION    The commission decided that there had been no sufficient lack of due diligence to justify state responsibility; it therefore rejected the American claim.

REASONING    The commission agreed that the Durango and local authorities might have acted more vigorously in seeking to apprehend the culprits in the slaying of Neer. However, the commission also recognized that the local authorities were handicapped by the fact that Mrs. Neer, the only prosecution eyewitness to the murder, had not overheard the exchange of words between Neer and his killers and that she could not supply the authorities with any helpful information, such as a description of the individuals involved.

In view of the steps taken by the authorities, such as the investigations carried out and the examination of arrested suspects, the commission held that whatever lack of vigor had been displayed did not constitute a lack of diligence serious enough to charge the Mexican government with an international delinquency. For this reason the claim of the United States was disallowed.

MORE EXAMPLES OF LACK OF DUE DILIGENCE    Other cases, mostly dating to the same period as the Janes and Neer claims, show the lack of or the existence of due diligence. Thus, in the well-known Youmans case,[14] an American claim for $50,000 was allowed to the extent of $20,000 for the death of an American citizen who, together with two other United States nationals, was the victim of a mob attack in Angangues, state of Michoacán, Mexico.

The three men were hiding in a house following a wage dispute between one of them and a Mexican citizen, involving the sum of twelve cents. The killings had been accomplished under rather unusual circumstances: when a mob attacked the house in question, the local mayor, failing to quiet the crowd, had ordered a lieutenant in the state troops to use his men to quell the riot. The soldiers, arriving at the scene of the disturbance, instead of dispersing the mob, opened fire on the house, killing one of the Americans. The two others, driven from their refuge when part of the mob entered it from the rear, were killed by the troops and members of the mob. Their bodies were dragged through the streets, mutilated, and left under a pile of rocks by the side of a road.

The next morning Mexican federal troops arrived and restored order. Court action was started against twenty-nine members of the mob, but only eighteen of them were arrested. Several of this number were then released on nominal bail and were never troubled again. Five persons were sentenced to death, but their sentences were commuted, with no real effect, however, for one had died in the meantime and the other four had left town before

[14] United States (T. H. Youmans Claim) v. United Mexican States, United States–Mexico General Claims Commission, 1926 (Opinions of Commissioners, 1927, 150).

they were even arrested. Seven were acquitted; the cases against six others were discontinued; and the charges against the remaining eleven were still left open as late as 1887, seven years after the riot had taken place, just in case they were apprehended and could be prosecuted.

The General Claims Commission decided that the Mexican government had to assume responsibility for failing to exercise due diligence to protect Youmans and to take proper steps for the apprehension and punishment of the guilty parties. The participation of troops of the state of Michoacán aggravated the responsibility laid on the government of Mexico.

Frequently, a charge of denial of justice forms the basis of a claim against a state, generally when an alien is brought to court and later claims irregularity in proceedings, cruel treatment, or a clearly unjust sentence. The following case, despite its bizarre elements, may illustrate some of the meanings of denial of justice:

### UNITED STATES (B. E. CHATTIN CLAIM) v. UNITED MEXICAN STATES

*United States–Mexico, General Claims Commission, 1927*
*(Opinions of Commissioners, 1927, 422)*

FACTS    Chattin, an American citizen, had worked since 1908 as a conductor for the Ferrocarril Sud-Pácifico de México (Southern Pacific Railroad of Mexico). He was arrested on July 9, 1910, at Mazatlán, state of Sinaloa, on a charge of embezzlement. It appeared that Chattin and a Mexican brakeman employed by the railroad had been engaged in the fraudulent sale of railroad tickets and had kept the proceeds of their enterprise for themselves. Chattin was kept in prison until January 1911, pending trial. He was tried in that month, convicted on February 6, 1911, and sentenced to two years' imprisonment. He was released from the jail in Mazatlán in May or June 1911, when the revolutionary forces of General Madero entered the town and liberated all prisoners.

Chattin returned to the United States and filed a claim with the Department of State, alleging that the arrest, trial, and sentence had been illegal; that he had suffered inhuman treatment in jail;

and that all this merited damages to the amount of $50,000.

ISSUE    Had a denial of justice taken place in the judicial proceedings and imprisonment involving Chattin? If such denial had occurred, did responsibility devolve on the government of Mexico?

DECISION    The General Claims Commission decided in favor of the United States and ordered Mexico to pay to the United States, on behalf of Chattin, the sum of $5,000 as damages for denial of justice sufficiently grave to create state responsibility for Mexico.

REASONING    [Note: There appears to have been no question as to Chattin's guilt on the charge of embezzlement: he and the brakeman had been guilty as charged.]

The commission found that Chattin had been legally arrested, although the procedure used differed from that normally employed in the United States. On the other hand, the evidence produced indicated grave irregularities in the court proceedings, such a lack of proper investigation, insufficient confrontation with witnesses and evidence, failure to acquaint the accused with all the charges brought against him, undue delay in starting judicial proceedings that rendered the hearings in open court a mere formality, and a proven intentional severity of the judgment (without, however, proof of unfriendliness on the part of the judge, as claimed by Chattin). Mistreatment in the prison was not proved, in the opinion of the commission.

In view of the foregoing and of the fact that Chattin had stayed in prison for eleven months instead of the two years, the commission allowed damages on his behalf to the extent of $5,000.

[Note: It should be mentioned that Chattin and his fellow embezzler had appealed the decision of the Mazatlán court up to the Supreme Court of Mexico but had lost the appeals; so local remedies had been exhausted before the claim was submitted to the U.S. Department of State.]

In regard to the courts, international responsibility of the state would arise if the judicial acts in question had been incompatible with international law, represented a denial of justice in a strict sense (no access to courts, undue delay, and so on), or created an obvious injustice—if, for instance, the acts were flagrant, were the work of the highest court in the land, and were done in bad faith and with intent to discriminate.

Enactments of national legislative bodies are considered acts of state. Therefore direct responsibility is created by the acts themselves, and foreign states are held to be entitled to protest against legislation clearly injurious to their citizens or their property.

SUMMARY OF STATE RESPONSIBILITY    In summarizing the law of state responsibility as covered thus far, it can be said that a state is internationally responsible for an act or omission that, under international law, is wrong, is attributable to that state, and causes an injury to the alien. The latter is entitled to present an international claim to his own government only after he has exhausted the local remedies provided by the state allegedly responsible for the alien's injury. The host state is not internationally responsible if an alien suffers injury through violation of the laws of that state or through resistance offered to law-enforcement officers engaged in their lawful duties. State responsibility is created through the acts of public officials, but the degree of responsibility and the redress to be granted vary with the nature of the officials and the acts committed by them. Ratification of an unauthorized official act makes that act a responsibility of the state. And denial of justice, including the failure to use due diligence to prevent injury to an alien or to punish those guilty of punishing him, may, depending on the circumstances, create an international responsibility for the delinquent state.

On the other hand, state responsibility for injuries to alien persons or their property ends through what is termed "prescription": failure to assert a claim over a very long (excessively long) period of time. Thus in *United States (William Bader)* v. *Venezuela* (1903), a claim had failed to be lodged in over 43 years and in Italy (Gentini) v. Venezuela (1903), the claim was not filed for 31 years.[15]

## INTERNATIONAL RESPONSIBILITY FOR PRIVATE ACTS

Under normal conditions a state does not assume international responsibility for injuries suffered by aliens in their persons or property at the hands of the state's own private citizens, unless the state fails to provide local remedies capable of supplying effective and adequate redress of the injury sustained at private hands (draft Article 11). If a given government, subsequent to the commission of private acts against aliens or their property, endorses (promotes or ratifies) such acts, state responsibility is created. This was the case in Iran after "student militants" seized the U.S. embassy and took hostages on November 4, 1979.

Outbreaks of mob violence resulting in injuries to alien persons or property also may create state responsibility. In this case, a claim's lawfulness centers on the presence of preventing efforts as well as on the adequacy of redress. What matters is whether the state used due diligence to prevent the outbreak and, later, to punish the persons guilty of injuring alien persons or property.

There is no generally applicable definition of *due diligence*, for the circumstances of each particular incident have to be utilized to determine whether or not such diligence was lacking.

## RESPONSIBILITY FOR ALIEN PROPERTY

Property owned by an alien is subject to the same laws and regulations as apply to the property of citizens. This general principle does not exclude the issuing of laws or regulations prohibiting ownership of certain kinds of property by aliens or the acquisition of certain kinds of property in specified geographic areas by aliens. It would therefore be lawful to prohibit an alien from owning real estate within, say, ten miles of an important naval or missile base. Security considerations would or might justify such a prohibition, and so long as all aliens were affected by it, no valid exception to it could be taken by any government.

On the other hand, the deliberate destruction of or damage to alien property would have to be considered unlawful unless such action were based on the judgment of a competent domestic court or, perhaps, of sanitation or health authorities, did not violate the laws of the host country on a discriminatory basis, and did not violate a treaty.

---

[15] For the *Bader* case, see Ralston, *Venezuelan Arbitrations of 1903* (1904), 161; for the *Gentini* case, *id.*, 720, 724–30.

**• RIGHT OF EXPROPRIATION OF ALIEN PROPERTY**   Lay opinion to the contrary, every government has the right of expropriation, that is, of eminent domain. The law of nations demands respect for private property, but it recognizes the state's right to derogate from this principle when its superior interest so requires. Thus the law allows expropriation for reasons of public utility in time of peace and requisition in war.[16] Expropriated property may be foreign or domestic: no distinction need be drawn by the seizing government, except in the case of foreign-owned public (state-owned) property. This principle has been affirmed again and again by international tribunals.[17]

Such taking of property can be either a forcible transfer of title or a mere deprivation of the owner of the use of the property. In either case, as long as the following conditions outlined hold true, the action of the state does not create an international responsibility. Much as some may decry the taking away of private property by any state, there can be no question that every independent political entity has an undoubted and lawful right to exercise the power of eminent domain.

Expropriation of foreign private property must, generally, satisfy all of the following conditions if the question of basic state responsibility is to be avoided:

1. The taking must be by a foreign sovereign government.
2. The property must be within the territorial jurisdiction of that government.
3. The government in question must exist and must be recognized by the state of which the affected owners are citizens.
4. The taking must not violate any treaty obligations.
5. Prompt, effective, and adequate compensation must be paid, and the capacity to pay and to effect transfer of funds has a legitimate place in determining the promptness and effectiveness of compensation.
6. No discrimination must exist in the taking.
7. The taking in question should be based on reasons of public utility, security, or national interest of a nature sufficiently great to override purely individual or private interests.

In December 1974 the General Assembly of the United Nations adopted a controversial instrument entitled Charter of Economic Rights and Duties

[16]Portuguese–German Arbitration (1919), *Award II* (1930), in United Nations, *Reports of International Awards, II*, 1039. See also the explanation offered by the U.S. Supreme Court in *Banco Nacional de Cuba* v. *Sabbatino* (376 U.S. 398, 1964, at 428) that "the Judicial Branch will not examine the validity of a taking of property within its own territory by a foreign sovereign government . . . even if the complaint alleges that the taking violates customary international law."

[17]See *Norwegian Claims against the United States of America*, Permanent Court of Arbitration, 1922, in Scott, ed., *Hague Court Reports, II*, 40–44, 70, as well as *German Interests in Polish Upper Silesia (Germany* v. *Poland)*, Merits, P.C.I.J., 1926, Ser. A, No. 7, esp. p. 22.

of States, by a vote of 120 to 6, with 10 abstentions.[18] Under the assumption that the charter represented merely a resolution and not newly created principles of international law, the document, reflecting the views of almost all Third World countries on a variety of topics, has led to substantial disagreement since its adoption. The cause of most of the irritation voiced in industrialized countries of the world was Article 2 of the charter:

1. Every State has and shall freely exercise full permanent sovereignty, including possession, use and disposal, over all its wealth, natural resources, and economic activities.

2. Each State has the right:

(a) To regulate and exercise authority over foreign investment within its national jurisdiction in accordance with its laws and regulations and in conformity with its national objectives and priorities. No State shall be compelled to grant preferential treatment to foreign investment;

(b) To regulate and supervise the activities of transnational corporations within its national jurisdiction and take measures to ensure that such activities comply with its laws, rules and regulations and conform with its economic and social policies. Transnational corporations shall not intervene in the internal affairs of a host State. Every State should, with full regard for its sovereign rights, co-operate with other States in the exercise of the right set forth in this subparagraph;

(c) To nationalize, expropriate or transfer ownership of foreign property in which case appropriate compensation should be paid by the State adopting such measures, taking into account its relevant laws and regulations and all circumstances that the State considers pertinent. In any case where the question of compensation gives rise to a controversy, it shall be settled under the domestic law of the nationalizing State and by its tribunals, unless it is freely and mutually agreed by all States concerned that other peaceful means be sought on the basis of the sovereign equality of States and in accordance with the principle of free choice of means.

Article 2 (by design, it must be assumed) omits all reference to what is termed public utility or public purpose—see Condition 7 listed above. It also contains no mention of the "doctrine of alien nondiscrimination," that is, the assertion that resident aliens are entitled at least to the same protection of persons and property as local law grants to nationals.[19]

There have been cases in which the taking of alien property has been held to be "wrongful," regardless of whether compensation was paid: such cases hinged on the fact that the act of the state involved in the seizure violated a valid treaty. In such circumstances, restitution or replacement

---

[18]GA Res. 3281 (XXIX), 29 UN GAOR, Supp. (No. 31) 50, UN Doc. 9631 (1974). Text in full in 69 *AJIL* (1975), 484 and 14 *ILM* 251 (1975). Voting against the Charter were Belgium, Denmark, the Federal Republic of Germany, Luxembourg, the United Kingdom, and the United States.

[19]See the lengthy analysis in Weston, "The Charter of Economic Rights and Duties of States and the Deprivation of Foreign-Owned Wealth," 75 *AJIL* 437 (1981); and Dolzer, "New Foundations of the Law of Expropriation of Alien Property," *id.*, 553.

in kind was held to constitute the acceptable remedy. The classic example in this category is the *Case Concerning the Factory at Chorzów*,[20] in which the court held that restitution was the appropriate remedy. The German-Polish Convention Concerning Upper Silesia, the treaty applicable to the dispute in question, specifically authorized expropriation of certain kinds of property but excluded categorically the taking, even against payment of compensation, of other properties. The *Chorzów* case was the latest case before an international tribunal in which restitution was ordered; there have been, however, similar decisions by national courts and international claims commissions.

In April 1949, by a "supervening expression of Executive Policy," the government of the United States suspended the act-of-state doctrine for U.S. courts in regard to forcible transfers of property under the laws of the former National Socialist government of Germany.[21] Similar steps had been taken by several members of the wartime United Nations.

NATIONALIZATION OF ALIEN PROPERTIES    Confiscation without payment of compensation has frequently reached enormous proportions in terms of the monetary value of the seized alien properties. Noteworthy instances relate to Russia's nationalization of alien properties immediately after the November Revolution of 1917; the seizure of American oil properties in Mexico on March 18, 1938 (eventually agreement was reached on the payment of what must be termed token compensation); the confiscation of foreign properties by the Russian satellite bloc in Eastern Europe following the end of World War II; and the wholesale expropriation of foreign properties by the Cuban government in 1959 and 1960.

From a legal point of view, the two outstanding modern instances of nationalization were the Iranian seizure of the Anglo-Iranian Oil Company in 1951 and the Egyptian taking of the Suez Canal in 1956. (See "Suggested Readings," Chapter 14.)

Following the granting of assent by the Shah on May 1, 1951, to two laws concerning seizure of the Anglo-Iranian Oil Company passed by the Iranian majlis and senate, a dispute arose between Iran and Great Britain. The British government, owning 35 percent of the company's stock, took the side of the corporation and on May 26 filed an application with the International Court of Justice. The Court decided that it lacked jurisdiction. Regrettably the Court never ruled on the Merits in this case, for Article 21 of the 1933 Concession to the then Anglo-Persian Oil Company provided:

[20]*P.C.I.J.*, 1928, Ser. A, No. 17.
[21]Department of State Release No. 296, April 27, 1949, "Jurisdiction of U.S. Courts re Suits for Identifiable Property Involved in Nazi Forced Transfers"; *Menzel* v. *List*, United States, N.Y. Supreme Court, N.Y. County, February 10, 1966, reported at length in 60 *AJIL* 851 (1966); Cheeseman, "Note on *Menzel* v. *List*" (United States, Supreme Court of New York, 1966, N.Y.S. 2nd 804) in 8 *Harvard Int'l L. Jl.* 130 (1967); and the following decisions by the Foreign Claims Settlement Commission: *In the Matter of the Claim of Hugo Schlessinger and Eugene Schlessinger*, Decision No. W-16119, 1966, reported in 61 *AJIL* 823(1967), and *In the Matter of the Claim of Arnold Bernstein*, Decision No. W-21545, 1967, *id.*, 1069.

This Concession shall not be annulled by the Government and the terms thereof shall not be altered either by general or special legislation in the future, or by administrative measures or any other acts whatsoever of the executive authorities.

The British government had contended that Article 21 in effect stopped the Iranian government from either altering or ending the concession. Subsequently an international oil consortium worked out a scheme whereby it operated the oil properties in Iran as an agent of the Iranian government and paid annual sums to the previous owners as installments compensating them for the seizure of the properties in question. [22]

The Iranian seizure of the British oil properties gave birth to several interesting cases in national courts, centering on the question of the recognition of foreign expropriation decrees. The Iranian government, deprived of the tankers necessary to transport its newly acquired oil to the world's markets when British oil and shipping companies collaborated in a "tanker boycott" of Iran, arranged for the sale of the oil to foreign companies, which in turn used their own or chartered tankers to fetch the oil from Iran.

In *Anglo-Iranian Oil Co.* v. *Jaffrate et al.*,[23] the company sued to obtain possession of a cargo of Iranian oil from the master (Italian citizen) of a tanker, against the Honduran corporation owning the vessel (registered in Panama), and the Swiss charterer of the vessel. The last had purchased the cargo of 700 tons of oil from the National Iranian Oil Company, the new agency operating the company's oil properties in Iran. The Aden court ordered transfer of the oil to the plaintiffs because of the Iranian government's failure to pay compensation for the expropriated oil properties of the British company.

A decision conflicting with that handed down in the Aden case resulted when the Anglo-Iranian Oil Company sought to establish its ownership rights in a cargo of Iranian oil brought to Italy by an Italian company that had purchased the oil from the Iranian government agency. In *Anglo-Iranian Oil Company* v. *Società Unione Petrolifera Orientale*,[24] the court rejected the defendants' assertion that the Italian courts had no jurisdiction and then rejected the plaintiff's claim to the oil in question, pointing out that the Iranian nationalization law provided for compensation in principle and set forth a procedure for arriving at its amount, even though the plaintiffs had rejected that procedure.

Nationalization can take effect immediately within the territory of the taking state. As soon as properties located beyond its jurisdiction are to be included in any expropriation, there are bound to be conflicts with

---

[22] The initial order of the court, of July 5, 1951, was reprinted in 45 *AJIL* 789 (1951); the excerpted judgment in *Anglo-Iranian Oil Company Case (Jurisdiction)*, *United Kingdom* v. *Iran*, International Court of Justice, July 22, 1952, *I.C.J. Reports, 1952*, 93, is found in 46 *AJIL* 737 (1952).

[23] Colony of Aden, Supreme Court, January 9, 1953, reported in 47 *AJIL* 325 (1953).

[24] Italy, Civil Tribunal of Venice, March 11, 1953, summarized in 47 *AJIL* 509 (1953).

the state in whose jurisdiction such properties are located. The general rule is that confiscations will not be given effect by a court in a foreign country with respect to assets located in that country unless the act of seizure is in accordance with the public policy of that foreign state.[25] On rare occasions, however, particular political agreements and considerations result in deviations from this general rule.[26]

OTHER MEANS OF DEPRIVING ALIENS OF PROPERTY    Thus far only the actual expropriation—that is, the assumption of title—of alien property has been considered. But there are other ways of depriving an alien of property, and such methods deserve brief comment.

Governments have attempted, for instance, to limit an alien's control or use of property. Entrances to a factory have been barred on grounds of preserving public order; wage legislation and labor courts have lifted the wages of the employees of an alien enterprise to prohibitively high levels; entrance visas have been denied to vitally needed foreign technical personnel; allocations of required foreign exchange have been curtailed or stopped entirely; importations of replacement parts for machinery have been prevented; portions of buildings have been prohibited for use by the alien enterprise; conservators, managers, or inspectors have been introduced by government order into an enterprise and then prevented free use and direction by the nominal foreign owners; or, by a simple prohibition on the sale of the property, the value of the assets has been sharply reduced.[27]

Such interference in the utilization of an alien's property could easily bring about a decision to sell the property to the government in question or, in extreme cases, to the closing or even the abandonment of the property. In many instances, the depreciation resulting from such state harassment has been so great that sale to the government on its own terms has brought far less than fair compensation for expropriation would have brought at the outset of the whole process. As yet, there is no generally accepted rule of law to deal with such deliberate harassment of foreign-owned or -controlled properties.

[25] See especially the famous case of *United States* v. *Pink, Superintendent of Insurance*, U.S. Supreme Court, 1942, 315-U.S. 203, and also *Bandes* v. *Harlow & Jones, Inc.*, U.S. Court of Appeals, 2d Cir., 1988, 852 F.2d 661, reported by Calabrese in 82 *AJIL* 820 (1988).

[26] Nonrecognition of nationalization of assets located outside the territory of the taking state is illustrated in *Carl Zeiss Stiftung* v. *V.E.B. Carl Zeiss Jena*, U.S. Court of Appeals, 2d Cir., 1970, 433 F.2d 686, reported in 65 *AJIL* 611 (1971) in *United Bank Limited* v. *Cosmic International, Inc.*, U.S. Court of Appeals, 2d Cir., 1976, 542 F.2d 868, reported in 71 *AJIL* 351 (1977); and in *Republic of Iraq* v. *First National City Bank*, U.S. District Court, S.D.N.Y., 1965, 241 F. Supp. 567, dismissal affirmed, Court of Appeals, 2nd Cir., 1965, 353 F.2d 47, and *certiorari denied*, Supreme Court, 1966, 86 S.Ct. 556; that interesting case is discussed in a *Note* by Horlings in 7 *Harvard Int'l Law Club Jl.* (1966), 316. See also the Netherlands case of *Svit, N.P.* v. *Bata-Best B.V.*, Netherlands, District Court, 'S-Hertogenbosch (First Chamber), 1975; an *Explanatory Note* by MacCrate and the decision are found in 15 *ILM* 669 (1976).

[27] The list has been adapted from Lewis B. Sohn and R. R. Baxter, "Responsibilities of States for Injuries to the Economic Interests of Aliens," 55 *AJIL* 545, 559 (1961).

GUARANTEES TO FOREIGN INVESTORS    In response to the increasing risks of nationalization facing American investors in foreign countries, the United States government inaugurated an unusual program of guarantees to such investors in countries willing to sign relevant agreements with the United States. Beginning with the Marshall Plan in 1948, the program initially covered only the problem of currency convertibility, but subsequently, not only expropriation but losses caused by war were included in the guarantees.

By the end of April, 1962, such agreements had been concluded, on a bilateral basis, between the United States and fifty-five countries.[28]

In 1970 another federal agency, the Overseas Private Investment Corporation (OPIC), began to sell political-risk insurance to U.S. firms operating in Third World countries. In 1981, OPIC registered a record profit of $76.2 million, while issuing $1.5 billion in insurance. Major payments over the years included $315 million to fifteen U.S. companies whose properties in Chile had been taken in 1971, and $14.5 million or more paid out for losses suffered in Iran in 1979.[29]

In 1985, the World Bank launched a new plan to assure investment guaranties by drafting and transmitting the Convention Establishing the Multilateral Investment Guarantee Agency.[30] The procedure used was somewhat unusual. The draft of the instrument was first approved by the Bank's Executive Directors, then by its Board of Governors at a meeting in Seoul (October 11, 1985). The Board then transmitted the draft to all member states of the Bank and to the government of Switzerland for signature (and eventual ratification). Ecuador, Korea, and Turkey signed immediately, and Ecuador was the first state to ratify the convention.

PROTECTION OF FOREIGN INVESTMENT    The increasing frequency of expropriation of alien property and of disputes concerning foreign investments prompted the executive directors of the International Bank for Reconstruction and Development (World Bank) to submit to governments, in March 1965, the Convention on the Settlement of Investment Disputes Between States and Nationals of Other States. This instrument was signed by forty-six governments and had been ratified by twenty-one of them when it entered into force on October 14, 1966.[31] It established the International Center for

---

[28]See also Martin, "Multilateral Investment Insurance: The OECD Proposal," 8 *Harvard Int'l L. Jl.* 280 (1967). The following decisions or awards illustrate some of the problems encountered in the investment guarantee program: *Valentine Petroleum & Chemical Corporation* v. *U.S. Agency for International Development*, United States, Arbitration Tribunal, 1967, reported in 9 *ILM* 889 (1970); and *Revere Copper and Brass, Inc.* v. *Overseas Private Investment Corporation*, Arbitration Award, 1978, reprinted in 17 *ILM* 1321 (1978).

[29]See *Time*, Sept. 27, 1982, 49 for more details on OPIC.

[30]Text in 24 *ILM* 1605, with introduction 1598–1605. See also Shihata, *Origins, Operations, Policies and Basic Documents of the Multilateral Investment Guarantee Agency* (1987). The convention is not in effect at the time of writing, with only one ratifying state and too few signatories.

[31]Text in 60 *AJIL* 892 (1966).

Settlement of Investment Disputes, located in the bank, which is available to settle, by conciliation or arbitration, investment disputes between private foreign investors and the sovereign states in which investments have been made. The center maintains panels of qualified persons from which arbitrators and conciliators may be selected. Its services are available to a contracting state and its nationals only after that state has become a party to the convention. Once a contracting state and a foreign investor have agreed to arbitrate a dispute or settle it by conciliation, that agreement becomes binding, and neither party may lawfully withdraw from it unilaterally. The United States ratified the convention on June 1, 1966.

LUMP SUM SETTLEMENTS OF EXPROPRIATION CLAIMS    On many occasions, the wholesale expropriation of foreign property has been followed, usually after a long interval, by a lump-sum settlement given by the taking state to the home country or countries of the deprived alien owners. The proceeds of such settlements have then been distributed, on a pro-rata basis, among those owners.[32] Thus the Soviet Union agreed to repayment amounting to some $300 million in 1933 to American owners of properties confiscated in the Soviet Union. The government of Mexico eventually agreed to a minimal payment to the owners of American oil companies expropriated by Mexico. In 1973, the United States reached an agreement with Hungary for a lump-sum payment by Hungary of $18.9 million to cover a variety of claims by American interests.[33] In May 1976, the government of Sri Lanka agreed to pay $13.7 million to British owners of tea, rubber, and coconut plantations expropriated only a year earlier. In May 1979, a lump-sum settlement agreement was reached between the United States and the People's Republic of China concerning expropriations of American properties. According to the agreement, China would pay to the United States a total of $80.5 million over the following six years. That sum represented a settlement at a rate of about forty-one cents on the dollar of the $197 million in claims against China. In return, the People's Republic was promised U.S. government assistance in recovering some $80 million in assets frozen in the United States.

A more recent lump-sum settlement was the agreement with Czechoslovakia. The settlement was originally worked out in November 1980; Congress approved it in a bill passed on December 16, 1981; and procedural details were completed in January 1982. In the middle of February 1982, each party fulfilled the obligations assumed under the agreement. The Czech government paid to the United States $81.5 million (plus some additional minor sums), and the United States government agreed to the return to Czechoslo-

---

[32]Consult Lillich and Weston, *International Claims: Their Settlement by Lump Sum Agreements* (1975), the most comprehensive treatment of the subject available.
[33]Text in 12 *ILM* 407 (1973); see also Lillich, "The United States-Hungarian Claims Agreement of 1973," 69 *AJIL* 534 (1975).

vakia of the remainder of the latter's monetary gold reserves that had been looted by Germany and recovered by Allied forces at the end of World War II. The sums paid to the United States were to be given to the holders of claims arising out of Czech nationalization measures. There were to be future negotiations regarding claims arising out of defaulted Czech government bonds.[34] The 1981 agreement was the latest in such settlements of claims lodged against Eastern European governments by the United States: Yugoslavia (1948, 1964), Hungary (1956, 1976), Poland (1960), Rumania (1960), and Bulgaria (1963). Typical of modern compensation agreements is that concluded between the United States and Ethiopia on December 19, 1986, arising out of long-standing claims and counterclaims concerning the Kalamazoo Spice Extraction Company.[35]

## CONTRACTS BETWEEN A STATE AND ALIENS

A common source of international claims is that part of a state's general obligation to protect aliens that pertains to alleged breaches of contracts made between a state and an alien. The problem posed is not really one of state responsibility as such, for the state itself is one of the parties to the agreement and thus is involved directly from the beginning. The issue in question is the right, or lack thereof, of the alien's own state to assume his claim for breach of contract and to present a claim on his behalf to the state alleged to have violated the agreement.[36]

Although some governments have been most willing to press such claims by their citizens, many more have been rather reluctant to do so. This hesitation is based in part on the idea that anyone entering into contractual relations with a foreign state can be presumed to do so with a clear conception of the risks involved. Because many such contracts provide exceedingly large returns to the alien, he is presumed to have weighed the profits expected against the risks taken in dealing with a sovereign state. Enough claims based on contract violations have been presented, however, to make this sphere of state–alien relations one of the most contentious ones in the realm of international law.

A state that arbitrarily violates the terms of a contract or concession to which it and an alien are parties is clearly in the wrong and has committed a wrongful act. The opinion of most writers and international tribunals has

---

[34]See Vratislav, Pechota, "The 1981 U.S.–Czechoslovak Claims Settlement Agreement" 76 *AJIL* 639–53 (1982), as well as the extensive documentation in 21 *ILM* 371–95, 414–19 (1982).
[35]Text (and stipulation, plus 2 Minutes) in 25 *ILM* 56–62 (1986); see also 80 *AJIL* 344 (1986).
[36]Mann, "State Contracts and State Responsibility," 54 *AJIL* 572 (1960); and particularly Whiteman, vol. 8, 906–15. See also Delaume, "State Contracts and Transnational Arbitration," 75 *AJIL* 784 (1981).

been that the alien must first exhaust the available local remedies. Only when this has been done and no adequate redress has been obtained does he have a right to present a claim to his own government with the expectation that the latter will press the claim against the delinquent state. It should be noted, however, that the local law of the state alleged to have violated the contract might be of such a nature as to deprive the alien, through judicial action supporting the violation of the contract, of property rights or actual property.[37] In that case the alien's own government might conclude properly that a denial of justice had taken place, that arbitrary acts had injured the alien, and that an international claim might be lawfully pressed.

, THE CALVO CLAUSE    It was to be expected that governments would view with disfavor appeals by aliens to their own governments to institute international claims based on an alleged violation of contract terms. Hence it could have caused no great surprise when a number of Latin American states began to write into contracts made with aliens a provision called the *Calvo Clause*. This clause stipulated that the alien agreed that any dispute arising out of the terms of the contract was to be settled by the national courts of the contracting state in accordance with the latter's national law and was not to cause the lodgment of any international claim by the alien's government. A number of such clauses contained the additional provision that, for purposes of the contract, the alien was to be considered a national of the contracting state.[38]

The introduction of the Calvo Clause gave rise to strong protests by other states because, taken literally, the clause not only attempted to deprive the alien of the right to appeal to his own government after exhausting available local remedies but, in fact, declared the new doctrine that an individual citizen could, on his own responsibility, deprive his state of protecting its interests abroad. No major state outside Latin America—in particular, the United States—could agree to such a private restriction on the undoubted right of every sovereign state to assume the protection of the rights of its citizens, even over the written objections to or waiver of such protection by those citizens. When the Calvo Clause appeared as a material ingredient of cases and claims before international courts and arbitration tribunals, some decisions accorded validity to the clause, but the majority of recorded

---

[37] See the unusual instance of the 1957 Israeli–USSR (*Jordan Investments and Delek Israel Fuel Corporation* v. *Sojuzneftexport*) arbitration, detailed in Domke, "The Israeli–Soviet Oil Arbitration," 53 *AJIL* 787 (1959), as well as the more recent and directly relevant (to the intrusion of local—Polish—law) case of *C. Czarnikow, Ltd.* v. *Centrala Handlu Zagranicznego "Rolimpex"* [*Czarnikow, Ltd.* v. *Rolimpex*], United Kingdom, House of Lords, July 6, 1978, reproduced in 17 *ILM* 1384 (1978). See also the *ELSI* case cited *supra*, n. 11.

[38] Freeman, "Recent Aspects of the Calvo Doctrine and the Challenge to International Law," 40 *AJIL* 121, 130 (1946).

opinions appears to have denied the validity of a contractual agreement to set aside a right of protection by the alien's government.[39]

Generally, it must be assumed today that most states will not agree to be bound by a restrictive covenant by one of their citizens, such as is represented by the Calvo Clause, and would not hesitate to take proper steps to protect the rights of a citizen, provided always that the local remedies could be shown to have been exhausted.

PUBLIC BONDS    The situation is somewhat different, however, in the case of a particular kind of contractual obligation: public bonds. A bond issued by a state is normally a bearer obligation, freely marketable and transferable; interest and amortization payments are made to the holder of record at a particular time, and that holder more often than not is different from the original purchaser of the bond. Hence governments, in general, have adopted the attitude that a public bond represents a much looser and more impersonal contract than one drawn up directly between an alien and a state. Also, because many individuals and institutions buy public bonds not for investment but for speculative purposes, with the degree of risk usually indicated by a rather high rate of interest, governments tend to agree that the old rule of *caveat emptor* applies to all holders of such securities.

On the other hand, when default occurs in any obligation attached to a public bond, the holder of that instrument quite often is barred from all local remedies by the immunity from suit claimed and enforced by the state that had issued the bond in question. This regrettable situation leads the holder of the bond to seek the aid of his own government. Although most states will not normally intervene on behalf of the bondholder for the reasons previously stated, the majority will do so if the facts indicate discrimination by the foreign debtor. If no such discrimination can be shown, official support is not likely to be forthcoming for the investor. For instance, U.S. private interests purchased some $75 million of Imperial Russian government bonds before 1917. The Soviet government disclaimed all responsibility for imperial or provisional government obligations, and the bonds in question must be regarded as, at best, very decorative wallpaper.[40]

Other breaches of good faith likely to lead to international claims are such practices as diverting revenues pledged for the interest and redemption payments of bonds to other purposes, thereby depriving the bondholders of the security behind the public obligations held by them; payment of sums,

---

[39] See *United States (North American Dredging Co. of Texas)* v. *United Mexican States*, United States–Mexico General Claims Commission, 1926 (*Opinions of the Commissioners*, 1927, 21), in which the Claims Commission agreed that an alien might sign a contract containing the Calvo Clause, but that he could not deprive his own government of the right of "applying international remedies to violations of international law committed to his damage."

[40] In 1986, the Soviet Union and Great Britain agreed to Russian payment of certain Czarist debts in return for the release of Russian funds impounded in London since 1917: see *CSM*, July 16, 1986, at 2 and *Time*, July 28, 1986, at 49.

promised in gold or "gold-currency," in depreciated paper money;[41] and paying interest to selected groups of bondholders while defaulting with respect to all others. Any of these actions appear to constitute valid grounds for international claims.

**•THE DRAGO DOCTRINE**    Failure to pay compensation to injured aliens or to meet legitimate obligations to foreign bondholders has led on occasion to the threat of and even to the use of force by the governments of the injured aliens against delinquent states.

Dr. Luis Drago, then the foreign minister of Argentina, evolved the so-called Drago Doctrine when he wrote on December 29, 1902, to the Argentine minister in Washington that "a public debt cannot give rise to the right of intervention, and much less to the occupation of the soil of any American nation by any European power."[42]

The Drago Doctrine was interpreted by its framer as a logical supplement to the Monroe Doctrine, and as such, as well as on its presumed own merits, it attracted much support among Latin American states.

## RESPONSIBILITY OF STATES FOR THE ACTIONS OF REBELS AND INSURGENT GOVERNMENTS

The discussion of international claims arising out of the treatment of aliens has centered thus far only on acts undertaken, directly or indirectly, by the lawful, recognized government of a state. Frequently, however, aliens suffer injuries in their persons or property at the hands of rebels or insurgent governments. The rules governing such injuries are fairly simple; yet there have been numerous controversies between states as a result of incidents connected with civil wars and uprisings.

In the event of a rebellion, the assumption of state responsibility centers on the concept of the exercise of "due diligence." Almost by definition, every government is concerned with using all available means to prevent an outbreak of rebellion and, if one occurs, to suppress it as effectively and as quickly as possible, with subsequent punishment of the rebels. If it can be demonstrated that reasonable precautions were taken to prevent a rebellion and that after an uprising began, prompt measures were taken to subdue the rebels and to punish them, then the lawful government has no international responsibility for the acts committed by rebels against aliens.[43]

This principle was illustrated in the

---

[41]Failure to honor the so-called gold clause has led to a number of important decisions by international tribunals. Noteworthy are the *Case of the Serbian Loans Issued in France (France v. Kingdom of the Serbs, Croats and Slovenes), P.C.I.J., 1929*, Ser. A, No. 20, in which the court held that the gold clause involved had to be honored by Yugoslavia.

[42]Moore, vol. 6, 592; the complete "text" of the doctrine may be found in *U.S. Foreign Relations, 1903*, 1–5.

[43]See also "Articles," n. 2, nos. 14 and 15.

## HOME MISSIONARY SOCIETY CASE
## (UNITED STATES v. GREAT BRITAIN)
*United States–Great Britain, Claims Arbitration, 1920*
*(Claims Arbitration under a Special Agreement*
*of August 8, 1910—Nielsen's Report, 421)*

FACTS    The United States presented a claim for $78,068.15, together with interest thereon from May 30, 1898, against Great Britain on behalf of an American religious body known as the "Home Frontier and Foreign Missionary Society of the United Brethren in Christ." This claim was in respect of losses and damages sustained by that body and some of its members during a rebellion in 1898 in the British protectorate of Sierra Leone.

The British administration in Sierra Leone had imposed in 1898 a new tax, known as the *hut tax*, on the indigenous population of the protectorate. On April 27, as a result of the levy, a serious revolt broke out in the Ronietta district, accompanied by indiscriminate attacks on the persons and properties of Europeans.

All of the society's missions in the district were attacked and either destroyed or damaged. Several of the missionaries were killed.

The British authorities summoned troops to the district and quickly and firmly suppressed the revolt. In September, October, and November, as many of the natives guilty of attacks on white property and persons as could be located were arrested, tried, and on conviction punished by the British law-enforcement agencies in the protectorate.

On February 21, 1899, the United States government called the losses sustained by the society to the attention of the British government. The latter, on October 14, 1899, repudiated all liability for the acts of the rebels, expressing only its regret that no funds were available from which compensation could be paid as an act of grace.

The United States government then submitted its claim to arbitration under a special agreement signed by the two countries on August 10, 1910, alleging lack of due diligence on the part of the British authorities in Sierra Leone.

ISSUE    Did state responsibility devolve on Great Britain, with consequent liability for compensation, as a result of lack of due diligence in suppressing the revolt in Sierra Leone?

DECISION    The Arbitration Tribunal found no evidence of lack of due diligence by the British authorities in question and therefore rejected the American claim, in the absence of British state responsibility.

REASONING    The hut tax was a lawful exercise of British authority in the protectorate and was a tax quite generally encountered at the time in African colonies and protectorates.

The widespread levy of the tax in other parts of Africa did not suggest that its imposition in Sierra Leone would lead to an indigenous uprising.

Investigation by a Royal Commissioner indicated clearly that the British authorities had done everything in their power to protect lives and property as soon as the revolt took place. Despite heavy losses, the number of troops in the affected areas was increased continuously. Difficulties in communications and the simultaneous outbreak of risings in widely separated localities made it impossible to have troops available at all points where losses of life or property occurred.

Repression of the revolt proceeded with the greatest possible dispatch, and the hunting down, trial, and punishment of as many persons guilty of crimes as could be found were prompt and adequate.

The tribunal could not, therefore, uphold the contention advanced by the United States government that the British authorities had failed to act with due diligence.

• **THE CALVO DOCTRINE**    The Sierra Leone case dealt with a native uprising, quickly suppressed. What, on the other hand, would be the situation as related to alien claims when a revolt assumed such proportions that a civil war could be said to exist, that is, when a revolutionary government had come into being and had troops and other appurtenances of an organized civil society at its disposal?

Under such conditions, could the lawful government be held responsible for injuries suffered by aliens when they, together with segments of the local population, were actually removed from the authority of the legitimate government and were placed under the temporary authority of an insurgent or rebel government?

The general principle applicable under such circumstances would still be the same: the legitimate government of the state in question could be held responsible for injuries suffered by aliens at the hands of insurgents only if it could be demonstrated that the government had failed to exercise due diligence in preventing or suppressing the rebel movement. Latin American states have adopted a more restrictive view under the so-called Calvo Doctrine, named after the inventor of the Calvo Clause.

According to the Calvo Doctrine, *no* state can accept responsibility for losses suffered as a result of insurrection or civil war, because such acceptance would tend to menace the independence of weak states by virtually asking for intervention by stronger states whose citizens have suffered losses, and also because acceptance of such a responsibility would place aliens in a more favorable position than would be true for the citizens of the state beset by civil war. The Calvo Doctrine, today, must be regarded as constituting at best a principle of regional international law.

Many cases, some of them very well known, show under what conditions international responsibility may be imputed to a state for the acts of insurgents.[44] The classic decision cited most commonly is that in

---

[44]Thus especially *Italy (Sambiaggio Claim)* v. *Venezuela*, Italy–Venezuela, Claims Arbitration, 1903, in Ralston, *Venezuelan Arbitrations of 1903*, 679; see also Hyde, vol. 2, 979–84; Hackworth, vol. 5, 666–81.

## UNITED STATES (ROSA GELBTRUNK CLAIM)
### v. SALVADOR
Arbitral Tribunal, 1902
(U.S. Foreign Relations, 1902, 876)

FACTS    In 1898 Maurice Gelbtrunk & Co., a partnership firm owned by two United States citizens, carried on a mercantile business in the Republic of El Salvador. In November of that year, a revolution broke out in that state, and a revolutionary force occupied the city of Sensuntepeque, where a quantity of goods valued at $22,000 and belonging to the Gelbtrunk enterprise was stored. The soldiers of the rebel army looted the goods in question and sold, appropriated, or destroyed them. This action was not done under the orders of any officer or as an act of military necessity but was an act of lawless violence by the soldiers in question.

The firm assigned its claim against El Salvador to Rosa Gelbtrunk, the wife of one of the two partners. She, in turn, appealed to the United States government to intervene on her behalf in claiming indemnification for the lost property. The government accepted her appeal but failed to arrive at a settlement through diplomatic negotiations. The claim was then submitted to an arbitration tribunal already handling other United States claims against El Salvador.

ISSUE    Did state responsibility devolve on the lawful government of El Salvador for losses suffered by aliens as a result of the activities of insurgents?

DECISION    The tribunal rejected the American claim, holding that the government of El Salvador could not be held responsible for the action of the insurgents in question.

REASONING    An alien moving into another state to engage there in business must be regarded as "having cast in his lot with the subjects or citizens of the state in which he resides and carries on business. ... The state to which he owes national allegiance has no right to claim for him as against the nation in which he is resident any other or different treatment in case of loss by war — either foreign or civil — revolution, insurrection, or other internal disturbance caused by organized military force or by soldiers, than that which the latter country metes out its own subjects or citizens."

The tribunal concluded that in the case in question, the Gelbtrunk firm had not been treated any less favorably than had the citizens of El Salvador themselves.

What if the rebel government wins control over the territory of the entire state and replaces the lawful government against which it rose in the first place? In that case, the new government may be held responsible by other states for whatever injuries were caused to aliens from the very beginning of the existence of the then insurgent group. Likewise, the new government would not assume responsibility for whatever injuries were suffered by aliens at the hands of the overthrown previous administration of the state during the course of the civil war.

In other words, a lawful government is usually not responsible internationally for the acts of unsuccessful rebels, provided that due diligence in preventing or suppressing the revolt can be demonstrated. A successful insurgent group may be held responsible internationally for all acts undertaken under its authority from its inception. No responsibility can be imputed to the group for the acts of the vanished government as long as those acts were of a political or military nature, incidental to the civil war, and undertaken for public ends.

## DETERMINATION OF COMPENSATION FOR INJURIES TO ALIENS

No international claim can be presented by one state against another if the state pressing such a claim cannot show that the claimant is entitled to its protection, that is, had already possessed its nationality at the time the injury occurred, and continued in that nationality until the claim is presented.[45]

In this connection we encounter again the problem of the place of the individual in international law. According to traditional practice and theory, only a state possessed the right to present claims for damages or injuries suffered by its citizens in the jurisdiction of another state. This exclusive right was passed, of course, on the notion that an individual was not a subject of international law.

A government normally refuses to support a claim by an individual who became its national only after the claim had accrued or by one who enjoyed its protection and then assumed foreign nationality after the claim had ac-

---

[45] See Hackworth, vol. 5, 802–51; Moore, vol. 6, 628–42. Concerning the requirement of the nationality of the claimant state at the time the injury occurred, see the valuable collection of facts and documents by Myers, "Nationality of Claims," 908–15, in his "Contemporary Practice of the United States Relating to International Law," 53 *AJIL* 896 (1959); Whiteman, vol. 8, 1246–47; the long and detailed explanatory letter from the then Assistant Secretary of State for Congressional Relations (August 5, 1982) in 76 *AJIL* 836 (1982); "United States–Israel Claims Settlement" (1980), reported in 75 *AJIL* 368 (1981), and n. 46 below.

For cases illustrating the nationality aspect of the claimant, see *United States (Agency of Canadian Car & Foundry Co.)* v. *Germany*, United States–Germany, Mixed Claims Commission, 1939, digested in Hackworth, vol. 5, 833; *United States (Romano-American Claim)* v. *Great Britain* in Hackworth, vol. 5, 702–05, 840–44. See also the *Case Concerning the Barcelona Traction, Light and Power Company, Ltd.* (New Application, 1962; *Belgium* v. *Spain*), *Preliminary Objections, I.C.J. Reports,* 1964, 6; excerpted at length in 59 *AJIL* 131–60 (1965); *Second Phase. I.C.K. Reports,* 1970, 3; *Judgment of February 5, 1970,* digested by Bishop, in 64 *AJIL* 653 (1970). See also the *Note* by Susman in 12 *Harvard Int'l L. Jl.* 91 (1971). This decision, involving a judgment of 48 pages, has 306 pages of declarations, individual and — one — dissenting opinions, and has already produced a growing body of commentary, mostly critical in nature: see, *inter alia,* Briggs, "Barcelona Traction: The *Jus Standi* of Belgium," 65 *AJIL* 327 (1971); Lillich, "The Rigidity of Barcelona," *id.,* 522–32; Mann, "The Protection of Shareholders' Interests in the Light of the Barcelona Traction Case," 67 *AJIL* 259 (1973).

crued.[46] It must be pointed out in connection with the nationality issue that general principles of international law do not apply to expropriation by a state of the property of its own nationals.[47]

Assuming that the claimant possesses the required nationality and that state responsibility for injuries suffered by him has been established, how is the compensation due him through his government established?

The general practice appears to be that the measurement of damages is not based on the degree or kind of delinquency shown to have been exhibited by the state held to be responsible; rather, it is based on the loss caused to the claimant by whatever injury was done.

Thus, in the *Janes* case, to cite an example, once state responsibility was established by the claims commission, the determination of damages for compensation purposes was switched back to the original injury sustained.

❡ An area of constant dispute about compensation is that arising out of the nationalization of alien property.[48] It has already been mentioned that most claims originating in the taking of such property revolve around the inadequacy or total lack of compensation rather than any question about the right of a state to engage in the nationalization as such of alien property. In regard to the actual compensation for nationalized property, the U.S. government enunciated its point of view through a statement in January 1972:

With regard to current or future expropriations of property or contractual interests of U.S. nationals, or arrangements for "participation" in those interests by foreign governments, the Department of State wishes to place on record its view that foreign investors are entitled to the fair market value of their interests. Acceptance by U.S. nationals of less than fair market value does not constitute acceptance of any other standard by the United States Government. As a consequence, the United States Government reserves its rights to maintain international claims for what it regards as adequate compensation under international law for the interests nationalized or transferred.[49]

It should be noted, in passing, that when the debtor (delinquent) state does not pay compensation promptly, it may become liable for moratory

[46]See Articles 1 and 4 of the resolution on the "National Character of an International Claim Presented by a State for Injury Suffered by an Individual" (September 10, 1965), of the *Institut de Droit International,* in 60 *AJIL* 521 (1966); consult also Copithorne, "International Claims and the Rule of Nationality," *Proceedings* 30–35, (1969); Kerley, "Nationality of Claims—A Vista," *id.,* 35–42, and comments on the foregoing, *id.,* 42–53; see also n. 45, above.

[47]See *Case of Lithgow and Others,* 102 Eur. Ct. H.R. (1986), European Court of Human Rights, July 8, 1986, reported in 81 *AJIL* 425 (1987), in which the plaintiffs—all of British nationality—had filed a complaint against the United Kingdom.

[48]Lillich, ed., *The Valuation of Nationalized Property in International Law,* 3 vols. (1975), still represents the most comprehensive coverage of the subject.

[49]U.S. Department of State *Press Release No. 630* of December 30, 1975.

interest, and that the first "Hickenlooper amendment" requires suspension of aid to all nations in which United States property has been expropriated without "adequate compensation" if the expropriating state fails within six months to take steps to make quick and equitable payment to the former owners in convertible currency.[50]

EX GRATIA PAYMENTS    One other form of compensation has to be mentioned briefly: payments made by a state to aliens for injuries suffered—not as the result of a judicial or arbitral award but because of humanitarian reasons, including the perception that a wrong had been done. Such compensation, termed an *Ex Gratia Payment*, has been made on occasion. The most recent and well-publicized example was caused by the downing of Iran Air Flight 655 by the U.S.S. *Vincennes* (July 3, 1988), with a loss of all 290 persons aboard the civilian aircraft.[51] Many experts, including the Legal Adviser of the Department of State, while denying U.S. liability, have proposed an *ex gratia* payment to the families of the persons killed. Such payment has been delayed, however, because the U.S. Government ruled out any role for the Iranian government in settling the claims. In consequence, Iran filed a claim against the United States (May 19, 1989) in the International Court of Justice. Iran asked the Court to assert U.S. responsibility for compensation, the amount of the latter to be determined by the Court.

In the case of an earlier modern example, the U.S.S. *Stark* had been attacked (accidentally, it appears) by an Iraqi Air Force Mirage, with a loss of 37 lives. After initial presentation of a large bill by the United States, lengthy negotiations resulted in a reduced claim settlement of $27,350,274, or $739,199 per crew member killed. In that instance, as on most previous occasions for *ex gratia* payments, it was assumed that the government at fault did not have a *legal* liability to make a settlement but did so for compassionate reasons.[52] Not resolved as yet has been a U.S. Government claim for $82.9 million for costs of repairing the ship and a request for compensation for sailors injured in the attack.

[50]See 57 *AJIL* 749 (1967), for text, but also Lillich, "Requiem for Hickenlooper," 69 *AJIL* 97 (1975), on the "defusing" of the amendment. The United States' view about payment still is that payment must be "prompt, adequate and effective." Payment in a non-convertible currency would not be an effective payment.
[51]See the collection of official documents and private views in 83 *AJIL* 318 (1989); *Current Policy Nos. 1092* and *1093* (both July 1988); International Court of Justice, Application Instituting Proceedings in *Case Concerning Aerial Incident of 3 July 1988 (Iran v. United States).* May 17, 1989, in 28 *ILM* 842 (1989); International Court of Justice, Order in the *Case Concerning the Aerial Incident of July 1988 (Iran v. United States)*, Dec. 13, 1989, in 29 *ILM* 123 (1990).
[52]Text of compensation agreement in 28 *ILM* 644 (1989); Documents on the *Stark* incident in *id.*, 26, 1423 (1987).

## SUGGESTED READINGS

### Responsibility of States: General

Lauterpacht's *Oppenheim*, vol. 1, 338–69; Lillich, *International Claims: Their Adjudication by National Commissions* (1962); Silvanie, *Responsibility of States for Acts of Unsuccessful Insurgent Governments* (1939); Garcia-Amador, *The Changing Law of International Claims*, 2 vols (1984); covers both the traditional and the proposed NIEO systems; China: Foreign Economic Contract Law (Effective July 1, 1985), Text and Introductory Note in 24 *ILM* 797–800 (1985); Lillich, ed., *The International Law of State Responsibility for Injury to Aliens* (1983).

CASES

*United States (Harry Roberts Claim)* v. *Mexico*, General Claims 1926, *Opinions of Commissioners* 100, 4 U.N. Rep. Int'l Arb. Awards 77.
*United States (P.W. Shufeldt)* v. *Guatemala*, in Hackworth, vol. 5, 485.
*United States (Noyes)* v. *Panama*, General Claims Arbitration, 1933, Hunt's Rep. 155, 190.
*Claim of Finnish Shipowners (Finland* v. *Great Britain)*, 1934, 3 U.N. Rep. Int'l Arbitral Awards 1479.

### Contracts

CASES

*United States (El Triunfo Co. Claim)* v. *Salvador*, 1902, in *U.S. Foreign Relations*, 1902, 859.
*Liberian Eastern Timber Corporation (LETCO)* v. *The Government of the Republic of Liberia*, Arbitral Tribunal Award (Int. Centre for Settlement of Investment Disputes), March 31, 1986, Rectification, May 14, 1986, in 26 *ILM* 647 (1987). [Recovery of Damages for Breach of a Concession Agreement]

### Expropriation of Alien Property

See, *inter alia*, Lillich, *The Protection of Foreign Investment* (1965); Mooney, *Foreign Seizures: Sabbatino and the Act of State Doctrine* (1967); Lowenfeld, ed., *Expropriation in the Americas* (1971); Cassad & Montagné, *Expropriation in Central America and Panama* (1975); Baklanoff, *Expropriations of U.S. Investments in Cuba, Mexico, and Chile* (1975); Akinsanya, *The Expropriation of Multinational Property in the Third World* (1980); the monographic treatment by von Mehren and Kourides, "International Arbitration Between States and Foreign Private Parties: The Libyan Nationalization Cases," 75 *AJIL* 476 (1981); Peru–United States: *Exchange of Notes on the Distribution of Proceeds Received under the Agreement on Compensation for Expropriated Properties of United States Nationals*, December 18–31, 1974, in 14 *ILM* 36 (1975); Petras, Morley, Smith, *The Nationalization of Venezuela Oil* (1977). France: *Law of Nationalization* (February 11, 1982), in 21 *ILM* 815 (1982); Sornarajah, *The Pursuit of Nationalized Property* (1985); Lillich, ed., *The Valuation of Nationalized Property in International Law* (Vol. IV, 1987); Venezuela, "Decree No. 717 on Foreign Investment, Technology Licensing and Foreign Credit Regulations," Jan.

18, 1990, in 29 *ILM* 273 (1990); Belgium–Luxembourg–Union of Soviet Socialist Republics: "Agreement Concerning the Promotion and the Reciprocal Protection of Investments," Feb. 9, 1989, in *id.* 299; France–Union of Soviet Socialist Republics: "Agreement for the Promotion and Reciprocal Protection of Investments," Feb. 9, 1989, in *id.* 299; France–Union of Soviet Socialist Republics: "Agreement for the Promotion and Reciprocal Protection of Investments," July 4, 1989, in *id.*, 317; Federal Republic of Germany–Poland: "Treaty Concerning the Promotion and Reciprocal Protection of Investments, Nov. 10, 1989, in *id.*, 333; Federal Republic of Germany–Union of Soviet Socialist Republics: "Treaty of Promotion and Reciprocal Protection of Investments," June 13, 1989, in *id.*, 351.

CASES

*Present* v. *United States Life Insurance Co.*, New Jersey Supreme Court, 1967, 232 At2d 863, reported in 62 *AJIL* 494 (1968).

*F. Palacio y Compania, S.A.* v. *Brush*, U.S. Dist. Court, S.D.N.Y., 1966, 256 F. Supp. 481, excerpted in 61 *AJIL* 601 (1967).

*Alberti* v. *Empresa Nicaraguense de la Carne*, U.S. Court of Appeals, 7th Cir., April 18, 1983, 705 *Fed. Reporter*, 2d Series 250–57 (1983), in 22 *ILM* 835 (1983).

Arbitration Tribunal: *Award in the Matter of an Arbitration Between Kuwait and the American Independent Oil Co. (AMINOIL)*, March 24, 1982, in 21 *ILM* 976 (1983).

*Case Concerning the American International Group, Inc./American Life Insurance Company and the Islamic Republic of Iran/Central Insurance of Iran*, Iran–United States Claims Tribunal, December 19, 1983, reproduced in full in 23 *ILM* 1 (1984).

*Shareholders* v. *Compagnie de Saint-Gobin*, Commercial Court, Namur, October 14, 1986 (with introductory note by Feldman), 26 *ILM* 1251 (1987).

*Kalamazoo Spice Extraction Company* v. *The Provisional Military Government of Socialist Ethiopia*, U.S. Dist. Court, W.D. Mich. (Southern Div.), August 26, 1985, in 24 *ILM* 1277 (1985).

*INA Corp.* v. *The Islamic Republic of Iran*. AWD 184-161-1, Iran–United States Claims Tribunal, The Hague, August 13, 1985, reported in 80 *AJIL* 181 (1986).

*AMOCO International Finance Corp.* v. *Islamic Republic of Iran*. AWD 310-56-3. Iran–United States Claims Tribunal, The Hague, July 24, 1987, reported in 82 *AJIL* 358 (1988). The 'Partial Award' in this case, of July 14, 1987, is found in full in 27 *ILM* 1314 (1988).

and the unusual

*Claim of Silberg and Mogilanski*, Foreign Claims Settlement Commission of the United States, Decisions Nos. PO 62 and 63, 1961, reported in 56 *AJIL* 544 (1961).


Protection of Investments

Meron, *Investment Insurance in International Law* (1976); Panama–United States: "Treaty Concerning the Treatment and Protection of Investments" (Oct. 27, 1982), and supporting documents, 21 *ILM* 1227 (1982).

# 12

# Extradition

## EXTRADITION AND INTERSTATE RELATIONS

The escape of an alleged fugitive from justice from the territory of the state in which his offense was claimed to have been committed into the jurisdiction of another state leads to a temporary halt of an effort to punish the individual in question. Under the prevailing doctrine of the independence of states, the pursuing state is stopped at the boundary of another state's sovereignty: its own authority has no effect within that foreign sovereignty. Because states are still very jealous of their territorial integrity, they will not normally consent to the intrusion of the authority of another entity. At times this strict construction may lead to rather extraordinary consequences, as was shown in a famous old case:

### THE SAVARKAR CASE: FRANCE–GREAT BRITAIN

*Tribunal of the Hague Permanent Court
of Arbitration, 1911*

FACTS    Vinayak Damodar Savarkar, a British Indian, was in custody aboard the English mail steamer *Morea* on his way to India for trial in connection with a murder case. On July 8, 1910, while the vessel was in the port of Marseilles, Savarkar succeeded in making his way ashore. He was arrested shortly by a member of the French maritime *gendarmerie* (the British authorities had previously warned the French police that an escape attempt might be made at Marseilles) and returned to the ship. On July 9, the *Morea* left Marseilles with Savarkar aboard. It developed later that the arresting policeman did not know the identity of the escapee and believed him to be a member of the ship's crew, escaping after committing some offense on the vessel.

The French government then demanded the return of Savarkar to France, alleging that he had been removed from French territory without authorization; this request was followed by a formal demand for Savarkar's extradition to France. When Great Britain rejected both demands, the French government brought the dispute in 1911 before an arbitral tribunal of the Hague Permanent Court of Arbitration.

ISSUE    Should Vinayak Savarkar be restored or not restored to France by the British government, in accordance with existing rules of international law?

DECISION    The arbitral tribune decided that Great Britain was not required to return Savarkar to France.

REASONING    The evidence presented showed that the local (Marseilles) French police authorities had placed themselves at the disposal of the captain of the *Morea* and had placed an agent aboard to assist the officer in charge of the prisoner. The return of the fugitive to the ship was done in good faith and did not represent recourse to fraud or force in order to obtain possession of an individual who had taken refuge in a foreign country. The act of the officer who returned Savarkar to the ship was not disowned before the *Morea* left the port,

and thus the British police were left under the impression that the French officer had acted under instructions or that his action had received the approval of his superiors.

Although it had to be admitted that Savarkar's return to the ship had been somewhat irregular, there was no rule of international law imposing, under the circumstances cited, an obligation on Great Britain to restore Savarkar to France—merely because a mistake committed by the agent of the maritime police.

EXTRADITION    A common interest in preventing flight abroad from foiling the apprehension and punishment of a fugitive from justice has led to interstate cooperation and to the development of procedures by which fugitives can be returned to the state in which the alleged crime was committed. The process, always including a formal request for the surrender of the persons wanted, together with certain well-defined conditions for surrender, is called *extradition*.[1] In *Terlinden* v. *Ames* (184 U.S. 270, 289, 1902), extradition was defined as "the surrender by one nation to another of an individual accused or convicted of an offence outside of its own territory, and within the territorial jurisdiction of the other, which, being competent to try and to punish him, demands the surrender." Extradition today is normally based on a bilateral treaty, in the absence of a generally accepted convention on the subject. In *Factor* v. *Laubenheimer* (290 U.S. 276, 287, 1933), the U.S. Supreme Court stated the general rule: "The principles of international law recognize no right to extradition apart from treaty. While a government may, if agreeable to its own constitution and laws, voluntarily exercise the power to surrender a fugitive from justice to the country from which he has fled, and it has been said that it is under a moral duty to do so, . . . the legal right to demand his extradition and the correlative duty to surrender him to the demanding country exist only when created by treaty."

Although most provisions for extradition are, as already mentioned, based on bilateral treaties, a sufficient similarity in state practices has developed to support the view that by now a series of customary rules has been developed or that such rules are in the final stages of their development.

PROBLEM OF FLIGHT ABROAD    The problem of alleged fugitives is actually a very complicated aspect of interstate relations. In all, there are five divisions:

1. Recovery of fugitive criminals in violation of international law.

[1]On the general subject of extradition, consult Whiteman, vol. 6, 727–1122; Hackworth, vol. 4, 1–241; Harvard Research in International Law, "Extradition," in 29 *AJIL* Sp. Supp. 16–434 (1935); Shearer, *Extradition in International Law* (1971).

2. Capture of a fugitive criminal in the territory of the sheltering state, with the connivance of its officials, by private citizens of the seeking state.
3. Capture of the fugitive in the sheltering state, without the knowledge of its officials, by private citizens of the seeking state (the case of Eichmann comes to mind as a celebrated example).
4. Irregular apprehension of a fugitive criminal by officials of the sheltering state before extradition takes place.
5. Wrongful (mistaken) surrender of a fugitive by officials of the sheltering state to the seeking state.

The limitations of a general text preclude a detailed analysis of all the preceding possibilities, and so only those aspects that have figured prominently in the recent history of extradition can be covered.

## Extradition Treaties

The surrender of wanted fugitives was not transformed into a legal duty until the members of the community of nations created a network of bilateral extradition treaties. These fall into either of two categories: the older, traditional type, which contains a specific list of offenses for the commission of which a fugitive will be surrendered, and the newer type, of twentieth-century origin, which contains no such list but which provides for extradition in all cases in which the offense in question is punishable in both countries involved in a given case. Thus, for an offense to give rise to extradition, it must either be included specifically in the treaty, or be regarded as a crime under the laws of the contracting parties, or both (*Rule of Double Criminality*). The operation of the Rule was illustrated in the case of Adnan Khashoggi in 1989. The Saudi financier, at one time held to be the world's wealthiest man, was arrested in April 1989 in Bern (Switzerland) at the request of the United States, which promised to send necessary documentation within 60 days. Khashoggi had been indicted in the U.S. District Court in New York for helping Ferdinand Marcos and his wife in real estate transactions involving funds stolen from the Philippine Treasury and also for a variety of racketeering charges. He was extradited to the United States in July 1989 and faced charges for mail fraud and obstruction of justice (contained also in the request for extradition). He was not tried on the racketeering charges: the latter were punishable in the United States but were not punishable under Swiss law.

The practice of states varies a great deal as to whether they conclude a traditional or a more modern type of extradition treaty. For example, the new Japan–United States extradition treaty approved by the Japanese parliament on February 19, 1980, replacing an agreement of 1886, lists 47 offenses (compared with 15 in the older treaty), including hijacking, narcotics violations, and, in a catch-all provision, any crime punishable by "death, imprisonment, or deprivation of liberty for a period of more than one year" under the laws of either country.

It should be pointed out that in modern times at least, international law knows no duty to extradite apart from treaties. A state may voluntarily decide to surrender a fugitive from justice, but a legal right to demand such surrender and a correlative duty to acquiesce in such a demand can exist only where created by treaty. In the United States, official opinion denies the existence of any authority to surrender a fugitive in the absence of a treaty. On a few occasions, the surrender of a fugitive from another country was achieved when no relevant treaty existed, but in such instances the United States explained carefully that this government could not reciprocate the favor.

Until recently, all extradition treaties were bilateral in nature. On April 18, 1960, however, the European Convention on Extradition, drawn up in Paris in December 1957, entered into force and was supplemented by two additional protocols, one on October 15, 1975, and a second one on March 17, 1978.[2] By 1985, the original convention was in force for 18 countries, including Cyprus, Israel, and Turkey. In Latin America an earlier regional Convention on Extradition, adopted at the Seventh International Conference of American States in 1933, represents another effort to substitute uniformity in extradition practices through multilateral treaties for the prevailing diversity in practice based on bilateral agreements.

Up to about the middle of the eighteenth century, extradition treaties covered primarily the surrender of *political* fugitives. Gradually, ordinary crimes began to be included as reasons for the surrender of an alleged offender. By the second half of the last century, however, the revolution in transportation had made the speedy escape of criminals ever easier; hence extradition treaties became increasingly general in character. Interestingly enough, as the scope of these agreements expanded to include more categories of criminal offenses, political offenses ceased to play a part, and today they no longer form a basis for the surrender of fugitives.[3]

FORMAL PROCEDURE FOR EXTRADITION    Although extradition treaties vary considerably in regard to the offenses listed in them as the basis of surrender, the actual procedure utilized in extradition has been standardized fairly well all over the world.[4]

---

[2]Text in 17 *ILM* 813 (1978). The 1975 Additional Protocol excluded war crimes from the definition of political offenses, while the 1978 Protocol dealt with fiscal offenses. Other primarily European instruments covering related matters are The European Convention on Mutual Assistance in Criminal Matters (1959) and its 1978 Protocol (18 countries); The European Convention on the International Validity of Criminal Judgments (1970), obligating six countries; and the European Convention on the Transfer of Proceedings in Criminal Matters, of 1972 (five countries).

[3]For the effect of war on extradition treaties, see *Argento* v. *Horn*, United States, Court of Appeals, 6th Cir., 1957, 241 F.2d 258, reported in 51 *AJIL* 634 (1957); for subsequent developments, see 54 *AJIL* 409 (1960).

[4]On July 16, 1981, the U.S. Department of State issued to all Foreign Service posts the revised Directive on International Extradition. Excerpts are in 76 *AJIL* 154 (1982), and constitute a concise summary of modern extradition procedures. See also M. Cherif Bassiouni, *International Extradition: United States Law and Practice*, vol. 1 (1982), which includes the 1982 U.S. Draft Extradition Act.

A request for the surrender of an alleged fugitive criminal must be presented to the foreign state through the diplomatic agent of the seeking government. When such a request is received, the foreign government institutes an investigation through its judicial agencies to determine whether there is sufficient evidence, in accordance with the local law, to warrant an arrest of the fugitive.[5] If sufficient evidence is submitted and accords with the local law requirements, the fugitive is held pending the arrival of law-enforcement agents of the seeking state. The agents then receive the fugitive into their custody and return him to the state in which the crime was committed.

When the fugitive has been surrendered and is tried, the *principle of speciality* requires that he must be tried *only* for the specific offense or offenses mentioned (in list or by penalties involved) in the request for his extradition—unless the asylum state permits otherwise. In other words, the fugitive may only be tried for offenses committed before extradition and for which he was surrendered. Examples of the operation of this principle abound in the history of the law; the case of *United States* v. *Rauscher*[6] is considered a classic example. Rauscher had been surrendered by Great Britain on a charge of manslaughter, but was tried in the United States on the charge of inflicting cruel and unusual punishment.

In the *Case of Blackmer*,[7] the United States government had requested the extradition of Henry Blackmer on a charge of perjury in connection with certain income tax returns. The French court held that the penalty for the offense differed in the two countries and that the corrective penalty for the offense specified by French law had been barred through prescription (expiration of a time limit of three years prevailing under French law).

---

[5] It should be noted that so-called common-law countries require such a showing of sufficient evidence, whereas civil-law countries frequently view such a showing as a usurpation of domestic jurisdiction by a foreign court. The United States and Iran do not have, at the time of writing, a treaty of extradition. Thus, although the deposed Shah of Iran lived briefly in the United States (1979–1980), his country made no attempt to present a formal demand for his extradition. But after the Shah had moved to Panama, Iranian authorities prepared a formal request for his detention and subsequent extradition. The 450-page document was to be presented by a French attorney representing Iran to the Panamanian government on March 24, 1980. The Shah, however, elected to leave Panama, with his family, on March 23, 1980, and moved to Egypt, at the invitation of President Anwar Sadat. Panamanian laws would have required the arrest of the Shah as soon as the extradition request had been filed with the host country's foreign ministry.

[6] United States Supreme Court, 1886, 119 U.S. 407; however, the surrendered fugitive *may* be tried also for another offense if sufficient evidence is sent to the country that surrendered the individual and if that country agrees to a trial for the second offense. See *United States* v. *Berenguer et al.*, United States, Dist. Court, S.D.N.Y., 1976, No. 76-2829, reprinted in 74 *AJIL* 161 (1980). Its sequel, *Berenguer* v. *Vance*, United States, Dist. Court, D.C., 1979, 473 F. Supp. 1195, in *id.*, 674.

[7] France, Court of Paris, Chambre des Mises en Accusation, 1928, in Hudson, 514–15.

SAMUEL INSULL CASE    There was a great amount of publicity in the well-known *Samuel Insull* case decision of the Greek Court of Appeals in 1933.[8] In that instance, the United States requested the extradition of the former Chicago banker Samuel Insull, Sr., on charges of embezzlement and larceny. The Greek court ruled twice that the evidence submitted by the United States was insufficient under Greek law to prove that the fugitive had deliberately intended to evade laws of the United States when he concealed or transferred certain assets, and it ordered the release of the detained Insull. The government of the United States asserted that the Greek court had exceeded its proper functions and notified Greece of the termination of a brand-new extradition treaty concluded between the two states. Amusingly enough, Insull was incautious enough to leave his Greek sanctuary and to venture in a chartered Greek vessel into Turkey. The United States filed a request for his extradition with the Turkish government, and the latter removed Insull from the ship and permitted his transportation to the United States. At the time in question, no extradition treaty was in force between the United States and Turkey.

Insull's case illustrates the frequently forgotten fact that an extradition treaty does not have to be in existence for a country to surrender an alleged fugitive from justice. That can always be done on the basis of comity (or courtesy) if the sheltering country is willing to extradite. The United States, unlike its earlier practice in the case of Samuel Insull, no longer asks for surrender on the basis of comity.[9] It asks extradition only from countries with which the United States has an applicable treaty and only for an offense specified in some manner in that treaty. It must be suspected that the reverse situation would also be true: the United States would not normally surrender an alleged fugitive in the absence of an extradition treaty (see the instance of the deposed Shah of Iran, n.5, *supra*). The United States' attitude toward comity in extradition was illustrated in the instance of two citizens of the Republic of China (Taiwan) who were accused of murdering a Chinese-American writer in California in October 1984. There being no extradition treaty between the ROC and the United States, the American refusal to demand extradition on the basis of comity caused the Ministry of Justice in Taipei to file preliminary murder charges against the two alleged killers (February 4, 1985); the Republic of China asserts that it has the right to try its own citizens for crimes committed abroad. The two received life sentences. The court also convicted a fellow gang member, Tung Kuei-sen, *in absentia*; he was subsequently captured in Brazil and extradited to the United States. Tung was convicted of first-degree murder by a California court (May 16, 1988). Earlier, in 1985, a Taiwanese court had sentenced

---

[8] *United States* v. *Insull*, 8 F. Supp. 310. U.S. Dist. Court, N. D. Ill. 1934.
[9] An illustration of comity is supplied by *Fioconni* v. *Attorney General of the United States*, United States, Court of Appeals, 2nd Cir., 1972, 462 F.2d 475, reported 67 *AJIL* 346 (1973). *Certiorari denied* by Supreme Court, 1972, 409 U.S. 1059.

the head of the Military Intelligence Agency in Taiwan's Department of Defense to life imprisonment for plotting the California murder, and two subordinates were convicted as accessories to murder.

Naturally, because a fugitive might decide to leave his current place of refuge at the first hint of the start of extradition proceedings, most treaties provide for his or her arrest after informal—say, telegraphic—request, pending the preparation and sending of a formal extradition request. Normally the agreements limit such temporary detention to a relatively brief period of time, such as forty days.

The return of a surrendered alleged fugitive to the seeking state through the territory or airspace of third countries requires permission for such transit. Normally no difficulties are encountered in securing such permission in the case of charges of homicide or other serious crimes. On the other hand, offenses in the sphere of fraud may lead to problems for the seeking state. Many countries, particularly those following Roman-law systems, have varying definitions of fraud, and quite often the arresting officers escorting the surrendered individual to the seeking state have to plan circuitous routes of travel to avoid the airspace of such countries.

DOCTRINE OF RECIPROCITY    Another complicating factor in extradition is the manifest unwillingness of most states to surrender their own citizens to another state when those individuals have fled back into their country. Most states in continental Europe as well as in Latin American hold to the concept that a crime committed by one of their citizens anywhere in the world constitutes a violation of their own law just as much as the law of the state in which the offense took place.[10] These countries then proceed to reserve for themselves the trial and punishment of the offender when he comes within their jurisdiction, refusing to honor extradition requests for the person of the fugitive. By contrast, Anglo-American practice follows the principle that crimes must be tried where they have been committed and that criminal courts lack jurisdiction over crimes that took place outside the territory of the state in question. This means that if, say, the United States refused to surrender an American citizen who is charged with the

---

[10]Useful illustrative cases include *Charlton* v. *Kelly*, United States, Supreme Court, 1913, 229 U.S. 447, 33 Sup. Ct. 945, and *Coumas* v. *Superior Court of San Joaquin Country*, United States, Supreme Court of California, 31 Cal. 2d. 682 (1948). See also *NYT*, January 31, 1952, and 47 *AJIL* 150 (1953), for details of the fascinating case of *In re Lo Dolce* (United States, Dist. Court W.D. N. Y. 1952, 106 F. Supp. 455), which involved an Italian demand for surrender by the United States of two U.S. nationals for the murder of another American (Major William V. Holohan) by poisoned soup and shooting, while all three were behind enemy lines, and the embezzlement of $100,000 in gold and currency. The murder had taken place in Italy in 1944, behind the German lines, while the three men were engaged in carrying the valuables in question to Italian partisans; see Fink and Schwartz, "International Extradition: The Holohan Murder Case," 39 *American Bar Association Journal* 297, 346 (1953). See also the decision of the (West) German Federal Constitutional Court, First Division, of July 10, 1958, reported in 54 *AJIL* 419 (1960).

commission of a crime in France and who had fled to this country, he would not be tried and punished for what he did.

This paradoxical situation has led to the widespread adoption of the doctrine of reciprocity. If the requesting state is shown to be willing, by past performance, to surrender its own citizens for trial by the courts of another country, the "detaining" state is normally willing to surrender its own citizens. But this system does not operate in certain countries in which the local constitution prohibits the extradition of nationals to other countries, such as in the case of the Federal Republic of Germany (Art. 16, par. 2, of the constitution).

Numerous extradition treaties provide specifically that neither of the contracting parties will surrender its own nationals to the other party. This is true, for instance, in several such treaties to which the United States is a party; these agreements supersede the principles laid down in a number of earlier court decisions, considered at one time of great importance. [11]

A new extradition treaty concluded between Italy and the United States became effective on September 25, 1984. It provides, among other things, for the extradition of citizens from each country to the other (reciprocity), as well as for the abandonment of the "probable cause" requirement under which Italian authorities had had to prove in advance the probable guilt of a suspect. Under the new treaty, a "reasonable basis" for belief in the individual's guilt is sufficient for extradition purposes. The treaty also permits a person convicted in one of the two countries to be extradited for trial in the other before his full prison term had been served. As a result of that provision, the day the treaty came into effect saw the extradition to Italy of Michele Sindona, an Italian financier serving a 25-year term in a U.S. federal prison for various fraud charges in connection with the failure of an American bank. In Italy Sindona faced trial for fraud in relation to an Italian bank failure as well as for ordering the 1979 murder of an Italian lawyer in charge of the Italian bank after its failure. Even if Sindona was convicted on any charge in Italy, he had to be returned to the United States to serve the rest of his American prison term before being sent to Italy to serve an Italian sentence.

Because the principle of reciprocity may lead to nonpunishment of guilty parties, efforts have been made by legal experts as well as by governments to add to the principle an obligation by his own government to prosecute the accused person for the offense with which he was charged by the state denied surrender of his person. Thus the Montevideo Convention on Extradition (1933), a regional instrument, imposed this obligation (Art. 2) on the parties to the agreement, subject to certain conditions surrounding the crime in question.

[11]See the careful analysis by Evans, "The New Extradition Treaties of the United States," 59 *AJIL* 351 (1965), and the key case on the subject, *Valentine* v. *United States ex rel. Neidecker*, U.S. Supreme Court, 1936, 299 U.S. 5.

An interesting series of events concerning the extradition of nationals took place in Colombia during the effort to end the reign of the "narcoterrorists," the drug cartels operating in Colombia. Two bilateral extradition treaties with the United States (1888, 1941) did not allow the extradition of nationals to the other party. A modern treaty with the United States (1979), however, provided for the extraditing country's own citizens to be surrendered, thereby departing from the traditional international rule of exempting one's own from extradition to another state. The Supreme Court of Colombia, however, threw out the treaty (June 25, 1987) because of claimed procedural faults in presidential approval of the treaty. The United States maintained, on the other hand, that the agreement was still in force. In August 1989, Colombian President Barco revived the treaty in invoking emergency powers, and on October 4, 1989, Colombia's Supreme Court upheld the relevant presidential decree, asserting that the previous procedural faults relating to the treaty had now been remedied. By July 2, 1990, 17 leading Colombian drug traffickers indicted in the United States were arrested and extradited to the United States at the latter's request. However, on September 5, 1990, President Cesar Gaviria offered immunity from extradition and cuts in sentences to any "drug barons" who would turn themselves in, conditions laid down by the traffickers the previous January.

A somewhat unusual problem in the sphere of extradition, a conflict between a law-making treaty and a bilateral extradition treaty, was illustrated in the recent *Soering Case*:

## THE SOERING CASE[12]

### European Court of Human Rights, July 7, 1989

FACTS    Jens Soering, 22, a German national, son of a German diplomat, was accused of murdering his girlfriend's parents in Virginia. He and the girl were arrested in the U.K. on a charge of check fraud, and Soering confessed to the murders, claiming to have been under the influence of the girl. The latter currently was serving multiple life sentences in Virginia as an accessory to the murders.

The U.S. requested extradition of Soering under the U.K.–U.S. Extradition Treaty of 1972. The U.K. attempted to obtain American assurances that the death penalty, if imposed, would not be executed. The U.S. replied that the U.K. position would be communicated to the sentencing judge. Soering thereupon lodged a complaint with the European Human Rights Commission which brought the case before the European Court of Rights.

The complaint charged that the U.K., if extraditing Soering to the U.S., would be in violation of Article 3 of the European Convention for the Protection of Human Rights and Fundamental Freedoms. ["No one shall be subjected to torture or to inhuman or degrading treatment or punishment."]

Soering claimed that if he were returned to Virginia and sentenced to

---

[12]Text of decision, including *ILM* Content Summary, in 28 *ILM* 1063 (1989).

death, he would face years in death row under extreme conditions while appealing his sentence. His contention therefore centered, not on the merits of capital punishment (allowed under certain conditions laid down in the Human Rights Convention), but on the conditions experienced by prisoners awaiting execution and the outcome of appeals.

ISSUE    Could the U.K. deny extradition of Soering to the U.S. despite the U.K.–U.S. Treaty whose provisions did cover the crime of murder?

DECISION    The Court ruled unanimously against Soering's extradition to the United States.

REASONING    "Having regard to the very long period of time spent on death row in such extreme conditions, with the ever present and mounting anguish of

awaiting execution of the death penalty, and to the personal circumstances of the applicant, especially his age and mental state at the time of the offense, the applicant's extradition to the United States would expose him to a real risk of treatment going beyond the threshold set by Article 3." [Several minor issues have been omitted in this Abstract.]

NOTES:    The European Human Rights Convention, to which the U.K. was a party, represented a law-making treaty and as such took precedence over the bilateral U.K.–U.S. extradition treaty.

A unanimous verdict by the full court, representing all 23 members of the Council of Europe, is rare.

It was expected, after the verdict by the Court, that Soering would be extradited to the German Federal Republic to stand trial there on the murder charges.

By 1990, very few countries (including the United States) still utilized the death penalty, except under very special conditions such as wartime treason or espionage, etc. This development has affected the extradition of fugitives from justice, and the current view is illustrated by Section 8 of the Law on International Assistance in Criminal Matters (December 23, 1982)[13] of the Federal Republic of Germany: "If the act is punishable by death under the law of the requesting state, extradition shall be granted only if the requesting state gives assurances that the death penalty will not be imposed or carried out."

Some extradition treaties as well as the laws of some states stipulate that the offense in question (re extradition) must have been committed "within the jurisdiction" of the requesting state. Such provisions obviously impede, in some cases, the attainment of justice. In consequence a considerable number of extradition treaties have been amended in order to remove the impediment. For example, the new Paragraph (2) of Article 3 of the 1971 Canada–United States Treaty on Extradition, as amended on January 11, 1988, reads:

"(2) When the offense for which extradition is requested was committed outside the territory of the requesting State, the executive or other appropriate authority of the

[13]Text in 74 ILM 945 (1985).

requested State shall grant extradition if the laws of the requested State provide for jurisdiction over such an offense committed in similar circumstances. If the laws in the requested State do not so provide, the executive authority in the requested State may, in its discretion, grant extradition."

## Political Offenses

The most interesting aspect of extradition from a general point of view and the one receiving the greatest amount of publicity in the press has to do with political offenders.

It has been pointed out already that a virtually complete reversal in state policy took place during the nineteenth century, when political offenses were removed from the list of crimes for which individuals might be extradited. Modern extradition treaties specifically exempt political offenses, most likely because liberal and democratic governments have developed a strong antipathy toward the idea of surrendering political offenders into the hands of despotic or dictatorial governments. But it must be kept in mind that there is no generally recognized rule of international law prohibiting the extradition of political offenders.

Extradition being asserted to be a matter of domestic jurisdiction, the nonextradition of political offenders is also a domestic practice, and each state is free to determine the extent to which it will adhere to the practice. Japan, for instance, does not grant asylum to alleged political offenders, as a matter of long-standing policy, and so the problem does not arise there at all. The Japanese government will send political defectors or seekers of political asylum to third countries of their choice. In the absence of a treaty, a state is therefore free to surrender a person accused of a political offense without violating any principle of international law. Even if a treaty does exist, a state may choose to surrender a political offender if the surrender should be dictated by national policy. This relatively new interpretation, found originally in a few court decisions,[14] gained acceptance through the provisions of the 1957 European Convention on Extradition.

Practically all extradition treaties and relevant national laws contain a reservation on non-extradition for political offenses, starting with the French–Belgian Treaty on Extradition of 1834 (Art. 5). Some states have even included the principle in their constitutions, such as in the *Grundgesetz* (Art. 16, section 2) of the Federal Republic of Germany. In the *Castioni case* (see below), the court held that to qualify as a political crime or offense, "the act is done in furtherance, with the intention of assistance, as a sort of overt act in the course of acting in a political matter, a political rising, or a dispute between two parties in a state."

MEANING OF POLITICAL OFFENSE    The question then arises: What is a political offense? In general terms, it is an act directed against the security of

[14]See *Chandler* v. *United States*, U.S. Court of Appeals, 1st Cir. 1948, 171 F.2d 921; *cert. denied* 336 U.S. 918 (1949), in Chapter 10.

a state. Until recently, treaties as well as court decisions tended to define such an offense in relatively narrow terms. In order to be political in nature, it was maintained, the action in question had to satisfy the following conditions:

1. It had to be an overt (open) act.
2. It had to be done in support of a political rising.
3. The rising had to be connected with a dispute or struggle between two groups or parties in a state as to which one was to control the government.

In other words, a political offense may be an act that although it is in itself a common crime, acquires a predominantly political character because of the circumstances and motivations under and for which it was committed.[15] The injury done is generally held to have to be proportionate to the results sought. By that is meant that the stakes at issue must be sufficiently important to justify, or at the very least to excuse, the impairment that the act in question has caused to private legal values.

On the other hand, war crimes (see Chapter 27) do not fall within the sphere of political offenses and therefore represent acts that do give grounds for extradition.[16] One of the most publicized recent instances of extradition for such crimes was the surrender of Klaus Barbie by Bolivia to France in February 1983. Barbie, the Nazi "Butcher of Lyons," had lived in Bolivia since 1951 under the alias of Klaus Altmann, under which name he had been granted Bolivian citizenship in 1957. He had been jailed in early 1983 on charges of fraud stemming from a debt owed to a mining company. After extradition requests by the Federal Republic of Germany and by France, Barbie paid the sum in question ($10,000 plus interest), was stripped of his Bolivian nationality, and turned over to the crew of a French military jet. The French government planned to prosecute Barbie again under a new French law (intended to deal with cases involving war crimes and genocide) on charges of crimes against humanity. He had already been twice sentenced to death *in absentia* by military courts in Lyons in the early 1950s. France, however, abolished the death penalty in 1981.

In any case, the earlier convictions were no longer valid because a 20-year statute of limitations had expired. But there was no such limit, under a 1964 French law, for crimes against humanity. After a delay of four years, Barbie went on trial in May 1987, before a three-judge court and a jury

[15] See Evans, "Reflections upon the Political Offense in International Practice," 57 *AJIL* 1 (1963).
[16] See the relevant case *In re Bohne*, Argentina, Supreme Court, 1966, *Jurisprudencia Argentina, 1966–V*, 339 (September–October 1966), digested in 62 *AJIL* 784 (1968). On the other hand, see the exceptional instance of Gustav Franz Wagner, an alleged Nazi criminal, who found asylum in Brazil and whose extradition to the German Federal Republic, Poland, Austria, and Israel (all of which had requested it individually) was, for different reasons advanced in each case, denied by the Brazilian government: *NYT*, June 24, 1979, 12.

of nine citizens. He was convicted on July 3, 1987, and sentenced to life imprisonment. He was 73 years old at the time.[17]

Andrija Artukovic (The "Butcher of the Balkans"), former Interior and Justice Minister of the German puppet "state" of Croatia during World War II, disappeared when Yugoslav partisans ended the regime. He appeared in the United States in 1948. Soon afterward rumors began to blame Artukovic for the killing of hundreds of thousands in Croatia. Official efforts to return him to Yugoslavia continued sporadically, although his extradition had been formally demanded by the Belgrade government. Finally, in February 1986, the U.S. Court of Appeals in the Ninth Circuit affirmed a District Court finding him a proper subject for extradition and Judge Rehnquist of the U.S. Supreme Court denied a requested stay. On February 12, 1986, Artukovic was deported to Yugoslavia. There he was charged with crimes against civilians and prisoners of war while serving as Interior Minister of Croatia. On May 14, 1986, he was convicted of ordering the deaths of 231,000 Jews, Gypsies, Serbs, and political prisoners. He was sentenced to death by firing squad. At the time, Artukovic was 86 years of age.

John Demjanjuk, born in the Ukraine (USSR), had been admitted to the United States in 1952 and was naturalized in 1958. In 1981 it was claimed that he was "Ivan the Terrible," a guard who had tended the gas chambers at the Treblinka death camp where 850,000 Jews were killed in 1942–43. Demjanjuk at this time was a retired autoworker, living in Ohio. The U.S. District Court (N.D. Ohio) found that his certificate of naturalization had been procured by "willful misrepresentation of material facts,"[18] and he was stripped of his citizenship. Israel then asked to have Demjanjuk extradited on war crimes charges. The District Court certified that he was indeed subject to extradition.[19]

After a variety of unsuccessful legal maneuvers,[20] including a claim that the appellant was not subject to extradition under the terms of the U.S.–Israel extradition treaty, Demjanjuk lost his case in the U.S. Court of Appeals[21] and was found subject to extradition. The Court concluded that the term "murder" in the treaty included the mass murder of Jews. The court also pointed out that a United States court cannot *order* the extradition of a person. It can only certify that a person is properly subject to extradition, whereupon the executive branch determines whether or not the individual is to be extradited.

---

[17] See the valuable article by Wiesel, "Was He Normal? Human? Poor Humanity," *Time*, May 11, 1987, 93–94, as well as *id.*, May 18, 1987, at 49; *id.*, July 13, 1987, at 40; and *U.S. News & World Report*, May 18, 1987, 35–36.

[18] *United States* v. *Demjanjuk*, 518 F.Supp. 1362 (N.D. Ohio 1981), *aff'd per curiam*, 680 F.2d 32 (6th Cir.), *cert. denied*, 459 U.S. 1036 (1982).

[19] *In re Extradition of Demjanjuk*, 612 F.Supp. 544 (N.D. Ohio 1985).

[20] See 80 *AJIL* 656 (1986).

[21] *Demjanjuk* v. *Meese*, 784 F.2d 11, U.S. Ct. of Appeals (D.C. Cir. 1986), *cert. denied*, 106 U.S. 1198 (1986).

Demjanjuk's main defense argument had been his claim of mistaken identity: he was not the person styled "Ivan the Terrible" at Treblinka.

He was flown to Israel in late February 1986. During the ensuing 14-month trial his claims were proven to be false and on April 25, 1988, he was sentenced to be hanged for his crimes. He was then 67 years old. In May 1990, he appealed the verdict.

There have been a few modern cases in which convicted war criminals have not been extradited on request One such instance involved Herbert Kappler, whose wife had smuggled him in a suitcase out of an Italian prison hospital (shades of Hugo Grotius!) and had transported him to West Germany (August 1977). Inasmuch as Kappler was a German national (extradition of such is forbidden by the West German constitution), as no supporting documents for a war crimes charge had been filed, and as Kappler was dying of cancer, the West German authorities rejected Italy's extradition request and permitted him to stay in West Germany to die.

"PURELY POLITICAL OFFENSES" VERSUS "RELATIVE POLITICAL OFFENSES"    The problem of political offenses has been immensely complicated because the term has been used by two distinct meanings. The so-called purely political offenses embrace all definite acts aimed at the state without involving the commission of an ordinary crime, whereas so-called relative political offenses involve the commission of an ordinary crime connected with a political act aimed against the state in such an intimate manner that both have to be viewed as a single "political offense." It is obvious that determination of the first category represents few obstacles to a court, but the determination of the existence of a relative political offense of a nature to prevent the extradition of the fugitive in question still bedevils judges in most countries.[22] On the other hand, the circumstances in a given case may be of such a nature that the determination of a relative political offense is relatively easy, as shown in the classic case of

## IN RE CASTIONI

Great Britain, Queen's Bench Division, 1890
{1891} 1 Q.B. 149

FACTS    Angelo Castioni, a Swiss citizen, had participated on September 11, 1890, in an uprising in the canton of Ticino. The revolt had been caused by the refusal of the cantonal government to revise the Ticino constitution or to hold a plebiscite on this question. A large group of citizens, including Castioni, seized the arsenal of the town of Bellinzona, disarmed the police, caught

[22]Consult the exemplary study by Garcia-Mora, "The Nature of Political Offenses: A Knotty Problem of Extradition Law," 48 *Virginia Law Review* 1226 (1962); see also Gold, "Non-extradition for Political Offenses: The Communist Perspective," 11 *Harvard Int'l Law Jl.* 191 (1970). See also McCreary, "Court Ruling Strains Anglo-Irish Relations," *CSM*, April 10, 1990, 2, for an unusual decision by the Supreme Court of Ireland concerning terrorist charges held to be political in nature.

and bound several persons connected with the cantonal administration, and forced them to march in front of the armed crowd to the municipal "palace." A number of government officials, including a M. Rossi, barred access to the building, whereupon the crowd forced the gates and rushed into the structure.

Castioni, armed with a revolver, was among the first to enter. Rossi was shot and died a little while later; witnesses later identified Castioni as the person who fired the fatal shot. The crowd captured the palace and organized a provisional government, which functioned briefly until it was dispersed following the arrival of Swiss federal troops.

Castioni fled to Great Britain, where he had lived for seventeen years, having returned to Ticino only one day before the uprising.

The Swiss government formally requested the arrest and extradition of Castioni on charges of having committed willful murder. After his arrest, his legal representative asked for the issuance of a writ of habeas corpus and for the freeing of Castioni, claiming that he had been guilty only of a political offense.

ISSUE    Was Castioni's act in the nature of a political offense?

DECISION    The court ruled in favor of Castioni, and his extradition to Switzerland was therefore denied.

REASONING    The court held that Castioni had committed an overt act; that is, Rossi was shot in plain view, as part of an attack on the "palace"; that the act was connected with an uprising aimed at the cantonal government; and that the uprising was part of a struggle between two groups, one seeking to hold onto the control of the government and the other seeking to gain control. In view of these findings, Castioni (who had not known Rossi and hence held no personal feelings against him) was held to have shot Rossi in the promotion of a political uprising. His act thus constituted a political offense, for which he could not be surrendered to the Swiss authorities.

A companion case, of equal interest to students of law and political theory, dealt with the offenses committed by a certain Meunier:

### IN RE MEUNIER

*Great Britain, High Court of Justice,*
*Queen's Bench Division, 1894*
*(L.R. {1894}, 2 Q.B. 415)*

FACTS    Meunier, a French citizen, by political belief an anarchist, took it upon himself in March 1892 to cause two explosions, one at the Café Véry in Paris, which caused the death of two persons, the other at the Lobau military barracks in the same city. Both outrages represented part of an anarchist effort to avenge the execution of the anarchist Ravachol.

After committing the two attacks, Meunier fled to Great Britain. A French court tried him *in absentia* and, on convictions on charges of murder, sentenced him to death. The French government made formal application for his arrest and extradition. Meunier was arrested on April 4, 1894, in the Victoria Station in London. He protested his arrest and pending deportation to France, and his counsel, citing the *Castioni* case, claimed that although the bombing of the barracks had been a reprehensible act, it was possessed of political character. His counsel also asserted that insufficient evidence had been produced in the case of the attack on the Café Véry to lay the blame for the two deaths on Meunier.

ISSUE     Did Meunier's acts in Paris correspond to the accepted definition of a political offense?

DECISION     The court rejected Meunier's contention that his acts constituted political offenses and ordered his continued detention until he could be surrendered to agents of the French government.

REASONING     The attacks on the Café Véry and on the military barracks did not constitute political offenses. There was no struggle between two parties in the French state, each seeking to impose the government of its choice on the state. The group with which Meunier identified was the enemy of all governments and desired to abolish them, rather than to control them. The terrorist acts of anarchists, furthermore, were not directed primarily at governments (which might have given them a semblance of political character) but were usually aimed at private citizens (the attack on the Café Véry was cited as an example by the court).

"The party of anarchy is the enemy of all Governments. Their efforts are directed primarily against the general body of citizens. They may secondarily and incidentally commit offences against some particular Government; but anarchist offences are mainly directed against private citizens."

Under the circumstances, Meunier's acts did not represent political offenses within the meaning of the British Extradition Acts of 1870 and 1873.

[NOTE:     After Meunier had been taken back to France, the death sentence imposed on him in his absence was carried out.]

•  The two preceding cases illustrate the attempt made in the nineteenth century to separate acts committed in the preparation or commission of revolutions or revolts (viewed as political acts) from individual acts of violence not in any manner conducive to a change in the political system and therefore logically denied recognition as political offenses. In the latter category belonged all terrorist acts perpetrated by any kind of radical as well as acts of violence characterized by their especially atrocious nature.

Lest the criteria mentioned previously and brought out so clearly in the *Castioni* case be taken to be universal standards, it should be pointed out that no generally accepted standards have yet been evolved, even though the concept of the political offense is directly related to the protection of human rights. The Universal Declaration of Human Rights (see Chapter 10) states (Art. 14) that

Everyone has the right to seek and enjoy in other countries asylum from persecution. This right may not be invoked in the case of prosecutions genuinely arising from non-political crimes or from acts contrary to the purposes and principles of the United Nations.

Purely political offenses usually have been limited to three categories of acts: treason, sedition, and espionage. So-called relative political offenses involve political acts as well as "acts connected therewith." A relative political offense is therefore characterized by the existence of one or several common crimes closely connected with a political act; the concept is illustrated by the *Castioni* case. Such offenses always pose a delicate problem for national courts, as the desire to see a crime punished conflicts with the obligation not to surrender a political offender. The obvious but frequently difficult-to-achieve solution is to determine the degree of connection between the common crime and the political act.[23] Here again, national determination and national standards come into play.[24] But fundamentally it is true that acts which have the character of an ordinary crime and appear in a list of extraditable offenses may, because of the motive and the object of the act, become political crimes or offenses. As such they render the perpetrator immune from extradition—if the political motivation is deemed to outweigh the criminal action.[25]

**TERRORISM AND EXTRADITION**    A rapid increase in the number of terrorist acts in the late 1970s led several Western countries, and in particular the United States, to narrow the scope of the "political offense exception." This was done by negotiating agreements amending existing extradition treaties to exclude terrorist acts from the political offense category.[26]

An example of the older and broader interpretation was the case of *United States* v. *Mackin* (668 F.2d 122, U.S. Court of Appeals, 2d Cir., 1981). Desmond Mackin, a member of the Provisional Irish Republican Army (PIRA), was wanted by the United Kingdom for the attempted murder of a British soldier. A Federal Magistrate decided that at the time of the alleged offense, the PIRA was conducting an armed uprising in the area in which Mackin was an active member, and that the attack on the soldier was incidental to Mackin's role in the PIRA's political uprising. Hence Mackin's extradition was denied. That decision subsequently was affirmed in a U.S. District Court and the Second Circuit Court of Appeals. The latter court held that the refusal of a court to grant extradition under certain conditions was not an appealable order.[27]

---

[23] See Garcia-Mora, *op. cit.*, n. 22 *supra*, for a scholarly and fascinating analysis of national tests and standards; a relevant case of interest is *In re Gonzalez*, U.S. Dist. Ct. S.D.N.Y., 1963, 217 F. Supp. 717, digested in 58 *AJIL* 191 (1964).

[24] See *United States* v. *Macklin*, U.S. Court of Appeals, 2nd Cir., 1981, 668 F.2d 122, reported in 76 *AJIL* 391 (1982), see *infra*.

[25] See also Foighel, "Political Crimes and Extradition," *Israel Yrbk on Human Rights* (1971) 51–60.

[26] Such as the Supplementary Treaty Concerning Extradition of 1987 to the 1986 U.S.–Federal Republic of Germany Extradition Treaty, in 81 *AJIL* 935 (1987), and the U.S.–U.K. Supplementary Extradition Treaty of 1985, in 80 *AJIL* 338 (1986).

[27] Based on a Statement by the then Legal Adviser of the Department of State, in *Current Policy No. 762* (November 1985), at 2.

The new trend in favor of exclusion was first illustrated in the United States in *In the Matter of the Extradition of McMullen*,[28] when a Federal Magistrate in San Francisco refused to recommend the extradition of Peter Gabriel McMullen, an admitted member of the Irish Republican Army (IRA), who had been charged with the attempted murder related to the bombing of a military barracks in England. The Magistrate considered McMullen's alleged offense to be political in nature.

Considerably greater publicity attached to the second major "terrorist extradition" case, the extradition of Abu Eain from the United States to Israel.[29] The accused Abu Eain, a Palestinian resident of Ramallah in the Israeli-occupied West Bank, had traveled to Chicago shortly after the May 14, 1979 bombing of a marketplace in Tiberias that had killed two and injured thirty-six others. He claimed that the purpose of his trip was to visit his sister in Chicago. Israel sought his surrender under the 1963 U.S.–Israel Extradition Treaty.

Eain asserted that he was in his Ramallah workshop during the entire day of the bombing, and produced affidavits from a dozen friends and relatives to that effect. Ramallah is a two-hour drive from Tiberias. The Israeli charges were based primarily on the uncorroborated testimony of one Jamil Yasmin, an admitted member of the PLO, who had built the bomb used in Tiberias and who had claimed that Eain was his accomplice and had carried out the actual bombing. By the time Eain was arrested in Chicago, Yasmin had recanted his involvement of Eain, claiming that he had signed a confession written in Hebrew, a language of which he was ignorant.

The Federal Magistrate ruled that there was "probable cause" to believe that Eain was guilty and held that the conflicting evidence should best be examined by an Israeli court. The Court of Appeals then confirmed the decision of the Magistrate and held that Eain was properly subject to extradition.

It should be noted that the reasoning of the Appeals Court included a thoroughgoing and instructive analysis of the process of extradition for a crime and the often complex operation of the "political offense exemption."

Unusual and considerable outside efforts on Eain's behalf failed to prevent his eventual extradition: Amnesty International and other human rights organizations invoked the alleged Israeli use of torture to extract confessions; 17 Arab governments asked the U.S. Government not to surrender Eain;

---

[28]N.D./.Cal., May 11, 1979 (Magistrate No. 3-78-1099 MG) memorandum decision, reported in 74 *AJIL* 434 (1980).
[29]*In the Matter of the Extradition of Eain*, U.S. District Court, N.D. Ill., 1979 (Magistrate No. 79 M175), reported in 74 *AJIL* 435 (1980); *Abu Eain* v. *Peter Wilkes*, U.S. Court of Appeals, 7th Cir., 1981, 641 F.2d 504, in full in 21 *ILM* 342 (1982) and also reported in 75 *AJIL* 662 (1981). *Cert. denied* by Supreme Court in October 1981. See also the relevant UN General Assembly Resolution 36/171, Dec. 16, 1981, in 21 *ILM* 442 (1982), including related documents. See commentaries on this case: *Time*, Jan. 4, 1982, 64; *CSM*, Jan. 30, 1981, 11; and Wingerter in *The Link*, Sept. 1985, 1–13, at 4–5.

and the UN General Assembly adopted a Resolution (Res. 36/171, 12 Feb. 1982) deploring Eain's pending extradition and *demanding* that he be released immediately.

After altogether two years under arrest in Chicago, Eain was deported to Israel. He was tried, convicted of the charges against him, and sentenced to life imprisonment. He was freed in a prisoner exchange with the PLO in May 1984, but was rearrested in August of that year, on suspicion that he planned to hijack an Israeli bus. He was placed in administrative detention which is done without a trial in the territories occupied by Israel.

It is of interest that the U.S. Government had contended in *Abu Eain* v. *Peter Wilkes*[30] that the determination of whether the crime in question fell within the political offense exception under the U.S.–Israel Extradition Treaty was a matter within the exclusive discretion of the executive branch. The Court of Appeals, however, rejected this claim and held that since political offenses were excluded from extradition by the treaty, the judiciary (the judicial branch) could determine whether the political offense exception applied in a given case because U.S. courts had the right to construe applicable treaty provisions. The Appeals Court was supported in this view by reference to the Supreme Court decision in *Baker* v. *Carr* (369 U.S. 186, 211–13, 1962) in which the Court had ruled in like manner.

The problem of the applicability of the political offense exception to terrorist acts was summarized succinctly by William P. Clark, then Deputy Secretary of State, in a Memorandum of January 4, 1982, in connection with the *Abu Eain* case before the UN General Assembly[31]:

The standard relied upon by United States courts in determining applicability of the Political Offense Exception is the 'political incidence' test. Under that test, a common crime cannot be considered a political offense unless two conditions are first satisfied: the act must have been committed during a political uprising, involving a group of which the accused was a member, and the act must have been "incidental to" that uprising, that is, done in furtherance of or with the intention of assisting it. The placing of a time bomb in a market place with intent to kill civilians cannot be deemed to be "incidental to" a political uprising.

That is and must be the position of the United States. It is hoped that it would be the position of all nations.

ACT-OF-STATE DOCTRINE    A modern example of the act-of-state doctrine in regard to extradition was supplied by the case of Marcos Perez Jimenez. Venezuela instituted proceedings in the United States for the extradition of its former president to stand trial for financial offenses allegedly committed while he was dictator of his country. After a finding of probable cause as to each offense charged against him, he was arrested and confined, pending action by the U.S. Secretary of State.

[30]U.S. Ct. of Appeals, 7th Cir. 1981, 641 F.2d 504, in 75 *AJIL* 662, 663 (1981). [Peter Wilkes was a U.S. Marshal.]
[31] Text in 21 *ILM* 445, 448 (1982).

The accused contended in a habeas corpus proceeding that his acts in Venezuela constituted acts of state and that consequently the acts were not subject to the jurisdiction of United States courts. The Court of Appeals, in affirming the denial of the writ of habeas corpus, held that the acts in question (embezzlement, breach of trust, fraud, and receiving money and securities while knowing that they had been obtained illegally) were not acts of state but acts undertaken by the accused in his personal capacity and for his own private benefit. Hence the act-of-state doctrine was not a bar to extradition proceedings. Jimenez was subsequently surrendered to agents of the Venezuelan government and returned to his country for trial, after the U.S. Supreme Court denied *certiorari*.[32]

ATTENTAT CLAUSE    During the second half of the nineteenth century, a number of assassination attempts (several of them successful) were made on the persons of heads of states. Such attacks did not constitute part of organized uprisings or struggles for the control of governments but had to be viewed as the acts of individuals or of small terrorist groups. In 1856, following an unsuccessful attempt to extradite Celestin Jacquin, who had tried to blow up a train carrying the French emperor Napoleon III, Belgium adopted into its extradition law the so-called *attentat* clause. This provision excluded from the category of political offenses the attempt (whether or not successful) to kill the head of another state or a member of such a head's family. The United States, after the assassination of President James Garfield, inserted the clause in its extradition treaty with Belgium (1882), and the 1933 Montevideo Convention included a similar provision. Many modern extradition treaties have been equipped with the restrictive clause, and either by direct provision or by interpretation, it extends not only to crowned heads of state but to any head of a government as well as to the members of the latter's family.

At times, political considerations outweigh legal obligations, and this is true also in the case of extradition, even when the *attentat* clause is involved. An example is the well-known *In re Pavelić* case.[33] Ante Pavelić and an accomplice killed King Alexander of Yugoslavia and the French foreign minister, Louis Barthou, and wounded a French general, in an attack in Marseilles, France, in October 1934. Pavelić fled to Italy, and the French government demanded his extradition. The Italian government refused to honor that request, and although the court in question cited rather dubious interpretations of the Italo-French Extradition Treaty then in force, it appears quite obvious that the Italian government, then already striving for a breakup of Yugoslavia, would not permit the extraditon of an individual

---

[32] *Perez Jimenez* v. *Aristeguita*, U.S. Court of Appeals, Fifth Cir., 1962, 311 F.2d 547; *certiorari* denied, Supreme Court, May 13, 1962. Accused was convicted on August 1, 1968, by the Supreme Court of Venezuela of embezzling $13 million of government funds. Because he had already spent more time in detention than his four-year sentence, he was released and permitted to depart for Spain; see also 57 *AJIL* 670 (1963), and 58 *AJIL* 185 (1964).

[33] See Kirchheimer, "Asylum," 53 *APSR* 985, esp. 1002–3 (1959).

who was active in efforts to dismember that kingdom. Pavelić later became head of the puppet state of Croatia and then fled to Argentina, but a Yugoslav demand for extradition on charges of war crimes and murder was rejected by the Argentine government. Pavelić eventually found territorial asylum in Paraguay and died in 1960.

EXPANSION IN MEANING OF POLITICAL OFFENSE    The second quarter of the twentieth century saw an expansion in the meaning of *political offense* as a result of the ideological divisions of mankind and in the rise of radical and conservative dictatorships. The Harvard Draft Convention of 1935, reflecting existing world conditions, included under political offenses such acts as the commission of treason, sedition, and espionage, even if each of these were undertaken by only one person. It also included any offenses connected with the activities of an organized group directed against the security or governmental system of the requesting state.

The appearance of the Cold War expanded still further the meaning of *political offense*. In 1952, a Swiss court ruled that three Yugoslavs who had diverted a passenger plane from its destination in their own country and had caused it to be landed in Switzerland were guilty of a political offense and hence not subject to extradition.[34] A similar ruling was handed down in 1954 by a British court in the case of seven members of the crew of a Polish trawler. The men, fearing that they were suspected by their government of harboring anti-Communist opinions and that they would be subject to trial on their return, subdued the captain and other members of the crew, wounded the political officer aboard the vessel, and brought the ship to a British port. They were held to be political refugees and were given asylum in Great Britain.[35]

## TERRITORIAL ASYLUM

The question of the treatment of foreign political offenders leads logically to the more extensive problem of territorial asylum and the conditions under which it ought to be granted. Asylum or refuge is granted without question when a particular state denies a request by another state for the extradition of an individual adjudged to have committed a political offense. This was, in most instances, the normal limit of a grant of asylum.

During the nineteenth century, a few occasions were marked by the appearance of large groups of refugees or exiles, usually the remnants of the supporters of lost revolutions, such as participants in the Paris Commune. Then the twentieth century became the era of the political escapee. At times the number of seekers of asylum ran into thousands or even tens of thousands: White Russian refugees, both civilian and military; Jewish persons escaping from Hitler's Germany and later from countries dominated by him; the

---

[34]*In re Kavic, Bjelanovic and Arsenijevic*, reported in 1 *International Law Reports* 371 (1952).
[35]*In re Kolczynski et al.*, 1 Q.B. 540 (1954), 1 All E.L.R. 31 [1955], digested in 49 *AJIL* 411 (1955); consult also Garcia-Mora, *op. cit.*, n. 22, at 1242–44.

remnants of the Spanish Republican armies; the remnants of Russian ethnic minorities; escapees from Chinese-occupied Tibet; the countless voluntary exiles from Iron Curtain countries and Castro's Cuba; and more recently the multitudes leaving portions of Indochina, as well as thousands of African refugees. (See also Chapter 9.) The Federal Republic of Germany was faced by 1986 by the *Asylantenflut* (flood of asylum seekers), a large proportion entering with ease from East Berlin with the connivance of the German Democratic Republic (and, in some African instances, of the Soviet Airline *Aeroflot*). Just before a tightening of West German asylum rules on October 1, 1986, some 27,000 Turkish *Asylanten* boarded about 600 buses in Istanbul, bound for East Berlin, then points beyond. Canada, also in 1986–87, was besieged by some 1,000 foreigners a week, all claiming refugee status and asking for asylum. Some of these were in fact "fake" refugees, such as several hundred Sri Lankans who landed in Newfoundland, being ferried ashore by the lifeboats of a West German ship, after having lived for several years in West Germany.[36] In 1989, over 60,000 asylum seekers filed claims with the Immigration and Naturalization Service to remain legally in the United States; that total was reached by the first five months of 1989.

One of the more bizarre episodes in the history of modern territorial asylum had its beginning in the form of diplomatic asylum: the saga of the "Mariel Cubans."

On March 19, 1980, six Cubans crashed their way by means of an electric utility truck into the 20-acre Peruvian embassy compound in Havana, bringing to 15 the number of Cuban citizens inside the grounds; that total was soon raised to 30. When Cuban guards were withdrawn from outside the embassy, 10,800 Cubans seeking asylum and new homelands crowded into the embassy compound over the weekend of April 6, 1980. Peru offered to accept 1,000 of this crowd, and Costa Rica indicated its willingness to absorb up to 10,000 individuals; the United States planned to accept 3,500. A limited number of the prospective refugees were flown out of Havana by Costa Rican aircraft before the Cuban government halted the airlift. Then that government designated the Cuban port of Mariel as an official departure point, and a fleet of small and large boats (more than 1,000 at one time), mostly chartered by or manned by Cuban exiles in the United States, began to move refugees to Key West, Florida. By June 10, 1980, the exodus ended when the last vessels of the "Freedom Flotilla" left Mariel. By that time, nearly 112,500 individuals had been brought from Mariel to the United States; about 790 of these, suspected of being true criminals from Cuban jails and under "final order of exclusion," were held in U.S. jails pending the outcome of exclusionary hearings or a resolution of the problem of how any or all of these persons were to be repatriated to Cuba. Out of the total of 125,000, a total of 2,555 were classified as

[36]*CSM*, Feb. 17, 1987, at 9.

excludable. On December 14, 1984, Cuba and the United States agreed that 2,746 refugees considered to be "dangerous" by the United States would be returned to Cuba. The Agreement also called for the resumption of normal emigration of Cubans to the United States.[37]

Cuba, however, suspended the Agreement after the U.S. station "Radio Marti" (Florida), aimed at Cuba, became operative. By that time 201 Cubans had been deported under the 1985 Agreement. This left 2,545 still to be sent back.

In August 1985 the U.S. Department of Justice announced continuation of its policy of taking into custody Mariel refugees who were released from Florida jails and who were to be deported.

In November 1987, after Cuba and the United States announced the "reimplementation" of the 1984 instrument, the Cuban detainees at the Oakdale and Atlanta federal prisons rioted. Public attention again focused on the deportation or granting of parole for Mariel excludables. "Excludable" meant a person who either had a criminal record or a history of mental illness before arrival in the United States, or who had committed a serious crime or repeated misdemeanors after his arrival. In December 1987, the Attorney General of the U.S. approved new procedures for repatriation, review, and parole for Mariel detainees. The revived 1984 Agreement provided for the release of 1,149 Cubans from Federal prisons. By October 18, 1988, over 2,000 detainees had been set free, but more than 1,500 were still in detention. On December 2, 1988, the first five Mariel Cubans, who had been imprisoned for crimes, were deported by air to Cuba. They had become excludable by their offenses and, after completing their prison sentences, entered detention by the Immigration and Naturalization Service until they could be returned to Cuba.

## Conditions for Granting Asylum

Which of such individuals or groups should be admitted by another country and granted a haven of refuge, that is, political asylum? Most democratic states in the West have been willing to grant asylum, provided the individuals seeking a refuge satisfied the host authorities that they were indeed political or racial persecutees. And once asylum had been granted, demands for extradition from the refugee's government were denied on grounds of the commission of political offenses. This modern attitude meant that the original concept of such offenses had been expanded greatly and now included anyone who, for reasons of political or racial persecution, had felt the need to escape from the authority of his own state.

[37]*NYT*, March 20–June 30, 1980, *passim.*; *Newsweek*, April 21, 1980, 53; April 28, 1980, 38–43; and especially the documentary materials listed in n.40 *infra*. See also the important statement on current U.S. policy on the granting of diplomatic asylum by the Dupty Legal Adviser (William Lake) on April 29, 1980, in 75 *AJIL* 142–47 (1981). See Cuba—United States: Agreement on Immigration Procedure and the Return of Cuban Nationals (Done at New York, December 14, 1984), in 24 *ILM* 32–37 (1985).

This new interpretation of who could be accorded asylum has been defined quite adequately in Article 1-A (2) of the Geneva Convention of July 28, 1951, on the Status of Refugees, which stated that a refugee was a person who

as a result of events occurring before January 1, 1951 and owing to well-founded fear of being persecuted for reasons of race, religion, nationality, membership of a particular social group or political opinion, is outside the country of his nationality and is unable or owing to such fear unwilling to avail himself of the protection of that country; or who, not having a nationality and being outside the country of his former habitual residence as a result of such events, is unable or, owing to such fear, unwilling to return to it.

A fairly recent example illustrates the expanded concept of *refugee:* on May 26, 1973, the Italian government granted political asylum to the commander as well as to 30 officers and men of the crew of the Greek Navy destroyer *Velos.* The vessel had dropped out of NATO maneuvers off Sardinia, and when it reached the port of Fiumcino, the crew members in question came ashore and requested political asylum. The grant of asylum was especially interesting because mutiny normally represents an extradition offense.

Even if a refugee does not meet the conditions laid down in the Geneva Convention, in full or in part, he would still qualify in many states for political asylum, because general international law knows of no rule limiting political asylum to "political criminals." In fact, it is rather difficult to be precise in the terminology applicable to this special sphere of the rules governing extradition. As Evans pointed out, "the terms 'political refugee', 'political offender,' or 'political fugitive' are rather flexible in usage. United States statues are not specific as to the meaning of 'political offender' or 'political offense.' The legislation on extradition does not define either term."[38]

This writer prefers the application of the term *political refugees* to the groups and individuals mentioned above. They do not fit into either of the two major categories of political offenders (purely political offenses and relative political offenses), and in almost all instances, they fall instead under the provisions of Article 33 of the 1951 UN Convention Relating to the Status of Refugees and of the 1967 UN Protocol Relating to the Status of Refugees (see Chapter 9 concerning both instruments). Paragraph 1 of Article 33 of the convention reads as follows:

Prohibition of Expulsion or Return 1. No Contracting State shall expel or return ("refouler") a refugee in any manner whatsoever to the frontiers or territories where his life or freedom would be threatened on account of his race, religion, nationality, membership of a particular social group or political opinion.

[38]Evans, "Observations on the Practice of Territorial Asylum in the United States," 56 *AJIL* 148, 149 (1962).

Examples of the positive (grant of asylum) or negative (denial of asylum) handling of real or alleged political refugees are so plentiful that only a small number of examples can be cited here. In late July 1976, the Netherlands granted asylum to Viktor Korchnoi, a Soviet grandmaster and at the time the world's second-ranked chess player; in July 1977, Boris Itaka, a Soviet embassy official in Uganda, defected to the United States and was granted asylum; in June 1978, First Lieutenant Viktor I. Belenko of the Soviet air force defected in his MIG-25 to Japan and was granted asylum in the United States; in the same month, Vladimir Rezun, a Soviet diplomat in Geneva, defected and was granted asylum in the United Kingdom; and in April 1978, amidst much publicity, Arkady N. Shevchenko, UN Undersecretary General for Political and Security Affairs, refused to return, as ordered, to the Soviet Union and defected to the United States, where he was granted asylum.

The lack of generally accepted rules governing the granting of territorial asylum prompted the General Assembly of the United Nations to request the International Law Commission on November 21, 1959, to begin work on the codification of the "principles and rules of international law relating to the right of asylum." Eventually a UN conference (Geneva, January 1977) considered a draft convention on the subject. Pending the completion of codification, the General Assembly had adopted unanimously on December 14, 1967, the Declaration on Territorial Asylum, recommending guidelines for the granting of such asylum and excluding, incidentally, individuals suspected of war crimes, crimes against peace, or crimes against humanity.[39]

The grant of residency to illegal aliens seeking political asylum in the United States was made considerably easier through the decision of the U.S. Supreme Court in *Immigration and Naturalization Service* v. *Cardoza-Fonseca*[40] on March 9, 1987. This case involved a Nicaraguan woman living in Nevada who claimed that the Sandinista government would prosecute her if she were forced to return to her homeland. The Immigration Judge decided that she had not established "a clear probability" of persecution, as deemed necessary under United States immigration laws. He therefore rejected her petition for withholding deportation and for asylum. The Board of Immigration Appeals agreed with the Judge, and Cardoza-Fonseca appealed. The U.S. Court of Appeals (9th Cir.) ruled that the previous decisions had wrongly applied the narrow "clear probability of persecution" standard. The Supreme Court affirmed and held that applicants for asylum did not have to establish a "clear probability of persecution" if they were deported.

The Court outlined in careful detail that there were *two* means for an asylum seeker to prevent deportation, not just the claim of "clear probability" espoused by the Immigration Service: (a) the already mentioned presumption

[39]Text in 62 *AJIL* 822 (1968). On the general subject of refugees and of territorial asylum, consult Whiteman, vol. 8, 660–696.
[40]107 S.Ct. 1207, U.S. Supreme Court, March 9, 1987, reported in 81 *AJIL* 654 (1987) and in full in 26 *ILM* 396 (1987).

of a clear probability of persecution, and (b) the showing of "a well-founded fear" of prosecution of the applicant were deported to his or her homeland. The Court observed that a well-founded fear would be easier to demonstrate for an alien than a clear probability of persecution. It expressly refused, however, to define the precise meaning of "a well-founded fear." The Court also pointed out that the ultimate decision on an asylum seeker remained with the Attorney General who could give concrete meaning to the standard only through a process of case-by-case adjudication. Thus Cardoza-Fonseca won the case, based on her "well-founded fear" of persecution if deported.

It is interesting to note that the Supreme Court relied in this case without any reservation on international refugee law, that is, on the 1967 "UN Protocol Relating to the Status of Refugees" (606 UNTS 267), in arriving at its interpretation of U.S. immigration law. In fact, it appeared to suggest that the Immigration and Naturalization Service should, in the future, be guided by the relevant international law rules.

Denial of territorial asylum has occurred less frequently in recent years but has produced some interesting situations from a legal point of view. Thus the Swedish government, which had granted asylum to some 500 antiwar American citizens, shut its doors to American deserters who left their military posts after the Vietnam cease-fire; Iran denied asylum to Lieutenant Valentin I. Zasimov of the Soviet Air Force (under the terms of an antihijacking agreement signed by Iran and the USSR in August 1973) and returned the pilot to the Soviet Union in October 1976; and the United States refused to grant political refugee status to some 2,000 fugitive Haitians who arrived in small groups since December 1972: the American government's reason for denial of asylum has been its charge that the Haitians came to the United States to seek jobs and therefore should be classified as economic rather than political refugees.[41]

In June 1984, Egypt denied political asylum to four Iranian defectors who had comandeered an Iranian navy plane to Cairo but permitted the four to go to France. Later in the same month, Egypt also rejected a request for asylum by two other Iranian citizens who had hijacked an Iranian Boeing 727 jetliner. The two were permitted to travel to Iraq on an Iraqi commercial aircraft. Both Iranian planes were returned promptly to Iran.

## Diplomatic Asylum

The general subject of asylum includes a fascinating and well-publicized special form known as *diplomatic asylum*.

[41]See United States, Public Law 96–212, March 17, 1980: "The Refugee Act of 1980," 19 *ILM* 703 (1980), with supporting documents, *id.*, 713; *Haitian Refugee Center* v. *Carter*, U.S. Court of Appeals, 11th Cir., May 24, 1982, *id.*, 21 603 (1982); U.S. Department of Justice, Immigration and Naturalization Service, "Regulation on Refugee and Asylum Procedures" (Final Rule, October 12, 1981), *id.*, 20 1259 (1981); Haiti–United States, "Agreement to Stop Clandestine Migration of Residents of Haiti to the United States," (September 23, 1981), *id.*, 20 1198 (1981); and United States, "Proclamation 4865 of September 29, 1981; High Seas Interdiction of Illegal Aliens," *id.*, 20 1263 (1981).

On hundreds of occasions, individuals either guilty of political offenses or qualifying as political persecutees have chosen (or have been forced by a time element) to stay in their own country and to seek asylum in foreign embassies or legations.

The passage of time saw the growth of a conviction by the receiving states that an unlimited grant of asylum by foreign diplomatic missions represented, in essence, an unwarranted intervention in the internal affairs of the missions' host state. As a result, the sphere of diplomatic asylum was circumscribed little by little, and many states abandoned the practice entirely, normally by issuing suitable prohibitory instructions to their diplomatic agents. Today extensive practice of the grant of diplomatic asylum appears to be restricted to the Latin American republics where the practice has been employed so consistently that it can be said to represent by now a principle of regional international law.

The policy of the United States government with respect to diplomatic asylum has been fairly consistent over many decades. Beginning in the nineteenth century, American diplomatic agents were instructed not to grant such asylum except temporarily to persons whose lives were threatened by mob violence. The American attitude is based on a belief that diplomatic asylum does not represent a valid principle of international law but merely a usage. At most, therefore, diplomatic asylum is viewed as a "permissive local custom," acceptable merely as a temporary measure.

It was therefore quite logical for the United States to enter a reservation to this effect when signing the 1928 Havana Convention on Asylum[42] and to refuse to sign a new interpretative convention agreed on by the Latin American delegations at the 1933 Montevideo Conference.

On the other hand, practice has occasionally departed from stated policy, and United States diplomats have granted asylum in embassies and legations on various occasions not involving mob violence: to deposed presidents in Peru (1870), the Dominican Republic (1906), also Haiti (1911), and Chile (1914), as well as to rival politicians (Chile, 1891). More recently, a notable departure from traditional abstention was recorded when asylum was granted in the U.S. embassy in Budapest to Jószef Cardinal Mindszenty, from the Hungarian uprising of 1956 to September 28, 1971.

In June 1978, seven Russian Pentecostal dissidents rushed into the U.S. embassy in Moscow and were granted an unofficial and temporary asylum pending Soviet acceptance of a U.S. proposal for assurances of nonpunishment. After 15 months of stalemate, the Soviet Interior Minister offered to the U.S. ambassador consideration of granting exit visas to the seven dissidents, provided they first returned to their homes in Siberia. That offer was accompanied by assurances that the individuals in question would not be persecuted for their actions on June 27, 1978 (flight into the embassy). One of the group, after a hunger strike, was removed, with United States'

[42]Text in 47 *AJIL* 446 (1953).

consent, from the embassy to a hospital, eventually returned to her home, and then was permitted to emigrate. The others remained in their diplomatic haven until April 1983 and finally left the Soviet Union in July 1983 with other family members (a group of fifteen altogether). On another occasion (1959), a brief diplomatic asylum was granted by the U.S. embassy in Burma to a defecting Russian diplomat, until, after protests by the Burmese government, he was brought to the United States in a military aircraft.[43]

Among the recent instances of diplomatic asylum was the action taken when the U.S. embassy was seized in Iran. The Canadian government quietly granted diplomatic asylum to five U.S. consular employees and one U.S. agricultural attaché; the six had escaped via a back door of the U.S. embassy when it was seized on November 4, 1979, by a band of "student militants." At least one of the six was hidden away for a while in the Swedish embassy, and other countries may also have provided temporary asylum for some of the six, until all were gathered in the Canadian embassy. All of the individuals in question were spirited out of Iran with forged Canadian passports and Iranian visas when Canada closed its embassy in Teheran on January 28, 1980. Ironically, the Iranian foreign minister, Sadegh Ghotbzadeh, denounced the Canadian operation as a "flagrant violation of international law" at a time when the so-called Iranian militants were still holding some 50 American diplomats and private citizens as hostages in the embassy and when three other American diplomats were held in "protective custody" in the Iranian Ministry of Foreign Affairs, all these acts being in violation of international law. (See also Chapter 13 under "Terrorism.")

One of the relatively rare examples of diplomatic refuge granted by the United States was that to Fang Lizhi and his wife. Fang, a Chinese astrophysicist and dissident, had fled to the U.S. Embassy in Beijing during the put-down of the pro-democracy demonstrations in Tiananmen Square (June 5, 1989). A year later the Fangs were allowed to leave China for England (June 25, 1990) aboard a U.S. Air Force jet. A heart attack suffered a month earlier by Fang turned out to be the face-saving event that permitted the Chinese government to cite "humanitarian reasons" for allowing the Fangs to leave.

When the United States invaded Panama ("Operation Just Cause") on December 20, 1989, a major object of the incursion was the capture of the country's leader, General Manuel Antonio Noriega, and bringing him to trial in the United States. Earlier he had been indicted in Miami on federal drug-related charges: he and others were charged with acceptance of $4.6 million in bribes from Colombia's Medellin drug cartel to protect drug

---

[43]On Latin American instances, see Evans, "The Colombian-Peruvian Asylum Case: The Practice of Diplomatic Asylum," 46 *AJIL* 142, esp. 144 (1952); for the Soviet Pentecostals, see *NYT*, June 24, 1979, 3; Sept. 22, 1979, 2; and the *Times-Colonist* (Victoria, B.C.), July 17, 1983, D-15. For the Burmese instance, consult Kaznacheev, *Inside a Soviet Embassy (Experiences of a Russian Diplomat in Burma)* ed. with introd. by Wolin (1962).

shipments, launder money, supply drug laboratories, and protect traffickers from law-enforcement agencies. A separate indictment in Tampa charged him with accepting another $5.4 million from the cartel.

Noriega hid from capture for four days and then found diplomatic asylum in the Vatican Embassy in Panama City. Panama and the Vatican are not parties to an extradition treaty. If Noriega had been caught by agents of the new Panamanian government, his extradition to the United States would have been forbidden by the Panamanian constitution. If he wanted to leave for a third country, he would have had to receive asylum from the Vatican Embassy and safe passage from Panama to a country willing to accept him. Before Noriega entered the Embassy, a number of his top aides and their families had already found refuge therein.

One day later (December 25), the U.S. Government, without success, asked the embassy to turn Noriega over to American custody. Embassy personnel, in the meantime, were equally unsuccessfully attempting to find a country willing to grant him asylum. On the 26th, the United States took steps to freeze Noriega's foreign bank accounts, estimated at over $10 million, and Spain officially denied him asylum.

The American troops surrounding the Embassy now proceeded to set up loudspeakers blaring rock and roll music, aimed at the Holiday Inn where many journalists were staying. It was alleged that the noise was to prevent those journalists from listening with electronic devices to the negotiations in the Embassy, but greater credence should be given to another purpose of the harassment: to render life difficult in the Embassy.

On December 31st, Panama's new attorney general stated that charges of murder were being prepared against Noriega for the deaths of 10 officers killed during a failed coup attempt on October 3rd. He also asserted that the Vatican Embassy would be asked to surrender Noriega to Panama for trial.

Finally (January 3, 1990), Noriega left the Vatican Embassy and turned himself over to U.S. troops. He was taken to a plane and ferried from the (American) Howard Air Force Base in Panama to Florida and eventual trial. Technically he was not under arrest until the aircraft entered international airspace. A few days later the papal nuncio said that he granted asylum to Noriega because the latter threatened to order massacres if not granted sanctuary.[44]

---

[44]See Lowenfeld's heavily documented study, "U.S. Law Enforcement Abroad: The Constitution and International Law, Continued," 84 *AJIL* 444 (1990); Nanda, "The Validity of United States Intervention in Panama under International Law," *id.*, 494; Farer, "Panama: Beyond the Charter Paradigm," *id.*, 503; D'Amato, "The Invasion of Panama was a Lawful Response to Tyranny," *id.*, 516; and Rubin, "Is Noriega Worth Subverting US Law?" *CSM*, March 19, 1990, 18. Examine *United States* v. *Verdugo-Urquidez*, U.S. Supreme Court, Feb. 28, 1990, in 29 *ILM* 441 (1990), in which the Court ruled that the Fourth Amendment did not apply to aliens in foreign territory or in international waters. Any restrictions on foreign searches or seizures had to be imposed by Congress, based on diplomatic negotiations, or found in the provisions of treaties.

On January 9, 1990, the Peruvian government announced that it had granted diplomatic asylum to 12 of Noriega's top associates who had taken refuge in the Peruvian ambassador's residence in Panama City. That facility had then been surrounded by U.S. troops. The Peruvian government said that the twelve would be allowed to come to Peru, but no negotiations to that effect had started as yet.

General acceptance of diplomatic asylum led, in turn, to efforts aimed at providing adequate regulation of the granting of such asylum. Beginning with a conference in Montevideo in 1889, a series in Latin American conventions have been devoted to the subject (Caracas, 1911; Havana, 1928; Montevideo, 1933 and 1939). In 1948 the Ninth Conference of American States, meeting in Bogotá, drafted the American Declaration of the Rights and Duties of Man, which provided, in Article 27, that

Every person has the right, in case of pursuit not resulting from ordinary crimes, to seek and receive asylum in foreign territory, in accordance with the laws of each country and with international agreements.[45]

This provision could be interpreted to include the "foreign territory" represented by foreign embassies and legations.

At times the exercise of the doctrine of diplomatic asylum has produced striking results, as to either the number of individuals involved or the publicity received from the actions taken. Thus during the early phases of the Spanish Civil War, some 12,000 opponents of the Republican government of Spain found shelter in various embassies and legations in Madrid,[46] while a great amount of bitter denunciation, culminating in two cases laid before the International Court of Justice, was caused by the granting of diplomatic asylum by the Colombian Embassy in Lima to Victor Raúl Haya de la Torre, the leader of the Peruvian Aprista party.[47]

Following the Chilean military coup of September 11, 1973, the National Committee for Aid to Refugees was formed under the auspices of the UN High Commissioner for Refugees. This body was to find safe havens for thousands of foreign and Chilean political refugees—some of whom had already fled to foreign embassies. Chilean authorities created four sanctuaries, and over 3,000 persons moved into them. The government then issued about 6,500 safe-conduct passes, and gradually the refugees left the country, once other states agreed to admit them. By January 3, 1974, almost 1,500 non-Chilean refugees had left the country; 1,800 registered foreign refugees

[45]Text in 43 *AJIL* 133 (1949, supp.).
[46]Norman J. Padelford, *International Law and Diplomacy in the Spanish Civil Strife* (1939), 157–68.
[47]*Haya de la Torre Case:* for the decisions of the Court, see *ICJ Reports, 1950,* pp. 266, and *ICJ Reports, 1951,* 71, or the (excerpted at length) first decision of November 20, 1950, in 45 *AJIL* 179 (1951), and the digested second decision of June 13, 1951, *id.,* 781. For discussions of the cases, see Evans, *op. cit.* (n.38), 147–57.

remained (455 of whom were in safe havens, 112 in embassies, along with 500 Chilean exiles-to-be); 1,210 other foreigners were living as refugees in private homes; and 23 were known to be in prison.[48]

A number of instances in which grants of diplomatic asylum were given took place in 1990. On July 3 some 600 Albanians, seeking asylum and passage out of the country, found refuge in foreign embassies in the capital of Tirana. The Albanian government decided on July 5 to grant passports to the asylum-seekers, who had been reinforced by large crowds around the embassies, seeking to exit from Albania. By July 8 more than 5,000 people were sheltered in foreign diplomatic missions, with 2,200 in the West German embassy and its grounds and 1,000 in the Italian mission. On the next day 51 refugees from the Czechoslovak embassy were flown to Prague. On July 12 an Italian-chartered ferry sailed for Albania to pick up refugees, and by July 15 some 4,500 Albanians had been ferried to Italy in vessels chartered by the Italian and West German governments. Some 3,200 of these persons entrained for West Germany. And a French-chartered ferry carried 545 Albanians from their country directly to Marseilles.

In July 1990 a number of mostly working-class Cubans found refuge in foreign embassies in Havana (Czechoslovakia, 12; Italy, 4; Spain, 18; and Switzerland, 5). Their intent was to find asylum until they would be permitted to leave Cuba. Their government demanded that they leave the embassies without any guarantees by Cuba. On July 16 all 12 refugees left the Czechoslovak embassy voluntarily after assurances that no prosecution would be undertaken. On September 27 the four Cubans in the Italian embassy gave up their quest for departure from Cuba and left the mission's premises. Later the five in the Swiss mission surrendered. But the 18 Cubans in the Spanish embassy were still holding out by the middle of August 1990.

The latest instance of a grant of diplomatic asylum, at the time of this writing, took place in Lebanon. Rebel general Michel Aoun's forces suffered a decisive defeat at the hands of Syrian troops, and the general fled to the French embassy in Beirut (October 13, 1990). The French authorities granted him and his family asylum, despite the refusal of the Lebanese government to allow Aoun to leave the country. Lebanon wanted to try Aoun on a number of charges, including a claim that he stole some $75 million in state funds. The French demand for Aoun's safe conduct to leave the country and the Lebanese demand for his surrender by the French ambassador had not been resolved at the time of this writing.

## PROBLEMS OF EXTRADITION AND ASYLUM

INFORMAL EXTRADITION   A problem connected with both the process of extradition and the granting of asylum is posed by what is termed *informal*

---

[48]See *NYT*, September 29, 1973, 3; October 3, 1973, 11; October 5, 1973, 7; and, in particular, January 12, 1974, 6.

*extradition*. This term refers to any of a great variety of devices and practices utilized by states to secure the apprehension of civil, criminal, and political offenders who have managed to escape beyond the frontiers of the seeking state—all without the formality of the procedural details characteristic of normal state practice under the terms of an extradition treaty.

Modern history is filled with examples of informal extradition, some of them interesting. Although they cannot be presented in detail, the subject can be summarized as follows: From a legal point of view, a state willing to surrender a political offender to the seeking state by some informal method rather than through formal procedures does not commit a wrong: all it does is to abandon the assertions and claims it has made or invoked, openly or tacitly, in the particular case when it accepted the refugee and by doing so initially denied extradition. The existence of an extradition treaty between the two countries concerned in such a transaction might well lead to a substantial defense of the fugitive when tried before the courts of his own state—on the concept that a treaty by incorporation is the law of his land—but in practice such a defense, while valid in theory, might not produce much in the way of results. Even in the United States, citizens have been prosecuted successfully after they have been delivered without due process and in violation of extradition treaties, by countries in which they had sought refuge in order to escape what might be termed *politically motivated criminal prosecution* at home.[49]

FORCIBLE ABDUCTION    In regard to fugitives abducted and returned against their will to their own country, the judicial attitude in the United States appears to be that "the power of a court to try a person for a crime is not impaired by the fact that he had been brought within the court's jurisdiction by reason of a 'forcible abduction,' " whether from another state[50] or from another country.[51] Thus a defendant cannot dispute the jurisdiction

---

[49] Kirchheimer, *op. cit.*, n.33 998–99; the following cases might be cited as illustrative specimens: *United States* v. *Sobell*, U.S. Dist. Court, S.D. of N.Y., 1956, 142 F. Supp. 515; *Chandler* v. *United States*, 1948, 171 F. (2d) 921; see also *NYT*, April 16, 1972, 12.

[50] *Frisbie* v. *Collins*, U.S. Supreme Court, 1952, 342 U.S. 519.

[51] *Ker* v. *Illinois*, U.S. Supreme Court, 1886, 119 U.S. 437. United States courts have, in fact, referred to a *Ker-Frisbie Rule*, such as in *United States* v. *Toscanino*, U.S. Court of Appeals, 2d Cir., May 15, 1974, 500 F.2d 267, as amended on denial of rehearing, August 21, 1974, reported in 69 *AJIL* 406 (1975); in *United States* v. *Lira*, U.S. Court of Appeals, 2d Cir., 1975, 515 F.2d 68, reported 70 *id.*, 142 (1976); and in *United States* v. *Lara*, U.S. Court of Appeals, 5th Cir., 1976, 539 F.2d 495, reported 71 *id.*, 537 (1977). See also the interesting case of *United States* v. *Postal*, U.S. Court of Appeals, 5th Cir., 1979, 589 F.2d 862, covered at length in Riesenfeld, "The Doctrine of Self-Executing Treaties and *U.S.* v. *Postal:* Win at Any Price?" 74 *AJIL* 892 (1980), with relevant comments concerning the Ker-Frisbie Rule. See also *United States ex rel. Lujan* v. *Gengler*, U.S. Court of Appeals, 2d Cir., 1975, 510, F.2d 62, reported 69 *AJIL* 895 (1975), concerning forcible abduction and its sanctioning by American courts; "Kidnapping Drug Lords," *U.S. News & World Report*, May 14, 1990, 28–30; and especially "Irregular Apprehension of Criminal Suspects," 84 *AJIL* 725 (1990).

of a federal court simply because his arrest was unusual or even illegal. What really matters is that the defendant has, somehow, come under the authority of that court.

The defense of illegal entry into a court's jurisdiction is therefore rejected, generally on the plea that the supposed violation in question was not that of the individual's interests but of the interests of the state whose rights were violated. This principle is supported by the laws of the overwhelming number of all states; once a prisoner is under the authority of a given court and has been properly charged in accordance with the local law, he may be tried and, if convicted, sentenced by that court regardless of the mode by which he was brought originally under the authority of that court.

The whole question of abducting a fugitive from his refuge for trial elsewhere came into worldwide prominence through the seizure on May 11, 1960, of Adolf Eichmann by "private" Israeli citizens in Argentina and his transportation to Israel on an Israeli aircraft to face trial as a Nazi war criminal. Eichmann had been removed in violation of international law, a fact emphasized formally by the UN Security Council, to which Argentina brought a complaint about the incident.[52] After Israel tendered an official apology, Argentina waived further action on the abduction. The matter was declared closed in a joint communiqué issued by the two states on August 3, 1960.

Illustrative of some of the problems occasionally encountered in extraditing fugitives from justice was the case of Ronald Biggs, sentenced to 30 years in prison for his part in the robbery of $7.2 million from a British mail train in 1963. He escaped in 1965 and fled, first to Australia and then to Brazil. There he fathered a child, and the Brazilian government refused to surrender him to the United Kingdom on the grounds that a Brazilian law bars the extradition of anyone with a Brazilian dependent. In March 1981, several men, later labeled in the press as "kidnappers for hire," seized Biggs at a restaurant in Rio de Janeiro. Biggs was found, some time later, under guard on a yacht drifting off Bermuda. Both the United Kingdom and Brazil filed requests with Barbados for the extradition of Biggs; in one case because he was an escaped felon and in the other case because he had been kidnapped from Brazil—which also demanded the extradition from Barbados of his kidnappers. In April 1981 the Barbados Supreme Court, reversing the decision of a lower court, ruled that Biggs could not be extradited to England because the Barbados Parliament had not yet ratified an extradition treaty with the United Kingdom. As a result, Biggs returned to Brazil as a free man.

[52] On the question of Eichmann's abduction, consult Silving, "In Re Eichmann: A Dilemma of Law and Morality," 55 *AJIL* 307 (exhaustive bibliographical and background notes) (1961); see also Cardozo, "When Extradition Fails, Is Abduction the Solution?", *id.*, 127; Schwarzenberger, "The Eichmann Judgment," 237–251, in his *International Law and Order* (1971); *NYT*, November 26, 1972, 14; and, concerning Israel's attitude toward abduction, *Time*, August 20, 1973, 31. Also see Argentina's complaint to UN Security Council, in Henkin, 449–51.

BRINGING HIJACKERS TO JUSTICE   Alleged hijackers can be tried in the country where they were captured or, under a treaty, in the country whose citizens were injured or killed by the hijackers. When such "normal" procedures fail, then, in the case of the United States, an alleged hijacker being sought under American laws and indictments may be arrested abroad by U.S. law-enforcement agents and taken to the United States for trial. As early as July 1985, unidentified State Department officials asserted that in the absence of either a fair trial by local authorities or extradition under a treaty, the only valid alternative was abduction of hijackers.[53] And, as pointed out earlier, the means by which an accused party was brought into U.S. jurisdiction has been largely irrelevant as far as U.S. federal courts have been concerned.

A case of primary importance in this connection was *United States* v. *Younis*.[54] Fawad Younis, a former Lebanese car dealer, was accused of being the mastermind behind the hijacking of a Jordanian airliner (June 11, 1985). The aircraft was seized at Beirut, Lebanon, and flown twice all over the Mediterranean, returning each time to Beirut. Both Syria and Tunisia denied access to their airspaces, but the aircraft was refueled on Cyprus and in Sicily. After the first trip, five passengers were set free and the rest were threatened if the demands of the hijackers were not met. Those demands centered on the expulsion of all Palestinians from Lebanon. Ultimately the crew and the rest of the passengers were set free and the plane was blown up.

Younis' whereabouts on Cyprus were discovered and after a brief period of surveillance he was lured aboard a yacht manned by FBI agents off Cyprus, on promises of a drug deal. (In 1986, Congress had authorized the FBI to investigate all terrorist acts against Americans and to apprehend the perpetrators abroad for trial in the United States.) Younis was interrogated aboard a U.S. Navy munitions ship, then was transferred to the U.S. aircraft carrier *Saratoga* and flown to Washington, D.C. without the plane touching down in any foreign country. He had been indicted of conspiring with others in the June 11th seizure of the Jordianian airliner. He was the first overseas terrorist seized abroad for trial in the United States.

The proceedings in the District Court began with charges based on Section 32(a) of the U.S. Aircraft Piracy Act being dismissed because that section gave no jurisdiction over aircraft piracy lacking connection to American territory. The Court held, however, that traditional principles of international law provided sufficient grounds for asserting both subject matter and personal jurisdiction over the other crimes charged and that the U.S. Hostage Taking Act and also Section 32(b) of the Aircraft Piracy Act created liability for the offenses allegedly committed by Younis.

[53]*CSM*, July 22, 1985, 6. See also Case History No. 3, below.
[54]681 F. Supp. 896. U.S. Dist. Court, D.D.C., Feb. 12, 1988, reported in 83 *AJIL* 94 (1989).

The defense and prosecution based their respective stands on the five traditional bases of jurisdiction over extraterritorial crimes under international law: (1) territorial, the place where the offense was committed; (2) national, the nationality of the offender; (3) protective, the potential harm to the national interest; (4) universal, the commission of crimes considered particularly evil and harmful to humanity; and (5) passive personality, the nationality of the victim.[55]

The Court agreed with the prosecution and held that both the universal and the passive personality principles confirmed a basis for jurisdiction in this case. It emphasized the existence of conventions against aircraft piracy and hostage taking. It noted that a majority of all states had become parties to the Tokyo, The Hague, and the Montreal Conventions and that the Convention against the Taking of Hostages, in its Article 5(1)(d), gave each signatory state discretion to exercise extraterritorial jurisdiction when an offense was committed "with respect to a hostage who is a national of the State, if that State considers it appropriate."[56] The Court also held that the much debated passive personality principle was recognized by the family of nations as a legitimate principle of international law. Although not really accepted by the United States, recent years showed that the principle had received U.S. approval when applied to universally condemned crimes, such as piracy and hostage taking. An example cited was the reliance of the U.S. Government on the principle in issuing an arrest warrant for Muhammed Abbas, mastermind of the hijacking of the *Achille Lauro* (see Case Study No. 3, below).

In answer to other arguments brought on by the defense, the Court noted that the Hostage Taking Act set forth in clear and unambiguous terms the intent of Congress to hold liable offenders who took American nationals hostage, regardless of where the seizure took place. Overall, the Court's reasoning and ruling strongly affirmed the applicability of the universal and passive principles by any government attempting to impose liability in the case of such offenses.

Younis was found guilty of both aircraft piracy and hostage taking.[57]

It is only fair to admit that not all governments view with approval a reliance on the universal and passive personality principles when a given state attempts to pursue criminals extraterritorially; the troublesome issue of national sovereignty is raised, not surprisingly. The latter, being almost by definition a highly sensitive issue in all countries, has therefore been used

---

[55] The defense cited *Hanoch Tel-Oren* v. *Libyan Arab Republic et al.*, 726 F.2d 774, 781 n.7 (D.D.Cir. 1984) [24 *ILM* 370–426 (1984)], *cert. denied* 470 U.S. 1003 (1985), several other cases all *cert. denied* by the U.S. Supreme Court; Henkin, 447 (1980); and D'Amato, *International Law and World Order* 564 (1980).

[56] See Chapter 13, *sub* Aerial Hijacking and also Peacetime Hostage Taking, on the conventions mentioned.

[57] The above condensation is based in part on the comprehensive report on the Younis Case by Clarizia in 83 *AJIL* 94 (1989).

on occasion to thwart or at least to protest against attempts to seize alleged offenders in the spheres of aircraft hijacking and hostage taking, as well as in the instance of other types of terrorist acts. The more a given state is still conscious of past outside interventions, the more likely it will be to resent acts which in other countries, including the United States, may be held to be justified, legal, and desirable.

Recent examples of various forms of forcible extradition included Israel's seizure in Rome of Mordechai Vanunu (charged with revealing Israeli nuclear secrets), Iranian airline officials attempting to kidnap an Iranian passenger on a plane at the Frankfurt airport, the United States' attempt to seize the captors of the Italian cruise ship *Achille Lauro* (See Case History No. 3, below.), and, of course, the case of General Manuel Noriega.

STATUS OF PREWAR EXTRADITION TREATIES    One of the many problems connected with formal extradition treaties arises at the end of a war. Do the prewar extradition agreements concluded between opposing belligerents survive the war? Judging on the basis of numerous court decisions, it appears that such agreements are not terminated by the outbreak of war but are merely suspended. They come into effect again after the end of the conflict, as soon as relevant notifications have been exchanged between the former belligerents.[58]

## SUGGESTED READINGS

### Extradition in General

CASES

*Rivard* v. *United States*, U.S. Court of Appeals, 5th Cir., 1967, 375 F.2d 882, reported in 61 *AJIL* 1065 (1967).
*Royal Government of Greece* v. *Governor of Brixton Prison ex parte Kotronis*, United Kingdom, House of Lords, 1969 [1969] 3 W.L.R. 1107, reported in 64 *AJIL* 714 (1970).
*Atkinson* v. *United States of America Government*, United Kingdom, House of Lords, 1969, [1969] 3 W.L.R. 1074, reported in 64 *AJIL* 711 (1970).
*In re Kam-shu*, U.S. Court of Appeals, 5th Cir., 1973, 477 F.2d 333, reported in 68 *AJIL* 125 (1974).
*United States* v. *Cordero*, U.S. Court of Appeals, 1st Cir., 1981, 668 F.2d 32, in 76 *AJIL* 618 (1981).
*Sabatien* v. *Dabrowski*, U.S. Court of Appeals, 1st Cir., 1978, 586 F.2d 866, reported 73 *AJIL* 510 (1979).
*In re Extradition of David*, U.S. Dist. Court, E.D. Illinois, 1975, 395 F. Supp. 803, reported 70 *AJIL* 361 (1976).

[58] Illustrative cases include *Society for the Propagation of the Gospel in Foreign Parts* v. *Town of New Haven*, U.S. Supreme Court, 1823, 8 Wheaton 464; *Terlinden* v. *Ames*, U.S. Supreme Court, 1902, 184 U.S. 270; and *Clark* v. *Allen*, U.S. Supreme Court, 1947, 331 U.S. 503.

*In re Magisano*, U.S. Court of Appeals, 9th Cir., 1976, 545 F.2d 1228, reported 71 *AJIL* 533 (1977).

For accounts of the attempts on the part of the United States to secure the extradition of one *Robert Vesco* for wire fraud and other charges (covering attempts in the Bahamas, Argentina, and Costa Rica, all of which denied extradition), consult *inter alia*, *NYT*, June 23, 1973, 1, 13; November 4, 1973, 1, 81; December 7, 1973, 20; December 8, 1973, 1, 24; June 12, 1977, 2; March 25, 1978, 5. See also *Time*, December 24, 1973, 74–75; October 2, 1978, 31; *Newsweek*, June 13, 1977, 47; March 27, 1978, 62; A.P. Dispatches, December 30, 1980; January 1, 1981; July 27, 1981; May 13, 1982. See also *Time*, November 28, 1983, 28, according to which Vesco, after being expelled from the Bahamas, settled in Cuba.

## Political Offenses

Green, "Political Offenses, War Crimes and Extradition," 11 *Int'l and Comp. L.Q.*, 329 (1962); Epps, "The Validity of the Political Offender Exception in Extradition Treaties in Anglo-American Jurisprudence," 20 *Harvard Int'l Law Jl.* 61 (1979).

CASES

*In re Ezeta*, U.S. Dist. Court, N.D. Cal., 1894, 62 Fed. 972.
*In the Matter of Ktir*, Switzerland, Supreme Federal Court, 1961, digested in 56 *AJIL* 224 (1962).
*Ornelas* v. *Ruiz*, U.S. Supreme Court, 1896, 161 U.S. 502.
*Cheng Tzu-tsai* v. *Governor of Pentonville Prison*, United Kingdom, House of Lords, 1973, [1973] 2 All E.R. 204, reported in 68 *AJIL* 135 (1974).
*Garcia-Guillern* v. *United States*, U.S. Court of Appeals, 5th Cir., 1971, 450 F.2d 1189, reported 66 *AJIL* 629 (1972).

## Eichmann Case

Whiteman, vol. 6, 105–9; Rogat, *The Eichmann Trial and the Rule of Law* (1961); Hausner, *Justice in Jerusalem* (1966); Robinson, *And the Crooked Shall Be Made Straight* (1966); Leavy, "The Eichmann Trial and the Role of Law," 48 *American Bar Assoc. Jl.* (1962), 820–25 (1962); *Attorney-General of the Government of Israel* v. *Eichmann*, District Court of Jerusalem, December 11, 1961, excerpted at length in 56 *AJIL* 805 (1962); see *Israel Digest*, June 5, 1962, 1, for the summary of the dismissal (May 29, 1962) of Eichmann's appeal to the Supreme Court of Israel; see also *NYT*, November 26, 1972, 14. Eichmann was executed by hanging on May 31, 1972.

## Asylum

Sinha, *Asylum and International Law* (1971); Grahl-Madsen, *Territorial Asylum* (1980); Martin, "Large-Scale Migrations of Asylum Seekers," 76 *AJIL* 598 (1982).

# Case Study No. 3

## The *Achille Lauro* Affair

A state, victim of international terrorism, has three options in attempting to bring the guilty parties to justice; it may rely on an extradition treaty, covering the offense, with the asylum state to have the offenders returned for trial; it may persuade the asylum state to try the offenders under its own laws in its own courts; or, all else failing, it may try to capture of offenders and abduct them to its own jurisdiction for trial.

The terrorist seizure of the Italian cruise ship *Achille Lauro* and its sequel illustrates both procedures and problems encountered in practice. It also represents the first time the United States officially employed the third option listed.

On October 7, 1985, five Palestinian hijackers seized control of the Italian cruise ship *Achille Lauro*, en route from Alexandria, Egypt to Port Said. Some 600 passengers had left the vessel in Alexandria for a day-long land tour, but some 400 persons, including about 160 passengers, were still aboard the ship when it was seized. The hijackers demanded the release of 50 prisoners held by Israel and threatened to destroy the vessel if attacked. They claimed to be members of the Palestine Liberation Front, a dissident splinter group of the Palestine Liberation Organization (PLO).

The hijackers attempted to have the *Achille Lauro* enter Syrian territorial waters, but were denied permission to do so. The vessel was then directed to return to Egypt. While under the control of the hijackers, one of the ship's passengers, an American citizen, was shot and thrown overboard with his wheelchair.

On October 9 the ship, its crew, and all passengers aboard were released when the *Achille Lauro* reached Egypt. The hijackers surrendered to a PLO representative, were taken to Cairo and the next day placed aboard a chartered Egyptian airliner. Soon afterward four U.S. Navy fighter-interceptor jets met the airliner over international waters; it was bound from Cairo's Al Maza military airport for Tunis. The jets forced the airliner to land at an Italian NATO airbase on Sicily. There Italian forces took the hijackers and Muhammed Abbas, a known terrorist and alleged mastermind of the affair, into custody. Before interception, the pilot of the Egyptian aircraft had radioed both Tunis and Athens, requesting permission to land; both requests were turned down.

A dispute quickly developed between Italy and the United States concerning the exercise of criminal jurisdiction over the hijackers and Abbas.[1] And ruffled feelings abounded about other aspects of the events: Egypt's president demanded a public apology from President Reagan for forcing down the aircraft carrying the hijackers; legal experts wrangled over the legitimacy of the American action, and so on.

On October 11 a judge of the U.S. District Court in the District of Columbia had issued an arrest warrant for Abbas (a.k.a. Abu el-Abas and Muhammed Zaydan), in which Abbas was charged with hostage taking, piracy on the high seas, and conspiracy. The Italian judicial authorities, faced with an American request to arrest Abbas and eventually extradite him (and the hijackers) to the United States, demurred on the grounds that there existed a lack of sufficient evidence to arrest Abbas. The latter left for Yugoslavia where he traveled under the protection of an Iraqi diplomatic passport, then left for elsewhere in the Middle East. The United States had asked Yugoslavia to arrest Abbas, who was well-known as a terrorist, but the Iraqi passport was cited in response, plus the fact that by that time he was gone.

However, on July 11, 1986, an Italian court in Genoa convicted Abbas (*in absentia*) and the five hijackers of the hijacking and of the killing of the American passenger. Abbas and two others were given life in prison sentences, the others 15- to 30-year terms in prison. This action meant, moreover, that under a "double jeopardy" provision in the 1963 U.S.–Italy extradition treaty, the six could not be tried again in the United States for the cited offenses. That treaty is a modern instrument devoid of the traditional list of offenses but calling for extradition for any crime punishable under the laws of both parties. A most interesting feature of that treaty is its Article 3 which does not limit extraditable offenses to such as were committed on the territory of the requesting state but permits extradition for *extraterritorial* crimes, so long as the offense met the criterion of double criminality. Article 7 of the treaty, which also featured in the U.S.–Italy dispute, provides that extradition could be refused if the authorities of the requested (asylum) state were proceeding against the wanted persons for the same offense for which extradition had been requested.

As far as the interception of the Egyptian airliner was concerned, a number of legal scholars have expressed the belief that the American action could be viewed as akin to the maritime visit and search doctrine. Inasmuch as an aircraft could not be stopped on the high seas for visit and search, it was argued that forcing the plane in question to land for visit and search by Italian authorities was legitimate "by extension." On the other

---

[1]See the extensive collection of documents and treaty texts on the whole affair in 24 *ILM* 1509 (1985) and the heavily documented study by Halberstam, "Terrorism on the High Seas; The Achille Lauro, Piracy and the IMO Convention on Maritime Safety," 82 *AJIL* 269 (1988).

hand, one scholar maintained that not only was the airliner diverted illegally without Egypt's consent, but the action was illegal under the American Fourth Amendment; it represented violation of the hijackers' rights against an illegal search and seizure.

If Lauterpacht's definition of piracy[2] is accepted as correct, then the seizure of the *Achille Lauro* was an act of piracy. As such, the pirate was beyond the law (in German: *vogelfrei*, "free as a bird") and could be brought to justice by the military authorities (here U.S. Navy jets) of *any* country. Under this interpretation, the American diversion of the airliner should viewed as legally correct. This view of the seizure of the cruise ship as piracy was echoed by the Legal Adviser of the Department of State,[3] and also when that Department secured arrest warrants charging the hijackers with hostage taking, conspiracy, and *"piracy on the high seas."*[4]

### Suggested Readings

McGinley, "The Achille Lauro Affair—Implications for International Law," 52 *Tenn. L. Rev.* 691 (1985); Paust, "Extradition of the *Achille Lauro* Hostage-Takers: Navigating the Hazards," 20 *Vanderbilt J. Transnat'l L.* 235 (1987); Fenwick, " 'Piracy' in the Caribbean," 55 *AJIL* 426 (1961); "Getting Even," *Newsweek*, Oct. 21, 1985, 20–39; *Time*, Oct. 21, 1985, 22–33.

[2]See Chapter 13, n.9 and related text.
[3]*NYT*, Dec. 30, 1985, A-1.
[4]24 *ILM* 1554–57 (1985).

# 13

# International Criminal Law

## INTRODUCTION

It was pointed out earlier (Chapters 1 and 10) that the individual normally does not represent a subject of international law. Certain crimes, however, have such international significance that their perpetrators have become increasingly subject to action taken under rules of international law: they can be pursued, indicted, tried, and punished in accordance with international criminal law (French: *droit penal international*; German: *Völkerstrafrecht*). The offenses covered by that law fall into two categories. The first includes the slave trade, piracy, air hijacking, terrorism, peacetime taking of hostages, genocide, torture, and Apartheid: a grouping covered in this Chapter. The second category includes the waging of war (if such be indeed illegal), war crimes, crimes against peace, aggression, and the group of somewhat ill-defined acts styled crimes against humanity. That category will be covered in Chapters 19 and 27, for its components represent acts commonly associated with warfare.[1]

Some writers include still other offenses as crimes against international law: counterfeiting currency, government securities, and postage stamps (see Chapter 7); unlawful human experimentation, destruction or theft of national treasures, environmental degradation, theft of nuclear materials, crimes against internationally protected persons (See Chapter 19), and bribery of foreign public officials.[2] Others also include as international crimes "oppression" and "politicide."[3]

## THE SLAVE TRADE

Great Britain abolished slavery within its realm in 1807 and then ordered its navy to stop and search vessels suspected of being engaged in the slave trade.

---

[1] Most aspects of both rather traditional categories of international crimes are covered comprehensively in Bassiouni and Nanda, eds., *A Treatise on International Criminal Law* (2 vols, 1973), although some material is now dated.

[2] Bassiouni, *International Crimes: Digest/Index of Conventions and Relevant Penal Provisions* (2 vols, 1985).

[3] Paust, "Aggression Against Authority: The Crime of Oppression, Politicide And Other Crimes Against Human Rights," 18 *Case W. R. Res. J. Int'l Law* 283 (1986).

At the Congress of Vienna (1815), the British government proposed the creation of economic boycotts against any country refusing to abolish slavery (Sweden had done away with the institution in 1813, the Netherlands in 1814). That suggestion was not received with any enthusiasm by the assembled delegations, as only the British Navy would have been able to enforce such collective measures as a boycott, and no one at Vienna harbored any desire to strengthen British rule of the oceans. Hence only a solemn condemnation of "the trade in negroes" was passed, with no enforcement detailed.

The British government then concluded a series of bilateral agreements with several countries, providing in each case for reciprocal rights of visit and search by public ships and private vessels flying the flag of the other party. The United States, incidentally, was prevented by Article I, section 9, of its Constitution from barring the importation of slaves into its territory until 1808. In that year, Congress prohibited the further importation of slaves and in 1820 labeled a pirate any person engaged in the slave trade.[4] After 1840, a number of multilateral conventions were developed, culminating in the Convention of St. Germain (1919), which provided for the complete abolition of slavery and any trade in slaves on land or by sea. Another treaty, the Convention to Suppress the Slave Trade and Slavery (Geneva 1926, amended by a Protocol in 1953) entered into force in 1927 (for the United States in 1929) and is still securing accessions.[5] That instrument reaffirmed in much more emphatic terms and for many more countries the contents of the St. Germain agreement. It was updated and enlarged through the Supplementary Convention on the Abolition of Slavery, the Slave Trade, and Institutions and Practices Similar to Slavery (Geneva 1956), in force April 30, 1957 (for the United States since 1967). It must be pointed out that none of the foregoing agreements contains realistic enforcement provisions.

In consequence of the international prohibitions' weakness, slavery has not disappeared. Its extent is highly debatable, for no accurate statistics are available, and even the governments within whose territories indisputable evidence of slavery has been found deny that such an institution exists and, in some instances, point to solemn governmental prohibitions of the practice. But slavery does appear to continue in a broad belt of states extending from northwestern Africa to the eastern borders of the Arabian peninsula, and possibly in isolated pockets beyond into the Asian mainland.[6] For example, a report based on an inquiry by the Anti-Slavery Society of London, under study by the UN Human Rights Commission, charged that as many

---

[4] See Sheikh, *International Law and National Behavior* (1974), 18–19.
[5] See Lauterpacht's *Oppenheim*, vol. 1, 620; Higgins-Colombos, 310; Reiff, 125–27.
[6] Consult Rosenberg, "The Middle East Slave Trade," 9 *Middle East Review* 58–62 (Winter 1976–1977), as well as the related rebuttal by the secretary of the Anti-Slavery Society (London), and the author's response, both 9 *Middle East Review* 67–70 (Summer 1977).

as 100,000 persons in Mauritania represented what was very likely the largest slave group in the world in 1981. Corroborating the charge was the admission, in the fall of 1980, by the Mauritanian foreign minister that slavery "still exists in our country . . . it will take a long process before we are finally rid of this hateful practice."[7]

Since then, despite frequent official denials, the major types of slavery (chattel slavery, debt bondage, child bondage, and prostitution) have continued to flourish. In fact it has been said by the director of the Anti-Slavery Society that more individuals can be said to be enslaved today than when the Society was founded in 1839. And it has been claimed that in some parts of the world, such as the western Sudan, slavery has made a reappearance on a limited tribal basis.[8]

The 1982 UN Convention on the Law of the Sea (UNCLOS III) provides in Article 99:

Every State shall take effective measures to prevent and punish the transport of slaves in ships authorized to fly its flag, and to prevent the unlawful use of its flag for that purpose. Any slave taking refuge on board any ship, whatever its flag, shall *ipso facto* be free.

And Article 110 (1-b) of the same convention reaffirms the right of *all* public vessels to stop, visit, and search any merchant vessel on the high seas when there is reasonable ground for suspecting that the ship in question is engaged in the slave trade (Emphasis added). (The 1982 articles correspond, in essence, to Articles 13 and 21 (1-b) of the 1958 Geneva Convention on the High Seas.)

## PIRACY

Piracy, an age-old occupation of certain enterprising individuals, has not yet disappeared completely from the world's oceans. Generally, piracy may be of two kinds, *statutory piracy* and *piracy jure gentium*. The former variety is piracy as it is defined in the statutes of individual states and is of no concern to us here. The second variety is piracy under international law. The traditional definition of such piracy corresponds to Oppenheim's:

Piracy in its original and strict meaning, is every unauthorized act of violence committed by a private vessel on the open sea against another vessel with intent to plunder (*animo furandi*).
If a definition is desired which really covers all such acts as are in practice treated as piratical, piracy must be defined as *every unauthorized act of violence against persons*

[7] *International Herald Tribune* (Paris), August 28, 1981, 5; see also Omaar, "The Forgotten Slaves [Mauritania]," *CSM*, Aug. 14, 1990, 19.
[8] See Will's revealing column in *The Washington Post*, June 21, 1990, and the Sudan report in *CSM*, Aug. 31, 1987, 9.

*or goods committed on the open sea either by a private vessel against another vessel or by the mutinous crew or passengers against their own vessel* (Emphasis in original).[9]

A shorter definition is found in the classic case of *In re Piracy Jure Gentium* when the court endorsed as "nearest to accuracy" the definition of "piracy is any armed violence at sea which is not a lawful act of war."[10]

It should be pointed out that "authorized" acts of a nature that today is called *piracy* (then known as *privateering*) were abolished and declared illegal by Article 1 of the Declaration of Paris in 1856.[11]

**PIRACY IN 1982 UN CONVENTION ON THE LAW OF THE SEA**    The 1982 United Nations Convention (UNCLOS III) deals with piracy in Articles 101 through 107 and 110(a). (Articles in parentheses are the corresponding and virtually identical articles in the 1958 Geneva Convention on the High Seas):

### ARTICLE 101 (15)

Piracy consists of any of the following acts: (a) any illegal act of violence, detention or any act of depredation, *committed for private ends* by the crew or the passengers of a private ship or a private aircraft, and directed: (i) on the high seas, against another ship or aircraft, or against persons or property on board such ship or aircraft; (ii) against a ship, aircraft, persons or property in a place outside the jurisdiction of any State; (b) any act of voluntary participation in the operation of a ship or of an aircraft with knowledge of facts making it a pirate ship or aircraft; (c) any act of inciting or of intentionally facilitating an act described in subparagraph (a) or subparagraph (b) of this article. (Emphasis added)

### ARTICLE 102 (16)

The acts of piracy, as defined in article 101, committed by a warship, government ship or government aircraft whose crew has mutinied and taken control of the ship or aircraft are assimilated to acts committed by a private ship or aircraft.

### ARTICLE 103 (17)

A ship or aircraft is considered a pirate ship or aircraft if it is intended by the persons in dominant control to be used for the purpose of committing one of the acts referred to in article 101. The same applies if the ship or aircraft has been used to commit any such act, so long as it remains under the control of the persons guilty of that act.

[9]Lauterpacht's *Oppenheim*, vol. 1, 608–9. See Rubin, *Piracy, Paramountcy and Protectorates* (1974) and his *The Law of Piracy* (1988), the most comprehensive study available; Whiteman, vol. 4, 648–67; Higgins-Colombos, 329–34; and for historical background, de Montmorency, "The Barbary States in International Law," 87–94 in *Transactions of the Grotius Society* (1919).
[10]*In re Piracy Jur Gentium*, Great Britain, Judicial Committee of the Privy Council, 1934 [1934] A.C. 586, reprinted in 3 *Brit. Int'l L. Cases* 236, 842 (1965).
[11]Consult Sohn and Buergenthal, *International Protection of Human Rights* (1973), 23–40, concerning the "private reprisals" in question.

## ARTICLE 104 (18)

A ship or aircraft may retain its nationality although it has become a pirate ship or aircraft. The retention or loss of nationality is determined by the law of the State from which such nationality was derived.

## ARTICLE 105 (19)

On the high seas, or in any other place outside the jurisidiction of any State, *every State* may seize a pirate ship or aircraft, or a ship taken by piracy and under the control of pirates, and arrest the persons and seize the property on board. The courts of the State which carried out the seizure may decide upon the penalties to be imposed, and may also determine the action to be taken with regard to the ships, aircraft or property, subject to the rights of third parties acting in good faith. (Emphasis added)

## ARTICLE 106 (20)

Where the seizure of a ship or aircraft on suspicion of piracy has been effected without adequate grounds, the State making the seizure shall be liable to the State the nationality of which is possessed by the ship or aircraft, for any loss or damage caused by the seizure.

## ARTICLE 107 (21)

A seizure on account of piracy may be carried out only by warships or military aircraft, or other ships or aircraft clearly marked and identifiable as being on government service and authorized to that effect.

## ARTICLE 110 (22)

1. Except where acts of interference derive from powers conferred by treaty, a warship which encounters on the high seas a foreign ship, other than a ship entitled to complete immunity in accordance with articles 95 and 96, is not justified in boarding it unless there is reasonable ground for suspecting that: (a) the ship is engaged in piracy. . . .

The phrase "for private ends" in Article 101(15) above has proven to be troublesome since it first appeared in the conventions. It has never been defined officially in the Geneva instruments or their predecessors, except that the preparatory meetings of several treaties indicate that the phrase was meant to exclude acts of unrecognized rebels who restricted their attacks to the state from which they sought independence. [12]

Modern interpretations of piracy differ also from the older definitions in that the intention to rob, mentioned in Oppenheim's definition of piracy, is

---

[12] Halberstam, "Terrorism on the High Seas: The Achille Lauro, Piracy and the IMO Convention on Maritime Safety," 82 *AJIL* 269, at 277–84.

no longer required. It is now recognized that acts of piracy may be prompted by feelings of hatred or revenge and not merely by a desire for gain. But even today an act must be committed for *private ends* in order to be classified as piratical.

RIGHT OF SUPPRESSION OF PIRACY   In earlier times, even private individuals were tolerated as enforcers of the prohibition on piracy. Today any state may seize, on the high seas or in any other place outside the territorial waters of another state, a pirate ship or aircraft, or a ship taken in piracy and under the control of pirates, and arrest the persons and seize the property on board. The craft and prisoners are supposed to be taken to the nearest appropriate court of the arresting state, and that court decides on the penalties to be imposed and on the disposition of the craft and its contents. Although private craft are not to hunt down pirates today, should a merchant vessel overpower its attacker, the "arrest" of the pirate craft and crew by the merchant vessel would be lawful. Normally the merchant vessel would then summon a warship to its assistance and turn the captured craft and crew over to the custody of that warship. Essentially, the capture of pirate craft may today be undertaken only by warships or military aircraft, unless other ships or aircraft on government service have been authorized to undertake such capture.

If an individual is found guilty of piracy, the state of which he is a national or citizen has, under customary international law, no right to defend or represent him in further proceedings that may take place. If, on the other hand, a ship, an aircraft, or individuals on suspicion of piracy have been seized without adequate grounds, the state making the seizure is liable to the state whose nationality is possessed by the craft or individuals in question, for any loss or damage caused by the seizure.[13]

STATUS OF SUBMARINES AND AIRCRAFT   The failure of many German submarines during World War I to observe certain laws of war led to charges of piracy against the new type of warship. Such accusations were ill founded, especially because of the absence of a "private end" by the submarine commander and his crew. Nevertheless the views held during World War I regarding submarines were echoed again in 1937 when an "arrangement" was signed at Nyon, France, by a number of maritime states as the result of attacks by submarines of "unknown" or undeclared nationality on Spanish and neutral vessels during the Spanish Civil War. The agreement provided for the treatment as pirates of the crew of any submarine attacking a vessel belonging to neither party in that conflict.

MODERN PIRACY   The mere fact that a ship sails without displaying a flag or an aircraft travels without identifying markings is not sufficient to give such craft the character of a pirate.

A pirate craft has the nationality of the state in which it is registered, except in the case where the national laws of that state view piracy as a

[13] See the celebrated case of *The Virginius*, in Moore, vol. 2, 895–903, and, for comparison, the well-known case of *The Marianna Flora*, U.S. Supreme Court, 1826, 11 Wheaton 1.

ground for the loss of nationality; in the latter case, the ship would be regarded by all countries as being stateless.

Piracy in municipal law is determined by the statutes of each individual state. This fact assumed some importance when airlines and private owners of aircraft in the Western Hemisphere began to be plagued by an increasing incidence of hijacking of planes. After 1960, dozens of passenger planes were diverted to Cuba, with such incidents on occasion occurring as often as twice a day. Planes, crews, and passengers were always permitted to return to their scheduled routing, with the captor remaining in Cuba.

In 1961 President John F. Kennedy signed a bill declaring the hijacking of aircraft an act of piracy, with penalities for the offense ranging up to death. The law also provided for a $1,000 fine for carrying concealed weapons aboard an aircraft and for sentences of up to five years in prison for giving false information on plane hijacking. Application of such legislation proved to be almost impossible, however, for in almost all instances the "pirates" remained in Cuba, beyond the jurisdiction of American courts. In a few instances, on the other hand, the hijackers were subdued before the aircraft left the United States or reached Cuba. In such cases, prosecution of the individuals in question took place. In February 1973, the United States and Cuba negotiated an understanding on hijacking (both of aircraft and of vessels) that provided for either prosecution or extradition.[14] The agreement was allowed to lapse in April 1977. (See also "Air Hijacking" below.)

Piracy, old style, as portrayed in countless motion pictures, has not yet been eliminated altogether. Thus 1977 saw piratical raids in and off the port of Lagos (Nigeria). Since 1978, true acts of piracy have occurred with embarrassing frequency off the western coast of Thailand, in the Gulf of Thailand, the Sulu Sea, and the Celebes Sea.[15] The majority of the recent pirate attacks have been launched at the so-called boat people or refugees in the South China Sea and in the Gulf of Thailand, according to representatives of the UN High Commissioner of Refugees. It is believed that since 1980 more than 2,000 boat people have been killed and hundreds of young women abducted by pirates, to be sold to brothels in Thailand and elsewhere on the mainland. In the first seven months of 1989 alone, 271 boat people were killed or missing. In one of the worst incidents, off Malaysia, on April 16, 1989, 130 refugees were killed, leaving only one survivor of the attack.

Not all recent attacks by pirates have aimed at small native craft filled with boat people. In 1983, for instance, there were 74 attacks on merchant

---

[14]U.S.–Cuba "Memorandum of Understanding on Hijacking and Vessels and Other Offenses" (February 15, 1973): text in *NYT*, February 16, 1973, 4; see also the memorandum's relation to the right of asylum, as analyzed by the U.S. Department of State, 67 *AJIL* 535 (1973).
[15]See, *e.g.*, *NYT*, Nov. 23, 1977, A-6; *Time*, July 31, 1978, 35; *The Washington Post*, Sept. 2, 1980, A-14; *Time*, Nov. 9, 1981, 56; *CSM*, Jan. 7, 1982, 8, Feb. 9, 1984, 13, Feb. 28, 1984, 3, June 9, 1986, 18, and especially Armstrong in *id.*, April 30, 1985, at 3–4; AP Dispatches of April 24, 1985, Dec. 25, 1985, Nov. 8, 1986, May 5, 1989, Aug. 8, 1989, and April 6, 1990.

ships, and while the totals have declined over the years since then, such attacks still take place. They have been located along the West Coast of Africa (emphasis on the looting of container ships), in the South China Sea, and, on very rare occasions, in the Caribbean.

Piracy off Singapore has increased recently: whereas there were only three cases of piracy in the area in 1989, not less than 17 cases were reported by September 10, 1990.

SANTA MARIA CASE    January 1961 saw an instance in which the concepts of insurgent, pirate, and criminal were interwoven almost inextricably: the famous incident of the *Santa Maria*. The vessel, a 21,000-ton Portuguese cruise ship sailing the Caribbean, was seized on January 24 at gunpoint by a band of "patriot pirates," led by Henrique Galvão, a former Portuguese army captain. Seventy heavily armed members of the band, after killing the third officer of the liner, ordered the vessel, with its crew of 370 and more than 600 passengers, to proceed eastward from Martinique. A widespread search by British and American warships and aircraft "failed to locate" the liner for a day, although radio messages from both hijackers and passengers continued to be received in New York.

The purpose of the seizure of the vessel was to call attention to the dictatorial nature of the Portuguese government. By January 28, with the liner heading for northern Brazil, U.S. navy authorities arranged negotiations for the release of the passengers. Eventually the ship reached Brazil, and the rebel group was granted asylum there as political offenders.[16]

From a legal point of view, the brief capture of the *Santa Maria* posed interesting questions.[17] Captain Galvão denied that he was a pirate, and certainly the seizure of the vessel was not inspired by private ends. He insisted that he was an insurgent, engaged in an attempt to overthrow the government of Portugal on behalf of Salazar's chief enemy, General Humberto Delgato. Unfortunately for his claim of insurgent status, Galvão's group had not been recognized as insurgents by any state; hence he could not enjoy any privileges accruing to the leader and armed forces of a belligerent community. A private citizen, even when he has a handful of followers, does not qualify as head of an "insurgent" community, especially when the latter lacks a territorial base.

Lacking status as an insurgent band and not qualifying as a pirate crew because they were not seeking private gain or private ends, the Galvão group had to be legally classified as ordinary criminals, having committed murder and seized private property and private persons against their will.

---

[16]*NYT*, Jan. 24–31, 1961; see also *Time*, Feb. 3, 1961, 19–20, for a detailed account of the events, including a useful map.

[17]Fenwick, " 'Piracy' in the Caribbean," 55 *AJIL* 426 (1961); Forman, "The International Law of Piracy and the Santa Maria Incident," 15 *JAG Journal*, October–November 1961, 143, 166, 168; Váli, "The Santa Maria Case," 56 *Northwestern University Law Review* 168 (March–April 1961); Franck, " 'To Define and Punish Pirates'—The Lessons of the Santa Maria: A Comment," 36 *N.Y.U.L. Rev.* 839 (1961).

The Brazilian government erred in granting political asylum to the group, for although the band's basic motives may have been political, its actions were wholly criminal.

On the other hand, straight piracy in the old-fashioned (acting-for-gain) sense appears to have been involved in the plot hatched by four men arrested in May 1978; they had planned to take over the SS *Emerald Seas*, a 24,000-ton cruise vessel out of Miami, and to hold the ship and its 800 passengers for $6 million in ransom.[18] Before the seizure could be attempted, the quartet was arrested through the work of a federal agent who posed as a weapons supplier to the plotters.

The *Tabarzin* affair gained much notoriety in 1981. On August 13, three new French-built, 160-foot missile-launching patrol boats on their way to Iran were cruising off the Spanish port of Cadiz, pursued by a Spanish-registry tugboat. When the latter reached one of the Iranian vessels (the *Tabarzin*), twenty Iranian commandos opposed to the Khomeini government boarded and captured the *Tabarzin*, hauled down the Islamic Republic's flag, and hoisted the flag of the former Imperial Government. A passing yacht radioed for help from Spain, but the *Tabarzin* headed toward Tangiers and later to Toulon, France. The other patrol boats, escorted by Spanish naval units, sailed to Algiers on their way to Iran. On August 17 the *Tabarzin* reached French waters and two days later was turned over to French naval authorities in Toulon. The captors, headed by ex-Admiral Kamal Habibollahi, a former commander of the Imperial Navy, were given political asylum in France, despite an Iranian request for extradition. The vessel was turned over to Iranian naval officers flown to France and eventually reached Iranian jurisdiction.[19]

A direct result of the seizure of the *Achille Lauro* (See Case History 3 following Chapter 12) was a convention developed by the International Maritime Organization (IMO) and adopted at a diplomatic conference in March 1988: the Convention for the Suppression of Unlawful Acts Against the Safety of Maritime Navigation.[20]

It should be kept in mind that the connections existing in many instances between cases of modern piracy, air/sea hijacking, and terrorist acts create an interwoven complex of international criminal activity. Their present division in this chapter should not serve to obscure the fact of their frequently intimate relationship.

## AIR HIJACKING

One of the peculiar and distressing accompaniments to the successful development of air transportation has been the forcible seizure of aircraft (hi-

[18]*NYT*, May 2, 1978, 13.
[19]*Time*, August 24, 1981, 35; *NYT*, August 14–20, 1981, *passim*.
[20]See Halberstam, *op. cit. supra*, n. 12, 291–309.

jacking). Incidents of this nature took place occasionally in connection with large-scale disturbances in various countries (Czechoslovakia in 1950, China, Cuba) in the late 1940s and the 1950s, but the writer agrees with Gary N. Horlick[21] that modern hijacking, on a large scale, began on May 1, 1961. On that day Antulio Ramirez Ortiz, a Cuban using the pseudonym of Elpirata Cofrisi, the name of an eighteenth-century Spanish pirate, diverted a National Airlines plane and forced the pilot to land in Havana. The resulting publicity surrounding this and subsequent hijackings with Cuba as their destination increasingly focused public and governmental attention on the problem of hijacking.

The motivation behind air hijackings varies from case to case. In some instances (the diversions to Cuba are the best examples), individuals either harbor some grudge against their own government or have other and quite personal reasons for wishing to leave their country of residence and to go to another place. In other instances, ransom for the plane and passengers plays a major role, either for the hijacker's personal enrichment or to finance some underground or rebel movement (many hijackings by Middle Eastern groups are examples of this variety of motivation). Again, aircraft have been hijacked as a lever with which to bring about the release of certain political (or other types of) prisoners, or, quite frequently, to draw attention to a political or social cause through the publicity engendered by the hijacking. In still other instances, hijackings have been caused by the desire of an individual or small groups to escape from a regime that is objectionable to them (most of the hijackings of Eastern European and one People's Republic of China planes were examples).

During the early period of modern air hijackings, those guilty of the acts in question pleaded for asylum on the grounds that they were political offenders. That defense of the seizure of aircraft held true in many cases, but increasingly the courts and governments of many countries became cognizant of the danger to the safety of the aircraft, its crew, and its passengers and of the fact that this danger was most clearly out of proportion to the claims of personal endangerment, persecution, and so on brought forward by hijackers. It was thus become gradually accepted that the dangers posed to property as well as to innocent people should not be overshadowed by real or alleged political aspects.[22] In consequence, a large proportion of more recent air hijackings have been classified by such bodies as the Organization of American States as "common crimes," particularly when the seizure of hostages has been involved in the act.

International reaction to criminal acts connected with aircraft began in a rather modest way when the Convention of Offenses and Certain Other

[21]Horlick, "The Developing Law of Air Hijacking," 12 *Harvard Int'l Law Jl.* 33, n. 1 (1971).
[22]*Id.*, 49–50. See also the statements relating to asylum for hijackers, relative to the 1973 agreement (n.14 supra) between the United States and Cuba, by then Secretary of State Rogers and then Deputy Assistant Secretary of State Hurwitz, in 67 *AJIL* 535 (1973).

Acts Committed on Board Aircraft was signed in Tokyo on September 14, 1963, at the end of a conference called by the International Civil Aviation Organization (ICAO). Representatives of sixteen countries, including the United States, signed the agreement.[23]

A great increase in air hijackings in the late 1960s (thirty instances were recorded in 1968, eighty-one cases in 1969), after relatively few such acts had taken place between 1963 and 1967, caused ICAO to draft an appropriately updated agreement. Adopted by the organization at The Hague on December 16, 1970, the (Hague) Convention for the Suppression of Unlawful Seizure of Aircraft entered into force on October 14, 1971.[24]

Unlike the Tokyo convention, the Hague instrument made air hijacking a distinct separate crime and gave the receiving state no real discretion on the issue of prosecution of a hijacker: motivation was excluded from consideration, at least by the wording of the convention.[25] Dinstein was somewhat critical of several provisions of the Hague agreement: he felt (correctly in the view of the present writer) that Article 4 of the treaty could have based jurisdiction simply on the "universality principle," arguing that when certain crimes against international law have been committed, jurisdiction is vested in any state able to secure possession of the guilty party or parties, regardless of where the offense in question has taken place or of the nationality of the apprehended individual.[26]

In September 1971, the ICAO held its Diplomatic Conference on Air Law in Montreal, at which still another agreement was concluded: the Montreal Convention to Discourage Acts of Violence Against Civil Aviation (1971),[27] unanimously accepted by the representatives of thirty countries, agreed that hijackers could be tried if found in the territory of a state other than the state in which the aircraft in question had been registered (Art. 4, par. 3). Enforcement provisions in the new agreement again were weak, even in the view of the sponsoring ICAO. Consequently, a special subcommittee met in Washington, D.C., in September 1972, in order to consider a convention providing for the cutting off of air service and for other boycott activity against states that failed to comply with the rules laid down in the Tokyo, Hague, and Montreal conventions. Afterwards, the ICAO Council decided to

---

[23]Text in 2 *ILM* 1042 (1963); see also the detailed analysis of the convention in Shubber, *Jurisdiction over Crime on Board Aircraft* (1973). The convention entered into force on December 4, 1969.

[24]Text in 10 *ILM* 133 (1971), and in 65 *AJIL* 440 (1971 Supp.). The key articles of the agreement are nos. 4 and 7. The United States is a party to the treaty.

[25]See also Brooks, "Skyjacking and Refugees: The Effect of the Hague Convention upon Asylum," 16 *Harvard Int'l Law Jl.* 93-97 (1975); referring to the wording and the U.S. government's understanding of the crucial Article 7 of the treaty.

[26]Dinstein, "Criminal Jurisdiction over Aircraft Hijacking," 7 *Israel Law Review* 195-197 (1972). The "universality principle" underlay the judgment of the Israel Supreme Court in the well-known *Eichmann* case; see also Buergenthal & Maier, 169–70.

[27]Text in 10 *ILM* 1151 (1971); the Montreal convention entered into force on January 26, 1973; the United States is a party

convene an extraordinary session of its assembly and a diplomatic conference in Rome in August–September 1973 and to submit all proposals to that conference. The twenty-five–day meeting ended on September 21, 1973, after voting down all the proposals calling for tougher action against air hijackers.

On December 27, 1985, Palestinian terrorists attacked the Israeli airline (El Al) desks at both the international airports in Rome and Vienna. Eighteen persons, including four of the terrorists, were killed and more than a hundred were injured. In consequence of those episodes and of others, particularly in the Mediterranean area, the ICAO moved to supplement the coverage of offenses against aircraft by the Montreal Convention of 1971. It drafted the Protocol for the Suppression of Unlawful Acts of Violence at Airports Serving International Civil Aviation. That instrument was signed at Montreal on February 23, 1988, by 46 countries.[28] The signatories included not only most states in which hijacking episodes involved airports, but also the Byelorussian S.S.R. and the Ukrainian S.S.R. (See Chapter 4 on the somewhat dubious international status of these entities.)

The record of the United Nations in dealing with the problem of air hijacking has been less than impressive over the years. Following General Assembly Resolution 2551 (XXIV) of December 12, 1969, in which the dangers of hijacking were recognized and prosecution of all guilty persons was recommended, the Security Council, called into urgent session by the United States and the United Kingdom, met briefly and passed its Resolution 286 (1970) on September 9, 1970, consisting of three sentences, the last of which called on states to take all possible legal steps to prevent further hijackings or any other interference with international civil air travel. This was followed by General Assembly Resolution 2645 (XXV) of November 25, 1970, in which the General Assembly, in essence, endorsed the declarations adopted at the 1970 Montreal meeting of the ICAO and subsequent instruments developed by that agency. After there had been several hijackings and after a twenty-four hour strike by airline pilots, the Security Council adopted by consensus on June 20, 1972, a "decision" in which it urged states to put an end to hijacking by adopting cooperative international efforts. Needless to say, that decision had no measurable effects on the problem. Then, following a renewed outbreak of hijacking, forty-two countries (mostly Western nations) jointly asked the General Assembly, on October 22, 1977, to schedule a debate on safety of international civil aviation. The 149-member Special Political Committee approved by consensus a resolution that was then adopted by the General Assembly, without a vote, on November 3, 1979.[29] One of the interesting Arab- and African-sponsored amendments to the resolution stressed the importance of the concept of national sovereignty. This amendment implied, according to observers, that

[28] Background, content summary, and text in 27 *ILM* 627 (1988); entered into force Aug. 6, 1989. The U.S. Senate gave advice and consent to ratification on Nov. 22, 1989.
[29] Text in 16 *ILM* 1545–46 (1977).

the 1977 West German rescue of crew and passengers of a hijacked Lufthansa craft in Somalia was acceptable, in view of Somalia's approval of the action to be taken, whereas Israel's 1976 rescue of hostages from Entebbe in Uganda was not acceptable, in view of Ugandan opposition.[30] (See "Unusual Hijacking Cases with Special Legal Implications.")

Lastly, it should be mentioned that the Council of Europe, through its Consultative Assembly, adopted a recommendation from its Legal Affairs Committee (September 24, 1970) in which it called on the UN General Assembly to condemn air hijacking and recommended that the Council's Committee of Ministers establish by common agreement sanctions, among other proposals, in the area of civil aviation, such as boycotting airports or airlines and refusing landing rights to the airlines operated from states on whose territory organized terrorism in the air or hijacking is tolerated and that have refused either to extradite or to punish offenders severely.[31]

The failure of international agencies to develop effective measures aimed at air hijackers resulted in regional, bilateral, and unilateral plans of action. Thus thirteen countries, including the United States, Israel, and the Federal Republic of Germany, had created, by the middle of October 1977, commando units trained to rescue hijacked hostages.[32] In July 1978, representatives of the United States and six other major non-communist industrial countries, attending an economic summit in Bonn, West Germany, resolved to act jointly in suspending air traffic to and from states that failed to turn over hijacked aircraft and hijackers quickly.[33]

On a bilateral basis, the United States and Cuba arrived at the Memorandum of Understanding on the Hijacking of Aircraft and Vessels (February 15, 1973).[34] That agreement provided for the return of hijackers to the country in which the aircraft or vessel in question had been registered or for their trial in the country whose territory the hijackers had reached. Both parties also agreed to provide severe punishment for the promoters of, and participants in, hostile expeditions of any kind from either state to the other state. In the fourth part of the memorandum, it was agreed that the receiving country

may take into consideration any extenuating or mitigating circumstances in those cases in which the persons responsible for the acts were being sought for strictly political reasons and were in real and imminent danger of death without a viable alternative for leaving the country, provided there was no financial extortion or physical injury to the members of the crew, passengers, or other persons in connection with the hijacking.

[30] See *NYT*, Nov. 4, 1977, A-3.
[31] Text reproduced in 9 *ILM* 1247–49 (1970).
[32] See *NYT*, Oct. 22, 1977, 7, for a survey of the types of units then in existence and of some of the actions in which several had been involved; consult also *Time*, Oct. 31, 1977, 44.
[33] *NYT*, July 18, 1978, A-1, A-6; and Aug. 2, 1978, A-7.
[34] Text *NYT*, Feb. 16, 1973; 4, and 12 *ILM* 370–76 (1973).

The agreement was to be in force for five years. However, on October 15, 1976, Prime Minister Fidel Castro denounced the memorandum because of claimed American complicity in the crash of a sabotaged Cuban airliner off Barbados, a charge denied by the United States government.[35] On September 16, 1980, the Cuban government announced that it would either punish or return to the United States any person hijacking an aircraft to Cuba from the United States. The announcement was made after nine U.S. planes had been hijacked to Havana since August 10, 1980. It was stated at the time that all of the hijackers in question had been arrested at once and had been sentenced to prison terms, ranging from two to fifty years. On January 28, 1981, two Cubans who had earlier taken over a Delta Air Lines flight and who had been returned by Cuba were sentenced in Columbia, South Carolina, to forty-year prison terms after having pleaded guilty to charges of air piracy. A number of agreements similar to the United States–Cuba one were signed by other countries, such as one between France and the United States (February 1970) and between Cuba and Mexico (June 1973).

On a unilateral basis, country after country has amended its domestic legislation in order to provide for the trial and punishment of air hijackers. To cite a few examples only, this took place in Cuba as early as September 1969, in the Soviet Union in January 1973, in the German Democratic Republic in July 1973, in the Republic of China in 1973, and in Belgium in 1976. In the United States, Congress had passed an antihijacking law as early as October 14, 1970 (the Act to Implement the Convention on Offenses and Certain Acts Committed on Board Aircraft, P.L. 91–449, 84 Stat. 921).[36] Congress later passed Public Law 93-366 on August 5, 1974, which amended the Federal Aviation Act of 1958[37] in order to implement the Hague Convention of 1970. It is interesting to note that Public Law 93–366 refers to *air piracy*, a term used in the domestic legislation of several countries, though not in international agreements. The 1974 law also provided for the death penalty (or life imprisonment) if the death of another person resulted from the commission or attempted commission of an air hijacking. But attempts to seize aircraft in the United States continued.

UNUSUAL HIJACKING CASES WITH SPECIAL LEGAL IMPLICATIONS    Several cases of hijacking during the past decade have provided unusual and interesting problems, as well as unorthodox solutions, in the sphere of international law. In the *Brazinskas* case, two Lithuanian citizens of the Soviet Union hijacked a Russian aircraft in a domestic flight and forced the pilot to land in Turkey (October 15, 1970). A Russian stewardess was killed, and the

---

[35]*NYT*, Oct. 16, 1976, 1, 4.
[36]See Lissitzyn, "In-Flight Crime and United States Legislation," 67 *AJIL* 306 (1973), for an analysis of the law.
[37]Text in 13 *ILM* 1515 (1974). See also *NYT*, Sept. 14, 1976, 1, 32, for an arraignment of "air pirates."

two pilots were wounded during the affair. A Turkish court of first instance had originally freed the two Brazinskas (Pranas and his teenage son), ruling that their offense was of a political nature and that they therefore could not be extradited to the Soviet Union, as demanded by the latter. However, the Soviet government charged that the two had committed crimes within the Soviet Union and should be returned for trial. The Trabzon district court, upon examining the evidence sent from Russia, then found father and son guilty of manslaughter and sentenced them to prison. They were released in July 1976 and left for Italy, whence they eventually entered the United States illegally by way of Venezuela. The Soviet Union then demanded their extradition from the United States. The U.S. government replied (April 27, 1977) that both Brazinskas had been denied political asylum in the United States because they had committed a "serious nonpolitical crime" and that they would both be deported to Venezuela.[38]

In the famous episode referred to as the Entebbe Raid, the problems raised were carried, unsuccessfully, before the UN Security Council. The facts were fairly clear: On June 28, 1976, an Air France plane in a flight from Israel to France with a crew of 12 and 256 passengers aboard, was hijacked by a group of PLO terrorists after the aircraft left Athens. After a detour to Libya, the plane was finally landed at Entebbe airport in Uganda. The hijackers demanded the release of over 150 terrorists jailed in several European countries, in Israel, and in Kenya. Just 164 passengers were released, the remainder being held as hostages. The Ugandan government appears to have done nothing to assist the crew to regain control of the craft and to proceed to France. On July 3, an Israeli military commando unit liberated the surviving hostages (3 had died) and flew them to Israel. The crew remained with the plane. During the fighting involved in the rescue operation, one Israeli soldier, seven terrorists, and a number of Ugandan military personnel were killed, and much of the Entebbe airport was wrecked, as were a number of Ugandan military aircraft found on the ground.[39] On July 12, 1976, two draft resolutions were introduced in the Security Council: one by Tanzania, Libya, and Benin condemning Israel for violating the territorial integrity and sovereignty of Uganda; the other by the United Kingdom and the United States, condemning hijacking, though affirming the need to respect the territorial integrity and sovereignty of all states.[40] When the matter came up for a vote on July 14, 1976, the U.K.–U.S. resolution failed to obtain the nine affirmative votes needed, and

[38]*NYT*, Nov. 22, 1970, 24; July 12, 1976, A-2; April 17, 1977, 41; May 14, 1977, 3.
[39]See the *Introductory Note* by McDowell, 15 *ILM* 1124 (1976), on which much of the above account has been based, as well as *NYT*, July 5, 1976, 1, 4, for French charges of Ugandan collusion with the hijackers; and also *Newsweek*, July 19, 1976, 42–43, for a detailed account of the rescue operation.
[40]Texts in 15 *ILM* 1226 (1976); see *id.*, 1228–34, excerpts from the most interesting presentations of various members of the Security Council. See also *Time*, July 26, 1976, 39–40.

the African resolution was not pressed for a vote. On July 22, 1976, President Idi Amin of Uganda informed the French government that he would release the hijacked aircraft. Its crew thereupon took it back to France.

The legal implications of the Entebbe Raid touch mostly on the subject of an expanded right of self-defense, that is, the claimed right of a state to intervene by the use or threat of force for the protection of its citizens suffering injury in the territory of another state. The defenders of this claim usually point out that when such intervention (self-defense) violates the sovereignty and territory of the state in which the citizens in question are located, then the intervention must be exceptional in nature and must be limited to instances in which no other measure of protection is left to the intervening state.[41] Legal writers as well as governments have justified resorting to the use of force on many occasions in which the "host state" proved to be unwilling or unable to protect the lives and property of foreign citizens. Thus Bowett pointed out that the United States employed military forces on at least forty-six occasions between 1813 and 1899 and on at least twenty-four occasions between 1900 and 1927.[42] More recently, the United States sent 200 marines to Tang Island, off the shores of Cambodia, to rescue the crew of the American containership *Mayaguez* (May 14, 1975), which had been seized by the Khmer Rouge in Cambodian waters.[43] The Cambodian action was likened, at the time, to piracy, and the counteraction by the United States was characterized as legitimate defense against the seizure of its citizens.

A series of events in many respects similar to the Entebbe Raid was the Mogadishu Raid of October 1977.[44] On October 13 of that year, a Lufthansa aircraft was hijacked and eventually landed (after traveling over much of the Middle East) at the airport of Mogadishu, Somalia. It had been trailed for some time by two planeloads of West German specialist troops of the Border Protection Force (also trained to act against hijackers). Some 110 hours after the hijackers had taken control of the aircraft, the German units attacked and captured the plane, killing three of the four hijackers in the process. In contrast with the Entebbe incident, the Mogadishu recapture was undertaken with the full knowledge and explicit approval of the Somalian government.

[41]Consult Bowett, *Self-Defense in International Law* (1958), 87, and Brierly, 427; also the valuable internal memorandum by the Legal Adviser (Department of State) to the Secretary of State, in 1976, on the legality of Israel's action: 73 *AJIL* 122 (1979).

[42]Bowett, *op. cit.*, 97.

[43]For a day-by-day account of the *Mayaguez* incident, see *NYT*, May 13, 1975, 1, 19; May 14, 1975, 1, 18; May 17, 1975, 1, 11; May 19, 1975, 1, 4; May 20, 1975, 1, 14; and May 21, 1975, 16. For the legality of the *Mayaguez* affair, under American law and with justifications under international law, see *NYT*: May 15, 1975, 18 Lewis, "The Laws Under Which Mr. Ford Took Action," May 18, 1975, E-2, Berger, "The *Mayaguez* Incident and the Constitution," May 23, 1975, 35, See also Rowan, *The Four Days of Mayaguez* (1975).

[44]A detailed account, with map, of the entire incident may be found in *Time*, Oct. 31, 1977, 42-44.

On other occasions, commandos brought in by permission of the country in which the hijacked aircraft was located attacked the airliner and liberated the hostages: in April 1981, Indonesian commandos stormed an Indonesian plane at the Bangkok (Thailand) airport, and in July 1984, Venezuelan commandos took a hijacked Venezuelan aircraft at the airport in Willemstad, Curacao.

On November 23, 1985, Egyptian hijackers seized an Egypt-Air Boeing 737 jetliner, with more than 100 people aboard, in Greek airspace and forced it to land at Valetta, Malta. (The aircraft by coincidence was the same that had been intercepted by U.S. Navy jets a month earlier in connection with the *Achille Lauro* affair (see Case History No. 3, following Chapter 12). One of the three Americans aboard was killed and her body thrown from the plane at the Valetta airport. The hijackers' demand for fuel was rejected by the Maltese government because the murder had been committed while the aircraft was already on Maltese soil. The hijackers finally released 11 women passengers to Malta. The following evening the plane was attacked and captured by *Egyptian* commandos flown in *with the consent of the Maltese government*. However, 56 people, including nine children, were killed during the taking of the aircraft, as were three of the four hijackers. Twenty-six passengers and the surviving hijacker were hospitalized. Egypt then requested the extradition of that last individual, but Malta refused to comply with the request, intending to try the man in its own courts. In 1989 he was sentenced to 25 years imprisonment—the maximum sentence under Maltese law.

In November 1981, a group of more than forty mercenaries under the command of Col. "Mad Mike" Hoare had flown to the Republic of the Seychelles in the Indian Ocean in an attempt to overthrow the local government. Foiled by discovery of their weapons on arrival at the airport, they hijacked an Air-India passenger jet and had it flown, with all passengers aboard, to South Africa where they surrendered. When only a few of the commandos were charged by South Africa, the signatories of the Bonn Declaration of July 17, 1978 (Canada, France, West Germany, Italy, Japan, the United Kingdom, and the United States) pointed out that they had agreed to halt their national air services with any country that refused either to extradite or prosecute those who had hijacked an aircraft, or refused to return that aircraft. South Africa rearrested all the mercenaries and placed them on trial. Hoare and 41 of the group were convicted of air piracy and sentenced to prison terms of varying length. Four months later the mercenaries were given time off for good behavior and released (Hoare in May, 1985). Several other mercenaries captured at the time of the attempted coup were tried in the Seychelles. Four were sentenced to death (but those sentences were later commuted to life imprisonment) and one was given 20 years in prison. (see also Chapter 24, *sub* Mercenaries)

On September 4, 1986, four Arab hijackers dressed as airport security guards seized a Pan American Boeing 747 at the Karachi, Pakistan, airport and demanded to be ferried to Cyprus. The aircraft had just arrived from Bombay and was bound for New York via Frankfurt. Its cockpit crew escaped through an emergency hatch as soon as the first gunshots of the hijackers were heard. The next evening all lights on the plane went out when the generator ran out of fuel, and a number of passengers opened several doors. That allowed *Pakistani* commandos waiting outside to storm the plane. Twenty-one passengers, as well as two of the hijackers, were killed, and more than 100 were wounded. Earlier the hijackers had shot an American passenger, had thrown his body on the tarmac, and also shot and wounded three airport workers. The American casualty died in a Karachi hospital. The two surviving hijackers were captured. On January 5, 1988, those two and three other Palestinians went on trial in a Pakistani court; the defendants admitted comandeering the aircraft but insisted that the Pakistani commandos had killed the 21 passengers. All were found guilty of hijacking and murder.

On April 5, 1988, nine Arab hijackers seized an Air Kuwait 747 aircraft bound from Bangkok to Kuwait. They demanded the release of 17 terrorists jailed in Kuwait for bombing the U.S. and French embassies there in 1983. The plane was diverted to Mashhad, Iran, where 57 hostages were released. It then proceeded to Beirut where permission to land was refused, and the aircraft was directed to Larnaca, Cyprus, where reluctant consent for refueling was granted in exchange for the release of 13 more hostages. Five days later the plane was flown to Algiers. Protracted negotiations resulted in the Algerian Interior Minister's announcement that "a solution settling all the issues of the hijacking has been reached" (April 20). The hijackers wiped off all their fingerprints in the plane and left quietly, followed by the rest of the passengers and the crew. (However, two Kuwaiti security guards had been killed and dumped from the plane at Larnaca.) According to the Kuwaiti official news agency, safe passage to either Beirut or Tehran had been assured the hijackers by the Algerian authorities. The official Algerian spokesman, on the other hand, spoke about Algeria's "meditation" of the dispute between Kuwait and hijackers.

On December 1, 1988, five armed Soviet hijackers seized a busload of schoolchildren in Ordzhonikidze in Southern Russia and traded them for use of a plane and $3.3 million in ransom. They asked to be flown to Israel, South Africa, or Pakistan. Soviet Authorities ordered the plane's crew to fly to Israel. That country's Defense Minister termed the five non-Jewish hijackers (an Armenian couple and three other men, armed with four pistols and a hunting knife) "thieves" and stated that Israel would honor a Soviet request for extradition. That request was transmitted as soon as the aircraft had begun its flight to Ben Gurion Airport in Israel. After the Soviet Union had agreed in writing that the hijackers would not be executed, the five were returned on the Soviet plane to their country. Interestingly enough, Israel deported them as "illegal immigrants," not as hijackers. The somewhat puzzling Soviet strategy in allowing the five to depart after they had surrendered their hostages contrasted sharply with that used in an earlier (March 1988) domestic Soviet hijacking episode. Then soldiers attacked and captured a Russian aircraft held by members of a family jazz band from Irkutsk. Five of the hijackers, three other passengers, and a stewardess died in the attack; the plane was destroyed by a bomb set off at the last minute by the hijackers.

## PEACETIME HOSTAGE TAKING

The peacetime taking of hostages is not a mere byproduct of aircraft or ship hijacking or of other types of terrorists activities: it has been recognized, at least since 1979, as a separate international crime. The intention of hostage takers has been either to enable them to bring pressure to bear on those against whom their activity is aimed or to protect themselves against attack or reprisal. In the latter case, either the hostage taking by itself or coupled with another terrorist act would be the reason for any antiterrorist action.

Thus a takeover of the Dominican Republic's embassy of Bogotá, Colombia, by Colombian terrorists during a Dominican independence day celebration (February 28, 1980) led to the capture of thirteen ambassadors who were held as hostages for almost two weeks. On February 14, 1981, a group of Cubans seized the Ecuadorian embassy in Havana and held hostage at first two and then one diplomat and a Cuban office worker. Eight days later, at the request of the Ecuadorian government, a Cuban army assault team stormed the building and freed the hostages. In September 1982, ten Honduran guerrillas held two cabinet ministers and seventy-eight businessmen hostage in the Chamber of Commerce building in San Pedro Sula, Honduras. The less important hostages were released in batches, and eventually, eight days after the incident began, the guerrillas were flown to Havana aboard a Panamanian Air Force plane.

A widely publicized recent instance of hostage taking followed the takeover of the U.S. embassy complex in Tehran, Iran, on November 4, 1979, by a group alleged to consist of students (subsequently referred to as "militants"). Some one hundred hostages were seized initially, including 63 American citizens, mostly members of the embassy staff. Later those individuals who were not American citizens, and still later a few of the American personnel, were released, with some 50 remaining as hostages. Major demands of the hostage takers centered on the return of the former Shah to Iran to stand trial for his "crimes" and on the return of the fortunes allegedly removed from Iran by members of the royal family. The Iranian government had done nothing to prevent the seizure of the embassy, nor did it afterward try to liberate the hostages. It, in fact, approved what had taken place. In addition to the fifty, three members of the embassy staff, including Bruce Laingen, the U.S. *chargé d'affaires* in Tehran, were kept in "protective custody" in the Ministry of Foreign Affairs, where they had happened to be at the time of the embassy takeover.

On November 29, 1979, the United States filed its application with the International Court of Justice in the *Case Concerning United States Diplomatic and Consular Staff in Tehran (United States* v. *Iran)*, seeking an Order of Interim Measures in connection with the seizure of its Tehran Embassy and the taking of diplomatic hostages (November 4, 1979). The United States charged Iran with violating Articles 22 (immunity of diplomatic premises) and 29 (inviolability of diplomatic personnel) of the 1961 Vienna Convention; relevant provisions of the 1963 Vienna Convention on Consular Relations; and Articles 2, 4, and 7 of the 1973 UN Convention on the Prevention of Crimes Against Internationally Protected Persons, Including Diplomatic Agents. The United States and Iran were parties to those three instruments.

The court issued its Order for Interim Measures on December 15, 1979,[45] unanimously instructing Iran to give all U.S. diplomatic and consular personnel the full protection, privileges, and immunities guaranteed under international law and not to put the hostages on trial. The court also ordered Iran to file a counterbrief by February 18, 1980. Iran ignored both the order and the counterbrief. The continuation of the hostages' detention ignored the January 7, 1980, deadline for the release of the hostages set by the UN Security Council on December 31, 1979. That decision had been based on the vote of 11 to 0 in the Council, with 4 countries (including the Soviet Union) abstaining.

On March 20, 1980, the United States formally presented its case before the Court, requesting a decision in its favor. The Court handed down its Judgment (Merits) on May 24, 1980. The judgment emphasized that Iranian governmental responsibility had been created by repeated official endorsement of the hostage taking (and of the embassy seizure). The court stated that because of the endorsement, "the militants, authors of the invasion and jailers of the hostages, had now become agents of the Iranian state for whose acts the state itself was internationally responsible." The decision went on to point out that "the facts of the present case, viewed in light of the applicable rules of law, thus speak loudly and clearly of successive and still continuing breaches by Iran of its obligations to the United States under the Vienna Conventions of 1961 and 1963 (on diplomatic and consular relations) as well as under the (U.S.–Iran) treaty of 1955." The judges also ruled unanimously that the American embassy had to be returned to the United States, that normal diplomatic privileges had to be restored, and that no hostages were to be put on trial or on a witness stand.

The Court decided that Iran had violated the obligations owed to the United States under international conventions between the two parties and under rules of general international law; that the violations in question engaged the responsibility of the Iranian government; that Iran had to take immediately all steps to redress the situation (free the hostages, see to it

---

[45] *International Court of Justice* (1979), *I.C.J.* 7; text in Henkin, 570–78.

that they left Iran, and place into the hands of a Protecting Power the U.S. embassy and consulates in Iran); that none of the hostages could be kept in Iran to face judicial proceedings or to act as witness in such; that Iran was obligated to make reparations to the United States; and that if the two parties failed to agree, the form and amount of such reparations would be settled by the Court. The justices from the Soviet Union, Poland, and Syria dissented from the majority ruling that the United States was entitled to reparations. With respect to the aborted American military attempt to free the hostages (April 24–25, 1980), the court stated that the mission was "of a kind calculated to undermine respect for the judicial process in international relations." But, continued the court, the rescue attempt had no direct bearing on the case. Iran ignored the judgment.

Ultimately the government of Algeria served as an intermediary in the dispute and helped resolve the crisis. The United States freed the frozen assets of Iran, requiring all the banks holding them to transfer them to the Federal Reserve Bank in New York for further transfer to Iran, as ordered by the Secretary of the Treasury. One billion dollars of those assets, however, were deposited in a security account in the Bank of England, to the account of the Algerian Central Bank, to be used to satisfy awards rendered against Iran by a special arbitration tribunal. The United States also restricted the transfer of property of the late Shah. Iran, in turn, agreed to permit the hostages to return home via Algeria.

Once the financial details had been arranged, Iran allowed the remaining fifty-two hostages to depart, about one hour after Ronald Reagan had succeeded Jimmy Carter in the American presidency, January 20, 1981. On May 12, 1981, the president of the International Court of Justice ordered the discontinuance of the case filed by the United States.

The taking of the hostages was, of course, in violation of both customary and conventional international law, as it involved the illegal seizure of the embassy and its staff; it was followed by approval by the Iranian government, an approval that created international responsibility for the government (see Chapter 11); and it was done by private individuals in violation of international law without any attempt by the Iranian government to intervene (see Chapter 11). Furthermore, the continued detention of the hostages was in violation of the orders for interim measures (including an immediate release of the hostages) handed down by the International Court of Justice.

While these events were taking place, the UN General Assembly drafted and then approved a convention (December 17, 1979) that for the first time prohibited the taking of hostages in time of peace: "The International Convention against the Taking of Hostages."[46] However, this instrument

---

[46]Text in 18 *ILM* 1456 (1979) and in 74 *AJIL* 277 (1980). The convention went into force after ratification by 22 states; for the United States on Jan. 6, 1985. See also Verwey, "The International Hostages Convention and National Liberation Movements," 75 *AJIL* 69 (1981), and esp. Lambert, *Terrorism and Hostages in International Law* [A Commentary on the Hostages Convention 1979] (1990).

has a few loopholes to which France and Poland added reservations before granting approval.

Although the convention provides that any state apprehending a hostage taker is bound either to extradite such a person on request or to try that person under the apprehending state's own laws, Article 9 of the treaty states that extradition need not be undertaken

if the requested state has substantial ground for believing that, among other things, the request for extradition has been made for the purpose of prosecuting or punishing a person on account of his race, religion, nationality, ethnic origin or political opinion.

And Article 12 of the treaty states that

the convention shall not apply to any act of hostage-taking committed in the course of armed conflicts as defined in the Geneva Conventions of 1949 . . . in which people are fighting against colonial domination and alien occupation and against racist regimes in the exercise of their right of self-determination.

In the years since the Tehran Embassy affair, a number of other long-term hostage takings have taken place, but mostly on an individual taking basis. Thus by March 1990, seventeen hostages (including 8 U.S. citizens) were still held in various parts of Lebanon, apparently by a number of splinter terrorist groups allegedly under Iranian influence.

The taking of foreign hostages by Iraq in 1990 was history's largest in scope. On August 15, 12 days after the invasion of Kuwait, Iraq announced that it would hold all (male) foreigners from "aggressive nations" until the threat of war against Iraq had ended. American and British citizens in Kuwait were ordered to move into central Kuwait City hotels. Some 600 foreigners in Kuwait and Iraq were transported to key installations, mostly of a military or weapons manufacturing nature, to serve as deterrence against U.S. attack.

It was believed at the time that more than 21,000 Westerners were in Iraq and Kuwait, including 700 Canadians, some 4,000 British citizens, and 3,100 American citizens. On August 19 the UN Security Council demanded unanimously that Iraq allow the immediate departure of the thousands of foreigners trapped there. It also insisted that consular officials be permitted to see the hostages (called "guests" by Iraq's leaders) and that nothing be done to jeopardize the safety and health of the hostages. The relevant resolution of the Security Council invoked the mandatory provisions of Chapter VI of the UN Charter.

Illustrating the fact that the foreign hostages were intended to serve as part of a bargaining position, Iraqi President Saddam Hussein offered fruitlessly to free all foreigners in Iraq and Kuwait if the United States promised to withdraw its forces from Saudi Arabia and guaranteed the lifting of the international economic boycott against Iraq (August 19). As time passed, a selective system of releasing hostages developed. Foreign women and children were allowed to leave, as were elderly or sick foreign males. Thus about 2,000 U.S. citizens were released between August 15 and December 8, 1990. Then foreign male citizens could depart after prominent personages from their country, or family members, had come to intercede on their behalf with President Hussein. At times entire national contingents of hostages were freed, such as the 263 French citizens on October 29. On November 18, Iraq announced that all remaining foreign hostages could leave over a period of time starting at Christmas, unless something marred "the atmosphere of peace." However, on December 6, President Hussein told the Iraq National Assembly that all foreign hostages in both Iraq and Kuwait were to be freed immediately. At that time there remained more than 2,000 Westerners (including 88 "human shields") and Japanese in Iraq and Kuwait, as well as 3,200 Soviet citizens. Most of the Soviet group had served on a contract basis in Iraq's oil industry. An Associated Press survey at the time indicated that the total number of foreigners awaiting departure from Kuwait and Iraq numbered over a million, including large contingents of Egyptians, Pakistanis, and Lebanese citizens. There can be no question about the fact that Iraq's 1990 hostage taking represented a violation of norms of international law.

The liberation of all hostages has been affirmed on numerous occasions by resolutions of the UN Security Council.[47] Regrettably, those endorsements had proven to be devoid of results at the time of this writing.

## TERRORISM

In the twentieth century, terrorist activities have increased in number, scope, and geographic locale from relatively limited manifestations in earlier decades. A very large number of terroristic acts have been aimed at bringing about changes in the government (and sometimes also of the socioeconomic order) of a given country, but nationalism, particularly in non-European countries, has also produced a variety of terrorist organizations that have become active on the world scene. The modern varieties of terrorists are numerous: Puerto Rican nationalists, Basque separatists, Greek Cypriots, Armenian nationalists, South Moluccan nationalists, groups under the shadowy umbrella (or outside of it) of the Palestine Liberation Organization, the Irish Republican Army, Croatian nationalists, the Armenian Secret Army for the Liberation of Armenia, the Armenian Revolutionary Army—the list could go on almost endlessly. All these groups have had a hand in terrorist activities of one kind or another during the past few dozen years. Simulta-

---

[47] Such as UN Security Council Resolution 579 (1985), of Dec. 18, 1985; text in 80 *AJIL* 437 (1986) and in 25 *ILM* 243 (1986). The resolution followed a unanimous vote in the General Assembly on a resolution which condemned all acts of terrorism as "criminal."

neously, these terrorist groups have collaborated on intelligence, training, finances, and operation. The international linkages among various terrorist groups were allegedly demonstrated in the case of the Japanese Red Army group in 1972: the unit (Rengo Sekigun-ha), composed of Japanese citizens, was said to have been trained in North Korea, to have picked up funds in West Germany, to have had further training in both Syria and Lebanon, to have picked up its arms and ammunition in Italy, and then to have attacked the Lod Airport in Israel on behalf of the Popular Front for the Liberation of Palestine!

A major problem connected with what is commonly called "terrorism" is the determination of the meaning of the term. What may appear to one to be the work of a criminal may appear to another as the heroic deed of the freedom-fighter. And no two major calculations of the total number of terrorist acts committed in a given year agree because the calculators disagree as to what is a terrorist act.

Whitehead's definition represents the view of the present writer: "Terrorism is a sophisticated form of political violence. It is neither random nor without purpose . . . [it] is a strategy and tool of those who reject the norms and values of civilized people everywhere."[48] Other definitions of interest are "Terrorism is any violent activity conducted by a non-state organization to attain political objectives (Jaffee Center for Strategic Studies, Tel Aviv University); "The unlawful use or threatened use of force or violence by a revolutionary organization against individuals or property with the intention of coercing or intimidating governments or societies for political or ideological purposes" (U.S. Department of Defense, 1983); terrorism is "Premediated, politically motivated violence perpetrated against noncombatant targets by subnational groups or clandestine state agents (U.S. Department of State, 1984); terrorism is "The unlawful use or threat of violence against persons or property to further political or social objectives. It is usually intended to intimidate or coerce a government, individuals, or groups or to modify their behavior or policies" (U.S. Vice-President's Task Force on Combating Terrorism, 1986).[49]

Terrorism is not new, contrary to popular belief. The Barbary Pirates operated along terrorist lines; the modern car bomb had its origin in the days of Napoleon as the cart bomb, and assassination punctuated the history of almost all major countries, notably in the 19th century with the activities of the Nihilist persuasion of Anarchism.

While much of modern terrorism has been carried out by individuals or groups on their own, there also exists state-supported terrorism, that is,

---

[48]John C. Whitehead, Deputy Secretary of State, quoted in *Current Policy No. 900* (Dec. 1986), 1. See also Dugard, "Towards the Definition of International Terrorism," 67 *AJIL* 94 (1973); Abu-Lughod, "Unconventional Violence and International Politics," *id.*, 100–4; Schwarzenberger, "Terrorists, Guerrilleros, Mercenaries," 219–236 in his *International Law and Order* (1971).

[49]*CSM*, April 18, 1986, 12.

terrorist policies and acts sponsored and supported directly or indirectly by states. President Reagan, on July 8, 1985, listed five "outlaw" states which he called "a new, international version of Murder, Inc." His list of principal terrorist backers included Iran, Libya, North Korea, Cuba, and Nicaragua.[50]

While the key element in all terrorist activity is a deliberate effort to create fear in order to persuade the ultimate target to accede to the terrorist's demands, it is not easy to determine culpability of a given state in promoting and supporting the acts creating such fear. Does Iran really control and direct the terrorist group known as Islamic Jihad? To what extent did Libya "control" various "rejectionist" Palestinian and Egyptian groups which it is said to have supported generously over the years? In some instances it has been possible to prove that certain acts sponsored by a supporting state could indeed by termed state terrorism and thus create direct liability for the sponsoring state. But in all too many instances it has been impossible to point a finger at some faction within a government or, indeed, within a given terrorist organization and claim that there existed state responsibility. But "well-founded" suspicions, proven government-sponsored activities, and at times acknowledged responsibility for offenses may be combined to present a believable indictment of a country.[51]

The methods by which terrorists have struck include bombing, attacks on government, military, or industrial facilities (especially airports), assassinations, kidnappings and other hostage takings, and maimings, roughly in the order given as far as utilization has been concerned over the past twenty years. Hijacking has been discussed earlier in this chapter and it must be emphasized that not all hijackings have been truly terroristic acts but have been instituted in some cases for personal or piratical reasons. The subject of hostage taking follows this section of Chapter 13.

Bombings have occurred in roughly 46 percent of terroristic acts while attacks on various facilities total about 31 percent. Targets for assassination have included every conceivable occupation, with diplomats and government officials (including police) topping the list.

For a long time, bombings appear to have been selective, that is, the purpose was the death of a specific person or persons. During the past few years, however, a disturbing trend toward indiscriminate bombing has been observed. Examples include the bombing of the U.S. Marine facility in Beirut, the bombing of Pan American Flight 103 over Lockerbie, Scotland (December 1988), and more recently the destruction of UTA Flight 772 (a DC-10) over Niger in West Africa (September 1989). A striking illustration of this new trend was the terrorist attack by Palestinians on the Greek

---

[50]This American list has varied over the years: in Sept. 1985, it read Iran, Libya, Syria, Cuba, and Nicaragua; in 1987 it listed Syria, Libya, Iran, Cuba, and South Yemen. On Syria, see *Current Policy No. 1019* (Nov. 1987), 2–3.

[51]See the "Chronology of Libyan Support for Terrorism 1980–85" (U.S. Dept. of State) in the valuable collection of "Documents Showing the Evolution of Sanctions Against Libya," 25 *ILM* 173, 186–89 (1986); also found in *Special Report No. 138* (Jan. 1986).

cruise ship *City of Portos* on July 11, 1988. Four terrorists opened fire with automatic weapons and hand grenades on the other nearly 500 passengers before the vessel had returned to the port of Piraeus. The attackers then fled in a speedboat which had pulled up, by obvious prearrangement, next to the cruise ship. Nine persons, including one of the attackers, died and 98 passengers were wounded. Several Palestinian terrorist organizations, some known, others hitherto unknown, claimed credit for the attack. One of the three escaped attackers was caught, even though all of them had been identified eventually. The one terrorist caught was convicted in Athens on false passport charges (July 14, 1988), clearing the way for a U.S. extradition request to be heard. The new trend toward lack of discrimination was first recognized when, on July 27, 1984, a new dimension in terrorism made its appearance: the mining of portions of the Red Sea by unknown hands. As of August 12, fourteen ships had struck mines (none were sunk), and Egypt asked Italy to join in efforts to clear the Red Sea of mines as a convoy of five British and French minesweepers and two support ships arrived to help. The United States also sent the U.S. Navy transport *Shreveport*, carrying four mine-sweeping helicopters, to the scene; on August 19 the search was joined by two Soviet minesweepers to which were later added another minesweeper and a helicopter cruiser. By September 25, however, only three suspected mines had been found, by which time a total of nineteen vessels had been damaged. No definite responsibility for the mining could be assigned, but a circumstantial case was built against Libya after a Libyan freighter was examined by French authorities in Marseilles where the vessel was undergoing repairs. (See Chapter 25 concerning the employment of mines in war at sea.)

The growth in the number of terroristic activities has been assisted by three special conditions: (1) the availability of an almost instant audience—hence publicity for the act, the person, and the cause of the terrorist—through television, radio, and newspaper coverage; (2) the tacit or overt endorsement—and often support—of certain governments for certain terrorist groups; and (3) the availability of new types of weapons, adding to the aggressive and defensive capabilities of terrorists. Some commentators have feared that since security at airports and embassies has increased greatly, some terrorists might be tempted to resort to chemical weapons either to attain goals or simply to attract attention. This fear was based on the fact that certain types of chemical weapons are not only relatively inexpensive, but can also be produced in almost any corner of the world. Another development in the field of weaponry has been the ability to construct bombs with long-delay timing features, that is, bombs that can be set to explode in days rather than hours—by which time the terrorists would be long gone. Such a bomb was used in the 1985 attempt to assassinate British Prime Minister Thatcher and much of the leadership of the British Conservative Party. And constant "improvement" has been noted in the development of ever more powerful plastic explosives usable by terrorists.

INTERNATIONAL LAW AND TERRORISM    Dugard[52] listed four components of an ideal antiterrorist convention which, he believed, should

(1) reaffirm that all states have the duty in all circumstances to refrain from encouraging guerilla activities in another state;
(2) prohibit acts of terrorism which disturb the international order and clearly identify the international element which brings the act within the jurisdiction of international law;
(3) oblige states to extradite or to punish offenders under the Convention;
(4) reaffirm the international community's abhorrence of state-controlled terrorism as expressed in the Nuremberg principles, the Genocide Convention, and the human rights provisions of the Charter.

The earliest international effort to create treaty law to combat terrorism was the abortive League of Nations Convention for the Prevention and Punishment of Terrorism (1937), drafted in consequence of the assassination of King Alexander of Yugoslavia. That instrument, receiving only one ratification to date, never entered into force. It was followed by conventions aimed against air hijacking: the ICAO Convention on Offenses and Certain Other Acts Committed on Board Aircraft (Tokyo, 1963), the ICAO Convention for the Suppression of Unlawful Seizure of Aircraft (The Hague, 1970); the ICAO Convention to Discourage Acts of Violence Against Civil Aviation (Montreal, 1971)—concerning all of which consult *supra, sub* Hijacking. In addition, treaty law was amplified by the IMO Convention for the Suppression of Unlawful Acts Against the Safety of Maritime Navigation (1988). In 1971, the Organization of American States (OAS) had adopted the Convention to Prevent and Punish the Acts of Terrorism Taking the Form of Crimes Against Persons and Related Extortion That Are of International Significance (1971). That instrument, aimed primarily at the kidnapping of diplomats, became law in 1973. Insofar as the United Nations was concerned, the General Assembly passed by consensus the UN Convention for the Protection and Punishment of Crimes Against Internationally Protected Persons, Including Diplomatic Agents (December 14, 1973), which entered into force on February 20, 1977. The second United Nations instrument in the battle against terrorism was the UN International Convention Against the Taking of Hostages (1979), which entered into force on June 3, 1983, for the U.S. on January 6, 1985. Mention should also be made of a second regional instrument, the Council of Europe's "Convention on the Suppression of Terrorism" (1977), ratified since then by a majority of the members of the Council.[53]

[52] Dugard, *op. cit. supra*, n. 45.
[53] Text in 15 *AJIL* 1272 (1976). On January 15, 1982, the Council's Committee of Ministers adopted its "Recommendations concerning International Terrorism;" text in 21 *AJIL* 199 (1982).

In addition to its two legislative contributions, the United Nations General Assembly repeatedly passed resolutions condemning all acts of terrorism (1972, 1976, 1977, 1979, 1981, 1983), and stronger terms—acts are criminal—in 1985.

The United States, for its part, supported all ICAO and United Nations measures aimed at international terrorism. In addition, much domestic legislation supported its antiterrorist stand. In 1984, two laws were enacted: under Public Law 98-533, rewards of up to $500,000 would be paid for information leading to the arrest or conviction of any person for conspiring to commit terrorist acts against U.S. citizens or property; under Public Law 98-473, persons convicted of taking U.S. citizens as hostages or committing terrorist acts in or outside the United States could be sentenced to life imprisonment, while a sentence of up to 20 years in prison and $100,000 in fines could be imposed for attempted sabotage of airliners or airports.[54] The Omnibus Diplomatic Security and Anti-Terrorism Act of 1986 provided for United States jurisdiction over terrorist crimes committed against U.S. citizens overseas, established a counter-terrorism witness protection fund to reimburse other governments for expenses related to security for those who provided testimony or evidence in terrorist cases, and also increased funding for the protection of U.S. diplomats and embassies against terrorists. L. Paul Bremer III, then U.S. Ambassador at Large for Counterterrorism, speaking about this law, said, "The United States now has on the books a law which enables our law enforcement agencies to better combat terrorism. Popularly called a "long arm" statute, the law makes it a federal crime to kill, injure, threaten, detain, or seize an American citizen anywhere in the world in order to compel a third person or government to accede to a terrorist's demand."[55]

If the American Secretary of State designates a given country as a state sponsor of terrorism, the provisions of Section 6(j) of the Export Administration Act are applied to that country. This was done, for example, after the bombing of KAL [Korea Air Lines] Flight 858 on November 29, 1987, with a loss of all 155 aboard.[56] The U.S. Government had become convinced by evidence and testimony that the North Korean Government was linked directly to the bombing of the South Korean airliner.

Under Section 6(i) of the Export Administration Act, U.S. exports of goods or technology that would make significant contributions to the military potential of a state supporting terrorism or would enhance the terrorist support ability of such a state are restricted. Under Section 38 of the Arms Export Control Act, the State Department will not permit the export of defense articles and services to the list of terrorist-supporting states.

[54]Text of 98–533 in 24 *ILM* 1015 (1985).
[55]*Current Policy No. 1135* (Dec. 1988), 1.
[56]For the destruction of Flight 858, see especially *Current Policy No. 1042* (March 1988), with its account of the tracking of the terrorists to their capture.

In the sphere of overall U.S. policies relating to international terrorism, the United States will not accede to the demands of terrorists, will not make any concessions, will not pay a ransom, will not permit a release of prisoners demanded by terrorists. Under the new legislation, it will try to impose the rule of law on terrorists by identifying, tracking, apprehending, prosecuting, and punishing them. If such a process is found to be blocked, or if the "hosts" of an identified terrorist are unwilling either to surrender the individual or to have local courts undertake prosecution, the United States now reserves the right to resort to forcible abduction to this country (see Chapter 12 *sub* Forcible Abduction).

On occasion, domestic issues interfere with a country's efforts to combat terrorism. As mentioned above, both the ICAO and the IMO had worked diligently in 1986 to draft international conventions for the protection of vessels or aircraft, respectively. The United States had supported those efforts from their beginnings but budget cuts then prevented the United States "from meeting the relatively modest sums assessed" as dues to members of the two international agencies.[57]

Other countries also have increased, through legislation, their ability to deal with the phenomenon of international terrorism. Thus, for example, France ordered the trials of terrorists to be heard by professional judges in order to decrease the chance of jury intimidation, and doubled the time a person charged with terrorism could be held for interrogation.

Other techniques adopted by states individually or bilaterally include improved screening of airline passengers, the issuing of "watch lists" of terrorists to border police, increased cooperation between INTERPOL, the FBI, and other law-enforcement agencies, and "measures to sow dissension within terrorist groups through black and gray covert operations" [obviously but unfortunately not explained].[58]

Specific techniques adopted by the United States or other countries include closing one's embassy in a state supporting terrorism; ordering that state's embassy to be closed; limiting the size of diplomatic and consular missions and other official bodies of states suspected of supporting terrorism; control of travel of members of such missions and bodies; denial of entry to all persons, including diplomatic personnel, who have been expelled or excluded from a state of suspicion of involvement in international terrorism or who have been convicted of a terrorist offense[59] (see also Chapter 19). After a rash of terrorist bombings in Paris in 1986, the French Government

[57] From a Jan. 23, 1987, speech by Secretary of State Shultz, in *Current Policy No. 909* (January 1987).
[58] *Current Policy No. 1023* (Nov. 1987).
[59] These and additional methods were reaffirmed at the Tokyo Economic Summit (May 5, 1986) "Statement on International Terrorism," reprinted in 25 *ILM* 1005 (1986). The Statement was signed by the leaders of the U.S., Great Britain, Canada, France, Japan, Italy, and West Germany. Neither the U.S. bombing raid on Libya nor a proposed oil boycott of terrorist supporters was endorsed.

imposed a visa requirement on all foreigners coming to France, except for citizens of the European Community and Switzerland.

One obvious weapon in the arsenal against international terrorism has been the employment of economic sanctions (see also Chapters 19 and 22). The United States, France, the Council of Europe, the European Community, and many other members or groupings of members of the Family of Nations have resorted to the imposition of sanctions against states claimed to be supporters of terrorism. A detailed list of what has been embargoed, forbidden, or limited in exports (see the U.S. examples *supra*) and financial transactions, operations of enterprises, and so on would look formidable indeed,[60] yet many commentators have expressed serious doubts about the true efficacy of such antiterrorist measures.

Another weapon developed to combat terrorism has been the creation of commando-type armed units, already mentioned earlier (see *supra, sub* Hijacking, *re* the Entebbe, Mogadishu and Karachi incidents.). Great Britain had formed its Special Air Service Regiment (SAS) in 1941, the United States established a commando unit in 1978 and now has the U.S. Army's Delta Force, based in Fort Bragg, N.C. According to unverified reports, a Delta unit was flown to the Eastern Mediterranean (Cyprus?) during the June 1985 TWA jet hijacking but did not take action when Flight 847 was in Beirut because in most instances it is virtually impossible to stage a rescue operation without some cooperation from the country in which a plane is on the ground. Italy created its Special Agents for Security Operations in 1979, and France, West Germany, several other European states, Israel, and some Asian states established special antiterrorist units. All of these were designed primarily for service abroad, but on occasion participated in emergencies at home, such as when the British SAS and police stormed the Iranian Embassy and rescued 19 hostages, and when Italian Special Agents freed a kidnapped U.S. general (January 1982), and an incident in Venezuela in August 1984.

The use of armed force beyond the limits of commando operations has been made rarely. Thus the United States, on April 14, 1986, launched a number of air strikes against "terrorist-related targets" in Libya. Justification of the action was based on Article 51 of the UN Charter, through a claim of the inherent right of self-defense. Its avowed purpose was to deter future terrorist acts by Libya. It was asserted officially that this self-defense became necessary after "quite diplomacy, public condemnation, economic sanctions and demonstrations of military force failed to persuade Colonel Qaddafi."[61] In April 1986, Libya had requested the Security Council to condemn the U.S. raids but the measure was killed by vetos cast by the United

---

[60]See, for example, the list of the key provisions of President Reagan's Executive Orders of Jan. 7 and 8, 1986, in 80 *AJIL* 949 (1986), and the collection of documents on U.S. Sanctions imposed on Libya, *op. cit. supra*, n. 51.
[61]Statement before UN Security Council by the U.S. Permanent Representative, April 15, 1986, in "Self-Defense against Terrorism," 80 *AJIL* 632, 633 (1986).

States, Great Britain, and the Soviet Union. On November 20, 1986, the UN General Assembly voted 79 to 28 to condemn the United States for its raids on Tripoli and Benghazi.

A relatively new variety of terrorism is *narcoterrorism*, the utilization of terrorist acts in association with narcotics trafficking, primarily to undermine or at least intimidate local governments.[62] Until the time of writing, this new form of terrorism has operated for the most part in the Andean countries, especially in Colombia. While many nations, besides the United States, have passed anti-narcotic legislation, international action had depended on extradition treaties and on the United Nations. The latter's Commission on Narcotic Drugs had urged in 1988 the calling of an international conference to adopt the draft of a convention intended to supplement and to reinforce two earlier UN instruments. That diplomatic conference met in Vienna in late 1988 and succeeded in adopting the new "UN Convention Against Illicit Traffic in Narcotic Drugs and Psychotropic Substances."[63]

The 1988 instrument contains a long list of internationally recognized offenses, related to the traffic in drugs, that are to be treated as crimes under the domestic laws of states which are parties to the convention. It also contained detailed provisions for international cooperation to bring both traffickers and those who gained for drug traffic to justice. Each party to the treaty is to establish jurisdiction over offenses when the latter were committed in its territory or on board of a vessel flying its flag or an aircraft registered under its laws at the time the offense was committed. The convention also provides that each of the offenses listed are to be deemed to be included as an extraditable offense in any extradition treaty existing between parties to the agreement.

Virtually all commentators on the phenomenon of international terrorism have agreed with Waterman[64] that while terrorists may have won small victories, they have rarely, if ever, achieved any given main goals. No real progress in combating hijacking, hostage taking and other terrorist activities can be expected until three basic concepts have been incorporated in global conventions and are then implemented without exception: (1) the states of the world must agree not to permit their territories to be used as places of asylum by terrorists, regardless of the nationality of the latter;[65] (2)

---

[62]See "Narcotics: Terror's New Ally," *Time*, May 4, 1987, 30–37, and U.S. Dept. of State, *International Narcotics Update* (Nov. 1989).

[63]Text of 1988 convention in 28 *ILM* 497 (1989); text of the "UN Single Convention on Narcotic Drugs" (1961), as amended by a 1972 Protocol, in 11 *ILM* 804 (1972); text of the earlier "UN Convention on Psychotropic Substances" (1971) in 10 *ILM* 201 (1971). See also McCaffrey, "The Forty-second Session of the International Law Commission," 84 *AJIL* 930, at 935 (1990), on the Commission's proposed Draft Article X (Illicit Traffic in Narcotic Drugs) for a revision of the 1954 version of the UN Draft Code of Crimes against the Peace and Security of Mankind.

[64]See Waterman's perceptive analysis in *CSM*, Dec. 3, 1986, 14.

[65]See also McCaffrey, *op. cit. supra*, n. 63, at 933.

extradition of individuals charged with terrorist offenses must be granted on submission of evidence of presumed guilt; and (3) if no extradition is granted, the receiving (or host) state must prosecute the alleged terrorists. Underlying all three of the above concepts must be the clearly defined characterization of terrorist as criminals. However, in view of the political overtones associated with so many terrorist acts, realization of the above principles appear to be utopian as far as the near future is concerned.

## GENOCIDE

*Genocide* means an act committed with the intent to destroy, in whole or in part, a national, ethnical, racial, or religious group. The word itself was coined by Dr. Raphaël Lemkin in his *Axis Rule in Occupied Europe.*[66]

The practices of the German government before and especially during World War II, pertaining to the attempt to eliminate entire groups of its own citizens and later citizens of occupied states, led to the question of whether such acts of destruction could be regarded any longer as domestic acts or whether they constituted crimes against humanity.

Genocide, in practice, went beyond the killing of people: it covered such related acts as the practice of abortion, sterilization, artificial infection, the working of people to death in special labor camps, and the separation of families or of sexes in order to depopulate specific areas. None of these activities was carried out with the approval of the individuals concerned and, in every sense of the term, had to be regarded as criminal in intent as well as in execution, even under the laws of the German Reich.

### The Genocide Convention

On December 13, 1946, the General Assembly of the United Nations unanimously adopted Resolution 96 (I), in which it condemned genocide as a crime under international law. The Assembly also requested the Economic and Social Council to begin studies toward the eventual drawing up of a draft convention on genocide. The Council, in turn, asked the Secretary-General to prepare a first draft and to circulate it among the members for comment. In 1948, the Economic and Social Council appointed an *ad hoc* committee consisting of seven members to revise the original draft. When that project had been completed, the Council, after a general debate, decided on August 26, 1948, to send the draft to the General Assembly for the study and action. After further study in Paris by the Legal Committee of the General Assembly, action followed in the parent body. On December

[66](1944), 79: Chap. 9 (79–95) dealt with the subject in question in detail, particularly as to Axis practices; consult also Lemkin's "Genocide As a Crime Under International Law," 41 *AJIL* 145 (1947).

9, 1948, the General Assembly adopted the Convention on the Prevention and Punishment of the Crime of Genocide.[67]

The convention affirms the criminality of genocide in time of peace as well as in time of war (Art. 1). The offense itself is defined in Article 2:

In the present Convention, genocide means any of the following acts committed with intent to destroy, in whole or in part, a national, ethnical, racial or religious group, as such:

(a) Killing members of the group;
(b) Causing serious bodily or mental harm to members of the group;
(c) Deliberately inflicting on the group conditions of life calculated to bring about its physical destruction in whole or in part;
(d) Imposing measures intended to prevent births within the group;
(e) Forcibly transferring children of the group to another group.

Article 3 provides that all of the following acts are punishable: genocide; conspiracy to commit genocide; direction and public incitement to commit genocide; attempts to commit genocide; and complicity in genocide.

Persons committing any of the acts listed in Article 3 are punishable, whether they are constitutionally responsible rulers, public officials, or private individuals (Art. 4).

The parties to the convention undertook to enact the necessary domestic legislation to give effect to the convention and, in particular, to provide effective penalties for persons guilty of the forbidden acts (Art. 5).

Persons charged with any of the enumerated acts are to be tried by a competent tribunal of the state in which the act was committed or by such international penal tribunal as may have jurisdiction with respect to those contacting parties that have accepted its jurisdiction (Art. 5).

Under Article 7, genocide and all other acts prohibited by the convention are not to be considered political crimes for the purpose of extradition, and the parties to the convention have pledged to grant extradition in accordance with their laws and treaties in effect.

Article 8 provides that any party to the instrument can call on the competent organs of the United Nations to take such action under the UN Charter as they would consider appropriate for the prevention and suppression of acts of genocide.

Under Article 9, any dispute between the parties relating to the convention is to be submitted to the International Court of Justice at the request of any of the parties to the dispute.

The Genocide Convention, originally signed by 25 states, came into force on January 12, 1951. By January 1985, ninety-six ratifications, adherences, or successions had been deposited with the UN Secretary-General. The United States had thus far refrained from ratification. The legislative

[67]Text in 45 *AJIL* 7 (1951 Supp.). Consult also Kunz, "The United Nations Convention on Genocide," 43 *AJIL* 738 (1949), and Whiteman, vol. 11, 848–74.

history of the ratification, while not exemplary, is rather interesting. By the end of 1985, the Convention had been pending in the U.S. Senate (intermittently because of lapses in presidential submissions during the John Foster Dulles era) for almost thirty-six years. On December 6, 1978, President Carter repeated his earlier efforts and again asked the Senate to give consent to ratification, but to no avail. On September 15, 1984, President Reagan had urged the Senate to quickly give its consent to the ratification of the Convention, but senatorial opposition buried the consent again in committee. The Senate gave its consent to the ratification of the convention on February 19, 1986, by a vote of 83–11, but it took two more years to gain Congressional passage of legislation needed to implement the treaty by making genocide punishable under federal laws and setting penalties for violators. The House then passed the implementing legislation in April, 1988, and the Senate did so on October 15, 1988. The Senate version of the bill was officially called "The Proxmire Act" in honor of Senator William Proxmire (Wis.) who with unmatched dedication had delivered over 3,300 speeches in favor of ratification. His call to action had been repeated on every day the Senate was in session, since January 11, 1967.

President Reagan signed the Genocide Implementation Act of 1987 on November 4, 1988,[68] and then deposited the instrument of ratification; the convention entered into force for the U.S. on February 23, 1989. As of May 16, 1989, a total of 105 states had ratified, acceded to, or succeeded to the Genocide Convention.

American objections to the Convention were based in part on domestic constitutional questions, such as the belief that by undertaking to "prevent and punish" acts of genocide (Art. 1 of the Convention), the federal government might usurp functions constitutionally reserved for the individual states. Senators opposed to ratification also objected to having the U.S. government compelled either to extradite or try offenders against international rules when the acts in question might not be clearly illegal under domestic law. There has also existed a vocal and continuing opposition on the part of some citizens to the idea that American nationals could be tried before some foreign tribunal under procedures alien to the American judicial system. While such objections might seem to be at best farfetched indeed, every presidential effort to secure Senate ratification had produced bitter opposition in some circles.

A number of states made reservations at the time they signed the convention, and others, such as Bulgaria and the Philippines, entered reservations at the time of ratification, mostly dealing with Article 9.[69] These reservations

---

[68]Text, with Joyner's Introductory Note and the "Lugar Report," in 28 *ILM* 754 (1989).
[69]See Finch, "The Genocide Convention," 43 *AJIL* 732 (1949), which covered early criticism in American legal circles. Consult also Kuhn, "The Genocide Convention and State Rights," *id.*, 498, on the relation of the instrument to the concept of national sovereignty; the Note by Bryant and Jones, 16 *Harvard Int. Law Jl.* 683 (1975); extremely important are the excerpts from Senate committee hearings (Sept. 1984) on the convention, in 79 *AJIL* 116 (1985).

caused strong objections by other members of the United Nations that were parties to the convention.

Returning to the convention itself, history has seen instances of acts of genocide after the drafting of the instrument and has thereby shown the need for universal acceptance and enforcement of its provisions. In the Korean War, there were an appalling number not only of war crimes but also of acts of genocide.[70] Other recent examples of genocide not directly connected with international war are supplied by the intermittent (1959–1973 and 1988) massacres taking place in Burundi during intertribal fighting between the Tutsi and Hutu groups; the reported slaughter of large numbers of Ugandans during the rule of former president Idi Amin; the reported slaying of dissidents in Equatorial Africa in the decade after independence was secured from Spain in 1968; the wholesale killing of Cambodians at the hands of their own government during the reign of Pol Pot; and the reported mass killings of members of the Muslim minority in Chad in 1979. (See "Suggested Readings" for a brief list of sources for the above and other instances of genocide.)

## TORTURE

Government-sanctioned torture of prisoners has become "a way of life" in several dozen countries since World War II and has been on the increase in many others. Amnesty International, as early in 1974, listed sixty-one states in which barbarous tortures were the order of the day.[71] In consequence of this ever-spreading phenomenon, the UN-sponsored Congress on Crime Prevention and Treatment of Offenders (Geneva, 1975) drafted a declaration banning torture. That draft was subsequently approved by the General Assembly in November 1975 as the Declaration on the Protection of All Persons from Being Subjected to Torture and Other Cruel, Inhuman or Degrading Treatment or Punishment (G.A. Res. 3452. 30 GAOR, Supp. [No. 34] 91, UN Doc. A/10034-1975).[72] The instrument, comprising twelve articles, did not impose (as a mere declaration) any obligations on UN members; it was designed merely as a series of rather specific guidelines. It has had no noticeable practical effects. On the other hand, the European Human

---

[70]Consult, *inter alia*, "Atrocities in Korea—How Bad? *U.S. News & World Report*, May 1, 1953, 16–17; "Red China: The Mask Comes Off," *id.*, Nov. 6, 1953, 25, which summarizes the report of the war crimes division of the U.S. Army in Korea, of June 30, 1953; and see "Genocide Charged by South Koreans," *Presbyterian Life*, July 7, 1951, 21, as well as *Voice of Korea*, January 14, 1954, 4, for a summary of the debate in the General Assembly and the text of the latter's resolution of November 20, 1953.

[71]See *NYT*, August 4, 1974, E-5; and Amnesty International, *Report on Torture* (1975) as well as its *Torture in the Eighties* (1984), listing abuses in 98 countries.

[72]Text in 19 *ILM* 972 (1980); see also UN "Draft Convention Against Torture and Other Cruel, Inhuman or Degrading Treatment or Punishment" [1984], 23 *ILM* 1027 (1984). See also *Time*, Aug. 16, 1976, 31–34, for an illuminating account of the modern use of torture.

Rights Convention (also condemning torture) has served to produce a very important and interesting decision by the European Court of Human Rights in *Ireland* v. *United Kingdom* (January 18, 1978).[73] The complaint in that case centered on the (successful) Irish contention of mistreatment of arrested persons by British forces in Northern Ireland. The court relied heavily on the UN Declaration on Torture in interpreting the European Convention of Human Rights.

The Council of Europe approved (November 26, 1987) its European Convention for the Prevention of Torture and Inhuman or Degrading Treatment or Punishment.[74] Within less than a year, 15 European countries had ratified the treaty. One of the interesting features of this instrument is provided by its Article 5, under which the Committee of Ministers elected the 15 members of the Special Committee that is empowered under the treaty to visit any place of detention operated by a public authority (in the ratifying states) and to make recommendations for greater protection of detainees from torture or inhuman and degrading treatment or punishment. The first meeting of the Special Committee was scheduled for late 1989.[75] It goes without saying that one obvious result of the recommendations would be hoped-for adverse publicity concerning the offending public authority or state.

The Organization of American States (OAS) had adopted (December 9, 1985) its Interamerican Convention to Prevent and Punish Torture.[76] This instrument holds guilty of the crime of torture a public servant or employee who orders, instigates, or induces the use of torture, as well as any person who does so at the instigation of the above. Acting under the orders of a superior does not provide exemption from criminal liability under the convention.

In November 1984 the Greek Parliament unanimously passed a law outlawing torture and providing imprisonment for offenders: prison for life if the victim died, and imprisonment for 20 years in the case of survival of the victim. The law represented the first instance in which a specific prohibition of torture has been included in a national penal code.

The UN General Assembly adopted the Convention against Torture and Other Cruel, Inhuman or Degrading Treatment or Punishment.[77] The United States did not sign it, harboring strong reservations concerning certain provisions of the convention.

---

[73]Text of judgment in 17 *ILM* 680 (1978). See also the following related materials: *NYT*, February 9, 1977, 3; Spjut, "Torture Under the European Convention on Human Rights," 73 *AJIL* 267 (1979); and the earlier but most valuable and heavily documented study by O'Boyle, "Torture and Emergency Powers Under the European Convention on Human Rights: Ireland v. The United Kingdom," 71 *AJIL* 674 (1977).

[74]Text in 27 *ILM* 1152 (1988), see also 82 *AJIL* 806 (1988). The convention entered into force on Feb. 1, 1989.

[75]*Id.*, 28 (1989) at 1341.

[76]Text in 25 *ILM* 519 (1986).

[77]Text in 23 *ILM* 1027 (1984), with changes at 24 *ILM* 535 (1985).

The convention, which entered into force on June 26, 1987, called for a Committee Against Torture to be set up, similar to the provisions of the anti-*Apartheid* convention. The Committee consists of ten experts and all parties to the treaty have to report regularly to the Committee on measures taken to put the provisions of the convention into effect.

In the United States, a case of more than academic interest was decided in 1980: *Filartiga* v. *Peña-Irala*.[78] This case originated in 1976 when the son of a Paraguayan dissident was abducted and tortured to death in prison by Américo Peña-Irala, the police inspector general in Asunción. After arrest and disbarment, following an attempt to commence a criminal action in the Paraguayan courts, the father of the youth, together with his daughter, emigrated to the United States. In 1978, Peña entered the United States on a visitor's visa. But when the Filartiga daughter learned of his presence, she informed the Immigration and Naturalization Service, which arrested Peña and a female Paraguayan companion. Dolly Filartiga had Peña served with a summons and civil complaint while he was being held in the Brooklyn Navy Yard, claiming that he caused her brother's death and demanding $10 million in compensatory and punitive damages. Peña moved to dismiss the complaint on the ground that subject-matter jurisdiction was absent. The Filartigas (father and daughter) submitted affidavits by noted legal scholars, who upheld unanimously that international law absolutely prohibited the use of torture as alleged. Peña's lawyer asked for dismissal on the ground of *forum non conveniens*, in particular that Paraguayan law provided adequate remedies for the wrong alleged. On May 15, 1979, the court (U.S. District Court, ED N.Y.) dismissed the complaint on jurisdictional grounds. Shortly afterward Peña and his companion returned to Paraguay.

The plaintiffs appealed, and on June 30, 1980, the Circuit Court of Appeals decided in their favor, reversed the decision of the District Court and remanded the case for further proceedings.

The Court of Appeals relied heavily on a most interesting and heavily documented Memorandum, filed at the court's request by the United States Department of Justice jointly with the Department of State. The Memorandum, asserting that official torture violated international law, centered on the interpretation of Section 9 of the Judiciary Act of 1789 (1 Stat. 76 [1789]), now Section 1350 of the U.S. Code (28 U.S.C. 1350), which reads:

The district courts shall have original jurisdiction of any civil action by an alien for a tort only, committed in violation of the law of nations or a treaty of the United States.

---

[78]U.S. Court of Appeals, 2d Cir., Docket No. 79-6090, June 30, 1980, reproduced in 19 *ILM* 966 (1980); see also the *Memorandum* filed by the United States, 19 *ILM* 585 (1980); and Blum and Steinhard, "Federal Jurisdiction over International Human Rights Claims: The Alien Tort Claim Act After *Filartiga* v. *Peña-Irala*," 22 *Harvard Int'l Law Jl.* 53 (Winter 1981).

The Memorandum pointed out that the view that a state's treatment of its own citizens was beyond the purview of international law was once widely held. However, in consequence of changing standards of behavior in the community of nations, an international law of human rights had begun to develop. This did not mean that all such rights could be judicially enforced. But one thing became clear: the assumption that a state had no obligation to respect the human rights of its citizens was incorrect. Through both treaties and the continuing development of customary law, states had accepted as law a duty to observe basic human rights, and that customary law had been upheld in decisions of the International Court of Justice (*Nuclear Tests {Australia* v. *France}*, 1974; Advisory Opinion on *Legal Consequences . . . of Continued Presence of South Africa in Namibia*, 1970).

Among the fundamental human rights protected by every relevant multilateral treaty was freedom from torture, just as customary international law condemned torture. Every state accused of torture has denied the accusation, and none has tried to justify torture. Hence it could be asserted correctly that official torture was a tort "in violation of the law of nations."

In January 1984, the same District Court (ED N.Y.) awarded the plaintiffs $10 million in compensatory and punitive damages.

## APARTHEID

South Africa had persevered in its policy of *apartheid* (racial discrimination) despite increasing protests by many countries and the imposition of economic sanctions by some of them. It was therefore not overly surprising when the UN General Assembly, after several years of preparatory work adopted in November 1973 the International Convention for the Suppression and Punishment of the Crime of Apartheid.[79] It thereby added one more to the growing list of international crimes. The convention established the international criminal responsibility of individuals, members of organizations and institutions, as well as of representatives of states, whenever they committed or were involved in the commission of the crime of *apartheid*.

Scores of states ratified the Convention but of all the major Powers, only the Soviet Union did so. The major reason for abstentions and later refusals to accede to the instrument was the widespread belief that many of its provisions represented undue (read: illegal) interference in the domestic affairs of member states. Such interference was prohibited in the UN Charter.

An unusual aspect of the "operation" of the convention made its appearance in 1985. At the request of the UN Commission on Human Rights, an

[79] Text in 13 *ILM* 51 (1974). The vote was 91 in favor and 4 against (Portugal, South Africa, the United Kingdom, the United States), with 26 abstentions. See also Howard and Rita Taubenfeld, "Human Rights and the Emerging International Constitution," 9 *Hofstra Law Review* 475 (482–509 discuss the Apartheid Convention) (1981); and Bassiouni and Derby, "Final Report on the Establishment of an International Criminal Court for the Implementation of the *Apartheid* Convention and Other Relevant International Instruments," *id.*, 523.

*Ad Hoc Working Group of Experts on Southern Africa* compiled for the Centre for Human Rights a list of persons deemed responsible for *apartheid* under the provisions of the convention.

The United States abstained repeatedly from anti-*apartheid* votes in both the General Assembly and the UN Security Council. This was not because the United States favored the institution of *apartheid* but because of objections to "violent rhetoric" and "excesses of language" in the measures under consideration. In any case, the resolutions did not have the slightest effect on South Africa's policies. Heavy outside pressures, the spectacle of the weakening of Communist control in Eastern Europe, and continued application of economic sanctions finally resulted in a limited retreat by the South African government from some of the more obnoxious manifestations of *apartheid* (1989–1990).

In the United States, the passage overriding a Presidential veto of the Comprehensive Anti-Apartheid Act of 1986[80] marked a major response of the U.S. Government to the continuing practice of *apartheid* by South Africa. The Act imposed important economic sanctions, including a ban on new investments, on steel and certain other imports, and cancellation of landing rights in the United States for South African airlines.

APARTHEID IN SPORTS    In an action virtually ignored in the Western press, the UN General Assembly adopted on December 10, 1985, by a vote of 125 to 0 (24 abstentions) an "International Convention against Apartheid in Sports." The convention entered into force on April 3, 1988, after 27 "instruments of ratification, acceptance, approval or accession" had been deposited. By December 22, 1989, 45 countries or entities had deposited such instruments, but the only major state on the list was the Soviet Union. The rest of the list comprised the Ukraine, Byelorussia, and an array of Latin American, African, and Asian countries. In accordance with the provisions of the convention, a 15-member Commission against Apartheid in Sports was established. It submitted its first report to the General Assembly on October 23, 1989.[81]

## SUGGESTED READINGS

### International Criminal Law —General

Bassiouni, *International Criminal Law*, 3 vols (1986), and Bassiouni (ed.) *A Draft International Criminal Code and Draft Statute for an International Criminal Court* (1987).

### Piracy

Moore, vol. 2, 951–79; Hackworth, vol. 2, 681–95; Johnson, "Piracy in Modern International Law," 43 *Transactions of the Grotius Society* 63 (1957).

[80]Text and related documents in 26 *ILM* 77 (1987).
[81]29 *ILM* 466 (1990).

CASES

*The Le Louis*, Great Britain, High Court of Admiralty, 1817, 2 Dobson 210.
*The Magellan Pirates*, Great Britain, High Court of Admiralty, 1853, 1 Spinks 81.
*United States* v. *Smith*, U.S. Supreme Court, 1820, 5 Wheaton 153.

## The Slave Trade

CASES

*United States* v. *The Schooner La Jeune Eugénie, Rabaud and Labatut, Claimants*, U.S.
   Court of Appeals, 1st Cir., 1822, 2 Mason 409.
*The Antelope*, U.S. Supreme Court, 1825, 10 Wheaton 66.

## Air Hijacking

McWhinney, *Aerial Piracy and International Terrorism (The Illegal Diversion of Aircraft
and International Law)* (2nd rev. ed., 1987); Stern [U.S. judge in the *Tiede Case*],
*Judgment in Berlin* (1984); Evans, "Aircraft Hijacking: What Is Being Done," 67
*AJIL* 641 (1973).

CASE

*Husserl* v. *Swiss Transport Co., Ltd.* U.S. District Court, S.D.N.Y. 1972, 351, F.Supp.
   702, reported in 67 *AJIL* 549 (1973).

## Terrorism

Mewhouse, "A Freemasonry of Terrorism," *The New Yorker*, July 8, 1985, 46–63;
Murphy, *Punishing International Terrorists: The Legal Framework for Policy Initiatives*
(1985) and his "Recent International Legal Developments in Controlling Terrorism," 4 *Chinese Yearbook* [CYILA], 97 (1985); Yonah and Nanes (eds.), *Legislative
Response to Terrorism* (1986), survey of 17 countries; Yonah and O'Day, *Ireland's Terrorist Dilemma* (1986); Ra'anan, Pfaltzgraff, Shultz, Halperin, and Lukes (eds.), *Hydra
of Carnage: The International Linkages of Terrorism and Other Low-Intensity Operations:
The Witnesses Speak* (1986); Evans and Murphy, *Legal Aspects of International Terrorism* (1978); Friedlander, *Terrorism: Documents of International and Local Control*, 4 vols
(1978–80); Alexander, Carlton, and Wilkinson, *Terrorism: Theory and Practice* (1979);
Lillich (ed.), *Transnational Terrorism: Conventions and Commentary* (1982); Bassiouni
(ed.), *Legal Responses to International Terrorism: U.S. Procedural Aspects* (1988); Erickson,
*Legitimate Use of Military Force Against State-Sponsored International Terrorism* (1989);
Ronzitti (ed.), *Maritime Terrorism and International Law* (1990). See also the informative Special Report by Kidder, "Unmasking Terrorism," *CSM* May 13, 1986,
17; May 14, 17; May 15, 18; and May 21, 15, as well as *Current Policy No. 792*
(February 1986).

CASES

*Pan American World Airways* v. *Aetna Casualty and Surety Co.*, U.S. Court of Appeals,
   2nd Cir., 1974, 505 F.2d 989, in 13 *ILM* 1376 (1974). See also the relevant
   *Note* by Breckenridge in 16 *Harvard Int'l L. Jl.* 445 (1975). The District Court
   decision, in full, is in 12 *ILM* 1445 (1973) and reported briefly in 68 *AJIL*
   119 (1974).

*United States* v. *Busic*, U.S. Court of Appeals, 2nd Cir., 1978, 592 F.2d 13, reported in 73 *AJIL* 685 (1979).

## Genocide

Kuper, *The Prevention of Genocide* (1986); Paris, *Genocide in Satellite Croatia, 1941–1945* (1961); Arens (ed.), *Genocide in Paraguay* (1976). For Burundi, see *NYT*, Oct. 24, 1965, 9; June 11, 1972, 1, 3; July 2, 1972, E-9; July 30, 1972, E-5; May 15, 1973, 5; June 5, 1973, 12; June 17, 1973, 1, 14; June 23, 1973, 3; Dec. 21, 1976, 10, as well as Williams, "Slaughter in Burundi," 1 *World*, Nov. 2, 1972, 20–24. For Equatorial Africa, see *NYT* Jan. 25, 1978, A-5; Feb. 16, 1978. For Uganda, see *NYT* May 27, 1973, 9, *et seq.* For Cambodia, see *NYT* July 31, 1978, 39–40; Oct. 2, 1978, 45, *et seq.* For Chad, see *NYT* April 10, 1979, A-1, A-4. For Bangladesh, see *NYT* April 11, 1974, 3; June 29, 1974, 1, 4. For Afghanistan, see Girardet, "Afghanistan: Soviet 'Migratory Genocide'," *CSM* Dec. 6, 1983, 22–23.

## Torture

Cassese, "A New Approach to Human Rights: The European Convention for the Prevention of Torture," 83 *AJIL* 128 (1989); Burgers and Danelius (eds.), *The United Nations Convention against Torture* (1988).

## Apartheid

Bassiouni and Derby, "Final Report on the Establishment of an International Criminal Court for the Implementation of the [UN] *Apartheid* Convention and Other Relevant International Documents," 9 *Hofstra L. Rev.* 523 (1981); H. and R. Taubenfeld, "Human Rights and the Emerging International Constitution," *id.*, 9, 475 (1981); Bindman (ed.) for the International Commission of Jurists, *South Africa: Human Rights and the Rule of the Law* (1988).

PART IV

Territorial Questions

# 14

# Title to Territory, Air, and Space

A state has an unquestioned right to exercise sovereign authority throughout the extent of its territory. Territory therefore has become in the legal order "the point of departure in settling most questions that concern international relations."[1]

In the earliest states of Western history, effective control of a territory, together with the ability to defend it, represented the title that counted. Soon, however, additional title requirements of a more legal nature entered into the picture, such as treaties of cession, marriage settlements, and occasionally claims based on an asserted hereditary right to succession. Over time, a considerable number of titles to particular areas or territories received express or tacit recognition by the majority of states.

Beginning with the Age of Discovery, a more systematic approach to the problem of title to territory became necessary in view of the sometimes sweeping claims based on discovery and of the claims by certain seafaring nations to jurisdiction over enormous expanses of the world's oceans.

## METHODS OF ACQUIRING TITLE
## TO TERRITORY TODAY

Title to territory has been obtained by states through the transfer of land from one owner to another or through the acquisition of land not belonging to any other state. In the former case, a "derivative" title was obtained, whereas in the latter instance the owner received an "original" title.

Generally, six methods of acquiring title to territory are recognized by states today: occupation, accretion, prescription, voluntary cession, treaties of peace, and forced cession or conquest (the last with reservations, to be sure).

Discovery is the oldest and, historically, the most important method of acquiring title to territory. Up to the eighteenth century, discovery alone sufficed to establish a legal title, but since then such discovery has had to

---

[1]Judge Max Huber in the *Palmas Island Arbitration* (United States–Netherlands), 1928; see 22 *AJIL* 867 (1928).

be followed by an effective occupation in order to be recognized as the basis of a title to territory. The history of Spanish exploration (as an example) abounds with the landing of explorers in new territories and the establishment of claims to title by a proclamation of annexation, coupled with the performance of such symbolic acts as the burying of inscribed lead or brass tablets.

The doctrine of the sufficiency of mere discovery to establish a valid title was asserted as late as 1823 by Chief Justice John Marshall in *Johnson and Graham's Lessee* v. *M'Intosh* (Supreme Court of the United States, 1823, 8 Wheaton 543), but the learned judge did qualify his dictum by adding that the "title might be consummated by possession." In fact, during the next year, the United States government maintained in its negotiations with Russia concerning territorial questions that "dominion cannot be acquired but by a real occupation and possession, and an intention to establish it is by no means sufficient."

OCCUPATION    *Occupation* means a state's settlement of a territory hitherto not belonging to any other state, for the purpose of adding the land in question to the national territory. Such "vacant" land (*terra nullius*) exists even if it already has a native population—provided the latter consists of nomads or of a people judged to possess a civilization inferior to that of the standard prevailing in Europe (the Aztec Empire in Mexico is an example). The actual settlement has to be made if the, at best, vague claim based on discovery is to be transformed into a legal, recognized title. Such settlement must be made within a "reasonable" time after discovery and must assume a permanent character. Mere visits by fishermen or the maintenance of seasonal fishing settlements are not held to constitute occupation in the legal meaning of the term.

One of the most interesting modern cases dealing with title to territory on the basis of discovery and claimed occupation was the dispute between France and Great Britain regarding sovereignty over the tiny islands in the English Channel called the Minquiers and Ecrehos groups. By a special agreement of September 24, 1951, the disputants asked the International Court of Justice to determine who was the sovereign of the islets in question.[2] The court decided in favor of the British claim, denying the validity of alleged French occupation and exercise of sovereign acts in the islands. What makes this decision especially interesting is not only the reasoning of the court but also the examination of historical evidence going back to the Norman Conquest in the case of England and, in the case of the evidence submitted by France, to A.D. 933.

Title (sovereignty) to territory based on occupation lapses on abandonment by the owner (see the Case Study No. 4, on the Falklands Islands War, at the

---

[2] *Minquiers and Ecrehos Case (France–United Kingdom)*, International Court of Justice, November 17, 1953, *I.C.J. Reports, 1953,* 47, digested by Bishop, in 48 *AJIL* 316 (1954); see also Johnson, "The Minquiers and Ecrehos Case," 3 *Int'l and Comp. L.Q.,* 189 (1954).

end of this chapter). A number of cases of territorial titles claimed on alleged or actual abandonment have been recorded during the past four centuries, such as the island of Santa Lucia, the area around Delagoa Bay in Africa, and the Atlantic island of Ilha da Trinidade. Recent disputes, not yet resolved at the time of writing, involve disagreements among France, Madagascar, and Mauritius over Tromelin Island and also among Vietnam, the People's Republic of China, the Republic of China, and the Philippines over title to the Spratly Islands.[3]

In the relatively few cases in which the fact of occupation was important, the extent of settlement needed to assert a valid title became a crucial issue. Generally, a single permanent settlement, even if located along the fringes of an unappropriated area, has been held to constitute sufficient evidence of occupation. Exceptions are on record, of course, and the interested reader might profitably investigate problems connected with the Louisiana Purchase, the boundary questions incidental to the Anglo-American Oregon controversy, and several of the disagreements centering on European territorial claims along the Western coasts of Africa. For modern disputes, the disagreement between Norway and Denmark over title to Eastern Greenland, won by Denmark through a ruling by the Permanent Court of International Justice in 1933,[4] and the French-Mexican dispute over Clipperton Island in the Pacific might be cited.

In December 1971, the United States settled its last territorial dispute of any consequence by ceding to Honduras the two tiny Swan Islands, located 100 miles offshore from that republic. Honduras had periodically renewed its claim, basing it on the original Spanish conquests in Central America. The American claim was founded on Spanish lack of occupation, hence lapse of title, followed by U.S. occupation in 1863, after the passage in 1856 of the Guano Islands Act (justifying occupation of unclaimed islands rich in guano).

In order to prevent a recurrence of repeated "discoveries," with resultant claims, the major powers agreed in the Final Act of the Berlin Conference of 1885 (Art. 34) that any occupation of African territory should be followed by the notification of all signatory states so that any other claims to the area in question could be voiced and settled before a dispute could arise.

In this connection, the doctrine of the *Hinterland* should be mentioned, even if it, like discovery and occupation, has only historical interest today. Because of the problems in arriving at interior boundaries in the Americas, the major powers involved in the partition of Africa in the last quarter of the nineteenth century concluded a number of bilateral agreements delimiting the territorial zones contiguous to the initial settlements set up along the coasts. Such interior zones were termed the *Hinterland* (backcountry), and although not occupied in the sense of actual permanent settlement, they

[3]See *CSM*, January 3, 1979, 3, concerning the Spratly Islands.
[4]*Legal Status of Eastern Greenland Case (Denmark–Norway), P.C.I.J., 1933,* Ser. A/B. No. 53.

were recognized as constituting spheres of interest of the state based on the coastal settlement.

ACCRETION    A second but minor mode of acquiring title to territory is through accretion, the gradual deposit of soil by a river flowing past a shore or by an ocean along its coasts. The rule governing accretion dates back to Roman days and is quite simple: a thing that is added follows the fate of the principal thing. Soil added to a river bank represents an addition to the territory of the riparian state; islands built up within a riverbed become a part of the territory of the state within whose boundary lines the flats or islands are formed.[5]

Mud flats or islands built up within a state's territorial waters not only become the property of that state but also cause an outward extension of the maritime frontier from the new islands to a distance normally claimed along its shores by the state in question (the baseline of the territorial sea being determined by reference to the low-water mark). The classic case dealing with accretion is

### THE ANNA

*Great Britain, High Court of Admiralty, 1805*
*(5 C. Robinson 373)*

FACTS    The *Anna*, a vessel flying the American flag (although some authors claim that the ship was actually a Spanish one), carried a cargo of logwood as well as $13,000 from Spanish ports in the Caribbean to New Orleans. It was captured by the British privateer *Minerva* near the mouth of the Mississippi River, during the war then in progress between Great Britain and Spain. The American minister filed a claim to the vessel and cargo, stating that the capture had taken place within the territorial waters of the United States.

The *Anna* had been taken outside the three-mile limit if that limit was measured from the Balise, an ex-Spanish fort at the edge of the mainland, but within a three-mile limit if the latter was measured from a few small mud islands composed of earth and driftwood, formed by the Mississippi River. The islands were uninhabitable because of the consistency of their soft soil.

ISSUE    Could uninhabited mud islands formed by action of a river be claimed by the coastal state and serve to extend the latter's territorial sea limits?

DECISION    The court ruled in favor of the United States; the ship and cargo were ordered released because of their capture within neutral American waters. The islands were a part of American territorial jurisdiction and extended the boundaries of the American territorial sea for three miles beyond the islands.

REASONING    The islands, formed by accretion, had to be taken to be "natural appendages of the coast on which they border. Their elements are derived immediately from the territory. . . . " If they did not belong to the United States, any other state could occupy them, fortify them, and through them control all traffic to and from the mouth of the Mississippi. But they had

[5] See Lauterpacht's *Oppenheim*, vol. 1, 563; Whiteman, vol. 2, 1084.

been formed of American soil and American driftwood, as both shores of the Mississippi were in the United States, and hence they were a part of American territory. As such, they formed the outermost land off their shore and served to extend American territorial waters by three miles away from shore and into the ocean. Under these conditions, the *Anna* had been captured in American neutral waters. Such capture was a violation of neutral rights and was illegal.

PRESCRIPTION    *Prescription* is a legal term related to title to territory; it means continued occupation, over a long period of time, by one state of territory actually and originally belonging to another state. In essence, this circumstance corresponds to abandonment, but technically there is a difference. *Abandonment* implies a withdrawal, a kind of open retreat from a territory. *Prescription* means that a foreign state occupies a portion of territory claimed by a state, encounters no protests by the "owner," and exercises rights of sovereignty over a long period of time. Eventually the original title lapses, and the "squatter state" acquires legal title to the territory.

Most early writers on international law wrestled with the problem of the actual length of time required to validate a title founded on prescription, but none of them arrived at a generally acceptable number of actual years of occupation. Unlike the common-law rules found in many states on this essential factor of continued adverse holding, there still exists no international standard that defines precisely how long the occupant must hold on to an area before acquiring title. In one of the few arbitral decisions available on the subject, the *Island of Palmas* arbitration, a slight clue was supplied, however:

## THE ISLAND OF PALMAS (MIANGAS) ARBITRATION
### (United States—The Netherlands), Tribunal of the Permanent Court of Arbitration, 1928

FACTS    The treaty of peace ending the Spanish-American War included the cession by Spain of the Philippine Islands to the United States. The island of Palmas, also known as Miangas Island, was an isolated island located about midway between the southern tip of Mindanao in the Philippines and the northernmost island of the Nanoesa group in the (then) Dutch East Indies. The island, a small one (two miles by three-quarters of a mile) then had a population of about 750 and no economic resources to speak of.

The American governor of the province of Moro visited the island on January 21, 1906, and was astonished to see the Dutch flag flying above Palmas. His maps, and the peace treaty of December 10, 1898, indicated that the island was located twenty miles inside the boundaries of the Philippine Islands as ceded by Spain to the United States.

A long diplomatic dispute then arose between the United States and the Netherlands about the status of Palmas. In 1925 the two governments agreed to submit the question of title to the island to arbitration, and a sole arbitrator, M. Max Huber, was selected.

ISSUE    Is a valid title to foreign territory obtained through exercise of acts of sovereignty when the lawful owner fails to protest such acts?

DECISION    The island was awarded to the Netherlands: despite original Spanish title to Palmas, the Dutch government had exercised sovereign rights for more than two hundred years and had obtained title by prescription.

REASONING    "The principle that continuous and peaceful display of the functions of State within a given region is a constituent element of territorial sovereignty" is a recognized principle of international law.

Spain could not cede in the 1898 treaty more rights than Spain possessed. If the original Spanish title to the island of Palmas was valid in 1898, then that title had been transferred by the peace treaty to the United States. But the Dutch government submitted undeniable evidence to the effect that since 1700 the island had formed a part of successive native states on the Island of Sangi, which native states, since 1677, had been connected with the Dutch

East India Company. The vassal states or the Dutch government had occasionally exercised "acts characteristic of State authority" on the island of Palmas, not only between 1700 and 1898, but also between 1898 and 1906. The evidence was clear that at least since the middle of the nineteenth century, the Dutch government had considered the island of Palmas a part of its lawful possessions.

No Spanish protests concerning Dutch acts or claims had been forthcoming since the Spaniards, withdrawing from the Moluccas in 1666, had made express reservations as to the continuation of their sovereign rights. No other power had attempted any display of sovereignty until the United States claimed the island in 1906. Thus an uncontested exercise of Dutch sovereignty was shown to extend from 1700 to 1906. The Dutch title, acquired by continuous and peaceful acts of state authority, over two hundred years, and uncontested by the original holders of title to the island, held good.[6]

A much shorter period of adverse and uninterrupted possession than the 200 years cited in the *Island of Palmas* arbitration was specified in the interesting case centering on title to the privately owned Palmyra Island: *United States* v. *Fullard-Leo et al.*[7] The concept of a privately owned island with title conferred by occupation was revived in recent years when a search for islands in international waters, unclaimed by a state, came into being. The purpose of most such endeavors appears to have been either to create tax havens or to create a base of laundering money derived from criminal pursuits. It was, of course, possible that tourism opportunities or

---

[6]See also Jessup, "The Palmas Island Arbitration," 22 *AJIL* 735 (1928); Jennings, *The Acquisition of Territory in International Law* (1963), which contains, additionally, the full text of the *Palmas* award.

[7]U.S. Circuit Court of Appeals, Ninth Cir., February 1, 1943, as amended March 4, 1943, 133 F.2d 743; *certiorari denied* by the Supreme Court, May 10, 1943, reported in 37 *AJIL* 520 (1943). See *id.*, 526, for a well-reasoned dissenting opinion by Circuit Court Judge Healy. In August 1979, it was reported that the U.S. Government might *buy* Palmyra Island in order to use it for the storage of nuclear waste from Asian reactors. The island, still owned by the Fullard-Leo family, was then legally under the jurisdiction of the city and county of Honolulu, 1,110 miles away; see *NYT,* August 19, 1979, 22.

the understandable fantasy wish to be the lord of one's own island played a part in other searches. Two particularly interesting treatments are found in the legal literature or in court records: The "Republic of Minerva"[8] and the "Grand Capri Republic."[9] In the latter instance, the United States secured an injunction against the terra-forming of a reef into an island, outside the territorial waters of Florida.

VOLUNTARY CESSION   *Cession* means the formal transfer of title (sovereignty) over territory from one state to another. Voluntary cession conveys a lawful title to the new owner. Normally cession is formulated through the provisions of a treaty of cession that specifies precisely (if such is possible at the time) the area to be transferred as well as the conditions under which the transfer is to be accomplished. All kinds of related provisions may be encountered in such instruments, regarding the nationality of the inhabitants, of the territory, the adjustment of public debts connected with the area, the establishment or fate of servitudes therein, and so forth.

Cession may take one of a number of forms. A common and simple type, particularly popular in past centuries but not unknown in modern times, is a *treaty of sale*. This form of conveyance of title was utilized by the United States in such well-known acquisitions as the Louisiana Purchase (1803), the Florida Purchase (1819), the Gadsden Purchase (1853), the Alaska Purchase (1867), and the purchase of the Danish West Indies (Virgin Islands) in 1916. In a recent instance, Australia purchased from their private British owner the 27 atolls comprising the Cocos Islands, for $7 million.

Another form of voluntary cession is the exchange of one piece of real estate for another, such as the transfer of the island of Heligoland by Great Britain to Germany in 1890 in exchange for areas adjacent to German East Africa.

Again, cession has been effected by means of a gift—in past centuries as part, say, of a royal dowry or, in more modern times, as illustrated by the donation of a portion of a reef in Lake Erie by Great Britain to the United States (1850), subject to the condition that the latter would assume responsibility for the construction and maintenance of a lighthouse on the reef in question.

Cession has, on rare occasions, been accomplished by a conveyance of title by demise. That term here means a legal transfer of property or real estate by a monarch (not necessarily by the latter's death). One famous example was the transfer of title to the Congo Free State to Belgium (1908) by King Leopold II, who was sovereign of the Congo in his personal capacity, in addition to being king of the Belgians.

Among relatively recent examples of voluntary cession were the cession of Ifni, a Spanish enclave in North Africa, by Spain to Morocco in 1969

---

[8]Comment: "To Be or Not to Be: The Republic of Minerva—Nation Founding Individuals," 12 *Columbia J. Trans. L.* 520 (1973).

[9]*United States* v. *Ray*, U.S. Court of Appeals, 5th Cir., 1970, 423 F.2d 16.

and the United States' relinquishment of its territorial claims to several of the Line and Phoenix islands, including Christmas, Canton, and Enderbury, to the Republic of Kiribati. The latter cession was included in a Treaty of Friendship with Kiribati after the ex-British protectorate (Gilbert Islands) had attained independence in 1979.

One modern cession led to a full-scale armed conflict and still was listed as unresolved at the time of writing: the Spanish cession of the Western Sahara (see Case Study No. 5, The Western Sahara Dispute, at the end of this chapter).

A minor but interesting case of voluntary cession is that of Macao. This "colony" of Portugal, consisting of two small islands linked by a peninsula with mainland China, comprises only six square miles of land inhabited by an estimated 400,000 people, almost all Chinese. Macao was occupied by Portugal in 1557; its control by the latter was confirmed in a Sino-Portuguese treaty in 1887, and in 1951 Macao was transformed into an overseas province of Portugal, similar to the status of, say, Martinique in relation to France. After the basic change in Portugal's government in 1974, the status of Macao received a new and unusual designation: Chinese territory under Portuguese administration. That step was followed by the gradual withdrawal of Portugal's minuscule military forces. China had repeatedly requested the return of Macao, and after lengthy negotiations, agreement was reached with Portugal on April 13, 1987. The terms signed provided for a return of Macao to Chinese rule on December 20, 1999. Local autonomy is to be preserved, together with a free market economy, for 50 years after the change in control. The plan resembles that for the return of Hong Kong to China in 1997 (see below, *sub* Leased Territories).

INVOLUNTARY CESSION BY CONQUEST    Involuntary cession has been accomplished most commonly through military conquest. A country defeated in war is subjugated; that is, its government and armed forces cease to exist, and its territory is occupied by the victorious enemy, who then achieves legal title to the territory of the defeated state by annexation. Or portions of enemy territory are occupied and then retained as part of the occupant's territory without the formal confirmation of annexation in any peace treaty. Title in the latter case is based on abandonment by the former owners. This practice disappeared during the nineteenth century but was revived once more when Turkey "abandoned" two provinces in 1912 (Tripoli and Cyrenaica) and Italy subsequently annexed them. The peace treaty ending the Italo-Turkish War (Treaty of Lausanne, October 18, 1912) did not mention the cession of either province to Italy.

Subjugation reappeared during the twentieth century with the annexation of Ethiopia after conquest by Italy (1936), with the conquest and annexation of Poland by the Soviet Union and Germany, and with the Allied subjugation (not followed, however, by the usual step of annexation) of Germany by the Western Allies and Soviet Union in May 1945.

Involuntary cession of territory through subjugation followed by annexation, whether by wartime "abandonment" or peace treaty, had always been regarded as conveying a lawful title to the new holders of the areas involved. The establishment of the League of Nations, followed by the Kellogg-Briand Treaty (Pact of Paris) of 1928, appeared to have changed the traditional pattern and to have eliminated conquest as a source of valid title to territory.

Article 10 of the League of Nations Covenant, it has been asserted, implied an obligation of member states to deny recognition of the seizure of territories from other members. It does not appear to have had similar implications relating to territorial losses suffered by nonmembers, nor was the article interpreted meaningfully (as related to nonrecognition of title to territory) in practice when the Assembly decided, in December 1939, to expel the Soviet Union for its aggression against Finland. Previous instances of forceful acquisition of territory (Manchuria, Ethiopia, Austria, Czechoslovakia, Albania, and all portions of Poland) all failed to secure implementation of Article 10.

Neither the Covenant of the League nor the Pact of Paris contained express provisions obligating states to deny recognition of the results of "unlawful acts of conquest." In view of this lack of specificity, it was asserted by some writers as well as by the Permanent Court of International Justice that denial of title by conquest *ought* to take place but did *not have* to take place.[10] The Japanese seizure of Manchuria in 1931–1932, however, led the American Secretary of State, Henry Stimson, to issue a series of pronouncements (subsequently endorsed by the Assembly of the League) denying the validity of the acquisition of territory by the use of force. The Latin American states in particular strongly condemned the conquest as a lawful means of territorial aggrandizement, especially after the outbreak of the Chaco War between Bolivia and Paraguay, and again at the Inter-American Conferences in 1933, 1936, and 1938, as well as at the Foreign Ministers' Conference in Havana in 1940.[11]

The Stimson doctrine of nonrecognition therefore represents a basic principle of regional inter-American law, but not general international law.

It should be noted, moreover, that individual or multilateral declarations concerning the invalidity of conquest as a source of territorial titles have been more than counterbalanced by the contrary practices of states when viewed on a global basis. In consequence of the numerous annexations carried out in the decades between the end of World War I and the founding of the United Nations, it must be concluded that the Covenant, the Pact of Paris, and the Inter-American declarations all failed to create a new and generally applicable principle of international law with respect to cession by conquest.

[10]See Gerson, "Trustee-Occupant: The Legal Status of Israel's Presence in the West Bank," 14 *Harvard Int'l Law Jl.* 1 at 5 (1973), and the *P.C.I.J.* cases cited there.

[11]See Wright, "The Legal Foundations of the Stimson Doctrine," 8 *Pacific Affairs* 439 (1935); see Whiteman, vol. 2, 1145, 1157, on the Stimson doctrine and its status in regional Western Hemisphere law; and see the specific coverage of the doctrine, *id.*, vol. 5, 8/4.

The coming into force of the United Nations Charter ended, in this writer's opinion, the legality of the acquisition of title to territory through conquest. The relevant provisions of the instrument (especially Art. 2, par. 4) make it abundantly clear that, from a *legal* point of view, the threat of or the use of force, in violation of obligations assumed under the charter, to obtain territory from another state is clearly prohibited to all member states of the organization. [12] But, as has been pointed out, those same members have acquiesced on several occasions in the forcible seizure of territory by one of their number or by a nonmember, and by tacit acceptance or mere mild protest, they have created situations in which the continued possession of seized territory ended in a valid title of the possessor. Examples include the aggression committed by India against the state of Hyderabad and, in 1961, against the Portuguese enclaves in India; the repeated refusal of the Soviet Union to return a part of the Kurile Islands seized from Japan at the end of World War II;[13] and the seizure of East Timor by Indonesia in 1975. East Timor was a Portuguese colony until Portugal, then in the midst of political upheavals, gave up its sovereignty over the area in August 1975. On December 7 of that year, shortly after the local group called Fretilin proclaimed the independence of East Timor, Indonesian troops invaded the region, and Indonesia annexed East Timor early in 1976. Since then a struggle between Indonesian forces and a determined group of rebels continued until, in March 1983, an informal cease-fire began, only to break down in August of the same year. The U.S. Department of State has estimated that between five and six hundred guerillas are still operating in East Timor. Beginning in early 1984 the United States, Australia, and the Vatican have put diplomatic pressure on Indonesia, primarily out of concern about human rights violations since the start of the Indonesian invasion and annexation of East Timor in November 1975. The Vatican interest was demonstrated by a papal visit in October 1989 and was based, at least in part, on the fact

---

[12]See also Lauterpacht's *Oppenheim,* vol. 1, 574, on this point; Lauterpacht stressed (574, n. 4) that this interpretation represented a personal opinion, as is also true for the present writer. Consult the thoughtful analysis by Schwebel, "What Weight to Conquest?" 64 *AJIL* 344 (1970).

[13]Contrary to media claims, the Kurile archipelago *per se* has not been at issue at all, having been ceded by Japan to the Soviet Union at the end of World War II. What has been in dispute are the four "Northern Islands" lying between the Kuriles and the northernmost Japanese island, Hokkaido. The Soviet Union has consistently maintained that the four are a part of the Kuriles; Japan (and many geologists) have asserted the contrary view. The Soviet Union offered to return two of the islands after a Russo-Japanese peace treaty had been signed; Japan demands the return of all four islands in question before signing a peace treaty. See also 55 *AJIL* 153 (1961), and Sneider, "Moscow Seeks Foreign Investment in Kuriles," *CSM,* Sept. 12, 1989, 5. See also the detailed commentary on the dispute by Myers, 55 *AJIL* 153 (1961); the text of the relevant Yalta Agreement is reproduced, with commentary, in Briggs, "The Leaders' Agreement of Yalta," 40 *AJIL* 376 (1946), with vigorous criticism of the legal weaknesses in the instrument. See also *NYT,* October 11, 1973, 3; October 23, 1973, 2; January 31, 1979, A-6; and May 16, 1979, A-3; *Time,* October 22, 1973, 58.

that Roman Catholics, comprising only 2.5 percent of Indonesia's population of 187,000 million, are most heavily concentrated in East Timor (600,000 out of the East Timor's population of 650,000). Other foreign concerns have centered on the mass killings reported since 1975 (60–100,000 slain out of East Timor's population) and numerous reported human rights violations. It has been asserted that intermittent Portuguese-Indonesian negotiations about East Timor have taken place at UN headquarters since 1983 under the guidance of the Secretary-General, but that no progress has been achieved. It has also been claimed that the United Nations continues to recognize a residual Portuguese claim to East Timor.[14]

Two annexations by Israel have not only caused much criticism of that state but are replete with interesting legal implications:

*The Case of East Jerusalem.* During the hostilities of 1948 and 1949, Jordan assumed control over East Jerusalem, and Israel absorbed West Jerusalem. In 1950 Jordan annexed East Jerusalem, together with "eastern Palestine," that is, the West Bank. In 1967, Israel occupied the Eastern part of the city during the Six-Day War; the seizure claimed to be on the right of self-defense. The correctness of that assumption depends, of course, on whether the start of the 1967 conflict represented a legitimate resort to self-defense, such as has been claimed for preemptive or, as some have referred to them, anticipatory strikes. (See also Chapter 23.) On June 28, 1967, the Knesset (Israel's parliament) passed a law annexing East Jerusalem, and soon afterward measures such as the following were taken in that part of the city: (1) abrogation of the Arab Municipal Council; (2) elimination of certain municipal services and the amalgamation of others with their Israeli counterparts; (3) application of all Israeli laws to the Arab inhabitants; (4) transfer of all Arab public schools to the authority of the Israel Ministry of Education, which then led to the use of Israeli curricula; (5) issuance of Israeli identification cards to all inhabitants; (6) nonrecognition of the Jerusalem Islamic courts; (7) closure of Arab banks and exclusive use of Israeli currency; and (8) physical transfer to East Jerusalem of a number of Israeli ministries and government departments. In the meantime, beginning in July 1967, the UN Security Council passed numerous resolutions concerning Israel's annexation, with all of them stressing that acquisition of territory by military conquest was inadmissible.[15]

Finally, on July 30, 1980, the Knesset enacted a law declaring that "complete and united Jerusalem is the capital of Israel,"[16] thus formalizing for a second time the annexation of East Jerusalem. At the time, 10 Latin American countries and the Netherlands had their embassies in East Jerusalem, other countries having located their diplomatic missions in Tel Aviv. Soon after the passage of the July 30 law, Venezuela, Uruguay, Chile, Ecuador,

---

[14]See *CSM*, August 21, 1986, 12, and Oct. 11, 1989, 4.
[15]Such as Resolution 298 (1971), September 25, 1971, in 10 *ILM* 1294 (1971).
[16]*NYT*, July 31, 1980, A-1.

and the Netherlands moved their embassies to Tel Aviv, after the Security Council had adopted its Resolution 478 (April 19, 1980) by a vote of 14–0, with the United States abstaining. That resolution called on countries with embassies in Jerusalem to remove them. Other Latin American countries at once began considering such a move, besides the ones listed above.[17] The present writer believes that ultimately only the embassies of Costa Rica and El Salvador remained in Jerusalem.

Israel's annexation of East Jerusalem not only violated the principle of lack of title through conquest, but also was in conflict with a number of provisions of the international humanitarian law of war. The major reason for nonrecognition of the claim to sovereignty over East Jerusalem is that jurisdiction *de facto* was acquired through the use of force. Resolutions of the UN Security Council [Res. 242 (1967), 252 (1968), 267 (1971), 476 (1980)] repeatedly reaffirmed that the acquisition of territory by force was inadmissible and in violation of international law. They also drew no distinction between territory acquired by the *lawful* use of force and the *unlawful* use of force.[18] The United Nations therefore refused to accept the Israeli argument that territory was lawfully acquired as the result of action taken in lawful self-defense. The latter *per se* only permits states to repel an armed attack—it does *not* legitimize the acquisition of territory.[19]

Similarly rejected must be the argument that Israel could exercise lawful sovereignty over East Jerusalem because its action taken in self-defense was better founded than Jordan's control over the city, acquired by aggressive war in 1948.[20]

The administrative measures undertaken by Israel in East Jerusalem in consequence of "annexation" violate provisions of the Fourth Geneva Convention Relative to the Protection of Civilian Persons in Time of War (1949), such as Articles 47, 50, 54, 64, and others, because under applicable international law East Jerusalem remained occupied belligerent territory, no matter what Israel called it. Both Jordan and Israel are parties to the 1949 Fourth Geneva Convention.

Lack of title to territory through conquest alone also was for some time a rule of customary international law, as well as a rule of conventional law since

[17]See Crane, "Middle East: Status of Jerusalem," 71 *Harvard Int'l Law Jl.* 784 (1980).

[18]The refusal to draw that distinction was fully in line with the Declaration on Principles of International Law Concerning Friendly Relations and Co-operation among States in Accordance with the Charter of the United Nations (General Assembly, 1970, Res. 2625-XXV); see also Bowett, "International Law Relating to Occupied Territory: A Rejoinder," 87 *Law Quart. R.* 473 (1971), and Whiteman, vol. 10, 548.

[19]See Jennings, *The Acquisition of Territory in International Law* (1963) at 55; Cassese, "Legal Considerations on the International Status of Jerusalem," 3 *Palestinian Yrbk of Int. Law* (1986), 14, esp. at 23, 26. See also Stone, *Israel and Palestine—Assault on the Law of Nations* (1981), at 51–53, and Shapira, "The Six-Day War and the Right of Self-Defense," 6 *Israel Law R.* 65 (1971).

[20]See Schwebel, "What Weight to Conquest?" 64 *AJIL* 344 (1970); Blum, "The Missing Reversioner: Reflections on the Status of Judea and Samaria," 3 *Israel Law R.* 279 (1968).

1949 through the law-making treaty cited. It was affirmed clearly in the case of *United States* v. *Alstotter et al.*[21]: "The so-called annexed territories in Poland were in reality nothing more than territory under belligerent occupation of the military forces of Germany."

Also, as Crane pointed out, under international law two criteria are needed to establish sovereignty over a territory: a demonstration of the intention and will to act as the sovereign power and an exercise of actual sovereign rights over the area in question (*The Legal Status of Eastern Greenland* [1933], *P.C.I.J.*, Series A/B, No. 53.). However, that rule is qualified by the old maxim that the law will not recognize a wrong (*ex injuria jus non oritur*). And if the area is an inhabited one, the acquisition of valid sovereignty requires that the state in question have a demonstrably stronger claim to the territory than has any other claimant state.[22]

In consequence of Security Council Resolution 478 (*supra*), all states concerned eventually moved their embassies from Jerusalem to Tel Aviv. But Costa Rica, followed in April 1984 by El Salvador, shifted its embassy back to Israel's capital. These reversals of the previous exodus prompted Egypt to break diplomatic relations with both countries as a gesture of protest (April 21, 1984). The Egyptian decision followed a call for such a break by all Muslim states, issued by the Islamic Conference Organization at a meeting in Fez, Morocco.

*The Case of the Golan Heights.* The annexation of East Jerusalem by Israel was followed in 1981 by the annexation, in violation of international law, of Syria's Golan Heights. The Golan area, lying outside the former Palestine Mandate, had been an integral part of Syria since the latter's founding. Israel had seized the strategic Heights (1967) from which Syria had intermittently shelled Israeli settlements. Subsequently, in accordance with a military disengagement agreement, Israel had consented to hand back about one-third of the Heights, including the town of Quneitra. But two weeks before the withdrawal had been completed (1974), the Israeli forces destroyed the remainder of the town with dynamite (the inhabitants had all fled at the outset of the 1967 war). Syria preserved surviving ruins as a monument and continued until now to demand a return of all seized Golan territory. In the time since 1967, several score Israeli settlements have been created in the area that is shared with some 1,000 ethnic Druzes who stayed in 1967.[23]

On December 12, 1981, the Knesset approved the Golan Heights Law—5742/1981.[24] The key paragraph read simply: "1. The law, jurisdiction and

---

[21]U.S. Military Court, Nuremberg, 1947, in 6 *UN War Crimes Commission Reports* 1, 92. See also Mallinson and Mallinson, "Moving U.S. Embassy: What's the Law?" *CSM*, June 1, 1984, 14; the commentary by Schwarzenberger, "The Law of Belligerent Occupation: Basic Issues," 30 *Nordisk Tidsskrift for Inter. Ret* (1960), 10 at 12–18 (1960); and Land Warfare, 140.

[22]Crane, *op. cit. supra* n. 17, at 788 n. 29.

[23]See Moffett in *CSM*, Feb. 3, 1989, 4.

[24]Text with map in 21 *ILM* 163 (1982).

administration of the State shall apply to the Golan Heights, as described in the appendix." It should be noted that "annexation" was not used in the wording of the law, possibly because the drafters did not want to use annexation in its legal meaning, for that would have appeared to require the incorporation of a part of a country to be accompanied by some agreement between the two parties involved—and in the cases of East Jerusalem and the Golan Heights, there was no such an agreement. The December 12 law was preceded and followed by protests by many countries. The United States and Egypt asserted that Israel's action violated the 1979 Camp David accords as well as international law. The French foreign minister charged that the annexation violated the provisions of the 1907 Convention on the Laws and Customs of War on Land (Hague IV), Articles 43 and 56, which demanded respect for local law in occupied territory. Syria drafted a resolution for the Security Council to declare the annexation "null and void" and called on Israel to reverse its action. (The General Assembly had already voted on December 17, 1981, to adopt a similar resolution, 121–2, with the United States and Israel voting against it.) The next day, however, the Security Council unanimously adopted Resolution 497 (1981), the "Syrian Resolution."[25] And on December 18 the United States suspended implementation of a new strategic cooperation agreement with Israel. On the other hand, the United States then vetoed (January 20, 1982) a Security Council resolution sponsored by Syria and calling for voluntary sanctions against Israel by members of the United Nations. On June 12, 1984, the Prime Minister of Israel, Yitzhak Shamir, declared during a cornerstone laying in a West Bank settlement: "We now are in the same state. Israel extends up to the Jordan River."[26]

Returning once more to the validity, or lack thereof, of title by conquest, it should be remembered that several writers have pointed out an interesting and paradoxical aspect of conquest as related to the Charter of the United Nations. Although individual recognition of the fruits of aggression appears to be forbidden by the Charter, the United Nations as an organization may, or so it appears, itself accept a situation that it considers beneficial, even if that situation had an illegal origin. This has been true, one must assume, in the case of Israel, which in 1948 occupied by military force territory considerably in excess of the areas allocated to it by the United Nations resolution adopted in 1947. Similarly, the United Nations suffered without effective action the partitions of both Kashmir and Korea, even though a policy of unification by plebiscite had been formulated.

On the other hand, numerous American court decisions reflect the conviction held by the United States government that conquest alone does not

---

[25] Text in 21 *ILM* 214 (1982); see also *Time*, December 28, 1981, 54–55, for an analysis of the Golan Heights annexation.
[26] AP Dispatch, June 12, 1984.

confer valid title. Thus, in *Brunell* v. *United States*,[27] the court held that Brunell, an entertainer injured in an army vehicle while touring the island of Saipan, could not bring suit against the United States under the Federal Tort Claims Act, which excludes any claims arising in a foreign country. The court cited a letter from the Legal Adviser of the Department of State to the Attorney General of the United States, which stated that the island was an area under military occupation by forces of the United States but was not American territory because no treaty of cession covering the island had been concluded with Japan nor had Congress enacted any legislation incorporating the island into the United States.

A minor but irritating dispute concerning title to territory was settled in 1989: the Egypt–Israel contention over Taba. That area comprises a one-half square mile beach on the Gulf of Aqaba, containing a luxury hotel, a holiday village, and a few service buildings. Taba had been under Egyptian sovereignty until it was captured by Israel in 1967. The latter refused to relinquish control when it evacuated the rest of the Sinai in accordance with the 1979 peace treaty, claiming that Taba had been part of the former British Palestine Mandate.

After a post-1979 re-demarcation of the border between the disputants, disagreement persisted about nearly 100 "boundary pillars." After repeated negotiation sessions, the two parties ultimately agreed to submit their differences to arbitration. The agreed-upon five-member arbitration tribunal made its award on September 29, 1988, in favor of the Egyptian claim.[28]

On February 26, 1989, the two parties agreed that the Taba beach was to be returned to Egypt by March 15 of that year. The delay since the date of the award had been caused by the need for intricate negotiations concerning access by Israeli tourists, compensation for the hotel and holiday village, etc. Egypt agreed to purchase the Sonesta Hotel for $37 million and the village for $1.5 million. On March 14, 1989, Egypt assumed sovereignty (and control) over Taba.

## POLAR REGIONS

National claims to areas in the Arctic and Antarctic regions did not raise any considerable international problems until a few decades ago. Careful exploration beginning in the nineteenth century was followed in many instances by claims based exclusively on discovery, but because of an assumed lack of resources and difficulties in travel and transport, no crises developed from these asserted rights.

---

[27] U.S. Dist. Court S.D. of N.Y., 1948, 77 F. Supp. 68.
[28] Text and content summary in 27 *ILM* 1421 (1988) summary in 83 *AJIL* 590 (1989); text of the *Arbitration Compromise* of Sept. 11, 1986, in 26 *ILM* 1 (1987). See also *CSM*, June 8, 1988, 11, and Sept. 30, 1988, 11, and final agreements in 28 *ILM* 611 (1989).

Only the coming of the long-distance aircraft and the belief that sizable deposits of valuable minerals and coal might be found under the Antarctic ice have caused a sudden interest in polar claims.

## Arctic Claims

Exploration had determined the absence of land near the North Pole, and claims on subsurface ocean resources could at best be based on the somewhat vague claim of contiguity, that is, on an extension of some part of the continental tableland. Occupation took form only in the shape of numerous weather stations and air bases, particularly during and after World War II.

ARCTIC SECTOR THEORY    Existing territorial claims in the Arctic were based on discovery, occupation, and especially on a variation of the doctrine of contiguity, expressed more fortuitously as the Arctic Sector Theory. A state whose territory lies close to the Arctic claims all land to be found between a line extending from its eastern extremity to the North Pole and another line extending from its western extremity to the pole. The Russian government, originally relying on the older version of the doctrine—extensions of the continental tableland under the ocean surface—switched to the sector theory in 1926. Other northern nations have also adopted the sector theory (United States, Canada, Denmark, Norway).[29] This writer does not know whether the Danish claim has been reduced by the emergence of an Icelandic sector following the separation of Iceland from Denmark in 1944 but believes that such has been the case. Within the sector claimed by the Soviet Union lie Nansen Land, claimed by Norway, and Wrangel Island, whose sovereignty has repeatedly been asserted by the United States.

It is doubtful that the "sector theory" represents a rule of international law.[30] It should probably be characterized as an accommodation device elaborated by the states concerned.

The Arctic regions emerged briefly into the limelight in 1970 when Canada claimed jurisdiction over all *waters* within 100 miles of its northern coast, for the admittedly limited purpose of preventing pollution of the Arctic.[31]

The question of Canadian Arctic jurisdiction was not involved in two agreements reached by the United States and Canada after two years of negotiations: an Agreement on Arctic Cooperation (January 11, 1988) and

[29]See *Life,* January 20, 1947, 55–62, for an instructive survey of the polar regions, especially note the map on 55 delineating the various national sectors claimed; Whiteman, vol. 2, p. 1267.
[30]See also Svarlien, *The Eastern Greenland Case in Historical Perspective* (1964), on this point.
[31]Consult Henkin, "Arctic Anti-Pollution: Does Canada Make—Or Break—International Law?" 65 *AJIL* 131 (1971). See *NYT,* August 31, 1969, 23; Sept. 14, 1969, 26; Feb. 22, 1970, 7. The United States has rejected the validity of Canada's extension of its Arctic jurisdiction.

an exchange of Notes Concerning Transit of the Northwest Passage (October 10, 1988).[32]

## Antarctic Claims

The existence of a landmass in the Antarctic prompted a development of territorial claims quite unlike that experienced in the Arctic regions. Numerous and conflicting claims have been set forth over the decades by the United Kingdom, Argentina, Norway, Australia, New Zealand, France, and Chile. Most of these claims were based exclusively on discovery, but in the Palmer Peninsula region, a degree of permanent settlement has been achieved through bases maintained by Great Britain, Argentina, and Chile over a number of years.[33]

The United States has not asserted any official claims to territory in the Antarctic. This policy, first enunciated by Secretary of State Hughes in 1924, is based on the theory that no claims in Antarctica could be recognized until discovery had been followed by effective occupation or control, including settlement as well as development. This abstention from the announcement of definite territorial claims has not always met with the unqualified support of every element in the United States. As Hanessian pointed out,[34] the 1950s saw the introduction of a number of resolutions in Congress declaring United States sovereignty over specified portions of Antarctica. None of these proposed declarations passed, however, and as yet no formal United States claims have been communicated to other states.

By contrast, other countries have not only asserted such claims but in several instances have also recognized one another's claims as valid. Thus, in 1927 when France laid claim to Adélie Land and certain islands near Antarctica, placing them under the administration of the governor-general of Madagascar, Great Britain specifically recognized those claims at the time it asserted the sovereignty over the large sector assigned to Australia.[35]

On the other hand, overlapping territorial claims have at times caused considerable bitterness between rival claimants, leading even to firing by competing national groups on one another. The Chilean claim, based on the sector theory, overlaps a British claim and almost half of the Argentine claim. The latter, in turn, covers most of the Chilean-claimed areas as well as most of the British sphere, called the Falkland Island Dependencies, including a substantial portion of the Antarctic continent itself. French Adélie Land is

[32] Texts and content summary in 28 *ILM* 141 (1989).

[33] Hanessian, "Antarctica: Current National Interests and Legal Realities," *Proceedings* (1958), 145, at 161; see also Hayton, "The 'American' Antarctic," 50 *AJIL* (1956), 583; Lt. Cmdr. and Mrs. Fiske, "Territorial Claims in the Antarctic," 85 *U.S. Naval Institute Proceedings* 82 (1959); see also the extensive bibliography in Bishop, 356, n. 18; and consult Whiteman, vol. 2, 1232–67. A map of the claims may be found in *Time,* Feb. 22, 1982, 65, and in *CSM,* Jan. 18, 1983, 12–13.

[34] Hanessian, *op. cit.,* 161–62.

[35] See especially Hayton, *op. cit. supra,* n. 33, 584, for the bases of national claims.

inserted between the two portions of the British (Australian) claim on Wilkes Land, and so on. Despite these confusing claims and counterclaims, the sector theory generally applies to the Antarctic as it does to the Arctic. But in the cases of Argentina, Australia, Great Britain, and Chile, claims have been advanced to a greater area than that bounded by the projection of the outer limits of mainland domains adjacent to the Antarctic. The application of the sector theory to the Antarctic should be regarded, moreover, primarily as a method of asserting territorial claims and not as conferring a "right" of acquisition or sovereignty in lieu of continuous settlement. The necessary proof, for a lawful title, must remain, under existing international law, the power and the disposition on the part of a claimant to maintain control of Antarctic areas by continuous settlement. As the Norwegian government correctly stated in 1929 in reference to Roald Amundsen's "acquisition" of Antarctic territory in the name of the king of Norway, "the said discovery and annexation constitute a valid basis for a claim of priority to acquire such territories whenever the requirements of international law as to effective occupation of a new territory shall have been fulfilled."[36]

ANTARCTIC TREATY   On May 2, 1958, the United States invited eleven other nations to a conference on Antarctica; the meeting was held in Washington from October 15 to December 1, 1959. The participating countries in addition to the United States were Argentina, Australia, Belgium, Chile, France, Japan, New Zealand, Norway, South Africa, the Soviet Union, and the United Kingdom. At the conclusion of the conference, the Antarctic Treaty was signed by the delegates of all participating states. The instrument entered into force on June 23, 1961.[37] Poland, West Germany, Brazil, China, Uruguay, and also India subsequently became additional "consultative members" (voting members) of the Antarctic Treaty. Adhering to the instrument but lacking voting privileges are the "acceding" members: Austria, Papua-New Guinea (as a successor state), Bulgaria, Czechoslovakia, Denmark, East Germany, Finland, Hungary, Italy, the Netherlands, Rumania, Spain, Sweden, Cuba, Peru, Finland, Ecuador, Greece, South Korea, and North Korea.

The treaty provided that Antarctica was to be used exclusively for peaceful purposes: no military bases were to be established there, and no military maneuvers or the testing of any type of weapons were to be carried out, but military personnel and equipment could be used for scientific research. Other provisions of the instrument called for the free exchange of information regarding plans for scientific programs in Antarctica, for an exchange of

---

[36] Hackworth, vol. 1, 453–54.

[37] See *The Conference on Antarctica* (Department of State Publication 7060) (1960); texts of the final act and of the treaty may also be found in 54 *AJIL* 476 (1960 Supp.); and the text of the treaty alone in 19 *ILM* 860 (1980). Consult also the monographic study of Hanessian, "The Antarctic Treaty 1959," 9 *Int. and Comp. Law Quart.* 436 (1960); Hayton, "The Antarctic Settlement of 1959," 54 *AJIL* 348 (1960); and see especially Auburn, *Antarctic Law and Politics* (1982).

scientific personnel, and for an unhindered sharing in scientific observations made in Antarctica. All nuclear tests in the region and the disposal of radioactive waste materials there were prohibited unless, with reference to such disposal, subsequent treaties were concluded. In the latter case, such treaties should also apply to Antarctica.

Each contracting party was given the right to appoint observers to carry out inspections under Articles VII and IX of the treaty. These provided for complete freedom of inspection in all parts of Antarctica, of all installations and equipment, as well as of ships and aircraft at points of discharge of both cargoes and personnel in the region. Aerial observation was permitted at any time over any or all of Antarctica.

Disputes between contracting parties concerning the interpretation or application of the Antarctic Treaty were to be settled by peaceful means of their choice. If such disputes could not be resolved by normal methods, provision was made for submission to the International Court of Justice for settlement.

On the other hand, the agreement contained a specific statement to the effect that it could not be interpreted as a renunciation, by any contracting party, of previously asserted rights or claims to territorial sovereignty in Antarctica or as prejudicing the positions of any such party in regard to its recognition or nonrecognition of any other state's rights of, or claims or bases of claims to, territorial sovereignty in Antarctica. No activities taking place while the Antarctic Treaty was in force were to constitute a basis for asserting, supporting, or denying a claim to sovereignty in the regions in question or to create there any rights of sovereignty. No new claim, or enlargement of any existing claim, to territorial sovereignty in Antarctica was to be asserted while the treaty was in effect.

The entire system established by the treaty was to be subject to review after thirty years (1989) by a conference of all the parties to the agreement. And after 1991, any full (voting) member of the treaty can propose revisions of it.

Annual meetings among the 16 consultative parties to the treaty have dealt with a variety of Antarctic problems.

For example, a ban on sealing was established in 1972, coming at a time when commercial sealing had almost ended. In 1980 the Convention on the Conservation of Antarctic Marine Living Resources was adopted by a conference held at Canberra.[38] In June 1982, in Wellington, New Zealand, and again in July 1982 in Bonn, conferences of the 16 voting members of the Antarctic Treaty, plus the acceding members, worked on the preliminary stages of a "minerals regime," a legal framework for mineral exploitation in the Antarctic. The project proceeded slowly, however, and by December 1983 the UN General Assembly had adopted by consensus a

[38]Text of Final Act and of Convention in 19 *ILM* 837 (1980); see also the brief commentary by Stone in 22 *Harvard Int'l Law Jl.* 195 (1981).

resolution that requested the Secretary-General to prepare a "comprehensive, factual, and objective study of the Antarctic Treaty and other relevant factors." The passage of that resolution indicated the degree of dissatisfaction felt in many (especially Third World) countries with the alleged secretiveness of the voting members of the Antarctic Treaty, in holding closed sessions and providing only scant information about their decisions. There was also a question about the applicability of the 1982 Law of the Sea Convention to the oil and mineral (and gas) resources of the Antarctic, should such resources be found to exist and to be exploitable.[39]

Beginning in 1982, a number of multilateral negotiating sessions aimed at creating an orderly administration of the exploration and exploitation of Antarctic minerals were held by the Consultative Members group of the Antarctic Treaty. As Joyner pointed out in his investigation of the matter,[40] those preliminary sessions attracted wide attention because of disagreements within the United Nations as to whether Antarctica represented a part of the "common heritage of mankind."[41] If such was held to be true, then Antarctica's resources would belong, at least in theory, to all mankind. (See also *infra, sub* Moon Treaty, *re* the heritage concept.)

Potential resources of Antarctica include oil and gas, coal, as well as a considerable variety of metals.[42]

The Antarctic Treaty Consultative Party group (ATCPs) had considered the subject of mineral resources exploitation at several meetings since 1970. Ultimately a treaty, the Convention on the Regulation of Antarctic Mineral Resources Activities, was adopted at a special meeting of the ATCPs on June 2, 1988.[43] Representatives of the 13 Contracting Parties to the Antarctic Treaty that were not Consultative Parties participated by invitation in the discussions during the special meeting.

The convention calls for the establishment of a formal regime for Antarctic mineral exploration and exploitation under an Antarctic Mineral Resources Commission (Arts. 18–22), which is to hold its first meeting within six months after the treaty enters into force. The functions of the Commission are to include, among others, the power to designate areas in which resource

[39]See *CSM* Dec. 2, 1983, 15; Nov. 19, 1984, 21–23; Dec. 17, 1984, 17; Parfit, "Nations Are Debating the Future of the Antarctic's Frozen Assets," *Smithsonian,* November 1984, 46–59; and the excellent account by Wiznitzer, "Who Owns Antarctica?", *CSM,* Feb. 14, 1985, 16–17. See also Joyner (ed.), *The Antarctic Legal Regime* (1988); Bush, *Antarctica and International Law: A Collection of Inter-state and National Documents* (3 vols., 1982 and 1988); and Peterson, *Managing the Frozen South: The Creation and Evolution of the Antarctic Treaty System* (1988).

[40]Joyner, "The Antarctic Minerals Negotiating Process," 81 *AJIL* 888 (1987).

[41]Joyner, "Legal Implications of the Common Heritage of Mankind," 35 *Int'l & Comp. L. Q.* 190 (1986); Joyner and Theis, "The United States and Antarctica: Rethinking the Interplay of Law and Interest," 20 *Cornell Int'l L.J.* 65, 93 (1987).

[42]See the map of suspected resources in *Time,* June 20, 1988, 38.

[43]Text of Final Act, of the Convention, and a content-summary, in 27 *ILM* 859 (1988).

activities are prohibited or restricted, to adopt measures to protect the environment and to regulate measures relating to prospecting for resources. Also included are provisions for an Advisory Committee to the Commission (Arts. 25–27).

The convention also provides for the creation of a Mineral Resources Regulatory Committee for each area identified by the Commission as acceptable for resource development and exploitation (Arts. 29–32), and for the establishment of a permanent Secretariat.[44]

The operating rules laid down in the convention are very definite: all 20 ACTPs must agree to open an area for exploration/exploitation; specific requests for mineral development must then be approved by a 10-country regulatory committee; if accidents harmful to the environment do take place, the mining operator is liable for all costs to return the area involved to pre-accident conditions.

Soon afterward, doubts about the wisdom of the 1988 Convention surfaced. In order to enter into force, the instrument must be ratified by all seven countries with Antarctic territorial claims. By early 1990, five (Great Britain, Argentina, Chile, Norway, and New Zealand) had approved the convention, but then Australia and France refused to do so, raising the prospect of renegotiation. The objections centered primarily on environmental conservation questions.[45]

## LEASED TERRITORIES

Leases of territory, regardless of the length of time specified in the relevant agreements, do not confer title or create changes in sovereignty. Thus the major Chinese leases of Port Arthur and Dalny to Russia; Kiao-chao to Germany; Wei-hai-wei, Tientsin, and the so-called New Territories on the mainland opposite the island of Hong Kong to Great Britain; and Kwang-chao-wan to France—none transferred legal title to the areas involved from the lessor to the lessee.[46] The same doctrine applied to the former lease of the Canal Zone granted by Panama to the United States.

All of the above leases, except the one affecting Hong Kong, have been canceled. The one exception, however, has recently become the subject of intense negotiation and speculation. What is called the British Crown Colony of Hong Kong consists of three separate parts: Hong Kong island itself, containing the core of the metropolis, was ceded by China in perpetuity following the Opium War of 1841; the tip of the Kowloon Peninsula, ceded

---

[44]See also the valuable accounts in *Time*, Oct. 24, 1988, 64–65; *CSM*, June 7, 1988, 9–10; and *U.S. News & World Report*, Oct. 24, 1988, 64–66.

[45]See *Time*, May 24, 1989, 4; Jan. 15, 1990, 56–62; Feb. 7, 1990, 19.

[46]See *In re Ning Yi-Ching and Others*, Great Britain, Vacation Court, Aug. 23, 1939, 56 *Times L.R.*, No. 1, 3, reprinted in 34 *AJIL* 347 (1940). On leased territories in general, consult Whiteman, vol. 2, 1216.

similarly in 1860, following an Anglo-French intervention in China; and the "New Territories" (comprising more than 90 percent of the total territory) were leased in 1898 rent-free from China for a period of 99 years. All experts agree that Hong Kong would not be economically viable without the New Territories.

July 1982 saw the opening round of Sino-British negotiations on the future of Hong Kong after 1997. In the same year, Article 31 was inserted into the Chinese constitution. This article permits the crown colony, once sovereignty has been transferred to China, to change into a "special administrative zone." As such, Hong Kong will remain a free port and retain its own currency, local Chinese will run the administration and courts as well as issue Hong Kong's own passports and visas. In view of the nonviability of the ceded parts (after 1997) and the Chinese emphasis on a return of a sovereignty over all portions of Hong Kong obtained through "unequal treaties," all three parts of the colony will fall under Chinese sovereignty in 1997.

On May 25, 1984, the Chinese Premier, Deng Xiaoping, stated that China would station a limited number of troops in Hong Kong after the end of British rule. And then, after 23 rounds of talks, a final draft agreement on the transfer of Hong Kong was initialed at Peking on September 26, 1984, providing for the colony to become a Special Administrative Region of the People's Republic on July 1, 1997. The present civil rights of the population as well as other facets of the colony's life, mentioned earlier, are to remain unchanged for fifty years after the transfer. The House of Commons and the House of Lords unanimously approved the agreement in early December, and the treaty was signed in Peking on December 19, 1984, by the British Prime Minister and the Premier of China. The next step leading to the transfer was the Chinese drafting of the Basic Law for the government of the Special Administrative Region.[47]

In February 1989, the Chinese government released the text of a draft Basic Law (constitution) for post-1997 Hong Kong. Immediate protests by concerned Hong Kong citizens centered on three provisions which appeared to violate a British-Chinese declaration made in 1984. That joint statement said that after 1997 Hong Kong would enjoy "independent judicial power, including that of final adjudication," whereas the draft Basic Law asserted that "the power of interpretation . . . shall be vested in the standing committee" of China's parliament (the Chinese National People's Congress), not in the courts of Hong Kong. Again, the city had been promised in 1984 that its "executive authorities shall . . . be accountable to the [H.K.] legislature," but the draft Basic Law granted the chief executive, appointed by China until at least the year 2012, power to dissolve the Hong Kong legislature and to veto bills. Finally, the draft granted the Chinese government

---

[47] See Wesley-Smith, *Unequal Treaty, 1898–1997: China, Great Britain and Hong Kong's New Territories* (1980); the text of the 1984 treaty is found in 23 *ILM* 1366 (1984).

veto power over laws passed by the Hong Kong legislature that were "not in conformity . . . with the relationship between" China and Hong Kong.

A "Final Draft" of the Basic Law by China (January 20, 1990) did not lessen the apprehension felt by many Hong Kong residents about their future under China. Apparently little of importance had been changed between the two versions recorded here. But then China's parliament passed a bill (April 3/4, 1990) that provided for a high level of autonomy for Hong Kong after 1997, except in the fields of defense and foreign affairs. The law also contained the definite assurance that Hong Kong's present capitalist system would remain intact for a period of 50 years after 1997.

After much British and Hong Kong criticism about an alleged limit of British citizenship to Chinese residents of Hong Kong (supposedly limited to less than 10 civil servants), the British Prime Minister proposed that 50,000 selected Hong Kong Chinese, including key officials, and their families would receive British citizenship (and thereby the right to emigrate and live in England) after the 1997 changeover in control in Hong Kong. That proposal, accounting for an estimated total of 225,000 Chinese immigrants, created massive public opposition in England to such an influx of "Asian citizens." France made a commitment to offer up to 1,500 passports to Hong Kong employees of French companies. Sixteen other governments, such as West Germany, Belgium, and Luxembourg, were expected to follow suit.

The legal position of the lessor has never been very strong in any of the instances cited. Transfers of control over a leased territory have been made repeatedly without consultation with or the consent of the nominal territorial sovereign. Thus the Russian leases of Port Arthur and Dalny were assigned to Japan after the Russo-Japanese War of 1904–1905, and the German rights in Kiao-chao were turned over to Japan by the treaty of Versailles without consultation with the Chinese government (in 1922 Japan agreed to the return of Kiao-chao to China).

Authorities and diplomats have agreed that the conclusion of a lease treaty effects only a transfer of jurisdictional rights and does not at all effect an alienation of territory. In other words, sovereign *rights* are exercised by the leasing state, but *title* to the territory remains indisputably with the state granting the lease. This is true even when the lease entails use of the territory as a naval or military base by the leasing state, such as Guantánamo Bay in Cuba, leased but not ceded to the United States.[48]

[48]See Lazar, "International Legal Status of Guantánamo Bay," 62 *AJIL* 730 (1968), and his "'Cession in Lease' of the Guantánamo Bay Naval Station and Cuba's 'Ultimate Sovereignty',", 63 *AJIL* 116 (1969), as well as the critique by Maris, "Guantánamo: No Rights of Occupancy," *id.*, 114. A nominal rent of $3,386.25 was paid annually by the United States until 1960, when the Cuban government refused to accept further payments on the grounds that the base should not be allowed to remain in U.S. hands (*NYT,* Feb. 4, 1964, 14; Aug. 30, 1977, 4). The most recent U.S. offer of rent amounted to $4,085. See also Scheina, "The U.S. Presence in Guantánamo," 4 *Strategic Review* 81 (Spring 1976), and *CSM,* Dec. 3, 1985, 3.

The leases of air and naval bases in Bermuda and Newfoundland obtained by the United States from Great Britain under the executive agreements and other arrangements of 1940–1941 have figured in a number of judicial decisions that, in turn, have given rise to considerable discussion in legal circles.

Thus, in *Vermilya-Brown Co.* v. *Cornell et al.*,[49] the Supreme Court of the United States affirmed a judgment of the Circuit Court of Appeals by holding that for purposes of the Fair Labor Standards Act of 1938, the air base leased in Bermuda was a "possession" of the United States.

Such a decision did not appear to be in accordance with the international legal status of a leased territory, but the majority on the Supreme Court succeeded in distinguishing the *Vermilya-Brown* case from the legal situation presented in 1949 in *United States* v. *Spelar*,[50] when it held that the U.S. air base in Newfoundland, acquired under conditions identical with those in the case of the Bermuda base, was a "foreign country" within the provisions of the Federal Tort Claims Act. The basis of the distinction on which the 1949 decision was based had to do with the language of the claims act, as compared with that of the Labor Standards Act of 1938. It is, however, somewhat difficult to see how leases derived from similar instruments can constitute "possessions" and "foreign countries" at the same time.

The leased territories in existence are the British-controlled New Territories facing Hong Kong, the minor American leases at Guantánamo and Bahia Honda from Cuba and the Great Corn and Little Corn Islands from Nicaragua, and the major American installations in the Philippines. In addition there is a minor American-leased area in Bahrain. The United States also pays to the Republic of the Marshall Islands (see Chapter 4) almost $10 million annually for the lease of 11 Kwajalein atolls as a missile testing range. There exists one subleased territory, the atoll of Diego Suarez in the Indian Ocean, leased by Mauritius to the United Kingdom, which in turn leased it (1966) to the United States for use as a naval base for a period of 50 years.[51]

## SERVITUDES

The otherwise complete sovereignty of a state over the territory under its jurisdiction may be limited or impaired by the existence of a *servitude*, which represents a binding obligation by a given state to permit specified uses to be made of all or parts of its territory by or in favor of another state or

[49]U.S. Supreme Court, 1948, 69 Sup. Ct. 140.
[50]U.S. Supreme Court, 1949, 338 U.S. 217.
[51]On lease renewals in the Philippines, see AP Dispatch, July 27, 1988; on Bahrain, see 87 *U.S. News & World Report,* Nov. 5, 1979, 30 (map on 29); on Diego Suarez, see *Time,* July 14, 1980, 5; on Kwajalein Atolls, see *CSM,* June 8, 1989, 6.

states. A servitude may also include an obligation not to undertake certain acts.[52]

A servitude is tied directly to the territory in question and remains as an obligation, regardless of any change in the form of the government of the state concerned, and it remains intact even when another state takes over. In the latter instance, the successor state assuming sovereign rights over the territory affected by a servitude is bound by that servitude until a different arrangement has been worked out, by treaty or exchange of diplomatic notes, with the state or states benefiting from the servitude as established at the time succession took place.

CLASSIFICATION OF SERVITUDES    Servitudes can be classified in two ways: The most common is a distinction between negative (passive) and affirmative (active) servitudes, depending on whether the state in question agrees to suspend the exercise of one or several of its foreign rights over the territory or whether a foreign sovereign is suffered (permitted) to enter the territory of the state. An example of a negative servitude is the assumption of an obligation not to fortify specified areas of a state's territory or to limit the strength of one's armed forces to a specified total number of effectives. Among affirmative servitudes are fishing rights granted by one state in its coastal waters to the citizens of another state and transit rights to citizens of another state.

A second distinction among servitudes is based on the purpose of the obligation in question. A common separation is between military servitudes and economic servitudes. An example of the former is an obligation to permit the armed forces of another state to traverse one's own territory, to permit the permanent stationing on such territory of armed forces of another state, or to demilitarize certain areas permanently. On the economic side, numerous examples in the spheres of transportation and communications come to mind. In both classifications, modern practice favors the establishment of military over economic servitudes.

The foundation of most kinds of servitudes is found in a bilateral or multilateral treaty, with only a few based on custom or tradition.

METHODS OF TERMINATING SERVITUDES    Servitudes can be terminated in a number of ways. First, and very common, is a treaty by which the beneficiary or beneficiaries of a servitude agree with the burdened state to end the special situation in question. As has already been pointed out, this method would also normally be used to end a servitude assumed with territory in a case of state succession (universal or partial, as the case might be).

A second method for terminating a servitude is a unilateral declaration to that effect issued by the state or states benefiting from the obligation involved, without any participation in such a step by the burdened state

[52]On both general and specific aspects of servitude, consult the most comprehensive treatment available in English, Váli, *Servitudes of International Law: A Study of Rights in Foreign Territory* (2nd ed. 1958). See also Whiteman, vol. 2, 1173, particularly 1183–84, for the text of an internal Department of State memorandum, "State Servitudes Under International Law" (August 11, 1956).

itself. A third method occurs when the benefiting state acquires the obligated state, or vice versa; in either case, an end of the servitude takes place by domestic enactment. Finally, a servitude ends with the physical disappearance of either party to the agreement establishing the servitude.

Among the areas of territorial jurisdiction circumscribed, on occasion, by the existence of servitudes have been, or are, navigation on certain rivers,[53] navigation on oceans, and the flow and diversion of waters.[54]

It is generally accepted that customary international law, now reinforced by Article 14 of the 1958 Convention on the Territorial Sea and the Contiguous Zone, and especially by Articles 17 to 26 of the 1982 UN Convention on the Law of the Sea, imposes a servitude on all states fronting on an ocean: the right of ships of all nations to innocent passage through territorial waters as well as their right to use such waters as a refuge in the case of storms or distress.

This very important servitude is subject to several modifications or limitations. The littoral state is entitled to issue regulations for the protection of navigation and for the enforcement of its domestic legislation in such areas as quarantine and customs, and under certain conditions, it is also entitled to bar innocent passage from specific portions of its waters for security reasons. The servitude may be constricted greatly in time of war, that is, when the littoral state assumes either neutral or belligerent status. This restriction is particularly noticeable as it relates to the passage and activities of belligerent warships in the territorial waters of any state.

RIGHT-OF-WAY SERVITUDES   On rare occasions, special servitudes relating to rights of way for the transit of persons and goods have been granted by treaty to some foreign state on the territory of the state obligated by the servitude. The peace treaties ending World War I created a whole series of right-of-way servitudes, relating particularly to transit across Germany and Austria and also, for the benefit of the latter, across territories formerly a part of the Austro-Hungarian empire and lying between Austria and the Adriatic. The free zones in the German ports of Stettin and Hamburg granted to Czechoslovakia should also be regarded as right-of-way servitudes.

More recently, such a servitude was the core of a case before the International Court of Justice: the *Case Concerning Right of Passage over Indian Territory (Portugal v. India)*.[55] The dispute centered on a claim by Portugal to possess a right of passage for its nationals across Indian territory between

---

[53] See Higgins-Colombus, 166–189, on the international control of rivers.

[54] Consult Hirsch, "Utilization of International Rivers in the Middle East—A Study of Conventional International Law," 50 *AJIL* 81 (1956); see also Bishop, 391, for key excerpts from a Department of State Memorandum dated April 21, 1958, by William L. Griffin, "Legal Aspects of the Use of Systems of International Waters"; and the important summary of key principles in Brierly, 231.

[55] International Court of Justice, *Judgment on Preliminary Objections,* Nov. 26, 1957, *I.C.J. Reports, 1957,* 125, digested in 52 *AJIL* 326 (1958); *Judgment,* April 17, 1960, *I.C.J. Reports, 1960,* 6, digested at length in 54 *AJIL* 673 (1960) and also in Henkin, 56.

the enclaves of Dadra and Nagar-Aveli and between those enclaves and the coastal district of Damão (one of three Portuguese districts in India, the other two being Goa and Din, in addition to the two inland enclaves). The court found that Portugal indeed possessed such a right of passage "to the extent necessary for the exercise of Portuguese sovereignty over the enclaves and subject to the regulation and control of India, in respect of private persons, civil officials and goods in general." On the other hand, according to the court, Portugal did not, in 1954, "have a right of passage in respect of armed forces, armed police, and arms and ammunition." The court also found that India had "not acted contrary to its obligations resulting from Portugal's right of passage in respect of private persons, civil officials, and goods in general."[56]

Most famous of all right-of-way servitudes was that based on a 1903 agreement between the United States and Panama, by which the former was granted a perpetual monopoly to construct a canal across Panamanian territory. The agreement did not take the form of a lease, to be sure, but this technicality had no effect on the legal character of the obligation created for Panama: it was a servitude.

The terminology of the 1903 instrument left much to be desired in regard to the classification of the question of sovereignty over the Canal Zone. The United States was empowered to act as "if it were sovereign" in the zone "in perpetuity" and "to the entire exclusion of the exercise by the Republic of Panama of any such sovereign rights, power or authority." In return for the control in question, the United States promised an immediate payment of $10 million, plus annual rental payments of $25,000 beginning nine years after ratification of the agreement (1904). In the course of time, the payments of "rent" have been increased on several occasions, and since 1955 the compensation to Panama has amounted to $1.9 million per year.

CANALS    When a canal is located within the territory of a state and does not connect two seas or oceans, it is viewed as being under the exclusive jurisdiction of the sovereign in question, and no servitude of innocent passage exists. Normally, too, even when a canal does serve as a connecting link between seas, it is not burdened with a servitude. The state in whose territory the canal is found may offer the use of the canal to the vessels of other states, provided fixed tolls and possibly other service charges are met by the users; but such offers represent purely voluntary action by the sovereign involved (Corinth Canal in Greece, Kiel Canal in Germany until 1919).

*Kiel Canal.* The Treaty of Versailles provided that the Kiel Canal, linking the North Sea with the Baltic, should be open to the vessels (public and

---

[56]See the excellent study of this specialized subject by Krenz, *International Enclaves and Rights of Passage* (1961), and Merani, "The Goa Dispute," 14 *Jl of Public Law* 143 (1965). After India took over the Portuguese enclaves, the remaining example of this territorial paradox are Büsingen and Veronahof, Campione, and Llivia, all in Europe.

private) of all states at peace with Germany, and that complete equality with German nationals, vessels, and cargoes should be granted to the nationals, vessels, and cargoes of such other states.

A test of the nature of this servitude arose in connection with the attempt of the British vessel SS *Wimbledon* to traverse the waterway in 1921:

## THE SS WIMBLEDON
### Permanent Court of International Justice, 1923,
### P.C.I.J., Ser. A, No. 1

FACTS    The SS *Wimbledon,* a British merchant vessel, had been chartered by a French armament firm to carry war materials from France to the port of Danzig. The cargo was destined for the Polish government, then at war with the Russian state. On March 21, 1921, the vessel arrived at the western entrance to the Kiel Canal and was refused access by the German authorities on the grounds that under the terms of its neutrality regulations, Germany could not permit the ship with its cargo to proceed through the canal. To grant such permission would expose Germany to a charge of performing an unneutral service, according to the German statements issued at the time.

The British, French, Italian, and Japanese government filed suit against the German government before the Permanent Court of International Justice, claiming that the German action violated obligations arising from Article 380 of the Treaty of Versailles, the section that had imposed the canal servitude on Germany.

ISSUE    Did a servitude such as applied to the Kiel Canal override domestic neutrality legislation of the state obligated by the existence of the servitude?

DECISION    Decision against Germany. Article 380 of the treaty of Versailles prevented Germany from applying to the canal a neutrality order promulgated by the German government on July 25, 1920. The German government was ordered to compensate the charterers of the vessel for the losses sustained as a result of the German action in barring the vessel from traversing the Kiel Canal.

REASONING    Article 380 of the Treaty of Versailles read: "The Kiel Canal and its approaches shall be maintained free and open to the vessels of commerce and of war of all nations at peace with Germany on terms of entire equality." The terms of the article were clear and categorical. The canal had ceased to be an internal and national navigable waterway, the use of which might have been left to the discretion of the riparian state. Instead, the canal had become an international waterway intended to provide under treaty guarantee easier access to the Baltic for the benefit of all nations of the world. The only condition applicable to any closing of the canal related to the requirement that all vessels permitted to use it had to belong to nations at peace with Germany. The SS *Wimbledon* was owned by English interests and was registered in Great Britain, a country at peace with Germany. The vessel had been chartered by a firm domiciled in France, a country at peace with Germany. Hence the vessel could not be barred from access to the Kiel Canal.

The only limitation permitted under the servitude created by Article 380 related to the right of Germany to defend itself and to bar the use of the canal by enemy vessels.

Germany was perfectly free to declare and regulate its neutrality in the Russo-Polish war, but subject to the condition laid down in Article 380 of the Treaty of Versailles.

The Permanent Court of Justice did not define the provisions of Article 380 as a servitude; only the (German national) Judge Schücking, in a separate opinion, argued that a servitude had been created.

The weight of legal opinion appears to have favored the view that Article 380 of the Versailles instrument did create a servitude for Germany and that barring the advent of the Hitler era, Germany would quite likely have continued carrying out the obligation imposed by Article 380 even after the other provisions of the Treaty of Versailles had been set aside in one manner or another.

*Panama Canal.* One of the two major interoceanic canals, the Panama Canal, had become the subject of a self-imposed servitude by the United States, an obligation that assured the members of the community of nations the right of innocent passage through the waterway, subject to the payment of tolls and to certain formal conditions.

The international status of the Panama Canal was based on the Hay–Pauncefoote Treaty (United States–Great Britain) of November 18, 1901, which superseded the Clayton–Bulwer agreement of 1850. The 1901 instrument replaced the previously anticipated joint control of a canal through the Isthmus of Panama with a plan for the construction, regulation, and management of such a canal under the sole authority of the United States. That canal was to be open to the use of vessels of commerce and war of all states on a basis of equality, and the United States was to protect the canal against acts of hostility by belligerents in time of war and to prevent its use by belligerents for strategic purposes.

The United States subsequently assumed that no discrimination in tolls or charges was permissible; that assumption may also be taken to represent a self-assumed servitude.

The major legal problem posed by the canal after its construction centered on its use in time of war. The United States adopted the rather logical position that the use of the waterway by enemies of the United States did not represent a part of the self-imposed servitude and proceeded in 1912 to construct fortifications to defend the canal against possible enemies of the United States. During both world wars, belligerent warships passed freely through the canal as long as the United States claimed a neutral status. As soon as the United States officially became a belligerent, the canal was closed to enemy ships of every kind.

Today the Canal is operated in accordance with the provisions of two U.S.–Panama agreements: the Panama Canal Treaty of 1977 (operation and defense of the canal) and the Treaty Concerning the Permanent Neutrality and Operation of the Panama Canal, of 1977 (international status).[57]

Because of the international importance of the Panama agreements, the contents of the two instruments are outlined here. According to the Canal Treaty, Panama will assume full responsibility for the management, operation, and maintenance of the canal on the termination of the treaty on December 31, 1999. Until then, the canal is being operated (beginning October 1, 1979), by a new United States agency, the Panama Canal Commission, whose board will include five Americans and four Panamanians until 1990, when a Panamanian administrator assumed control. Panama assumed jurisdiction over the 533-square-mile Canal Zone when the treaty entered into force, but the zone was to be integrated into Panama over a thirty-month transition period. On March 31, 1982, all U.S. laws and regulations ceased to apply in the 5-mile-wide zone. The United States continues to have primary responsibility for the defense of the canal until the end of 1999. The Neutrality Treaty provided that the United States and Panama each have the right (after the treaty goes into effect on December 31, 1999) to defend the canal against threats to its security (peaceful passage of ships) or neutrality. Panama pledged to keep the canal open to the "peaceful transit" of all vessels, including warships. Another provision, added by the U.S. Senate, gives to the United States the right to use all needful measures, including the use of military force, to reopen the canal or restore its operation, should this be necessary. Ratifications were exchanged on June 16, 1978.[58] Two Senate additions were of interest: one spelled out in greater detail the right of the United States to use military force to protect the neutrality of the canal after 1999, and the other specified that U.S. warships could go "to the head of the line" in order to traverse the canal in time of war. The president of Panama interpreted these last two additions as being included among the various guarantees embodied in the treaty, thus avoiding the necessity of a second Panamanian referendum.

Finally, nondefense installations in the Canal Zone, owned by the U.S. government at the time the treaties went into effect, were transferred gradually to Panama at no charge to the latter.

*Suez Canal.* The Suez Canal, connecting the Mediterranean and the Red Sea, figured prominently in the history of servitudes until it was seized by the Egyptian state in 1956. Space, however, does not permit an account of the checkered fortunes of this vital waterway. (See "Suggested Readings.")

[57] Text of the Panama Canal Treaty in 16 *ILM* 1022 (1977), in 72 *AJIL* 225 (1978), and in *NYT,* Sept. 7, 1977, A-16-17. Text of the Neutrality Treaty, with a relevant Protocol and other documents, in 16 *ILM* 1040–98 (1977); text of Treaty and Protocol only, in 72 *AJIL* 238 (1977) and in *NYT,* Sept. 7, 1977, A-17.

[58] Three documents were involved: "Protocol of Exchange of Instruments of Ratification on the Panama Canal Treaties," the "Panama Understanding Concerning the Panama Canal Treaty," and the "United States Amendments, Conditions, Reservations and Understandings" on the Neutrality Treaty. The texts of all three instruments are reprinted in 17 *ILM* 817 (1978). Consult also the interpretative *Note* by Hamlin, in 19 *Harvard Int'l Law Jl.* 278–328 (1978).

OTHER TERRITORIAL DISPUTES    Among remaining territorial disputes should be included the question of sovereignty over Gibraltar and the issue of Iraq's claim to the Shatt-al-Arab waterway and some Iranian territory seized near the end of the Iraq–Iran conflict, and the claims to the Spratly Islands. (Other territorial claims are listed in the "Suggested Readings.")

GIBRALTAR.    Gibraltar, a 2 1/2-square-mile territory connected by an isthmus to the mainland at the entrance to the Mediterranean, had been seized by Great Britain in 1704. The dependency has a population of about 30,000, which, in a plebiscite in 1967, voted 12,138 to 44 to remain under British rule. In 1966, Spain had requested "substantial sovereignty" of Gibraltar and had also imposed a partial blockade of the "Rock." That blockade lasted until the Franco government was replaced by the present monarchy in Spain. A new constitution (1979) granted increased domestic authority to an elected House of Assembly. The UN General Assembly had adopted a resolution requesting an end of British rule over Gibraltar by October 1, 1969, but nothing happened in the way of implementation.[59] The current (at the time of writing) British Prime Minister (Thatcher) was reported to have adopted the view that it was up to the Gibraltarians to decide their own political future.

SHATT-AL-ARAB.    Iraq and Iran had concluded an agreement in 1975 under which the Shatt-al-Arab waterway was designated as their common border. That arrangement left the Shatt-al-Arab as Iraq's only route to the Persian Gulf. Intermittent skirmishing over the waterway began in 1979, and on September 17, 1980, Iraq abrogated the 1975 agreement. The president of Iraq announced that he wished to return to the Constantinople Accords of 1913 which, he claimed, recognized the Shatt-al-Arab as being entirely within Iraqi territory.[60] On September 22, 1980, Iraqi forces began an invasion of Iran and thereby an eight-year-long war. The latter ended on August 20, 1988, when Iraq, the victor, accepted a UN resolution calling for a ceasefire. In June 1989 Iraq secured the backing of the Arab Cooperation Council (ACC) for its long-standing claim to the Shatt-al-Arab waterway. The ACC also supported Iraq's request to the United Nations to arrange for the clearing of war debris from the waterway. It is of interest that in 1990 Iraq voluntarily gave up all Iranian territory seized during the 1980–1988 war. It has been claimed that the reason for this unusual step was an Iraqi resolve to promote better relations with Iran after the imposition of UN sanctions against Iraq for the conquest of Kuwait.

In 1961, Iraq had claimed all of the Emirate of Kuwait, six days after the British protectorate had ended. Other Arab states and Great Britain sent troops to the Iraqi border and no invasion took place. In 1990, however, Iraq began to denounce Kuwait, charging it with the "theft" of oil from an

[59]See Levie, *The Status of Gibraltar* 1983).
[60]See Kaikobad, *The Shatt-Al-Arab Boundary Question: A Legal Reappraisal* (1988); Haldane in *CSM*, Nov. 14, 1989, 10; AP Dispatch, Nov. 18, 1989.

oil field straddling the Iraq-Kuwait border. It also demanded control over two small islands (Warbah and Bublyon), possession of which would guarantee Iraq direct access to the Persian Gulf. Iraq also voiced again a claim to Kuwait, based on asserted historical foundations. While negotiations about the Iraqi complaints were under way, Iraqi forces entered Kuwait (August 2, 1990) and quickly conquered the emirate. On August 8, Iraq announced that it had formally annexed Kuwait "at the request of the provisional government" (which it had installed earlier). It should be noted that Iraq acceded on February 14, 1956, to the Fourth Geneva Convention of 1949 Relative to the Protection of Civilian Persons in Time of War. By its accession, Iraq was bound by the treaty provisions prohibiting its annexation of Kuwait.

*The Spratly Islands.* The Spratly Islands in the South China Sea comprise some 500-plus small islands and coral reefs, yet have been for decades the object of territorial claims by China, Vietnam, the Philippines, the Republic of China (Taiwan), and Malaysia. The two chief reasons for the disputes are the strategic location of the group and the suspected presence of significant oil reserves around the group.[61]

Recent years have seen evidence of the militarization of the Spratly Islands: the Philippines has placed troops close to Palawan Island in the easternmost part of the group; the Republic of China is said to maintain a small garrison on Itu Aba, the largest island. In March 1988, 110 Chinese marines and surveyors, escorted by warships, landed on a coral reef near the island of Sinh Cow. That act led to a 30-minute exchange of fire with nearby Vietnamese naval components. The Chinese frigates won the brief battle, setting three Vietnamese vessels on fire and wounding or killing 79 men. The Chinese were reported to have captured six reefs during that month, while Vietnam earlier had taken ten other islands or reefs. It was reported at the time that China was engaged in creating and manning military outposts in the Western part of the Spratly Islands, whereas naval forces from Vietnam and Malaysia also had been stationed on various atolls for at least a year.[62]

## LAND, RIVER, AND LAKE BOUNDARIES

The extent of the territory subject to the jurisdiction of any state is determined by definite boundary lines, as in the case of the domestic real property of any citizen.

[61]See Ritterbush, "Marine Resources and the Potential for Conflict in the South China Sea," 2 *Fletcher Forum* 64–85 (1978).

[62]Park, "The South China Sea Disputes: Who Owns the Islands and the Natural Resources?" 5 *Ocean Dev. and Int'l Law Jl.* 27 (1978); Chiu & Park, "Legal Status of the Parcel and Spratly Islands," 3 *id.,* 1 (1975–76); Cheng, "Dispute over the South China Sea Islands," 10 *Texas Int'l Law Jl.* 265 (1975), and his "The Sino-Japanese Dispute over the Tiao-yu-tai (Senkaku) Islands and the Law of Territorial Acquisition," 14 *Virginia Jl Int'l Law* 221 (1971).

Most of the existing boundaries on land have been fixed by international conventions, in particular by peace treaties. Such general settlements as the Treaty of Westphalia (1648), the various agreements reached at the Congress of Vienna (1815), and the peace treaties of 1919 and 1947 have redrawn the frontiers of European states on a wholesale basis, whereas more limited agreements, both in Europe and elsewhere, have determined new or old but disputed boundary lines.

Other instances of determination—say, by prescription—abound in Europe, Africa, Asia, and the Americas, with no specific document available to certify as to the origin of a particular line of demarcation between two states.

Although there has been much loose talk in discussions of natural frontiers when topography alone was cited in violation of other "natural" frontiers based on race, language, culture, or religion, it is true that certain basic rules have been evolved in the practice of states to assist in determining land boundaries.

A common device is to fix a border at the water divide or watershed when a chain of hills or mountains forms an approximate boundary between states. Although a convention may prescribe such a line as the boundary in general terms, the exact location of the frontier would then have to be made through surveys by a designated body, such as a boundary commission. But when the area's topography is such that the water divide is not coincidental with the highest elevations in the hills or mountains in question, there is likely to be trouble.

THE GROTIAN RULE    Rivers have frequently been included as part of a boundary line between states, either because they serve as a strategic natural barrier or because a broad waterway appears to all concerned parties to represent an obvious dividing line between them. The exact determination of the boundary in the river originally followed the Grotian rule that the frontier should be located in the middle of the river. This long-standing principle posed, in the case of navigable streams, a number of unanticipated problems when the main channel of navigation wandered back and forth across the political frontier, so that a vessel proceeding along the course of the stream was now in one country and now in the other.

THE RULE OF THE THALWEG    In view of the customs problems involved, coupled with the difficulties of collecting tolls and preventing the escape of subjects intent on departing against a sovereign's will, the old rule was modified early in the nineteenth century to read that in the case of navigable rivers, the boundary would follow the middle of the principal channel or the path of the strongest downstream current, technically known as the *Thalweg.*

The major advantage of the change was that the border would henceforth coincide with the main route of river commerce, allowing each of the riparian states an equal share of this route within its own territory. The rule of the *Thalweg* has been accepted generally among nations for the redetermination of river boundaries (in the case of navigable streams only) and has also become the principle applicable to possible domestic disputes between political subdivisions of a state.[63]

Should the *Thalweg* gradually shift, either by erosion or accretion, along the banks of the river, the boundary line will shift with the channel in question.[64] If, however, the shift is not gradual but sudden and extensive (*avulsion*), the boundary line will remain unchanged from its previous location. Should one of the riparian states yield either a part of its river domain or even a part of its shore domain to the other riparian state under a form of prescription, the doctrine of the *Thalweg* will, of course, be superseded in time and can no longer be cited in support of riparian or shore claims by the deprived state.[65]

UNITED STATES–MEXICO CHAMIZAL TRACT DISPUTE    The United States was involved with Mexico in a controversy centering on avulsion and title to the Chamizal Tract, a piece of land adjoining the Rio Grande between El Paso, Texas, and Juarez, Mexico. The dispute dated back to 1864, in which year the Rio Grande changed its course and thereby placed the Chamizal Tract on the United States side of the border. After decades of fruitless argument, a convention was signed on June 24, 1910, for the arbitration of the two governments' rival claims.

In 1911 the arbitrators awarded the greater part of the Tract to Mexico. This holding was proper from a legal point of view, because the prevailing rule was then, as now, that if a boundary river deserts its original bed and creates a new channel, the boundary will remain in the middle (or, on occasion, in the middle of the former main channel) of the deserted riverbed. The United States, however, rejected the award, charging that the commissioners had exceeded their powers in making the award. The original United States claim to the Tract was based on the doctrine of prescription: undisturbed and unchallenged adverse possession. The commission, however, decided that the conditions required for the application of prescription had not been met.

[63] *New Jersey* v. *Delaware,* U.S. Supreme Court, 1934, 291 U.S. 361, which contains a most valuable history of the doctrine of the *Thalweg; Arkansas* v. *Tennessee,* U.S. Supreme Court, 1940, 311 U.S. 1. Re Grotian rule, see *Texas* v. *Louisiana,* U.S. Supreme Court, 1973, 83 S.Ct. 1215 in 67 *AJIL* 784 (1973). See also Rhee, "Sea Boundary Delimitation Between States Before World War II," 76 *AJIL* 555, esp. 559–65 (1982).

[64] *Kansas* v. *Missouri,* U.S. Supreme Court, 1944, 322 U.S. 213; see the opinion in some detail in 39 *AJIL* 122 (1945). See also *Mississippi* v. *Arkansas,* U.S. Supreme Court, 1974, 94 S.Ct. 1046, reported briefly in 69 *AJIL* 181 (1975).

[65] See *Nebraska* v. *Iowa,* U.S. Supreme Court, 1892, 143 U.S. 359; *Arkansas* v. *Tennessee,* U.S. Supreme Court, 1970, 397 U.S. 88; and *Anderson-Tully Co.* v. *Franklin,* U.S. District Court, N.D. Miss., 1969, 309 F. Supp. 539, the latter two cases digested in 64 *AJIL* 957 (1970).

The controversy concerning title to the Tract continued to simmer and then emerged into prominence again in 1962. Then, after weeks of negotiation, the Convention for the Solution of the Problem of the Chamizal was signed at Mexico City on August 29, 1963.[66]

The respective transfers of title to the disputed lands took place on October 28, 1967. Mexico acquired 630.3 acres, and the United States obtained the former Mexico enclave of Cordoba Island, covering 193.2 acres north of the Rio Grande. The two governments shared equally the cost of constructing a new riverbed, along the middle of which the new frontier now runs.

By means of the U.S.–Mexican agreement of August 21, 1970, a formula for settling other past (and future) boundary disputes along the Rio Grande was laid down, and 319 tiny river islands were divided between the two states. Over two hundred cases of border shifts through avulsion have been recorded along the course of the river since it became an international frontier by the treaty of Guadeloupe Hidalgo (1848).

PRINCIPLE OF THE MIDDLE OF A BRIDGE BOUNDARY     Paradoxically, the emergency of the *Thalweg* doctrine has not universally changed the principle according to which the middle of a bridge represents the boundary line between two states, regardless of the location of the main channel of navigation in the river itself or of the path of the strongest downstream current. The only logical reason for clinging to the middle of the bridge as a dividing line above the waters of a navigable stream is the common practice of riparian states of dividing equally the cost of bridge construction. On the other hand, some practical and amusing problems have developed, such as when a vessel, traveling in the water of one riparian state, collides (with its mast, its stack, or its superstructure in general) with a part of bridge located in the jurisdiction of the other riparian state. In such instances, the cause of the damage is found in one country, which the actual consequences— namely, injury to the structure of the bridge—took place in the other one.

Some states have adapted the *Thalweg* principle also for the bridge boundary, notably the United States and Mexico in their convention of 1884 for determining boundaries, should a bridge be built across the Rio Grande. In the latter case, however, it was provided that the boundary line on such a bridge, once fixed, would not be moved even if the main channel of the river should be subject to a gradual shift toward the territory of one or the other of the parties.

---

[66] Text in 58 *AJIL* 336 (1964). See also Gregory, "The Chamizal Settlement: A View from El Paso," 1 *Southwestern Studies* 1–52 (1963); Jessup, "El Chamizal," 67 *AJIL* 423 (1973); Liss, *A Century of Disagreement: The Chamizal Conflict 1864–1964* (1964); and Jacobini, "Mexican-American Studies: A Case-Study—The Chamizal Settlement," 48 *Il Politico* [Univ. Pavia, Italy] 235 (1983).

PROBLEMS IN THE USE OF WATER    A problem relating to both river boundaries and servitudes is the question of the use of water of boundary rivers, international rivers, and international drainage basins.[67] A discussion of the many troublesome questions in this sphere exceeds the scope and purpose of a general text, but it should be pointed out that more than one hundred treaties govern the use of water around the world. Problems posed and causing the conclusion of such agreements pertain not only to the actual use of water by affected states but also to the diversion of water, the variations in water level in adjacent countries caused by obstructions, the effect of water flow on hydroelectric installations, the pollution of boundary rivers by citizens of a riparian state, and many more aspects of boundary rivers and of drainage basins.[68]

LAKE BORDERS    Legal theory and state practice agree on the principle that if a lake or a landlocked sea is enclosed entirely by a given state's territory, the body of water is a part of that state's territory. On the other hand, if such bodies of water are surrounded by the territories of a number of states, no agreement prevails. The majority of writers and governments agree that under such circumstances the lake or sea forms part of the surrounding states and that international agreements are needed to delimit the specific portions of the lake or sea belonging to each of the bordering or littoral states.

Examples of the lakes in question include Lake Constance, Lake Geneva, and most of the Great Lakes in North America (Huron, Erie, Ontario, and Superior).[69] The Black Sea is an example of a landlocked sea, but it is regarded as part of the open or high seas (except for territorial waters along its shores) under the Peace Treaty of Paris (1856) and subsequent agreements, the latest of which was the Montreaux Convention of 1936. An example of a "national" landlocked sea is the Aral Sea in the Soviet Union.

RECENT BOUNDARY DISPUTES    Although almost all land boundaries have been set for a long time and cause no international rifts, a number of borders remain in dispute. Disagreements about them have even led to warfare on occasion, for the passage of time has invested such quarrels with a high degree of bitterness. Some disputes about land borders have been settled fairly recently, but quite a few are still in existence.

---

[67]See Henkins, 410–17; Griffin, "The Use of Waters of International Drainage Basins under Customary International Law," 53 *AJIL* 50 (1959); Witmer (ed.), *Documents on the Use and Control of the Waters of Interstate and International Streams: Compacts, Treaties, Adjudications* (U.S. Govt. Ptg. Office, 1956); the *Lake Lanoux Case,* Arbitration between France and Spain, [1957] *Int. Law Reports* 101; Moffett, "If Jordan Valley Wells Run Dry . . . ," *CSM,* March 14, 1990, 4.

[68]See, *inter alia,* LeMarquand, *International Rivers: The Politics of Cooperation* (1977); Bangladesh–India," Agreement on Sharing the Ganges' Waters (1977)," in 17 *ILM* 103 (1978) (for the background, see *NYT,* Oct. 6, 1976, 2).

[69]For details on the latter four, consult Piper, *The International Law of the Great Lakes* (1967).

For example, a 54-year-old quarrel between Nicaragua and Honduras was finally settled in November 1960 by a decision of the International Court of Justice. The area in dispute, called Mosquitia, is a wedge-shaped, sparsely populated region extending about 150 miles along the Caribbean coast and 175 miles inland. A long dispute between the two countries concerning the location of boundaries in this region had been offered for arbitration by King Alfonso XIII of Spain, who in 1906 had recommended that the main course of the boundary should follow the Segovia River (also called the Coco River). The basic question to be settled by the court was the validity of the arbitral award of 1906, an award asserted by Nicaragua as early as 1912 to be null and void.[70] When the court handed down its decision on November 17, 1960, it ruled in favor of Honduras and declared that Nicaragua was obligated to give effect to the 1906 award, declared to be valid and binding on both disputing countries.[71] The border was then demarcated in accordance with the court's decision and with the collaboration of a mixed commission set up through the InterAmerican Peace Committee.

The 120-year-old controversy between Belgium and the Netherlands concerning the sovereignty over 30 acres of land inside Dutch territory was finally decided in favor of Belgium by the International Court of Justice on June 20, 1959.[72]

A recently settled boundary dispute between Argentina and Chile went back to an arbitral award made in 1902 by King Edward VII of Great Britain. One particular region, Palena/Río Encuentro, comprising 260 square miles in the Andes, remained in contention after the award. In 1964, after the bitterness increased between the disputants about this area, Chile invited the United Kingdom to arbitrate the location of the border remaining unsettled after a 1955 decision handed down by the Argentina–Chile Mixed Boundary Commission. Argentina agreed to the Chilean arbitration proposal, and on November 24, 1966, Queen Elizabeth II handed down her award.[73] The final boundary determination left about 71 percent of the disputed area in Argentina, the rest being allocated to Chile. (See also Chapter 18 on the dispute between Argentina and Chile over the boundary in the Beagle Channel.)

---

[70] For details consult Fenwick, "The Honduras–Nicaragua Boundary Dispute," 51 *AJIL* 761 (1957).
[71] *Case Concerning the Arbitral Award Made by the King of Spain on 23 December 1906* (*Honduras v. Nicaragua*), International Court of Justice, November 18, 1960, *I.C.J. Reports, 1960*, p. 192; Whiteman, vol. 3, 633–48; see Johnson, "*Honduras* v. *Nicaragua*—Decision of the International Court of Justice," 10 *Int. and Comp. Law Quarterly* 328 (1961).
[72] *Case Concerning Sovereignty over Certain Frontier Lands* (*Belgium–Netherlands*), *I.C.J. Reports, 1959*, 209, digested in some detail by Bishop, in 53 *AJIL* 937 (1959). See also Gross, "The Jurisprudence of the World Court: Thirty-Eighth Year (1959)," 57 *AJIL* 751, esp. 771–78 (1963); and Whiteman, vol. 2, 1090–93, and vol. 3, pp. 626–33.
[73] Text of award, excerpted at length, in 61 *AJIL* 1071 (1967).

The acrimonious dispute between Thailand and Cambodia concerning the national location of the Temple of Preah Vihear was settled in 1962 by the International Court of Justice in favor of Cambodia.[74]

The delimitation of the border dividing the "neutral zone" between Kuwait and Saudi Arabia, by an agreement of July 7, 1965, with an exchange of ratifications on July 25, 1966, ended one of the most complicated border problems of modern times, one that was made difficult to resolve because of both by the question of the international status of Kuwait and the nature of the neutral zone itself.[75] In Europe, the lingering dispute (or perhaps better, disagreement) between the Federal Republic of Germany and the People's Republic of Poland over the western borders of the latter was resolved at last by a treaty on November 18, 1970.[76] An agreement between the Soviet Union and the Federal Republic that had been concluded on August 12, 1970, contained these interesting provisions of Article 3 concerning boundaries:

In accordance with the foregoing purposes and principles the Federal Republic of Germany and the Union of Soviet Socialist Republics share the realization that peace can only be maintained in Europe if nobody disturbs the present frontiers.
—They undertake to respect without restriction the territorial integrity of all States in Europe within their present frontiers;
—they declare that they have no territorial claims against anybody nor will assert such claims in the future;
—they regard today and shall in future regard the frontiers of all States in Europe as inviolable such as they are on the date of signature of the present Treaty, including the Oder–Neisse line which forms the western frontier of the People's Republic of Poland and the frontier between the Federal Republic of Germany and the German Democratic Republic.[77]

Other border disputes existing at the time of writing include one involving limited military action between Thailand and Laos about a portion of their common border.[78] A much more important border dispute between India and China had not been settled at the time of writing. After relatively large buildups of troops along the disputed border (1987), the two parties decided to shift to negotiations. The disagreement centers on the so-called McMahon Line, drawn by Great Britain in 1914 to demarcate the

---

[74]*Case Concerning the Temple of Preah Vihear* (*Cambodia* v. *Thailand*), International Court of Justice: *Preliminary Objections,* Judgment of May 26, 1961, *I.C.J. Reports, 1961,* 17, excerpted in 55 *AJIL* 978 (1961); *Merits,* Judgment of June 15, 1962, *I.C.J. Reports, 1962,* 6, excerpted in 56 *AJIL* 1033 (1962). See also Whiteman, vol. 2, 1093–97, and vol. 3, 648–61.

[75]See Hosni, "The Partition of the Neutral Zone," 60 *AJIL* 735 (1966).

[76]Text in 10 *ILM* 127 (1971); see also Gelberg, "The Warsaw Treaty of 1970 and the Western Boundary of Poland, 76 *AJIL* 119 (1982).

[77]Full text of treaty in 18 *The Bulletin* (Bonn) (1970), 212.

[78]*CSM,* Feb. 5, 1988, 2 and April 4, 1988, 12, as well as AP Dispatch, Feb. 18, 1988.

Indo-Tibetan border. China has repeatedly questioned the validity of that demarcation and also has claimed title to India's Arunachal Pradesh State.[79]

India has also been involved in a border plus territorial title dispute with Pakistan since the two countries achieved independence. The border dispute over the line separating the two states on the Siachem Glacier in northern Kashmir has led repeatedly to fighting, in 1971, 1984, and 1987. Cease-fires ended hostilities in each case. The problem arose when the peace negotiators after the 1971 India-Pakistan war failed to mark the boundary line on the large glacier. In 1990 the border dispute became linked to the Kashmir Muslim Revolt against the administration of the Indian part of Kashmir. Although few people had been killed at the time of writing, both states began to greatly increase troop concentrations in the area. Kashmir has not known true stability since India and Pakistan became independent.[80] (See "Suggested Readings" for additional listings.)

## JURISDICTION OVER AIR AND SPACE

### NATIONAL AIRSPACE

The invention of the balloon and more especially the airplane made it necessary to clarify a state's rights in the air above its territory. Initially a number of theories came into being, according to which (1) there prevailed complete freedom in airspace, just as on the high seas; (2) a nation could claim territorial jurisdiction in airspace up to about one thousand feet above the ground, with the upper air again free, as in the case of the high seas; (3) the entire airspace above a state, with no upper limit, was national air, with a servitude of innocent passage granted to all aircraft registered in friendly foreign countries; and (4) a nation had absolute and unlimited sovereignty over national airspace, with no upper limit.[81]

The last-mentioned theory received general approval when the outbreak of World War I led all belligerent states to assert immediately full sovereignty over their national air. Neutrals, in turn, denied all right of passage to belligerent aircraft, thus aligning national airspace with the rules applying to the land surface rather than with those applicable to neutral territorial waters. In fact, both the Swiss and the Dutch armed forces, maintaining the integrity of their neutral airspaces, brought down a number of belligerent aircraft that had penetrated their national airspaces. By the end of the con-

---

[79]*CSM,* May 7, 1987, 16; June 12, 1987, 10; June 17, 1987, 2.

[80]*CSM,* Oct. 2, 1987, 7, Feb. 2, 1990, 4; *Time,* Oct. 12, 1987, 45; AP Dispatch, March 15, 1990.

[81]"The United States Government has not recognized any top or upper limit to its sovereignty." —From a speech by the Legal Adviser to the Department of State, May 14, 1958, reported in 38 *Department of State Bulletin* 962 (1958). Consult also Jacobini, "International Aviation Law: A Theoretical and Historical Survey," 2 *Jl. of Politics* 314 (1953); and the excellent legal and historical survey by Dula, "Frontier Law 1977," 97 *Analog* (August 1977), 60–74.

flict, national sovereignty over airspace was accepted, and only the question of innocent passage remained to be settled, particularly with respect to the problem of whether such passage, if permitted, represented a right or a special grant under some form of treaty.

There can be no question today about the legal status of national airspace: states have complete and exclusive sovereignty over the air above their territories (including the territorial sea but not the contiguous zone). This statement not only is declarative of a rule of customary law but has been affirmed in numerous conventions.[82]

RIGHT OF INNOCENT PASSAGE    The major problem traditionally encountered in the enforcement of a claim of absolute sovereignty over national airspace is the innocent passage of foreign aircraft. It is clearly permissible for any state to assign entry and exit lanes, if only for purposes of control induced by considerations of national defense, and to delineate routes or lanes over its territory through which planes in innocent passage may traverse the national airspace. Equally lawful is a designation of specified areas as closed to foreign aircraft, again in the interest of national security. In fact, many countries require that foreign commercial airlines obtain (normally one-time) permission to cross national territory and, in many cases, pay a standard overflight charge per flight.[83]

Again, there is no right of innocent passage through the national airspace: permission for such passage is granted, either unilaterally or, more commonly, through conventions, to foreign *civil* aircraft. Most countries insist, however, on such passage taking place through designated corridors and, frequently, only after notification, including flight plans and so on, has been supplied to the relevant air-defense authorities. Specific permission is normally required if foreign *military* aircraft are to be permitted to enter the national air.

The right to penetrate national airspace and to land on national territory in the event of distress or of unfavorable weather conditions has been generally accepted and is based on analogous rights of vessels in distress. National regulations govern the rights of aircraft in this category of intrusion into the national airspace.

The airspace above the high seas is controlled by no one and hence is free for the use of all states (1982 United Nations Convention on the Law of the Sea—hereafter UNCLOS III—Arts. 87(1b) and 88).

---

[82] See Whiteman, vol. 2, 1270–85; Hackworth, vol. 7, 550, 552, 555–56; and vol. 9, 309–312; see also the references supplied by Lissitzyn, "The Treatment of Aerial Intruders in Recent Practice and International Law," 47 *AJIL* 559 at 567 (1953), and, *inter alia,* the Convention for the Regulation of Aerial Navigation (Paris, 1919) and the Convention on International Civil Aviation (Chicago, 1944), and the 1982 U.N. Convention on the Law of the Sea (hereafter: UNCLOS III), Art. 2 (2).

[83] See Perdomo-Escobar, "Aeronautical Servitudes: A Comparative Study," 44 *Michigan Law Review* 1013 (1946). In most parts of the world, bilateral treaties regulate commercial overflight privileges.

It should be mentioned that aircraft have to be registered, like ships, and possess the "nationality" of the "flag state."

The global intergovernmental organization charged with supervision of airlines is the International Civil Aviation Organization (ICAO; see also Chapter 13), with more than 140 members. However, the International Air Transport Association (IATA) is the trade organization of the world's scheduled airlines.

The "height" of the air subject to national sovereignty has been a topic of much concern to states interested in establishing a legal regime for outer space. Although no agreement has as yet been reached as to the exact boundary between national air and outer space, a maximum airspace height of 12 miles has been laid down in UNCLOS III for both land territory and territorial waters.[84]

## Aerial Intrusion

The penetration of national airspace by foreign aircraft has led to numerous disputes and claims between countries, to one case brought before the International Court of Justice and, in at least one instance, to a serious international crisis and the cancellation of a proposed "summit" conference.

PRINCIPLES    Under the doctrine of exclusive sovereignty over the national airspace, the territorial sovereign may adopt one of several actions when a foreign aircraft intrudes into that space without permission: he may ignore the intruder; he may attempt (in the event of a landing) to exercise administrative and possibly judicial authority over the craft and its occupants; he may attempt to destroy the craft after intrusion has become a fact; or he may attempt to force the craft to leave the sovereign's airspace, change course, or land in a designated area.

Oliver J. Lissitzyn, a specialist in air law, has pointed out that any nation may intercept foreign aircraft violating its airspace. That airspace, though currently varying from country to country, will probably correspond at some future time to the 12-mile border limit laid down in the UNCLOS III Convention. Any foreign aircraft that is intercepted can legally be escorted out of the airspace it is violating, or it can be ordered to land, either by radio contact or by accepted international signals (the most common signal is for the intercepting plane to fly alongside, in visual contact, and tip its wings). If the intruding aircraft refuses to be escorted out of the airspace or to land, the normal and traditional procedure is for the intercepting planes to fire a warning shot. If the intruder still refuses to leave the airspace or to land, the intercepting plane or planes may fire upon it.[85]

[84]Some states, such as Greece since 1931, have chosen a 10-mile airspace. See Whiteman, vol. 2, 1281–88. For earlier approaches to the problem, consult Fenwick, "How High Is the Sky?" 52 *AJIL* 96 (1958); the valuable analysis by Cooper, "Legal Problems of Upper Space," *Proceedings* (1956), 85–93; *id.*, 93–114, for varied and illuminating commentaries on Cooper's paper; Pépin, "Space Penetration," *Proceedings* (1958), 230 (commentary on 243–52).
[85]Cited in Harper's AP Dispatch, Sept. 2, 1983.

The procedures outlined above do not, however, distinguish between military and civilian planes. There could be no recriminations if a bomber from an unfriendly country were to intrude, refuse to land or turn back, and were attacked. On the other hand, what if a civilian plane, especially one carrying passengers, were to follow similar tactics after intruding into another country's airspace? Or what if the ostensibly civilian plane were actually a spy aircraft, manned by government personnel and engaged in an electronic survey of the country whose airspace had been violated?

UNITED STATES–YUGOSLAVIA DISPUTE    Firing at the intruder in an effort either to drive the craft out of national airspace or to down it in national territory has become a frequent occurrence and has led to serious diplomatic disputes. The first major incident of this sort took place on August 9, 1946. An unarmed American military air transport (C-47 type), on a regular flight from Vienna to Udine, Italy, was attacked over Yugoslav territory by Yugoslav fighter planes and forced to crash-land. All of the plane's occupants were detained by Yugoslav authorities and questioned repeatedly but were finally released on August 22. The United States government charged that the pilot had been instructed to avoid Yugoslav national air but had been forced to intrude because of adverse weather conditions. This existence of bad weather was denied by the Yugoslav government. The United States also claimed that no internationally accepted signal to land had been given and that the attack had begun without recognizable warning and had been repeated as the plane descended for a landing.

Before the occupants of the plane in the August 9 incident were released, a second American plane, of similar type and category, was shot down by Yugoslav fighter planes on August 19, with the loss of the five-man crew. This time the Yugoslav government claimed that a short time before firing on his plane commenced, the American pilot had been "invited" to land but had ignored the request. The United States government, in reply, cast doubts on the extension of such a request, stating that at the time in question, the pilot had reported himself as above the city of Klagenfurt, Austria. The United States also partially denied a Yugoslav charge of 278 unauthorized American intrusions into Yugoslav airspace between July 16 and August 29, 1946. The American reply acknowledged only 43 instances during this period in which United States planes had been close enough to the frontiers of Yugoslavia to lead to possible violations of those frontiers. Finally, the United States argued that the shooting down of the two planes constituted a clear violation of international law.[86]

After several exchanges of notes, the Yugoslav government agreed that military aircraft had a right of innocent passage when forced to intrude by stress of weather, and it expressed regrets about the loss of lives in the second of the two incidents. Eventually that government voluntarily paid

[86]See *NYT,* Sept. 4, and Oct. 10, 1946; the detailed documents are in 15 *Department of State Bulletin* 415–18; 502–4 (1946).

$30,000 to each of the families of the crewmen who died on August 19, 1946. The conclusion from these episodes appears to be that the Yugoslav government still claimed a right to down by force any intruding aircraft in time of peace, but only after the intruder had been given a chance to land after being clearly ordered to do so.

In 1948, the Yugoslav government, in a note to the secretary-general of the United Nations for circulation among the members of the Security Council, again charged the United States with numerous violations of Yugoslav airspace.

ISRAEL–BULGARIA DISPUTE    Between 1950 and 1953 there were several incidents similar to the 1946 episodes over Yugoslavia, this time taking place in Soviet or satellite airspace in Eastern Europe. A major occurrence, however, and the one that led to submission of the dispute to the International Court of Justice, took place on July 27, 1955, when a commercial aircraft belonging to the El Al Israel Airlines, on a flight between Vienna and Lydda (Israel), intruded over Bulgarian territory and was shot down by Bulgarian military aircraft. All seven crew members and the fifty-one passengers were killed in the crash of the burning plane.[87] When diplomatic negotiations failed to satisfy the demands of the Israeli government for compensation for the loss of the plane, its crew, and its passengers, Israel submitted the dispute to the court on October 16, 1957. The court sustained Bulgaria's objections to the jurisdiction of the tribunal, agreeing that the adherence of the Bulgarian state to the compulsory jurisdiction of the Permanent Court of International Justice had ceased to apply when that court was dissolved on April 18, 1946, and that Bulgaria had never ratified the optional clause of the new court's statute.

Protracted negotiations between Israel and Bulgaria over payment of compensation to the heirs of the passengers killed in the incident resulted in an agreement, announced on June 3, 1963. Bulgaria agreed to pay a total of $195,000, which, however, excluded compensation for the loss of the plane.

U-2 AND RB-47 INCIDENTS    The most publicized incidents of aerial intrusion during the 1960s centered on two United States planes over Russian territory: the U-2 and the RB-47 incidents. In the latter case, an American military patrol craft was shot down (July 1, 1960) over Soviet territorial waters off the northern coast after it had "intruded deliberately" into Soviet airspace and had disobeyed an order to land. The only two members of the crew who survived the crash of the bomber-type craft were jailed by the Russian authorities, pending trial, until they were released and permitted

---

[87] *Case concerning the Aerial Incident of July 27, 1955 (Israel v. Bulgaria)* [Preliminary Objections, Judgment of May 26, 1959], *I.C.J. Reports, 1959,* 127. Consult Gross, "The Jurisprudence of the World Court: Thirty-Eighth Year (1959)." 57 *AJIL* 751 at 753–71, and Caflisch, "The Recent Judgment of the International Court of Justice in the Case Concerning the Aerial Incident of July 27, 1955, and the Interpretation of Article 36 (5) of the Statute of the Court," 54 *AJIL* 855 (1960).

to leave, in January 1961. During the exchange of notes following this incident, as well as during subsequent debates in the UN Security Council, the main controversy centered on the location of the craft at the time it was attacked—the Soviet Union maintaining a location well over Russian territorial waters and the United States holding that the craft was at least 30 miles off the Russian shore.

The U-2 incident of May 1, 1960, was the most noteworthy of the postwar intrusion cases, from the point of view of both political results and legal arguments.

The U-2 (*U* stood for "utility"), a high-flying United States craft, was engaged in aerial reconnaissance over Russian territory. On May 1, 1960, while flying from Pakistan to Norway, the U-2 was brought to earth (by still undisclosed means) near Sverdlovsk, almost 1,300 miles inside the Soviet Union. Its pilot, Francis G. Powers, was arrested.

The flight of the U-2 was then only the latest in a series of reconnaissance penetrations of Soviet airspace carried on, over a period of four years, under the general orders of President Eisenhower and under the control of the Central Intelligence Agency.[88] The incident served as the Russian excuse for abandoning the planned Paris Summit Conference between President Eisenhower and Premier Nikita Khrushchev.

From a legal point of view, the Russian citations of the Paris (1919), Havana (1928), and Chicago (1944) conventions (the United States was a party to the latter two agreements), pointed up the unchallenged principle that sovereignty over its national airspace is a right of each state under international law, a principle supported even more dramatically by the fact that the United States did not protest the Russian downing of the U-2 and the trial and conviction of the pilot. Powers was released and permitted to return to the United States in 1962, under the terms of an exchange agreement under which a convicted Russian spy was permitted by the United States to return to the Soviet Union.

Summarizing the U-2 incident, and disregarding strategic and political factors, it must be held that in authorizing the craft's flights over Soviet territory, the United States violated international law and that the Soviet Union was justified in forcing the aircraft down and instituting criminal proceedings against its American pilot.

In March 1964, a U.S. RB-66 reconnaissance bomber was shot down by Soviet military forces over East Germany. This was the fourteenth U.S. aircraft brought down since 1950 adjacent to or inside the Iron Curtain

---

[88]See Wright, "Legal Aspects of the U-2 Incident," 54 *AJIL* 836 (1960); Lissitzyn, "Some Legal Implications of the U-2 and RB-47 Incidents," 56 *AJIL* 135 (1962), as well as the copious literature cited in those sources. For the aftermath of the incident, consult also Wise and Ross, *The U-2 Affair* (1962). See also "Legal Aspects of Reconnaissance in Airspace and Outer Space," 61 *Columbia Law R.* 1074 (1961); Stanger (ed.), *Essays on Espionage and International Law* (1963); and Powers with Gentry, *Operation Overflight* (1970), as well as *NYT,* August 2, 1977, 12.

countries, in addition to some 17 "incidents" involving U.S. military aircraft.

In April 1966, Turkey prohibited the use of United States airbases on Turkish soil for reconnaissance flights by the U.S. Air Force, asserting that such flights endangered Turkey's security.

Beginning around 1964, the airspace above mainland China began to be penetrated by pilotless American jet-powered reconnaissance aircraft. Most of these were launched from C-130 transports over the high seas, were under remote control during flight, and were afterward directed to a recovery zone where films exposed over China were removed.

Aerial intrusions, real or alleged, have been a regular feature of the world scene since the incidents detailed above. The following incidents were among those receiving considerable publicity.

It should be noted that amidst the enormous discussion of the 1962 blockade of Cuba, almost nothing was said about the aerial reconnaissance of the island that the United States had instituted sometime before the missiles and sites were discovered. Clearly, this was a repetition of the sort of activity, on a much more extensive and intensive scale, that had produced the U-2 crisis of 1960 between the Soviet Union and the United States. Again, the national airspace of an independent state had been violated, on a daily basis, by both high-level and low-level flights accompanied by photography of almost every square mile of Cuba's territory.

The only defense made in 1962 was by President John F. Kennedy, who simply stated that the overflights of Cuba were justified because the security of the United States was at stake.

Under traditional principles of law, such overflights (aerial intrusions) had to be viewed as illegal and justified Cuban military action to clear the Cuban national airspace of such intruders (one U.S. plane was shot down). To be sure, the Rio Treaty for Reciprocal Assistance (1947), to which Cuba was a party, had authorized the Organ of Consultation to agree by a two-thirds vote on measures for both the common defense and the maintenance of the peace and security of the hemisphere (Arts. 6, 8, 17). On January 31, 1962, the Organ of Consultation approved at Punta del Este a resolution that called on the member states to "strengthen their capacity to counteract threats or acts of aggression, subversion, or other dangers to peace and security resulting from the continued intervention in this hemisphere of Sino-Soviet powers." And on October 23, 1962, the Organ of Consultation of the OAS adopted a resolution that asserted that it was "desirable to intensify individual and collective surveillance of the delivery of arms to Cuba." Nevertheless, under existing rules, grave doubts must be maintained about the legality of the flights over Cuba.

In April 1969, North Korean MIGs shot down a U.S. Navy EC-121M reconnaissance plane, some 90 miles off the North Korean coast, with a total loss of the 31-man crew. In February 1973, Israeli military aircraft shot down a Libyan airliner that had strayed into the Sinai airspace, with a loss of

106 lives and only 7 survivors. The Assembly of the ICAO, in its Resolution A19-1, condemned the Israeli action, and the ICAO Council instructed the agency's secretary general to institute a fact-finding investigation. The latter was then undertaken by ICAO secretariat experts.[89] On March 21, Libyan jet fighters attacked a U.S. Air Force "transport plane" (really an electronic reconnaissance craft), claimed by the United States to have been, at the time in question, over 80 miles off the Mediterranean coast of Libya.[90] On August 10, 1973, Israeli military aircraft intercepted a civil airliner of Middle East Airlines in Lebanese airspace outside Beirut and forced it to land on a military air base in Israel. The claimed purpose of the act was to capture four leaders of Arab terrorist organizations. After two hours, the craft and all aboard were permitted to depart.[91] The resumption of U.S. photo reconnaissance flights over Cuba was announced on November 16, 1978. The aircraft to be used for the overflights, which must be considered illegal, was the highly sophisticated SR-71 "Blackbird" "spy" plane. Intelligence overflights of Cuba had been carried on intermittently since the Cuban missile crisis but had been suspended by presidential order in January 1977. The announced reason for their resumption was, initially, the presence of Soviet MIG-23 jet fighters on bases in Cuba and, in 1979, the presence of a Russian combat brigade in Cuba. In September 1981, Sudanese air defense forces shot down an intruding Libyan bomber, killing its two pilots. In 1982, the United States started an overflight program over Nicaragua.[92]

The U-2 was replaced (except for a few drone models) by the SR-71, which could reach very high speeds at 80,000 feet, thus being extremely difficult to down. The Blackbird was withdrawn from service in March 1990, because of high costs, danger from improved missiles, and advantages accruing from the utilization of satellites.[93] It has been rumored that more than 900 attempts have been made to shoot down the SR-71, only one of which was made public when on August 26, 1981, North Koreans fired a surface-to-air missile, which missed the aircraft. In mid-1981, production of the newest American spy plane, the TR-1, was begun. The TR-1 cruises at

[89]*NYT,* March 1, 1973, p. 7; text of the ICAO Council Resolution of June 4, 1973 in 12 *ILM* (1973), p. 1180.

[90]*NYT,* March 22, 1973, pp. 1, 9; March 24, 1973, p. 5; May 31, 1973, p. 2; "Letter Dated 18 June 1973 from the Permanent Representative of the United States of America to the United Nations to the President of the Security Council," in 12 *ILM* (1973), pp. 1277–78.

[91]*NYT,* August 11, 1973–August 16, 1974, *passim;* UN Security Council condemnation (15 to 0) of Israel in Resolution 337 (1973) on August 15, 1973, *NYT,* August 16, 1973, p. 13, and a second condemnation of Israel by the Council, August 20, 1973, in 12 *ILM* (1973), pp. 1280–81; see also 68 *AJIL* (1974), pp. 111-12, concerning the episode.

[92]See the informative account by Kim Willenson in *Newsweek,* November 19, 1984, p. 46.

[93]See Thatcher, "Bye-Bye (Supersonic) Blackbird," *CSM* July 26, 1989, 12 and *Time,* March 19, 1990, 25.

a relative low speed but has "Stealth" technology aboard to foil "unfriendly" radar and also has a much larger payload capacity than its forerunners did.

THE SOVIET UNION AND AERIAL INTRUSION    Between April 8, 1950, and September 1, 1983, Soviet military aircraft (except in the Powers incident of May 1, 1960, in which the means employed are not known) attacked at least 36 foreign aircraft, in the name of fending off aerial intruders: 16 military planes were attacked, another 16 downed, with a loss of 76 lives; 3 civilian planes were attacked, with a loss of 3 lives; and another civilian aircraft (KAL Flight 007) was downed, with a loss of 269 lives. The scene of these attacks varied greatly: some took place over the Soviet Union itself, others near the borders of that country (the Baltic, Poland, Czechoslovakia, East Germany, the Siberian coast); still other attacks were over the Japanese islands and others over clearly international waters (the Baltic, the Sea of Japan).[94]

The aerial intrusion that received truly worldwide publicity was the Korean airliner incident on August 31, 1983. On that day a Korean Airlines Boeing 747 en route from New York to Seoul (Flight 007) departed from Anchorage with 269 passengers (Korean, Japanese, and American). Some time later it was discovered by Soviet radar personnel and tracked by Soviet military authorities. The Korean aircraft strayed into Soviet airspace over the Kamchatka Peninsula, the Sea of Okhotsk, and Sakhalin Island. At least eight Soviet fighter planes were deployed in reaction to the intrusion. Eventually, after the alleged failure of attempts to communicate with the aircraft and after it had turned away from Soviet airspace, a Soviet fighter pilot destroyed the airliner with an air-to-air missile. All 269 persons aboard Flight 007 perished.[95] The Soviet Union subsequently claimed that the airliner at some time that night had been mistaken for a U.S. RC-135 spy plane and that the Soviet pilots had believed that the Korean plane had been collecting military intelligence.

It should be noted that any suits started in United States courts in the hope of obtaining compensation for lives lost in the KAL incident were subject to the Foreign Sovereign Immunities Act (see Chapter 7) and that such suits do not appear to be authorized by the terms of that Act. Any similar

[94]Based on a listing in *U.S. News & World Report*, September 12, 1983, 25.

[95]See 22 *ILM* 1109 1419, (1983), for a collection of the documents covering the incident, including Security Council meetings, ICAO deliberations, diplomatic notes to the Soviet Union, national actions taken by the United States and other states as a result of the downing of the airliner, actions by the International Federation of Air Line Pilots, as well as the "Rules of the Air," signals to be used in plane-to-plane communications, and so forth. For general accounts of the Korean Airlines (KAL) incident, see *Time*, Sept. 12, 1983, 10–18; and *Newsweek*, Sept. 12, 1983, 16–30, *passim*. See also Union of Soviet Socialist Republics, "Law on the State Boundary of the U.S.S.R." (entered into force on March 1, 1983), in 22 *ILM* 1055, esp. 1058, 1063 (1983); "Japan–U.S.–USSR: Memorandum of Understanding concerning Air Traffic Control" (Tokyo, July 29, 1985) in 25 *ILM* 74 (1986); Dallin, *Black Box, KAL 007 and the Superpowers* (1985).

claims against Korean Airlines would fall under the terms of the Warsaw Convention, an instrument imposing certain limits and conditions.[96] The United States government could have presented claims to the Soviet Union on behalf of the families of American citizens lost in the KAL incident, under the doctrine that a sovereign suffers damages when some government inflicted injuries or losses "upon the sovereign's subjects in violation of an internationally recognized duty."

## Satellites

Long-range overflights by manned aircraft have been rendered somewhat obsolete by the development of reconnaissance satellites by both the United States and the Soviet Union, craft capable of passing over states at such altitudes as to be practically invulnerable to normal defense measures.

The main arguments regarding high flights and satellites in foreign airspaces center on two concepts: the undoubted legal right of any state to engage in genuine self-defense and the equally undoubted exclusiveness of national airspace. In fact, the Soviet Union and the United States came to a tacit agreement, and other countries soon joined them, that satellites have to be tolerated, and in recent years, the United States government has made available, for purely nominal sums, to any country desiring them, satellite photographs showing agricultural development, locations of mineral deposits, and so on.[97]

On occasion the lofting of satellites has introduced the world to problems likely to multiply in the space age. Thus, for example, the U.S. Atomic Energy Commission admitted in May 1964 that 2.2 pounds of lethal plutonium-238 had been lost some weeks earlier when rocket failure prevented a navigational satellite from going into orbit. The payload came down, instead, into the earth's atmosphere off the west coast of Africa. There it burned up, but the radioactive material was dispersed in minute particles in the atmosphere at a height of about 120,000 feet.

## OUTER SPACE

The problems of the law of the air have not ended with the question posed by the increasingly common penetration of the upper layers of the earth's atmosphere: outer space has become one of the next targets for voyages

[96] *Gayda v. Polskie Linie Lotnicza (LOT)*, U.S. Court of Appeals, 2nd Cir., 1983, 702 F.2d 424.

[97] See Dula, *op.cit. supra* n. 81, at 64–66; Jordas, "Looking in on Us," 19 *Environment* 6–11 (Aug.-Sept. 1977); *U.S. News & World Report*, Sept. 12, 1983, 24, and Sept. 8, 1986, 59–60. Consult also Staple, "The New World Order: A Report from Geneva," 80 *AJIL* 699 (1986), and Thomas in *CSM*, Sept. 28, 1988, 3–4. The first artificial satellite went into orbit around the earth on October 4, 1957.

of discovery. Already the legal implications of space travel have begun to appear.[98]

UNITED NATIONS RESOLUTION (1961)    Late in 1961, the General Assembly adopted the Resolution on Peaceful Uses of Outer Space, which asserted that international law, including the Charter of the United Nations, applied to outer space as well as to celestial bodies and that both such space and such bodies were to be regarded as free for exploration and use by all states.[99]

These concepts were expanded in 1963 by the General Assembly's Declaration of Legal Principles Governing Activities in Outer Space. That declaration, though not a binding treaty, summarized neatly the consensus arrived at after serious debate in the General Assembly. It provided that (1) space exploration and the use of space were to be for the benefit of mankind; (2) states conducting activities related to space would be responsible for their acts; (3) all activity in space was to be guided by the principles of cooperation and mutual assistance; (4) states launching objects and personnel were to retain jurisdiction over them in space and also on their return to earth, no matter where they might land; (5) states were to be liable for any damages on earth, in the airspace, or in outer space caused by objects launched by them into outer space; and (6) astronauts were to be considered envoys of mankind and, in case of accident, all states were to be bound to render them all possible assistance and to return them promptly to the state in which their space vehicle was registered.

OUTER SPACE TREATY    On May 7, 1966, President Lyndon Johnson announced that the United States would seek a UN agreement to prevent any state from claiming title to the moon and other celestial bodies. The Legal Committee (on Outer Space, now composed of 28 members) quickly began to draft such an agreement, adding sections on the prohibition of weapons of mass destruction in outer space or on celestial bodies.

After reconciling the differences between the views of the United States and the Soviet Union, the draft was approved unanimously in the General Assembly on December 19, 1966.[100] On January 27, 1967, the treaty was signed at an unusual ceremony in the White House attended by representatives of sixty nations, and thereafter the treaty was open for ratification. The United States Senate gave its consent on April 25, and the United States then ratified the treaty, which entered into force on October 10, 1967.[101]

---

[98]See Whiteman, vol. 2, 1285–1321.

[99]Res. 1721 (XVI), UN General Assembly, 16th Session, reprinted in 56 *AJIL* 946 (1962 Supp.) see also Simsarian, "Outer Space Co-operation in the United Nations," 57 *AJIL* 854 (1963).

[100]G.A. Res. 2222 (XXI), 19 December 1966.

[101]Consult also the analysis of the agreement by Ambassador A. J. Goldberg, in 56 *Department of State Bulletin* 78 (1967), [or see 61 *AJIL* 586 (1967), for his views]; and Adams, "The Outer Space Treaty: An Interpretation in Light of the No-Sovereignty Provision," 9 *Harvard Int'l Law Jl.* 140 (1968). By the end of December 1984, a total of ninety-two states had ratified the treaty, but 30 signatories had failed to do so.

An examination of this Treaty on Principles Governing the Activities of States in the Exploration and Use of Outer Space reveals that despite the exaggerated claims put forth in 1967, the instrument represents little more than a declaration of "principles": in essence (in the absence of enforcement provisions), it is only a set of "self-denying" statements.[102]

One development in the sphere of outer-space law was the drafting of a treaty by the UN Committee on Outer Space on the Rescue of Astronauts, the Return of Astronauts and the Return of Objects Launched into Outer Space.[103] As soon as the General Assembly had approved the draft, the agreement was opened to signature and ratification. It came into effect on December 3, 1968. Of the six substantive articles in the treaty, one pertains to the recovery and the return of artificial space objects, one to the inclusion of international agencies as launching authorities affected by the agreement, and the other four pertained to the rescue and also the return of astronauts on Earth as well as in space. In contrast with the relevant provisions in the Outer Space Treaty, the 1968 instrument contains detailed and well-thought-out provisions concerning the duties and rights of states respecting the rescue and return of astronauts who have crash-landed on Earth, with no currently imaginable contingencies omitted. On the other hand, the treaty's provisions dealing with the rescue of astronauts who have encountered difficulties in space are incomplete. The situation appears logical because some of the problems likely to be encountered in such a contingency have not yet appeared in fact, and solutions are problematical at best. Among the problems left unanswered is the foremost question of who would meet the staggering monetary costs of an earth-to-space rescue effort. Next, the Convention on International Liability for Damage Caused by Space Objects was concluded in 1972.[104] In January 1979, this instrument was invoked for the first time by Canada as a result of damage claimed to have been caused by the *Soviet Cosmos 954*.[105]

By November 1974, the UN Committee on the Peaceful Uses of Outer Space had completed a draft treaty, the Convention on Registration of Objects Launched into Outer Space.[106] That draft was approved by the General Assembly on January 14, 1975, and the Secretary-General opened it for

---

[102]See the comprehensive survey of Lay and Taubenfeld, *The Law Relating to Activities of Man in Space* (1970), 63, on this point.

[103]*NYT*, Dec. 17, 1968, 1, 66 (for the text of the treaty, see *NYT*, 66, and 63 *AJIL* 382 (1969). Consult also Hall, "Rescue and Return of Astronauts on Earth and in Outer Space," 63 *AJIL* 197 (1969).

[104]Text in 66 *AJIL* 702 (1972).

[105]See 18 *ILM* 899 (1979), for the relevant diplomatic correspondence; and 20 *ILM* 689 (1981), for the protocol (April 2, 1981) on settlement of Canada's claim for damages caused by *Soviet Cosmos 954*. See also Christol, "International Liability for Damage Caused by Space Objects," 74 *AJIL* 346 (1980).

[106]Text in 14 *ILM* 44 (1975).

adherence; the convention entered into force September 15, 1976. A major reason for the enactment of that instrument was the ever-increasing number of artificial objects floating through space. After the American space shuttle *Challenger* lost a rendezvous balloon, two satellites, and two rockets in February 1984, a total of 5,173 objects were in space as of February 1984, according to the North American Defense Command at Colorado Springs, Colorado. A total of 3,785 of those objects were junk (burned-out rocket casings, shrouds, and other debris; 1,329 were Earth-circling payloads; and 59 were deep-space probes. According to a recent study by NASA and the U.S. Department of Defense, "space trash" by 1989 was composed of dust, tens of thousands of small bits, and some 7,000 larger objects, all of these orbiting at around 17,000 miles an hour. [107]

In July 1976, the Agreement on Cooperation in the Exploration and Use of Outer Space was concluded by nine Socialist countries (Bulgaria, Cuba, Czechoslovakia, the German Democratic Republic, Hungary, Mongolia, Poland, Rumania, and the Soviet Union); the agreement entered into force on March 25, 1977, and was scheduled to remain in force for 10 years from that date. [108] On October 30, 1980, the Convention for the Establishment of a European Space Agency, drawn up in Paris, entered into force; it was ratified by France, Belgium, Denmark, the Federal Republic of Germany, Italy, the Netherlands, Spain, Sweden, Switzerland, and the United Kingdom. [109]

Finally, the 47-member UN Committee on the Peaceful Uses of Outer Space approved (July 3, 1979), after seven years' work, a modified version of the Agreement Governing the Activities of States on the Moon and Other Celestial Bodies (commonly called the Moon Treaty); [110] the concept had been originally proposed by the Soviet Union in 1971. A major cause of the delay in arriving at a compromise solution had been the Soviet Union's unwillingness to express in treaty terms the idea that the resources of the moon were "the common heritage of mankind." The version finally approved by the committee states that neither the surface nor the subsurface of the moon shall become the national property of any country. The draft agreement was to become a binding convention upon passage by the UN General Assembly during its regular session in 1979 and ratification by a minimum of five members. At the time of writing, serious objections to U.S. ratification have been voiced in the United States, primarily by a number of business

---

[107] See *CSM*, March 1, 1989, 19, and March 21, 1989, 13. See also Baker, *Space Debris: Legal and Policy Implications* (1989); Reijnen and DeGraaff, *Pollution of Outer Space, in Particular of the Geostationary Orbit* (1989); He, "Environmental Impact of Space Activities and Measures for International Protection," 16 *Jl. of Space Law* 117 (1988); and Cowen, "Wanted: an International Accord Banning Space Junk," *CSM*, Jan. 5, 1988, 17.

[108] Text in 16 *ILM* 1(1977).

[109] Final Act of the 1975 meeting and the text of the convention appear in 14 *ILM* 855 (1975).

[110] Text in 18 *ILM* 1434 (1979); see also *NYT*, July 4, 1979, A-4, and July 8, 1979, E-18.

concerns as well as by the L-5 Society. On July 11, 1984, the Moon Treaty entered into force, following the fifth ratification of the agreement; 11 states have signed the treaty, with France representing the only major signatory.[111]

The most recent international instrument related to Outer Space was the USSR–US Agreement on Cooperation in the Exploration and Use of Outer Space for Peaceful Purposes, of April 15, 1987.[112]

## RADIO COMMUNICATIONS

The invention of wireless telegraphy at the beginning of the century resulted in discussions similar to those later posed by the advent of aircraft. In 1906, an International Wireless Telegraph Convention was signed in Berlin, superseded by the International Wireless Convention of London (1912). Both instruments dealt with technical aspects of radio communications. In 1927, a conference in Washington, D.C., resulted in the International Radio Convention, signed by representatives of 78 governments. That instrument expanded controls and required private radio stations to obtain government licenses, and it also provided for the use and allocation of radio frequencies and types of sending. As telecommunications expanded in scope, more modern methods of control became desirable. The Madrid Telecommunications Convention of 1932 created a new international agency, the International Telecommunication Union (ITU). This body was placed in control of all varieties of telecommunications, hitherto governed by separate treaties. For each mode of communication, a separate set of regulations was drawn up, and a central office of the union was established in Berne, supervised by the Swiss government. Subsequently the Union has convened a number of conferences and, in 1982, evolved the new Telecommunication Convention which came into force on January 1, 1984. Regional telecommunication conventions have evolved also in the Americas (Havana, 1937; Rio de Janeiro, 1945) and in Asia (Asian Broadcasting Union, 1964). The latest global convention (Malaga–Torremolinos, 1973) entered into force on January 1, 1975 (for the United States, April 7, 1976). In addition, global radio regulations (Geneva, December 6, 1979) entered into force on January 1, 1982 (except for certain provisions on February 1, 1983); for the United States on October 27, 1983.

One of the basic regulations adopted by the Telecommunication Union was the requirement that all radio stations must be operated in such a manner as to avoid interference with the communications services of all contracting governments or agencies authorized by them. This regulation

[111]See *CSM,* Feb. 20, 1980, 11; *Time,* March 24, 1980, 47; *Note* by Spitz in 21 *Harvard Int'l Law Jl.* 579 (Spring 1980) and especially Christol, "The Moon Treaty Enters Into Force," 79 *AJIL* 163 (1985).

[112]Text and Agreed List of cooperative projects in 26 *ILM* 622 (1987).

has been violated on a wholesale basis by the governments of the Soviet bloc states, which set up extensive systems of radio stations purposely designed to interfere with (jam) broadcasts from the BBC, the German Deutsche Welle, and the American Voice of America, Radio Free Europe, and Radio Liberty.[113]  The Soviet jamming of the Voice of America ended in late May 1987, as did interference with the broadcasts of Radio Free Europe and of British transmissions to Poland (January 1988). By the end of February of that year, only the Afghan service of the Voice of America and the broadcasts of Radio Free Europe were subject to East bloc electronic harassment. At the end of the year, Bulgaria was the last bloc state to end jamming Radio Free Europe. Soon after the Armenian earthquake in 1989, Radio Liberty began to broadcast interviews with eyewitnesses, supplying much greater detail than could be found in Russian network stations. All Soviet jamming of Radio Liberty had ended and it was permitted to station a "stringer" in Moscow to telephone daily news reports to Munich.

One of the more unusual stations that saw the end of its operations in February 1987 was "Radio 1st August," transmitting over eight years daily fraudulent reports of corruption, racism, and armed revolt to China. The obvious intent behind the programs was to create discord in the Chinese armed forces.

The same year also saw the first guerrilla AM station, Radio Liberacion, operated by the Contras against the Sandinista government of Nicaragua. Reports at the time claimed that the funding for this operation had been provided from U.S. contra-aid funds. The obvious purposes of the enterprise were to foment discontent about the Nicaraguan government and to keep the name of the Contra umbrella organization, the United Nicaraguan Opposition (UNO) before the non-Contra public.

The radio war-of-words had escalated in March/April 1984 when Radio Martí, a U.S. government-funded station in Florida, began sending programs concerning internal news and developments in Cuba to that island. Cuba replied through radio transmissions to the United States. On March 27, 1990, as a planned three-month $7.5 million test of a television station—TV Martí, also financed by the U.S. government and aimed at Cuba—was beginning, Cuba responded with massive jamming in the first 15 minutes of the first program.

In 1958 a new phenomenon in the communications sphere made its appearance and soon involved several aspects of international law: pirate broadcasting.

Privately owned radio stations, located on vessels anchored or sailing outside the territorial sea or established on artificial islands beyond territorial jurisdictions, began to broadcast to states whose governments did not permit, or controlled rigorously, the transmission of commercial advertising.

---

[113]See *NYT,* Sept. 30, 1977, A-6; von Glahn, "The Case for Legal Control of 'Liberation' Propaganda," 31 *Law and Contemporary Problems* (Duke University, Summer 1966), 554.

Under the rules of the Telecommunications Union, such commercial broadcasting from international waters was prohibited, but the responsibility for enforcement rested on the country in which the vessel in question was registered.[114]

In 1962, the "Voice of Slough" began operations off the English coast and was joined, in 1964, by Radio Caroline, a large-scale operation on a former ferry, staffed by two disc jockeys and a crew of ten. When the British government protested to the ITU, the flag state of the *Caroline,* Panama, was reminded by the ITU of its responsibilities, for on previous occasions Panama had agreed to withdraw its registration from vessels housing illegal radio stations off the Dutch and Danish coasts. Meanwhile the owners of the *Caroline* acquired a second vessel, which soon began to broadcast off the British coast near Liverpool.[115]

Two other pirate stations (Radio Invicta, later renamed Radio 390, and Radio City) were established on abandoned World War II antiaircraft towers (Marbelle Towers), resting on the seabed in the Thames estuary outside British territorial limits, and a third, Radio London, began operating from a former U.S. minesweeper that was anchored outside the three-mile limit.

Denmark took direct action in August 1964, when Danish police boarded the vessel housing another station, Radio Mercur, and closed the station. Similarly, Dutch police, in December of 1964, boarded and silenced TV Noordzee, the only known pirate television station, operating from a platform affixed to the North Sea bed five miles off the Dutch coast.[116]

In May 1971, violence erupted between the crews of the vessels housing Radio Noordzee and the competing Radio Veronica (the latter station having been so popular in the Netherlands that the Dutch government initially had refused to ratify the 1965 Council of Europe treaty — see below — fearing that such a step would cost it too many votes). After a truce had been arranged, Radio Caroline shifted its location (in January 1973) from off the English coast to the Dutch coast and began to broadcast to the Netherlands. In February 1974, the Dutch government at last ratified the 1965 treaty and then announced that it would silence the pirate stations off its coast. Radio Caroline, however, moved into the North Sea and continued operating until the vessel housing the station sank, without loss of life, in a storm on March 20, 1980.

Interference by the coastal state with pirate stations operating beyond the maritime border has been justified under Article 24(1) of the 1958 Geneva Convention on the Territorial Sea and the Contiguous Zone, as

[114]See *United States* v. *McIntyre,* U.S. Dist. Court, D. New Jersey, 1973, 365 F. Supp. 618, reported in 68 *AJIL* 339 (1974); *Newsweek,* Sept. 24, 1973, 93, on McIntyre's activities; Whiteman, vol. 9, 789–809, and Henkin, 384–85, on pirate stations.

[115]Consult *Time,* Jan. 14, 1973, 34; and *The Province* (Vancouver, B.C.), Aug. 2, 1978, 13, on Radio Caroline.

[116]*NYT,* Jan. 3, 1965, p. 14; consult also the detailed study by van Panhuys and van Emde Boas, "Legal Aspects of Pirate Broadcasting," 60 *AJIL* 303 (1966).

falling among the permitted activities of a coastal state in a contiguous zone, and might possibly be justified by stretching a point under Article 33 of the UN Convention on the Law of the Sea (1982). Stopping the operation of pirate radio (or television) stations on the high seas would be authorized by Article 109 of the same convention, which provides that offenders may be prosecuted before the court of the ship's flag state, the state of registry of the installation, the state of which the person is a national, any state where the transmissions can be received, or any state where authorized radio communication is causing interference (from the illegal station).[117]

On January 20, 1965, the Council of Europe opened to signature the European Agreement for the Prevention of Broadcasts Transmitted from Stations Outside National Territories.[118]  And in 1967, the United Kingdom enacted the Marine and Broadcasting Offenses Act, making it a criminal offense to assist a pirate station in any manner, after an earlier (1964) Territorial Waters Order in Council, aimed at the stations located on fixed tower sites.[119]

The most recent attempt at pirate broadcasting took place in August 1987 in international waters off Long Island, New York. It ended after four days with the arrest of the crew of the *Sarah* by the U.S. Coast Guard. The latter based its action on a violation of the relevant 1975 Geneva Convention.[120]

## SUGGESTED READINGS

### Title to Territory: General

Whiteman, vol. 2, 1028–1232; Shaw, *Title to Territory in Africa* (1986).

### Denial of Title by Conquest

Lauterpacht's *Oppenheim,* vol. 1, 451–60, 544–81; Briggs, "Non-Recognition of Title by Conquest and Limitations on the Doctrine," *Proceedings* (1940), 72–82; UN Security Council Resolution 242 (November 22, 1967) concerning the "inadmissibility of the acquisition of territory by war," reprinted in *NYT* May 6, 1978, together with Gwertzman's commentary on the resolution.
Concerning the West Bank of the Jordan: UN General Assembly, Res. 2799 (XXVI), December 13, 1971, in 11 *ILM* 214 (1972); Forward, Jay *et al.,* "The Arab-Israeli War and International Law," 9 *Harvard Int'l Law Jl.* 232 at 254–55, 257 (1968); Dinstein, "The Legal Issues of 'Para-War' and Peace in the Middle East," 44 *St. John's Law Review* 466 (1970), and see Chapter 24.

[117]UNCLOS III, Arts. 109(3) and 110(c).
[118]Text of treaty in 59 *AJIL* 715 (1965).
[119]See *Regina* v. *Kent Justices, Ex Parte Lye et al.,* Great Britain, Queen's Bench, 1966, (1966), 2 W.L.R., reported in 61 *AJIL* 1077 (1967), and noted, with elaborate documentation, by Watts in 9 *Harvard Int'l Law Jl.* 317 (1968).
[120]*Time,* Aug. 10, 1987, 17.

## Polar Regions

Hackworth, vol. 1, 399–476; Svarlien, "The Legal Status of the Arctic," *Proceedings* (1958), 136–43; Pharand, *Canada's Arctic Waters in International Law* (1988).

CASE

*Martin* v. *Commissioner of Internal Revenue,* Tax Court of the U.S., 1968, 50 T.C. No. 9, reported in 63 *AJIL* 141 (1969).

## Servitudes

Higgins-Colombos, 166–70; Lauterpacht's *Oppenheim,* vol. 1, 480–85; Baxter, *The Law of International Waterways* (1964).
The Suez Canal: Huang, "Some International and Legal Aspects of the Suez Canal Question," 51 *AJIL* 277 (1957), and Obieta, S.J., *The International Status of the Suez Canal* (1960). Consult also the following brief accounts, each of which, however, is supplied with copious documentation valuable for further study: Delson, "Nationalization of the Suez Canal Company: Issues of Public and Private International Law," 57 *Columbia Law R.* 755 (1957); "Suez Canal: Heads of Agreement, Signed at Rome, April 29, 1959," 54 *AJIL* 493 (1960 Supp.). The canal was closed to all shipping from the Six-Day War of 1967 to its reopening on June 5, 1975. The first Israel-bound cargo vessel to pass through the canal made the trip on November 2, 1975.

## Land Boundaries

## Borders

Luard, ed., *The International Regulation of Frontier Disputes* (1970); Hyde, vol. 1, 439–450, 489–510; Cukwarah, *The Settlement of Boundary Disputes in International Law* (1968); Whiteman, vol. 3, 1–871, vol. 9, 1132–43; Chang, *China's Boundary Treaties and Frontier Disputes* (1982).
*Case Concerning the Frontier Dispute (Burkina Faso* v. *Republic of Mali),* International Court of Justice, *1986 I.C.J. Reports* 554, Dec. 22, 1986. Text in 25 *ILM* 146 (1986) and an excellent summary in 81 *AJIL* 411 (1987). Text of the Special Agreement of Sept. 16, 1983 to submit the dispute to the ICJ in 22 *ILM* 1252 (1983).

## Rivers

Zacklin and Caflisch, eds., *The Legal Regime of International Rivers and Lakes* (1981).

## National Air

Lauterpacht's *Oppenheim,* vol. 1, 517–29; Whiteman, vol. 9, 312–441, 634–717; McWhinney and Bradley, *The Freedom of the Air* (1969).

## Aerial Intrusion and Overflights

CASE

*Appeal Relating to the Jurisdiction of the ICAO Council (India v. Pakistan), ICJ Reports,* 1972, 46, reported in 67 *AJIL* 127 (1973).

## Outer Space

Christol, *The Modern International Law of Outer Space* (1982); American Institute of Aeronautics and Astronautics, *Proceedings of the Twenty-Third Colloquium on the Law of Outer Space* (New York, 1981); Forkosch, *Outer Space and Legal Liability* (1982); Zwaan, "Some Reflections on the (Il-)legality of the Military Use of Outer Space," 21 *Postepy Astronautyki,* 107–118. van Fenema, "Space Law of the Future," 13 *Air Law* 286–294 (Dec. 1988).

## Radio Communications

Soley, "The Clandestine Radio Connection," (Part I), 219 *Stamps,* June 8, 1987, 778–79, (Part II), *id.,* 219, June 13, 1987, 838–39; also his *Clandestine Radio Broadcasting* (1987).

# Case Study No. 4

# The Falklands Dispute

Title (or sovereignty) based on occupation lapses when the territory in question is abandoned by its owner. A classic example of the operation of this doctrine has been supplied by the dispute between Argentina and Great Britain concerning sovereignty over the Falkland (Malvinas) Islands. In view of the fact that this perennial argument ended in a full-scale war, it appears desirable to furnish a condensed account of the background and current status of this matter.

The Falkland Islands were first discovered in 1592 by an English sea captain and rediscovered in 1594 by the Englishman Sir Richard Hawkins, who named the islands "Hawkins' Maiden Land" in honor of Queen Elizabeth I. In 1690, another Englishman, John Strong, actually landed and named the island group after the First Lord of the Admiralty, Viscount Falkland. Earlier, a Dutch captain, Sebald de Weert, also had found the islands and named them after himself: the Sebaldine Islands. French citizens were the first to settle, and they built a small fort in Port Louis on East Falkland in 1764. The total population amounted to twenty-two men, five women, and three children. In 1766 the British reappeared, claimed West Falkland, and started a settlement called Port Egmond. For two years the two groups were ignorant of each other's existence, but when the English discovered the French settlement, they ordered the inhabitants to leave. In the meantime, however, Spain asserted that the Papal Line of Demarcation of 1492 had awarded the entire region to Spain, and the French government sold the islands for the then equivalent of £24,000, and Port Louis was renamed Puerto de la Solidad. The Spanish government then sent troops which evicted the English from Port Egmond. In 1771, Spain permitted the English settlers to return to the Falklands, but the British government, preoccupied with its problems in North America, became convinced that the Falkland Islands were not economically viable and abandoned Port Egmond again in 1774. However, when departing, the English commander left "signs and marques," that is, he nailed up a lead plate that bore the inscription: "Be it known to all nations that the Falkland Islands are the sole property of his Most Sacred Majesty, George the Third, King of Great Britain, France and Ireland. . . . "

Some time later, a Spanish governor moved to the islands but abandoned them again in 1806 when British forces attacked Spanish units in

Buenos Aires. When in 1816, the Argentines declared their independence from Spain, they claimed that they had inherited Spanish sovereignty over the islands they now called Las Malvinas. During the next years few people settled in Puerto de la Solidad which, it should be mentioned, was attacked and sacked by the crew of the U.S. corvette *Lexington* at one time, after a minor dispute over sealing rights in the area. At this point the British government came to believe that reoccupation of the islands was desirable, sent H.M.S. *Clio* to the Falklands, ordered a tiny Argentine garrison to depart for home, and raised the British flag (1833). The fact that the United States did not protest by invoking the Monroe Doctrine appears to have indicated its silent approval of the British occupation of the island group. Argentina protested to London, to no avail, and periodically renewed its claims to the Malvinas. In the 1960s, several privately organized Argentine expeditions (one by aircraft) attempted to take possession of the Falklands, but all were unsuccessful. When Argentina took the dispute to the United Nations, the General Assembly voted in 1965 that the two claimants should settle their quarrel by negotiation. In 1971 the dispute was shelved temporarily when Argentina agreed to cease (for the time being) its claim in return for British assistance in creating better transportation and communication arrangements between the Falklands and the mainland. But in 1977 Argentina renewed its claim to sovereignty and held three exploratory conferences, but no settlement was achieved.[1]

On March 19, 1982, a group of Argentine scrap metal workers landed on the Falklands dependency of South Georgia to dismantle an old whaling station, and then promptly raised the Argentine flag over the island. The governor of the Falklands insisted that the workmen depart, asserting that they could return once proper permission had been obtained from the authorities at Port Stanley. On April 2, 1982, however, Argentine forces seized the main islands, capturing the rest within the next two days, and the Falklands War had begun. It ended on June 15, 1982, with the surrender of 15,000 Argentine troops in Port Stanley to the British forces that had landed during the retaking of the Falklands. (See also Chapter 19, on embargoes and Chapter 25 on blockades and war zones, for material related to the Falklands War.)

Argentina's claim to the Falklands Islands was based on two premises: on the historical claim, outlined above, and on the text of several UN General Assembly Resolutions relating to decolonization. In particular, Argentina relied on GA Resolution 1514 (the Declaration on the Granting of Independence to Colonial Countries and Peoples—G.A. Res. 1514 (XV), 15 GAOR Supp. 16, 1966). However, unlike other incidents of decolonization, the Falklands posed the peculiar problem of the inhabitants' race:

---

[1] For earlier, and sometimes farcical, developments in the dispute, consult *NYT*, September 6, 1964, 24; December 12, 1965, 23; October 2, 1966, E-2; February 17, 1977, 5; February 23, 1977, A-2; December 13, 1977, 9; *CSM*, July 20, 1977, 11; *Time*, October 6, 1966, 48; *Newsweek*, October 10, 1966, 60.

they were Caucasians (who, incidentally, wanted to remain British citizens), as were the British and the Argentines. Hence it was not surprising that the non-European members of the Security Council were not willing to apply GA Resolution 1514 to the case at hand. The Australian representative on the Security Council referred to "Argentine colonialism," and the representative from Kenya, Ambassador Maina, asserted that Argentina's claim was "a pure territorial claim against the United Kingdom based on history, in total disregard of the people who now live on the Falkland Islands."[2] British and Argentine representatives met briefly in July 1984 in Berne, Switzerland. Ignoring a formula worked out by Brazilian and Swiss diplomats who had acted as intermediaries, the British delegation refused to discuss the issue of sovereignty over the Falklands, whereas the Argentine team insisted that this issue was the reason they had come to the meeting. The Argentine delegation left the talks on the second day. In December 1984, the House of Commons Foreign Affairs Committee created embarrassment for the British government when it held that it was not possible to assert whether the United Kingdom or Argentina possessed great claim to the Falklands but that Argentina had prejudiced its claim when it resorted to armed force in 1982. Great Britain, however, held out for a formal Argentine declaration of peace, for such a statement (in the British view) would make possible the cancellation of the exclusion zone and a resumption of normal economic relations between the two countries.

At the end of May 1986, the Argentine Coast Guard sank a Taiwanese trawler and by this act brought the attention of the world to the problem of South Atlantic fishery resources as well as the issue of sovereignty over the Falklands. As mentioned earlier, Great Britain, after the Argentine surrender, had imposed a 150-mile exclusion zone around the islands, applicable only to Argentine vessels. Argentina protested the fact that when foreign fishing vessels were detected fishing in Argentine coastal waters, they fled to the exclusion zone as a haven of refuge. On May 27, 1986, Argentina officially informed the diplomatic representatives of countries engaged in fishing in the South Atlantic that any foreign trawlers found violating Argentine waters would be severely penalized, with fines of $250,000, the confiscation of catch and gear, and, in the case of really serious violations, of the vessel itself.

A few days earlier, a Japanese and a Polish vessel were detained for fishing within the 200-mile coastal zone created by Argentina. The Taiwanese case was different: the trawler had operated outside the Argentine 200-mile zone but within a 200-mile perimeter around the Falklands. Argentina claimed that inasmuch as the Malvinas (read: Falklands) belonged to it, the 200-

---

[2]Claude, "The Use of the United Nations in the Falklands Crisis," 1 *Global Perspectives* (Spring 1983), 64, 67. See also Franck, "Dulce et Decorum Est: The Strategic Role of Legal Principles in the Falklands War," 77 *AJIL* (1983), 109; Moore, "The Inter-American System Snarls in Falklands War," 76 *AJIL* 830 (1982) and the ensuing correspondence (Cárdenas and Moore, 77 *AJIL* 606 (1983), as well as Raphael Perl, *The Falkland Islands Dispute in International Law & Politics: A Documentary Sourcebook* (1983).

mile coastal zone applied to the islands as well. The British government thereupon decided to impose a 150-mile fisheries-protection zone around the Falklands, with an option to extend it to 200 miles. If that option had been exercised, the new British zone would have overlapped the Argentine coastal zone.

The British Prime Minister approved (August 1989) direct talks with Argentina, after the latter's new President had made it clear that talks could be held without the issue of sovereignty over the Falklands being raised. In late October 1989 two days of talks in Madrid resulted in an announcement by Argentina that it was formally ending its "state of hostility" with Great Britain. Other significant developments of the meeting were immediate resumption of consular relations, restoration of air and sea links between London and Buenos Aires, and the lifting of all financial restrictions imposed between the former belligerents. Great Britain also ended its prohibition on the presence of Argentine merchantmen and fishing vessels in the 150-mile fisheries protection zone around the Falklands by the end of March 1990. On February 15, both countries announced the restoration of full diplomatic relations, which took place 13 days later. The issue of sovereignty over the islands, omitted from discussion at the Madrid meetings, was not resolved and remains dormant at the time of writing.

## SUGGESTED READINGS

Coll and Arend (eds.), *The Falklands War: Lessons for Strategy, Diplomacy and International Law* (1985); Gustafson, *The Sovereignty Dispute over the Falkland Islands* (1988); Argentina–United Kingdom: Joint Statement on Relations and a Formula on Sovereignty with Regard to Falkland Islands, South Georgia and South Sandwich Islands, Madrid, October 19, 1989, in 29 *ILM* 1291 (1990); Argentina–United Kingdom: Joint Statement on Confidence-Building Measures, Madrid, February 15, 1990, in 29 *id.* 1296 (1990). Claude, "The Use of the United Nations in the Falklands Crisis," 1 *Global Perspectives* 64, esp. at 67 (Spring, 1983).

# Case Study No. 5

# The Western Sahara Dispute

One recent case of voluntary cession has resulted in a small but bitter armed conflict. On August 21, 1974, the Spanish government announced that it would arrange for a referendum in 1975 to enable the people of the then Spanish Sahara to determine their political future. The Spanish colony, now called the Western Sahara, encompassed the territories of Sakiet el-Hamra and Río de Oro, with a population of about 72,000. The government of Morocco, the northern neighbor of the Spanish Sahara, promptly appealed to the United Nations, claiming that the entire Spanish colony had been a part of Morocco at one time and should be returned to that kingdom. However, on November 14, 1974, Spain, Morocco, and Mauritania (the southern neighbor of the Spanish Sahara) agreed that the Spanish colony would be divided between Morocco and Mauritania. The former would receive the far larger portion, including some 62,000 people and rich phosphate deposits, and the latter would receive a much smaller part, with some 10,000 inhabitants. In order to satisfy the spirit of the UN Declaration on the Granting of Independence to Colonial Countries and Peoples of 1966 (G.A. Res. 1514 [XV], 15 GAOR Supp. 16, 1966), the agreement included a provision for a vote, not by the people of Western Sahara, but by the territory's Assembly (comprising about 100 members). It was reported, incidentally, that as soon as news of the agreement reached the colonial capital, almost 70 of the members of the Assembly disappeared by choice. The government of Algeria, which has a 35-mile common border with what was then a Spanish colony, protested against the agreement because Algeria had not been invited to participate in the negotiations.

The UN General Assembly, perturbed about the cession to Morocco and Mauritania, passed a resolution on December 13, 1974, requesting an advisory opinion from the International Court of Justice on two questions:

I. Was Western Sahara (Río de Oro and Sakiet el-Hamra) at the time of colonization by Spain a territory belonging to no one (*terra nullius*)?
   If the answer to the first question is in the negative,
II. What were the legal ties between this territory and the Kingdom of Morocco and the Mauritania entity?

The court's *Advisory Opinion on the Western Sahara* was delivered on October 16, 1975.[1]  In brief, the court felt that at the time of colonization by Spain, Western Sahara was not a territory belonging to anyone. On Question II, the court decided that there were legal ties between the territory and the kingdom of Morocco and also the Mauritanian entity but that those legal ties were not of such a nature "as might affect the application of Resolution 1514 (XV) in the decolonization of Western Sahara and, in particular, of the principle of self-determination through the free and genuine expression of the will of the people of the Territory. . . . "

In the meantime, the UN General Assembly had adopted (December 10, 1975) two resolutions: 3458A (XXX), which requested Spain to assure the Saharan population self-determination under UN auspices and urged all parties to desist from unilateral action, and 3458B (XXX), which noted the Madrid Agreement of November 14, 1974, and also asked the three interim governing parties (Spain, Morocco, and Mauritania) to ensure that the population could and would exercise their right to self-determination.[2] These resolutions had, of course, no effect in view of the Madrid Agreement and also because, as Spain later pointed out correctly, a popular vote would have posed insuperable problems owing to the presence of strong Moroccan military contingents in much of the territory and smaller Mauritanian military components in the south.

On February 26, 1976, the last Spanish officials left the territory, apparently slightly earlier than planned, in view of Spain's implied desire not to be burdened with any responsibility for the vote to take place in the colony's Assembly. Spain officially indicated that it would not accept the vote, when cast, inasmuch as it had not been supervised by the United Nations. (It should be mentioned that the Organization of African Unity also had attempted repeatedly to introduce some form of popular vote into the transfer process, but without success; the latest of such proposals came, rather belatedly, in August 1981.)

Fighting had erupted: the Polisario Front, a highly mobile and relatively small but well-armed (through Algeria and Libya, according to reliable sources) independence movement, were fighting primarily against Moroccan units in the northern two thirds of the former Spanish colony, but also against Mauritania in the south.[3]  In the middle of July 1979, the Polisario movement announced an end to a year-long cease-fire with Mauritania and a resumption of fighting to the south. On August 6, 1979, Mauritania

---

[1][1975] *I.C.J.* 12, text in 14 *ILM* 1355 (1975); consult also Janis, "The International Court of Justice: Advisory Opinion on the Western Sahara," 17 *Harvard Int'l Law Jl.* 609 (1976) and Franck, "The Stealing of the Sahara," 70 *AJIL* 694 (1976).

[2]Texts, with relevant documents, in 14 *ILM* 1503 (1975).

[3]*Polisario* is a Spanish acronym for The Popular Front for the Liberation of Sakiet el-Hamra and Río de Oro, *i.e.,* of the pre-1975 Spanish Sahara. The Polisario Front was the military arm of the Saharan Arab Democratic Republic (SADR), the self-proclaimed Western Saharan government-in-exile, in Algeria. It was eventually recognized by 71 countries as the government of the Western Sahara.

renounced all claims to any part of Western Sahara and agreed to withdraw forthwith from the southern third of the territory, in favor of the Polisario movement. Morocco promptly occupied the ex-Mauritanian sector, and a bitter and at times bloody war began. By late 1982, the Polisario Front had formed the Saharan Arab Democratic Republic (SADR), an inchoate government which from its beginning aspired to become a full member of the Organization of African Unity (OAU), representing the Western Sahara. Morocco and 18 other African members bitterly opposed that admission. The eighteenth annual meeting of the OAU ended in a deadlock because of differences in regard to the admission of the Polisario movement, and the latter was persuaded to temporarily shelve its application for membership at the twentieth annual meeting in 1983 in order to prevent a repetition of the stalemate.[4] The twenty-first meeting, however, saw a majority of the 50 members of the OAU vote to seat the Polisarios as a full member (November 12, 1984). Morocco withdrew in protest against that decision. In the meantime, moreover, Libya had formally recognized Morocco's title to the Western Sahara (August 1984) by signing a treaty with Morocco and withdrawing all support for the some 3,500 Polisario guerrillas fighting for the independence of the area in question.

UN Secretary-General Javier Pérez de Cuéllar had tried to mediate the Western Sahara dispute in 1986, and the United Nations had proposed a referendum to be held in the territory to determine its future status. Morocco had accepted the proposal, insisting, however, that its troops had to remain in place during the voting process. The Polisario Front also agreed, subject to the departure of Moroccan forces before the referendum. The Secretary-General returned to the plan in February 1987, this time proposing that the Organization of African Unity (OAU) and the United Nations should administer the Western Sahara on an interim basis while referendum plans were worked out. No positive response was elicited from the disputants.

In the meantime, Morocco, in order to end Polisario incursions, had constructed a 1,400 mile, extremely expensive wall of sand and barbed wire, manned by some 160,000 soldiers. It was supplemented with sophisticated electronic equipment and a variety of alarm systems. The wall extended from west of Tindouf (Algeria) to the Atlantic Ocean, its last western segment meant to help to protect fishermen and fishing vessels operating in an excellent fishing area. The completion of that last segment also meant that future Polisario attacks in that region would have to come from neutral Mauritanian soil. It was feared that if the weak available forces proved incapable of stopping such encroachments, Moroccan troops might pursue their enemies into Mauritania.[5]

[4]Consult *Time*, December 10, 1979, 68–69; May 31, 1982, 41–42; and the detailed analyses in *CSM*, March 28, 1983, 7; May 16, 1983, 13; May 26, 1983; 13; June 10, 1983, 3; July 27, 1983, 23; November 1, 1983, 13; Hodges, *Western Sahara: The Roots of a Desert War* (1984).
[5]See Blackburn in *CSM*, June 9, 1987, 24.

In May 1987, King Fahd of Saudi Arabia sponsored a brief meeting of Moroccan and Algerian representatives to discuss the threat of an escalation of the conflict. The Polisario Front had claimed all along that Saudi Arabia had been the major financier of Morocco's war effort, with the latter spending about $1.7 million a day on the conflict.

Heavy fighting along the wall marked the rest of 1987 and continued well into 1988. In May of that year, however, Morocco and Algeria restored diplomatic relations and later signed, with three other countries, a treaty calling for greater North African political and economic unity. The UN Secretary-General supplied the belligerents with a detailed plan for settling the dispute (August 11, 1988). The scheme included a cease-fire, peace negotiations under the auspices of the OAU and the United Nations, and Algeria and Mauritania to act as observers. Finally, a referendum on self-determination was to be held under U.N. and OAU supervision. By that time Algerian assistance to the Polisario Front had begun to decline drastically,[6] in consequence of the conclusion of the treaty mentioned above, and military stalemate developed.

Both the Polisario Front and Morocco agreed "in principle" to accept the UN peace plan (August 30, 1988), and the United Nations was considering sending some 2,000 peacekeeping troops to the Western Sahara. But problems about the peace plan multiplied quickly. The Polisario Front demanded the withdrawal of all Moroccan troops as well as that of all but low-level administrators before a referendum. It also argued that all Moroccan settlers in the region behind the wall, estimated at 100,000, should be evacuated from urban environments in the Western Sahara area before the UN referendum took place. Both sides, however, agreed on the delicate issue of voter eligibility: only Saharawis registered in a Spanish census in 1974 and their descendants over the age of 18 were to be allowed to vote on the political future of the Western Sahara.

It should be noted in passing that by this time 71 states had recognized the Saharawis' claim to the Western Sahara; no nation had backed Morocco in its claim.

On September 21, 1988, the UN Security Council unanimously approved an independence referendum for the Western Sahara, despite the different views of the parties concerning the operation of the plan. A special representative of the UN Secretary-General was chosen to monitor the referendum in which either independence or affiliation with Morocco was to be decided.

An unfortunate incident on December 8, 1988, distracted attention from peace maneuvers: a U.S. government anti-locust–spraying DC-7, of the U.S. Agency for International Development, was downed by a ground-to-air missile over Mauritania, with a loss of all five persons aboard, and a second DC-7, although damaged by a missile, managed to land in Morocco. The Polisario Front admitted the downing, asserting that it was done in the

[6]See Moffett, "Morocco Winning Hearts and Minds," *CSM,* April 12, 1989, 3.

mistaken belief that it was a Moroccan military aircraft. It recovered the bodies and took them to Algeria for return to the United States.

To no one's surprise, the August 1988 UN peace plan had to be tabled (including the peacekeeping force and the referendum) because of the lack of agreement on the part of the two belligerents. Brief exchanges of views between Morocco's King Hassan and Polisario representatives ended without results. But the United Nations persisted in its efforts to end the conflict over the Western Sahara. A UN committee had been appointed, preparing plans for the reduction in Moroccan troop strength along the wall from 80,000, which compared with an estimated Polisario force of 7,000, to 8,000 men. Consultation also took place with Spanish experts who had prepared the 1974 census that had listed 74,000 Saharawis. It was also determined that, officially, 165,000 Saharawi refugees were in Tindouf, an Algerian border town.[7]

In June 1989, the UN Secretary-General paid a visit to Morocco, Mauritania, Algeria, and Mali; a major part of the agenda of the meetings was the UN peace plan for the Western Sahara. The contending parties began to show increasing signs of being willing to accept a settlement, so that the UN Security Council at the end of June 1990 authorized final preparations for a peacekeeping operation in the Sahara. It was decided then to send a UN technical team to the scene for an assessment of the requirements of what promised to be a large-scale and expensive operation.[8]

[7]See Houk, "Stalled Referendum Gets a Push," *CSM*, June 15, 1989, 4, and *id., loc.cit.,* "Among the Refugees in Tindouf."
[8]See Houk, "Western Saharan Peace Prospects Improve, UN Says," *CSM*, July 3, 1990, 6.

# 15

# The Law of the Sea

## 1. NATIONAL VESSELS

INTRODUCTION   Under certain conditions, a state may lawfully extend its effective jurisdiction beyond its normal territorial limits. For instance, citizens' allegiance to their state is a personal one and is preserved no matter how far they may travel into the world. If and when they return to the territory of their state, the state may hold them responsible for what they did while abroad. If citizens are aboard a vessel flying their country's flag, they are legally in the same position as if they were back home in the actual territory of their state; hence that state may apply its domestic law to them. It is in this sense that a national vessel and, incidentally, a national plane (registered in a particular country) may be thought of correctly as a kind of an extension of a nation's territory. The term *national vessel,* as used here, refers to a ship registered in a particular state and flying the flag of the latter, a national vessel of that state possessing its nationality. Although several readers have objected to the term *national vessel,* because they believe that all vessels are national vessels (excluding pirates and other stateless vessels), the term has been retained because this chapter deals with the flag state's authority over its own national vessels.

NATIONALITY   Every state has the right to sail ships under its flag on the high seas. In the past, this privilege was reserved to coastal or island states.[1] This tradition was first set aside in the various peace treaties ending World War I, which provided for the international (maritime) recognition of the flag of the Allied and Associated Powers. Soon afterward, in 1922, the states participating in the Barcelona Conference agreed to extend recognition of national flags for maritime purposes to all countries adhering to the declaration resulting from the conference's deliberations. During World War II, the major belligerents agreed to recognize the flag of Switzerland on the oceans of the world, and the old jibe about a Swiss navy became obsolete. It might be mentioned that by agreement among the opposing belligerents a portion of the Italian port of Genoa was set aside as a Swiss port-of-entry and guaranteed immunity from attack. Sealed freight trains conspicuously

---

[1]See McDougal, Burke, and Vlasic, "The Maintenance of Public Order at Sea and the Nationality of Ships," 54 *AJIL* 25, esp. 66–70 (1960).

displaying the Swiss white cross on the sides and roofs of cars carried goods between Switzerland and its Genoese terminal zone. Currently an estimated total of 30 vessels ply the oceans under the Swiss flag. The recent practice in granting rights concerning registration and flags by landlocked states was approved in Article 90 of the 1982 United Nations Convention on the Law of the Sea (hereafter UNCLOS III):[2]

"Every State, whether coastal or land-locked, has the right to sail ships flying its flag on the high seas."

Each state determines for itself the conditions for the grant of its nationality to vessels, for the registration of ships in its territory, and for the right of ships to fly its flag. And ships have the nationality of the state whose flag they fly.[3]

Generally, once a vessel has been registered in a given state, it is regarded by that state and other states as constituting a legal person; it may be sued and it may sue. Its nationality determines, at least on the high seas, the national location of most acts taking place aboard it.

The concept that vessels flying the flag of a given state represent a sort of floating extension of the territory of that state was taken quite literally in earlier days. Many decisions handed down, especially by British and American courts, affirmed this fiction of extraterritoriality. In the twentieth century, the view has been adopted that ships shall sail under the flag of one state and, save in exceptional cases expressly provided for in treaties, shall be subject to its exclusive jurisdiction on the high seas. This means that its laws and regulations apply to most acts undertaken aboard the vessel but that the latter cannot be regarded as part of the territory of the flag state, except for public warships, ships owned or operated by states and used only for government noncommercial service, and ships serving certain international organizations.

As was pointed out, the exclusive jurisdiction in question here must be viewed with minor reservations: in time of peace, the public vessels of all maritime states have rights of visit and search when there are grounds for suspicion that a given ship may be engaged in piracy, in the slave trade, and the like. An example occurred in May 1982 in connection with the *Evergreen,* a freighter sailing under the Panamanian flag (of convenience). While on the high seas, a minor mutiny took place, involving two Filipino crew members who killed the first officer (a citizen of India). The Israeli captain of the vessel sailed it into U.S. territorial waters and radioed for help, but when FBI agents and members of the coast guard boarded the ship, the crew had already subdued the mutineers. When the *Evergreen* reached Houston, the two sailors were handed over to private security guards hired by the local Panamanian consul general. The sailors were then flown, aboard commercial

[2]Text in 21 *ILM* 1261 (1982).
[3]See Herman Meijers, *The Nationality of Ships* (1967); Whiteman, vol. 9, 1–51; and UNCLOS III, Art. 91(1).

aircraft, to Panama via Miami, for trial in the flag state. In that particular instance, no criminal prosecution in the United States was possible, as no U.S. laws had been violated, the vessel had been on the high seas at the time of the killing, and no U.S. citizens had been involved. Furthermore, a state has an undoubted right, under self-defense, to seize a vessel flying a foreign flag when it is suspected that the flag is being used fraudulently or that the vessel is being used by rebels or insurgents in an attack on the arresting state. And, finally, in time of war, belligerent warships possess extensive powers of visit and search to enforce contraband and blockade regulations. (See Chapter 25.)

FLAGS OF CONVENIENCE    The national right to register vessels has led several states, particularly Panama, Cyprus, and Liberia, to enact rather liberal legislation enabling the registration of ships owned and operated by foreign companies. The tonnage now under the flags of these companies and of a number of small states (for the convenience of the shipowners, hence the origin of the term *flag of convenience*) has increased sharply in recent decades, until today both Panama and Liberia rank ostensibly among the top five maritime nations in the world. By the middle of 1989, more than 500 vessels were registered under the flags of Panama, Liberia, Honduras, and Vanuatu. American military authorities consider such ships, if American-owned, to be part of the "effective controlled fleet" of the United States because they can be used, legally, in time of war.

The reasons for adopting a flag of convenience are numerous and include such considerations as low taxes; legislation providing for lower wages to seamen than those prevailing in the country in which the owners of the vessels do business; the absence of, or minimal, social security contributions by the vessel's owners under the laws of the registering state; and possibly the absence of, or weakness of, labor unions in that country. The registering states appear to lack the administrative machinery to enforce whatever legislation they may have enacted for vessels flying their flags, and furthermore, most of the ships in question never call at the ports of their "home" state. In consequence, real or fancied abuses have led repeatedly to the picketing of such vessels when they arrive in the ports of the country in which the owners are domiciled, and labor disputes have punctuated the maritime history of several Western nations, particularly the United States.

Despite the traditional rule about granting a vessel the right to fly the flag of the registering state, Article 5(1) of the 1958 Convention of the High Seas imposed a rather interesting limitation on the freedom of a state to grant nationality to a vessel:

There must exist a genuine link between the state and the ship; in particular, the state must effectively exercise its jurisdiction and control in administrative, technical and social matters over ships flying its flag.

The UNCLOS III Convention, however, in its Article 91(1), refers to this linkage only in these words: "There must exist a genuine link between the

State and the ship." This wording might be interpreted to mean that in the absence of such a genuine link, another state might feel free to deny recognition to the asserted nationality of a vessel flying a flag of convenience and to treat it, in other words, as a stateless vessel and bar it from its ports. (See below about the two conventions.)

The inclusion of the limitation in the final version of the convention did not, of course, settle the problem. To date, recognition of nationality never has been denied because of the absence of a genuine link, and until one takes place, a state's traditional right to decide who shall be entitled to its nationality will remain unchanged in practice. On the other hand, one major legal precedent regarding the "genuine link" has been recorded in another connection and may help in a future court decision about vessels flying a flag of convenience without a genuine link to the registered state.[4]

An interesting variation on the traditional use of flags of convenience occurred in 1987: in an attempt to protect Kuwaiti tankers against attack during the Persian Gulf hostilities, the United States agreed to reflag 11 such tankers by putting them under the U.S. flag and to escort them with U.S. Navy vessels during their sojourns in the Persian Gulf.[5] The tankers were given new names (such as from Al Puntas to Middletown), but there was no genuine link in existence during the episode.

Ships can sail under the flag of only one state and on the high seas are under the jurisdiction of that state alone. No ship can change its flag during a voyage or while in a port of call, except in the event of a real transfer of ownership or a change in registry.

If a vessel sails under the flags of two or more states, using them as convenience dictates, that vessel is treated as a stateless vessel. This is also true for a ship displaying a flag not attributable to a member of the family of nations.[6] The mere fact that a vessel has no right to fly a flag or uses

---

[4] *Nottebohm Case* (*Liechtenstein* v. *Guatemala*), International Court of Justice, 1955, *ICJ Reports, 1955,* 4. See the detailed and annotated discussion of a "genuine link" and "flags of convenience" in McDougal, Burke, and Vlasic, *op. cit. supra,* n. 1, 28–40 and esp. 104–11. Consult also Dye, "Flags of Convenience: Maritime Dilemma," 88 *United States Naval Institute Proceedings* 76 (Feb. 1962) and Romans, "The American Merchant Marine: Flags of Convenience and International Law," 3 *Virginia Jl. of Int'l L.* 121 (1963). The most extensive study of flags of convenience still is Boczek, *Flags of Convenience: An International Legal Study* (1962).

[5] See M.H. Armacost (U.S. Under Secretary for Political Affairs), "The U.S. Plan to Protect Kuwaiti Ships in the Gulf by Putting Them under U.S. Flags," (June 16, 1987), and related documents, in 26 *ILM* 1429 (1987); *Current Policy No. 958,* "International Shipping and the Iran–Iraq War"(May 1987); and Lamar, "Rough Seas and New Names," *Time,* June 29, 1987, 13.

[6] See also UNCLOS III, Art. 92(2). Jurisdiction over stateless vessels on the high seas was involved in two interesting American cases: *United States* v. *Cortes,* U.S. Court of Appeals, 5th Cir., 588 F.2d 106, 1979, reported in detail in 20 *Harvard Int'l Law Jl.* 397 (1979); and *United States* v. *Marino-Garcia* (two consolidated cases), U.S. Court of Appeals, 11th Cir., 679 F.2d 1373, 1982, reported in 77 *AJIL* 630 (1983). These cases brought out the fact that all nations have the right to assert jurisdiction over stateless vessels on the high seas, even if there is no direct connection between the vessel and the state asserting jurisdiction.

an "unknown" (unattributable) flag does not mean, however, that the ship in question would be treated as a pirate vessel, unless it had engaged in piratical acts. Normally a stateless vessel will not be admitted to the ports of any country. It may be stopped, searched, arrested, and taken into port for examination and/or trial by the naval or coast-guard vessels of any member of the family of nations.[7] On the other hand, a ship may lawfully fly the flag of an international organization (hence not to be connected to an individual country) under the provisions of Article 7 of the 1958 Geneva Convention. Such organizations include the United Nations, its specialized agencies, and the International Atomic Energy Agency.[8] If and when a vessel legitimately flies, say, the flag of the United Nations, the question of a "genuine link" in the meaning of the 1958 convention emerges in totally new surroundings and has interesting new interpretations. On the other hand, a rather unusual departure from the accepted norms took place in December 1983, when, with the unanimous support of the Security Council, UN Secretary-General Pérez de Cuéllar agreed that for "strictly humanitarian reasons," the ships that were to evacuate Yasser Arafat and some four thousand soldiers of the PLO would be allowed to run the UN flag alongside the flag of their country of registration (France, Greece, Italy). The ships, chartered by Saudi Arabia, were to be escorted by French warships in order to deter any Israeli or Syrian attacks.

Prompted by the problems created by the concept of a "genuine link" at a time when the use of flags of convenience increased and "linkage" was increasingly absent, a UN international conference in Geneva drafted a new UN Convention on Conditions for Registration of Ships (1986).[9] The avowed intent of the drafters of the instrument was to define the minimum elements of a genuine link that should exist between a ship and its flag state. Those minimum elements included: (a) the flag state was to have a competent and adequate national maritime administration subject to its jurisdiction and control; (b) that administration was to ensure that ships flying the flag of that state complied with its law and regulations; (c) that such ships were to be surveyed periodically to ensure compliance with applicable international rules and standards; and (d) a "satisfactory part" of the complement [officers and crew] was to consist of nationals of the flag state.

It should not have surprised anyone knowledgeable about conditions on ships flying flags of convenience or the absence of genuine links that, as of

---

[7] See *Naim-Molvan* v. *Attorney General for Palestine,* Great Britain, Privy Council, 1948, reported in 42 *AJIL* 953 (1948); and *United States* v. *Cortes,* U.S. Court of Appeals, 5th Cir., 1979, 588 F.2d 106, reported in 73 *AJIL* 514 (1979). See also the case of *United States* v. *Escamilla* in view of the fascinating and most unusual circumstances surrounding it (murder committed on a floating ice island in the Arctic—a floe manned by U.S. citizens working for the U.S government. The Department of Justice termed the "island" a "vessel on the high seas"), reported in detail in *Time,* September 28, 1970, 58.

[8] See also UNCLOS III, Art. 93.

[9] Text and content summary in 26 *ILM* 1229 (1987).

August 31, 1987, only 13 countries had signed the convention; that this group did not include any of the major suppliers of flags of convenience, and that no country had ratified the convention by that date. The instrument was to enter into force when ratified by 40 states representing 25 percent of the relevant gross registered tonnage. At the time it was estimated that the ratification process would take up to five years, a case of gross underestimation based on either ignorance or, more likely, on an unwillingness to face facts in the real world of shipping.

JURISDICTION OVER NATIONAL VESSELS    The law of the flag state governs matters relating to internal affairs aboard a vessel, including discipline. However, if the "shipping articles" signed by crew members stipulate the application of the law of a state other than the flag state, then the stipulated law would apply, say, to injury claims. [10] Because qualification standards for masters, other officers, and several categories of crew members of oceangoing ships have varied widely and have been of minimal quality, or virtually nonexistent in the case of some of the "flag-of-convenience" vessels, it is interesting to note that in recent years a number of international agreements have been drawn up to remedy these conditions. Among them are the International Labor Organization's Convention Concerning Minimum Standards in Merchant Ships (October 29, 1976), the same agency's supplementary Recommendations Concerning the Improvement of Standards in Merchant Ships (October 29, 1976), and a new instrument adopted by the Intergovernmental Maritime Consultative Organization on July 1, 1978, on regulations and minimum requirements for masters and crews of merchant vessels, the Convention on Standards of Training, Certification and Watchkeeping for Seafarers. The latter instrument has been supplemented by 23 resolutions recommending additional procedures. The convention is scheduled to become effective upon ratification by 25 maritime countries. And, finally, the International Labour Conference of the International Labour Organisation (ILO) adopted four conventions at its seventy-fourth (Maritime) Session in Geneva in 1987 (attended by representatives of 77 countries): the Convention on Seafarers' Welfare at Sea and in Port; the Convention on Health Protection and Medical Care of Seafarers; the Convention on Social Security for Seafarers (Revised); and the Convention on Repatriation of Seafarers (Revised). [11]

LAW ABOARD SHIPS    As mentioned earlier, a vessel is subject to the laws of the flag state. It is true that while in foreign waters, a ship owes what might be termed a limited allegiance to the foreign state in question; that is, it must obey the host country's navigation and similar regulations. But once the vessel returns to high seas, it is bound by the law of the state

---

[10] See the relevant American cases of *Tjonaman* v. *A.S. Elittre,* U.S. Court of Appeals, 2nd Cir., 1965, 340 F.2d 290; *Shahid* v. *A/S J. Ludwig Mowinckeles Rederi,* U.S. District Court, S.D.N.Y., 1964, 236 F. Supp. 751; and especially *Kontos* v. *S. S. Sophie C.,* U.S. District Court, E.D. Pa., 1964, 236 F. Supp. 664. See also Whiteman, vol. 9, 51–83.
[11] Text and content summary in 27 *ILM* 631 (1988).

in which it is registered.[12] This principle was illustrated convincingly in a classic case in 1860:

## REGINA v. LESLIE
### Great Britain, Court of Criminal Appeal,
### 1860, 8 Cox's Criminal Cases 269

FACTS    Leslie was captain of the British private merchant vessel *Louisa Braginton*. When the ship came to the Chilean port of Valparaiso, the Chilean government contacted Leslie and persuaded him to sign a contract whereby he undertook to transport several Chilean citizens to Liverpool. The individuals in question had been banished from Chile for political reasons. They were taken under military guard to the port and placed aboard the *Louisa Braginton*. Whenever that vessel then touched a port on the voyage around South America and on to Liverpool, the exiled Chileans demanded to be set ashore, but Leslie insisted on the fulfilment of his contract and brought the entire group to Liverpool. There the Chileans sued Leslie on charges of false imprisonment. The lower court ruled in favor of the plaintiffs, and Leslie appealed to the Court of Criminal Appeals.

ISSUE    Was Leslie liable to an indictment in Great Britain for fulfilling his contract concluded in Chile with the government of that country?

DECISION    The conviction of Leslie was affirmed: he had been under the rule of English law as soon as he quit Chilean territorial waters.

REASONING    The conviction could not be sustained for what Leslie had done in Chile. It had to be assumed that in Chile the action of the local government toward its citizens was lawful; in consequence, Leslie was correct in what he did in Chile as an agent of the Chilean government.

However, the conviction had to be sustained for what Leslie did outside of Chilean territorial waters. As soon as he left them, he and his ship were subject to the laws of England, as were all persons, English and foreign, aboard the vessel. His activities subsequent to the departure from Chilean jurisdiction amounted to false imprisonment, for he took the Chileans without their consent to England, denying them the right to depart when they desired to leave his ship in other states. A Chilean captain and vessel would have acted correctly under the circumstances, but Leslie had violated the law of England.

REGULATIONS FOR SAFETY AT SEA    Every state is obligated to adopt measures for the ships under its flag to ensure safety at sea, such as the use of signals, the maintenance of communications, and the prevention of collisions.

In the event of a collision or any other incident of navigation concerning a ship on the high seas, involving the penal or disciplinary responsibility

[12]See *Lauritzen v. Larsen*, U.S. Supreme Court, 1953, 345 U.S. 571, reported in 47 *AJIL* 711 (1953).

of the master or of any other person in the service of the ship, no penal or disciplinary proceedings may be instituted against such person except before the judicial or administrative authorities of either the flag state or the state of which such a person is a national. This doctrine, accepted generally in recent decades and now affirmed in Article 97(1) of UNCLOS III (UN Convention on the Law of the Sea, 1982), stands in sharp contrast with the decision in the *Lotus* case, at one time considered a classic. *The S.S. Lotus, P.C.I.J.,* (1927, Ser. A, No. 10). That adjudication by the Permanent Court of International Justice centered on a collision on the high seas between the French steamer *Lotus* and a Turkish collier, the *Boz-Kourt.* The main issue that the court had to settle was whether Turkey had a right, under international law, to institute criminal proceedings, under Turkish law in a Turkish court, against the French officer in charge at the time of the collision. The court found that all vessels on the high seas are under the law of their flag state and that each state should be able to exercise jurisdiction and to do so with respect to an incident as a whole. Thus there existed, in this case, an instance of concurrent jurisdiction; that is, there was no rule of international law in regard to collision cases, to the effect that criminal proceedings were exclusively within the flag state's jurisdiction.

A diplomatic conference meeting in Brussels in 1952 disagreed with the conclusions of the Permanent Court in the *Lotus* decision and in consequence drafted the International Convention for the Unification of Certain Rules relating to Penal Jurisdiction in Matters of Collision and Other Incidents of Navigation, signed in Brussels on May 10, 1952. That instrument contained the provisions concerning the trial of alleged offenders in connection with collisions on the high seas later reiterated in the 1958 Geneva Convention on the High Seas (Art. 11). The UNCLOS III convention, in its Article 97(3), also pertaining to collisions or other incidents on the high seas, affirmed that "no arrest or detention of the ship, even as a measure of investigation, shall be ordered by any authorities other than those of the flag State." Thus the *Lotus* case today is purely of historical interest.

## 2. THE MARITIME BORDER

Coastal states benefit from certain specific derogations (detractions) from the concept that the ocean and seas of the world represent a common heritage and, so to speak, communal property of all nations. (See below, *sub* The High Seas.)

### A. THE TERRITORIAL SEA

The early writers in international law realized that the boundary of a coastal state should extend beyond the low-tide mark along the shore. Such an extension appeared to be dictated by the logic of defense as well as by the obvious necessity of protecting in some reasonable manner the rights of the coastal state to fishery resources along its own shores.

It should be kept in mind that there is a difference between a particular width of territorial sea that represents a portion of a nation's domain and over which *sovereignty* is asserted, and the waters beyond this territorial sea, that is, adjacent portions of the high seas (contiguous zones, conservation zones, customs zones), over which *protective* or *preventive rights* are asserted.

## Methods of Determining Extent of Territorial Sea

THREE-MILE LIMIT    The states concerned in determining the precise extent of their sovereignty over what is now called the *territorial sea,* or *marine sovereignty zone,* or *territorial waters* appear to have based their agreement on a compromise between two different views. Denmark—controlling, in the seventeenth and eighteenth centuries, Norway, Iceland, and the Faroe Islands—promoted the concept of a territorial sea of measured width. The Netherlands, on the other hand, maintained that control by the coastal state should extend the distance commanded by artillery on the shore, that is, cannon range. The resulting compromise was the principle that the territorial sea comprised an area of water to a line three miles from the low-tide mark. [13]

At the time in question, the approximate limit of the range of coastal cannon was said to have been three miles, and the governing concept adopted seems to have been that a state could claim ownership over such waters as it was able to command with its armament. [14]

It should be noted parenthetically that the "miles" referred to in connection with territorial seas, contiguous zones, and so on are nautical (or marine, or geographical) miles: 1 such mile equals approximately 1.15 common or statute miles.

Over time, the three-mile limit was accepted by the major maritime nations, in particular by Great Britain and the United States. [15]

## Problem of the Breadth of the Territorial Sea

The problem of the breadth of the territorial sea came into fore in the twentieth century when the unilateral establishment of fishing and conservation zones called attention to the varying limits set by coastal states for their territorial waters. The first major (and unsuccessful) attempt to arrive at a generally acceptable and uniform breadth of the territorial sea was made at

---

[13] See Kent, "The Historical Origins of the Three-Mile Limit," 48 *AJIL* 537 (1954); consult also Higgins-Colombos, 70–76.

[14] See Bynkershoek, *De Domino Maris* (1702), in the *Classics of International Law* translation, 44: "the power [control] over the lands ends where the power of weapons ends" (*potestam terrae finiri, ubi finitur armorum vis*). A convenient summary of the historical background may be found in Dean, "The Second Geneva Conference of the Law of the Sea: The Fight for Freedom of the Seas," 54 *AJIL* 751, esp. 756–62 (1960).

[15] For different claims, see the FAO 1971 study in 10 *ILM* 1255 (1971).

The Hague in 1930. No agreement could be reached then, the differences in views being so pronounced that not a single proposal of a limit was even put to a vote.

In discussing the problem after World War II, the International Law Commission of the United Nations had decided that international law did not call for an extension of the territorial sea beyond 12 miles, justifying its stand by the opinion that any greater breadth jeopardized the principle of the freedom of the high seas. On the other hand, the commission did not succeed in fixing the limit between 3 and 12 miles.

The problem came up next for discussion at the 1958 Geneva Conference on the Law of the Sea, but again there were no conclusive results. It was this particular failure to reach agreement that prompted the calling of the Second Geneva Conference on the Law of the Sea in 1960.

The second meeting soon bogged down in a welter of conflicting claims to both territorial waters and fishing zones. Acceptance of a unilateral extension, however, in order to be generally valid, had to be by such a large number of states that the dissenters comprised but a minority as against those who consented openly or tacitly.[16]

At the 1958 Geneva Conference, the United States sponsored a proposal for a six-mile fishing zone beyond a six-mile territorial sea limit. That startling American reversal of a traditional insistence on a three-mile limit failed to be adopted at the time. During the 1960 conference, the Soviet Union proposed a "flexible" rule. Other proposals, including a U.S.–Canadian compromise, went down to defeat. After this the Conference eventually terminated without having decided on a general limit to the width of the territorial sea.

No international agreement having been reached, the coastal states proceeded in larger numbers to announce new limits for their territorial seas. The United States shifted to the support of a 12-mile territorial sea limit: in February and again in May 1970, it was announced that a 12-mile limit for all coastal states would be deemed acceptable, in exchange for free transit privileges through and over all straits used for international navigation. Ultimately the United States on December 28, 1988, expanded its territorial sea limits from the traditional three miles to the 12-mile breadth already adopted by that date by 104 other countries,[17] and called for in UNCLOS III, Art. 4.

"NORMAL" BASELINE SYSTEM    Traditionally, the outer boundary of territorial waters was determined by the low-tide mark along the coastline, called the *normal baseline,* at whatever distance had been fixed for the width of the territorial waters.

STRAIGHT BASELINE SYSTEM    The 1958 Geneva Conference on the Law of the Sea instituted a significant innovation regarding the concept of the ter-

---

[16]On this point, see the lucid analysis in Lauterpacht's *Oppenheim,* vol. 1, 17.
[17]See Newsom, "Why the Three-Mile Limit Sank," *CSM,* Jan. 26, 1989, 18; see also Henkin, 307–11.

ritorial sea: the straight baseline system for delimiting that sea. Eventually more and more states claimed that the baseline from which the territorial sea was measured should not necessarily be the actual coastline but might be a system of straight lines drawn from points on or near the shore over areas of water to some other points on or near the shore.

The first major dispute over this system of determining the extent of the territorial sea resulted in the well-known *Anglo-Norwegian Fisheries* case, decided by the International Court of Justice in 1951.[18] Beginning in 1911, British fishing vessels operating in waters off the coast of Norway were seized and condemned by Norwegian authorities for violating regulations of the coastal state governing fishing in waters allegedly part of the Norwegian territorial sea. The dispute not being amenable to other methods of settlement, the British government instituted proceedings before the International Court of Justice in 1949, the main argument being that the seizures occurred more than four miles off the Norwegian coast (Norway's territorial waters extend to a distance of four miles from shore); hence they took place, illegally, on the high seas, or so it was claimed.

The court decided by a vote of 10 to 2 in favor of Norway, approving the Norwegian practice of drawing an outer boundary for its territorial sea that was based on straight baselines following the general directions of the coast but not the indentations of that coast.

The court's opinion dwelt at length on the extraordinary geographic peculiarities of the Norwegian coastline and appeared to have sanctioned the straight baseline method for exceptional use rather than a principle of universal applicability.

When the International Law Commission drafted a convention on the territorial sea, prior to the 1958 Geneva Conference, it attempted to embody this method as an exceptional approach in determining the boundaries of a state's territorial waters. The conference accepted the commission's proposals in virtually unchanged form, and Article 4 of the 1958 Geneva CTSCZ reads:

1. In localities where the coast line is deeply indented and cut into, or if there is a fringe of islands along the coast in its immediate vicinity, the method of straight baselines joining appropriate points may be employed in drawing the baseline from which the breadth of the territorial sea is measured.
2. The drawing of such baselines must not depart to any appreciable extent from the general direction of the coast, and the sea areas lying within the lines must be sufficiently closely linked to the land domain to be subject to the regime of internal waters.
3. Baselines shall not be drawn to and from low-tide elevations, unless lighthouses or similar installations which are permanently above sea level have been built on them.

[18] *United Kingdom* v. *Norway (Norwegian Fisheries Case)*, *I.C.J. Reports 1951*, No. 1, reported in detail in 46 *AJIL* 348 (1952). Consult also Evensen, "The Anglo-Norwegian Fisheries Case and Its Legal Consequences," 46 *AJIL* 609 (1952). The text of the Anglo-Norwegian agreement of 1960 may be found in 57 *AJIL* 490 (1963).

4. Where the method of straight baseline is applicable under the provisions of paragraph 1, account may be taken, in determining particular baselines, of economic interests peculiar to the region concerned, the reality and the importance of which are clearly evidenced by a long usage.
5. The system of straight baselines may not be applied by a State in such a manner as to cut off from the high seas the territorial sea of another State.
6. The coastal States must clearly indicate straight baselines on charts, to which due publicity must be given.

The provisions of Article 7 of UNCLOS III virtually duplicate the 1958 stipulations, except for the addition of Article 7 (2), which covers the problem of unstable coastlines such as may be found in a delta.

The utilization of the straight baseline method means that areas of water previously part of the high seas may be assimilated into the territorial waters of a coastal state and thus come under the exclusive jurisdiction of that state, subject to a right of innocent passage for foreign vessels. It should be noted that straight baselines are still applicable in exceptional circumstances only, such as in the case of Canada's Arctic coast,[19] so that states with only slightly irregular coastlines are bound by the traditional method of delimiting the outer boundaries of their territorial sea.

VARYING BREADTHS OF A CONTINENTAL SEA    Neither customary law nor the 1958 Geneva Convention on the Territorial Sea and the Contiguous Zone prohibit a variation in the breadth of a country's territorial sea, and the as yet not in force UNCLOS III provides in its Art. 3 that " Every State has the right to establish the breadth of its territorial sea up to a limit not exceeding 12 nautical miles." Thus Turkey has adopted the 12-mile limit in the Black Sea and the Mediterranean but a 6-mile limit in the Aegean, and Japan and South Korea adopted a 12-mile limit in the Strait of Korea except in its western channel where a 3-mile limit prevails.

ARCHIPELAGO THEORY    A new method of determining a territorial sea was developed unilaterally by the Philippines and Indonesia: the so-called archipelago theory. Each of the two states claimed the right to draw a perimeter around its outermost islands and to term all waters within that perimeter *historic internal waters*. Their territorial waters would then extend outward from the straight baselines envisioned by the two states.[20] Indonesia proposed a 12-mile limit for its territorial sea, whereas the Philippines put forth a varying limit, ranging from three miles at some points to more than 12 miles at others. A glance at a map reveals the immense extent of the internal seas claimed under the archipelago theory. Indonesia's perimeter extends over 3,000 miles from east to west and about 1,300 miles in a north–south direction, and the Philippines cover an area roughly 600 miles

[19] See map in 18 *Canada Today/d'aujourd'hui,* 3 (Jan. 1987).
[20] See Dean *op. cit. supra* n.14, 753, 765–67, concerning the precise wording of these Philippine and Indonesian claims, particularly notes 4, 53, and 54, which document those claims and their discussion both at Geneva and in the General Assembly of the United Nations. See also the official U.S. view in 1989, in 83 *AJIL* 559 (1989).

wide and 1,000 miles long, from north to south. If the original archipelago theory were accepted by other states, the proclaimed internal-waters status of the seas enclosed within the perimeters in question would abolish rights of free passage, the right of submarines to enter and travel submerged, and all rights of foreign aircraft to fly over the waters involved, unless special treaty rights were granted to the citizens and craft of particular nations ("conditionally innocent passage").

UNCLOS III hence limits the length of archipelagic baselines to a normal maximum of 100 nautical miles (Articles 46–51), which would prevent the closure of enormous areas as internal waters. In the case of very large archipelagos, up to 3 percent of the total number of baselines may exceed the limit to a maximum of 125 miles.

The traditional doctrine, opposing the archipelago theory, was upheld in the interesting American case of *Civil Aeronautics Board* v. *Island Airlines, Inc.,*[21] in which it was held that the channels separating the Hawaiian Islands beyond the three-mile limit are international waters: the boundaries of Hawaii, therefore, are represented by a three-mile belt of territorial sea surrounding each individual island.

## General Rules

When the coasts of two states are opposite or adjacent to each other, neither of the two states is entitled, failing their agreement to the contrary, to extend its territorial sea beyond a median line every point of which is equidistant from the nearest points on the baselines from which the breadth of the territorial seas of each of the two states is measured (Art. 12, 1958 Geneva Convention on the Territorial Sea and Art. 15 of UNCLOS III). This rule would not apply, of course, where, by reason of historic title or some other special circumstance, it is necessary to delimit the territorial waters of the two states in some other manner.

In the case of rivers, no problem is posed when a stream flows directly into the sea (both banks belonging to the same state), for in such a case both the 1958 Convention on the Territorial Sea (Art. 13) and UNCLOS III (Art. 9) call for drawing a straight line across the mouth of the river as the baseline for the delimitation of the territorial sea. But if a river empties into a bay or estuary and the banks are controlled by different states, then any attempt to use a different approach to that delimitation must be viewed as violating the accepted rules of international law. Such an attempt was made by Argentina and Uruguay in January 1961 when the two countries attempted to delimit in a novel manner the borders in the Rio de La Plata. The effort resulted in strong protests by the United States.

---

[21]U.S. Dist. Court (U.S.), Hawaii, 1964, 235 F. Supp. 990, excerpted in 59 *AJIL* 635 (1965), and noted with citation of much relevant literature by Nafziger in 7 *Harvard Int'l Law Club Jl.* 143 (Winter 1965). The decision of the District Court was affirmed by the Court of Appeals, 9th Cir., 1965, 352 F.2d 735. See also Whiteman, vol. 4, 281.

## Special Rules for Gulfs and Bays

Thus far the discussion of the maritime border—that is, of the seaward limit of the territorial sea—has dealt with the usual coastline. The border thus would follow the convolutions of the coast at some uniform distance from the low-tide mark along the coast. But the facts in the Gulf of Aqaba dispute, discussed below, indicate that special rules apply to gulfs and bays. Whenever there are indentations along the coast of a state, the delimitation of the maritime frontier becomes more difficult. A strictly logical interpretation of the rules governing the territorial sea would leave all bays and gulfs within that sea inside a line drawn from shore to shore at points six miles apart (assuming a *three-mile* limit of the sea).[22]

There are, however, certain bays that are considerably wider than six miles at the mouth or entrance, and some of these inlets run deep into the territory of the coastal state. It is not surprising, therefore, that the coastal state lays special claim to complete sovereignty over such bays or gulfs, and many such claims have received the tacit approval of other maritime states. Some of the best-known examples of such a claim are the historic ones supported by the United States over the Delaware and Chesapeake bays (the former ten miles wide at its entrance, the other nine and one-half miles wide) and the Canadian claim to Conception Bay in Newfoundland. Unique is the situation of the Gulf of Fonseca, which was ruled, in 1917, by a decision of the Central American Court of Justice, to be a historic bay and a closed sea, part of the territories of El Salvador, Costa Rica, and Nicaragua, the three states constituting the coastal states fronting on the gulf.

The 1958 Geneva Convention on the Territorial Sea and the Contiguous Zone changed the traditional rule governing sovereignty over bays by stating (Art. 7, par. 5) that where the distance between the low-water marks of the natural entrance points of a bay exceed 24 miles, a straight baseline of 24 miles should be drawn within the bay in such a manner as to enclose the maximum area of water that is possible with a line of that length. Paragraph 1 of Article 7 of the convention reads, "This article relates only to bays and coasts of which belong to a single state." The particular language used was adopted in order to avoid the necessity of taking a position on the Gulf of Aqaba and access to it through the Straits of Tiran.[23] This area had been the source of a bitter and continuing dispute between Israel on the one hand and the Arab states on the other.[24]

---

[22] See Higgins-Colombos, 131–46, for an extensive analysis of specific problems in connection with bays and gulfs.

[23] Bishop, 49, n. 84; see also the U.S. position on gulfs and bays (1973) in 68 *AJIL* 107 (1974).

[24] Consult *inter alia*, Gross, "The Geneva Conference on the Law of the Sea and the right of Innocent Passage Through the Gulf of Aqaba," 53 *AJIL* 564 (1959), with extensive documentation; Porter, *The Gulf of Aqaba: An International Waterway* (1957). On May 23, 1967, the United Arab Republic closed the Straits of Tiran and the gulf to Israel shipping, an act partly responsible for the outbreak of the subsequent Six-Day War.

UNCLOS III retains the provisions of the 1958 Convention on the Territorial Sea but provides a bit more elaboration (Article 10). It should be noted that if a bay or gulf somehow involves the application of straight baselines, the limit of 24 miles on such baselines would not apply, and in any event the limitation would exclude all so-called historic bays, that is, bodies of water along the coasts of countries that have been traditionally regarded as part of those states' territorial waters (see above). This last concept was illustrated in the interesting case of

## THE PEOPLE v. STRALLA AND ADAMS
*United States, Supreme Court of California, 1939*
*(98 California Decisions 440)*
*{Reproduced in full in 34* AJIL *143 (1940)}*

FACTS    Stralla and Adams operated the *Rex,* a gambling ship anchored in Santa Monica Bay, four miles from the city of Santa Monica and six miles landward from a line drawn between the headlands of the bay. Those headlands are separated by a distance of 25 nautical or about 29 statute miles. The depth of the bay from a line connecting the headlands is about ten miles.

The authorities of Los Angeles County raided the ship and arrested its owner-operators, who were convicted of operating a gambling ship, in violation of the laws of California. Conviction was appealed from the Superior Court of Los Angeles to the District Court of Appeal and, in turn, came before the California Supreme Court.

ISSUE    Was Santa Monica Bay part of the territory of California, or was the vessel anchored in the high seas and thus immune from seizure by California authorities?

DECISION    The Supreme Court affirmed the previous conviction. All of Santa Monica Bay was held to be within the jurisdiction of the state of California.

REASONING    Santa Monica is a "historic" bay, title to which has been claimed by California over a long period of time. The state constitution claims all bays and harbors along the coast. The bay is part of California territorial waters, the outer limits of which extend seaward at a distance of three miles parallel to a line drawn between the headlands of the bay. Within the bay, the state of California may exercise its jurisdiction for all lawful purposes, including the prosecution of violators of the state's penal law.

**THE GULF OF SIDRA INCIDENT**    In March 1986, clashes between the armed forces of the United States and Libya centered attention on the legal problems connected with Libya's claim to the Gulf of Sidra. That body of water covers an area of some 22,000 square miles, bordered on three sides by Libyan territory. Libya had by law extended its territorial sea breadth to 12 nautical miles (February 18, 1959). In 1973 the Libyan government announced that all of the Gulf constituted an integral part and internal waters of the country. Foreign vessels (private or public) henceforth were to enter the Gulf only after receiving permission from Libya. The seaward limit of the Gulf was set by a straight-baseline of about 300 miles, from "headland" to "headland."

The United States (and other countries, such as Italy) rejected this Libyan claim (February 11, 1974), pointing out that the baseline in question was more than 12 times the permissible closing line of a bay or gulf (24 miles). It also rejected the concept that the Gulf of Sidra was a historic bay of Libya. Libya had not claimed jurisdiction beyond territorial waters before 1973, thus lacked the "historic" aspect of a possible claim by failing to claim the Gulf over an extended period of time. Libya also had failed to exercise effective jurisdiction over the Gulf beyond the territorial sea limits, and the maritime community of the world had not recognized, or at least acquiesced in, a Libyan claim to a historic bay or gulf.

When a three-carrier U.S. naval group penetrated the Gulf after crossing the Libyan baseline (March 23, 1986), Libya fired surface-to-air missiles at U.S. planes, U.S. planes fired missiles at a Libyan patrol boat (lost with its crew) and launched missiles at a Libyan missile site at Sirte, the U.S. cruiser *Yorktown* fired a missile at a Libyan patrol boat outside the Gulf, and the carrier *Saratoga* launched a second attack on the Sirte missile base. On March 25, U.S. planes hit another Libyan patrol sailing in the Gulf beyond Libyan territorial waters.[25]

## National Sovereignty over Territorial Waters

Within the limits of a state's territorial waters, the jurisdiction of the coastal (littoral) sovereign is as complete as it is over its territory on land. Any existing limitations, whether they refer to a "right of innocent passage" or to privileges and immunities granted to foreign vessels, represent voluntary concessions that do not touch the essential principle of complete sovereignty. Vessels do, however, enjoy the right to enter and even to anchor in territorial seas when in distress or danger from threatening weather. The coastal state has the right not to admit foreign ships that do not meet the safety standards prescribed by the coastal state and by international law. It has been stated that Sweden, in 1758, was the first country to assert this modern doctrine of national sovereignty over its territorial sea.

RIGHT OF INNOCENT PASSAGE   A foreign vessel, on entering the territorial sea of the coastal state, has a right of innocent passage. This right includes stopping and anchoring, but only insofar as the same are incidental to ordinary navigation or are rendered necessary by *force majeure* or by distress. Passage of a foreign fishing vessel is not considered innocent if it fails to observe the laws and regulations issued by the coastal state in order to

---

[25] See Blum, "The Gulf of Sidra Incident," 80 *AJIL* 668 (1986); *Gist,* December 1986; and the AP and UPI Dispatches of March 23, 1986, to March 27, 1986.

prevent such a vessel from fishing in the territorial sea.[26] Thus the Bahamian patrol boat *Flamingo* acted correctly when on May 10, 1980, it chased and then arrested two 60-foot Cuban fishing vessels caught fishing in the territorial waters of the Bahamas. On the other hand, Cuba was acting irresponsibly, to say the least, when two of its military jets bombed and sank the *Flamingo,* with the loss of four lives. The Cuban defense, which was soon followed by an apology, was that one of the two Cuban vessels had radioed that it was being attacked by a "pirate ship."

If the national security of the coastal state is felt to justify it, that state may suspend temporarily, in specified areas of its territorial sea, the right to innocent passage of foreign ships, provided there is no discrimination among vessels of different nationalities. Such a suspension of the right of innocent passage normally takes effect only after it has been publicized.[27] However, a coastal state may not suspend the innocent passage of foreign vessels through straits that are used for international navigation between one part of the high seas and another part of the high seas or the territorial sea of a foreign state.[28] On their part, foreign ships exercising their right to innocent passage are bound to comply with the laws and regulations of the coastal state, in conformity with international law, particularly with such rules as relate to transport and navigation.[29]

In short, the passage of a foreign vessel through the territorial sea is not considered innocent if it is prejudicial to the peace, order, or security of the coastal state.

Finally, the coastal state has complete sovereignty over the airspace above its territorial sea. The right of innocent passage through the sea does *not* include the passage of foreign aircraft, and indeed a foreign vessel may not

---

[26]See Selak, "Fishing Vessels and the Principle of Innocent Passage," 48 *AJIL* 627 (1954). Ecuador had claimed inability to control foreign shipping and had prohibited innocent passage of fishing vessels. On the other hand, UNCLOS III includes in Article 19 (2) a long list of practices deemed to be in violation of innocent passage and lists, among other items, "any fishing activities," any act "aimed at collecting information to the prejudice of the defence or security of the coastal state," as well as acts of willful or serious pollution, and so on; the list concludes with item 2-1: "Any other activity not having a direct bearing on passage." In 1979, Ecuador enacted a law banning all fishing by foreign tuna boats within 100 miles of the Ecuadorian coast, extending thereby the old limit of 60 miles.

[27]See notice of suspension because of an underground nuclear test explosion (1971) by the United States: 65 *Department of State Bulletin* 599 (1971).

[28]Article 16 (4) of the 1958 (Geneva) Convention on the Territorial Sea and the Contiguous Zone, 52 *AJIL* 838 (1958 Supp.). The International Law Commission, in its draft of this paragraph, had used the expression "normally used for navigation," based on the decision of the International Court of Justice in the *Corfu Channel Case:* see 51 *AJIL* 196 (1957 Supp.). UNCLOS III Article 38 (1) omits the word *normally.*

[29]See *Payne* v. *S.S. Tropic Breeze,* U.S. Court of Appeals, 1st Cir., 1970, 423 F.2d 236, reported in 64 *AJIL* 953 (1970). See also Union of Soviet Socialist Republics–United States: "Joint Statement with Attached Uniform Interpretation of Rules of International Law Governing Innocent Passage," Sept. 23, 1989, in 28 *ILM* 1444 (1989), and Butler, "Innocent Passage and the 1982 Convention: The Influence of Soviet Law and Policy," 81 *AJIL* 331 (1987).

launch, land, or take aboard any aircraft while that vessel is in territorial waters (1982 UN Convention on the Law of the Sea, Art. 19(2)(e)0.) Both the 1958 Geneva Convention and the 1982 United Nations Convention agree on these points.

## Jurisdiction over Foreign Merchant Vessels

A foreign merchant vessel leaving the high seas and entering the territorial waters (and ports) of another state automatically creates a conflict between the jurisdiction applying to the vessel by virtue of its nationality and the physical jurisdiction into which it has come. This conflict has been adjusted, on the whole, by custom and treaty law, so that side by side there now exist a continuing but limited jurisdiction by the flag state and a rather extensive but *not* unlimited jurisdiction by the state into whose territory the vessel has entered.[30]

CRIMINAL JURISDICTION    Internal discipline aboard a foreign vessel passing through the territorial sea is normally subject to the laws and regulations of the flag state, unless the captain of the vessel or a consul of the flag state requests the assistance of the coastal state's authorities.

The coastal state may not take any steps on board a foreign ship passing through the territorial sea to arrest any person or to conduct any investigation in connection with any crime committed before the ship entered the territorial sea, if the ship, proceeding from a foreign port, is only passing through the territorial sea without entering internal waters.

When a foreign vessel is passing through the territorial sea, the criminal jurisdiction of the coastal state *should not* be exercised on board that vessel to arrest any person or to conduct any investigation in connection with any crime committed on board the ship during its passage, except if the consequences of the crime somehow extend to the coastal state, if it is of a nature to disturb the peace of the country or the good order of the territorial sea, or if it is necessary for the suppression of illegal traffic in narcotic drugs (Art. 19, par. 1, 1958 Convention on the Territorial Sea; Art. 27, UNCLOS III).

The same articles also rule that the preceding provisions do not affect the right of a coastal state to take any steps authorized by its law for the purpose of an arrest or investigation aboard a foreign ship passing through the territorial sea after leaving internal waters. Thus are conferred on a coastal state greater powers over ships passing through the territorial sea after leaving that state's internal waters than over ships merely passing through the territorial sea. The logic behind this differential treatment appears to be that a coastal state's interests are more directly affected by ships stationary in the territorial sea or passing through it after departing from a port than by those engaged in mere innocent passage through the sea.

---

[30]On the general subject, consult Higgins-Colombos, 239–51.

Finally, according to Article 20, paragraph 1, of the 1958 Geneva Convention (Art. 28 par. 1, UNCLOS III Convention) the coastal state should not stop or divert a foreign ship passing through the territorial sea for the purpose of exercising civil jurisdiction in relation to a *person* on board the ship. On the other hand, the *ship* itself may be arrested or seized as the result of events occurring in the waters of the coastal state during the voyage in question as, for example, a collision or a salvage operation.

When a foreign merchant vessel enters a port of a coastal state, the Anglo-American view has been that the host state has the right to enforce not only various safety and navigation regulations but also its criminal laws when the tranquility of its port (or "its peace," in the terminology of UNCLOS III Convention) is disturbed by events aboard ship. The European view, on the other hand, has affirmed that all matters and events *aboard* the vessel represent an exclusive concern of the flag state.

The Anglo-American interpretation of the coastal state's authority was laid down in the following case:

## MALI v. KEEPER OF THE COMMON JAIL (WILDENHUS' CASE)
### United States, Supreme Court, 1887, 120 U.S. 1

FACTS   The Belgian steamer *Noordland* was docked in the port of Jersey City, New Jersey. On October 6, 1886, a Belgian member of the crew, Joseph Wildenhus, fought below decks with another Belgian crew member, by the name of Fijeus, and stabbed him with a knife. Fijeus died as a result of the wound.

The police of Jersey City boarded the vessel and arrested Wildenhus, who was then committed by a police magistrate to the common jail of Hudson County, New Jersey, pending trial for murder. The Belgian consul (M. Charles Mali) for New York and New Jersey then asked for a writ of habeas corpus, claiming that by international law and under the provisions of the Belgian–United States Consular Convention of 1880, the offense with which Wildenhus had been charged was to be handled under the laws of Belgium and that the state of New Jersey lacked proper jurisdiction.

Article 11 of the convention invoked stated, among other things, that

"The local authorities shall not interfere [with the internal order of merchant vessels], except when the disorder that has arisen is of such a nature as to disturb tranquility and public order on shore or in the port, or when a person of the country, or not belonging to the crew, shall be concerned therein."

The Belgian case rested in the assertion that no outside persons had been involved, that slayer and victim, both Belgian citizens, had been members of the crew of the *Noordland,* and that the commission of the crime, aboard ship and below deck, had not disturbed the tranquility of the port and public order.

The U.S. Circuit Court for the District of New Jersey refused to deliver the arrested individuals (Wildenhus and two witnesses, both members of the ship's crew) to the consul. The consul then appealed that decision.

ISSUE   Does murder aboard a foreign vessel in port, affecting only members of the foreign crew, constitute a disturbance of the tranquility of the port and thereby justify assertion of jurisdiction by the local law enforcement agencies?

DECISION    For the Keepers of the Common Jail, judgement of the Circuit Court affirmed.

REASONING    The crime of murder, by its commission, disturbs tranquility and public order on shore or in a port so that it has to be regarded as falling within the exceptions provided for in the treaty of 1880, in which the local authorities have a right to interfere.

A foreign merchant vessel in port may be subject to civil suit by a citizen of the host state, and its officers and crew may be sued individually, just as they are subject to criminal prosecution if they violate the laws of the host state.

An act committed on board a ship may sometimes be subject to the concurrent jurisdiction of several states: the state in which the vessel is registered, the state in whose territory the ship happens to be at the time, and the state or states of which the individuals concerned are citizens or subjects. Naturally, only one of those concurrent jurisdictions can be exercised at a given time.

One of the classic cases exemplifying this problem of concurrent jurisdiction is the following:

### REGINA v. ANDERSON
*Great Britain, Court of Criminal Appeal, 1868*
*11 Cox's Criminal Cases, p. 198*

FACTS    James Anderson, an American citizen, was indicted for murder on board a vessel belonging to the port of Yarmouth, Nova Scotia, and registered in Great Britain. At the time the offense was committed, the ship was moving up the river Garonne, on its way to the French city of Bordeaux, some 90 miles from the coast. The vessel, at the time, was therefore on the internal waters of the French Empire.

The accused was detained on the ship until it returned to England and was charged with murder in the Central Criminal Court in London. He was convicted of manslaughter, despite his plea that the court lacked jurisdiction to try him, as the offense had been committed in French territory, aboard a colonial vessel, by an American citizen. The judgement of the Criminal Court was appealed.

ISSUE    Which country had jurisdiction to try the accused under the conditions described?

DECISION    Conviction affirmed: British courts had jurisdiction to try offenses committed aboard British ships.

REASONING    The Court of Criminal Appeal found that the accused was subject to American jurisprudence as an American citizen, to French jurisprudence for having committed an offense in the territory of France, and also to British jurisprudence, for the jurisdiction of British law and of British courts extends to the protection of British vessels, no matter where those vessels might be at a given time. The court held that the French authorities could have enforced French law by arresting Anderson and placing him on trial for his offense.

France had not asserted its undoubted right to prosecute Anderson for disturbing the tranquility of a port and public order. Great Britain, in control of the vessel, then exercised its authority and prosecuted Anderson. This procedure was wholly approved by the Court of Criminal Appeal.

A more recent case, *Regina* v. *Governor of Brixton Prison, ex parte Minervini,*[31] illustrates the modern application of this principle. Minervini, an Italian seaman, was accused of having murdered a fellow crew member aboard a Norwegian merchant vessel. The Norwegian government instituted extradition proceedings when Minervini was located in England. The accused was arrested and, after a hearing before the Metropolitan Magistrate, committed to prison to await execution of an extradition order issued by the British Secretary of State of Foreign Affairs. Minervini then applied for a writ of habeas corpus, claiming that because the location of his ship at the time of his alleged offense had not been determined, the Anglo-Norwegian extradition treaty of 1873 was inapplicable because it referred only to crimes committed on Norwegian territory. The court ruled that the term *territory* had to be construed as the equivalent of *jurisdiction,* and because the alleged offense had been committed on board a Norwegian vessel—that is, under Norwegian jurisdiction—the treaty applied. Hence Minervini's application was denied.[32]

GRANTING OF ASYLUM    Before leaving the subject of "normal" foreign merchant vessels in the territory of a coastal state, it must be pointed out that such ships cannot serve as places of asylum, either for alleged fugitives from criminal justice or for political refugees. There is no question that the local authorities have a legal right to board foreign merchant vessels in the port of the coastal state and remove from them such fugitives or refugees. It also appears that the commander of such a vessel can be tried in the courts of the host state for violating the rule prohibiting the granting of asylum on merchant vessels.

It is not established, on the other hand, whether the authorities of a coastal state have the right to remove from a foreign merchant vessel coming into their port a passenger who, as a political refugee from the authorities of the coastal state, boarded the vessel in question in a third state. Inconclusive evidence appears to support the view that such a right does exist, on the assumption that the refugee voluntarily reentered the jurisdiction of the country whose authorities were attempting to apprehend him. However, not all extant cases confirm this interpretation.

The coastal state may not, except under highly abnormal conditions (such as an appeal for help from the captain of a vessel), take any steps on board a foreign ship passing through the territorial sea (to arrest any person or to

---

[31] W.L.R. 559 Queen's Bench Div. Court, Oct. 7, 1958.
[32] Still more recent is the unusual case of *United States* v. *Reagan,* U.S. Court of Appeals, 6th Cir., 1971, 453 F.2d 165, reported in 66 *AJIL* 874 (1972).

conduct any investigation in connection with any crime committed before the ship entered the territorial sea) if the ship, proceeding from foreign port, is only passing through the territorial sea without entering internal waters. In regard to civil jurisdiction, a coastal state may not stop or divert a foreign ship passing through the territorial sea for the purpose of exercising such jurisdiction in regard to a person on board the ship. This prohibition does not apply in the case of a ship lying in or passing through the territorial sea after leaving the internal waters of the coastal state. (See the 1958 Convention on the Territorial Sea and the Contiguous Zone, Art. 20, and UNCLOS III, Art. 28, concerning civil jurisdiction.)

### Jurisdiction over Foreign Public Vessels

The position of foreign public noncommercial vessels in the ports and waters of a coastal state is quite different, in most respects, from that occupied by merchant vessels, essentially because there is a close and immediate relationship between a state and its public ships. This section deals with the rules applicable in time of peace. For those prevailing during a war, see Chapter 29.

First, a foreign warship entering the territorial sea of another state is expected to comply not only with all applicable rules of international law but also with all regulations of the coastal state in regard to navigation. Should such a foreign warship fail to follow those regulations, the coastal state may require the warship to leave the territorial sea.

RIGHT OF INNOCENT PASSAGE    Although the right of innocent passage through territorial waters extends to public vessels as well as private craft, a number of states have recorded reservations to the 1958 Geneva Convention on the Territorial Sea. The Soviet Union, Bulgaria, the Byelorussian Republic, Hungary, Rumania, and the Ukranian Republic all require prior authorization or consent by the coastal state before passage of a foreign warship is permitted through the territorial sea. The Republic of Colombia made a declaration amounting to a corresponding reservation because of a provision in the Colombian constitution. Other countries do not require such prior authorization, and all proposals to include state consent in the convention were rejected during the relevant meetings. Only the requirement that submarines that are warships must show their flag and proceed at the surface was accepted as a reasonable requirement by the coastal state for passage through territorial waters.

Beyond these reasonable and proper limitations, the foreign public vessel, regarded as a floating portion of the territory of its flag state, is completely exempt from all jurisdiction of the coastal state.

Sweden, more than any other country, has been plagued by violations of its territorial waters by mostly unidentified submarines. It has been stated semiofficially that since 1962, over 200 foreign submarines, both full-sized and midget types, have penetrated Swedish waters without obeying the rule of traveling on the surface.[33] The most spectacular incident involved the Soviet whiskey-class submarine 137 which ran aground on a reef in a restricted Swedish military zone some nine miles from the Karlskrona naval base. The grounding took place on October 28, 1981, and the submarine was not towed from the reef until November 6, after lengthy Swedish-Russian negotiations. The Soviet Union apologized for the incident, blaming it on faulty navigation, and paid Sweden $658,000 for the salvage operation. Following repeated incidents off its coast, Sweden officially warned the Soviet Union in April 1983 that it would destroy any submarines found submerged in Swedish waters, and since then the Swedish navy has used depth charges as well as antisubmarine missiles whenever the occasion appeared to demand it. In May 1983, Norway had a frigate fire 15 antisubmarine missiles and a depth charge on a suspected Soviet submarine, and in the previous year Italy claimed in February that a Soviet victor-class submarine had violated its territorial waters near the Taranto naval base. In all instances except that involving submarine 137, the Soviet Union has denied that its vessels had penetrated foreign waters.

The status of a foreign warship in the territorial sea attracted worldwide attention in 1968 through the North Korean seizure (January 23, 1968) of the USS *Pueblo,* an intelligence vessel operating off the coasts of North Korea. Being a part of the U.S. Navy, the *Pueblo* was entitled to the immunities recognized by Article 8 of the 1958 Geneva Convention on the High Seas. Even though North Korea was not a party to that agreement, the immunity of a foreign warship has long been a part of customary international law. Under Article 23 of the convention, the only authority possessed by North Korea, had it been a party to the treaty, would have been an order to the vessel to leave the territorial sea.

The United States government claimed to have no official knowledge of the breadth of the North Korean territorial sea but assumed that a claim of 12 miles, corresponding to that of other socialist states, was in effect. It maintained that the *Pueblo* was captured 15 miles offshore.[34] On the other hand, if the ship did penetrate North Korean territorial waters, then two factors should be taken into consideration in judging the action of the North Korean authorities in seizing the vessel (but not excusing the apparently barbaric treatment of the crew until it was released in December 1968):

---

[33]See Stanglin, "A Cold-War Hangover," *U.S. News & World Report,* Feb. 19, 1990, 41. See also Union of Soviet Socialist Republics, "Rules for Navigation and Sojourn of Foreign Warships in the Territorial and Internal Waters and Parts of the U.S.S.R.," 24 *ILM* 1715 (1985).

[34]See telegram from U.S. Department of State to all U.S. diplomatic missions (February 8, 1968) in 62 *AJIL* 756 (1968); the U.S. "admission of espionage," signed to obtain the release of the crew, 8 *ILM* 199 (1969); and related documents in 63 *AJIL* 682 (1969). See also the lengthy account by Hersh on alleged U.S. submarine espionage in Soviet territorial waters, *NYT,* May 25, 1975, 1, 42.

the nature of the activities reportedly carried on by the *Pueblo* ("intelligence gathering") and the fact that the 1953 armistice did not end the Korean War, insofar as its legal status as a war was concerned (see Chapter 22), so that, in effect, the *Pueblo* could have been classified by North Korea as an enemy warship.

A public vessel in a foreign port is immune from civil suits *in rem,* at least as far as warships and naval auxiliary vessels are concerned.[35]

The "fiction" of the extraterritorial character of public vessels has been challenged repeatedly in modern times. One of the most vigorous denunciations of the doctrine was made in the judgment in the following British case:

## CHUNG CHI CHEUNG v. THE KING

*Great Britain, Judicial Committee of the
House of Lords, Dec. 2, 1938.
{1939} A. C. 160*

FACTS    Chung, a British subject, was a cabin boy on the Chinese maritime customs cruiser *Cheung Keng* when that vessel was in Hong Kong territorial waters. On January 11, 1937, he shot and killed Douglas Lorne Campbell, the captain of the cruiser and a British national. Both men were, at the time, in the service of the Chinese government. After killing the captain, Chung wounded the acting chief officer of the vessel and then shot and wounded himself. The chief officer ordered the cruiser to proceed at once to Hong Kong and to hail a police launch. A few hours later, a police launch was sighted and came alongside in answer to the cruiser's signal. The police took the wounded officer and Chung to a hospital in Hong Kong.

On February 5, 1937, the chairman of the provincial government of Kwangtung requisitioned the extradition of Chung to China on charges of murder and attempted murder on board the Chinese customs cruiser "within the jurisdiction of China while the said cruiser was approximately one mile off Futau-

mun (British waters)." It later was determined that the shootings took place in British territorial waters. After several adjournments, the magistrate in charge of the extradition proceedings decided that the accused was a British subject and that the proceedings therefore failed. Chung was promptly arrested again and charged with murder "in the waters of this Colony." At his trial, the chief officer of the cruiser and three of the crew were called as witnesses for the prosecution. Chung was convicted and sentenced to death.

By appeal the case came before the Judicial Committee of the Privy Council in London.

ISSUE    Did a British court have a right to try the accused Chung?

DECISION    The local British court in Hong Kong had jurisdiction to try the appellant. Appeal dismissed.

REASONING    (1) "A public ship in foreign waters is not, and is not treated as,

---

[35] The classic case, still prevailing today, is *Schooner Exchange* v. *MacFaddon,* U.S. Supreme Court, 1812, 7 Cranch 116: see abstract in Chapter 7.

territory of her own nation. The domestic courts in accordance with principles of international law will accord to the ship and its crew and its contents certain immunities, some of which are well settled, though others are in dispute. In this view the immunities do not depend on an objective extraterritoriality, but on implication of the domestic law. They are conditional, and can in any case be waived by the nation to which the public ship belongs."

(2) "Their Lordships have no hesitation in rejecting the doctrine of extraterritoriality expressed in the words of Mr. Oppenheim, which regards the public ship 'as a floating portion of the flagstate.' However the doctrine of extraterritoriality is expressed, it is a fiction, and legal fictions have a tendency to pass beyond their appointed bounds and to harden into dangerous facts.... Immunities may well be given in respect of the conduct of members of the crew to one another on board ship.... But if a resident in the receiving state visited the public ship and committed theft, and returned to shore, is it conceivable that when he was arrested on shore . . . the local Courts would have no jurisdiction?"

(3) " . . . it appears to their Lordships as plain as possible that the Chinese Government, once the extradition proceedings were out of the way, consented to the British Court exercising jurisdiction. It is not only that, with full knowledge of the proceedings, they made no further claim, but at two different dates they permitted four members of their service to give evidence before the British court in aid of the prosecution."

The immunity granted to a foreign warship in the territorial waters of the host state extends also to the members of that vessel's crew when they are on shore *on duty*.[36] On the other hand, if a member of such a crew commits a violation of the host's laws while on shore and off duty, the individual in question normally does not enjoy immunity from local jurisdiction.[37] (See Chapter 7 for the lack of immunities of publicly owned vessels engaged in commercial activities.)

ASYLUM ABOARD FOREIGN PUBLIC VESSELS    The question of asylum aboard foreign public vessels has arisen frequently in every part of the globe. Earlier centuries saw the granting of asylum to both ordinary criminals and political fugitives. This generous interpretation of the immunity of foreign public vessels has been curtailed decisively since the middle of the last century, and today only a customary right of asylum for political offenders is recognized. The government of the United States, traditionally averse to a broad grant of asylum rights, has restricted the use of American public vessels to occasions on which the life of the political refugee is in immediate danger by mob violence.[38] Latin American states, on the other hand, have laid down by

[36] *Georges Triandafilou* v. *Ministère Public,* Mixed Courts in Egypt, Court of Cassation, June 29, 1942, reprinted in translation in 39 *AJIL* 345 (1945).
[37] *Malevo Manuel* v. *Ministère Public,* Mixed Courts in Egypt, Court of Cassation, March 8, 1943, reprinted in translation, *id.,* 349.
[38] See Hackworth, vol. 2, 639–42, and Whiteman, vol. 6, 498–502, for examples.

convention (1928) a rule by which asylum may be granted aboard public vessels to political offenders in "urgent cases."[39]

## B. INTERNATIONAL STRAITS

STRAITS   Straits connecting territorial bays or seas with an ocean are subject to the same rules as is the territorial bay or sea itself. The only major problems arising in this connection involve straits connecting two oceans or seas. Among the few examples available is the former privilege of Denmark to levy a toll on traffic between the Baltic and the North Sea, abolished in 1857.[40] Another example is the Argentina–Chile agreement of 1881 for the perpetual neutralization of and guarantee of free navigation in the Straits of Magellan. (But see Chapter 22 concerning the Beagle Channel dispute.) On the other hand, Indonesia and Malaysia announced on November 20, 1971, that the Strait of Malacca and Singapore Strait were "not international straits" but that both states recognized free use of the waterways for international shipping on "the principle of innocent passage."

Other straits connecting seas have been regulated by multilateral international instruments, notably the Dardanelles and the Bosporus, connecting the Black Sea with the Mediterranean and bordered exclusively by Turkey. Beginning in 1809, regulation of travel through these straits was attempted, and after an almost unbelievably complicated series of conferences, each resulting in some form of agreement, a presumably final settlement was achieved in the Montreux Convention of 1936, by which all previously existing international supervision was terminated, and recognition of exclusive Turkish sovereignty over the straits was granted, including a Turkish right to militarize the straits. The only restriction remaining was a limit of 10,000 tons for offensive naval units passing through the straits. The convention expired in 1977.

It has been claimed that there are at least 120 straits in the world 24 miles in width or less.[41] In addition to those mentioned above, other important straits are the Korean Strait, the Strait of Dover, the Baltic Strait, the Gulf of Aden, the Strait of Gibraltar, the Strait of Hormuz, the Northwest Passage (termed a strait by the United States, an inland waterway by Canada), and the Strait of Corfu.

---

[39] Hackworth, vol. 2, 646–49.

[40] On straits in general, see Whiteman, vol. 4, 417–80; Kheng-Lian, *Straits in International Navigation: Contemporary Issues* (1982). Moore, "The Regime of Straits and the Third United Nations Conference on the Law of the Sea," 74 *AJIL* 77(1980); Reisman, "The Regime of Straits and National Security: An Appraisal of International Lawmaking," *id.*, 47; and Articles 34 to 44 of the 1982 UN Convention on the Law of the Sea, in 21 *ILM* 1276–1278 (1982).

[41] Coll, "Functionalism and the Balance of Interests in the Law of the Sea: Cuba's Role," 79 *AJIL* 891, at 901 (1985).

If two states border a strait 24 miles wide or less and fail to reach agreement on a dividing line midway between the two shores, a problem will have arisen. A width of exactly 24 miles would likely leave no high seas corridor available for shipping. The example cited lately in the literature is the Strait of Korea: Japan and South Korea extended their territorial seas to a breadth of 12 nautical miles each in 1977, but agreed to retain the earlier 3-mile limit in the western channel of the Strait. At its narrowest point, that channel has a width of 23.2 miles, and thus 12-mile limits could not be established without creating what Pak termed a "territorial strait." Keeping the old limit along the channel meant, on the other hand, a high seas corridor almost 17 miles wide.[42]

A major international incident involving a strait took place in the Strait of Corfu in 1946. Following the end of World War II, the victorious powers (with the help of many vessels and crews recruited from among their defeated opponents) engaged in a large-scale attempt to remove anchored and floating mines around the coasts of Europe. British vessels cleared the Strait of Corfu between the Greek Island of Corfu and the mainland shores of Greece and Albania. Shortly afterward, two British destroyers struck mines while traversing the Strait. Great Britain then sent minesweepers into the Strait, in accordance with a decision of the International Mine Sweeping Commission, and this action was protested by Albania on the grounds of invading Albanian territorial sovereignty.

When the dispute, which also involved a British claim for compensation arising out of the destroyer incident, was brought before the Security Council of the United Nations, it decided on March 25, 1947, that Albania must have been cognizant of the presence of mines, a decision that implied a degree of Albanian responsibility for the placement of the mines in the Straits. The majority vote of the Security Council was rendered ineffective, however, by a Soviet Union veto. The dispute was then brought before the International Court of Justice by Great Britain:

### THE CORFU CHANNEL CASE
### (GREAT BRITAIN–ALBANIA)

*I. C. Reports, 1949, pp. 4, 244; Judgment {Merits}, April 9, 1949; Assessment of Amount of Compensation, December 15, 1949.*[43]

FACTS    In October 1944, the North Corfu Channel was swept by the British navy and no mines were found; as a result of this operation, Great Britain announced in November 1944 the existence of a safe route through the channel. In January and February 1945, the channel was checked again, with nega-

---

[42]Pak, *The Korean Strait,* 75 (1988).

[43]For texts of relevant documents, consult 42 *AJIL* 690 (1948) [Ruling on Preliminary Objection]; 43 *AJIL* 558 (1949) [Merits]; 44 *AJIL* 579 (1950) [Assessment of Compensation].

tive results. In May 1946, two British cruisers went through the channel and no mines were discovered, nor were special precautions taken.

On October 22, 1946, a squadron of British warships (the cruisers *Mauritius* and *Leander* and the destroyers *Saumarez* and *Volage*) left the port of Corfu and proceeded north through the channel. Outside the Bay of Saranda, the *Saumarez* struck a mine and was heavily damaged, and the second destroyer was ordered to render assistance and to take the damaged vessel in tow. While towing the *Saumarez*, the *Volage* struck a mine and also was badly damaged. Both destroyers succeeded, however, in reaching the port of Corfu.

Three weeks later (November 13), British minesweepers swept the channel and cut the cables of 22 moored mines. Two of these were taken to Malta for examination and were found to be of the German GY type.

The damage to both destroyers occurred in Albanian territorial waters. Expert analysis of the damage sustained by the two vessels excluded all possibility of its having been caused by floating mines or by ground mines—both of which had been suggested by Albanian authorities as likely causes.

The Albanian government had also suggested that the mine field discovered on November 13 might have been laid after October 22, so that the damage sustained by the destroyers would not have been caused by the contents of the field. But no evidence supporting this suggestion was produced; instead, the experts at Malta concluded that the damage suffered had been caused by mines identical with those found in the field.

Great Britain demanded compensation for damage to its ships and for the loss of life on the latter. Albania rejected the claim, and Great Britain instituted proceedings in the International Court

of Justice on May 22, 1947, against the People's Republic of Albania. On December 9, 1947, the court rejected the objection filed by Albania.

Great Britain claimed that the mine field had been laid by or with the connivance and knowledge of the Albanian government or, alternatively, that the Albanian government had known that the mine field was in its territorial waters and, in violation of the Eighth Hague Convention of 1907, had failed to warn other countries of the existence of the mine field. Furthermore, according to the British claim, Albanian authorities had observed the approach of the British naval units and had failed to warn them of the existence of the mines, and the existence without notification of the mine field was a violation of the right of innocent passage by foreign vessels through an international waterway such as Corfu Channel. In reparation, Great Britain asked for £825,000 to cover the repair of the damages to the two destroyers and £50,000 for pensions and other expenses resulting from the loss of life and injuries suffered by the crews of the two vessels.

Albania contended that no proof had been submitted that the mines responsible for the damage to the British ships had been laid by Albania; that no proof had been submitted that the mines had been laid by a third party on behalf of Albania; that no proof had been submitted that the mines were laid with the help, acquiescence, or knowledge of Albania; that a coastal state was entitled, under exceptional circumstances, to regulate the passage of foreign warships through its territorial waters and that this rule applied to the Corfu Channel; that the required exceptional circumstances existed at the time in question, so that foreign warships should have obtained prior authorization to pass through Albanian territorial waters; that passage of the vessels on October 22,

1946, without previous authorization constituted a breach of international law; that the British passage in question was not an innocent passage; and that the sweeping operations of November 12–13, 1946, had not been permissible in Albanian waters and constituted a breach of international law. For these reasons, Albania maintained, no compensation was owed to Great Britain, but instead the latter should give to the Albanian government satisfaction for the breaches of law committed.

ISSUES    (1) Was Albania responsible under international law for the explosions that occurred on October 22, 1946, in Albanian waters and for the damage and loss of human life that resulted from them?

(2) Was there any duty on the part of Albania to pay compensation if such responsibility was established?

DECISION    The court ruled that Albania was responsible under international law for the explosions and for the damage and loss of life resulting from them, and that Albania owed a duty to Great Britain to pay compensation.

REASONING    Based on all the evidence submitted, the court found that the two ships had been mined in Albanian territorial waters in a previously swept and check-swept channel. As far as the laying of the mines was concerned, the court noted the Albanian government's formal statement that it had not laid the mines and was in no position to have done so, as Albania possessed no navy. However, the British reply had indicated that on or about October 18, 1946, two Yugoslav warships carrying contact mines of the German GY type had sailed south from Sibenik and had entered the Corfu Channel. The British contention was that Yugoslavia had laid the mine field with the knowledge and connivance of the Albanian government; that is, collusion between the two states. The court, after examining testimony about the alleged Yugoslav mine-laying operations, felt that proof of the British charge had not been shown.

The court ruled, therefore, that the authors of the mine laying remained unknown. It then proceeded to examine whether Albania had had any knowledge of the existence of the mine field. It decided that the Albanian government constantly kept a close watch over the waters of the North Corfu Channel, a watch occasionally reinforced by the firing of shots at passing vessels. All evidence indicated that the mine-laying had to have taken place during the time Albanian authorities kept a close watch over the channel and were insisting that their permission had to be obtained before a foreign vessel should proceed through the channel. The court held, further, that the actions of the Albanian government during and after the sweeping operations in November 1946 indicated its knowledge of the existence of the mines. Expert testimony insisted that if any close watch had been kept over the channel—and Albania insisted equally strongly that this had been the case—the coastal guards had to have noticed the mine-laying operations.

The court held that it had been a duty of the Albanian government to notify the world in general of the existence of the mine field and to warn the approaching British naval units of their imminent danger. This duty was not incumbent on Albania because of the provisions of the Eighth Hague Convention of 1907, which was applicable in war, but because of elementary considerations of humanity, because of the principle of the freedom of maritime communication, and because of the obligation, resting on every state, not to knowingly allow its territory to be used for acts contrary to the rights of other states.

Because nothing had been done by the Albanian authorities to prevent the disaster, this omission gave rise to the international responsibility of Albania.

In the final submissions, Great Britain asked for damages amounting to £875,000, but Albania asserted that the court had no jurisdiction to assess the amount of compensation.

On December 15, 1949, the court set damages to the destroyer *Saumarez* at £700,087 (its replacement cost); the damage to the destroyer *Volage* at £93,812 (the sum asked by the British government); and costs for pensions and other grants resulting from loss of life and injuries suffered on the part of the two crews at £50,048. The total amount of compensation due Great Britain from the People's Republic of Albania was therefore set at £843,947.

[NOTE:    Albania ignored the award of compensation, and no workable suggestion has come forth as to how the judgment can be satisfied.[44]]

A more recent controversy over a strait and a gulf centered on the Straits of Tiran and the Gulf of Aqaba. The latter, from 10 to 30 miles wide, is bordered by four states and is connected to the high seas by the straits in question. On May 22, 1967, the United Arab Republic announced a blockade of the gulf, an action denounced by Israel as an open violation of international law as well as an act of aggression. President Johnson of the United States, in a statement on May 24, reflected the views of the Department of State in holding the gulf and the straits to be international waters.[45]

More recently, beginning in February 1984, the Strait of Hormuz in the Persian Gulf became prominent in the news as the Iraq–Iran conflict began to turn in favor of Iran. The strait in question is quite narrow (about 30 miles wide, with two shipping channels), and a considerable portion of oil going to Europe and the Far East from the Gulf producers has to be shipped through the strait. It began to be feared that Iraq, almost bankrupt and unable to get Iran to agree to an end to the conflict (which was begun by Iraq on September 20, 1980) would in desperation strike against the oil terminals in Kharg Island, the main exporting point for Iranian oil. Iran,

[44] For an abortive attempt on the part of Great Britain to collect from Albania, see the *Case of the Monetary Gold Removed from Rome in 1943* (*Italy* v. *France, United Kingdom, and the United States of America*)—*Preliminary Question,* International Court of Justice, 1954, *ICJ Reports, 1954,* 19, digested and excerpted in 48 *AJIL* 649 (1954). The text of the arbitral award figuring in the case may be found in 49 *AJIL* 403 (1955). See also Oliver, "The Monetary Gold Decision in Perspective," *id.,* 216; and *NYT,* Oct. 21, 1979, E-2; *CSM,* May 19, 1983, 12, and Aug. 22, 1984, 10. As of June 30, 1990, Great Britain still held 230,000 ounces of the prewar Albanian gold reserve (seized in Germany at the end of World War II), pending satisfaction of the *Corfu Channel* case claim of more than $1.7 million. See also Cooley, *CSM,* Aug. 26, 1985, 11.

[45] *NYT,* May 24, 25, 1967; see also Gross, "The Geneva Conference on the Law of the Sea and the Right of Innocent Passage Through the Gulf of Aqaba," 53 *AJIL* 564 (1959); El Baradei, "The Egyptian-Israel Peace Treaty and Access to the Gulf of Aqaba: A New Legal Regime," 76 *AJIL* 532 (1982).

in turn, threatened to close the Straits by means of some sort of blockade. The United States government then indicated that it would use its naval forces to prevent disruption of the oil shipments through the Strait.

## 3. ZONES OF SPECIAL JURISDICTION

### CONTIGUOUS ZONES

A generally recognized rule of customary international law holds that a coastal state may exercise protective as well as preventive control over a strip or belt of the high seas contiguous (or adjacent) to its territorial waters.[46]

The United States has on many occasions asserted jurisdiction for limited purposes over adjacent waters. Thus, since 1790, it has claimed jurisdiction for customs purposes up to a distance of 12 miles from shore. Under a number of special "liquor treaties" with Great Britain and other states during the prohibition era, the United States had the right to stop, board, search, and seize vessels of the contracting states within one hour's sailing distance from the shore. When the Eighteenth Amendment to the Constitution had been repealed, the Anti-Smuggling Act was adopted in 1935, which authorized the president to establish at need so-called customs-enforcement areas up to 50 nautical miles beyond the 12-mile limit and 100 miles in each lateral direction from the "place of hovering."

The 1958 Geneva Conference on the Law of the Sea dealt with the question of contiguous zones in Article 24 of the Convention on the Territorial Sea and the Contiguous Zone.[47] The convention provided that in a zone of the high seas contiguous to its territorial sea, a coastal state could exercise the controls necessary to prevent infringement of it customs, fiscal, immigration, or sanitary regulations within its territory or territorial sea and that the coastal state had a right to punish violations of such regulations committed in the contiguous zone.[48]

More important, the convention provided that a contiguous zone could not extend beyond a limit of 12 miles from the baselines from which the breadth of the territorial sea was measured. This provision presupposed, therefore, that the width of the territorial sea was fixed at a distance of less than 12 miles.

The 1958 United Nations Conference on the Law of the Sea thus reaffirmed the traditional customary-law concept of a contiguous zone, despite the then inability of the participating states to agree on the equally important question of the width of the territorial sea. On the other hand, the new

[46]See Whiteman, vol. 4, 480–98.
[47]Text in 52 *AJIL* 840 (1958). The convention entered into force on September 10, 1964; by December 1968, 34 states had ratified it or acceded to it.
[48]See *United States* v. *Baker,* U.S. Court of Appeals, 5th Cir., Jan. 2, 1980, 609 F.2d 134, reported in 74 *AJIL* 678 (1980).

convention denied the demands of several states for exclusive and special fishery rights in the contiguous zone.

The 1982 UN Convention on the Law of the Sea (UNCLOS III), however, has somewhat different provisions for the nature and breadth of the contiguous zone in its Article 33:

1. In a zone contiguous to its territorial sea, described as the contiguous zone, the coastal State may exercise the control necessary to:
    (a) prevent infringement of its customs, fiscal, immigration & sanitary laws and regulations within its territory or territorial sea;
    (b) punish infringement of the above laws and regulations committed within its territory or territorial sea.
2. The contiguous zone may not extend beyond 24 nautical miles from the baselines from which the breadth of the territorial sea is measured.

The 1982 convention, for those states ratifying it, now takes into account the 12-mile limit provided for in the instrument for the territorial sea of a coastal state. The waters of the contiguous zone, beyond the outer limits of a given country's territorial waters, are considered integral parts of the high seas, except for the grant of law-enforcement controls in that zone, mentioned above.

## THE CONTINENTAL SHELF

Beginning with the proclamation issued by the President of the United States on September 28, 1945, claims have been advanced by many states to what is termed the *continental shelf*.[49] That shelf is the gentle slope from the edge of the land down to a point where there is a sudden increase in its steepness, to ocean depth. The width of the shelf varies enormously, from less than one mile to 80 miles, with an average width of about 30 miles. Owing to such divergent widths, in 1956 the International Law Commission of the United Nations limited the shelf to "a depth of 200 metres (approximately 100 fathoms), or, beyond that limit, to where the depth of the superjacent waters admit of the exploitation of the natural resources of the said areas." This language was adopted without change into the 1958 Geneva Convention on the Continental Shelf, ratified by May 1971 by 47 states (but not by Canada, Chile, Iceland, Indonesia, Iran, and Peru, among others).[50]

In essence, the various national claims have asserted that the seabed and subsoil of the land under the sea that extend as a sort of appendage of the

[49]Text, with the related executive order, reprinted in 40 *AJIL* 45 (1946 Supp.).
[50]Text in 52 *AJIL* 858 (1958 Supp.). However, Art. 76 omitted all mention of water depth and instead called for a 200-mile outer limit (maximum) for the shelf, in regard to exploitation by the coastal state.

landmass are under national jurisdiction of the littoral (coastal) state for exploitive purposes. The waters and the air above the continental shelf, on the other hand, are not claimed beyond the limits of the territorial sea of each of the states concerned.

The history of the concept of the continental shelf goes back to 1898, when the expression was first used by a geographer. Then "it made a fleeting appearance on the legal stage in 1916: but passed over it with 'printless feet'."[51] Although a 1942 treaty between Great Britain and Venezuela concerning spheres of influence in the Gulf of Paria could be said to have hinted at the concept of the continental shelf, this concept entered into the sphere of international law proper only with the Truman proclamation of 1945. That proclamation was implemented in turn, somewhat belatedly, by the passage of the Outer Continental Shelf Lands Act of August 7, 1953, which reserved for the United States all "political" and civil jurisdiction both in the subsoil and the seabed of the shelf beyond the seaward boundaries allowed to the states under the terms of the Submerged Lands Act of May 22, 1953.

The present writer believes that the new rule of international law dealing with national rights in the continental shelf evolved in an extremely short period of time as a result of the rapid issuance of claims, with 20 states, plus the United Kingdom on behalf of a dozen dependencies, asserting such claims in the space of 17 years. Although this new rule may not have been general in application, it is taken to have constituted a part of particular international law. This view was challenged vigorously, however, for the period antedating the 1958 Convention on the Continental Shelf. The new treaty has made the whole argument somewhat academic, of course, as all parties have agreed that since 1958, the position of the continental shelf in international law has been regularized.

## 1958 Convention on the Continental Shelf

The 1958 Convention recognizes exclusive sovereign rights to the seabed and subsoil resources of any continental shelf to a depth of 200 meters, or, beyond that limit, to where the depth of the "superjacent" waters permits the exploitation of the natural resources of the shelf. If a coastal state chooses not to exploit such resources, its sovereign rights will prevent any other state from undertaking such exploitation without its express consent. The 1982 UN Convention on the Law of the Sea (UNCLOS III) has, however, a somewhat different definition of the continental shelf in its Article 76(1):

1. The continental shelf of a coastal State comprises the sea-bed and subsoil of the submarine areas that extend beyond its territorial sea throughout the natural prolongation of its land territory to the outer edge of the continental margin, or to

---

[51]Footnote by the umpire, Lord Asquith of Bishopstone, in the *Arbitration Between Petroleum Development (Trucial Coast) Ltd. and Sheikh of Abu Dhabi,* Award of August 28, 1951, Paris, France, 1 *Int. and Comp. Law Quarterly* 247 (1952), digested in 47 *AJIL* 156, esp. 157 (1953). The award supplies amusing reading, in view of the umpire's many pithy comments.

a distance of 200 nautical miles from the baselines from which the breadth of the territorial sea is measured where the outer edge of the continental margin does not extend up to that distance.

Article 76(2–5) provides for certain extensions of the continental shelf of a coastal state through a system of straight lines, not to exceed 60 nautical miles in length, where the margin extends for more than 200 nautical miles. Article 76(6) states that the outer limit of a coastal state's continental shelf shall not exceed 350 nautical miles from the baselines from which the breadth of the territorial sea is measured.

Inasmuch as the 1982 Convention on the Law of the Sea is not yet in force at the time of this writing, the provisions of the 1958 instrument are still binding on states parties to it, and once the 1982 agreement is in force, each state will be bound by whichever instrument it ratified. In the event that a given state ratified both the 1958 and the 1982 agreements, the latter would prevail in governing continental shelf claims by the state in question.

The treaties further provide that the coastal state's rights over the shelf do not depend on occupation or any express proclamation.

The coastal state is not permitted to impede the laying or maintenance of submarine cables or pipelines on the continental shelf, subject to its right to take reasonable measures for the exploration of the shelf and the exploitation of its resources (1958: Art. 4; 1982: Art. 7).

Subject to these restrictions, the coastal state is entitled to construct and operate on the continental shelf installations of various sorts necessary for its exploration and the exploitation of its natural resources. Safety zones may be established by the coastal state. For obvious reasons, any installations constructed by the coastal state on the shelf are denied the status of islands. They thus lack any territorial sea of their own, and their existence cannot affect of delimitation of the territorial waters of the coastal state. Such installations are forbidden altogether where their presence would interfere with the use of recognized sea-lanes in international navigation.[52]

If another state should wish to sponsor or undertake research on the continental shelf, the consent of the coastal state is required (Art. 5).

Where the continental shelf is adjacent to the territories of two or more states whose coasts are opposite each other, the boundary of the shelf belonging to such states has to be determined by agreement between them. Failing such agreement, the boundary line is normally the median line, equidistant at every point from the nearest points of the base lines from which the breadth of the territorial sea of each state is measured. Where the shelf is adjacent to the territories of two adjacent states, the boundary of the shelf is determined by agreement between the states in question. In the absence of such agreement, the boundary is determined by the

---

[52]Article 60 of UNCLOS III spells out in detail the rights and duties of the coastal state concerning artificial islands, structures, and installations on the continental shelf.

application of the principle of equidistance from the nearest points of the relevant baselines. (Art. 6, 1958 Convention)

The provisions of UNCLOS III read somewhat differently in its Article 83:

1. The delimitation of the continental shelf between States with opposite or adjacent coasts shall be effected by agreement on the basis of international law, as referred to in Article 38 of the Statute of the International Court of Justice, in order to achieve an equitable solution.

2. If no agreement can be reached within a reasonable period of time, the States concerned shall resort to the procedure provided for in Part XV.

The procedures referred to include settlement of the dispute by peaceful means and, if need be, by submission to the International Tribunal of the Law of the Sea (outlined in the 1982 Convention), the International Court of Justice, or an arbitration tribunal.

As a point of interest, each coastal state has a perfect right to exploit the subsoil of the seabed by means of tunneling, regardless of the depth of the water above the subsoil (1958: Art. 7; 1982: Art. 85).

It should be obvious that whenever the coastal state is mentioned in a discussion of the right to exploit the resources of a continental shelf, this coastal state may conduct the exploration and exploitation through its own governmental agencies or may, at its discretion, grant the necessary concessions for such undertakings to private individuals or corporations.

A last comment needs to be added about the rights of the coastal state to exploit resources consisting of living organisms on the bottom, that is, atop the surface of the continental shelf. The desire of many states, particularly those with pearl fishery interests outside their territorial sea, to preserve exclusive control over such resources was met by the inclusion of "living organisms belonging to sedentary species" (1958: Art. 2, par. 4; 1982: Art. 77, par. 4) among the resources reserved by the 1958 Convention for the coastal state.[53]

Finally, in both conventions (1958 and 1982), the rights of the coastal state over the continental shelf do not affect the legal status of the superjacent waters or of the airspace above those waters.

A fairly recent case before the International Court of Justice must be regarded as important to the concept of the continental shelf: the *North*

---

[53] On this point, consult Young, "Sedentary Fisheries and the Convention on the Continental Shelf," 55 *AJIL* 359 (1961). Early in 1963, Brazil objected strongly to the French government against the continuing fishing for lobsters by French fishermen on the continental shelf off the Brazilian coast. See also the 1974 U.S. guidelines to foreign flag vessels fishing above the continental shelf, 69 *AJIL* 149 (1975).

*Sea Continental Shelf* cases, decided on February 20, 1969.[54] The parties had asked the court to state the applicable principles of international law concerning the North Sea continental shelf. The court rejected the Dutch and Danish claim that the boundaries on the shelf had to be drawn in accordance with the principle of equidistance, as laid down in Article 6 of the 1958 Geneva Convention on the Continental Shelf. It held, instead, that the Federal Republic of Germany (not being a party to the treaty) was not bound by the 1958 agreement and also that the principle of equidistance was not a rule of customary international law.

Some years after the North Sea problems had been resolved, a new dispute erupted between Greece and Turkey about the continental shelf (shelves) in the Aegean Sea. The trouble began after Greece discovered oil near one of its 3,049 islands off the Turkish coast and asserted that according to the 1958 Convention on the Continental Shelf, Greece could claim exploration and exploitation rights under the continental shelf on which the islands were located. Turkey, however, claimed that it enjoyed similar rights under the Anatolian Shelf, which, of course, could be said either to overlap with the Greek claim or to be identical with the shelf claimed by Greece. The dispute became increasingly bitter as both countries sent exploration vessels into the disputed area and as Turkey asserted other charges against Greece, such as the (apparently correctly stated) militarization of the Greek Dodecanese Islands, forbidden under a number of international agreements. Turkey also pointed out that it had never signed the 1958 UN Convention in question and hence could not be held to be bound by it.[55] Greece, in turn, charged Turkey with harboring designs on the sovereignty over the Dodecanese Islands.

On August 10, 1976, Greece took two steps: it brought the dispute before the UN Security Council and it unilaterally submitted an application to the International Court of Justice, asking for interim measures of protection. The Security Council adopted a resolution on August 25, 1976, asking both countries to resume direct negotiations. The court issued an order on September 11, 1976,[56] in which the court found that the circumstances

---

[54] *North Sea Continental Shelf Cases (Federal Republic of Germany/Denmark; Federal Republic of Germany/Netherlands),* International Court of Justice, February 20, 1969, *ICJ Reports,* 1969, 3, in 8 *ILM* 340 (1969), and digested in 63 *AJIL* 591 (1969). See also Friedman, "The North Sea Continental Shelf Cases—A Critique," 64 *AJIL* 229 (1970); Griesel, "The Lateral Boundaries of the Continental Shelf and the Judgment of the International Court of Justice in the North Sea Continental Shelf Cases," *id.,* 562; also the agreements between plaintiff and defendant in the case, 10 *AJIL* 600 (1971), and the Netherlands/Denmark/Germany agreements with the United Kingdom on the shelf, 11 *AJIL* 723, 731, 744 (1972).

[55] For the background of the dispute, consult Rozakis, *The Greek–Turkish Dispute over the Aegean Continental Shelf* (1975); Gross, "The Dispute Between Greece and Turkey Concerning the Continental Shelf in the Aegean," 71 *AJIL* 31 (1977); Karl, "Islands and the Delimitation of the Continental Shelf: A Framework for Analysis," *id.,* 642.

[56] Text of UN Security Council Resolution 395 (1976) in 15 *ILM* 1235 (1976); the text of the *ICJ* Order in the *Aegean Sea Continental Shelf* case (*Greece* v. *Turkey*) is reproduced in *id.,* 985.

did not require the issuing of interim measures of protection and held that the question of jurisdiction remained reserved for a future judgment, after the parties had had time to plead points of law. In essence, therefore, the court threw the problem back to the disputants, with the implied counsel to resume negotiations toward a solution. After a few months, Greece and Turkey did emerge with the so-called Berne Agreement on the Continental Shelf (November 11, 1976),[57] in which the two countries agreed to resume serious negotiations on the issue at hand and, in the meantime, not to undertake any acts likely to prejudice the success of negotiations.

On December 19, 1978, the International Court of Justice held that it lacked jurisdiction in the dispute, asserting that a joint communiqué issued by the prime minister of Greece and Turkey on May 31, 1975, did not furnish a basis for establishing the court's jurisdiction in the proceedings at hand.[58] In June 1982, Turkey accused Greece of violating the Berne Agreement, by exploring for oil in the eastern part of the area in dispute.

The dispute continued despite efforts on the part of the United States, NATO, and the United Nations to reduce the danger of a possible armed conflict. The alleged cause of the disagreement, the exploitation of apparently meager oil resources, was depreciated by many analysts who pointed to the 60-year history of squabbling between the two states over territorial waters, seabed mining rights on the shelf, airspace rights, and the militarization of islands.[59]

In March 1987, Greece staged a five-day military exercise in the area in which a Turkish research vessel was to engage in oil exploration, near the Greek islands of Samothrace, Lemnos, and Mitilini. Turkey claimed that the islands were part of the Turkish continental shelf and that, at the very least, any mineral rights should be shared. Greece claimed control over most of the Aegean continental shelf, asserting that each island had its own continental shelf. By the end of 1988, belligerence had diminished somewhat and top-level talks on the delimitation of the shelves began at the end of January. No solution had been found, however, at the time of writing in 1990.

In 1977, a five-member court of arbitration handed down a most interesting award in the *United Kingdom–France Continental Shelf Arbitration of 1977*.[60] The dispute in question centered on the continental shelf boundary between the two countries at two separate points. The tribunal decided that

---

[57] Text in 16 *ILM* 13 (1977). See also the retrospective *Note* by Robol in 18 *Harvard Int'l Law Jl.* 649 (1977).

[58] *Aegean Sea Continental Shelf Case* (*Greece* v. *Turkey*) (*Jurisdiction*), [1978] *ICJ Reports* 1, December 19, 1978, digested with copious excerpts by Evans in 73 *AJIL* 493 (1979).

[59] See Shutt, *CSM*, March 30, 1987, 11.

[60] See Colson, "The United Kingdom–France Continental Shelf Arbitration," 72 *AJIL* 95 (1978), and his "The United Kingdom–France Continental Shelf Arbitration: Interpretative Decision of March 1978," 73 *AJIL* 112 (1979).

for the areas near the Channel Islands, the boundary should be established so as not to violate the islands' established twelve-mile fishery zone; and for the Atlantic area commonly termed the Western Approaches, the award stated that the equidistance method should be used except near the Scilly Islands.

The next decision of the International Court of Justice dealing with the continental shelf was the 1982 *Case Concerning the Continental Shelf (Tunisia/Libyan Arab Jamahiriya)*.[61] That case centered on the delimitation of the boundary between the disputants on the Mediterranean continental shelf. The court followed the theory that *equitable principles* formed the base of the law of maritime boundary delimitation, just as it had in the *North Sea* cases and as the arbitration tribunal had in the *United Kingdom– French Continental Shelf* case. The Court declined to consider the equidistance method and, instead, ruled that "delimitation is to be effected in accordance with equitable principles and taking account of all relevant circumstances" (*Judgment,* par. 133).

In July 1984, Tunisia requested a revision of the Judgment handed down in 1982, an interpretation of a part of that Judgment, and a correction of what was regarded by Tunisia as an error in it. Libya in turn requested a denial of the Tunisian application. The alleged error had to do with the boundaries of an oil concession granted by Libya; Tunisia claimed that they were different from what had been presented in Libya's original submission. The Court found inadmissible the request for revision, found the request for interpretation admissible, and held that the request for correction of an error was without object and the Court was therefore not called upon to give a decision thereon. It then clarified (interpreted) the section (Par. 124) of the 1982 Judgment.[62]

In 1981, Malta applied to the International Court of Justice for permission to intervene in the *Case Concerning the Continental Shelf (Tunisia/Libya),* because its own continental shelf touched those of the parties in that case. The Court, however, denied such permission on April 14, 1981.[63] In response, Libya and Malta together filed a *Special Agreement for the Submission to the International Court of Justice of a Continental Shelf Dispute* (entered into force on March 20, 1982) with the Court on July 19, 1982.[64] The two

---

[61] *Case Concerning the Continental Shelf (Tunisia/Libyan Arab Jamahiriya),* 1982, *Judgment,* February 24, 1982, in full, in 21 *ILM* 225 (1982). See also the concise and instructive analysis by Feldman, "The Tunisia–Libyan Continental Shelf Case: Geographic Justice or Judicial Compromise," 77 *AJIL* 219 (1983).

[62] *Application for Revision and Interpretation of the Judgment of 24 February 1982 in the Case Concerning the Continental Shelf (Tunisia/Libyan Arab Jamahiriya,* International Court of Justice, *Judgment of December 10, 1985,* in 25 *ILM* 152 (1986) and briefly in 80 *AJIL* 645 (1986).

[63] *Application* of Malta, January 28, 1981, in 20 *ILM* 329 (1981); *Case Concerning the Continental Shelf (Tunisia/Libyan Arab Jamahiriya), Application by Malta for Permission to Intervene,* April 14, 1981, *Judgment, id.,* 569.

[64] Text of Agreement in 21 *ILM* 971 (1982).

parties asked the Court to inform them as to the rules and principles of international law applicable to determining the areas of the continental shelf appertaining to Malta and Libya respectively and how those rules could be applied by them in practice. The judgment in the *Case Concerning the Continental Shelf* (*Libyan Arab Jamahiriya* v. *Malta*) was delivered in June 1985. The Court reviewed the principles and rules applicable to the delimitation of a continental shelf between opposite coasts, as it had been requested to do. It invoked the principle of equity as it had done in the Libya–Tunisia case in 1982. ("Equity as a legal concept is a direct emanation of the idea of justice. The Court whose task is by definition to administer justice is bound to apply it."). It held that the delimitation line should be closer to Malta than to Libya, primarily because of the great disparity in the lengths of the relevant coasts of the two parties, then laid down the line of demarcation.[65]

Canada and the United States had disagreed for a number of years about delimitation of their fisheries jurisdictions in the Gulf of Maine, after both countries had extended those jurisdictions to 200 nautical miles in 1977. A treaty by which both sides agreed to binding arbitration of delimitation of the maritime boundary in the Gulf had been signed in 1979 but had been connected with another instrument relating to fisheries. Subsequently it was agreed to separate the two agreements and to postpone consideration of the fisheries question until the Gulf of Maine delimitation had been achieved. The treaty relating to the latter subject then came into effect on November 20, 1981.

## EXCLUSIVE ECONOMIC ZONES

Most analysts of UNCLOS III (UN Convention on the Law of the Sea, 1982) appear to agree that its treatment of the so-called Exclusive Economic Zone (EEZ) represented a major legal as well as political achievement, one that may remove most of the sources of such conflicts as the "Codfish Wars." (See the Case Study No. 6 at the end of this chapter.) The concept of such zones was not new when the Third Conference on the Law of the Sea began, as will be shown later, even though for the most part such early zones dealt only with fisheries questions. What emerged from the many sessions of the Law of the Sea Conference was a broad consensus on a far greater scope.

Articles 55 through 75 in UNCLOS III deal with the EEZ, which is defined in Article 55 as follows: "The exclusive economic zone in an area beyond and adjacent to the territorial sea, subject to the specific legal regime established in this Part, under which the rights and jurisdiction of the coastal State and the rights and freedoms of other States are governed by the relevant provisions of this Convention." According to Article 56, the coastal state possesses sovereign rights for the purposes of exploiting, conserving, and managing the natural resources, whether living or nonliving, of the

---

[65]Text of Judgment in 24 *ILM* 1189 (1985).

waters above the seabed, of the seabed, and of the subsoil of the same. The coastal state also has the exclusive right to build and use artificial islands, installations, and structures in the EEZ, subject to certain other provisions of the convention. The EEZ shall not extend beyond 200 nautical miles from the baselines from which the breadth of the territorial sea is measured. The coastal state also has the exclusive right to determine the allowable catch of the living resources in its EEZ. Other states may enjoy rights of navigation, overflight, and the laying of submarine cables and pipelines. An interesting proposition is outlined in Articles 69 and 70 of the UNCLOS III Convention: geographically disadvantaged as well as landlocked states are to have the right to participate equitably in the exploitation of an appropriate part of the surplus of the living resources of the EEZs of coastal states in the same subregion or region. On the other hand, Article 71 provides that the preceding articles (69 and 70) shall not apply in the case of a coastal state whose economy is overwhelmingly dependent on the exploitation of the living resources of its own EEZ.

The United States originally established not an exclusive economic zone but what were then termed *conservation zones*. On September 28, 1945, President Harry Truman proclaimed the establishment of conservation zones in the high seas contiguous to the coasts of the United States. In areas where only American nationals had been fishing, such zones were to be controlled by the United States on a unilateral basis; in areas where fishing had been shared with the nationals of other states, conservation zones were to be set up by agreement with the governments concerned.[66]

The initial American step toward conserving the resources of the high seas was followed shortly by similar conservation measures proclaimed by other countries for specified areas of the high seas off their coasts. In a number of instances, no question of joint control or even consultation was involved, but in some other cases, outright discrimination against foreign fishermen became established policy for the new conservation zones. It was therefore interesting to note that the United States supported a 200-mile outer limit for conservation zones (economic zones) at the 1974 Caracas Third UN Conference on the Law of the Sea, *provided* that such an extension of coastal states' control included guarantees of freedom of navigation, permission for fishing by foreign fleets, and compulsory third-party settlement of disputes.

U.S. FISHERMAN'S PROTECTIVE ACT   In response to the frequent seizures of American fishing vessels and to the imposition of heavy fines on their captains or owners, the Congress of the United States passed on August 27, 1954, the Fisherman's Protective Act. This law provides that the United States government will reimburse fishermen for all fines imposed on them by foreign states for fishing within zones or territorial sea limits not recognized by the United States. The government then will attempt to recover the sums

---

[66]The text of the proclamation may be found in 40 *AJIL* 46 (1946 Supp.). See also White-man, vol. 4, 932–1240.

in question from the foreign states involved. In addition, the United States has repeatedly assisted American shipowners in presenting their claims for losses and damages sustained in the seizures of fishing vessels.

In 1967–1968, Congress reviewed the original law and passed a revision (really, an addition to the previous legislation) introduced in a bill by the Department of the Interior. The new feature is voluntary participation by the fishing industry, together with the United States government, in an insurance program designed to compensate certain losses arising from arrests, fines, and seizures in waters claimed illegally in the view of the United States (P.L. 90-482, 1968). In 1972 the insurance program addition was extended by Congress, through Public Law 92-569, on October 26, 1972.

Subsequently Congress enacted the Pelly Amendment, directing the Secretary of Commerce to certify to the President if nationals of a foreign country were conducting fishing operations in such a manner as to "diminish the effectiveness" of an international fishery conservation program. The President, in his discretion, could then direct the imposition of sanctions (embargos?) on the certified country.

On April 13, 1976, after extensive debate had preceded congressional approval, President Ford signed Public Law 94-265, the Fishery Conservation Management Act of 1976, which went into effect on March 1, 1977.[67] That law expanded what had been a contiguous zone of a breadth of 12 miles around the coasts of the United States to a breadth of 200 nautical miles. The law did not prohibit all foreign fishing in the economic zone: it gave U.S. fishermen first chance at existing resources and explained in considerable detail that foreign vessels could collect only such excess stock as could not be harvested domestically. Conservation of marine resources was required under the law, and control was exercised by eight regional fishery-management councils.

After the 1976 law entered into effect on March 1, 1977, the U.S. Coast Guard found 97 foreign vessels in violation of the law during the month of March 1977; of these, 53 were Soviet ships. After several high fines were imposed by the United States, the Soviet government announced (April 14, 1977) that the captains of all Soviet fishing vessels had been ordered to abide by the United States zonal regulations. Nevertheless, the Russian violations of the zone continued: in September 1980, the Soviet Union agreed to $400,000 in fines rather than have the trial for violations continued. Three months earlier (June 1980), the largest fine ($700,000) up to then had been collected from the Hoko Fishing Company of Tokyo: the company paid rather than forfeit a major fishing vessel.

---

[67] Text in 70 *AJIL* 624 (1976), and in 15 *ILM* 635 (1976). Many critics of the law, including U.S. government officials, held that its provisions violated the clear wording of the 1958 Convention on Fishing and the 1958 Convention on the Conservation of the Living Resources of the Sea: see *NYT*, July 20, 1976, 4, and Windley "International Practice Regarding Traditional Fishing Privileges of Foreign Fisherman in Zones of Extended Maritime Jurisdiction," 63 *AJIL* 490 (1969).

More recently, an *ad hoc* Arbitration Tribunal composed of three members of the International Court of Justice issued an award delimiting the maritime boundary between Guinea and Guinea-Bissau (February 14, 1985). This dispute was caused by the fact that oil companies had been granted off-shore concessions but were unwilling to commence operations as long as the sovereignty over the area in question had not been settled.[68]

In connection with the delimitation of maritime boundaries, the decision of a Chamber of the International Court of Justice in the Gulf of Maine case should be mentioned. Canada and the United States had disagreed for number of years about the delimitation of their fisheries jurisdictions in the Gulf of Maine, after both states had extended their economic zonal jurisdictions to 200 nautical miles in 1977. A treaty calling for binding arbitration of the issue had been signed in 1979 but was connected to another instrument also related to fisheries. The two agreements were separated and the delimitation treaty came into effect on November 20, 1981.[69] Five days later the two governments notified the International Court of Justice of the agreement which provided for submission of the delimitation to a *Chamber* of the Court, as provided for in the Statute of the latter. This was to be the first time that a Chamber rather than the full court was to consider a dispute. The Chamber handed down its decision on October 12, 1984, awarding to the United States approximately three-quarters of the Georges Bay fishing grounds in the Gulf of Maine. That meant that the United States was given about two-thirds of the Gulf and three-fourths of the total fishing grounds therein.[70]

An interesting example of the extremes to which legal provisions may drive states was supplied by Japan in 1988: 17 Japanese vessels and a labor-force of 200 men engaged in a five-month endeavor to build concentric rings of 9,000 steel blocks plus concrete around Okino Tori Shima (Island of the Offshore Birds). Several tiny islets, barely two feet above high tide, lying about 1,110 miles from Tokyo in the Pacific, were being given protective

---

[68]Text of award (English transl.) in 25 *ILM* 252 (1986).

[69]*Delimitation of the Maritime Boundary in the Gulf of Maine Area (Canada/United States)*, International Court of Justice, *1984 ICJ Reports* 246, *Judgment* of October 12, 1984: see Legault and Hanley, "From Sea to Seabed: The Single Maritime Boundary in the Gulf of Maine Case," 79 *AJIL* 961 (1985).

[70]For the background of the dispute and award, see Purcell in *CSM*, Oct. 16, 1984, 5; text of the Treaty and related documents in 20 *ILM* 1371 (1981); text of the Court's Order (January 20, 1982) providing for the creation of the Chamber, and other documents relating to the *Case Concerning Delimitation of the Maritime Boundaries in the Gulf of Maine Area (Canada/United States)*, 21 *ILM* 69 (1982); the complete documentation of the case, including separate opinions, the technical report, and charts, is to be found in 23 *ILM* 1197 (1984). See also Rhee, "Equitable Solutions to the Maritime Boundary Dispute Between the United States and Canada in the Gulf of Maine," 75 *AJIL* 590 (1981); Schneider, "The Gulf of Maine Case: The Nature of an Equitable Result," 79 *AJIL* 539 (1985); and Robinson, Colson, and Rashkow, "Some Perspectives on Adjudicating Before the World Court: The Gulf of Maine Case," *id.*, 79, 578 (1985).

outer walls to prevent the islets from being eroded. As long as the rocks were above sea level at all times, they enabled Japan, in accordance with the provisions of UNCLOS III, to claim a 160,000-square-mile exclusive economic (fishing) zone. The project, slated for completion by March 1990, would keep legally valid the southernmost marker-point of the zone.

The United States thus had exercised since 1976 the management and conservation authority over fisheries resources (except for highly migratory species of tuna) within 200 nautical miles of the U.S. coasts. Inasmuch as 56 countries had proclaimed 200-mile Exclusive Economic Zones and 23 others, including the United States, had established 200-mile fisheries zones, the United States was not out of step when President Reagan, on March 10, 1983, proclaimed a 200 nautical mile EEZ.[71] That zone not only was established along the North American, including Alaska, coasts but also applied to Guam, the Northern Marianas, Johnston Island, Hawaii, Midway Island, American Samoa, several Pacific atolls, and Puerto Rico. In his announcement of the zone, Reagan reiterated his main reason against signing the UNCLOS III Convention (the deep-seabed–mining provisions) but averred that the treaty also contained provisions regarding traditional uses of the oceans, such as those dealing with exclusive economic zones. Interestingly enough, he did not assert a right of jurisdiction over marine scientific research in the EEZ: he affirmed that international law provided for such a right by the coastal state but that the United States wished to encourage such research in its zone and therefore did not desire to limit it.

Other bilateral agreements concluded by the United States in anticipation or as a consequence of the creation of the 200-mile economic zone were with Japan (February 10, 1977) and with the Soviet Union (November 26, 1976).

Many coastal states, ignoring the 1958 treaty limitations on the boundaries of economic zones, began to proclaim such zones with an almost standard breadth of 200 nautical miles. To name but a few, such was the case with India, Sri Lanka, Canada, Mexico, Vietnam, North Korea, New Zealand, Norway, both Germanys, Cuba, Sweden, Poland, and South Africa. The establishment of a 200-mile zone by the Soviet Union in 1977 caused strong protests by Japan, because the original Soviet proposal would have applied the new limit also to the four southernmost Kurile Islands, claimed by Japan since 1945 but actually held by the Soviet Union. (See Chapter 14.) After extended discussions, a Soviet-Japanese agreement signed in May 1977 provided for the elimination of the wording that would have been prejudicial to the Japanese territorial claim and also allowed Japanese fishing vessels limited access to the Soviet economic zone.

A recent dispute between Canada and France centered on French claims of a 200-mile exclusive economic zone around the French islands of St.

---

[71]Proclamation No. 5030, text in 77 *AJIL* 621 (1983), and, with relevant statements and an interesting map, in 22 *ILM* 461 (1983); another map is in *CSM*, March 31, 1987, 21.

Pierre and Miquelon, off the southern coast of Newfoundland. Canada, on the other hand, recognized only a limit of 12 miles for the islands. In 1977 Canada asserted, under the provisions of UNCLOS III, a claim of an economic zone of 200 miles. The conflicting claims embraced an area rich in cod and fished by both countries. In January 1987 Canada offered increased temporary quotas for French boats fishing cod in offshore waters in exchange for French agreement to have the territorial dispute settled by binding arbitration. After much haggling and a temporary recall of the French ambassador to Canada, the "Agreement Establishing a Court of Arbitration for the Purpose of Carrying Out the Delimitation of Maritime Areas between France and Canada (March 30, 1989)" was reached.[72]

## CONSERVATION ZONES

1958 CONSERVATION CONVENTION    The fact that the numerous earlier conventions did not represent a unified system, despite the obvious relationships among their several subject matters, led the delegates to the 1958 Geneva Conference to adopt a new Convention on Fishing and Conservation of the Living Resources of the High Seas.[73] In summary, the new convention reaffirms the freedom of citizens of all states to fish in and on the high seas, subject, however, to certain rights and interests of coastal states. A state whose nationals alone fished a certain stock in a certain area of the high seas can, at its discretion, adopt for its citizens any and all conservation measures deemed necessary. If the nationals of two or more states fish the same stock or stocks of fish or other living marine resources in a particular area of the high seas, the states concerned must, at the request of any of them, enter into negotiations for an agreement applying conservation regulations, each to their nationals. If, on the other hand, nationals of different states fish different stocks in the same area, the provisions calling for negotiation of an agreement among the the states will not apply.

If negotiations fail to result in an agreement called for by the convention, any of the states concerned can initiate proceedings terminating in a binding decision by an impartial body (the word *arbitration* was not used in the instrument). This body is to be a special commission of five members, appointed in accordance with the provisions of Article 9 of the convention.

The special rights and interests of the coastal states, mentioned above, merit brief comment. Under Article 7 of the convention, any coastal state

[72]Text in 29 *ILM* 1(1990); text of the same-day agreement on temporary fishing quotas in *id.*, 7.
[73]The text has been reprinted in 52 *AJIL* 851 (1958 Supp.). The convention has been in force since March 20, 1966.

is entitled to undertake unilateral conservation measures in any area of the high seas adjacent to its territorial sea, provided that negotiations with other states whose nationals are fishing there have not led to an agreement within six months. The real weakness of the article in question is that no details are supplied as to the lawful extent of the conservation zones established by coastal states acting under the convention's provisions, nor are there given any clear-cut indications as to rights of enforcement of conservation regulations.

In retrospect, the convention is badly dated today: witness the growth in the number of 200-mile exclusive economic zones, detailed earlier.

## MILITARY ZONES

NORTH KOREA'S MILITARY BOUNDARY ZONE    No discussion of economic or other high seas zones would be complete without a mention of the innovation announced on August 1, 1977, by North Korea. That country has a 12-mile territorial sea limit and proclaimed an economic zone 200 nautical miles wide, to go into effect on August 1, 1977. However, on that date, the North Korean government proclaimed also the establishment of a 50-mile-wide military boundary zone.

Examination of the text of the proclamation reveals a series of interesting and unusual provisions. The third and fourth paragraphs of the brief announcement read as follows:

In the military boundary (on the sea, in the sea and in the sky) acts of foreigners, military vessels and foreign military planes are prohibited and civilian ships and civilian planes (excluding fishing boats) are allowed to navigate or fly only with appropriate prior agreement or approval.

In the military boundary (on the sea, in the sea and in the sky) civilian vessels and civilian planes shall not conduct acts for military purposes or acts infringing upon the economic interests.

These provisions, applicable beyond the territorial sea, are the most exclusive limitations on foreign ships and aircraft, quite abnormal when compared with the usual regulations applicable to exclusive economic zones. Moreover, the wording of "excluding fishing boats" led Japanese negotiators working out a fishing agreement with North Korea to assume that fishing vessels could enter the military zone without the otherwise called-for approval by North Korea. They were informed, however, that foreign fishing was banned entirely in the military boundary zone, which meant that the Japanese negotiators could negotiate only about the remainder of the economic zone of North Korea.[74]

[74]See Park, "The 50-Mile Military Boundary Zone of North Korea," 72 *AJIL* 866 (1978).

## 4. THE HIGH SEAS

## ORIGINS OF THE LAW OF THE SEA

The term *high seas* refers to all areas of the world's oceans located outside the limits of national waters and the territorial seas of coastal states.[75]

Beginning in the seventh century, a number of compilations of rules applicable on the seas began to circulate in Europe. Several of these purely private compendiums gained such widespread acceptance and authority that the rules laid down in them achieved in time the status of customary law. In the Mediterranean area, the earliest generally accepted rules were collected in the *Lex Rhodia* (the Rhodian sea law), whose various existing versions were probably collected in the seventh century. It was followed by the much better known collection of rules known as the *Consolato del Mare* (the consulate of the sea).[76] The title of the work is derived from its compilers, the official judges of the ports who were designated *consuls,* and assorted captains and prominent merchants. The date of the *Consolato* is not certain, but it probably was in the late thirteenth or early fourteenth century. Written in the Catalan language, its original title was *The Laws of Barcelona,* and although several authorities claim that the code originated in Marseilles, the oldest existing printed version, dated 1494, came from Barcelona.

In the Atlantic area, the basic rules of the sea were collected in the *Rolles d'Oléron* (the rules of Oléron), a compilation probably set down in the twelfth century in Old French.[77] Oddly enough, the rules contained in this work are not the laws of the island of Oléron but those of several ports in western France. Many of the concepts embodied in this code are still found in modern French and English rules applicable to the seas.

In England, the ancient *Black Book of the Admiralty,* compiled during the reigns of Edward III, Richard II, and Henry IV, was a collection of rules for use in the Admiral's Court. Originally written in Norman French, the regulations were translated into English during the reign of Charles II in the seventeenth century.

In northern Europe, the *Sea Code of Wisby* may be taken to have been the most important collection of generally accepted rules.[78] Its first portion was merely a Flemish translation of the 24 oldest articles of the *Rolles d'Oléron;* its second half, the *Ordinancie,* compiled probably in Amsterdam in 1407, added numerous principles adopted by the Hanseatic cities. The first printed

---

[75] See Reiff for a basic reference work on the rules governing activities on the oceans of the world. Other useful works on the subject are McFee, *The Law of the Sea* (1950); the highly informative study by Higgins-Colombos; and McDougal and Burke, *The Public Order of the Oceans* (1962).

[76] Text of Rhodian law in McFee, *op. cit.,* 299–305, and 37–46 for a discussion of the background of the Rhodian law and, on 55–60, its contents; on *Consolato,* see Jados trans., *Consulate of the Sea and Related Documents.* (1975)

[77] McFee, *op. cit.,* 305–10.

[78] See McFee, *op. cit.,* 75–77 for the Code of Wisby and 68–75, for the Amalfi Code.

edition of the work (Copenhagen, 1505) was entitled *Gothlantic Sea Law* and, it is assumed, is the handwritten compilation used officially by the Maritime Court at Wisby, on the island of Gothland.

Subsequent centuries witnessed the growth of conventional laws of the sea through the conclusion of many multilateral treaties, such as the London Convention of 1841 Concerning the Closing of the Dardanelles, modified in 1856 and again in 1871; the London Convention of 1841 for the Supression of the Slave Trade; the 1856 Declaration of Paris Concerning War at Sea (and the abolition of privateering); the numerous treaties governing the construction, use, and protection of submarine cables; and many conventions relating to maritime war, the protection of fishing rights, and so on. The culmination of a large part of international efforts to arrive at a common law of the sea by convention came with the three UN Conferences on the Law of the Sea in 1958, 1960, and 1973–1982.

In sharp contrast with the majority of national attitudes prevailing until the early part of the nineteenth century, legal authorities as well as governments agreed increasingly that the high seas were common property and open to the use of all states. All former national claims over large areas of the world's oceans have been abandoned, even though controversy continues over economic zones and fishery rights.

This "freedom of the seas" was essentially an achievement of the nineteenth century, even though the roots of the doctrine reach back at least to 1604 and the appearance of the well-known *Mare Librum* by Hugo Grotius.[79] Though late in time, the general acceptance of the doctrine of the free seas had its basis in a common recognition of the desirability of preventing one state, or a group of states, from asserting a legal right to bar other members of the community of nations from the use of any portion of the high seas. But in recent decades, the freedom has begun to be limited to some extent. This trend is particularly noticeable in two significant conventional definitions. Article 2 of the 1958 UN Convention on the Law of the Sea (Geneva) asserts that

The high seas being open to all nations, no State may validly purport to subject any part of them to its sovereignty. Freedom of the high seas is exercised under the conditions laid down by these articles and by other rules of international law. It comprises, *inter alia* . . .

1. Freedom of navigation;
2. Freedom of fishing;
3. Freedom to lay submarine cables and pipelines;
4. Freedom to fly over the high seas.

These freedoms, and others which are recognized by the general principles of international law, shall be exercised by all States with reasonable regard to the interests of other States in their exercise of the freedom of the high seas.

[79]Whiteman, vol. 4, 501–42; and Allen, "Freedom of the Sea," 60 *AJIL* 814 (1966).

On the other hand, note the subtle but important and more restrictive changes in the wording of Articles 87 to 89 of the 1982 United Nations Convention on the Law of the Sea (hereafter: UNCLOS III):

ARTICLE 87
FREEDOM OF THE HIGH SEAS

1. The high seas are open to all States, whether coastal or land-locked. Freedom of the high seas is exercised under the conditions laid down by this Convention and by other rules of international law. It comprises, *inter alia,* both for coastal and land-locked States:

   (a) freedom of navigation;
   (b) freedom of overflight;
   (c) freedom to lay submarine cables and pipeline, subject to Part VI [Part VI of the convention refers to the continental shelf];
   (d) freedom to construct artificial island and other installations permitted under international law, subject to Part VI;
   (e) freedom of fishing, subject to the conditions laid down in section 2;
   (f) freedom of scientific research, subject to Parts VI and XIII [Part XIII deals with marine scientific research];

2. These freedoms shall be exercised by all States with due regard for the interests of other States in their exercise of the freedom of the high seas, and also with due regard for the rights under this Convention with respect to activities in the Area [the "Area" refers to the mineral resources on or under the seabed outside territorial waters].

ARTICLE 88
RESERVATION OF THE HIGH SEAS FOR PEACEFUL PURPOSES

The high seas shall be reserved for peaceful purposes.

ARTICLE 89

No State may validly purport to subject any part of the high seas to its sovereignty.

1958 CONVENTION ON THE HIGH SEAS    The 1958 United Nations Conference on the Law of the Sea (Geneva), attended by representatives of 86 states, drafted, among other instruments, a Convention on the High Seas.[80] The major provisions of this agreement summarize many of the basic rules of today's law of the high seas.

RIGHTS OF NATIONS    The high seas being open to all nations, no state may validly assert sovereignty over any part of them. Freedom of the high seas means, for both coastal and noncoastal states, freedom of navigation, fishing, laying submarine cables and pipelines, and flying over the high seas (see above).

States having no seacoast have a right of free access to the sea (Art. 2). To this end, states interposed between the sea and an inland state should,

---

[80]Text of the convention in 52 *AJIL* (1958), supp., pp. 842–51. The convention entered into force on September 30, 1962.

by treaty, grant to the landlocked state (on a basis of reciprocity) freedom of transit through their territory and accord to vessels flying the flag of the landlocked state treatment equal to that accorded to their own ships.[81]

This principle has been the underlying cause for a quarrel of long standing between Bolivia and Chile, which led to a severance of diplomatic relations between the two countries in 1962. Bolivia, landlocked since a defeat in 1879 by Chile, has demanded repeatedly that the small Chilean port of Mejillones, 35 miles north of Antofagasta, should be ceded to Bolivia, together with a small enclave. Bolivia did not insist on the acquisition of a corridor linking the port with its territory, being apparently content to use an existing railroad to transport goods from the coast inland. In return for the cession of the port and enclave, Bolivia offered to divert water from five small rivers in the upper Andes to assist in the irrigation of Chile's northern desert region.

After years of protest against being a landlocked state, it appeared in September 1977 that Bolivia might be granted a corridor, to be ceded jointly by Peru and Chile. No action was taken on the project, and hence Bolivia expressed its displeasure by breaking off diplomatic relations with Chile on March 17, 1978. However, in July 1976, Argentina gave to Bolivia a good-sized (1200 yards of mooring frontage) free-port zone at Rosario on the Paraná River. That zone, complete with warehousing and other facilities, enables Bolivia to ship goods from its eastern provinces to Rosario and thence by oceangoing vessels (Rosario being a deep-water port) to the outside world.

The right of access granted to landlocked states was reinforced by the signing on July 8, 1965, of the Convention on Transit Trade of Landlocked Countries, negotiated at a UN conference on this subject in New York.[82] This instrument provides, besides duty-free access to the sea for the goods of landlocked countries—except for a small, nondiscriminatory service charge—for "free, uninterrupted and continuous traffic in transit." The treaty is to stay in force in time of war so far as "the rights and duties of belligerents and neutrals" permit. A maritime state is ensured specifically of the right to keep out such goods as arms, narcotics, and diseased animals and plants, as well as "persons whose admission into its territories is forbidden, on grounds of public morals, public health or security."

The 1982 UN Convention on the Law of the Sea (UNCLOS III)[83] contains, in Article 124 through 132, an expanded list of rights of landlocked states (access, transit privileges, and the like). Article 69 ensures such states the right to participate equitably in the exploitation of an *appropriate part* of the *surplus* of the living resources of the exclusive economic zones of coastal states of the *same subregion or region* (see also below).

---

[81]On access in general, see Whiteman, vol. 8, pp. 1143–63.

[82]*NYT,* July 9, 1965, 7; the convention was approved by forty-six countries, with none opposed but with seven abstentions: text in Whiteman, vol. 9, 1156–61.

[83]Text of UNCLOS III in 21 *ILM* 1261 (1982).

## POLICE ACTIVITIES ON THE HIGH SEAS

RIGHT TO VISIT AND SEARCH    A warship encountering a foreign merchant vessel on the high seas may stop the vessel for purposes of investigation if one of the following suspicions is harbored by the commander of the warship or if other causes for such a "visit and search" are authorized for him by special treaty arrangements: (1) that the ship is engaged in piracy; (2) that the ship is engaged in the slave trade; or (3) that the vessel, although flying a foreign flag or refusing to show its flag, is in reality of the same nationality as the warship.[84]

These suspicions are a limitation on the normal rule that a merchant vessel on the high seas can be boarded only by members of the crew of a warship flying the same flag as the merchant ship. Should the captain of the warship receive permission of the government to search a vessel flying the flag of that foreign government, such a search would not be regarded as violating the conventional law of the sea.[85]

Article 110 of the UNCLOS III Convention of 1982 adds two reasons for boarding a suspicious vessel: if the vessel is stateless ("without a nationality") and if the vessel is engaged in unauthorized broadcasting and the warship's flag state has jurisdiction under Article 109 of the convention in question.

The above provisions of either convention apply not only to warships but also to military aircraft. Article 110(5) of UNCLOS III states that these provisions also apply to any other duly authorized ships or aircraft clearly marked and identifiable as being on government service.

The suppression of unauthorized broadcasting from the high seas represents a new police authority sanctioned under Article 109 of the UNCLOS III Convention. The article defines such broadcasting as the transmission of radio or television broadcasts from a ship or installation on the high seas for reception by the general public, contrary to international regulations but excluding the transmission of distress calls. Any person engaged in such unauthorized activity may be prosecuted before the court of the ship's flag state, the state of registry of the installation, the state of which the person is a national, any state where the transmission can be received, or any state whose authorized radio communication is suffering interference from the illegal transmissions. Any of the states possessing such jurisdiction may arrest any person or ship engaged in unauthorized transmissions and seize the broadcasting apparatus.

---

[84]See van Zwanenberg, "Interference with Ships on the High Seas," 10 *Int. and Comp. Law Jl.* 785 (1961); Whiteman, vol. 4, 633–40, 667–77; and UNCLOS III, Art. 110. See also the account of the seizure of the *Don Emilio* in 71 *AJIL* 345 (1977); the earlier capture of the *Miss Connie* in *NYT*, Dec. 29, 1977, A-16; and the interesting "stateless vessel" case of *United States* v. *Cortes,* U.S. Court of Appeals, 5th Cir., 1979, 588 F.2d 106, reported at length by Voth in 20 *Harvard Int'l Law Jl.* 397 (1979).

[85]*United States* v. *Green,* U.S. Court of Appeals, 1st Cir., 1982, 671 *Federal Reporter* 2d 46.

According to both conventions, should the suspicions prove to be unfounded, the state to which the warship belongs must compensate the owners of the merchant ship for any delay (loss, damage, and so on) caused by the actions of the warship.

Another aspect of police activity on the high seas pertains to the continuing problem of illicit trade in narcotics and psychotropic substances. Article 108 of UNCLOS III reads that all states shall cooperate in suppressing such illicit trade engaged in by ships on the high seas in violation of international conventions. Any state that has reasonable grounds for believing that a ship carrying its flag is engaged in such illicit traffic may request the cooperation of other states in suppressing the activity in question. Some states have gone further and have authorized other states to board and search, arrest and try perpetrators of drug smuggling, and so on, when the vessels in question fly their own flag. Such was the case when the United Kingdom, by a note of November 13, 1981, informed the United States that such boarding of vessels flying the British flag would not be objectionable (provided that the United Kingdom were subsequently notified of such actions), if the boarding took place in waters clearly specified in the document (the Caribbean, the Gulf of Mexico, other areas of the U.S. Atlantic coast within 150 miles of that coast, and so on).[86] In other instances, where boarding takes place relatively close to the shore of the policing country, the vessel's flag state has given specific authority for the seizure of the ship and the trial of the persons engaged in the illicit traffic.[87]

**RULE OF HOT PURSUIT**    One of the more spectacular rules governing the high seas pertains to what is termed *hot pursuit*.[88] This means the pursuit into the high seas of a foreign vessel suspected of having committed an infringement of a coastal state's laws or regulations. To be lawful, hot pursuit has to commence when the foreign vessel or one of its boats is within the national waters, territorial sea, or contiguous zone of the pursuing state. The pursuit may be continued outside the territorial sea or contiguous zone only if the pursuit has not been interrupted; once the pursuit has been broken off, it cannot be resumed. The beginning of the pursuit normally has to be preceded by hoisting a visual signal or by giving an audible command, not by radio, to stop for visit and search.

If the foreign vessel is within the contiguous zone at the time that the pursuit is begun, the pursuit is lawful only if there has been a violation of the rights for the protection of which the zone was established. In other

---

[86] Text of note in 21 *ILM* 439 (1982).
[87] *United States* v. *Dominquez*, U.S. Court of Appeals, 4ht Cir., August 10, 1979, 604 F.2d 304, reported in 74 *AJIL* 437 (1980).
[88] Hackworth, vol. 2, 700–709; Higgins-Colombos, 123–28; Whiteman, vol. 4, 677–87; Poulantzas, *The Right of Hot Pursuit in International Law* (1969); and Williams, "The Judicial Basis of Hot Pursuit," 16 *BYIL* 83 (1939).

words, an alleged violation of customs regulations may not justify a pursuit begun in a contiguous zone created to protect, say, fishing rights. Hot pursuit ceases as soon as the ship pursued enters the territorial waters of its own country or of a third state.

In order to prevent possible abuses, the right of hot pursuit may be exercised only by warships, military aircraft, or other ships or aircraft or government services specifically authorized to engage in this activity. If the allegations of unlawful activity are found to be without foundation, the arresting state is obligated to compensate the vessel's owners for any loss or damage caused by the hot pursuit and arrest of the ship.[89]

Article 111 of UNCLOS III, which covers hot pursuit, specifies that the ship giving the order to stop to a vessel in territorial waters or a contiguous zone does not itself have to be, at the time, in those waters or that zone.

By applying the principle of "constructive presence," the doctrine of hot pursuit has been expanded to cover cases of vessels that remain or "hover" on the high seas—beyond territorial waters—but maintain contact with the shore through small craft.

OTHER POLICE ACTIVITIES    The suppression of piracy and the trade in slaves is a well-known police activity on the high seas, discussed in Chapter 13.

Finally, there is one other area in which the public ships of one state may lawfully interfere with the normal freedom of the seas enjoyed by the vessels of other states: offenses specified by treaty.

An illustration of this category was the Convention Concerning the Abolition of the Liquor Traffic Among the Fishermen of the North Sea, signed in 1887 by Great Britain, Belgium, Denmark, France, Germany, and the Netherlands. The purpose of that agreement was to prohibit the sale of liquor to the crews of fishing vessels in the North Sea, as well as to license and regulate the so-called bumboats that brought provisions to the fishing vessels.[90]

STATUS OF WARSHIPS    Warships on the high seas enjoy complete immunity from the jurisdiction of any foreign state. In order to be included in this category, a vessel must belong to the naval forces of a state, bear the external markings distinguishing warships of its nationality, be under the command of an officer commissioned by the flag state's government, and be manned by a crew under regular naval discipline. An equal unlimited immunity is enjoyed on the high seas by vessels owned and operated by a state, provided they are used only on government noncommercial service. Both of these rules were reaffirmed in the UNCLOS III, Articles 95 and 96.

---

[89]See also Bishop, 530–31, and the famous old case of *The I'm Alone* (*Canada* v. *United States*) [1929], *id.,* 531 and Hackworth, vol. 2, 703.
[90]Whiteman, 645–48.

SECOND GENEVA CONFERENCE (1960)    The UN General Assembly had called a second conference on the Law of the Sea in 1960 to resolve certain problems not settled in 1958, but the meeting failed to achieve any part of that goal.

THIRD LAW OF THE SEA CONFERENCE (1973–1982)    In view of the 1960 experience, the General Assembly scheduled a third meeting, beginning with an organizational session in New York in December 1973. That Third Conference met in various locations 11 times; the final session took place in Montego Bay, Jamaica, on December 6–10, 1982. The end product of those sessions was the United Nations Convention on the Law of the Sea (UNCLOS III), signed at Montego Bay on December 10, 1982, by the representatives of 117 states (including Namibia, signed by the UN Council for Namibia) and two other entities.[91] By December 9, 1984, (the closing date) the signatures of states numbered 159 (including Mali, which signed as a landlocked state—the Holy See and Switzerland, also landlocked, had not signed the convention), together with three more entities. Among the states that chose not to become signatories were the United States (see below), the United Kingdom, the Federal Republic of Germany, Israel, Ecuador, Peru, Brazil, and Venezuela. Also by December 1984, only nine countries had ratified the convention, which is to enter into force 12 months after the date of the deposit of the sixtieth instrument of ratification or accession.

The 1982 Convention is a mammoth agreement, both in size and in the scope of its subject matter: 320 articles and 9 annexes to the basic document, covering almost every conceivable aspect of the high seas as well as territorial waters, archipelagos, continental shelves, and the like. Once in force, the convention is to prevail, as between parties to the agreement, over the Geneva Conventions on the Law of the Sea of April 29, 1958, according to Article 311(1). In addition to "old" topics previously found in agreements and remaining virtually unchanged, the new instrument expanded coverage of specific subjects, such as in Article 19 (under "innocent passage"), a long list of activities deemed to be prejudicial to the peace, good order or security of the coastal state, and, in Article 21 (again under "innocent passage"), a slightly shorter list of laws and regulations permissible to the coastal state in the sphere of innocent passage.

But besides these unchanged or expanded concepts, the 1982 instrument contains provisions dealing with new topics, and that is what has caused the refusal of certain countries, notably the United States, to become parties to the convention.

The bulk of the additional subject matter is found in Articles 133 through 191, a grouping headed "The Area." The Area, in simplified terms, comprises the deep seabed and its subsoil, including all of the kinds of minerals and metals to be found there. Articles 136 through 155 cover basic principles relating to the Area, which is regarded as the common heritage of all mankind. Articles 156 through 191 describe in detail, the "Authority"

[91]Text in 21 *ILM* 1261 (1982).

and its components: the International Seabed Authority, to be located in Jamaica, which is to supervise and also exploit the Area. Finally, Annex III to the convention formulates the basic conditions of prospecting, exploring, and exploiting the Area. Annex IV details the structure and operations of the "Enterprise," the agency that is to exploit the Area, and Annex VI contains the Statute of the International Tribunal for the Law of the Sea, intended to settle disputes between parties to the convention.

It is beyond the scope of a general text to describe in detail the provisions of Articles 156 through 191, but because it is part of the convention that, with its related annexes, has caused much controversy, a brief outline is desirable.

The Authority is to have three major agencies: an Assembly, the legislative organ of the Authority, composed of all parties to the convention; a Council of 36 members, the executive organ, and a Secretariat, to operate in the traditional manner of such a unit. The members of the Council are to be selected by a somewhat complicated system, based in part on the percentage of consumption or imports of the commodities to be produced from minerals to be derived from the Area, investments in activities in the Area, "special interests" from developing states, and an "equitable geographic distribution of seats" in the Council. All members are to be elected by the Assembly. Below the Council are to be an Economic Planning Commission of 15 members and a Legal and Technical Commission of 15 members. The "Enterprise," the organ through which the Authority is to carry out its economic functions in the Area (transporting, processing, and marketing of minerals recovered from the Area) in part by itself and in part in association with the Authority by states that are party to the convention, state enterprises, or natural or juridical persons defined in Article 153 of the convention. The headquarters of the Enterprise are to be in Jamaica.

The International Tribunal for the Law of the Sea, to be located in Hamburg, West Germany, is to consist of 21 independent members elected for nine-year terms, with no two to be nationals of the same state. The first election of the judges is to be done by the states in question and afterwards by procedures to be determined by those states. The Seabed Disputes Chamber of the International Tribunal is provided for by Articles 186 through 191.

Finally, the Authority is to have international legal personality and such legal capacity as may be necessary to exercise its functions, to fulfill its purposes (Article 176), and to enjoy immunity from legal process unless such be waived by it (Article 178). In addition, the Authority is to enjoy a variety of privileges and immunities, including immunities for its delegates and staff, as long as the acts in question are performed in the exercise of their functions.

Annex I, Resolution I, to the Final Act of the Third UN Conference on the Law of the Sea, December 10, 1982, provides for the Preparatory Commission for the International Seabed Authority and for the International

Tribunal for the Law of the Sea. The commission is to consist of the states (and Namibia) that have signed or acceded to the convention. The Secretary-General of the United Nations is to convene the commission upon signature of or accession to the convention by 50 states. The first actual session of the preparatory commission took place, however, in April 1983. Among other actions taken, it was agreed that all important decisions by the commission were to be taken by consensus, in order to avoid the rule by a "tyrannic majority." Detailed regulations for seabed mining were to be drawn up at future meetings of the body.

The objections voiced by the United States (and echoed in part by a number of the nonsignatories) center on the following real or assumed points:[92] (1) the convention placed under burdensome international regulation the development of all resources of the seabed and subsoil beyond the limits of national jurisdiction; (2) the convention would establish a supranational mining company (the Enterprise) which would benefit from discriminatory advantages over companies from industrialized countries; (2a) it could eventually monopolize the production of seabed minerals; (2b) funding of the initial capitalization of the Enterprise would be required from the United States and other countries in proportion to their contributions to the United Nations; (3) through its transfer of technology provisions, the convention would compel the sale of proprietary information and technology now largely in U.S. hands; (3a) the convention also guaranteed similar access to privately owned technology by any developing country planning to go into seabed mining (except for national security–related technology); (4) the convention limited the annual production of manganese nodules from the deep seabed, as well as the amount that any one company could mine for the first twenty years of production; (5) the convention created a one-nation, one-vote international organization. In its Council, the Soviet Union and its socialist allies would be guaranteed three seats, but the United States would have to compete with its allies for any representation; (5a) the Assembly was characterized as the "supreme" organ, and the Council's specific policy decisions had to conform to the Assembly's general policies; (6) the convention provided for a review of its provisions after 15 years of production of minerals from the Area. If the United States, for example, were to disagree with duly ratified changes, it would nevertheless be bound by them, unless it exercised its options to denounce the entire treaty; (7) the convention imposed revenue-sharing obligations on seabed mining corporations that would sig-

[92] Combined testimony by Ambassador James M. Malone before the Subcommittee on Oceanography of the House Merchant Marine and Fisheries Committee, April 28, 1981, reproduced in Oxman, "The Third United Nations Conference on the Law of the Sea: The Tenth Session (1981)," 76 *AJIL* 1, esp. 9–10 (1982); and the explanation by President Ronald Reagan (July 9, 1982) of why the United States would not sign the convention, reported in Department of State, Bureau of Public Affairs, *Gist,* November 1982. See especially the reasoning outlined in Department of State, *Current Policy No. 617,* Freedom and Opportunity: Foundations for a Dynamic National Oceans Policy (September 24, 1984).

nificantly increase the cost of seabed mining; (8) the convention imposed an international revenue-sharing obligation on the production of hydrocarbons from the continental shelf beyond the 200-mile limit; (9) the convention lacked any provisions for protecting investments made prior to the convention's entry into force; (10) the production provisions limited the availability of minerals for global consumption; (11) the convention contained a discriminatory limit on the number of mining operations that could be conducted by any one country; (12) the convention would not ensure national access to seabed resources by current and future qualified entities: applicants would not be granted contracts based exclusively on whether they satisfied objective qualification standards; (13) the decision-making process in the Seabed Authority would not reflect the realities of the world's economic system, in which some nations had much more far-reaching interests, more ability to consume, and more ability to invest than others did; for example, the convention would make American access to seabed resources dependent on the voting of competitors and on those countries that did not wish to see the resources produced.

On September 2, 1982, the United States, the United Kingdom, the Federal Republic of Germany, and France concluded a formal instrument, effective at once, the Agreement Concerning Interim Arrangements Relating to Polymetallic Nodules of the Deep Sea Bed.[93] That agreement made provisions for avoiding overlaps in areas to be claimed and conflicts in license applications and for reciprocal recognition of mining sites. It was preceded and followed by a spate of national legislation in the various countries, all designed to provide interim measures for deep-seabed mining.

On August 3, 1984, eight industrialized countries signed at Geneva a new agreement intended to prevent disputes over sites among companies mining minerals from the seabed outside territorial waters. Those involved in the scheme were Belgium, the United Kingdom, France, Italy, Japan, the Netherlands, West Germany, and the United States: several of these states had also signed UNCLOS III. On August 15, in Geneva, a group of 77 developing countries denounced the eight-country accord as illegal, claiming that "the convention of the Law of the Sea is the only legally acceptable international regime applicable to the seabed and its resources."

According to D'Amato, the four-power agreement of 1982 should have gone beyond mere deep-seabed–mining questions and included other topics also found in UNCLOS III, so that the "universality of desirable Convention

[93]Text in 21 *ILM* 950 (1982). National legislation on interim measures for deep-seabed mining proliferated since 1980, and the relevant laws may be found as follows: Japan, 22 *ILM* 102 (1983); France: 21 *ILM* 808 (1982); Federal Republic of Germany: 20 *ILM* 393 (1981), and 21 *ILM* 832 (1982); United Kingdom, 20 *ILM* 1217 (1981); Soviet Union: 21 *ILM* 551 (1982); and United States: 19 *ILM* 1003 (1980), 20 *ILM* 1228 (1981), and 21 *ILM* 867 (1982).

norms" could be ensured.[94] However, as he pointed out, this led to the interesting speculation as to whether nonsignatory states (that is, those that had not signed and ratified the UNCLOS III) could then legally engage in deep-seabed mining after UNCLOS III came into force. In any case, it would seem to the present writer that considering the number and, in many instances, the technological development of the nonsignatories to the 1982 convention, it might be to their advantage at some future time to be parties to a separate and comprehensive sea law treaty.[95]

STATUS OF THE 1982 CONVENTION (UNCLOS III)    As of May 31, 1989 (latest total available at the time of writing), 40 states had ratified the 1982 Convention on the Law of the Sea. That figure did not include any of the major maritime countries of the world. According to Article 308, the convention will enter into force 12 months after the sixtieth instrument of ratification or accession has been deposited.

CONSERVATION TREATIES    Excessive unilateral acts are at best doubtful legality when measured against the rules of international law, particularly against the principle of the freedom of the sea. On the other hand, numerous treaties have been concluded between regional groupings of states for the purpose of conserving certain species of marine life or of all species in a particular portion of the high seas. A somewhat larger number of international agreements provide for the operation of commissions, either of an advisory type or of an administrative nature; examples are the Northwest Atlantic Fisheries Convention (1949) and the North Pacific High Seas Fisheries Convention (1952).

INTERNATIONAL WHALING COMMISSION    On a still broader basis, both in scope of activities and in the area of the seas involved, is the work of the International Whaling Commission, established by convention in 1946.[96] This body not only sets quotas for whaling but also has the authority to end a particular season as soon as the quotas have been filled. In recent years the United States has been defeated repeatedly in the annual whaling conference when it has proposed a ten-year moratorium on the killing of whales in order to save them from extinction. Japan and the Soviet Union, the only two countries still operating large whale fleets, have refused to accept such a moratorium. In 1976, 1977, and again in 1980, however, both accepted reduced kill quotas. In 1979 the commission had approved a ten-year whale sanctuary in the Indian Ocean (including the Red Sea, the Arabian Sea, and the Persian Gulf). In 1981, over Japanese objections, a "zero quota"

[94]D'Amato, "An Alternative to the Law of the Sea Convention," 77 *AJIL* 281, at 281 (1983). D'Amato asked in this article a number of intriguing questions as to possible rulings to be expected if the issue of nonsignatory seabed mining ever came up for decision by the International Court of Justice.

[95]See the thoughtful analysis by Lee, "The Law of the Sea Convention and Third States," 77 *AJIL* 541 (1983).

[96]The text of the basic convention may be found in 40 *AJIL* 174 (1945 Supp.); see also Reiff 293–397.

on all sperm whaling was set for the Southern Hemisphere and the North Atlantic, but an Australian proposal to phase out all commercial whaling was blocked when the necessary three-fourths majority of votes could not be achieved. In July 1982, however, the commission (by then consisting of 38 members) succeeded in voting a ban on commercial whaling worldwide for an indefinite period, beginning January 1, 1986. Japan, Norway, Peru, the Soviet Union, Brazil, Iceland, and South Korea opposed the ban. Peru and Brazil, however, dropped their objections in 1983, leaving only the Soviet Union, Norway, and Japan opposed. The latter two states asserted that they would continue whaling despite the ban.

Japan, under pressure from the United States, agreed in November 1984 through an executive agreement with the United States to end sperm whaling by 1988. When Norway persisted in whaling in the North Atlantic, the Secretary of Commerce sent to the President the certification called for under the amended Fisherman's Protective Act of 1967.

It should be noted that Japan, Norway, Iceland, and South Korea were still entitled to hunt several hundred whales each "for scientific research purposes." At the 1987 annual meeting of the Whaling Commission, both Japan and Norway reacted strongly against a move inspired, it was claimed, by the United States to end the "research" quota, which still existed at the time of this writing.

Japan finally agreed to abide by the moratorium on commercial whaling; the Soviet Union had already announced (May 26, 1987) a ban on commercial whaling, but Mauritius announced its withdrawal from the Commission's convention on August 27, 1987, an action duplicated by Belize on December 30, 1987. The following three years witnessed a continued killing of whales in the name of research by Japan, Norway, and Iceland, but the totals involved represented but a fraction of the pre-moratorium kills.

## Nuclear Weapons on Seabed

One of the feared consequences of the development of nuclear weapons systems has been the danger arising from the emplacement of a variety of missiles on the seabed, to be launched electronically at predetermined targets on shore. As demand for the control or prohibition of such possible installations proliferated, the Geneva disarmament meetings quickly discovered that although the United States and the Soviet Union were quite willing to work out an agreement on the matter at hand, they differed widely in what each would propose to abolish. The Soviet Union urged that all military activity on the seabed should end. The United States, on the other hand, already utilizing the ocean floor in submarine surveillance and reconnaissance activities, desired to abolish only the placement of nuclear weapons on the ocean floor.[97]

[97] See Sullivan, "Extending the Arms Race to the Ocean Deeps," *NYT*, March 10, 1969, E-7; and Hamilton, "Some Slow Progress Toward Disarming the Ocean Floor," May 25, 1969, E-4.

The point of view of the United States prevailed: on February 11, 1971, the UN Treaty on the Prohibition of the Emplacement of Nuclear Weapons and Other Weapons of Mass Destruction on the Seabed and the Ocean Floor and the Subsoil Thereof was signed is Moscow, London, and Washington.[98] It entered into effect on May 18, 1972. In addition to the prohibition on emplacement, the treaty also forbids "structures, launching installations, or any other facilities *specifically designed* for storing, testing or using such weapons" (italics added). The prohibitions in the instrument all relate to the high seas beyond the 12-mile outer limit (contiguous zone) as defined in the 1958 UN Convention on the Territorial Sea and the Contiguous Zone.

## Sea Cables and Pipelines

A more traditional segment of the law of the sea pertains to submarine cables and pipelines on the bed of the high seas. All states have an undoubted right to lay such pipelines and cables. No coastal state may impede the laying or maintenance of such installations by a foreign state, subject to an obvious modern right to take reasonable measures for the exploration and exploitation of the continental shelf and its resources.[99] The Iranian delegation, in signing the 1958 Convention on the High Seas, added a reservation to this principle (which appeared in Article 26, paragraph 2, of the instrument), emphasizing that the laying of submarine cables and pipelines was to be subject to authorization of the coastal state, in regard to the continental shelf area.

Whenever a state undertakes to lay undersea cables or pipelines, it must pay due attention to any cables or pipeline installation already in position in the seabed.

## Status of the Air Above the High Seas

It appears advisable at this point to outline the status of the air above waters outside the territorial sea. The details concerning this subject, previously based on several treaties as well as customary law, have been collected by the drafters of the UNCLOS III Convention, and the reference to the relevant articles is appended after each item below.

In straits used in international navigation, the bordering states have sovereignty over the airspace above their waters (Art. 34-1), and in such straits transit passage includes overflight solely for the purpose of continuous transit (Art. 38-2). Aircraft over such straits owe certain duties to the coastal states while in transit (Art. 39-1).

---

[98] Text, and the relevant U.N. General Assembly Resolution 2660 (XXV) of December 7, 1970, in 10 *ILM* 145 (1971). By the end of December 1984, a total of 81 states had ratified the treaty while 28 signatories had failed to do so.

[99] See Whiteman, vol. 4, 727–39, and also UNCLOS III, Arts. 112–15.

Archipelagic states have sovereignty over the airspace above archipelagic waters (Art. 49-2), and all aircraft enjoy the right of archipelagic sea-lanes passage (Art. 53-2, 4, 5, 12). Articles 39 and 40 apply also to archipelagic sea-lanes passage.

Above all exclusive economic zones, there is freedom of overflight (Art. 58). In regard to artificial islands and structures, it appears that the coastal state in question apparently enjoys no privileges in the relevant airspace, rather, such space is open to all overflight (Art. 56-1b, Art. 61-1). And, finally, any rights of the coastal state over its continental shelf do not affect the legal status of the airspace above the shelf: that airspace is open to overflight to all.

## SUGGESTED READINGS

### Jurisdiction over Vessels: General

Whiteman, vol. 9, 1–308.

CASES

*Cunard Steamship Co.* v. *Mellon,* U.S. Supreme Court, 1923, 262 U.S. 100.
*Strathearn Steamship Co.* v. *Dillon,* U.S. Supreme Court, 1920, 252 U.S. 348.
*United States* v. *Flores,* U.S. Supreme Court, 1933, 289 U.S. 137.
*Payne* v. *S.S. Tropic Breeze,* U.S. Court of Appeals, 1st Cir., 1970, 423 F.2d 236, digested in 64 *AJIL* 953 (1970).
*United States* v. *Conroy,* U.S. Court of Appeals, 5th Cir., 1979, 589 F.2d 1258, reported in 73 *AJIL* 696 (1979).
*United States* v. *Postal,* U.S. Court of Appeals, 5th Cir., 1979, 589 F.2d 862, reported in 73 *AJIL* 698 (1979).

### Flags of Convenience

Osieke, "Flags of Convenience Vessels: Recent Developments," 73 *AJIL* 604 (1979).

CASES

*McCulloch, Chairman, National Labor Relations Board, et al.* v. *Sociedad Nacional de Marineros de Honduras; McLeod, Regional Director, National Labor Relations Board* v. *Empresa Hondurena de Vapores, S.A.; National Maritime Union of America, AFL-CIO* v. *Empresa Hondurena de Vapores, S.A.,* U.S. Supreme Court, 1963, 372 U.S. 10.
*Hellenic Lines, Ltd. et al.* v. *Zacharias Rhoditis,* U.S. Supreme Court, June 8, 1970, in 9 *ILM* 769 (1970); decision of U.S. Court of Appeals (July 3, 1969) digested in 64 *AJIL* 703 (1970).
*Windward Shipping (London), Ltd.* v. *American Radio Association,* U.S. Supreme Court, 1974, 415 U.S. 104, 94 S. Ct. 959, reported in 16 *Harvard Int'l Law Jl.* 500 (1975).

## Territorial Waters

Hackworth, vol. 1, 642–45, 651–53; Lauterpacht's *Oppenheim,* vol. 1, 487–504; Whiteman, vol. 4, 1–480; Strohl, *The International Law of Bays* (1963); Cuba–United States, "Maritime Boundary Agreement (December 16, 1977)," in 17 *ILM* 110 (1978); Burmester, "The Torres Strait Treaty: Ocean Boundary Delimitation by Agreement," 76 *AJIL* 321 (1982); Union of Soviet Socialist Republics: "Law on the State Boundary of the U.S.S.R." (entered into force March 1, 1983), 22 *AJIL* 1055 (1983); Jagota, *Maritime Boundary* (1985); Kaikobad, *The Shatt-al-Arab Boundary Question* (1988); Prescott, *The Maritime Political Boundaries of the World* (1986).

CASE

*Treasure Salvors, Inc.* v. *Abandoned Sailing Vessel,* U.S. Dist. Court, S.D. Florida, 1976 (amended February 4, 1976), 408F. Supp. 907, reported in 71 *AJIL* 151 (1977).

## Gulfs and Bays

Colombia–Venezuela dispute concerning the Gulf of Venezuela: see *NYT,* April 29, 1973, 11; for copious excerpts from a U.S. *Note* to the Libyan Arab Republic (February 11, 1974), protesting announcement of a Libyan extension of boundaries in the Gulf of Sirte, see 68 *AJIL* 510 (1974). Consult Westerman, *The Juridical Bay* (1987).

CASE

*People* v. *Foretich,* United States, Appellate Dept., Superior Court, Los Angeles County, Calif., December 31, 1970, reported in 66 *AJIL* 192 (1972) (another case dealing with Santa Monica Bay).

## Territorial Sovereignty

Lee, "Jurisdiction over Foreign Merchant Ships in the Territorial Sea: An Analysis of the Geneva Convention on the Law of the Sea," 55 *AJIL* 77 (1961); Simmons, *The Pueblo, EC-121, and Mayaguez Incidents: Some Continuities and Changes* (1978).

CASES

*United States* v. *Dixon,* U.S. Dist. Court, E.D.N.Y., 1947, 73 F. Supp. 683, noted in 42 *AJIL* 493 (1948).
*Lauritzen* v. *Larsen,* U.S. Supreme Court, 1953, 345 U.S. 571, reported in 47 *AJIL* 711 (1953).
*United States* v. *Postal,* U.S. Court of Appeals, 5th Cir., 1979, 589, F.2d 862, covered at length in Stefan Riesenfeld, "The Doctrine of Self-executing Treaties and U.S. v. Postal: Win at Any Price?" 74 *AJIL* (1980), pp. 892–904, and reported 73 *AJIL* (1979), pp. 698–701.
*United States* v. *Flores,* U.S. Supreme Court, 1933, 289 U.S. 137, in Hankin, 341–43.

## Straits

Alexandersson, *The Baltic Straits* (1982); Lapidoth-Eschebacher, *The Red Sea and the Gulf of Aden* (1982); Ramazani, *The Persian Gulf and the Strait of Hormuz* (1979); Truver, *The Strait of Gibraltar and the Mediterranean* (1980); Leifer, *Malacca, Singapore and Indonesia* (1978); Cuyvers, *The Strait of Dover* (1986); Butler, *Northwest Arctic Passage* (1978); Pharand, *Northwest Passage: Arctic Straits* (1984); Rozakis and Stagos, *The Turkish Straits* (1987); Pak, *The Korean Straits* (1988).

## Contiguous Zones

CASES

*Cook* v. *United States,* U.S. Supreme Court, 1933, 288 U.S. 102.
*The Grace and Ruby,* U.S. Dist. Court, Mass., 1922, 283 F. 574.

## The Continental Shelf

Whiteman, vol. 4, 740–931; Richardson, "Jan Mayen in Perspective," 82 *AJIL* 443 (1988); Chiu, "Some Problems Concerning the Application of the Delimitation of Maritime Boundary Provisions of the 1982 United Nations Convention on the Law of the Sea," 4 *Chinese Yearbook of International Law and Affairs* [CYILA] 66 (1984).

CASES

*Guess* v. *Read,* U.S. Court of Appeals, 5th Cir., 1961, 290 F. (2d) 622, digested in 56 *AJIL* 211 (1962).
*Bonser* v. *La Macchia,* Australia, High Court, 1969 (43 *Austral. L.J.R.* 275), in 64 *AJIL* 435 (1970).
*Occidental of Umm al Qaywayn, Inc.* v. *A Certain Cargo of Petroleum Laden Aboard the Tanker Dauntless Colocotronis,* U.S. Court of Appeals, 5th Cir., Aug. 9, 1978, in 17 *ILM* 1190 (1978).
*United States* v. *Ray,* U.S. Dist. Court, S.D. Florida, January 3, 1969 in 63 *AJIL* 642 (1969); and see also *Time,* Jan. 24, 1969, 55, on this case.
*United States* v. *California,* U.S. Supreme Court, 1965, 381 U.S. 139, reported in 59 *AJIL* 930 (1965), and its supplementary decree, January 31, 1966, 382 U.S. 448, excerpted in 60 *AJIL* 588 (1966). See also the *Note* by Moreau in 7 *Harvard Int'l Law Club Jl.* 339 (1966), on this case and its background.
*Continental Oil Company* v. *London Steam-Ship Owners' Mutual Insurance Association, Ltd.,* U.S. Court of Appeals, 5th Cir., 417 F.2d 1030, reported in 64 *AJIL* 695 (1970).
*United States* v. *States of Maine, New Hampshire, Massachusetts, Rhode Island, New York, New Jersey, Delaware, Maryland, Virginia, North Carolina, South Carolina, Georgia and Florida,* U.S. Supreme Court, October Term, 1968, reproduced in 8 *ILM* 850 (1969).

## Exclusive Economic Zones

Attard, *The Exclusive Economic Zone in International Law* (1987); Kwiatkowska, *The 200 Mile Exclusive Economic Zone in the Law of the Sea* (1989); Dahmani, *The Fisheries*

*Regime of the Exclusive Economic Zone* (1987); Smith, *Economic Zone Claims: An Analysis and Primary Documents* (1986).

## The High Seas: General

Lauterpacht's *Oppenheim,* vol. 1, 567–608; Whiteman, vol. 4, 631–33 (on landlocked states); Reiff, 363–68; Bowett, *The Legal Regime of Islands in International Law* (1979); Sohn and Gustafson, *The Law of the Sea in a Nutshell* (1984); Hailbronner, "Freedom of the Air and the Convention on the Law of the Sea," 77 *AJIL* 490 (1983); McDougal and Burke, *The Public Order of the Oceans* (1987); O'Connell (Shearer, ed.), *The International Law of the Sea* (2 vols., 1983 and 1984); Churchill and Lowe, *The Law of the Sea* (2nd, rev. ed., 1988); Vicuña, *The Exclusive Economic Zone* (1989).

## Police Activities at Sea

"International Convention Relating to the Arrest of Sea-Going Ships" (Brussels, May 10, 1952; in force November 20, 1955), text in 53 *AJIL* 539 (1959); Higgins-Colombos, 334–41 (on insurgent vessels).

CASE

*United States* v. *Warren,* U.S. Court of Appeals, 5th Cir., 1978, 578 F.2d 1058, reported in 73 *AJIL* 143 (1979).

## Hot Pursuit

CASES

*Church* v. *Hubbart,* U.S. Supreme Court, 1804, 2 Cranch (6 U.S.) 187 ["Hovering" Vessels].

*The I'm Alone,* U.S. Department of State, *Arbitration Series,* No. 2 (1-7), 1931–1935 [Hot Pursuit].

*The Katina,* Egypt, Mixed Court of Appeal of Alexandria, 1929, in 24 *AJIL* 175 (1930) [Hot Pursuit].

*United States* v. *F/V Taiyo Maru,* U.S. Dist. Court, 1975, 395 F. Supp. 413, reported in 70 *AJIL* 138 (1976); see also Fidell, "Hot Pursuit from a Fisheries Zone: *United States* v. *Fishing Vessel Taiyo Maru No. 28; United States* v. *Kawaguchi,*" 70 *AJIL* 95 (1976); and Ciobanu, "Hot Pursuit from a Fisheries Zone: *United States* v. *Fishing Vessel Taiyo Maru No. 28; United States* v. *Kawaguchi,*" 70 *AJIL* 549 (1976).

## Accidents and Collisions

CASES

*The Heleanna Case,* Italy, 1971, reported in Dicke, "Heleanna Case and International Lawmaking Treaties: A New Form of Concluding a Treaty?" 69 *AJIL* 624 (1975).

*Sobonis* v. *Steam Tanker National Defender,* U.S. Dist. Court, S.D.N.Y., 1969, 298 F. Supp. 631, discussed by Wadlow in a *Note,* 11 *Harvard Int'l Law Jl.* 239 (1970).

## Third Conference on the Law of the Sea

Simmonds, ed., *The UN Convention on the Law of the Sea* (1983); Allott, "Power Sharing in the Law of the Sea," 77 *AJIL* 1 (1983); Wertenbaker, "The Law of the Sea," *New Yorker,* Aug. 1, 1983, 38–65, *passim,* and Aug, 8, 1983, pp. 56–83, *passim.*

## Deep Seabed Resources and Mining

Oda, *The International Law of the Ocean Development* (2 vols., 1972, 1975); Kronmiller, *The Lawfulness of Deep Seabed Mining,* (2 vols., 1979); Friedman, *"Selden Redivivus—*Towards a Partition of the Seas" 65 *AJIL* 757 (1971); Arrow, "The Proposed Regime for the Unilateral Exploitation of Deep Seabed Mineral Resources by the United States," 21 *Harvard Int'l Law Jl.* 337 (1980).

Consult also the documents in Deep Sea Ventures, Inc. [United States]: "Notice of Discovery and Claim of Exclusive Mining Rights, and Request for Diplomatic Protection and Protection of Investment," filed November 15, 1974, in 14 *ILM* 51 (1975); U.S. Department of State, "Statement on Claim of Exclusive Mining Rights by Deepsea Ventures, Inc.," *id.,* 66; Comments by Government of Canada (re Deepsea Ventures Claim), *id.,* 67–68; "Reply of the Australian Government," *id.,* 795; "Reply of British Government," *id.,* 796; and Hopson, "Miners Are Reaching for Metal Riches on the Ocean's Floor," *Smithsonian* (Jan. 1981), 51–59.

Expert Panel on the Law of Ocean Uses, "Exchange between Expert Panel and Reagan Administration Officials on Non-Seabed–Mining Provisions of LOS Treaty," 79 *AJIL* 151 (1985), its Statement on "U.S. Policy on the Settlement of Disputes in the Law of the Sea," 81 *AJIL* 438 (1987); and its Statement on "Deep Seabed Mining and the 1982 Convention on the Law of the Sea," 82 *AJIL* 363 (1988); Adede, *The System for Settlement of Disputes under the United Nations Conventions on the Law of the Sea* (1987).

## Whaling

Birnie, *International Regulations of Whaling* (2 vols., 1984).

# Case Study No. 6

# The Codfish War

The most publicized dispute concerning offshore economic zones was the three-part "Codfish War" between Iceland and the United Kingdom. Originally, in its first phase, the dispute had been caused by Iceland's unilateral decision in 1958 to extend its territorial waters to a 12-mile limit and to bar all foreigners from fishing within that area. The United Kingdom indicated a willingness to let Iceland claim an exclusive economic zone for two miles beyond the earlier four-mile territorial sea limit, with additional concessions to be made in certain key fishing areas. However, because the sea surrounding the country represents the key factor in its economy, Iceland refused to retreat. Clashes between British trawlers and Icelandic coast guard vessels erupted quickly. However, in March 1961, the United Kingdom accepted the Icelandic 12-mile limit for its territorial sea, and in return the Icelandic government permitted British fisherman to pursue their calling, in specified area, up to six miles offshore.

The second phase of the "war" came in 1971, when Iceland announced the imposition, by September 1, 1972, of a 50-mile conservation or economic zone, measured from straight baselines, closed to all foreign fishing vessels. Iceland claimed that this action was based on the extent of the Icelandic continental shelf. In reply, the United Kingdom unilaterally instituted proceedings (April 14, 1972) before the International Court of Justice, claiming that Iceland was not entitled to the unilateral extension ordered and that the conservation of fish stocks off Iceland should be subject to bilateral arrangements between the two countries.[1]

The court issued orders for interim measures of protection on August 17, 1972, which temporarily enjoined Iceland from enforcing the extension of the fishing limits, while also imposing limits on British catches.[2] Iceland denied the validity of the orders, inasmuch as it had not been a party before the court and ordered its coast guard vessels to cut the nets and trawls of all foreign fishermen violating the area composing the new economic zone.

On February 2, 1973, the International Court of Justice found (14–1) that it possessed jurisdiction to entertain the application filed by the United

---

[1]Iceland Althing, "Resolution on Fisheries Jurisdiction, February 15, 1971," in 11 *ILM* 643 (1972); Icelandic Regulations on Fishery Limits, of July 14, 1972, *id.*, 112.
[2]Text, *id.*, 1069, and in 67 *AJIL* 145 (1973).

Kingdom.[3] Clashes between Icelandic and British vessels continued unabated, however, accompanied ashore by bizarre incidents reminiscent of the better efforts of Messrs. Gilbert and Sullivan. The United Kingdom finally resorted to the dispatch of frigates to protect British fishermen. On May 25, 1973, demonstrators attacked the British embassy in Reykjavik, and Iceland appealed to the North Atlantic Treaty Organization to order a removal of British warships from the economic zone, hinting at a withdrawal from NATO. On May 30, 1973, Iceland expelled a British diplomat on charges of having divulged secret information on the movements of Icelandic ships. Finally, on July 10, 1973, Iceland concluded an agreement with Norway whereby Norwegian vessels of a specified maximum length would be allowed to obtain fishing licenses for a zone between 12 and 50 nautical miles around Iceland, measured from outside baselines, and on November 13, 1973, a similar but interim agreement was concluded with the United Kingdom — in the latter case, however, the number of British vessels was also specified.[4] Meanwhile, the court handed down (July 12, 1973) an order continuing the interim measures of protection originally issued in 1972.[5] An order was issued concerning a similar German–Icelandic dispute. Then, on October 16, Phase II of the "war" supposedly ended when negotiators of both parties settled the major issues of the dispute, with the United Kingdom agreeing to a limitation on British fishing in the 50-mile economic zone and limitations relating to the number and size of British vessels, restriction of British fishing to designated areas, and limitation of the maximum British catch set at 130,000 tons per year, a reduction of about 50,000 tons from previous total catches.[6]

On July 25, 1974, the International Court of Justice ruled against Iceland and in favor of the United Kingdom (after Iceland had refused to plead its case, maintaining that the court lacked jurisdiction in what Iceland held to be a purely domestic issue). The court found that "Iceland is not entitled unilaterally to exclude United Kingdom fishing vessels from areas between the 12-mile and 50-mile limits, or unilaterally to impose restrictions on their activities in such areas." In both cases (United Kingdom and Federal Republic of Germany), the court held that the interests of both plaintiffs in fishing off the coast of Iceland dated back for a long time, that both of their economies depended heavily on such fishing, and that a mandated loss of access to the fishing grounds would substantially affect entire communities in both countries.[7]

---

[3] Judgment (and related documents, including Judgment on a similar application filed unilaterally by the Federal Republic of Germany), in 12 ILM 290 (1973).
[4] Texts, with map, id., 1313.
[5] Text, id., 743.
[6] NYT, Oct. 17, 1973, 8.
[7] Fisheries Jurisdiction Case (United Kingdom v. Iceland), (Merits), I.C.J. Reports 1974, text in 13 ILM 1049 (1974); (including the German case); also excerpted in 69 AJIL 154 (1975). A convenient abstract is represented by Weill's Note in 16 Harvard Int'l Law Jl. 474 (1975).

Iceland refused to heed the court's judgment, for reasons explained earlier, and Phase III of the Codfish War commenced in the fall of 1975. By late November of that year, the British Admiralty had ordered frigates back to the Icelandic economic zone to protect British trawlers, just about at the time that both Belgium and the Federal Republic of Germany accepted the 200-mile limit in question through agreements concluded with Iceland on November 28, 1975.[8]

Owing to the British naval action, Iceland threatened repeatedly to withdraw from NATO unless the British frigates were recalled. Minor ramming incidents began to multiply after Icelandic coast guard vessels cut trawl wires and gunfire was exchanged. On November 26, 1975, Iceland closed its airspace and airports to aircraft of the Royal Air Force, and on January 13, 1975, it threatened to break off diplomatic relations within 48 hours unless all British warships were withdrawn from "Icelandic waters." Even though the time limit was not met, the British frigates were withdrawn from the economic zone, beginning on January 20, 1976, and British trawlers were ordered to stop fishing in the zone. As a result, negotiations were reopened four days later, even though they were soon accompanied by new incidents off Iceland when British trawlers were instructed by the British government to resume fishing following a dispute between one of them and an Icelandic law-enforcement vessel. On February 5, 1976, two British frigates were ordered back into the zone to protect trawlers, whereupon Iceland broke off diplomatic relations with the United Kingdom (February 19, 1976). Eventually, the British naval units were withdrawn (May 31, 1976), and negotiations were resumed the next day, by means of which, at long last, the long dispute was settled by means of the Agreement Concerning British Fishing in Icelandic Waters.[9] That treaty, to run for six months, permitted limited fishing by British vessels, of specified length and gross registered tonnage, up to a distance of 20 miles from Icelandic coastal baselines—with a few specified exceptions. After the expiration of the six months, British vessels were allowed to fish in Icelandic waters defined in the Icelandic Regulations of July 15, 1975,[10] only to the extent provided for in arrangements agreed with the Icelandic government. Iceland had won the Codfish War.

The latest development in the Icelandic fishery situation came on June 1, 1979, when Iceland's legislature passed law 41, the Law Concerning the Territorial Sea, the Economic Zone and the Continental Shelf.[11] That law fixed the outer limit of territorial sea at 12 nautical miles and placed the outer limit of the economic zone at a distance of 200 nautical miles beyond the territorial sea.

[8] Texts in 15 *ILM* 1 (1976), (Belgium) and 43 (FRG).
[9] Text, with related documents, in *id.*, 878. On March 10, 1976, a similar agreement had been concluded between Iceland and Norway; its text is found in *id.*, 875.
[10] Text, with map, 14 *ILM* 1282 (1975).
[11] Text, 18 *ILM* 1504, including map (1979).

# PART V

# International Transactions

# 16

# Agents of International Intercourse

## DIPLOMATIC AGENTS

BACKGROUND    International relations between friendly states have been characterized from the beginning of recorded history by a need for special organs of communications. For millennia, however, these organs, called *ambassadors* (diplomatic agents), did not possess the character of permanent representatives; instead, they were used only on occasion for the purpose of achieving certain tasks. In other words, an ambassador would be sent to a certain country to conclude an alliance, to make a trade agreement, to seek the hand of a princess for his king, to arrange for a marriage dowry, or to carry out whatever special purpose was at hand. Once he succeeded or failed in his mission, he returned home. Nevertheless, classical antiquity, particularly among the Greek city-states, witnessed the development of firm rules governing the sending of such agents, such as their inviolability, which still prevail today.

Permanent representatives did not appear at foreign capitals until the middle of the fifteenth century–the city of Milan usually being cited as the originator of the practice, around A.D. 1450. After a while, the occasional placement of permanent agents abroad was supplanted slowly by a general acceptance of the system. Among the various obstacles to a rapid and universally applied system of permanent representation was a major one: the distrust with which courts viewed a foreign ambassador, for all too many of them saw in him nothing but a spy—noble of birth, to be sure—of the sending state. Thus Russia, until the reign of Peter the Great, resisted successfully all attempts to locate permanent foreign representatives in its capital. Western Europe, on the other hand, quickly realized the many advantages accruing from the permanent presence of representatives abroad, and the custom quickly spread in that portion of the continent. Some states persisted for quite a while in ensuring, by means of bilateral agreements, each other's right to send ambassadors, but the majority regarded such a right as an aspect of sovereign independence. After the Treaty of

Westphalia (1648), the establishment of permanent diplomatic missions became the rule in Europe.

## Diplomatic Relations

RIGHT OF REPRESENTATION    The right of diplomatic intercourse is divided into an *active* and a *passive* right. The active right is the authority to send diplomatic agents abroad, an unquestioned right of every independent member of the family of nations. The problem of who is to exercise this right of representation in any given state is an internal constitutional question. As a rule, it is the monarch in a monarchy and the president in a republic (alone or in conjunction with some legislative body) who exercise the right. In the case of a confederation, the individual states usually have the right of representation, although a paramount member may be granted the right also, on either a sole or a concurrent basis. Corresponding to the right to send diplomatic agents is the passive right: the right to receive such agents. Normally an international person having the former right also has the latter. Generally, however, the right of representation, being a common attribute of sovereign states, posed questions only in the relatively few instances when it had to be determined whether or not a given community was entitled to this right. On rare modern occasions, an entity that is neither a recognized member of the community of nations nor a legal person in the form of an international organization has been accorded by a few countries a right of diplomatic representation. Thus India, on January 9, 1975, granted full diplomatic status to the representative of the Palestine Liberation Organization (PLO), the first time this had been done by a non-Arab state.

CODIFICATION OF RULES    Until 1815, the rules governing diplomatic intercourse were based primarily on customary international law, supplemented by practices founded on courtesy among nations. The classification of diplomatic ranks achieved at the Congress of Vienna and amended in the Protocol of Aix-la-Chapelle (1818) did not add materially to the existing rules, and it was not until 1927 that a possible codification of those rules was seriously considered. In that year, the League of Nations Committee of Experts for the Progressive Codification of International Law reported to the Council of the League that it regarded the subject of diplomatic privileges and immunities as "sufficiently ripe for international regulation." The Council, however, rejected the committee's conclusion. On the other hand, the Sixth Conference of American States (Havana, 1928) adopted the Convention on Diplomatic Officers.[1] This instrument, subsequently ratified by 12 American states, was signed but not ratified by the United States, which objected to the inclusion of provisions approving the granting of diplomatic asylum.

The International Law Commission of the United Nations selected the subject of diplomatic intercourse and immunities as one of 14 topics for

---

[1] Text of the convention in 22 *AJIL* 142 (1928).

codification, but did not give it any priority standing at the time the list was drawn up (1949). At its seventh session, in 1952, however, the General Assembly passed a resolution requesting the commission to codify the subject. In 1954, the commission initiated a study of diplomatic intercourse and immunities. Work on a proposed draft convention proceeded, and the commission succeeded in completing a final and excellent draft by 1959.

On December 7, 1959, the General Assembly, by Resolution 1450 (XIV), decided to convene an international conference to consider the question of diplomatic intercourse and immunities. This gathering, the United Nations Conference on Diplomatic Intercourse and Immunities, met at the Neue Hofburg, Vienna, from March 2 to April 14, 1961. It prepared three instruments: (1) Vienna Convention of Diplomatic Relations, (2) Optional Protocol Concerning Acquisition of Nationality, and (3) Optional Protocol Concerning the Compulsory Settlement of Disputes.[2] Of these, the Convention on Diplomatic Relations, of April 14, 1961, is the most important (hereafter Vienna Convention). Although it followed to a large extent the draft convention prepared by the International Law Commission, there were significant departures in several articles of the Vienna Convention. On April 18, 1961, the representatives of 75 states signed the convention, and the instrument entered into force on April 24, 1964 (for the United States, December 13, 1972).

Although the Vienna Convention does not show basic deviations from hitherto existing customary law, the fact it had at last been codified marked an advance in the development of international law. The subject matter of the Vienna meeting was not encumbered with too many contentious matters: the disputes at the conference arose out of questions of balance and emphasis rather than conflicting national interests. This writer believes that by now the provisions of the Vienna Convention are generally accepted components of conventional international law and has treated the convention's contents accordingly.

It is interesting that the final paragraph of the preamble to the convention declares that the signatory states affirm "that the rules of customary international law should continue to govern questions not expressly regulated by the provisions of the present Convention."

## Representation

From a legal point of view, each sovereign state is completely free to decide whether, and in which foreign states, it wishes to be represented by diplomatic agents. Should a state decide, for some reason, to deviate from what certainly has become a general custom and endeavor to live in solitude, such deviation would be regarded by other states, at the very least, as an international incivility. And if the state in question resolved also to bar all

---

[2]The texts of the convention, the protocols, and resolutions are reprinted in 55 *AJIL* 1062 (1961 Supp.).

foreign diplomatic agents from its jurisdiction, it would remove itself from further membership in the community of nations.

On the other hand, few states maintain diplomatic representation at all capitals of the world.[3] A given country might not be able to afford the relatively enormous sums needed for such an enterprise, or it might properly decide that it had so few interests in maintaining relations with a given foreign state that they would not warrant the expense of a diplomatic mission. Hence some states content themselves with being represented in certain capitals through the diplomatic mission of a friendly third state or with maintaining an ambassador at one capital who acts as their accredited representative to a number of other states. Thus Western Samoa, independent since 1962, decided for reasons of economy not to join the United Nations and not to establish diplomatic missions abroad. Its limited foreign relations were entrusted by special agreement to the embassies maintained by New Zealand in various parts of the world.

Somewhat different is a state's right to break off diplomatic relations with another state on a temporary basis, that is, to recall its diplomatic agents. Such an occurrence does not dissolve all relations between the states in question, because normally both states arrange to be represented through a third state, which then acts as an intermediary for purposes of communication. Thus, by early December 1972, the Swiss ambassador to Cuba represented his own state as well as nine others (including the United States) in Havana.

Ruptures of diplomatic relations occur with greater frequency than might be suspected, quite commonly because one of the parties involved has pursued a foreign policy contrary to the aims of the other party or, fairly frequently, because of misconduct (real or alleged) by diplomatic personnel. In the 1970s, diplomatic ruptures averaged three a year, ranging from one to eight. On April 7, 1980, the U.S. government broke off diplomatic relations with Iran. All but one of the remaining 15 Iranian diplomats and all 36 Iranian consular officials were given 36 hours to leave the United States. The one staff member in question was to remain until the Algerian government assumed custodianship of the embassy building. It should be pointed out that the Iranian diplomats assigned to the United Nations (and their families) were not affected by the expulsion order. They were, however, restricted to a 25-mile radius of New York City. Also expelled by the presidential order of April 7, 1980, were 207 Iranian air force personnel training in the United States, as well as about 140 Iranian students at American military colleges (see below for an earlier expulsion order). During the rest of 1980, Iraq broke off diplomatic relations with Syria; in October, Saudi Arabia did the same with Libya. In May 1981, the United States severed diplomatic relations with Libya.[4] In June 1981,

---

[3] In 1985 there were 131 embassies in Washington, D.C., and the United States maintained 140 embassies in other countries.

[4] Regarding the "People's Committee of the Socialist People's Libyan Arab Jamahiriya," see 74 *AJIL* 921 (1980); regarding the break with Iran, see 74 *AJIL* 663 (1980).

the Sudan and Libya mutually broke off relations, and in August, Somalia broke off relations with Libya. In October, Australia followed suit in its relations with Lebanon, and in the same month, Jamaica broke off relations with Cuba. Subsequent years have witnessed ruptures at similar rates. (See Appendix 1.)

On the other hand, full normal diplomatic relations were resumed in the same time period, often after ruptures of great length, for example, between the United States and Egypt, 1973 (after six years); between Rumania and Portugal, 1974 (after 25 years); between India and Portugal, 1975 (after almost 20 years); between India and the People's Republic of China, 1976 (after 14 years); between Spain and Yugoslavia, 1977 (after 22 years); between Spain and the Soviet Union, 1977 (after almost 40 years); between the Soviet Union and Egypt (after 12 years); between the United States and the People's Republic of China, January 1, 1979, (after almost 30 years); between the United States and Iraq on November 26, 1984 (after 17 years); Egypt and Jordan on September 25, 1984 (after 5 years);[5] . . . . . . and Egypt and Syria in 1989 (after 12 years). (See Appendix 2.)

SPECIAL INTERESTS SECTIONS     The official rupture of diplomatic relations is mitigated, on occasion, by the establishment of special interest sections by the two states involved. This may take one of two forms: sections are created on the onset of a "limited exchange" of diplomats, preceding an eventual full resumption of diplomatic relations, or sections are established on the rupture of such relations. An example of the former variety came into being when, after a seven-year break, relations were resumed between the United States and Syria in 1974 on a "limited exchange" basis. The former American embassy building in Damascus (hitherto in the custody of Italy) was redesignated the "Embassy of Italy: Section for the Protection of the Interests of the United States of America," with the American flag flying above it, and a similar name change took place with respect to the former Syrian embassy building in Washington. When the 16-year-old rupture of diplomatic relations between the United States and Cuba ended in 1977, a similar strategy was adopted: Switzerland had had custody of the U.S. embassy building in Havana, and Czechoslovakia of the Washington embassy building of Cuba. Special Interest Sections were established in the respective facilities, still designated as the "protecting power's" embassy, and limited relations began.

The best-known example of the second form appeared when the United States and Iran severed diplomatic relations in 1980. The United States established a Special Interests Section in the Swiss Embassy in Tehran, with no U.S. citizens employed therein. Iran set up the Iranian Special Interests Section as a part of, but not physically in, the Algerian Embassy in Washington. It was staffed by ethnic Iranians who were either naturalized Americans

---

[5]See documents in 17 *ILM* 272 (1979), and also the coverage of Chinese recognition in Chapter 5.

or resident aliens. Algeria permitted the section to use its diplomatic bag or pouch. In 1987, Switzerland operated a British Special Interest Section in Buenos Aires, besides representing 14 other states around the world (Iran in Israel, etc.).

In neither case are staff members of such Special Interest Sections regarded as diplomats in the legal sense. They lack diplomatic privileges and immunities and must pay taxes to the host state, but in the case of the United States, they must register with the Department of State. The business undertaken in such Special Interests Sections involves the granting of visas, communication with relatives, renewal of expiring passports, assistance in obtaining birth certificates, and so on. When diplomatic relations are broken at a time when there has been no change in government in the "offending" state, it does *not* mean the withdrawal of recognition of the government in power in that state. After the rupture of diplomatic relations with the Castro administration in Cuba, the government of the United States continued to accord to the Cuban government such rights as accrue to the government of a sovereign state under international law.

On some occasions, only the top-level diplomats are withdrawn by governments as a gesture of protest against some host government policy or act: the United States and Sweden were without ambassadors in their respective capitals, because of Swedish criticism of the U.S. bombing of Hanoi and Haiphong, from 1972 until ambassadors were finally exchanged again in March 1974. Great Britain conducted its diplomatic relations with the People's Republic of China through respective missions, each headed by a chargé d'affaires for 20 years until ambassadors were finally exchanged by both countries in 1971. In 1975, 15 European countries temporarily recalled their ambassadors from Madrid to protest the Spanish execution of five terrorists. Mexico, then having no embassy in Spain, expressed its displeasure with the executions by cutting off postal communications with Spain.

## Beginning and Termination of a Diplomatic Mission

ACCEPTANCE OF AN AGENT    No state is required to accept every individual proposed as the agent of a foreign state. The agent must enjoy the confidence of the receiving state's government. Should the latter decide that a given nominee, for any reason, is not suitable as the representative of his government, it may reject the appointment.

Hence it is the rule that the sending state, before a diplomatic agent is appointed, inquires of the receiving state whether the nominee is acceptable to it, that is, if he is persona grata. If such notification is not given, the receiving state normally refuses to admit the nominee. Rejection of the nominee as persona non grata may or may not be accompanied by reasons for the decision. Traditionally no reason is given or expected. Nevertheless, the United States and Great Britain for a long time not only insisted on being given reasons for the rejection of one of their nominees but indeed asserted their right to approve or reject those reasons as valid. This attitude had to be abandoned by both the United States and Great Britain, for in practice any receiving state can simply refuse to accept an individual whom it has judged to be persona non grata.

On the other hand, when Iran rejected (June 1979) the U.S. ambassador-designate Walter Cutler, a reason was cited: alleged American intervention in Zaire at a time when Cutler was the American ambassador there. In February 1982, Afghanistan asked the United States to withdraw the visa application of Archer Blood, its chargé d'affaires–designate, on the grounds that while posted in New Delhi, Blood had been in contact with Afghan citizens hostile to the regime. The United States unsuccessfully protested the request as being unacceptable and labeled the explanation as "irrelevant and immaterial." In August 1983, Kuwait apologized to the United States for rejecting Ambassador-designate Brandon Grove, Jr., who had served as consul general in Jerusalem, claimed by Israel as its capital. The United States, again unsuccessfully, objected, asserting that locating a consulate general in Jerusalem did not mean American recognition of Israel's claim to the city as its capital. It then indicated to Kuwait that the ambassadorship would remain unfilled indefinitely.

When the United States in 1885 appointed a Mr. Keiley as minister to Italy, without previous inquiry, he was denied reception for the interesting reason that some 14 years earlier he had protested at a meeting in the United States against the Italian absorption of the Papal States. Secretary of State Bayard viewed this as a sufficient reason for Keiley's rejection. But then the same individual was appointed, without previous nomination, as American minister to Austria-Hungary and was rejected again. This time, however, the reason given did not satisfy the United States government: "The position of a foreign envoy wedded to a Jewess by civil marriage would be untenable and even impossible in Vienna."[6] President Grover Cleveland contradicted his Secretary of State, who had held that each state had a right to exercise its discretion in receiving or rejecting diplomatic agents, and in protest refused to make a new nomination, leaving the affairs of the United States legation for two years in the hands of the secretary of the legation. It might be mentioned, in passing, that beginning with the appointment of the first United States ambassadors to foreign posts in 1893, the Department of State has been careful to inquire about the acceptability of a proposed diplomatic agent before the actual appointment. Although advance notification and inquiry by the sending state are not required by law for subordinate staff members of a diplomatic mission, courtesy has prompted most states to apply the practice to such individuals.

The legal basis of each diplomatic office is the agreement of the receiving state to the admission of a foreign mission. The receiving state therefore lays down the rules governing the legal position and activities of foreign diplomats, but in each instance the state is bound by the valid and applicable

[6]Moore, vol. 4, 480–83.

principles of international law.[7] In effect, the receiving state concedes to the foreign diplomat certain rights, privileges, and spheres of activity, subject to international law. Thus each diplomatic activity carried out by an agent of a state rests on a kind of double basis or title: the agreement (concession) of the receiving state and the instructions issued to him within the framework of that concession by the sending state.

The appointment of a diplomatic agent is a constitutional act of the sending state. His rights and duties begin formally with the handing over and acceptance of his credentials (*lettre de créance*) in the receiving state, which, by its acceptance of that document, recognizes the position of the individual concerned as the agent of his government. The credentials are accepted, depending on the rank of the agent, by either the chief of state or the minister of foreign affairs (in the United States, the Secretary of State) or through some specially designated protocol officer or functionary.

TERMINATION OF A MISSION    Because the accrediting of a diplomatic agent is a personal act—from the sender to the receiver—it terminates when one of the two parties ceases to represent his or her state. Therefore, when there is a change in monarchs, one or the other party has to accredit again the ambassadors and other diplomats. A renewal of the credentials is also called for by a change in rank of the diplomat in question and, normally, when there is a change in the form of government in either state. There are, however, many exceptions to the last rule. For instance, the United States ambassador to Russia, David R. Francis, reported to the Department of State on March 17, 1917, that the imperial government of Russia had been overthrown by revolution. He requested authorization to recognize the new government, which he received two days later from Secretary of State Lansing. On March 22, Francis called on the new Council of Ministers and presented his new credentials as United States ambassador. When the Provisional Government was in turn ousted on November 7, 1917, Ambassador Francis did not receive new credentials, and presumably his diplomatic mission terminated with the overthrow of the provisional government. He did remain in Russia, however, and until he left on July 25, 1918, he continued in his privileges and immunities.

On the other hand, a mere change in the person acting as chief of state in a republic or in the person acting as foreign minister does not require a renewal of diplomats' credentials.

Formally, the office of a diplomat ceases whenever one of the preceding conditions requiring renewal of accreditation takes place. Other reasons for the termination of a diplomatic office are the following:

• In the case of a nonpermanent diplomatic mission, the completion (success or failure) of the task entrusted to the mission ends its existence.

---

[7] See also the U.S. Department of State *Memorandum* of Dec. 12. 1974, setting forth the requirements for accreditation by the United States; relevant excerpts in 69 *AJIL* 394 (1975).

• The diplomatic agent may be recalled by the sending state. The replacement of the departing diplomat, in handing his own credentials to the head of the receiving state, also hands over the letter of his predecessor's recall.

The reasons for which diplomats are recalled are many and varied: they may be founded on interstate relations; rest on the relationships between the diplomat and the government of the receiving state; or be of purely domestic origin, such as when a diplomat is transferred.

The diplomatic mission may also end with the agent's dismissal. If a diplomat somehow offends the government of the receiving state, he may be declared persona non grata, and the recall is requested of the sending state. Thus, in late January 1980, New Zealand declared the Soviet ambassador, Vsevolod Sofinsky, persona non grata for paying Soviet funds to a small pro-Soviet political party; and in July 1980, the United States recalled Ambassador Frederic L. Chap from Ethiopia at the request of the latter's revolutionary government. (See also below, on violations of the law of the host government.)

On many recent occasions the dismissal of diplomatic agents represented merely a retaliatory action, caused by a similar dismissal (usually for purely political reasons) of agents by the sending state. The British government ordered (September 24, 1971) 105 Soviet embassy and trade agency staff members to leave within two weeks, accusing them of espionage and attempting to infiltrate saboteurs. In turn, the Soviet Union expelled 13 British embassy staff members on October 6, 1971. In February 1977, Norway expelled six Russian diplomats, whereupon the Soviet Union expelled one Norwegian and refused another one permission to return to his post in the Soviet Union. On December 18, 1979, the U.S. Department of State announced that at least 183 Iranian diplomatic staff members would be expelled within five days, leaving only 35 Iranian diplomatic personnel in the country. This action was announced to be a reprisal for the seizure of the American embassy and hostages in Tehran. However, the steps taken and the words spoken did not agree: by January 18, 1980, only 51 of the individuals asked to leave had actually departed; 77 had dropped from sight and could not be located by the U.S. Immigration and Naturalization Service; about 40 had been granted a "new status" and were allowed to remain; and some 15 persons were "under study" to determine their final status.[8]

A somewhat peculiar expulsion of "diplomats" took place in the United States. On May 4, 1980, the U.S. Department of State announced the expulsion of four Libyan "diplomats" (none of whom had diplomatic credentials), ordering them to leave within 72 hours. The reason given was a series of intimidating activities aimed at Libyan dissidents in the United States. Earlier, on April 17, 1980, the United States disclosed the expulsion of two other Libyan diplomats for distributing literature calling for

[8] Shaplen, "Eye of the Storm," *New Yorker,* June 9, 1980, 48–111, *passim.,* esp. 82.

the "liquidation" of Libyan dissidents. On May 8, the U.S. government threatened to break off diplomatic relations unless the four agents named in the May 4 order left the country immediately and the remaining embassy staff registered as diplomats. The Libyan staff, however, denied that any of the mission members were diplomats or that there was a Libyan embassy: it claimed that Libya had converted its embassies into "people's bureaus," staffed by "people's committees." This action, it was claimed, was in accord with the Libyan president's egalitarian reforms. That may have been correct, but the action was also in violation of international law and conventions. The Libyan claim of lack of diplomatic status resulted in a demand for the granting of due process, arrest, and placement of any accused on trial, with proof of the charges laid against them. The "people's committees" then took over nine Libyan embassies around the globe, and Libya expelled 25 American citizens and arrested several more. In the United States the impasse ended in part when Libya recalled the four "diplomats," and they left the country on May 11, 1980.

The tempo of dismissals picked up dramatically in 1983, however: at least 236 diplomats (excluding journalists and one ambassador's wife, charged with "bugging" other embassies) were expelled, including six Americans. Of that astonishing total, 147 Soviet diplomats were asked to leave because of charges of spying, 18 Soviet diplomats were expelled en masse by Bangladesh for "meddling in internal politics," and 18 other Russian diplomats were asked to leave Iran for "working with treacherous and mercenary agents." In February 1984, four U.S. diplomats were asked to leave Ethiopia, charged with espionage, and in March Ethiopia expelled two Soviet diplomats, and Norway ordered five Soviet diplomats to leave and barred four others from reentering the country: all of the Russians in question were accused of having engaged in subversive activities. On April 26, 1984, 140 expelled Libyans left London, and 30 British citizens (diplomats and their families) arrived home from Tripoli. The reason for that mass exodus was the breaking off of diplomatic relations between the United Kingdom and Libya, following the April 17 incident at the Libyan embassy in London.

On September 13, 1985, Great Britain expelled 25 Soviet citizens, including six diplomats, on charges of espionage; two days later, the Soviet Union ordered 25 British diplomats, journalists, and businessmen to leave. This mass expulsion ended a few days later when the total for each side reached 31. A few days earlier, Libya began to expel foreign workers, including almost 60,000 Tunisians, and Tunisia in turn ordered the expulsion of 153 Libyans, including 30 diplomats, and closed the Libyan consulates and cultural centers in the country. In May 1986, Great Britain expelled three Syrian diplomats after their embassy refused to waive their immunity, which would have exposed them to police interrogation concerning a failed attempt to bomb an Israeli airliner. Syria reacted on the same day by expelling three British diplomats. The Soviet Union expelled five U.S. diplomats on October 19, 1986, for engaging in "impermissible activities" (read: spying). Two days later, the United States ordered the departure of 55 Soviet officials from both the Soviet embassy and the Soviet consulate in San Francisco. In March 1987, the Soviet Union expelled a U.S. diplomat a week after the United States had ordered cutbacks in personnel at the Soviet UN mission in New York. And in September of that year, Kuwait ordered the expulsion of five Iranian diplomats after three missiles had landed in four days along the Kuwait coast.

In June 1988, charges of spying and retaliatory expulsions involved a total of 32 Canadian and Soviet diplomats and officials. Much publicity resulted July 11, 1988, when Nicaragua ordered the U.S. ambassador and seven other embassy officials to leave after they were accused of "state terrorism." [On January 20, 1989, the Nicaraguan government announced that the United States could replace these diplomats.] The United States retaliated immediately by expelling Nicaragua's ambassador and seven other Nicaraguan officials. In this instance, an unusual factor intruded: the ambassador to the United States was also Nicaragua's ambassador to the Organization of American States (OAS) in Washington, D.C. The OAS permanent council held a special meeting in which it was pointed out that the 32 OAS member states had the right to attend OAS meetings "independent of their bilateral relations with the host government." It was also mentioned that those rights were protected, albeit inadequately, in a 1975 U.S.–OAS agreement governing the obligations of the host country.[9] Yugoslavia expelled three Australian diplomats December 5, 1988, after Australia had closed the Yugoslav consulate in Sidney and expelled its staff. The Australian action had followed a Yugoslav refusal to surrender to police a consulate guard who had shot a Croatian émigré.

Another major reduction in British and Soviet embassy personnel occurred in May 1989. First, Great Britain expelled eight Soviet diplomats and three journalists accused of espionage, and the Soviet Union responded with a matching set of expulsions. Then the Soviet Union ordered Great Britain to reduce its official staff at the Moscow Embassy from 375 to 170 persons, in order to match the maximum permitted the Soviet Union at its London Embassy.

In 1990, Panama expelled the Peruvian chargé d'affaires and recalled its own diplomat of that rank from Peru. The reasons advanced for this action were "scornful remarks" by Peruvian leaders following the U.S. invasion and a Peruvian delay in recognizing the new Panamanian government.

In March 1990 the Panamanian government expelled the Cuban ambassador after Cuba had questioned the legitimacy of the new government of Panama. Later in that year, the developing Persian Gulf crisis led to a multitude of expulsions of diplomats. On August 27, the United States ordered the departure of two-thirds (36) of the staff of the Iraqi embassy because of Iraq's treatment of diplomats in Iraq and occupied Kuwait. The remain-

[9]AP Dispatch, July 15, 1988.

ing 19 staff members were restricted in travel to within a 25-mile radius of Washington, D.C. On September 18 the 12 European Community governments agreed on the expulsion of Iraqi military attachés, and Iraq retaliated two days later by ordering the expulsion of dozens of American, European, and Arab diplomats, including 11 military attachés. France alone had 11 of its diplomats expelled from Iraq. The United States, Spain, and Egypt responded immediately with the expulsion of a number of Iraqi diplomats. And on September 22, 1990, Saudi Arabia ordered most of the diplomatic staffs of Iraq, Yemen, and Jordan to leave the country.

A diplomat who is no longer persona grata may or may not be given a time limit within which to leave the receiving state's jurisdiction. Should the diplomat refuse to leave, he may be placed under detention and escorted to the frontier for expulsion.

The outbreak of war between two states ends their direct diplomatic relations. In each of them, the ambassador or minister transfers limited representation rights to the agents of a third (neutral) state, through which are maintained, for the duration of the conflict, whatever diplomatic relations there remain between the belligerents.

An unusual set of circumstances caused the closing of six diplomatic missions in one country. Within the 12 months beginning in February 1979, the governments of the Federal Republic of Germany, Great Britain, Israel, Japan, South Africa, and Switzerland suspended operations of their embassies in El Salvador because of the growing incidence of political violence in that country. The occupation of embassies and government buildings and the taking of hostages by leftist groups had become routine, and the Salvadoran government had proved incapable of protecting the diplomats and their diplomatic premises.

Finally, a diplomatic mission ends with the disappearance of the sending or receiving state. An unusual exception to this normal and logical rule took place in the case of the diplomatic representatives of the Republic of Latvia following that country's absorption into the Soviet Union in 1940. Because most of the world's governments refused to recognize the annexation of Latvia, Estonia, and Lithuania by the Soviet Union, the diplomatic agents of the three Baltic republics continued to occupy their posts in all nonrecognizing states. The Latvian envoy in London, as the senior diplomatic agent of Latvia abroad, assumed the emergency powers of his government. [10] Thus a diplomatic representative assumed the status of a government-in-exile and claimed sovereignty over all Latvian citizens living in Western countries. Such jurisdiction naturally was limited to states in which Latvian diplomatic agents were still accredited. In a more normal example, the staff of the South Vietnamese embassy in Washington, from the ambassador down, lost its diplomatic status when the embassy was closed down in May 1975

---

[10] See *Mrs. J. W.* v. *Republic of Latvia,* Germany, Landgericht, Berlin, Oct. 3, 1953, digested in 48 *AJIL* 161 (1954).

after the fall of Saigon to the forces of North Vietnam. The last ambassador asked the United States government to act as the protecting power for the premises, which was done, pending a decision on the request of the new Saigon authorities that the government of Algeria be appointed caretaker.

## Diplomatic Rank

When there were no permanent representatives abroad, distinctions between diplomatic agents depended almost entirely on the relative strength and importance of the sending state. But as soon as there were permanent representatives, bitter quarreling ensued between the representatives of various powers stationed in the same capital. It was generally accepted that the representatives of monarchs (*ambaxatores*) occupied the highest category in rank. Besides such "ambassadors," there was one other class of representatives— the ministers, or residents, entitled, since the middle of the seventeenth century, *envoyés* (envoys). After some time, this second group was divided into two classes—ordinary and extraordinary envoys—and the latter began to claim special privileges and higher rank than the former had. More and more states named *envoyés extraordinaires* and insisted that these constituted a class distinct from ambassadors and residents, even when their duties and powers corresponded in every detail to those of the residents.

The protracted negotiations leading to the peace treaties of 1648, which ended the Thirty Years' War, illustrate the difficulties under which early modern diplomacy operated. The eight-year span of time required to settle the war was due primarily to a lack of rules governing diplomatic ceremonial and etiquette. Thus an offer by Venice to mediate was ignored completely because the offer addressed Queen Christina of Sweden as *Serenissime* without adding *Très-Puissante* to her official title. A little later, Sweden refused to send delegates to any peace conference at which Sweden's good friend and ally, France, would have precedence over Swedish diplomats.

One was reminded of these rather picayune incidents when, in 1968– 1969, protracted maneuvering (10 weeks) preceded the decision to use a round-table seating arrangement for the Paris talks designed to bring an end to the war in Vietnam. [11]

CATEGORIES OF DIPLOMATIC REPRESENTATIVES    At the beginning of the eighteenth century, three basic classes were recognized: ambassadors, envoys extraordinary, and residents (soon called *ministers resident*). By the end of the century, a fourth category had made its appearance, *chargés d'affaires,* occupying the bottom rank among diplomatic agents.

The emergence of definite categories did not, however, end the disputes among diplomats, for within each class, quarrels concerning precedence continued. The Congress of Vienna finally cleared up a totally confused state of affairs when it adopted, on March 19, 1815, the *Règlement sur le Rang Entre les Agents Diplomatiques,* a document supplemented later by the

[11]See *Time,* Jan. 24, 1969, 36.

*Protocol* of Aix-la-Chapelle of November 21, 1818. The categories set up by these two instruments still exist today, even though still another class of diplomats, added by the 1818 Protocol, has disappeared from the world scene and is not listed anymore in the Vienna Diplomatic Convention of 1961 (Art. 14). There are, then, four classes, or categories, of diplomatic representatives:

1. Ambassadors (ambassadors extraordinary, ambassadors plenipotentiary, and papal nuncios).
2. Ministers (envoys extraordinary, ministers plenipotentiary, and papal internuncios).
3. Ministers resident.
4. Chargés d'affaires and chargés d'affaires ad interim.

The first three categories are accredited by and to chiefs of state; the fourth is accredited by and to ministers of foreign affairs.

States customarily exchange diplomatic agents of the same rank, even though there have been exceptions to this practice. In the past, ambassadors were exchanged only between the Great Powers, but in the past 40 or so years, this custom has been abandoned in most cases, notably by the United States. Sending an ambassador to a small country supposedly ranks the latter equal with a powerful nation—and, regardless of the facts, appears to flatter sometimes very susceptible egos in the small country's government. Thus the United States, in pursuance of the "good neighbor" policy adopted during the presidency of Franklin Roosevelt, elevated its heads of missions in all Latin American states to the rank of ambassador.

The vexatious question of precedence within each class has been settled, since 1815, by ranking the various agents in accordance with the date of their accreditation in a particular capital—a kind of seniority system, as it were.

Nuncios (papal ambassadors) by custom act as the deans (*doyens*) of the diplomats accredited to a given government: they act as their spokesmen, particularly on ceremonial occasions.

Ministers (diplomatic agents of the second class) are not technically representatives of the head of their state, even though their credentials are signed by the latter and are presented to the head of the receiving state. This technical inferiority has been ignored, however, in the twentieth century, and today a minister, as well as the second class of papal diplomat, the internuncio, is regarded as equal to the ambassador in the ability to speak for the head of his state.

The chargé d'affaires is accredited by and to a minister of foreign affairs (in the United States, the secretary of state). Whereas he was once customarily sent only to small, backward, unimportant states (*ad hoc*), he is today primarily an assistant, with specified administrative functions, to an ambassador or minister. Normally he assumes, on an acting basis (*ad interim*), the functions of his superior during the latter's absence from the diplomatic mission or until a replacement is sent to the mission.

Below the ambassador or minister, a diplomatic mission may contain hundreds of persons. On occasion, distinctions are drawn between the official and nonofficial personnel of such a mission. The official personnel include all persons employed by the sending state or the chief of mission, to whom they are subordinate. This group comprises all of the mission's various functionaries, including the affiliated military or technical *attachés,* as well as the clerical staff (typists, secretaries, file clerks, interpreters, code clerks, and so forth).

The family of the chief of mission is definitely part of his official retinue. The nonofficial personnel are the servants of the chief of mission and the embassy (ambassador) or legation (minister), such as chauffeurs and gardeners. The legal position of this unofficial personnel has been, at times, the subject of much dispute. In most states, individuals in this category enjoy, by courtesy, diplomatic privileges and immunities as long as they are in the employ of the embassy or legation and are listed as employees with the foreign office (Department of State) of the receiving state. In other states, such employees do not enjoy any special standing (Soviet Union).

## Functions of Diplomatic Agents

The functions of the diplomat may be classified under six main headings:[12]

1. *Negotiation.* The original reason for having diplomats—the intention of having a representative in a foreign capital empowered to negotiate agreements with the receiving state—was to "deal" directly with the foreign government. This basic function has been downgraded considerably in the past half century or so, in part because of progress in communications, which makes the diplomat more of a spokesman than a true negotiator, and in part because of a tendency to substitute foreign ministers' meetings or summit meetings for negotiation at the ambassadorial level.

2. *Representation.* The diplomatic agent is the representative of the government of his state. He acts as such on ceremonial occasions but also files protests or inquiries with the receiving government. A diplomatic agent presents the policies of his government to the host state.

3. *Information.* A diplomat's basic duty is to report to his government on political events, policies, and other related matters. He is not a spy in the orthodox meaning of the term—even though a few heads of missions have been spies in the true sense of the word, and others have acted as paymasters to spies.

4. *Protection.* The diplomat has a duty to look after the interests, persons, and property of citizens of his own state in the receiving state. A diplomat

---

[12]See Sen, *A Diplomat's Handbook of International Law and Practice* (1988).

must be ready to assist them when they get into trouble abroad, may have to take charge of their bodies and effects if they happen to die on a trip, and in general act as "troubleshooters" for his fellow nationals in the receiving state.

5. *Public relations.* The diplomat continually tries to create goodwill for his own state and its policies. This propaganda–public relations function means giving and attending parties and dinners; giving lectures and other speeches; attending dedications of monuments, building, and (lately) foreign assistance projects; and so on. The effectiveness of such public relations activities is questionable, however, because it is difficult to measure. Only one thing is certain: if the diplomat refrains from participating in such activities, it creates ill will.

6. *Administration.* The chief of a diplomatic mission is the administrative head of the group, even though, in a large mission, he may have a subordinate personnel office and department heads. In the last resort, the ambassador or minister is responsible for the operation and administration of the embassy or legislation.

In the absence of consular relations (see below) between two countries, diplomatic officers customarily perform various functions normally performed by consular officers, always provided that the host (receiving) state does not object to the practice.

## Diplomatic Privileges and Immunities

A diplomatic person enjoys a considerable range of privileges and immunities based on customary as well as conventional international law. The obvious intent behind the grant of these privileges has been the desire to enable a diplomatic agent to exercise his duties and functions without being impeded by the authorities of the receiving state.

The extent of such diplomatic privileges has varied considerably during the past five centuries. Today the following are generally recognized as valid:

PERSONAL INVIOLABILITY    The person of the diplomatic agent is inviolable. This, his oldest privilege, was mentioned in the earliest records extant. Originally a diplomatic agent's sacred character was a question of practical necessity, because in many parts of the ancient world a foreigner had no rights whatsoever and, in many instances, the injury or even the killing of an alien was not punished by the local authorities. But ambassadors were not ordinary foreigners; they were always regarded as the representatives of their state. Hence any attack on an ambassador was an attack on his state and as such could lead to war; therefore, one had to surround the ambassador with privileges in order to give him special protection.

In recent times privileges have been viewed in proper perspective: diplomatic inviolability today means little more than that the diplomat enjoys a somewhat greater protection under criminal legislation than other aliens do. This protection is guaranteed by the law of the receiving state; hence it is a question of domestic law, not international law. The latter only obligates each state to promulgate and enforce the inviolability—that is, the protection—of the diplomat. As should be obvious, such inviolability is not absolute or unconditional: if a diplomat acts in such an illegal manner that measures of self-defense or police action are needed to restrain him, he cannot stand on the privilege of inviolability.

On the other hand, during the past 16 years, attacks on diplomats, consuls, and other government representatives have continued on a scale never witnessed before (see also Chapter 13 *sub* Peacetime Hostage Taking). Ambassadors have been kidnapped and then murdered; ambassadors have been kidnapped and later released; and ambassadors have been wounded in attacks. At times such incidents have occurred on a weekly basis. These attacks on diplomatic personnel have been found, furthermore, around the world, although most of the incidents have taken place in Europe.

In the United States, harassment of certain foreign diplomats and inconsequential attacks on foreign mission buildings, particularly those of the USSR, led to the passage of the Protection of Diplomats Act (1972), Public Law 92-539.[13] Because that new law did not appear to meet fully the needs of the times, another act was passed by Congress in 1976 and signed into law by the President on October 8, 1976: the Act for the Prevention and Punishment of Crimes Against Internationally Protected Persons, Public Law 94-467.[14] The purpose of that legislation was to bring Title 18 of the United States Code into conformity with two international conventions ratified by the United States: the 1971 OAS Convention to Prevent and Punish the Acts of Terrorism Taking the Form of Crimes Against Persons That Are of International Significance,[15] and the 1973 UN Convention on the Prevention and Punishment of Crimes Against Internationally Protected Persons, Including Diplomatic Agents.[16]

The UN Convention, which entered into force on February 20, 1977, provides in its Article 7 that "the State Party in whose territory the alleged offender is present shall, if it does not extradite him, submit, *without exception whatsoever* and without undue delay, the case to its competent authorities for the purpose of prosecution, through proceedings in accordance with the laws of that State"[italics added]. In other words, the defense of political offense was eliminated from the convention—only, however, after prolonged and somewhat heated debate in the UN General Assembly: the overwhelming majority of member governments agreed that the offenses in question

---

[13] Text of the Act for the Protection of Foreign Officials and Official Guests of the United States in 67 *AJIL* 622 (1973). For accounts of some of the events leading to the passage of the law, consult *NYT,* Jan. 17, 1971, 1, 65; Apr. 25, 1971, 23. See *NYT,* Nov. 21, 1971, 12; Nov. 26, 1971, 12; June 17, 1974, 29; Dec. 17, 1975, 1, 33; and April 2, 1976, 3, for continuation of the problems that the law was supposed to have cured.

[14] See 71 *AJIL* 134 (1977).

[15] Text in 10 *ILM* 255 (1971).

[16] Text in 67 *AJIL* 383 (1974), and in 13 *ILM* 41 (1974).

represented crimes under international law rather than political activities that were in some manner excusable.[17]

IMMUNITY OF EMBASSY AND LEGATION BUILDINGS    The embassy or legation quarters, as well as the residence of a diplomatic agent, are inviolable. The agents of the receiving state may not enter them, except with the consent of the head of the diplomatic mission. This rule was exemplified in the events regarding the Libyan embassy in London in April 1984. In February of that year, a group of Libyan revolutionary students asserted that they had staged a successful coup in the embassy, that there now was a "people's bureau" in accordance with the tenets of the Libyan leader, and that the 22 accredited Libyan diplomats in the embassy were no longer relevant. The British government ignored these announcements and continued to deal only with the accredited members of the Libyan staff. On April 17, 1984, Libyan exiles mounted an anti-Khaddafi demonstration across the street from the embassy, and an occupant of the building fired on the dissidents. Eleven of the latter were injured, and one British policewoman was killed. British police and commandos of the Special Air Service sealed off the embassy, and Libyan troops surrounded the British embassy in Tripoli. The British government proceeded to sever diplomatic relations with Libya, but continued to honor the immunity of the embassy building under the terms of the Vienna Convention, after permission to enter the building had been denied by the Libyan mission. Eventually the standoff was resolved by an agreement under which each country expelled the diplomats of the other. Only after the departure of the Libyan staff and the students did British security personnel enter the embassy building to search for weapons and information as to the identity of the departed killer.[18]

Following its invasion and occupation of Kuwait, the Iraqi government on August 20, 1990, ordered all foreign embassies in Kuwait to be closed by August 23. The United States and 20 other governments refused to comply with that order and kept their embassies open, albeit with reduced staffs. After three Canadian naval vessels sailed for the Persian Gulf, Iraqi troops surrounded first the Canadian, then the rest of the foreign embassies, with troops. Iraq also announced that Canadian and other diplomats in Iraq would be prohibited from leaving because their embassies in Kuwait remained open. The U.S. Department of State denounced this step as "an outrageous breach of international law." On August 25, water and electric-

---

[17]Consult also Bloomfield and FitzGerald, *Crimes Against Internationally Protected Persons: Prevention and Punishment* (1975), for a detailed analysis of the provisions of the UN Convention; and Kearney, "The Twenty-Fourth Session of the International Law Commission," 67 *AJIL* 84 esp. 85–92 (1973). See also Bayles, "Hostage Crisis Still Haunts Nation," AP dispatch, Oct. 28, 1984, and Chapter 13.

[18]See the following about security problems of diplomatic premises: "Can U.S. Buy Embassy Safety?" *U.S. News & World Report,* Apr. 14, 1986, 22–23; Moffett, "US Embassies under Siege of Terrorism," *CSM,* Jan. 29, 1986, 14–15; *Current Policy No. 788,* "Enhancing Diplomatic Security" (Feb. 1986), and *No. 923,* "How Much Security is Enough?" (Mar. 1987).

ity were cut off to several of the open embassies, and Iraq maintained that since midnight of August 24 the diplomats of the remaining embassies had lost their immunity and were to be detained as hostages. By September 3, telephone communications had been severed to most of the embassy compounds. As time went on, one country after another evacuated its embassy and consular staffs until only the British and American missions remained. They were able to leave for home in December, after Iraq had let foreign hostages ("guests") depart (see Chapter 13).

The normal inviolability of diplomatic and consular premises was not observed when, on September 15, 1990, Iraqi soldiers invaded the residence of the French ambassador in Kuwait City and seized four French citizens, including the military attaché, who was released later. Iraqi military personnel also entered the Belgian and Dutch embassy compounds and the residence of the Canadian ambassador. Iraq denied the incidents, labeling the foreign compounds as "former diplomatic missions." At that time, 17 foreign embassies in Kuwait City had refused to obey the Iraqi order to close. The UN Security Council unanimously condemned the raids on diplomatic missions in occupied Kuwait (September 16, 1990).

The fiction that the diplomatic quarters are actually located in the territory of the sending state has been abandoned in modern legal theory.[19] Any offense against local law committed in such quarters is committed in the receiving state.[20] But the latter cannot *enforce* its laws in connection with the offense committed. Immunity also applies to the contents of diplomatic quarters, including archives and correspondence files, and to the means of transportation owned by the diplomatic mission.

The much-publicized case of *Rose* v. *The King*[21] indicates, however, that there may be a limit to the immunity of the contents of diplomatic archives. In discussing an appeal from the conviction of a member of the Canadian parliament for conspiracy to commit offenses against the Official Secrets Act of 1939, in connection with supplying information to Soviet agents in Canada, the appeal court had to deal at some length with the defendant's objection that documents taken from the Soviet embassy by an embassy employee could not lawfully be used in evidence against him. The court held that when the acts of accredited diplomats were contrary to the laws

---

[19]See *Time*, July 21, 1958, 20–21, for the lively tale of Sam Sary, Cambodian ambassador to Great Britain, who wrongly maintained that he had every right under Cambodian law to whip a concubine with the assistance of his No. 1 wife; Sary justified his action by asserting that his embassy was "Cambodia in London." See also the *Asylum Case (Colombia-Peru), ICJ Reports, 1950,* 274.

[20]See *Fatemi* v. *United States,* U. S. Dist. Court, D.C., 1963, At. 2d 525, in which the court stated correctly "(1) that a foreign embassy is not to be considered the territory of the sending state; and (2) that local police have the authority and responsibility to enter a foreign embassy if the privilege of diplomatic inviolability is not invoked when an offense is committed there in violation of local law."

[21]Quebec, Court of King's Bank, Appeal Side, 1946 (1947, 3 D.L.R. 618), digested in 42 *AJIL* 945 (1948).

of the receiving state, there was no longer any immunity of the documents to be found in diplomatic quarters. If by some means such documents were turned over to a court for the prosecution of a crime committed by a citizen of the receiving state, the court could not give immunity.

RIGHT OF PROTECTION—BUILDINGS    Part and parcel of the immunity of embassy and legation buildings is a special duty of protection by the host (receiving) state. When a German mob attacked the British embassy in Berlin after the outbreak of World War I, the German government formally expressed its regrets to the British government and paid for all damages. There lately have been an increasing number of attacks on diplomatic premises. At least 17 embassies or mission headquarters were attacked, and in some cases demolished, between 1971 and the end of 1984. In addition, more and more cultural centers and consulates were attacked—even destroyed. In February 1980 alone, five embassies were attacked or occupied (in Mexico, Libya, Guatemala, and Colombia). Apologies usually followed those incidents, but only in rare cases did the host state even offer to pay compensation (Libya did so).

Two of the more recent incidents involving the seizure or invasion of diplomatic premises took place in London and in Monrovia, Liberia. On April 30, 1980, five Iranian militants captured the Iranian embassy in London and demanded the release of 91 Iranian Arab political prisoners, as well as some degree of autonomy for the province of Khuzistan. The Iranian government not only rejected those demands, but insisted that the British government free the building and the hostages. After laying siege to the embassy for several days, an attack was mounted by members of the British Special Air Service Regiment when the militants began to execute their hostages. Four of the militants were killed, and the remaining 19 hostages were freed.

On June 14, 1980, Liberian troops invaded the French embassy in Monrovia and arrested Adolphus B. Tolbert, son of the late Liberian president William R. Tolbert, Jr., who had been assassinated during the April 12, 1980, coup that overthrew the existing government. France protested strongly the invasion of its embassy, but the Liberian defense ministry denounced the asylum granted to Tolbert as a "grave situation." The French government had cited "evident humanitarian reasons" for granting the asylum status to Tolbert.

EXTRATERRITORIALITY    A second privilege of diplomatic persons is characterized as *extraterritoriality*. This concept involves a number of exemptions from local jurisdiction to which the diplomat is entitled under international law. Literally, as was mentioned, extraterritoriality means that the person or thing in question has to be viewed as not being in a given territory or jurisdiction. Although this assumption is obviously a fiction, it is nevertheless a daily observance in the conduct of states.

Many persons confuse the two terms *inviolability* and *extraterritoriality*, but they are not identical, even though both terms serve an identical purpose: extraterritoriality is a more recent development than inviolability is. It was unknown in classical antiquity and appeared only in the time of Grotius. The "fiction" of a diplomat's being outside the jurisdiction of the receiving state was abandoned some decades ago by continental writers, even though it was defended with spirit and vigor by Anglo-Saxon commentators on the law of nations. Today both publicists and governments around the world agree that under no condition is the diplomatic person to be considered *extra territorium;* instead he is subject to the application of the local law of the receiving state but enjoys immunity from the *enforcement* of that law as long as his privileged status lasts. This exemption from enforcement of the local law operates in a number of spheres:[22] the person of a diplomat is virtually exempt from the jurisdiction of the receiving state. No civil or criminal action can be taken against him except as noted below under "Restraints on Diplomatic Agents."[23] Furthermore, a diplomat cannot be required to appear as a witness in a court.

WAIVER OF IMMUNITY    Diplomats may not themselves waive their immunity; this may be done only by the sending state in the case of heads of missions; subordinate staff members may have their immunity waived, in specific instances, by their authorized superior. National regulation of the sending state, however, governs such waivers of immunity.

Common exceptions to the immunity from the civil and administrative jurisdiction of the receiving state include (1) a real action relating to private immovable property situated in the receiving state, unless the diplomatic agent holds it on behalf of the sending state for the purposes of the mission; (2) an action relating to succession in which the agent is involved as executor, administrator, heir, or legatee as a private person and not on behalf of the sending state; and (3) any action relating to any professional or commercial activity exercised by the diplomatic agent in the receiving state outside his official functions (Art. 31, par. 1). In regard to the third of these exemptions, the Vienna Convention prohibits such outside professional or commercial activity for personal profit (Art. 42).

EXEMPTION FROM TAXES AND PERSONAL SERVICES    The head of a mission is exempt from certain fiscal obligations normally payable in or to the receiving state. Thus he does not have to meet any direct national, regional, or municipal dues and taxes relating to the premises of the mission (Art. 23,

---

[22]Dinstein, "Diplomatic Immunity from Jurisdiction *Ratione Materiae*," 15 *Int'l. and Comp. Law Q.* 76 (1966). See also the U.S. note to the Republic of the Congo (Brazzaville) in 1965, notifying the latter of the withdrawal of the U.S. diplomatic and consular personnel because of harassment, arrests, and so on: text of note in 60 *AJIL* 91 (1966).

[23]See, as an example, the Federal Republic of Germany "Circular Note on Sovereign Immunity in Civil Proceedings (1973)," in 13 *ILM* 217 (1974), and especially the case of *Founding Church of Scientology* v. *Lord Cromer and Mr. Brian L. Crowe,* U.S. Supreme Court, 1971, *id.,* 1051.

par. 1).[24] And all diplomatic agents are exempt from all dues and taxes, personal or real, in the receiving state, except for indirect taxes normally included in the cost of goods or services;[25] taxes on real estate in the receiving state owned privately by the agent; estate, succession, or inheritance duties on personal property (except in the event of the agent's death, when his movable property is treated as tax-exempt); taxes on private income and on investments made in commercial enterprises in the receiving state; and certain fees and duties relating to real estate (Art. 34 and Art. 39, par. 4).

Minor immunities include exemption from all personal services and from such military obligations as those connected with requisitioning, military contributions, and billeting (Art. 35). Subject to local regulations and laws, the receiving state waives payment of customs duties and similar charges on all incoming articles for the official use of a mission and for articles brought in for the personal use of a diplomatic agent or his family (Art. 36, par. 1). The baggage of diplomats is normally exempt from inspection. However, if it is strongly presumed that it contains articles that by law cannot be imported or exported, as the case may be, the receiving state may insist on inspection in the presence of the diplomatic agent or his authorized representative (Art. 36, par. 2).

IMMUNITIES OF FORMER DIPLOMATS    The immunities of a diplomat who is no longer accredited as such are governed by Article 39(2) of the Vienna Convention on Diplomatic Relations. When the functions of such a person have ended, a diplomat's privileges and immunities "normally cease . . . when he leaves the country, or on expiry of a reasonable period in which to do so, but shall subsist until that time, even in the case of armed conflict." It has been asserted by the U.S. Department of State (1987) that, under the Convention, the immunities of ex-diplomats do not survive if acts performed during the performance of diplomatic functions were *not* performed in the exercise of functions as a member of the diplomatic mission.

U.S. DIPLOMATIC RELATIONS ACT 1978    In order to remove conflicts between existing United States law and the 1961 Vienna Convention on Diplomatic Relations, Congress passed and the President of the United States signed (September 30, 1978) Public Law 95-393, the Diplomatic Relations Act of 1978.[26] The act, following the example of the 1961 Vienna Convention,

---

[24]See *United States* v. *City of Glen Cove,* U.S. Dist. Court, E.D.N.Y., 1971, 322 F. Supp. 149, reported in 65 *AJIL* 832 (1971); and also *United States* v. *County of Arlington, Virginia,* U.S. Court of Appeals, 4th Cir., Feb. 1, 1982 in 21 *ILM* 109 (1982).

[25]The U.S. Department of State introduced a new policy (February 1985) on sales tax for foreign diplomats living in the United States to reflect the treatment of American diplomats living abroad. The new system is one of "reciprocity" and reflects foreign collection of sales and value-added taxes from U.S. embassies and diplomatic staffs.

[26]Text in 17 *ILM* 149 (1979); Department of State regulations concerning compulsory liability insurance for diplomats, 18 *ILM* 871 (1979).

divides the members of a diplomatic mission into three groups: head of mission and diplomatic staff, administrative and technical staff, and service staff. The act also relates to the families of the first two of these groups, the service staff being excluded because the families of service staff members have never enjoyed diplomatic immunity. Another provision of the act brought missions to the United Nations, the Organization of American States, and similar organizations under its regulations.

This immunity issue, now brought into harmony with the convention, can be summarized as follows: Heads of missions and diplomatic staff and their families have full criminal and civil immunity (but see "Restraints on Diplomatic Agents"); administrative and technical staff, and their families have full immunity in criminal matters but civil immunity only in the performance of official duties; service staff members have immunity from criminal and civil prosecution in the performance of official duties only; and private servants, their families, and the families of service employees have no immunity at all. One of the Act's innovations is found in Sections 6 and 7, which authorize a new requirement that foreign diplomats and their families must obtain liability insurance against the risks arising from the operation of automobiles (beginning in 1984, at least $1 million per car), vessels, and aircraft in the United States. These two sections, furthermore, apply regardless of whether or not a given individual diplomat is immune from suit, and such immunity cannot be pleaded in court either by the diplomat, by his insurers, or by anyone else. Suits arising out of the new liability of diplomats have to be brought in the federal district courts, which serve as courts of original and exclusive jurisdiction in such cases. On the other hand, the perennial and frustrating problem of parking tickets issued to and ignored by diplomats is outside the scope of the act because parking violations in most parts of the United States are classified as criminal, not civil, offenses.[27]

INVIOLABILITY OF MEANS OF COMMUNICATION    Diplomats enjoy complete secrecy, in regard to their correspondence and other communications. Their correspondence is immune from seizure, search, and censorship by the receiving state. A mission may employ codes and ciphers in its communications, but the installation and operation of radio transmitters may be undertaken only with the consent of the receiving state. Diplomatic couriers, traveling on diplomatic passports, cannot be arrested or impeded, and the contents of their pouch or baggage cannot be inspected or confiscated. The International Law Commission initiated work on a convention on the diplomatic courier and the diplomatic bag in 1977. In 1986, 33 draft articles had

[27]On all these details, consult John P. Rieser's *Note* on diplomatic immunity in 19 *Harvard Int'l. Law Jl.* 1019 (1978); 73 *AJIL* 125 (1979); *NYT,* Feb. 2, 1976, 25; Aug. 12, 1977, A-4; Aug. 14, 1977, E-4; April 4, 1979, A-3.

been completed and comments from governments were solicited. A second reading of the draft took place at the 1989 session of the Commission.[28]

NATIONALITY OF CHILDREN    It is interesting that the exemption of a diplomat from the territorial jurisdiction of the receiving state also covers the nationality of any children born to the diplomat while holding his or her official position. Such children are regarded as born on the territory of the diplomatic person's home state, subject to it *jure soli.* This would be true even if the diplomat and his or her spouse were in transit through the territory of a third state.

STAFF OF A DIPLOMATIC MISSION    Equally, the usual privileges and immunities apply to the staff of a diplomatic mission other than diplomatic agents. This exemption was somewhat general until fairly recently, when a rather logical limitation appeared: many states assert a right to exercise jurisdiction in the case of private (nonofficial) acts of administrative functionaries attached to foreign embassies or legations, as long as the officials also perform nondiplomatic duties for their own government.[29] Thus the Tribunal of Rome held on July 13, 1953, in *Soc. Arethusa Film* v. *Reist*[30] that the defendant, chancellor at the U.S. embassy in Rome, could be held subject to the civil jurisdiction of the Italian courts with regard to his unofficial acts. The tribunal cited a number of international agreements that rule that administrative personnel of foreign diplomatic missions are subject to the jurisdiction of the receiving state.

A mission's service staff enjoys diplomatic privileges and immunities in the execution of official functions and duties. However, a basic requirement is that such service staff members must be registered for such immunity with the foreign ministry (or corresponding agency) in the receiving state. When their service with the foreign mission ends, these individuals are usually granted a period of grace of about 30 days, during which they continue to enjoy immunity and are expected to settle their affairs before leaving the receiving country.

A slightly different situation arises when a national or resident of the receiving country obtains employment in a foreign embassy and legation. A few countries permit such persons to be listed on the roster of employees entitled to diplomatic immunity, but such individuals do not enjoy a period of grace following termination of their employment. They then may be held responsible for any and all offenses committed if they had been cloaked with diplomatic immunity.

The 1961 Vienna Diplomatic Convention provides that the private ser-

---

[28]See McCaffrey, "The Thirty-Sixth Session of the International Law Commission," 79 *AJIL* 755, at 757 (1985), his "The Thirty-Eighth Session of the I. L. Commission," *id.,* 81, 668, at 676 (1987), and his "The Forty-First Session of the I. L. Commission," *id.,* 83, 937 (1989); *Time,* Sept. 22, 1986, 57.

[29]Vienna Diplomatic Convention, Article 37 (2 and 3).

[30]Reported in 49 *AJIL* 102 (1955).

vants of members of diplomatic missions, if such servants are not nationals of or permanent residents in the receiving state, are to be exempt from taxes on their salaries or wages. Any other grant of immunity depends on the generosity of the receiving state (Art. 37, par. 4); the Diplomatic Relations Act of 1978 of the United States does not grant any immunity to such private servants.

STATUS OF DIPLOMATIC PERSONS IN TRANSIT    All rights and privileges pertaining to diplomatic persons lawfully apply to them only in the receiving state because no legal relationship exists between a diplomat and a third state. However, as a matter of courtesy and because it is a question of interest and convenience to all states, diplomats traveling through third states are usually granted the same privileges as would be their due in the receiving state.

The classic modern case in this area of diplomatic immunities is *Bergman* v. *De Sieyes.*[31] The defendant had been served with process in a tort action in New York while on his way to Bolivia, to which country he had been accredited as the French minister. The District Court had dismissed the complaint, holding that although De Sieyes was not entitled to immunity under Title 22, section 252, of the U.S. Code, that section was declaratory of existing international law, and hence, under that law, the French diplomat should be granted immunity—and the dismissal was upheld by the Circuit Court. The latter reviewed previous New York State court decisions in point and concluded that as a result of changing concepts of diplomatic immunity and changing conditions of travel, "the courts of New York would today hold that a diplomat *in transitu* would be entitled to the same immunity as a diplomat *in situ.*"

However, a diplomat apparently must be en route on an official mission in order to enjoy immunity: the Guatemalan ambassador to Belgium and the Netherlands flew to New York from Europe on a personal visit and was arrested on a narcotics charge. His motion to dismiss because of diplomatic immunity was denied because of the nature of his trip. Similarly, Ludovicus Vastenavondt, chancellor of the Belgian Embassy in New Delhi, India, was arrested with seven others in New York City (May 26, 1985) after he delivered 22 pounds of heroin to an FBI agent. He apparently served as a courier for a smuggling ring.[32]

RESTRAINTS ON DIPLOMATIC AGENTS    The primary prohibition laid by international law on all diplomatic agents is abstention from all interference—by word or deed—in the internal affairs of the receiving state. This prohibition is all-inclusive: diplomats may not discuss pending legislation, may not comment on political controversies, and may not endorse or criticize

---

[31]U.S. Court of Appeals, 2d Cir., 1948, 170 F.2d 360, digested in 43 *AJIL* 373 (1949).
[32]*United States* v. *Rosal,* U.S. Dist. Court, S.D.N.Y., 1960, 191 F. Supp. 663, reported briefly in 55 *AJIL* 986 (1961); see AP Dispatch, June 6, 1985, re Vastenavondt. See also *CSM,* May 18, 1988, 2.

the host government, political parties, or party platforms.[33] They may not correspond with the press and other news media on any matter that is still a subject of communication between their own government and the host government. They may not make public a communication from their government to that of the receiving state before the latter has received it nor publish any correspondence from the latter without obtaining prior authorization. Equally prohibited but difficult to prove are the use of an embassy or a legation as a center for the dissemination of propaganda on a matter on which the two governments concerned may be in disagreement and the conversion of any diplomatic mission into a center of subversive or spy activities in favor of the ideological or national interests of the sending state. And, of course, spying is prohibited to diplomats,[34] as is the smuggling of goods.[35]

A very modern and quite obvious prohibition in regard to diplomatic activities is assistance to or participation in terrorist activities in the host country.[36]

A minor violation of some of these restraints on the diplomat's activities may be overlooked or lead to a protest by the appropriate authorities of the receiving state. But if the violation is repeated or is of a serious nature, the receiving state is fully within its rights if it requests the recall of the offender or, as quite often happens, expels him at once.

Among the classic relevant instances found in the history of the law, two are quite well known.

In 1871, the United States government requested the recall of the Russian minister, M. Catacazy, because he had seen fit to indulge in personal criticism of President Ulysses S. Grant. The American note in question asserted that Catacazy's behavior was of such a nature as "materially to impair his usefulness to his own government and to render intercourse with him, for either business or social purposes, highly disagreeable."[37]

More striking was the American demand on September 9, 1915, for the recall of the ambassador of Austria-Hungary, Count Dumba, for acting as virtual paymaster for agents of the Central Powers engaged in sabotage activities in the United States and for using an American citizen to carry offi-

---

[33]See *Time,* Feb. 1, 1960, 28, for an amusing example, and *NYT,* July 1, 1976, 4, for another illustration of the rule.

[34]Typical examples may be found in *NYT,* Jan. 20, 1974, 1, 9, and Jan. 21, 1974, 5 (China); Aug. 9, 1975, 3 (Laos); Oct. 17, 1976, 7 (France); Jan. 11, 1977, 3, and Jan. 13, 1977, 6 (Canada); Jan. 29, 1977, 4 (Norway); Feb. 20, 1977, 7 (France); Feb. 10, 1978, A-1, A-10 (Canada); and Apr. 13, 1979, A-1, A-4 (South Africa).

[35]See *NYT,* Oct. 16, 1976, 5; Oct. 21, 1976, 4; Oct. 23, 1976, 5; and Oct. 26, 1976, 5 (all dealing with Scandinavian investigations of smuggling by North Korean diplomats); Dec. 30, 1976, 5 (Peru); the *Globe & Mail* (Toronto), July 29, 1983, 4.

[36]*NYT,* Aug. 15, 1973, 6 (Norway); July 11, 1975, 1, 6 (France); July 28, 1978, A-2 (Great Britain).

[37]Moore, vol. 4, 501.

cial dispatches secretly through Allied lines to the ambassador's own country. Three months later, on December 4, 1915, the Department of State notified the German government that the German naval attaché, Captain Boy-Ed, and the military attaché, Captain von Papen, were considered personae non gratae following the discovery of incriminating documents relating to German espionage and sabotage activities in the United States.

It might be assumed that diplomatic personnel automatically enjoy freedom of movement in the receiving state, for such would appear to be essential to the performance of diplomatic duties. However, the receiving state may create by its law or regulations zones, entry into which is prohibited or restricted for reasons of security. Recent decades have seen such restrictions imposed on diplomats as a reprisal (more correctly, as retorsion: see Chapter 19) for delicts of their own government. Thus, from July 1966 to August 5, 1967, the United States curbed travel by Russian diplomats in retaliation for a similar Russian action. Subsequent U.S. travel curbs on diplomats from all Socialist states were eased for representatives of the People's Republic of China in November 1971 and for Soviet diplomats in March 1974.[38] In August 1967, Great Britain limited the embassy personnel of the People's Republic of China to an area five miles from the center of London. One of the most extensive travel limitations on record was imposed in January 1952, when the Soviet government converted 80 percent of the area of the Soviet Union into a forbidden zone, including incidentally the capitals of the allegedly independent Ukrainian and Byelorussian republics, both members of the United Nations. The ban was reduced in extent in 1974 and again later.[39] The most drastic restrictions on the movement of diplomats were those imposed in Cambodia under the Pol Pot government: members of the 11 foreign missions accredited to Cambodia lived under virtual house arrest, being forbidden to venture more than 200 yards from their compounds; missions were not permitted to operate automobiles; and meals had to be ordered daily through Khmer Rouge military personnel, who then delivered them to each mission.[40]

Restrictions on movement based on security needs resulted at one time in an unprecedented action by the British government: on April 18, 1944, in order to prevent any disclosure of second-front plans or military movements, foreign ambassadors and other diplomats and their staffs were temporarily forbidden to leave Great Britain. The United States and Soviet embassies were excluded from this restriction, which had originated in a request by General Dwight Eisenhower, Allied Commander-in-Chief. The British regu-

---

[38]66 AJIL 387 (1972).

[39]Liang, "Diplomatic Intercourse and Immunities as a Subject for Codification," 47 AJIL 439, at 443 (1953); see NYT, Feb. 20, 1974, 6, and Feb. 3, 1977, 2 (with maps showing 1977 restricted areas in both the United States and the Soviet Union); also Feb. 2, 1977, A-2, on travel by UN diplomats from governments not recognized then by the United States.

[40]See Time, Oct. 24, 1977, 58; and Müller, "Scenes from Hermetic Cambodia," 28 Swiss Review of World Affairs 6–7 (May, 1978).

lations also included the assertion of a temporary right to censor the contents of all diplomatic mailbags and a denial, to all except the two embassies mentioned, of the right to send coded telegrams, cables, or radio messages from foreign missions unless encoded either by the British Foreign Office or the staffs of the two exempted embassies.

Two more recent examples of travel restrictions took place in the United States, one in December 1981, when the movements of diplomats at the Polish embassy in Washington, D.C., and the staff at the two consulates, in Chicago and New York, were limited to those cities (in retaliation for surrounding with police the equivalent facilities in Poland), and the other in November 1983, when the Department of State announced a new list of areas in the United States open or closed to Soviet Union diplomats and journalists. Newly closed areas included Dallas and Houston, the "Silicon Valley" in California, Denver, Minneapolis–St. Paul, and Seattle.[41]

In 1985, the U.S. Secretary of State, in order to reduce spying, ordered some 300 Soviet nationals employed by the United Nations to report almost all travel outside of a 25-mile radius of Columbus Circle in New York City. The Soviet contingent, together with 20 Afghans, 30 Cubans, 50 Iranians, 40 Libyans, and 15 Vietnamese employees, also were ordered to make all their future airline and hotel reservations through the Department of State's Office of Foreign Missions. In late 1985 and early 1986, the Department of State notified the UN missions of Bulgaria, Czechoslovakia, the German Democratic Republic, and Poland of the same report and reservation requirements for their nationals employed by the United Nations.

Another restriction, this time on diplomats, was imposed by the United States when, on March 7, 1986, it notified the Soviet UN mission to cut its staff by 38 percent over the next two years, from 275 to 170 by April 1, 1988. (At the time, the United States UN mission staff totaled 126 and the Chinese mission totaled 116 members.) The United States mission declared to reporters that the then current size of the Soviet UN mission was "not warranted by the staffing needs for official UN business. . . . Moreover, it poses a threat to U.S. national security." In the opinion of the UN Legal Counsel, the reduction ordered by the United States did appear to meet the test laid down in Article 14 of the 1975 Vienna Convention on the Representation of States in Their Relations with International Organizations:

The size of the mission shall not exceed what is reasonable and normal, having regard to the functions of the Organization, the needs of the particular mission and the circumstances and conditions in the host State.

(See also 80 *AJIL* 783, 1986). On September 18, 1986, 25 Soviet UN mission members, specifically selected by the United States, were ordered expelled in consequence of the order of March 7.

[41]*Time*, Dec. 28, 1981, 19; *News-Tribune & Herald* (Duluth, Minn.), Nov. 21, 1983, 8-A.

# SPECIAL CATEGORIES OF AGENTS

## Special Officers

Several countries, notably the United States, have on occasion utilized the services of special officers of various types, in addition to the generally recognized categories of diplomatic personnel. Almost invariably the sending states attempted to secure diplomatic status, with its attendant privileges and immunities, for such special officers, whereas the receiving states generally opposed such efforts. In essence, whatever status is granted to such officers depends on the decision of the receiving state, and none of the categories is covered by either customary or conventional rules of law.

The United States Treasury Department has employed a group of officers attached to embassies and legations in Europe and styled, at different times, special commissioner, customs attaché, customs representative, and treasury attaché. Despite repeated efforts to have these individuals accorded diplomatic status, only France has accepted the Treasury Department's agents as full-fledged diplomats. Other countries have been willing to grant to them only an exemption from income taxes on their salaries.

Other United States special officers abroad include assistant commercial attachés under the Secretary of Commerce, later under the Department of State, and agricultural attachés. The latter have been accorded diplomatic status in a few states.

## Commissioners and Special Envoys

An innovation in diplomatic practice was recorded on February 22, 1973, when the United States and the People's Republic of China announced agreements to establish liaison offices in Peking and Washington, in order to speed up the normalization of their relations. What made the announcement remarkable was the fact that the United States had not then recognized the Chinese government. Staff members of both missions were to have diplomatic privileges, including the right to communicate in code with the respective home governments.[42]

Special envoys are usually granted temporary diplomatic status and, in recent decades, have been, in fact, equipped with a diplomatic rank. Thus heads of delegations to international conferences are commonly styled ambassadors or envoys extraordinary. Similarly, members of arbitration tribunals and boundary commissions are on occasion granted diplomatic privileges and immunities.

## Agents of International Organizations: Privileges and Immunities

The development of international organizations has been accompanied by more problems connected with the privileges and immunities of the of-

---

[42]See 67 *AJIL* 536 (1973); full text of joint communiqué in 12 *ILM* 431 (1973).

ficials and agents of the agencies in question. As long as there was no generally applicable body of rules, court decisions and increasingly uniform practice created a new sphere of international law, the law of international organizations as related to diplomats and agents.

LEAGUE OF NATIONS    Article 7(4) of the Covenant of the League of Nations conferred on the representatives of the member states and the agents of the League diplomatic privileges and immunities. In some respects, the paragraph in question included definite innovations compared with earlier practices. Thus, for instance, the representatives of the International Labor Organization (ILO) were entitled to full diplomatic status even when they represented states that were not members of the League. And at the same time, diplomatic privileges were given to delegates representing workers and employers at the General Conferences of the ILO. Switzerland, as host country to the League, granted diplomatic status, privileges, and immunities to the permanent delegates accredited to the League, even though the same individuals were not accredited to Switzerland.[43]

UNITED NATIONS    In contrast with Article 7 of the Covenant, the corresponding Article 105(2) of the United Nations Charter grants to the representatives of the member states "such privileges and immunities as are necessary for the independent exercise of their functions in connection with the Organization." [44]

On February 13, 1946, the General Assembly adopted the General Convention on the Privileges and Immunities of the United Nations.[45] Because the headquarters of the new organization was to be located in the United States, arrangements had to be worked out with the prospective host government. The initial step was passage by Congress on December 29, 1945, of the Statute Extending Privileges, Exemptions, and Immunities to International Organizations and to the Officers and Employees Thereof (International Organizations Immunities Act).[46] The negotiations between the Secretary-General and the United States resulted in the definitive Headquarters of the United Nations: Agreement between the United States of America and the United Nations of June 26, 1947 (in force November 21, 1947), and an interim agreement of December 18, 1947, applying relevant provisions of the June 26 agreement to the temporary headquarters of the United Nations at Lake Success, New York.[47]

DIPLOMATIC PRIVILEGES AND IMMUNITIES OF MEMBER STATES    Article 4 of the General Convention details the diplomatic privileges and immunities

[43] Consult Hackworth, vol. 4, 419–23, on League questions.
[44] On the general subject of the immunity of UN officials, consult the excellent and heavily documented summary in Bishop, 614-20.
[45] Text in 43 *AJIL* 1 (1949 Supp.).
[46] Text 40 *AJIL* 85 (Apr. 1946 Supp.); see 68 *AJIL* 316 (1974), on 1973 amendments relative to the OAU and the OAS.
[47] Texts of agreements, together with notes and the required joint congressional resolution of Aug. 4, 1947, in 43 *AJIL* 8 (1949 Supp.).

of representatives of member states. These rights apply to delegates to the principal and subsidiary organs of the United Nations and to conferences convened by that organization, but only while these representatives exercise their functions and during their travel to and from the place of meeting. The privileges listed include immunity from arrest or detention and seizure of personal luggage; immunity from legal process of every kind for all acts (and words spoken or written) in their capacity as representatives; inviolability of all papers and documents; the right to use codes and receive correspondence and papers by courier or in sealed bags; exemption for representatives and their spouses from immigration restrictions or national service obligations en route or while visiting in the exercise of their functions; and equality of treatment as respects currency or exchange restrictions with representatives of foreign governments on temporary official missions.

In acknowledgment of the theory of functional necessity, section 14 of Article 4, states that

privileges and immunities are accorded to representatives of Members not for the personal benefit of the individuals themselves, but in order to safeguard the independent exercise of their functions in connection with the United Nations. Consequently a Member not only has the right but is under a duty to waive the immunity of its representative in any case where in the opinion of the Member the immunity would impede the course of justice, and it can be waived without prejudice to the purpose for which the immunity is accorded.

Officials of the United Nations falling into categories to be specified by the Secretary-General are to enjoy substantially the same privileges and immunities as representatives of member states, under Article 5 of the convention. And experts performing missions for the United Nations are also to be accorded substantially the same privileges (Art. 6, sec. 22).

The Headquarters Agreement with the United States outlines the rules governing the Headquarters District in New York City (see also Chapter 7). The federal, state, and local laws of the United States and the jurisdiction of the federal, state, and local courts of the United States apply within the district, except as specified in the General Convention or in the Headquarters Agreement. Normally, however, the United Nations makes regulations for the district, and no federal, state, or local law of the United States conflicting with such regulations can be applied in the district (Art. 3, sec. 8).

The district is inviolable. Federal, state, or local officers or officials of the United States, whether administrative, judicial, military, or police, cannot enter the district without the consent and under the conditions agreed to by the Secretary-General. On the other hand, the district may not become a place of asylum (Art. 3, sec. 9-b).

The various levels of United States authorities may not impede travel to or from the district by the representatives of members; by the families of such persons; by experts performing missions for the United Nations; by representatives of media of mass communications who have been accredited by the United Nations or one of its agencies at its discretion after consultation with the United States; or by other persons summoned to or having official business with the United Nations and its Specialized Agencies (Art. 4, sec. 11).

Henrique Galvão, who had seized the *Santa Maria* in 1961 (see Chapter 13 *sub* Piracy) and who had been convicted *in absentia* in Portugal of involuntary manslaughter during the seizure, asked (November, 1963) for a hearing before the Fourth Committee of the UN General Assembly. The reason for his request was that he offered to provide a "solution" to the problems encountered by Portugal in its then colony of Angola.

The Fourth Committee, realizing that there existed an extradition treaty between Portugal and the United States that might be invoked in Galvão's case, asked the UN Secretariat for a Legal Opinion on Galvão's immunity, should he be invited to come to New York. The Legal Opinion, relying heavily on the 1947 United States–UN Headquarters Agreement, pointed out that Galvão was completely immune from any U.S. action or interference while coming to the headquarters District as a UN invitee. On the other hand, the Opinion stated, there was no precedent that would indicate whether or not Galvão could be stopped by United States agencies, while departing from the District, as a result of proceedings against him and unrelated to his UN appearance.

The Fourth Committee approved Galvão's visit, and he appeared before the Committee on December 9, 1963, and left the United States the next day. The Portuguese government had requested his extradition by the United States just prior to his arrival in New York. When Portugal subsequently protested that he had not been confined pending surrender to Portuguese officials, the Department of State explained (lamely or "with a straight face"?) that the processing of the extradition request had taken longer than had been anticipated—hence no arrest before Galvão slipped back to Brazil.

The resident representatives to the United Nations, as specified in Article 5, section 15 of the agreement, are entitled in the territory of the United States to the same privileges and immunities as are enjoyed by diplomatic agents accredited to the United States. In the case of member states whose governments are not recognized by the United States, such privileges and immunities need be extended to such representatives only within the Headquarters District, at their residences or offices outside the district, in transit between the district and their residences or offices, and in transit on official business to and from foreign countries.

In regard to diplomatic immunity in general, the Headquarters Agreement took from the International Organizations Immunities Act of 1945 four categories of governmental representatives and conferred diplomatic immunity on them—leaving, however, United Nations officials and employees within the narrower ambit of limited immunity granted by the Act of 1945.

However, on April 29, 1970, the United States deposited an instrument of accession to the Convention on the Privileges and Immunities of the United Nations, thereby modifying numerous provisions of both the Headquarters Agreement and the Act of 1945.[48]

UN PROBLEMS IN IMMUNITIES    Almost as soon as the United Nations began its operations in the United States, cases pertaining to the immunities of representatives, officials, and servants of both categories began to be reported.[49]

In most recent decisions dealing with such immunities, the functional-necessity theory influenced the courts' holdings. This was particularly true in the Advisory Opinion of April 11, 1949, on *Reparations for Injuries Suffered in the Service of the United Nations*,[50] in which the International Court of Justice clearly based on functional necessity the inviolability of persons serving the United Nations.

Soon, however, clarification of the status and immunities of delegates and others accredited to international organizations became more urgent. The International Law Commission drew up successive draft articles on the subject, and finally an international conference on the subject, called by the UN General Assembly, met in Vienna from February 4 to March 14, 1975. That conference adopted a new convention, the Vienna Convention on the Representation of States in Their Relations with International Organizations of a Universal Character.[51]

As Fennessey[52] and others pointed out, one of the unusual features of the convention is the high level of privileges and immunities granted to the representatives concerned, as well as the fact that the service staff and the private staff of mission members are exempted from taxes on their salaries. To detail the various immunities exceeds the limits of a general text; suffice it to state that representatives to international organizations of the kind involved are to enjoy the same privileges as were given to their colleagues under the Vienna Convention on Diplomatic Relations. Thus Thiam Tidjani, chief of Chad's UN mission, and another member of that mission could not be charged by the New York City police with rape, sodomy, and robbery (September 29, 1979) because of their full diplomatic immunity.

---

[48]See also Secretary of State William Rogers's report on the effect of U.S. accession to the convention, 64 *AJIL* 409 (1970).

[49]See *Westchester County on Complaint of Donnelly* v. *Ranollo*, 187 Misc. 777, 67 N.Y.S.2d 31 (City Ct. New Rochelle 1946); see also the analysis of early instances in Oreuss, "Immunity of Officers and Employees of the United Nations for Official Acts: The Ranallo [*sic*] Case," 41 *AJIL* 555 (1947); *People* v. *Von Otter*, 114 N.Y.S. (2d) 195 (City Ct. New Rochelle, July 30, 1952), reported in 47 *AJIL* 151, n. 1 (1953); *Tsiang* v. *Tsiang* (1949), 194 Misc. 259, 86 N.Y.S. (2d)556; and Wright, "Responsibility for Injuries to United Nations Officials," 43 *AJIL* 95 (1949).

[50]*ICJ Reports, 1949*, 174.

[51]Text in 69 *AJIL* 730 (1975); see also Fennessy's analysis of the convention, 70 *AJIL* 62 (1976).

[52]Fennessey, *op.cit.* nos. 50, 65.

The problem of spying by UN employees and mission staff members has been a knotty one. Two cases in this sphere have attracted considerable attention and may illustrate some of the questions involved. The earlier of the two, *United States* v. *Coplon and Gubitchev,*[53] had its beginning in 1949. Valentin A. Gubitchev, a Soviet national, was employed in the headquarters planning office of the UN Secretariat. He was indicted for a number of violations of the United States espionage laws and made a motion to dismiss on the grounds of diplomatic immunity. This motion was dismissed. Gubitchev had come to the United States on a diplomatic passport. The U.S. District Court denied the immune status of the accused because he had not been accredited to the United States government, and the International Organizations Immunities Act did not apply to him because it conferred immunity only for acts performed in an official capacity and falling within the functions of officers or employees of the United Nations. The offenses charged against the accused did not fall within such categories.

Gubitchev retained counsel of his own choice and the court granted reargument of the case. This time the Soviet embassy sent an official communication to the court, testifying to Gubitchev's diplomatic rank before his arrival in the United States and asserting that "the Soviet Government has not revoked the diplomatic status of Mr. Gubitchev V. A. and up to the present time he remains an officer of the Ministry of Foreign Affairs of the USSR, with the diplomatic rank of Third Secretary."

The court regarded the presentment of the affidavit as being without precedent and forwarded it to the Secretary of State. The court then found that Gubitchev was not a member of the Soviet embassy and that his name had not been submitted by the Secretary-General for inclusion in a list of members of delegations entitled to diplomatic privileges under the Headquarters Agreement, and the court was notified by the U.S. Secretary of State that the latter rejected Gubitchev's claim of diplomatic immunity; his diplomatic visa had been issued as a matter of courtesy.

The court properly denied again the claim of the accused.

In 1960, the case of *United States* v. *Melekh*[54] attracted considerable attention. Igor Y. Melekh, a Russian national, had been attached since June 10, 1955, to the UN Secretariat as chief of the Russian Language Section, Office of Conference Services. He resisted removal to Illinois to stand trial on three counts of espionage, asserting that he enjoyed diplomatic immunity and that his immunity applied also to the preliminary proceeding of removal.

The U.S. District Court found that although Melekh was a second secretary of the Ministry of Foreign Affairs in the Soviet Union and had arrived

---

[53]U.S. Dist. Court, S.D.N.Y., 1950, 88 F. Supp. 915, digested in 44 *AJIL* 586 (1950); the first hearing of the case, May 10, 1949 (84 F. Supp. 472), was digested in 43 *AJIL* 810 (1949).

[54]U.S. Dist. Court, S.D.N.Y., 1960, 190 F. Supp. 67, digested at length in 55 *AJIL* 734 (1961); see also *Chicago Daily Tribune,* Mar. 21, 1961, 1, 2.

in the United States with a Soviet diplomatic passport, he had not been granted a diplomatic visa by the United States. His work in the United Nations was of a nondiplomatic character, he had never been attached to the Soviet embassy, he had never been accredited as a diplomatic officer to any government, nor was he a member of the Soviet delegation to the United Nations.

The court, after a careful analysis, held that Melekh was not entitled to diplomatic immunity. Hence Melekh was ordered to be removed to Illinois to stand trial.

In November 1962, a group of agents of the Cuban government, reported to have planned terrorist acts and acts of sabotage in the New York–New Jersey area, were arrested by agents of the United States government. Among those detained was one Casanova, a resident member of Cuba's permanent mission to the United Nations, who was charged with conspiracy to commit sabotage and to violate the Foreign Agents Registration Act. He sought release from detention under habeas corpus, claiming that he was either entitled to diplomatic immunity under the Charter, the Headquarters Agreement, and international law, or that the Supreme Court of the United States had exclusive and original jurisdiction to try his case. The U.S. District Court dismissed the writ of habeas corpus, holding that Article 105 of the Charter did not confer diplomatic immunity on the representatives of member states, and that even if the article were held to be self-executing with respect to the functional activities of such representatives, a conspiracy to commit sabotage against the United States could not be held to be a proper function of any such representative; that the government of the United States did not, by issuing a nonimmigrant visa and a landing permit, give its consent to entitle Casanova to diplomatic immunity; that under international law Casanova was not entitled to diplomatic immunity from the time of his arrival pending determination of his status, because his position was not comparable to that of a diplomat awaiting acknowledgment by a government to which he was accredited (international law could define the nature and scope of immunity only when it had been determined that an individual was entitled to such immunity); and that Casanova was not an ambassador or other public minister of a foreign state accredited to the United States within the meaning of the constitutional or statutory provisions vesting original and exclusive jurisdiction in the Supreme Court of the United States.[55]

A rather unusual recent case centered on Alicja Wesolowska, a Polish citizen employed as a secretary at UN headquarters in New York. While on home leave in Poland and en route to a new UN post in Mongolia, Wesolowska was arrested by Polish authorities. She was using United Nations travel documents and under the terms of the 1946 UN General Convention, was immune from arrest, even by her own government, in the

---

[55] *United States ex rel. Casanova v. Fitzpatrick*, U.S. Dist. Court, S.D.N.Y., 1963, 214 F. Supp. 425, reported in 57 *AJIL* 920 (1963).

performance of her official UN duties. The Polish government, however, claimed that the accused had spied in New York on behalf of an unidentified NATO official. Despite protests form the UN Secretary-General, a Warsaw military court sentenced the accused to seven years in prison (March 7, 1980).[56]

More recently, several members of the Cuban mission to the United Nations were involved in illegal activities. In April 1983, a third secretary and an attaché were caught in spying activities and ordered to leave the United States. After an appeal against the expulsion order by the Cuban mission failed, the pair was given 48 hours to leave the country. And in early July 1983, a second pair, a second secretary and an attaché, was caught attempting to purchase certain types of high-technology electronic equipment. Both were expelled "expeditiously" from the United States.

Again, in April 1983, Aleksandr N. Mikheyev and Oleg V. Konstantinov, both on the staff of the Soviet UN mission, were detained on charges of spying. Both left the United States as soon as released.

UN OBSERVER MISSION STAFF    Several governments maintain observer missions at the United States. Staff members of such units possess only "functional immunity," regardless of their rank or title. In other words, they have protection from prosecution only in regard to acts related directly to their work at the mission. (See Case Study No. 7A.) Thus O Nam Chol, a third secretary in North Korea's observer mission, who had avoided arrest for almost 11 months by hiding in the mission premises, surrendered on July 26, 1983, and pleaded guilty to a reduced charge of third-degree sexual abuse, a misdemeanor (the original charge had been a felony charge). The judge in the Westchester, New York, Criminal Court announced then that O would be freed, inasmuch as he had indicated that he would leave the country and never return.[57]

OTHER INTERNATIONAL AGENCIES    The judges of the International Court of Justice enjoy diplomatic privileges and immunities when engaged in official business, under the provisions of Article 19 of the Statute of the Court. Lesser staff members and employees of the court are treated in the same manner as are the comparable ranks among the members of diplomatic missions at The Hague. Similar rights and privileges are accorded to members of the Permanent Court of Arbitration (under Article 46 of the 1907 Hague Convention for the Pacific Settlement of International Disputes) when such members are on official duty outside their own country.

It was pointed out earlier that the European Economic Community (EEC) and the European Atomic Energy Community (EURATOM) have the right to deal with the representatives of individual states. These representatives enjoy the customary diplomatic privileges and immunities in the state in

---

[56]Concerning the Wesolowska case, see *NYT,* Oct. 7, 1979, 1, 21, and *Newsweek,* Mar. 17, 1980, 52.
[57]AP dispatches, Jan. 30, 1983, 4-A; July 27, 1983, 5-C.

which the headquarters of the respective communities are located (Article 19 of each charter). By the middle of 1962, 48 states had opened diplomatic relations with the communities, and 41 of them had already sent accredited diplomatic agents to them. A whole specialized system has evolved for ranking these agents.

A functional type of diplomatic immunity similar to that provided under Article 105 of the UN Charter was made available under Article 40 of the Statute of the Council of Europe for that organization itself, as well as for the representatives of members and for the staff of the council's Secretariat.

In the United Kingdom, officials of the European Commission of Human Rights enjoy diplomatic immunity for official acts under an act and an order-in-council of 1950.

## CONSULAR AGENTS

BACKGROUND     Classical antiquity developed certain institutions resembling the modern consul in a number of details. In the Greek city-states could be found officials (*proxenai*) responsible for the welfare of resident aliens in a given state, and Rome developed the office of the *praetor peregrinus*. All of these officials, however, were citizens of the territorial sovereign and not of the states whose nationals were in their charge. The end of Greek independence, followed eventually by the collapse of the Roman Empire, meant the disappearance of these predecessors of the modern consul.

The modern consulate had its true beginning in the medieval period, in the Mediterranean area. Alien merchants settling in a port received the permission of the host state to establish a sort of corporation with a limited right of self-government and jurisdiction over its members. This function soon ended up in the hands of judges who, beginning in the eleventh century, were chosen by the merchants from among their own number. The competence of these judges extended primarily into the sphere of commercial disputes. Their titles varied, with *consules mercatorium (consuls de commerce, juges consuls)* being the most commonly used. In the twelfth century, these officials were increasingly regarded not only as the heads of the foreign merchants' guild, but also as officials (frequently appointed) of the territorial sovereign.

The usefulness of specialized agents to deal with commercial matters became so apparent after a short time that the consular institution began to spread from Italy into other parts of the Mediterranean world, particularly to the Near East and North Africa. As increasing numbers of merchants established branches there, the home government sent out agents (*consules missi*) to take charge of the settlers' interests and to exercise both criminal and civil jurisdiction over them. Most historians of consular institutions point out that a number of these consuls, now stationed abroad, were elected by the emigrant merchants (*consules electi*), but that such personages had, in general, less authority than did those sent abroad by governments.

In the thirteenth century, the concept of *consules missi* was expanded to cover the ports of southwestern Europe and, by the fifteenth century, had spread to western and northern Europe. The Western consuls in Africa and the Near East did enjoy considerably greater authority, in every respect, than did their colleagues elsewhere. The consuls in the Near East received special privileges from the local (Muslim) sovereigns, privileges centering on judicial prerogatives and the right to try cases involving their own nationals under their own, Western, law. The fact that such extraterritorial privileges devolved on the consuls by treaty (capitulations) or by local concession and that they were achieved in most instances by negotiation and in a few cases by threats of force is immaterial. The essential fact was that under Islamic law, Christians were not allowed to be subjects of that law, which was based on the Koran. Hence, regardless of the method used, the special rights granted to Westerners represented an act of grace to individuals who otherwise would have been "lesser breeds without the law." To the Muslim of that time, it did not matter where the infidel found his law—if he desired to apply his own law to himself and his fellows, no objection would be made. All vestige of such preferential treatment of aliens has disappeared, and the multitude of treaties, which began with a Turkish-Genoese agreement in 1453, by which extraterritorial privileges were established have been abrogated in one way or another.

In the Western states themselves, the expansion of the practice of stationing permanent diplomatic representatives in foreign capitals tended to minimize the institution of the consul until the growth of international commerce around the early part of the eighteenth century, when it became apparent to many governments that the presence of commercial representatives in other countries might indeed be advantageous. Soon scores of consuls appeared and began to fulfill important nonpolitical functions abroad. Since then, the institution has proliferated, until today several thousand consuls of various ranks are scattered all over the world.

## Consular Relations

Consuls are *not* diplomatic representatives of their state. They are not accredited, in the diplomatic meaning of the term, to a foreign government. The only "normal" situation in which a consul would be automatically entitled to diplomatic privileges and immunities would be if he were accredited also as chargé d'affaires to the receiving state. This, however, would be a most unusual situation today. A consul is appointed by a state and is a member of the foreign service of that state. He is recognized by the receiving state as an official agent of his government and, as such, he is permitted to undertake certain functions that would normally be entrusted to the agents of the state in which the consul resides (the receiving state). But generally the consul's duties are more commercial than political (diplomatic) in their nature.

The greater part of a consul's functions—and rights—have been based up to now on special bipartite agreements (consular treaties) between the state whose agent he is and the state within which he performs his functions.[58]

CODIFICATION OF RULES   The UN International Law Commission, at its seventh session in 1955, decided to begin the study of consular relations and appointed a special rapporteur for it. After several delays, his report was followed by the drawing up of the Draft Convention on Consular Relations. It was submitted to the General Assembly with the recommendation that the assembly convene an international conference of plenipotentiaries to study the draft and to conclude one or more conventions on the subject.

The General Assembly concurred in this recommendation, and as a result the United Nations Conference on Consular Relations met at the Neue Hofburg in Vienna from March 4 to April 22, 1963. The conference was attended by representatives of 92 states and by observers from Bolivia, Guatemala, Paraguay, the International Labor Organization, the Food and Agriculture Organization, the International Atomic Energy Agency, and the Council of Europe.

The conference, in addition to adopting a number of resolutions, prepared the following instruments: (1) the Vienna Convention on Consular Relations; (2) the Optional Protocol Concerning Acquisition of Nationality; and (3) the Optional Protocol Concerning the Compulsory Settlement of Disputes.[59] Of these, the Convention on Consular Relations obviously was the most important. On April 24, 1963, the representatives of the participating states signed the convention; the treaty entered into force on March 19, 1967 and, for the United States, on December 24, 1969. The Optional Protocol entered into force on the same dates.

The International Law Commission had already pointed out that consular intercourse, together with related privileges and immunities, had been governed partly by municipal law and partly by international law. The commission had decided to base its draft articles not only on rules of customary international law but also on the material furnished by international conventions, especially on consular treaties. The following discussion, therefore, draws heavily on the Vienna Convention of 1963 as evidence of the rules applicable to consular matters.

The establishment of consular relations between states takes place by mutual consent. Normally the consent required for the establishment of

[58]See, as an example, the *Consular Convention (France–United States)*, signed on July 18, 1966 (in force Jan. 7, 1968), reprinted in 62 *AJIL* 551 (1968 Supp.); the *Consular Convention of U.S.–USSR*, 1964, in force since 1968; text in 50 *Department of State Bulletin* 979 (1964); see also Lay, "The United States–Soviet Consular Convention," 59 *AJIL* 876 (1965), and the *Consular Convention between the United States of America and the People's Republic of China* (Sept. 17, 1980), and related letters, in 19 *ILM* 1119 (1980).

[59]The texts of the convention and of the protocols are reprinted in 57 *AJIL* 993 (1963); and see Lee, *The Vienna Convention on Consular Relations* (1966), and his brief but useful "Vienna Convention on Consular Relations," *International Conciliation* (January 1969), 41–76. The convention will be cited hereafter as Vienna Consular Convention.

diplomatic relations also implies consent to the establishment of consular relations. On the other hand, a severance of diplomatic relations does not, *ipso facto*, mean a breaking off of consular relations. It is also possible to establish consular relations between states that do not have diplomatic relations with each other. In this situation, the consular relations represent the only permanent official relations between the states in question. In most instances of this sort, the consular relations constitute a preliminary to diplomatic relations.

Consular relations are normally exercised through consular posts (Vienna Consular Convention, Art. 3), but it is possible for them to be carried out through diplomatic missions. If members of such a mission are assigned to consular functions, they may continue to enjoy diplomatic privileges and immunities (Art. 15; see also Art. 3(2) of the 1961 Vienna Convention on Diplomatic Relations).

It is only logical that the location of consulates or branches thereof and the boundaries of the districts assigned to each of them are determined by mutual agreement between the sending state and the receiving state; subsequent changes in either sphere must receive the consent of the receiving state (Vienna Consular Convention, Art. 4).

## Functions of Consular Agents

The major functions exercised by consuls may be summarized as follows:

1. Protecting in the receiving state the interests of the sending state and its nationals within the limits set by international law.
2. Promoting trade and also the development of economic, cultural, and scientific relations between the two states in question.
3. Reporting to the government of the sending state on conditions and developments in the economic, cultural, and scientific life of the receiving state and also giving such information to interested persons and firms.
4. Issuing passports and travel documents to nationals of the sending state and visas or similar documents to persons desiring to go to that state.
5. Assisting in all legitimate ways the nationals of the sending state.
6. Acting as notary and civil registrar and performing certain administrative functions, particularly in the safeguarding of the interests of nationals of the sending state in cases of succession (caused by death) in the territory of the receiving state.
7. Representing nationals of the sending state before the courts and other authorities of the receiving state when, for some reason or other, those nationals are unable to assume the defense of their rights, so as to preserve, on a provisional basis, those rights in accordance with the law of the receiving state.
8. Serving judicial documents or executing commissions to take evidence for the courts of the sending state in accordance with existing treaties or, in their absence, in accordance with the laws of the receiving state.

9. Exercising rights of supervision and inspection, under the laws and regulations of the receiving state, in respect of vessels having the nationality of the sending state and of aircraft registered in that state, and in respect of their crews; examining the stamping ships' papers, conducting investigations into any incidents that have occurred during the voyage, and settling disputes between the master, the officers, and the seamen to the extent that such settlement is authorized by the laws of the sending state (Vienna Consular Convention, Art. 5).

It is possible, incidentally, for a sending state to entrust a consulate located in a particular state with the exercise of consular functions in a third state. However, this may be done only with the consent of both other states (Art. 7).

## Beginning of a Consular Commission

ACCEPTANCE OF HEADS OF CONSULAR POSTS    Heads of consular posts are appointed by the sending state and are admitted to the exercise of their functions by the receiving state (Vienna Consular Convention, Art. 10). The head is supplied by the sending state with a *commission,* or notice, setting out in detail his category and class, the consular district, and the seat of the consulate (Art. 11, par. 1). Vice-consuls and consular agents are furnished with a similar document, usually known as a *brevet.*

Acceptance of the commission is followed by the granting of an authorization by the receiving state. Until and unless the head of a consular post receives this document, known as an *exequatur,* he may not enter on duty (Art. 12). In other words, the granting of the *exequatur* is the official act whereby the receiving state grants admission to the consul and confers the right to exercise his consular functions. Municipal law determines which organ of the state is competent to grant the *exequatur;* in most states, this is done by the Ministry of Foreign Affairs. The granting of an *exequatur* to the head of a consular post may automatically cover the members of the consular staff working under his orders and responsibility.

## Classes of Consuls

State practice has settled fairly uniformly on four classes of heads of consular posts: (1) consuls general, (2) consuls, (3) vice-consuls, and (4) consular agents (Vienna Consular Convention, Art. 9). No country would be obligated, of course, to adopt all four titles, and indeed the class of consular agent is seldom utilized today.

A few countries, such as West Germany, use the title of consular attaché, even though this is not mentioned in the convention. The U.S. Department of State, for its part, announced on November 24, 1980, that it would henceforth refuse to grant recognition to this fifth title and would, despite earlier exceptions, from then on accept only the titles found in the convention.

A few states still follow the formerly common practice of permitting their consular officials, especially those of the lower two ranks, to engage in business activities in the receiving state. When such is the case, the official in question does not enjoy any privileges or immunities for such activities, because the latter are completely outside his official functions. The Vienna Consular Convention, on the other hand, forbids career consular officers to carry on for personal profit any professional or commercial activity in the receiving state (Art. 57, par. 1).

HONORARY CONSULS    Many portions (notably Arts. 58–68) of the Vienna Consular Convention refer in whole or in part to so-called honorary consuls. In contrast with career consuls, who are always nationals of the sending state, honorary consuls, and on a few occasions vice-consuls, are recruited from among the nationals of the receiving state. Most honorary consuls carry on a private gainful activity in additional to their consular functions, and indeed some states classify as an honorary consul any consular official, regardless of nationality, who engages in such private activity. Consular officials, as a rule, possess the nationality of the sending state. However, such officials may be appointed from among the nationals of the receiving state or of a third state, subject to the consent of the receiving state, which may be withdrawn at any time (Art. 22). It is still fairly common for smaller or new states to follow these practices. Thus, for example, in 1971, El Salvador appointed a Chinese citizen as its (honorary) consul to the Republic of China, and Bolivia followed suit by selecting a naturalized American citizen of Chinese descent to act as its (honorary) consul in Taipei (Taiwan). Thus, always based on local acceptance, such honorary consuls are still found here and there; for instance, Austria, El Salvador, and Uruguay all have such officials in Spain. Generally, honorary consuls enjoy the same privileges and immunities as do career consuls, but there are differences. The interested reader is referred to the relevant portions of the Vienna Consular Convention.

## Termination of a Consular Commission

If a consular official's conduct gives serious grounds for complaint, the receiving state may notify the sending state that this person is no longer acceptable. In that case, the sending state is bound either to recall the individual or to end his connection with the consulate. If the sending state refuses this obligation or fails to carry it out within a reasonable time, the receiving state has a right, either to withdraw the *exequatur* from the person in question or cease to regard him as a member of the consular staff.

The importance of a valid *exequatur* was shown clearly in the unusual case of *Dominican Republic* v. *Peguero*[60] in 1963. A consul of the Dominican Republic sued to prevent his vice-consul from acting as consul. Both

[60]U.S. Dist. Court, S.D.N.Y., 1963, 225 F. Supp. 342, reported briefly in 58 *AJIL* 1012 (1964).

had been appointed by the then defunct government of President Bosch. The U.S. District Court ruled, correctly, that the end of the Bosch government did not end the defendant's authority to act on behalf of his country but that what mattered was the status of the two parties' *exequaturs*. Inasmuch as the *exequatur* of Peguero had not been canceled by the United States, whereas the plaintiff consul's had been revoked, the latter had no standing in the courts of the United States to bring an action on behalf of the Dominican Republic.

A person may, of course, also be declared unacceptable before arriving in the territory of the receiving state. In such a case, the sending state must withdraw the individual's appointment (Vienna Consular Convention, Art. 23). As in the instance of a diplomat held to be persona non grata, the receiving state does not have to give any reasons for rejecting an appointee to a consular post.

Under all conditions, including a case of armed conflict, the receiving state must grant facilities to enable consular personnel (other than its own nationals) and the members of their families to leave the state with their property at the earliest possible moment (Art. 26).

A rare termination of consular relations occurs when a given state strongly disapproves of an act of another state and to indicate such disapproval closes its consular facilities in the offending state. Such was the case after the Soviet Union invaded Afghanistan. On January 4, 1980, President Jimmy Carter stated that his administration would delay opening any new Soviet or American consular facilities, and a few days later construction work on the Kiev consulate was stopped, and the American Embassy in Moscow announced that the staff of seven and their dependents would be reassigned and that the Soviet staff would leave New York in a matter of days. In February 1984, it was rumored that in the not too distant future, American consulates in Kiev and Tashkent would be opened and Soviet consulates would be activated in New York and Chicago. Nothing further had taken place, however, by the time of this writing.

If consular relations between two states are severed, the receiving state must, even in cases of armed conflict, respect and protect consular premises and their contents. The sending state may entrust the premises and their contents to the care of a third state acceptable to the receiving state, just as it may entrust the protection of its interests and those of its nationals to a third state acceptable to the receiving state (Art. 27, par. 1).

## Privileges and Immunities

INVIOLABILITY OF CONSULAR PREMISES    Consular premises are inviolable, and the agents of the receiving state may not enter them except with the consent of the head of the consular post. The receiving state is under a special duty to take appropriate measures to protect the consular premises, which are immune from any search, requisition, attachment, or execution (Vienna Consular Convention, Art. 31). These premises are also exempt, under international law, from state and local real estate taxes.[61] A few consular treaties and the municipal law of some states also recognize inviolability of a consul's residence, but this is an innovation that has not gained widespread acceptance.

Consular archives and documents, wherever they may happen to be, are inviolable (Art. 33).

INVIOLABILITY OF MEANS OF COMMUNICATION    The receiving state permits a consulate free communication for all official purposes. The consulate may employ diplomatic or consular couriers and the diplomatic or consular bag and may send and receive messages in code or cipher. It may install and use a wireless transmitter only with the express consent of the receiving state. The official correspondence of a consulate is inviolable from all interference, including inspection and censorship (Art. 35).

FREEDOM OF COMMUNICATION    The nationals of the sending state are to be free to communicate with the consulates of their state, and, in turn, the consular officials of that state are to be free to communicate with the nationals of their state located in the receiving state (Art. 36, par. 1-a). The competent authorities of the latter are to notify the consulate of a sending state without undue delay if in the relevant district a national of the sending state is committed to prison or to custody pending trial or is detained in any other manner. Equally, any communication from such nationals is to be forwarded to the relevant consulate without undue delay (Art. 36, par. 1-b). Consular official are to have the right to visit any national of the sending state who is in prison, custody, or detention, for the purpose of gaining information about the case and of arranging for his legal representation (Art. 36, par. 1-c). Obviously these rights would have to be exercised in accordance with the laws and regulations of the receiving state, provided that the laws or regulations do not nullify the rights of consular officials.

TAX EXEMPTIONS ON FEES AND CHARGES    The fees and charges collected by consulates in the performance of authorized functions are exempt from all dues and taxes in the receiving state (Art. 39). This rule is based on the concept that the moneys collected are the property of the sending state.

RIGHTS OF PROTECTION    As in the case of diplomatic agents, the receiving state is under a duty to accord special protection to consular officials by reason of their official position and to treat them with respect. It must take all appropriate steps to prevent attacks on their person, freedom, and dignity (Art. 40). This duty applies as soon as a consular official enters the territorial jurisdiction of the receiving state.

PERSONAL INVIOLABILITY AND IMMUNITY FROM LOCAL JURISDICTION    Consular officials are not liable to arrest or detention pending trial, except in the case of a grave crime and in accordance with the decision of the competent judicial authorities. If, however, criminal proceedings are instituted against a consular official, he must appear before the competent authorities

[61]See letter from Legal Adviser, U.S. Department of State, dated Jan. 27, 1969, excerpted in 63 *AJIL* 559 (1969).

(Art. 41). The purpose of this provision is to settle the question of the personal immunity of consular officials.

This question has been controversial, both in theory and in state practice, as many states have refused to recognize the personal inviolability of consular officials, certainly not for any acts not a part of the official duties of these officials.

The relevant provisions in the bulk of consular treaties exclude from personal inviolability those consular officials that are nationals of the receiving state and consular officials engaged in commercial activities in regard to such activities, and they specify what ranks or categories of consular officials are to enjoy inviolability: some grant it only to heads of posts, others to all consular officials, and still others generously extend inviolability to specified categories of consular employees.

In all instances, however, members of a consulate enjoy immunity from the jurisdiction of the receiving state's administrative and criminal authorities with respect to any act performed in the exercise of consular functions (Art. 43).

The classic instance illustrating the liability of a consular official for nonofficial acts is the celebrated case of

### BIGELOW v. PRINCESS ZIZIANOFF

*France, Court of Appeal of Paris, 1928*
*Gazette du Palais, March 4, 1928 (No. 125)*

FACTS  Bigelow was director of the Passport Service at the American Consulate General in Paris. He appealed from the judgment of the Conventional Tribunal of the Seine of April 5, 1927, which asserted its competence in a prosecution of Bigelow for defamation.

Princess Zizianoff, a White Russian resident in France, had requested a visa in order to travel to the United States. Bigelow had refused to grant her the visa. The princess protested against his decision, and Bigelow proceeded to furnish information about her at a press conference, apparently to justify his refusal of the visa.

On September 5, 1926, the *Boston Sunday Post* carried a story over the by-line of Robert Johnson, in which the essential sentences read:

"Did Beauty Spy on U.S.? Princess Zizianoff is an international spy. She worked for the Germans in Russia during the World War and was deported to Siberia when she was caught. She was sent to America by Zinovieff last year to do espionage work among the American patriotic organizations, and her anti-Bolshevik activity is only a blind. In the past week she has twice secretly visited the Soviet embassy in Paris."

As a result of this publication, Princess Zizianoff filed a suit before the Twelfth Correctional Tribunal of the Seine against Mr. Kahn, the Paris representative of the newspaper, and Mr. Bigelow, the latter being named an accomplice for having furnished the elements of the article, on grounds of abusive language and libel. [*Princess Zizianoff* v. *Kahn and Bigelow,* reprinted in 21 *AJIL* 811 (1927).] Bigelow denied the competence of the tribunal but was overruled by the court, which declared itself competent in respect to him.

Bigelow's contentions were, first, that French tribunals had no jurisdiction over consuls of the United States, by reason of the provisions of both the Consular Convention of February 23, 1853, between France and the United States, and the Consular Convention of January 7, 1876, between France and Greece, applicable to American consuls by virtue of the "most-favored-nation" clause in the former convention; and, second, that under a general principle of international law, it was not permitted, even in the absence of a consular treaty, to cite a foreign consul before a court of the receiving state for acts done in the performance of his duties, not even for misdeeds committed in the exercise of his functions.

ISSUE    Is a consul immune from the jurisdiction of the receiving state in respect of a libel committed by his giving information as to his reasons for denying a visa, that is, for an act outside his official duties?

DECISION    The Court of Appeal rejected Bigelow's contentions and ruled that the French courts were competent to try him for his private act. The court confirmed the judgment of the Correctional Tribunal and ordered Bigelow to pay the costs of the appeal.

REASONING    Each state has the right to interpret international treaties, and its interpretation is final for all courts under its jurisdiction. The French government had decided on earlier occasions (cited in the judgment) that its consular convention, in which it dealt with the immunities of consular officials, meant that "the personal immunity granted to consuls by the convention does not exclude the competence of our courts in penal matters." Hence Bigelow's argument based on the convention was rejected.

His second contention, based on a presumed rule of international law, also had to be rejected. Now, Bigelow had been well within his functions when he explained the reasons that led him to refuse the visa requested by Princess Zizianoff. Even the issuing of a communiqué or the calling of a press conference for such a purpose was legitimate and within the scope of consular functions.

But the nature of the remarks made by Bigelow, as reproduced in the press, injured the private interests of Princess Zizianoff and were divorced from his administrative acts. His statements accusing the princess of having acted as a German spy and later as a Russian spy, of having visited the Soviet embassy in Paris, and so on were unsubstantiated and did not constitute the performance of an official act. Hence Bigelow stepped outside his functions in a manner that excluded the application of the immunity asserted by him under international law:

"Whereas, moreover, as the judgment below declares, the defendant is prosecuted, not for refusal of a passport, which would be an act in his consular capacity and would consequently be outside any jurisdiction of the courts, but only for having, in his communication of that decision of his country, delivered himself on the subject of said refusal of the above-described comments, which were not its necessary and indispensable corollary; and as in these comments, viewed as apart from or included in the official act itself, there is a serious wrong susceptible of injuring private interests and having a personal character; and this wrong, which is clearly unconnected with the duty performed by Bigelow and is not at all required in the examination of the said official act, would, if it is established, involve him in penal liability by reason of the criminal elements which it appears to contain."

On occasion, consuls are accused, rightly or wrongly, of having engaged in spying—an activity obviously outside the scope of their normal and legal functions. Thus Sweden expelled Albert Liepa, a Soviet vice-consul, in April 1982 on a charge of spying against Latvian exile groups in Sweden, and the Soviet Union expelled (September 12, 1983) Lon David Augustenborg, a vice-consul at the American consulate general in Leningrad, and his wife Dorothy, on charges of engaging in intelligence work. At the time, American sources hinted that the expulsion might have been in retaliation for a similar action by the United States a month earlier against two Soviet diplomats.

One of the most instructive modern American cases touching on the exercise of consular functions, immunity of consular premises, amenability of consuls to legal process, and other aspects of consular agents was the famous *Kasenkina* case.[62] It illustrated, among other consul-related topics, that consular premises may not be used lawfully to detain citizens of the consul's state against their will.

Members of a consulate may be called on to attend as witnesses in the course of judicial or administrative proceedings. If they decline to do so, however, no penalty can be imposed on them. On the other hand, members of a consulate are not obliged to give any evidence on matters connected with the exercise of their functions, nor are they obligated to produce official documents and correspondence relating to such matters (Vienna Consular Convention, Art. 44).

WAIVER OF IMMUNITY    The sending state alone may, of course, waive its consular officials' immunity, but such a waiver must in all cases be express. If the sending state waives the immunity of its officials, for the purpose of civil or administrative proceedings, the waiver does not constitute a waiver of immunity from measures of execution resulting from a judicial decision. A separate waiver, again express in nature, would be required for such measures (Art. 45). A consular official who initiates proceedings in a matter in which he might normally enjoy immunity is precluded from invoking such immunity from local jurisdictions in respect of any counterclaim directly connected with the principal claim.

SPECIAL EXEMPTIONS    Members of the consulate, their families, and their private staff are exempt from regulations and laws of the receiving state in regard to the registration of aliens, residence permits, and work permits (Art. 46).

EXEMPTIONS FROM TAXES AND PERSONAL SERVICES    Members of a consulate and members of their families are exempt from all dues and taxes, personal or real, national, regional, or municipal, except

---

[62]*Emmet* v. *Lomakin,* U.S. Superior Ct., Special Term, New York County, 1948, 84 N.Y.S. (2d) 562, reported in 43 *AJIL* 381 (1949). Consult also Preuss, "Consular Immunities: The Kasenkina Case (U.S.–USSR)," *id.,* 37, and *NYT,* Aug. 21, 1948, as well as 19 *Department of State Bulletin* 251 (Aug. 29, 1948).

1. Indirect taxes normally included in the price of goods and services.
2. Dues and taxes on private immovable property in the territory of the receiving state, unless held on behalf of the sending state for purposes of the consulate.
3. Estate, succession, or inheritance taxes, but not in the case of those concerning the succession of a member of the consulate or of a member of his family.
4. Dues and taxes on private income having its sources in the receiving state and capital taxes on investments made in commercial or financial enterprises in that state.
5. Charges levied for specific services rendered.
6. Registration, court or record fees, mortgage dues, and stamp duties (Art. 49).

Excluded from all these provisions are members of the consulate and members of their families who carry on a private gainful occupation, members of the consulate and members of their families who are nationals of the receiving state, honorary consular officials, and the service staff of the consulate (Art 57).

Members of a consulate, except the service staff, and members of their families are exempt from all personal services and military obligations such as those connected with requisitioning, military contributions, and billeting (Art. 52). Other common exemptions of this kind are based on customary international law and cover such matters as military service, service in a militia, the function of jury member or law judge, or personal labor service ordered by a local authority in connection with a public disaster.

STATUS IN TIME OF WAR    The status of consular officials in time of war presents numerous especial problems. The receiving or sending state may move consulates to different locations. An invading belligerent decides whether or not neutral consulates are to remain and operate in occupied enemy territory. If the consuls are allowed to remain, they do not require new *exequaturs* from the occupant's government. Any misconduct of a neutral consul subjects him to the same penalties as would be visited on the indigenous inhabitants by the occupant.[63]

## SUGGESTED READINGS

Documentation of the *Case Concerning*
*United States Diplomatic and Consular Staff*
*in Tehran (United States v. Iran)*

International Court of Justice, *United States Application and Request for Interim Measures of Protection in Proceeding against Iran* (Nov. 29, 1979). Text in 74 *AJIL* 258 (1980),

---

[63] See von Glahn, 88–90, for further details on the treatment of neutral consuls in occupied territory; cf. Hackworth, vol. 4, 683, 689–91, 713–14.

and in 18 *ILM* 1464" (1979). The oral argument presented before the Court, as well as the Order below, are reproduced in U.S. Department of State, "Selected Documents No. 15: World Court Rules on Hostage Case" (1979), as well as in 18 *ILM* 1464 (1979), and in 19 *ILM* 248 (1980).
International Court of Justice, *Case Concerning United States Diplomatic and Consular Staff in Tehran: Order of Provisional Measures* (December 15, 1979), in 19 *ILM* 139 (1980). International Court of Justice, *Order of the Court Setting Dates for Memorials* (Dec. 24, 1979), *id.*, 147. See also Gross, "The Case Concerning United States Diplomatic and Consular Staff in Tehran: Phase of Provisional Measures," 74 *AJIL* 395 (1980).
United Nations Security Council, *Resolution 457 (1979) of December 4, 1979* (Calling for the immediate release of the hostages), reproduced in 18 *ILM* 1644 (1979).
International Court of Justice, *Case Concerning United States Diplomatic and Consular Staff in Tehran: Judgment* (May 24, 1980), in 19 *ILM* 553 (1980) (including one separate and two dissenting opinions), and in 74 *AJIL* 746 (1980) (Judgment only).
Government of the Democratic and Popular Republic of Algeria, *Declaration on the Settlement of the Iran Hostage Crisis* (Jan. 20, 1981), in 20 *ILM* 224 (1981), in 75 *AJIL* 418 (1981), and in *Department of State Bulletin*, No. 2047, Feb. 1981, 1.
Algeria, Text of the *United States Government–Iran Government Settlement of Claims Agreement* and *Escrow Agreement* (Jan. 19, 1981), in 20 *ILM* 229 (1981), and in 75 *AJIL* 431 (1981).
United States, *Executive Order 12283* (Non-Prosecution of Claims of Hostages and for Actions at the United States Embassy and Elsewhere), Jan. 19, 1981, in 75 *AJIL* 430 (1981).
United States, *Executive Orders 12276–12281,* Jan. 19, 1981, in 20 *ILM* 286 (1981).
United States, *Executive Order 12284* (Restrictions on the Transfer of Property of the Former Shah of Iran), Jan. 19, 1981, in 75 *AJIL* 431 (1981), and in 20 *ILM* 292 (1981).
International Court of Justice, *Case Concerning United States Diplomatic and Consular Staff in Tehran, Order on Discontinuance* (May 12, 1981), in 20 *ILM* 889 (1981). See also Gerhard Wegen, "Discontinuance of International Proceedings: The Hostages Case," 76 *AJIL* 717 (1982).

## Diplomatic Agents: General

Dembinski, *The Modern Law of Diplomacy* (1988); Hevener, ed., *Diplomacy in a Dangerous World: Protection for Diplomats under International Law* (1986); McClanahn, *Diplomatic Immunity: Principles, Practices, Problems* (1989); Brierly, 254–67; Lauterpacht's *Oppenheim*, vol. 1, 769–838; Steele, ed., *The Iran Crisis and International Law* (1981); Przetacznik, *Protection of Officials of Foreign States According to International Law* (1983); Bassiouni, "Protection of Diplomats under Islamic Law," 74 *AJIL* 609 (1980).
(a) U.S. Tehran Embassy Seizure: Consult the excellent and instructive chronological analysis by Shaplen, "Eye of the Storm," I, *New Yorker,* June 2, 1980, 43–89, *passim;* II, June 9, 1980, 48–111, *passim* (almost entirely on Tehran question); and III, June 16, 1980, 44–95, *passim* (also covers Pakistani and South Korean issues).
(b) United States: Department of State, "Guidance for Law Enforcement Officers with Regard to Personal Rights and Immunities of Foreign Diplomatic and Consular Personnel" (Feb. 1988), in 27 *ILM* 1617 (1988), with *ILM* Content Summary.

CASES

*Dickinson* v. *Del Solar,* Great Britain, King's Bench Division, 1920, [1930] 1 K.B. 376.

*Holbrook, Nelson & Co.* v. *Henderson,* United States, Supreme Court of the City of New York, 1839, 6 N.Y. Super. Court (4 Sandford 619).

*The Magdalena Steam Navigation Company* v. *Martin,* Great Britain, Court of Queen's Bench, 1859, 2 Ellis & Ellis, 94.

*Regina* v. *Madan,* Great Britain, Court of Criminal Appeal, 1961, 1 All E.R. 588, reported briefly in 55 *AJIL* 991 (1961).

*Hellenic Lines, Ltd.* v. *Moore,* U.S. Court of Appeals, D.C. Circuit, 1965, 345 F.2d 978, reported in 59 *AJIL* 927 (1965).

*Shaffer* v. *Singh,* U.S. Court of Appeals, D.C. Cir., 1965, 343 F.2d 324; see also the extensive *Note* on this case by Levit, *Harvard Int'l. Law Jl.* 153 (Winter 1965).

*Anonymous* v. *Anonymous,* United States, N.Y. Family Court, N.Y. County, 1964, 252 N.Y.S. 2d 913, noted, 59 *AJIL* 391 (1965).

*United States* v. *Butenko,* U.S. Court of Appeals, 3rd Cir., 1967, 384 F.2d 554, reported in some detail in 62 *AJIL* 777 (1968).

*Regina* v. *Governor of Pentonville Prison, ex parte Teja,* United Kingdom, Queen's Bench Division, 1971, [1971] 2 W.L.R. 816, reported in 66 *AJIL* 193 (1927). Petition to appeal to House of Lords denied, Feb. 24, 1971.

## Special and U.N. Missions

Waters, *The Ad Hoc Diplomat: A Study in Municipal and International Law* (1963).

CASE

*United States* v. *Egorov,* U.S. Dist. Court, E.D.N.Y., 1963, 222 F. Supp. 106, reported in 58 *AJIL* 513 (1964).

## Consular Agents: General

Lauterpacht's *Oppenheim,* vol. 1, 829–45; Roosaare, "Consular Relations between the United States and the Baltic States," *Baltic Review* (Jan. 1964), 11–36; Donaldson, "Soviet Consular Conventions: Post-Vienna," 10 *Harvard Int'l. Law Jl.* 360 (1969).

CASES

*Fenton Textile Association* v. *Krassin,* Great Britain, 1921, 38 Times L.R. 259.

*Rocca* v. *Thompson,* U.S. Supreme Court, 1912, 284 U.S. 30.

*Santovincenzo* v. *Egan,* U.S. Supreme Court, 1931, 223 U.S. 317.

*United States* v. *Trumbull,* U.S. Dist. Court, S.D. of Cal., 1891, 48 Fed. 94.

*Bliss* v. *Nicolaeff,* United States, New York, Appellate Division, 1948, 79 N.Y.S. (2d) 63, reported in 42 *AJIL* 944 (1948).

*Kita* v. *Matuszak,* U.S. Court of Appeals, Michigan, 1970, 21 Mich. App. 421, 175 N.W. 2d 551, reported in 65 *AJIL* 620 (1971).

*Radwan* v. *Radwan,* United Kingdom, Probate, Divorce, and Admiralty Division, May 11, 1972, reported in 66 *AJIL* 875 (1972).

*Heaney* v. *Spain and Gomero,* U.S. Court of Appeals, 2d Cir., July 2, 1971, reported in 10 *ILM* 1038 (1971).

## APPENDIX I: MEDIA-REPORTED RUPTURES
## OF DIPLOMATIC RELATIONS, 1973–1990

| | | | |
|---|---|---|---|
| 1973 | Libya–Egypt | 1981 | Australia–Lebanon |
| | Cent. Afr. Republic–Israel | | Jamaica–Cuba |
| | U.S.A.–Uganda | 1983 | Surinam–Cuba |
| 1976 | Gt. Britain–Uganda | | Grenada–Cuba |
| | Equat. Guinea–U.S.A. | | Grenada–USSR |
| | Egypt–Syria | | Grenada–Libya |
| 1977 | USSR–Somalia | | Burma–North Korea |
| | Cuba–Somalia | 1985 | Liberia–USSR |
| | Egypt–Syria | | Tunisia–Libya |
| | Iraq–Egypt | 1986 | Great Britain–Syria |
| | Libya–Egypt | 1987 | France–Iran |
| | Algeria–Egypt | | Australia–Libya |
| | South Yemen–Egypt | | Egypt–Iran |
| 1980 | Syria–Iran | 1988 | Tunisia–Iran |
| | Saudi Arabia–Libya | | Saudi Arabia–Iran |
| 1981 | U.S.A.–Libya | 1989 | El Salvador–Nicaragua |
| | Sudan–Libya | 1990 | Kenya–Norway |

APPENDIX II: MEDIA-REPORTED RESUMPTIONS
OF DIPLOMATIC RELATIONS, 1973–1990

| | | | |
|---|---|---|---|
| 1973 | U.S.A.–Egypt | 1987 | Morocco–Egypt |
| 1974 | Romania–Portugal | | North Yemen–Egypt |
| 1975 | India–Portugal | | West Germany–Albania |
| 1976 | India–China | 1988 | Australia–Fiji |
| 1977 | Spain–Yugoslavia | | Iran–Kuwait |
| | Spain–USSR | | Iran–Canada |
| | USSR–Egypt | | Iran–France |
| 1979 | Israel–Egypt | | Iran–Great Britain |
| | U.S.A.–China | | Ethiopia–Somalia |
| 1984 | U.S.A.–Iraq | | Ecuador–Nicaragua |
| | Egypt–Jordan | | Algeria–Morocco |
| 1985 | Ivory Coast–Israel | 1989 | Egypt–Syria* |
| | Liberia–Israel | | Kenya–Israel |
| | Zaire–Israel | | Cent. Afr. Republic–Israel |
| | Iran–Sudan | | Ethiopia–Israel |
| 1986 | Great Britain–Guatemala | 1990 | Indonesia–China |
| | Israel–Cameroon | | Great Britain–Iran |
| | Poland–Israel | | USSR–South Korea |
| 1987 | Libya–Tunisia | | USSR–Israel** |
| | Bahrain–Egypt | | Iran–Iraq |
| | Saudi Arabia–Egypt | | USSR–Saudi Arabia |
| | Kuwait–Egypt | | Great Britain–Syria |

*At that point Egypt again had diplomatic relations with 28 of 29 Arab states.
**Consular relations only.

# Case Study No. 7

## A. The PLO Observer Mission to the United Nations; B. The Arafat Visa Denial

### A. THE PLO OBSERVER MISSION

The attempt of the United States to close the Palestine Liberation Organization (hereafter PLO) Observer Mission to the United Nations in 1987 resulted not only in interesting diplomatic maneuvering, but also brought illuminating decisions by a U.S. District Court and by the International Court of Justice.

In 1987, several bills were introduced in Congress to require, among other things, the closing of the PLO Permanent Observer Mission to the United Nations. Although the U.S. Department of State opposed those measures on the grounds that they violated provisions of the 1947 U.S.–U.N. Headquarters Agreement,[1] the proposed ban on the PLO UN Mission became a part of the Foreign Relations Appropriation Act for 1988 and 1989, as the "Anti-Terrorist Appropriation Act of 1987" (ATA).[2]

The UN concerns about the ATA were discussed in the UN General Assembly Committee on Relations with the Host Country, where the U.S. representatives admitted that the closing of the Mission would be a violation of the Headquarters Agreement. Eventually the General Assembly itself voted (December 17, 1987, Res. 42/210 B), 145–1 (Israel), the United States abstaining, requesting the United States to observe the obligations assumed under the Headquarters Agreement.

True to a promise made by the Attorney General, the Department of Justice on March 22, 1988, filed a complaint against the PLO, its UN Mission, and all members of the same in the U.S. District Court (S.D.N.Y.): *United States of America* v. *Palestine Liberation Organization, et al.* (88 Div. 1962).[3] In response, on March 23, 1988, a group of 65 U.S. citizens and organizations filed a Complaint against the Attorney General: *Mendelsohn*

---

[1] Text of relevant portions in *Time*, Dec. 12, 1988, 36.
[2] Text in 27 *ILM* 756 (1988). See the informative collection of "Documents Concerning the Controversy Surrounding the Closing of the Palestine Liberation Organization Observer Mission to the United Nations," 27 *ILM* 712 (1988).
[3] Text in 27 *ILM* 789 (1988).

v. *Meese,* in the same District Court (88 Civ. 2005), asking that the ATA not be enforced. The reasons for this request were based essentially on the provisions of the 1947 Headquarters Agreement and the Bill of Attainder Clause. Interestingly enough, both cases were assigned to the same District Court judge.

It should be mentioned that a separate litigation, begun before the passage of the ATA, was going on relative to a closing of the Palestine Information Office in Washington, D.C. The claimed authority of the U.S. Government in this action was the Foreign Missions Act: *Palestine Information Office* v. *Shultz,* 674 F. Supp. 910 (D.D.C. 1987), No. 87–5898 (D.C. Cir.).

The ATA having by then become law but not yet in effect, the UN Secretary-General requested of the U.S. representative that the law not be applied in such a manner as to interfere with the operations of the PLO Mission. As was to be expected, the United States refused that request, whereupon the Secretary-General invoked the settlement-of-disputes provisions of the Headquarters Agreement. The General Assembly also passed two resolutions (143–1, 143–0), the United States abstaining), one calling again on the United States not to violate its treaty obligations, the other asking the International Court of Justice for an Advisory Opinion as to whether the United States was obliged to enter into arbitration under the Headquarters Agreement's provisions for dispute settlement.

The United States then informed the UN Secretary-General that the Attorney General had decided that under the ATA he had to close the PLO Mission and that submission to arbitration "would not serve a useful purpose." The Attorney General also notified the Permanent Observer of the PLO Mission that maintenance of that Mission after March 21, 1988, would be unlawful. The UN General Assembly reconvened and, after considerable debate, passed Resolution 42/230 (1988) by a vote of 148–2 (Israel, United States), repeating its previous stand about the United States and violation of the 1947 Agreement.

On March 9, the International Court of Justice (hereafter ICJ) issued an Order[4] requesting information on the issue from both the United States and the United Nations.[5] This was done, with the German Democratic Republic and Syria also submitting written statements of their views. At the Oral Hearings, however, only the UN Legal Counsel appeared.

The ICJ handed down its Advisory Opinion[6] on April 26. It held unanimously that the United States was obliged to arbitrate the dispute about the PLO Mission.

The decision of the District Court in *United States* v. *Palestine Liberation Organization* came on June 29, 1988.[7] The Court ruled that the *final decision*

[4]*ICJ Reports, 1988,* 3, in 27 *ILM* 803 (1988).
[5]For U.S. statement, see *id.,* 806.
[6]*ICJ Reports, 1988,* 11, in *id.,* 808; see 82 *AJIL* 833 (1988) for a detailed summary. The full decision, including notes, is found in 4 *Palestinian Yrbk. of Int'l. Law* 170 (1989).
[7]Text and *ILM* content summary in 27 *ILM* 1055 (1988).

on the manner in which the United States would honor its treaty obligations had to be left to the U.S. Executive Branch. Hence the Court interpreted the ATA and the Headquarters Agreement itself instead of waiting for the ruling of an as yet nonexistent arbitration tribunal.

The Court held that the closing of the PLO Mission would be contrary to the manner in which the United States dealt with other Observer Missions and, under the provisions of the Headquarters Agreement, the United States should not interfere with the PLO Mission. The Court then concluded after an analysis of the ATA that it could not find any expression of a congressional intent to violate U.S. obligations under the Headquarters Agreement, hence did not require a closing of the PLO Mission. The Court decided that the ATA applied to PLO activities except for those connected with the UN Mission. The latter existed by invitation of the United Nations [since 1974] and was therefore protected by the Headquarters Agreement. In effect, the District Court's decision also represented a decision in the *Mendelsohn* v. *Meese* litigation.

On August 29, 1988, the Department of Justice announced that it would not appeal the decision of the District Court, asserting that "on balance, the interests of the United States are best served by not appealing."

It is of interest to note, in view of the U.S. opposition to arbitration of this controversy, that in February 1988 the UN Secretary-General had appointed a former president of the ICJ, Eduardo Jimenez de Arechaga of Uruguay, as the UN arbitral tribunal member (out of a total of three). The Tribunal was, of course, never constituted.

The closure of the Palestine Information Office in Washington, D.C., which was not connected with the United Nations, took place legally under the provisions of the Anti-Terrorist Act.

## B. THE ARAFAT VISA DENIAL

A second controversy between the United States and the Palestine Liberation Organization (PLO) took place in 1988, when the United States denied a visa to PLO chairman Yassir Arafat. The latter had planned to address the UN General Assembly after the PLO had decided whether or not to declare an independent Palestinian state.

On November 24, 1988, the U.S. Department of State received an application from Arafat for a visa to attend the UN General Assembly session of December 1 as an invitee. The application was denied after Secretary of State Shultz decided not to recommend a waiver of ineligibility.[8] The reason given for the denial was an assertion of PLO terrorism and the fact that Arafat, as chairman, "knows of, condones, and lends support to such acts" and was "an accessory to such terrorism."

---

[8]US Dept. of State, "Statement on the Visa Application of Yassir Arafat," 83 *AJIL* 253 (1989).

The denial of the visa appeared, however, to violate the 1947 United States–United Nations Headquarters Agreement which provided, *inter alia*, that it preserved

the right of the United States to safeguard its own security and completely to control the entrance of aliens into any territory of the United States *other than the headquarters district and its immediate vicinity* (emphasis added).[9]

Thus U.S. law excluded members of the PLO from entering the United States because the organization practiced terrorism. But Arafat wanted to come as a UN invitee and hence should have been protected against exclusion. The UN Secretary-General denounced the U.S. action as incompatible with the obligations of the host country under the 1947 Agreement, and similar views were voiced by other UN officials. The Department of State responded by claiming that its decision was "firm and final. It is not the physical presence that is the issue here. . . . This is a question of terrorism . . . and the security of American citizens." On November 29, the UN General Assembly's Legal Committee, by a vote of 121–2, urged a reversal of the American position, as did the General Assembly itself by a vote of 151–2.

On December 2, the General Assembly voted 154–2 (Great Britain abstaining) to move a meeting to Geneva, Switzerland. That session was scheduled for December 13–15, 1988, and would enable Arafat to address it. The United States then announced that it would attend and participate in the Geneva session.

### SUGGESTED READINGS

Reisman, "The Arafat Visa Affair: Exceeding the Bounds of Host State Discretion," 83 *AJIL* 519 (1989).

[9]See the relevant portions of the Agreement in *Time,* Dec. 12, 1988, 36.

# 17

# International Agreements

## TYPES OF TREATIES

BACKGROUND    Treaties and other forms of international agreements have been in evidence throughout recorded history. In modern times, beginning with the writings of Grotius, writers and diplomats have depended mostly on rules of law governing contractual relations between private individuals in developing the principles regulating contractual arrangements between states. Only in the last few decades have there been serious attempts to develop international codes governing treaties and other interstate agreements. Although but two such major conventions have been completed, the general principles applied by states in actual practice have achieved such a degree of uniformity that the rest of the law of interstate agreements should not prove too difficult to codify.[1]

BILATERAL TREATIES    The functions served by international agreements can best be understood by examining the various types of such instruments utilized by states. One distinction commonly emphasized is that between bilateral and multilateral treaties. Bilateral agreements are between only two states or parties. They are closely related, at least by analogy, to contracts between individuals. Normally a bilateral treaty is concluded between two states desiring to promote or regulate interests or matters of particular interest to them alone. As of January 1, 1982, the United States was a party to 255 bilateral treaties.

MULTILATERAL TREATIES    States also conclude multilateral (multipartite) treaties, that is, agreements negotiated by and involving more than two parties. Some of these agreements do not create new principles or rules of international law, but are merely an expanded version of a bilateral (bipartite) treaty. Examples are particularly numerous in the area of multilateral military or political alliances (for instance, the North Atlantic Treaty Organization (NATO) and the Warsaw Pact). Other state interests served by multilateral instruments not characterized as lawmaking are in the economic and social areas, in which a common aspect of multilateral treaties is the establishment of some form of international administrative agency to carry out the common interest agreed upon in the treaty. Others, however, must

---

[1]On the general subject of treaties, consult Hackworth, vol. 4, 1–433; Moore, vol. 5, 155–870; and Lord McNair, *The Law of Treaties* (reiss. 1986).

be regarded as lawmaking treaties in the true sense. (See Chapter 1.) As of January 1, 1982, the United States was a party to 600 multilateral treaties. These fall again into two major categories: true treaties and so-called declarations.

DECLARATIONS    Declarations are a peculiar type of lawmaking agreement resulting from inter-American conferences and meetings of foreign ministers. They produce statements of legal principles applying, on a regional basis, in the Western Hemisphere. Thus the Preamble of the Act of Chapultepec (Conference on Problems of War and Peace, Mexico City, 1945) states that "the American States have been incorporating in their international law, since 1890, by means of conventions, resolutions and declarations, the following principles." The governments of states in Latin America do not differentiate, in regard to legal status or binding force, between rules laid down in formal treaties and those found in resolutions or declarations, regarding all as having equal standing.

CLASSIFICATION OF TREATIES    All writers, from Hugo Grotius onward, have pointed out that the names or titles of international agreements included under the general term *treaty* have little or no legal significance. Certain terms are, to be sure, useful, but they furnish little more than mere description. A so-called simple treaty refers to an absolute obligation, a conditional treaty to a qualified one. Finally, there is an important distinction between an executed treaty and an executory treaty. The former type deals with a single matter that, when performed or taken care of, is disposed of. Good examples are agreements delimiting a boundary between two states and also the numerous treaties dealing with voluntary cession. Executory treaties, by contrast, provide for continuous or occasional subsequent action or performance or application. Examples are instruments governing commercial relations between states, extradition treaties, agreements establishing administrative organization, treaties of alliance, and so on.

A treaty in the accepted sense of the term may be characterized in the words of Sir Gerald G. Fitzmaurice, the third rapporteur on the law of treaties for the UN International Law Commission, of March 14, 1956:

A treaty is an international agreement embodied in a single formal instrument (whatever its name, title or designation) made between entities both or all of which are subjects of international law possessed of an international personality and treaty-making capacity, and intended to create rights and obligations, or to establish relationships, governed by international law.[2]

Oppenheim's definition is more to the point: "International treaties are agreements, of a contractual character, between States, or organisations of States, creating legal rights and obligations between the Parties."[3]

[2]Myers, "The Names and Scope of Treaties," 51 *AJIL* 574, 575 (1957).
[3]Lauterpacht's *Oppenheim*, vol. 1, 877.

NOMENCLATURE    The variety of names given over the years to treaties (and portions of multilateral instruments) is astounding. Besides the common varieties, such as *convention, agreement, protocol, treaty,* and the less common *final act, general act,*[4] and *declaration,* a bewildering array of relatively rare terms confronts the student. Among them, to list but a few, are *arrangement, accord, code, compact, contract, regulation, concordat,* and *statute.* "Statements of intent" are not international agreements, all claims to the contrary notwithstanding.[5]

EXECUTIVE AGREEMENTS    Executive agreements represent a uniquely American practice in conducting relations with other states. Unlike a treaty concluded by the President (or his agents, such as the Secretary of State and his subordinates) with another country, which requires submission to the United States Senate for the constitutional two-thirds "advice and consent" before ratification, an executive agreement does not require the Senate's final approval. It is a binding international obligation made by the executive branch on the basis of prior congressional authorization and within the limits set by Congress or, on occasion, without prior congressional authority within the powers generally recognized as vested in the presidential office.

On August 22, 1972, President Richard Nixon approved the Case Act (Public Law 92-404), which requires that international agreements, other than treaties, thereafter entered into by the United States be transmitted to Congress within 60 days after the agreements have been executed (that is, concluded).[6] The Case Act covers, of course, executive agreements, as was made clear preceding passage during the hearings by a written statement by the Legal Adviser, as well as by instructions from the acting Secretary of State to all executive-branch departments and agencies.[7] The act was amended by Public Law 95-426 (Foreign Relations Authorization Act, Fiscal Year 1979, of October 7, 1978) as follows:

REPORTING AND COORDINATION OF INTERNATIONAL AGREEMENTS
Sec. 708. Section 112b of title 1. United States Code, is amended—
(1) by inserting "(including the text of *any oral international agreement* [emphasis added], which agreement shall be reduced to writing)" immediately after "international agreement" in the first sentence;
(2) by inserting "(a)" immediately before the first sentence; and          Presidential
(3) by adding at the end thereof the following new subsections:          report,

---

[4]These all have the same binding force; *id.,* pp. 898–99; as mentioned above, declarations are *regional* treaties.
[5]See 72 *AJIL* 391 (1978) on this point.
[6]Text of the law in 11 *ILM* 1117 (1972), see also the statement by the Legal Adviser, Department of State (May 18, 1972), excerpted in 66 *AJIL* 845 (1972), and letters from the acting Secretary of State (Jan. 26, 1973), 67 *AJIL* 544 (1973); and (Sept. 6, 1973), 68 *AJIL* 117 (1974). The transmittal is only for purposes of information.
[7]Consult also, *inter alia,* Borchard, "Shall the Executive Agreement Replace the Treaty?" 38 *AJIL* 637 (1944), McDougal and Lans, "Treaties and Congressional-Executive or Presidential Agreements: International Instruments of National Policy," 54 *Yale Law* 181 543 (1945); and Borchard's rejoinder to the above, "Treaties and Executive Agreements—A Reply," *id.,* 616.

"(b) Not later than March 1, 1979, and at yearly intervals thereafter, the President shall, under his own signature, transmit to the Speaker of the House of Representatives and the chairman of the Committee on Foreign Relations of the Senate a report with respect to each international agreement which, during the preceding year, was transmitted to the Congress after the expiration of the 60-day period referred to in the first sentence of subsection (a), describing fully and completely the reasons for the late transmittal.

*transmittal to Speaker of the House, and Senate committee.*

"(c) Notwithstanding any other provision of law, on international agreement may not be signed or otherwise concluded on behalf of the United States without prior consultation with the Secretary of State. Such consultation may encompass a class of agreements rather than a particular agreement.

*Consultation.*

"(d) The Secretary of State shall determine for and within the executive branch whether an agreement constitutes an international agreement within the meaning of this section.

"(e) The President shall, through the Secretary of State, promulgate such rules and regulations as may be necessary to carry out this section."

*Rules and regulations.*

The proportion of executive agreements out of the total number of agreements concluded by the United States testifies to the continuing emphasis on this mode of arriving at international concords: from 1789 to the end of 1974 (latest available figure), 1,254 treaties were concluded, 7,809 executive agreements were signed, and over 400 "secret" additional agreements were concluded.

The Department of State has held that executive agreements ought to be subject to certain limitations; in its Circular No. 175, (1955 as revised 1966), the department stated that

Executive agreements shall not be used when the subject matter should be covered by a treaty.[8] The executive agreement form shall be used only for agreements which fall into one or more of the following categories:

a. Agreements which are made pursuant to or in accordance with existing legislation or a treaty;
b. Agreements which are made subject to Congressional approval or implementation; or
c. Agreements which are made under and in accordance with the President's Constitutional Power.[9]

In an executive agreement has not been authorized by prior legislation or does not fall within the sphere of constitutional presidential authority, the

---

[8]See the instructive collection of memoranda from various U.S. officials and agencies (Senate Legislative Counsel, Legal Adviser of the State Department, and so on) on the question of whether certain secret agreements and commitments made by the United States with Israel should have been in the form of treaties; 14 *ILM* 1585 (1975), and 15 *ILM* 187 (1976).
[9]50 *AJIL* 784, 785 (1956 Supp.)

agreement is regarded as void.[10] This is particularly true if the agreement contravenes the provisions of a federal statute dealing with the matter in the executive agreement.

A not well known but important use of the executive agreement has been the settlement of claims of U.S. nationals against foreign countries. The executive agreement has been used in this way at least 10 times since 1952, without protest by Congress. The issue arose again in connection with the suspension of claims against Iran (see Chapter 16 in reference to the *Hostage* case), particularly after the issuance of President Carter's executive orders (ratified on February 24, 1981, by an order of President Reagan), when even attachments resulting from claims against Iran were suspended.[11]

What is the duration of an executive agreement? The question is superfluous because such instruments constitute binding obligations of the United States and in many instances specify a definite duration, expressed in terms of years, such as the 50-year minimum agreement of April 6, 1939, concluded with the United Kingdom for the joint control of the Canton and Enderbury islands.

The United States has never really denied binding effect to an executive agreement on the grounds of presidential succession, for in international law an executive agreement is regarded as a form of treaty.

The most famous and controversial modern executive agreement is the Far Eastern Agreement signed at Yalta on February 11, 1945. Pan demonstrated convincingly[12] that President Roosevelt regarded the document as an executive agreement, yet did not admit this in his actual verbal report to Congress on March 1, 1945. Pan also pointed out the instrument's unique and unprecedented features, down to the use of the signatories' titles (or lack thereof) and the immense political implications, which involved most unusual duties by one party (the United States) in regard to an Allied but nonsignatory power (China).

An interesting sidelight on the history of the Yalta Agreement was that President Roosevelt requested Congress to "concur in the general conclusions" reached at Yalta, yet Congress could take no such action because the agreement's actual text was not released by the Department of State until February 1946. In the meantime, however, the United States government, through the executive branch, undertook to carry out the measures called for in the agreement.

---

[10]See *United States* v. *Guy W. Capps, Inc.*, U.S. Court of Appeals, 4th Cir., 1953, 204 F.2d 655, digested in 48 *AJIL* 153 (1954).

[11]See *Dames & Moore*, v. *Regan, Secretary of Treasury, et al.*, U.S. Supreme Court, July 2, 1981, slip opinion reproduced in 20 *ILM* 897 (1981).

[12]Stephen C. Y. Pan, "Legal Aspects of the Yalta Agreement," 46 *AJIL* 40, 48 (1952); the essentially opposing views of Briggs, "The Leaders' Agreement of Yalta," 40 *AJIL* 376 (1946) (text of the agreement is reprinted in full in both sources); and Schachter, "The Twilight Existence of Nonbinding International Agreements," 71 *AJIL* 296 (1977).

## CODIFICATION OF THE LAW

The International Law Commission developed draft articles on the Law of Treaties at its fourteenth, fifteenth, sixteenth, and seventeenth sessions, culminating in January 1966 in a draft convention, complete with an elaborate commentary.[13] That draft was discussed at the first session of the United Nations Diplomatic Conference on the Law of Treaties, held in Vienna from March 26 to May 24, 1968. Sixty-five of the original 75 articles in question were adopted (many with relatively minor changes) by the committee of the whole; action was deferred on 9 articles; 4 new ones were added; and 1 (Art. 38) was deleted.

The revised draft was discussed again, in its entirety, and then voted on, article by article, at the second session of the conference, April 9 to May 22, 1969, in Vienna. Thus a convention was produced for submission to governments. That agreement, the Vienna Convention on the Law of Treaties (hereafter referred to as the Vienna Convention) was adopted on May 22, 1969, by a vote of 79 in favor, one against (France), with 19 abstentions (including all members of the Soviet bloc). The convention entered into force on January 27, 1980. At this time, the United States has not become a party to the agreement, but the Legal Adviser of the Department of State asserted in a letter (September 12, 1980) that 'while the United States has not yet ratified the Vienna Convention on the Law of Treaties, we consistently apply those of its terms which constitute a codification of customary international law. Most provisions of the Vienna Convention, including Articles 31 and 32 on matters of treaty interpretation, are declaratory of customary international law."[14]

In order to complete coverage of the subject of treaties, the International Law Commission adopted at its twenty-ninth session (1977) Draft Articles on Treaties Concluded between States and International Organizations or between International Organizations. This comprehensive set of more than 60 carefully drafted articles, now in the form of a convention done at Vienna on March 21, 1986, was not yet in force at the time of this writing.[15]

## FORMATION OF TREATIES

The treaty-making process generally has four stages, several of which may, however, occur concurrently:

1. Negotiation (including the drawing up and authentication of the text).
2. Provisional acceptance of the text, normally through the affixing of the signatures of the negotiators.

---

[13] Text and elaborate commentary in 61 *AJIL* 263 (1967 Supp.); text of convention and related documents in 63 *AJIL* 875 (1969), and in 8 *ILM* 679 (1969).
[14] Quoted in 75 *AJIL* 147 (1981).
[15] Text in 25 *ILM* 543 (1986).

3. Final acceptance of the treaty, normally through ratification.
4. The treaty's entry into force.

## Negotiation

A treaty is normally drawn up by a process of negotiation that may be carried on by any duly authorized persons or agencies. Diplomatic or other official channels may be utilized, a meeting of representatives may be arranged, or an international conference may be called. For treaties negotiated under the auspices of an international organization, the text may be drawn up either in an organ of that agency or at a conference convened by the agency.

There are no basic general limitations as to the actual persons entitled to negotiate a treaty. On occasion, a head of state may do so himself or herself (President Woodrow Wilson at the Paris Peace Conference is an example), or the head of the government, the minister of foreign affairs, or diplomatic offices may undertake the task.[16]

Representatives negotiating a treaty must be duly authorized to carry out their tasks and normally are required to have available credentials to that effect. On the other hand, heads of states and of governments, as well as foreign ministers and heads of diplomatic missions (in the case of bilateral treaties), are presumed to have an *ex officio* capacity to negotiate and to sign, although they do not need to exhibit credentials to that effect (Vienna Convention, Art. 7, par. 2). The principle in the case of foreign ministers was illustrated through the ruling of the Permanent Court of International Justice in the well-known *Eastern Greenland Case (Denmark-Norway)*.[17] The court ruled that a valid and binding international agreement resulted from an official conversation between a foreign minister and a diplomatic agent of another state; the undertaking made by the foreign minister in the conversation, while he acted within his normal official authority, was binding on his state.

## Adoption and Authentication

ADOPTION    Once the text of a treaty has been drafted in formal form by the negotiation, it is adopted by the parties in one of several ways: for bilateral agreements, by mutual consent of the two parties; for treaties negotiated between a limited number of states, usually by unanimous consent; for multilateral instruments negotiated by an international conference, by the voting rules adopted by that conference; and for treaties drawn up in an international organization or at a conference convened by such an organization, according to the voting rules provided either by the constitution of the organization or by the decision of an organ or agency competent to issue such rules.

[16]See the *Memorandum* (Oct. 15, 1973) of the acting Legal Adviser, U.S. Department of State, on the functions of the Secretary of State with respect to treaties, excerpted in 68 *AJIL* 322 (1974).
[17]*P.C.I.J.*, 1933, Ser. A/B, No. 53.

AUTHENTICATION/SIGNATURE    Adoption of a final text by the negotiators is followed by authentication. This step may take place in a number of ways: the negotiators may simply initial the text on behalf of their states; the text may be incorporated in the final act of the conference at which it was drawn up; the text may be incorporated in a resolution adopted by an organ of an international organization; or most commonly, the negotiators may append their signatures to the text of the agreement. Any of these procedures confirm that the text of the treaty is in its final form (Vienna Convention, Art. 10). The obvious purpose of authentication is to supply to all parties (states) a settled text so that each will know definitely what the commitments are in the event of ratification. On rare occasions in modern times, dwindling into insignificance today, treaties have become effective on signature, and in such a case, the authentication of the text assumes vital importance to all parties concerned, for it marks not only agreement on the wording but also an act of binding acceptance of that wording.

Who may sign a treaty? Obviously, only persons who have the capacity *ex officio* to do so—such as heads of states or of governments and ministers of foreign affairs—or representatives of states to whom full (plenary) powers to negotiate and sign have been issued may sign.

Article 18 of the Vienna Convention contains the logical assertion that once a state has signed a treaty, it is obliged to refrain from all acts that would defeat the treaty's object and purpose, at least until that state has ratified the agreement or has indicated that it does not intend to become a party to the agreement.

## Ratification

PROCESS OF RATIFICATION    Most modern international treaties become effective only on ratification. Virtually every state has developed detailed domestic regulations spelling out the process of treaty ratification, and although the constitutional provisions vary greatly from country to country, there is some common agreement. Thus ratification is generally held to be an executive act, undertaken by the head of the state or of the government, as the case may be, through which the formal acceptance of the treaty is proclaimed. Until such acceptance is forthcoming, a treaty does not create obligations for the state in question—except in the rare instance of an agreement that becomes effective and binding on signature alone. In other words, a treaty normally is "concluded" as soon as mutual agreement has been manifested by the act of signature by the duly authorized agents of the parties, but the binding force of the instrument is suspended until ratification has been completed.

It is the parties' intention that is decisive in determining whether a nonratified treaty is to be regarded as binding. In many states, executive ratification must be preceded by some action by the legislative branch of the government—commonly an action expressing the granting of consent to ratification. In the United States, a treaty must receive the "advice and consent of two-thirds of a quorum of the Senate. This, normally, is followed by the ratification act by the President.[18]

UNCONSTITUTIONAL RATIFICATION    The unconstitutional ratification of a treaty should not be regarded as voiding the international obligations and responsibilities of the ratifying states. The Permanent Court of International Justice observed in the case of the *Treatment of Polish Nationals in Danzig*[19] that "a State cannot adduce as against another state its own Constitution with a view of evading obligations incumbent upon it under international law or treaties in force." Such an interpretation appears most reasonable and fully in accord with the principles of international law, for receipt of a notice of ratification would lead a state to expect that an agreement would be honored in good faith.

Another problem with ratification pertains to its possible retroactive effects. A traditional American view held that a treaty became effective on the date of signature, once it had been ratified; that is, the act of ratification was assumed to have a retroactive force. This point of view was not shared by other states, and there was a gradual shift in opinion in the United States. Beginning with the decision of the Supreme Court of the United States in *Haver* v. *Yaker*,[20] in which the Court held that the rule of retroactivity did not apply when a treaty affected private rights, the retreat from the old position proceeded apace. Today the view of all governments is that a treaty does not become effective until it has been ratified—unless the instrument itself provides otherwise (Vienna Convention, Arts. 12–17).

Nowadays, following the official acceptance of a treaty, ratifications are exchanged by the parties to the agreement, and the agreement is announced to be in effect.

ACCESSION/ADHERENCE    Related to both signature and ratification is the subject of *accession/adherence:* the formal act of a third party, one that had not signed or ratified a treaty, by which that third party assumes the obligations and possible privileges of a treaty and considered itself bound by its provisions. On occasion the permission of the original parties to the treaty is required before nonsignatories may join in the agreement, and commonly accession is involved only in originally multipartite agreements.[21] To cite some recent examples of variations in the terminology used for accession: on May 5, 1978, Nauru "deposited its signature" to the Vienna Convention on Diplomatic Relations; on April 13, 1978, Laos "signed" the 1977 UN Convention on the Prohibition of Military or Any Other Hostile Use of Environmental Modifications Techniques, and on July 18, 1972, sent to the UN Secretariat a "notification it considers itself bound" by the 1967 Outer Space Treaty; on October 7, 1981, Luxembourg "deposited its accession" to the Genocide Convention.

[18]See Glennon, "The Senate Role in Treaty Ratification," 77 *AJIL* 257 (1983).
[19]*P.C.I.J.*, 1932, Ser. A/B, No. 44, at 24; see also Hyde, vol. 2, 1385.
[20]1869, 9 Wallace 32; for utilization of the old rule, see Moore, vol. 5, 244.
[21]Hyde, vol. 2, 1447–48; see also Hackworth, vol. 5, 74–84.

SUCCESSION   On occasion, a newly independent state, formerly part of another entity (such as an ex-British colony) joins a multipartite agreement to which its former government (say, the United Kingdom) had been a party. In such a case, for example, Kiribati on April 2, 1982, deposited with the UN Secretariat its *notification of succession* to the Vienna convention on Diplomatic Relations.

NON-SELF-EXECUTING TREATIES   Treaties may be either self-executing or non-self-executing in nature. In the United States, a self-executing treaty becomes domestic law as soon as the instrument enters into force internationally. Non-self-executing agreements require implementing legislation before they come into effect domestically. In the United States and elsewhere, the courts look at that implementing legislation in arriving at decision in relevant cases. Legal scholars are virtually unanimous (Israeli publicists excepted) in the belief that whether a treaty falls into one or the other of the two categories is immaterial as far as the legal obligations of a party to that treaty are concerned. Naturally, if a country fails to adopt implementing legislation in the case of a non-self-executing treaty, it cannot carry out its obligations under that agreement. But internationally, it is still obligated by that instrument.

The decision as to which category a given treaty falls into is usually made by the judicial branch of a government, based on the intentions of the parties as shown in the wording of the treaty,[22] or, in some instances, it is based on national policy. On other occasions, statements by a chief executive or legislative body have helped in determining the nature of a given agreement.

Decisions of the Israeli Supreme Court (and statements by a former attorney general) have repeatedly emphasized the need for implementing legislation for such agreements as the 1949 Geneva Convention IV for the Protection of Civilian Persons in Time of War; the court refused acceptance of that agreement as binding on Israel, even though signed and ratified by the latter. At most, Israel has promised to honor the "humanitarian portions" of the Convention, even though the *entire* treaty is regarded elsewhere as a basic part of the modern humanitarian law of war, and also as a self-executing agreement, binding without implementing legislation. In the United States, the Senate insisted on implementing legislation for the Genocide Convention, delaying the deposit of a document of ratification until Congress had passed the required domestic legislation. (See Chapter 13 *sub* Genocide.)

## Rejection of Treaties

Except in the case of treaties effective on signature, a state is not bound by a treaty until ratification has taken place. It is therefore possible for

---

[22]See *Foster and Elam* v. *Neilson,* U.S. Supreme Court, 1829, 27 U.S. (2 Pet.) 253. See also the valuable study by Paust, "Self-Executing Treaties," 82 *AJIL* 760 (1988).

a prospective party to an agreement to refuse to consent to ratification, in accordance with its constitutional requirements. Thus the United States Senate is free to deny its consent to a treaty negotiated by the executive branch, and although such an action might generate ill feeling among the other parties to the agreement, it falls within the Senate's proper sphere of authority. Under such conditions, the treaty could not be ratified by the President and hence would remain inoperative in regard to the United States. Among the major treaties rejected by the Senate are the agreements with Great Britain and Colombia of 1824 (suppression of slave trade); Texas, 1844 (annexation of Texas); Belgium, 1853 (extradition); Denmark, 1867 (acquisition of St. Thomas and St. John); Colombia, 1869 and 1870 (canal); Great Britain, 1869 (Alabama claims); Dominican Republic, 1870 (proposed purchase of the country by the United States); Great Britain, 1889, and France, 1892 (extradition); the seven Kasson treaties of 1902 (commerce); and the rejection of the Versailles Treaty. An interesting attempt to enable a country's voters to reject a treaty negotiated by their government was defeated overwhelmingly in a national referendum in Switzerland in 1977 by a vote of 1,153,594 to 351,749.

## Understandings

"Understandings" are statements attached to the ratification of a treaty by means of which a party to the agreement specifies its own interpretation of certain provisions of the instrument.[23] This is a quite common practice, by means of which states are enabled to place on the record what would be called advance interpretations, particularly with respect to intent. If and when these interpretations are found acceptable by the other party or parties to the agreement, they may serve as highly useful commentaries in the event of subsequent disagreement over the meaning of treaty provisions.

## Reservations

MEANING OF RESERVATIONS    Reservations are changes or amendments inserted into a treaty by one party as an implied or specified condition of ratification (Vienna Convention, Arts. 19–23). A reservation must be accepted by the other parties to the agreement if the agreement is to come into force and have legal effect. Normally a reservation has limiting effects; the state making reservation denies the applicability of a portion of the treaty to relations of that state with the other state or states that may be parties to the instrument. Occasionally reservations assume the character of "nullifying reservations," changing the text of the treaty itself. A famous example was provided by several of the reservations proposed in 1919 by Senator Henry Cabot Lodge of Massachusetts, which would have affected the conditions under which the League of Nations operated.

[23] See Hackworth, vol. 5, 144–53, for an extensive commentary on this topic.

**BILATERAL AGREEMENTS**    If the treaty is a bilateral agreement, few problems arise over a reservation: the other party either ratifies the original agreement as altered by the reservation or refuses to ratify it and thus kills the agreement.

**MULTILATERAL TREATIES**    Multilateral treaties, however, pose grave problems in connection with reservations.[24] It is generally agreed that two schools of thought prevail among the nations of the world. In the Americas, the view is held that a treaty is in force on a strictly national basis: those countries that accept another state's reservation are bound by it, whereas others may declare not to do so and are not bound by it as altered but only in its original form. The Governing Board of the Pan American Union expressed the inter-American view in this manner:

1. The treaty shall be in force, in the form in which it was signed, as between more countries which ratify it without reservations, in the terms in which it was originally drafted and signed.
2. It shall be in force as between the governments which ratify it with reservations and the signatory States which accept the reservations in the form in which the treaty may be modified by said reservations.
3. It shall not be in force between a government which may have ratified with reservations and another which may have already ratified, and which does not accept such reservations.[25]

A different point of view is generally held among European states and has been shared by the secretariats of both the League of Nations and the United Nations. It has been outlined as follows:

A State may make a reservation when signing, ratifying or acceding to a convention, prior to its entry into force, only with the consent of all States which have ratified or acceded thereto up to the date of entry into force; and may do so after the date of entry into force only with the consent of all States which have therefore ratified or acceded.[26]

The interesting feature of this conflict of views is that the International Court of Justice supported a theory essentially identical with the inter-American view in the Advisory Opinion on *Reservations to the Convention*

---

[24]See Fitzmaurice, "Reservations to Multilateral Conventions," 2 *Int'l. and Comp. Law Q.* (1953), and Hackworth, vol. 5, 130–31 (one of the clearest statements on this point). See also the unusual approach adopted in Gamble, "Reservations to Multilateral Treaties: A Macroscopic View of State Practice," 74 *AJIL* 372 (1980). The new standard work on the subject is Horn, *Reservations and Interpretive Declarations to Multilateral Treaties* (1988).

[25]See 45 *AJIL* 111 (1951 Supp.); refer also to Fenwick, "Reservations to Multilateral Treaties," 45 *AJIL* 145 (1951).

[26]45 *AJIL* 110 (1951 Supp.).

*on the Prevention and Punishment of the Crime of Genocide in 1951.*[27] On the other hand, the International Law Commission tended to follow the League of Nations–United Nations point of view in its own recommendations.[28] Sensibly enough, however, the commission also recommended a practice already encountered frequently in the states' actual usages: it suggested that each treaty should contain its own specifications of the status to be granted to reservations made on the occasion of the various steps in the formation of the treaty (signature, ratification, accession—in the case of multilateral agreements).

Article 20 of the Vienna Convention provides that

1. A reservation expressly authorized by a treaty does not require any subsequent acceptance by the other contracting States unless the treaty so provides.
2. When it appears from the limited number of the negotiating States and the object and purpose of a treaty that the application of the treaty in its entirety between all the parties is an essential condition of the consent of each one to be bound by the treaty, a reservation requires acceptance by all the parties.
3. When a treaty is a constituent instrument of an international organization and unless it otherwise provides, a reservation requires the acceptance of the competent organ of that organization.
4. In cases not falling under the preceding paragraphs and unless the treaty otherwise provides:
    (a) acceptance by another contracting State of a reservation constitutes the reserving State a party to the treaty in relation to that other State if or when the treaty is in force for those States;
    (b) an objection by another contracting State to a reservation does not preclude the entry into force of the treaty as between the objecting and reserving States unless a contrary intention is definitely expressed by the objecting State;
    (c) an act expressing a State's consent to be bound by the treaty and containing a reservation is effective as soon as at least one other contracting State has accepted the reservation.
5. For the purposes of paragraphs 2 and 4 and unless the treaty otherwise provides, a reservation is considered to have been accepted by a State if it shall have raised no objection to the reservation by the end of a period of twelve months after it was notified of the reservation or by the date on which it expressed its consent to be bound by the treaty, whichever is later.

And Article 21 of the same treaty states that

1. A reservation established with regard to another party in accordance with articles 1, 20 and 23:

---

[27] *ICJ Reports, 1951* (Pleadings, Oral Arguments), May 28, 1951, in 45 *AJIL* 579 (1951); see also Liang, "The Third Session of the International Law Commission: Review of Its Work by the General Assembly—I," 46 *AJIL* 483 (1952), for a detailed analysis of the opinion.
[28] 45 *AJIL* 106 (1951 Supp.); and Liang, "The Practice of the United Nations with Respect to Reservations to Multipartite Instruments," 44 *AJIL* 117 (1950).

(a) modifies for the reserving State in its relations with that other party the provisions of the treaty to which the reservation relates to the extent of the reservation; and

(b) modifies those provisions to the same extent for that other party in its relations with the reserving State.

2. The reservation does not modify the provisions of the treaty for the other parties to the treaty *inter se*.

3. When a State objecting to a reservation has not opposed the entry into force of the treaty between itself and the reserving State, the provisions to which the reservation relates do not apply as between the two States to the extent of the reservation.

On January 12, 1952, the General Assembly of the United Nations adopted a set of recommendations dealing with reservations to multilateral treaties.[29] The first of the three points brought out was a recommendation that the organs of the United Nations, specialized agencies, and states should, in preparing multilateral agreements, consider inserting provisions declaring the admissibility or nonadmissibility of reservations and the effects to be given to such reservations if they are permitted.

The second recommendation, relating to the Convention on the Prevention and Punishment of the Crime of Genocide, was that states should be guided by the relevant Advisory Opinion of the International Court of Justice. However, in the opinion the court failed to indicate who should decide whether a given reservation to the particular instrument in question was or was not compatible with its object and purpose.

Finally, the General Assembly requested the Secretary-General, in registering treaties deposited with the Secretariat, to accept future documents containing reservations or objections, without passing on the legal effects of such additions.

## Proclamation of Treaties

The constitutional requirements of many countries demand some further step beyond ratification of a treaty or the conclusion of an executive agreement in order to create as binding a force on natural and legal persons as domestic law is. In Belgium, for instance, promulgation of a treaty is required, and in Switzerland, a treaty must be published in the official government journal before it acquires domestic effects.

In this connection, it must be emphasized that certain treaties require the passage of domestic legislation before they have any effect on or apply to citizens in a given country. This requirement is always present in the case of non-self-executing treaties.[30]

---

[29] Text reprinted, 46 *AJIL* 66 (1952 Supp.)

[30] See Evans, "Self-Executing Treaties in the United States of America," 30 *BYIL* 178 (1953). Refer also to the decisions in the *Sei Fujii* case (1952), in Chapter 7, nos. 19, 20.

The domestic nature of the actions mentioned (proclamation, promulgation, publication, legislation) means that failure to carry out the implementary acts subsequent to ratification of a treaty does *not* free a state from any responsibilities incurred through ratification. The treaty stands for the ratifying government, and that government's obligations toward the other parties to the agreement continue in force despite the nonperformance of the domestic acts called for.

## Registration

The registration of international treaties is not a new idea. The practice of states, on the other hand, was governed to a large extent by the concept of secret diplomacy. The search for the causes of World War I, however, led to strong criticism of secret diplomacy, and President Woodrow Wilson emerged as the leader of a segment of international public opinion favoring not only open diplomacy but also the registration of treaties as a means of ensuring publicity for their conclusion as well as for their contents.[31]

Although the expectation of open diplomacy and full public knowledge concerning the making and contents of all kinds of agreements among nations has proved to be illusory, the idea of registering treaties has actually been implemented, largely as the result of Wilson's crusade.

LEAGUE OF NATIONS' PROVISIONS FOR REGISTRATION    Article 18 of the League Covenant provided that "every treaty or international engagement entered into hereafter by any Member of the League shall be forthwith registered with the Secretariat and shall as soon as possible be published by it. No such treaty or international engagement shall be binding until so registered."

UNITED NATIONS' PROVISIONS FOR REGISTRATION    The Charter of the United Nations provides in Article 102 for the compulsory registration of international treaties and agreements:

(1) Every treaty and every international agreement entered into by any Member of the United Nations after the present Charter comes into force shall as soon as possible be registered with the Secretariat and published by it.
(2) No party to any such treaty or international agreement which has not been registered in accordance with the provisions of paragraph 1 of this Article may invoke that treaty or agreement before any organ of the United Nations.

The significant change in the Charter from the provisions of Article 18 of the Covenant is the avoidance of the principle that unregistered treaties would lack binding force for the parties in question. The wording of Article 102 (2) of the Charter is, of course, specific in that it provides that "no party" (member or nonmember) may invoke an unregistered agreement before organs of

---

[31]Note the wording of the first of Wilson's "Fourteen Points" "Open covenants of peace, openly arrived at, after which there shall be no private international understandings of any kind, but diplomacy shall proceed always frankly and in the public view."

the United Nations. The regulations adopted by the General Assembly in 1946 for the registration of treaties under Article 102 of the Charter also take into account the new and important field of agreements concluded by and among international organizations. Coverage of this subject, however, exceeds the scope of a general text on international law. [32]

## Effective Date of a Treaty

Modern treaties increasingly contain a provision specifying the date or the acts that will bring them into force. The best-known recent example is that of the Charter of the United Nations, which provided in Article 110 (3) that it would come into force when ratified by the five permanent members of the Security Council and "by a majority of the other signatory states." On a few occasions, treaties have specified that they would enter into force on signature: such was the case with the Agreement for the Promotion and Protection of Investments, concluded on June 19, 1980, between the United Kingdom and the People's Republic of Bangladesh.

In the absence of specific internal provisions, an international treaty is generally regarded as coming into force (1) after ratification by the parties and (2) after such ratifications have been exchanged or deposited, as the case may be. In the case of adhering states rather than original parties to an agreement, receipt by the depository agency of the notice of adherence is taken to be the effective date of the treaty for the adhering party, unless either the treaty specifies some other date or the notice or adherence itself contains a contrary date for the coming into force of the agreement.

## THE INTERPRETATION OF TREATIES

PRINCIPLES    Once an international agreement comes into force, the interpretation of its meaning may be questioned. In order to discover just what obligations or privileges are involved in such an instrument, writers on international law, beginning with Hugo Grotius, have attempted to formulate rules and principles. Until the appearance of international tribunals having obligatory jurisdiction, the chief value of such private endeavors has been their recognition by national courts in settling disputes. [33] The decisions and pronouncements of international courts, on the other hand, must be regarded as supplying more reliable and authoritative guides for the interpretation of treaties.

---

[32] The interested reader will find suggestive materials in Jessup, "Modernization of the Law of International Contractual Agreements," 41 *AJIL* 378, 381–85 (1947); see also Vienna Convention, Articles 76–80.

[33] The literature on the subject is extensive and diversified in its approach. Consult, *inter alis,* Lauterpacht's *Oppenheim,* vol. 1, 950–58 (which, incidentally, lists an unusually large total of 16 rules to be applied to the interpretation of treaties), and the illuminating opinions of the Legal Adviser of the Department of State concerning the 1963 Nuclear Test Ban Treaty, reprinted in 58 *AJIL* 175 (1964).

Most modern writers agree that two principles govern all commentaries in the interpretation of treaties: (1) the subject of interpretation is to determine the real meaning of the parties' accepting the instrument; and (2) unless there is evidence to the contrary, a treaty must be assumed not to be intended to be without effect or even to be absurd (see Vienna Convention, Arts. 31–33).

WORDING OF THE TREATY    A fundamental objective of interpretation is, therefore, to discover just what the parties to a treaty understood the agreement to mean when they entered into it. If one is to discover this, the treaty's actual wording must be regarded as taking priority over all other considerations. If the instrument's terms are clear and specific, no contrary intent can be asserted by either party to the agreement. A commonly cited example illustrates this principle. Article III, sec. 1, of the Hay–Pauncefote Treaty of 1901 provided that the Panama Canal should be "free and open to the vessels of commerce and war of all nations observing these Rules, on terms of entire equality." The United States asserted, however, that the term *all nations* did not include the United States, because that country had built the canal and was its owner and could not have had any intention to yield preferential treatment of its own ships, to wit, exemption from payment of tolls under the Panama Tolls Act. Elihu Root, one of the most prominent international lawyers in the United States, sided with the British government in its protest that the clear terms and intentions of the treaty had been violated by the exemptions in question. After much discussion in Congress, the exemptions were eventually repealed in 1914.

The words used in the agreement are interpreted in their usual, ordinary meaning unless, by some chance, such an interpretation would produce absurd, contradictory, or impossible consequences.[34] Because a treaty is expected to reflect the intentions of the parties involved, it may be necessary in interpretation to depart from the literal meaning of certain words, in order to avoid conclusions quite obviously contrary to the treaty's intent.

Gould cited the interesting problem posed for Poland by the Leaders' Agreement at Yalta.[35] Winston Churchill told the House of Commons on February 27, 1945, that the Yalta Agreement for an independent Poland obligated that country to be friendly to the Soviet Union: "The Poles will have their future in their own hands, with the single limitation that they must honestly follow, in harmony with their Allies, a policy friendly to Russia." Because independence would appear to imply a right to be unfriendly to anyone else at one's own discretion, the intentions of the leaders

---

[34]See *Sumitomo Shoji America, Inc.* v. *Avagliano et al.*, U.S. Supreme Court, June 15, 1982, slip opinion reproduced in 21 *ILM* 791 (1982), and digested in 76 *AJIL* 853 (1983), in which the Court relied on the "literal language" of the Japanese-American Treaty of Friendship, Commerce and Navigation.

[35]Gould, 335.

at Yalta appear to have been expressed poorly through the choice of the word *independence* with regard to Poland.

Treaties can also be interpreted, on occasion, in the light of other conventions covering the same subject matter. This was done, for example, by the Permanent Court of International Justice in the *River Oder Commission* case.[36]

RULES FOR INTERPRETATION OF MULTILINGUAL TREATIES    When a treaty is concluded in two or more languages, all texts being authentic, there may be considerable difficulties in interpretation. For instance, a given term may have a broad, liberal meaning in one of the languages, and its equivalent in another language may have a restrictive, narrow meaning. Under such conditions, the tendency has been to use the narrower meaning in interpreting the treaty. As in the case of virtually all other rules applicable to the subject, there may be limitations to this one, the most commonly cited being the decision of the Permanent Court of International Justice in the *Mavrommatis Palestine Concessions* case.[37] A question about the narrower meaning of *contrôle public* and the more extensive meaning of *public control* was decided in favor of the meaning of the English term.

On occasion a term in a treaty has a different meaning in the countries that are parties to the agreement; one commonly employed solution is to apply the meaning prevalent in the country where the action contemplated by the treaty is to take place. If, of course, such action is scheduled for, say, both parties to such agreement, then the application of this rule might result in the rather odd—and perhaps unacceptable—spectacle of different procedures or actions being taken in two countries under the terms of the same instrument.[38] An example that has caused much bitter debate since 1967 (concerning Israeli authority in the West Bank and Gaza) has been a phrase in Article 43 of the 1907 Hague Regulations, which apply to that occupation as customary international law. In the original and governing French text of Article 43, the phrase reads *l'ordre et la vie publics,* whereas the English translation (found in all texts) reads *public order and safety.* The two phrases are *not* identical in meaning, and the controversy has centered on the precise meaning of the French version in the English language.

LOGICAL INTERPRETATION    If grammatical analysis should prove insufficient to interpret a treaty, logical interpretation may be called into play. In other words, a given term or provision in an international instrument may be given a meaning that is logical and in harmony with the other parts of

---

[36] *River Oder Commission Case* (Six Gov'ts v. Poland), *P.C.I.J.,* 1929, Ser. A, No. 23, at 26 of the *Judgment* of Sept. 10, 1929.

[37] *P.C.I.J.,* 1924, Ser. A, No. 2.

[38] See Vienna Convention, Article 33, and Germer, "Interpretation of Plurilingual Treaties: A Study of Article 33 of the Vienna Convention on the Law of Treaties," 11 *Harvard Int'l. Law Jl.* (1970).

the agreement.[39] Such an interpretation seeks to construe dubious passages or terms in their context—a principle with which one can find little quarrel.

HISTORICAL INTERPRETATION    Again, courts have applied a historical interpretation to certain treaties, although this method appears to require considerable caution in its application. As long as a court restricts itself in this sphere to an examination of records concerned with the negotiation of the agreement and related documents, the historical approach to interpretation appears quite reasonable. But once a court accepts previous history (historical relations among the parties, for example), it begins to tread on highly questionable ground.[40]

PURPOSES AND FUNCTIONS    Still another approach to treaty interpretation—all others having failed—is to relate one's inquiry to the function intended to be served by the treaty. A court may attempt to interpret the instrument on the basis of its purposes.[41]

## Special Problems

EFFECT ON THIRD PARTIES    Certain special problems with the interpretation of international agreements should be mentioned at this point. One of these is the effect of such instruments on third parties. Many agreements, by their positive terminology, have been clearly intended to benefit third parties. This is particularly true when a treaty contains an adhesion or accession clause, enabling third states to become parties to the instrument and to acquire by such a step a variety of legal privileges that otherwise might or might not have been conceded to them. On the other hand, no treaty can create legally binding obligations or rights for a third party without the latter's consent. If that consent is stated expressly, then the third party accepts the obligation established intentionally by the treaty. A legal right is created if the parties to the treaty intend to grant that right to a third party, to a group of states to which that party belongs, or to all states, but in every instance, the third party must assent to the right. That assent, however, need not be expressed specifically (as would be the case for a treaty-created obligation); as long as the third party does not voice an objection to the right granted, assent is assumed by the parties to the treaty.

[39]See such pertinent opinions of the Permanent Court as the one on the *Interpretation of the Statute of Memel, P.C.I.J.,* 1932, Ser. A/B, No. 49, on the *Minority Schools in Upper Silesia,* 1928, Ser. A., No. 15; the *Mosul Case,* 1925, Ser. B, No. 12; and the opinion on the *Postal Service in Danzig,* 1925, Ser. B, No. 11.

[40]See Lauterpacht, "Some Observations on the Preparatory Work in the Interpretation of Treaties," 48 *Harvard Law* 549 (1935); also the Advisory Opinion of the Permanent Court of International Justice in *Jurisdiction of the European Advisory Commission of the Danube between Galatz and Braila, P.C.I.J.,* 1927, Ser. B, No. 14, p. 18.

[41]See Permanent Court of International Justice Advisory Opinions on the *Acquisition of Polish Nationality,* 1923, Ser. B, No. 7; on the *Competence of the International Labour Organization to Regulate, Incidentally, the Personal Work of Employers,* 1923, Ser. B, No. 13; on *Interpretation of the 1919 Convention Concerning Employment of Women during the Night,* Ser. A/B, No. 50; in the judgment on *Certain German Interests in Polish Upper Silesia,* 1926, Ser. A, No. 7; and in the *Chorzów Factory* case, 1928, Ser. A, No. 17.

If an obligation or a right is created for a third party, then this obligation or right cannot be terminated or modified without the consent of the third party. However, if a given treaty contains a rule already accepted as a part of customary international law, that rule would automatically be binding on all third parties, except for such parties as had objected to that rule from its very beginning.[42]

CHARTERS AND CONSTITUTIONS OF INTERNATINAL ORGANIZATIONS    Special problems of interpretation may arise in connection with the charters or constitutions of international organizations. The majority of such instruments, certainly in the case of most contemporary specialized agencies of the United Nations, contain provisions specifying how any disputes concerning interpretation are to be settled. But the Charter of the United Nations lacks such a precise formulation, even though it does contain a number of hints as to various possible methods of interpretation. The absence of specific provisions might indicate that unilateral interpretation is permissible. Again, designation in Article 92 of the International Court of Justice as "the principal judicial organ of the United Nations" could lead to the logical conclusion that the court should serve as the agency of interpretation. Finally, the provision of Article 10, which grants competence to the General Assembly to "discuss any questions or any matters ... relating to the powers and function of any organs provided for in the present Charter," could be viewed as authority for the General Assembly to interpret at least certain aspects of the Charter.

The factual development of Charter interpretation in the United Nations appears to have emphasized interpretation by the political organs of the United Nations, but on occasion not only the International Court of Justice but also the Secretary-General have handed down rulings as to the meaning of the applicability of the Charter.

## VALIDITY OF TREATIES

One of the oldest principles in international law is usually rendered as *pacta sunt servanda:* "treaties must be observed."[43] But as in the case of domestic contracts as well as of domestic legislation, there may be circumstances or conditions that will invalidate either. Hence we must examine not only the validity of the principle itself but also the conditions under which treaties are valid or invalid, as the case may be. It is not sufficient to verbally condemn

---

[42] Based on Vienna Convention, Articles 34–38, on the effect of treaties on third parties. See also Permanent Court of International Justice, *Free Zones of Upper Savoy and Gex, P.C.I.J., 1932,* Ser. A/B, No. 46.

[43] See the excellent historical analysis of the maxim in Wehberg, "Pacta Sunt Servanda," 53 *AJIL* 775 (1959), as well as the heavily documented study of Kunz, "The Meaning and the Range of the Norm *Pacta Sunt Servanda,*" 39 *AJIL* 180 (1945), and Vienna Convention, Article 26.

an international agreement, as did Pope Innocent X in the instance of the Treaty of Westphalia, as "null, void, invalid, iniquitous, unjust, damnable, reprobate, inane, empty of meaning and effect for all times." Rather, specific events or situations affect the validity of an agreement, or, put differently, validity is determined by the existence, or lack thereof, of binding force on the parties involved. Many considerations play a part in this matter, any or many of which may nullify an international agreement.[44]

1. *Capacity to contract.* A treaty is invalid if one of the parties to a bilateral agreement lacks the capacity to contract. That capacity is among the characteristics commonly ascribed to international persons. It does not mean that every state has a right to join in any treaty arrangement made between other states, but it does mean that every fully sovereign entity (and many international legal persons) has a right and an ability to conclude binding agreements with others of its kind. To be sure, a few states have been prevented in some manner from concluding specific kinds of agreements (neutralized states are unable to conclude treaties of alliance), but this circumstance would be no bar to concluding other valid agreements.

But if one of the parties to a treaty lacks the capacity to contract, the treaty is not valid. Thus, if a party—such as a nomadic tribe—is not a member of the family of nations, no treaty recognized as such under international law could be concluded with that party. To bring the matter closer to home, each of the 50 states that comprise the United States of America lacks the capacity to contract internationally, to enter into valid agreements with foreign states, under the provisions of the United States Constitution (Art. I, sec. 10, par. 3), which properly reflects the situation as it ought to exist in a federal state.[45] In a confederation the member units may or may not have the capacity to enter into treaties with foreign states, depending on domestic constitutional factors. In Switzerland, for example, the various cantons may conclude treaties with foreign states, but only with respect to "local matters."

Certain international organizations have the right to conclude valid international agreements with states and/or among themselves. This ability adds a new aspect to the problems of capacity to contract: in the case of such organizations, the governing statues, charters, or constitutions may have to be checked carefully in order to determine whether a given organization has the capacity to conclude a certain agreement or to commit itself to specific obligations.

---

[44] Validity, invalidity, and termination of treaties are dealt with in the Vienna Convention, Articles 26–75; consult also the authoritative study by Briggs, "Procedures for Establishing the Invalidity or Termination of Treaties under the International Law Commission's 1966 Draft Articles on the Law of Treaties," 61 *AJIL* 976 (1967).

[45] See Rodgers, "The Capacity of the States of the Union to Conclude International Agreements: The Background and Some Recent Developments," 61 *AJIL* 1021 (1967). On the other hand, see New York–Quebec: "Agreement on Acid Precipitation" (July 26, 1982), in 21 *ILM* 721 (1982), as well as Chapter 4 *sub* Federal States.

*2. Authority granted to agents.* The validity of an international agreement depends in part on the authority granted by their respective governments to the agents entrusted with its negotiation. As mentioned earlier, although binding agreements have on occasion resulted from the subsequent ratification of negotiations by unauthorized or improperly authorized agents, such occurrences are very rare. Normally a treaty negotiated by an unauthorized agent is not to be regarded as representing any obligation to the state on whose behalf he claimed to act. Also, if an agent exceeds the powers conferred on him, any agreement representing the use of such excess authority cannot be presumed to create any obligation for his state if the other parties have been notified beforehand of the restrictions on his authority (Vienna Convention, Art. 47).

On the other hand, a state would most likely be held responsible for any injury suffered by another state when the latter reasonable assumed that the negotiating agent or organ of the first state was indeed competent to conclude an agreement.

*3. Duress or coercion (on party or parties).* A treaty is not necessarily invalid if it is accepted by one or several parties under duress or coercion. This sounds like an unreasonable dogma, and its practical application may be the cause of untold difficulties. Obviously a treaty, to be valid, must receive the assent or acceptance of two or more parties; a unilateral declaration by one state is not binding (in the legal sense, although it may be so in the political sphere) on other states and does not create legal obligations. *Assent* or *acceptance,* furthermore, is usually modified by writers by the adjective *voluntary*—a necessary modification, they believe. Yet, and this is where the problem arises: Are there many treaties that lack this voluntary aspect? Is not every peace treaty at the end of a war imposed by the victors on the vanquished on a involuntary basis, under duress? However, the same writers who stress the need of free assent also maintain that the particular duress involved in a peace treaty does not negate its validity, and thus they place peace treaties in an essentially separate category.[46] The traditional view—that the consent of the defeated state is required to make a peace treaty legally valid—though observed in the case of Japan in 1951, has been replaced in some modern instances by a new attitude: the consent of Italy was not required for the coming into effect of the Italian peace treaty after World War II, and although Italy, Bulgaria, and Finland did sign their respective peace treaties, Hungary and Romania did not—yet no one has claimed that the latter peace treaties were not valid.

*4. Personal duress or intimidation.* A treaty is invalid when personal duress has been brought to bear against the negotiators of one party (Vienna Con-

---

[46]Brierly, 319, 332. See Vienna Convention, Art. 42, which reads "A treaty is void if its conclusion has been procured by the threat or use of force in violation of the principles of international law embodied in the Charter of the United Nations." Consult also the pioneer study by Malawer, *Imposed Treaties and International Law* (1977), as well as McNair, "The Legality of the Occupation of the Ruhr," 5 *BYIL* 17 (1924).

vention, Art. 51). The classic example cited throughout the relevant literature is Napoleon's threat in 1807 to have Ferdinand VII of Spain arraigned at
a trial for treason unless he abdicated. After Napoleon's defeat at the Battle
of Leipzig, the invalidity of the agreement was confirmed.

An instance of the use of intimidation, not so much against the person of
a head of state but involving the threat of wholesale bombing, took place in
1939. On March 14 of that year, German Chancellor Adolf Hitler summoned
President Hacha of Czecho-Slovakia to Berlin. When Hacha and his foreign
minister arrived at the Reich chancellery at 1 A.M. on the 15th, Hitler and
a group of advisers demanded the immediate surrender of Czecho-Slovakia.
Hacha was informed that unless he signed an instrument of surrender by
5 A.M., 800 German bombers would attack Prague and other cities in Czecho-
Slovakia without warning. At 4 A.M., President Hacha yielded and signed
an agreement creating the Protectorate of Bohemia and Moravia. Technically
the instrument placed the Czechs under German protection, with assurances
of "autonomous development of indigenous life in accordance with their
character."[47] Hacha, who then served as "president" of the protectorate, was
regarded as a traitor by the postwar "National Front" in Czechoslovakia and,
without a trial, was allegedly beaten to death in a Prague jail in 1945.

5. *Use of fraud in negotiation.* A treaty whose negotiation involved fraud
would be considered invalid. Modern history can show very few instances
in which outright fraud was a part of treaty negotiation, but this does
not preclude the possibility of such instances occurring in the future.[48]
However, mere failure to disclose some facts during negotiation when such
disclosure would weaken the case or argument of one of the negotiating
parties should not be taken as a case of fraud. Only deliberate fraudulent
misrepresentation during the course of negotiation, such as the use of falsified
maps or documents or false statements as to facts, would have the effect of
invalidating the resulting agreement.

6. *Corruption of a state agent.* At the insistence of several Third World
delegations at the 1969 Vienna Conference, Article 50 was added to the
Vienna Convention. It provides that if the expression of a state's consent
to be bound by a treaty has been procured through the corruption of its
representative directly or indirectly by another negotiating state, the first
state may invoke this corruption as invalidating its consent to be bound by
the treaty.

7. *Substantial error.* A treaty is voidable—or, in some instances, void *ab
initio*—if it can be shown that the agreement was concluded as a result
of substantial error concerning the facts. In other words, if in the course
of negotiation and ratification an incorrect assumption is made by one of
the parties, then the treaty may be considered void, or the party in question

---

[47] *NYT,* Mar. 15 and Mar. 22, 1939).
[48] The interested reader is referred to Gould, 321, n. 1, for two nineteenth-century instances
of fraudulent practices. See Vienna Convention, Art. 49; and also Hackworth, vol. 5, 159–
60.

may consider it "voidable"—or, at the very least, refuse to be bound by the agreement. An illustrative instance might be the use of an incorrect map— note that in this case it would be an *erroneous* map, not one deliberately falsified to defraud the other party (see Vienna Convention, Art. 48).

8. *Conformity to other agreements.* A treaty is not necessarily invalid if its provisions do not conform to earlier agreements concluded among the same parties. In the event of inconsistency between a new treaty and earlier agreements between the same parties, the general principle that applies is that the latest agreement prevails.

If a new treaty violates the rights of a third state under an earlier agreement with one of the parties to the new instrument, the obligations of the older treaty take precedence over those in the newer treaty.[49] Most authorities agree that under such circumstances the newer treaty is not necessarily invalid. Only obligations affecting a third party (that is, *not* a party to the new agreement) prevail over the text of the new treaty. In other words, both treaties would seem to be in force, and if inconsistencies between the two result in loss or damage to a third party, appropriate remedies or damages ought to be provided for by the parties to the new agreement, which, after all, is the cause of the inconsistency existing.

9. *Inconsistency with provisions of UN Charter.* A treaty inconsistent with the provisions of the Charter of the United Nations has to yield to the Charter, provided that all parties to the agreement are members of the United Nations.[50]

10. *Conflict with international law.* Is a treaty invalid if its provisions contradict principles of general customary or conventional international law? A majority of writers believe such is the case. Their attitude reflects a conviction that a combination of the rules of customary law and the rules laid down in law-making treaties constitutes a body of principles to which treaties between states must conform, even if one of the parties to the agreement has not ratified or acceded to a specific law-making treaty touching on the subject matter of the agreement in question. Opinion is still divided as to whether international law recognizes the existence within its legal order of rules from which the law does not permit any derogation (peremptory norms). The International Law Commission, in drafting the Vienna Convention on the Law of Treaties, held that the law of the Charter prohibiting the use of force in reality presupposed the existence in international law of peremptory rules and concluded that a treaty would be void if it conflicted with a peremptory norm of general international law "from which no derogation was permitted and which could be modified only by

---

[49]See Gould, 325–26; Hackworth, vol. 5, 161–62, and especially Lauterpacht's *Oppenheim,* vol. 1, 894–95.
[50]See the Charter, Art. 103; consult also Lauterpacht's *Oppenheim,* vol. 1, 895–96. Gould, 326, believed that Art. 103 meant that the Charter would also take precedence over any treaties concluded with nonmembers "if only before United Nations organs."

a subsequent norm of general international law having the same character" (Vienna Convention, Art. 53).[51] The Convention itself defines a peremptory norm of general international law as a "norm accepted and recognized by the international community of states as a whole as a norm from which no derogation is permitted and which can be modified only by a subsequent norm of general international law having the same character."

The concept of *jus cogens*, or peremptory norms, was subsequently introduced in a number of other agreements, notably in the 1986 Convention on Treaties between States and International Organizations or between International Organizations.

The current widely accepted view asserts that peremptory norms do exist. It appears that to be *jus cogens* norms, rules must satisfy at least four criteria: they must be norms of *general* international law; they must be accepted by the community of states *as a whole*; they must not be capable of derogation; and there must not exist any possibility that such norms can be modified in any way except by the appearance of new peremptory norms of the same character.[52]

It is, of course, difficult to pinpoint the peremptory norms in existence today. Although some scholars still debate the very existence of such norms,[53] a majority of scholars now appear to support the existence of *jus cogens*. Many commentators on the law believe that all main principles laid down in the UN Charter qualify as peremptory norms and cite Article 103 of the Charter in support of their views. That Article specifies that obligations of states under that instrument enjoy precedence over all other national commitments. That provision alone appears to be sufficient to place those principles above any other principles or norms. Thus Article 103 appears to define a group of rules of peremptory character.

In addition, the traditional rule of the inviolability of diplomatic agents appears to qualify as a peremptory norm. Hannikainen listed at least five other categories of such norms possessing peremptory character: (1) the prohibition on the use of aggressive force between states, (2) respect for the self-determination of peoples, (3) respect for basic human rights, (4) respect for the rules guaranteeing the international status of sea, air, and space beyond the limits of national jurisdiction, and (5) respect for the basic in-

---

[51] Article 64 of the Vienna Convention provides that "if a new peremptory norm of general international law of the kind referred to in Article 53 emerges, any existing treaty which is in conflict with that norm becomes void and terminates."

[52] See Hannikainen, *Peremptory Norms* (jus cogens) *in International Law: Historical Development, Criteria, Present Status* (1988), at 21–22.

[53] See Sztucki, *Jus Cogens and the Vienna Convention on the Law of Treaties: A Critical Appraisal* (1974) for a carefully researched denial of the existence of peremptory norms; Hannikainen, *op. cit. supra*, n. 52, 315 ff.; and Stephens, *Enforcement of International Law in the Israeli-Occupied Territories* (Al-Haq, Occasional Paper No. 7, 1989), at 31, 34, for defenses of the existence and importance of peremptory norms. Consult also Meron, "On a Hierarchy of International Human Rights," 80 *AJIL* 1, at 13–21 (1986).

ternational rules governing armed conflicts.[54] Proponents of the existence of the *jus cogens* concept also commonly cite the dissenting opinion of Judge Schucking in the *Oscar Chinn* case.[55]

It should also be pointed out that the Vienna Conference was cognizant of the strong criticisms voiced against the concept of *jus cogens* and added in Article 66(a) of the Vienna Convention the provision that "any one of the parties to a dispute concerning the application or the interpretation of Article 53 or 64 may, by a written application, submit it to the International Court of Justice for a decision unless the parties, by common consent, agree to submit the dispute to arbitration." As Zacklin pointed out,[56] this provision means that the convention provided a procedure by which, at least in theory, rules of *jus cogens* could emerge from judicial or arbitration decisions as well as from the practice of states.

*11. Immoral object.* Is a treaty void or voidable because it has an immoral object as its substance? Lauterpacht has given a most persuasive affirmative answer.[57] But dissent must be registered: to grant validity to the position taken by Lauterpacht implies not only that whatever is immoral is *ipso facto* illegal but also that states generally agree on what may be considered immoral. Certainly there are grave doubts about both assumptions. As yet, morality and legality have not been united in marriage, as far as states are concerned, and definitions of immorality may, and indeed do, differ greatly, not only among different civilizations in the world but even among the member states of the "Western" group.

*12. Oral agreement.* An agreement is not invalid because it is an oral agreement rather than a written instrument.[58] An agreement reached verbally between agents of states who are capable of binding their respective governments is quite sufficient—provided that the individuals in question intend at the time to conclude a binding agreement. Nevertheless, a written instrument is preferable to a verbal agreement, if only to prevent subsequent disputes about the nature of the understanding that has been reached.

*13. Intention.* Finally, a unilateral declaration, if conceived as being a treaty, is as binding an international obligation as if it were a negotiated instrument. Thus the unilateral declarations made by certain European states to the League of Nations on their treatment of minority groups or the declarations relating to the Optional Clause by which states accept in advance

---

[54] *Id.*, 315 ff.

[55] *Oscar Chinn Case (Belgium v. Great Britain)*, P.C.I.J., 1934, Ser. A/B, No. 63, 148.

[56] Zacklin, "Challenge of Rhodesia: Toward an International Policy" *International Conciliation*, Nov. (1969), 18, n. 25.

[57] Lauterpacht's *Oppenheim*, vol. 1, 896–97. See also von Verdross, "Forbidden Treaties in International Law," 31 *AJIL* 57 (1937).

[58] *Eastern Greenland Case (Denmark-Norway)*, P.C.I.J., 1933, Ser: A/B, No 53; Garner; "The International Binding Force of Unilateral Oral Declaration," 27 AJIL 493 (1933).

the jurisdiction of the International Court of Justice for certain categories of disputes were binding obligations of a treaty nature.

## TEXTUAL ELEMENTS

There are no generally accepted regulations as to the actual format of a treaty; however, most treaties follow an established pattern in regard to their textual elements. Many agreements are prefaced by a preamble stating the reasons the agreement was concluded and the results expected to arise from it. Other treaties incorporate such a statement of purpose in the opening paragraphs of the agreement's actual text.

Next comes the substantive part of the agreement, containing the detailed provisions of the treaty. This is followed by a number of sections dealing with mechanical but quite important matters, such as details of the ratification process (or whether this process is not required), the method by which the agreement is to enter into force, the duration of the treaty if it is not stated to have indefinite duration, the method by which the treaty may be terminated, and, lately, provisions governing the registration and deposit of the instrument. In some bilateral and most multilateral treaties, there also is a provision in this concluding portion that specifies whether the agreement is to remain open for signature and how accession by states other than the signatories is to be handled (if such accession is to be permitted). This last part is quite often omitted from the actual treaty and is found in an ancillary protocol.

A highly desirable procedural provision that ought to be included in every modern treaty is an article outlining whatever method or agency has been agreed upon by the parties for the interpretation of the agreement.

## TERMINATION OF TREATIES

Most writers agree that there are six basic ways in which a treaty may be terminated: (1) in accordance with the terms of the treaty itself; (2) by explicit or tacit agreement of the parties concerned; (3) through violation of the provisions of the agreement by one party, the second party then asserting, if it so desires, that it considers the treaty abrogated by the violation; (4) by one party on the grounds that fundamental conditions on which the treaty rests have changed; (5) through the emergence of a new peremptory norm of general international law conflicting with the treaty; and (6) through the outbreak of hostilities between parties to the agreement (Vienna Convention, Arts. 54–64). A seventh, and obvious, cause of termination—particularly true in the case of bilateral agreements—is the disappearance (extinction) of one of the parties, by annexation or possibly by a natural disaster: all of Sri Lanka might sink beneath the Indian Ocean, and at once all bilateral treaties made by other states with that state would come to an abrupt end.

The fact that so many ways of termination are listed indicates that it is unrealistic to believe that any treaty will last forever. Even if a given instrument provides in its text that its duration shall be "in perpetuity," such an agreement will come to an end, sooner or later.

Let us now examine the methods of termination.

TERMS OF THE TREATY    Many treaties contain in their text specific details about their termination. In general, such provisions envisage three causes for the end of the agreement: performance, arrival of a fixed termination date, and denunciation of the agreement as outlined therein.

Executed treaties end when the acts called for by the agreement have been performed by the parties involved. Most examples are in the sphere of voluntary cession of territory by sale. When the purchasing state has transmitted the appropriate sums to the selling state, the title to the affected area is transferred and the treaty is terminated. The actual documents remain, of course, as evidences of the transaction and may help settle any disputes about the performance of the acts involved.

Many treaties contain a specific expiration date. On that date, the treaty is terminated unless there has also been a provision for extending the life of the agreement and the parties concerned have acted in accordance with that provision to extend their agreement's duration.

Again, many treaties contain provisions permitting denunciation (sometimes termed *renunciation*) of the agreement. Usually such provisions set a minimum duration of the agreement. After the date on which this minimum life comes to an end, the treaty continues in force but may terminate when denounced by a party. Commonly termination, in regard to the denouncing party, does not occur immediately but after a time interval (six months or a year are periods frequently utilized) between the time the notice of denunciation was filed and the effective termination of the agreement for the denouncing party. Normally no reason has to be given for denouncing a treaty when the action is taken in accordance with the relevant provisions of the instrument.

Treaty termination in accordance with the terms of the instrument was the method chosen by President Carter when he invoked Article X of the 1954 Mutual Defense Treaty with the Republic of China: termination after one year's notice by either party. This was fully in accord with Article 67(2) of the Vienna Convention (treating that instrument, prior to its coming into effect, as an expression of generally accepted rules of international law), which reads:

Any act declaring invalid, terminating, withdrawing from or suspending the operation of a treaty pursuant to the provisions of the treaty or of paragraphs 2 or 3 of Article 65 shall be carried out through an instrument communicated to the other parties. If the instrument is not signed by the Head of State, Head of Government or Minister for Foreign Affairs, the representatives of the state communicating it may be called upon to produce full powers.

The arguments voiced concerning the legal aspects of the termination of the Mutual Defense Treaty with the Republic of China did not really touch on the international law aspects of the matter. Rather, they related to certain foreign policy issues and particularly to a domestic question: whether the President should have obtained congressional or senatorial approval before terminating the treaty, that is, whether he was correct in assuming that he had the unilateral authority claimed to terminate an agreement originally approved through consent of the Senate.[59]

It must be pointed out that there is no rule of international law requiring that all treaties with a "derecognized" government terminate automatically with the end of recognition, provided the agreements in question relate to the area (territory) actually under the control of the derecognized government. Hence it was legal for the United States government to announce, some time after the denunciation of the Mutual Defense Treaty, that the slightly fewer than 60 other agreements concluded earlier with the Republic of China would be regarded as in force.[60]

**EXPLICIT OR TACIT AGREEMENT**    Any agreement between states may end by agreement of the parties to the instrument. Such agreement may take the form of a written declaration by which the parties abrogate a treaty. This method is most often encountered when a new treaty between them contains a provision terminating prior accords between them—referring to such earlier instruments by title and other details and announcing the effective date of their termination.

Similarly, states may terminate a treaty by implication, that is, through the conclusion of a treaty that obviously supersedes prior agreements among the same parties without mentioning such agreements in the text of the new instrument. And on occasion, it appears that a treaty has been terminated by a tacit agreement among the parties involved to let the treaty lapse through nonobservance. In other words, each in turn fails to comply with the terms of the treaty, and no one protests such nonobservance, because all are in

---

[59]*Goldwater et al.* v. *Carter et al.,* U.S. Court of Appeals, D.C., Nov. 30, 1979, 617 F.2d 697, reproduced in 18 *ILM* 1488 (1979). See especially 1501–2 on the presidential power to recognize governments and to void a treaty without congressional action. On appeal, the Supreme Court vacated the judgment of the Court of Appeals and remanded the case to the District Court with directions to dismiss the complaint: U.S. Supreme Court, No. 79–856, Dec. 13, 1979, reported in 19 *ILM* 239 (1980) and in 74 *AJIL* 441 (1980). On the other hand, see the *Memorandum, Termination of Treaties: International Rules and Internal United States Procedure,* by the Deputy Assistant Legal Adviser for Foreign Affairs, Department of State, in Whiteman, vol. 14, 461, in which the author asserted that "matters of policy or special circumstances may make it appear to be advisable or necessary to obtain the concurrence or support of Congress or the Senate."

[60]*NYT,* Dec. 18, 1978, A-1, A-10; see also U.S. Public Law 96-8, the "Taiwan Relations Act" of April. 10, 1979, in 18 *ILM* 873 (1979).

tacit agreement that they no longer wish to be bound by the provisions of the instrument.

VIOLATION OF PROVISIONS    In the event of a violation of the provisions of a treaty by one of the states that is party to it, the treaty is not *ipso facto* invalid or void, but must be considered voidable at the discretion of the other party or parties to the agreement. Such a voidance would most likely occur if the other parties regarded the violation as having injured them or as having eliminated the bases of the entire agreement.

The Charter of the United Nations contains a harsh-sounding approach to the question of unilateral violation. The relevant provision, Article 6, states that

a Member of the United Nations which has persistently violated the Principles contained in the present Charter may be expelled from the Organization of the General Assembly upon the recommendation of the Security Council.

It might be mentioned, as a matter of some interest, that the Charter (unlike the League Covenant) does not contain any provisions for the voluntary withdrawal of any member; thus the Charter (a treaty) lacks the denunciation feature found in so many international agreements.

CHANGED CIRCUMSTANCES    Is a treaty void or voidable because fundamental circumstances have altered since the agreement's inception? This question represents one of the most irritating problems in the realm of international agreements. Unilateral denunciation of a treaty on the grounds of changed circumstances has been justified, though often regretfully, by almost all modern writers on international law.

Since Vattel's time, the correctness of the concept of *rebus sic stantibus* has been recognized quite generally, not only by writers,[61] but also by the Secretary-General of the United Nations, in commenting on the termination of European treaties protecting minorities (between 1939 and 1947) through basic changes in conditions.[62] Numerous modern court decisions have also referred to the doctrine,[63] so that it may now be invoked by states. The International Court of Justice itself affirmed the doctrine of *rebus sic stantibus* in the *Fisheries Jurisdiction* case (*United Kingdom* v. *Iceland, Jurisdiction, ICJ Reports,* 1973, 18) when it held that "this principle and the conditions and exceptions to which it is subjected, have been embodied in Art. 62 of the Vienna Convention . . . which may in many respects be considered as a codification of existing customary international law." It should be pointed out, however, that these views have been disputed vigorously by a number

---

[61]See Vienna Convention, Article 62. Consult Brierly, 335–43; cf. Jessup, 151–52, 250–54; Lauterpacht's *Oppenheim,* vol. 1, 844.

[62]UN Document E/CN. 4/367, 36–38, 71 cited by Gould, 340.

[63]Thus the Permanent Court of International Justice, in *Nationality Decrees Issued in Tunis and Morocco,* 1927, Ser. B, No. 4, and partially in the case of the *Free Zones of Upper Savoy and the District of Gex,* 1932, Ser. A/B, No. 46.

of modern publicists. Thus Briggs referred to the doctrine of *rebus sic stantibus* as an "alleged principle of international law."[64] Unfortunately, some of the attacks on the doctrine's applicability departed from legal considerations and questioned the need for or the wisdom of the application of the doctrine in specific instances. Approaches like these have vitiated much of the validity of the legal criticisms with which such considerations of expediency and policy were intermixed. The present writer believes, however, that more recent practices and studies support the view that the doctrine of *rebus sic stantibus* represents a valid principle of international law.[65]

The real problem in the doctrine of *rebus sic stantibus* arises when invocation is sought in actual practice.[66] Few writers and fewer diplomats appear to be able to agree on when the doctrine could be justifiably invoked. Brierly observed that "there seems to be no recorded case in which its application has been admitted by both parties to a controversy."[67]

Interestingly enough, numerous governments opposed the inclusion of *rebus sic stantibus* in the final version of the draft code to go before the 1968 Vienna Conference (including such states as Colombia, Turkey, and the United States). The International Law Commission decided, however, to preserve the doctrine in the draft submitted to the conference.

Article 62 of the Vienna Convention contains two conditions for the application of the doctrine: (1) the existence of the circumstances subsequently changed "must have constituted an essential basis of the consent of the parties to be bound by the treaty" (that is, a fundamental change), and (2) the effect of the changes must have been such as "radically to transform the extent of obligations still to be performed under the treaty."

The same article also states that a fundamental change of circumstances may not be invoked if (1) the treaty established a boundary or (2) if the change was the "result of a breach by the party invoking it either of an obligation under the treaty or of any other international obligation owed to any other party to the treaty." Qualified authorities as well as courts also have concluded that the doctrine of *rebus sic stantibus* does not apply to treaties creating rights of passage[68] or treaties creating other property rights.[69]

It is clear that unless the entire fabric of international treaties is to be doomed to disintegration at the whim of any state invoking the doctrine of *rebus sic stantibus* to avoid obligations presumably assumed in good faith, the doctrine must somehow be limited. Because neither party to a treaty susceptible to invocation of the clause should self-judge the evidence, the

---

[64]Briggs, "The Attorney General Invokes Rebus Sic Stantibus," 36 *AJIL* 89, 93 (1942).

[65]See also the *Report* of the International Law Commission, in 2 *Yrbk Int'l. L. Comm.* 169, 256–58 (1966).

[66]Examples are few: the end of a number of concordats between the Vatican and several states (1861), the lapse of cultural agreements between Germany and a number of European states, concluded in the 1930s, and a few others.

[67]Brierly, 335; see also Corbett, 83–89.

[68]Lauterpacht's *Oppenheim*, vol. 2, 938–44.

[69]*Free Zones of Upper Savoy and the District of Gex, P.C.I.J.*, 1932, Ser. A/B, No. 46, 157.

decision about the nature of the changes and their effect on the treaty in question should be left to a competent international authority or tribunal.

IMPOSSIBILITY OF PERFORMANCE    Is a treaty void because one of the parties finds itself unable to perform the obligations called for? The answer must be in the affirmative, for impossibility of performance renders meaningless any attempt to perpetuate the existence of the instrument in question (Vienna Convention, Art. 61). A commonly cited illustration of this principle is a state that has concluded defensive alliances with two other states. Should those two then go to war against each other, the first state will obviously be unable to honor its commitments and its alliance treaties will be void. In such circumstances, it would be proper to assert not only a physical impossibility but also a legal impossibility of performance. Another condition under which impossibility could be advanced in defense of voidance would be if a state faced grave danger to its continued existence if it carried out the military, economic, or other obligations called for in a treaty—if, in other words, honoring the agreement would represent a real danger of self-destruction.

EXTINCTION OF ONE OF THE PARTIES    Finally, a bilateral treaty terminates with the physical disappearance of one of the two parties. This requires no comment. On the other hand, what happens if several states merge into a new unit? A treaty concluded prior to union by one of the states with an outside state commonly remains in force and, by agreement, binds the new union. Thus the treaty of peace, amity, navigation, and commerce, signed in 1846, and the consular convention, signed in 1850, between the United States and New Granada continued in effect despite the constitutional changes through which the Republic of New Granada became the Confederation Granadina, then the United States of Granada, and later the Republic of Columbia. Similarly, the treaties in force in 1918 between the United States and the Kingdom of Serbia did not terminate at the formation of the Kingdom of the Serbs, Croats, and Slovenes, but were applicable to the new entity.

UNUSUAL ABROGATIONS    Two unusual abrogations of treaties might be noted: On February 9, 1952, Italy "disowned" its peace treaty obligations (a partial abrogation?) to the Soviet Union, citing as the reason repeated Soviet vetoes in the Security Council that had barred Italy from membership in the United Nations. And on March 5, 1984, the president of Lebanon announced the abrogation of the May 17, 1983, accord with Israel. The present writer has not seen the text of that abrogation, but believes that the real reason (besides the pressure exerted by Syria on Lebanon) was the inability of the Lebanese government to fulfill its obligations under the agreement.

## Revision of Treaties

If unilateral denunciation of an international agreement, whether on grounds of changed conditions or for other reasons, is regarded as an undesirable practice because of the frequent intrusion of political considerations and because it undermines the principles of good faith and *pacta sunt servanda,* there still remains a need to provide procedures for the peaceful revision of treaties.

The literature on *peaceful change,* which was a common term in the legal literature of the 1930s, is vast, yet much of it is permeated with purely political arguments.

A fundamental assumption underlying any discussion of treaty revision is that whatever instrument is being considered came lawfully into existence and that all parties to it agree that the treaty is valid under international law.

Once this assumption has been established, the revision procedures may be discussed with some promise of success. The trouble that arises at this point is that the reasons advanced by a party desiring revision tend to be exclusively political in nature. This fact complicates revision, for though the lack of validity can be traced to legal causes and can be remedied by legal means, the intrusion of political issues renders impossible a juridical solution to the demand for revision.

Recognition of this, together with the realization that treaties (especially peace treaties) may require revision, led in 1919 to the incorporation of the problem of revision in Article XIX of the Covenant of the League of Nations. Unfortunately, political considerations prevailed in the postwar period, and the revision question was quietly shelved by the League's members.

What can effect peaceful revision of treaties? One obvious answer, illustrated by many modern instances, is to incorporate revision clauses in international agreements. Such clauses would be increasingly effective as their procedural provisions increased in detail as well as comprehensiveness. (For the effect of war on treaties, see Chapter 22.)

## SUGGESTED READINGS

### Treaties: General

Brierly, 317–45; Lauterpacht's *Oppenheim,* vol. 1, 877–976; Note: from United States Representative to the UN to the Secretary-General, on Reservations to Treaties, May 24, 1971, in 65 *AJIL* 810 (1971); U.S. Ratification of Tokyo Convention, Sept. 5, 1969, 64 *AJIL* 1 (1970); Bolintineanu, "Expression of Consent to be Bound by a Treaty in the Light of the 1969 Vienna Convention," 68 *AJIL* 672 (1974); Reisenfeld, "The Doctrine of Self-Executing Treaties and *U.S.* v. *Postal:* Win at Any Price?" 74 *AJIL* 892 (1980).

CASES

(1)Power to Conclude Treaties:
*United States* v. *Belmont,* U.S. Supreme Court, 1937, 301 U.S. 324.
*United States (Claim of United States and Venezuelan Co.)* v. *Venezuela,* 1909, in Hackworth, vol. 5, 156–57.

(2) Effect of Treaties:

*Haver* v. *Yaker,* U.S. Supreme Court, 1869, 9 Wallace (76 U.S.) 32.

*Whitney* v. *Robertson,* U.S. Supreme Court, 1888, 124 U.S. 190.

*Jurisdiction of the Courts of Danzig,* Advisory Opinion, *P.C.I.J.,* 1928, Ser. B, No. 15.

*Asakura* v. *City of Seattle,* U.S. Supreme Court, 1924, 265 U.S. 332.


## Vienna Convention on Treaties

Sinclair, *The Vienna Convention on the Law of Treaties* (2nd ed., 1984); Rosenne, *The Law of Treaties: A Guide to the Legislative History of the Vienna Convention* (1971); Kearney and Dalton, "The Treaty on Treaties," 64 *AJIL* 495 (1970); the "Letter of Transmittal" (Vienna Convention to the U.S. Senate), Nov. 22, 1971, together with State Department, "Letter of Submittal," in 11 *ILM* 234 (1972); Vierdag, "The Law Governing Treaty Relations between Parties to the Vienna Convention on the Law of Treaties and States Not Party to the Convention," 76 *AJIL* 779 (1982).


## Executive Agreements

CASE

*Aris Gloves,Inc.* v. *United States,* U.S. Court of Claims, 1970, 420 F.2d 1386, reported in detail in *Note* by Liverman in 12 *Harvard Int'l. Law Jl.* (1971), also in 64 *AJIL* 948 (1970).


## Treaty Interpretation

McDougal, Lasswell, and Miller, *The Interpretation of Agreements and World Public Order* (1967); Liacouras, "The International Court of Justice and Development of Useful 'Rules of Interpretation' in the Process of Treaty Interpretation," *Proceedings* 161 (1965); Gross, "Treaty Interpretation: The Proper Role of an International Tribunal," *Proceedings* 108 (1969); Gottlieb, "The Interpretation of Treaties by Tribunals," *id.,* 122.

CASES

*Interpretation of the 1919 Convention Concerning Employment of Women during the Night,* Advisory Opinion, *P.C.I.J.,* 1932, Ser. A/B, No. 50.

*Nielsen* v. *Johnson,* U.S. Supreme Court, 1929, 279 U.S. 47.

*Case Concerning Rights of Nationals in the United States of America in Morocco* (*France* v. *United States*), International Court of Justice, 1952, *I.C.J. Reports, 1952,* 176; reported at length, in 47 *AJIL* 136 (1953).

*United States of America ex rel. Treves* v. *Italian Republic,* U.S.–Italy Conciliation Commission, Case No. 95, Sept. 24, 1956; digested in 51 *AJIL* 436 (1957).

*Dole* v. *Carter,* U.S. Court of Appeals, 10th Cir., 1977, 569 F.2d 1109, reported in 72 *AJIL* 665 (1978).

*Advisory Opinion on Interpretation of the Agreement of 25 March 1951 between the WHO and Egypt* (*December 20, 1980*), International Court of Justice (1980) 20 *ILM* 88 (1981); *Weinberger, Secretary of Defense, et al.* v. *Rossi, et al.,* U.S. Supreme Court, March 31, 1982, slip opinion 21 *ILM* 660 (1982).

## Validity and Invalidity of Treaties

Sinha, *Unilateral Denunciation of Treaty Because of Prior Violations by Other Party* (1966); von Verdross, "Jus Dispositivuum and Jus Cogens in International Law," 60 *AJIL* 55 (1966); Schwelb, "Some Aspects of International *Jus Cogens* as Formulated by the International Law Commission," 61 *AJIL* 946 (1967). See also Nahlik, "The Grounds of Invalidity and Termination of Treaties," 65 *AJIL* 736 (1971), and also Schwarzenberger, "International Jus Cogens," 27–56 in his *International Law and Order* (1971).

## Termination of Treaties

Wright, "The Termination and Suspension of Treaties," 61 *AJIL* 1000 (1967); Lissitzyn, "Treaties and Changed Circumstances," *id.,* 895, one of the best brief studies of *rebus sic stantibus* known to the present writer. See also the text of the German-Czechoslovak Treaty (1973) voiding the Munich Agreement of Sept. 29, 1938, in 13 *ILM* 19 (1974); Briggs, "Unilateral Denunciation of Treaties: The Vienna Convention and the International Court of Justice," 68 *AJIL* 51 (1974).

CASES

*Terlinden* v. *Ames,* U.S. Supreme Court, 1902, 184 U.S. 270.

*Charlton* v. *Kelly,* U.S. Supreme Court, 1913, 229 U.S. 447.

*Van der Weyde* v. *Ocean Transport Co., Ltd.,* U.S. Supreme Court, 1936, 297 U.S. 114.

*Akins* v. *United States,* U.S. Court of Customs and Patent Appeals, 1977, 551 F.2d 1222, in 71 *AJIL* 791 (1977) (Customs Court decision [1976, 407 F. Supp. 748] *id.,* 357).

## Termination of 1954 Mutual Defense Treaty

Cohen, Remarks on "Legal Implications of Recognition of the People's Republic of China," *Proceedings* 240 (1978); remarks by Chiu, *id.,* 250 Scheffer, "The Law of Treaty Termination as Applied to the United States De-Recognition of the Republic of China," 19 *Harvard Int'l. Law Jl.* 931 (1978) (heavily documented); Henkin, "Litigating the President's Power to Terminate Treaties," 73 *AJIL* 647 (1979).

## Unusual Agreements

(A) The 1952 "Contractual Agreements" with West Germany

J. Bishop, Jr., "The 'Contractual Agreements' with the Federal Republic of Germany," 49 *AJIL* 125 (1955), Wright, "Some Legal Aspects of the Berlin Crisis," 55 *AJIL* 959 (1961); and on the legal status of Germany between May 8, 1945 and 1952, von Glahn, 273–90.

(B) The Israel–Federal Republic of Germany Reparation Agreement

Honig, "The Reparation Agreement between Israel and the Federal Republic of Germany," 48 *AJIL* 564 (1954).

# 18

# Peaceful Settlement
# of Disputes

## INTRODUCTION

One of the major purposes of law at any level is to deal with disputes: either to prevent them altogether or to settle them. This is certainly true of international law, and throughout its long history it has been concerned with disputes between states.

In the course of time, diplomats and legal writers realized that disputes are not all of the same kind and thus that different procedures had to be developed to deal effectively with a given type of problem.

CLASSIFICATION OF DISPUTES   The common classification of disputes divided them into two categories: political and legal; and in recent decades a third category has made its appearance: technical disputes. Almost by definition, each subdivision of this new type of dispute tends to be settled or handled by specialized agencies conversant with the problems and providing the special rules required by those questions.

Writers on international law have long been concerned with attempts to draw some kind of boundary line by which political disputes might be distinguished from legal disputes. The former were commonly referred to as *nonjusticiable,* the latter as *justiciable.* This distinction became an accepted part of positivist legal thinking and was enshrined in the provisions of several arbitration treaties.

The basic difference, using this terminology, appears to be that nonjusticiable disputes are those in which nonlegal considerations—political (such as "vital national interests"), economic, psychological, and so on—play such an important role that the application of legal rules would not settle the dispute. Justiciable disputes, on the other hand, are those in which there is not only a question of law, but the law also is truly relevant to the dispute and can be utilized to settle it. From a practical point of view, however, the distinction is all too often an academic one, for it is frequently very difficult to separate political and legal considerations.

Today most writers tend to view the difference between "legal" and "political" disputes as dependent on the attitudes of the parties involved. If, regardless of subject matter, the parties seek only their *legal* rights, then the dispute is classified as justiciable, as a "legal" dispute. If, however, one or both of the parties demand not only legal rights but also the satisfaction of some special interests, even though satisfaction would require changes in the prevailing legal situation, then the dispute is nonjusticiable, that is, a "political" dispute.[1] Needless to say, a distinction arrived at in such a manner merely reiterates the fact that in our existing world society, states sometimes view a decision based on law as a satisfactory device for settling international disagreements; at other times, they do not choose to adopt such a view.

One approach to the whole problem recommended by a number of authorities is to leave the determination of the nature of the dispute to the appropriate United Nations organ or specialized agency for referral to the International Court of Justice. Then, if the question of the nature of the dispute is raised again before the court, the court can itself make a final decision on the matter, using objective criteria.[2]

## DIPLOMATIC NEGOTIATIONS

The oldest and most common method of settling disputes and the least encumbered with procedural details is that of diplomatic negotiation. Classical antiquity already recognized a legal obligation to negotiate before resorting to the use of force. Thus the College of Fetials in Rome sent agents or heralds who presented the demands of their government to the other party in a dispute and asked for redress of Roman grievances before a state of war ensued. It may be argued that this procedure was nothing more than a formality, but the important thing is that the technical obligation to negotiate was present. The medieval period produced elaborate and wearisome discussions by canonists and theologians about the nature of a just war, and again, the need for negotiation before the use of force was agreed on by everyone. Hugo Grotius and his followers continued this tradition and insisted on the necessity of negotiation.

In later centuries, negotiation has been deemed to constitute one of the prior conditions necessary to grant any designation of justice to the use of force. Even if one and all could see that whatever negotiation was carried on had all the earmarks of pretense, that pretense had to be undertaken in order to satisfy the generally accepted standards. Resort to force without negotiation, attack without warning, continued to be condemned. But even when morality and justice were left out of the picture altogether, negotiation had one highly desirable feature: it was an inexpensive means by which a state might conceivably achieve its aims without going into the risks and

---

[1] Based on the reasonable analysis of the question found in Brierly, 367–68.
[2] This was done by the Court, for instance, in the *Advisory Opinion Concerning Conditions of Admission of a State to the United Nations*, *ICJ Reports, 1948,* 61.

expenses of a war. Hence it would have been foolish, so the thought would have run, to resort to force at once before trying negotiation first.

In our own time, hardly a week passes without one or more agreements being reached through negotiations between foreign offices, particularly since the number of sovereign states has increased so greatly during the past few decades. Because most diplomatic negotiations are conducted on the old basis of secrecy or at least relative privacy, the general public is not likely to realize the extent of current diplomatic negotiations. The United States alone concludes about 200 agreements (treaties and executive agreements) a year, and the United Nations, the international depository of treaties, has published since 1946 several hundred volumes containing thousands of international agreements. And in addition, many disputes are settled each year by negotiations that do not lead to a formal treaty. No one can tell how great this aspect of negotiation is today, but each major state annually settles scores or even hundreds of moot points with other states through letters and memoranda as part of its continuing diplomatic negotiations.

If additional evidence were needed to prove the importance of negotiation, one would only have to check on the provisions of some of the many international treaties for the peaceful settlement of disputes: almost every one of those instruments restricts is applicability to disputes that have not been possible to settle by diplomatic negotiation. The Permanent Court of International Justice discussed this principle in some detail in the *Mavrommatis Palestine Concessions (Jurisdiction)* case[3] and stated that "before a dispute can be made the subject of an action at law, its subject matter should have been clearly defined by means of diplomatic negotiations." The court admitted that it would have to decide in each case whether sufficient negotiation had preceded the submission of a dispute but said it would not overlook the views of the states concerned "who are in the best position to judge as to political reasons which may prevent the settlement of a given dispute by diplomatic negotiation."

## GOOD OFFICES

When the parties to a dispute find that it cannot be settled by diplomatic negotiation but that the conflict of rights or claims appears to be of sufficient importance, the technique of *good offices* may be invoked.

Some writers refer to this as a form of intervention; yet this term, having a specialized meaning in international law, does not appear appropriate in most instances. Only when armed force is used would *intervention* be the correct name for the process, such as when the Great Powers intervened in the Greco-Turkish quarrel over Crete in 1868. The normal meaning of *good office* is more adequately represented by *intercession* (the act of interceding — by a third state, a group of states, or even an individual of such standing

[3]*P.C.I.J.*, 1924, Ser. A, No. 2

as the Secretary-General of the United Nations—in an effort to bring the disputants together and to induce them to start or resume negotiations). The offering of good offices may, of course, be declined by either or both of the disputants, and that would be the end of the matter: such was the case with the 1981 Saudi Arabian peace proposals for the Middle East, with President Reagan's 1982 peace plan for the Middle East; and with the 1983 Contadora Declaration, in which Colombia, Mexico, Panama, and Venezuela proffered their good offices in seeking peaceful solutions to the problems of Central America.

Good offices may be exercised only with the agreement of both parties to a dispute. The third party is then allowed to attempt to bring the parties together so as to enable them to reach an adequate solution between themselves. Normally the profferer of good offices meets separately with each of the disputing parties; seldom, if ever, does the third party attend a joint meeting. The practice is particularly important when the two disputing states have reached the point that they have broken off diplomatic relations. Then the third party (always with the consent of the disputants) may act as a go-between, transmitting messages and suggestions in an effort to soothe the feelings of the aggrieved states and to restore an atmosphere in which the parties finally agree to negotiate together. For instance, the United States proffered, successfully, its good offices to Israel and Egypt and persuaded them (October 27, 1973) to agree to a meeting of military representatives in order to implement the cease-fire called for by the Security Council. Neither party regarded the U.S. action as unfriendly.[4] There is no obligation for any state to offer its services in this connection, nor are any of the parties to a dispute obliged to accept the proffered good offices.

The good offices normally terminate as soon as the disputing parties have been persuaded or assisted to resume negotiations. There are instances on record, however, in which both parties have invited the third state, whose proffer of good offices has been accepted or whose assistance for such purpose has been sought, to be present during the negotiations.

## MEDIATION

Often confused with good offices, mediation as a procedure to achieve the peaceful settlement of a dispute goes further than does the utilization of good offices: the mediator actively participates in the settlement itself. Mediation may be undertaken by a third state, a group of states, an individual, or an agency of an international organization.

Regardless of the nature of the mediator, he is expected to offer concrete proposals for settling substantive questions instead of merely contenting

---

[4]Both Hague Conventions for the Pacific Settlement of Disputes (1899 and 1907) emphasized in Article III that the right to offer good offices "can never be regarded by either of the parties in dispute as an unfriendly act." Consult also Moore, vol. 6, 239.

himself with making negotiation possible. The mediator therefore assists the parties directly and may meet with the parties either jointly or separately. His functions come to an end when the dispute is settled or when one of the parties (or the mediator) decides that the proposals are not acceptable. The proposals submitted by a mediator represent nothing more than advice; under no condition can they be taken to have any binding force on either party to the dispute.

Modern examples of mediation are numerous. Frequently cited examples include the U.S. mediation of 1866 between Spain, on the one hand, and Bolivia, Chile, Ecuador, and Peru, on the other; the mediation by Pope Leo XIII of the German-Spanish dispute over the Caroline Islands group in the Pacific; U.S. mediation between Russia and Japan in 1905 to end their war; U.S. mediation, in 1906, between France and Germany concerning their respective rights in Morocco; the mediation efforts of Dr. Ralph Bunche to end the phase of active hostilities between Israel and its Arab neighbors in 1948–1949; the (ineffective) U.S. attempt to mediate in 1965 between Great Britain and Guatemala in the dispute over the latter's claim to British Honduras (Belize); UN mediator Gunnar V. Jarring's mediation efforts in 1971 to end the Mideast dispute; the U.S. offer of mediation among Turkey, Greece, and Cyprus in an effort to end the island's crisis; and the mediation by the President of the United States between Egypt and Israel in 1978 (to bring about a peace treaty).

Since the beginning (September 1980) of the Iraq-Iran war, there were numerous efforts to end the conflict through mediation. The President of the UN Security Council appealed to both parties during that month to settle the dispute peacefully after ceasing to fight. The Security Council then adopted a resolution calling on both states to "refrain immediately from any further us of force." Then Olof Palme, former Swedish prime minister, was appointed by the Secretary-General to act as his special emissary to try to end the conflict, but he failed in his task. The 42-member Organization of the Islamic Conference attempted to use mediation to end the war, beginning in September 1980: Iraq then accepted a mediation commission plan, but Iran balked at the concept. The Conference finally ended its efforts in October 1982. Numerous groups and individual countries then proffered mediation plans to the antagonists: the Nonaligned Movement, the Gulf Cooperation Council, a mediation team of the Islamic Conference Organization, the Islamic Foreign Ministers Conference, and proposals for mediation by Saudi Arabia, India, Algeria, Turkey, and Japan. All these efforts failed after one or both parties turned down the offers, in almost all instances because Iraq refused to accept Iran's preconditions to ending the conflict. Eventually a special UN mediator, the Swedish UN ambassador, working under the Secretary-General, succeeded in laying the groundwork for a cease-fire between the two belligerents. The mediation by the UN Secretary-General himself was the key element in bringing about the cease-fire in the eight-year-old war. Acting under the authority of the UN Security Council, the

Secretary-General employed the 1987 Council's Resolution 598[5] demanding a cease-fire and bringing the two belligerents to meet and discuss an end to the war. The Secretary-General finally set the cease-fire for August 20, 1988. In July 1990 Iran and Iraq agreed to seek a permanent peace settlement through mediation by the UN Secretary-General.

The well-known recent problems and hostilities in Central America led several groups to offer their services as mediators. In 1981 El Salvador rejected a proposal by the Socialist International (through its Canadian vice-president) to mediate in the civil war in El Salvador by charging that mediation by outsiders was deemed to be "an act of intervention." In August/September 1984, four Central American states (Costa Rica, Nicaragua, Honduras, and Guatemala), in consequence of the 1983 Contadora Declaration, developed a peace plan for the area calling for free elections and total removal of all foreign troops and advisers, coupled with continuing efforts on the part of the four countries involved in the 1983 document.[6] Nicaragua accepted the 21-point plan on September 21, provided the "United States would halt its aggression against Nicaragua," but the United States reportedly urged its allies and friends in Central America to reject the scheme, and then appeared to have prompted Costa Rica, El Salvador, and Honduras to demand extensive changes in the proposal. The United States and Nicaragua proceeded to hold nine meetings in Manzanillo, Mexico, but on January 18, 1985, the United States suspended those bilateral talks, denying that any progress had been made in the preceding months. The United States intimated that any result from such talks would eventually be incorporated in a comprehensive settlement of Central American problems within the Contadora framework.

The Central American presidents, however, continued their peace efforts, as did the 13-member Contadora group.[7] On February 15, 1987, Costa Rica put forward a full-fledged peace plan for the consideration of the Central American presidents.[8] That scheme was supported in the U.S. Senate in a nonbinding resolution by a vote of 97–1. The five presidents endorsed the Costa Rican proposal and, on August 22 at Caracas, agreed to the creation of a 15-member committee of Latin American states to monitor the fulfillment of the peace plan. Nicaragua, however, rejected the plan as long as the U.S.-backed Contra insurgency continued.

Finally, Nicaragua's President Ortega offered a peace proposal of his own (November 14), based on a month-long cease-fire and amnesty. For the

[5] UN Sec. Council Res. 598 (1987) of July 20, 1987, text and related documents in 26 *ILM* 1479 (1987).
[6] See the collection of 12 documents, "The Contadora Process for Peace in Central America (June 9, 1984–January 10, 1985)," in 24 *ILM* 182 (1985), including U.S. statements on *Nicaragua* v. *United States;* also *CSM,* Apr. 11, 1985, 9. See U.S. Department of State, Special Report No. 115, *U.S. Efforts To Achieve Peace in Central America* (March 15, 1984).
[7] See Volman in *CSM,* June 6, 1986, 9–10.
[8] Text and *ILM* content summary in 26 *ILM* 573 (1987). For Nicaragua's reaction, see *id.,* 580.

ending of the U.S.-Nicaragua controversy, see the Case Study No. 2, following Chapter 8. It should be noted here, however, that the OAS assigned in
1989 a team of mediators to achieve a democratic transfer of power following
a democratic election in Nicaragua.

Elsewhere, Saudi Arabia's King Fahd agreed in late 1988 to act as me-
diator in a lingering boundary dispute between Bahrain and Qatar; former
U.S. President Carter and former Tanzanian President Nyerere were invited
to act as "comediators" in the civil war between Eritrea and Ethiopia; an
Arab League mediation team had reached a "dead end" in its efforts to end
Lebanon's continuing civil war; an OAS team had tried unsuccessfully to
end Panama's political crisis before the U.S. invasion, as the President of
Costa Rica had done, acting as a mediator; and on September 28, 1989,
the Soviet foreign minister offered to act as mediator between Israel and the
PLO.

A major modern employment of mediation in dispute settlement resulted
on April 14, 1988, in the signing of the Geneva Accords ending the Soviet
military role in the Afghan conflict. The United Nations had endeavored for
seven years to mediate a settlement involving a withdrawal of Soviet forces
from Afghan territory. One of the accords established a UN Good Offices
Mission in both Afghanistan and Pakistan to monitor the implementation
of the other accords.[9]

The most recent instances of actual or proposed mediation occurred in
May 1990. A Salvadorean government commission traveled to Venezuela
for UN-sponsored peace discussions with Salvadorean rebels, and Colombian leftist guerrillas asked former U.S. President Carter and Venezuelan
President Andrés Pérez to act as mediators in peace talks with the Colombian government.

On rare occasions, mediation of a civil war is offered by other states. One
example of this practice occurred in August 1947, when the 20 states represented at the Inter-American Defense Conference meeting in Brazil adopted
unanimously a proposal for joint mediation of the civil war then in progress
in Paraguay. More recently (1978), the United States, Guatemala, and the
Dominican Republic attempted unsuccessfully to arrange for Nicaraguan
President Somoza to engage in substantive negotiations with the rebel Sandinista leadership.

As with good offices, either or both parties to a dispute are free to reject
an offer to mediate, as was done in 1898 when the United States rejected
such offers by the Pope, Austria, France, and Great Britain, and in 1972,
when both sides in the Vietnam war rejected UN Secretary-General Kurt
Waldheim's offer of mediation. (See also below, *sub* "Arbitration," for the
*Beagle Channel Arbitration* and the settlement of that dispute reached through
papal mediation.)

---

[9] Afghanistan/Pakistan/USSR/United States, *Accords on the Peaceful Resolution of the Situation in
Afghanistan*, Geneva, Apr. 14, 1988, in 27 *ILM* 577 (1988).

# COMMISSIONS OF INQUIRY

Some international disputes have involved an inability or unwillingness of the parties concerned to agree on points of fact. In consequence, a number of bilateral agreements were concluded during the late nineteenth century, under which *ad hoc* fact-finding commissions were appointed to report to the parties in question on the disputed facts. Such commissions proved to be of particular value in determining boundary lines.

HAGUE CONVENTIONS (1899, 1907)    The Hague Peace Conference of 1899 established commissions of inquiry as a formal institution through Convention I for the Pacific Settlement of International Disputes. That instrument provided for the maintenance of a permanent panel of names, from which five were to be selected for specific cases. Each party to a dispute was entitled to select two commissioners, only one of whom was to be taken from its own appointees to the panel; the fifth commissioner was to be named by the other four. The report of such a commission was to be limited to a finding of facts and had in no way the character of an award. It was not expected, therefore, that the report would include proposals for settling the dispute in question. [10] The Second Hague Conference of 1907 expanded the procedural details in the earlier convention by prescribing such matters as the place of meetings, the languages to be used, and the filling of vacancies on a commission. One important innovation was the requirement that three neutrals had to sit as members of each commission of inquiry.

Commissions of inquiry, despite the obvious advantages for the disputants, have been used very rarely in the twentieth century. The best-known instance was in the famous *Dogger Bank* case. [11] This was a dispute between Great Britain and Russia, arising out of an attack in 1904 on British fishing vessels in the North Sea by Russian warships on their way to the Far East. On a foggy day, the Russians had opened fire on the British ships under the misapprehension that the latter were Japanese torpedo boats. One fishing vessel was sunk, and another was damaged seriously. Because the facts of the incident were in dispute between the two countries, the French government suggested using a commission of inquiry. A commission consisting of admirals from the British, Russian, French, Austrian, and American navies was selected to investigate and, interestingly enough, to fix responsibility for the incident. The group therefore was empowered to be more of an arbitration tribunal than a commission of inquiry, but it is nevertheless usually listed as an example of the latter. The commission met in Paris from December 22, 1904, until February 26, 1905, when it reported that no Japanese vessels had been anywhere in the North Sea and that the attack by the Russian fleet had been completely unjustified. The report was accepted by the parties to the dispute, and Russia paid an indemnity of £65,000 to Great Britain.

[10]See Hill, "International Commissions of Inquiry and Conciliation," *International Conciliation,* No. 278 (Mar. 1932), esp. 9–94.
[11]Scott, ed., *The Hague Court Reports* (1916), 403–13.

Unlike European states, the American republics have concluded numerous treaties calling for inquiry into disputes; most of these instruments have tended to emphasize conciliation more than the investigation. Among them are a six-country agreement concluded at the Conference on Central America Affairs (Washington, 1922–1923) and the so-called Gondra Treaty, which was one of the results of the Pan-American Conference in Santiago in 1923 and which was enlarged at two meetings in 1928 and 1929 to include conciliatory provisions. The last-mentioned instrument was used successfully in an investigation of the facts in the Gran Chaco conflict between Bolivia and Paraguay.

Recent instances of the use of fact-finding bodies include an "outside" commission to investigate (1969) the dispute between the St. Kitts/Nevis/Anguilla federation and the inhabitants of the island of Anguilla, and a UN fact-finding mission appointed in November 1970 to investigate the charge by the Republic of Guinea that Portuguese forces based on Portuguese Guinea had repeatedly invaded the republic's territory, on one occasion even the very capital of the country.[12] And see the report of the ICAO fact-finding investigation in the downing of Iran Air Flight 655 (1988).[13]

Before leaving the subject of commissions of inquiry, it should be mentioned that the League of Nations made use of such fact-finding bodies on at least six occasions.[14]

On December 18, 1967, the General Assembly of the United Nations adopted unanimously a resolution (2329 [XXII] 1967) urging member states to make more effective use of the existing methods of fact finding in accordance with Article 33 of the Charter. The General Assembly also requested the Secretary-General to prepare a register of experts whose services might be utilized for fact-finding purposes.

One of the more bizarre instances in the history of commissions of inquiry occurred in connection with the "Corfu incident" in 1923, in which the Italian general Tellini was assassinated on Greek territory while acting as a member of a commission sent to the Greek-Albanian border by the Conference of Ambassadors in order to delimit that border. The conference sent a commission of inquiry to the area in question (consisting of a representative of each of the four Great Powers) to report on Greek responsibility for the murder. The commission found by a 3-to-1 vote that Greece had exercised due diligence to discover and punish the guilty persons and hence was not responsible, even though the assassins were not discovered (Greece

---

[12]See *NYT*, May 25, 1969, 24 (Anguilla), Nov. 29, 1970, 29 and Dec. 16, 1971, E-5 (Guinea).

[13]Excerpted in 83 *AJIL* 332 (1989); see Chapter 13 *sub Ex Gratia* Payments.

[14]The commissions investigated disputes involving Sweden and Finland in 1920, Yugoslavia and Albania in 1921, the Allied Powers and Lithuania in 1923, Great Britain and Turkey in 1923, Greece and Bulgaria in 1925, and China and Japan (Manchurian crisis) in 1931.

stated that the murderers were Albanian bandits). The Conference of Ambassadors, however, suppressed the request of its own commission of inquiry and laid responsibility for the crime at the doorstep of Greece, which then was coerced into paying a 50-million-lira penalty to Italy.[15]

One of the most publicized modern commissions of inquiry was that appointed by UN Secretary-General Waldheim to investigate Iran's grievances against the United States and the deposed Shah of Iran. The five UN commissioners stayed in Tehran from February 23 to March 11, 1980, and then returned to New York without having been allowed to see any of the hostages in the U.S. embassy in Tehran. The commissioners announced that because of their failure to see the hostages, they would not issue a report on their investigation of the various Iranian charges. The Secretary-General then issued a statement saying that the commission of inquiry had suspended its work in Tehran but was prepared to return after consultation at United Nations headquarters. The inquiry never resumed.

## COMMISSIONS OF CONCILIATION

The procedure of peaceful settlement of disputes through conciliation means submitting a given dispute to an already-established commission or a single conciliator for the purpose of examining all facets of the dispute and suggesting a solution to the parties concerned. Either or both parties are, of course, free to accept or reject proposals of the conciliators (styled, in the case of an organized group, "commission of investigation and conciliation" or "commission of conciliation"). As in the case of mediation, conciliators may meet with the parties jointly or separately.

The decades since the end of World War I have seen the establishment, by bipartite or multipartite conventions, of scores of such bodies. Many of these treaties provide for the establishment of permanent commissions, which, in some instances, are even authorized to offer their services to the parties in dispute without being requested to do so. Others of the instruments in question call for the establishment of *ad hoc* commissions only after there has been a dispute. More recently, a number of agreements, some of considerable importance, have contained provisions for the creation of conciliation commissions, such as the Pact of Bogotá (1948) and the Treaty of Brussels (March 17, 1948). And respectable numbers of disputes have been submitted to the consideration of such bodies: in 1949, a dispute between Rumania and Switzerland; in 1947, a boundary dispute between France and Thailand; in 1952, a Danish-Belgian dispute; in 1955, two disputes between France and Switzerland; and in 1956, a disagreement between Greece and Italy.

[15]See the detailed account of the entire episode, including bombardment of the Greek island of Corfu by the Italian navy and occupation by Italian troops, in Barros, *The Corfu Incident of 1923: Mussolini and the League of Nations* as well as Chapter 19.

On the other hand, although such listings are quite impressive, the actual use of conciliation procedures represents an extremely rare phenomenon on the international scene. It has been suggested that other procedures for the settlement of disputes (arbitration, adjudication) are preferred because they provide for the issuance of a binding award of judgment, rather than leaving each party free to reject mere recommendation, as in the case of conciliation. It would be possible, of course, to expand already existing machinery and to provide conciliation services on a global basis.[16]

## ARBITRATION

EARLY DEVELOPMENT OF ARBITRATION    The procedure known as *arbitration* is one of the oldest methods used by Western countries to settle international disputes.[17] The Greek city-states not only evolved comprehensive procedural details for arbitration, used in the peaceful solution of many disagreements, but also concluded many treaties under which the parties agreed in advance to submit either all or specified categories of disputes to arbitration. In the medieval period, there was occasional recourse to the procedure, usually in the form of a papal arbitration, and almost every one of the classical writers on international law, from Vitoria and Suárez through Grotius to Vattel, endorsed arbitration. Some of these writers, notably Grotius, even advocated arbitration of disputes by assemblies or conferences of the Christian powers.

But although arbitration began to be used increasingly as a civil procedure, particularly between merchants, it did not play a prominent part in modern international relations until 1794, when Jay's Treaty provided for the use of arbitration to settle disputes between the United States and Great Britain. One single arbitration under the provisions of the treaty resulted in more than 500 awards to private claimants.

American interest in arbitration has continued ever since that agreement. Thus the New York Society of Peace (founded in 1815) and the Massachusetts Peace Society carried on consistent propaganda campaigns and, in 1820, appealed to Congress to promote arbitration of disputes as a permanent aspect of American foreign policy. Their efforts bore some fruit: Article 21 of the Guadeloupe-Hidalgo treaty with Mexico (1848) provided for the arbitration of all future disputes before either country had recourse to war. Another Anglo-American arbitral tribunal, operating under the provisions of the Treaty of London in 1853, settled more than 100 claims. On the other hand, an American-Mexican commission established under a treaty concluded in 1868 handled more than 2,000 claims, but dismissed about 1,700 of these.

---

[16]See the optimistic presentation in Clark and Sohn, *World Peace through World Law* (1958), 321–30, and the definitive work by Cot, *International Conciliation* (1972).
[17]Consult the standard historical treatment of the subject in Ralston, *International Arbitration from Athens to Locarno* (1929), and see Stuyt, *Survey of International Arbitration, 1794–1970* (1972, 2nd printing, 1976), for a modern analysis.

The single event that suddenly called attention to the usefulness of the procedure was the successful arbitration under the Washington Treaty of 1871 of the *Alabama* claims (Geneva, 1872) in which the United States won an award of $15.5 million in compensation for the direct losses caused by Confederate cruisers illegally supplied to the South by British interests. At once, great interest in the procedure was manifested in many places. As early as 1875, the private Institute of International Law drafted a body of arbitral procedure rules. At the First International Conference of American States (Washington, 1889–1890), a comprehensive Plan of Arbitration was elaborated but not ratified.

HAGUE PEACE CONFERENCE (1899)     The acceptance of arbitration on a large-scale basis came at the Hague Peace Conference of 1899. The Convention for the Pacific Settlement of International Disputes (revised in 1907) established the Permanent Court of Arbitration. Actually this title is a misnomer, for the treaty did not create a tribunal in the orthodox sense of the term. Instead, the "court" consisted of a panel, a list of four names of individuals submitted to a central office in The Hague by each signatory to the convention. When a dispute was referred to the court, each party (unless it had agreed to some other procedure) selected two arbitrators from the panel. Only one of the two could be a national of the state in question. The four arbitrators then selected an umpire. Thus there was a permanent panel of arbitration, but the court itself had to be constituted anew for each case. In order to bring the Hague machinery into operation, however, a network of bipartite arbitration treaties was required to supplement the 1899 convention.

Despite the relative simplicity and inexpensiveness of the Hague procedure, only a very small number of disputes (such as 14 awards between 1902 and 1914) have been settled by reference to it, notably the Newfoundland Fisheries dispute between the United States and Great Britain in 1910.[18]

Although the nations of the world have bypassed the institution of the Hague Court, they have nevertheless used its procedure, arbitration, to an increasing extent during the twentieth century, and hundreds of bipartite compulsory arbitration treaties have come into existence.

The largest accumulation of claims (over 70,000) were handled by the more than 40 mixed arbitral tribunals established after World War I to cover claims by nationals of the Allied and Associated Powers against the three Central Powers.

---

[18]See Levie, "Final Settlement of the *Pious Fund Case*," 63 *AJIL* 791 (1969); also study the rather plaintive Circular Note of the Secretary General, Permanent Court of Arbitration, of March 3, 1960, in 54 *AJIL* 933 (1960 Supp.), which contains a plea for more extensive utilization of the facilities of the court. Today the major "practical" function of the Permanent Court appears to occur whenever there is a vacancy on the International Court of Justice. The "national groups" of the Permanent Court nominate candidates from among whom the General Assembly and the Security Council of the United Nations elect new judges to the International Court of Justice.

PROCEDURE OF ARBITRATION    The first characteristic of arbitration is the free selection of arbitrators—quite different from judicial settlement by a permanently established true court.

Second, arbitration treaties generally specify that the arbitrators must respect the rule of international law and must attempt to come as close as possible in their award to what would normally be regarded as a legal decision. Obviously some disputes submitted to arbitration center not on legal principles and issues but on facts. In that case, the arbitrators come rather close to the functions of a commission of inquiry—except for the feature of *a binding award* in arbitration.

Because not all rules of international law are clear beyond a doubt, the parties to a dispute frequently stipulate in the agreement (*compromis*)—that is, the instrument under which a dispute is submitted to arbitration—that the award is to be made on the basis of either specified rules of law or general principles of equity. On occasion, the *compromis* even lays down special rules that are to apply only to the case on hand.

Third, the procedure of arbitration assumes, explicitly or implicitly, an agreement by both parties to accept the award of the arbitration tribunal and to carry out its provisions. Only if the arbitrators disregard the instructions laid down in the *compromis* by not following specified rules and principles or by exceeding the terms of the document may the party against which the award has gone rightfully claim not to be bound by the latter. This, as most texts point out, was the case in the famous award in the Northeastern Boundary Dispute in 1831. Both parties, the United States and Great Britain, rejected the award on the grounds that the arbitrator, the king of Holland, had exceeded the instructions given to him in the *compromis*.

Except under such unusual circumstances, the awards of arbitral tribunals settle the dispute definitely and without a right of appeal. However, the arbitrators may revise and even reverse an award if new facts pertinent to the dispute are discovered or disclosed later. A UN Convention on the Recognition and Enforcement of Foreign Arbitral Awards has now been in force since June 7, 1959 (for the United States since December 29, 1970).

EFFORTS TO MAKE ARBITRATION A BINDING OBLIGATION    The creation of the League of Nations placed emphasis on the procedure of arbitration because the latter had been mentioned expressly and repeatedly in the Covenant (Arts. 13 and 15, in particular). Because states found "gaps" in the Covenant and desired to devise means whereby resort to peaceful methods would be a binding obligation, there appeared a number of international agreements. In 1924, the Geneva Protocol, stillborn because of the signers' failure to ratify it, was the first of such efforts. It was followed in 1925 by the Locarno Treaties, a series of bipartite agreements concluded between Germany, on the one hand, and Belgium, Czechoslovakia, France, and Poland on the other, which called for the submission of appropriate disputes to either arbitration or judicial settlement. Then, in 1928, the Assembly of the League adopted the General Act. That instrument, submitted to all members for ratification, dealt in considerable detail with conciliation, judicial settlement, and arbitration as methods of peaceful settlement.[19]

Concurrently, a series of regional agreements for the peaceful settlement of disputes were concluded: the Gondra Treaty (Santiago Inter-American Conference of 1923); the General Convention of Inter-American Conciliation and the General Treaty of Inter-American Arbitration (both at the Washington Conference of 1929); the Anti-War Treaty of Non-Aggression and Conciliation (Saavedra Lamas Treaty, 1933)—which, incidentally, limited the scope of the conciliation procedure stressed in the Gondra Treaty—and the Buenos Aires treaties of 1936, which attempted to correlate earlier instruments, particularly through the Treaty to Coordinate Existing Treaties.

One of the claims handled by the German-American Tribunal involved an element hitherto unknown in the history of international arbitration: on June 15, 1939, Justice Owen T. Roberts, umpire of the commission, found Germany guilty of sabotage and responsible for the Black Tom and Kingsland disasters in 1916 and 1917. The unusual added feature of the decision was the umpire's finding that Germany had also been guilty of fraud and collusion in the presentation of its defense against the charge of responsibility. This was the first time that a major power had been adjudged guilty of fraud before an international arbitration tribunal.[20]

A unique arbitral award took place in 1932: the *Arbitration of the Aaroo Mountain.* The mountain in question is situated on the boundary line between the kingdom of Saudi Arabia and Yemen. The armed forces of Yemen occupied the mountain, claiming that they had been invited to do so by the inhabitants of Aaroo. Negotiations failed to settle the question of territorial sovereignty over the mountain, and the Imam of Yemen finally telegraphed a request for settlement by arbitration to King Abdul Aziz (Ibn Saud), agreeing that the latter should be the sole arbitrator and that he would accept the king's decision as final. Ibn Saud accepted and decided against himself.[21]

Two recent instances of the use of arbitration—one supplying a rare example of the rejection of an award, the other successful—were the *Beagle Channel Arbitration* (Argentina-Chile) and the *Arbitration on the Delimitation of the Continental Shelf* (United Kingdom–France).

A dispute had been simmering for over a century between Argentina and Chile over title to three tiny islands (Nueva, Pictón, and Lennox) at the eastern entrance to the Beagle Channel at the southern tip of South America. On July 22, 1971, the disputants agreed to have the British government

---

[19]Text in 25 *AJIL* 204 (1931).

[20]*United States (Lehigh Valley R.R. Co.)* v. *Germany,* United States–Germany Mixed Claims Commission, 1939, *Opinions and Decisions, 1939,* 310; see 33 *AJIL* 770 (1939); and also *NYT,* June 16, 1939, 1, 16, for the text of the decision and an analysis thereof.

[21]For texts of telegrams and of the award, see Wright, "The Arbitration of the Aaroo Mountain," 33 *AJIL* 356 (1939).

arbitrate the controversy under the terms of a 1902 General Arbitration Treaty.[22]

Argentina denounced the 1902 Argentina-Chile treaty (under Art. 15 of that instrument) on March 11, 1972. The treaty therefore terminated on September 22, 1972. In the meantime, however, the two governments signed the new Agreement on Judicial Solution of Disputes on April 5, 1972.[23] The British government thereupon appointed a five-member Court of Arbitration (composed of citizens of the United States, the United Kingdom, France, Nigeria, and Sweden, all judges of the International Court of Justice). The decision, dated February 18, 1977, was announced by Queen Elizabeth II on April 18, 1977.[24] It awarded the three islands to Chile. On January 25, 1978, Argentina issued a "declaration of nullity," rejecting the awards as "insuperably null and void, in accordance with international law."[25] It must be suspected, however, that Chilean sovereignty over the three islands was deemed by Argentina to represent an encroachment on Argentina's South Atlantic and Antarctic claims. In any event, the presidents of the disputing countries met in Argentina in late February 1978 and signed a *Minute* providing for a three-stage process (involving mixed commissions of citizens of Argentina and Chile) to settle the entire controversy.[26] After numerous meetings based on the *Minute,* no productive consequences were forthcoming. On November 8, 1978, Argentina accepted a Chilean proposal for the selection of a neutral mediator.[27] This sensible step followed a strengthening of the respective military forces near the disputed area. Hope for an early settlement faded, however, by December 15, when Argentina withdrew from the Chilean plan, whereupon Chile suggested submission of the dispute to the Organization of American States and also invited foreign military observers from the United States and from Europe. A few days later Pope John Paul II announced that Chile and Argentina had accepted his proposal to send a personal envoy to try to mediate the dispute, after an earlier attempt to secure papal mediation had failed. Cardinal Antonio Samorè was then sent to confer in turn with Argentinian and Chilean officials. On January 8, 1979, the disputants agreed formally, at Montevideo through their foreign ministers, to accept papal mediation, asking Pope John Paul II to be the mediator,[28] and the pontiff agreed to personally mediate the Beagle Channel dispute.

After Chile and Argentina signed a declaration of peace and friendship at

[22] Text of the 1971 Argentina/Chile/United Kingdom Agreement (really the *compromis*) in 10 *ILM* 1182 (1971).

[23] Text 11 *ILM* 691 (1972).

[24] Text of the Queen's Declaration, 17 *AJIL* 632 (1978); textual excerpts from the award, *id.,* 634 (including appended maps). See also *id.,* 1198 for additional documents from the president of the Arbitration Court.

[25] Texts of the diplomatic notes exchanged between Argentina and Chile, *id.,* 738.

[26] Text of *Minute, id.,* 793.

[27] *NYT,* Nov. 9, 1978, A-3.

[28] Text of agreement in 17 *ILM* 1 (1979); see also *NYT,* Jan. 10, 1979, A-3.

the Vatican on January 23, 1984, an agreement on the islands and the Beagle Channel boundary was reached on March 5. Argentina accepted Chilean sovereignty over the three islands and an east-west course for the Channel, in line with the 1978 arbitration award. Chile, in return, yielded its claim to waters on the Atlantic side of Cape Horn, except for a 12-mile jurisdiction around the three islands and other Chilean territory in the region. In October, final details of the settlement were announced. The agreement still had to be ratified by the people as well as by Argentina's legislature, as well as by the ruling Chilean junta. The Argentina popular referendum on November 25, 1984, showed overwhelming public support for the pact, and both parties as well as the Pope signed the agreement on May 2, 1985.[29]

The *Continental Shelf Arbitration (United Kingdom–France)* centered on the delimitation of the shelf in parts of the English Channel, in the area of the Scilly Islands and in areas to the north and northwest of the Channel Islands. This arbitration required two decisions, the second one asked for by the United Kingdom under the terms of the *compromis* of July 10, 1975, concerning the scope and meaning of a decision.[30]

The most active arbitration tribunal in recent years has been the Iran–United States Claims Tribunal, created in 1981 as part of the settlement of the hostage controversy between the two countries. The purpose of the Tribunal was to arbitrate the hundreds of claims arising out of U.S. and Iranian actions and brought by each party against the other.

By September 1989, the Tribunal had awarded more than $5.9 billion to U.S. citizens and banks and $632 million to the government of Iran and Iranian citizens. Those sums, however, represented only a part of the total claims lodged by both countries.[31] On May 9, 1990, the United States and Iran reached a tentative agreement to settle 2,370 pending small U.S. claims for $105 million and to settle 108 Iranian claims for $400,000.

The largest settlement reached through the Tribunal was the result of Iran's agreement (June 15, 1990) to pay two claims totaling $600 million to the Amoco Oil Company for facilities taken by Iran.[32]

[29] See *CSM*, Mar. 11, 1981, 13; Jan. 25, 1984, 7; Mar. 6, 1984, 2; Mar. 9, 1984, 10; Nov. 28, 1984, 14; Dec. 21, 1984, 15; for background, see F. V., "The Beagle Channel Affair," 71 *AJIL* 733 (1977). Consult Teubal de Alhadeff, "Introductory Note," and documents: "Argentina-Chile: Negotiation and Conclusion of Border Dispute Agreement (Feb. 20, 1978–Jan. 14, 1985)," in 24 *ILM* 1 (1985).

[30] Text of first decision (June 30, 1977) in 18 *ILM* 398 (1979); text of second decision (Mar. 14, 1978), *id.*, 462 (including appended map).

[31] See the valuable tabulation, supplied by the Department of State, of the various classes of claims, including military claims, then outstanding, in *U.S. News & World Report*, Aug. 28/Sept. 4, 1989, at 89.

[32] A considerable literature about the Tribunal has emerged: see Lillich, *The Iran–United States Claims Tribunal 1981–1983* (1984), the references cited therein and in Crook, "Applicable Law in International Arbitration: The Iran–U.S. Claims Tribunal Experience," 83 *AJIL* 278 (1989) as well as *id.*, 915; and the authoritative, heavily documented monograph by Caron, "The Nature of the Iran–United States Claims Tribunal and the Evolving Structure of International Dispute Resolution," 84 *AJIL* 104 (1990).

## ADJUDICATION

The first serious attempt to create an international court, in the true meaning of the term, for the settlement of international disputes through judicial processes (adjudication) took place in 1907. In accordance with the Treaty of Washington of that year, the five Central American states situated between Mexico and Panama created the Central American Court of Justice. That court, consisting of five judges, sat at the city of Cartago in Costa Rica. It had jurisdiction over international questions submitted to it by means of a special agreement between any one of the five states and a foreign state, over cases between any of the contracting states and individuals if such a case was submitted to the court by agreement between both parties, and over claims by nationals of one of the five states against one of the other states, provided local remedies had been exhausted and a denial of justice had been proved. The court lasted only a short time, for it was unable to enforce an award handed down against Nicaragua in a case dealing with the rights of other states bordering on Fonseca Bay.

### Permanent Court of International Justice

The desirability of having a true international court to settle legal disputes between states was reflected in Article 14 of the Covenant of the League of Nations, which called on the Council to "formulate and submit to the members of the League for adoption, plans for the establishment of a Permanent Court of International Justice." As a result of this provision, the Advisory Council of Jurists was appointed and met in The Hague in June 1920 to draft the basic instrument (statute) of such a tribunal. The result of the meeting, called a *draft scheme,* was submitted to the Council and Assembly. After certain changes had been incorporated in the scheme, it was approved by the Assembly on December 13, 1920; it was to be binding on states only if they signed and ratified the Protocol of Signature dated December 16, 1920. Certain amendments adopted in 1928–1929 were submitted to member states for ratification in the form of a second protocol in 1929.[33] By December 1942, the original protocol had been ratified by 51 states, including all major powers except the United States.

After the end of World War II, the statute was revised still further. The remaining judges of the Permanent Court resigned in January 1946, and the former Assembly of the League of Nations dissolved the court. The new International Court of Justice was then established as the successor to the League agency. In most details, the statute of the new court duplicates that of the old one, but there are certain significant differences, one of which centers on the fact that all member states of the United Nations are automatically parties to the statute of the new court, whereas in the case of

[33] The major documents relating to the court are found in "Instruments Relating to the Permanent Court of Justice" (with an introduction by Hudson), *International Conciliation,* No. 388, March 1943, 137–93.

the 1920 statute, only those states were bound by it that ratified the 1920 Protocol of Signature.

Because the old Permanent Court has been abolished, the following discussion is based on the statute and operations of the current court, whose first regular session began on April 18, 1946.

## International Court of Justice: Its Structure and Operations

STRUCTURE OF THE INTERNATIONAL COURT    The court consists of 15 judges qualified to hold the highest judicial offices in their own countries or recognized as experts in international law. Candidates are nominated, as mentioned previously, by the "national groups" of the Permanent Court of Arbitration. In recent years, these groups have been either national groups in the Permanent Court appointed in accordance with the provisions of the Hague Conventions of 1898 and 1907 for the Pacific Settlement of International Disputes or special groups appointed by governments that are not parties to those conventions. The special groups are selected under the conditions laid down in the conventions. Normally, national and special groups consist of four individuals.[34] From the list thus obtained, judges are elected by the General Assembly and the Security Council, voting separately.

Judges are elected for a term of nine years (five every three years) and may be reelected. They may be dismissed only when the other members of the court are convinced that they have ceased to fulfill the required conditions of holding office as a judge. No two judges may be nationals of the same state.[35]

In a given case in which a party to a dispute before the court does not have a national sitting on the court, an appropriate *ad hoc* judge is appointed to sit with the regular court. Thus Nicaragua chose a French judge as the *ad hoc* judge in its 1984 case against the United States. Nine judges, excluding such *ad hoc* national judges, constitute a quorum.

As in the case of the old Permanent Court, states that are not members of the United Nations may become parties to the Statute of the International Court of Justice. However, in each instance, conditions are laid down by the General Assembly, and the state in question may become a party to the statute only on recommendation of the Security Council. This has happened in a few cases: Switzerland in 1947, Liechtenstein in 1950, and Japan and San Marino in 1954.

AD HOC CHAMBERS OF THE COURT    The use of an *Ad Hoc* Chamber of three or five judges by the Court was authorized by Articles 26–29 of the Court's Statute, but it was not utilized until the case of the *Delimitation of the Maritime Boundary in the Gulf of Maine Area* [Constitution of Chamber, 1982

---

[34]Baxter, "The Procedures Employed in Connection with the United States Nominations for the International Court in 1960," 55 *AJIL* 445 (1961).
[35]See also Rosenne, "The Election of Five Members of the International Court of Justice in 1981," 76 *AJIL* 364 (1982).

*ICJ Reports* 3 (Order of January 20)]. (See Chapter 15.) This use of a Chamber followed an earlier agreement to that effect (1979) by the litigants.[36] The Chamber procedure was used again in *Frontier Dispute* (*Burkina Faso* v. *Mali*) [Constitution of Chamber, *ICJ Reports, 1985,* 6 (Order of April 3)], in *Elettronica Sicula S.p.A.* (*ELSI*) (*U.S.* v. *Italy*) [Constitution of Chamber, *ICJ Reports, 1987,* 3 (Order of March 2)], and in *Land, Island and Maritime Frontier Dispute* (*El Salvador* v. *Honduras*) [Constitution of Chamber, *ICJ Reports, 1987,* 10 (Order of May 8)].[37]

The cited articles of the Statute provide that the Court may from time to time form one or more Chambers, composed of three or more judges, dealing with particular categories of cases, or it may form a Chamber to deal with a particular case. A judgment given by a Chamber is to be considered as rendered by the Court. The Chambers may sit elsewhere than at The Hague with the consent of the parties. And (Art. 29) the Court, with a view to the speedy dispatch of business, is to form annually a Chamber composed of five judges who, at the request of the parties, may hear and determine cases by summary procedure.

The Revised Rules adopted by the Court provide (Art. 17) that a request for the formation of a Chamber may be filed at any time until the closure of the written proceedings. If the other party then agrees, a Chamber would be formed. Both parties are to be consulted to determine their views regarding the composition of the Chamber.[38]

The major advantage accruing from the use of a Chamber is that such enables the Court to handle a much greater caseload than would otherwise be possible. Also, if a Chamber were to sit physically close to the litigants, the procedure may well be much less expensive than if everyone had to journey to The Hague. And finally, Article 17 of the Rules permits input by the parties concerning the composition of the Chamber.

OPERATIONS OF THE INTERNATIONAL COURT    The competence of the court is outlined in Articles 34 through 38 of the statute. Only states may be parties in cases before the court. If, therefore, an individual desires to bring a case before the court, he must depend on his own government to take up the case or claim before it can be heard by the court. The court may request of public international organizations information relevant to cases under consideration and may receive such information presented by such agencies on their own initiative. Also, and this has been extremely useful and important, the United Nations may request advisory opinions on legal questions, as may be done by other organs authorized to do so by the United Nations. The General Assembly has granted this privilege to all Specialized

[36]See the authoritative coverage by Schwebel, *"Ad Hoc* Chambers of the International Court of Justice," 81 *AJIL* 831, 844 (1987).

[37]Oda, "Further Thoughts on the Chambers of the International Court of Justice," 82 *AJIL* 556, 557, n. 6 (1988).

[38]Schwebel, *op. cit. supra.,* 838–39, n. 35.

Agencies, except the Universal Postal Union. In the case of the United States, a provision of the 1947 Headquarters Agreement, which calls for arbitration of differences between the United States and the United Nations, also calls for an advisory opinion by the International Court, which is to be taken into consideration by the arbitral tribunal.

In connection with advisory opinions, the Permanent Court had established a very important precedent in the *Eastern Carelia* case[39] when it refused to give such an opinion because the League of Nations had not obtained the consent of the Soviet Union before requesting the advisory opinion. To be sure the Soviet Union was not a member of the League at the time, but, on the other hand, was an interested party to the dispute. Because the *Eastern Carelia* quarrel was between the USSR and Finland and because an advisory opinion would have been, in view of the facts in question, a decision of the dispute, the issuance of advisory opinion by the court would in effect have imposed the court's jurisdiction on the Soviet Union.

On the other hand, in the instance of the International Court of Justice, it should be noted that if the optional clause is not applicable to both parties in a dispute, the consent of both must be obtained if the dispute is to be submitted to the court.

The court is open to all states that are parties to the statute, and it may also be open to other states, subject to special provisions contained in treaties in force and subject to conditions laid down by the General Assembly. When a state that is not a member of the United Nations is a party to a case, the court fixes the amount that this state is to contribute toward the expenses of the court, unless the state in question is doing so already.

The court's jurisdiction comprises all cases that the parties refer to it and all other matters especially provided for in the UN Charter or in treaties in force.

However, not only must a submitted dispute be capable of being settled by a court (justiciable dispute), but the dispute also must have arisen between the parties in question. The South-West Africa cases (see Case History No. 1) involved a dispute, not between the applicants (Ethiopia and Liberia) and the respondent (South Africa), but between the respondent and the General Assembly. And the two member states could not appear before the court as either representatives or agents of the General Assembly.

The states that are parties to the statute may at any time declare that they recognize as compulsory, *ipso facto* and without special agreement, in relation to any other state accepting the same obligation, the court's jurisdiction in all legal disputes concerning (1) the interpretations of a treaty; (2) any question of international law; (3) the existence of any fact that, if established, would constitute a breach of an international obligation; and (4) the nature or extent of the reparation to be made for the breach of an international obligation.

---

[39] *Legal Status of Eastern Carelia, P.C.I.J.,* 1923, Ser. B, No. 5.

The declarations mentioned (adherence to the "optional clause") may be made unconditionally or on condition of reciprocity by several or certain states, or for a specified length of time, and are to be deposited with the Secretary-General of the United Nations. Any declarations made under Article 36 of the statute of the Permanent Court of International Justice and still in force in 1946 were deemed, as between the parties to the new statute, to be acceptances of the compulsory jurisdiction of the International Court of Justice in accordance with their terms. The question of the "renewal" of an acceptance of compulsory jurisdiction made in accordance with the statute of the Permanent Court and carried over under the statute of the International Court came up in two cases before the latter tribunal. In the case of the *Aerial Incident of July 27th, 1955 (Israel* v. *Bulgaria)*[40] the court found that Bulgaria's declaration of acceptance of compulsory jurisdiction, made in 1921, had lapsed in 1946 and that Bulgaria had taken no steps to indicate either its renewal of the declaration or its acceptance of the compulsory jurisdiction of the International Court. The court therefore was forced to conclude that Bulgaria was not obligated to submit to its jurisdiction.

In the *Judgment on Preliminary Objections* in the *Case Concerning the Temple of Preah Vihear (Cambodia* v. *Thailand)*, May 26, 1961,[41] a dispute as to territorial sovereignty over the region of the Temple of Preah Vihear, Thailand asserted that because of the decision in *Israel* v. *Bulgaria,* Thailand was no longer bound by its renewal of its declaration of acceptance of compulsory jurisdiction.

The government of Thailand had accepted that jurisdiction (then relating to the Permanent Court of International Justice) on September 20, 1929, for a period of 10 years. This declaration was renewed in 1940 and was scheduled to expire on May 6, 1950. Thailand, however, sent a new declaration of acceptance under date of May 20, 1950. In the case on hand, the Thai government contended that the court's decision in *Israel* v. *Bulgaria* revealed that the assumptions on which the language of the Thai 1950 declaration was based were incorrect and that the declaration, in the light of the court's decision, was meaningless. Thailand admitted that it had fully intended to accept the court's compulsory jurisdiction, but now asserted that its declaration of 1950 had been revealed as having been ineffectual to achieve Thailand's purpose.

The court ruled against Thailand's objection, holding that the renewal of acceptance of jurisdiction of the Permanent Court had expired on May 6, 1950; that the new declaration of May 20, 1950, was a new and independent instrument; and that the new declaration had, in fact, no relation to the

---

[40]*ICJ Reports, 1959,* 127, digested by Gross in 57 *AJIL* 753 (1963), with special emphasis on the optional clause. See also the *Case Concerning Right of Passage over Indian Territory,* Chapter 14, *sub* Right-of-way Servitudes.

[41]*ICJ Reports, 1961,* 17, digested in 55 *AJIL* 978 (1962).

defunct Permanent Court and had relation only to the International Court, whose compulsory jurisdiction had thereby been accepted.

On June 15, 1962, the court handed down its judgment in the case, awarding the contested territory to Cambodia.[42] The lengthy decision was based primarily on an analysis of the reports and maps produced by boundary commissions in the early twentieth century and on Thailand's prolonged failure to assert a claim to the area in dispute. Judge Alfaro, concurring in the award, added an extensive discussion of "preclusion," the doctrine that a state that is a party to an international litigation is bound by its previous acts or attitudes when they contradict its claims in the litigation. He concluded that a state's failure to assert its right when that right was openly challenged by another state meant abandonment of the right in question.

A slightly different problem was raised by Guatemala in the *Nottebohm* case. By application, Liechtenstein had instituted proceedings against Guatemala. The latter, however, contended in 1953 that the time limit of five years provided for in its declaration (accepting compulsory jurisdiction of the International Court) of January 27, 1947, had expired at midnight on January 26, 1952, and that from that moment the International Court of Justice had no jurisdiction to treat or decide cases that would affect Guatemala, unless Guatemala extended the duration of its declaration, submitted a new declaration to the Secretary-General, or signed a special protocol of submission with any interested state.

The court ruled, however, that when an application was filed at a time when the law in force between the parties entailed the compulsory jurisdiction of the court, the latter had to deal with the claim. It had jurisdiction to deal with all of its aspects, and the subsequent lapse of a declaration of one of the parties owing to the expiration of a time limit or to denunciation could not deprive the court of the jurisdiction already established.[43]

CONNALLY AMENDMENT   The question of the optional clause has agitated many governments as well as jurists. Most states that have ratified the clause have done so not only by attaching a time limit after which their acceptance of compulsory jurisdiction would expire but also by including in their ratifications numerous reservations that can be referred to against the reserving state by the other party in a dispute. Most famous of all the reservations is that of the United States, the so-called Connally amendment, according to which the United States excluded from its acceptance of the compulsory jurisdiction of the court "disputes with regard to matters which are essentially within the domestic jurisdiction of the United States of America *as*

---

[42] *Case Concerning the Temple of Preah Vihear (Cambodia v. Thailand), Merits.* June 15, 1962, *ICJ Reports, 1962,* 6; the opinion is reproduced at length in 56 *AJIL* 1033 (1962 Supp.).

[43] *Nottebohm* case (*Liechtenstein v. Guatemala*), *Preliminary Objection,* International Court of Justice, Nov. 18, 1953, *ICJ Reports, 1953,* 111, digested and excerpted in 48 *AJIL* 327 (1954).

*determined by the United States of America*" (italics added; the italicized words are the portion referred to as the Connally amendment).[44]

One of the major arguments advanced by critics of the amendment is that it has discouraged use of the court and thus has lessened its importance. It is true, of course, that the existence of the amendment or equivalent reservations has tended to keep disputes out of the court, in part because of the principle of reciprocity. This principle applies not only in a general sense, in that a country that accepts the court's jurisdiction cannot be sued without its consent by a country that has not done so, but also specifically. Thus France, which earlier had filed a reservation very similar to the Connally amendment, sued Norway in 1957 over the latter's refusal to pay off certain bonds in gold. Norway invoked France's own reservation, and claimed that the matter was "domestic," and that was the end of the matter.[45] And Bulgaria invoked the Connally amendment against the United States in the case of the *Aerial Incident of 27 July 1955.* The case was withdrawn on May 30, 1960, as a result of the United States' acceptance of Bulgaria's preliminary objection based on the Connally amendment.[46]

Of all the states that have accepted the court's jurisdiction, only five (Liberia, Mexico, Pakistan, Sudan, and South Africa), aside from the United States, have filed what may be termed a *self-judging reservation.* India and France, both of which have asserted similar self-judging privileges, have abandoned them, India completely in September 1959, and France by replacing its original reservation in July 1959 by a somewhat more circumscribed reservation exempting from the court's jurisdiction "disputes arising out of any war or international hostilities and disputes arising out of a crisis affecting the national security or out of any measure or action relating thereto." The wording indicates that France did not completely discard self-judgment.

It may be instructive to recall, in connection with the "optional clause," that by the end of 1979 a total of 147 states, including Liechtenstein, San Marino, and Switzerland, were parties to the statute of the Court, but only 46 of them regarded the jurisdiction of the Court as obligatory. And a number of these had attached, just as the United States had done, reserva-

---

[44]Text of U.S. declaration of Aug. 14, 1946, in 41 *AJIL* 11 (1947). The literature on the amendment is enormous; consult the valuable ideas in D'Amato, "Modifying U.S. Acceptance of the Compulsory Jurisdiction of the World Court," 79 *AJIL* 385 (1985); DeCain, "The Connally Amendment," 10 *National Review,* Mar. 11, 1961, 143–47; Preuss, "The International Court of Justice, the Senate, and Matters of Domestic Jurisdiction," 40 *AJIL* 720 (1946). See also the monographic study of the subject by Briggs, "Reservations to the Acceptance of the Compulsory Jurisdiction of the International Court of Justice," 93 *Hague Academy Recueil des Cours* (1958, I), 223–367.

[45]*Certain Norwegian Loans (France v. Norway), ICJ Reports, 1957,* No 9, 22.

[46]See Gross, "Bulgaria Invokes the Connally Amendment," 56 *AJIL* 357 (1962), and his subsequent analysis, 57, *id.,* 767 (1963).

tions to their acceptance of the Court's jurisdiction. The People's Republic of China had repudiated, by letter, in September 1972 the acceptance of compulsory jurisdiction by the Republic of China in 1946. As of January 1985, only 44 of the then 162 parties to the statute had accepted the compulsory jurisdiction of the Court and all but seven had attached reservations to their acceptances. In April 1984, the United States announced that it rejected the authority of the Court over Central American questions for the next two years (see the Case Study No. 2). This American action had been bolstered by a number of well-known precedents, including denial of jurisdiction by the United Kingdom in a commercial disagreement with Saudi Arabia, by India in its dispute with Portugal over rights of passage in several of the latter's enclaves in India, by Australia in a fishing dispute with Japan, and by Canada in an effort to bar claims for marine pollution by Canada.[47]

MAJOR PROCEDURAL ISSUES    Major procedural issues meriting mention in connection with the International Court of Justice are:

The court has the power to indicate, if it considers that conditions warrant it, any provisional measures that ought to be taken to preserve the respective rights of either party.

A decision by the court has no binding force except between the parties and in respect of the particular case in question (Art. 59). A judgment of the court is final and without appeal. An application for the revision of a judgment can be made only when it is based on the discovery of a fact of such a nature as to be decisive and that must have been unknown to the court and to the party claiming revision at the time when the judgment was given.

Article 38 of the statute instructs the court to apply (1) international conventions, both general and particular; (2) international custom, as evidence of a general practice accepted as law; (3) the general principles of law recognized by civilized nations; and (4) subject to Article 59, judicial decisions and the teachings of publicists, as subsidiary means for determining the rules of law. Finally, if both parties of a dispute agree, the court can also decide a case *ex aequo et bono*. That phrase, in Anglo-Saxon practice, means "equity," but in the case of the International Court is apparently means that the Court can use its own judgment, even if this means disregarding the existing rules of law, in order to arrive at a fair decision.[48]

NON-APPEARANCE BEFORE THE ICJ    *The Case of Military and Paramilitary Activities in and against Nicaragua (Nicaragua v. United States)* (see the Case Study No. 2) created a great deal of interest in the phenomenon of nonappearance of a party before the International Court of Justice. The problem has been anticipated as a result of the experience of the Permanent Court of International Justice and was intended to be covered by Article 53 of the ICJ Statute:

[47] AP dispatch, April 9, 1984; *CSM,* April 16, 1984, 18.
[48] See Whiteman, vol. 1, 98–103.

1. Whenever one of the parties does not appear before the Court, or fails to defend its case, the other party may call upon the Court to decide in favour of its claim.

2. The Court must, before doing so, satisfy itself, not only that it has jurisdiction in accordance with Articles 36 and 37, but also that the claim is well founded in fact and law.

There cannot be any doubt that UN members and parties to the Court's Statute have agreed in advance that they will respect the judgments of the Court in cases to which they are a party (Art. 94, par. 1 of the UN Charter an Arts. 59 and 60 of the Statute). This does not mean, however, that such members and parties have given specific consent to the jurisdiction of the Court.[49]

The Court pointed out in *Nicaragua* v. *United States (Merits, ICJ Reports, 1986, 25, par. 31)* that

Though formally absent from the proceedings, the party in question frequently submits to the Court letters and documents, in ways and by means not contemplated by the [Court's] Rules . . . the Court has to emphasize that the equality of the parties . . . must remain the basic principle for the Court . . . The party which declines to appear cannot be permitted to profit from its absence, since this would amount to place the party appearing at a disadvantage.

Non-appearance of one of the parties has been involved thus far in 13 cases before the Permanent Court of International Justice and the International Court of Justice. The technique did not enhance the ability of either court to exercise obligatory jurisdiction. This was especially true of the actions of the United States in the *Nicaragua* case: it did not only withdraw from the proceedings, but also canceled its Article 36(2) Optional Clause declaration.[50]

**WEAKNESSES OF ENFORCING JUDGMENTS**     One major problem left for brief examination is the question of enforcing both arbitral awards and judicial decisions.

Most judgments of the Permanent Court of International Justice were executed without difficulty because no major international problems were submitted to the court. There were, as could be expected, a few exceptions to the rule of execution: In the *SS Wimbledon* case,[51] the court decided in favor of France, but the judgment was not executed. The Reparations Commission, of which France was a member, ruled that damages should not be paid, even though Germany, against which the damages were assessed, asked to

---

[49]Highet, 81 *AJIL* 239, n. 49 (1987).

[50]The non-appearance problem is covered well in Highet's review-article of Elkind, *Non-appearance before the International Court of Justice: Functional and Comparative Analysis* (1984) and Thirlway, *Non-appearance before the International Court of Justice* (1985), in 81 *AJIL* 237 (1987).

[51]*P.C.I.J.*, 1923, Ser. A, No. 1: see Chapter 14.

be allowed to pay as ordered by the court. In the *Sociéte Commerciale de Belgique* case,[52] the court decided that Greece had to honor awards made against that country in a 1936 arbitration; Greece, however, failed to do this.

After the establishment of the International Court of Justice, greater obstacles to the execution of judgments were encountered. Albania refused to pay the compensation awarded to Great Britain in the *Corfu Channel* case, and Iran failed to institute the interim measure of protection ordered in the *Anglo-Iranian Oil Company* case, just as it did in the *Case Concerning United States Diplomatic and Consular Staff in Tehran.* (See Chapter 16.)

In the case of arbitration, very few instances are known in which a party has refused to accept an award and carry out its provisions. Among such examples are the *Pelletier* case (United States–Haiti, 1885), the *Chamizal Tract* case (United States–Mexico, 1911), and a few others, some of which did not involve the United States, such as the *Beagle Channel* case.

The principle that an arbitral award or a judicial decision is binding on the parties and must be carried out in good faith is accepted without dissent, in regard to legal theory. In arbitration treaties, the *compromis* normally specifies that the award is to be binding on both parties—a safeguard only, for it is a rule of customary law that the losing side shall honor the award in an arbitration. In the case of adjudication, there is no question that the decisions of the International Court of Justice are binding on all members of the United Nations (Art. 94 of the Charter). If nonmember states adhere to the statute of the court or become plaintiffs in a case before the court, they are burdened with the same obligation to comply with decisions of the court.

When a state objects to carrying out an award or a decision, it tends to advance the doctrines of nullity or impossibility of performance. Usually there are three reasons for such nullity: (1) excess of power, (2) corruption of a member of the tribunal, or (3) a serious deviation from the rules of procedure in making the award or decision.

The most common assertion centers on an excess of power, that is, the charge that the arbitral tribunal or the court in question exceeded the powers granted to it. Coupled with this assertion, or, at times, found separately, is an assertion of an impossibility to carry out the award or decision.

What may the "winning" party in a dispute do when the losing state refuses to comply with an arbitral award or a judicial decision? This is where self-help short of war enters, which is discussed in the following chapter.

Because self-help procedures, particularly those employing force short of war, are somewhat risky with respect to preserving peace and because, as will be seen later, such measures may easily degenerate into armed conflict,

---

[52]*P.C.I.J.*, 1939, Ser. A/B, No. 78; see also *Socobel and the Belgian State* v. *Kingdom of the Hellenes,* Brussels Civil Tribunal, 1951, digested in 47 *AJIL* 508 (1953).

attention has been focused for some time on international organizations as enforcement agencies.

The Convenant of the League of Nations provided in Article 13 (4) for the joint enforcement of awards and decisions. In the case of the United Nations, Article 94 (2) of the Charter represents the corresponding provision:

2. If any party to a case fails to perform the obligations incumbent upon it under a judgment rendered by the Court, the other party may have recourse to the Security Council, which may, if it deems necessary, make recommendations or decide upon measures to be taken to give effect to the judgment.

The notable difference between the provisions of the Charter and the Covenant is that the former refers only to judgments of the court, whereas the latter referred to "awards or decisions," thus including arbitration in the enforcement text.

Again, Article 94 (2) does not specify what measures may be taken by the Security Council to enforce a judgment of the court, nor do the records of the San Francisco Conference indicate that any restrictions were intended to be imposed on actions contemplated by the Security Council in seeking to give effect to a judgment.

Thus far, Article 94 (2) has been invoked only once, in the "interim-measures-of-protection" decision in the *Anglo-Iranian Oil Company* case. Great Britain brought the case before the Security Council on a contention that the latter had the right to take action to deal with interim measures ordered by the court but not carried out by Iran. The Security Council, however, decided to postpone any action until the International Court of Justice had decided whether it was itself competent to handle the case, and when the court decided that it lacked jurisdiction, the order for the measures of protection lapsed and with it all question of enforcement by the Security Council.

The Security Council, therefore, has not thus far acted against a defendant country that balked at carrying out a ruling by the International Court of Justice. The question became pertinent again when Iran denounced as "meaningless" the decision of the court (May 24, 1980) in the U.S. hostages case. (See Chapter 16.) Iran, it should be noted, was not the only country which refused to appear and then ignored a decision of the court: France, Iceland, and Turkey have done the same thing, as has the United States in the Nicaragua case.

One of the more promising methods of securing compliance with a judgment has been evolved by the framers of the treaty creating the European Coal and Steel Authority: a member state failing to carry out obligations of that treaty, including compliance with judgments of the authority, may be fined effectively by a suspension of payments due to it from the other member states.[53]

[53] Article 88, Treaty Establishing the European Coal and Steel Authority, 261 *U.N. Treaty Series,* 221; the court, open to litigants on March. 7, 1953, was reconstituted as the Court of Justice of the European Communities on Oct. 7, 1958.

In conclusion, the basic weakness of enforcing judgments of international tribunals must be pointed out. In a national system of adjudication, the effectiveness of the courts in restraining citizens is derived, at least in part, from the hierarchy of courts established there. A decision at one judicial level can be appealed to a higher level, and eventually a supreme court of some kind will state with authority what is the law in the case at hand.

But in the international sphere, a heterogeneous collection of courts, including the International Court of Justice (which can in no way be compared with a national supreme court), hands down judgments but does not manifest legal connections between the individual courts. This decentralization, characteristic of much of international law, is reflected in the difficulties in the securing of compliance with judgments, particularly because the "clients" of international courts are, mainly, sovereign states.

## INTERNATIONAL ORGANIZATIONS

Although it cannot be maintained seriously that international organizations per se can be treated as "methods" for settling international disputes, a number of such agencies have developed *procedures* for achieving such settlements. Thus Article 12 of the Covenant of the League of Nations provided in its original form that all members of the League would submit a dispute either to arbitration or to inquiry by the Council; judicial settlement was added later as an alternative method for arbitration. Article 13 held that all matters suitable for submission to arbitration should be so dealt with and listed such suitable matters, although the list was somewhat vague and general (the interpretation of a treaty, questions of international law, questions of fact having a bearing on a breach of an international obligation, and the reparation to be made for such a violation). All members of the League obligated themselves not to resort to war until three months after the arbitral tribunal had made its award or the Council had reported on its inquiry.

The United Nations and regional organizations such as the Organization of American States have been active in providing such procedures, usually combining the functions of investigation and conciliation. The United Nations has also appointed numerous special commissions to deal with specific disputes and situations.

The United Nations appears also to have adopted at times a rather novel approach to certain situations demanding peaceful solution. Repeatedly faced with national intransigence, the organization has proceeded to evolve what Claude called "instances of not-quite-pacific settlement and pacific nonsettlement."[54] A number of disputes have been resolved into what may be described as "peaceful perpetuation": no real settlement has been achieved

---

[54]See Claude, 242–44, for an analysis of several actual examples.

through investigation and conciliation procedures. Instead, provisional pacification measures have been extended indefinitely, with occasional attempts to discover whether an actual resolution of the dispute might be possible. A good example of this mode of handling quarrels by ending the actual violence and then maintaining a degree of supervision until reconciliation might be possible is the Kashmir dispute between India and Pakistan.

The Charter of the United Nations imposes on all its members a duty to "settle their international disputes by peaceful means in such a manner that international peace and security, and justice, are not endangered" (Art. 2, par. 6). It appears that the members have an unconditional obligation to settle their disputes peacefully, whereas the organization has an obligation limited to the settlement of disputes or situations "which might lead to a breach of the peace." Chapter VI of the Charter, which pertains to the peaceful settlement of disputes, is expressly limited to disputes "the continuance of which is likely to endanger the maintenance of international peace and security" (Art. 33, par. 1).

If a given dispute falls within the proper competence of an organ of the United Nations, that organ is not to deal with the merits involved but is to decide which method of procedure or of settlement is best adapted to the dispute (Art. 33). When the parties have failed to achieve a settlement by methods of their own choice and then by the methods recommended by the organ of the United Nations in a dispute, the dispute is to be referred to the United Nations again for additional recommendations; only then can the UN organ recommend actual terms of settlement. Further action by the United Nations is contingent on a finding that the dispute is "in fact" likely to endanger peace.

On the other hand, if all parties to a dispute so request, the United Nations is authorized to make recommendations for a pacific settlement, regardless of the limitations of the other provisions of Chapter VI of the Charter (Art. 28).

The whole process has been designed deliberately to permit a gradual approach to each dispute and to distinguish between disputes involving "compulsory jurisdiction" by the United Nations (disputes whose continuance are likely to endanger peace) and those involving "contingent jurisdiction" (minor disputes submitted for recommendation at the request of all parties involved).

Most of the Charter's provisions dealing with disputes or situations entailing dangers to peace confers jurisdiction over these matters on the Security Council, in accordance with the basic assumption that the Council has primary responsibility for the maintenance of international peace and security (Art. 24, par. 1). Because the Security Council is in permanent session, speedy action on such disputes and situations was anticipated at the San Francisco Conference.

The General Assembly, under Article 12(2) of the Charter, has unlimited jurisdiction over all questions not brought before the Security Council or no longer being handled by the Security Council. In such instances, the General Assembly is free not only to discuss but also to make recommendations on the matter in question. Such recommendations may be addressed to the parties involved, to the Security Council, or to both at the same time (Art. 11, par. 2). Thus the General Assembly was within its legal rights when, on January 14, 1980, it passed by a vote of 104 to 18 a resolution calling for the immediate and total withdrawal of all foreign (that is, Russian) troops from Afghanistan, after the Soviet Union had vetoed a similar resolution in the Security Council on January 7, 1980.

Can the General Assembly take action itself if the Security Council fails to act in accordance with its responsibilities? Secretary-General Dag Hammarskjöld held, in 1957, that only the Security Council had authority to order the use of force. The General Assembly could recommend, investigate, and pronounce judgment, but it lacked the power to compel compliance with recommendations.[55]

On the other hand, some recommendations of the General Assembly have indeed been held to possess definitely binding effects. The Secretary-General pointed out in his report on the Middle Eastern question on February 11, 1957, that it appeared "appropriate to distinguish between recommendations which implement a Charter principle, which in itself is binding on Member States" and other recommendations.[56] In other words, if a recommendation of the General Assembly represents a reiteration in specific form of an obligation assumed by members under the Charter, then such a recommendation would have a binding effect on all members.

Still another avenue of reaching a peaceful settlement of a dispute through the United Nations is the adoption by the Security Council of a recommendation to refer a dispute to the International Court of Justice or to request an advisory opinion on a dispute or question. The fundamental restriction imposed here is that such disputes or questions must be "legal" in character. This limitation raises the question of what yardstick is to be employed in order to determine the "legal" character of a dispute or question.

It should be mentioned that the five permanent members of the UN Security Council drafted a comprehensive peace plan designed to end the 12-year-old Cambodian civil war (November 25, 1990). The United States, the Soviet Union, China, Great Britain, and France, along with Indonesia, co-chairman with France of the Paris Conference on Cambodia, jointly urged the parties to the civil war to agree to the proposed settlement. It was expected that the Paris Conference would be reconvened after it had recessed in September 1989 without achieving success.

---

[55] Text of the "Uniting for Peace" Resolution of Nov. 3, 1950, 45 *AJIL* 1 (1951 Supp.); 1957 statement in Kunz, "The Secretary-General on the Role of the United Nations," 52 *AJIL* 300 (1958); cf. Andrassy, "Uniting for Peace," 50 *AJIL* 563 (1956).
[56] *General Assembly, Official Records, 11th Session,* Annexes, Agenda Item 66, 59.

The new plan called for the creation of a transition government and administration by the United Nations to monitor a cease-fire, free elections, and disarmament. It also provided for the withdrawal of foreign troops from Cambodia, repatriation of Cambodian refugees, and even basic principles for a new Cambodian constitution. In addition, the five permanent members also prepared a draft agreement on the sovereignty, independence and territorial integrity, and neutrality of Cambodia.

## PEACEFUL SETTLEMENT OF DISPUTES THROUGH REGIONAL ORGANIZATIONS

DEVELOPMENT OF REGIONAL ORGANIZATIONS     The peaceful solution of international disputes has been achieved not only through the employment of traditional procedures and "universal" international organizations, but also through a multitude of regional arrangements frequently cast in the form of permanent institutional frameworks.

The concept of regional organization is not a new one at all. Thucydides described what today would be termed *mutual security groupings* among the Greek city-states in his *History of the Peloponnesian Wars*. Beginning with the close of the medieval period, numerous peace projects supplied blueprints for a European community of states, complete with joint institutions and, in some cases, even collective security arrangements. Still later, regional agencies such as the European Danube Commission (1856) were established. And in the Americas, a slow but steady development was observed, from the forerunners of the Pan American movement through the Conferences of the American Republics into the Organization of American States (OAS) created through the Bogotá Charter of 1948. However, the period since 1945 has witnessed an almost incredible growth in the number and scope of regional organizations.

One of the reasons for this expansion has been a belief in the common interests and aims of the members of such a grouping. The Soviet Union has been inclined to remove or lessen tensions and strains in the Communist bloc by procedures involving only the members of that bloc. The United States has pursued a similar policy in Europe (NATO) and in Latin America (OAS). Such resort to an intrabloc resolution of disputes does not necessarily represent a deliberate flouting of a world organization such as the United Nations, but reflects, in effect, a commendable alternative method to bring about desired results without exposing the members of the bloc in question to interference by members of other blocs.

UN EMPHASIS ON REGIONAL AGENCIES     The UN Charter itself emphasizes regional arrangements before a dispute is submitted to the United Nations. Article 33 (1) of the Charter states that "the parties to any dispute, the continuance of which is likely to endanger the maintenance of international peace and security, shall, first of all, seek a solution by . . . resort to regional agencies or arrangements, or other peaceful means of their own choice." And paragraph 2 of the same article provides that "the Security Council shall, when it deems necessary, call upon the parties to settle their dispute by such means." These obligations are detailed at length in Chapter VIII of the Charter ("Regional Arrangements," Arts. 52–54).

One of the unresolved problems in the pacific settlement of disputes is the relationship between the provisions cited and the rules governing the relevant powers of the Security Council. The Charter states that the provisions on regional arrangements shall not impair the applications of those portions of the Charter that deal with the submission of disputes and situations to the Security Council and with the latter's authority to investigate such disputes or situations (Art. 52, par. 4). This lack of clarity led to unexpected and considerable difficulties in the Guatemala Crisis of 1954.[57]

INTER-AMERICAN REGIONAL ARRANGEMENTS    Disregarding the various inter-American instruments drawn up in the course of the nineteenth century, the modern practice of creating regional arrangements in the Western Hemisphere began with the Treaty to Avoid or Prevent Conflicts between the American States (Santiago, 1923, generally called the Gondra Treaty—commissions of inquiry). This convention, eventually ratified by 18 states, was followed by the General Treaty of Inter-American Arbitration (Washington, 1929), supplemented by the Protocol of Progressive Arbitration (arbitration of disputes of legal character); the General Convention of Inter-American Conciliation (Washington, 1929—conciliation commissions); and the Anti-War Treaty of Non-Aggression and Conciliation (Rio de Janeiro, 1933, usually termed the Saavreda Lamas Treaty—conciliation commissions); and culminated in the Treaty on the Prevention of Controversies (Buenos Aires, 1936—bilateral mixed commissions).

ORGANIZATION OF AMERICAN STATES (OAS)    The charter of the OAS, of April 30, 1948, contains only very general provisions relating to the settlement of disputes, with emphasis on listing and recommending peaceful procedures (Arts. 20–23), in a manner similar to Article 52 (3) of the UN Charter.[58] Significantly, Article 1 of the OAS charter declares that "within the United Nations, the Organization of American States is a regional agency." The separate American Treaty on Pacific Settlement (Pact of Bogotá), signed at the same time, established detailed procedures for the settlement of disputes between the American states.[59] The Pact of Bogotá was

---

[57] See Fenwick, "Jurisdictional Questions Involved in the Guatemalan Revolution," 48 *AJIL* 597 (1954).

[58] Text of Charter in 46 *AJIL* 43 (April 1952 Supp.); 1967 amendments (Protocol of Buenos Aires), 64 *AJIL* 996 (1970); 1985 amendments (Cartagena), 25 *ILM* 527 (1986). Consult also the excellent study by Fenwick, *The Organization of American States* (1963), as well as Thomas and Thomas, *The Organization of American States* (1963); Rubin, "The Falklands (Malvinas), International Law, and the OAS," 76 *AJIL* 594 (1982).

[59] Text of the Pact of Bogotá in 30 *UN Treaty Series* 84 (English text).

intended to replace all eight of the earlier instruments listed previously. Because it has been ratified by only a minority of the American states, however, the older agreements may still be applied to disputes in the Western Hemisphere. The problem arising in the event of any dispute is therefore first to ascertain whether the parties are bound by any of the agreements in question, then to determine in what order applicable treaties are to be used by the parties to the dispute.

This difficulty has been avoided on a number of occasions by referring to the provisions of still another agreement, the Inter-American Treaty of Reciprocal Assistance (Rio de Janeiro, 1947).[60] This agreement was drafted in a form that relates it explicitly to Articles 52–54 of the Charter of the United Nations. Article 5 of the instrument states that

the High Contracting Parties shall immediately send to the Security Council of the United Nations, in conformity with Articles 51 and 54 of the Charter of the United Nations, complete information concerning the activities undertaken or in contemplation in the exercise of the right of self-defense or for the purpose of maintaining inter-American peace and security.

Articles 7 and 8 of the treaty provide for procedures for the reestablishment and maintenance of peace in the hemisphere system, whereas Article 2 outlines the commitments of the contracting parties to settle local disputes — in a manner intentionally reminiscent of Article 52 (2) of the charter.

The Rio Treaty has not, on the whole, been as effective as its drafters assumed it would be. In recent years, the instrument was not helpful in bringing about hemisphere action to block support by Cuba for Salvadoran guerrillas, nor did it lead to a peaceful settlement of the Falklands conflict[61] or the American activity in Grenada.

One of the most common and useful procedures adopted by the American states has been consultation. This concept has been embodied in a series of treaties, beginning with the Convention for the Maintenance, Preservation and Reestablishment of Peace (Buenos Aires, 1936), and normally functions through consultative meetings of ministers of foreign affairs. Currently the procedure is invoked when a dispute threatens: the Council of the OAS convokes a meeting of the Organ of Consultation but does not actually hold such a meeting at all; the council can, after such a call, operate itself as a provisional organ and is empowered to take such steps as may be necessary; if required, an investigating committee is dispatched to the scene of the dispute, and the recommendations contained in the committee's report commonly represent the basis of the decisions made by the council acting as

[60]Text in 43 *AJIL* 53 (1949 Supp.).
[61]See Moore, "The Inter-American System Snarls in Falklands War," 76 *AJIL* 830 (1982), and Organization of American States, two resolutions (Apr. 29, 1982, and May 29, 1982) on the Falklands War, 21 *ILM* 669 (1982).

a provisional organ of consultation. Most of the decisions have been accepted as binding by the parties to the dispute.

The most promising inter-American instrument for the peaceful settlement of disputes may yet be the Pact of Bogotá, which codifies all the various methods adopted in the Americas between the two world wars. The parties to the treaty agree to settle their controversies by regional pacific procedures before referring them to the United Nations (Art. 2). Once such a procedure has been initiated, no other can be started until the earlier one has been concluded (Art. 4). Although none of the procedures supplied through the treaty can be applied to matters in states' domestic jurisdiction, either party to a dispute may submit to the International Court of Justice the preliminary question, whether or not the controversy concerns a matter of domestic jurisdiction (Art. 4). Article 7 provides that the parties will not

make diplomatic representations in order to protect their nationals, or to refer a controversy to a court of international jurisdiction for that purpose, when the said nationals have had available the means to place their case before competent domestic courts of the respective State.

This provision was rejected by the United States by means of a reservation.

The treaty contains the expected detailed provisions not only for commissions of investigation and conciliation but also for arbitration and judicial procedure and also establishes a permanent panel of American conciliators. In the event of a dispute, each party is to select two members from that panel, and the four conciliators are then to choose a fifth one (Art. 19). Arbitral tribunals are to be chosen from a list of 20 names chosen from the general panel of members of the Permanent Court of Arbitration in The Hague (Art. 40).

In the event conciliation fails to resolve the dispute and if the parties have not agreed on arbitration, the dispute is to go to the International Court of Justice at the referral of either party (Arts. 31–32). If the court decides that it has no jurisdiction because the dispute is not a legal one, then the parties are required to resort to arbitration (Art. 35). In case a party fails to comply with the court's decision or with an arbitral award the other party is entitled to request a meeting of consultation of the ministers of foreign affairs, who are to decide on measures to ensure compliance with the decision or award (Art. 50).

The latest development in Latin American regional organization was the creation of a new court in Quito, Ecuador, the Court of Justice of the Cartagena Agreement. That agreement established the so-called Andean Group (1969) and was supplemented 10 years later by the Treaty Creating the Court of Justice of the Cartagena Agreement (Cartagena, May 28,

1979).[62] The agreement in question deals with regional economic integration, and the court is to handle such problems as actions of nullification or noncompliance by signatories to the agreement.

REGIONAL ARRANGEMENTS IN EUROPE    The development of regional arrangements and organization in Europe has been even more extensive and also perhaps more important than it has been in the Americas.

The earliest important regional arrangement following World War II was the Treaty of Economic, Social and Cultural Collaboration and Collective Self-Defense (Brussels Treaty) of March 17, 1948. The contracting parties agreed to settle all legal disputes between them by referring to the International Court of Justice, subject only to such reservations as had been made by them when each accepted that court's jurisdiction. All nonlegal disputes are to be subject to conciliation procedures. If a dispute between parties to the treaty includes both legal and nonlegal matters (a "mixed dispute"), either party will be conceded the right to "insist that the judicial settlement of the legal questions shall precede conciliation" (Art. 8). The Brussels Treaty itself lacks detailed provisions as to the conciliation procedures to be employed; instead, all contracting parties are to observe the conciliation provisions of the Geneva General Act for the Pacific Settlement of Disputes (1928).[63] Two territorial disputes between parties to the Brussels Treaty have been submitted thus far to the jurisdiction of the World Court: the Franco-British dispute concerning title to the Minquiers and Ecrehos islets and the Belgian-Dutch dispute over certain lands in the communes of Baerle-Duc and Baale-Nassau. In both instances, the parties in question complied with the court's judgments.

The Council of Europe did not have any provisions in its constitutional instruments for settling disputes among its members. After much urging by its consultative assembly, the European Convention for the Peaceful Settlement of Disputes was drawn up and signed on April 29, 1957.[64] This instrument provides for referring all legal disputes between the contracting parties to the International Court. Nonlegal disputes are to be settled through conciliation and, if this fails, by arbitration. The provisions for settling mixed disputes are patterned after the corresponding portions of the Brussels Treaty.

EUROPEAN COAL AND STEEL COMMUNITY    The Treaty Establishing the European Coal and Steel Community (Paris, April 18, 1951) created a Court of Justice "to ensure the rule of law in the interpretation and application" of the convention and of the regulations issued for its execution.[65] This court

---

[62] Text of 1969 Agreement in 8 *ILM* 910 (1969), and text of the 1979 Treaty, 18 *ILM* 1203 (1979). Consult also García-Amador, *The Andean Legal Order: A New Community Law* (1978).
[63] Text of the Brussels Treaty in 43 *AJIL* 59 (1949 Supp.)
[64] Text in *International Court of Justice, Yearbook,* 1958–1959, 228; see also Kaplan-Katzenbach, 329–30.
[65] Text in 46 *AJIL* 107 (1952): see Articles 31–45; see also Kaplan-Katzenbach, 323–24.

was granted jurisdiction over appeals by any of the six member states or by the Council of Ministers of the Community "for the annulment of decisions and recommendations of the High Authority on the grounds of lack of competence, major violations of procedure, violation of the treaty or of any rule of law relating to its application, or abuse of power" (Art. 33). Interestingly enough, enterprises as well as producers' associations were also given a right of appeal. The court has the authority to assess damages against the Community when injuries result from "an official fault" of the Community in violation of the treaty (Art. 40), to assess damages against any official of the Community in cases in which injury results from "a personal fault" in the performance of his duties, and against the Community if the injured party is unable to recover from the official (Art. 40). The court has the right to decide disputes among member states concerning the application of the treaty only when the dispute cannot be settled by another procedure provided for in the treaty (Art. 89).

More significant than the fact that the Court of Justice commenced operations on an apparently satisfactory basis is the extensive expansion on its jurisdictional responsibilities that took place in 1957. In that year the Treaty Establishing the European Economic Community (Rome, March 25, 1957)[66] and the Treaty Establishing the European Atomic Energy Community (Euratom), of the same date,[67] both incorporated the jurisdiction of the Court of Justice.

THE EUROPEAN COMMUNITY    The structure of the European Community is divided into three branches. The executive part consists of the Commission of the European Communities. Its members are appointed for four-year terms by the respective governments. Below the Commission is found a large civil service (22 departments) under a Secretary-General. The legislative branch embraces the Council of Ministers and the European Parliament. The Council is composed of ministers from each member state, selected according to topics scheduled for discussion at the next session, with meetings taking place once a month. On certain subjects, a system of weighted voting has been developed, under which the larger (industrial) states enjoy more votes than each of the rest. Twice a year, the government leaders of the member states meet to monitor the progress of the economy. The 518 members of the Parliament are elected directly by the voters of their respective countries. The Parliament, despite its name, is basically an advisory unit rather than a true legislative body. It meets once a year in Strasbourg, with committee meetings at Community headquarters in Brussels. The judicial branch is represented by

---

[66] Kaplan-Katzenbach, 324–27; the text of the treaty with related agreements may be found in 51 *AJIL* 865 (1957 Supp.).

[67] Text with related agreements, 51 *AJIL* 955 (1957 Supp.); consult also Hahn, "Euratom: The Conception of an International Personality," 71 *Harvard Law Review* 1001 (1958), and Kaplan-Katzenbach, 327–29.

the European Court of Justice, with 13 judges and six advocates-general, all appointed for renewable six-year terms by the governments of the member states. The major function of the court is, of course, the settlement of disputes between member states of the Community. The European Community expects to complete the development of a unified common market for its members in 1992.

NORTH ATLANTIC TREATY ORGANIZATION    The North Atlantic Treaty Organization (NATO) (Washington, April 4, 1949)[68] does not contain specific provisions for settling disputes among the contracting parties. All reference to the question is limited to a general obligation (Art. 1) to settle international disputes by peaceful means in such a manner that international peace and security are not endangered. Because of the lack of procedural details in the treaty, the North Atlantic Council decided in December 1956 that disputes not settled directly (by negotiation) should be submitted to good-offices procedures within the NATO framework before member states resorted to any international agency.

The North Atlantic Council itself has dealt directly with a number of disputes among the member states, and the Secretary-General of NATO offered his good offices to conciliate in the acrimonious dispute, over the island of Cyprus, among Greece, Turkey, and the United Kingdom. The Greek government felt itself unable to accept the offer, which therefore was abandoned; in 1958, however, a renewal of the offer was accepted by the three parties, and with the assistance of both the Secretary-General and the Council of NATO, a mutually satisfactory agreement was achieved in February 1959. The resulting Cyprus settlement lasted without major crises until the outbreak of civil war in 1964 and the despatch of international peacekeeping forces under UN auspices.

Other regional organizations have proved to be ineffectual in settling internal or international quarrels and conflicts. Thus the Organization of African Unity (OAU) could not settle the civil wars in Ethiopia, Nigeria, and Zaire, nor was it able to help resolve the conflict between the Polisario-backed Saharan Arab Democratic Republic and Morocco, Its one major contribution to peace in Africa has been the agreement among its members (with the exception of Libya) to respect the political boundaries inherited from the former colonial powers.

The Arab League has been incapable of settling peacefully such Middle Eastern problems as the activity of Palestinian guerrillas, the several wars fought by Israel, or the recent civil war in Lebanon. And the Association of South-East Asian Nations (Malaysia, Singapore, Thailand, the Philippines, and Indonesia) was not able to resolve peacefully a variety of conflicts in the region.

[68] Text in 43 *AJIL* 159 (1949 Supp.).

# SUGGESTED READINGS

## Peaceful Settlements: General

Merrills, *International Dispute Settlement* (1984); Oellers-Frahm and Wühler, *Dispute Settlement in Public International Law: Texts and Materials* (1984); Brierly, 345–96; Young, *The Intermediaries: Third Parties in International Crises* (1967); Shore, *Fact Finding in the Maintenance of International Peace* (1970); Fisher, *International Mediation: A Working Guide* (1978).

## Good Offices

Ramcharan, "The Good Offices of the United Nations Secretary-General in the Field of Human Rights," 76 *AJIL* 130 (1982), and his *Humanitarian Good Offices in International Law* (1983); Probst, *'Good Offices' in the Light of Swiss International Practice and Experience* (1989).

## Arbitration

Stuyt, ed., *Survey of International Arbitrations 1794–1989* (1990); Schwebel, *International Arbitration: Three Salient Problems* (1987); Elias, "The Doctrine of Intertemporal Law," 74 *AJIL* 285 (1980); Damrosch, "Retaliation or Arbitration—Or Both? The 1978 United States–France Aviation Dispute," *id.*, 785; Convention on the Settlement of Investment Disputes Between States and Nationals of Other States (March 18, 1965), entered into force in 1966: text in 4 *ILM* 532 (1965).

CASES (AWARDS)

*Southern Pacific Properties (Middle East) Ltd.* v. *Arab Republic of Egypt*, Netherlands, Dist. Court of Amsterdam, July 14, 1984, with introductory note by Van den Berg, in 24 *ILM* 1040 (1985).

*Award of Her Majesty Queen Elizabeth II for the Arbitration of a Controversy between the Argentine Republic and the Republic of Chile Concerning Certain Parts of the Boundary between Their Territories* (Nov. 24, 1966), reported in 61 *AJIL* 1071 (1967).

*Chaco Arbitral Award* (Oct. 10, 1938), text in 33 *AJIL* 180 (1939); excerpts, with useful map, in 49 *Current History* (Dec. 1938), 52.

*Czech-Hungarian Boundary Award* (Nov. 2, 1938), text in 33 *AJIL* 180 (1939).

International Centre for Settlement of Investment Disputes, Arbitration Tribunal; Award in the Case of *AGIP Company* v. *Popular Republic of the Congo*, Nov. 30, 1979, in 21 *ILM* 726 (1982).

International Centre for Settlement of Investment Disputes, Arbitration Tribunal: Award in the Case of *Benvenuti et Bonfant* v. *People's Republic of the Congo*, Aug. 8, 1980, text in 21 *ILM* 740 (1982).

*Note:* See also the Court of Appeals of Paris Judgment of June 6, 1981, concerning the recognition and enforcement of the above award, 20 *ILM* 877 (1981).

## Adjudication

Rosenne, *The World Court* (1989); Singh, *The Role and Record of the International Court of Justice* (1989); Elias, *The International Court of Justice and Some Contemporary Problems*

(1983); Rosenne, *The Law and Practice of the International Court* (1985); Fitzmaurice, *The Law and Procedure of the International Court of Justice* (1986); Chinkin, "Third-Party Intervention before the International Court of Justice," 80 *AJIL* 495 (1986); Gross, "Limitations upon the Judicial Function [Re: *Case Concerning the Northern Cameroons (Cameroons* v. *United Kingdom), Preliminary Objections,* International Court of Justice, *ICJ Reports, 1963,* 15]," 58 *AJIL* 415 (1964), and Gross, ed., *The Future of the International Court of Justice* (2 vols., 1976); McWhinney, *The World Court and the Contemporary International Law-Making Process* (1979).

CASE

*Appeal Relating to the Jurisdiction of the ICAO Council (India* v. *Pakistan), ICJ Reports, 1972,* 46, in 10 *ILM* 452 (1972,).

## Enforcement of Judgments

Nantwi, *The Enforcement of International Judicial Decisions and Arbitral Awards in Public International Law* (1966); Reisman, *Nullity and Revision: The Review and Enforcement of International Judgments and Awards* (1971).

CASES

*The Dogger Bank Case (Great Britain–Russia),* Commission of Inquiry, 1905, in James B. Scott, *Hague Court Reports,* 403.

*N. V. Algemene Transporten Expeditie Onderneming van Gend & Loos* v. *Netherlands Fiscal Administration,* Court of Justice of the European Communities, 1963, Case No. 26/62, digested in 58 *AJIL* 194 (1964), and see the extensively documented analysis of this decision by Riesenfeld and Buxbaum, *id.,* 152.

*Commission of the European Economic Community* v. *Government of the Republic of Italy,* Court of Justice of the European Communities, Dec. 19, 1961, digested in 57 *AJIL* 431 (1963).

## International Organizations

Raman, *Dispute Settlement through the United Nations* (1977); Bailey, *The Procedure of the UN Security Council* (2d ed., 1988).

# 19

# Self-Help Short of War

The absence of a central authority able and willing to assist a state in obtaining justice and the satisfaction of a legitimate claim has meant that when peaceful methods of settling a dispute fail, the state resorts to self-help. This means that a universal need to rely on one's own efforts continues to exist. There is no doubt that each instance of self-help, whether it occurs in pursuit of legitimate goals, in the protection of legal rights, or as an accompaniment of aggression, creates tensions, confusion, and a depreciation of the effectiveness of both law and peaceful settlement. On the other hand, the presence of methods of self-help short of war, in the twentieth century, is a characteristic reflection of the state of transition in which international law and the community of nations are today.*

Although the Charter of the United Nations would seem to condemn methods of self-help based on the use of force short of war, the fact remains that such methods are still in use, precisely because the condition stated in the opening sentence of this chapter continues to prevail. Most of the methods of self-help described below can be applied only by a stronger state against a weaker state; however, in most instances, the idea has been to relate, in some fashion, the degree of pressure or even force to the offense or wrong committed. Third states tend to be unaffected by the procedures in question and to assume the position of watchful bystanders unless or until their own particular interests are involved.

The employment of self-help obviously represents an anomaly in view of the fact that since 1918 a number of multipartite treaties have called for the peaceful settlement of disputes, a trend climaxed by the explicit formulations found in the Charter of the United Nations. The reasons for the continued use of self-help techniques are (1) the failure of the leading powers to take seriously the commitments mentioned; (2) a paralysis, on too many occasions, of the League of Nations and, later, of the United Nations machinery for the peaceful resolution of international differences; and (3) an apparent conviction by many states that at least minor disputes can be settled efficiently by means of self-help measures. This last attitude appears

---

*The terminology used by the present writer, "self-help short of war," was replaced by Zoller with the more legal sounding "peacetime unilateral remedies" (see "Suggested Readings" *sub* Self-Help: General).

to be based either on the belief that peaceful measures have been exhausted without success or on the suspicion that the employment of such measures would result in a decision or solution favoring the other party involved.

## SELF-HELP TECHNIQUES

CONDEMNATION    The least forceful and perhaps the least effective method of self-help is the condemnation of a state for its policies and acts. This is being done almost routinely around the world, all in an effort to attract and marshal public opinion as well as the attention of the target state so as to bring about a desired change. The manner of voicing the condemnation is well known through statements and declarations by national leaders and legislative bodies, resolutions adopted by the UN General Assembly or Security Council, and the sending of diplomatic notes to the government being criticized.

RUPTURE OF DIPLOMATIC RELATIONS    Breaking off diplomatic relations with another state should be mentioned at this point, for it frequently precedes some other technique in an effort to settle a dispute or to obtain justice.[1] It therefore is a warning by one state to another that matters have reached the point at which normal relationships are no longer possible and beyond which harsher methods are likely to be applied. The ironic result of this step is, of course, that peaceful negotiation is made extremely difficult, unless outsiders proffer their good offices or indicate their willingness to mediate the dispute. In other words, at the very time when discussion and negotiation appear to be most needed, a rupture of diplomatic relations makes such negotiations virtually impossible. Examples abound in recent history, such as when New Zealand broke off diplomatic relations with Argentina (April 4, 1982) after the latter's invasion of the Falkland Islands.

On occasion, an act displeasing to a given country or felt to be injurious to it is answered by a partial (and usually temporary) rupture of diplomatic relations, such as when, in March 1981, the People's Republic of China protested the sale of several Dutch submarines to the Republic of China by recalling its ambassador from The Hague, demanding that the Netherlands recall its ambassador to Beijing, and also requesting that diplomatic relations between the two states be reduced from the embassy level to that of an office headed by a chargé d'affaires. Japan reacted in a different manner against the October 9, 1983, bomb attack that killed four members of South Korea's Cabinet in Burma and for which North Korea was blamed. On November 8 of that year, Japan indicated its disapproval of such terrorist tactics by ordering its officials to "restrict contacts" with North Korea.

On May 14, 1963, the United States government inaugurated a "limited diplomatic boycott" of the Haitian government of President François

[1]See Whiteman, vol. 2, 30–34.

Duvalier. In an effort to express disapproval of the unconstitutional extension of Duvalier's tenure of office, the "boycott" introduced a no-contact policy between the U.S. embassy officials in Port-au-Prince and Haitian officials. The gesture obviously and admittedly represented a temporary, halfway measure, falling short of a suspension of diplomatic relations between the two countries. The policy was abandoned on June 3, 1963.

WITHDRAWAL FROM ORGANIZATIONS    One method of indicating disagreement with someone else's acts or policies is to withdraw from an organization of which both parties are members. Such a step not only attracts a considerable amount of publicity—and thus draws attention to one's grievances—but may actually hurt the offending group by the loss of funding resulting from the withdrawal. Thus the United States left the International Labor Organization (ILO) in November 1977, charging it with violating its basic tripartite principle, a selective concern for human rights, a growing disregard for due process, and an increasing politicization. But in early February 1980, a special advisory committee recommended to President Carter that the United States rejoin the ILO, following the resolution of most of these issues. On February 18, 1980, therefore, the United States rejoined the organization.[2]

In November 1984, Poland withdrew from the ILO. Poland had protested against the formation of a special ILO commission in June 1983 to investigate labor conditions in Poland, and the withdrawal was announced after the governing council of the ILO accepted the report of the commission. The latter had concluded that Poland had violated two ILO conventions to which it was a party: one provided for freedom of association, the other for the right to organize and to bargain collectively.

On December 28, 1983, the United States notified the 161-member UN Educational Scientific and Cultural Organization (UNESCO) of its intention to withdraw after the end of a 12-month period, charging UNESCO with anti-American and anti-Western policies as well as with questionable budget and personnel policies. Other criticisms centered on the Director-General's backing of the Palestine Liberation Organization and his proposal to restrict media coverage of Third World countries through the creation of a "new world information order." At the time, the United States contributed 25 percent of UNESCO's $374 million budget. A financial crisis similar to that implied by the American notice of withdrawal had faced UNESCO in 1974, when President Ford withheld the American contribution for two years after UNESCO had decided to withhold funds from Israel and to exclude it from its European group. On that occasion the director-general of the agency borrowed money from the Organization of Petroleum Exporting Countries (OPEC). This time, he announced, he would attempt to borrow from international money markets to make up for the impending loss of

---

[2]Relevant texts and documents in 14 *ILM* 1582 (1975), 16 *ILM* 1561 (1977), and 19 *ILM* 552 (1980).

the U.S. contribution.[3] Withdrawal from UNESCO was confirmed by the United States on December 19, 1984.

Soon afterward the Department of State established a formal observer mission to UNESCO.[4] The United States, however, continued to administer the International Conventions and Scientific Organizations Fund of the agency and remained a member of the latter's Universal Copyright Convention as well as participating in its Intergovernmental Copyright Committee.

On January 28, 1985, the Director-General of UNESCO sent to the organization's Executive Board his illuminating report on "Consequences of the Withdrawal of a Member from UNESCO."[5]

In October 1987, the incumbent Senegalese Director-General withdrew his bid for reelection and was replaced in November by a Spanish biochemist. Although the latter stated that the United States' return was absolutely essential to the agency, no such step had been taken by the time of this writing.[6]

On November 22, 1984, the United Kingdom announced that it would follow the lead of the United States and withdraw from UNESCO unless that organization undertook management and budget reforms by the end of 1985, and on December 28, 1984, Singapore gave notice of withdrawal from UNESCO, citing the existence of priority objectives for the country's limited resources. (See also Chapter 14 for Morocco's withdrawal from the Organization of African Unity.)

REFUSAL TO SEAT DELEGATES    A rarely used technique of self-help consists of the refusal by the members of an international organization to seat the duly accredited delegates of a member state deemed guilty of a delict. This, in essence, corresponds to an expulsion of the party in question. The best-known instance has been the continuing rejection by the UN General Assembly, since 1973, of the credentials of the delegates intended to represent South Africa. The reason for this action has been the continued existence of the crime of *apartheid* in that country.[7] On October 25, 1986, the Conference of the International Red Cross in Geneva ousted its South African delegation. Related have been repeated attempts by a number of

---

[3] Text of message delivered to the Secretary-General of the United Nations on Dec. 29, 1983, in 23 *ILM* 218 (1984); text of the U.S. letter to the Director-General of UNESCO, *id.*, 220; text of UNESCO reply, *id.*, 224; text of U.S. letter of Dec. 20, 1984, in 24 *ILM* 489 (1985), as well as *Gist*, Feb. 1985. See also Department of State, *Current Policy No. 634, Perspectives on the U.S. Withdrawal from UNESCO* (Oct. 31, 1984).

[4] Letters concerning the establishment of the mission are reproduced in 24 *ILM* 491 (1985).

[5] 24 *id.*, 493 (1985).

[6] See *Current Policy No. 1201*, "U.S.–UNESCO Relations," Sept. 1989, and also Ross and Luck in *CSM*, Oct. 27, 1989, 19.

[7] See also Alden, Augusti, Brown, and Rode, "The Decredentialization of South Africa," 16 *Harvard Int'l. Law Jl.* 576 (1975); Bissell, *Apartheid and International Organizations* (1977); Heunis, *United Nations versus South Africa* (1986); Ciobranu, "Credentials of Delegations and Representation of Member States at the United Nations," 25 *Int'l. and Comp. Law Q.* 351 (1976).

Arab governments to oust Israel from its UN membership (1982).[8] The Arab states represented in the United Nations abandoned on November 19, 1990, their eight-year attempt to oust Israel from the organization. The chairman of the group stated that the Arab states would move to accept Israel's credentials as long as Israel did not represent occupied Arab territories, *i.e.*, "Jerusalem, Gaza, the West Bank and Golan Heights." The Israeli UN Mission asserted that it rejected any answer to the problem of seating Israeli delegates that singled out Israel with special conditions. The Arab approach to the credentials question was termed the "Portuguese formula," a reference to the approach African states had taken in 1973, when the question of the credentials of Portuguese delegates had arisen. The General Assembly had then voted to seat the Portuguese delegation provided that they did not represent their country's African colonies, which were then engaged in wars of liberation against Portugal.

RETORSION   The traditional definition of *retorsion* is the commission of an unfriendly but *legal* act, undertaken in response to a prior, equally unfriendly but legal act by the other party to the dispute. However, a legal response to an *illegal* and unfriendly prior act would also be entitled to the label of *retorsion*. Retorsion, in effect, is a lawful act undertaken in answer to an act in the legislative, administrative, or judicial sphere to which another state objects. Because retorsion involves no illegal action, both parties have to see to it that the activities in question violate neither general international law nor their respective treaty obligations.

The actual steps comprising retorsion vary from case to case; their severity normally depends on the initial act to which exception is taken. Among the causes of retorsion frequently cited in the literature are discriminatory tariff rates, discriminatory treatment of aliens, and similar acts not governed by treaties. Retorsion may involve methods of self-help commonly classified separately, such as an embargo or a boycott, but generally, until quite recently, it consisted of retaliation in kind: if state A withdraws non-treaty concessions or privileges from the nationals of state B, the latter will duplicate this action against the nationals of state A living in the territory of B. A good example of retorsion was supplied by the United States at the beginning of 1955, when, in response to travel restrictions imposed by the Soviet Union on foreign diplomats, the United States government barred Russian diplomats from travel in large portions of the United States. In early 1977, the Soviet Union had refused to grant visas to the members of a congressional committee intending to check on Russian performance in carrying out the provisions of the Helsinki Accords, whereupon the United States retaliated by denying an entry visa to the editor of the weekly *Literaturnaya Gazeta,* who was a member of a Soviet committee on carrying out the accord's provisions. In a more serious vein, Egypt seized (February 16,

---

[8]See Halberstam, "Excluding Israel from the General Assembly by a Rejection of Credentials," 78 *AJIL* 179 (1984) and AP Dispatch, Nov. 20, 1990.

1978) two Kenyan airliners in retaliation for forcing down and capturing an Egyptian cargo aircraft flying over northern Kenya with a load of munitions destined for Somalia.

More recently, after relations between the United States and Iran had deteriorated following the November 4, 1979, seizure of the U.S. embassy and most of its staff, the Iranian government threatened to withdraw its deposits from U.S. banks (November 14, 1979). President Carter at once ordered a "freeze" on almost all Iranian public funds, estimated at the time to amount to about $6.5 billion. Subsequent estimates were much smaller: it was reliably stated that only $2.7 billion was actually within U.S. territory. The main reason for the presidential action was a desire to protect current and future American claims (debts, contracts, and so on) against Iran's refusal to pay. Such claims were believed to total approximately $2.45 billion. (See Chapter 18 *sub* Iran–U.S. Claims Tribunal.) "Frozen" Iranian assets totaling $567 million were released on November 7, 1989, in the hope that Iran might use its influence in freeing American hostages in Lebanon. More along traditional lines was the United States' decision, as an act of retorsion against Iran, not to purchase Iranian oil (embargo). On April 7, 1980, the United States took further measures against Iran: (1) the United States broke off diplomatic relations and expelled the remaining Iranian diplomatic and consular staffs, as well as military personnel training in the United States and cadets in military schools; (2) all exports to Iran, except food and medicines exempted from earlier sanctions attempts, were prohibited (embargo); (3) the Secretary of the Treasury was instructed to make an inventory of all outstanding claims of U.S. citizens (including the hostages and their families) and corporations against the government of Iran, with the aim of seizing Iranian governmental assets in the United States to finance settlement of the claims in question; (4) all visas issued to Iranians for entry into the United States were declared invalid, and no visas were to be issued or renewed except for compelling and proven humanitarian reasons or when required by the American national interest. On April 17, 1980, the United States banned all imports from Iran, ordered the freeing for U.S. use or sale of impounded military equipment purchased by Iran, barred financial transactions with anyone in Iran except those involved with journalism (embargo), and prohibited U.S. citizens from traveling to Iran without U.S. government permission. In mid-June, the visa policy was eased to permit genuine students to remain until their studies had been completed.

Normally, retorsion is employed against a country that has caused an injury to the one applying retorsion. It was therefore unusual for the United States to apply a series of retorsion measures against the Soviet Union after the latter had launched an invasion of Afghanistan on December 27, 1979, as the Soviet act had not constituted an international delict directly affecting the United States. The United States adopted, in January 1980, the following measures against the Soviet Union: (1) a decision to ban exports of American grain to the Soviet Union beyond the quantities already un- der contract (the U.S. ban affected more than 17 million tons of grain); (2) cancellation of the opening of the U.S. consulate in Kiev and the Soviet con- sulate in New York City; (3) curtailment by the Civil Aeronautics Board of flights by the Soviet airline Aeroflot into the United States; (4) a moratorium on cultural and other exchanges; (5) a curb on Soviet fishing in specified American waters; and (6) a ban on the delivery of advanced technology to the Soviet Union. In addition to all these steps, President Carter, backed by appropriate resolutions passed in both houses of Congress, appealed to all countries to boycott the 1980 Moscow Summer Olympic Games unless Soviet troops were withdrawn from Afghanistan.

In regard to the last step, 81 national teams competed in the Games, with 55 abstaining, largely because of the protests against the Soviet action in Afghanistan. (The Soviet Union retaliated in 1984 by boycotting the Summer Olympic Games in Los Angeles.) Similarly, the Olympic Council of Asia voted in September 1990 to ban Iraq from participating in the upcoming Asian Games and to suspend it from the Council. These actions were in response to the Iraqi invasion and conquest of Kuwait on August 2, 1990. The suspension was to last until Kuwait's national Olympic committee was again functioning in its country.

The other measures that the United States took against the Soviet Union proved to be relatively ineffective: the trade restrictions did not seriously injure the Soviet Union, and the sanctions on cultural and educational ex- changes were difficult to evaluate. On the other hand, it was claimed that American farmers suffered losses they would not have encountered without the cutback in trade.

Undeterred, however, the United States instituted (December 23, 1981) a number of sanctions against the Soviet Union as a result of the imposition of martial law in Poland: barring new licenses for an expanded list of oil and gas equipment; suspending the issuance and renewal of licenses for the export of electronic equipment, computers, and other high-technology equipment; postponing discussions on a long-term grain treaty; requiring Soviet ships seeking permission to dock at U.S. ports to give 14 days' notice, instead of four days'; suspending Aeroflot's landing rights in the United States; closing the Soviet Purchasing Commission, a ten-member Soviet team in New York; and refusing to renew U.S.-Soviet exchange agreements in the fields of energy, science, and technology. Similarly, on the same day, the United States imposed sanctions against Poland, including the suspension of credit guarantees for the export of farm commodities, the suspension of Polish civil aviation privileges in the United States, and the suspension of the right of Polish fishing vessels to operate within the 200-mile zone. The sanctions against Poland were eased when Polish fishing rights were restored in November 1983, talks were reopened on Poland's large debt to the West, and the Polish national airline LOT was permitted to operate charter flights to the United States (January 19, 1984).

The United Kingdom also adopted sanctions against the Soviet Union and Poland (February 5, 1982) after the imposition of martial law in Poland, including barring new financial credits to Poland, restricting the movement of Soviet and Polish diplomats, and not licensing Soviet fishing in British waters.

A rather unusual example of retorsion occurred on March 4, 1983, when the United States announced that, effective June 30 of that year, Romania would lose its most-favored-nation status for trade with the United States. The reason for this was Romania's passage of the Decree on the Obligations of Persons Emigrating to Repay Debts and Expenses for Education (November 1, 1982).[9] That law was deemed to be an obvious violation of the 1975 Helsinki Accords, imposing, as it did, a tax from $4,000 to $5,000 in "hard" currency for each year of higher education.

REPRISALS    Modern reprisals may be defined as illegal acts undertaken in retaliation against a state to compel it to agree to a satisfactory settlement of a dispute originating in an earlier illegal act. In earlier centuries, going back to the Middle Ages, private citizens (usually merchants) who had suffered injury or loss at the hands of aliens compensated themselves by seizing the property of foreigners who were fellow nationals of the offender. When this practice led in time to grave abuses, the governments of many states intervened and regularized this form of self-help by issuing letters of marque and reprisal. Armed with these instruments of authority, the injured parties could then lawfully prey on the nationals of the state whose citizens had caused the original injury in order to make good the losses suffered by the seizure of goods and ships. The obvious consequence was, of course, that the owners of the seized items secured similar authority from their own government—and the process continued almost indefinitely. The process of seizing private alien property under government authority was termed *special reprisals* but in essence was a modern resumption of the medieval practice of private warfare.

Special reprisals were abolished initially on an individual-country basis and then by all the states that had signed the Treaty of Paris in 1856. Since that year, reprisals by private individuals have been illegal, and only states may have recourse to this method of self-help. Such action must then be taken either on behalf of the state itself, if it believes itself to have been injured illegally, or by the state on behalf of its injured citizens.

It may be surprising that such remedies still exist, but their great and overriding advantage lies in the fact that it brings an immediate response. The hostilities that sometimes ensue are usually carefully characterized as reprisal, and most states have been rather reluctant to create a state of hostilities incommensurate with the original wrong claimed. The limitations commonly associated with the acts of reprisal are that (1) such acts are to cease as soon as the offending state has made reparations for its illegal

[9]Text in 22 *ILM* 667 (1983); see also *CSM,* Mar. 8, 1983, 3.

act (or has ceased its practice, as the case may be); (2) reprisals may not be instituted against reprisals; (3) they must not be employed when their application would injure third parties; and (4) acts of reprisal must not be out of proportion to the original injury suffered. Some commentators have insisted that a fifth limitation should be recognized. Inasmuch as reprisals are justified only if their purpose is to bring about a satisfactory settlement of a dispute, they should not be employed unless and until negotiations to secure redress from the delinquent state have failed.

Modern reprisals have taken many forms. On occasion they have been nonperformance of treaty obligations, invasion of the other party's territory, capture of some of the offending party's nationals, freezing the other party's assets, and seizure of any property belonging to the offending state. At times even the bombardment of the other party's territory and towns has been undertaken in reprisal, such as the Italian bombardment and subsequent temporary occupation of the island of Corfu in 1923 when Greece refused to admit responsibility and to pay compensation for the death of an Italian general serving on a boundary commission.[10]

The classic case of modern reprisal, complete with explanations of the limitations surrounding the concept, was the Naulilaa incident of 1914:

## NAULILAA INCIDENT ARBITRATION

*Portugal–Germany, Arbitral Decision of July 31, 1928 concerning the Responsibility of Germany for Damage Caused in the Portuguese Colonies of South Africa. (2 UN Reports of International Arbitral Awards [1949], 1011)*

FACTS     In October 1914, when Portugal was still a neutral, a German official and two German officers of South-West Africa were killed and two others interned by members of the Portuguese frontier garrison at Naulilaa in Portuguese Angola. The governor of the German colony ordered reprisals to be undertaken and sent German military forces into Angola. In the course of a short period of fighting, the fort of Cuangar and four minor posts along the Angola border were attacked and destroyed. The invaders also compelled the Portuguese garrison to evacuate Naulilaa. The indirect result of the Portuguese reverses was a minor native uprising, accompanied by a considerable amount of looting and pillaging. The German forces retreated into South-West Africa as soon as the Portuguese frontier garrisons had been defeated.

Subsequent investigation showed that the original incident has been caused by the inability of the German officials and officers to understand Portuguese. The commander of the Naulilaa post, receiving no acceptable reply from the group,

---

[10]Consult Barros, *The Corfu Incident of 1923: Mussolini and the League of Nations* (1965), in which he pointed out that the Commission of Jurists appointed by the Council of the League did not commit itself unequivocally on the legality, under the League Covenant, of reprisals involving the use of force, a legality asserted by the Italian government.

believed himself to be in danger of attack and ordered his men to open fire.

After some acrimonious exchanges, Germany and Portugal agreed to submit the question of responsibility to arbitration. The length of the war and other factors delayed the arbitral decision until July 31, 1928.

ISSUE    Was the German governor correct in ordering an invasion of Angola in the name of reprisal? If not, was Germany responsible for damages?

DECISION    The (three-member) tribunal found Germany responsible for all damages done by way of reprisal.

REASONING    1. Reprisals "are an act of appropriate justice of the injured state, in retaliation for an unredressed act of the offending state contrary to international law. They have for an object to suspend temporarily, in the relations between the two states, the observance of such or such a rule of international law. ... They will be illegal unless a previous act in violation of international law has furnished the justification. They tend to impose on the offending state reparation for the offense or a return to legality and avoidance of new offenses."

2. The arbitrators held that because the death of the German officials was not the consequence of an act contrary to international law by the Portuguese authorities, the justification for reprisals was lacking.

The disarming and interning of German officials was a lawful right—and, indeed, a duty of the neutral Portuguese, because the Germans were "belligerents under arms" who had intruded into neutral territory.

The German authorities in South-West Africa had not attempted to secure a peaceful settlement before resorting to reprisals—thus the reprisals were illegal.

The accidental death of the German officials was disproportionately smaller than a military campaign of almost three weeks and the destruction of six Portuguese posts. In other words, the German authorities had violated the necessity of a proportionality between the reprisal and the offense alleged to have been committed. Although "international law does not require such proportionality... reprisals out of all proportion to the act which has motivated them" had to be considered excessive and consequently illegal.

According to compilations of the U.S. Department of State, some 48 instances of the use of military force in peacetime reprisals were recorded between 1811 and 1911. The United States thus utilized this form of self-help on numerous occasions, such as in 1854 when the USS *Cyane* bombarded and then burned the Nicaraguan port of Greytown (San Juan). [11] On one celebrated occasion, American marines were landed at the Mexican port of Veracruz in 1914, after General Huerta had refused to apologize for the arrest of several American sailors. In this instance, Congress had passed a joint resolution authorizing the use of military force. Mexican charges that the occupation of Veracruz was an act of war were denied by the Department of State, which insisted that no state of war existed and that, instead, a temporary occupation represented an act of redress, a reprisal.

[11]Most of the fascinating details are to be found in *Perrin* v. *United States,* U.S. Court of Claims, 1868, Ct. Cl. 543.

A more recent well-known case of reprisals occurred in 1937 during the Spanish Civil War. On the morning of Saturday, May 29, Spanish government aircraft sighted the German pocket battleship *Deutschland,* which was engaged in international "neutrality patrol" duties, lying off the island of Iviza in the Mediterranean. Angry at German aid to the Franco forces, the crews of the aircraft were unable to resist the temptation to attack the warship. They proceeded to bomb it without warning and succeeded in killing a number of ship's officers then eating breakfast.

On May 31, the sister ship of the damaged craft, the pocket battleship *Admiral Scheer,* and four destroyers bombarded the Spanish (government-controlled) seaport of Almeria at dawn. Almeria was a fortified port, and its coastal batteries returned the fire of the German ships, which withdrew about three-quarters of an hour after the attack began. Germany notified the International Non-Intervention Committee in London on the same day that the action had been taken in reprisal for the attack on the *Deutschland.* [12]

There are several recent examples of reprisals involving the use of force in the continuing "informal hostilities" between Israel and its Arab neighbors, following the Six-Day War of 1967. [13] Terrorism, sabotage, artillery duels, air strikes, and plain murder have created mounting tensions in the Middle East. Often the retaliation has appeared to be out of proportion to the initial offense charged, but on occasion each side has argued that its retaliatory act was in response to a number of prior acts of the other side. The most publicized reprisal was an attack by Israel on the airport at Beirut, Lebanon, with an estimated damage to Lebanese aircraft of $100 million, in reprisal for an Arab terrorist attack on an Israeli passenger plane at Athens and several bombing attacks on Israel itself. [14]

. The philosophy behind many of these reprisals, beyond mere retaliation, was expressed lucidly by the former chief of Israeli intelligence, Vivian Herzog: "The very presence of terrorists near our borders is a provocation. No longer will we wait for them to strike use before we strike them. This is not a matter of a reprisal, we are engaged in a continuing war." [15] Preventive

---

[12]*NYT,* June 1, 1937, 1, 2. Although the German "reprisal" did take place during a conflict, its nature appears closer to orthodox reprisals than to wartime reprisals undertaken by "official" belligerents.

[13]Concerning the Arab-Israel conflict in general, see the excellent summary by Forward *et al.,* "The Arab-Israeli War and International Law," 9 *Harvard Int'l. L. Jl.* 232 (1968); see also UN Security Council Resolution 262 (1968) of Dec. 31, 1968, in 63 *AJIL* 681 (1969).

[14]*NYT,* Dec. 29, 1968, *et seq.; Time,* Jan. 3, 1969, 26–27; Jan. 10, 1969, 27–28; Falk, "The Beirut Raid and the International Law of Retaliation," 63 *AJIL* 415 (1969); Blum, "The Beirut Raid and the International Double Standard—A Reply to Professor Richard A. Falk," 64 *AJIL* 73 (1970); UN Security Council Resolution 262 (1968), Dec. 31, 1968, condemning the raid, in 8 *ILM* 445 (1969).

[15]See Tucker, "Reprisals and Self-Defense: The Customary Law," 66 *AJIL* 586 (1972); Bowett's heavily documented study "Reprisals Involving Recourse to Armed Force," *id.,* 1. See also the report on a study of reprisals "in self-defense" by Julia W. Willis, Deputy Legal Adviser for European Affairs, Department of State, 73 *AJIL* 489 (1979).

self-defense? Who can really determine whether a strike against guerrilla bases in a neighboring state (following repeated attacks launched from those bases) should be categorized as an act of lawful self-defense or as a punitive reprisal designed also to inhibit further attacks? Also, and this is relevant to a number of actual situations, suppose that ground intelligence or aerial surveillance detects a massing of prospective invaders (guerrillas or regular units of a neighbor's armed forces) next to one's borders: Would a strike against such "prospective" enemies represent an act of illegal aggression or preventive self-defense or an "anticipatory reprisal"? Recent years have seen the emergence of several euphemisms for this kind of action, including "preemptive raids" and "anticipatory counterattacks." The present writer prefers "anticipatory reprisals" for the kind of thing Mr. Herzog had in mind.

Other recent examples of "peacetime" reprisal raids include the Israeli air attack on the PLO headquarters near the capital of Tunisia (October 1985). It is difficult for the writer to label that raid an act of self-defense, as claimed by Israel, because that concept was never meant to include retaliation by armed force against a neutral country unless that country harbored active enemy forces in time of war. On the other hand, White House spokesman Larry Speakes described the enterprise as a "legitimate response to terrorist attacks . . . as long as you pick out the people responsible." Into the category of reprisals must also be fitted the U.S. air strikes against Libya, the cause of much scholarly debate. (See also Chapter 13.) Those Libyan raids should be labeled an armed reprisal that is normally strictly punitive in character. On the other hand, the UN Security Council condemned the American raids "as an act of armed aggression perpetrated . . . in flagrant violation of the Charter of the United Nations, international law, and norms of conduct."[16] It is interesting that at the time (April 16, 1986), the White House announced that the United States would no longer retaliate against specific acts of terrorism, but would wage preemptive strikes to deter future terrorist attacks.

## Anticipatory Reprisals

On very rare occasions, a state has employed force—without the intention of going to war—against another state in order to prevent a future delinquency by the latter. The most famous instance was the Israeli bombing raid on Iraq's Osirak nuclear reactor (June 7, 1981). The successful attack on the French-built installation involved six F-15 interceptors and eight F-16 fighter bombers. Israel's justification for the attack centered on the belief that the reactor would be used to produce weapons-grade plutonium. Even though both Iraq and France insisted that there had been no such intention, there was much doubt at the time about the need of an oil-rich country for the speedy completion of a large nuclear reactor. The UN Security Council unanimously condemned Israel's action and urged payment of "appropriate re-

[16]See "Reprisals," 80 *AJIL* 165 (1986).

dress." Israel, however, rejected that resolution (of June 19, 1981) as "biased and one-sided."[17] From a legal point of view, the preemptive strike appears to have been in violation of the Charter, except perhaps in situations like that on the eve of the 1967 Six-Day War, when every indication pointed to the immediacy of an attack on Israel, and Israel struck first. It should be remembered, however, that the latter example refers to a war, whereas the preemptive strike discussed above does not refer to an intent to fight a war.

Lest anyone come to believe that only Israel and, on occasion, the United States have engaged in military reprisals indistinguishable from war except for the absence of an intent on either side to refer to one's conduct as a war, the following represents a much abbreviated listing of some modern reprisals of the kind under discussion: On February 8, 1958, French ground forces from Algeria attacked and destroyed the *fellagha* (Algerian rebel) base at Sakiet-Sidi-Youssef in Tunisia, after repeated attacks on French forces in Algeria had been launched from Tunisia, beginning in August 1957. In March and April 1964, after prior warnings, British aircraft attacked targets in Yemen, after repeated attacks had started there against the South Arabian Federation. Rhodesia (now Zimbabwe) repeatedly attacked its neighbors Zambia and Mozambique in an effort to eliminate guerrilla camps located in those states. In early May 1978 and on subsequent occasions,[18] South Africa invaded Angola briefly in what it termed a "limited military operation" against SWAPO guerrillas in response to numerous border raids into South-West Africa. Angola, which had given shelter to the guerrillas for some time, promptly asked for an emergency meeting of the UN Security Council. And returning once more to Israel's actions, it launched repeated military strikes into Jordan in 1968 and 1969 in an effort to destroy guerrilla bases. These activities were condemned again and again in the UN Security Council.[19] Last but not least should be mentioned the U.S. rescue of the merchant vessel *SS Mayaguez* after its seizure of Cambodian forces in May 1975. (See "Suggested Readings" for materials on this much-debated incident.)

The current legal status of peacetime reprisals is not entirely clear. The Covenant of the League of Nations did not prohibit coercive measures of self-help short of war. On the other hand, the Charter of the United Nations requires its members to settle their disputes by peaceful means and to refrain from the threat or use of force.

[17]See *NYT,* June 8–19, 1981, *passim.; Newsweek,* June 22, 1981, 20–29 *passim.; Time,* June 29, 1981, 37; *CSM,* June 24, 1981, 12–13; and also D'Amato, "On the Degradation of the Constitutional Environment of the United Nations," 77 *AJIL* 569 (1983); AP dispatch, Nov. 13, 1981, on the details of a strongly worded resolution passed by the UN General Assembly.
[18]See *NYT,* Nov. 2, 1976, 3; June 5, 1977, E-1; Mar. 8, 1978, A-1, 7; Aug. 2, 1978, A-9; and *Time,* June 13, 1977, 24–25.
[19]Res. 248 (1968), of Mar. 24, 1968; Res. 256 (1968), Aug. 16, 1968; Res. 265 (1969), Apr. 1, 1969. None of the resolutions had any effects. See also "Suggested Readings" under "Reprisals" concerning the continuing reprisal acts by Israel against suspected guerrilla bases in Lebanon.

The question that remains to be settled is whether the reprisals undertaken by one member against another member fall under the Charter prohibition if force in the military sense is not used. Presumably, reprisals involving force can be said to be legal only if undertaken under the authority of some organ of the United Nations, such as the Security Council under Articles 41 and 42 of the Charter. Here we see one of the paradoxes of modern international law. Under customary international law, states have the unquestioned right to use military force as sanctions in the case of a delict, either in the form of war or of military reprisals, in additional to the equally unquestioned right to use such military force for self-protection by way of self-help. And on the other hand, nonmilitary reprisals can by thought of as sanctions because they presuppose a delict by the "offending" state—even if the existence of that delict or delinquency has been determined by the state carrying out the reprisals in a given case. The Charter prohibits resort to force except temporarily in self-defense, in the event of an armed attack, a prohibition extending, at the time of this writing, to 159 states. But force has been employed by member states in the exercise of reprisals. The least that can be said about such acts is that they violate the spirit, if not the letter, of Article 2 (3–4) of the Charter. Expediency appears to prevail, in this case, over the letter of the law, and states generally utilize reprisals involving the use of force in disregard of the Charter.

Reprisals not involving force appear to be legitimate as long as they do not threaten the peace. And it should be kept in mind that reprisals involving force are normally stipulated not to correspond to a state of war and are (normally) ended as soon as the objective in question has been achieved, namely, the ending of the delict (and sometimes reparation for the injury or damage caused by the delict).

This writer believes that in the case of serious delicts, peacetime reprisals are legitimate, even if they involve the use of force, provided they meet the two conditions laid down in the *Naulilaa Incident Arbitration* award: (1) the act of the offending state must have been illegal, and (2) a reasonable degree of proportionality must be shown to exist between the initial offense and the retaliatory action.[20] Although the justification of peacetime reprisals employing forces may appear to many as unorthodox, this writer believes that the members of the United Nations have, in practice (consensus by action), suspended the application of the Charter to reprisals meeting, in essence, the previously listed conditions.

EMBARGO    An embargo represented at one time a specialized form of reprisal. Its early form, following the disappearance of the special reprisal, was the detention in port of vessels flying the flag of the offending state,

[20]See Tucker, "Reprisals and Self-Defense: The Customary Law," 66 *AJIL* 586 (1972); and Derek Bowett, "Reprisals Involving Recourse to Armed Force," *id.,* 1. A third condition, failure to achieve redress before resorting to a reprisal, found in the *Naulilaa Arbitration,* has no authority to be found in customary international law and is not encountered in modern practice.

in order to coerce the latter into remedying the wrong done. Seldom did such detention represent the prelude to confiscation, but the latter did take place on occasion when the offending state refused to grant redress for the wrongs done. The best-known American example of this type of embargo was established by Congress in the Act of December 1807. That measure applied to all vessels, foreign as well as domestic, found in American ports; however, an exemption was granted to any foreign vessel willing to leave in ballast only.

Some states went further in applying the older version of the embargo. In certain instances, vessels flying the flag of a particular foreign state were detained in port when the outbreak of war with that state was foreseen: detention made the subsequent arrest and condemnation as prizes of war much easier and assured the detaining state of a ready supply of every ship available for seizure. The legality of such a maneuver was highly questionable, however.

On the other hand, certain states were not content to detain vessels of an offending state in their ports, but sent their warships out on the high seas to hunt down, arrest, and bring home for detention those vessels flying the flag of the offending state. Many sources use such action by Great Britain in 1839 as an example. In that year, Great Britain, then involved in a quarrel over alleged violations of treaty rights and obligations by the Kingdom of the Two Sicilies, placed an embargo on all vessels of that state found in ports under British authority and, in addition, ordered the British navy to seize all Neapolitan and Sicilian ships found in their own national waters or on the high seas and to bring them into British-controlled ports for detention. When the Two Sicilies settled the dispute in a manner satisfactory to Great Britain, all of the seized ships were returned to the control of their rightful owners. (See Chapter 26 for a discussion of wartime embargoes.)

The twentieth century saw the birth of new forms of the embargo, either as an action by a single state or as a collective act of a number of states to prevent an alleged or potential aggressor from increasing its stockpiles of essential war matériel and supplies.

This meant that on the outbreak of a conflict, individual neutral states could prohibit the export of war matériel to either or both belligerents by placing an embargo on such exports. An example was the French arms embargo to Middle Eastern countries following the 1967 Six-Day War; the embargo was ended in August 1974. Similarly, embargoes have been used to prevent shipments of arms, munitions, and so forth to countries in a state of civil war, such as when the United States prohibited the export of war goods to Mexico in 1912.

More recently, embargoes in the form of export or import prohibitions have been undertaken, individually or collectively, to force states to cease illegal or undesirable activities or to prevent them from using certain categories of goods, mostly war matériel, for purposes objected to by the states instigating the embargoes. Among the early examples were the recommendations of the Coordinating Committee of the League of Nations in 1935. The group, acting in accordance with Article 16 of the Covenant, recommended a wide variety of measures of nonintercourse aimed at Italy, including a prohibition of arms shipments to Italy, the floating abroad of Italian public and private loans, and an extension of credit to Italian agencies or corporations, a prohibition on the importation of goods from territory under Italian control, and an embargo on the exports of specified goods, mostly war matériel.

In May 1951, the UN General Assembly recommended to all members the creation of a "strategic" embargo against mainland China and North Korea, involving arms, ammunition, atomic energy materials, petroleum, and any other commodity usable in the production of arms. Each member state was to determine which of its exports to China fell into the proscribed categories and then place an embargo on its shipment. The main reason behind the embargo was the increasing Chinese participation in the Korean War.[21]

SANCTIONS II    The term commonly used for most measures of self-help short of war is "sanctions." The nature and aim of those measures was discused in Chapter 1 (*sub* Methods of Enforcing the Law—Sanctions I), but additional comment is necessary at this point. Even if sanctions are employed by only one country against another, this method may embrace several techniques, such as embargoes, boycotts, a peacetime blockade, and so on. Traditionally those procedures are covered separately, as in this chapter, but any combination of them is likely to be employed in a self-help effort by one state, several states, or regional/global international organizations.

It should again be noted here that sanctions may have one, two, or a combination of purposes: to cause an offending party to cease whatever it is doing that is offensive or illegal, to punish an offending party for what it has done or is doing, or both aims together. Despite their popularity with parties imposing them, economic sanctions have not proven to be very effective unless the target state depends heavily on trade with the sanctioning state. This was demonstrated in a striking manner in the controversy between the Soviet Union and Lithuania over the latter's unilateral declaration of independence in the spring of 1990.

The most common technique used in the imposition of economic sanctions is the trade embargo. Unfortunately, the most notable uses of economic sanctions were also notable failures. The UN mandatory but limited sanctions against Rhodesia in 1966 failed to prevent the target state from locating sufficient trade partners abroad with which to offset the efforts of the United Nations. The 1973–1974 OPEC oil embargo failed to indirectly compel Israel to withdraw from Arab lands seized during the Six-Day War in 1967. A U.S. grain embargo and an effort to persuade other countries not to participate in the construction of the Siberian oil pipeline failed to achieve their

---

[21]See *Time,* May 28, 1951, 28, for an analysis of the loopholes in the measure as passed.

purpose in the target state, the Soviet Union. And economic sanctions created in protest have failed thus far to topple the white government in South Africa.[22]

A recent situation illustrated one of the problems encountered in imposing economic sanctions. The U.S. government had investigated a possible embargo on South African exports of gold, but found that most of that gold entered the United States in the form of jewelry, mostly from Italy, worth $800–900 million each year. The problem, not solved at the time of writing, was that it was and is difficult to establish the source of gold in imported jewelry.[23]

One of the best-known economic sanction attempts centered on Southern Rhodesia. That British colony had unilaterally proclaimed its independence in 1965. Thirteen months later, in December 1966, the United Nations Security Council resorted to the imposition of mandatory selective economic sanctions. It placed an embargo on about 90 percent of Rhodesian exports; banned the sale of oil, arms, motor vehicles, or aircraft by UN members to Rhodesia; and forbade all "financial or other economic aid" to Rhodesia. South Africa promptly announced its intention to ignore the sanctions imposed on a country of which it was the principal trading partner. On May 29, 1968 (Security Council Resolution 25, 1968), these sanctions were broadened to cover additional items. Rhodesia, however, refused to bow to the pressure brought on it by the United Nations and, on March 2, 1970, proclaimed its status as a republic, an action condemned as an illegal proclamation by the Security Council on March 18, 1970. One day earlier, a draft resolution in the Security Council requiring members to cut all communications with Rhodesia and also condemning the United Kingdom for refusing to use force to end the Rhodesian "rebellion" was rejected through vetoes cast by the United Kingdom and the United States. That vote represented the first use of the veto by the United States in the almost 25 years of the existence of the United Nations.

The Security Council (Res. 314 and 320, 1972) twice reaffirmed the continuation of mandatory sanctions in 1972, and, effective November 29, 1972, the U.S. Office of Export Controls placed a virtually total embargo on exports of both commodities and technical data from the United States to Rhodesia.

By May 1973, further measures appeared to be necessary in the view of the Security Council's Committee on Southern Rhodesia. On another

---

[22]See Nincic and Wallensteen, eds., *Dilemmas of Economic Coercion: Sanctions in World Politics* (1983); Daoudi and Dajani, *Economic Sanctions: Ideals and Experience* (1983); Jenkins, "Why Sanctions Are a Failure," *U.S. News & World Report*, Sept. 21, 1987, 40; Newsom, "For All Their Huff, Sanctions Don't Work," *CSM*, May 13, 1988, 14; Magnuson, "Assessing the Impact of Sanctions," *Time*, Aug. 4, 1986, 20–21; Askin, " 'Sanctions Busting': Schemes to Skirt South African Embargoes," *Time*, Aug. 8, 1988, 10; Watson and Gibson, "Economic Sanctions: In Small Ways, They Work," *Newsweek*, June 23, 1986, 36–37. See also *infra*, Appendix I.
[23]AP dispatch, Oct. 29, 1989.

front, Arab chiefs of state, at the end of a conference in Algeria, announced on November 28, 1973, an embargo on oil shipments to Rhodesia, South Africa, and Portugal.

At long last the U.S. Senate voted on December 18, 1973, to restore the UN ban on chrome imports to the United States, an action followed eventually by the House on March 14, 1977. The House Resolution became law on March 18, 1977.

From the beginning of the Rhodesian sanctions, certain countries (South Africa and Portugal) had openly defied the bans imposed, whereas others (such as Botswana, Malawi, and Zambia) found themselves unable to cut all economic links with Rhodesia. For a long time, still others closed their official eyes to sporadic violations of sanctions (the United Kingdom in the instance of several oil companies).

On December 12, 1979, the Rhodesian parliament repealed the 1965 unilateral declaration of independence and adopted legislation providing that "Zimbabwe Rhodesia shall cease to be an independent state and shall become part of Her Majesty's dominions." The same law repealed the 1979 constitution and replaced it with a new instrument approved by the 1979 Lancaster House peace conference.

On December 16, 1979, the United States lifted economic sanctions against Rhodesia, and on December 21, the UN Security Council voted to call on all member nations to lift these sanctions.[24]

The most recent example of the use of the embargo as a sanction resulted from Iraq's invasion and conquest of Kuwait on August 2, 1990. On that day, the United States froze all assets of the Iraqi government found in the United States, exempting, however, those of Iraq's diplomats in the United States. That measure enabled them to buy food and other supplies and, if necessary, aircraft tickets to return to Iraq. It also imposed a ban on Iraqi imports, including oil. The Soviet Union immediately halted its arms shipments to Iraq, and the European Community imposed an oil embargo on Iraq on August 4.

On August 6, the UN Security Council, by a vote of 13–0 (Cuba and Yemen abstaining), ordered a compulsory economic and arms embargo against Iraq and occupied Kuwait. That global embargo, however, exempted humanitarian shipments of food in conditions of famine.

Those developments were supported by the pledge of military forces (land and sea) to be sent to Saudi Arabia in order to protect it against an anticipated Iraqi attack or to implement the U.S. embargo. The United States, Great Britain, France, Egypt, Canada, Australia, Syria, Pakistan, Morocco, Belgium, the Netherlands, Bangladesh, Argentina, and Bulgaria, among others, contributed to a multinational force. Poland, Czechoslovakia, Ro-

---

[24]See Hawkins's analysis and comparison with sanctions against South Africa in *CSM*, Oct. 20, 1986, 10. For a more recent attempt aimed at an "illegal" government, see Leigh, "Economic Measures against the Illegal Noriega Regime in Panama," 82 *AJIL* 566 (1988).

mania, and Japan offered medical facilities for the ground forces, and Turkey assured the United States that its air bases could be used to launch strikes against Iraq, should war come. Turkey also joined the UN embargo and cut two pipelines carrying oil from Iraq.

The two reasons for cautious optimism about the success of the embargo were Iraq's likely loss of oil-export revenues if the embargo held and Iraq's dependence on food imports. Previously these had amounted to 70–80 percent of consumption—and in Kuwait's case, to 95–97 percent.

On August 11, President Bush admitted that a *de facto* U.S. naval blockade was in place to prevent shipment of Iraqi-Kuwaiti oil from the Persian Gulf. On August 13, an Iraqi oil tanker was denied docking and loading privileges at a Saudi Arabian port and another Iraqi tanker was denied access to a Portuguese ship repair yard.

The U.S. blockade of the Persian Gulf then began officially on August 17. The United States insisted that its "interdiction" of Iraqi trade was legal, even though the UN Security Council had not authorized the use of force to back its sanctions. To bolster its claim of legality of the blockade, the United States kept referring to Article 51 of the Charter as justifying U.S. action as self-defense. In fact, the UN Secretary-General had warned the United States on August 17 that unilateral action by U.S. naval vessels in the Gulf would be in violation of the Charter. The same interpretation was voiced by a number of prominent Canadian international lawyers, who also pointed out that a "peacetime blockade" could not be effected lawfully against third parties. The United States had been meticulous in its official statements to use the term "interdiction" to describe its "blockade" of Iraq, inasmuch as the action applied also to third parties and, if called a blockade, would have been a "hostile blockade," an act of war.

Approval of the Anglo-American naval blockade had to represent a Security Council decision as to whether and when force should be used to enforce its sanctions. If such approval were granted to individual member states, the need for setting up a UN joint command would not arise. On August 25, for the first time in its history, the Security Council authorized the use of minimum military force to ensure observance of the economic sanctions. Agreement was also reached to have the almost defunct Military Staff Committee of the United Nations coordinate naval activities in the Gulf region. The Committee consists of the chiefs of staff of the five permanent members of the Security Council.

On August 27, all Iraqi commercial vessels were instructed by their government not to challenge the blockade in the Gulf. This order eased the task of naval vessels enforcing the blockade to stop and search suspicious ships.

The next development in the embargo came on September 15, when the Security Council ordered an *air embargo* of Iraq by a vote of 14–1 (Cuba opposing). The new embargo prohibited Kuwait- or Iraq-bound air traffic, unless they were called for approved humanitarian considerations. In essence, the new order involved a denial of landing or refueling rights to an aircraft suspected of trying to evade the economic embargo. However, an attempt to attack or destroy such a plane would be unlawful under a number of lawmaking treaties. The Security Council also decided that secondary economic sanctions would be considered against any country helping an Iraqi violation of either embargo.

The UN embargo was now complete and in place. However, seven weeks after economic sanctions had been imposed, Iraq was still receiving some military supplies as well as "war matériel." Much of this influx was said to come through the Jordanian port of Aqaba, thence by truck to Iraq, although the Jordanese government persisted in claiming it was abiding by the UN embargo. And in the Gulf, after 20 vessels had been boarded by the US Navy to check compliance, the first authentic blockade runner had been caught on September 4: an Iraqi freighter loaded with Sri Lankan tea.

In line with its earlier repeated demand for an Iraqi departure from Kuwait, the UN Security Council on October 29 adopted a resolution holding Iraq liable for all war damages and human rights violations committed during its occupation of the emirate. On the same day the five permanent members of the Security Council convened an "informal" meeting of the UN Military Staff Committee.

After much lobbying by the United States and much discussion among governments, the UN Security Council finally authorized the use of military forces unless Iraq withdrew from Kuwait by January 15, 1991 (Resolution 678-1990, November 29, 1990). The vote to grant authority to use force by the 28 states with military forces in the Gulf area was 12–2, with Cuba and Yemen voting against the resolution and China abstaining.

The interesting aspect of the UN action was the setting of a precise deadline after which a presumed failure of economic sanctions would be replaced by the use of force. Military action began on January 17, 1991.

BOYCOTT    A boycott is a form of retaliatory action involving the suspension of business and trade relations by nationals of the injured state with the citizens of the offending state. As long as this concerted action is truly voluntary and does not involve any pressure or persuasion from the government or any official act in its support, the boycott does not involve state responsibility and is, indeed, outside the purview of international law. If, on the other hand, the government of the injured state is involved in any way in the boycott, the involvement creates state responsibility and represents a method of self-help. If the state at which a boycott is aimed has not committed any offensive act involving the boycotting state, the action in question would have to be considered an unfriendly one and would give rise to legitimate protests.

One well-known example of the modern boycott was the widespread suspension by Chinese citizens of trade and business relations with Japan in 1931. The Japanese government protested the action as a violation of international law, but the Chinese government took the official attitude that prior acts undertaken by Japanese authorities constituted far more serious violations of that law. The Committee of Nineteen, appointed by the League of Nations to investigate the findings of the Lytton Commission (which had inquired into the facts of the Manchurian invasion by Japan), decided that the Chinese boycott was a lawful reprisal.

Best known among recent boycotts established through governmental auspices is the one organized by the "Office of the Arab Boycott," created by the now 22-member Arab League after the first Arab-Israeli War of 1948. The agency coordinated a ban on trade with Israel or any foreign businessmen or companies (such as Ford and RCA) investing in or granting franchises to or trading with Israel. (Israel reacted by setting up the "Political-Economic Planning Division," an antiboycott agency, to thwart the efforts of the Arab League; that Israeli agency had been established in 1960.) The Arab League Office then proceeded in 1974 to draw up a "blacklist" of over 2,000 foreign companies and businessmen, of which more than 1,800 were American.

On February 5, 1980, the Egyptian parliament approved a law ending 30 years of economic boycott against Israel. In conformity with the provisions of the Israel–Egypt peace treaty, the law canceled the boycott law of 1955, which had formally imposed sanctions against Israel and against any companies that had dealings with it. (Egyptians had observed an "unofficial" boycott before 1955). Under the terms of the peace treaty, Egypt was obligated to end all forms of economic sanctions against Israel and to allow Israeli ships to call at Egyptian ports after diplomatic relations had been established between the two countries. During the last week of February 1980 those relations became fact.

The U.S. government reacted sharply to the Arab boycott. Congress, in the Tax Reform Act of 1976, provided penalties for U.S. taxpayers who participated in or cooperated with an international boycott based on race, nationality, or religion. That was followed by the Export Administration Act of 1979, which, among other provisions, authorized the President to prohibit, if need be, any "United States person" from complying with international boycotts.[25]

As noted earlier, boycotts that are not supported, approved, or sponsored by governments do not create international responsibilities for the governments in question. Hundreds of such boycotts have been recorded, some of great scope and impact, others of little effect and of short duration. The group includes the enormous private boycott movements, in the United States and other countries in the 1930s, aimed at the importation and sale of goods produced in Germany during the Nazi era or in Japan; a 1973 boycott of American shipping by Australian maritime unions in response

---

[25] A summary of the relevant provisions of the 1976 Act is found in 71 *AJIL* 347 (1977); for the 1979 Act, see *Briggs & Stratton Corporation* v. *Baldrige*, U.S. Dist. Court, E.D. Wis., May 10, 1982, 539 F. Supp. 1307, reported 77 *AJIL* 310 (1983); U.S. Court of Appeals, 2d Cir., 1984, 728 F.2d 915, in 78 *AJIL* 904 (1984); *certiorari* denied, 105 S.Ct. 106.

to the American bombing of North Vietnam; and a boycott attempted in 1974 by U.S. wildlife and conservation groups against products from the Soviet Union and Japan, because those countries had refused to accept a 10-year prohibition on whaling. One of the more bitter private boycotts of recent years was that engineered against the Swiss-based Nestlé Company in a controversy over sales of infant formula in the Third World (1977–1982). The company finally agreed to observe voluntarily the Code of Marketing of Breastmilk Substitutes (1981) of the World Health Organization. And at the time of writing, the most recent private international boycott was the short-lived ban on flights to Moscow, instituted in 1983 by the International Federation of Airline Pilots Association after the downing of Korean Airlines Flight 007.

OCCUPATION OF FOREIGN TERRITORY    Occupation of foreign territory is another method of self-help short of war, and it frequently follows a naval demonstration off the coasts of a delinquent state. (A show of military force has been adopted on a few modern occasions, such as the combined naval demonstration by fleet units of the Great Powers against Turkey in 1880, by the Allied Powers against Greece on September 1, 1916, and by the Netherlands against Venezuela in 1908.)

Occupation by military force has also played a part in modern history. In 1895, Great Britain landed naval personnel at the port of Corinto in Nicaragua and took control of the local customs house, which it held until the Nicaraguan government agreed to pay indemnities for injuries suffered by British nationals residing in Nicaragua. In 1901, a French force occupied the then Turkish island of Mytilene in order to force Turkey to pay sums owed to two French nationals and to fulfill its treaty obligations concerning the Constantinople dues. In 1914, the United States occupied Veracruz in Mexico. In 1923, Italy bombarded and occupied Corfu, justifying this action, however, as a reprisal.

BLOCKADE    There are two traditional types of blockade: a pacific block-ade and a hostile blockade. A pacific blockade is a highly effective method for settling a dispute by coercive measures short of war, provided it is ap-plied by a strong state against a weaker state. This procedure made its first appearance in 1827, when France, Great Britain, and Russia established a joint blockade of certain sections off the coasts of Greece in order to induce Turkey to grant independence to Greece. The blockade, originally intended to be pacific, did not remain so, however, for the fleets of Great Britain and Egypt fought a battle at Navarino, ending in a decisive victory for Great Britain. Since 1827, there have been many pacific blockades, some engineered by individual states, others undertaken as a joint action. Most publicized were the British-French blockade of the Netherlands in 1832 in an effort to secure Dutch recognition of Belgian independence; the British blockade of Greek ports in 1850 to secure compensation for the burning, in an Easter riot, of the house of Don Pacifico, a native of Gibraltar and a British subject; the blockade of Greece by a combined fleet of the Great

Powers to prevent Greece from going to war against Turkey; and a similar action by the Powers in 1897 when the blockaded the coasts of Crete in order to prevent the inhabitants of the island from joining with Greece by means of self-annexation.

Later, during the First Balkan War, the Great Powers blockaded the port of Antivari in order to prevent a Montenegran annexation of the city of Scutari, which the Powers had intended to make a part of Albanian territory.

The best-known early pacific blockade in the Western Hemisphere was the joint effort in 1902 by Great Britain, Germany, and Italy against Venezuela in an attempt to force that country to honor a long list of claims filed against it by citizens of the three countries. In accordance with the Monroe Doctrine, the claimant states first sought the consent of the United States for their joint action. That consent was granted, subject to certain conditions and limitations. Because no state of war existed, other states did not feel obligated to declare their neutrality. The United States, however, eventually protested vigorously after the allied fleet of the three powers exercised the traditional practices of a hostile blockade and stopped the vessels of third parties. The American contention that such acts were illegal in the absence of a state of war was met by the three powers' assertion that such a state did actually exist—but then the stoppage of the vessels of third parties ceased, and the blockade resumed the characteristics of a pacific blockade.

A pacific blockade differs from a hostile one in two respects: in the former situation a formal state of war does not exist, and (in modern times) the pacific blockade is applied only to the ships of the blockaded state. Third states are not affected by the blockade and, because no formal war exists, do not achieve the status of neutrals. The United States in particular has insisted again and again that a pacific blockade can affect only the vessels of the blockaded (and, obviously, of the blockading) state; this point of view has prevailed in the community of nations. As was pointed out earlier, this was why the United States chose to refer to "interdiction" when it started its blockade of Iraq in 1990. The UN Security Council's call for compulsory sanctions against Iraq in 1990 was unique: it aligned 158 countries against Iraq and, at least in theory, left scarcely any entities able to play the part of traditional blockade runners (see *supra*). Thus the old problem as to whether a given blockade (embargo, too, in this case) was hostile or pacific in nature was avoided. The Security Council's approval of the use of the minimum force necessary to enforce its sanctions did not constitute creation of a traditional hostile blockade, in the opinion of this writer, nor did it conform to the characteristics of a traditional pacific blockade.

## Evolution of a New Type of Blockade

The reported arrival in Cuba, in the summer of 1962, of Soviet military equipment accompanied by large numbers of technicians and other apparently military groups led to a widespread demand in the United States for the establishment of a unilateral pacific blockade of Cuba. Even then, it was interesting to note that many proponents of this step advocated application of the blockade to Russian and other foreign vessels, because Cuba itself had almost no merchant marine of its own. This position ignored the restriction characteristic of a pacific blockade: it does not apply to vessels of third parties. Because the application of the second traditional type of blockade, the belligerent or hostile variety, would enable the United States to bar access to Cuba to all ships, adoption of this type was also considered. But under the rules of traditional international law, such a blockade was lawful only in time of war.

A two-day conference of the American foreign ministers (October 2–3, 1962) in Washington agreed that further economic and security measures were required in order to cope with the Cuban armament buildup, and an invitation was drafted to non-Communist states, asking them to tighten controls over ships flying their flags and carrying Soviet goods to Cuba. The United States, for its part, took three initial steps: it closed its ports to all ships carrying arms to Cuba; it closed its ports to ships sailing between a Communist-bloc port and Cuba; and it prohibited all vessels registered in the United States from engaging in any Cuban trade.

MISSILE CRISIS    Discovery through the United States' aerial reconnaissance of the installation of medium-range (1,000 nautical miles) ballistic missiles and of the construction of sites for intermediate-range (about 2,000 nautical miles) missiles in Cuba brought the whole matter to a high-crisis level. On the evening of October 22, 1962, President Kennedy initiated seven steps:

1. A strict "quarantine" on all offensive military equipment bound for Cuba; all ships so bound, from whatever nation or port, were to be turned back by the United States Navy if found to be carrying offensive weapons.
2. A continued and increased aerial surveillance of Cuba, in line with the communiqué of the meeting of American foreign ministers, which had rejected secrecy in such matters for the Western Hemisphere.
3. Proclamation of a United States policy that regarded "any nuclear missile launched from Cuba against any nation in the Western Hemisphere as an attack by the Soviet Union on the United States requiring a full retaliatory response upon the Soviet Union."
4. Reinforcement of the garrison of the U.S. Naval Base at Guantánamo, Cuba, from which United States dependents had been evacuated.
5. A call for an immediate meeting of the Organ of Consultation under the OAS to consider the Cuban situation and to invoke Articles 6 and 8 of the Rio de Janeiro Treaty.
6. A request for an emergency meeting of the United Nations Security Council "to take action against Soviet threat to world peace."
7. A call to Soviet Premier Nikita Khrushchev to "halt and eliminate this clandestine, reckless and provocative threat."

On October 23, 1962, the Council of the OAS met and constituted it-self as the Provisional Organ of Consultation. This body then studied the evidence submitted by the United States of the presence of Russian strate-gic missiles in Cuba and concluded logically that a situation existed that could endanger hemisphere peace in the meaning of Article 6. The Organ then adopted a resolution that recommended that the member states, col-lectively and individually, take measures, including, the use of armed force, to prevent further receipt by Cuba of military matériel and supplies capable of endangering hemisphere peace. The OAS decision was communicated at once to the UN Security Council.

The resulting U.S. presidential proclamation of the defensive quarantine was based on the action of the Consultative Organ. To be sure, the American announcement of intent to establish the quarantine preceded the action of the OAS, but the actual establishment of the quarantine followed that action. On October 24, the quarantine went into effect, implemented by naval and air force units of the United States only; a total of 183 U.S. naval vessels were employed.

The ensuing events are now history: the avoidance of trouble when com-ponents of the United States Navy actually stopped Russian ships; the di-version of Soviet-bloc vessels from the Cuba run; the attempt of the Acting Secretary-General U Thant to prevail on the United States to suspend the blockade of Cuba and on Khrushchev to halt shipments to the island; the rejected Russian proposal of October 27 to withdraw offensive weapons from Cuba in exchange for American withdrawal of rockets from Turkey; and the Russian agreement on October 28 to dismantle the Cuban missile sites and to transport the missiles back to the Soviet Union.[26]

Aerial surveillance of Cuba continued after the blockade was lifted and disclosed the continuing presence on the island of large quantities of Russian conventional weapons as well as of great numbers of Soviet technical and some military personnel (estimated at 17,000 as of February 6, 1963).

The order instituting the blockade of Cuba, signed on October 23, 1962, is rather interesting in view of the new aspects of the blockade in ques-tion. The document, entitled "Interdiction of the Delivery of Offensive Weapons to Cuba," listed these weapons as offensive: surface-to-surface mis-siles; bombers, bombs, air-to-surface rockets, and guided missiles; warheads for such weapons; mechanical or electronic support equipment; and any other weapons designed at a later time "for the purpose of effectuating this procla-mation."[27]

The term *quarantine* used initially to describe the action adopted indicated the realization that this was a new method of blockade. Analysis revealed

---

[26] A selection of major published documents (Sept. 2–Oct. 28, 1962) is conveniently available in Foreign Policy Association, *The Cuban Crisis: A Documentary Record.* Headline Series No. 157 (1963); see also "Suggested Readings."

[27] The text of the proclamation may be found in 57 *AJIL* 512 (1963 Supp.)

that it fell somewhere between the two traditional types of blockade. It was a pacific blockade in that neither the element of intent for war nor a "state of war" existed, but at the same time, it was a hostile blockade in that the quarantine was applied to vessels of a third state.

## Legal Status of Blockades and Forcible Self-Help

The legal status of a traditional pacific blockade has engendered a great deal of controversy among jurists. If, say, the League of Nations, acting under Article 16 of the Covenant, had called on its members to institute a collective pacific blockade against a state held to have violated its obligations under the Covenant, such a joint effort would have proved to be ineffective if one of the major maritime states had refused to tolerate interference with its shipping bound for or coming from the blockaded state. When the Charter of the United Nations was written, Article 42 appeared to prohibit unilateral institution of a pacific blockade as an enforcement action.[28] Most writers concur that a pacific blockade would be legal today only under one of two conditions: (1) if it were adopted by the United Nations as a collective enforcement action, or (2) if it were instituted by a state not bound by the obligations of the Charter, that is, by a state that is not a member of the United Nations. The argument is not a mere academic one, for it revolves around the touchy subject of unilateral enforcement of both the Charter and the rules of international law.

Outside the two conditions mentioned, it is difficult to reconcile a traditional pacific blockade with the applicable provisions of the Charter (Art. 2, pars. 3 and 4), nor can such a blockade be found among the resolutions for an international dispute listed in Article 33 of the instrument.

If one is to assume that the Charter's prohibition of the use of military force as a unilateral sanction is binding, then states against which violations of international law not representing an armed attack have been committed may on occasion be without a really adequate remedy. In addition to the absence of a workable but forcible method of self-help, it is conceivable that the machinery of the United Nations might not be able to secure redress for injuries suffered and that the various methods of peaceful settlement might be rejected by the offending state.

The attitude found in certain states—namely, that Article 2, paragraph 4 of the Charter does not prohibit unilateral action by the threat or use of military force (and, by implication, of a blockade) to enforce international rights if their exercise is illegally denied—was directly responsible for the French-British attack on Egypt in 1956. The British and French governments defended that attack as legitimate, and this position was emphasized by the vetoes cast by the two states in the Security Council.

The Anglo-French position, maintained even after military operations

---

[28] See Kunz, "Sanctions in International Law," 54 *AJIL* 324, 331 (1960) on this point.

failed owing to United Nations opinion and pressure from both the United States and the Soviet Union, was condemned by both the Secretary-General of the United Nations and most writers on international law. But a staunch defense of a total prohibition of the unilateral threat or use of military force still appears, to this writer to be not only an unrealistic but also a highly dangerous attitude. What the Charter's provisions have done, in effect, is to deprive states of valuable tools of self-help and the enforcement of international rights, without substituting a really workable method for achieving the same ends. It remains to be seen whether states will stand by the prohibition if and when their interests or rights are affected and peaceful methods of settlement or sanction have failed.

Two eminent jurists pointed out that if reprisals or limited retaliation remained politically feasible and practically effective without collective retaliation, then the prohibitions presumably imposed by the Charter would either fade into unimportance or would have to be altered.[29] At the present time, the prohibitions are "on the books." But it appears that when a state comes to believe that a vital interest or survival (or at least self-defense) justifies forcible measures short of war and hopes to escape total war despite the utilization of such measures, they will be undertaken, despite the existence of the Charter.

Returning once more to the subject of a pacific blockade: such an action obviously remains "pacific" only as long as both parties involved choose to treat it as such. The blockaded state can, at its discretion, regard itself as being in a state of war, can supply naval escorts for its vessels, and can attempt to "shoot its way" through the blockading fleet. And if the blockading state attempts to bar the vessels of third parties from reaching the blockaded ports, those parties can supply escorts for their ships and, if need be, attempt to force passage to the blockaded ports. This risk of conversion into a state of war is inherent in many measures of self-help and has to be faced by any state contemplating the use of such measures in the assertion of its international rights.

## APPENDIX I

A Representative List of Modern Embargoes (in Addition to Those Covered in Chapters 1 and 19).

1955 U.S. arms embargo against Egypt (to 1976).
1956 U.S. oil embargo against Western Europe (Anglo-French-Isreali invasion of Egypt.)
1964 U.S. embargo on military equipment to South Africa (earlier there had been an embargo on all such equipemnt that could be used to enforce segragation in South Africa or South-West Africa).

---

[29] Kaplan-Katzenbach, 217.

1964 OAS trade embargo against Cuba (to July 29, 1975).

1965 U.S. limited arms embargo against India and Pakistan (to February 24, 1975).

1975 U.S. limited arms embargo against Turkey (invasion of Cyprus; to 1978.)

1975 U.S. trade embargo against Vietnam (after the defeat of South Vietnam.)

1976 U.S. military aid embargo against Indonesia (takeover of East Timor; ended after six months).

1976 French embargo on exports of nuclear fuel-processing plants able to produce weapons-grade plutonium.

1977 U.S. arms embargo against Guatemala (to 1983).

1977 U.N. Security Council mandatory arms embargo against South Africa.

1978 U.S. trade embargo against Uganda (after genocide charges had been brought against President Idi Amin Dada).

1980 U.S. partial grain embargo against the Soviet Union.

1980 U.S. embargo on exports of computers and raw materials, products and data in "process technology" such as petrochemical plants.

1980 U.S. embargo on trade with Iran [See 74 *AJIL* 668 (1980)].

1980 U.S. limited grain embargo against the Soviet Union (invasion of Afghanistan.)

1980 U.S. embargo on military aid and equipment against Argentina (to April 24, 1981; human rights violation).

1981 U.S. embargoes against Poland and the Soviet Union (martial law in Poland).

1982 U.S. embargo on sale of U.S. energy technology (to companies supplying such for the Soviets' Siberian natural-gas pipeline).

1982 U.S. embargo on Libyan oil imports and sale of U.S. oil and gas equipment to Libya.

1982 West Germany, Belgium, France, the Netherlands: arms embargo against Argentina (invasion of Falklands); Sweden and Switzerland arms embargo against both Argentina and the United Kingdom.

1982 All 10 members of the European Communities (and most other Western European states): embargo on imports of Argentine goods (to May 17, 1982).

1982 U.S. economic santions against Argentina (to July 12, 1983).

1982 United Kingdom arms embargo against Israel (invasion of Lebanon).

1983 U.S. embargo against 90 percent of sugar imports from Nicaragua.

1983 U.S. embargo on all business ties between U.S. airlines and the Soviet Aeroflot (and closure of the latter's New York and Washington offices). Caused by downing of the Korean Airlines Flight 007.

1985 U.S. embargo on all trade with Nicaragua (except for goods destined for Contras; embargo on all Nicaraguan vessels and aircraft; abrogation of 1956 friendship treaty.
U.S. embargo on imports of South African Krugerrands.

1986 Italian arms export embargo against Libya.

U.S. trade embargo against Libya.

U.S. tightening of trade embargo against Cuba and prohibition on Cuban immmigration from Third World countries.

European Community trade embargo (except for coal) against South Africa.

Great Britain embargo against Libyan landing rights.

European Community trade embargo against Syria.

U.S. trade embargo against Syria.

U.S. "Comprehensive Anti-Apartheid Act of 1986" codified almost all earlier U.S. embargoes against South Africa.

1987 Norway embargo on most trade with South Africa.

U.S. embargo on all imports from Iran.

1988 U.S. embargo on all payments to Noriega regime in Panama.

U.S. extended authority for embargoes against Libya for six months.

1989 U.S. embargo in military sales to China.

U.S. trade embargo against Noriega's Panama.

1990 U.S. trade embargo against Iraq and occupied Kuwait.

U.N. trade embargo against Iraq and occupied Kuwait.

## SUGGESTED READINGSS

### Self-Help: General

Elegab, *The Legality of Non-Forcible Counter-Measures in International Law* (1988); Zoller, *Peacetime Unilateral Remedies* (1984).

CASES

*The Boedes Lust,* Great Britain, High Court of Admiralty, 1804, 5 C. Robinson 233 [Embargo].

*United States* v. *Curtiss-Wright Export Corporation,* U.S. Supreme Court, 1936, 299 U.S. 304 [Embargo].

*Gray, Administrator* v. *United States,* U.S. Court of Claims, 1886, 21 Ct. Cl. 340 [Reprisals].

### Reprisals

Onuf, *Reprisals, Rituals, Rules, Rationales* (1974).
(a) Anticipatory Reprisals: *NYT,* Oct. 22, 1972, E-5; Dec. 3, 1975, 1; June 10, 1978, 1, 4; *Time,* July 10, 1972, 33.

### Sanctions

Malloy, *Economic Sanctions and U.S. Trade* (1990); Collection of Documents, United States, "Economic Sanctions against Nicaragua," 24 *ILM* 809 (1985); Documents, Canada, "Sanctions against South Africa," 25 *ILM* 1164 (1985); *Current Policy No.*

*1081,* "The Potential Impact of Imposing Sanctions against South Africa" (June 1988); Carter, *International Economic Sanctions* (1988); *Current Policy No. 780,* "Libyan Sanctions" (Jan. 1986); Renwick, *Economic Sanctions* (1982); Strack, *Sanctions: The Case of Rhodesia* (1977).

## Boycotts

(A) General: Maw, "Historical Aspects and the U.S. Involvement in Boycotts," *Proceedings* 170 (1977).

(B) The Arab Boycott of Israel (Oil Embargo and U.S. Reaction): Chill, *The Arab Boycott of Israel* (1976); Turck, "The Arab Boycott of Israel, 55 *Foreign Affairs* 472 (1977); *NYT,* Feb. 24, 1975, 8; Feb. 27, 1975, 1, 16 (includes list of American names on the Arab blacklist); Feb. 28, 1975, 8; Mar. 6, 1975, 17; and Aug. 8, 1977, 8; *Time,* Dec. 2, 1966, 93–94; Moore, "United States Policy and the Arab Boycott," *Proceedings* 174 (1977); "Arab Boycott," 69 *AJIL* 658 (1975); Paust and Blaustein, "The Arab Oil Weapon—A Threat to International Peace," 68 *AJIL* 410 (1974); Shihata, "Destination Embargo of Arab Oil: Its Legality under International Law," *id.,* 591; Blum, letter *re* Shihata's article, 69 *AJIL* 635 (1975); Smith, "Re 'The Arab Oil Weapon': A Skeptic's View," *id.,* 136; Paust and Blaustein, letter *re* Smith's article, *id.,* 637.

CASE

*United States* v. *Bechtel Corporation,* United States, U.S. Dist. Court, N.D.Cal., Jan. 10, 1977, in 16 *ILM* 95 (1977). See also Archer, "Overview of the Bechtel Litigation," *Proceedings* 190 (1977). The case was also reported by Feinerman in 18 *Harvard Int'l. Law Jl.* 699 (1977).

## The Cuban Missile Crisis (1962)

Whiteman, vol. 4, 523–24; Larson, *The "Cuban Crisis" of 1962: Selected Documents and Chronology* (2nd ed., 1986); Chayes, *The Cuban Missile Crisis: International Crises and the Role of Law* (1974); Mallison, "Limited Naval Blockade or Quarantine— Interdiction and Collective Defense Claims Valid under International Law," 31 *George Washington L. Rev.* 335 (1962); Alford, "The Cuban Quarantine of 1962: An Inquiry into Paradox and Persuasion," 4 *Virginia Jl. of Int'l. Law,* 35 (1964); Meeker, "Defensive Quarantine and the Law," 57 *AJIL* 515 (1963); Christol, "Maritime Quarantine: The Naval Interdiction of Offensive Weapons and Associated Matériel to Cuba, 1962," *id.,* 524; Fenwick, "The Quarantine against Cuba: Legal or Illegal?" *id.,* 588; McDougal, "The Soviet-Cuban Quarantine and Self-Defense," *id.,* 597; and the dissenting views of Wright in "The Cuban Quarantine," *id.,* 546; McDevin, "The UN Charter and the Cuban Quarantine," 17 *JAG Jl.* 71 (April–May 1963); *Time,* Sept. 27, 1982, 85–86; *Newsweek,* Oct. 11, 1982, 120.

# Case Study No. 8

## The United States and the U.N. Budget Crisis

The United Nations experienced a period of serious financial crisis, resulting in large part from certain U.S. measures taken in Congress during the 1985–1986 sessions. As Nelson pointed out,[1] the United States' withholding of payments to international organizations fell into one of three categories: (1) specific cuts in funds of particular programs; (2) contingent withholding, becoming a reality only if certain conditions were or were not realized; and (3) nonspecific across-the-board cuts, such as those mandated under the Gramm-Rudman-Hollings legislation.

The cuts in question reduced the total U.S. contribution to the UN budget by a sum equal to the 25 percent U.S. share for the activity or program authorized by the General Assembly.

Specific cuts were applied primarily to programs involved with Palestinian questions, with SWAPO in Namibia (prior to 1990), and with the "Second Decade to Combat Racism and Racial Discrimination (GA Res. 3379-XXX). A specific but nonlegislative cut affected the Preparatory Commission implementing the Law of the Sea Convention (UNCLOS III), a treaty not signed by the United States.

Contingent withholding of funds on materialization of a specific condition was required by the 1986 Kassebaum Amendment to the U.S. Foreign Relations Authorization Act for FY 1986 and 1987 (hereafter Kassebaum Amendment). Involved was a reduction of the assessed U.S. contributions to the UN and its specialized agencies, from 25 to 20 percent, *unless* weighted voting based on the size of a member's contribution was introduced in all UN budgetary questions. That reduction, scheduled to begin with the fiscal year 1987, was mandated "in order to foster greater financial responsibility" by the various agencies and the United Nations itself. Jeane Kirkpatrick, U.S. ambassador to the United Nations in 1985, put the American attitude in a succinct manner when she said, "There is a terrible disjunction in the United Nations between responsibility and power. This is what is at the root

---

[1] Nelson, "International Law and U.S. Withholding of Payments to International Organizations," 80 *AJIL* 973 (1986).

of the problems in the UN administration and budget."[2] The Kassebaum Amendment[3] stated U.S. reasoning as follows: "The Congress finds that the United Nations . . . [has] not paid sufficient attention [in developing its budget] to the views of the member governments who are major financial contributors to those budgets." It provided that if UN financial matters were not reorganized, United States contributions were to fall to 20 percent of the "total annual budget of the UN and its specialized agencies."

It should be noted that introduction of weighted voting in the UN would require an amendment of Article 18 of the Charter. That article provides for one vote for each UN member. Weighted voting, it has been argued, would also violate the provision of Charter Article 2(1) calling for the "principle of the sovereign equality of all its Members."

An overwhelming majority of legal scholars have agreed that the United States was in violation of its treaty (Charter) obligations in cutting assessed contributions and that such action could in turn lead to the loss of its vote in the General Assembly.[4]

From a material, factual point of view, the withholding of substantial U.S. monetary contributions was bound to critically affect the extent of UN personnel, for about 75 percent of normal UN budgetary receipts have annually been in the sphere of personnel. In terms of numbers, it was estimated at the time that 1,600 out of 11,400 staff positions supported by the regular budget were at issue.[5]

By March 1986, the United Nations had a deficit of $265 million, the bulk of which was owed for Middle East peacekeeping debts, the Soviet Union being the major debtor. In addition, South Africa, denied seating since 1973, had withheld $24.5 million from the regular UN budget. On the other hand, China notified the UN in September that it would pay $4.4 million in dues withheld over the years for a variety of reasons.

The size of the proposed U.S. cut in contributions amounted to $70 million annually, *i.e.*, a cut of one third of the U.S. annual assessment of $210 million (25 percent of the 1986 UN budget). In August 1986, the chairman of a UN-appointed 18-member Group of High-Level Inter-governmental Experts stated that the UN should cut its staff sharply to streamline the organization and make it more efficient. The suggested reduction amounted to over 1,700 UN Secretariat positions to be cut over the course of three years. On the other hand, UN Secretary-General Pérez de

---

[2] *Newsweek,* Oct. 28, 1985, 52.

[3] Text in 25 *ILM* 27 (1986). See also the Mar. 14, 1986, "Memorandum to the United States Concerning the Financial Situation of the United Nations," by the 12-member European Community, 25 *ILM* 482 (1986).

[4] See Chapter 20, *sub* International Armed Forces, for an earlier U.S.–USSR confrontation about this issue.

[5] Martin and Berard, rapps., UN *Budgetary and Financial Impasse* [The Stanley Foundation] (1986), 11.

Cuéllar had persuaded the General Assembly to approve $60 million worth of total cuts in the UN budget.

In late October 1986, the United States announced that its annual contribution to the UN budget would be *$100 million* instead of the assessed $210 million. The General Assembly, alarmed by that statement, prepared an elaborate and serious resolution (including the report of the Group of Experts mentioned earlier): Resolution Concerning the Efficiency of the Administrative and Financial Functioning of the UN."[6]

Excellent as the GA Resolution was—and Senator Kassebaum admitted that the United Nations had done "quite a fine job in meeting the intent" of her amendment—the United Nations had failed, as anticipated, to meet the amendment's central demand, the introduction of weighted voting in UN budgetary matters. Zoller pointed out that a statement by the President of the General Assembly on December 19, 1986, indicated clearly that in the matter of budgets, nothing more than a "gentlemen's agreement" had been reached: the member states had tacitly agreed that budgetary decisions would not be taken against the will of the major contributors and that UN budgetary "law" had not been changed.[7]

By September 1987, the United States owed more than $360 million in assessed contributions (not including $61 million for Middle East peacekeeping operations), even though the U.S. Ambassador to the United Nations (Walters) had publicly supported the restoration of the cuts made.

At last, the United States paid *$90 million* to the United Nations, but by then U.S. arrears totaled $320 million. On September 15, 1988, the United States had held back $520 million of its assessed contributions; that amount represented a major portion of the total of $691 million owed by its members to the UN. Moreover, the $520 million did *not* include $111.8 million owed by the United States for peacekeeping operations. Two days earlier, President Reagan had authorized the release of $188 million of UN-assessed contributions, at which time 102 delinquent states owed the UN regular budget $602 million in unpaid contributions and assessments. President Reagan also asked the Department of State to develop a plan for the gradual payment of remaining U.S. assessments and peacekeeping expenses.

President Reagan had promised in October 1988 that the United States would begin payment of its bills to the United Nations and repay past debts over a six-year period, a promise repeated by President Bush. The U.S. Congress in 1989 appropriated $206 million of the $215 million in then-current dues only. In 1990 the U.S. House of Representatives approved full

---

[6]Resolution 41/213, adopted without a vote on Dec. 19, 1986, text and *ILM* background content analysis, in 26 *ILM* 137 (1987). See also *ASIL Newsletter* (Jan.–Feb. 1987), 1–2, and Zoller, "The 'Corporate Will' of the United Nations and the Rights of the Minority," 81 *AJIL* 610 (1987).

[7]Zoller, *op. cit.* 634, n. 6.

payment of the 1990 U.N. dues and 20 percent of the $288 million owed to the U.N. on the regular budget from the past. The U.S. Senate then considered similar legislation for payments to the United Nations.

The whole affair reflects a perhaps justified desire on the part of the major contributors to the United Nations to improve the efficiency and financial responsibility of the organization as well as its member states. At the same time, however, the United States tried to ignore the inescapable fact that under the Charter, as it stands, it was unequivocally obliged to pay assessments approved and apportioned by the UN General Assembly.[8] No member of the United Nations can legally cut its obligations to the UN on a unilateral basis, no matter how meritorious its real or alleged motivation may be.

It should be mentioned that in another budgetary crisis, the Organization of American States (OAS) faced a possible lay-off of about 300 of its 1,000 member staff in 1988. This was the result of a decision of the U.S. government to reduce its 1988 contribution to the OAS by $10 million and by the same amount in 1989. Since other members, including Chile and Venezuela, had already fallen behind in their annual contributions, the U.S. action greatly aggravated an already serious OAS problem.

[8]See the report of the ASIL Special Working Committee on UN Relations, "The United States Is Obligated to Pay Its United Nations Assessments," *ASIL Newsletter* 3–6 (July–Sept. 1989).

# PART VI

## Armed Conflicts

# 20

# Legal Nature of War Today

War in the traditional sense may be defined as a contention, through the use of armed force, between states, undertaken for the purpose of overpowering another.[1] True, such a definition does not cover the modern development of what has been called a *status mixtus*[2] or intermediacy concept. The latter is supposed to be a condition between peace and war, but the concept has not yet become a part of accepted international law, despite its advocacy by several well-known jurists.[3] In view of the fact that a large number of modern armed conflicts have taken place without an official declaration of a state of war, the term *armed conflict* has been used, when deemed to be desirable, in the discussion to follow. It should be noted, however, that hostile relations between state may assume a variety of forms.

The right to go to war was regarded for hundreds of years by both writers and the heads or governments of states not only as a lawful course of action for a sovereign state but indeed as one of the characteristics of such an entity.[4] War served two purposes in international society: it provided an effective method of self-help to achieve the enforcement of rights in the absence of competent international tribunals, and it also supplied states with a method, again of the self-help type, to change the rules of international law and to adopt them to basically changed conditions. The latter function, which by analogy could be compared with a domestic revolution carried on to change laws no longer considered tolerable, appeared to be particularly justified in the continuing absence of any agencies of international legislation.

[1] See Lauterpacht's *Oppenheim*, vol. 2, 201–10. There appear to be as many definitions as there are writers on the subject: see, *inter alia*, Hyde, vol. 3, 1686; Moore, vol. 7, 154; Kelsen, *Principles of International Law*, 26–28; the collection of many different ones in Eagleton, "The Attempt to Define War," *International Conciliation*, No. 291 (June 1933), 237–87.
[2] Schwarzenberger, "Jus Pacis ac Belli?" 37 *AJIL* 460 (1943).
[3] Jessup, "Should International Law Recognize an Intermediate Status between Peace and War?" 48 *AJIL* 98 (1954). See also McDougal and Feliciano, "International Coercion and World Public Order: The General Principles of the Law of War," 67 *Yale Law Jl.* 774 (1958); the position of the two authors is clarified at length in their heavily documented basic study, "The Initiation of Coercion: A Multi-Temporal Analysis," 52 *AJIL* 241 (1958).
[4] "To declare war is one of the highest acts of sovereignty"—Secretary of State Lansing to President Woodrow Wilson, Aug. 16, 1919; quoted in Lauterpacht, *Recognition in International Law* (1947), 5, n. 1.

International law did not prohibit war; rather, it viewed the institution as a normal function of sovereign states. The rights claimed did not have to have legal or moral merits: it was regarded as sufficient that a sovereign state asserted its rights. Failing to enforce them by peaceful means, it was free to pursue its aims by recourse to force.

Under such conditions, the functions of international law were conceived of as dealing primarily with the relations of states in time of peace, emphasizing the independence of every member of the family of nations. However, once a state decided to go to war, it was regarded as having been released from the obligations imposed by the law, except those few that regulated the conduct of armed conflicts and could proceed "lawfully" to impair or even to extinguish the same independence of the opponent that had been preserved so jealously in time of peace under the rules of the law.

## ATTEMPTS TO RENOUNCE WAR

The arrival of the mass army and the continuing discoveries of more efficient weapons led in the late nineteenth century to the first serious attempts to limit war as a legally accepted method of enforcing legal rights and changing the rules of law. The Hague Conference of 1899 represented the official realization of many privately conducted studies and draftings of conventions designed to surround the institution of war with legal restrictions. The Second Hague Conference of 1907 served the same purpose, with greater effectiveness because of the lessons learned from the results of its predecessor. Thus the Hague Convention of 1907 Respecting the Limitation of the Employment of Force for the Recovery of Contract Debts, while limited in its scope and purpose, illustrated the trend well under way by then of using law-making treaties to limit the hitherto virtually unlimited rights of sovereign states.

Still later, and more important, the Covenant of the League of Nations provided in its preamble an acceptance by the contracting parties of obligations not to resort to war and denied them the right to go to war except under certain conditions (Art. 12, part. 1; Art. 13; Art. 15, par. 7; Art. 17).

All these attempts were made with the intent to limit the use of war as a tool of law. More spectacular, in some respects, were the efforts made to establish aggressive war as an illegal enterprise. As early as 1923, the Treaty of Mutual Assistance—which never came into force—attempted to identify wars of aggression as an international crime. The equally abortive Geneva Protocol of 1924 similarly labeled aggressive war a crime (preamble) and in its Article 2 imposed an obligation on all parties to the agreement to refrain from war except in the specific circumstances listed in the treaty. In 1927, the Assembly of the League passed a resolution under which all wars of aggression were said to be prohibited and only pacific means were to be employed to settle international disputes of every kind, an approach reflecting the provisions of the Treaty of Mutual Guarantee (Locarno Treaty) of 1925. And in 1928, the Sixth Pan-American Conference adopted a resolution asserting that a "war of aggression constitutes a crime against the human species . . . all aggression is illicit and as such is declared prohibited."

**KELLOGG–BRIAND PACT (PACT OF PARIS)**    The culmination of these efforts to "outlaw" aggressive war—the adjective is necessary, for none of these proposals really prohibited every kind of war—was represented by the General Treaty for the Renunciation of War (Kellog–Briand Pact, or Pact of Paris) signed in Paris on August 27, 1928, by representatives of 15 states and ratified or adhered to by 65 nations. The key parts of the text of this famous instrument read as follows:

ART. 1. The High Contracting Parties solemnly declare in the names of their respective peoples that they condemn recourse to war for the solution of international controversies, and renounce it as an instrument of national policy in their relations with one another.

ART. 2. The High Contracting Parties agree that the settlement or solution of all disputes or conflicts of whatever nature or of whatever origin they may be, which may arise among them, shall never be sought except by pacific means.

The preamble of the instrument contained a statement by the signature states in which they affirmed that "all changes in their relations with one another should be sought by pacific means and be the result of a peaceful and orderly process, and that any Signatory Power which shall hereafter seek to promote its national interests by resort to war should be denied the benefits furnished by this Treaty."

Interestingly enough, the pact contained no provision for denunciation and did not state a date of termination. It thus is one of the extremely rare modern instances of a perpetual agreement. This latter fact alone may be taken as an indication of the instrument's optimistic and unrealistic aspects.

The purpose of the agreement was obviously to renounce war both as a tool of self-help to right an international wrong and as a rightful act of national sovereignty to change existing rights.[5] It was not intended to abolish the institution of war as such, for under its terms, resort to war was still allowed in legally permissible self-defense and as an instrument of collective action to restrain an aggressor. The treaty also did not abolish resort to war between a party to the agreement and a country not party to the agreement. The treaty, furthermore, did not prohibit the resort to war against a country that had violated the treaty's provisions.

The Pact of Paris failed to provide a means of enforcement and, even more importantly, did not define the measures and methods through which relations between states might be changed without resorting to force.[6]

---

[5] For a dissenting view, see Kaplan-Katzenbach, 210.

[6] See Morris, "The Pact of Paris for the Renunciation of War: Its Meaning and Effect in International Law," *Proceedings* 88–91 (1929), and discussion of that paper, *id.*, 91–109; consult also Wright, "The Meaning of the Pact of Paris," 27 *AJIL* 39 (1933) and especially Borchard, "The Multilateral Treaty for the Renunciation of War," 23 *AJIL* 116 (1929).

*This is*
*still law.*
*What*
*really is.*

The sad truth was that the statesmen of the world had ignored the principle underlying the whole system of positive international law: any rule, to be effective, must correspond to the needs of states and must equally correspond to the practice of states. De Visscher expressed this concept very well when he wrote, "A normative (lawmaking) treaty the content of which is too far in advance of development in international relations is stillborn, just as a treaty that ceases to be exactly observed in the practice of governments is no longer valid in its formal expression."[7] Or, as the translator of De Visscher's book observed, "Law cannot be built upon a heedless sacrifice of reality."[8] In regard to the failure of the pact's signatories to provide methods of enforcement, the words of Justice Oliver Wendell Holmes in the case of *The Western Maid* come to mind: "Legal obligations that exist but cannot be enforced are ghosts that are seen in the law but that are elusive to the grasp."[9]

The present writer does not believe that war, except in self-defense, was outlawed by the Pact of Paris. He believes, instead, that the document represented nothing more than a moral preachment, despite the trappings of a treaty surrounding it. The states that had signed it denied validity to the doctrine, and armed conflicts in the ensuing decade were both more numerous and more serious than they had been between 1919 and 1928.

As McLaughlin pointed out,[10] the renunciation of war was a "statement of principle" that provided no criteria for testing compliance with the concept. The use of the pact by the Nuremberg (International) Tribunal to assert that acts initiating an aggressive war constituted a crime should be viewed as exceeding the original intention of those who drafted the pact.

Wright came to believe that the proponents of the outlawing of war did not expect immediate effects from the pact; rather, they were thinking in terms of generations.[11] This may have been true—and if true, it casts some interesting light on the pact as a treaty in the normal meaning of that term—but those same proponents later criticized the violations of the pact when wars occurred within a few years after its ratification. In any case, the "legal" effect claimed for the pact was not in consonance with the practical interpretation of it by the parties to the agreement.

Typical of the attitude of national leaders was their failure to label as wars many of the conflicts of the 1930s. If such a label were omitted, so the reasoning appears to have been, then no war existed; hence no one could be blamed for breach of promises under the pact. Or, if a war had to be declared, it became at once a war in self-defense.

Even a war presumed to be illegal under the Pact of Paris would require the application of a body of rules to the hostilities; otherwise, a return

---

[7]De Visscher, *Theory and Reality in Public International Law* (1957), 133.
[8]Corbett, *id.,* viii.
[9]*The Western Maid, The Liberty, The Carolinian,* U.S. Supreme Court, 1922, 257 U.S. 159.
[10]Mills and McLaughlin, *World Politics in Transition* (1956), 351.
[11]Wright, "The Outlawry of War and the Law of War," 47 *AJIL* 365, 369 (1953).

to barbarism would be the consequence of such a resort to force. And the body of rules to be applied in an "unlawful" war, to be applied to both aggressor state and to its victim, during the conduct of hostilities must be the customary and conventional laws of war. [12]

Yet the tribunal at Nuremberg asserted that the Pact of Paris meant that an aggressive war was henceforth illegal under general international law and that therefore those who planned and waged such a war committed a crime in so doing: "War for the solution of international controversies includes a war of aggression, and such a war is therefore outlawed by the Pact." [13]

The present writer does not agree with that interpretation of the Pact of Paris. [14]

LEAGUE OF NATIONS    How was peace to be preserved and enforced under these early instruments? The Pact of Paris did not broach this subject. On the other hand, Article 16 of the Covenant provided for the imposition of sanctions against a member of the League of Nations that had resorted to war in violation of its obligations under the Covenant. The article was applied in only one of the five major instances in which such a violation did take place. When Japan invaded Manchuria in 1931, the Assembly concluded that "without any declaration of war, part of the Chinese territory has been forcibly seized and occupied by the Japanese troops." [15] Nevertheless, the Assembly decided, Japan had not resorted to war in violation of the Covenant, and therefore Article 16 did not apply.

In 1934, in connection with the Chaco War between Bolivia and Paraguay (1932–1935), many members of the League, each deciding that Paraguay had violated the Covenant, began an arms embargo, originally imposed on both belligerents, to Paraguay alone. The Japanese invasion of China proper, in 1937, led to a decision by the Assembly that Japan had violated the Nine-Power Treaty of 1922 as well as the Pact of Paris and that consequently Article 16 of the Covenant now applied to the dispute. Each member state, however, was judged to be free to apply such individual enforcement action against Japan as it saw fit—and none of them took any action. When the Soviet Union attacked Finland in late 1939, the Assembly did act under Article 16(4) and expelled the Soviet Union from the organization. Expulsion was not implemented by collective enforcement action, however.

Only in the case of the Italian invasion of Ethiopia, in 1935, did the Assembly conclude that the invasion represented resort to war in violation of the Covenant and that Article 16(1) was applicable. Collective economic

---

[12] Views similar to the one expressed by the present writer have been criticized by several commentators; their best and most reasonable defense may be found in H. Lauterpacht, "Rules of Warfare in an Unlawful War," in Lipsky, 89–113.

[13] *Trial of the Major War Criminals Before the International Tribunal, Nuremberg, 14 November 1945–1 October 1946*, I (1947), 220.

[14] See Stone, 302 for views similar to those held here.

[15] League of Nations Assembly, "Report on the Sino-Japanese Dispute," 27 *AJIL*. 146 (1933 Supp.).

sanctions were therefore authorized against Italy. These were not enough, however, and the failure to adopt the obviously effective measures of an embargo on oil shipments and a closing of the Suez Canal led to Italy's successful defiance of the League and to the conquest of Ethiopia. It should be pointed out, in passing, that the closing of the Suez Canal, which was urged on the League by prominent private persons in many countries, would have constituted a clear violation of the 1888 Constantinople Convention.

THE UNITED NATIONS    The experience of World War II and the approaching abolition of the League of Nations combined to bring out a renewed attempt to circumscribe resort to force by the provisions incorporated in the Charter of the United Nations. Article 2 of that document contained the relevant key regulations:

3. All Members shall settle their international disputes by peaceful means in such a manner that international peace and security, and justice, are not endangered.
4. All Members shall refrain in their international relations from the threat or use of force against the territorial integrity or political independence of any state, or in any other manner inconsistent with the Purposes of the United Nations.

The Charter, therefore, went beyond the provisions of the Pact of Paris in that the members of the United Nations renounced not only their right to go to war—except in instances of individual or collective self-defense—but also their right to resort to the threat or the use of force. It is, in fact, interesting to note that the only reference to war in the Charter occurs in its preamble ("determined to save succeeding generations from the scourge of war"). Elsewhere, "threat or use of force" and "threat to the peace, breach of the peace, or act of aggression" are used in reference to situations in which the new organization, through the Security Council, could take action under specified conditions.

Taking the Charter's provisions at face value, it would appear as if at long last legal controls had been established over the right of states to resort to the use of force.

Unfortunately, not only have the cited portions of the Charter been qualified extensively through other provisions of that instrument, but the operating mechanisms intended to make the legal controls work have broken down or have been violated on numerous occasions since 1945. And the United Nations itself resorted to force in the Congo for purposes that many governments, as well as individuals, felt difficult to locate in the avowed purposes of the organization, as outlined in the Charter.

This brings us back to the status of war under the Charter. As mentioned earlier, various qualifications surrounded the optimistic provisions of Article 2 (3–4).[16] First, Article 51 guarantees to all members the inherent right

---

[16]See Franck, "Who Killed, Article 2(4)? or: Changing Norms Governing the Use of Force by States," 64 *AJIL* 809 (1970); Henkin, "The Reports of the Death of Article 2(4) Are Greatly Exaggerated," 65 *AJIL* 544 (1971).

of individual or collective self-defense in the event of an armed attack. In theory, the Security Council may assume responsibility for an attacked member state and defend it against the attacker—but only if the Permanent Members of the Council are in agreement, a situation not yet realized. Until such agreement is reached, a state may continue to use force in its own defense.

Second, the Security Council may make "decisions" (determining the existence of a threat to the peace, a breach of the peace, or an act of aggression) of facts and action to restore the peace only if the concurrence of the same permanent members can be obtained. Until such concurrence is achieved, wars involving member states may continue. Third, even if the Security Council acted in either of the preceding instances, it would not enforce its decisions or act as a defender of a member unless adequate military forces were made available through voluntary action by the member states. Until such forces were placed at the Council's disposal, the wars could go on without check.

Treaty law (this includes the Covenant of the League of Nations, possibly the Pact of Paris, and the Charter of the United Nations) is particular international law based on general international law. When the particular treaty rules, created in derogation of general law, cease to be effective, they are replaced, automatically and instantly, by the relevant or corresponding rules of general international law. Hence the return of the community of nations to traditional notions of neutrality and warfare appears to have been well founded, in this writer's view.

As matters stand now, there are two categories of war: defensive war and aggressive war. The former is clearly permissible, for as Article 51 of the Charter declares:

Nothing in the present Charter shall impair the inherent right of individual or collective self-defense if an armed attack occurs against a Member of the United Nations, until the Security Council has taken the measures necessary to maintain international peace and security.

Aggressive war, on the other hand, has been asserted to be illegal, a position reinforced in the judgment of the International War Crimes Tribunal at Nuremberg when the tribunal asserted that

To initiate a war of aggression, therefore, is not only an international crime; it is the supreme international crime differing only from other war crimes in that it contains within itself the accumulated evil of the whole.[17]

Unfortunately, the actual situation is not as clear-cut as such a statement appears to indicate. Many states have resorted to war (international armed

---

[17]"International Military Tribunal (Nuremberg) Judgment and Sentences," 43 *AJIL* 168 (1949); consult also Wright, "The Prevention of Aggression," 50 *AJIL* 514 (1956).

conflict) since 1945 and usually justified their action on grounds of self-defense, either by citing that cause directly or by implying it. To give an example: On June 6, 1982, the armed forces of Israel invaded neighboring Lebanon, justifying their invasion as an effort to subdue Palestine Liberation Organization forces who had carried out terrorist attacks against Israel in the past. The initially announced plan of driving PLO forces from a relatively narrow belt of territory next to the Israeli border was abandoned, and Israel's military forces finally penetrated the Muslim half of Beirut itself, after the PLO had been evacuated from West Beirut in 12 days in early September 1982.

Furthermore, there have been serious problems of definition in connection with attempts to define the term *aggression*.[18] Until now, the present writer believes, no generally *binding* definition of what is meant by aggression has come into being, despite the General Assembly's approval of its Special Committees definition of *aggression* (see below).

Until it can be shown that states indeed honor that definition as valid and pursue the logical courses of action dictated by such an acceptance, the statement above should not be regarded as stating a rule. To illustrate the point made: How did the Soviet incursion into Afghanistan (December 27, 1979) relate to Offense No. 1 of the General Assembly's definition of aggression? Although many of the war crimes tribunals sitting after World War II were concerned with aspects of aggression, they did not arrive at an acceptable definition.[19] In view of general realization that aggression did constitute an illegal act but could not be punished unless it were known just which acts constituted an offense against international law, the General Assembly of the United Nations moved to settle the issue. On December 11, 1946, it requested the International Law Commission to incorporate the principles of the Charter of the Nuremberg Tribunal and of the latter's judgment in the draft of an international criminal code.

The commission then drew up such in instrument, the Draft Code of Offenses against the Peace and Security of Mankind. The latest (1954) version of this code listed nine specified offenses related to the issue of aggression.[20]

---

[18]The complicated problem of definition has been summarized very well in Gould, 606–18, with special emphasis on the activities of war crimes tribunals. See also Wright, "The Outlawry of War and the Law of War," 47 *AJIL* 365 (1953), which enters also into the persistency of the ancient concept of a just war (*bellum justum*). On the latter, see Tucker, *The Just War: A Study in Contemporary American Doctrine* (1960). See also Nussbaum, "Just War—A Legal Concept," 42 *Michigan Law Rev.* 453 (1943); and the important study by von Elbe, "The Evolution of the Concept of the Just War in International Law," 33 *AJIL* 665 (1939).

[19]See Gould, 610–18, and Stone, 330–34, for brief but admirable accounts of the problem and its difficulties; see also Glueck, "The Nuremberg Trial and Aggressive War," 59 *Harvard L. Rev.* 396 (1946).

[20]"Report of the International Law Commission, 1954," 49 *AJIL* 21 (1955 Supp.). Consult also Johnson, 'The Draft Code of Offenses against the Peace and Security of Mankind," 4 *Int'l. and Comp. Law Q.* 445 (1955), Ferencz, "The Draft Code of Offences against the Peace and Security of Mankind," 75 *AJIL* 674 (1981).

For a while, little was done in the General Assembly to try to define *aggression* for a lawmaking treaty. One reason for this lack of progress was a desultory debate in the Assembly (and also among writers on international law) as to whether a precise definition of *aggression* was possible or even desirable. Many opposed such a definition on the reasonable grounds that it would enable potential aggressors to evade culpability by circumventing precisely defined formulations. Also, no agreement was achieved on whether any definition of *aggression* ought not to include what might be termed *indirect aggression,* such as conspiracies organized abroad or ideological propaganda.

Eventually the General Assembly resumed its endeavor to establish a generally acceptable definition of aggression when, on December 18, 1967, it authorized the appointment of its 35-member Special Committee on the Question of Defining Aggression.

On April 12, 1974, the Special Committee adopted, by consensus, an eight-article definition of aggression developed by the committee's Working Group. Aggression was defined as "the use of armed force by a State against the sovereignty, territorial integrity or political independence of another State, or in any other manner inconsistent with the Charter of the United Nations, as set out in this Definition." Seven offenses were categorized as qualifying as acts of aggression:

(1) The invasion or attack by the armed forces of a State of the territory of another State, or any military occupation, however temporary, resulting from such invasion or attack, or any annexation by the use of force of the territory of another State or part thereof;

(2) Bombardment by the armed forces of a State against the territory of another State or the use of any weapons by a State against the territory of another State;

(3) The blockade of the ports or coasts of a State by the armed forces of another State;

[(4) An attack by the armed forces of a State on the land, sea or air forces, of another state;]

(5) The use of armed forces of one State, which are within the territory of another State with the agreement of the receiving State, in contravention of the conditions provided for in the agreement or any extension of their presence in such territory beyond the termination of the agreement;

(6) The action of a State in allowing its territory, which it has placed at the disposal of another State, to be used by that other State for perpetrating an act of aggression against a third State;

(7) The sending by or on behalf of a State of armed bands, groups, irregulars or mercenaries, which carry out acts of armed force against another State of such gravity as to amount to the acts listed above, or its substantial involvement therein.[21]

---

[21]Report of the Working Group, including explanatory comments, in 11 *ILM* 710 (1974); see also *NYT,* Apr. 13, 1974, 1, 6, in which the reporter, Pace, had already referred to the definition as "hazy."

The bracketed fourth offense was subsequently eliminated, when the General Assembly approved the definition and its appendices (December 14, 1974) through its Resolution 3314 (XXIX) without vote, by "consensus."[22] It should be kept in mind that General Assembly resolutions do not create obligatory rules of international law (see Chapter 1).

What about the legitimacy of a so-called preventive war (preemptive attack), an example of which was the opening of hostilities by Israel in the Six-Day War of 1967? It may well be that what Secretary of State Daniel Webster admitted in 1842 in the *Caroline* incident to be "instant and overwhelming necessity" should justify counteraction prior to impending attack, in the name of justified self-defense.[23]

Such an interpretation might be applied to the Charter's provisions prohibiting threats of the use of armed force and would justify striking the first blow at an enemy gathering forces for an impending attack, particularly if appeals to international organizations had failed to produce actions designed to remove the threats. Under traditional international law, a clear-cut case for self-defense could be made, even if no attack had been launched, when there was a definite threat of injury. "Under the Charter, alarming military preparations by a neighboring state would justify resort to the Security Council, but would not justify resort to anticipatory force by the state which believed itself to be threatened."[24] Well and good, but what if it could be anticipated with good reason that the Security Council would not act or if the threat of attack was so imminent that a nation's survival could not be made dependent on discussion, debate, and possible Security Council action at some future date? In that case, it is submitted, a preventive use of force by the threatened state would be justified.

## INTERNATIONAL ARMED FORCES

The subject of the status of war in the modern world cannot be concluded without considering the emergence of international military commands. Logically this subject might have been left to the chapter dealing with participants in a modern war, but the topic is so fundamental to the status of war itself that it will be discussed at this point.

[22]Text, with explanatory comments by the Special Committee, in 69 *AJIL* 480 (1975). See also Cassin, Debevoise, Kailes, and Thompson, "The Definition of Aggression," 16 *Harvard Int'l. L. Jl.* 589 (1975); and two excellent and also critical studies: Stone, "Hopes and Loopholes in the 1974 Definition of Aggression," 71 *AJIL* 224 (1977), and Ferencz, "The United Nations Definition of Aggression: Sieve or Substance?" 2 *World Issues*, April–May 1977, 26–28. See also *Time*, Nov. 14, 1983, 32, quoting a number of eminent legal scholars on "What Is Aggression?"

[23]On this point, see Wright, "Power Politics or a Rule of Law?" 147 *New Republic*, Dec. 29, 1962, 11–12; see also Chapter 7, under "Right of Self-defense."

[24]Jessup, "Force under a Modern Law of Nations," 25 *Foreign Affairs* 90–105, at 96 (1946).

The question of the legal basis for United Nations armed forces posed immense and practical problems for the organization's future work in keeping the peace.[25]

The authority of the United Nations to create armed forces is found in the UN Charter in Articles 1(1), 39, 41, and 42; the last of these is the most important one:

Should the Security Council consider that measures provided for in Article 41 would be inadequate or have proved to be inadequate, it may take such action by air, sea, or land forces as may be necessary to maintain or restore international peace and security. Such action may include demonstrations, blockade, and other operations by air, sea, or land forces of Members of the United Nations.

Note that the Security Council is the agency mentioned in Article 42, not the General Assembly. And the first "peacekeeping" experience of the United Nations was indeed launched by the Security Council. Post-World War II boundary disputes between Greece, Bulgaria, Albania, and Yugoslavia led in December 1946 to the Security Council's creation of a Commission of Investigation. However, in September 1947, the Council shifted the disputes to the General Assembly, and a month later the Assembly established in fact the first nonmilitary peacekeeping unit, a Special Committee (UNSCOB) which lasted from 1947 to 1954.[26] The General Assembly acted later to establish the first of the UN Emergency Forces (UNEF I) and the West Irian Security Force, but outside those particular occasions, the organization of peacekeeping activities by the United Nations has remained in the hands of the Security Council.

UNITED NATIONS COMMAND (SOUTH KOREA)    After the attack by North Korean forces on South Korea in June 1950, the Security Council voted (in the absence of the Soviet Union) to create a "unified Command under the United States" and recommended that the members of the United Nations make military forces and other aid available to that command. Sixteen states supplied combat units, and five others sent medical units.

Despite argument to the contrary, there can be no doubt that the Korean operation was a measure taken by the United Nations and one taken in accordance with the provisions of the Charter. The Security Council had officially determined that there had been a breach of the peace (June 25, 1950), and its resolution of July 27, 1950, recommended effective assistance to the Republic of Korea "to repel the armed attack and to restore international

[25]See especially Halderman, "Legal Basis for United Nations Armed Forces,' 56 *AJIL* 971 (1962).

[26]See Higgins, *United Nations Peacekeeping. Documents and Commentary, Vol. IV: Europe 1946–1979* (1981). The series of Higgins' coverage of UN peacekeeping activities is the accepted standard reference work on the subject.

peace and security in the area."[27] Further proof of the official character of the steps taken in the Korean situation is found in the resolution of the General Assembly of May 18, 1951, recommending an embargo of arms and strategic matériels against both the North Korean and the Communist Chinese regimes. The reader should note, however, than in the Korean instance, the United Nations created only a "unified command." The term *United Nations Command* was introduced, it must be suspected, for propaganda purposes. It achieved wide usage, but did not correspond to the technical fact that only a unified command under the United States could be attributed juridically to the United Nations. The forces operating in Korea were not, legally speaking, a United Nations expeditionary force. The command has been replaced by a mutual defense agreement between the United States and South Korea (1976).

UNITED NATIONS EMERGENCY FORCE (UNEF GAZA)    The UNEF was established in connection with the Suez Crisis of 1956 and represented action by the General Assembly rather than by the Security Council. The inability of the latter to act because of the threat of vetoes by several permanent members brought the first application of the "Uniting for Peace" Resolution.

The actual force was created by a variety of devices: the command was established by the General Assembly Resolution of November 5, 1956; the commanding officer and the initial group of officers were taken from the United Nations Truce Supervision Organization in Palestine; and the remainder, some 5,000 men, were supplied by a group other than the permanent members of the Security Council. In regard to the legal basis for these methods and for the establishment of UNEF itself, the General Assembly relied entirely on the provisions of the Charter as developed by the 1950 "Uniting for Peace" Resolution.[28]

All units of UNEF were withdrawn from Egyptian territory on May 19, 1967, at the request of the government of the United Arab Republic, and the entire Sinai Peninsula along the Israeli border was declared by the UAR military command to be a "forbidden area" to foreign military personnel. A few days later the Six-Day War erupted. Today the 1956 force is usually referred to as UNEF I, to distinguish it from the 1973 expeditionary force, UNEF II.

UNITED NATIONS (WEST IRIAN) SECURITY FORCE (UNSF)    From October 1, 1962 to May 1, 1963, the United Nations Security Force (UNSF), composed of Pakistani troops, was stationed in Western [Dutch] New Guinea.

---

[27]Consult Kunz, "Legality of the Security Council Resolutions of June 25 and 27, 1950," 45 *AJIL* 137 (1951); Pye, "The Legal Status of the Korean Hostilities," 45 *Georgetown L. Jl.* 45 (Feb. 1956). See also Bishop, 759–770, for a selection of relevant documents.
[28]See Goodrich and Rosner, "The United Nations Emergency Force," 11 *Int'l. Organization* 413 (1957), for materials relating to the Suez crisis of 1956 and UNEF. The text of the "Uniting for Peace" Resolution has been reprinted in 45 *AJIL* 1 (1951 Supp.), and in Bishop, 770–71. See also the important study by Garvey, "United Nations Peacekeeping and Host State Consent," 64 *AJIL* 241 (1970). See also Friedman, 930–33.

In addition to the Pakistan units, the force included observers from six countries and small U.S. and Canadian air force components. This force supported the operations of the UN Temporary Executive Authority (UN-TEA), which supervised the former Dutch New Guinea. The security force had been requested by the Netherlands and Indonesian and operated at their expense. It was replaced by Indonesian troops after all Dutch forces had been withdrawn.

UNITED NATIONS FORCES IN THE CONGO   The creation of the Organisation des Nations Unies au Congo (ONUC) was different, procedurally, from the instances already mentioned and has remained a subject of some continuing controversy among analysts. The initial step leading to the establishment of ONUC was a request from the new Congolese government (July 12–13, 1960) to the UN Secretary-General for military assistance. In accordance with a recommendation from the Secretary-General, the Security Council on July 14, 1960, authorized him to furnish the asked-for assistance to the Congo until the country's own security forces were able to fulfill their own tasks. The Secretary-General thereupon supervised the creation of ONUC, which consisted of troops voluntarily supplied by members and which served under a United Nations Command. ONUC (1960–1964) was built into a force of over 20,000 men, supplied by 29 countries; in addition, large numbers of civilians sent by the United Nations carried out a variety of technical assistance programs.

Of key importance in the role played by ONUC during 1961 and to the end of January 1962, when the rebellious province of Katanga surrendered to the control of central Congolese authorities (after some sharp fighting between Katanganese forces and ONUC units) was the Security Council Resolution of February 21, 1961. In that resolution the Security Council urged that the United Nations take all appropriate measures to prevent the occurrence of civil war in the Congo, including, if necessary and in the last resort, the use of force. Findings of a threat to the peace were contained in a report by the Secretary-General on February 27, 1961, and in a General Assembly resolution adopted on April 15, 1961.

ONUC's status as a collective measure had been doubted by many. Not a single theory advanced to explain the basis of ONUC in the Charter had been entirely satisfactory. The problem was complicated by the fact that both before and after the Security Council action authorizing ONUC to use force, if need be, to prevent civil war in the Congo, the Secretary-General specifically denied that the operation was under the provisions of Articles 41 and 42 of the Charter—which would have overridden the domestic jurisdiction limitations found in Article 2(7).

On April 17, 1961, the Secretary-General stated to the Fifth Committee of the General Assembly that the operation of ONUC represented

the use of military personnel or contingents for essentially internal security functions in the territory of a Member State at the invitation of the Government of that State.

. . . The measures themselves did not constitute "sanctions" or enforcement action directed against a State as contemplated by Articles 42 and 43 of the Charter.[29]

A study of the relevant documents establishes clearly that ONUC was a legal subsidiary organ of the United Nations whose personnel was subject to Article 100 of the Charter.[30]

CYPRUS PEACEKEEPING FORCE    The next UN peacekeeping effort followed outbreaks of violence between the Greek and Turkish elements of the population of the island of Cyprus. In March 1964, the Security Council established a new unit, the UN Peacekeeping Force in Cyprus (UNFICYP), originally set at 4,500 men and ultimately expanded to a total of 6,500, including limited numbers of foreign police.[31] That force was financed jointly by the states providing military contingents as well as by voluntary contributions by various member states. After depletion of the Cyprus force through the manpower needs of the new Mideast Force (UNEF II), the invasion of Cyprus by Turkey (July 1974) required an increase of UNFICYP to 5,000 men in order to supervise the truce finally arranged between Turkish forces and Cypriot forces of the Greek community on the island. At the time of writing, the Cyprus force of 2,122 men was still on guard at a cost of about $25 million a year.

UNITED NATIONS EMERGENCY FORCE (UNEF II)    The so-called Yom Kippur War of 1973 resulted in the creation of still another UN peacekeeping force, styled the Mideast Emergency Force. This was established by the Security Council on October 25, 1973 (Res. 338, 339 and 340—1973). The force, to total about 6,000 men, was to be composed of personnel drawn from member states, excepting permanent members of the Security Council. The force, the first units of which, detached from Cyprus, reached the Egyptian-Israeli cease-fire lines within 24 hours after the force was created, were interposed between the military forces confronting each other near the Suez Canal.

Because the new Mideast force had the backing of both the United States and the Soviet Union, financing problems remained at a minimum. On December 11, 1973, the General Assembly approved financing arrangements for the estimated $60 million annual expenses of the new operation. Under the Assembly resolution in question, each of the five permanent members of the Security Council was to be assessed on the same scale by which they contributed to the regular UN budget, but with a surcharge of 15.57 percent

---

[29]UN Doc. A/C.5/864, quoted in Halderman, *op. cit. supra,* n. 26, 988–89.

[30]See the excellent analysis of ONUC in E.M. Miller, "Legal Aspects of the United Nations Action in the Congo," 55 *AJIL* 1 (1961), on this point. See also Lefever, *Crisis in the Congo: A U.N. Force in Action* (1965); Linda Miller, *World Order and Local Disorder: The United Nations and Internal Conflict* (1967); Abi-Saab, *The United Nations Operation in the Congo, 1960–1964* (1978); 934–38.

[31]See 3 *ILM* 371, 451, 545 (1964), for documents on the creation of UNFICYP.

(the U.S. share was therefore estimated at $17.2 million), with other UN members assessed higher percentages of their regular dues.[32] China had indicated at the time of the Assembly action that it would not pay for Mideast peacekeeping operations and was one of 23 countries absent at the time of the vote on the financing question. The Soviet Union, which had initially balked at sharing expenses for UNEF II (and which had refused to pay its special assessments for UNEF I earlier), finally agreed to pay the sums due for the new force, provided its operations were "lawful."[33] However, on December 30, 1976, the Soviet Union sent a note to the Secretary-General notifying him that it would not pay its assessment for UNEF II because the Soviet Union had not participated in drawing up the second Egyptian-Israeli agreement on troop disengagement in the Sinai Peninsula (1975). The U.S. Department of State referred to the Soviet Union's refusal to pay its share of the expenses as "illegal." UNEF II ceased to exist on July 25, 1979. Its demise was an indirect result of the Israel-Egypt peace treaty of March 26 of that year, even though that instrument envisaged a continuation of the UN force, interposed between the ex-enemy forces in the Sinai. The direct cause of the end of the UNEF II was the Soviet Union's refusal to agree to a continuation of UNEF's mandate from the Security Council. The Secretary-General had made it clear that the original role of UNEF II could not be changed to supervision of the phased withdrawal of Israel under the terms of the peace treaty without authority from the Security Council. That authority lacking, the force had to be disbanded and sent home.[34] After unsuccessful negotiations, a final compromise was reached whereby Israel and Egypt were assigned primary responsibility for monitoring the treaty. (See also "Observer Missions," below.)

GOLAN HEIGHTS DISENGAGEMENT FORCE    On May 31, 1974, the Security Council approved a joint U.S.–Soviet resolution establishing the UN Disengagement Observer Force (UNDOF) for the Golan Heights between Israel and Syria. Despite its official title, this was more than an observer group: the unit of some 1,250 (1990 total: 1,327) men was designed to be inserted between the belligerent forces and to keep them separated.[35] The life of the Golan Heights unit has been extended regularly by the six-month periods called for in the original instrument creating the force. Its cost has been almost $35 million a year.

UN INTERIM FORCE IN LEBANON    Unlike earlier UN military forces interposed between combatant forces in order to preserve a truce or an armistice,

---

[32]See relevant Security Council documents in 68 *AJIL* 193 (1974), and the report of the Secretary-General on his establishment of UNEF II in *NYT,* Oct. 27, 1974, 11, as well as "Financing" in 68 *AJIL* 320 (1974).

[33]*NYT,* Oct. 30, 1973, 19.

[34]See *NYT,* Jan. 7, 1977, A-3, and Jan. 8, 1977, 7, on Russian refusal to pay part of the costs of UNEF II; and *NYT,* June 17, 1979, 8, and July 19, 1979, A-10.

[35]*NYT,* June 1, 1974, 10, for the text of the Syria-Israel "separation of forces" agreement signed at Geneva on May 31, 1974; see also *CSM,* July 2, 1984, 9.

the next UN force was intended from the beginning to be a barrier between military units not tied down by any formal or informal agreement to stop active hostilities. This is the UN Interim Force in Lebanon (UNIFIL), established by the UN Security Council through Resolution 425 (1978) on March 19, 1978.[36] The resolution called on Israel to withdraw its military forces from southern Lebanon and authorized the creation of the new UN force. This force, a body of 5,850 men in late 1990, cost approximately $138 million in 1988. It has had to contend with numerous problems not faced by other UN military forces[37] and is still in existence at the time of this writing.

The Soviet Union helped pay the costs of UNIFIL, beginning in 1986.

UN TRANSITIONAL ASSISTANCE GROUP, NAMIBIA    The approach of independence in Namibia led the United Nations to create the Transitional Assistance Group (UNTAG). Its purpose was to supervise elections (1989) and the transition period to full independence. The Group was composed of 4,650 peacekeeping troops, 500 police supervisors, and 1,000 civilians. The estimated cost of the Group was $700 million. (See also the Case Study No. 1 for details).

The approaching official end of the Nicaraguan civil war brought into being the UN International Commission of Support and Verification (CIAV), the first contingent of which (170 Venezuelan soldiers) arrived in Nicaragua on April 22, 1990. The purpose of the military units was to oversee the demobilization, disarming, and repatriation or resettlement of some 10,000 Contras located in Honduras. CIAV was planned to include troops from Canada, Spain, West Germany, Colombia, and Venezuela. Resettlement was to be under the auspices of the Office of the UN High Commissioner for Refugees.

UN PEACEKEEPING FINANCIAL CRISIS    THE 1956 General Assembly resolution to assess members for the costs of UNEF was approved by an affirmative vote of 64 to 0, with 12 abstentions; the assembly resolution establishing assessments for ONUC in 1960 had been approved 70 to 0, with 11 abstentions. Despite such support for the operations, it soon became apparent that many members were in arrears in paying their assessments. By the fall of 1962, only 29 states had paid what they owed for UNEF, 25 others had made partial payments but were still in arrears, and 24 had not paid at all. In the case of the maintenance costs of ONUC, only 27 members had met their assessments by September 1, 1962, 10 were in arrears for part of their contributions, and 63 had failed to make any payment whatsoever.

Under the authority of the Security Council, the Secretary-General issued, in 1961, about $170 million worth of UN bonds, repayable at 2 percent

---

[36]Text of resolution, *NYT*, Mar. 20, 1978, A-10; see also 17 *ILM* 491, 772 (1978) and 21 *ILM* 908, 1173 (1982) for this and other official UN documents relating to the creation and operation of UNIFIL, as well as 72 *AJIL* 911 (1978).

[37]See, *inter alia, Newsweek*, Apr. 3, 1978, 39, 41, 42, and Aug. 31, 1981, 34; *U.S. News & World Report*, Jan. 10, 1983, 25–26; and *CSM*, Jan. 18, 1983, 9, and Oct. 16, 1984, 18.

interest over a period of 25 years. The proceeds from the sale of the bonds were used to meet current (and past) expenses of the United Nations.

The General Assembly also adopted a resolution, by a vote of 52 to 11, with 32 abstentions, requesting an advisory opinion from the International Court of Justice as to whether the expenses authorized in the assessment resolutions covering UNEF and ONUC were "expenses of the organization" within the meaning of Article 17 of the Charter. If such was the case, then Article 17 provided that such expenses "shall be borne by the Members as apportioned by the General Assembly."

Two months later, the International Court of Justice handed down its opinion, holding, by a vote of 9 to 5, that the expenses in question were indeed "expenses of the Organization" in the meaning of Article 17 of the Charter.[38]

Several states—some large, some small—refused to comply with the assessment resolutions, and by the end of 1963, accumulated arrearages of assessments totaled $150 million (in addition to the $151 million of bonds issued and not yet repaid at that time).

What were the reasons for nonpayment? The Soviet Union and France, to cite only two examples, both maintained that the Security Council alone had the authority to establish peacekeeping forces, including their financing; that accordingly the General Assembly had exceeded its powers in passing the assessment resolutions for UNEF and ONUC; and that in consequence neither resolution bound member states. The Soviet Union in particular led the continuing opposition of members to paying the peacekeeping assessments, and on at least two occasions (June 27, 1963, and March 21, 1964), the Soviet delegation at the United Nations issued statements of its government's views, namely, refusal to contribute any funds for the peacekeeping operations.

ARTICLE 19 OF THE CHARTER   The fascinating legal aspect of these continued refusals to meet certain assessed expenses was found in the possibility that Article 19 of the Charter might be applied against members in arrears. That article reads:

A Member of the United Nations which is in arrears in the payment of its financial contributions to the Organization *shall have no vote in the General Assembly* if the amount of its arrears equals or exceeds the amount of the contributions due from it for the preceding two full years. The General Assembly may, nevertheless, permit such a Member to vote if it is satisfied that the failure to pay is due to conditions beyond the the control of the Member [italics added].

---

[38]*Certain Expenses of the United Nations (Article 17, Paragraph 2, of the Charter)*, Advisory Opinion, International Court of Justice, 1962, *I.C.J. Reports, 1962,* 151, in 56 *AJIL* 1053 (1962). Consult also Gross, "Expenses of the United Nations for Peace-Keeping Operations: The Advisory Opinion of the International Court of Justice," 17 *Int'l. Organization* (1963), 1–35; Claude, "The Political Framework of the United Nations' Financial Problems," *id.,* 831–59; and Henkin, 977–83.

By March 1964, the Soviet Union owed the United Nations a total of $52.6 million. Six countries had owed more than two years' contributions when the seventeenth session of the General Assembly was about to meet, and 10 states were in the same position just before the special session of the assembly in the spring of 1963. In all but one case, sufficient payments were made in each instance at the last moment to avoid an invocation of Article 19.

Only Haiti was in arrears for more than the total of two years' contributions when the 1963 special session began. When the Assembly convened on May 14, the Secretary-General informed the president of the General Assembly by letter that Haiti owed more than the amount specified in Article 19. At the opening plenary session, the Haitian delegate was absent. The president of the General Assembly then replied to the letter of the Secretary-General, stating that

I would have made an announcement drawing the attention of the Assembly to the loss of voting rights in the Assembly of the Member State . . . , under the first sentence of Article 19, had a formal count of votes taken place in the presence of a representative of that State at the opening plenary meeting.[39]

In 1964, the Soviet Union's arrearages made the provisions of Article 19 of the Charter applicable to that country because the General Assembly, by formal resolution on December 19, 1962, had accepted the advisory opinion of the World Court and because the language of Article 19 appeared to impose an obligatory loss of voting rights on delinquent members.

The 1964–1965 session of the General Assembly witnessed scenes worthy of the talents of Messrs. Gilbert and Sullivan. In order to avert the crisis over the prospective loss of the Soviet Union's vote, the device of not taking any votes was adopted. After weeks of frustrating debate, punctuated by attempts by Albania and others to force a vote and hence a showdown over Russian arrears, the General Assembly adjourned. As one of its last acts, the session created, on February 18, 1965, without a vote, a special committee (33 members) to study the subject of peacekeeping operations and the coverage of their costs. The committee met 14 times, yet was unable to reconcile fundamentally opposing views on the payment crisis.

Finally, on August 16, 1965, the United States yielded and declared that it "recognizes, as it simply must, that the General Assembly is not prepared to apply Article 19 in the present situation, and that the consensus of the membership is that the Assembly should proceed normally. We will

[39]Chayes, "The Rule of Law-Now," excerpted in 57 *AJIL* 912, at 916 (1963). In 1980, the Sudan was $65,000 behind in its contributions and could raise only $40,000 before the General Assembly's vote condemning the Soviet invasion of Afghanistan (Jan. 14, 1980). In consequence, the Sudan became a victim of Article 19 and lost its vote: see *Time,* Jan. 28, 1980, 21.

not seek to frustrate that consensus."[40] Consequently, the special committee could agree that Article 19 would not be raised again relative to UNEF and ONUC and that the financial problems of the United Nations should be solved by means of voluntary contributions.

Thus far, however, no way has been found of paying outstanding obligations arising out of the UNEF and ONUC operations. All creditors were notified by the Secretariat in September 1968 that any payment on these debts had to be postponed indefinitely.

The Soviet Union, long the most vocal opponent of payment for UN peacekeeping operations, finally announced in October 1987 that it would pay a total of $197 million in debts for Middle East expenses dating back to 1975. It then paid $25 million in early 1988 and promised to pay the balance owed during the next four or five years.

All other UN Peacekeeping activities have been financed by voluntary contributions by member states. It should be remembered that after the UN General Assembly did not enforce their Charter obligations against members in arrears regarding peacekeeping operations, the United States declared in 1965 in the so-called Goldberg Reservation that "if any member can insist on making an exception to the principle of collective financial responsibility with respect to certain activities of the organization, the United States reserves the same option to make exceptions if, in our view, strong and compelling reasons exist for doing so."

NON-UN PEACEKEEPING FORCES   Three multinational peacekeeping forces have thus far been formed outside the framework of the United Nations. The first was the Inter-American Peacekeeping Force sent by the Organization of American States to the Dominican Republic in 1965 (see Chapter 8). The second was the Inter-Arab Deterrent Force sent into Lebanon in 1976 by the Arab League. Consisting of small units from Saudi Arabia, the Yemens, the Sudan, Algeria, and the United Arab Emirates (withdrawn in April 1979), with the bulk of the force constituted of units of the Syrian army, the Arab force (30,000 men) was intended to police the armistice that ended the 1975–1976 civil war between Lebanon's Christians and Muslims and to restore a measure of order into the chaos called Lebanon. The first (Sundanese) unit arrived in Beirut on June 10, 1976, but in reality it merely supplemented the large Syrian force (22,000 men) already then located in Lebanon. The cost of the entire operation was estimated at about $90 million every six months. Unlike most other international forces, this one has sometimes been involved in heavy combat in attempting to halt fighting among the various factions in Lebanon. The Arab force was still in existence at the time of this writing and was composed entirely of Syrian units, estimated at 40,000 men in 1990.

Originally it was to be financed by the Arab League and was to act under the command of the President of Lebanon. The mandate of the Force

[40]UN Doc. A/AC.121/PV.15.

was renewed several times before it officially expired on July 27, 1982, at the time of the Israeli siege of Beirut.[41] The Lebanese government refused to request that the mandate be renewed by the Arab League. Instead, in September 1986, Lebanon requested an end to the Syrian presence in Lebanon. It would appear that, lacking legal authority from both Lebanon and the Arab League, Syria's military forces had to be regarded henceforth as illegal occupants of Lebanon.

In December 1979, a 1,300-man monitoring force arrived in Southern Rhodesia (newly reestablished temporarily as a British colony and formerly known as Rhodesia, now as Zimbabwe) from British Commonwealth countries, including Great Britain, Australia, New Zealand, Kenya, and Fiji. The purpose of this peacekeeping force was to oversee the cease-fire agreement ending the guerrilla war and to help supervise the elections scheduled for February 1980. Until independence as Zimbabwe had been achieved, Southern Rhodesia was governed by a British governor-general, Lord Soames.

MULTINATIONAL FORCE (LEBANON) I    After Israel's armed forces had routed the PLO contingents from Lebanon, a withdrawal of Palestinian units from Beirut was arranged through the efforts of the Secretary-General of the United Nations.[42] In order to supervise the evacuation of the Palestinians and such units of the Arab force as were in or near Beirut, it was arranged to station a Multinational Force in Beirut. This was not a United Nations peacekeeping force, even though its creation was tied to the United Nations. The various units of Multinational Force I were under their own national commands, not under a UN command. The force arrived in Beirut between August 21 and 26, 1982, and was composed of 860 in the French contingent, 575 in the Italian contingent, and 850 U.S. Marines. Force I was withdrawn again between September 10 and 13, 1982. During its stay in Beirut, it supervised the evacuation (by land and sea) of 16,059 persons from Beirut: 12,068 members of the PLO and similar Palestinian groups, 378 of their noncombatant dependents and relatives, and 3,613 members of the Arab Deterrent Force.

An enlarged Multinational Force (Lebanon) II, however, returned after a brief interval, owing to renewed violence in Lebanon. This second force was intended to preserve a fragile cease-fire and to give the Lebanese government time to try to strengthen its control over the country and to build up the Lebanese armed forces to the point that peace could be restored and then maintained. The second force consisted, at its maximum strength, of a 2,100-member French contingent, 2,200 Italian military personnel, a token force of 100 British army personnel, and 1,800 U.S. Marines. Losses

---

[41]See Mallison and Mallison, *The Palestine Problem in International Law and World Order* (1986), 278–79; Farah, in *CSM,* Sept. 4, 1986, 16; Hottelet, *id.,* Feb. 7, 1989, 18; and letter from Sobieski, *id.,* July 20, 1989, 20.
[42]See 21 *ILM* 1165 (1982) for an extensive collection of relevant documents.

during attacks in the same night on the American and French headquarters amounted to 241 American and 58 French dead, plus many wounded. American dead during the existence of the second force totaled 265. Time soon proved that the second force could not carry out its mandate: civil strife in Lebanon escalated; control by the Lebanese government weakened day by day; and eventually the second force had to be withdrawn. The British contingent left on February 8, 1984; the Italians embarked on February 19 and 20; the last 500 French soldiers left on March 31; and the last American combat units (leaving behind an embassy guard and a few instructors for the Lebanese army) went aboard their vessels on March 31 and April 1, 1984. In the words of an editorial writer in the *Christian Science Monitor* (October 24, 1983), "The troops in Lebanon from the beginning were not so much peacekeepers as time-buyers."

INDIA PEACEKEEPING FORCE, SRI LANKA    Sri Lanka (formerly Ceylon) had been plagued for several years by ethnic violence in certain of its provinces. Tamils, representing about 13 percent of the population of 16 million, rebelled in favor of a separate Tamil state. India, with 50 million Tamils in its South, lent some support to the rebels and, despite an attempt to mediate in the conflict, had permitted the Tamil rebels to maintain "exile headquarters" in one of its southern Tamil states.

Eventually the two countries reached the "Agreement to Establish Peace and Normalcy in Sri Lanka" (Colombo, July 29, 1987).[43] The treaty provided for abandonment of Tamil demands for independence in favor of autonomy for the Tamil (northern) portions of the island. One of the key provisions of the Agreement, however, was its Article 2.16(c), which read:

In the event that the Government of Sri Lanka requests the Government of India to afford military assistance to implement these proposals the Government of India will co-operate by giving to the Government of Sri Lanka such military assistance as and when requested.

The first 2,000 Indian soldiers landed on Sri Lanka on July 31, 1987, to carry out the Agreement and to disarm the Tamil rebels. A few weeks later, the size of the peacekeeping force was 4,500 and it ultimately reached a total of 45,000. Following Tamil attacks on the Sinhalese majority, the force launched a military offense (October 10, 1987). Sporadic bitter fighting continued, and in June 1989 the Sri Lankan government requested an immediate withdrawal of the Indian troops. The Indian government, however, asserted that a withdrawal depended on "full implementation" of the 1987 Agreement. Sri Lanka then settled for a token reduction of the force by 600 men (July 29, 1989). On September 9, India's Prime Minister announced that the peacekeeping force would be withdrawn from Sri Lanka by the end

[43] Text and ILM background/content summary in 26 *ILM* 1175 (1987); see also Tenorio in *CSM*, July 28, 1987, 9–10. See also Chapter 8 *sub* Military Intervention.

of the year. That action had not taken place by early February 1990, however, and the Sri Lankan government accused the force of "violating the island's sovereignty."

ONE-PARTY PEACEKEEPING FORCE    There have also been on record a limited number of one-country peacekeeping forces, normally present with the permission, if not by the invitation, of the host country. Thus, in June 1978, the United States transported Moroccan troops to Zaire's Shaba (Katanga) Province and evacuated French Foreign Legion troops to Corsica on the return flights of the aircraft involved. The offer of Moroccan troops had been the sole positive response to a Belgian-sponsored proposal to Zaire for an all-African peacekeeping force. In March 1979, Nigerian troops on peace-keeping duties in Chad were called upon to enforce the observance of an agreement between the contending parties, ending Chad's civil war. That war continued, however, and after the Nigerian units withdrew again, a French 1,200-man peacekeeping force attempted to prevent a recurrence of the bloodshed that had left 40,000 dead in 1979.

WEST AFRICAN PEACEKEEPING FORCE (ECOMOG)    A civil war had erupted in Liberia when a rebel force entered the country from the Ivory Coast on December 24, 1989. In the conflict, which ultimately involved three Liberian groups, some 10,000 people, mostly civilians, were killed. In August 1990 about 2,100 U.S. Marines were on four Navy ships off the coast of Liberia, and on August 5 about 235 of them were airlifted to the capital of Monrovia to rescue several hundred American citizens. On August 7 the Economic Community of West African States (ECOWAS) approved a Nigerian proposal to send a multinational peacekeeping force into Liberia. The purpose of the force was not only to rescue foreign citizens, many of whom were being detained as hostages in Liberia, but also to put an end to the civil war. The force, with an initial strength of about 3,000 men, was composed of soldiers from Ghana, Guinea, Nigeria, Sierra Leone, and Gambia. It arrived off Monrovia on August 25 and, on landing, was soon embroiled in fighting with Charles Taylor's rebel group, the National Patriotic Front.

Sporadic fighting continued, and by the middle of September 1,000 additional Nigerian troops were sent to reinforce the peacekeeping force. In the meantime Liberian president Samuel Doe had been killed and the chairman of ECOWAS requested the peacekeeping force to rescue and evacuate hundreds of Doe loyalists. ECOWAS had met in Ghana to select a Liberian interim government, to be led by Amos Sawyer, a political scientist. Prince Yormie Johnson, leader of a second rebel group, agreed to that choice, but Taylor vowed to keep on fighting. By October 11, the peacekeeping force, now 6,000 men strong, had captured the capital of Monrovia from Taylor's followers.

Finally, on November 28, 1990, the three factions (followers of the late Doe, Johnson, and Taylor) signed a cease-fire in Mali, with the leaders of

13 African states in attendance. The president of Nigeria announced that a regional military task force would remain in Liberia indefinitely to monitor the cease-fire.

OBSERVER MISSIONS    In addition to international or national peacekeeping forces, a number of useful international (and, in a case or two, national) observer missions have served in various parts of the world. Under United Nations auspices were UN Military Observers in Greece (UNMOG), 1952–1954, investigating incidents along the borders of Albania, Bulgaria, and Yugoslavia, and the UN Military Observer Group in India and Pakistan (UNMOGIB), stationed primarily in Kashmir Province from 1948 to date with 39 observers; in 1965–1966 it included UNIPOM, the UN India-Pakistan Observer Mission monitoring the cease-fire between the two countries. UN observers were stationed in Indonesia from 1947 to 1950. From 1948 to the present, the UN Truce Supervision Organization in Palestine (UNTSO), with 298 men, has been stationed in "Palestine" and has supplied, on occasion, officer components for other UN Mideast operations, most recently (1982) when at first 10 and eventually 50 officers were sent to Beirut. Also there was a UN Observer Group in Lebanon (UNOGIL) along the Lebanese-Israeli frontier (June-December 1958). In 1963–1964, the UN Yemen Observation Mission (UNYOM) operated in the Arabian peninsula.

The cessation of hostilities in the Iran-Iraq conflict resulted in the creation (August 9, 1988) of UNIIMOG, the UN Iran-Iraq Military Observer Group, composed of 350 observers. The Russian military withdrawal from Afghanistan was monitored by the 50 observers of UNGOMAP, the UN Good Offices Mission in Afghanistan and Pakistan. And the Cuban military withdrawal from Angola is being corroborated by UNAVM, the UN Angola Verification Mission, 70 observers, at a total estimated cost of $20.4 million. The UN Observer Group in Central America (ONUCA), an unarmed multinational force of several hundred military officers, was created in November 1989. Located throughout the five Central American republics, its purpose was to verify two key provisions of the Nicaraguan peace settlement: the end of military aid to guerrillas sited in Honduras and El Salvador, and the non-use of national territory to stage attacks on neighboring states.

NON-UNITED NATIONS OBSERVERS    A small group of observers (28) was sent by the Organization of American States (OAS), in conformity with a decision on July 31, 1976, to supervise a demilitarized zone between Honduras and El Salvador, following a renewal of border incidents. The original quarrel in question dated back to the five-day war (the "Soccer War") and its antecedents in 1969.

The U.S. Sinai Field Mission (SFM), a team composed of 150 U.S. civilian technicians and support personnel, was stationed in the Sinai Peninsula from February 1976 to May 1982. The purpose of the team was to operate and monitor an early-warning electronic system in connection with the Second

Egypt-Israel Accord of 1975, that is, to monitor the Gidi-Mitla Pass areas in the Sinai for possible military movements by either Egypt or Israel.[44]

The Sinai Multinational Force and Observers (MFO) originally was to be created by Israel and Egypt under the terms of their peace treaty of March 26, 1979, that is, a multinational force to supervise the implementation of Annex I to the treaty, the Protocol Concerning Israeli Withdrawal and Security Arrangements.[45] The Security Council of the United Nations, called upon to create the needed force, failed to reach an agreement, and in consequence Egypt, Israel, and the United States drew up their own Protocol for the creation of the multinational force and observers (June 17, 1981).[46]

The combination (force and observers) began to arrive in the Sinai on March 17, 1982. Truly international, its components have come from the United States (1,100), Fiji (500), New Zealand and Australia (140), Uruguay (74), Colombia (500), the Netherlands (105, including 100 military police), Italy (90), France (42), and a small number of personnel from the United Kingdom. In April 1985, Canada announced that it would replace the Australian units. The total strength of the force and observers (50 U.S. civilians) in 1984 was 2,600. The United States currently is paying 60 percent of the annual costs of the enterprise, the balance being split between Israel and Egypt. The military portion of the entity, under the command of Lieutenant General Frederik Bull-Hansen of Norway, patrols a 300-mile zone between Israel and Egypt.

At the request of the Lebanese government, a 45-man French truce observation team began to function in March 1984, positioned at the main crossing between the Christian east and Muslim west Beirut. The French government, asserting that the unit no longer could carry out its mission, ended the operation on April 1, 1986. After a six-state Arab League committee plan for a multinational observer group in Lebanon (April 1989) to monitor a cease-fire was not implemented, the cease-fire ended abruptly.

## SUGGESTED READINGS

### Legal Nature of War: General

The excellent study by Greenwood, "The Concept of War in Modern International Law," 36 *Int'l. and Comp. Law Q.* 283 (1987); Cassese, ed., *Restraints on the Use of Force 40 Years after the UN Charter* (1986); Dinstein, *War, Aggression and Self-Defence* (1988); Kalshoven, *Constraints on the Waging of War* (1987); Singer and Small, *The Wages of War, 1816–1965* (1972); Ferencz, *Defining International Aggression—The*

---

[44]See *Time,* Mar. 1, 1976, 25–26; *Newsweek,* May 17, 1976, 53–54; and U.S. Department of State, General Foreign Policy Series, No. 9321, *U.S. Sinai Support Mission* (June 1980).
[45]See 18 *ILM* 362 (1979) for the text.
[46]Text of this protocol and related documents in 20 *ILM* 1190 (1981) and 21 *ILM* 196, 456 (1982). See also 76 *AJIL* 613 (1982).

*Search for World Peace* (2 vols., 1975) and *An International Criminal Court: A Step toward World Peace* (2 vols., 1980); Farer, "Humanitarian Law and Armed Conflict: Toward the Definition of 'International Armed Conflict,' " 71 *Columbia Law Rev.* 37 (1971); Time Essay, "On War as a Permanent Condition," *Time,* Sept. 24, 1965, 30–31.


## Wars of National Liberation

Hodges and Abu Shanab, eds., *NLF: National Liberation Fronts, 1960–1970* (1970); von Glahn, "The Case for Legal Control of 'Liberation' Propaganda," 31 *Law and Contemp. Problems* [Duke University] 553–88 (1966).


## Peacekeeping Forces

Siekmann, *Basic Documents on United Nations and Related Peacekeeping Forces* (2nd rev. ed., 1989); Örn, "Soldiers of Peace," 2 *World Monitor* 20 (Oct. 1989); Wainhouse, *International Peacekeeping at the Crossroads* (1973); Higgins, *United Nations Peace-keeping 1946–1967. Documents and Commentary.* vol. 1: *The Middle East* (1969), vol. 2: *Asia* (1970), vol. 3: *Africa* (1980), vol. 4: *Europe, 1946–1979* (1981); Williams, *Intergovernmental Military Forces and World Public Order* (1971); Wiseman, ed., *Peacekeeping: Appraisals and Proposals* (1983); Whiteman, vol. 13, 586-610; Henkin, 967–75.

CASE

*Attorney-General* v. *Nissan,* Great Britain, Court of Appeal, Civil Div., 1967 [1967] 2 All E.R. 1238, reported in 62 *AJIL* 511 (1968) and, more extensively, in 8 *ILM* 588 (1969).


## UN Payments Crisis

Department of State, Office of the Legal Adviser, "Memorandum of Law: Article 19 of the Charter of the United Nations," 58 *AJIL* 753 (1964); Whiteman, vol. 13, 307–39; the revealing collection of UN documents in 8 *ILM* 434 (1969); People's Republic of China: "Letter Transmitting the First Contributions to the United Nations (Feb. 20, 1972)," 11 *ILM* 652 (1972); Geib, *The Origins of the Soviet-American Conflict over United Nations Peacekeeping: 1942–1948* [Emporia State Research Studies, vol. 22, no. 3] (Kansas State Teachers College, 1974); *CSM,* Jan. 6, 1983, 6.

# 21

# The Laws of War

## GENERAL DEVELOPMENT

International law has always been concerned as much with the conduct of states engaged in war as with their relations in time of peace. Indeed, the authors of the classics in the law gave priority in space and attention to hostile relations among nations, a practice justified by the "normality" of such relations, compared with the relative abnormality of peace among the states of Europe. The gradual development of a stable international order favored the growth of rules governing the rights and duties of states in time of peace, and in modern times, the "law of peace" occupies the bulk of any treatise on international law.

Beginning with the Thirty Years' War (1618–1648), isolated instances of humane practice in the conduct of hostilities acquired in the course of time the status of usages and came to be regarded as customs, as binding legal obligations to be observed by states at war with one another. To some, it may appear paradoxical, even ridiculous, that the killing of human beings, facilitated increasingly by the development of more effective instruments of death, should be regulated equally increasingly by rules designed to introduce a measure of humaneness into a bloody business.

The answer to such observations is that many people in many countries have achieved pride in the fact that they have achieved a degree of civilization in which it is possible to show some decency even to a mortal enemy. Also, leaving aside such cultural, as well as any moral or religious, considerations, there are some practical values in the regulation of warfare. Moderation and humaneness have, at times, not only prevented retaliation by the enemy but also have led forces to surrender instead of fighting to the bitter end, thus dispensing with the heavy losses to both sides involved in such a suicidal course of action.

"THE LAWS OF WAR" Lauterpacht pointed out that three principles have determined the growth of the "laws of war": the principle that a belligerent is justified in applying any amount and any kind of force considered necessary to achieve the goal of a conflict—the defeat of the enemy; the principle that because of humanitarian considerations, any violence not necessary for the achievement of that goal should be prohibited; and the principle that a certain amount of chivalry, of the spirit of fairness, should prevail in the

694

conduct of hostilities, that certain practices smacking of fraud and deceit should be avoided.[1]

The "laws of war," as mentioned, took the initial form of rules of customary law, beginning even before the sixteenth century. Their modern development, however, has taken place through the application of conventional law, through the conclusion of a number of multilateral treaties.

EARLY ATTEMPTS TO DEVELOP THE LAWS OF WAR    The middle of the nineteenth century witnessed the birth of this stage in the growth of the law. First among the major instruments dealing with modern war was the Declaration of Paris (1856), under which privateering was abolished, regulations were formulated concerning the status of noncontraband goods, and the rule was created that a blockade had to be effective in order to have legally binding force. There followed the Geneva Convention of 1864, concerned with the wounded in the field. The original treaty was replaced by a revision, signed in Geneva on July 6, 1906. In 1868, the Declaration of St. Petersburg prohibited the use of small (under fourteen ounces in weight) explosive or incendiary projectiles.

THE HAGUE CONFERENCES    In 1899, the First Peace Conference at The Hague resulted in the signing of the Convention with Respect to the Laws and Customs of War on Land, derived from the *Instructions for the Government of Armies of the United States in the Field,* issued during the Civil War (April 24, 1863) and based on a draft by Dr. Francis Lieber of Columbia.[2] The Second Peace Conference, which met in 1907 in The Hague, revised the earlier convention, and the new version is known as Convention IV (Convention Respecting the Laws and Customs of War on Land, The Hague, October 18, 1907). The drafters of the document realized full well that many aspects of the conduct of hostilities had not been covered fully or had been omitted from the document altogether. Hence the preamble of the convention included toward its end the significant statement:

It has not, however, been found possible at present to concert Regulations covering all the circumstances which arise in practice.

On the other hand, the High Contracting Parties clearly do not intend that unforeseen cases should, in the absence of a written undertaking, be left to the arbitrary judgment of military Commanders.

Until a more complete code of the laws of war has been issued, the High Contracting Parties deem it expedient to declare that, in cases not included in the Regulations adopted by them, the inhabitants and the belligerents remain under the protection and the rule of the principles of the law of nations, as they result from the usages established among civilized peoples, from the laws of humanity, and the dictates of the public conscience.[*]

[1]Lauterpacht's *Oppenheim,* vol. 2, 227.
[2]See von Glahn, 8–16; see also the "Suggested Readings" for this chapter for the general and detailed background of the laws of war.
[*]The last paragraph above is the so-called Marten's Clause, frequently cited as demonstrating the humanitarian aspect of the law of war.

It should be noted that both Hague conventions declared or stated principles and rules that, in essence, represented then existing customary international law. A basic weakness, found in both instruments, is the general participation clause, which provides that the Regulations annexed to each treaty would apply only as long as all parties to a conflict were also parties to the convention in question; if a noncontracting state were involved in a war, the Regulations were not to be binding. Much ink has been spilled in discussing these clauses, the one in the 1907 convention having been invoked by Germany in 1914. But the argument was essentially academic, because the two instruments were declaratory, for the most part, of customary rules of law that would have applied to all parties to a conflict irrespective of the applicability of a Hague convention.

Annexed to the Fourth Convention of 1907 (Convention Respecting the Laws and Customs of War on Land) were Regulations detailing the conduct of hostilities. Those regulations, of key importance even today (hereafter referred to as HR) must be distinguished from the Fourth Geneva Convention of 1949 (Relative to the Protection of Civilian Persons in Time of War, hereafter referred to as Geneva-IV, see Chapter 24) and the two Protocols Additional to the Geneva Conventions of 12 August 1949, of 1977 (hereafter referred to, respectively as PR-I and PR-II).

The 1907 conference resulted also in a number of additional instruments relating to the conduct of hostilities: a declaration concerning expanding bullets (dumdum bullets, named after a British arsenal in India in which such bullets had first been mass-produced), a declaration dealing with projectiles and explosives dropped from balloons, a declaration concerning projectiles diffusing gases of various kinds, a convention adapting to maritime warfare the principles of the Geneva convention (wounded) as revised in 1907, and conventions dealing with the opening of hostilities, the status of merchant vessels at the outbreak of hostilities, the conversion of merchant vessels into warships, the laying of automatic contact mines, bombardment by naval forces in time of war, and restrictions on the right of capture in maritime war and on the rights and duties of neutral states and persons in land warfare and in naval warfare.

ATTEMPTS TO DEVELOP LAWS OF WAR AFTER WORLD WARS I AND II    After World War I, a number of additional instruments were negotiated. The arrival of effective air warfare was intended to be covered by a new convention drafted by a representative group of jurists at The Hague in 1922, but this convention again failed to be ratified; on the other hand, there came into existence in 1925 the Protocol on the Use in War of Poison Gases, the 1929 Geneva conventions on the treatment of the sick and wounded as well as of prisoners of war, and the London Protocol of 1936 concerning the use of submarines against merchant ships. On the regional level, the Sixth Conference of American States at Havana in 1928 adopted the Convention on Maritime Neutrality (ratified by the United States in 1932), and in 1938 a group of regulations termed the Scandinavian Rules of Neutrality was adopted by Sweden, Norway, Denmark, Finland, and Iceland.

World War II was followed by extensive efforts to enact new lawmaking treaties in order to benefit from the bitter lessons in lawlessness learned during that conflict and to fill at least some of the major gaps in the laws of war. Thus the Geneva Diplomatic Conference of 1949 succeeded in drafting four conventions: Amelioration of the Condition of the Wounded and Sick in Armed Forces in the Field (Geneva-I); Amelioration of the Condition of Wounded, Sick and Shipwrecked Members of Armed Forces at Sea (Geneva-II); Treatment of Prisoners of War (Geneva-III); and Protection of Civilian Persons in Time of War (Geneva-IV).[3] By June, 1977, the four conventions had been ratified by 142 countries.

Customary laws of war are binding on all belligerents. The Hague conventions of 1899 and 1907 are binding on all belligerents to the extent that they represent customary law and are binding wholly in the event that all belligerents in a given war are signatories of the convention in question. The treaties concluded since 1907 are binding wholly only on ratifying or adhering states. There is some question whether a binding rule may be disregarded in the case of reprisals adopted by one belligerent in retaliation against prior illegal acts committed by an opposing belligerent.

One of the bitterest arguments connected with the laws of war has centered on the traditional German assertion, adopted by other states on occasion, that the laws of war may be set aside in the case of extreme necessity — such as when only a violation of the laws would enable a country or a military force to escape from deadly danger or to achieve the purpose of the war, the defeat of the enemy.

An unlimited doctrine of military necessity (*Kriegsraison*) cannot be supported easily today. Its acceptance without qualification would reduce all the laws of war to mere dogmas of military convenience. Each particular instance in which the doctrine is invoked must therefore be judged on its own merits. If honest conviction and corroborating factual evidence can be marshaled in support of a given application of the concept, well and good; but if it can be shown that there was no dire urgency or that the violation undertaken did not materially and immediately contribute to military success, then any tribunal judging the case on hand would be bound to rule that a war crime had been committed.[4]

Subsequent developments in the effort to expand the scope of the law of war have been centered in the United Nations and in the International

---

[3]See subsequent chapters for most of the key provisions of the 1949 conventions; consult also Kunz, "The Chaotic Status of the Laws of War and the Urgent Necessity for their Revision," 45 *AJIL* 37 (1951), and Meron, "The Geneva Conventions as Customary Law," 81 *AJIL* 348 (1987).

[4]See the illuminating study by Dunbar, "Military Necessity in War Crimes Trials," 29 *BYIL* 442 (1952), and his "The Significance of Military Necessity in the Law of War," 67 *Juridical Review* 201 (1955), as well as the appraisals of the problem by Downey, "The Law of War and Military Necessity," 47 *AJIL* 251 (1953), and in Lauterpacht's *Oppenheim,* vol. 2, 231–233. The history of the concept has been well developed in Weiden, "Necessity in International Law," 24 *TGS* 105–132 (1939).

Committee of the Red Cross (ICRC). In the United Nations, two important documents were produced: the Secretary-General's first "Report on Respect for Human Rights in Armed Conflicts" (GA Doc. A/7720, November 20, 1969) and its identically titled sequel (GA Doc. A/8052, September 18, 1970). These presented a superb analysis of certain major gaps in the existing law governing armed conflicts (guerrilla and internal warfare, wars of national liberation, certain methods of warfare, treatment of prisoners of war in unusual circumstances, and so on), together with some most promising, as well as some rather debatable or quite impractical, recommendations. Some important aspects of warfare, not all directly related to human rights, were not mentioned in the two reports (for example, conflicts at sea, economic warfare, and neutrality).[5]

The International Committee of the Red Cross organized two sessions of a Conference of Government Experts (1971 and 1972) in Geneva, to draft additional concrete rules applicable to armed conflicts (primarily in the form of additional protocols to the 1949 Geneva conventions), followed by the Diplomatic Conference on Reaffirmation and Development of International Humanitarian Law Applicable in Armed Conflicts (1974–1977).

On June 8, 1977, the Conference adopted by consensus two conventions: "Protocol Additional to the Geneva Conventions of 12 August 1949, and Relating to the Protection of Victims of International Armed Conflicts (Protocol I)" and "Protocol Additional to the Geneva Conventions of 12 August 1949, and Relating to the Protection of Victims of Non-International Conflicts (Protocol II)." Both treaties amplify many of the rules developed in the 1949 Geneva Conventions and also add some new regulations. The two treaties are referred to in this text as PR-I and PR-II. Both entered into force on December 7, 1978.[6] By the end of ten months after that date, PR-I had been accepted (ratified or acceded to) by 71 states and PR-II by 64. However, at the time of writing, the United States and several other Powers had not become parties to either Protocol.[7] The basic objection on the part of the United States to PR-I centered on its Article 1(4) which touched on the subject of so-called wars of national liberation. Until the appearance of PR-I, no distinction had previously been made under the law of war based on the cause, the motive, for which one party allegedly fought. A second major objection centered on a provision which in effect guaranteed members of irregular forces status as prisoners of war, even if their group disregarded laws and customs of war.

---

[5]See von Glahn, "The Protection of Human Rights in Time of Armed Conflict," in *Israel Yrbk. of Human Rights,* vol. 1, 208–227 (1971).
[6]Texts in 16 *ILM* 1391 (1977) and 72 *AJIL* 457 (1978).
[7]See Sofaer [Legal Adviser, Dept. of State], "The U.S. Decision Not to Ratify Protocol I to the Geneva Conventions on the Protection of War Victims," 82 *AJIL* 784 (1988), and President Reagan's letter of transmittal to the Senate (Jan. 29, 1987), transmitting PR-II for advice and consent and stating the reasons why PR-I would not be so transmitted, 81 *AJIL* 910 (1987).

A somewhat different interpretation of the causes for the American rejection of PR-I was detailed in Gasser's study of the question.[8]

Despite the codification since 1907 of the rules governing armed conflict, it must be admitted that realistically the "laws of war" ignore the inability of international law to prevent war and instead concentrate on the permissible use of force and the prohibition of certain weapons and methods of warfare. It will become obvious in succeeding chapters that the advance of technology has made obsolete a number of the older rules codified in 1907, and it is certain that if there should be a major nuclear conflict, the last vestiges of the old differentiation between combatants and noncombatants will disappear instantaneously.

## THE LAWS OF WAR AND INTERNATIONAL FORCES

The development of a global collective security system in the shape of the United Nations and various regional defense arrangements has posed numerous new problems in the laws of war. Those laws developed in the context of armed struggles between individual states. Because collective security systems were not known at the time the customary and conventional rules governing warfare were drawn up, no provisions governing international armed forces were included. Even the most modern conventions on the subject, the 1949 Geneva instruments and PR-I are concerned with national and not international forces.

Thus far no "official" answer has been found to the question of the extent to which international commands are bound by the existing rules. The fact that such forces operated in South Korea, in the Near East, in the Congo, on Cyprus, and elsewhere and may be called into activity under such organizations as NATO, raises the question of the extent to which such forces are bound by the laws of war.[9]

The problem posed above has been aggravated by the assumption implied in the formation of international armed forces, on a global or regional basis, that one side in the conflict has violated solemn treaty obligations and, as an aggressor, is fighting an unlawful war. If the laws of war are to apply to such a conflict, should they apply to the aggressor alone or both sides?

The present writer is convinced that both customary and conventional laws of war apply equally and unrestrictedly to both sides in a modern war, even if the conflict involves an international command (or a peacekeeping

---

[8]Gasser, "The U.S. Decision Not to Ratify Protocol I to the Geneva Conventions on the Protection of War Victims," 81 *AJIL* 912 (1987), and 83 *id.*, 345 (1989).

[9]See Jessup, 188–221, and Bivens, "Restatement of the Laws of War as Applied to the Armed Forces of Collective Security Arrangements," 48 *AJIL* 140 (1954). Consult also the Report of the Committee of the American Society of International Law on the Study of Legal Problems of the United Nations, " Should the Laws of War Apply to United Nations Enforcement Actions?" *Proceedings* 216–220 (1952); International Committee of the Red Cross, *Annual Report, 1961* (1962), 47–49.

force) and that one of the opposing parties may have been guilty of aggression.[10] Similarly, the tribunal in *U.S.* v. *List et al. (The Hostage Case)* pointed out that "international law makes no distinction between a lawful and an unlawful occupant in dealing with the respective duties of occupant and population in occupied territory . . . . Whether the invasion was lawful or criminal is not an important factor in the consideration of this subject."[11] Lauterpacht asserted that "a war is still a war in the eyes of International Law, even though it has been illegally commenced."[12] And the Korean conflict proved quite definitely that both sides were regarded as being bound by the customary and conventional rules of war.[13]

LAW OF NON-INTERNATIONAL WARS   At the 1974–1977 Diplomatic Conference, the West German delegate stated that 80 percent of the victims of armed conflicts after World War II were the victims of non-international conflicts, and the Soviet delegate asserted that the figure should be raised to 90 percent.[14] Moreover, until December 1978 when Protocol II of 1977 came into force, the only conventional (treaty-based) international law rule applicable to internal war was the common Article 3 of the four Geneva conventions of 1949 (see below), which was, in Farer's felicitous phrase, a statement of "affectionate generalities."[15] Nevertheless, Article 3 was the first example of a worldwide rule of international law requiring a state to treat its own citizens—rebels though they might be—in accordance with the minimum standards laid down by the "family of nations."

## ARTICLE 3

In the case of armed conflict not of an international character occurring in the territory of one of the High Contracting Parties, each Party to the conflict shall be bound to apply, as a minimum, the following provisions:

(1) Persons taking no active part in the hostilities, including members of armed forces who have laid down their arms and those placed *hors de combat* by sickness, wounds, detention, or any other cause, shall in all circumstances be treated humanely, without any adverse distinction founded on race, colour, religion or faith, sex, birth or wealth, or any other similar criteria.

To this end, the following acts are and shall remain prohibited at any time and in any place whatsoever with respect to the above-mentioned persons:

[10] See also Morgenstern, "Validity of the Acts of the Belligerent Occupant," 28 *BYIL* 291 at 321, n. 1 (1951), and see Whiteman, vol. 10, 43–50, 51–54, 63–64.

[11] *Trial of War Criminals Before the Nuremberg Military Tribunals* (1948), 1247, cited in Cunningham "Civil Affairs—A Suggested Legal Approach," *Military L. Rev.* October 1960, 115–137, at 125, n. 29.

[12] Lauterpacht's *Oppenheim,* vol. 2, 299.

[13] See Whiteman, vol. 10, 58–63, for relevant documents.

[14] In Forsythe's illuminating and heavily documented "Legal Management Internal War: The 1977 Protocol on Noninternational Armed Conflicts," 72 *AJIL* 272, at 272 (1978).

[15] Farer, *The Laws of War 25 Years After Nuremberg (International Conciliation* No. 538 1971), 31. See also Luard ed., *The International Regulation of Civil Wars* (1972); and Moore, ed., *Law and Civil War in the Modern World* (1974).

(a) violence to life and person, in particular murder of all kinds, mutilation, cruel treatment and torture;

(b) taking of hostages;

(c) outrages upon personal dignity, in particular humiliating and degrading treatment;

(d) the passing of sentences and the carrying out of executions without previous judgment pronounced by a regularly constituted court, affording all the judicial guarantees which are recognized as indispensable by civilized peoples.

(2) The wounded and sick shall be collected and cared for.

An impartial humanitarian body, such as the International Committee of the Red Cross, may offer its service to the Parties to the conflict.

The Parties to the conflict should further endeavour to bring into force, by means of special agreements, all or part of the other provisions to the present Convention.

The application of the preceding provisions shall not affect the legal status of the Parties to the conflict.

The relevance of common Article 3 was admitted unofficially in several instances of non-international conflict by both parties involved (France and the Algerian National Liberation Front, 1956, and the Cuban government and Fidel Castro's rebel movement, 1959).[16]

Protocol II of 1977 itself is a rather interesting document. It reaffirms the common Article 3 of 1949 (Preamble); disavows the legitimacy of any form of discrimination in its application (Art. 2-1); supplies a list of fundamental guarantees for those not taking a direct part or who have ceased to take part in hostilities, including a categorical prohibition of taking hostages and committing acts of "terrorism" (Art. 4); provides additional minimum safeguards for those whose liberty has been restricted (Art. 5); offers detailed guidelines for the prosecution and punishment of criminal offenses related to the armed conflict, including a prohibition of punishment except after trial before an independent and impartial court (Art. 6); outlines procedures to be applied concerning the wounded, the sick, and the shipwrecked (Arts. 7–12); and supplies minimum protection directives for the civilian population, relative to the latter's being bombed or shelled, its survival requirements, and installations containing "dangerous forces," for example, dams, dikes, and nuclear electric-generating stations—even if such should be genuine military objectives—if such attacks would cause severe civilian losses (Arts. 13–18).[17]

---

[16]Forsythe, *op. cit. supra*, n. 14, at 274. See also *id.*, 275–76 for a surprisingly long list of internal conflicts (1949 through 1978) in which at least one party accepted Article 3 or in which the International Red Cross contacted detainees.

[17]See also Aldrich, "Human Rights and Armed Conflict," *Proceedings* (1973), in 67 *AJIL* 141 (1973).

Because almost all countries participating in the formulation of PR-II were opposed to incorporating any sort of enforcement mechanism in the instrument, the determination of its applicability still rests, in essence, with the governments and other agencies (including rebel movements) involved in any given non-international armed conflict.[18] But the fact that such an admittedly "weak" treaty dealing with such an explosive and emotionally upsetting topic as internal wars could come into being and achieve ratification by enough countries to enter into force gives hope for the future of the international regulation of internal wars. This is especially true in view of the evidence so carefully marshaled by Forsythe, namely, that in a very considerable proportion of the post-World War II civil wars, either or both parties involved accepted the obligations imposed by the common Article 3 of the Geneva conventions of 1949.[19] On the other hand, George H. Aldrich, head of the U.S. delegation to the Diplomatic Conference, was not overly optimistic about PR-II. Said he:

My government sought a protocol with a low threshold of violence required to bring it into effect. We are disappointed that the conference adopted a protocol with a relatively high threshold. We fear ... the high threshold required by article 1 will serve as a convenient excuse to refuse to admit its applicability except in very limited situations.[20]

He also stated, on other occasions at about that time, that he expected only about 50 of the 109 participants in the Diplomatic Conference to ratify PR-II and that he believed that the Protocol would seldom be recognized by governments as applicable to a conflict because they would be reluctant to admit that they had a full-scale rebellion on their hands.

## PARTICIPANTS IN A WAR

Legal participation in a war has always been traditionally restricted to sovereign states. Semi-sovereign states and entities not included in the community of nations were not entitled to become lawful belligerents. A neutralized state such as Switzerland could become a lawful belligerent in view of its character as a sovereign state. If such a neutralized state participated in a war purely in defense against an attack aimed at it, it did not lose its character as a neutralized state; if, on the other hand, it entered a conflict by undertaking offensive operations against another state, it lost its status as a neutralized entity. The foregoing remarks are, of course, based on purely legal reasoning. The fact that a given entity was not a fully sovereign state has not necessarily prevented it from becoming a belligerent if it had the requisite military forces and resources.

[18]See also Forsythe, *op. cit. supra*, n. 14, at 294, on this point.
[19]*id.*, 275.
[20]*Air Force Times,* July 4, 1977, 17.

RECOGNITION OF A BELLIGERENT COMMUNITY    It is this distinction between legal qualifications and the actual ability to go to war that explains
why rebels (insurgents) may become belligerents, equipped with certain
rights as well as duties.[21] Once recognition as a belligerent community
has been extended by other states to an insurgent group, in answer to the
existence of certain factual elements, the community enjoys temporarily a
limited status as a belligerent. The facts that have to be proved before such
recognition should be lawfully extended would include such considerations
as the existence of a civil war beyond the scope of a mere local revolt (existence of a "state of general hostilities"); occupation of a substantial part of
the national territory by the rebels, together with the existence of a degree
of orderly and effective administration by that group in the areas under its
control; and observance of the rules of war by the rebel forces, acting under
the command of some responsible and ascertainable authority.

If those conditions of fact do not prevail or cannot be ascertained, recognition of the insurgents as a belligerent community is to be regarded as
premature and an unlawful intervention in the internal affairs of the lawful
and recognized government of the state in question.

When an outside state recognizes a rebel group as a belligerent community, this essentially political act does not normally bind the parent state
against which the rebels are fighting. Although writers differ widely on this
question, it appears that the parent state may treat the rebels as traitors even
after they have received foreign recognition as a belligerent community. The
modern tendency, on the other hand, appears to be that once such recognition has been received, the members of the rebel armed forces should be
treated, when captured, as prisoners of war, entitled to the usual protection
and rights of the latter under the laws of war.[22]

## Participants: Persons

Lawful combatants were defined in some detail in the first three Geneva
Conventions of 1949 and were divided into six categories:[23]

(1) Members of the armed forces of a Party to the conflict, as well as members of
militias or volunteer corps forming part of such armed forces.
(2) Members of other militias and members of other volunteer corps, *including those
of organized resistance movements,* belonging to a Party to the conflict and operating
in or outside their own territory, even if this territory is occupied, provided that

[21]See Whiteman, vol. 10, 31–32, esp. 150–72, on this question.
[22]See Lauterpacht's *Oppenheim,* vol. 2, 252–54, for a discussion of the intricate problems posed
by the recognition of subjects of an enemy state as "cobelligerents" or as "allied belligerents"
by a state engaged in war against the parent state of the individuals in question.
[23]Geneva I (Wounded and Sick in Armed Forces), Art. 13; Geneva II (Wounded, Sick and
Shipwrecked at Sea), Art 13; Geneva III (Prisoners of War), Art. 4(A). Article 4 (B-2) applies
the terms of Geneva III to interned members of the armed forces of an occupied country,
and also to anyone in the six categories who has been received by neutral or non-belligerent
states on their territory and whom these states are required to intern under international law.

such militia or volunteer corps, including such organized resistance movements, fulfill the following conditions [emphasis added]:

(a) that of being commanded by a person responsible for his subordinates:

(b) that of having a fixed distinctive sign recognizable at a distance;

(c) that of carrying arms openly;

(d) that of conducting their operations in accordance with the laws and customs of war.

(3) Members of regular armed forces who profess allegiance to a government or an authority not recognized by the Detaining Power.

(4) Persons who accompany the armed forces without actually being members thereof, such as civilian members of military aircraft crews, war correspondents, supply contractors, members of labour units or of services responsible for the welfare of the armed forces, provided that they have received authorization from the armed forces which they accompany, who shall provide them for that purpose with an identity card similar to annexed model.

(5) Members of crews, including masters, pilots and apprentices, of the merchant marine and the crews of civil aircraft of the Parties to the conflict, who do not benefit by more favourable treatment under any other provisions of international law.

(6) Inhabitants of a non-occupied territory, who on the approach of the enemy spontaneously take up arms to resist the invading forces, without having had time to form themselves into regular armed units, provided they carry arms openly and respect the laws and customs of war [*levée en masse*].

The second category listed above is the crucial one as far as resistance movements are concerned. It represents the first mention of such movements in any international treaty dealing with the laws of war.

IRREGULAR FORCES    In addition to the recognized armed forces, many conflicts have seen the utilization of what are commonly termed *irregular forces*. Such groups may have been authorized by a belligerent, or they may have originated privately and may be acting without special authority and on their own initiative. Until recently, the laws of war granted no legal status to the private variety of irregular forces; if captured, the members of such organizations were viewed as war criminals and commonly were executed without much ceremony. However, beginning with the Spanish guerrilla war against Napoleon, the irregular force became an increasingly important factor in modern war. Known under a variety of names—such as guerrillas, partisans, resistance groups, and "the underground"—these groups lacked the technical status of lawful combatants. During World War II, most of such irregular forces (Albania, Greece, France, Belgium, Norway, Burma, China, Malaya, and the Philippines) operated with the approval of their own government and received supplies and arms from it. In fact, in several countries, notably in the Soviet Union, they were on the payroll of their sovereign.[24]

[24]See the excellent historical study of Nurick and Barrett, "Legality of Guerrilla Forces Under the Laws of War," 40 *AJIL* 563 (1946); Baxter, "The Privy Council on the Qualifications of Belligerents," 63 *AJIL* 290–96 (1969); von Glahn, 51–52.

Both The Hague Regulations of 1907 (Art. 1) and the Third Geneva Convention of 1949 (Treatment of Prisoners of War, Art. 4-A, par. 2) reflect the "modern" view that under specified conditions, irregular forces are to be entitled to the rights and privileges of normal armed forces. Unfortunately for the members of such groups, however, the specified conditions under both conventions would be tantamount to suicide if obeyed literally: the treaties in question require that irregular forces, in order to enjoy the status of legal combatants, have to (1) be under the command of a person responsible for his subordinates; (2) wear distinctive insignia recognizable at a distance; (3) carry weapons openly; and (4) conduct their operations in accordance with the laws and customs of war. Such requirements would be extremely difficult for most irregular forces to meet, and so-called part-time partisans would find it literally impossible to qualify under these regulations.

The situation for most countries today, therefore, is that irregulars operating in groups may possibly meet the conditions under which they are granted combatant status. Individuals operating as partisans and "part-time" guerrillas are still, for practical purposes, beyond the law and may be shot as war criminals when captured by the opposing belligerent.

It should be remembered, however, that until the status of a person suspected of being a guerrilla is settled by a competent tribunal, the benefit of the doubt must operate in favor of the prisoner, according to Geneva Conventions I, II, and III (1949).[25]

The legal status of "freedom fighters" engaged in a war of national liberation was changed rather drastically through the provisions of PR-I of 1977 (Arts. 43, 44, and 45), for all countries ratifying it. PR-I states that wars of liberation are international, not internal, conflicts and, for ratifying countries, removes most of the former restrictions affecting guerrillas. However, the requirement that combatants be distinguishable from the civilian population was retained, and guerrillas were required to bear arms openly, but only during a military engagement and during the immediately preceding deployment of their force. The wording of the relevant articles, however, is not so precise as to prevent evasive interpretations. In regard to the nonratifying states (of PR-I), they are still bound by Art. 3 (1d) of the four Geneva conventions (1949) which guarantees a minimum standard of international law to guerrillas, regardless of whether or not their external or internal enemies have recognized them either as insurgents or as belligerents.[26]

---

[25] This is also true in the case of PR-I (Art. 45) for international armed conflicts, but only by rather vague implications in Art. 6 of PR-II for internal armed conflicts.
[26] See the interesting Israeli case of *Military Prosecutor* v.*Omar Mahmud Kassem et al.*, Military Court, Ramallah, April 13, 1969, reported in 65 *AJIL* 409 (1971), and comment on same by W. T. Mallison in *Proceedings* 156–57 (1976). The court had ruled that irregular forces had to be under state control in order to qualify for protection as lawful belligerents, an interpretation clearly at variance with the provisions of the Geneva Prisoner of War Convention of 1949.

MERCENARIES    According to generally accepted customary and conventional international law, mercenaries fall into the same category as do other regular or irregular combatants; provided they obey the rules (Hague, Geneva 1949) by which they are entitled to be treated as prisoners of war. The UN General Assembly attempted on several occasions to prescribe discriminatory treatment for such mercenaries as fought against freedom fighters and so on,[27] but the resolutions, by their nature, did not change the rules of law. However, PR-I of 1977, in Article 47, states (par. 1) that "a mercenary shall not have the right to be a combatant or a prisoner of war" and then outlines a six-part definition of a mercenary. Therefore, for those states ratifying PR-I, mercenaries are outlawed and in the category of criminals, if not worse. (See also "Suggested Readings.")

Mercenaries have appeared on the world scene on few occasions during the past decade: in 1975 such a group, under the leadership of Robert Denard, overthrew the government of the Federal and Islamic Republic of the Comoros, only to return three years later, overthrowing the government he had helped put into place originally and restoring the pre-1975 coup president to office. Later Denard was apparently involved in the assassination of Comoro President Ahmad Abdallah and ran the country with his mercenaries. In December 1989, however, French paratroopers were called in from the island of Mayotte by the Comoro Interim President, and Denard fled to South Africa. In 1981 (March and May), U.S.-financed Asian mercenaries unsuccessfully went twice into Laos in order to find surviving American captives from the Vietnam War. And in late 1981, a band of mercenaries under the command of Colonel Mike Hoare flew from South Africa to the Seychelles to overthrow the government of that country and return to office a former president deposed in a 1977 coup. Unconfirmed reports in early 1982 claimed the presence of 30 to 40 Westerners, most of them said to be Americans, serving with the forces of the late Major Saad Haddad in Southern Lebanon. The group was said to have been provided with uniforms, weapons, and pay by Israel. In the fall of 1989, media reports asserted that foreign mercenaries of Israeli and British nationality had been training armed paramilitary units for the Colombian drug cartels since 1987.[28]

In November 1988, a band of some 60 mercenaries tried to overthrow the government of the Republic of Maldives. The latter is located in the Indian Ocean, has an area of about 115 square miles, is divided into 19 atolls

---

[27] Such as GA Res. 2548 (XXIV), December 11, 1969; and GA Res. 3103 (XXVII), December 12, 1973 (the latter reprinted in 68 *AJIL* 379 1974.)

[28] For the Comoros incident, see McDowell, "Crosscurrents Sweep a Strategic Sea," *National Geographic,* Oct. 1981, 422, esp. 455, 457; for Laos, see AP Dispatch, May 22, 1981; for the Seychelles coup attempt, see the story in Chapter 13 and also *Time.* Dec. 7, 1981, 49, and Dec. 14, 1981, 56, Aug. 6, 1982, 30–31, as well as *Newsweek,* Dec. 7, 1981, 60, and *CSM,* Jan. 6, 1982, 4; for Lebanon, see *Newsweek,* March 8, 1982, 10; for the Colombia reports, see *CSM,* Sept. 22, 1989, 4.

with 1,087 islands, and has a population of about 195,000. The invaders, landing in speedboats from a freighter offshore, seized a number of government buildings and battled security forces in rather bloody encounters. The Indian High Commissioner in the capital of Male reported that the attackers were Sri Lankans. The President of the Maldives requested military intervention from India, the United States, and Great Britain. India dispatched 1,600 troops to restore order. The mercenaries fled to their mother ship and surrendered after an Indian frigate fired on the latter vessel. The prisoners were turned over to the Maldives for trial.

On December 4, 1989, the UN General Assembly adopted an "International Convention against the Recruitment, Use, Financing and Training of Mercenaries." This interesting and detailed instrument had not been opened for signature, however, as of January 31, 1990.[29]

PRIVATE ENEMY CITIZENS   Private citizens taking up arms against an invading enemy may, however, achieve combatant status and thus be entitled to treatment as prisoners of war if they happen to belong to a *levée en masse*. This means an armed mass-rising of the private citizenry in advance of an invading army. Provided that such a rising does take place on the approach of the enemy, and *not* behind his lines, the participating private individuals are entitled to combatant status under both the 1907 Hague Regulations and the 1949 Prisoners of War Convention if the individuals in question carry arms openly and observe the laws and customs of war.

FOREIGN VOLUNTEERS   A new development made its appearance in the Korean War of 1950–1953: the *recognized* appearance of foreign volunteers. The Spanish Civil War had already seen the participation of organized groups of Russian and other left-wing sympathizers on one side and German and Italian groups on the other. During World War II, Spanish and other volunteers fought against the Soviet Union on the side of the Axis Powers. But in the Korean War, large and organized bodies of Chinese "volunteers" took a most active part. The novelty was the Chinese participation in the negotiations leading to the armistice of July 27, 1953, which was concluded between "the Commander-in-Chief, United Nations Command, on the one hand, and the Supreme Commander of the Korean People's Army and the Commander of the Chinese People's Volunteers, on the other hand." This marked the first time in modern history that ideological "volunteers" became officially recognized cobelligerents in a war.

The government of the United States adopted the view that these Chinese forces, despite their volunteer label, were official forces of the People's Republic of China. This was shown clearly in a note of October 11, 1955, dealing with the downing of a Russian plane on July 27, 1953, the date on which the Korean armistice was signed.[30]

[29]Text and ILM content-summary in 29 *ILM* 89 (1990).
[30]For partial text, see *Note* by Myers on "Armed Intervention," 54 *AJIL* 656 (1960); consult also Brownlie, "Volunteers and the Law of War and Neutrality," 5 *Int. and Comp. Law Quarterly* 570 (1956). See also text of armistice in 47 *AJIL* 186 (1953 Supp.)

## Concept of Enemy Character

The modern laws of war do not restrict the concept of *enemy* to the armed forces of an opposing belligerent. Rather, one of the consequences of a state of war between two countries is that every national of one state becomes the enemy of every national of the other state. Citizens of neutral countries may acquire an enemy character if they enlist in the armed forces of a belligerent or commit hostile acts against a belligerent. A logical result of such a change in status is that a belligerent may apply the same measures against such ex-neutrals as he would apply against the nationals of an enemy state.

NEUTRAL CITIZENS LIVING IN ENEMY TERRITORY    Many commentators have pointed out, however, that neutral citizens residing in enemy territory do not enjoy special status or privileges, in regard to another and opposing belligerent. They will be treated in the same manner as is the indigenous enemy population, sharing their fate in every respect, and belligerents have a perfect legal right to treat such neutrals in a manner identical with their treatment of the enemy population.

Until World War I, enemy citizens residing in neutral countries lost their enemy character by identification with the neutral state expressed through their residence therein. This doctrine, defended particularly in Great Britain and the United States, was not, however, universally accepted. France and other European countries asserted that enemy character was not lost through neutral residence.

The Anglo-American attitude was abandoned as World War I progressed. The British government, as early as 1915, forbade its nationals to trade with any person (physical or legal) in foreign countries whose enemy nationality or enemy association called for such prohibition. In order to make clear who was to be regarded as possessed of enemy aspects, "blacklists" were issued, listing individuals and firms in neutral countries. British nationals could, of course, continue trade with anyone not featured on these lists. The British Trading with the Enemy Act of 1939 similarly regulated commercial intercourse during World War II. On that occasion, both Great Britain and France departed from the concept that enemy nationality automatically gave enemy character to an individual. Residence of such a person in enemy territory would, of course, make him an enemy; but if the individual resided in a neutral state, then inclusion of his name on a blacklist was necessary for a finding of enemy character.

STATUS OF CORPORATIONS    The status of legal persons, such as corporations, in time of war has proved to be even more complex and confusing than in the instance of physical persons. International law does not offer any general rules on the subject, and national practices have varied greatly. There has been general agreement for many decades that a corporation chartered in an enemy state possessed enemy character. There were some doubts as to the status of a firm not incorporated in an enemy country but carrying on business there, but eventually the general view prevailed that such activities conferred enemy character on the firm in question. The classic case dealing with this problem is the famous British case of *Daimler Co., Ltd.* v. *Continental Tyre and Rubber (Great Britain) Co., Ltd.* [1916], 2 A. C. 307. A more recent case illustrating the application was

## THE UNITAS

Great Britain, Privy Council (In Prize), May, 8, 1950,
2 All Eng. L. R. 219

FACTS    The *Unitas* was a whaling factory ship, registered in Germany and flying the German flag. The vessel was captured in a German port by British forces in June 1945, after the German surrender. Two Dutch companies contested the seizure, asserting that they, through Dutch subsidiaries, were the only stockholders in a German company controlled from Rotterdam. The two companies owned considerable properties in Germany and, in order to transfer some of those assets from the Reich, had arranged in 1936 for the construction, in Germany, of a German whaling fleet. The *Unitas* was one of the components of that fleet, chartered (after completion) by the German subsidiary to still another German company in which the former had less than 50 percent interest.

The outbreak of World War II caused no separation of the Dutch companies from their German subsidiaries, at least not as long as the Netherlands remained neutral. The Dutch companies asserted that the *Unitas* had been registered in Germany under duress, being constructed only because of pressures exerted by the German government, and that the British prize court should look behind the facade of German ownership to the true—that is, Dutch—ownership of the vessel.

The British court (Probate, Divorce and Admiralty Division, February 20, 1948. 1 All Eng. L. R. 421) ruled against the alleged Dutch owners and condemned the *Unitas* as a lawful prize taken from the enemy and possessed of

enemy character. The reason behind the court's decision was that the nationality (in this case, the enemy character) of a ship was determined by its flag. In addition, the court pointed out that the Dutch companies had "a house of trade" in enemy territory and had not severed their connections with it after the outbreak of the war. The Dutch companies appealed the condemnation of the vessel. The Privy Council handed down its decision on May 8, 1950.

ISSUE    Did Dutch ownership, as expressed through stock control, override the fact that the vessel was registered in Germany?

DECISION    The Privy Council rejected the appeal and affirmed the condemnation of the vessel as a lawful prize taken from an enemy.

REASONING    "The flying of an enemy flag alone is in this and in most cases sufficient to dispose of the matter at issue." The alleged economic pressure exerted on the appellant companies by the German government was rejected as insufficient to overrule the conclusive evidence that the ship was registered in Germany and flew the German flag.

Lord Porter, the presiding judge, commented that the building of the whaling fleet and its registration in Germany was not involuntary, as alleged by the appellants: "In truth, it was not involuntary in the sense of being unintentional: it was a deliberate choice taken between two distasteful alternatives. . . . Their Lordships accept the view that there may be circumstances which make the flying of the enemy flag inconclusive as a reason for condemning a ship in Prize, but such circumstances must be very exceptional." The court then cited the few instances of such inconclusiveness, one of the more unusual of which revolved around the *Palme*. That vessel had been a German ship, purchased by the Swiss Red Cross from German owners. Both the Swiss and French governments refused to permit the Red Cross to use their flags; hence the vessel continued to fly the German flag for want of a more legitimate insignia. When the *Palme* was stopped by the British navy, the German flag was held, quite properly, not to constitute conclusive proof of the vessel's enemy character.

Similarly, it is generally agreed that a company incorporated in or doing business in territory under enemy occupation should be regarded as possessed of enemy character.[31]

The United States held the view, until World War II, that a company not incorporated in an enemy country nor doing business there should not be regarded as possessing enemy character. This traditional American attitude was abandoned during World War II, when the United States government decided to follow the French practice, which applied the test of registration as well as control: the United States henceforth regarded enemy control, even when exercised indirectly through some form of holding company, as creating enemy character for a corporation.

STATUS OF VESSELS IN TIME OF WAR    The question of enemy character applies also to vessels in time of war. In time of peace, the nationality of a ship is determined by the flag it flies; that is, it possesses the nationality of the state in which it is registered. In time of war, this is still the test applied to any vessel displaying an enemy flag, even if the ship's actual owners happen to be citizens of a neutral landlocked state without a maritime flag. Regardless of ownership, any vessel flying the flag of an enemy state is regarded as an enemy vessel and is subject to capture or destruction.

The situation is not as clear, however, in regard to an enemy-owned vessel flying a neutral flag. Most writers agree that even before World War I, the display of a neutral flag determined the neutral character of a vessel only if the ship was actually entitled to fly the flag through registration in the neutral state. A genuinely neutral ship would still acquire enemy character by participating in hostilities, by being utilized for the transportation of enemy troops, by serving in some manner for the transmission of information on behalf of an enemy state, or by resisting the exercise of any belligerent's lawful right to visit and search.

Since World War II, the "control test" of the nationality of business enterprises has been extended to vessels and aircraft, at least in Anglo-American practice. This changed attitude is reflected in Section 501 of the current U.S. Navy manual:

[31]See *Part Cargo ex M.V. Glenroy*, Great Britain, Privy Council, 1945, 61 Times L.R. 303, reported in 39 *AJIL* 599 (1945).

Any merchant vessel or aircraft owned or controlled by or for an enemy State, enemy persons, or any enemy corporation possesses enemy character, regardless of whether or not such a vessel or aircraft operates under a neutral flag or bears neutral markings.[32]

## SUGGESTED READINGS

### Laws of War: General

Pictet, *Development and Principles of International Humanitarian Law* (1985); Swinarski, ed., *Studies and Essays on International Humanitarian Law and Red Cross Principles* (1984); Schindler and Toman, eds., *The Laws of Armed Conflict* (3rd ed., 1988); Cassese, ed., *The Current Legal Regulation of the use of Force* (1986); Levie, *The Code of International Armed Conflicts* (2 vols., 1986); Sandoz, Swinarski, Zimmermann, eds., *Commentary on the Additional Protocols of 8 June 1977 to the Geneva Conventions of 12 August 1949* (1987); Whiteman, vol. 10, 1–27, 28–47; Friedman, ed., *The Law of War: A Documentary History* (2 vols., 1972); Moore, *Law and the Indo-China War* (1972); Roberts, ed., *Documents on the Laws of War* (2nd ed., 1989); Solf, *New Rules for Victims of Armed Conflicts* (1982).

### Internal War

Cassese, "The Status of Rebels under the 1977 Geneva Protocol on Non-International Armed Conflicts," 30 *Int'l and Comp. L Quarterly* 416 (1981); Levie, ed., *The Law of Non-International Armed Conflict: Protocol II to the 1949 Geneva Conventions* (1987); Meron, *Human Rights in Internal Strife: Their International Protection* (1988); Wilson, *International Law and the Use of Force by National Liberation Movements* (1988); Falk, ed., *The International Law of Civil War* (1970).

### Irregular Forces

Laquer, *The Guerrilla Reader* (1978); Armstrong, ed., *Soviet Partisans in World War II* (1967); U.S. Dept. of the Army, *Special Forces Operation* ("unconventional" and counterinsurgency warfare), *Training Manual* (TM 31-21), June 1965; Whiteman, vol. 10, 32–38; Trainin, "Questions of Guerrilla Warfare in the Law of War," 40 *AJIL* 534 (1946); Dougherty, " The Guerrilla War in Malaya," 84 *U.S. Naval Institute Proceedings* 40 (Sept. 1958); Suter, *An International Law of Guerrilla Warfare: The Global Politics of Law-Making* (1984).

### Mercenaries

Burmester, " The Recruitment and Use of Mercenaries in Armed Conflicts," 72 *AJIL* 37 (1978); Van Deventer, "Mercenaries at Geneva," 70 *id.,* 811 (1976); Schwarzenberger, "Terrorists, Guerrilleros, Mercenaries," 219–36 in his *International Law and Order* (1971).

---

[32]U.S. Department of the Navy, Chief of Naval Operations, NWIP 10-2, *Law of Naval Warfare* (September 1955, as amended July 1959); see Whiteman, vol. 10, 685–86. For further details concerning vessels in time of war, see Chapter 25.

# 22

# Modern War: Commencement, Effects, Termination

## COMMENCEMENT OF WAR

UNDECLARED WARS   Wars have begun with a declaration of war, with pronouncements or announcements by a state to the effect that it considers itself to be at war with another state, or simply through the commission of hostile acts employing military forces by one state against another state. Beginning with Hugo Grotius, many writers on international law asserted that a declaration of war was required before the commencement of hostilities, but the practice of states proved beyond doubt that they did not accept this rule. Thus a British report in 1870 showed that between 1700 and 1870, a total of 107 conflicts had been initiated without the formality of a declaration of war. The United States, too, has conducted wars without a declaration: an undeclared war with France from 1798 to 1801, the invasion of Florida in 1811 under Generals Jackson and Matthews, the brief Mexican invasion in 1916, the undeclared war with the Soviet Union in 1918–1919, and, of course, the Vietnamese conflict from 1947 onward (for the United States, from March 7, 1965, to March 29, 1973).[1] A different and unorthodox approach to the matter was voiced by U.S. Under Secretary of Defense Fred C. Iklé, who told the House Armed Services Committee (January 24, 1984) that President Reagan did not consider it "appropriate or necessary" to ask Congress to declare war before U.S. forces invaded Grenada on October 25, 1983. Iklé stated that a declaration of war was limited to conflicts of larger scope and longer duration than the Grenada "rescue mission."

To the list of conflicts not preceded by a formal declaration of war can be added the German and Soviet invasions of Poland in 1939, the Korean military operations in 1950, the Japanese attack on Hawaii in 1941, the Chinese invasions of India (1962) and Vietnam (1979), Israel's three wars (1948, 1967, 1973), the Iraq–Iran war in 1980, and the U.S. invasions of Grenada in 1983 and of Panama in 1990.

[1] See Howard, *Fourteen Decisions for Undeclared War* (1978).

Virtually all writers have agreed that a dispute has to precede hostilities, that an unprovoked attack by one state on another is illegal, and that the outbreak of war has to be preceded by unsuccessful efforts to solve the quarrel between the parties to the conflict. Once such efforts have failed, however, general opinion has sanctioned a commencement of hostilities without issuing a declaration of war or other formal notice of intent to resort to the use of force.

THIRD HAGUE CONVENTION OF 1907    The absence of any customary or conventional rules governing the commencement of a war was finally remedied by the adoption at the Second Hague Peace Conference of Convention No. III Relative to the Opening of Hostilities (October 18, 1907). The immediate cause of the drafting of this instrument was the unannounced attack by Japanese torpedo boats on Russian warships at Port Arthur in 1904.

Article 1 of the convention stated:

The Contracting Powers recognize that hostilities between themselves must not commence without previous and explicit warning, in the form either of a reasoned declaration of war or of an ultimatum with conditional declaration of war.

Because the article did not specify any time interval between the declaration and the outbreak of hostilities, the former could immediately precede an attack, and there would be no violation of the convention: surprise attacks were therefore not eliminated from the legal practices of states. Also, because only a few states ratified the instrument and its application was limited to conflicts among the contracting parties, any war between non contracting states or between a contracting state and a non-contracting state did not require a declaration of war.

A declaration of war can be issued only by a member of the family of nations recognized as capable of such a sovereign action.

The "ultimatum" mentioned in Article 1 of the Third Hague Convention of 1907 means final demands, normally specifying a time limit, that one state makes on another. In order to satisfy the wording of Article 1, such an ultimatum must contain a conditional but definite threat that hostilities will begin when the time limit has expired and the demands in question have not been met.

Writers agree that if a war commences with the outbreak of hostilities and the hostilities are followed by a declaration of war, the legal beginning of the conflict dates to the time at which the declaration was issued. This traditional attitude is reflected in a number of American court decisions centering on the beginning of war with Japan in 1941.[2] However, the

---

[2]*Savage* v. *Sun Life Assurance Co. of Canada*, U.S. District Court, 1944, W. D. of La., 57 F. Supp. 620; *Pang* v. *Sun Life Assurance Co.*, Circuit Court, 1st Jud. Circ., Terr. of Hawaii, 1944, appeal, 37 Hawaii 208 (1945); and *Rosenau* v. *Idaho Mutual Benefit Association*, 145 Pac. (2d) 227. See also Borchard, "When Did the War Begin?" 47 *Columbia L. Rev.* 742 (1947).

famous case of *Louise C. Bennion* v. *New York Life Insurance Co.*[3] appears to have reversed the doctrine in regard to United States. Captain Bennion, the commander of the USS *West Virginia,* was killed in the Japanese attack on Pearl Harbor on December 7, 1941. The insurance company paid the principal of $10,000 due on his policy but refused to pay an additional sum of $10,000 asked for as double indemnity in case of death by accident. The refusal was based on a provision of the policy that excluded an accident that took place in "war or an act incident thereto." The District Court awarded its decision to Mrs. Bennion, but the Court of Appeals reversed that verdict, holding that the attack on Pearl Harbor commenced the war with Japan. The Supreme Court refused *certiorari* and also denied a petition for a rehearing.

The Court of Appeals based its reversal in part on the text of the President's address to Congress, on December 8, 1941, requesting a declaration of war: "I ask that Congress declare that since the unprovoked and dastardly attack by Japan on Sunday, December 7, a state of war has existed between the United States and the Japanese Empire." In other words, the court took the reasonable view that an attack by one sovereign state on another with intent to wage war and resistance by the attacked state created a state of war without any formal declaration.

The military operations in Korea under the United Nations Unified Command have been held to have been a war, in regard to insurance policies.[4] The status of war for the conflict was also asserted by General Douglas MacArthur in a statement made on December 2, 1950: "A state of undeclared war between the Chinese Communists and the United Nations forces now exists."[5]

The practice of states since 1907 has demonstrated amply that preference is given to a commencement of hostilities without a declaration of war, even when the parties involved have ratified or adhered to the Third Hague Convention of 1907.[6] Apparently such a course of action represents the real will of governments. The convention, in the view of many writers, thus should by now be regarded as obsolete. This attitude is not shared, however, by the United States Department of the Army: in its field manual, *The Law of Land Warfare,*[7] the department cites the Third Hague Convention as operative. This point of view was also emphasized in the indictment of major German war criminals by the International Military Tribunal at

---

[3] U.S. Court of Appeal, 10th Cir., 1946, 157 F. 2d 260, *certiorari* denied by Supreme Court, 1947, 331 U.S. 811. Text of Circuit Court opinion in 41 *AJIL* 680 (1947); see also McDougal and Feliciano, "The Initiation of Coercion: A Multi-Temporal Analysis," 52 *AJIL* 241 esp. n. 30 for a long list of "war clause" cases (1958).

[4] *Weissman* v. *Metropolitan Life Insurance Co.,* U.S. District Court, S.D. California, 1953, 112 F. Supp. 420, digested in 48 *AJIL* 155 (1954).

[5] UP dispatch from Tokyo, Dec. 2, 1950.

[6] See Whiteman, vol. 10, 66–85.

[7] FM 27–10, Washington, July 1956, 15 [FM 27–10 has not been updated since 1956].

Nuremberg, which cited the violation of Article 1 of the convention among Germany's breaches of treaty obligations.

The outbreak of hostilities between two states, without a declaration of war or a qualified ultimatum, would normally be regarded as a war in the legal sense, unless both parties indicated clearly that they did not recognize the existence of a state of war. A mere attack by the armed forces of one on the inhabitants or armed forces of the other has been held by some courts not to constitute war, unless the government of the attacked state accepted or recognized the existence of a state of war.[8]

On the other hand, some courts have asserted that for purposes of time charters of vessels, military operations lacking a declaration of war may be regarded as constituting a war and thereby bring "war clauses" of a charter into effect.[9]

## SOME LEGAL EFFECTS OF WAR

The principles of natural law asserted that the outbreak of war extinguished all legal relations between belligerents and reduced the latter to an anarchical condition of complete lawlessness, of a *bellum omnium contra omnes.* That view assuredly does not correspond to current attitudes toward conflict, or it would be useless even to contemplate the idea of a law of war. The employment of armed force by states, even in the nuclear age, cannot be said to be totally anarchical.

Although numerous deviations may be cited, it can be asserted that in general, the commencement of a war between two states has the following effects.[10]

DIPLOMATIC RELATIONS    The outbreak of war causes at once the breaking off of any continuing diplomatic relations between the belligerents. The diplomats of both sides are recalled and leave for home as soon as the necessary arrangements for their safe return can be made. If conditions appear to make it desirable, enemy diplomatic personnel may be safeguarded in some particular location to ensure observance of its immunity and safety—such as was done in the case of Japanese diplomats in the United States in December 1941. The embassy or legation building is entrusted to the protection of a neutral state. Similarly, consular relations between belligerents end with the commencement of war.

EFFECT OF WAR ON TREATIES    Legal writers differ greatly in their views of the effect that the outbreak of war between parties to a treaty has on that instrument.[11] A general statement on the subject would have to mention

---

[8]See *West* v. *Palmetto State Life Insurance Co.,* U.S. Supreme Court, 1943, 202 Sup. Ct. 422; consult the valuable survey by Young, "Meaning of 'War' in Insurance Policies," 52 *Michigan Law Rev.* 884 (1954).

[9]See *Kawasaki Kisen Kabushiki Kaisha of Kobe* v. *Bantham S. S. Company, Ltd.,* Great Britain, Court of Appeal, 1939, [1939] 2 K. B. 544, reproduced in 34 *AJIL* 533 (1940).

[10]See also Whiteman, vol. 10, 95–101.

[11]See, *inter alia,* Hyde, vol. 2, 1529–1535, and especially Stone, 447–50.

that certain treaties, such as those regulating the conduct of hostilities, actually come into full effect at the outbreak of war; that treaties of friendship or alliance, as well as all other agreements classifiable as political, concluded between opposing belligerents prior to a war, come to an end at the beginning of the conflict; that nonpolitical agreements are suspended for the duration of the conflict; and that a certain few types of treaties involving matters such as private property rights and possibly also boundary agreements not related to frontiers involved in the conduct of hostilities remain in force during the war.[12] Similarly, agreements that by their very nature were final in character would not be affected at all by the outbreak of war. Thus the Anglo-American Treaty of 1783, by which the independence of the United States was acknowledged by Great Britain, was not touched by the subsequent War of 1812. Treaties of cession are also normally beyond the effects caused by the coming of war, except that a peace settlement might reverse the transfer of territory accomplished by the earlier instrument. Even such a cursory survey as the preceding indicates at once one obvious problem: which treaties are to be considered political? On occasion, the text of an agreement shows clearly that it is political, although in many instances, the subject or object of the agreement reveals its obviously nonpolitical character.

Generally it can be said that treaty provisions, or even entire treaties, not incompatible with a state of war are not suspended or terminated by the outbreak of hostilities.[13]

Multilateral agreements pose far fewer problems than do bilateral treaties, in regard to the effects of war. It is generally agreed that multilateral treaties continue in effect during a war, except between opposing belligerent parties (when the agreement's provisions are incompatible with the existence of a state of war). So-called law-making treaties do not lose their validity or applicability at the onset of a conflict.

ENEMY PUBLIC PROPERTY    Enemy public property is subject to confiscation, but under normal circumstances, enemy embassy or legation buildings are not seized: they are left under neutral control for the duration of the conflict. On a few occasions, this practice has been varied by confiscation of the buildings concerned: during World War I, a number of Austro-Hungarian embassies were taken over by the Allied states, and the German embassy building in Rome was confiscated by Italy.

NATIONAL BORDERS    National borders do not change lawfully during modern conflicts, in contrast with past practice, when occupation of en-

---

[12]See *Argento* v. *North,* U.S. District Court, N. District of Ohio, E. D., 1955, 131 Supp. 538, digested in 50 *AJIL* 140 (1956); and the subsequent and more authoritative *Argento* v. *Horn,* 241 F. 2d 258; other relevant cases include the well-known *Techt* v. *Hughes,* New York, Court of Appeals, 1920, 229 N.Y. 222. The classic case is *Society for the Propagation of the Gospel in Foreign Parts* v. *Town of New Haven,* U.S. Supreme Court, 1823, 8 Wheaton 464; cf. esp. *Karnuth* v. *United States ex rel. Albro,* U.S. Supreme Court, 1929, 279 U.S. 231.
[13]See the important decision in *Clark* v. *Allen,* U.S. Supreme Court, 1947, 331 U.S. 503, on this point.

emy territory was taken to be tantamount to annexation, completed with a change in the nationality of the enemy inhabitants. Any shifting of frontiers has to await the end of the conflict and whatever settlement may be arrived at either through a peace treaty or through subjugation of the enemy.

ENEMY PRIVATE MERCHANT VESSELS    The question of enemy private vessels found in national waters was regulated, from the end of the seventeenth century until World War I, by the principle of "days of grace" (*délai de faveur*): after the outbreak of hostilities, such vessels were granted a limited period of time during which they were allowed to leave without hindrance. This concept, based on comity and not on international law, was applied during the Crimean War, the Austro-Prussian War of 1866, the Franco-Prussian War of 1870–1871, the Spanish-American conflict of 1898, and the Russo-Japanese War of 1904–1905. Some of the time limits were extremely generous: the English Order-in-Council of March 29, 1854, gave Russian merchant vessels six weeks to load and depart from ports under English control.

When World War I came, Germany proposed to the governments of France, Belgium, Great Britain, and Russia that both sides grant periods of grace to enemy merchant vessels. No agreement was reached. Consequently, no party on either side in the conflict granted such delays but seized any and all enemy merchant vessels within reach, except for France, which, on August 4, 1914, granted a period of seven days of grace to German ships found in French ports at 6:45 P.M. on that day or afterward arrived in such ports.

RELATIONS BETWEEN CITIZENS OF HOSTILE STATES    In the absence of customary and conventional law, domestic legislation and public policy in each country determines the ending or continuation of relations between citizens of countries at war with one another. The Anglo-American practice, maintained unchanged until today, has been that the outbreak of war severs all legal and commercial relations between citizens of hostile states. [14] European states, which had long opposed that interpretation, all have gradually come to accept the Anglo-American approach.

In regard to contracts between the citizens of warring states, the Anglo-American judicial attitude has been that contracts concluded during a war are null and void *ab initio,* unless special permission for such agreements has been granted by appropriate authority. Contracts entered into before the outbreak of the war are equally void if the time element is essential and requires execution of the contract after the commencement of the war. If execution can be delayed without impairing the contract, the latter is held to be suspended for the duration of the conflict. [15]

[14] *The Hoop,* Great Britain, 1799, 1 C. Rob, 196; *The Rapid,* U.S. Supreme Court, 1814, 8 Cranch 155.
[15] See *New York Life Insurance Co.* v. *Statham,* U.S. Supreme Court, 1876, 93 U.S. 24. Consult also Diamond, "The Effect of War on Pre-Existing Contracts Involving Enemy Nationals," 53 *Yale Law Jl.* 700 (1944).

World War I witnessed significant changes in the traditional approaches to the problem of relations with enemy citizens. The British government not only forbade trade with any person residing or doing business in the German Reich but followed this prohibition, on December 23, 1915, with a new regulation prohibiting all trade with persons of enemy nationality engaged in business in neutral countries. In order to make certain that all concerned would know the identities of all such persons (natural as well as legal), blacklists were drawn up, listing all individuals and firms with whom British individuals and firms could not conduct business relations. The United States, after protesting this British action while it was still officially a neutral, reversed its stand as soon as it became itself a belligerent and adopted both British policies as its own. During World War II, virtually all belligerents followed the practices evolved during the earlier conflict: enemy character was presumed to exist not only in all persons and firms in enemy territory but also in all persons controlled by the enemy or incorporated under the laws of the enemy, as well as natural and legal enemy citizens in neutral countries.

FROZEN ASSETS    The United States went several steps further during its phase of nominal neutrality in World War II. By executive orders, the assets of neutral countries invaded by Germany, as well as those of Latvia, Estonia, and Lithuania, were "frozen." A little later, the assets in the United States of China, Japan, Italy, and Germany were included under similar orders. The purpose of these measures was rather obvious: the government of the United States wished to prevent the use of American financial facilities in a manner deemed detrimental to America's interests, the liquidation of certain assets suspected of having been looted by Axis conquests, and the misuse of such assets for subversive activities in the United States. On July 17, 1941, the President authorized the drawing up of blacklists of persons and firms deemed to act on behalf of Germany or Italy. When Japan went to war against the United States, Japanese names and the names of other firms held to be acting in the interests of Japan were added to these lists.

ENEMY PROPERTY    Property located in a belligerent state and belonging to private enemy citizens not residing in that state was generally held to be subject to confiscation by the state in which such property was found. This doctrine was upheld by the Supreme Court of the United States in *Brown* v. *United States* as late as 1814.[16] But within a few years after that decision, state after state swung to the contrary view and maintained that private enemy property could not be confiscated by the belligerent on whose territory it was located. As long as the "property" was that of natural persons—consisting of bank deposits, titles to real estate, and so on—this new and liberal attitude could not be contested. But the coming of World War I showed that a significant development had taken place: private property owned by nonresident enemy citizens belonged to a large extent to corpora-

[16]8 Cranch 110; see also Hyde, vol. 2, 1726–43.

tions carrying on business in the belligerent state but controlled from abroad by boards of directors consisting entirely or largely of enemy citizens. Great Britain started a new trend by appointing a custodian of enemy property on November 27, 1914. This step meant not confiscation but a kind of receivership by court action in order to prevent hostile misuse of property located in Great Britain. The custodian was entitled to appoint controllers, who were placed in actual charge of enemy-owned or enemy-controlled enterprises, the operation of which was considered necessary, however, by the British government. Soon the British innovation was copied by France and Germany, as well as by the United States (beginning with the Act of October 6, 1917) after the latter's entry into the war. In the United States, the custodian was specifically authorized to sell any property entrusted to his custody, and, in fact, most of this property was disposed of to the highest bidders. [17]

On the other hand, modern states tend to refrain from seizing the property of enemy aliens residing in their territory, a trend that is in sharp contrast with the practices prevailing a few hundred years ago. In fact, it can be asserted that by the development of a rule of customary law, confiscation of such property under normal circumstances would now be considered a violation of international law. This does not mean that such property may not be placed under some form of government control for the duration of a conflict if it is suspected that it might otherwise be misused on behalf of the enemy. But it does mean that enemy alien property, even if seized temporarily, ought to be returned at the conclusion of the war. [18]

STATUS OF ENEMY ALIENS    The outbreak of war creates for any belligerent state a host of problems concerning enemy aliens found in its territory. Grotius believed that such aliens could be lawfully detained for the duration of the conflict, the idea being that their absence would weaken the enemy state. He asserted, however, that such internees should be released as soon as the war had ended. In 1758, Vattel took a more moderate view of the problem, contending that the admission of aliens meant a tacit acknowledgment by the receiving state that they could leave again in full freedom and safety. The great influence of Vattel on the legal thinking of the late eighteenth century gave much weight to this argument.

It is now generally agreed that under customary international law, enemy alien residents must be granted a reasonable time and an opportunity to leave a belligerent's territory. This act of grace does not apply, however, to such enemy aliens as are actual or potential members of the enemy's armed

---

[17] For practices during World War II, consult Carroll, "Legislation on Treatment of Enemy Property," 37 *AJIL* 611 (1943); Cohn, "German Enemy Property," 3 *Int. Law Quarterly* 530 (1950).

[18] Jessup, "Enemy Property," 49 *AJIL* 57 (1955); and see the legal reasoning outlined in Eder, "Confiscation of Enemy Alien Property Held Unconstitutional by Colombia Supreme Court," 54 *AJIL* 159 (1960), as well as Whiteman, vol. 10, 101–118.

forces (active or reserve officers and other reservists); such individuals may be detained for the duration of the war as prisoners of war. (But see note 22.)

Naturally, any belligerent may permit enemy aliens to remain in its territory during the entire course of a war, and this has been the practice of most states during the past 150 years or more. On a few occasions during that period, however, wholesale expulsions of enemy aliens took place: France forced all German nationals to leave in 1870; the South African states expelled almost all British citizens in 1899; Russia required all Japanese to leave the Far Eastern provinces in 1904; and Turkey expelled most Italians from Turkish territory in 1911.

Once enemy aliens are permitted to remain in the territory of a given belligerent, the latter may then decide whether to intern all of them or only some of them or to leave them at liberty in their normal place of residence, subject to registration and a varying amount of regulation and control. During World War I, France, Germany, and eventually Great Britain resorted to general internment of enemy aliens; the United States did not follow suit. The outbreak of World War II led again to wholesale internment, but after a relatively short time, only a few enemy aliens were detained in this manner, at least in England. In the United States a short-lived internment of 113,000 or so aliens as well as of Americans of Japanese descent took place following the Japanese attack on Pearl Harbor. The detainees were placed in relocation centers for the duration of their internment. After the war, Congress eventually appropriated funds to compensate these internees for a few of their losses suffered as the result of an extremely ill-considered, undemocratic, and unconstitutional action.

The rules applied in Anglo-American courts, as well as in many other countries in modern wars, hold that any individual (or firm) of nonenemy nationality voluntarily resident or carrying on business in enemy territory is an alien enemy by the territorial test; on the other hand, an enemy citizen allowed to remain in a belligerent's territory, to register himself, and to carry on business there is not an enemy alien by the territorial test — even if he is interned as an enemy alien. For example, President Truman signed (October 19, 1951) a congressional resolution ending the state of war with Germany: as of that date, German citizens in the United States were no longer enemy aliens.

As this may seem confusing, let us examine it briefly. During World War II, an American or Swiss citizen residing voluntarily in Germany or doing business there would have been regarded as an enemy alien in an American court; United States businessmen would not have been permitted to make contracts with such a person or to deal with him. But a German national permitted to remain in the United States after the commencement of war between the two countries would not have been an enemy alien in the eyes of the courts. United States nationals could have done business with him, and he would have been able to sue or be sued in United States courts.[19]

Resident enemy aliens could not sue in English courts until 1698, when a court finally granted them this right in time of war. Since then, alien enemies have been permitted access to English courts. In the United States, the Supreme Court ruled in 1813 that "a lawful residence implies protection, and a capacity to sue and be sued. A contrary doctrine would be repugnant to sound policy, no less than to justice and humanity."[20] This policy has been reaffirmed many times since then.

Logically enough, a belligerent state permitting the continued residence of "harmless" enemy aliens in its territory has a perfect right to surround those individuals with all kinds of necessary restrictions. The persons in question may be restricted in their freedom of movement, they may be forbidden to possess arms, radio transmitters, or carrier pigeons or to use code in their written communications; they may be removed from restricted areas for reasons of military security; and they may be barred from certain jobs or even from entire occupations relating to the national war effort.

Abuses of resident enemy aliens, many of whom were prevented from leaving the territory of a belligerent and thus were unable to escape persecution and at times outrageous mistreatment, resulted in the incorporation of many new safeguards in the 1949 Geneva Convention on the Protection of Civilian Persons in Time of War.[21]

This instrument (in force for the United States since February 2, 1956) goes in many respects beyond the previously existing rules of customary law in regard to enemy aliens in belligerent territory. The convention, however, does not protect the nationals of a state that is not a party to the agreement by ratification or adherence. A detailed analysis of the relevant portions of the convention exceeds the limits of a general text; suffice it to state that one specific section of the agreement (Sec. II, Arts. 35–46) deals specifically with the treatment of enemy aliens in belligerent territory and assures these individuals, classified as one of several groups of "protected persons" under the Convention, of extensive safeguards against arbitrary acts of their "hosts." Such topics as permissible departure (Arts. 35, 36),[22] ability to

---

[19]See Whiteman, vol. 10, 118–127; Lauterpacht's *Oppenheim*, vol. 2, 310–313; consult also Wilson, "Recent Developments in the Treatment of Civilian Alien Enemies," 38 *AJIL* 397 (1944), and his earlier "Treatment of Civilian Alien Enemies," 37 *AJIL* 30 (1943). See especially the interesting decision in the case of *Ex parte Kumezo Kawato*, U.S. Supreme Court, 1942, 317 U.S. 69, reprinted in 37 *AJIL* 336 (1943).

[20]*Clark* v. *Morey*, U.S. Supreme Court, 1813, 10 John. 69.

[21]Text in 50 *AJIL* 724 (1956 Supp.).

[22]It should be noted, however, that Article 35 of the Fourth (Civilian) Convention, though authorizing voluntary departure of enemy aliens at the outbreak of hostilities, permits the belligerent in whose territory they then happen to be to prohibit their departure when it believes such to be "contrary to the national interest." This really voids the guarantee of departure and allows the belligerent to detain any and all enemy aliens if it so desires.

receive relief shipments (Art. 38), employment opportunities and categories of permissible as well as prohibited work (Arts. 39, 40), place of residence (Art. 41), internment (Arts. 42–44), and transfer of protected persons by a belligerent to the territory of another state (Art. 45) are dealt with from a humane and liberal point of view as a result of the lessons taught by the experiences of World War II.

Finally, the Fourth Geneva Convention of 1949 contains detailed provisions for remedies available to the individuals in question, that is, recourse to the "Protecting Powers," to the International Committee of the Red Cross, and to the national Red Cross (Red Crescent) societies (Arts. 30 and 142), as well as extremely detailed regulations of the treatment of internees (Arts. 79–141). If—and this is, of course, the big question—in a future war, belligerent states bound by this convention carry out its provisions faithfully, the lot of enemy aliens, both in belligerent states and in occupied enemy territory, will be far better than the lot of such persons in earlier wars.

## THE TERMINATION OF CONFLICTS

WAYS OF ENDING HOSTILITIES    A conflict may end in one of several ways: (1) by a simple cessation of hostilities, (2) by subjugation, or (3) by a treaty of peace.[23]

Termination of a conflict by a simple cessation of hostilities is a rather uncommon occurrence. States generally prefer to avoid this method of ending a war because it proposes a number of practical postwar problems, particularly those that center on the precise time at which the conflict came to an end. The best-known instance of such a termination was the ending of the Franco-Mexican War of 1867, which came to an informal conclusion when the last French troops left Mexican territory to return to France. Other modern examples include the ending of the Polish-Swedish War of 1716, the Spanish-French War of 1720, the Russo-Persian war in 1801, the Spanish attempt to reconquer the lost American colonies (begun in 1810 and terminated in 1825), the state of war between Prussia and Liechtenstein that began in 1866, and the Spanish-Chilean "war" of 1865–1868, which came when Spain abandoned its efforts to fulfill its demands on Chile. After Argentina's forces on the Falkland Islands surrendered (June 14, 1982) to British forces, Argentina refused to declare a formal cessation of hostilities but recognized only a *de facto* halt to the fighting. The British government then announced (July 12) that it was satisfied with the Argentine acknowledgement and that the remaining 593 Argentine prisoners of war would be returned. But the United Kingdom continued to maintain, pending "further consideration," the 200 nautical-mile war zone around the islands, as well as the 12-mile blockade along the coast of Argentina and the

---

[23]Consult also Whiteman, vol. 10, 85–95.

sanctions imposed by the British government against Argentina. On the same day, President Reagan lifted the economic sanctions imposed by the United States against Argentina after the latter's invasion of the Falkland Islands.

Courts have often to deal with the end of a war. Thus, in an action to collect on an insurance policy on the life of a correspondent killed by Egyptian forces on November 20, 1956, during the "Suez Incident," an American court decided that the "war" had ended when the cease-fire agreement took effect on November 6, 1956, stating that "the resolution of the United Nations is to be considered here as having the same effect of terminating the war and restoring peace as a traditional treaty of peace." The court pointed out that in interpreting private contracts, many courts have viewed the actual cessation of hostilities as synonymous with the cessation of war.[24] To this writer, the court's view appears to be in error and in contradiction of accepted rules of the law.

MEANING OF SUBJUGATION    *Subjugation* means the firm military conquest of the enemy state following *debellatio*, the disintegration and eventual disappearance of its government and the total absence of organized resistance by citizens and soldiers of the defeated state. As Lauterpacht correctly emphasized,[25] subjugation and conquest are not necessarily identical, even though there can be no subjugation without conquest. Partial occupation of an enemy state and even its complete conquest may not be subjugation, as long as the enemy has forces in the field, either on its own territory or on that of allies. Subjugation takes place only when the conqueror, in effect, destroys, abolishes, and annihilates the existence and legal personality of the defeated enemy state by annexation. Hence "subjugation . . . may be correctly defined as extermination in war of one belligerent by another through annexation of the former's territory after conquest, the enemy forces having been annihilated."[26]

Obviously subjugation as defined above means the termination of the war for the two belligerents in question. The situation of Germany from its defeat in May 1945 to September 20, 1949—a subject of incredibly elaborate legal discussion—was not, however, subjugation in the classic sense, because conquest was not followed by annexation.[27] On the other hand, a country may be subjugated but still maintain (colonial or other) forces in the field—such as Poland during World War II.

UNCONDITIONAL SURRENDER    World War II saw the introduction of a new term relative to the end of a state of hostilities, *unconditional surren-*

---

[24]*Schneiderman* v. *Metropolitan Casualty Co.*, United States, Sup. Court (N.Y.), App. Div., 1st Dept., Nov 9. 1961, 220 N.Y.S. 2d 947.

[25]Lauterpacht's *Oppenheim*, vol. 2, 600; the general subject of subjugation is covered in considerable detail by Lauterpacht on 599–605.

[26]*Id.*, 600.

[27]See von Glahn, 273–284; Lauterpacht's *Oppenheim*, vol. 2, 602–605.

*der*. The legal consequences of such a surrender might or might not be the termination of a war *ipso facto*, depending on the situation at the time and on the subsequent conduct and intentions of the victors.[28]

The conventional laws of war did not encompass the concept of unconditional surrender. Unconditional surrender has nothing in common with an armistice; instead, it corresponds to what Grotius termed "pure surrender" in the *Three Books on the Law of War and Peace*, in his account of the surrender of Carthage at the end of the second Punic War. Grotius, like the leaders of the wartime "United Nations" in World War II, believed that such a surrender granted to the victor full authority, legal and actual, to do as he pleased with the defeated.

The absence of true modern precedents for unconditional surrender before 1945 meant that there was no traditional formula for such an act.[29] The "unconditional surrender" of Japan (September 2, 1945) was, technically, not unconditional at all: decrees changing the Japanese constitution and certain basic institutions were passed in the name of the emperor, not the military government. The wording of the surrender document indicates clearly the conditional nature of the surrender:

We . . . hereby accept the provisions set forth in the declaration issued by the heads of the Governments of the United States, China and Great Britain on 26 July 1945, at Potsdam, and subsequently adhered to by the Union of Soviet Socialist Republics, which four powers are hereafter referred to as the Allied Powers. . . .

The authority of the Emperor and the Japanese Government to rule the state shall be subject to the Supreme Commander for the Allied Powers who will take such steps as he deems proper to effectuate these terms of surrender.[30]

Authorities now seem to agree that the Hague Regulations of 1907 applied to the Japanese occupation, were subject to such greater powers granted to the occupant specifically in the instrument of surrender and in the Potsdam Declaration.

There can be no doubt that an unconditional surrender does not result in a termination of a war unless the victor clearly indicates that termination will accompany the submission of the defeated state.[31] This was illustrated strikingly in the note of July 9, 1951, from the British government to the Chancellor of the Federal Republic of Germany:

---

[28]Consult Balling, "Unconditional Surrender and a Unilateral Declaration of Peace," 39 *APSR* 474 (1945).

[29]For the text of the unconditional surrender instruments signed in May 1945 by Germany and Italy in Caserta and by German representatives in Rheims and Berlin, See 39 *AJIL* 168 (1945 Supp.). For the texts of the U.S. Proclamation and Joint Resolution terminating the state of war with Germany (October 19, 1951), see 46 *AJIL* 12 (1952 Supp.).

[30]Whiteman, vol. 1, 315; see also von Glahn, 285–286.

[31]See *Schiffahrt-Treuhand* v. *Procurator-General*, United Kingdom, Privy Council, 1953, 1 All Eng. L.R. 364, excerpted in 47 *AJIL* 722 (1953).

His Majesty's Government in the United Kingdom, bearing in mind that on 3rd September, 1939 a state of war was notified with the German Reich, that active hostilities were ended by the Declaration regarding the Surrender of the German Reich issued on the 5th June, 1945, but nevertheless the formal state of war with Germany has continued to subsist so far as the municipal law of the United Kingdom is concerned, and will so continue until the appropriate action is taken by His Majesty's Government to terminate it,
that through circumstances beyond German control it has as yet proved impossible to conclude a treaty which would dispose of questions arising out of the state of war with the German Reich, have determined that, without prejudice to the Occupation Statute, or to the decision of question the settlement of which must await the conclusion of a treaty, the formal state of war between the United Kingdom and Germany shall be immediately terminated.

A **notification** is, therefore, being published that the formal state of war with Germany has terminated as from four o'clock p.m. on the 9th July, 1951.[32]

GENERAL ARMISTICE    An *armistice* is a war convention, that is, an agreement or contract concluded between belligerents. Its primary and traditional purpose is to bring about a *temporary* suspension of active hostilities. A truce, to all intents and purposes, is identical with an armistice, although in former days it usually had a shorter duration. Whereas *particular armistices*, more commonly termed *truces* call for the cessation of hostilities in a portion of a theater of war, *general armistices* cause a general temporary cessation of hostilities between the belligerents. The following discussion centers on such general instruments.

From the days of Greece and Rome until today, writers, diplomats, and military men have agreed that neither type of agreement results in the termination of a state of war (*Land Warfare*, par. 749). The courts of numerous states have affirmed equally that the conclusion of an armistice does not end a war.[33]

No customary rules prescribe what may be written into an armistice agreement, and several modern examples have been referred to as *capitulatory armistices*, such as those that ended the active hostilities in World War I. The term is apt, for the agreements in question involved troop movements, evacuations, and surrender of defensive positions by the Central Powers, notably Germany, which rendered a resumption of hostilities hopeless, if not impossible, and thus constituted a capitulation or surrender, in fact if not in name. But *normally*, armistices envisage a future resumption of hostilities, because they represent merely a suspension of warfare.

After the first Arab-Israeli war in 1948–1949, the United Nations in 1949 established a Lebanese-Israeli Mixed Armistice Commission. Israel maintained, logically, that the commission became defunct when Lebanon declared war against Israel in 1967. Lebanon, on the other hand, asserted

---

[32] *London Gazette*, July 6, 1951, Suppl. (Nr. 39279).
[33] Such as *Kahn* v *Anderson, Warden*, U.S. Supreme Court, 1921, 255 U.S. 1.

on October 1984 and again at the beginning of negotiations for an Israeli withdrawal (January 8, 1985) that the Mixed Armistice Commission should be viewed as the most desirable basis for future Lebanese-Israeli relations.

Hostilities in the Korean conflict ended, under the provisions of an armistice, on July 27, 1953. Since then, no formal legal end of that conflict has been achieved. The Military Armistice Commission, composed of UN observers and U.S. and North Korean officers, has met about 380 times at Panmunjom, in the demilitarized zone created in 1953.

What legal situation prevails during the life of an armistice agreement? The state of war continues, beyond question, and not only between the belligerents themselves but also "between the belligerents and neutrals on all points beyond the mere cessation of hostilities."[34]

Problems commonly arise in connection with the interpretation of an armistice as to what may be permitted and what has been prohibited. Modern practice indicates that during a general armistice, the belligerents must abstain from undertaking only those acts that have been expressly prohibited by the armistice agreement.[35]

The contents of a typical armistice agreement were outlined in paragraph 487 of the current American manual *The Law of Land Warfare.* An armistice instrument includes provisions as to the effective date and time, duration, lines of demarcation, and possible neutral zones to be established, relations with the indigenous population, prohibited acts, status of prisoners of war during the armistice, and possibly various political and even economic matters involved in the temporary suspension of hostilities.[36]

If one of the parties to an armistice agreement commits a "serious" violation of one of the provisions agreed upon, the other party appears to be free to denounce the agreement and to resume hostilities, but this recourse to hostile acts may not be commenced without notice unless a case of urgency exists (Art. 40 of the Hague Regulations of 1907). The obvious difficulty inherent in this principle is the definition of what constitutes a "serious" violation and a "case of urgency."

CEASE-FIRES AND TRUCES    The terms *truce* and *cease-fire* have been used interchangeably in recent conflicts to denote a temporary cessation of hostilities.[37]

---

[34]Lauterpacht's *Oppenheim,* vol. 2, 546.

[35]*Law of Land Warfare,* par. 487e; and see Levie, "The Nature and Scope of the Armistice Agreement," 50 *AJIL* 880 (1956).

[36]For details of the individual topics, with historical examples, consult Levie, *op. cit.,*n.35 889–901.

[37]Such as the UN-arranged cease-fire that ended hostilities in the "Six-Day War" (June 10, 1967); the "Egypt–Israel Cease-Fire Agreement" (Nov. 11,1973) in 12 *ILM* 1312 (1973), which was followed by a "Separation of Forces Agreement" (Jan. 18, 1974) in *NYT*, Jan. 19, 1974, 11; Nicaragua–Nicaraguan Resistance [Contras] "Preliminary Cease-Fire Agreement" (March 23, 1988) in 27 *ILM* 954 (1988)—see also Dept. of State, *Regional Brief: Central America* (July 1988) and *Time,* April 4, 1988, 26–27.

Despite the supposedly temporary character of a cease-fire, several modern armed conflicts have "ended" in fact when hostilities were terminated through the conclusion of a cease-fire which was not followed by a peace treaty. Examples include the recent Iraq–Iran war, the Nicaraguan civil war, the Angolan civil war, and Israel's three wars with Arab states (although the cease-fire with Egypt was followed eventually with a formal peace treaty).

NAVAL ARMISTICE    In regard to war at sea, little is found in the literature, but the governing principles are clear. A naval armistice (or a general armistice, which, of course, would apply also to the naval segment of hostilities) precludes a naval battle as well as naval bombardments. Most writers, however, are silent on the subject of how an armistice would affect a blockade and of the relations between a blockading belligerent and neutrals. It appears that the blockading party may continue its activities during an armistice, including capturing enemy vessels, stopping neutral vessels, and carrying contraband, unless the armistice agreement contains specific provisions to the contrary.[38]

TREATY OF PEACE    A treaty of peace is the normal and greatly preferred mode of terminating a war. It must be reemphasized at the outset that a cease-fire, a truce, an armistice, or even preliminary peace negotiations do not represent the *legal* termination of a war, despite much lay misunderstanding on the point. Thus the Korean War is still legally in effect, because the relevant armistice agreement only ended hostilities but did not restore peace; the same is true of the Arab-Israeli conflicts of 1948, 1956, and 1967 (except between Israel and Egypt).

One of the more unusual aspects of the few recent peace treaties was in the background of the Treaty of Peace and Friendship Between the People's Republic of China and Japan (entered into force October 23, 1978).[39] As Teixeira pointed out,[40] Japan insisted that peace had been restored through the treaty that Japan had concluded in 1952 with the Nationalist Government on Taiwan (Treaty of Peace, Republic of China–Japan, entered into force August 5, 1952 — 138 U.N.T.S.3.), at the time recognized by many states as the lawful government of all of China. But the People's Republic insisted that a new peace treaty be concluded, based mostly on the 1972 Chou–Tanaka Communiqué of September 29, 1972, that restored diplomatic relations between the People's Republic and Japan.[41]

A treaty of peace has the primary effect of restoring a condition of peace between the ex-belligerents. As soon as the treaty becomes effective, all

[38] See Levie, *op. cit. supra* n. 35, 904–906, with historical examples, including the interesting relevant provisions of the Korean armistice of July 27, 1953. As regards the latter instrument, consult also the complete texts in *U.S. News & World Report*, Aug. 7, 1953, 85–91; and Joy, "The Korean Truce," *U.S. News & World Report*, Oct. 28, 1955, 131–62.
[39] Text in 17 *ILM* 1054 (1978).
[40] Teixeira, *Note on International Agreements*, 20 *Harvard Int'l. Law Jl*, 412, at 415 (1979).
[41] Text of the communiqué in *NYT* Sept. 30, 1972, 12.

normal peacetime rights and duties go back into effect between the parties to the agreement. Acts deemed legitimate in time of war cease to be lawful. Diplomatic and consular relations are resumed. Unless the treaty provides to the contrary, each ex-belligerent retains movable public property seized from the other belligerent.

An important effect of a peace treaty has been, traditionally, the release of all prisoners of war by all parties to the agreement. Such a release did not have to be immediate but was to take place as soon as possible. However, Article 118 of the 1949 Geneva Convention on Prisoners of War changed the existing customary and conventional law by requiring the immediate release and repatriations of all prisoners of war as soon as active hostilities has ceased. As Lauterpacht pointed out,[42] this provision appears to relate to the end of hostilities brought about by total surrender or by an armistice couched in such terms as to make resumption of warfare impossible for the defeated party. It grew out of the continued detention of prisoners of war long after the actual end of hostilities in World War II. (See also Chapter 23.)

The repatriation provisions of the Geneva Convention became a major reason for the delay in the United States' ratification of all four Geneva conventions of 1949, as a consequence of the end of hostilities in Korea (see also Chapter 23). After a large number of North Korean and Chinese prisoners of war, as well as a handful of American prisoners, refused to be repatriated, the Agreement on Repatriation of Prisoners of War (June 8, 1953) and the Supplementary Agreement on Prisoners of War had to be worked out between the representatives of North Korea and the United Nations Command (July 27, 1953).[43]

The Pakistan–India Cease-Fire Agreement (see n. 36, above) could also be viewed as a peace treaty, inasmuch as its terms indicated clearly that the instrument was intended to end the conflict, not merely end active hostilities.

The "Cease-fire Agreement" of January 27, 1973, concerning the Vietnam War, was a peace treaty, despite its media title, as was clearly indicated in its official title (Agreement on Ending the War and Restoring Peace in Vietnam) and in its preamble.[44]

STATUS OF PREWAR TREATIES     The resumption of the effectiveness or the validity of prewar treaties between ex-belligerents after the end of a war has been a much-discussed question.

Normally, peace treaties are used to reactivate economic and technical agreements suspended during the conflict, although reactivation, particu-

---

[42]Lauterpacht's *Oppenheim*, vol. 2, 613.

[43]Texts in 47 *AJIL* 178 (1953 Supp.).

[44]Text of agreement and relevant protocols in *NYT*, Jan. 25, 1973, 15–18; also in 12 *ILM* 48 (1973) (including details and maps relating to the Four Party Joint Military Commission), and in 67 *AJIL* 389 (1973). See also the Act of the International Conference on Viet-Nam (March 2, 1973). *id.*, 621, and "Suggested Readings" at the end of this chapter.

larly of economic agreements (commercial treaties, tariff agreements, and so on), commonly includes changes from the prewar stipulations and so in effect amounts to a renegotiation of the agreements. Sometimes, however, a party to the conflict refuses to revive the prewar agreements, as Spain did in 1898 when it declared that the war had ended all agreements between Spain and the United States. If the war ends with a decisive victory of one side over the other, then usually it is left to the victorious side to determine which treaties are to be regarded as still valid.

If a peace treaty is silent on the question of treaty validity, then all agreements that had been abrogated by the outbreak of the war (alliances and other political agreements) are dead (null and void) on the return of peace. On the other hand, under such conditions, treaties merely suspended by the coming of the war would have to be regarded as revived and in full force on the effective date of the peace treaty.

The 1947 peace treaties concluded with Italy and other European Axis countries each contained identical articles relating to prewar bilateral agreements. The provisions in question called for each of the victorious powers to give notice to the defeated state, within six months from the coming into effect of the respective peace treaty, as to which of its prewar bilateral treaties were to be maintained in effect or were to be reactivated. Any bilateral treaties not included on the lists to be sent to each defeated nation were to be considered abrogated.

The Japanese peace settlement of 1951 also contained in the treaty provisions the reactivation of prewar treaties, both bilateral and multipartite, in addition to a supplementary declaration relating exclusively to the continuing effects of the multilateral agreements.[45]

ENEMY PROPERTY    A final, difficult problem related to the restoration of peace pertains to the return or retention by states of seized enemy property. As was pointed out earlier, a rapid change in the applicable rules of law during the last fifty years has led to the general acceptance of the idea that a belligerent is entitled to seize enemy private property located in his own territory, provided that the enemy owners are not resident in the belligerent's jurisdiction. As mentioned then, during World War II, the anti-Axis belligerents seized all such enemy properties and entrusted them to the care of officials usually called *alien property custodians*.

What should become of such properties at the termination of a war when a treaty of peace does not call for their return to the former owners? Because the properties were held by governments, the obvious answer would be that they could be retained or sold and that in the latter case, the sums realized might be treated as a kind of reparation for war damage suffered by the seizing state and its citizens.

Eighteen Allied states adopted this view in the Paris Agreement on German Reparation of January 24, 1946, deciding that

---

[45] Text of the Japanese peace treaty in 46 *AJIL* 71 (1952 Supp.), and of the declaration, *id.*, 86.

each Signatory Government shall, under such procedures as it may choose, hold or dispose of German assets within its jurisdiction in manners designed to preclude their return to German ownership or control.[46]

The Bonn Convention of May 26, 1952, provided specifically that the Allies would waive all claims for governmental reparations from Germany and that the latter would agree never to contest the retention of seized assets by the Allies and furthermore would compensate the former owners of the seized properties.[47] For the United States, the War Claims Act of 1948 provided for the retention of seized enemy property, and if it were sold, the proceeds were to be used to settle war claims of American nationals, the net balance remaining to go into the Treasury of the United States.

Many of the enemy properties seized in this country were eventually sold. The largest remaining vested enterprise, the General Aniline and Film Corporation, valued at $35 million when seized and worth $100 million by 1956, became the object of the celebrated *Interhandel* case. (See "Suggested Readings" in Chapter 9 for sources on the case and on the eventual disposal, by sale, of the properties in question.)

In 1956, a movement began in the United States to return all properties vested in the custodian to the former, now ex-enemy, owners.[48]

Lack of space prohibits an analysis of the complicated arguments that evolved from the suggestions that the seized properties be returned. One point, however, must be stressed: legally the United States was correct in retaining the property vested in the custodian or the proceeds from its sale. Any reliance on alleged contrary rules of international law fails to take cognizance of the change in those rules that has taken place since 1918 and that has been reaffirmed in numerous treaties of undoubted validity.

## SUGGESTED READINGS

### General

United States, *Proclamations Regarding Alien Enemies* (Japan: No. 2525, December 7, 1941; Germany No. 2526, and Italy, No. 2527, December 8, 1941; Hungary, Bulgaria, Rumania, No. 2563, July 17, 1942), 36 *AJIL* 236 (1942 Supp.).

---

[46]Text in 40 *AJIL* 117 (1946 Supp.), see also *NYT,* April 20, 1973, 3.
[47]Relevant textual excerpts in Ely "Return of Enemy-owned Property," *Proceedings* 59–65, at 61, n. 5 (1958); see also Schisgall, *The Enemy Property Issue* (1957), 4.
[48]See, *inter alia,* Schisgall, *op. cit.,* 6–11; Reeves, "Return of Enemy Property," *Proceedings* 48–53 (1958); Carston, "Return of Enemy Property," *id.,* 53–59; Ely *op. cit.,* 59–65; Folsom, "Return of Enemy-Owned Property," *Proceedings* 65–70 (1958); and the discussion of the preceding papers, *id.,* 70–79. The Office of Alien Property closed on June 30, 1966, after handling varied properties valued at about $900 million.

CASES

*Brown* v. *United States,* U.S. Supreme Court, 1814, 8 Cranch (12 U.S.) 110.

*Commercial Cable Co.* v. *Burleson,* U.S. District Court, S.D. of New York, 1919, 255 Fed. 99.

*The Eliza Ann,* Great Britain, High Court of Admiralty, 1813, 1 Dodson 244, 165 Eng. Rep. 1298.

*Kaufman* v. *Société Internationale,* U.S. Supreme Court, 1952, 343 U.S. 156.

*Porter* v. *Freudenberg,* Great Britain, Court of Appeal, 1915, [1915] 1 K.B. 857.

## Vietnam War

Wormuth, *The Vietnam War: The President Versus the Constitution* (Fund for the Republic, 1968)—a defense of the need for a formal declaration of war; for defenses of the policy adopted by the United States [Gulf of Tonkin Resolution and so on] see, *inter alia,* the analyses, in *U.S. News & World Report,* Dec. 20, 1965, 33; March 13, 1967, 43; and May 22, 1967, 31–33, the last item including the testimony of the then Secretary of Defense McNamara on the avoidance of a formal declaration of war by the United States.

## Undeclared Wars

Brown, "Undeclared Wars," 33 *AJIL* 538 (1939); Eagleton "Acts of War," 35 *AJIL* 321 (1941); Green, "The Nature of the 'War' in Korea" 4 *Int'l Law Quarterly* 462 (1951); Pye, "The Legal Status of the Korean Hostilities," 45 *Georgetown Law Jl.* 45 (Fall 1956); See also Salisbury, "Russians to Mark '39 Mongolia War," *NYT,* May 24, 1964, 8, concerning the undeclared border conflict of 1937–1939 involving the Soviet Union and Outer Mongolia against Japan, a "war'" ended by an "unofficial armistice" after a serious Japanese defeat.

CASES

*Navios Corporation* v. *The Ulysses II,* U.S. District Court, 1958, 161 F. Supp. 932, reported briefly in 53 *AJIL* 192 (1959).

*Broussard* v. *Patton,* U.S. Court of Appeals, 9th Cir., 1972, 466 F.2d 816, reported in 67 *AJIL* 345 (1973).

*Hammond* v. *National Life & Accident Insurance Co.,* U.S. Court of Appeals (Louisiana) 3rd Cir., 1971 (rehearing denied, Feb. 24, 1971), 243 So. 2d 902, reported in 65 *AJIL* 822 (1971).

## Treaties and War

Lord McNair and Watts, *The Legal Effects of War,* (4th ed., 1967); McIntyre, *The Legal Effect of World War II on Treaties of the United States* (1958); Castel, "Effect of War on Bilateral Treaties," 51 *Mich. Law Rev.* 566 (1953); Rank, "Modern War and the Validity of Treaties," 38 *Cornell Law Quart.* 321 and 511 (1953).

## Enemy Aliens

U.S. War Department, *Final Report: Japanese Evacuation from the West Coast* (1943); Bosworth, *America's Concentration Camps* (1967); Brandon, "Legal Control over Resident Enemy Aliens in Time of War in the United States and in the United Kingdom," 44 *AJIL* 382 (1950).

CASES

*Ex parte Kumezo Kawato,* U.S. Supreme Court, 1942, 317 U.S. 69, reported at length in 37 *AJIL* 336 (1943).
*Japanese Government* v. *Commercial Casualty Insurance Co.,* U.S. District Court, S.D.N.Y., 1951, reported in 46 *AJIL* 567 (1952).
*Gmo. Niehaus & Co.* v. *United States,* U.S. Court of Claims, 373 F.2d 944, reported in 61 *AJIL* 1061 (1967).
*Bonnar* v. *United States,* U.S. Court of Claims, 1971, 438, F.2d 540, reported in 65 *AJIL* 820 (1971).

## Armistices, Cease-fires, and Truces

Bailey, "Cease-fires, Truces, and Armistices in the Practice of the UN Security Council," 71 *AJIL* 461 (1977).
(a) Korean Armistice: *NYT,* March 26, 1974, 9; Sept. 7, 1976, 1, 2; Oct. 10, 1976, 7; July 29, 1978, 2.
(b) Egypt–Israel Cease-fire, 1973: 12 *ILM* 1312 (1973); 13 *ILM* 23, 880 (1974); 14 *ILM* 1450 and maps (1975); and also *Washington Post,* Aug. 15, 1973, A-2; Sept. 2, 1975, 16.
(c) India–Pakistan Cease-fire of 1971: *NYT,* Dec. 6, 1971, *passim;* 11 *ILM* 123 (1972).
(d) Laos–Pathet Lao Cease-fire of 1973: 12 *ILM* 397 (1973), for text; *NYT,* Feb. 22, 1973, 17.

## Termination of War

Texts of Hungarian and Rumanian Peace Treaties: 42 *AJIL* 255 (1948 Supp.). documents relating to the Italian Armistice of 1943, 40 *AJIL* 1 (1946 Supp.). Tashkent Declaration (India–Pakistan, 1966), in *NYT,* Jan. 11, 1966, C-15; Webster, "Patterns of Peacemaking," 25 *Foreign Affairs* 596 (1947); Kunz, "Ending the War with Germany," 46 *AJIL* 114 (1952); see also the extremely interesting and instructive Library of Congress Report on "Congress and the Termination of the Vietnam War" (April 1973), prepared for the U.S. Senate Committee on Foreign Relations by the Foreign Affairs Division of the Library of Congress, in 12 *ILM* 699 (1973); Baily, *The Making of Resolution 242* [Cease-fire "ending" the 1973 Israel–Arab state war] (1985).
(a) Israel–Egypt Peace Treaty: For "Camp David Agreements (September 1978)," see 17 *ILM* 1463 (1978), text of March 26, 1979, peace treaty (and annexes) in 18 *ILM* 362 and 530 (1979) and *NYT,* March 27, 1979, A-1, A-10, A-14, A-16; Sept. 25, 1975, 3; April 26, 1979, A-8.

## Reparations

See *CSM,* July 23, 1976, 2, on Japanese reparations payments.

# 23

# Laws of Land
# and Air Conflicts

## BACKGROUND

The legality of war was acknowledged by eminent writers on international law, beginning with Hugo Grotius. At the same time, both governments and military leaders recognized that a regularization of the conduct of hostilities was highly desirable, as was an avoidance of needless suffering and an unnecessary loss of property. It was therefore not surprising that a relatively elaborate set of customary rules concerning the behavior of states during war was evolved between the end of the Thirty Years' War and the middle of the nineteenth century.

The true beginning of present-day rules applicable to land warfare came in 1863, when Francis Lieber's *Instructions for the Government of the Armies of the United States in the Field* was issued to the Union Army on April 24, 1863, as General Orders No. 100. The thoroughness of Lieber's work impressed military men elsewhere, and the *Instructions* became the model for numerous national manuals (Italy, 1896 and 1900; Russia, 1904; and France, 1901 and 1912).

Concurrently, private and governmental efforts at codifying the laws of war on land proceeded on the Continent. An international conference, held in Brussels in 1874 at Russia's initiative and attended by representatives of 15 states, resulted in a draft declaration.[1] Although the instrument was not ratified by the participating states, it did influence the thinking of legal experts and apparently induced a number of states to base new military manuals on the provisions of the draft instrument.

Two private attempts at codification merit brief mention: in 1880 the Institute of International Law prepared the so-called *Oxford Manual (Manuel de Lois de la Guerre sur Terre)*, and in 1894 the German writer Geffcken prepared a private code, anticipating in it several important aspects of the 1894 and 1907 conventions.

---

[1] Text in Graber, *The Development of the Law of Belligerent Occupation, 1863–1914* (1949), 297–317; see also Graber's account of the conference, at 20–28, and the commentary on the draft, 28–30.

The *Oxford Manual* was such an excellent effort, considering the type of warfare then current, that it is still cited with approval by European writers.[2]

Far more important than those early attempts were the conventions and regulations produced at the two Hague Peace Conferences in 1899 and 1907. In particular, the Fourth Convention Respecting the Laws and Customs of War on Land (1907) and its annexed regulations formulated the rules that have been accepted subsequently by most nations of the world and that have been incorporated in almost all military manuals.[3]

Although both world wars showed the inadequacy of many of the 1907 rules as well as the great gaps in the body of law presumably governing war on land, repeated attempts to modernize the rules have failed (conferences at Madrid, Monaco, and Liège), until the four Geneva conventions of 1949 and the two protocols of 1977.

## LAWS OF CONFLICTS ON LAND

The actual rules in force in 1914 were based in part on custom, in part on the conventions adopted in 1899 at The Hague, and in particular on the regulations annexed to the Fourth Hague Convention of 1907.

Because of the limitations of space, only the relevant text of the Regulations is reproduced below, followed by brief comments on selected provisions.[4]

### REGULATIONS RESPECTING THE LAWS AND CUSTOMS OF WAR ON LAND

SECTION 1. ON BELLIGERENTS

*Chapter I. The Qualifications of Belligerents*

*Article 1.* The laws, rights, and duties of war apply not only to armies, but also to militia and volunteer corps fulfilling the following conditions:

1. To be commanded by a person responsible for his subordinates;
2. To have a fixed distinctive emblem recognizable at a distance;
3. To carry arms openly; and
4. To conduct their operations in accordance with the laws and customs of war.[5]

In countries where militia or volunteer corps constitute the army, or form part of it, they are included under the denomination "army."

---

[2]The text of the *Manual* may be found in excerpted form in Graber, *op. cit.*, 297–317, and complete in Scott, ed., *Resolutions of the Institute of International Law Dealing with the Law of Nations* (1916), 26–42. Geffcken's code may be found in his "Règlement des Lois et Coutumes de la Guerre," 26 *Revue de Droit International* 586 (1894).
[3]The Regulations are cited hereinafter as HR.
[4]Consult Chapter 24 on the subject of belligerent occupation.
[5]See Chapter 21, *supra*, and below, concerning the changes produced for ratifying countries by Protocols I and II of 1977, abbreviated as PR-I and PR-II.

*Article 2.* The inhabitants of a territory which has not been occupied, who, on the approach of the enemy, spontaneously take arms to resist the invading troops without having had time to organize themselves in accordance with Article 1, shall be regarded as belligerents if they carry arms openly and if they respect the laws and customs of war.

*Article 3.* The armed forces of the belligerent parties may consist of combatants and non-combatants. In the case of capture by the enemy, both have a right to be treated as prisoners of war.

### *Chapter II. Prisoners of War*

[Articles 4 to 20 omited.][6]

### *Chapter III. The Sick and Wounded*

*Article 21.* The obligations of belligerents with regard to the sick and wounded are governed by the Geneva Convention.[7]

SECTION II. HOSTILITIES

### *Chapter 1. Means of Injuring the Enemy, Sieges, and Bombardments*

*Article 22.* The right of belligerents to adopt means of injuring the enemy is not unlimited.

*Article 23.* In addition to the prohibitions provided by special Conventions, it is especially forbidden—

(a) To employ poison or poisoned weapons;

(b) To kill or wound treacherously individuals belonging to the hostile nation or army [see PR-I, Arts. 37–39];

(c) To kill or wound an enemy who, having laid down his arms, or having no longer means of defence, has surrendered at discretion [see PR-I, Art. 41–42];

(d) To declare that no quarter will be given [see PR-I, Art. 40];

(e) To employ arms, projectiles, or material calculated to cause unnecessary suffering [see PR-I, Art. 35 (2)];

(f) To make improper use of a flag of truce, of the national flag or of the military insignia and uniform of the enemy, as well as the distinctive badges of the Geneva Convention [see PR-I, Arts. 37–39];

(g) To destroy or seize the enemy's property, unless such destruction or seizure be imperatively demanded by the necessities of war;

(h) To declare abolished, suspended, or inadmissible in a court of law the rights and actions of the national of the hostile party.

A belligerent is likewise forbidden to compel the nationals of the hostile party to take part in the operations of war directed against their own country, even if they were in the belligerent's service before the commencement of the war.

---

[6]Articles 4–20 have been replaced by the Geneva Convention of August 12, 1949 Relative to the Treatment of Prisoners of War and, for ratifying states, by PR-I and PR-II; see below.
[7]The reference is to the Geneva Convention of August 22, 1864, revised in 1906, 1929, and 1949.

*Article 24.* Ruses of war and the employment of measures necessary for obtaining information about the enemy and the country are considered permissible.

*Article 25.* The attack or bombardment, by whatever means, of towns, villages, dwellings, or buildings which are undefended is prohibited [see PR-I, Arts. 59–60];

*Article 26.* The officer in command of an attacking force must, before commencing a bombardment, except in cases of assault, do all in his power to warn the authorities.

*Article 27.* In sieges and bombardments all necessary steps must be taken to spare, as far as possible, buildings dedicated to religion, art, science, or charitable purposes, historic monuments, hospitals, and places where the sick and wounded are collected, provided they are not being used at the time for military purposes [see PR-I, Art. 52].

It is the duty of the besieged to indicate the presence of such buildings or places by distinctive and visible signs, which shall be notified to the enemy beforehand.

*Article 28.* The pillage of a town or place, even when taken by assault, is prohibited.

## Chapter II. Spies

*Article 29.* A person can only be considered a spy when, acting clandestinely or on false pretences, he obtains or endeavors to obtain information in the zone of operations of a belligerent, with the intention of communicating it to the hostile party.

Thus, soldiers not wearing a disguise who have penetrated into the zone of operations of the hostile army, for the purpose of obtaining information, are not considered spies. Similarly, the following are not considered spies: Soldiers and civilians, carrying out their mission openly, entrusted with the delivery of dispatches intended either for their own army or for the enemy's army. To this class belong likewise persons sent in balloons for the purpose of carrying dispatches and, generally, of maintaining communications between the different parts of an army or a territory.

*Article 30.* A spy taken in the act shall not be punished without previous trial [see PR-I, Art. 46].

*Article 31.* A spy who, after rejoining the army to which he belongs, is subsequently captured by the enemy, is treated as a prisoner of war, and incurs no responsibility for his previous acts of espionage [see PR-I, Art. 46(4)].

## Chapter III. Flags of Truce

*Article 32.* A person is regarded as a parlementaire who has been authorized by one of the belligerents to enter into communication with the other, and who advances bearing a white flag. He has a right to inviolability, as well as the trumpeter, bugler or drummer, the flagbearer and interpreter who may accompany him.

*Article 33.* The commander to whom a parlementaire is sent is not in all cases obliged to receive him.

He may take all the necessary steps to prevent the parlementaire taking advantage of his mission to obtain information.

In case of abuse, he has the right to detain the parlementaire temporarily.

*Article 34.* The parlementaire loses his right of inviolability if it is proved in a clear and incontestable manner that he has taken advantage of his privileged position to provoke or commit an act of treason.

[Chapters IV and V deal with capitulations and armistices.]

## Comments on the Regulations

It must be emphasized, above all, that the Regulations adopted at The Hague in 1907 are now accepted as part of customary international law and thus as binding on all members of the family of nations. The sole exceptions to that statement are those portions of the Regulations that have been replaced, as indicated in the text above, by subsequent conventions: they are part of conventional law and only binding on the states that have ratified or acceded to those subsequent instruments. In view of the customary law status of the Hague Regulations, the formerly troublesome Article 2 of the Fourth Hague Convention (the general participation clause mentioned in Chapter 21) can be regarded as irrelevant; testimony to that effect can be found in the first of the two reports of the UN Secretary-General on human rights in armed conflicts.[8]

On the other hand, the binding nature of the Geneva Conventions of 1949 is based on their status as multilateral treaties. To be sure, some of the components of those four treaties are based on previously accepted customary law: such provisions would be binding on all states. Inasmuch as new concepts and old customary law principles are blended into those four instruments, a case-by-case approach is needed to discover whether or not a given provision is indeed binding on a state not a party to the Geneva conventions.

The 1977 Protocols Additional to the Geneva Conventions of August 12, 1949, have a different status from the previous treaties mentioned. Owing in part to a disagreement caused by some of the provisions of PR-I and PR-II, fewer countries have ratified the two agreements (by the end of 1982, PR-I had been ratified by 27 states, and PR-II by only 23).[9] It therefore must be expected that it will be a long time before the two Protocols enjoy the widespread acceptance of the 1949 conventions.

The reader of the 1907 Regulations will have noted that some of the provisions sound quaint — if not totally outdated — in this day and age, even though they still stand as a part of international law. An old and regrettable anecdote in the modern history of the law is that during the negotiations that eventually led to the drafting of the four Geneva conventions of 1949, it was suggested that the International Law Commission should modernize the rules laid down at The Hague. That proposal was turned down because "war having been outlawed [in the Charter of the United Nations], the regulation of its conduct has ceased to be relevant."

In consequence of such an unrealistic attitude, the comments that follow

---

[8] *Report of the Secretary-General on Respect for Human Rights in Armed Conflicts*, UN GA Doc. A/7720 (1969), 22; both of the reports are mentioned briefly in Chapter 21.

[9] See the thoughtful analysis (from which these ratification numbers have been taken), "On the Inadequate Reach of Humanitarian and Human Rights Law and the Need for a New Instrument," 77 *AJIL* 589 (1983).

necessarily refer, in the case of the 1907 Regulations, to a dated but still important portion of international law.

It was pointed out in Chapter 21 that the 1907 Hague instruments were supplemented by the four Geneva conventions of 1949 and that the latter in turn were updated and expanded by the two protocols of 1977.[10] PR-I pertains to the questions connected with international conflicts, and PR-II pertains to certain aspects of noninternational conflicts.

MEANS OF INJURING THE ENEMY    HR, Article 22, asserted that the right of belligerents to adopt means of injuring the enemy was not unlimited, a view echoed in PR-I, Article 35 (1)—but in both instances, the statements are couched in rather vague terms. Military necessity, discussed in Chapter 21, was disavowed in the Hague conventions of 1899 and 1907; yet it has been pleaded during and after recent conflicts[11] and frequently has involved new methods of injuring an enemy. What about starvation, for instance, as a weapon of war? Would this practice, common in several modern wars, represent an "unlimited" means, especially because almost by definition its application destroys the "grand distinction" between combatants and noncombatants as well as the narrow provisions of Article 23 of the Fourth Geneva Convention of 1949?[12] Writers insist that acts of war should be based on a "balanced relation . . . to a military end,"[13] but such a claimed proportionality would appear difficult to achieve under war conditions related to national survival.

KILLING TREACHEROUSLY    The prohibition of killing treacherously (HR, Art. 23-b; PR-I, Art. 37-1) means that it is illegal to assassinate, proscribe, or outlaw an enemy, or to place a price on his head, or to offer a reward for his delivery "dead or alive." It is believed that the prohibition was not aimed at "sneak attacks" or individual members of an opposing armed force.

Article 23, paragraph 2, of the Regulations is self-explanatory.[14]

KILLING AN UNARMED ENEMY    The provisions of HR Article 23-c, and PR-I, Article 42, do not imply a prohibition on firing on descending parachutists bound on hostile missions. Although such individuals are temporarily unable to defend themselves effectively, their opponents have a lawful right to try to kill them. If, however, the descending parachutist is not bound on a hostile mission (doctors, nurses, chaplains, members of the crew of a disabled aircraft), he or she may not be attacked. The practical difficulty lies in the problem of discerning the nature of the individual, particularly if the descent is made at night or in poor visibility.

---

[10]Texts in 72 *AJIL* 457 (1978) and also in 16 *ILM* 1391 (1977).

[11]See Moffitt, 5–7, on this point.

[12]*Id.*, pp. 15–18, including a discussion of an interesting post-World War II case. See also PR-I, Art, 54 (1): "starvation of civilians as a method of warfare is prohibited."

[13]See Moffitt, 4, for example.

[14]Cf. von Glahn, 81–85, concerning the meaning of the prohibition in occupied enemy territory.

DENIAL OF QUARTER    The prohibition on the denial of quarter (HR, Art. 23-d, and PR-I, Art. 42) has several recognized exceptions: no quarter need be granted to enemy troops that resume fighting after hoisting a white flag or other sign of surrender, and a denial of quarter would be legitimate in reprisal for a similar refusal by an opposing military force. It should be noted that these exceptions are not listed in the relevant conventions.

USE OF RUSES    The provisions of HR, Article 24, and PR-I, Article 37 (2), concerning the lawful use of ruses, apparently were left vague by intent: no general treaty could list all the ingenious devices used or yet to be invented to confound an enemy. On the other hand, certain practices are recognized as unlawful, either under HR, Article 24, or under customary law. Thus it is forbidden to misuse a flag of truce or the emblem of the Red Cross (HR, Art. 23-f; PR-I, Arts. 38 and 39). The enemy's uniform must not be misused: it may be worn by his opponents but must be discarded before hostilities commence. Such an attitude is not very consistent; it means that an enemy can be lured into an unfavorable situation by a form of legal disguise, which would then suddenly become illegal at a moment when the enemy could no longer extricate himself form the situation. Soldiers of most nations appear to be united in a silent compact that justifies their killing of any enemy misusing their own uniform — especially when that enemy, still in the opponent's uniform, appears behind the latter's lines. Examples abounded in the Battle of the Bulge in 1944.

On the other hand, an American war crimes tribunal at Dachau, in September 1947, acquitted Otto Skorzeny and seven aides of charges of war crimes. The accused had infiltrated American lines during the Battle of the Bulge wearing American uniforms. Although the accused had obviously violated the spirit of HR, Article 23-f, they had not been captured in the act of violation but had been arraigned years later. Such a contingency was not covered clearly in the Hague Regulations. [15]

PROHIBITION OF CERTAIN WEAPONS    In line with the prevailing concept that needless suffering should be avoided, pre-1914 laws of war specified certain prohibited categories of weapons that, by their nature, would aggravate the sufferings of the wounded. And Article 36 of PR-I represents an innovative addition to the law of war:

In the study, development, acquisition or adoption of a new weapon, means or method of warfare, a High Contracting Party is under an obligation to determine

---

[15] Consult Jobst, "Is the Wearing of the Enemy's Uniform a Violation of the Laws of War?" 35 AJIL 435 (1941); cf. U.S. Department of the Army (FM 27–10), Law of Land Warfare (July 1956), 23; see also Koessler, "International Law on Use of Enemy Uniforms As a Strategem and the Acquittal in the Skorzeny Case," 24 Missouri Law Rev. 16 (1959).

whether its employment would, in some or all circumstances, be prohibited by this Protocol or by any other rule of international law applicable to the High Contracting Party. [16]

HR, Article 23-e—and now also PR-I, Article 35(2)—forbids the employment of arms, projectiles, and other material calculated to cause unnecessary suffering. The prohibition is somewhat vague, leaving, in essence, each state free to decide whether or not to utilize a certain weapon because in its judgment the weapon possesses or lacks the prohibited effect. State practice has sanctioned the use of explosives in artillery shells, mines, and hand grenades. On the other hand, such weapons as lances with barbed heads, irregularly shaped bullets, shells filled with glass, and the application of some substance to bullets, intended to inflame a wound, have been accepted as forbidden. Correctly prohibited have been dumdum bullets, that is, bullets whose surface has been scored or nicked. [17] During World War I, both sides accused the other of using such bullets, but at most, only individual instances were substantiated, and it must be concluded that any dumdum bullets employed had been altered to that form by their individual users, without order or authority from their commanders.

Certain unissued weapons, privately acquired and then used occasionally by U.S. military personnel in the Vietnamese conflict, appear to have been, at the very least of dubious legality, particularly so in the case of hatchets and shotguns.

The drafters of the 1977 Protocols had decided at the time that the prohibition of certain specific weapons should be left to a future meeting, to be called by the United Nations and to be restricted to that particular subject. The General Assembly thereupon convened the UN Conference on Prohibitions or Restrictions of Use of Certain Conventional Weapons Which May Be Deemed to Be Excessively Injurious or to Have Indiscriminate Effects. The conference met in Geneva from September 10 to 28, 1979, and from September 15 to October 10, 1980. Eighty-five states participated, 82 at the 1979 session and 76 at the 1980 session.

On October 10, 1980, the conference adopted the Convention on Prohibitions or Restrictions of Use of Certain Conventional Weapons Which May Be Deemed to Be Excessively Injurious or to Have Indiscriminate Effects (hereafter: Geneva 1980 Convention), the Protocol on Non-Detectable Fragments (hereafter: 1980 PR-I), the Protocol on Prohibitions or Restrictions on the Use of Mines, Booby-Traps and Other Devices (hereafter: 1980 PR-

---

[16] Consult, *inter alia*, letters from the General Counsel, Department of Defense, to Chairman, Senate Foreign Relations Committee, in 66 *AJIL* 382 (1972); and the panel discussion by Matheson, Blix, Delessert, and Paust on "Should Weapons of Dubious Legality Be Developed?" *Proceedings* 26–50 (1978), as well as 69 *AJIL* 397 (1975).
[17] *Law of Land Warfare*, 18.

II), and the Protocol on Prohibitions or Restrictions on the Use of Incendiary Weapons (hereafter: 1980 PR-III).[18]

The 1980 Geneva convention and its protocols are to apply in the situations referred to in Article 2 common to the four Geneva conventions of 1949, including any situation described in paragraph 4 of Article 1 of PR-I (wars against colonial domination, alien occupation, and racist regimes).

The Protocol on Non-Detectable Fragments (1980 PR-I) contains but a single sentence: "It is prohibited to use any weapon in primary effect of which is to injure by fragments which in the human body escape detection by X-rays."

The 1980 PR-II relates to the use on land of mines, booby traps, and other devices, including mines laid to interdict beaches, waterways, or river crossings, but does not apply to the use of antiship mines at sea or in inland waterways. The protocol prohibits, in essence, the use of the instruments listed against the civilian population as such or against individual civilians, even by way of reprisals, and also the indiscriminate use of devices that could be expected to cause loss of life or injury to civilians, excessive in relation to the concrete and direct military advantage anticipated. The use of the weapons listed is also forbidden in any area primarily inhabited by civilians in which no combat between ground forces is taking place, unless the device is planted on or next to a military objective.

INCENDIARY WEAPONS    In accordance with the Declaration of St. Petersburg of December 11, 1868, 17 states had agreed to prohibit, for themselves and such other states as would adhere to the declaration, the use of any projectile weighing less than 14 ounces (400 grams) that was charged with some inflammable substance or was explosive in nature. By contrast, the use of weapons employing fire (tracer ammunition, flamethrowers, napalm bombs, or sprayers) is not prohibited by any rule or treaty.

Napalm, in particular—used extensively in World War II, the Korean War, and then in the Vietnamese conflict—has been attacked frequently as an illegal weapon. This charge, based on the asserted great number of injured said to result from the use of napalm, has not been accepted in all medical circles or in military circles. A commission of physicians, headed by Dr. Howard Rusk of the *New York Times*, toured Vietnamese hospitals and reported that the total number of civilian casualties traceable to the utilization of napalm was negligible.[19] On the other hand, the experts attending the 1972 Geneva Conference on Human Rights in Armed Conflicts recommended that napalm and other incendiary weapons be prohibited.[20]

---

[18]Final act and texts of all instruments in 19 *ILM* 1523 (1980), 1536; see also 20 *ILM* 567, 795, 1287 (1981). The convention and its annexed protocols were opened to signature on April 10, 1981; they entered into force on Dec. 2, 1983, but not for the United States.
[19]See *Time*, March 24, 1967, 63.
[20]UN Document A/8803, Oct. 9, 1972; and *NYT*, Oct. 18, 1972, 2, as well as *CSM*, Jan. 26, 1976, 2.

The 1980 PR-II, dealing with incendiary weapons, proved to be the most controversial of the protocols at the 1979–1980 sessions. Some of the non-aligned countries (Mexico, Syria, and others) insisted that restrictions against aerial bombardment with napalm or other fire bombs be included. The United States, the Soviet Union, and the other major military powers refused, on the other hand, to consider an absolute ban on incendiary weapons. A compromise finally resulted in 1980 PR-III: Incendiary weapons are not to be used to attack the civilian population, and it is forbidden to use air-delivered incendiary weapons against a military objective located in a concentration of civilians. And it also prohibited (Art. 2-2): "to make any military objective located within a concentration of civilians the object of attack by incendiary weapons other than air-delivered incendiary weapons, except when such military objective is clearly separated from the concentration of civilians."

POISON AND POISONED WEAPONS    Under the Hague Regulations (Art. 23-a), the use of poison or of poisoned weapons was outlawed. This did not mean that water supplies and waterworks could not be rendered unusable by diversion or destruction, or that crops intended solely for the use of the enemy's armed forces could not be rendered unfit for use by some chemical or bacterial means. The problem in the last instance was, of course, a difficult one: how would one determine that a given crop was destined for consumption by only the armed forces of one's opponent?

POISON GASES AND RELATED WEAPONS    The First Hague Conferrence (1899) adopted a declaration signed by 16 states that provided that the parties would not use shells used for the distribution of asphyxiating gases. This prohibition was, obviously, fully in accord with the outlawing of the use of poison and with the humane endeavor to avoid causing unnecessary suffering. The United States delegation refused to sign this prohibition as inconsistent with already-accepted methods of warfare.

When Germany used poison gas (chlorine, then mustard gas) in World War I (1917), the Allies retaliated in kind, justifying their action as a reprisal. Both sides stopped gas warfare when they discovered that they could not control the drift of clouds of poison gas. The peace treaties ending the conflict reiterated the prohibition on asphyxiating gases. On June 17, 1925, the Geneva Gas Protocol for the prohibition of the use in war of asphyxiating, poisonous, or other gases, as well as of bacteriological methods of warfare, was signed by the United States delegate as well as by the representatives of 28 states (in force April 3, 1928).[21] The United States Senate, however, did not give its consent to ratification until December 16, 1974 (by a vote of 90 to 0). In view of the fact that 128 countries

---

[21]Text in 64 *AJIL* 387 (1970). Consult also O'Brien, "Biological/Chemical Warfare and the International Law of War," 51 *Georgetown Law Jl*, 1 (Fall 1962); and the valuable, thoroughly documented study by Baxter and Buergenthal, "Legal Aspects of the Geneva Protocol of 1925," 64 *AJIL* 853 (1970).

are now bound by the Protocol, most writers today agree that the Geneva instrument is binding on all states, through the development of a general rule of customary international law springing from the provisions of the Protocol. (The United States had not been bound prior to Senate ratification because the U.S. government had objected since 1925 to the rules involved.)

The Geneva Protocol, it should be noted, does not prohibit the production, acquisition, stockpiling, or use for nonwar purposes of the forbidden substances of warfare, only their use in conflict! And the instrument does not contain any provisions for ensuring verification or compliance.

It is believed that gas and bacteriological warfare methods were not used to any extent during World War II, even though both sides in that conflict were prepared for such an eventuality. The major reason for their commendable abstention from using such weapons probably may be found in an inability to protect military and civilians alike against the retaliatory use of similar weapons by an enemy; hence there seems to have been a tacit agreement to refrain from the use of such methods of warfare.

Italy, it was claimed, used mustard gas against unshod enemy troops in its Ethiopian campaign (1935–36), and the Japanese Army used chemical weapons against Chinese troops and civilians in 1939–44.

During the Korean conflict, the Soviet Union, China, and North Korea accused the United States of having used chemical weapons as well as biological warfare against its enemies (1951–59), while in 1957 the East-bloc press accused Great Britain of using biological weapons in Oman. In the case of the war in Vietnam, the United States admitted the use of riot-control agents (tear gas) and herbicides (Agent Orange) but denied the use of lethal agents or biological warfare (1962–68). The use of herbicides was discontinued in 1967. The United States in turn charged the Viet Kong with the use of poison and biological warfare methods. In the mid- to late seventies, Vietnam reportedly used chemical weapons against Hmong resistance in Laos and Cambodia.

Egypt was found to have used chemical weapons against its royalist opponents in the Yemen civil war (1967). In 1980–84, Afghan resistance leaders and the United States charged the Soviet Union with using chemical weapons and biological toxins in Afghanistan, and in 1980 Ethiopian government forces were allegedly using chemical weapons against Eritrean rebel forces.

On the other hand, apparently valid tests in the Toxilogical Institute of Ghent (Belgium) have been asserted to confirm charges by Iran that Iraq used mustard gas, and possibly other chemical warfare agents, in the Gulf War in 1984 and 1985. Small numbers of Iranian soldiers had been flown to Stockholm and Vienna, and medical reports did indicate exposure to chemical weapons.[22] In consequence of the charges made, the United States

[22]See AP Dispatches of March 4, 5, and 10, 1984 and March 24, 1985; *CSM*, March 28, 2, 1984, and April 26, 1985, 2; *Time*, March 19,1984, 28–30; and Aug. 27, 1984, 47; *Newsweek*, March 19, 1984, 39–40; April 2, 1984, 55–56, and April 9, 1984, 71.

stopped the export to Iraq of a large quantity of chemicals that could be used to produce poison gas. In March 1988, Iraq used poison gas against the Kurdish town of Halabja, occupied by Iran. Some reports stated that almost 5,000 civilians were killed. And in August/September 1988, Iraq was charged with the use of chemical agents against rebellious Kurdish civilians.

On November 25, 1969, President Nixon renounced on behalf of the United States a first use of lethal chemical weapons and extended that renunciation to the first use of incapacitating chemicals. He also renounced any use of any method of biological warfare (restricting research in related subject matter to purely defensive measures) and ordered the disposal of existing stocks of bacteriological weapons. The President also urged the Senate to approve ratification of the Geneva Protocol.[23] On February 14, 1970, the president extended the ban on the production and use of biological weapons to cover military toxins, that is, poisons biologically produced but used as chemical warfare agents. On December 16, 1974, the U.S. Senate gave its consent to the ratification of the 1925 Protocol, and after presidential signature, the instrument entered into force for the United States on February 10, 1975.[24]

Following the development of numerous drafts after a basic one of British origin (1968), the UN General Assembly adopted on February 20, 1972, the Convention on the Prohibition of the Development, Production and Stockpiling of Bacteriological (Biological) and Toxin Weapons and on Their Destruction. The convention was signed by representatives of sixty-one governments on April 10, 1972, in ceremonies in Washington, London, and Moscow. It entered into force on March 26, 1975.[25] In this instance, alleged violations are to be taken to the Security Council for its investigation and report. The virtually unanimous support for the 1972 convention resulted from two factors: the splitting off of biological weapons from the general category of chemical weapons and the realization by the major powers that there could not be a defensible rationale for the use of biological weapons.

Since 1975, the use of chemical and biological weapons can be said to be prohibited by the 1925 Gas Protocol, the 1972 UN Convention, and by customary international law. None of these, however, includes any form of effective verification or enforcement.

On January 11, 1984, the Soviet Union, together with the Warsaw Pact states, proposed a worldwide ban on chemical weapons as well as existing

[23] Text in 64 *AJIL* 386 (1970). On the subject of chemical, bacteriological, and biological warfare, see the excellent analyses by Thatcher, "Poison in the Wind" [A Special Christian Science Monitor Report], *CSM*, Dec. 13, 1988, B1-16; December 14, 1988, B1-12; Dec. 15, 1988, B1-12; Dec. 16, 1988, B1-12.
[24] See *NYT*, Dec. 13, 1974, 1, 2; 120 *Congressional Record* (daily), Dec. 16, 1974, S21605–S216607; and 14 *ILM*, 299, 794 (1975), for relevant documents.
[25] Text on the convention (and related documents) in 11 *ILM* 309 (1972). The U.S. Senate gave its consent to ratification on December 16, 1974. By the end of 1984, a total of 104 states had ratified the convention.

stockpiles. The proposal was vague and included no verification procedures. The United States, on the other hand, offered on April 18, 1984, at the Conference on Disarmament (Geneva) a very detailed draft treaty banning the possession, production, acquisition, retention, or transfer of chemical weapons. The draft agreement contained an assortment of procedures to verify compliance with the treaty through mandatory systematic international on-site verification.[26]

In September 1986, the "Second Review Conference" of the UN biological convention of 1972 met in Geneva (the first review had taken place in 1980).[27] Following this, at the invitation of France, 150 states met for four days in Paris (January 1989) to reaffirm the 1925 Geneva Protocol and to give an impetus to seemingly endless negotiations being carried on at Geneva for a total ban on development, use, production, and stockpiling of all varieties of chemical weapons. The Final Declaration of the meeting expressed the strong opposition of all participants to all such methods of warfare.[28]

In a similar vein, President Bush proposed on September 25, 1989, that the United States and the Soviet Union move swiftly to eliminate at least 80 percent of their stockpiles of chemical weapons as an example to other states. The two countries had already signed, five days earlier, a verification agreement. That instrument had been preceded in November 1987 by an experimental exchange of Soviet and American inspection teams, before verification became "institutionalized" by the 1989 agreement.

While these developments took place, the 40-nation UN Disarmament Conference continued its deliberations on the problem of chemical and biological weapons. As far as several analysts could determine, at the time of this writing, there existed four confirmed possessors of chemical weapons: the United States, the Soviet Union, Iran, and Iraq. A much longer list included suspected possessors of chemical weapons: France, Libya, South Africa, Vietnam, Ethiopia, Laos, Taiwan, Vietnam, Czechoslovakia, Romania, Bulgaria, Yugoslavia, Syria, Israel, China, North Korea, and Indonesia.

The United States had accused Libya as early as 1988 of manufacturing mustard and nerve gases in a large factory complex at Rabta. Libya maintained that the plant would be used to produce pharmaceuticals when it was opened. The United States then persuaded several German suppliers to halt all technical assistance to the Rabta complex. By December 23, 1988, matters had reached a point at which the U.S. presidential spokesman said that the American administration was not only extremely concerned about the plant but had not ruled out the use of military force against the Rabta facility. In reply, the Council of Permanent Representatives of the Arab League backed Libya against a U.S. threat. On March 15, 1990, Libya

---

[26]For details, consult U.S. Department of State, *Current Policy No. 566* (April 18, 1984).
[27]Text of Final Declaration, with content-summary, in 26 *ILM* 196 (1987).
[28]Text, with content-summary, in 28 *ILM* 1020 (1989).

announced that fire had seriously damaged the Rabta plant and that Israeli or American sabotage could not be ruled out. Both countries denied the insinuation.

On April 2, 1990, Iraq's President declared that his country possessed binary nerve gas weapons and would use them against Israel if attacked— apparently a reference to a possible second Israeli attack on Iraq's nuclear reactor complex. Binary chemical weapons were among those prohibited by the 1925 Geneva Gas Protocol.

On May 19, 1990, the United States and the Soviet Union signed a long-anticipated chemical weapons accord. The agreement called for an immediate halt in the production of such weapons by both countries, each of which also agreed to destroy 80 percent of its chemical weapons stockpile within eight years. Should a global agreement to ban all such weapons materialize in response to the 1990 accord, the United States and the Soviet Union agreed to destroy the remaining 20 percent of chemical weapon stocks within 10 years. One of the interesting aspects of the new American policy was that the production of chemical-loaded artillery shells, begun in 1987, had already been suspended because the only two U.S. companies capable of producing the necessary thionyl chloride refused to do so.[29]

Chemical warfare also includes additional aspects, such as the use of herbicides, not specifically covered either by the 1925 protocol or the 1972 instrument. The United States extensively used herbicides (such as "Agent Orange") in the Vietnam War, and then insisted that such use was permitted under international law, even though some legal experts at the time held that the use of herbicides affected the health of human beings and thus fell under various legal prohibitions.[30] American scientific circles increasingly favored a ban on herbicides as a weapon of war, and on April 8, 1975, President Ford signed an executive order renouncing the first use of herbicides in war as well as the first use of riot control agents.[31] The American executive order conformed, in part, with the UN General Assembly Resolution 2603A (XXIV) of December 16, 1969, which had listed the use of the substances in question as contrary to international law as laid down in the 1925 Geneva Protocol. Riot control agents include tear gas, which, the U.S. government had insisted for a long time, did not fall under any prohibitory treaty provisions.

Related to the foregoing is much of the new wartime methodology involved in changing the environment, including modifying the weather. One of the earliest attempts to put theory into practice was the little-publicized but successful attempt by the United States to create rain for the purpose

[29]See *CSM*, May 15, 1990, 20 and, for the start of such weapons production, *Time*, Jan. 11, 1988, 28.
[30]See Baxter and Buergenthal, *op. cit. supra* n. 21, 866–67; *NYT*, March 29, 1972, 3; Dec. 17, 1973, 12; and March 25, 1974, 11.
[31]Text in 14 *ILM* 794 (1975).

of impeding enemy movement in the Vietnam War.[32] Now Article 35 (3) of the 1977 PR-I prohibits to all ratifying states methods of warfare that are intended, or may be expected, to cause widespread, long-term, and severe damage to the natural environment. (See also PR-I, Art. 55, on same subject.) In addition, the UN-developed Convention on the Prohibition of Military or Any Other Hostile Use of Environmental Modification Technique was signed by the representatives of 34 states in Geneva in May 1977. The new convention entered into force on Oct. 5, 1978 (for U.S. on Jan. 17, 1980).[33]

NUCLEAR WEAPONS    Most controversial, although undreamed of before 1939, has been the use of nuclear weapons, whether delivered by land, sea, or air forces. As yet there is no *specific* conventional rule outlawing or limiting the use of atomic or nuclear weapons.[34] Responsible authorities, notably the late Sir Hersch Lauterpacht, believe that the use of any of such weapons ought to be prohibited if it could be demonstrated that the aftereffects of their use would place them in the sphere of "biological" warfare, while at the same time not objecting to their use against strictly military objectives.[35]

Lauterpacht expressed deep concern over the abandonment—insofar as bombing was concerned—of the traditional distinction between combatants and noncombatants, writing that to admit the impossibility of preserving that distinction was "to admit that in modern conditions there is no longer room for one of the most fundamental aspects of the traditional law of war."[36] He then went on to state that even with the use of atomic weapons, the distinction would invariably be obliterated.

On the other hand, the present writer believes that the aftereffects resulting form the employment of nuclear weapons would violate Articles 23-a and 23-e of the 1907 Hague Regulations and also the 1925 Geneva Protocol. The fact, however, that major powers have continued to produce these weapons means that they have accepted the existing rules as obsolete and have concluded that nuclear weapons will be used only on a basis of reciprocity and will not be used if the other party to a conflict does not use them first. They may also have decided that nuclear weapons will be used only in the instance of direct and absolute military necessity.

---

[32]See Hersh's accounts, *NYT*, July 9, 1972, E-3, and especially May 19, 1974, 1, 11.

[33]Text in 16 *ILM* 90 (1977). The convention entered into force on October 5, 1978 (for the United States on January 17, 1980). See also the heavily documented *Note* by Muntz in 19 *Harvard Int'l Law Jl*. 384 (1978); *CSM*, May 18, 1977, 6.

[34]Thus the *United States Law of Naval Warfare* (current ed.) states in par. 613 that "there is at present no rule of international law expressly prohibiting states from the use of nuclear weapons in warfare. In the absence of express prohibition, the use of such weapons against enemy combatants and other military objectives is permitted." See also Chapter 8 concerning the Nuclear Test Ban Treaty.

[35]Lauterpacht's *Oppenheim*, vol. 2, 348–49.

[36]*Id.*, 350. This would be true in an all-out nuclear war, as distinct from tactical nuclear weapons' use in battlefield situations (present writer's comment).

There can be no doubt that the destruction of existing nuclear weapons, together with a working system of inspection to make certain that no more such weapons were being manufactured on the sly, would represent a great advance in the march of civilization. Unfortunately, all attempts to reach such an agreement have failed thus far. However, after years of negotiations, the Nuclear Non-Proliferation Treaty was signed by more than 60 states on July 1, 1968, at parallel ceremonies in Washington, London, and Moscow. [37] By 1991, 141 states had ratified the treaty.

The agreement specified that the sponsoring powers would not give nuclear weapons—or control over them—to other states, nor would they help others make such weapons. Parties to the treaty not possessing nuclear weapons waived their right (for 25 years) to acquire or manufacture such weapons for their own defense. One of the key articles (3) recognized the International Atomic Energy Agency as the authority exercising overall control over safeguards in all peaceful nuclear activities in any state a party to the treaty. Inspections were to be carried out by the agency. The nuclear powers also pledged to provide immediate assistance to any nonnuclear state facing nuclear aggression or threats of such aggression.

Despite the prohibitions found in the Non-Proliferation Treaty, however, the list of likely possessors of nuclear weapons grew by the inclusion of Israel and India, while Pakistan and South Africa have been ranked as possible possessors. At the present time (1990) there are five acknowledged nuclear weapons states: China, France, the United Kingdom, the United States, and the Soviet Union.

The Soviet Union and the United States proceeded to work out additional instruments to lessen the danger of a nuclear conflict.

On May 26, 1972, two new agreements resulted from the Strategic Arms Limitation Talks between the two countries: a formal treaty—of unlimited duration—(the ABM Treaty) limiting the deployment of antiballistic missile systems, and a five-year executive agreement limiting strategic offensive arms. On June 22, 1973, the Agreement on the Prevention of Nuclear War was signed by the two countries in Washington, D.C. [38]

In addition, on October 1, 1971, following ratification by twenty-two states, the new Treaty on the Prohibition of the Emplacement of Nuclear Weapons and Other Weapons of Mass Destruction on the Seabed and the Ocean Floor and in the Subsoil Thereof came into force. It had been proposed originally by the nuclear superpowers and had been signed by 83 states. (See also Chapter 9 on related agreements.)

The United States had proposed in November 1976 that the United Nations should consider drafting a treaty to ban the use of radioactive waste material to develop radiological weapons of mass destruction. Research on

---

[37] Text in 7 *ILM* 809 (1968).

[38] Texts and associated documents of the 1972 instruments, 11 *ILM* 923 (1972); text of the 1973 agreement in 67 *AJIL* 833 (1973) and (with lengthy excerpts from Secretary of State Kissinger's briefing) in *NYT* June 23, 1973, 8.

the possible use of such waste to produce a weapon that could spread high-intensity radioactive isotopes in a battle zone had been started in the United States in the 1960s and had apparently shown the possible realization of such new weapons. The United States, as well as the Federal Republic of Germany, possessed then (and now) very large stockpiles of these waste materials from the operation of power reactors. On July 10, 1979, the United States and the Soviet Union jointly submitted a 13-article draft treaty on a ban on radiological weapons to the Geneva Disarmament Conference. The parties to such an agreement, should it be implemented, would commit themselves "not to develop, produce, stockpile, otherwise acquire, possess or use radiological weapons."[39]

A little-known fact connected with the question of the use of nuclear weapons appears significant to this writer: when the 1977 Protocol I (PR-I, see Chapter 21) was signed, the United States explicitly declared that "It is the understanding of the United States of America that the rules established by this protocol were not intended to have any effect on and do not regulate or prohibit the use of nuclear weapons." Great Britain signed the Protocol with a virtually identical statement of understanding.

NUCLEAR-FREE ZONES    In 1983 the UN General Assembly appointed the UN Study Group on the Question of Nuclear Weapon-Free Zones. That 21-member panel, which included all five nuclear-weapon powers, attempted to plan nonnuclear zones in the Middle East, the Balkans, Northern Europe, Africa, South Pacific, and South Asia. After two years of fruitless discussion, the Study Group disbanded in February 1985.

On a regional basis, however, the Treaty for the Prohibition of Nuclear Weapons in Latin America (Treaty of Tlatelolco) was signed at Mexico City on February 14, 1967, by representatives of 14 Latin American states. The convention prohibited the manufacture, use, storage, or acquisition of nuclear weapons; it has been in force since April 22, 1968. It covers the Western Hemisphere south of the United States and required besides ratification by the negotiating states and states outside the zone involved but controlling territory within it, guarantees by the nuclear powers that they would not violate the terms of the agreement. Since then, all five nuclear powers have indicated that they would observe the treaty.[40]

As of May 2, 1989, 25 Latin American states (including a number of states independent since the agreement was signed originally) had ratified or acceded to the Tlatelolco instrument; only Argentina and Dominica had

---

[39]NYT, Nov. 11, 1976, A-2; and July 11, 1979, A-4; see also the instructive Release No. 103 (September 1979) of the U.S. Arms Control and Disarmament Agency dealing with the proposed multilateral treaty on a somewhat detailed basis.

[40]Text of the treaty in 6 ILM 521 (1967); see also 12 ILM 468 (1973). A detailed "Introductory Note" on the comprehensive instrument, by Schwab, is found in 28 ILM 1400 (1989), together with relevant documents concerning Protocol I and II. See also Robinson, "The Treaty of Tlatelolco and the United States: A Latin-American Free Zone," 64 AJIL 282 (1970).

not yet done so, the latter having signed the treaty only on May 2, 1989. The two Additional Protocols (I & II) to the treaty have entered into force, except for France.

The United States and the Netherlands have also negotiated safeguards agreements with the International Atomic Energy Agency in accordance with Additional Protocol I of the Tlatelolco Treaty.[41]

Several countries proposed similar nuclear-free zones, such as India for the Indian Ocean, Finland for a zone including the Nordic countries (1963) and the Soviet Union for a similar Nordic zone (1981). None of those proposals were adopted. On the other hand, Australia's 1983 plan for a nuclear-free zone in the South Pacific met with success. On August 6, 1985, the South Pacific Nuclear Free Zone Treaty was signed at Raratonga, Cook Islands, by 13 independent and self-governing states (Treaty of Raratonga).[42] Three Protocols to the treaty have since come into effect or are in the process of being approved. As of December 1, 1989, 11 members of the South Pacific Forum (the group eligible to be parties to the treaty) had ratified the convention. The latter, incidentally, does not ban passage or port calls in the zone by nuclear ships, apparently in deference to the views of the United States.

UNDEFENDED TOWNS AND BUILDINGS    Article 25 of the Hague Regulations of 1907 prohibited the attack or bombardment, by any means, of undefended towns, villages, dwellings, or buildings. This rule reflected the warfare of the nineteenth century, in which forts were used, in which cities or towns were surrounded by fortifications (if the fortifications were inseparable from the community, say, by reason of proximity, bombardment of the town would have been legal under Article 25), and when it was possible to pinpoint the limited number of factories, military warehouses, communications facilities used by armed forces, and so on, so as to isolate an attack on these from a general attack on the community in which they were located. Article 57 of the 1977 PR-I repeats the 1907 prohibition, in stronger terms and in much greater detail.

The rise of modern mass armies, with their staggering demands for every conceivable kind of supplies, and the distribution of production facilities of the "nation in arms" throughout communities rendered Article 25 virtually obsolete before the end of World War I. Although the rule still stands technically, it has had to be abandoned in practice and finds modern application only in instances of wanton destruction totally unconnected with an attempt to weaken the enemy's war potential. Hence the elaborate provisions of PR-I, mentioned above, appear quite anachronistic in terms of a modern major war.

A more appropriate rule to be cited against the party committing the acts in question, assuming one wished to establish the commission of a war

---

[41]Texts, with Schwab's Introductory Note, in 28 *ILM* 1345 (1989).
[42]Text, with Dalrymple's Introductory Note, in 24 *ILM* 1440 (1985); texts of protocols in 28 *ILM* 1599 (1989).

crime, would be Article 23-g of the Hague Regulations, which prohibits the destruction of enemy property unless such destruction appears to be imperatively demanded by the necessities of war.

German use of V-1 (*Vergeltungswaffe-1* — Retaliation Weapon No. 1) rocket bombs against London in 1944–1945 raised a storm of protest concerning the illegality of the weapon under Article 25 of the Hague Regulations. Most of the protests centered on the obvious inability of its makers to aim the V-1 at a specific target; instead, the fuel supply was doled out in such a manner and in such accordance with wind and atmospheric conditions that the bomb, properly aimed, would run out of fuel and descend somewhere into the sprawling metropolitan area of London, or, on occasion, some other British city. The speed of the V-1 was not very great — its approach could be seen and it could be pursued by fighter planes — but when the motor cut out, the city dwellers in the prospective target area had approximately ten seconds in which to find some kind of shelter. Thus no adequate warning was possible, despite the bomb's slow speed. Its successor, the V-2, traveling at supersonic speed, gave no warning at all of its approach; only after the great bomb had already hit and exploded was its presence known, and only then could its approach be heard.

FOREWARNING OF BOMBARDMENT    Again, Article 26 of the Hague Regulations required that "the officer in command of an attacking force must, before commencing a bombardment, except in cases of assault, do all in his power to warn the authorities" of the locality to be attacked. This rule, too, reflected the conditions of war in nineteenth century and did not anticipate the aerial bombardments of modern war, carried out, on most occasions, against strong defenses from the ground. To be sure, modern armies still insist that their ground commanders honor the provisions of Article 26 before bombarding a locality known to contain or suspected of still containing remnants of its civilian population, and on occasion the rule has actually been observed. But for air force commanders, any warning of an impending air strike might completely vitiate the effort and might result in heavy losses to the attacking force.

CLASSIFIED BUILDINGS    The provisions of Article 27 of the Hague Regulations, concerning the sparing of certain types of buildings, have been increasingly difficult to enforce. World War I saw a limited destruction of such exempt edifices, except for a deliberate German destruction of church towers in France, on the grounds that the French armies consistently misused such elevated structures as the hiding places of artillery spotters. World War II saw a comprehensive ignoring of the rule. Saturation and atomic bombing played no favorites, and the nature of a given building was commonly ignored. In addition, authenticated reports indicate that Germany, in particular, tended to locate genuine military targets near or next to an exempted building, hoping obviously that the military installation would benefit from the immunity of its neighbor. This, for instance, occurred before the Allied bombing (1944) of the Abbey of Monte Cassino in Italy; although the German forces were not holding the abbey itself, they had placed machine-gun nests and stored ammunition within a few yards of it. On the other hand, with one small lapse, the hospital-city character of Marburg, announced by Germany to the Allied armies and watched over by neutral observers as well as a daily aerial inspection, was maintained scrupulously. PR-I, in Articles 51 to 53 and 57 and 58, attempts to exempt cultural objects, places of worship, and so on from attack (or from military reprisals), but saturation bombing makes observance of these rules impossible, as in the case of HR, Article 23.

PR-I, In Article 60, expanded the exempt community status by the new concept of demilitarized zones, agreed upon by both sides in a conflict. Such zones are to be beyond any extension of military operations by a belligerent if such an extension contradicts the agreement creating the zone in question.

Novel also are the provisions of PR-I, Article 54, providing for protection of objects indispensable to the survival of a civilian population, prohibiting, in other words, the destruction, removal, or rendering useless of drinking-water installations, foodstuffs, farming areas for the production of foodstuffs, crops, livestock, and so on, in order to starve out civilians or for any other motive. The prohibitions do not extend, however, to the use of native foodstuffs by a hostile military force, provided that the removal and use of food do not expose the civilian population to starvation or force it to move.

Finally, PR-I contains a most interesting section (Art. 56, in seven parts, already discussed earlier) concerning their protection of works and installations containing "dangerous forces." This somewhat unusual term embraces dams, dikes, and nuclear electrical generating stations, which are to be exempt from attack.[43] The parties to a conflict are urged to avoid locating any military installations near the protected ones. In any case, the protection laid down shall cease for dams and dikes if they are used for other than normal purposes and if their military support can be ended only by an enemy attack. In the case of nuclear generating stations, if they supply power in regular, significant, and direct support of military operations and this support, again, can be ended only by means of an attack by the other party, they are no longer exempt.

HOSTAGES One of the traditional tactics employed by invading military forces has been taking civilian hostages to serve as guarantees against violations of the rules of the behavior of the indigenous population in enemy-controlled territory. This traditional device was employed in such exaggerated and also inhuman fashion by the Axis Powers during World War II (following lesser violations, mostly by Germany, in World War I), that Article 34 of the Fourth Geneva Convention of 1949 prohibits altogether and categorically the taking of any sort of hostage.

[43]See *U.S. News & World Report*, Aug. 14, 1972, 18, 52, on U.S. bombing of Red River dikes in the Vietnam war.

Following several significant peacetime acts of hostage taking, the Federal Republic of Germany took the initiative in spurring the UN General Assembly into drafting a new convention prohibiting the taking of hostages (1976). After several periods of the necessary preliminary work, the final product was the International Convention Against the Taking of Hostages (December 17, 1979).[44] (See also Chapter 13.)

ESPIONAGE    Spying represents a legitimate practice by a belligerent, yet when spies are captured behind enemy lines, they are regarded as having committed an act of illegitimate warfare and hence are subject to punishment. Under the provisions of Article 29 of the Hague Regulations of 1907, a person can be considered a spy only when, acting clandestinely or on false pretenses, he or she obtains or endeavors to obtain information in the zone of operations of a belligerent, with the intention of communicating it to the opposing hostile party. Thus soldiers not wearing a disguise who have penetrated the enemy's zone of operations, for the purpose of obtaining information, are not considered spies. A true spy, however, does not have prisoner-of-war status and hence does not enjoy the protection normally accorded to prisoners of war. (See also PR-1, Art. 46.)

Spies include persons of all classes, military or civilian, without regard to citizenship or sex. When they are punished, it is not because they have violated the laws of war—for spying is legal—but to make spying as dangerous, difficult, and ineffective as possible. When caught, a spy must be given a trial (HR, Art. 30), and on conviction, the normal penalty is death.

A spy who, after rejoining his or her own armed forces, is subsequently captured by the enemy must be treated as a prisoner of war and incurs no responsibility for his or her previous acts of espionage (HR, Art. 31).[45]

## RULES OF CONFLICTS IN THE AIR

The use of balloons to transport mail and newspapers from besieged Paris during the Franco-Prussian War had led to considerable speculation toward the end of the nineteenth century as to the possibilities of aerial warfare. At the Hague conference of 1899, a declaration, renewed at the Second Conference in 1907, prohibited until the end of a Third Peace Conference "the discharge of projectiles and explosives from balloons and by other new methods of a similar nature." Very few states signed the instrument in 1899. In 1907, France, Germany, Italy, Japan, and Russia refused to sign it, primarily, it appears, because these countries, impressed by the advance

---

[44]Text in 74 *AJIL* 277 (1980); see also Verwey, "The International Hostages Convention and National Liberation Movements," 75 *AJIL* 69 (1981). See also Chapter 13.

[45]On spies, see Whiteman, vol. 10, 150–53, 166–67, 177–95; Koessler, "The International Law on the Punishment of Belligerent Spies: A Legal Paradox," 5 *Criminal Law Review* 21 (1958); and *NYT*, Jan. 26, 1973, 3; March 26, 1973, 3; May 4, 1973, 10, for an interesting Israeli spy trial.

in aviation, desired to wait and see what promising and possibly legal use could be made of the newfound ability to fly. Italy then became a pioneer, using balloons in the Italo-Turkish War of 1911–1912, both for spotting enemy troops and from dropping explosives (bombs) on them.

AIR WARFARE IN WORLD WAR I    The outbreak of war in 1914 brought the airplane, and later the dirigible, into immediate prominence. Both sides not only fought each other in the air but proceeded to bomb enemy targets, which all too soon appeared to be "undefended" cities. Both sides, too, piously insisted that their aviators received strict orders to attack only points of military importance and, in the case of cities, to bomb only genuine military targets. The usefulness of such instructions, even if the willingness to carry them out could have been proved, was nil, for the speed of an airplane and the absence of bombsights or other aiming devices left the ultimate destination of a dropped bomb to chance and the aviator's skill. One did not have to be a cynic to say before the end of the war that every inhabited enemy community had become a legitimate target, and attitude reinforced by the concept of the *nation-in-arms*. The distinction between undefended and defended communities had become meaningless, except in the rare cases of genuine "hospital towns," declared to be such and subject to neutral inspection.[46]

PROBLEMS OF NEUTRAL AIRSPACE    One of the new problems created by the extensive use of planes and dirigibles pertains to neutral airspace. Because each country's national air is included in its territorial jurisdiction, no military activities may be carried on in neutral national air, and a neutral state has a perfect right to protect its sovereignty by attempting to keep belligerent planes out of its national air. If violations of its airspace continue, it has the legal right to try to bring down belligerent planes and to intern the crews for the duration of the conflict.[47]

REGULATION OF AIR WARFARE—POST-WORLD WAR I    The application of the rules of land warfare to the new weapon failed to prevent indiscriminate bombing. After World War I, therefore, the possibility of developing a separate code of air warfare was considered. Here, however, military considerations of the greatest magnitude intruded. The airplanes, as perfected by 1918, had become the weapon of the future to many military staffs, and they successfully opposed any code promising to cripple this new item in the military hardware closet. The 1919 Aerial Navigation Convention left all parties to the treaty complete freedom of action in wartime (Art. 38). The Washington Conference of 1921–1922 failed to produce a draft treaty on aerial war and had to be content to appoint a commission of legal experts to study the subject and make recommendations. That commission

[46] See Moffitt, 18–20, on general background.
[47] See Spaight, *Air Power and War Rights* (3rd ed., 1947), 420–60; Phillips, "Air Warfare and Law," 21 *George Washington Law Rev.* 311, 395 (1952–1953); and Chapter 26.

succeeded in writing two sets of draft rules, of which Part II dealt with air war.[48]

The failure of the Hague Rules of Air Warfare to achieve ratification left regulation of aerial conflict precisely where it had been at the end of World War I. The Spanish Civil War and the Japanese invasion of China showed, however, that new rules governing aerial bombardment were needed most urgently. In 1938 the Prime Minister of Great Britain, in a statement made in the House of Commons, asserted that three principles ought to be observed by all participants in future wars: (1) a deliberate attack on civilian populations was a clear violation of international law; (2) "targets which are aimed at from the air must be legitimate military objectives and must be capable of identification"; and (3) "reasonable care must be taken in attacking these military objectives so that by carelessness a civilian population in the neighborhood is not bombed."[49] Later that year, the Assembly of the League of Nations unanimously adopted a resolution embodying the three principles.

World War II saw the manned plane in its heyday, with even greater bombing of enemy locations, beginning with the German attack on Poland. Without going into details that would extend this section beyond reasonable limits, it can be stated that by 1945 it was generally accepted that strategic bombing from the air, without warning, was an accepted method of warfare and that those who attempted to punish the captured perpetrators of those raids by execution would end up as war criminals themselves. Since then, the manned bomber, at least, seems to be on the way out, and its replacement, the unmanned intermediate or intercontinental ballistic missile, together with its relatives aboard nuclear-powered submarines, has appeared on the scene.

Moreover, May 11, 1940, may be regarded as the very day on which virtually unrestricted air bombardment was "legitimized." It was on that date that the British Cabinet decided on strategic air attacks on the enemy's interior, a decision that resulted, on August 8, 1940, in the German "reprisal" raids against English nonmilitary targets, including the city of Coventry.

In a most unusual development, Iraq declared the air above Iran an "exclusion zone" as of March 19, 1985, and warned all commercial aircraft to avoid the zone lest they became targets. Iran lodged a complaint with the ICAO.

Even today there is no global treaty governing war in the air. Only by analogy with the rules laid down for hostilities on the ground can rules be detected that apply to air warfare, and they are relatively limited in number

---

[48]"General Report of the Commission of Jurists at The Hague, 1923," 17 *AJIL* 242 (1923 Supp.), and consult Lauterpacht's *Oppenheim*, vol. 2, 518–22. See also the instructive excerpts from the letter of the General Counsel of the Dept. of Defense (September 22, 1972), 67 *AJIL* 122 (1973), representing a rather typical outlook.

[49]Cited in Lauterpacht's *Oppenheim*, vol. 2, 523.

and scope. The U.S. Department of the Air Force, after some twenty years of research and planning, issued in 1976 its regulations for the conduct of air operations and, it must be added, in most admirable form in view of the scarcity of accepted international rules.[50]

The coverage of the regulations in this book (despite its title, the "pamphlet" is substantial in volume) is extensive and is divided into three main categories. Chapters 1 to 3 deal with airspace, combatants in the air, and aircraft. Chapters 4 to 9 cover in detail combat in the air and the utilization of airborne weaponry. Chapters 11 to 14 review, again in detail, the 1949 Geneva Conventions for the Protection of War Victims. The last chapter discusses command responsibility and the like.

Some of the more interesting "rules" include the assertion that urban areas containing military targets remain subject to attack (Chapters 5–8). Dikes, dams, and nuclear generating stations may also be attacked if "under the circumstances ruling at the time, they are lawful military objectives" (see also above, "Classified Buildings," on the provisions of PiR-I on this subject).[51] Area bombing is judged to be in accordance with existing international law rules (Chapter 1–15). In agreement with what has been stated before, the employment of nuclear weapons does not violate currently existing international law but should be used only at the direction of the president (Chapter 6–5). Interestingly enough, the Air Force manual justifies aerial overflights if they are based on the right of self-defense (Chapter 2–6) and also admits the undoubted right of every state to prevent (that is, attack and destroy, if possible) foreign military aircraft from unauthorized aerial intrusions (Chapter 2–6). Medical aircraft and their protection are covered in the U.S. Air Force manual in chapters 2, 4, 13, and 14, and now also in PR-I, Articles 24 to 31, in great detail. The American manual represents the first comprehensive official effort to describe, backed with impressive documentation, the subject of modern air war, from both a legal and a practical point of view. Despite some gaps and certain vague statements, the present writer believes that the manual could well serve as the basis for the negotiation of a global convention on the subject, perhaps through another Geneva diplomatic conference.

## PRISONERS OF WAR

Prisoners had fared in many different ways during past centuries. In antiquity, they were either killed or sold into slavery. After the coming of Christianity and until the sixteenth century, enslavement continued—St. Thomas Aquinas justified it by treating the reduction of prisoners to slaves

[50]U.S. Air Force, *International Law—The Conduct of Armed Conflict and Air Operations*, Pamphlet 110–31 (1976).
[51]See *supra*, n. 43.

as punishment for cowardice in combat and as a judgment of God under the concept of the ordeal by battle in which only the just side would win and then was entitled to enslave its surviving opponents. Noble prisoners, on the other hand, normally were released on payment of a ransom, the amount depending on their rank and resources. Still later, special cartel arrangements for the treatment and return of prisoners were concluded, either at the outbreak of hostilities or soon thereafter.

EARLY ATTEMPTS TO PROTECT PRISONERS OF WAR    The end of the Thirty Years' War saw also the end of enslavement, and gradually humane considerations began to govern the treatment of captive enemies. An American-Russian Treaty of Friendship, concluded in 1785, is now generally regarded as containing the first stipulations of the decent treatment of prisoners of war, prohibiting (Art. 24) confinement in convict prisons and the employment of irons, and guaranteeing facilities for exercise.

HAGUE CONFERENCES OF 1899 AND 1907    By the nineteenth century, the customary rules of law dictated the treatment of prisoners of war at a standard comparable to that of the captor's own troops. There were no conventional rules on the subject until the Hague Conferences of 1899 and 1907.

The 1907 Hague Regulations (Arts. 4–20) provided in detail for the humane treatment of prisoners. Unfortunately the actual practices of belligerents during World War I illustrated the inadequacy of the rules and the many gaps that needed to be filled.

1929 GENEVA CONVENTIONS    In July 1929, the representatives of forty-seven states met in Geneva at the invitation of the Swiss government in order to improve the earlier conventional law. The conference succeeded in drawing up two instruments, the Convention for the Amelioration of the Condition of the Wounded and Sick in Armies in the Field, and the Convention on the Treatment of Prisoners of War, consisting of 94 articles. Following widespread ratification, both conventions were in effect when World War II began. Only relations between Germany and the Soviet Union were not governed by those two instruments during the conflict. But again, belligerent practices indicated the need for further conventional safeguards for prisoners of war.

## 1949 GENEVA CONVENTION

One of the most serious violations of customary rules was committed by the Soviet Union through its failure to repatriate its prisoners of war at the end of World War II. (A report published at the beginning of July 1952 by the Information Section of the North Atlantic Treaty Organization indicated that of the more than 7 million prisoners taken by the Soviet Union, fewer than half had been repatriated by the middle of 1952; about 1 million were reported dead or still held in the Soviet Union; and some 2.5 million were completely unaccounted for, including about 370,000 members of the

Japanese forces in Manchuria, captured at the very end of the war.[52] Hence the Geneva Conference of 1949 produced the new Convention Relative to the Treatment of Prisoners of War, which incorporated, besides old material, many new provisions based on the experiences of the last war. This new instrument was ratified quickly and came into effect on October 21, 1950, replacing for its ratifiers all earlier instruments dealing with the treatment of prisoners of war.

Owing to the extreme length of the 1949 Convention (143 articles) and the details incorporated in its provisions, an exhaustive analysis of the instrument would exceed the proper limits of a general text.[53] Hence only a few significant features can be mentioned here, together with some illustrative case materials.

## Comments on the 1949 Convention

APPLICATION OF THE 1949 CONVENTION TO CONFLICTS    Under Article 2 of the convention, the instrument applies not only to all cases of declared war but also to all other armed conflicts that may arise between two or more of the contracting parties, even if the existence of a state of war is not recognized by one of them. The convention also applies to all cases of partial or total occupation of the territory of a contracting party, even if the occupation has not met with any armed resistance. Again, the convention applies in a war with a state that is not a party to the agreement, provided the latter accepts and applies the instrument's provisions.

PRISONERS OF WAR    Persons entitled to the protection of the convention and hence to treatment as prisoners of war include regular armed-forces personnel; members of militia forces; recognized or unrecognized volunteer corps (provided they satisfy the convention's somewhat unrealistic requirements); officers and crews of civil aircraft and the belligerent's merchant marine; individuals who formed part of a lawful *levée en masse*; authorized persons accompanying armed forces (war correspondents, contractors, and so on); under specified circumstances, former members of the armed forces of an occupied state; and high civil government personnel (Art. 4).

Prisoners of war are to be regarded as in the custody of the capturing state and not of particular armies or military units. They are entitled to humane

---

[52]For further details from the report, see *Time*, July 7, 1952, 33. See also excerpts from *Kamibayashi et al.* v. *Japan*. Japan, Tokyo Dist. Court, April 18, 1989, with Introductory Note by Adachi, in 29 *ILM* 391 (1990).

[53]See *Law of Land Warfare*, 25–82; and Lauterpacht's *Oppenheim*, vol. 2, 369–96, for two exhaustive analyses of the provisions of the 1949 convention. Consult also Pictet, "The New Geneva Conventions for the Protection of War Victims," 45 *AJIL* 462 (1951); Yingling and Ginnane, "The Geneva Conventions," 46 *AJIL* 393 (1952); and the thorough study Levie, "Prisoners of War and the Protecting Power," 55 *AJIL* 374 (1961). See also the "Suggested Readings" at the end of this chapter.

treatment.[54] They are entitled to the same maintenance as are troops of the same rank of the captor state. They are to be confined only to the extent that their detention is guaranteed and must not be punished except for acts committed by them after their capture.

The Iraqi government violated several provisions of the Geneva convention on January 21, 1991, when it telecast "interviews" with captured allied personnel and also announced that prisoners of war would be used as "human shields" agains allied air attacks. Under Article 17 of the convention, a prisoner of war, when questioned on the subject "is bound to give only his surname, first names and rank, date of birth, and army regimental, personal or serial number, or failing this, equivalent information." Article 17(4) provides that "No physical or mental torture, nor any other form of coercion, may be inflicted on prisoners of war to secure from them information of any kind whatsoever." Insofar as the use of prisoners of war as human shields is concerned, the 1949 convention provides in Article 19(1) that "Prisoners of war shall be evacuated, as soon as possible after their capture, to camps situated in an area far enough from the combat zone for them to be out of danger." In particular, Article 23(1) asserts that "No prisoner of war may at any time be sent to, or detained in, areas where he may be exposed to the fire of the combat zone, *nor may his presence be used to render certain points or areas immune from military operations*" (emphasis added).

On the other hand, Article 85 of the convention reads: "Prisoners of war prosecuted under the laws of the Detaining Power for acts committed prior to capture shall retain, even if convicted, the benefits of the present convention." The Soviet Union and its satellite states entered a reservation against Article 85 before and at the time of signature, to the effect that prisoners of war convicted by them of committing war crimes and crimes against humanity would be treated after such conviction like other criminals. However, an Italian decision in 1952 asserted that Article 85 bore no relevance to war crimes.[55] Until the United States' ratification of the convention in 1956, the American official attitude had been that prisoners of war tried for war crimes were not entitled to the judicial safeguards of the 1929 Geneva Convention; this was brought out in *In re Yamashita*.[56] An unsuccessful attempt to escape may result only in disciplinary punishment; on the other hand, force may be used against prisoners to prevent an escape, and it is considered lawful even to shoot at, and kill, an escaping prisoner.

If, on the other hand, an escaping prisoner commits criminal offenses not directly connected with his escape, he may be punished for those acts. This rule was illustrated clearly in the case of

---

[54]Contrast with the Soviet Union's official admission that the Soviet NKVD (now KGB) killed 15,131 Polish army officers captured in 1939—in the Katyn Forest and in NKVD camps: see AP Dispatch, April 14, 1990, and *CSM*, March 23, 1990,2.

[55]The *Case of Kappler*, Italy, Supreme Military Tribunal, 1952, digested in 49 *AJIL* 96 (1955).

[56]U.S. Supreme Court, 1946, 327 U.S. 1.

## REX V. BROSIG
### Ontario Court of Appeal, March 1, 1945
### 2 D. L. R. 232

FACTS    Brosig was a German prisoner of war, who was moved to Canada for detention. On December 21, 1943, he hid in a prisoner-of-war mailbag that was placed in the mail car of a Canadian train, next to a radiator in the car. The prisoner cut open the bag from the inside and then opened another mailbag containing parcels. From these he took some cigarettes, some chewing gum, and a bottle of perfume. He smoked some of the cigarettes and used some of the gum and also some of the perfume. He was later captured and charged with theft from the mails. The magistrate's court trying the initial case dismissed the charge, and the Crown appealed to the Court of Appeal.

QUESTION    Could an escaping prisoner of war be charged with the theft of goods stolen in the course of his escape and used by him?

DECISION    The appeal was allowed, and a conviction of theft from the mails was recorded. A jail sentence of two months' duration was imposed, after which Brosig was to be returned to his prisoner-of-war camp.

REASONING    The looting of the mailbag was not an act necessary to Brosig's escape. It served no military purpose and represented an offense against civil authority for the personal advantage of the prisoner of war. The court cited with approval the finding of the Magistrate's Court:

"With regard to the perfume, I have given him the benefit of the doubt and say that he used it in order to assist his escape by concealing the extreme odour of perspiration. With regard to the cigarettes and gum I am unable to see that they would assist his escape materially and I feel that he took them for his own comfort."

Enlisted personnel may be put to work not directly assisting the war effort of the captor state and are to be paid for such work. Officers cannot lawfully be forced to perform such work but may do so on a purely voluntary basis (Arts. 50–68). All prisoners are to be paid at the rate applicable to their rank at the time of capture, the actual terms of payment being outlined in the convention (Art. 69).[57]

Communication with relatives is to be allowed at periodic intervals, and agents of a "protecting" neutral state as well as of the International Committee of the Red Cross are to be permitted access to prisoners of war.

If a prisoner escapes and, at a later date, after rejoining his own forces, becomes a prisoner of war again, he may not be punished for his escape. Disciplinary and judicial punishments for prisoners guilty of offenses after capture are delineated in the convention in considerable detail to protect them against arbitrary denial of justice (Arts. 89, 99–108).

[57] Consult Levie, "The Employment of Prisoners of War," 57 *AJIL* 318 (1963).

The most recent official invocation of the Geneva Convention of 1949 came in January 1985 in connection with the Iraq–Iran conflict. A three-man UN mission from Geneva spent two weeks investigating the treatment of some 10,000 Iranian prisoners of war and 50,000 captured Iraqis.

TERMINATION OF CAPTIVITY    Particularly important are the new conventional rules governing the termination of captivity. Under the provisions of Article 118, prisoners of war are "to be released and repatriated without delay after the cessation of active hostilities," and elaborately detailed regulations now govern the earlier repatriation of sick prisoners of war (Arts. 109–117, 119).

The 1929 Geneva Convention had stipulated merely that the repatriation of healthy prisoners should be effected as soon as possible after the conclusion of peace. The importance of the new rule regarding the immediate release when *hostilities* have ended stemmed from the problems encountered at the end of World War II.[58] The experts at Geneva in 1949 had assumed that every prisoner of war would want to go home as soon as possible. This somewhat erroneous impression should not have prevailed, in view of certain events that had taken place at the end of World War II. Then, thousands of Russian citizens who had joined General Andrei A. Vlassov's anti-Communist army on the side of Germany and who had fled westward as the Soviet armies advanced into Germany were captured by the Western Allies. Despite pleas not to be repatriated because of their well-founded fears of being tried for treason, these Russians were forcibly repatriated by the Western forces. Many, including General Vlassov, were executed as traitors.

REPATRIATION PROBLEM (KOREA)    The Korean conflict posed a different problem. In the case of Korea, thousands of North Koreans as well as Chinese "volunteers" refused to be returned to their countries for ideological reasons. Concurrence in this request by the United Nations Command created a dilemma that proved to be a key reason for the delay until 1956 of the United States' ratification of the four Geneva conventions of 1949.[59] By then, those prisoners who were unwilling to return to North Korea or China had been screened and dispersed after release; by early 1954, slightly over 14,000 Chinese soldiers had already been transferred to Taiwan.[60]

It should be noted that the four Geneva conventions of 1949 were not in force in regard to the opposing parties in the Korean conflict. Both sides,

---

[58]See above, text and n. 50.

[59]See Chapter 22 for details concerning the arrangements finally worked out for the removal of the prisoners in question; see also Stone, 680–83.

[60]See the illuminating study by Mayda, "The Korean Repatriation Problem," 47 *AJIL* 414 (1953); Potter's Note on "Repatriation of Prisoners," 46 *AJIL* 508 (1952); and the valuable analysis by Charmatz and Wit, "Repatriation of Prisoners of War and the 1949 Geneva Convention," 62 *Yale Law Jl.*, 391 (1953).

however, had stated that they would honor the principles laid down in those agreements.[61]

OTHER RECENT CONFLICTS    In the case of the Vietnam conflict, all U.S. prisoners of war were repatriated within weeks after the conclusion of the Paris peace agreements of January 27, 1973. The exchange of captured personnel between the two Vietnams, on the other hand, was not completed until March 8, 1974. In the India–Pakistan conflict of 1971, however, repatriation was delayed for several years, until a series of complicated solutions had been worked out in the India–Pakistan Agreement on Repatriation of Prisoners of War (August 28, 1973) and an instrument on Repatriation of Prisoners of War and Civilian Internees (April 9, 1974).[62]

Treatment of prisoners of war in the above-mentioned recent conflicts led to a reiteration and also an expansion of the 1949 Geneva Convention's provisions governing these individuals in the new PR-I of 1977 (Arts. 44–45, 72–75). The major additions to the already existing regulations were represented by a much more carefully detailed description of the role and rights of an outside Protecting Power (the weakness of this feature of the treatment of prisoners is, of course, that no Protecting Power may be requested by the parties to the dispute or may be forthcoming by some other means, so that there would be no real outside supervision of the treatment of prisoners) and by a more detailed list of prohibited acts against prisoners of war.

Israel's 1982 invasion of Lebanon resulted in the capture of about 9,000 soldiers and guerrillas, more than 4,000 of which were confined in one large detention center, Ansar Camp, in southern Lebanon. The Israeli authorities considered the captured Syrians as prisoners of war but viewed the Palestinians—the bulk of the inmates—as terrorists not entitled to special rights under international law. As such, these guerrillas were not held to be prisoners of war but, in the words of the Israeli Minister of Justice, "They will be treated humanely, as called for by the Geneva Convention." Some of them were to be tried in Israeli courts and the rest were event ally released. Initially, during the last days of PLO resistance against the Palestinian rebel groups in the battle for Tripoli, a year-long series of negotiations ended with the arrangement of a prisoner exchange: Israel agreed to release about 4,700 Lebanese and Palestinian prisoners in exchange for 6 Israeli soldiers held for more than a year by the PLO. The 4,700 included about 100 Palestinians

---

[61]See von Glahn, 17–18; "Assurances to Respect Geneva Conventions," 9 *U.N. Bulletin* 101 (1950); "Report of the United Nations Command Operations in Korea, for the period of August 1–15, 1950," in 23 *Dept. of State Bulletin* (1950), 406; see *id.*, 287, 333 for details concerning the North Korean "adherence" and its observance; and also consult 33 *Dept. of State Bulletin* (1955), 69–79.

[62]Texts in 12 *ILM* 1080 (1973), and 13 *ILM* 501 (1974); see also Levie, "The Indo-Pakistani Agreement of August 28, 1973," 68 *AJIL* 95 (1974), as well as his 1973 article cited in the appended "Suggested Readings." Also see India–Pakistan, "Agreement on the Release and Repatriation of Detained Persons" (New Delhi, April 9, 1974), in 13 *ILM* 603 (1974).

released from Israeli jails. Details of the exchange are given in order to show the logistic problems of such undertakings: 1,100 prisoners, including the ones taken from jails in Israel, were flown to Lod Airport (outside Tel Aviv) and from there, on Air France 747 jetliners, to Algeria; at the same time, 120 Israeli buses left Ansar Camp with 3,600 Palestinians who chose to stay in southern Lebanon. The 6 Israeli prisoners were ferried from Tripoli on two fishing boats to a Red Cross vessel, then put aboard a French destroyer, and finally transported to Israel on an Israeli missile ship.[63] On June 28, 1984, Israel freed more than 300 Syrians (prisoners of war and 21 Syrian civilians held in Israel) in exchange for 3 Israeli soldiers and 3 civilian employees of Israel's liaison office in Lebanon. Another exchange of prisoners (3 Israeli soldiers held by Syria against 1,150 Lebanese and Palestinians held by Israel) took place on May 20, 1985, with the 3 Israelis and 394 Palestinians flown to and released in Geneva.

In the 1982 Falklands War, British forces took some 11,000 prisoners, all of whom were repatriated to Argentina rather than shipped to England.

In the American operation in Grenada, Cuban military and other prisoners were repatriated via Jamaica in early November 1983. An interesting sidelight to that development was a nonbinding Senate resolution, passed by a voice vote, urging President Reagan to "insist that as a condition for repatriation of Cuban nationals captured by U.S. armed forces in Grenada the government of Cuba should agree to the return to Cuba of all Cuban nationals in the U.S. who are found to be deportable under the immigration laws of the United States." The Cubans in question were, of course, the "undesirable elements" of the 1980 mass migration from Cuba to the United States (see Chapter 11).

In the case of the Afghanistan conflict between the Afghan government and Soviet forces versus native rebel movements, it has been asserted that at least one hundred Russian prisoners and deserters were in rebel hands. The Kabul authorities permitted the ICRC to monitor conditions in government detention centers for about two months in the summer of 1982, but then the Swiss representatives of the Red Cross were asked to leave. On the other hand, nine Soviet prisoners were interned in Switzerland in consequence of a 1982 agreement among the ICRC, the major Afghan rebel groups, and the Soviet Union. (A tenth prisoner escaped in 1983 and sought asylum in the Federal Republic of Germany.) The Soviet soldiers were to be interned for two years or the duration of the war, whichever came first. The nine internees eventually had to decide whether to return to the Soviet Union or to ask for asylum in Swiss military guard, and were visited every two months by Soviet diplomats—no other outside agencies were permitted to see them. In late May 1984, one of the men chose to return to the Soviet Union and two decided to remain in Switzerland on a basis of annual residence permits. In early August 1984, two more were returned to

[63]Based for the most part, on *Newsweek*, Dec. 5, 1983, 76–79.

the Soviet Union. In November 1986, the Canadian government brought five Red Army "deserters" from Afghanistan to be resettled in Canada, after spending three years as virtual prisoners with the Afghan guerrillas (mujeheddin). And in March 1988, at a secret meeting in Bonn, West Germany, Soviet diplomats and Afghan guerrilla representatives agreed to a prisoner exchange at the rate of 25 mujeheddin for each Soviet prisoner of war.

In a most unusual incident, two Iranian military pilots who had flown their F-4 jet to an Iraqi airport (August 30, 1984) were not taken prisoners, despite the ongoing war between the two countries. Both requested and were granted, after an initial denial of such, political asylum. At the same time the Iraqi Revolutionary Command Council urged other Iranians to defect and released a number of Iranian prisoners of war in honor of a religious celebration.

On January 12, 1985, the twelfth prisoner exchange took place between China and Vietnam since the two countries had been engaged in a six-week frontier conflict in 1979; 15 Vietnamese prisoners of war were exchanged for 71 Chinese, among the latter being some fishermen who had slipped inadvertently into Vietnamese waters.

The most recent release of prisoners of war, at the time of this writing, was that between Iraq and Iran, beginning in August 1990. Each of the parties had captured tens of thousands of its opponent's army during the 8-year war that began in 1980. Following the imposition of U.N. sanctions against Iraq following its August 2, 1990, invasion of Kuwait, Iraq and Iran reached agreement on the releaase and repatriation of the prisoners. On August 18 each party freed and repatriated 1,000 prisoners, and by August 25 each side had liberated about 16,000 men. According to the International Red Cross, there had been about 20,000 prisoners (POWs) registered in Iraq and 50,000 registered in Iran by the end of hostilities in August 1988. UN estimates of the number of POWs differed: officials said that there might have been as many as 35,000 Iranian POWs and 70,000 Iraqis in Iranian hands. In November 1990 Iraq claimed that more than 37,000 of its men were still held in Iran.

## SICK, WOUNDED, AND DEAD

Until 1864, only numerous bilateral agreements but no general conventional rules governed the care of captured sick or wounded members of an enemy's armed forces. In that year, however, the Geneva Conference adopted the first treaty on the subject, providing for the humane treatment of such prisoners.

In 1906, a revision of the Geneva Convention was undertaken at a conference called by the Swiss government in response to a request made at the First Hague Conference of 1899, and a new convention, signed by 35 states, resulted. The experiences of World War I convincingly demonstrated the need for further regulations, and the 1929 Geneva Conference accordingly formulated the 1929 Convention for the Amelioration of the Condition of the Wounded and Sick in Armies in the Field (the Red Cross Convention). The 1949 Geneva convention for the Amelioration of the Condition of the Wounded and Sick in Armed Forces in the Field somewhat belatedly updated the primitive rules of the nineteenth century and incorporated the lessons learned in World War II.

Space does not permit a detailed analysis of the regulations now in force,[64] but in summary, medical treatment and humane care are to be given by the captor state to wounded or sick prisoners, and enemy medical personnel are exempt from capture. If such personnel are detained, however, their members are to be used only for the care of the members of enemy armed forces. The personnel of relief agencies such as the Red Cross and Red Crescent societies are equally protected under the convention. Hospital facilities and areas are to be specifically marked: hospital zones are to be clearly designated and notified to the enemy and are subject to inspection by protecting powers and/or private relief agencies. The enemy state is to be notified, through designated channels, of the wounded and the sick in the hands of the captor state.

Protocol-I of 1977 greatly expanded the provisions of the 1949 Convention through the provisions of its Articles 8 through 22 and 32 through 34. Most of these recent additions pertain to the protection of military and civilian medical units. Another and very detailed section of PR-I covers the protection of medical aircraft on legitimate medical errands (Arts. 23–31).

In regard to the war dead of military forces, each belligerent is to try to make proper identification and to bury the bodies individually if at all possible under prevailing conditions. The dead are not to be robbed. The home state is to be notified, through designated channels, of the identity and disposal of the dead. (See also PR-I, Art. 34.)

## SUGGESTED READINGS

### Laws of Conflicts on Land and in the Air: General

Green, *Essays on the Modern Law of War* (1985); Bothe, Partsch, & Solf, *New Rules for Victims of Armed Conflicts* (1982); Cassesse, *The New Humanitarian Law of Armed Conflict* (2 vols. 1979); Levie, *Protection of War Victims; Protocol 1 to the 1949 Geneva Conventions* (4 vols. 1977–1981); Trooboff, ed., *Law and Responsibility in Warfare: The Vietnam Experience* (1975).

### Illegal Weapons

(a) Chemical-Bacteriological Warfare: Lundin, ed., *Non-Production by Industry of Chemical-Warfare Agents* (Technical Verification under a Chemical Warfare Conven-

---

[64]See Lauterpacht's *Oppenheim*, vol. 2, 353–55, for background information; and 355–64, for a summary of the relevant 1949 Convention, as well as *Law of Land Warfare*, 84–97.

tion) (1989); Sims, *International Organization for Chemical Disarmament* (1987); Van Wynen & Thomas, *Legal Limits on the Use of Chemical and Biological Warfare: A Study in Restraint* (1968); Meselson, Ed., *Chemical Weapons and Chemical Arms Control* (1978); U.S. Dept. of State, *Special Report No. 98* (March 1982), *No. 104* (Nov. 1982), *Current Policy No. 553* (Feb. 1984); UN, *Canadian Government Report* (on Southeast Asian Chemical Warfare), UN Doc. A/37/308 of June 25, 1982.

(b) Herbicides: Verwey, *Riot Control Agents and Herbicides in War* (1977); "U.S. Department of Defense Position with Regard to Destruction of Crops through Chemical Agents (April 1971)," 10 *ILM* 1300 (1971); Johnstone, "Ecocide and the Geneva Protocol," 49 *Foreign Affairs* 711–20 (1971); *Newsweek*, Aug. 7, 1972, 24–26.

(c) Nuclear Weapons: Alley, *Nuclear-Weapon-Free Zones: The South Pacific Proposal* (Stanley Foundation, 1977)—a plan different from the one adopted; Weston, "The 'Sources' of International Law Revisited: The Case of Nuclear Weapons," 4 *Chinese Yearbook of Int. Law* 7–37 (CYILA-1985), and his "Nuclear Weapons Versus International Law: A Contextual Reassessment," 28 *McGill Law Jl* 542 (1983); Singh & McWhinney, *Nuclear Weapons and Contemporary International Law* (2nd ed., 1988); Miller and Feinreider, eds., *Nuclear Weapons and Law* (1984); Boyle, "The Relevance of International Law to the 'Paradox' of Nuclear Deterrence," 80 *Northwestern U.L. Rev.* 1407 (1986); Firmage, "The Treaty on the Non-Proliferation of Nuclear Weapons," 63 *AJIL* 711 (1969); Willis, "Nuclear Non-Proliferation: Who's Next to Get the Bomb?" *CSM*, Feb. 25, 1983, 12–13.

## Conflicts in the Air

Littauer & Uphoff, eds., *The Air War in Indo-China* (Rev. ed., 1972); *NYT*, April 26, 1972, 16 (lengthy excerpts from the 1969 National Security Study of the Vietnam War), and Sept. 17, 1972, E-1.

CASES

*Holtzman* v. *Schlesinger*, U.S. Court of Appeals, 2nd Cir., 1973, 484 F.2d 1307, reported briefly in 68 *AJIL* 337 (1974).

*Drinan* v. *Nixon*, U.S. Court of Appeals, 1st Cir., Aug. 10, 1973, No. 73-1271, reported briefly *id.*, 336.

## Prisoners of War

Hingorani, *Prisoners of War* (2nd ed., 1982); Levie, *Prisoners of War in International Armed Conflicts (1978)*, and his (ed.) *Documents on Prisoners of War* (1979); Bethell, *The Last Secret* (1974); Rodley, *The Treatment of Prisoners Under International Law* (1987); United Nations Command—Korean People's Army—Chinese People's Volunteers, "Agreement on Repatriation of Sick and Wounded Prisoners (Panmunjom, April 11, 1953)," in 47 *AJIL* 178 (1953 Supp.); same parties, "Agreement on Prisoners of War (Panmunjom, June 8, 1953)," *id.*, 180; Casella, "The Politics of Prisoners of War," *NYT Magazine*, May 28, 1972, 9, 25–35 *passim.*; Levie, "Procedures for the Protection of Prisoners of War in Viet-Nam: A Four-Way Problem," 65 *AJIL* 209 (1971 *Proceedings*); Falk, "International Law Aspects of Repatriation of Prisoners during Hostilities,," 67 *AJIL* 465 (1973); Levie, "A Reply," *id.*, 693; Falk, "Reply,"

68 *AJIL* 104 (1974); Levie, "Legal Aspects of the Continued Detention of the Pakistani Prisoners of War by India," 67 *AJIL* 512 (1973).

CASE

*Rex* v. *Guenther Krebs*, Canada, Magistrate's Court, County of Renfrew, Ontario, Oct. 7, 1943, reprinted in 38 *AJIL* 505 (1944).

# 24

# Belligerent Occupation

## BACKGROUND

The present rules governing the occupation of enemy territory in time of war (belligerent occupation, hostile occupation, military occupation) were drawn up after centuries during which no distinction was made between mere occupation and conquest. The general assumption guiding heads of states was that conquest of enemy territory created annexation to the conqueror's own realm. Hence no restrictions on the invader's actions in the annexed territory were laid down, for it was his by right and in law.

As late as 1808, after Russian occupation of Swedish-owned Finland, Czar Alexander I forced the Finnish inhabitants to take an oath of allegiance to him, even though the official cession of Finland by Sweden was not accomplished until September 1809.[1] English practice as late as 1814 condoned the annexation of enemy territory as soon as occupation had taken place.[2] The United States, on the other hand, swung to the modern view as early as 1828, when Chief Justice John Marshall held that "the usage of the world is, if a nation be not entirely subdued, to consider the holding of conquered territory as a mere military occupation, until its fate shall be determined at the treaty of peace."[3]

• Today the accepted view is that the annexation of occupied territory is a violation of international law; that the title to the territory in question must not change until there is either complete subjugation (*debellatio*) or a peace treaty has been put into effect. As Roberts pointed out,[4] the ban on annexation is part of customary law, amply reinforced by judicial decisions and the writing of experts, but it is not explicitly laid down in the conventions dealing with occupation.

ARMY MANUALS    A considerable portion of the older rules stipulating the rights and obligations of a military occupant in enemy territory dates back

---

[1] Lauterpacht's *Oppenheim*, vol. 2, 432, n. 2.
[2] *Id.*, in the case of *The Foltina.*
[3] *American Insurance Company* v. *Peters*, U.S. Supreme Court, 1828, 1 Peters 542.
[4] Roberts, *Occupation, Resistance and Law* (1980), 39, n. 1.

to 1863, to the manual *Instructions for the Government of the Armies of the United States in the Field*, drafted by Professor Francis Lieber and issued, after minor revisions, on April 24, 1863, as General Orders No. 100.[5] The manual remained in force until 1914, when a successor, *Rules of Land Warfare*, was compiled by the War Department.

The military forces of other major nations, impressed by the *Instructions*, incorporated large sections of it into manuals they issued to their own armed forces.[6]

HAGUE CONVENTIONS (1899, 1907)     Following the drafting of private law codes outlining the rights and duties of both sides in a hostile occupation, the basic rules of the relevant modern law were developed at the Hague Peace Conferences of 1899 and 1907. The 1899 Convention with respect to the Law and Customs of War on Land laid the basis for most of today's rules governing military occupation in wartime. The later (1907) Fourth Convention Respecting the Laws and Customs of War on Land and its appended Regulations, especially Articles 23g, 23h, and 42 to 56, detailed the rules adopted officially by most of the states of the world in their military manuals. (The appended Regulations are hereafter cited as HR.) As mentioned earlier, it is accepted today that the *Regulations are part of customary international law* and thus *binding on all states*, unless they had objected to a particular rule from its very beginning.[7]

1949 GENEVA CONVENTIONS     The second global conflict produced such gross violations of customary and conventional law applicable to the occupation of enemy territory and resulted in such inhuman treatment of helpless enemy civilians caught in the hands of German, Japanese, and later Russian armies of occupation, that the need for a revision of the legal rules became undeniable.

The International Committee of the Red Cross emerged as the agency able to prod somewhat reluctant governments into action. After a number of preliminary meetings had been held, the Swiss government convened the Diplomatic Conference for the Establishment of International Conventions for the Protection of Victims of War. The conference met in Geneva from April 21 to August 12, 1949, and was attended by representatives of sixty-three governments as well as observers from many international organizations, and resulted in four conventions. The fourth of these, the Geneva Convention Relative to the Protection of Civilian Persons in Time of War

---

[5] See Graber, *The Development of the Law of Belligerent Occupation, 1863–1914* (1949), 14–20; the text of the *Instructions* is on 297–317.

[6] Von Glahn, *The Occupation of Enemy Territory: A Commentary on the Law of Belligerent Occupation* (1957), 8, 12–14. This chapter is based in part on the above study.

[7] See *Judgment of the International Military Tribunal* (Nuremberg), Cmd. 6963, 64, 125; *Judgment of the International Military Tribunal for the Far East* (1948), as shown in Lauterpacht's *Oppenheim*, vol. 2, 234–35; Supreme Court of Israel, *The Beit-El Case*. P.D. 33(2) 113, H.C. 606/78, 610/78 1979 33; Supreme Court of Israel, *Dwikat v. the Government of Israel*. H.C.J. 390-79, P.D. 34(1)1, October 22, 1979.

(hereafter cited as Geneva-IV),[8] is the one related most closely to the subject at hand.

LAW OF LAND WARFARE    After the United States had ratified the four conventions and they were in force for this country (February 2, 1956),[9] the U.S. Department of the Army revised its rather outdated 1940 military manual and issued (July 1956) a completely revised version, *The Law of Land Warfare*,[10] including the text of all four 1949 Geneva conventions, with much valuable supplementary commentary.

As mentioned earlier (Chapter 21) regarding conflicts, the two protocols resulting from the Geneva Diplomatic Conference of 1977 (Protocol I, relating to international armed conflicts, and Protocol II, relating to noninternational armed conflicts, hereinafter cited in PR-I and PR-II) supplement the four Geneva conventions of 1949. Although the United States, at the time of this writing, had not ratified the two protocols, their provisions will be, after ratification, incorporated in the next edition of *The Law of Land Warfare*.

FOURTH GENEVA CONVENTION AND PR-I    The major provisions of Geneva-IV are discussed in the remainder of this chapter. Article 2 of Geneva-IV merits brief comment, however, for it states that the convention applied not only in declared wars but also in all other armed conflicts between two or more of the contracting parties, even if a state of war was not recognized by one of them. The convention applied, furthermore, even if partial or total occupation of a party's territory met with no armed resistance. If, in a future conflict, one of the parties concerned was not a contracting party to the convention, it still applied to all other parties in their mutual relations. And if the noncontracting party to a war accepted and applied the convention's provisions, all contracting parties were bound to apply the instrument to the noncontracting party.

Article 2 of Geneva-IV is of particular relevance to the refusal of Israel (which had ratified the convention) to apply that instrument in its treatment of the inhabitants of the areas occupied since the 1967 Six-Day War. According to the Israeli view, the Fourth Convention does not apply to all cases of armed conflict, despite the wording of its second article. Israel has consistently relied on the wording of the *second* paragraph of Article 2

[8]See Pictet, "The New Geneva Conventions for the Protection of War Victims," 45 *AJIL* 462 (1951); Gutteridge, "The Geneva Conventions of 1949," 26 *BYIL* 294 (1949); Yingling and Ginnane, "The Geneva Conventions of 1949," 46 *AJIL* 393 (1952). The complete text of the Fourth Convention was reprinted in 50 *AJIL* 724 (1956 Supp.)

[9]See von Glahn, 18–19, for some of the reasons for the delay in American ratification.

[10]Department of the Army, Field Manual FM 27–10, *The Law of Land Warfare* (1956), hereafter referred to as *Law of Land Warfare*. It should be noted that on June 9, 1959, it was announced that the U.S. Department of the Army had authorized the deletion of the term *military government*: henceforth the term *civil affairs* has been used exclusively; see also Cunningham, "Civil Affairs—A Suggested Legal Approach," *Military Law Rev.* 115 (Oct. 1960).

(Geneva-IV): "The Convention shall also apply to all cases of partial or total occupation of the territory of a High Contracting Party, even if the said occupation meets with no armed resistance." Israel has asserted that the entire theory of the convention rested on an ouster of the legitimate sovereign and occupation of portions of the latter's territory. Israel has never recognized the legal rights of Syria, Jordan, and Egypt to the territories they occupied since 1948 in the former Palestine Mandate and has pointed out repeatedly that Egypt governed the Gaza Strip to 1967 under a military government, not as part of Egypt proper. Furthermore Israel has emphasized that no Arab government ever acknowledged the annexation of the West Bank to Jordan in 1950. (See "Right of Administration.") Thus, denying that its opponents had legal titles to Israeli-captured territories (including East Jerusalem), Israel maintains that its conquests in 1967 equaled, in validity, the rights of the Arab states in question.[11] On the other hand, Israeli spokesmen have maintained consistently, since 1971 (and possibly earlier), that in practice, the occupant has applied the humanitarian aspects of Geneva-IV; they always, however, refer officially and privately to the "administered territories" and not to the "occupied territories."

In other words, Israel has insisted that it has applied and is applying the Hague Regulations and Geneva-IV *de facto* but has not been obliged to do so *de jure* in view of the asserted absence of Jordanian sovereignty over the West Bank. In that connection it is interesting to note that only Great Britain and Pakistan recognized that sovereignty and that Jordan's King Hussein had, in effect, yielded Jordanian claims to the West Bank at the Arab League's 1974 Conference at Rabat. (See also below under "Right of Administration.")

In contrast, the UN Security Council in Resolution 465 (March 1, 1980), non-Israeli government officials, and almost all legal writers have held that the applicability of Geneva-IV to any occupation rests primarily on the wording of paragraph 1 of Article 2: "In addition to the provisions which shall be implemented in peacetime, the present Convention shall apply to all cases of declared war or of any other armed conflict which may arise between two or more of the High Contracting Parties, even if the state of war is not recognized by one of them." By that standard, Geneva-IV applied in full to the Israeli-"administered territories" during the hostilities and for a year after the general close of hostilities. Afterward, Articles 1 to 12, 27, 29 to 34, 47, 49, 51, 52, 53, 59, 61 to 77, and 143 still applied to the administered territories, in accordance with Article 6 of Geneva-IV. Overall

---

[11]The literature on this topic has grown to considerable proportions. Among the best brief analyses are Mallison and Mallison, *The Palestine Problem* (1986), 243, 252ff.; Gerson, "Trustee-Occupant: The Legal Status of Israel's Presence in the West Bank," 14 *Harvard Int'l Law Jl.* 1 (1973), his "War, Conquered Territory, and Military Occupation in the Contemporary International Legal System," 18 *Harvard Int'l Law Jl.* 525 (1977); and Meron, "Applicability of Multilateral Conventions to Occupied Territories," 72 *AJIL* 542 (1978). All four sources cited have impressive documentation.

coverage of occupation by the Regulations, on the other hand, is explained in beautifully simple language in paragraph 1 of Article 42: "Territory is considered occupied when it is actually placed under the authority of the hostile army." That simple sentence avoids all reference to legitimate sovereigns, to the previous legal status of the territory occupied, and so on. And as long as the word *legitimate* appears here, it should be noted that experts all agree today: the Regulations and all other instruments pertaining to occupations apply to both legitimate (lawful) and unlawful occupants. A better choice of words would be "displaced *de facto* government" or, simply, "displaced government."

Returning for a last time to the applicability of Geneva-IV to Israeli-occupied territory, a logical and unemotional view was propounded in 1986 by Rubinstein, a leading Israeli authority on constitutional law. He held that when one had to deal with a convention (Geneva-IV) not at all intended to be applied within the jurisdiction of a military occupant, not intended to influence internal law, and dealing entirely with territory and relations outside the occupant's own country, "a doubt arises in regard to the need for the process of 'absorption' into internal law." He believed that no alteration of domestic law was required under such conditions: the approval [ratification] of the convention was sufficient. He stated that a legislative body like Israel's Knesset could not legislate a convention, for its authority related to persons and property under its rule, which did not apply to occupied territory. Rubinstein concluded that this was the reason why Geneva-IV had not been 'legislated' into the domestic legal systems of states party to the convention.[12]

Both applicable modern instruments (Geneva-IV in Art. 9, PR-I in Arts. 5–7) require the utilization of a Protecting Power (or Powers) to watch over the implementation of the convention and the protocol. It is the duty of the parties to a given conflict to secure the designation and acceptance of such a power or powers, in accordance with specific provisions laid down in PR-I, Article 5, paragraphs 2 to 5.

Despite their many valuable additions to the hitherto existing rules governing military occupation, the Fourth Convention and PR-I have left untouched many important facets of the occupation of enemy territory, particularly in the economic sphere. Such gaps are mentioned below, but full discussion of the "missing rules" must of necessity be left to specialized treatments of the subject.

EFFECTS OF PROLONGED OCCUPATION    Israeli legal experts have long asserted that the long occupation of the West Bank and the Gaza Strip since the 1967 war rendered it unique and that in consequence not all legal restraints concerning a "normal" occupation should or could apply to Israel.[13]

---

[12] Rubinstein, "The Changing Status of the Occupied Territories," 11 *Eyunai Mishpat* [Legal Studies], 439 (1986).

[13] See Israel National Section of the International Commission of Jurists, *The Rule of Law in the Areas Administered by Israel* (1981), 95–97.

A similar view was adopted by the Supreme Court in the case of *The Christian Society for the Holy Places* v. *The Minister of Defense*,[14] in which it defended the adaptation of legal rules to temporal needs. The Israeli government itself also favored this concept in an official *Memorandum of Law*.[15]

The problem which arises in the case of the Israeli contention is that the appropriateness of permitted changes in rules must be judged by determining whether new or modified rules have developed through the historic and accepted lawmaking procedures of international law: custom or treaty. As mentioned earlier, the United Nations and the bulk of states outside of Israel have insisted on numerous occasions that the customary law of the Hague Regulations and the treaty law of Geneva-IV represent the rules applicable to the administration of the occupied territories. It appears, to this writer, impossible that new customary rules or changes in existing ones can develop through unitary declarations by an occupant: no rules of customary law can be born in that manner. In consequence, most legal scholars outside Israel agree that the HR and Geneva-IV rules, as laid down in 1907 or 1949, are binding on Israel.[16] It does not matter in the least that, in the view of some commentators, the rules were drafted for a short occupation. Those rules say nothing about changes due to duration, except in Article 6(3) of Geneva-IV, in which instance the key rules on occupation are to continue in force after some regulations cease to apply a year after the general close of military operations.

## RIGHTS AND OBLIGATIONS OF THE OCCUPANT

During the extraordinary length of the Israeli occupation of the West Bank, the Gaza Strip, and East Jerusalem a very large list of violations of the customary law HR as well as of Geneva-IV has taken place. In part, this happened because of Israel's rejection of the *de jure* character of Geneva-IV. A number of such violations are cited in this Chapter but should *not* be taken as evidence of anti-Israel attitudes: they are to be viewed as textbook illustrations of lawful restrictions and their violations, laid on a belligerent occupant by the humanitarian law of war. Many similar violations, but of course only of the Hague Regulations, were recorded during the belligerent occupations by Germany, the Soviet Union, and Japan during World War II.

LAWFUL OCCUPATION    Territory is considered occupied when it is actually placed under the authority of the hostile army, according to Article 42 of the 1907 Hague Regulations. Invasion, therefore, precedes but does not correspond to occupation, which occurs when the enemy government

---

[14] HCJ 337/71 P.D., vol. 26, Part 1 (1972) 582.

[15] See 17 *ILM* 432 (1978).

[16] See the erudite and heavily documented study by Roberts, "Prolonged Military Occupation: The Israeli-Occupied Territories since 1967," 84 *AJIL* 44 (1990), its criticism by Rostow in 84 *AJIL* 717 (1990), and Roberts' reply, *id*, 720.

has been rendered incapable of exercising its authority in a given area. The invader (occupant) then substitutes his own authority for that of the legitimate sovereign. So-called fictitious occupations, created by the dispatch of flying columns into enemy territory, are not lawful occupations.

THREE SYSTEMS OF LAW    The result of belligerent occupation, then, is that three distinct systems of law apply in territory under an enemy occupant: the indigenous law of the legitimate sovereign, to the extent that it has not been necessary to suspend it; the laws (legislation, orders, decrees, proclamations, and regulations) of the occupant, which are gradually introduced; and the applicable rules of customary and conventional international law.

MAINTENANCE OF OCCUPATION    Once occupation has been established on a *de facto* basis, it has to be maintained in order to continue in existence. If the invader is expelled by the forces of the invaded state or the latter's allies, occupation ceases. If the indigenous population revolts successfully and evicts the occupant, the occupation also ceases, and if, at a later date, it is restored, the native population should not be punished for its earlier and successful eviction of the occupant (*Land Warfare*, par. 360). If an invader fails to establish effective control over a portion of the enemy's territory, all orders issued by him are devoid of legal force.

RIGHTS OF ADMINISTRATION    Legal writers generally agree that the legitimate government of an occupied territory retains its sovereignty but that this sovereignty is suspended in the area for the duration of the belligerent occupation. The occupant, therefore, exercises a temporary right of administration on a sort of trusteeship basis until the occupation ceases in one way or another.[17] The occupant assumes international responsibility for the occupied territory, and in regard to neutrals, the occupant's legitimate acts possess the same degree of validity as if they had been the acts of the "lawful sovereign."

Belligerent occupation does not transfer sovereignty. Instead it transfers to the occupant the authority to exercise some of the rights of sovereignty. "The exercise of these rights results from the established power of the occupant and from the necessity of maintaining law and order [*l'ordre et la vie publics*] indispensable both to the inhabitants and to the occupying force."[18] It is unlawful under Article 47 of Geneva-IV for a belligerent occupant to annex occupied territory (Israel: Golan Heights, East Jerusalem) or to create a new state therein.[19]

---

[17] On this point, see *Law of Land Warfare*, pars. 281–82 and 358, as well as *United States* v. *Rice*, U.S. Supreme Court, 1819, 4 Wheaton 246. Consult also Whiteman, vol. 1, 947–51; Schwarzenberger, "The Law of Belligerent Occupation: Basic Issues," 30 *Nordisk Tidsskrift for International Recht* 10 (1960); and the *Case of Solazzi and Pace*, Italy, Court of Cassation (Penal), 1953, 37 *Riv. di Dir. Int.* 387, noted in 49 *AJIL* 423 (1955).

[18] *Law of Land Warfare*, 138, 140.

[19] See International Military Tribunal, *Trial of the Major War Criminals*, vol. 22, 411, 497–98. On Israel's early changes in the status of Jerusalem, see UN General Assembly Res. 2253 (ES-V) of July 4, 1967, asserting that "these measures are invalid" and were to be rescinded. The General Assembly repeated this demand in Res. A/2254 (ES-V) of July 14, 1967.

On the other hand, occupied territory is generally considered a part of the occupant's realm in regard to belligerent purposes (bombardment, contraband of war, and so on). This common view was expressed long ago by the Supreme Court of the United States in the well-known case of *Thirty Hogsheads of Sugar* v. *Boyle* (1815, 9 Cranch 191), when it held that

although acquisitions made during war are not considered as permanent until confirmed by treaty, yet to every commercial and belligerent purpose, they are considered as a part of the domain of the conqueror, so long as he retains the possession and government of them.

Any attempt to supplant the legitimate sovereign (displaced government) by absorption of occupied territory during the course of a war must be considered an unlawful premature annexation. The reference to the "legitimate sovereign" (displaced government) is important in view of the continuing disagreement concerning the future of the Israeli-occupied West Bank and East Jerusalem. Israel has maintained that inasmuch as Jordan occupied the territories in question in 1948 in violation of the partition plan arranged by the United Nations, Jordan was not the legitimate sovereign of these areas. Israel has also pointed out that Jordan's annexation was subsequently recognized only by Great Britain and Pakistan. Hence, so Israel's government holds, its title to East Jerusalem and any or all of the West Bank areas is as good as that of Jordan, being based equally and solely on conquest. It is thus argued that if the UN General Assembly holds "Arab" (Jordanese) titles to be valid—and they also were based on conquest—then consistency would demand an acceptance of Israeli title to conquered territory, despite any contradicting Charter provisions.

On July 31, 1988, King Hussein of Jordan announced that Jordan had discontinued its administration of the West Bank, captured in 1948 and annexed in 1971. That act was the only instance known to the present writer in which a "displaced government" of a territory under hostile belligerent occupation gave up its claim to sovereignty over that territory while the occupation was still in effect. In part in consequence of Jordan's action, the Palestinian National Council adopted on November 15, 1988, a political communiqué and declaration of independence for a Palestinian state.[20]

In view of the continuing disagreement about those points, it appears desirable to supply some background of the dispute. The Golan Heights, the Gaza Strip, East Jerusalem and the so-called West Bank (of the Jordan River) all were part of the Ottoman Empire before October 30, 1918. Prior to 1948, all were part of the British Palestine Mandate.

Before the Treaty of Lausanne came into force (August 6, 1924), the Gaza Strip was formally part of the Ottoman Empire, but then Turkey renounced title to the Strip in Article 16 of the treaty. That instrument, however, did not identify the country to which title was passed. It must be assumed

[20] Texts in question in 27 *ILM* 1638 and 1660 (1988).

that administration, as contrasted with title, passed to the parties to the agreement governing the Palestine Mandate. That agreement did not transfer any sovereignty. E. Lauterpacht referred to the I.C.J. *Advisory Opinion on the Status of South West Africa*[21] and pointed out that subsequently, in 1947–1948, no agreement to settle the fate of the Strip was reached between the General Assembly and the United Kingdom: the Partition Plan of November 29, 1947, was not implemented.

At the British withdrawal in May 1948, Syria took the Golan Heights, the then Kingdom of Trans-Jordan took East Jerusalem and the West Bank (annexing both on April 25, 1950), and Egypt occupied the Gaza Strip, administering it through a Military Government. Israel then assumed control of all territories in question during the Six-Day War of 1967. In the case of East Jerusalem and the West Bank, Israel insisted not only that Jordan had lacked sovereignty (see above) but that the Israeli occupation was the result of self-defense undertaken after Jordan opened hostilities against Israel on June 5, 1967. Israel had been at war with Egypt since the early hours of that day and had informed Jordan (an ally of Egypt) that Israel would not conduct hostile operations against Jordan unless the latter instigated such operations itself. When Jordan opened hostilities, Israeli military forces moved into Jordan and quickly occupied the West Bank and East Jerusalem. As far as the Gaza Strip was concerned, the Peace Treaty between Israel and Egypt (March 26, 1979) specified in Article II that "the permanent boundary between Egypt and Israel is the recognized international boundary between Egypt and the former mandated territory of Palestine as shown on the map at Appendix II, without prejudice to the issue of the status of the Gaza Strip."

Legislation enacted by the legitimate sovereign was, traditionally, denied all validity in territory under enemy occupation. However, a number of decisions arising out of events during World War II led to the conclusion that legislation by the lawful sovereign intended to interfere with the occupant's legitimate rule has no effective force in occupied territory. But if such legislation does not conflict with the legitimate rule of the occupying power, it may apply in the territory.

International law does not require the issuance of a formal proclamation of belligerent occupation, but recent practice has favored such an announcement to the indigenous population.

## RIGHTS AND OBLIGATIONS OF
## THE INDIGENOUS POPULATION

DUTY OF OBEDIENCE    Most older texts in international law asserted the existence of a "duty of obedience" by the local inhabitants toward a bel-

[21](*I.C.J. Reports, 1950,* at 83) E. Lauterpacht, "The Contemporary Practice of the United Kingdom in the Field of International Law—Survey and Comment IV," 6 *Int. and Contemp. Law Quarterly* 513 (1957).

ligerent occupant and thus favored the latter at the expense of the civilian population. Numerous justifications have been evolved for this claimed obedience, some of them highly ingenious indeed.[22] More recently, there seems to have been a change in point of view, and it can be said that, at the most, the inhabitants should give an obedience equal to that previously given to the laws of their legitimate sovereign and that, at the least, [they should obey the occupant to the extent that such a result can be enforced through the latter's military supremacy.] Articles 27, 64, and 65 of the Fourth Geneva Convention of 1949 appear at first glance to dictate a real duty of obedience for the native population. However, a careful perusal of these articles will show that subject to certain conventional restrictions, it is the occupant who may actually dictate the limits of obedience expected. In any case, an occupant may not force the local population to act in a manner that can be construed as aimed to injure their displaced government.

UNARMED BUT VIOLENT RESISTANCE    The most recent example of unarmed but violent resistance to an occupant has been the *intifadah* (Uprising) by the Palestinian population of the Israeli-occupied West Bank and Gaza Strip. Its origins went back to the fall of 1986 when Gaza students began to confront the Israel Defense Forces (IDF). The true beginning of the Uprising began on December 9, 1987, following a road accident in which four Palestinians were killed in a collision with an army vehicle in Gaza. After that date middle-class Palestinians, particularly the merchant class, joined the struggle, "turning the *intifadah* into a mass-based rebellion against Israeli rule."[23] The characteristic feature of the Uprising has been stone-throwing by young Palestinians at members of the IDF, but on numerous occasions Molotov Cocktails have taken the place of rocks. By February 25, 1991, a total of 797 Palestinians, including children, had lost their lives, as had 57 Israelis; in addition, 325 alleged Arab collaborators had been killed by Palestinians.

The most serious incident in the *intifadah* took place on October 8, 1990, when at least 20 Palestinians were killed during a riot on the Temple Mount in Jerusalem. Each side accused the other of responsibility for the violence. American diplomats then drafted a resolution for the UN Security Council, condemning "the violence in Israel and the excessive Israeli response." Before the document was debated in the Security Council, Israel appointed a panel to investigate the killings on the Temple Mount. On October 12 the Security Council unanimously adopted the resolution, which included a call for a UN commission of inquiry (Security Council Resolution 672-1990). The

---

[22] See Baxter, "The Duty of Obedience to the Belligerent Occupant," 27 *BYIL* 235, esp. 240–44 (1950); Roberts, *op. cit. supra*, n. 1, 120–215.

[23] Bernard Mills, quoted in Moffett, "Arab Uprising Brings Pain and Gain," *CSM*, Dec. 7, 1988, 1,36. One of the most comprehensive accounts from the Palestinian point of view of the first year of the Uprising is found in Al-Haq (Law in the Service of Man), *Punishing a Nation* (Human Rights Violations During the Palestine Uprising), December 1987–1988 (1988).

Israeli government rejected any effort of the Security Council to send an investigatory team as an infringement of Israel's sovereignty over Jerusalem. It also asserted that if a UN delegation of investigators were sent, the government would not cooperate with it. In response, the Security Council voted unanimously on October 24 to rebuke Israel for such rejection of a UN mission.

Two days later the three-member Israeli panel reported that Palestinians started the Temple Mount riot but also strongly criticized police commanders for ignoring warning signs of impending trouble.

In the meantime the Security Council asked the UN Secretary-General to submit a report on the October 8 incident. The report was to be based on the findings of an investigatory team and was to be completed by the end of October. In light of Israel's attitude, the Secretary-General insisted that he could not prepare the requested report unless he was supplied with first-hand information from a UN team. He also rejected an Israeli suggestion that such a team might enter Israel in the guise of tourists, not on an official basis. He asserted on October 19 that he would not send a team to Israel unless the government of the latter state cooperated.

On November 12 Israel indicated its acceptance of a single emissary of the Secretary-General, but not on the basis of the rejected Resolution 672. This announcement was followed by an invitation to Jean-Claude Aime, the Secretary-General's chief assistant for Middle East questions, to discuss various Israel-Arab questions but apparently *not* the October 8 incident.

After the failure to achieve investigation of the Temple Mount incident, a proposal concerning the Israeli-occupied territories was laid before the UN Security Council in early December 1990. Under this plan, the Council would order the Secretary-General "to monitor and observe the situation" in those areas and to submit reports to the Council on a regular basis. Observer teams would be composed of some of the UN relief workers based on the Gaza Strip and the West Bank. The Security Council had not acted on this proposal by the time of this writing.

UNARMED NONVIOLENT RESISTANCE     Often coupled with the previous variety of resistance under occupation is unarmed and nonviolent resistance to the policies (acts) of a belligerent occupant. The most common techniques employed include boycotts of the occupant's goods, general strikes shutting down all businesses and transportation, and a refusal to pay taxes and customs levied directly or indirectly by the occupant. All three have been used during the *intifadah* in East Jerusalem and also in the West Bank and the Gaza Strip: they will be covered briefly below.

ARMED RESISTANCE     Resistance by the indigenous population to a belligerent occupant has given rise not only to a great body of literature but also to acts of great brutality and many diplomatic protests. As was mentioned earlier (Chapter 23), a *levée en masse*—that is, armed resistance by civilians—is lawful under Article 2 of the Hague Regulations, provided this resistance is offered to an invader *from as yet unoccupied territory*. Unfortunately for those supporting such a view, few if any cases of genuine *levée en masse* in occupied territory are on record, after the 1911 Italo-Turkish War. The *intifadah* is, by definition, not a *levée en masse*.

An armed uprising inside the occupied territory is not forbidden by international law, but persons engaging in such an activity would be in a state of unprivileged belligerency: they would not enjoy the protection (privileges) extended to other inhabitants by the various instruments concerned with belligerent occupation. Presumably, however, those regulations applicable to guerrillas would also be applicable to participants in an armed uprising against an occupant. During the German invasion of the Soviet Union (World War II), several fairly large areas behind the German lines were not under the control of the German armed forces and instead became the homes of guerrilla groups of varying sizes. Such a situation, however, should not be confused with an armed uprising against a belligerent occupant. The areas in question were unoccupied Soviet territory, and in many instances, the guerrilla groups were supplied by air from behind the Soviet lines.

The occupant is entitled to detain or otherwise punish inhabitants who resist by one means or another his lawful orders, but penalties must be in accordance with specified procedures and within specified limits, such as when Article 68 of Geneva-IV states that imprisonment is to be proportionate to the offense committed. Thus, while the basic right of an occupant to punish resistance to his rule is noncontroversial, it must be exercised only within the legal framework created by the two instruments as yet regulating belligerent occupation: the Hague Regulations and the Geneva-IV Convention. It must always be kept in mind that since the end of the 19th century, resistance to an occupant has not been forbidden, nor supported, by rules of international law. It therefore cannot be viewed as an *ipso facto* violation of that law.[24]

RIGHT TO PROTECTION    The civilian inhabitants of an occupied territory have a right to protection, especially in regard to their personal rights. Initially and sketchily detailed in Article 46 of the Hague Regulations, these personal rights are outlined in considerably expanded form in Geneva-IV, Article 27, and have now been outlined in detail in PR-I, Articles 72 to 77, representing a long list of guarantees to the indigenous population. Briefly, civilian inhabitants are guaranteed respect for their persons, honor, family rights, religious convictions and practices, and manners and customs. Women are protected especially against any attack on their honor, in particular against rape, enforced prostitution, or any form of indecent assault.

Article 32 of the same treaty prohibits certain practices associated with the Axis treatment of civilians, such as extermination, murder, torture, corporal punishment, mutilation, medical or scientific experiments not required by the medical treatment of an individual, and any other measures of brutality.

[24]See Roberts, *op. cit. supra*, n. 1, 163, 169.

In connection with these guarantees to civilians, the extremely important Article 3 of the Fourth Convention must be noted. Prompted by the frequency of "normal" civil wars in certain parts of the globe and the intrusion of a new factor, subversive international movements, into world politics, the article provides for the protection of civilians, along the lines mentioned above, "in the case of armed conflict not of an international character occurring in the territory of one of the High Contracting Parties." (See also PR-II.)

NATIONALITY    The nationality of the inhabitants of an area under belligerent occupation does not change, as it would in the case of a shift in sovereignty. Under the laws of most states, therefore, children born in a territory under enemy occupation possess the nationality of their parents. Under American law, however, children born on United States territory occupied by enemy forces do not acquire citizenship under *jus soli*, for the occupied territory is deemed—and correctly so—to be outside the jurisdiction of the United States government at the time of their birth.

ARREST, PROSECUTION, OR CONVICTION    Article 70 of Geneva-IV prohibits the arrest, prosecution, or conviction of members of the indigenous population for acts committed or opinions expressed before the occupation or during a temporary suspension thereof, except for breaches of the laws and customs of war. Also, nationals of the occupying state who, before the outbreak of the conflict, sought refuge in the territory of the occupied state may not be arrested, prosecuted, or deported from the occupied territory, except for offenses committed after the outbreak of hostilities or for offenses under common law committed before the outbreak of hostilities that, under the law of the occupied state, would have justified extradition in time of peace. Concerning war crimes, see PR-I, Articles 75 (7) and 88.

RELIGION    The religious convictions and practices of the native inhabitants are to be respected, in accordance with Article 48 of the Hague Regulations and Article 27 of Geneva-IV. Logically, however, the pulpit must not be misused to discuss politics or to incite revolt or resistance among the population. Political meetings may not be disguised as religious assemblies.[25]

EDUCATION    The control of education by a belligerent occupant has been the subject of much disagreement. Both customary and conventional international law rules before 1949 had nothing to say about this matter. Writers generally agreed that the occupant could lawfully supervise the educational system in occupied areas but disagreed as to the precise limits of this control. Logically, any teaching promoting hostility toward the occupant and his cause could be stopped, as could be discussion of all political matters. Schools, it was agreed, could be closed temporarily if military necessity required it.

[25] See *NYT*, August 16, 1975, 4; July 1, 1976, 2; October 10–23, 1976, *passim.*

Both world wars saw wholesale interference in educational matters by belligerent occupants, contrary to the tolerant attitudes displayed by academic commentators. The United States' regulations for the control of occupied enemy territory had almost nothing to say on the subject of education, until the thirteenth proclamation of General Dwight D. Eisenhower (December 16, 1944) to the German people. That document announced the closing of all German educational institutions except orphanages and boarding schools, until Nazism had been eradicated. When the Allied forces moved into Germany, this provision was carried out and was followed by an intensive effort to eliminate National Socialist elements from all teaching staffs, to substitute democratically oriented texts for those produced in the Nazi period, and to lay the groundwork for a more democratic administration of the schools and universities.[26] In these endeavors the Allied education officers were still bound by whatever Hague Regulations could be deemed to apply to education, until Germany surrendered unconditionally. After that time, no restrictions appear to have applied.

Article 50 of Geneva-IV provides that the occupant should facilitate the proper operation of educational institutions, with the cooperation of the native authorities in the territory, but several authors have recently contended that the article does not apply to institutions of higher learning.

In the territories occupied by Israel, closure of schools became almost habitual on the part of the military government. Student rioting was the usual reason given for numerous partial or total closings of the educational system, particularly after the beginning of the Uprising. Repeatedly sections of the system were allowed to reopen, only to be shut down again in a matter of days. On occasion all schools were closed, such as in the West Bank on July 21, 1988, a month before the scheduled end of the school year, and again on January 20, 1989, when all 1,200 West Bank schools were closed down barely a month after they reopened. On other occasions, wholesale school closing by the military authorities followed the call for a Palestinian general strike.

Higher education in the West Bank and the Gaza Strip was affected greatly by the outbreak of the Uprising: all six Palestinian universities (14,000 students) and 16 small community or vocational colleges were ordered closed in December 1987 in order to help in the quelling of the *intifadah*. The colleges were finally permitted to reopen (3,000 students) in March 1990, with the universities intended to open later.

During the shutdown of the universities, many students met in "underground" classrooms in homes, offices, and mosques. Almost 40 percent of previously enrolled students participated and about 1,000 were said to have

---

[26]See *inter alia*, Zink, *The United States in Germany, 1944–1955* (1957), 193–214; and von Glahn, "Some Aspects of German Education in the U.S. Zone of Occupation," 33 *Science Education* 7 (1949).

been able to graduate. Financing for this limited activity was obtained from various Arab governments and foreign private organizations.[27]

REQUISITIONING OF SERVICES    One of the important rights of a belligerent occupant is requisitioning the services of the indigenous enemy population, providing such services are for the needs of the army of occupation. Under Article 52 of the Hague Regulations, requisitioned labor by the local inhabitants must not involve them in the operations of war against their own country. Anyone in the population is subject to such a call, either in his or her normal occupation or, in emergencies, as a common laborer for clearing debris and burying corpses.

Axis abuse of this right caused the inclusion of comprehensive safeguards for the civilian population in Articles 51 and 52 of Geneva-IV. The new rules set a minimum age limit of 18 years for requisitioned labor, prohibit the transportation of labor from occupied enemy territory, require payment of fair wages, and call for the application of the labor legislation prevailing in the occupied territory prior to the invaders' arrival.[28]

DEPORTATIONS    The deportation (expulsion) by the occupant of inhabitants from an occupied territory is strictly forbidden by Article 49(1) of Geneva-IV:

Individual or mass transfers, as well as deportations of protected persons from occupied territory to the territory of the Occupying Power or to that of any other country, occupied or not, are prohibited, regardless of their motive.

Earlier the International Military Tribunal [Nuremberg] had judged deportation of civilians from occupied territories to be illegal, a war crime, and a crime against humanity.[29] Again, Article 9 of the Universal Declaration of Human Rights as well as Article 12(4) of the International Covenant on Civil and Political Rights of 1966 prohibit deportation in the one case and denial of the right to enter one's own country in the other. A frequent Israeli claim that Article 44(1) of Geneva-IV reflected and referred only to World War II German practices is invalid in view of the clear wording of Article 44(1).

It is still lawful, however, under Article 44(2) for an occupant to undertake partial or total evacuation of a given area if the security of the population or imperative military reasons so demand.

[27]Moffett, "West Bank School Doors Open," *CSM*, March 15, 1990, 12. See also Roberts, Joergensen, Newman, *Academic Freedom under Israeli Military Occupation* (World University Service and International Commission of Jurists) (1984); *NYT*, March 14, 1973, 14; Dec. 12, 1974, 4; Jan. 14, 1976, 6; Nov. 4, 1979, 16. Concerning the licensing of colleges, see AP Dispatches of July 6, 1980, Dec. 9, 1980, July 8, 1982, Nov. 17, 1982. Also see *CSM*, April 2, 1982, 13 and April 1, 1983, 7.
[28]See von Glahn, 69–73, concerning deportation practices by belligerents in both world wars and other details relating to requisitioned labor.
[29]International Military Tribunal, *Trial of Major War Criminals*, vol. 1, at 227, 293, 296.

The Military Government of Israeli-occupied territory has frequently deported individuals from those areas, charging them with incitement to violence or accusing them of illegal entry into the territories.[30] The legal basis for such deportations is claimed to be based on one of two sources. "Infiltrators" are expelled in accordance with Military Orders 329 for the West Bank and 290 for the Gaza Strip. All other deportations have been based on the British Defense (Emergency) Regulations of 1945, even though those Regulations had been abolished by Great Britain in 1948.[31] Deportation from Israel itself was eliminated by law in 1979, but the British deportation policy was "reactivated" later for the occupied territories.[32]

On August 4 , 1985, the Military Government revived deportation (plus administrative detention and "other measures") to deter "terrorism and incitement" in the occupied territories. From 1967 to January 18, 1988, a total of 876 Palestinians had been deported by official count, and 63 had been expelled since the beginning of the *intifadah* until May, 1990. Jordan, Egypt, and Lebanon all refused to accept deportees from the occupied areas, but Israel has deported some to Jordan and the majority to southern Lebanon, particularly after the Lebanese government no longer exercised effective control of that area.

In 1987–88, three interesting deportation cases in the Israel Supreme Court (sitting as a High Court of Justice) centered on the respondent's (government's) argument that while deportations violated Article 49 of Geneva-IV, that treaty, as conventional and not customary international law, did not become part of Israeli law in the absence of adoption by legislation.[33]

In view of the prohibitory clauses of Geneva-IV and other international agreements, Israel's deportations caused strong protests abroad, particularly by the United States and by the UN Security Council. The protests, no matter how strongly worded, had no effect and Israel continued to deport Palestinians when such appeared to be desirable.

Israel had deported 60 Palestinians between the start of the *intifadah* and December 1990. In that month, the expulsion of four Palestinian fundamentalists from the Gaza Strip was ordered on a charge of having been key activists in a Moslem organization backing the uprising. On December 25 an appeal against deportation by the four Palestinians was rejected by the Military Appeals Court, and they were given 48 hours to carry their appeal to the Israeli Supreme Court. That body had never overturned an expulsion order, expecially because such orders had always been presented by the army as involving security matters.

[30]See de Zayas, "International Law and Mass Population Transfers," 16 *Harvard Int'l L.Jl.* 207 (1975); see also Protocol I of 1977, Art. 85(4a).
[31]See details in the study by Hilterman, "Israel's Deportation Policy in the Occupied Territories," 3 *Palestine Yrbk of Int'l Law*, 154, at 160–61 (1986).
[32]Text of the 1945 British Regulations, *id.*, 134–38, together with three unusual deportation cases at 90–125.
[33]All three cases, with *ILM* content-summary, in 29 *ILM* 139 (1990).

The UN Security Council, on December 20, unanimously approved a resolution urging Israel to end the deportation of Palestinians from the Gaza Strip and the West Bank.

◊    SETTLEMENT OF OCCUPIED TERRITORY    One of the more troubelsome questions delaying a lasting peace settlement in the Middle East has been Israel's creation of some 180 (at the time of writing) settlements in territories occupied during the Six-Day War of 1967. The first of these settlements were created in 1967 as paramilitary *nahals*, several of which became civilian settlements when they achieved economic viability. Truly civilian settlements have multiplied since 1968; only a minority without government approval and the majority with the approval and active support of the state, support that frequently has meant the confiscation of land for settlement purposes. Such transfers of population by an occupant (and, in this instance, tolerated as well as promoted by an occupant) into occupied territory are clearly in violation of Article 49, paragraph 6, of Geneva-IV and PR-I, Article 85 (4a), which read: "The occupying power shall not deport or transfer parts of its own civilian population into the territory it occupies." The illegality of the Israeli settlements has been pointed out by officials of the United States[34] and the International Committee of the Red Cross, as well as by the UN General Assembly[35] and, in at least one instance, by the Supreme Court of Israel sitting as a High Court of Justice.[36] In 1977 there were only about 5,000 settlers in the occupied areas, but by the end of 1983 they numbered in excess of 30,000. By June 1990 there existed 130 Israeli settlements in the Gaza Strip and on the West Bank, with 75,000 settlers.

In June 1990 Israel had bowed to Soviet pressure and announced that new immigrants would not be settled beyond the "green line," which marked Israel's pre-1967 borders with the Gaza Strip and the West Bank. Nothing, however, was said about Arab East Jerusalem. In October a minor dispute about new settlers arose between the United States and Israel after the latter announced plans to build 5,000 apartments for new Soviet immigrants in Arab East Jerusalem. The United States then made public a letter from the Israeli Foreign Minister, David Levy, to Secretary of State James A.

[34]See letter from Legal Adviser, Department of State, of April 21, 1978, in 17 *ILM* 777 (1978); quotations from President Carter and others, by Hodding Carter III in the State Department daily news briefing, July 26, 1977, and excerpted in 72 *AJIL* 138, 139 (1978); and *NYT*, Feb. 17, 1978, A-2; April 24, 1979, A-1, A-4.

[35]Such as in its Resolution 32/5, of October 28, 1977, reproduced in 16 *ILM* 1543 (1977); see also *NYT*, July 15, 1979, 7. The Security Council condemned the Israeli settlement policy in a resolution (March 1, 1980) that became famous because of the subsequent U.S. assertion that the affirmative American vote had been cast by mistake: *NYT*, March 3–13, 1980, *passim*; and *Time*, March 17, 1980, 37–38.

[36]*The Elon Moreh Settlement in the Occupied West Bank* (October 22, 1979), reproduced in 19 *ILM* 148 (1980). In that decision, the court also pointed out that the Regulations bound the military administrations in Judea and Samaria, being parts of customary international law.

Baker III in which it was promised that in return for $400 million in U.S.-backed housing-loan guarantees, Soviet Jewish immigrants would not be settled beyond the "greeen line." Israeli officials then stated that the letter was worded incorrectly, that it should have excluded the settlement of new immigrants from the West Bank alone, and Minister Levy added that he did not promise to refrain from settling Russians beyond the "green line" but only not to use U.S. funds for such settlement.

Israel's justification of its settlements in the occupied areas has centered on four arguments: (1) Geneva-IV did not fully apply, a position vigorously defended by the former Israeli Attorney General, Meir Shangar, and other officials; (2) the view expounded by Prime Minister Menachem Begin on July 27, 1977, when he rejected U.S. charges of illegality regarding the settlements, by holding that Israel was not an occupying power in a legal sense, at least not on the West Bank, because Jordan had acquired that area in 1948 by aggression; (3) the argument that the settlements were needed for national security reasons; and (4) the assertion that occupied areas—the West Bank, in particular—represented traditional parts of the ancient homeland of the Jewish people, hence could validly be reclaimed by Jewish settlers. From a legal point of view, all four arguments fail in view of the clear wording of Geneva-IV, to which Israel is a party, and of the reiteration of that wording in PR-I of 1977, Article 85 (4a).

It must be emphasized that the problem of an occupant's settlements in a territory under belligerent occupation is not a new one or one created by Israel. During World War II, Germany undertook a massive settlement of German citizens in the richest agricultural sections of the Soviet Union, and much later, to cite another example, Vietnam began in 1982 to bring sizable groups of Vietnamese settlers to occupied areas, rich in resources, of Cambodia (Kampuchea). By October 1983, the number of such settlers was estimated at a minimum of 400,000.

POSITION OF PRIVATE NEUTRAL CITIZENS    Private neutral citizens in territory under belligerent occupation are protected persons and the 1949 Convention (Geneva-IV) applies to them. Their protection, however, is more limited than that granted to the native inhabitants of the occupied area: they have a right to leave the territory unless the occupant opposes their departure as being against his national interest (Art. 48), and there is an absolute prohibition (Art. 49) against the inhabitants' forcible transfer from the occupied territory.

## ADMINISTRATION OF THE LAW

Article 43 of the 1907 Hague Regulations provides that an occupant

shall take all measures in his power to restore and insure, as far as possible, public order and safety, while respecting, unless absolutely prevented, the laws in force in the [occupied] country.

Likewise, Article 64 of Geneva-IV requires (subject to certain exceptions) that the penal laws of the occupied territory remain in force.

Normally an occupant would honor this rule because the administration of enemy territory would be greatly facilitated by using existing and known local laws and regulations.

An interesting example of the continued use of existing laws took place in the territories occupied by Israel since 1967. Article 53 of Geneva-IV prohibited destruction by an occupant of any property belonging to private enemy citizens in occupied territory, unless such destruction was absolutely necessary for military operations. Israel proceeded to demolish private houses in occupied areas if they were believed to have been used by terrorists, and such acts were termed legitimate under Regulation 119(1) of the British Mandatory's Emergency Regulations of 1945. (See above.) Needless to say, the demolitions in question violated the explicit and non-derogatory provisions of Geneva-IV. It could also be held that the destruction of such houses violated Article 33(3) of Geneva-IV: "Reprisals against protected persons and their property are prohibited." Or, perhaps even better, the destruction of the houses could be said to have violated Article 52 of the 1977 Geneva PR-I, which states: "Civilian objects shall not be the object of attack or reprisals." The statement by the then Attorney General of Israel, Meir Shamgar, at a Symposium on Human Rights in Time of War (Tel Aviv, July 2, 1971), opposed these views: "Personal punitive measures are not reprisals." It has also been maintained by some critics of demolition that the procedure involves the forbidden (Article 33, Geneva-IV) practice of collective punishment, inasmuch as the family of an alleged offender is punished with the loss of its home.

Since the beginning of the *intifadah*, the IDF has, on occasion, sealed homes of "suspected" throwers of stones or firebombs. In virtually all instances the demolition or sealing took place before the accused had been tried and convicted of his alleged offense. In other cases the owners unsuccessfully challenged Army demolition orders in Israel's Supreme Court (High Court of Justice). On July 30, 1989, the Court ruled that the IDF had to allow appeals before destroying houses and had to inform owners of houses slated for demolition that they had a right to appeal to a military commander and the Supreme Court. The latter also said that in some cases, a house could be sealed before the appeal hearing. On the other hand, however, the Court also ruled that the IDF had the right to demolish a house immediately in the case of "operational military necessity" such as combat. By that time, 227 houses, by official count, had been demolished in the territories under occupation since the beginning of the Uprising. Before that event, a house was demolished only in rare cases of crimes such as murder.

One of the largest mass demolitions undertaken by the Israeli Army since the beginning of the *intifadah* took place on September 24, 1990, in the Bureij refugee camp in the Gaza Strip. Some 12 shops were bulldozed before a court restraining order had been secured. That order was overturned the next day by the Supreme Court of Israel, which, however, ruled that completion of the demolition was contingent on both compensation and provision of alternate housing by the Army. A total of some 30 shops and homes were destroyed before the end of the incident. The latter followed the killing of an Israeli soldier in the refugee camp. The Army defended its actions as necessary in order "to widen the area for security and military reasons." Critics termed the incident another example of illegal collective punishment.

As in the case of deportations, demolitions of houses caused numerous but unsuccessful protests by other states and UN agencies.

The destruction or sealing of homes of alleged offenders against security regulations in the West Bank and the Gaza Strip must not be confused with the destruction of Palestinian homes by the occupant because the structures were built without a permit. This practice occurred rarely before the Uprising but increased greatly since December 1987. Since then, a total of 550 such houses had been destroyed by July 1989.[37]

COLLECTIVE PUNISHMENT    A belligerent occupant possesses the undoubted right, under the provisions of the Hague Regulations and Geneva-IV, to decree an extensive list of penalties for violations of his lawful orders and ordinances. He is forbidden, however, to impose collective penalties or punishment, under Article 33 of Geneva-IV:

No protected person may be punished for an offense he or she has not personally committed. Collective penalties and likewise all measures of intimidation or of terrorism are prohibited. Pillage is prohibited. Reprisals against protected persons and their property are prohibited.

Article 33 is written in absolute terms, compared with a similar prohibition found in Article 50 of the Hague Regulations.[38] Examples of collective punishment encountered in 1988 and 1989 in the Israeli-occupied territories include cutting of telephone lines between occupied areas and the outside; selective electric outages (in Gaza for the resignations of Palestine policemen); surrounding the commercial district of Gaza City with barbed wire entanglements; and imposition of curfews when such were not required as security measures.

SUSPENSION OF LAWS    The suspension of laws injurious to the interests of the occupant or to his war aims is legitimate. Conscription laws, travel regulations, the right to bear arms, suffrage legislation, and local rights of free speech and assembly are categories of legislation subject to immediate suspension, for obvious reasons.

[37] See Katz, "Israel Destroys 'Unlicensed' Houses," *CSM*, June 28, 1989, 4. See also the detailed report by Playfair, *Demolition and Sealing of Houses* [International Commission of Jurists] (Al-Haq, 1987).
[38] See Roberts, *op. cit. supra*, n. 1, at 161–62.

INTERNAL ADMINISTRATION    The occupant may not change the internal administration of occupied enemy territory—he may not introduce a new indigenous governmental structure.

LOCAL LAW    Although the local law should be retained in force to the greatest possible extent, the occupant is, of course, free to legislate in the occupied territory, as long as his ordinances are in accordance with conventional or customary international law. If native law conflicts with legitimate legislation by the occupant, the local law must yield to the occupant's rules.

CIVIL LAW    Most authorities agree that civil law, in the narrow sense, is normally immune from interference by the occupant: such laws as govern family life, property, debts, most contracts, inheritance, and so on fall into this group. The writer has long questioned the validity of this assertion, in view of the increasingly total nature of war; yet the weight of legal commentary supports this principle.

CRIMINAL LEGISLATION    Criminal legislation in occupied enemy territory is subject to extensive temporary alteration by an occupant. Many acts, lawful under peacetime conditions, constitute grave dangers to an occupying force; other acts, already prohibited by the lawful sovereign, would be punished more severely by an occupant when undertaken against members of his forces or against his property than they would be when committed against civilian inhabitants.

In addition to his admitted legal right to change existing legislation in the occupied territory, the occupant is apparently quite free to suspend or alter ordinances (as distinct from laws), decrees, and administrative regulations issued by the legitimate sovereign before the occupation.

## Judicial System

SUSPENSION OF INDIGENOUS COURTS    The Hague Regulations had little to say about the varieties and operations of courts in occupied territory. Customarily, indigenous courts continue to function with the same personnel and jurisdiction and under the same laws (unless suspended or supplemented by the occupant) as before the commencement of the occupation. The occupant has a right to dismiss judges, just as they have a right to resign if unwilling to serve under the invader. If a given judicial organ interferes through its functioning with the occupant's war aims, this organ may be suspended. Thus the Allies invading Germany in World War II were legally correct when they suspended the *Volksgerichtshöfe* (people's courts) and other special judicial agencies, such as the *Sondergerichte* (special tribunals) peculiar to the National Socialist government of the Reich. On January 25, 1985, the West German Bundestag (parliament) voted unanimously to declare invalid all verdicts of the former people's courts.

In fact, an occupant may close down all indigenous courts under conditions of real need.[39]

[39]See *Land Warfare*, par. 373, for the conditions involved.

JURISDICTION OF INDIGENOUS COURTS    Under Article 23 of the Hague Regulations of 1907, an occupant may not bar the native inhabitants from access to their own courts of law in order to assert or protect their civil rights. On the other hand, the same inhabitants may not use their own courts to bring suit against the occupant, even when a claim arising out of a contract entered into with the occupant or his agents is involved. The occupant is not subject to the courts or to the laws of the occupied enemy state, and indigenous courts do not have jurisdiction over members of the occupying forces.

The indigenous courts of an occupied territory have generally asserted their duty to enforce the orders and regulations of a belligerent occupant as long as they are in accord with the Hague Regulations. Although few native courts have escaped criticism for enforcing such lawful orders, in the case of World War II most of these orders were upheld even after liberation.

ESTABLISHMENT OF MILITARY COURTS    Modern belligerent occupants, even if they have permitted some or all of the native courts to function, have tended to establish their own tribunals in occupied enemy territory. This practice is based on customary law and the practice of states and has now been made a part of conventional law through the provisions of Articles 66 to 76 of Geneva-IV. Space does not permit a detailed examination of the new rules.[40] It should be pointed out, however, that an occupant may create his own tribunals when the local judicial system has disintegrated or has had to be suspended for good reasons. He may also establish his own courts to try offenses committed by local inhabitants against occupation personnel. And he may set up his courts to deal with all native violations of his orders, regulations, and occupation statutes. Naturally he may also create his tribunals to try offenses committed by his own armed forces or civil occupation administration. Such a court would not be called an occupation court, however, for its basis would be found in the occupant's own domestic law and not in international law.[41]

If a military government (occupation) court handles civil cases not connected with the occupant or his forces—a situation quite possible in the absence of functioning indigenous courts—the law applied by such a court in the cases mentioned would be the law of the occupied territory, unless suspended by the occupant.

CONVENTIONAL LAW BASED ON ANGLO-AMERICAN JURISPRUDENCE    Finally, the new conventional law governing occupation courts (Arts. 66–76 of

---

[40]The literature on military occupation courts is very extensive: see von Glahn, 111–13 and the sources cited in the relevant footnotes. For the latest (at the time of writing) study of the structure and operation of Israeli military courts in the occupied territories, see Paust, von Glahn, Woratsch, *Inquiry into the Israeli Military Court System in the Occupied West Bank and Gaza* [International Commission of Jurists, Geneva] (1990).

[41]See *Porter v. Freudenberg*, Great Britain, Court of Appeal, 1915, cited in Hackworth, vol. 6, 368, and digested at length in Pfankuchen, *A Documentary Textbook of International Law* (1940), 718–24.

Geneva-IV) has borrowed heavily from the procedures and judicial safeguards commonly encountered in Anglo-American jurisprudence. This fact represents a most fascinating adaptation of a quite alien system of judicial procedure by the European states ratifying Geneva-IV—states that, basically, follow a legal system based on Roman law and the Napoleonic Code, as adapted.

DEATH PENALTY    One controversial feature of the new rules is the concluding sentence in Article 68, paragraph 2, of Geneva-IV. The sentence in question states that the occupant may impose the death penalty only when the offense was punishable by the laws of the occupied country in force before the commencement of the occupation. Several states participating in the Geneva Diplomatic Conference of 1949, including the United States, opposed this provision. Opposition centered on two points: the fact that the new rule would deprive an occupant of a major deterrent to illegal acts and the possibility that the legitimate sovereign, as the last act before his ouster from the area by an invading enemy, would abolish the death penalty in his jurisdiction. In consequence of this view, the United States, joined by Canada, Great Britan, the Netherlands, and New Zealand, signed and later ratified Geneva-IV with a reservation against the application of the convention's death penalty clause.

REGIONAL AND LOCAL OFFICIALS    An occupant usually retains regional and local officials, provided their government has not instructed them to the contrary and they are willing to continue to serve. Should they decline to serve, or resign later, the occupant is now forbidden to coerce or punish them for their action, under Article 54 of Geneva-IV. (On March 5, 1988, several West Bank city councillors resigned, followed on March 12 by 450 Palestinian policemen in the West Bank and on March 14 by 150 policemen in Gaza.) If native officials are retained, they may be lawfully required to give an oath or a promise of efficient and unprejudiced service under the occupant. Salaries of these officials are met out of revenues collected by either the occupant or the remaining regional and local governmental organs in the occupied territory.

Occupation authorities have an unquestioned right to dismiss indigenous officials, particularly police officials, subject to the relevant provisions of Geneva-IV. Thus Israeli authorities dismissed the mayor of the city of Gaza in 1972 for refusing to obey an order to incorporate as part of the city 30,000 Palestinians in a nearby refugee camp; on October 22, 1975, the former mayer was reinstated in his office. Much greater publicity resulted from a decision by Israel's Cabinet (November 14, 1979) to deport the Palestinian mayor of Nablus, Bassam Shakaa, for allegedly condoning an attack by Arab terrorists in 1978 (near Tel Aviv). All 25 elected Arab mayors and the councilmen in the West Bank as well as the four appointed mayors in the Gaza Strip resigned in protest. Then the mayors proposed to meet at the Gaza Red Cross Center for a one-day hunger strike as a gesture of solidarity. (1972 was the first year in which Israel permitted the election of mayors in the West Bank.)

On November 16, the UN General Assembly approved (132 to 1, the one negative vote being Israel's) a resolution urging Israel to cancel the deportation order. That cancellation took place on December 5, 1979; Shakaa was set free and returned to office on condition that "his functions will be limited to municipal matters."

In March 1982, the three West Bank mayors of El Bireh, Nablus, and Ramallah were dismissed from their posts in order to permit the appointment of "people who are not bent on the destruction of Israel but who are willing to negotiate with Israel, to come to the fore." A wave of rioting followed. During the next five months, five other elected West Bank mayors were dismissed. The removal receiving the widest publicity, however, was that on July 9, 1982, of the appointed mayor of Gaza, Rashid a-Shawa, who had been appointed mayor under the Egyptian military administration and had then continued in office after the 1967 War. The ostensible reason for his firing was his leadership of a partial strike to protest Israeli policies, but the real reason was probably his well-known hostility toward the occupation of the Gaza Strip.

ADMINISTRATIVE DETENTION    Administrative detention (internment) is a procedure by which a government detains individuals without charges and without judicial trial. The practice has been surprisingly common: the laws of some 85 countries permit it and several of them practiced it as late as the early 1980s. In connection with belligerent occupation, HR Article 43 obliges an occupant to take all needed measures to maintain security, public order, and the civil life of the inhabitants; Article 27 of Geneva-IV reads "the Parties to the conflict may take such measures of control and security in regard to protected persons as may be necessary as a result of the war." The practice of administrative detention is covered in the Convention's Article 78: "If the Occupying Power considers it necessary, *for imperative reasons of security*, to take safety measures concerning protected persons, it may, at the most, submit them to assigned residence or to internment." Articles 66, 68, and 76–135 then cover the practice in very great detail.

It should be noted that under Geneva-IV, Article 133, internment shall cease as soon as possible after the close of hostilities, reflecting a general international understanding that internment is of importance only during the early post-hostilities months of occupation. Israel's continued use of administrative detention has led to the considerable criticism that it is illegal.[42] Administrative detention as applied by Israel is based on the British Defense (Emergency) Regulations and a number of Israeli Military Orders, the former being replaced by the Orders following the outbreak of the 1967 war. The last remaining internee was released in 1972. Administrative detention

---

[42]See U.S. Dept. of State, *Country Reports on Human Rights Practices in 1988* (1988), at 168–69; UN Human Rights Commission, Resolution of 15 February 1977, Sec. 4(e); the detailed report by Amnesty International, *Israel and the Occupied Territories: Administrative Detention during the Palestinian Intifada* (July 1989); and Paust, von Glahn, Woratsch, *op. cit. supra*, n. 41, at 50–58.

was resumed in August 1985, aimed at "terrorists." The reactivating Military Order has been supplemented since then by a number of similar Orders. At the beginning of the *intifadah* only 50 individuals were in administrative detention, but since then the number increased greatly. By July 1989, some 5,500 Palestinians had been subject to detention and about 1,500 were still detained then. These detainees were all kept in a camp called Ketziot (or Ansar III) in the Negev desert in Israel. In November 1990 four additional Palestinian leaders were placed in administrative detention.

The individuals detained were doctors, journalists, politicians, intellectuals of every kind. Referring to the permissive Article 78 of Geneva-IV, Pictet in his authoritative analysis of the convention commented that Article 78 relates only to persons not charged with any offense, hence precautionary detention represents only preventative, not punitive action.[43] They were arrested with no offenses charged, subject to initial detention periods of six months, renewable in similar increments without limit. In August 1989, the six-months period was changed to one year. The detainee normally did not find out the reasons for his arrest, since the "key" evidence was not disclosed to him or his lawyer. An appeal for release or shortening of the detention period has led to freedom for many detained Palestinians, but still is a slow process. Decisions concerning release, change in term, or renewal of the term of detention is in the hands of a military judge, normally overwhelmed with the number of such requests. It should be noted that administrative detention does not involve, at any stage, a regular judicial trial. What does take place is an initial hearing, followed in most cases by successive later hearings at lengthy intervals.

The location of the Ketziot Detention Center in Israel clearly violates Article 76 of Geneva-IV which calls for the detention of protected persons in the occupied territory. At one time General Dan Shomron, then IDF Chief of Staff, acknowledged that the location was a "contradiction" of Article 76.

## Restrictions on Activities of the Native Population

COMMUNICATION MEDIA    Many activities of the native population may be regulated or even forbidden by an occupant, even though the acts in question do not violate the laws of war. Thus severe restrictions on or even the closing down of newspapers and periodicals is lawful; strict censorship of all permitted publications is authorized; and censorship of the mails and telephone calls, radio broadcasts, telegraphic communications, telecasts, and control of the use of carrier pigeons is legal. Virtually all military manuals prohibit the use of codes or ciphers by the indigenous population. Normally the belligerent occupant assumes immediate control of all surviving media of communication and, once their use is authorized, supervises all operations and programs.

---

[43] Pictet, *Commentary, Convention Relative to the Protection of Civilian Persons in Time of War* (ICRC, 1958) 367–68.

PUBLIC MEETINGS    Public meetings, if not forbidden outright, are subject to permits issued by the occupant's organs, and, commonly, advance copies of speeches to be delivered have to be submitted for censorship and approval. Religious assemblies and processions traditionally did not require permission by the occupant, but this practice was abandoned, except for regular church services, by both sides during World War II.

CIRCULATING AND TRAVELING    For obvious reasons of security as well as control, a belligerent occupant may restrict the circulation of civilians in occupied enemy territory, including the imposition of curfews. Exceptions to this generally applied rule occur regularly in the case of medical personnel and members of fire-fighting agencies and now also any remaining civil defense agencies. (See PR-I, Arts. 63–64.) Travel prohibitions, usually setting maximum distances from one's normal place of residence, are common, and special passes for travel beyond those limits are seldom issued by occupation authorities.

VOTING PRIVILEGES    The voting privileges of the indigenous population are normally suspended for the duration of the occupation, with a few exceptions recorded in the case of purely local elections. Thus, on May 2, 1972, town council elections were permitted in 12 towns on the occupied West Bank.

NATIONAL ANTHEM AND DISPLAY OF FLAG    Modern practice sanctions prohibiting the playing or singing of all songs disrespectful of or hostile to the occupant, and the playing or singing of the native national anthem as well as the display of the flag of the lawful sovereign is usually forbidden.

ARMS AND AMMUNITION    Regardless of local laws pertaining to the ownership or use of firearms, occupants are permitted, for obvious reasons of security, to order the surrender of all arms and ammunition owned by the indigenous population.

HUMANITARIAN CONTROL    Self-interest, combined with observance of his duty to restore public order and safety, grants to an occupant wide powers in such areas of public life as control over local hospitals, supplies of drugs and medicines, the sale of alcoholic beverages, prostitution and other forms of vice, and the creation of adequate safeguards to prevent the rise and spread of epidemics. Bitter experiences from German and Japanese interpretations of these humanitarian controls led to the extensive codification of the necessary requirements, obligatory for future occupants, at Geneva in 1949. Articles 14 to 23 and 55 to 57 of Geneva-IV detail the required action for hospitals, hygiene, and public health; Articles 24 to 26 and 50 are devoted to child welfare and related matters; Articles 59 to 63, and 143 deal with the various aspects of relief (collective and individual) and Red Cross and other relief and welfare agencies. (See also PR-I, Arts. 14 to 16.)

In this connection, Articles 59 and 60 of the convention must be regarded as being of particular importance. Mindful of the faminelike conditions prevailing in many parts of the world occupied by the Axis powers during World War II, the drafters of the convention specified the conditions under which food and other outside relief were to be brought into territory under hostile occupation. One of the new aspects of these rules is a belligerent occupant's obligation to agree to relief schemes on behalf of the indigenous population and to facilitate such programs by all the means at his disposal. Article 60 categorically affirms that an occupant is not relieved of his responsibilities for the welfare of the civilian population by his acceptance of relief shipments into the territory and also forbids all diversion of such shipments, except under rather unlikely conditions specified. (See also PR-I, Arts. 67–71.)

## ECONOMIC SYSTEM

RATIONING    Rationing may be lawfully instituted by an occupant and, under the conditions of modern war, is a normal feature of belligerent occupation. Recent practice shows that actual administration of rationing tends to be delegated to remaining indigenous authorities, with direction and control vested in agencies of the occupant.

TAXES AND CUSTOMS REVENUES    The occupant is entitled, under Article 48 of the Hague Regulations of 1907, to collect all taxes and customs revenues imposed by and for the benefit of the legitimate sovereign. Most military manuals and the writings of jurists agree that all such revenues in excess of the sums needed to administer the occupied territory become the occupant's lawful spoils and may be used for whatever purposes he sees fit. Administrative expenses thus represent a first charge against tax and revenue collections. Quite frequently, occupants have decided to entrust the collection of national taxes (and possibly customs duties, if any foreign trade is permitted) to indigenous agencies.

An occupant is free to suspend the collection of certain "national" taxes if the remaining income from that source is sufficient to cover his administrative expenses and he should decide not to retain funds not needed for these purposes.

Taxes collected by local agencies for local needs are beyond the occupant's lawful reach—except if the purposes in question can be held to be inimical to the interest of the occupant. Naturally, if local agencies had acted as tax collectors for their national government before the occupation, then any sums they collected after the occupation commenced would be treated by the occupant as subject to seizure and would have to be used primarily for the administrative expenses of the occupant. This conclusion would not apply, of course, if the sums formerly collected for the enemy government had been intended for eventual redistribution among local units of government. In that case, the occupant would act illegally if he treated the sums in question as "national" taxes of the enemy state and seized them.

A few commentators have asserted that an occupant may impose new taxes in occupied enemy territory, and the Israeli authorities in the West

Bank area (and later in the Gaza Strip) did introduce an eight percent "value-added" tax in 1976 (such a tax had been in effect in Israel proper for several months). Imposition of the tax resulted in repeated business strikes called by the mayors of most of the communities on the West Bank. The value-added tax imposed in the Gaza Strip became the subject of a suit in which the plaintiffs unsuccessfully opposed the new tax as violating the provisions of the binding Regulations.[44]

The Israeli Supreme Court admitted that there was a divergence of opinion between various authorities concerning the imposition of a new tax in occupied territory but found no bar to the imposition of the value-added tax in question, particularly because the occupation was a long one. One controversial point in the opposing arguments in the case was the meaning of "public order and safety," a phrase found in several places in the Regulations. The authoritative version of the Regulations, however, is the French version, not the semiofficial English version. In the original, the corresponding phrase (HR-43) is "l'ordre et la vie publics." Various meanings have been read into that, from "the public order as well as the safety of the occupying forces" to "public life" (virtually without meaning) to "the social functions, the ordinary transactions, which constitute everyday life" (from Baron Lambermont, Belgian representative at the Conference of Brussels, session of August 12, 1874),[45] and to "the ordering and functioning of legal institutions."

Neither Geneva-IV nor PR-I mentions the subject of *new* taxes, but the American *Law of Land Warfare* states (par. 426-b) that "unless required to do so by considerations of public order and safety, the occupant must not create new taxes." That view appears to be shared by a majority of governments and commentators.

In view of the fact that "public order and safety" are now considered to include the needs and welfare of the indigenous population under the phrase of "civil life," a new tax may be introduced by a belligerent occupant only if it is designed to clearly further one of two lawful purposes: to meet financial needs of the occupation forces (security and administration) or the needs and welfare of the civilian population of the occupied territory. Any new "national" tax levied without genuinely meeting either purpose would be unlawful under the provisions of HR Article 43.

Non-payment of taxes was a Palestinian technique of civil disobedience adopted soon after the beginning of the *intifadah*, particularly in the West

---

[44] See *Abu Ita et al* v. *Commander of the Judea and Samaria Region et al*, Israel, Supreme Court, sitting as High Court of Justice, HCJ 69/81, and *Omar Abd el-Kader Kandil et al* v. *Customs Officers, Gaza District Region et al*, Israel, Supreme Court sitting as High Court of Justice, HCJ 493/81, in IV *Palestine Yearbook of International Law* 1987–88, 186–210; von Glahn, *Obiter Dictum: An Unofficial Expression of Opinion on the VAT Case Judgment, id.*, 210–21.

[45] See Schwenk, "Legislative Power of the Military Occupant under Article 43, Hague Regulations," 54 *Yale Law Jl.* 393, n. 1 (1954).

Bank. When this maneuver began to spread, Israeli authorities countered it with a variety of novel techniques. Thus, in February 1988, merchants had to prove tax payments before being allowed to trade with Jordan across the Allenby Bridge. Some months later, Israeli tax collectors were accompanied by several hundred troops when descending at dawn on Arab villages. They seized the identity cards of tax-delinquent inhabitants and informed them that the cards would not be returned until all taxes were paid in full. Later during such raids, cars were impounded for non-payment of vehicle licensing. And still later that year, the tax collectors impounded all cars, TV sets, radios, some appliances, and so on, belonging to tax delinquents. These goods were removed at once, and their return depended on payment of all taxes past due. In one much publicized case, the entire contents of a pharmacy in Beit Sahur were seized for the refusal to pay taxes.

An occupant is exempt from indigenous taxation of any kind, unless he takes the highly unlikely step of waiving his sovereign immunity. Practice shows that an early order is issued by the occupation authorities exempting the agencies, personnel, and property of the occupant from all direct taxes. The writer believes that indirect taxes, such as excise taxes or various indirect sales taxes, also would not apply to any instrumentality of a belligerent occupant.

DEBTS    One of the more confusing aspects of belligerent occupation is the status of enemy debts in occupied territory. An occupant may lawfully prevent all payments from the area to the enemy government. In accordance with one interpretation of Article 53 of the 1907 Hague Regulations, he may collect those debts owed to the displaced government, but the present writer stands with a majority of the legal commentators on the meaning of the relevant provision and does not believe that an occupant is entitled to collect debts owed to that absent entity and falling due during the period of hostile occupation.

Jurists generally agree that an occupant may not contract new debts on behalf of an occupied portion of enemy territory.

LEVYING OF MONEY CONTRIBUTIONS    An occupant, requiring additional sums for the expenses of his occupation forces or for the administration of the territory, may levy money contributions on the indigenous population under the provisions of Article 49 of the Hague Regulations of 1907. If such contributions are imposed, the law requires that receipts be issued. These rules mean that the collection of money would be illegal if it were for the general war effort of the occupant, for buying supplies abroad for the occupation forces, or for the expense of belligerent operations outside the occupied enemy territory in which the contribution was exacted.

The actual payment of monetary contributions is usually organized through the local native authorities after their quota has been set by the occupant's agencies. The actual individual assessment of payments is therefore left to the local officials, who simply transfer the total sum they collect to the occupant. It should be mentioned, too, that under Article 50 of the 1907

Regulations, no general penalty, pecuniary or otherwise, may be inflicted on the indigenous population on account of the acts of individuals for which they cannot be regarded as jointly and severally responsible. Thus collective punishment for hostile acts against the occupant may not take the form of monetary contributions levied on a community or an entire territory—a rule violated conspicuously by Germany on many occasions during World War II.

REQUISITIONS IN KIND    Levies on the local population in terms of commodities of every description—called *requisitions in kind*—may take the place of monetary contributions and have been esteemed highly by many modern occupants. Under the terms of Article 52 of the Regulations, requisitions in kind (as well as services of inhabitants) are not to be demanded from municipalities or individuals except for the needs of the army of occupation. Such requisitions are to be in proportion to the country's resources. Requisitions in kind are to be paid for in cash, as far as possible; if this is not done, a receipt must be given, and payment should be made as soon as possible.[46]

Both world wars witnessed extensive violations of these regulations, particularly in regard to the removal of requisitioned commodities from occupied enemy territory to the home country of the occupant for the use of the latter's armed forces or even civilian population. Also, military occupation commanders conveniently overlooked the proviso that contributions (requisitions) in kind were to be proportionate to the country's resources, and especially in the matter of food requisitions, some extremely crass violations are on record. In this connection, it must be emphasized that an occupant does not have to consider an individual's resources in levying contributions in kind. As Feilchenfeld phrased it pithily, an occupant "may take a farmer's last cow and piece of bread as long as by doing so he does not unduly exhaust the cattle and bread supply of the whole country."[47]

FOOD SUPPLY AND OTHER NECESSITIES    The vital matter of the food supply of an occupied territory is dealt with at some length in Article 55 of Geneva-IV. There it is stated that the occupant, to the fullest extent of the means available to him, has the duty of ensuring the population's food and medical supplies. He should, in particular, bring in the necessary food, medical stores, and other necessities if the resources of the occupied territory are inadequate. In regard to requisitioning, Article 55 specifies that such levies can be exacted for the use of the occupation forces and administrative personnel only after the requirements of the civilian population have been taken into account. (See also the provisions of PR-I, Art. 50, also mentioned in Chapter 23.)

---

[46]See the important case of *Bataafsche Petroleum Maatschappli & Ors.* v. *The War Damage Commission*, Singapore, Court of Appeal, April 13, 1956, 22 *Malayan Law Jl.* 155 (1956), opinion reprinted in 51 *AJIL* 802 (1957), for a clear explanation of the rights and duties of an occupant regarding the seizure of private property without formal requisitioning.

[47]Feilchenfeld, *The International Economic Law of Belligerent Occupation* (1942), 37.

The receipts mentioned in the Regulations in connection with monetary contributions and requisitions in kind were intended as evidence that money, goods, or services had been furnished and constituted a kind of deferred-payment voucher. This writer does not believe that they constituted a promise by the occupant to pay for whatever was supplied to him. But, because Articles 52 to 54 of the Regulations, Article 19 of the Fifth Hague Convention of 1907, and Article 55 of Geneva-IV provide for payment for requisitioned goods, there must be someone intended to make that payment. Modern practice seems to be to make the lawful sovereign of the occupied territory the one who is expected to make payment after the termination of the belligerent occupation.

STATE-OWNED IMMOVABLE PROPERTY    The lawful sovereign's immovable public property may not be appropriated by a belligerent occupant. Rather, the occupant is in the position of an administrator and usufructuary of such property under Article 55 of the Regulations. As a mere usufructuary, the occupant is bound to preserve the substance of the property in question but is entitled to seize as his own the product or proceeds arising out of the property. He may not sell land that is enemy public domain, but he is entitled to the crops raised on that land. Thus an occupant may use, for the duration of his stay, public buildings, real estate, forests, farmlands, docks, barracks, and all other immovable property of the enemy state.

World War II, which saw widespread violations of Article 55 of the Regulations, also witnessed a development totally unforeseen by the drafters of the Regulations: the seizure of state-owned business enterprises by a belligerent occupant. This new problem arose in particular in regard to the Soviet Union. Under the terms of the Soviet constitution of 1936, the Soviet Union recognized three kinds of property: personal property (Arts. 9 and 10), socialized property (Art. 5), and cooperative property, which included cooperative farms. Personal property was presumably safeguarded by the various protective clauses of the Hague Regulations, but the other two types posed the problem when the occupation authorities undertook to seize them.

A strict interpretation of the Regulations would have placed all Soviet state-owned enterprises in the category of immovable public property—and this would then have covered *all* enterprises of any kind in the Soviet Union. The German authorities denied the validity of such a view and proceeded to "abolish" officially most of the collective farms. Because implementation of the order would have ruined agricultural production in occupied territory, Germany actually permitted most of the farms to function as before, but under German control. Later, many collective farms were broken up, and the land was sold illegally to German settlers, just as many state-owned factories were sold to German companies, in some cases simply turned over to German nationals, and in many instances shipped bodily into Germany.

Charges of illegality arising out of such practices were met with references to the fact that the Regulations did not define what is meant by state property or explain how a test of state ownership is to be applied. Modern practice in other states appears to indicate that the general attitude is this: if there is doubt about the nature of the ownership of a given property, it is assumed to be public property until (or unless) private ownership can be proved. In the instance of "semistate" property, that is, property in which the enemy state has an interest but is not the absolute owner, modern practice favors treating it as public property.

A rather interesting dispute erupted in 1977 between the U.S. government and the government of Israel over the latter's plans to develop and exploit new oil fields in the Sinai and offshore in the Gulf of Suez. Exploitation was to be carried out by private agents (concessionaires), who would receive their concessions from the Israeli government. The United States maintained that an occupant had no legal right to develop new oil fields; that even if these fields could be lawfully developed, the oil could be used only for purposes of the occupation and not for the occupant's own country; that an occupant could not grant concessions of the sort involved; and that oil concessions granted by Egypt to American companies in the areas in question had to be respected even if they had been granted after the beginning of the occupation in 1967.

The relevant treaty provisions presumably governing this dispute are Article 23 of the Regulations and Article 52 of Geneva-IV. Unfortunately neither instrument is clear on the subject matter of the dispute. However, from a legal point of view, it appears that the two instruments do not forbid an occupant's exploitation of natural resources, including oil, except when such exploitation, in Gerson's term, represents a "wanton dissipation of the resources" involved. Exploration for resources by an occupant (including exploration in lawfully delimited offshore areas) normally cannot be considered a prohibited activity unless the exploration spoils in some manner (Gerson terms it "wasting") the land or other resources in the occupied area.[48]

STATE-OWNED MOVABLE PROPERTY    Public movable property of the enemy state, including cash and realizable securities owned by that state, may be lawfully appropriated by the belligerent occupant under Article 53

[48]See U.S. Department of State, "Memorandum of Law on Israel's Right to Develop New Oil Fields in Sinai and the Gulf of Suez (October 1, 1976)," in 16 ILM 733 (1977), and Israel Ministry of Foreign Affairs, " Memorandum of Law on the Right to Develop New Oil Fields in Sinai and the Gulf of Suez (August 1, 1977)," 17 ILM 432 (1978). [Amusingly, to this writer, both Memoranda cite von Glahn, 34, 177, 209.] See especially the cogent analysis by Clagett and Johnson, "May Israel As a Belligerent Occupant Lawfully Exploit Previously Unexploited Oil Resources of the Gulf of Suez?" 72 AJIL 558 (1978), in which the limitations on such exploitation by an occupant are carefully detailed. For another opinion, see the United Nations General Assembly Resolution A/Res/3175 (XXVIII) of February 7, 1974, in 13 ILM 241 (1974), in which the General Assembly "reaffirms that all measures undertaken by Israel to exploit the human and natural resources of the occupied Arab territories are illegal and calls upon Israel to halt such measures forthwith." See also NYT, Sept. 8, 1976, 5; Feb. 15, 1977, 1, 4; April 4, 1977, 4; Gerson, "Off-Shore Oil Exploration by a Belligerent Occupant: The Gulf of Suez Dispute," 71 AJIL 725 (1977).

of the Regulations. The only limitation is that all such property must be usable for military operations—a restriction without much meaning today, when virtually every commodity under the sun can somehow be fit into the category of permitted seizure.

Seized movable public property belonging to the enemy may be used up, shipped from the occupied territory, or utilized in any manner deemed necessary by the belligerent occupant. The writer does not agree with certain jurists who justify even the sale of such property, for Article 53 of the Regulations specifies that such property must be for military use. It should be noted here that illegal seizures of public property were held to constitute punishable war crimes under Article 6-b of the Charter of the Nuremberg War Crimes Tribunal.

PUBLIC RECORDS AND STATE ARCHIVES    Public records and state archives, although undoubtedly movable, have been held to be immune from seizure. The traditional interpretation was that the occupant might use the records during the occupation but had to restore them to their normal place of deposit. The one exception to this rule was the permitted seizure and retention of all materials directly relating to the war in progress. This widely accepted interpretation has been altered in recent times. Because of the extensive use of archival materials, possibly for propaganda purposes during a war and for the arraignment of war criminals at a subsequent date, the modern occupant is now quite generally conceded to have a right to seize and retain any and all enemy archives and records, with no requirement for an eventual return.

CULTURAL PROPERTIES    International law prohibits the confiscation, destruction, or damage of historical monuments, works of art, and institutions devoted to the arts and sciences, under the provisions of Article 56 of the Regulations and of the Hague Convention Relative to the Protection of Cultural Properties in Case of an Armed Conflict, of May 14, 1954. Regardless of ownership, such properties are to be treated as private property and as beyond the reach of the occupant—yet, in practice, the official looting of art objects and historical monuments from occupied territory has assumed staggering proportions in modern wars, especially by the Axis powers (and, later, the Soviet Union, in the name of reparations) in World War II.

On the other hand, the buildings of institutions presumably exempt under Article 56 of the Regulations may be utilized by an occupant, if necessary, for strictly military purposes.

PRIVATE ENEMY PROPERTY    In earlier centuries, belligerent states could seize and confiscate all private enemy property on the soil of occupied enemy territory. Since the early years of the nineteenth century, however, the exempt character of private enemy property has emerged slowly but definitely, and by 1899 the immunity of private property was generally acknowledged.

It was therefore not at all surprising that Articles 46 and 47 of the Regulations met with no opposition at either the 1899 or the 1907 conference. Article 46 states that "private property . . . must be respected. Private property cannot be confiscated," and Article 47 prohibits pillage (looting). Article 23 (g) states that enemy private property must not be destroyed unless absolutely necessary for reasons of the occupant's military operations, a prohibition reiterated in Geneva-IV, Article 53.

Not all private property enjoys immunity, however. An occupant is entitled under Article 53, paragraph 2, of the Regulations to seize any war materials or goods, including transport, suitable for war purposes with, however, an obligation to restore these items after the war and to pay compensation. Article 52 allows him to requisition private property required for the needs of the occupation forces, and monetary contributions may be levied in accordance with Article 49. Again, an occupant's right to quarter troops (and animals) in the homes (and stables) of the civilian population is an infringement on private property rights. Lastly, the occupant's duty to maintain public order and safety entitle him to expropriate both public and private property for the benefit of the indigenous population (see also *Law of Land Warfare*, par. 431, on this point).

Although most jurists agree that an occupant may not seize privately owned property and move it out of the occupied territory, both world wars were occasions for wholesale violations of this principle. Military necessity was the defense advanced whenever justification was felt to be necessary; yet such actions had to be classified as war crimes under Article 6-b of the Nuremberg Charter.[49]

During World War II, there was a development in the sphere of private property relations under occupation in many parts of Europe then under German occupation: in thousands of reported cases, titles to private properties (business enterprises or real estate or both) changed hands from the indigenous owners to either the government or nationals of the occupying state. Few of the instances in question represented a voluntary relinquishment of title. A number of the states allied against the Axis powers issued a joint declaration on January 5, 1943, reserving their individual right to declare any and all of such transfers invalid after regaining control of the occupied areas.[50]

In connection with the treatment of private property in occupied enemy territory, a source of continuing recriminations has been the Israeli practice of blowing up houses (especially on the West Bank) suspected of having been used to shelter Arab (Palestinian) terrorists. The practice of demolishing those houses suspected of having sheltered terrorists has continued to the time of writing, but clearly violates Article 23-g of the Regulations and Article 53 of Geneva-IV. (See above under Administration of the Law about Demolitions.)

---

[49]See also *NYT*, March 24, 1973, 1, 4, concerning alleged Israeli looting of industrial equipment in the Sinai in 1967.
[50]See relevant textual excerpt in von Glahn, 189, and discussion of the transfer of title abroad. *id.*, 193–96.

## Banks, Currency, and Business Operations

There is a great gap in the legal rules governing belligerent occupation in the general subject area of central banks, currency, exchange reserves, and business operations in general. Conventional law is virtually silent on these topics, despite their enormous importance for both the occupant and his enemy. During both world wars, occupants interfered on many occasions with the operations of central banks located in occupied enemy territory, with Germany even replacing banks of issue with new institutions serving primarily its own needs and the exploitation of the occupied territory. An occupant may, of course, create new banks of issue, in the absence of restrictive rules, provided they do not serve to accomplish forbidden ends.

REGULATION OF COMMERCIAL BANKS    Practice has sanctioned the regulation of commercial banks, despite the contrary views asserted by many legal commentators. In fact, one of the common initial steps taken during belligerent occupation is to close all banks and other financial institutions and to seal all vaults and safe deposit boxes. This measure usually accompanies an order instituting a general moratorium on all business payments. The reasons behind these financial moves are quite obvious: financial institutions must be safeguarded, records must be preserved, and funds subject to lawful seizure by the occupant must be protected until inventories of accounts can be taken in order to identify monies that may be acquired under conventional or customary law. Most moratoria on payments are lifted relatively early after their institution, and banks are permitted to reopen for business on a limited basis.

CURRENCY    Both practice and legal opinion have granted to the occupant far-reaching authority over the monetary system of an occupied enemy territory. Commonly a dual currency structure develops when an occupant pays his forces (and for requisitioned commodities) either in his own currency or in special occupation money.[51] Because in almost all cases the original native currency is permitted to circulate as before, two currencies exist side by side, and the occupant has the right to determine the rate of exchange between the two. As long as abuses designed for the occupant's ultimate enrichment are not introduced into such a situation, no fault can be found, from a legal point of view, with creating such a dual currency system in occupied territory.[52]

BUSINESS ENTERPRISES    The absence of rules of conventional law has enabled modern belligerent occupants to exercise sweeping powers over business enterprises (nonbanking) in occupied enemy territory. Supervision and regulation in any manner considered desirable from a military point of view

---

[51] See *Aboitiz & Co.* v. *Price*, U.S. District Court, Utah, 1951, 99 F. Supp. 602, digested in 46 *AJIL* 152 (1952), on the legality of issuing occupation currency.

[52] Consult *Land Warfare*, par. 430; Lemkin, *Axis Rule in Occupied Europe* (1944), 51–63; and *Hearings on Occupation Currency Transactions Before Committees on Appropriations, Armed Services and Banking and Currency* (U.S. Senate, 80th Congress, 1st Session, 1947), 72–84.

or in the interests of the native population are sanctioned by both custom and military manuals (for example, *Land Warfare*, par. 376). The occupant may force a business enterprise to stay open and continue in operation, or he may close it if it appears that its operations are against his interests or those of the indigenous population. If a given enterprise seems of sufficient importance for his needs or those of the civilian population, the occupant may place the business in question under his own direct control and management.

Needless to say, none of the steps mentioned may result in expropriation of the enterprise involved. Regardless of the amount of control exercised by the occupant, the title to the business must remain with its private owners if illegal procedures are to be avoided.

Most military manuals, a majority of jurists, and certainly the practices of all major occupants in modern wars have approved the right of a belligerent occupant to regulate prices in areas under his control. Conditions prevailing in such territories promote a rapid rise in price levels unless regulatory measures are adopted from the outset. Although not all modern occupants have succeeded in stemming inflationary tendencies in the areas they control, and black markets have been an inevitable accompaniment of recent occupations, price controls have always been tried, on a few occasions with notable success.

## Agriculture, Trade, Communication, and Transportation

REGULATION OF AGRICULTURE    Agriculture is another aspect of the economic sphere in which customary as well as conventional law has placed no restrictions on an occupant, except in the most general way, through the obligation to look after public order, public safety, and the general interests of the indigenous inhabitants. The normal but certainly not universal practice of modern occupants has been to leave intact, to the greatest possible extent, the regulations dealing with agriculture issued by the legitimate sovereign before the occupation. In some instances, notably in the practices of the Axis powers during World War II, regulation of agriculture was manipulated in such a way as to create a maximum benefit for the occupying state instead of for the local population. Such practices obviously violated the intent of Articles 52, 53, and 55 of the Hague Regulations of 1907.

FOREIGN TRADE    Little need be said about foreign trade under occupation. Conditions following entry into and conquest of enemy territory tend to render the existence of exportable surpluses highly doubtful, and the means of payment for imports are not normally available to the population.

COMMUNICATIONS    The means of communication are subject to seizure, control, and operation by an occupant if he wishes to exercise those powers. At the termination of the occupation, all such seized facilities must be restored to their owners. Even if communication media are left in native hands — a highly unlikely situation, especially during the early phases of a belligerent occupation — they are subject to rigid control and censorship by the occupant. Special provisions govern submarine cables terminating in occupied territory. If such cables connect the territory with a neutral country, they must not be seized or destroyed except in the case of absolute necessity; if they are, the properties must be returned at the end of the occupation, and compensation for loss will be fixed at that time. Geneva-IV (Arts. 23, 25–26, 38, 61–62, 98, 106–112, 128) now requires parties to the treaty to open or maintain certain types of postal communication between the occupied area and the outside world on behalf of the indigenous population, including internees.

TRANSPORTATION    Railroads may be seized and operated by a belligerent occupant, but all equipment and facilities have to be returned at the end of the war, at which time compensation is to be decided on.[53] Means of land transportation other than railroads (trucks, cars, buses, trolley cars, carts, and so on) may be seized by an occupant even when they are private property. Again, restoration at the end of the war is called for by the Regulations, and again, compensation is to be fixed then.

In all instances cited, the conventional law does not state who is to be held responsible for losses and damage and therefore ought to pay the compensation. The obvious answer seems to be that the occupant—who, after all, was the seizing state—ought to pay. But modern practice frequently shows that if the occupant turns out to be the victor in the conflict, he requires the losing state to assume the financial burden of paying its own citizens for communication and transportation losses or damage suffered at the hands of the occupant.

The case of public and private vessels found in enemy territory by an occupant is quite different from the situation affecting means of land transport. Prize courts established by occupants have succeeded, in modern times, in expanding the lawful capture of property at sea to include the territorial waters and navigable rivers of occupied enemy territory, and vessels have been seized in dry dock, in port, and in rivers.[54]

## THE TERMINATION OF BELLIGERENT OCCUPATION

WAYS OF TERMINATING OCCUPATION    The belligerent occupation of enemy territory may terminate in a number of different ways. The area may be set free by the forces of the legitimate sovereign or of his allies, liberated by a successful uprising of the indigenous population, and returned to the control of its legitimate sovereign under the terms of a peace treaty. It may also be annexed by the occupant under the provisions of such a treaty or, lastly, annexed by the occupant after the subjugation of the legitimate sovereign.

---

[53] Hague Regulations of 1907, Art. 53; see von Glahn, 217–20, on the complicated problems with public and private railroads in territory under belligerent occupation.
[54] See also *Law of Land Warfare*, par. 410 (a), detailing the now lawful seizure of various types of vessels; and *Schiffahrt-Treuhand* v. *Procurator-General*, United Kingdom, Privy Council, Jan. 12, 1953, 1. All Eng. L.R. 364, digested in 47 *AJIL* 722 (1953).

LAWS AND ORDINANCES    Most modern occupations have ended with the return of the occupied territory to its legitimate sovereign, but even this normal situation has been complicated by many problems. Thus what laws and ordinances issued by the occupant will lose their validity after his administration ceases? No clear-cut answer can be given. If any of his decrees or laws violate customary or conventional international law, they will be null and void in the eyes of the returning legitimate sovereign; if they correspond to what the occupant could do legally in the occupied territory, then the returning sovereign will decide whether or not to keep the occupant's legislation in force as his own.

ADMINISTRATIVE ACTS    Administrative acts undertaken by an occupant in accordance with the laws of war should be respected and upheld by the returning sovereign. The sovereign is, of course, free to set aside all such lawful acts; but such a course of action would tend to prompt future occupants to pay little attention to legal requirements and might injure the interests of many of the sovereign's own nationals who acted in accordance with the lawful steps taken by the occupant. The legitimate sovereign ought, instead, to be bound by lawful administrative acts of the occupant and by their material consequences, if any.

DECISIONS OF MILITARY TRIBUNALS    A number of writers have held that decisions of the occupant's military tribunals lose their validity at the termination of the occupation, unless a contrary provision is included in the treaty of peace.[55] After considerable reflection and study of relevant cases, the present writer has been forced to disassociate himself from this view formerly shared by him. It appears that a decision of a military government court, if made in a case falling within the jurisdiction lawfully granted to it by the occupant, ought to be treated by the returning sovereign like all other decisions of competent courts in the territory. Naturally this interpretation would not apply in the case of an individual who had violated the occupant's security regulations (lawful or illegal) and had been sentenced in an occupation court on criminal charges. In these circumstances, the judgment of the occupant's court would be set aside by the returning sovereign, and the individual would be set free, as a patriotic subject. For instance, a Greek court at Thebes ordered in 1951 that the record of conviction by a German military court in Athens be expunged. The reason given for this decision was that the judgment, even though valid when it was pronounced, automatically ceased to be so when the German occupation of Greece terminated.[56]

Normally, the returning legitimate sovereign regards the judgments and decisions of occupation courts as decisions of foreign courts, based on the occupant's power and authority. On occasion, a formal agreement between

---

[55] See De Visscher, "Enemy Legislation and Judgments in Liberated Countries: Belgium," 29 *Jl. of Comp. Legislation and Int. Law* (1947), pts. 3–4, 46–53.

[56] *Case of A.B.*, 6 *Revue Hellénique de Droit International*, 278, cited in 49 *AJIL* 423 (1955).

the occupant and the legitimate sovereign determines the future validity of the occupation courts' decisions. This was the case in the Convention on the Settlement of Matters Arising Out of the War and the Occupation, signed in Bonn on May 26, 1952, and in force on May 5, 1955, among the United States, the United Kingdom, France, and the Federal Republic of Germany. Article 5 (1) and Article 7 (1) of that instrument provide that "all judgments and decisions in criminal and noncriminal matters heretofore or hereafter rendered in Germany by any tribunal or judicial authority of the Three Powers or any of them shall remain final and valid for all purposes under German law, shall be treated as such by German courts and authorities and shall, on the application of a party, be enforced by them in the same manner as judgments and decisions of German Courts and authorities."[57]

DECISIONS OF INDIGENOUS COURTS    Decisions of indigenous courts, handed down during belligerent occupation, are normally kept in force by the returning sovereign unless the judgment can be shown to have been influenced by the occupant's authorities or to violate the laws of war.

DURATION OF APPLICABILITY OF THE CONVENTION    Until recently, there was no guide to the principles applicable in occupied enemy territory after the cessation of hostilities. This regrettable omission led to much confusion as to the status of Germany after its unconditional surrender in May 1945.[58] Article 6 of Geneva-IV has clarified, to some extent, the answer to the original question by asserting that the convention shall apply for one year after the general close of military operations and that certain of its basic provisions (Arts. 1–12, 27, 29–34, 47, 49, 51, 52, 53, 59, 61–77, 143) are to apply for the entire duration of the occupation.

The question of the duration of applicability of the 1907 Regulations has been raised on several occasions, both in the case of the German occupation and of Israel's "administered territories." On January 28, 1952, the chief of the Legal Services Division of the Office of the U.S. High Commissioner for Germany maintained in a letter that the

Hague Regulations were designed to define the powers of a belligerent occupant of enemy territory during, or shortly after, hostilities. As such, they cannot be considered literally applicable to the situation in Germany today. But . . . it has consistently been the position of the legal advisors to OMGUS and HICOG that whenever, in the light of the actual problem and all of the relevant factors, the Hague Regulations may be considered as expressing principles of international law which are pertinent to our situation, those principles should be observed by us.[59]

Technically, the chief of the Division was not quite correct, for nowhere in the Regulations or in the records of the 1907 Hague Peace Conference is there any definite statement as to the short-term or long-term applicability

[57]49 AJIL 73, 75 (1955 Supp.); see also the digests of two German cases hinging on the provisions of Art. 7, par. 1, in 52 AJIL 800 (1958) and 53 AJIL 459 (1959).
[58]See von Glahn, 273–90.
[59]Whiteman, vol. 10, 596, and vol. 1, 326–30.

of the Regulations. For want of such a statement, it must be assumed that the Regulations apply indefinitely, up to the termination of a belligerent occupation. No one in 1907 could have been expected to foresee the long term occupations that materialized after World War I, the Ruhr and the Rhineland, and Germany, after World War II, Japan, a Soviet garrison for years stationed in Finland, and so on. It must be pointed out again that there is no evidence whatsoever that the Regulations were intended to be a body of rules governing only a short-time occupation.

## Postscript

CIVILIAN CONTROL OVER BELLIGERENT OCCUPATION    The main heading of Section III of the Regulations reads: "Military Authority over the Territory of the Hostile State," and in various Articles, such as 51 and 52, reference is made to military officers. Such was consistent with past and subsequent practice: the authorities controlling the rear area behind the fighting front in an armed conflict, areas of the hostile state now under belligerent occupation, were logically enough military authorities. There was, of course, no reason that some other form of administration could not have been created in any given instance, but the military type prevailed down to our own day. When there were deviations, the courts varied in their reactions: a Dutch Special Court of Cassation ruled in 1949 in the case of *In re Rauter* that Germany had violated international law by creating in the Netherlands a civil administration functioning independently from a military commander.[60] On the other hand, the Dutch District Court at The Hague ruled in 1949, in *KNAC* v. *The Netherlands*,[61] that a separate civil administration should be viewed as permissible.

The entire matter might have been forgotten, had not Israel announced on September 22, 1981, a new policy for the administration of the West Bank and the Gaza Strip. The military government was to be phased out and replaced by a civilian governor directly responsible to the Prime Minister of Israel. The governor was to be in charge of all administrative affairs and would have both Arab and Israeli civilians working under him. The Israel Defense Forces (IDF) would be responsible solely for security in the occupied territories. The new governor was Menachem Milson, a professor of Arabic Literature at Hebrew University, an IDF colonel, and a former Arab affairs adviser to the military government.[62] But from the point of view of international law, the administrative reorganization changed nothing: the West Bank and the Gaza Strip continued in the legal condition known as belligerent occupation, subject to the hitherto and currently applicable rules of international law.

[60] Lauterpacht, ed., *Annual Digest and Reports of Public International Law Cases 1949* (1955), 540.
[61] *Id.*, 468.
[62] See *NYT*, Sept. 23, 1981, 8; and *Time*, Oct. 5, 1981, 32–33. In March 1982, Israeli military authorities removed three Palestinian mayors because of their refusal to recognize the Israeli civil administration in the West Bank.

## SUGGESTED READINGS

### Belligerent Occupation: General

Whiteman, vol. 1, 315–19, 325–38, 911–16, 946–96. For a fairly comprehensive listing of the extensive literature available, consult the bibliography of approximately 700 titles in von Glahn, 313–40; Draper, *The Red Cross Conventions* (1958); Kyre & Kyre, *Military Occupation and National Security* (1968).

### Specific Area Occupation

(a) Europe, World War II:
Warmbrunn, *The Dutch Under German Occupation* (1963); Dallin, *German Rule in Russia, 1941–1945: A Study of Occupation Policies* (1957); Whitcomb, ed., *France During the German Occupation, 1940–1944* (3 vols., 1959).

(b) Germany Under Occupation:
Gimpel, *A German Community Under American Occupation* (1961), and his *The American Occupation of Germany: Politics and the Military, 1945–1949* (1968); Willis, *The French in Germany, 1945–1949* (1961); U.S. Army, *The U.S. Army in the Occupation of Germany, 1944–1946* (1975); Backer, *Priming the German Economy: American Occupational Policies, 1945–1948* (1971) and his excellent *The Decision to Divide Germany* (1978); Zink, *The United States in Germany 1944–1955* (1957).

(c) Far East:
Oppler, *Legal Reform in Occupied Japan: A Participant Looks Back* (1976); Donnison, *British Military Administration in the Far East 1943–46* (1957); Baerwald, *The Purge of Japanese Leaders Under the Occupation* (1959); McCune, "The Occupation of Korea," 23 *Foreign Policy Reports* 186 (1947).

(d) Israel—Occupations, General:
Teveth, *The Cursed Blessing: The Story of Israel's Occupation of the West Bank* (1970); Gerson, *Israel, The West Bank and International Law* (1978); Moore, ed., *The Arab–Israeli Conflict* (vol. 2, 1975); State of Israel, Ministry of Defense, *Survey of the Administered Territories 1967–1975* (June 1975), and its *The Administered Territories 1971/1972, The Administered Territories, 1972/1973,* and *The Administered Territories, 1973/1974* (1972, 1973, and 1974, respectively); Mallison & Mallison, *The Palestine Problem in International Law and World Order* (1986); Roberts, "Prolonged Military Occupation: The Israeli-Occupied Territories since 1967," 84 *AJIL* 44 (1990); Israel National Section of the International Commission of Jurists, *The Rule of Law in the Areas Administered by Israel* (1981); Playfair, *Administrative Detention in the Occupied West Bank {Al-Haq}* (1986), Serrill, "In the Eye of a Storm," *Time,* Jan. 25, 1988, 30–34; Schwenk, "Legislative Power of the Military Occupant under Article 43, Hague Regulations," 54 *Yale Law Jl.* 393 (1945); Claggett & Johnson, "May Israel as a Belligerent Occupant Lawfully Exploit Previously Unexploited Oil Reserves of the Gulf of Suez?," 72 *AJIL* 558 (1978); Singer, "The Establishment of the Civil Administration in the Areas Administered by Israel," 11 *Israel Year Book of Human Rights,* 259 (1981); Stephens, *Taxation in the Occupied West Bank 1967–1989* [Al-Haq] (1990); Shehadeh, *The West Bank and the Rule of Law* (1980) and his *Occupier's Law: Israel and the West Bank* (rev. ed. 1988); Hiltermann, *Israel's Deportation Policy in the Occupied West Bank and Gaza* (1986); National Lawyers Guild, *International Human Rights Law and Israel's Efforts to Suppress the Palestinian Uprising* (1988);

Amnesty International, *Israel and the Occupied Territories: Administrative Detention During the Palestinian Intifada* (June 1989); A1-Haq, *Punishing A Nation — Human Rights Violations during the Palestinian Uprising* (American ed. 1988).

United Nations Documents: General Assembly "Resolution on the Uprising of the Palestinian People (Res. 43/21, November 3, 1988), with ILM Background/Content Summary, in 27 *ILM* 1680 (1988); UN Secretary-General, "Report to the Security Council on the Palestinian and Other Arab Territories Occupied by Israel since 1967" (January 21, 1988), *id.*, 1684–97.

(e) Israel — Title to Territory, Resources, Settlements:

United Nations General Assembly, Res. 3175 (XXVIII), December 17, 1973, in 13 *ILM* 241 (1974); panel discussion (Cummings, Clagett, Rogers, Gerson), *Proceedings* 118 (1978); UN General Assembly, Res. 3414 (XXX), December 5, 1975, in 15 *ILM* 182 (1976). On East Jerusalem, see UN Security Council, Res. 298 (1971), Sept. 25, 1971, in 10 *ILM* 1294 (1971); Israel Ministry of Foreign Affairs, *Jerusalem — Issues and Perspectives* (Jerusalem, 1972); Forward et al., "The Arab–Israeli War and International Law," 9 *Harvard Int'l Law Jl.* 232, esp. 255–57 (1968); Kollek, "Jerusalem," 55 *Foreign Affairs* 701–16 (1977). See, in particular, the two controversial reports (July 12 and December 4, 1979) of the Security Council Commission Established to Examine the Situation Relating to Settlements in the Arab Territories Occupied Since 1967 [under Security Council Resolution 446 (1979), March 12, 1979], reproduced, with annexes, in 19 *ILM* 46 (1980). pp. 46–108. The commission, like the Lytton Commission of the League of Nations (Manchuria, 1931–1932), was not permitted by Israel to enter the territories involved in its assignment.

(f) Human Rights in Israeli-occupied Territories: United Nations Documents: ECOSOC Doc. E/CN.4/1016, January 20, 1970, and its Adds. 1–5, February 11–20, 1970; ECOSOC Doc. E/CN.4/SR.1078, March 24, 1970, ECOSOC Res. 1505 (XLVIII), May 27, 1970; and esp. General Assembly Doc. A/8089, October 26, 1970; Commission on Human Rights, Res. 10 (XXVI), March 23, 1970; UN General Assembly Res. 2443 (XXIII), December 19, 1968; and UN Doc. A/7984, June 9, 1970. See also Anderson *et al.*, "Protection of Human Rights in Israeli-occupied Territories," 15 *Harvard Int'l Law Jl.* 470 (1974); Lawyers Committee for Human Rights [New York], *Detention of Human Rights Workers and Lawyers from the West Bank and Gaza* (1988); The Committee to Protect Journalists, *Journalism under Occupation* (Israel's Regulation of the Palestinian Press), Oct. 1988.

CASES

*Fleming & Marshall* v. *Page*, U.S. Supreme Court, 1850, 9 Howard 603.

*State of the Netherlands* v. *Federal Reserve Bank*, U.S. Court of Appeals, Second Cir., 1953, 201 F. (2d) 455.

*État Français* c. *Etablissements Monmousseau*, France, Cour d'Appel d'Orléans, 1948, reported in 43 *AJIL* 819 (1949).

*Haw Pia* v. *China Banking Corporation*, Philippines, Supreme Court, 1948, G.R. No. L.-554, reported in 43 *AJIL* 821 (1949).

*Agati* v. *Soc. Elettrica Coloniale Italiano*, Tripoli, Tribunal of Tripoli, 1950, reported in 49 *AJIL* 261 (1955), (see also six other occupation cases, briefly noted, *id.*, 262).

*Kent Jewelry Co.* v. *Kiefer*, United States, N.Y. Supreme Court, New York Country, 1952, 119 N.Y.S. (2d) 242, excerpted in 47 *AJIL* 503 (1953).

*Anton Schaffner* v. *International Refugee Organization*, U.S. Court of Appeals, Allied High Commission for Germany, 1951, Civil Case No. 11, Opinion No. 665, reported in 46 *AJIL* 575 (1952).

*Madsen* v. *Kinsella*, U.S. District Court, S.D. W.Va., 1950, 93 F. Supp. 319, reported in 45 *AJIL* 375–76 (1951).

*Japanese Government* v. *Commercial Casualty Insurance Co.*, U.S. District Court, S.D.N.Y., 1951, 101 F. Supp. 243, reported in 46 *AJIL* 577 (1952).

*Dwikat et al.* v. *Government of Israel et al.*, Israel, Supreme Court sitting as a High Court of Justice, Oct. 22, 1979, in 19 *ILM* 148 (1980).

# 25

# Laws of War at Sea

## ATTEMPTS TO FORMULATE RULES
## FOR NAVAL WARFARE

The rules governing warfare at sea appear to have survived the passage of two global wars to a far greater extent than have the rules applicable to land warfare, primarily because the character of naval war did not undergo the profound changes that have taken place in land war. To be sure, the battleship became obsolete, and the air forces of belligerents began to play an ever more important part in hostilities. But essentially, war at sea was at least similar in 1945 to the sort of conflict prevailing on the oceans of the world before 1914. At the same time, neutrals exerted far more pressure on belligerents to preserve the rules governing naval war than was the case with the rules governing land warfare, if only because the conflicts on land affected neutrals less directly than did interference with commerce on the high seas. And because many neutrals were not only militarily strong but were of great importance for belligerents from an economic point of view, their voice could be heard clearly in the case of naval warfare and its rules.

It appears today that many of the rules governing naval warfare are somewhat outdated and do not really reflect the reality of modern war at sea. Modernization was postponed deliberately when the 1977 Protocols to the Geneva Convention of 1949 were drafted: the conferees agreed to leave untouched naval warfare as well as the protection of noncombatants and property at sea.

DECLARATION OF PARIS (1856)  The first major international attempt to formulate rules for naval war took place in 1856 as a result of experiences in the earlier Napoleonic conflicts and especially the Crimean War. In 1856, the Allied powers and Russia adopted the famous Declaration of Paris,[1] which laid down four specific rules governing warfare at sea:

1. Privateering was abolished.
2. The neutral flag covered enemy's goods, with the exception of contraband of war.[2]

[1]Lauterpacht's *Oppenheim*, vol. 2, 460–64.
[2]In *The Dirigo*, Great Britain, Privy Council, 1919, 3 B. and C.P.C. 439, this rule was interpreted as representing a concept of general applicability, adopted not only for the benefit of the neutral vessel but also for that of the enemy owner.

3. Neutral goods, with the exception of contraband of war, were not liable to capture under the enemy's flag.
4. A blockade, in order to be binding, had to be effective; that is to say, it had to be maintained by a force sufficient to prevent access to the coast of the enemy.

All maritime states, with the exception of Venezuela and the United States, soon adhered to the declaration. The failure of American adherence was due to the refusal of the other countries to agree to an American proposal to abolish the right to capture any private property at sea. In practice, however, the United States saw fit to abide by the rules of the Declaration of Paris.

1907 HAGUE CONFERENCE    The First Hague Peace Conference of 1899 adopted a convention that extended at last the provisions of the 1864 Geneva instrument to naval war (revised in 1906). The 1907 Hague Conference, however, concentrated on naval questions and succeeded in drawing up several conventions dealing with maritime war: Hague VI, Status of Enemy Merchant Ships at the Outbreak of Hostilities; Hague VII, Conversion of Merchant Ships into War Ships; Hague VIII, Laying of Automatic Submarine Contact Mines; Hague IX, Bombardment by Naval Forces in Time of War; Hague X, Adaptation to Marine Warfare of Principles of the Geneva Convention; Hague XI, Restrictions with Regard to Right of Capture in Naval War; and Hague XIII, Rights and Duties of Neutral Powers in Naval War. Of these, Hague VIII, IX, and XI are perhaps the most important ones regarding this chapter's subject matter. (Hague XIII and several other conventions of 1907 will be discussed in Chapter 26.) The conference failed, however, to develop a code of naval warfare along lines similar to the Hague Regulations concerning land warfare. Hague Convention VII (Convention Relating to the Conversion of Merchant Ships to Warships) was not signed by the United States.

DECLARATION OF LONDON (1909)    The London Naval Conference of 1908 met from December 4, 1908, to February 26, 1909, when the Declaration of London was signed. This instrument "concerning the laws of naval warfare" contained fully seventy articles: blockade in time of war (1–21); contraband of war (22–44); unneutral service (45–47); destruction of neutral prizes (48–54); transfer to a neutral flag (55–56); enemy character (57–60); convoy (61–62); resistance to search (63); compensation (64); and final provisions (65–70). The Declaration was not ratified by Great Britain because the House of Lords refused to back the ratification of the House of Commons.

Significantly, the list of headings of the Declaration, given above, shows again a virtually complete absence of rules governing the behavior of hostile naval forces toward each other. Instead, most of the 70 articles dealt with economic questions and the relations between belligerents and neutrals: again, no naval equivalent of the Hague Regulations on land warfare was drawn up.

## RULES GOVERNING NAVAL WARFARE

Thus, when World War I came, naval warfare *per se* was governed primarily by the actual practices of the major belligerents rather than by a code of naval warfare adopted by international agreement. In fact, after the end of the war, the only phase of actual hostilities at sea "regulated" by treaty was the use of submarines against merchant vessels, by the abortive Treaty of Washington of 1922. The "rules" evolved from such national practices in the course of time may be summarized briefly as follows:[3]

*1. Laws of humanity.* Considerations of humanity are to prevail in naval war as they are in war on land.

*2. "Locale" of war at sea.* The locale normally would include the entire coastal area as well as the territorial sea and the national air of the belligerent states, in addition to the high seas, and the air above them. It may, on occasion, also include the belligerents' overseas colonies.

Any belligerent may choose to exclude certain territories or certain portions of the high seas from the locale of war, provided that strict neutrality is observed for the areas in question. (Crete and Egypt, in the Italo-Turkish War of 1911–1912, are good examples.) Special problems have been posed in this connection by the status of waterways. On occasion, all armed forces and warships of all belligerents were barred from such routes by mutual agreement among the belligerents (so-called negative neutralization), whereas on other occasions all belligerents were free to use such waterways, even for the shipment of troops and the travel of warships, but were forbidden to engage in any military or naval operations in the waterways (so-called positive neutralization).

War at sea is carried out not only in the territorial waters of belligerents but also on the high seas. Because the high seas are, however, free to neutral ships in war as in peace, belligerents have found it necessary to limit this traditional freedom of the seas in the interest of the exercise of belligerent rights connected with blockade and contraband of war, as well as unneutral service by neutrals (see Chapter 26).

One of the modern limitations on the freedom of the seas, the creation of defense zones and war zones, appeared just before the outbreak of the Russo-Japanese War of 1904. The Japanese government authorized its naval authorities to designate certain areas adjacent to the Japanese islands as "defense sea areas," with special restrictions to be imposed on all egress and ingress. Similarly, the United States, on entering World War I in April 1917, established by presidential order so-called defensive sea areas, controlling incoming and outgoing navigation in those areas.

---

[3] For an extended treatment of the subject, consult the excellent study by Tucker, *The Law of War and Neutrality at Sea* (1957). Tucker's volume also contains, in an appendix, the official U.S. Navy Manual, *Law of Naval Warfare*. See Whiteman, vol. 10, 614–18, 644–49, and vol. 11, 1–17, 115–26.

In contrast with those rather modest endeavors, certain European belligerents in World War I created vastly expanded "war zones." As early as November 3, 1914, the British government declared all of the North Sea to be a military area in which exceptional measures were to be taken in reprisal against the indiscriminate laying of mines by Germany. On February 4, 1915, Germany proclaimed all waters around Great Britain, including the English Channel, a war zone in which every ship was subject to destruction, irrespective of its nationality. In contrast with the British action, the German establishment of a war zone left no channels at all for neutral traffic. The German government gradually expanded the extent of its zone until, on January 31, 1917, all waters around Great Britain, France, and Italy, as well as the entire eastern Mediterranean, were included. The British retaliated against each expansion of the German zones by laying additional, duly notified, mine fields.

During World War II, the same conditions occurred again. In November 1939, Germany instituted a "blockade" of Great Britain by means of unmoored and uncharted mines and also announced that the Baltic would be closed to all shipments aiding Germany's enemies directly or indirectly. On November 21 of the same year, Great Britain retaliated ("in reprisal") by announcing that all exports of German origin or ownership would be seized, regardless of destination. This step resulted in a strong protest by the United States, citing the rules of international law as they pertained to neutral freedom to deal in noncontraband items with belligerent states.[4] On August 17, 1940, Germany, in turn, declared a "total blockade" of Great Britain and announced that all shipping, regardless of nationality, would be attacked in certain only vaguely defined "war zones" around the British Isles, extending westward to more than 375 miles beyond the Irish coast.

In the 1982 Falklands War, Great Britain declared a 200-mile "maritime exclusion zone" around the Falklands. A few weeks later this was replaced by a "total exclusion zone" of 200 miles around the islands. Any ships or aircraft found in the zone would be regarded as hostile and would be liable to attack. The next day, Argentina countered with its own war zone: British vessels or aircraft found within 200 miles of the Argentine coast or the Falklands would be considered to be hostile and treated accordingly.

In the Iraq–Iran conflict, Iraq announced in February 1984 an exclusion zone, embracing a 50-mile radius around Iran's Kharg Island oil terminal which lay within Iran's territorial waters. Iraq warned that vessels entering the zone would risk attack by Iraqi aircraft or naval units. A number of ensuing attacks took place, however, outside the 50-mile radius set by Iraq. On June 6, 1984, Iran in turn announced a war zone (also termed a "security zone") within which commercial shipping would be searched and Iraq-bound vessels seized.

[4]*NYT*, Dec. 9–11, 1939, *passim*.

It should be noted that Iran's war zone violated international law because it included the waters of the international Straits of Hormuz.

Like Iraq, so Iran on numerous occasions attacked foreign oil tankers and merchant vessels outside the limits of its zone. It appears that after Iraq had gradually built up new oil export facilities using pipelines in Turkey and Saudi Arabia, Iran was unable to stop those overland exports and retaliated by attacking non-belligerent shipping going to and from the ports of other Gulf states such as Kuwait, all of whom favored Iraq.

Oddly enough, the two antagonists, after seven years of war, were preparing in October 1987 to formally break diplomatic relations! Both approached Turkey with plans for a Turkish assumption of "consular duties" after the embassies, with only token staffs left, were closed.

By December 1987, 412 vessels had been attacked or damaged, according to London-based Lloyd's. More than 300 seamen had been killed. (93 vessels were trapped at Gulf ports, with 75 of them in the Shatt-al-Arab estuary, all unable to leave until the end of the conflict.) In the period to the 1988 cease-fire ending hostilities, numerous additional tankers were sunk or damaged, with heavy loss of life.

Most of the damaged or sunk ships were oil tankers, but others included ordinary merchant vessels, a West German oil field supply ship, as well as a tiny Kuwait supply vessel. The nationality of the ships attacked was totally disregarded by the two antagonists: among those attacked were vessels registered in Liberia, the Bahamas, Panama, Kuwait, South Korea, West Germany, Greece, Cyprus, Switzerland, Great Britain, and Norway. (See also Chapter 14 under "Straits" and Chapter 26 under Neutral Relations with Belligerents.)

It is possible for all or part of a neutral state to be included in a war's locale. This would be true in every instance in which neutral areas represent one of the objects for which the war is waged (Korea in the Russo-Japanese War of 1904–1905) and also when a belligerent attacks and invades a neutral state (Germany versus Denmark and the Netherlands in 1940). Equally, neutral territory is shifted into the locale of a war when a neutral state fails to prevent a belligerent from using its territorial waters or its territory as a base of military operations against an opposing belligerent.

3. *Hostile blockade.* A hostile or wartime blockade has been defined as "the blocking by men-of-war of the approach to the enemy coast, or a part of it, for the purpose of preventing ingress and egress of vessels or air-craft of all nations."[5] Unlike the situation encountered in the instance of a pacific blockade, the hostile version applies to all merchant vessels and to all cargoes, irrespective of character or nationality, that attempt to enter or leave the area declared to be under blockade. Any violators may be captured and their cargoes confiscated. This strict barring of all access is waived, occasionally, only as a matter of comity in the case of neutral warships and

---

[5]Lauterpacht's *Oppenheim*, vol. 2, 768; see also Chapter 19.

on grounds of humanity in the case of neutral merchant vessels in distress[6] or engaged in a strictly philanthropic mission not contrary to the war aims of the blockading state.[7]

The modern concept of a hostile blockade had its origin in the sixteenth century, when, in 1584, the rebelling Dutch provinces declared all ports of Flanders, then still under Spanish control, to be blockaded. Since then, the institution has been developed to a point that it has become a major weapon of a maritime power fighting against a coastal state.

Thus, although the initial application of a blockade was aimed only at fortified towns and ports along an enemy coast, the concept was broadened, and by the time of the Napoleonic wars, the entire coast of an enemy state was declared to be under blockade. The United States viewed this development with disfavor and defended repeatedly, as late as 1859, the total abolition of commercial blockade. This attitude changed drastically, however, with the beginning of the American Civil War, and the Union government promptly and quite successfully blockaded the entire coastline of the Confederacy.

In order to be legal, a hostile blockade must meet certain well-established tests: (1) declaration, that is, notification of the blockading state to all neutrals of the establishment of the blockade and (2) effectiveness of the blockade.

*3a. Declaration of a blockade.* A blockade may be declared only by a belligerent government or its naval authorities on its behalf and under its explicit authority.[8] The declaration must specify the date of the commencement of the blockade, the geographical limits of the blockaded area, and the period of grace normally permitted neutral vessels to come out of the blockaded area. In regard to the third point, no particular period of time has been specified in conventional law. Customarily, 15 days have been permitted during which neutral vessels in ballast or with cargoes bought and loaded before the beginning of a blockade have been allowed to leave unhindered.

*3b. Area of the blockade.* The blockade is limited to the area of operation of the participating warships (and planes). In view of modern methods of naval warfare, involving aerial and surface operations as well as submarines and mines, a blockading squadron or naval force tends to station its components at a considerable distance from a blockaded coast, and so the "area of operations" may assume extensive proportions.

*3c. Disposition of captured neutral vessels.* A neutral vessel seized for an attempted breach of a blockade, either upon ingress or egress, must not

---

[6]Article 7, Declaration of London (1909), under which a vessel permitted to pass through a blockading force under the conditions mentioned could not load or discharge cargo in the blockaded area. See also *The Fortuna*, Great Britain, 1803, 5 C. Rob. 27; and *The Nuestra Señora de Regla*, U.S. Supreme Court, 1872, 17 Wallace 29.

[7]See *The Rose in Bloom*, Great Britain, 1811, 1 Dodson 57.

[8]See *NYT*, August 18, 1940, for the text of the German announcement of the "total blockade" of Great Britain.

be destroyed; instead, it must be taken to the nearest port of the captor state (or of one of its allies where a prize court of the captor state may have been established) in order that there may be a proper trial before a prize court. Conviction on a charge of attempting to breach a blockade results in the vessel's condemnation. The cargo is also condemned if it belongs to the owners of the vessel. If the owners are not the same, the cargo is released only if its owners can prove that at the time of the shipment they did not know, or could not have known, of the vessel's intention to breach the blockade.[9]

In the Iraq–Iran war, few neutral ships were stopped for visit and search: in most cases an attack without warning took place. Furthermore the formality of announcing the establishment of a blockade had been abandoned in favor of announcing the creation of war zones.

*3d. Lawful blockades.* Article 18 of the 1909 Declaration of London specifically prohibited the blockading of neutral ports and coasts. On the other hand, there is no bar to a blockade of some of its own ports or coasts by a belligerent if such areas happen to be under enemy occupation. Although such a situation—that is, enemy occupation of coastal stretches—has occurred frequently, few belligerents have actually established a blockade such as was done by France in 1870 with respect to the ports of Rouen, Dieppe, and Fécamp.

Because of the resulting advantages, it was not all surprising that the major maritime powers quickly combined the doctrine of continuous voyage with the rules governing lawful hostile blockades. To be sure, Article 19 of the Declaration of London specifically prohibited applying the doctrine to a blockade, but World War I saw the end of that provision with the issuance of a number of British Orders-in-Council (1916) ordering the arrest of neutral vessels attempting to breach a blockade and suspected of carrying goods destined to arrive in enemy territory.

During World War I, the United States discussed with Great Britain the application of continuous voyage concepts to blockades and there were some rather strong diplomatic exchanges. But American entrance into the conflict changed the outlook of the United States government, and all hands appeared to agree that modern conditions of warfare made the old, limited concept of blockade inappropriate except in the instances of a few island states, such as Japan or Great Britain. Hence it is generally agreed today that the old "close" blockade is no longer useful in most instances, that long-range blockades are the only really effective ones, and that the doctrine of continuous voyage may be coupled lawfully with the rules governing blockades.

In connection with the Falklands War, Great Britain announced on May 8, 1982, a blockade 12 miles off the Argentine coast. The 200-mile ex-

---

[9]See the relevant English cases of *The Mercurius*, 1798, 1 C. Rob. 80; and *The Panaghia Rhomba*, 1857, 12 Moore P.C. 168; see the typical American case of *The Springbok*, 1866, 5 Wallace 1. Consult also Lauterpacht's *Oppenheim*, vol. 2, 789–90.

clusion zone mentioned earlier and the blockade remained in effect after the Argentine expeditionary forces had surrendered; Great Britain's price for ending those restraints was an Argentine "declaration of peace."

*3e. Paper blockade.* The question of effectiveness must be discussed briefly at this point. Jurists and diplomats agree that a blockade must be effective — that is, must not be a "paper blockade" — if it is to be lawful and binding on neutrals. A valid blockade requires not only naval supremacy on the seas by the blockading state but also the detachment of sufficient forces devoted to maintaining the blockade in order to make the latter effective. [10] But over and beyond the availability of blockading ships and planes, the effectiveness of a blockade is, and must be, a question of fact. Thus only a paper blockade came into being initially when President Abraham Lincoln declared, in 1861, a blockade of 3,000 miles of Confederate coastline when the Union had at its disposal only 42 ships, of which only three could be rated as frigates. Similarly, effectiveness was lacking during the Crimean War when a single allied warship claimed to blockade the Russian port of Riga while stationed 120 miles away from the only navigable channel leading to the port.

*3f. Civil wars and blockades.* Civil wars pose additional problems for the institution of a blockade. The United States and Great Britain have defended for a long time the concept that the *de jure* authorities of a country could not close, by a mere decree, ports under the control of rebels, for this would constitute a paper blockade. If the lawful government had sufficient naval strength at its command so that it could establish an effective blockade, then indeed could the ports in question be considered closed. [11]

Can rebels lawfully bar entrance to the ports and coasts of the *de jure* governments? This, like the previous topic, is the subject of much disagreement among legal experts. Many states refuse to recognize a rebel blockade and, on occasion, have used force to enable their merchant ships to go through such a blockade. Thus, in 1893 and 1894, British and United States warships intervened to prevent the rebel Brazilian naval units in the port of Rio de Janeiro from enforcing a blockade against merchant vessels flying the flags of the intervening powers.

However, most modern writers appear to favor the view that if a rebel force has sufficient naval strength to prevent the egress or ingress of merchant vessels at a given port, they have a right to stop supplies from reaching the *de jure* enemy forces. Even Great Britain has accepted this interpretation when in a given situation, it was clear that the necessary naval strength was present. For example, in Santiago, Chile, in 1891, Great Britain refused a naval convoy for a British ship attempting to breach the rebel blockade.

[10] See the case of *The Olinde Rodrigues*, U.S. Supreme Court, 1899, 174 U.S. 510, on this point.
[11] See Higgins-Colombos, 336–38; consult also Dickinson, "Closure of Ports in Control of Insurgents," 24 *AJIL* 69 (1930).

These considerations form in part the reason that it is so important for a rebel group to receive recognition of a state of belligerency or the status of a belligerent community. Such recognition removes the old suspicion of piracy from rebel vessels, and it justifies the application of most rules governing naval war and neutrality to the civil war at hand.

Recognition as a belligerent community grants to a rebel group the right to visit and search merchant ships on the high seas, to confiscate contraband goods, and to establish valid blockades. Such recognition does not mean, however, that the rebel authorities have been recognized as a successor government or as the government of an independent state.

The naval complications resulting from civil wars have been illustrated by two-well-known examples. The Confederate cruiser *Shenandoah* continued its belligerent operations near Cape Horn for some time after the end of the American Civil War. Obviously, under normal conditions, such behavior would constitute a clear case of piracy. When the *Shenandoah* was seized by British authorities, it developed that her officers and crew were ignorant of the capitulation of the Confederacy. The English authorities, properly, released the officers and crew, clearing them of all charges of piracy, and turned the vessel over to the United States.

During the Spanish Civil War, the attacks made by Italian and German submarines on neutral merchant vessels had led to a very confused situation. Finally, a Conference of the Mediterranean Powers was held at Nyon on September 14, 1937, resulting in an "arrangement" signed by Belgium, Egypt, France, Great Britain, Greece, Rumania, the Soviet Union, Turkey, and Yugoslavia. Italy subsequently indicated its willingness to abide by this pact. The instrument authorized the warships of the signatories, engaged on nonintervention patrol duty, to counterattack and, if need be, destroy any submarine found attacking a merchant vessel not belonging to either party in the Spanish Civil War. The patrol ships were also authorized to adopt the same course of action toward any submarine encountered so close to the scene of an earlier attack that no doubt of its guilt could be reasonably entertained. A supplementary agreement, signed by the same states on September 17, 1937, expanded the scope of the original instrument so as to make its rules applicable to surface vessels as well as to aircraft.

*4. Attack and seizure of vessels (enemy character).* The attack and seizure of enemy vessels is the most profitable tactic employed by a belligerent navy, for a belligerent seizes not only enemy individuals but also enemy goods, public and private.

This principle raises the issue of enemy character as it is defined in war at sea. None of the early statements of rules (Declaration of Paris, Declaration of London) provided any clue as to what constituted an enemy. British prize courts have long followed the interpretation that domicile determines enemy character. An individual, whether of neutral or enemy nationality, residing in territory under enemy control is regarded as possessing enemy character.

Goods owned by him are therefore enemy goods, in regard to the courts. [12] Domicile, in this connection, refers not only to the personal residence of an individual but also to the place where the latter's business is located. Thus, if countries A and B are at war and all others are neutral, a citizen and resident of C who conducts a business venture in country B would be viewed by the courts of A as possessing enemy character.

Similarly, because territory under enemy occupation is regarded as enemy territory, property belonging to persons or corporations residing in occupied areas is viewed as possessing enemy character. Thus, during World War I, British prize courts correctly treated German-occupied Belgium as enemy territory for the duration of the occupation. During the same war, Egyptian ports were treated as enemy ports by Austrian and German vessels, because Great Britain at the time was a military occupant of Egypt.

During World War II, the same practice was adopted by the states opposing the Axis powers. Thus, on July 30, 1940, Great Britain announced that all of France, as well as Algeria, Tunisia, and French Morocco, was to be treated, for purposes of contraband and enemy export controls, as enemy-controlled territory. Earlier, the German occupation of hitherto neutral Denmark on April 10, 1940, changed the status of Danish citizens and ships, in the British view, to that of enemies. Logically enough, however, the enemy occupation must be an effective one. Mere temporary presence of an enemy in a given territory in the course of military operations, without the incidental creation of an effective belligerent occupation, is not sufficient to endow the territory with enemy character.

The enemy character of goods normally continues to be in effect as long as their owner is domiciled in enemy territory and the goods are in transit. If, however, ownership of the goods is transferred during their voyage from an enemy owner to the neutral owner, the goods lose their enemy character. [13]

In regard to the nationality of a vessel, it will be recalled that the customary rule of law holds that the flag the vessel is authorized to display determines the ship's nationality. Hence enemy ownership does not create enemy character for a vessel registered in and carrying the proper papers of a neutral state. On the other hand, neutral ownership does not offset the enemy character created for a vessel properly displaying an enemy flag.

Private individuals cannot lawfully capture a vessel or its cargo as prize, unless they have received the appropriate authorization or ratification from some government. The issue did, however, come up on at least one occasion in a memorably styled case during World War II, in *Y. S. Ling et al.* v. *1,689 Tons of Coal Lying Aboard SS Wilhelmina.* [14]

---

[12] See *Part Cargo ex M. V. Glenroy*, Great Britain, Privy Council, 1945, 61 Times L.R. 303, reported in 39 *AJIL* 599 (1945).

[13] On this rather disputed point, see Higgins-Colombos, 437–38; for the American interpretation cited, see *The Circassian*, U.S. Supreme Court, 1864, 2 Wallace 135.

[14] U.S. Dist. Court, W.D. of Washington, October 7, 1942, 78 F. Supp. 57, digested in 42 *AJIL* 940 (1948).

*5. Enemy warships.* All enemy warships and all other enemy public vessels met on the high seas or in the territorial waters of either belligerent may be attacked at once.

*6. Enemy merchant ships.* Enemy merchant ships may be attacked lawfully only if they refuse to submit to visit and search after they have been requested to do so. (Both world wars witnessed countless violations of this rule.) Naturally such merchant vessels may refuse to honor the request and may choose to defend themselves. A merchant vessel of a belligerent attacking a public or private vessel of an opposing belligerent by taking the initiative would be regarded as a pirate, and its crew would be considered war criminals. Once an attack has been launched against it, however, a belligerent merchant vessel may pursue its attacker and even seize it, if this can be done.

*7. Submarines.* On the other hand, if a merchant vessel expects an attack without warning by a "lawless" enemy, it does not have to wait to be attacked before it itself resorts to the commission of hostile acts. This rule would apply, for instance, in the case of an enemy whose submarines had received instructions to attack merchant vessels of opposing belligerents without warning. Application of the rule raises the whole issue of submarine warfare, a subject about which an extensive literature has been written. Briefly, the problem posed has been this: A submarine by its construction is a rather fragile craft. If its commander abides by the rules applicable to normal warships and surfaces, signaling to an enemy merchant vessel to stop for visit and search, he exposes his ship and crew to the danger of attack, not only by the merchant vessel, by ramming or the use of "defensive" equipment such as artillery, but also by enemy aircraft, to which a surfaced submarine is a tempting and virtually defenseless target. Because the safety of his ship and crew is the commander's primary responsibility, he will most likely solve his predicament by ignoring the conventional rules and sinking the merchant vessel, without warning, by means of a torpedo. By so doing, he commits, technically, a war crime.

A submarine could abide by the traditional rules governing encounters with enemy merchantmen, including visit and search, as long as those vessels were not armed and had not been instructed to ram submarines on sight and as long as extended flights from shore or from carriers were not practicable. As soon as any of these three factors made its appearance, the submarine must abandon adherence to customary procedures.[15]

Lauterpacht was legally correct when he asserted that "the novelty of a weapon does not by itself carry with it a legitimate claim to a change in the existing rules of war." But he became naive, from a practical point of view, when after admitting that international law must adapt to the

[15] See Lauterpacht's *Oppenheim*, vol. 2, 468–71, and Higgins-Colombos, 384–88, for brief accounts of the measures adopted by the different belligerents during World War I in connection with submarine warfare; Mallison, *Studies in the Law of Naval Warfare: Submarines in General and Limited Wars* (1968); consult Whiteman, vol. 10, 650–66.

changes required by the appearance of new weapons, he outlined how the rules might be changed to accommodate the peculiar problems connected with submarines. [16] To propose seriously that in exchange for an abandonment of the arming of merchant vessels, submarines should be prohibited by treaty either from striking merchant vessels altogether or from sinking them anywhere except in certain areas close to shore was totally unrealistic. History has shown that almost every new weapon (the battle elephant, "Greek Fire," the longbow, the crossbow, the siege gun, the rifle, the balloon, the airplane, the dirigible, the submarine, and now nuclear weapons and ballistic missiles) has been initially greeted with outraged denunciation. If, however, the weapon proved effective and its users were able to defend themselves successfully against its retaliatory use, the use of the weapon was regarded, sooner or later, as lawful.

The best-known incident using a submarine against an enemy merchant vessel was the sinking of the British liner *Lusitania*.

On May 1, 1915, the *Lusitania* sailed from New York for Liverpool, with 1,257 passengers and a crew of 702 aboard. On May 7, 1915, the vessel was torpedoed by a German submarine off the coast of Ireland and sank in 18 minutes, with a loss of 1,198 lives. Contrary to German allegations, the British owners asserted that the *Lusitania* was not and had never been armed and had not carried any explosives aboard. It did carry 18 fuse cases and 125 shrapnel cases (empty shells, without powder charges), 4,200 cases of safety cartridges, and 189 cases of infantry equipment, such as leather fittings and pouches. [17] The question of whether the ship was armed has never been settled, but the vessel was designed to carry guns. The question of whether explosives or munitions other than those mentioned were aboard has remained a subject of continuing debate. In 1962 a team of divers descended to the wreck, and the pictures they took were shown in May of that year on television by the British Broadcasting Company. The leader of the team, an American (John Light), believed that the wreck had been tampered with since its loss in 1915. A section of steel deck appeared to have been cut away with torches, and a mooring wire was found to be roughly shackled into the flying bridge of the ship. An earlier private expedition to the wreck, in 1935, had not used such mooring wire. Also, holes and bent steel doors on the vessel appeared to indicate an explosion on the side away from the strike of the German torpedo. One of the survivors of the sinking remembered having heard three explosions, whereas only one torpedo had been fired at

---

[16] Lauterpacht's *Oppenheim*, vol. 2, 469–70.

[17] See *The Lusitania* (Petition of Cunard S.S. Co., Ltd.), United States District Court, S.D. of New York, 1918, 251 F. 715; Bailey, "The Sinking of the *Lusitania*," 41 *American Historical Review* 54 (1935). Consult *The Lusitania Cases*, U.S.-German Mixed Claims Commission, 1923, in 18 *AJIL* 361 (1924); the relevant collection of documents on the sinking in 2 *Current History* 613 (1915); "Lusitania," *Life*, Oct. 13, 1972, 58–80 *passim*; and Simpson, *The Lusitania* (1973), a valuable but flawed account. The 1982 expedition was reported on September 2, 1982, on the American television program "20/20."

the liner from the German submarine. The log of the submarine stated that the detonation of the torpedo had been followed by a heavier, internal explosion. In the summer of 1982, another investigation of the wreck was made by divers and with the help of a small unmanned submarine plus sonar. The divers reported that the vessel's forward area had been loaded with explosives and that the bow had been ripped out by an explosion. The divers claimed that someone had opened the hull to remove any evidence of explosives within the ship. That was denied by the British Ministry of Defense, which at one point attempted to stop further investigation because of "possible danger from explosives."

The London Naval Conference of 1930 resulted in a treaty signed by France, Great Britain, Italy, Japan, and the United States, which laid down, in Article 22, what were termed the "established rules of international law" governing submarines. These included, unrealistically, the renewed assertion that the same principles applied to submarines as applied to surface craft and the prohibition on the sinking of merchant vessels except if the latter refused to stop when ordered to do so or actively resisted visit and search.

Article 22 was to be in effect without a time limit. Therefore when the treaty of 1930 expired on December 31, 1936, Article 22 still remained valid and bound its signatories. In order to give this set of rules wider applicability, the original signatory states signed on November 6, 1936, the London Protocol, embodying verbatim the provisions of Article 22 relating to submarines.[18] The protocol included a provision for the adherence of additional states. Such adherence also to be without time limit, and by the outbreak of World War II, 48 states, including the Soviet Union and Germany, had formally indicated their adherence to the protocol.

By the time World War II began, there thus existed what Corbett termed a broad consensus,[19] condemning as in violation of international law the destruction of merchant vessels by submarines when such acts were not accompanied by the adequate protection of passengers as well as crews.

Yet World War II witnessed a repetition of the practices of 1914–1918, with an early resumption of submarines' sinking enemy vessels on sight. About ten hours after the official start of the war, a German U-boat torpedoed the British passenger liner *Athenia*; of the 1,400 passengers, 112 died, including 28 American citizens. The attack came while the German submarines were still operating in accordance with international law and agreements that prohibited attacks without warning on enemy merchant and passenger vessels, but the submarine commander ignored them. As before, retaliatory measures were promptly adopted by the opposing belligerents, particularly when it became apparent that no regard was being paid to the safety of the passengers and crews. In the Pacific area, in particular, both United States and British submarines began unrestricted campaigns

---

[18]See 31 *AJIL* 137 (1937 Supp.).
[19]Corbett, 224.

against Japanese merchant vessels. Unlike conditions in the Atlantic region, the operations in the Pacific led to a factual suspension of the Protocol of 1936.[20]

Enemy merchant vessels sailing in a convoy of warships or military aircraft may be attacked without warning, and this practice is lawful today.

Self-defense has now become the justification for the abandonment by submarines of the traditional rules still governing surface vessels. This new point of view was emphasized in the Opinion and Judgment of the International Military Tribunal at Nuremberg in the trial of Admiral Karl Doenitz (1947), in which he was absolved from guilt for his conduct of submarine warfare against British armed merchant ships. On the other hand, the German proclamation of operation zones and the sinking without warning of neutral vessels entering those zones were held to have constituted violations of the Protocol of 1936, and Admiral Doenitz was adjudged guilty of war crimes in this connection.[21]

An interesting item in the curiosity cabinet of history was the *Deutschland*, an unarmed commercial submarine used by Germany in 1916–1917. In an attempt to ease strains created by the Allied blockade, construction of a fleet of specially designed cargo submarines was begun in 1915–1916. Only one of these, the *Deutschland*, saw merchantman service on two voyages across the Atlantic. German agents purchased quantities of desperately needed Canadian nickel and shipped it to the neutral United States. There the submarine, bringing aniline dyestuffs to the United States, loaded the nickel for shipment to Germany. These trading voyages, which attracted much attention, ended when Germany resumed unrestricted submarine warfare and when the United States entered the war. The *Deutschland* and the then-unfinished boats of her class were converted into military submarines (*Deutschland* became the U-155) and went into naval service. U-155 survived the war, was towed to England, and became a tourist attraction in several ports before being scrapped.[22]

*8. Salvage Rules (Naval Vessels).* The salvage of sunken naval vessels does not pose difficult questions of law, despite contrary stories in the press. The rules are laid down quite unambiguously in the Salvage Convention (Brussels) of 1910. That instrument, which covers all kinds of wrecks, has been implemented in the United States by the Salvage Act of 1912. The central concept is that of public (state) property. It is part of the conventional law that state property remains the property of the owner unless expressly abandoned or captured by an enemy in time of war.

Hence when the U.S. Central Intelligence Agency (CIA) attempted to raise in early 1975 a sunken Soviet submarine in the Pacific, with its

---

[20]To illustrate: on Feb. 2, 1946, the U.S. Navy announced that it had sunk, through submarines, 1,944 major Japanese merchant vessels during the Pacific campaigns, with a loss of 276,000 crewmen: *NYT*, Feb. 3, 1946, 20.

[21]See relevant portions of the Judgment in Bishop, 810–12.

[22]Bessimer, *The Merchant U-Boat, Adventures of the Deutschland 1916–1918* (1988).

equipment and the bodies of the crew, it acted in violation of a law-making treaty: the Soviet Union had given no indication of abandonment of its title. Rubin, on the other hand, suggested quite untenably that relations between the United States and the Soviet Union were, in some respects, more like relations between belligerents (that is, an "intermediacy" state) and thus permitted the CIA's action.[23] The intermediacy concept has not, however, become a part of accepted international law, despite its advocacy by several renowned jurists.

During the battle of the China Sea (Russo-Japanese War, 1905), the Russian navy lost 20 of its 38 warships participating in the battle. One of these was the 8,524-ton cruiser *Admiral Nakhimov*, carrying a fortune in platinum and gold, estimated today at a value of between $1.4 and $4.5 billion. A private Japanese salvage expedition found the vessel in 1980, in 314 feet of water off Tsushima Island, in Japanese territorial waters. In September began the recovery of a substantial number of 22-pound ingots. The Soviet Union immediately filed a claim for all treasure found aboard the ship. Unlike merchant vessels, abandoned warships continue to belong to the government whose flag they flew. The Japanese Foreign Office, however, denied the Soviet assertion of a claim, holding that any treasure found belonged to neither the Soviet Union nor Japan.

The correctness of the Russian claim was shown, however, with the salvage of 5.5 tons of gold from the sunken British cruiser HMS *Edinburgh* in 1981. The *Edinburgh* was carrying the gold (payment by the Soviet Union to the United States for military supplies) from the Russian port of Murmansk (May 1942) when it was torpedoed by a German submarine and eventually sunk by a British destroyer in order to prevent German capture of the cruiser and its cargo. After several failed attempts, a private British salvage expedition found (in 1981) the *Edinburgh* and its cargo 800 feet below the surface of the Barents Sea. The total value of the salvaged gold was approximately $85 million. Under a tripartite agreement among the United Kingdom, the Soviet Union, and the salvagers, the latter received 45 percent of the salvaged gold, the Soviet Union about $30 million, and the British government the rest—a formula based on the amount of gold insured originally by the two governments. The United States had already been reimbursed by the Soviet Union for the military supplies.

*9. Status of armed merchant vessels relating to submarines.* Another aspect of submarine warfare, neglected by many modern commentators, pertains to the status of armed merchant vessels. During World War I, bitter disputes arose repeatedly between the opposing parties as to the legality of sinking, without warning, merchant ships armed for "defensive purposes only." It is somewhat difficult to see how a valid and precise differentiation can be made between "offensive" and "defensive" armament, particularly when

[23] Rubin, "Sunken Soviet Submarines and Central Intelligence; Laws of Property and the Agency," 69 *AJIL* 855 esp. 855 n. 3, (1975), for classic court decisions on the subject.

the enemy is in the vulnerable category of a submarine. Under international law, an armed enemy vessel may be sunk without warning if it carries offensive armament. The United States government, to cite a classic example, proposed to the Allied government on January 18, 1916, that all merchant vessels under belligerent flags should be prohibited from carrying any armament because "any armament . . . on a merchant vessel would seem to have the character of an offensive armament." Although the United States abandoned this position completely in March 1918 and accepted the British assertion that "defensively" armed merchant vessels were not war vessels and therefore should be immune from attack without warning, as well as from internment in neutral ports, the earlier position of the United States appears to have possessed much merit.[24] No change in this situation is foreseen for future conflicts. As long as both submarines and aircraft attack merchant vessels without warning, the latter are entitled, to use Lauterpacht's phrase, to employ "all modes of attack by way of defense."[25]

On the other hand, it must also be recognized that one of the traditional assumptions on which the older rules were based appears to be no longer applicable in modern war: the assumption that a clear distinction could be drawn between the naval forces of a belligerent and enemy merchant ships. Under modern conditions of warfare, merchant ships and their activities have tended increasingly to be integrated into the overall war effort, especially that part of it that takes place on the seas. The old rules must be held to apply today, to submarines as well as to merchant vessels, provided the latter are not incorporated into the military effort at sea. As soon as this condition fails to obtain—and increasingly this appears to be the case in modern war— a merchant vessel falls into a category permitting it to be attacked without warning, just as would be true if it tried to attack a submarine before the submarine had made any effort to halt and search the vessel.

The International War Crimes Tribunal at Nuremberg, in the *Doenitz Trial*, accepted as lawful unrestricted German submarine warfare in World War II, on the grounds that the British merchant marine had become an adjunct to, or an auxiliary of, the Royal Navy and hence, by assimilation, could be treated as if the vessels in question were in fact enemy public (war) ships.[26]

*10. Mines.* The Russo-Japanese War of 1904–1905 produced the first modern instance of the widespread utilization of mines. The resulting extensive damage to or loss of neutral ships quickly brought the realization that some form of regulation of this weapon was desirable. In consequence, Convention VIII Relative to the Laying of Automatic Submarine Contact Mines was adopted at The Hague in 1907. This instrument prohibited a

---

[24]See Higgins-Colombos, 397–403, for the background history of armed merchant vessels; Whiteman, vol. 10, 656–57, 670–76.

[25]Lauterpacht's *Oppenheim*, vol. 2, 471.

[26]See Whiteman, vol. 10, 665, as well as the letters by Evans and McDiarmid in 69 *AJIL* 859 (1975).

belligerent from laying unanchored automatic contact mines unless they embodied a mechanical feature rendering them harmless an hour after control over the mines was lost by those laying them. It also prohibited the laying of anchored automatic contact mines that would not be rendered harmless as soon as they broke from their anchoring devices. Article 2 of the convention forbade the laying of automatic contact mines off the ports and coasts of an enemy for the sole purpose of stopping commercial navigation—a rather unrealistic conception, because no one could assert conclusively that such mines had other than permitted objectives. Other provisions of the agreement covered such topics as belligerents' notification of danger zones to all governments and shipowners.

The widespread use of mines as well as new types of mines rendered much of the convention obsolete. It was mostly disregarded during both World Wars. During the first conflict, aircraft began to be used to deposit mines far off the shores of an enemy. During World War II, new forms of mines (acoustic and magnetic) appeared, capable of exploding after being drawn to the hull of a vessel. When that war had ended, a massive joint effort between Allied naval and German civilian vessels had to be organized to destroy almost all remaining mines.

On May 8, 1972, President Nixon announced that the entrances to North Vietnamese ports were being mined by U.S. forces with the intention of shutting off the flow of war supplies to North Vietnam. By deliberate intent, the U.S. action was not termed a blockade and, in order not to violate the 1907 Hague Convention, was stated to be motivated by a desire to prevent "North Vietnamese naval operations."[27]

The Iraq–Iran conflict brought about comparatively large-scale mining of the Persian Gulf, most by Iran. The latter, unable to stop Iraq's overland pipeline exports of oil, struck out in retaliation against foreign neutral vessels in the Gulf. This was done by clandestinely mining the major shipping lanes involved. Iran finally admitted its actions, asserting that it had sowed mines "to defend our coastlines" against the foreign warships protecting commercial shipping in the Gulf.

In time an international protection and minesweeping fleet of 32 ships operated in the Gulf, with one Belgian, three British, three French, two Italian and two Dutch mine sweepers, plus support ships, backed by 13 warships ranging from an aircraft carrier to small frigates. In addition, the United States maintained a 27-ship naval force in the Gulf. After hostilities ended with a UN-mediated cease-fire on August 20, 1988, the Iranian Navy joined the mine-clearing operations. By the end of the hostilities, 166 mines had been discovered in the Gulf since July 1987 when the United States assumed protective duties, and more than 200 mines were believed to be be left in the Gulf.

[27] See 66 *Dept. of State Bulletin* 750 (1972); *U.S. News & World Report*, May 22, 1972, 15–18, 21–22; *NYT*, May 8, July 7, 1972, *passim.*; and *Time*, May 22, 1972, 58.

The rules of international law applicable today to the use of mines in naval warfare are clear. Merchant ships generally are entitled to freedom of navigation, and a state has a right to protect and defend all vessels flying its flag lawfully. Belligerent governments have the right in time of armed conflict to use naval mines against other belligerents but may not endanger neutral shipping by the laying of mines. Commercial shipping and other vessels of neutrals must be warned of the location of mines.

Iran therefore violated the rules of international law when it secretly laid mines in international shipping channels with the specific intention of injuring neutral vessels, and without subsequent warnings.[28]

*11. Enemy ships immune from attack.*[29] Certain enemy vessels are immune from attack, under customary or conventional law. This category includes ships engaged in scientific exploration and research, under both customary law and Article 4 of Hague Convention XI of 1907, which expanded the category to include vessels with a religious, scientific, or philanthropic mission. Naturally, as soon as such a ship abandons its normal functions and either engages in hostilities or serves an enemy's commercial interests, its immunity comes to an end.

Small boats and fishing vessels engaged in local or coastal traffic were exempted from attack and seizure by one of the oldest rules of customary law and also, later, under Article 3 of Convention XI.[30] Germany was the first country to disregard this tradition during World War I, when a number of British coastal fishing vessels were sunk, and this practice was repeated during World War II, expanded, moreover, through the use of aircraft to bomb coastal vessels. At the same time, the Allies, on discovering that numerous Japanese fishing vessels were acting as observers and reporters for the Japanese navy, proceeded to sink them. Large vessels engaged in coastal trade and vessels devoted to deep-sea fishing have not been exempted from enemy attack by either customary or conventional international law.

Hospital ships enjoy immunity from attack under conventional law: Convention (X) for the Adaptation to Maritime Warfare of the Principles of the Geneva Convention (The Hague, 1907). During World War I, a number of Allied hospital ships were sunk on sight by German submarines, a practice repeated during World War II. Those sinkings were clearly illegal, particularly so because all vessels in question were clearly marked and identified in accordance with the requirements of the 1899 and 1907 Hague conventions; in addition, the Allies (in both wars) had communicated the names of all such hospital ships to the opposing side.

The Geneva Convention of 1949 for the Amelioration of the Condition of Wounded, Sick, and Shipwrecked Members of Armed Forces at Sea,

---

[28]Adapted from a letter by the Legal Adviser, U.S. Dept. of State, *CSM*, Nov. 13, 1987, 15. On mine warfare in general, see Whiteman, vol. 10, 676–81, and Levie, "Mine Warfare and International Law," 24 *Naval College Rev.* 27 (April 1972).

[29]Consult Whiteman, vol. 10, 624–43.

[30]See *The Paquete Habana; The Lola*, Chapter 3; consult also Higgins-Colombos, 417–19.

which greatly enlarged the earlier Hague Convention X of 1907, provided in Articles 22, 24, and 33 for the immunity of hospital ships of various categories from attack and seizure.[31] (See also PR-I of 1977, Arts. 22–23.)

In February 1966, through neutral diplomatic channels, the U.S. government requested the government of North Vietnam to respect the immunity of an American hospital ship operating in Vietnamese waters. No reply appears to have been received, because North Vietnam had consistently refused to recognize the applicability of Geneva conventions to the conflict on the grounds that no state of war had been declared.[32] Article 2 of the relevant 1949 agreement, however, specifies its applicability to both declared and undeclared wars.

*12. Mail ships.* Mail ships enjoy no general immunity from attack under either customary or conventional law, but a number of states have agreed on their immunity by means of special bilateral agreements. Mailbags, on the other hand, are exempted from enemy capture by Article 1 of Hague Convention XI (1907), provided the mail in question is not on its way to or from a blockaded port. It should be noted, too, that the immunity in question extends only to postal correspondence and not to parcel post. The latter is subject to confiscation when it contains contraband items, and correspondence is now regarded as subject to censorship even when found on neutral ships entering belligerent waters. Neutral protests against such censorship had no effect during either world war.[33]

*13. Position of enemy combatants.*[34] The position of enemy individuals in warfare at sea is analogous to that of enemy combatants on land. Under customary law, only those may be killed or wounded who resist capture. Sick and wounded men or those who surrender must be granted quarter. The 1949 Geneva Convention (II) amplified the older rules governing the treatment of wounded and sick enemy combatants, based on lessons learned from the naval phases of World War II.[35]

The practice has been, since 1914, to intern the officers and crews (enemy nationals) of captured enemy merchant vessels. If, however, an enemy merchant vessel resists arrest or defends itself against capture, the ship may be sunk, and the officers and crew, when taken, are treated as prisoners of war. As such, they are protected by the Geneva Convention of 1949 as soon as they are landed by their captors. As long as they are still aboard the capturing vessel, they are protected, though less adequately, by the principle of customary law that asserts that prisoners must be treated humanely.

[31]See Lauterpacht's *Oppenheim*, vol. 2, 479–80, esp. 502–5, including the valuable notes relating to incidents during World War II.
[32]*NYT*, Feb. 13, 1966, 4.
[33]Higgins-Colombos, 478–84; see also Whiteman, vol. 10, 769–78.
[34]See *Id.*, vol. 10, 618–24, 649.
[35]The text of Geneva-II is printed in U.S. Department of State Publication No. 3938 (August 1950); see also Yingling and Ginnane, "The Geneva Conventions of 1949," 46 *AJIL* 393 (1952).

*14. Enemy private citizens.* Enemy private citizens found aboard an attacked or captured enemy vessel may not be directly attacked or wounded if they are not members of the crew of the vessel or the enemy's armed forces—provided they do not take part in the fighting. Under certain conditions, such individuals may be made prisoners of war, say, if they are enemy officials of importance, such as heads of state or members of a cabinet.

*15. Position of neutral "combatants."* If a neutral merchant vessel resists a belligerent attempt to visit and search—that is, if the vessel resists arrest or seeks to escape (even though otherwise innocent)—its officers and crew become liable to detention as prisoners of war because of the ship's illegal conduct which gives it combatant or belligerent status. The vessel itself is subject to capture and condemnation by a prize court.

*16. Ruses.* Ruses are permitted in warfare at sea, to the extent that they are allowed on land. Thus, in World War I, the German cruiser *Emden*, easily recognizable by Allied warships at a great distance because of the smaller number of its smokestacks, was within its rights when it employed a canvas contraption resembling an additional stack, which was hoisted on occasion to create the impression that the *Emden* was a French or a British cruiser. The use of a neutral and even of an enemy flag by a belligerent warship has been endorsed as lawful by most writers whenever the ship in question is engaged in chasing an enemy ship, when trying to escape, or when attempting to lure an enemy vessel into action. On the other hand, it is universally agreed that immediately before an actual attack, the ship must display its own national ensign. Merchant vessels may use false colors at all times, although this ruse has given rise on many occasions to protests by neutrals whose flag has been used by merchant vessels registered to belligerent states.

*17. Naval bombardment.* The question of naval bombardment has been a highly controversial facet of warfare at sea. Under Article 3 of Hague Convention IX (1907), a naval force may bombard an undefended enemy community if the local authorities refuse to deliver requested provisions or supplies for the immediate use of that naval force. The requisitions must be proportionate to the community's resources; they must be requisitioned by the commander of the naval force; and they are to be paid for in cash, or if sufficient money is lacking, a receipt must be issued to the supplying authorities.

Defended enemy coasts may be lawfully bombarded by naval forces, acting either on their own or in support of a besieging or landing force. Until 1907, however, no generally accepted answer had been found to the question of whether the enemy's undefended coastal places could be lawfully bombarded. Hague Convention IX finally provided the rules applicable to this problem. Under Article I of that instrument, the bombardment of undefended ports, subject to the exception in the previous paragraph, is unconditionally prohibited. However, military works, depots of war materials or munitions, plants and other facilities usable for the enemy military forces, and warships in ports all may be lawfully bombarded, even when these targets are located in undefended localities.

A naval commander is supposed to give advance warning of such a bombardment to the local authorities to enable them to destroy the target facilities in question and thus to spare their community the damage incidental to a lawful naval bombardment. During a naval bombardment, all efforts are to be made to spare buildings devoted to public worship, art, science, and charitable purposes, as well as historical monuments and hospitals and other facilities for the sick and wounded. In order to enable the protection of these places, they are to be clearly indicated by visible signs (large rectangular panels, divided diagonally into two triangular portions, the upper one black, the lower one white) (Art. 5). It should be noted that from a practical point of view, these particular provisions are meaningless in most instances.

The convention was *technically inoperative* during World War I, because not all of the belligerents were parties to the instrument. During World War II, the convention was *ignored* in the practices of virtually all the belligerent naval powers, and naval bombardments did not discriminate.

*18. Armistice.* An armistice temporarily suspends hostilities, and it might be thought that such suspension would, logically, also apply to belligerent seizures on the high seas. Such an interpretation was, in fact, specifically included in a number of armistice instruments during the nineteenth century (The Franco-German armistice of January 28, 1871; the Sino-Japanese armistice of March 30, 1895; and the Greco-Turkish armistice of June 4, 1897). A complete reversal was recorded, however, in World War I. Article 5 of the naval section of the Allied Armistice Convention with Austria-Hungary (November 3, 1918) and Article 26 of the Armistice Convention with Germany (November 11, 1918) both specified that seizures of enemy ships and cargoes encountered on the high seas would continue until peace had been concluded. Consequently the Allied navies made many such seizures, and both ships and cargoes continued to be condemned by Allied prize courts.

Similarly, goods destined for Germany and seized after the 1918 Armistice became effective were condemned on the grounds of intention to serve hostile purposes. British Prize courts pointed out, correctly, that under the terms of Article 26, such procedures were lawful and also emphasized that technically, an armistice does not preclude an eventual resumption of hostilities.

Prize courts do not cease to operate even at the termination of a war. Their competence normally ends only when they have disposed of all matters and issues falling within their jurisdiction and arising during the conduct of hostilities. This explains why Allied prize courts continued to sit for many years after the end of World War I and were able to condemn ships and cargoes seized before the termination of that war. In fact, the last prize case arising out of the conflict was not decided until 1934![36]

19. *Submarine cables.* Some comment appears desirable on the subject of submarine cables in time of war. Part of the traditional principle of the freedom of the high seas is the undoubted right of states to lay submarine cables for telegraphic, and lately telephonic, communications with other states. Cables frequently are encountered where the depth of the ocean is not very great, and hence they are quite vulnerable to unintentional or intentional damage.

The only regulation applicable to cables known to this writer is Article 54 of the Regulations on Land Warfare (Fourth Hague Convention of 1907, Annex), which provides that

submarine cables connecting an occupied territory with a neutral territory shall not be seized or destroyed except in case of absolute necessity; they must also be restored and the indemnities for them regulated at the peace.

This regulation represents merely a minor limitation on the freedom of action of any belligerent, because the Regulations apply only to that portion of any cable found in the territorial waters and on the adjacent land surface of an enemy state, and then only to the extent that the coastal stretch is occupied by an opposing party in the war.

Belligerents, therefore, have felt free to interrupt cable communications as they saw fit. Chile cut a British cable between its territory and Peru in its war against Peru in 1883 but did pay full compensation to the owners. The United States, during the Spanish-American war in 1898, cut the cables connecting Cuba, Puerto Rico, and Manila with the rest of the world, even though the installations all were British property, that is, neutral. The severing of the Manila–Hong Kong cable interfered so greatly with commerce in Southeast Asian waters that violent protests regarding the action ensued. When the United States refused to pay compensation to the owners of British cables, claims were eventually brought before the American-British Claims Arbitration Tribunal in 1923.[37] The tribunal held that the United States was under no obligation to pay compensation, asserting that every belligerent had a legal right to deprive its enemy of communication over the high seas while preserving communication unimpeded for itself. The cutting of cables was not prohibited to a belligerent by any rule of law nor by any treaty. Furthermore the tribunal stated that the Manila–Hong Kong cable was under Spanish control to a degree that invested the installation with the character of a Spanish utility, despite British ownership. Basically, therefore, the rule applied was that a neutral whose business (cables, in this

[36] *The Bathori,* Great Britain, *Privy Council,* 1934, A.C. 91, cited in Higgins-Colombos, 436.
[37] *Great Britain* (Eastern Extension, Australasia and China Telegraph Co., Ltd.) v. *United States,* in *Nielsen's Reports,* 40.

instance) is located in belligerent territory cannot expect to receive compensation for losses sustained through belligerent operations that themselves are not prohibited by international law.

The outbreak of hostilities in 1914 was accompanied by an Allied severing of German-controlled submarine cables, partions of which were relaid later in order to provide additional lines of communication for the Allied countries with neutrals and also among themselves. At the end of the war, the Treaty of Versailles provided for the transfer of German government-owned cables to the Allied Powers without compensation; the value of German privately owned cables, also taken from their prewar owners, was credited (less depreciation) to Germany in the reparations accounts.

## SUGGESTED READINGS

Ronzitti, ed., The Law of Naval Warfare (1988); Kunz, "British Prize Cases, 1939–1941," 36 *AJIL* 204 (1942), containing many illustrative cases not available elsewhere; Stone, 585–607; Whiteman, vol. 10, 599–605, 610–14; O'Connell, "The Legality of Naval Cruise Missiles," 66 *AJIL* 785–94 (1972).

## Blockades

Mallison & Mallison, "A Survey of the International Law of Naval Blockades," 102 *U.S. Naval Institute Proceedings* 44 (Feb. 1976).

# 26

# Neutrality

## NATURE OF NEUTRALITY

**DEFINITION OF NEUTRALITY**  Neutrality by a state not a party to a war consists of refraining from all participation in the war and preventing, tolerating, and regulating certain acts on its own part, by its nationals, and by the belligerents. It is the duty of all belligerents to respect the territory as well as the rights of neutral states.[1]

**CONCEPT OF NONBELLIGERENCY**  Even though some current definitions omit the factor of impartiality, the later must be assumed to have been part of the traditional concept of neutrality and ought to play a role today. The difficulty is that modern practice indicates that numerous states somehow manage to remain outside a conflict, yet do not behave impartially toward belligerents. The term *nonbelligerency* has come into use to describe such behavior. It does not as yet have full standing in the vocabulary of the law, but it does describe the actual behavior of states and is often used. The term was apparently used for the first time in 1939 to describe the status of Italy before it became a normal belligerent. The use of the term spread rapidly—R. R. Wilson cited its invocation by President Inönü on November 1, 1940, to characterize Turkey's position in World War II.[2]

A state behaving as a nonbelligerent remains outside a war in regard to the actual hostilities and claims to be neutral, yet does not behave impartially but favors one side or the other. In consequence of such action, it does not enjoy the full status or the full rights of a genuine neutral. Impartiality and, equally, abstention from participation in a conflict are the characteristics of genuine neutrality; both must be present to support a claim of genuine

---

[1] Adapted from Department of the Army, FM 27-10, *The Law of Land Warfare* (July 1956), 185. It is interesting to note that the 1940 edition of that manual included a phrase to the effect that a neutral state had to exercise "absolute impartiality" in the prevention, toleration, and regulation of certain acts. Two general references on the subject of neutrality are Whiteman, vol. 11, 139–475; and Norton's heavily documented "Between the Ideology and the Reality: The Shadow of the Law of Neutrality," 17 *Harvard Int'l. Law Jl.* 249 (1976).
[2] Wilson, " 'Non-Belligerency' in Relation to the Terminology of Neutrality," 35 *AJIL* 121 (1941).

neutrality with full neutral rights.[3] Impartiality has been stressed in most major treaties applicable to neutrality—the Fifth Hague convention of 1907 (Art. 9), the Thirteenth Hague Convention of 1907 (Preamble), and the Havana Convention on Maritime Neutrality of 1928 (Preamble)—as well as in the draft conventions drawn up by the International Law Association in 1920 (Art. 9) and in 1928 (Art. 9) and by the Harvard Research itself (Art. 4).

However, in the past there really did exist on occasion a situation aptly described as "qualified" (imperfect) neutrality. This was the case when a given neutral rendered direct or indirect assistance to one of the belligerents in a conflict because of a treaty obligation contracted before the war, and not for that war in particular. Thus, in 1848, Great Britain, under a prewar treaty, prohibited the exports of arms to Prussia but permitted such exports to Denmark. Similarly, Denmark, in pursuance of a treaty obligations, supplied both warships and troops to Russia in 1788 during a war between Sweden and Russia. Sweden protested but eventually accepted Denmark's qualified neutrality.

Sometimes countries refuse to characterize hostilities as wars, primarily to avoid any application of the laws of neutrality. Thus it has been claimed that neither the Republic of China nor the Japanese government was willing to label as wars its protracted hostilities in the 1930s, for fear that third parties would stop the flow of military supplies to the two antagonists.

Nevertheless, *nonbelligerency* was the status assumed during World War II by Spain and the United States (in the latter case until December 7, 1941). Needless to say, the continuing enjoyment of this status depends almost entirely on the patience of the belligerents against which the nonbelligerent practices its discrimination, and a declaration of war may eventually end the anomalous status of the "neutral nonbelligerent." Nonbelligerency was the status adopted by France when, in 1981, it sold four French jet fighters to Iraq (then already embroiled in armed conflict with Iran), later exported up to 40 Exocet air-to-surface missiles to Iraq, and in 1983 delivered five Super Étendard fighter-bombers to Iraq—the latter were then to be armed with the missiles mentioned. Similarly, Algeria shifted into a state of nonbelligerency when, in 1981, it began to supply Iran with large shipments of Soviet-made arms, despite the Iran-Iraq conflict.

HARVARD RESEARCH PROPOSAL    The traditional emphasis on impartiality as a neutral duty began to be challenged seriously as early as 1939. In that year, the Harvard Research in International Law proposed that the concept be modified to read

---

[3]Consult also Harvard Research in International Law, "Rights and Duties of Neutral States, in Naval and Aerial War," 33 *AJIL* 169, esp. 232–35 (1939 Special Supp.). This document is hereafter referred to as Harvard Draft.

A neutral State, for the purpose of better safeguarding its rights and interests as a neutral or of better fulfilling its duties as a neutral, may, during the course of a war, adopt new measures or alter the measures which it has previously adopted.[4]

This proposal referred to the belief that changes in domestic neutrality legislation made in time of war would not necessarily violate the duty of impartiality.

CONTROVERSY OVER UNITED STATES NEUTRALITY LEGISLATION    The issue came fully into the open when the Congress of the United States revised American neutrality legislation in 1939 and President Franklin D. Roosevelt proposed repeal of the earlier mandatory arms embargo. Many critics pointed out that the purpose of this change was to assist the enemies of Germany and hence constituted a violation of international law.[5]

The controversy over nonbelligerency flared up again after President Roosevelt announced to Congress on September 3, 1940, that the United States had received from Great Britain 99-year leases on eight naval bases in the Caribbean in exchange for 50 overage destroyers.[6] This arrangement produced much disagreement among both members of Congress and jurists, even though the presidential message had been accompanied by a favorable opinion written by Attorney General Robert H. Jackson.[7]

That opinion maintained, among other things, that the relevant Article 8 of Hague Convention XIII (1907) did not apply, because that article pertained only to vessels originally "intended" to be used by a belligerent. Because the 50 destroyers had not been built with the intention of turning them over to Great Britain, the opinion held that neither Article 8 nor the Act of June 15, 1917 (40 U.S. Stat. 221), applied to the transfer of the vessels.

The present writer disagrees completely with the Attorney General's interpretation of the duties of a neutral: the article cited referred to the prevention of certain acts by private neutral citizens, and the pertinent reference should have been to the clear-cut prohibition imposed by Article 6 of Convention XIII: "The supply in any manner, directly or indirectly, by a neutral Power to a belligerent Power of warships, ammunition or war matériel of any kind whatever is forbidden." This prohibition had been acknowledged by the United States Department of State as early as October 15, 1917, when

[4]Harvard Draft, 316.
[5]See letter by Hyde and Jessup, NYT, Sept. 21, 1939, and the ensuing debate over the letter, NYT, Sept. 25, Oct. 1, 5, 7, 14, and 15, 1939, as well as the New York Herald Tribune, Oct. 25, 1939.
[6]See 34 AJIL 183 (1940 Supp.). The text of the Agreement of March 27, 1941 (and supplementary documents) for the American use of the bases was reprinted in 35 AJIL 134 (1941 Supp.).
[7]NYT, Sept. 9, 1940, 1, 10, 12, 16; and 34 AJIL 728 (1940). See also Borchard, "The Attorney General's Opinion on the Exchange of Destroyers for Naval Bases," 34 AJIL 690 (1940).

a department circular stated categorically that "for the Government of the United States itself to sell to a belligerent nation would be an unneutral act."[8]

The present writer also cannot accept Wright's conclusion that United States and Latin American abandonment of the canons of impartiality were justified because German aggression had violated international law as embodied in the Kellogg-Briand Pact and therefore exempted neutrals from the normal obligation of impartiality among belligerents.[9]

Attorney General Robert Jackson then added more fuel to the argument when he delivered a speech in Havana on March 27, 1941, in which he asserted that the United States was obliged as a matter of law to give Great Britain all aid "short of war," while at the same time it was "the declared determination of the government to avoid entry into the war as a belligerent."[10]

The inescapable conclusion seems to be that the United States abandoned its status as a neutral by the destroyer deal. It thereupon entered the status of a "nonbelligerent," or neoneutral.

LEND-LEASE BILL    A second and major step in the United States' shifting from traditional neutrality to an expanded version of nonbelligerency began with the presidential signature, on March 11, 1941, on the Defense Act of 1941, introduced as House Resolution 1776 on January 10 of that year and popularly known as the Lend-Lease Bill.[11] This remarkable example of unilateral deviation from accepted norms of neutral behavior asserted that a nonbelligerent had the right to discriminate among belligerents and to favor one side against the other by supplying one of them with military equipment.

The law itself authorized the president of the United States to grant various forms of aid to the "government of any country whose defense the President deems vital to the defense of the United States." Specifically, the chief executive was authorized to have manufactured in arsenals, factories, and shipyards any defense article for such governments and to sell, transfer title to, exchange, lend, lease, or otherwise dispose of, to any such government, any defense articles.[12]

Section 3 of the law authorized the president to inspect, prove, repair, outfit, recondition, or otherwise put into good working order any defense article for any such favored government or to produce any or all of such services by private contract. This, in turn, meant that henceforth belligerent warships, planes, and other matériel could be repaired or outfitted in American jurisdiction.

[8] 33 AJIL 238 (1939 Special Supp.).
[9] Wright, "Law and Politics in the World Community," in Lipsky, 3–14, at 8.
[10] Cited by Borchard, "War, Neutrality and Non-Belligerency," 35 AJIL 618 (1941).
[11] See Wilson, The International Law Standard in Treaties of the United States (1953), 234–39.
[12] See text of the law in 35 AJIL 76 (1941 Supp.). Consult also Kimball, The Most Unsordid Act: Lend-Lease, 1939–1941 (1969).

In April 1941 the United States assumed responsibility for defending the "orphaned" Danish colony of Greenland, and four months later a similar defense arrangement was announced for the then Danish colony of Iceland. On July 11, 1941, the U.S. Navy, in addition to its neutrality patrol duties off the Americas, assumed active convoy duty for merchantmen carrying lend-lease goods from the American coast to a point near Iceland, where the convoys were relieved by the Royal Navy. Westbound shipping in turn was convoyed from that point to the United States by the U.S. Navy. In consequence of the new policy, an undeclared naval war with German submarines ensued. Following several incidents, an American vessel, the U.S. destroyer *Kearny*, was torpedoed on October 17 while on convoy duty; though losing 11 of her crew, the *Kearny* managed to reach port. On October 31, another American destroyer, the *Reuben James*, was torpedoed in the North Atlantic and sank, with a loss of 115 men.

It is not surprising, then, that later most of the remaining parts of the Neutrality Act of 1939 were scrapped when Congress, in November 1941, authorized the defensive arming of American merchant vessels and their sailing into proclaimed war zones and belligerent ports. President Truman ended the Lend-Lease Program in August 1945.

## HISTORICAL BACKGROUND

EARLY DEVELOPMENT OF CONCEPT OF NEUTRALITY    The concept of neutrality has been closely connected with the development of another idea, that of the society or family of nations. It therefore came into being only when such a society was developing. The word *neutrality*, in its modern meaning first showed up in the fourteenth century.[13] By the end of the fifteenth century, the *Consolato del Mare* recorded definite rules concerning neutral rights at sea, and in the sixteenth century, diplomatic correspondence cited international law regarding neutrality.

Hugo Grotius, dealing only briefly with neutrality, supported a theory based on the doctrine of the just war, under which a state might claim to be neutral. Yet the state might judge the justice of a conflict and modify its conduct from impartiality toward not favoring the belligerent found fighting for an unjust cause:

It is the duty of those who have no part in the war to do nothing which may favor the party having an unjust cause, or which may hinder the action of one waging a just war and, in case of doubt, to treat both belligerents alike, in permitting transit, in furnishing provisions to the troops, in refraining from assisting the besieged. (*Three Books on the Law of War and Peace*, Book III, Chap. 17.)

Grotius thus came perilously close to the theory of nonbelligerency mentioned earlier.

[13] See Lauterpacht's *Oppenheim*, vol. 2, 624–42.

The rapid growth of the importance of international trade led the major neutral maritime states to resist ever more vigorously an increasing belligerent interference with neutral commerce. By the middle of the eighteenth century, it was generally agreed that belligerent states were legally bound to honor the neutrality of any state choosing to remain outside a given conflict and also that neutral status was characterized by a specific obligation of strict impartiality. Thus the basis of modern true neutrality was laid in the eighteenth century.

CONCEPT OF DUE DILIGENCE    Continuing belligerent interference with neutral persons and property has led neutral states, on numerous occasions since then, to resort to using force. Among the best-known examples are the "Armed Neutrality" of 1780, led by Russia; the "Second Armed Neutrality" of 1800; and the unofficial belligerent acts by the United States in 1798 in the Anglo-French War and from 1939 to December 1941.[14] An unofficial and amusing modification of "neutral ships make neutral goods" took place during the War of 1812, when some self-styled Scandinavians crossed the Canadian frontier into the United States, arguing that "neutral wagons made neutral goods." In the Declaration of Paris (1856), privateering was abolished, the law of blockade was laid down in fairly clear terms, and the rules of "free ships, free goods" and "free goods free even in enemy ships" were proclaimed. The American Civil War witnessed the basic neutrality of Great Britain (excluding isolated instances, such as the affair of the *Alabama*) and led through the experiences of that country to a much better understanding by all states of the rights and duties of a neutral. In addition, the Civil War contributed the rules of the Treaty of Washington of 1871, which asserted that a neutral must use "due diligence" to prevent evasion of its laws for the enforcement of its neutral duties.[15]

CONCEPT OF "MEANS AT ITS DISPOSAL"    The 1907 Hauge Peace Conference modified the concept of "due diligence" to read that the neutral had to use "the means at its disposal" (Arts. 8 and 25 of Hague Convention XIII of 1907). The *Alabama* award led to a recognition of the dangers inherent in permitting neutral private interests to outfit warships on neutral territory for the use of a belligerent state. Hence Article 8 of Hague Convention XIII of 1907:

A neutral government is bound to employ the means at its disposal to prevent the fitting out or arming of any vessel within its jurisdiction which it has reason to believe is intended to cruise, or engage in hostile operations, against a Power with which that Government is at peace. It is also bound to display the same vigilance

---

[14]See Deac, "America's Undeclared Naval War," 87 *U.S. Naval Institute Proceedings*, 70 (Oct. 1961).

[15]The phrase occurs in Article 6 of the Treaty of Washington. See *The Alabama Claims Award (United States–Great Britain)*, Arbitration under the Treaty of May 8, 1871. Consult also Wilson, *op. cit. supra*, n. 11, 191–223, for one of the best analyses available of the award and of the 1871 rules, as well as Lauterpacht's *Oppenheim*, vol. 2, 714–16.

to prevent the departure from its jurisdiction of any vessel intended to cruise, or engage in hostile operations, which had been adapted entirely or partly within the said jurisdiction for use in war.

The substitution of "means at its disposal" for the "due diligence" contained in Rules 1 and 3 of the Washington Treaty of 1871 reflected much more accurately the duties of a neutral state. Thus when the United States, before the outbreak of the war with Spain in 1898, purchased from Brazil two warships ordered by Brazil but still not completed in the yards of their British builders, the British government was correct in preventing both vessels from leaving British jurisdiction until the Spanish-American War had ended, and a similar policy was followed with regard to warships being built for Spain. The United States, for its part, adopted at a much earlier date the policies later followed by Great Britain. The Act of 1795 had already prohibited, among other practices, the fitting out and arming of warships intended to be employed by a foreign belligerent or the provision of increased armament by such vessels when already armed. The Supreme Court of the United States conscientiously applied these rules in all major cases. [16]

RULES GOVERNING NEUTRAL RIGHTS AND DUTIES    By the end of the nineteenth century, neutrality had been fully accepted as a legal status, but still lacking were clear and agreed-on definitions of both neutral rights and duties.

The major effort to fill this gap in international law was made at the Second Hague Conference in 1907. Two conventions on the subject were adopted, the Hague Convention V Respecting the Rights and Duties of Neutral Powers and Persons in Case of War on Land and the Hague Convention XIII Concerning the Rights and Duties of Neutral Powers in Naval War.

TESTING OF RULES BY WORLD WAR I    World War I tested beyond any expectations the new rules governing neutral status. Despite early proclamations of neutrality by most states remaining outside the conflict, belligerents quite early began to encroach on neutral rights, particularly in regard to the ancient doctrine of the freedom of the seas. Starting with the German invasion of Belgium, following that country's refusal to accede to a German demand for passage of troops through a neutral state, France and Great Britain proceeded to violate neutral rights on their part when, in 1915 and 1916, they landed troops in Greece (Salonika and Corfu) and used Greek neutral territory as bases of military operations. The Germans, in turn, brought captured enemy vessels into United States and Chilean ports and attempted to keep them there in violation of the strict and detailed rules laid down at The Hague. By the late fall of 1916, neutrals had been harassed by both sides almost to the point of fighting to protect what remained of their rights.

[16]Such as *The Santissima Trinidad*, 1822, 7 Wheaton 283; *The Bolivar*, in *United States* v. *Quincy*, 1832, 6 Peters 445; and *The Meteor*, 1866, 3 Wharton's *Digest*, 561.

COVENANT OF THE LEAGUE OF NATIONS     The Covenant of the League of Nations modified the traditional right of any state to remain neutral. Under the provisions of Article 16, any member resorting to war in violation of its obligation to settle disputes by peaceful means was deemed to have committed an act of war against *all* other members, which were then obligated to cut off all trade and financial relations with the aggressor.

On the other hand, it remained possible to be neutral, and neutrality continued to be practiced. The Covenant, after all, was only a treaty and therefore was binding only on the member states of the League or, as the British Foreign Office phrased it in 1929, "as between members of the League there can be no neutral rights because there can be no neutrals."[17] Outsiders were not bound by the provisions of the Covenant and were free to remain neutral in any conflict or dispute.

PACT OF PARIS OF 1928     The adoption of the Pact of Paris of 1928 (Kellogg-Briand Pact) for the Renunciation of War did not make any real change in the character of neutrality. The pact's signatories were expected not to observe toward a violator of the instrument such duties as international law prescribed for a neutral in regard to a belligerent, and were expected also to supply the attacked state with financial or material assistance, including munitions, and even to assist that state with armed forces.

REASSESSMENT OF THE PROBLEM OF NEUTRALITY     The failure of the League system of collective security to prevent Japanese aggression in China and the Italian conquest of Ethiopia led to a widespread reassessment of the problem of neutrality vis-à-vis the League. Many states decided that their own efforts had to be relied on to protect their neutrality, instead of entrusting the Geneva system with that task. Such examples as the Copenhagen Declaration of 1938 and extensive neutrality legislation passed in the Americas between 1935 and 1939 testified to a desire to ensure future neutrality, an attitude that culminated in 1939 in the General Declaration of Panama.

World War II saw wholesale violations of neutral rights by belligerents on both sides in the conflict. Belgium, Luxembourg, the Netherlands, Denmark, and Norway were invaded despite their neutral status; Swiss national airspace was violated by both sides; vessels were attacked, sunk, or captured in neutral waters; and the United States became a nonbelligerent participant in the conflict long before it joined the Western Allies after the attack on Pearl Harbor.

UN CONCEPT OF NEUTRALITY     The Charter of the United Nations did *not* cause the concept of neutrality to vanish. To be sure, Article 2, paragraph 5, states that

all Members shall give the United Nations every assistance in any action it takes in accordance with the present Charter, and shall refrain from giving assistance to any state against which the United Nations is taking preventive or enforcement action.

[17] Cf. Higgins-Colombos, 534–35; and see Taubenfeld, "International Actions and Neutrality," 47 *AJIL* 377, 378–83 (1953).

And the next paragraph of the same article asserts the rather amazing doctrine that

the Organization shall ensure that states which are not Members of the United Nations act in accordance with these Principles so far as may be necessary for the maintenance of international peace and security.

These provisions of the Charter merit brief comment. As Gould pointed out,[18] the Cold War had led many leaders to wonder whether a given collective action under the flag of the United Nations (Korea and Katanga came to mind at once) did not really represent political and military action by one side in the great power struggle against the other side. If this was so, then the members of the United Nations might easily come to believe that they did not have a duty to participate in such action and to remain neutral, for obviously it could be argued convincingly that the actions in question were not undertaken in support of the Charter's principles. Hence neutral status might be quite in order under certain conditions.[19]

The reality of such considerations was reflected not only in the slim support given to collective action in Korea, by the fact that the Soviet Union not only refused to participate on the side of the United Nations but also gave assistance to the North Korean and Chinese aggressors, but also by the more recent unwillingness of many members of the United Nations to contribute to the expenses of the Near East and Congo military missions under the UN flag.

In regard to Article 2 (6), any interpretation of the word *ensure* to mean coercion of nonmembers to abandon neutrality during United Nations collective actions would represent a gross negation of basic concepts of international law. At best, the paragraph can mean the use of "influence" on nonmembers. The present writer even believes that Gould erred when he suggested that *ensure* could mean "coerce" only if a nonmember actively and with prejudice assisted an aggressor.[20] Then, it is believed, a state of nonbelligerency could be claimed by a country assisting an aggressor; to interpret

---

[18]Gould, 624; see also Whiteman, vol. 11, 144–60, on a neutrality and the Charter of the United Nations.

[19]The late Charles G. Fenwick asserted for over 30 years that "the Covenant of the League of Nations put an end in principle to the traditional law of neutrality" (*International Law*, 2d ed., 1934, 613; 3rd ed., 1948, 613; 4th ed., 1965, 719) and later that "the adoption of the Charter of the United Nations . . . finally marked the end of neutrality as a legal system" (3rd ed., 621; 4th ed., 727). Even more recently, Fenwick criticized Whiteman for suggesting, in the latter's vol. 11, that something of neutrality was left: see his "Is Neutrality Still a Term of Present Law?" 63 *AJIL* 100 (1969). The reality is that the legal basis for a position of neutrality may indeed have been weakened but that the practice of states, motivated by self-interest and political goals, has denied the basis on which neutrality can be abandoned universally. See also Taubenfeld, "International Actions and Neutrality," 47 *AJIL* 377 (1953), on this important point. See also Norton, *op. cit. supra*, n. 1.

[20]Gould, 625.

the charter otherwise, it is felt, would grant legal rights to members that would not exist under international law as accepted today.

The failure to achieve the results planned for the Military Staff Committee under the Security Council produced a situation in the United Nations in which a general "call to arms," with emphasis on binding obligations under Article 2, has been out of the question. Every one of the collective military or peacekeeping actions carried out by the United Nations has been on the basis of leaving actual participation to the members' free choice.

On the other hand, the existence of the United Nations does not eliminate the concept of neutrality altogether, or even in the bulk of likely conflicts. Article 2 (5) of the Charter refers only to action undertaken by the United Nations. Judging from its past record, many conflicts "not endangering world peace" may occur without requiring collective action. Under such conditions, every member of the organization would be free to remain neutral, and the rules governing neutral status would apply.

This has been true in the limited wars in the former French Indochina, in the Soviet reinvasion of Hungary in 1956, in the fighting preceding the grant of independence to Algeria, in the Indian conquest of Goa, in the Chinese invasion of Tibet (1951) and of India (1962), and in dozens of other more recent invasions, including those of Czechoslovakia (1968), Cambodia (1979), and Afghanistan (1979). If, therefore, there is no collective action, either because of a veto in the Security Council or because of an unwillingness by the United Nations to intervene in a given dispute involving the use of force, then the traditional rules of law applicable to neutrality still apply.

STATUS OF NEUTRALITY AFTER ORGANIZATION OF THE UN   Finally, the major lawmaking treaties concluded after the establishment of the United Nations still frequently refer to neutrality as a legal status. Thus the four Geneva conventions of 1949 for the protection of war victims refer, in the sections on the treatment of prisoners of war and the protection of civilians, to "neutral state," "neutral power," and "neutral country," as well as, interestingly enough, to "neutral power or nonbelligerent."

Some commentators have insisted that neutrality is obsolete in view of the nature of modern war. Such a diagnosis ignores the important distinction between two different kinds of conflict. A "dual" war, fought between two states, can be fought even with the most modern weapons under conditions allowing outsiders to assert their rights as neutrals. On the other hand, a major or global conflict would make prolonged maintenance of a neutral position difficult if not untenable. Invocation of the Charter is not helpful on this point: it appears that this is another instance in which the membership of the United Nations has, by consensus, decided not to apply a principle of the Charter to the daily conduct of nations.[21] This has been true in scores of conflicts since 1946, and it must be concluded that neutrality is very much alive, even if not wholly well.

[21]Consult also Whiteman, vol. 11, pp. 163–74, on the ambiguity of the Charter provisions in question.

The following discussion of neutrality is centered mostly on the legal questions raised by naval warfare because most controversies involving belligerents and neutrals have occurred in that aspect of war. It should be kept in mind, too, that the so-called rights of neutrals have evolved by a long process of compromise between extreme demands by belligerents and equally extreme demands by neutral states.

## NEUTRAL RIGHTS AND DUTIES IN LAND WARFARE

HAGUE CONVENTION V OF 1907    The rights of a neutral state, formerly based on custom, were codified primarily in Hague Convention V of 1907. This instrument was, to a large extent, declaratory of the customary law of neutrality.

BASIC RIGHT OF INVIOLABILITY OF NEUTRAL TERRITORY    The basic right beyond any question is the inviolability of neutral territory. (V, Art. 1), and most writers agree that all other neutral rights really are mere corollaries to that fundamental principle governing territory. It is again affirmed in the Hague Convention dealing with neutrality in naval war.[22]

OTHER NEUTRAL RIGHTS    Corollary to the basic right, other neutral rights have been detailed in the Hague conventions:

A neutral state may expect that belligerent will not erect on its territory radio or other facilities for the purpose of communicating with belligerent forces on land, on the seas, or in the air (V, Art. 3-a); that belligerents will not use already existing facilities established by them before the war on now neutral territory for forbidden (military) purposes (V, Art. 3-b); and that they will not open recruitment offices or form military courts on neutral territory (V, Art. 4). A recent example was Libya's recruiting effort through its diplomatic missions in India, West-, and Central-African states for its Islamic Legion to fight in Chad (1985–1986). Most neutral states have been quick to close recruitment agencies or activities set up on their territory by a belligerent. The United States was therefore in accord with the already customary law when, in 1793, it ordered the French minister, Edmond C. Genêt, to cease issuing commissions on American soil. It is indeed, a neutral's duty to prevent the prohibited acts from being undertaken on its territory (V, Art. 5, par. 1). On the other hand, a neutral is not bound to prevent any of its citizens or residents from going abroad to offer their services to a belligerent (V, Art. 6). Thus the United States was not delinquent in its duties as a neutral when, in 1870, it permitted about 1,200 Frenchmen to leave on French vessels to join the armies of France

---

[22]Convention XIII, The Hague, 1907, Article 1: "Belligerents are bound to respect the sovereign rights of neutral Powers and to abstain, in neutral territory or neutral waters, from any act which would, if knowingly permitted by any Power, constitute a violation of neutrality." Article 1 of Convention V simply asserts: "The territory of neutral Powers is inviolable." See also Helmreich, "The Diplomacy of Apology: U.S. Bombings of Switzerland during World War II," 27 *Air University Review* (May–June 1977), 19–37.

against Prussia. Even though the ships carried considerable quantities of arms and ammunition aboard (96,000 rifles and 11 million cartridges), the group did not represent an organized hostile expedition; hence there was no question of violating the United States' neutrality. Similarly, Sweden was legally correct in permitting some 9,000 of its nationals to leave for service in the cause of Finland after that country was attacked by the Soviet Union on November 30, 1939. On the other hand, the Swedish government then virtually became a "nonbelligerent neutral" for a brief time when it permitted recruitment of such volunteers on its territory and then went on to allow its citizens to leave for Finland fully armed and equipped. When fighting broke about again between the Soviet Union and Finland in June 1941, several thousand Swedish volunteers crossed the frontier into Finland, but this time they received little official encouragement from their own government, and most of them were back home by the middle of 1944. The participation of several thousand Thai soldiers in the war in Laos in the early 1970s was similar to the employment of organized Chinese troops in the Korean conflict: a violation, in this case, of Thai neutrality. It must be assumed today that Article 6 of Hague Convention V is, and has been for decades, defunct under the principle of *rebus sic stantibus*.

## Neutral Trade

A neutral is not bound to prevent the export, on behalf of one or the other of the belligerents, of arms, munitions, or any other war matériel by private persons (V, Art. 7), unless, of course, it wishes to prohibit such exports at its own discretion.

RESTRICTIONS OF NEUTRAL STATES   A neutral state is prohibited from furnishing a belligerent supplies or munitions.[23] This rule has been of particular importance since 1917 in all cases in which production or trade are in the hands of states; the latter are prohibited from supplying arms, munitions, and/or implements of war in general, or war loans, to countries at war. If they insist on an alleged right to do so, they will lose their neutral status. Ships of such governments, except warships, are subject to the regulations applicable in the case of blockades, to the laws of contraband, and to other privileges exercised by belligerent states. Loans for military purposes cannot be granted by a neutral government. "Neutral" suppliers of military equipment and munitions risk the imposition of legal retaliation—at the very least—by the aggrieved party, such as economic sanctions.

RIGHT OF PRIVATE PERSONS TO TRADE WITH BELLIGERENTS   On the other hand, a neutral state may at its discretion permit private persons to make loans to either or both sides in a conflict or to sell war matériel to belligerents. This is true even in the case of rebellions. No state is bound

[23]But see, on the other hand, Smith, *Britain's Clandestine Submarines, 1914–1915* (1964), and note the U.S. supply of military matériel to Israel and the Soviet supply of similar goods to Arab states, both activities covering several decades in the absence of Middle East peace treaties and despite, or because of, repeated flare-ups of extensive hostilities.

to prevent its citizens from supplying war matériel to rebel groups—only the neutral government may not furnish such supplies. Thus Great Britain correctly refused to comply in 1817 with a Spanish demand to prohibit the export of arms and ammunition to the rebelling Spanish colonies in Latin America. Sir Christopher Robinson admirably expressed the legal picture when he wrote:

There is no obligation to enforce such prohibition and the remedy against the supply of arms, as contraband of war, is ordinarily found in the vigilance of the injured Government and the penalties it has a right to inflict in the confiscation of such articles.[24]

Somewhat later, on October 15, 1914, the U.S. Secretary of State, Robert Lansing, reiterated this classic approach to the problem of private neutral sales to belligerents:

It should be understood that, generally speaking, a citizen of the United States can sell to a belligerent government or its agents any article of commerce which he pleases. He is not prohibited from doing this by any rule of international law, by any treaty provisions, or by any statute of the United States. . . . Such sales by American citizens do not in the least affect the neutrality of the United States.[25]

In the case of civil wars, most governments tend to tolerate private exports of any kind of goods, including munitions and other war matériel, to the recognized government of the country afflicted with civil strife. To assist officially with such aid would also be correct, if done at the request of the recognized governments. Some states, however, desiring to preserve strict neutrality even in foreign civil wars, prohibit the export (embargo) of war matériel to either side in such a conflict. This was the policy adopted by the United States in the case of the Spanish Civil War. The Neutrality Act of 1937 was signed by President Roosevelt on May 1 of that year and was followed at once by two proclamations, one listing the commodities to be included under "arms, ammunition and implements of war" under the provisions of the Neutrality Act, and the second prohibiting trade in such commodities with Spain.

## Neutral Relations with Belligerent Forces

RIGHTS OF STATES TO PROTECT THEIR NEUTRALITY    If any neutral rights are threatened by a belligerent and the neutral state has to resort to force to preserve its lawful rights, such action cannot be regarded as a hostile act and an abandonment of neutrality (Convention V, Art. 10).

---

[24]Quoted in Higgin-Colombos, 515.
[25]Quoted in Wertenbaker, "The Price of Neutrality," 157 *Atlantic Monthly* (Jan. 1936), 100–108, 102.

On the other hand, if a neutral state is either unable or fails for any reason to prevent violation of its neutrality by the forces of one belligerent entering, or even passing through, its territory, then the other belligerent may be justified in attacking the enemy forces on the neutral territory. The degree to which such justification exists depends on the circumstances of any particular instance; above all, the neutral is obliged only to use the means at its disposal. If those means are insufficient to prevent a belligerent incursion into neutral territory, no blame can be attached to the neutral — provided the available means have actually been used to try to block the incursion.

During the Vietnam war, on April 30, 1970, the United States sent sizable U.S. forces into neutral Cambodia. The purpose of the incursion was to destroy Viet Cong bases along the Cambodian border. The American action did not represent an unlawful invasion of Cambodia, whose military forces would have been too weak to oust the Viet Cong. Rather, the incursion represented an American attack on an enemy that was misusing the territory of a weak neutral.

In the case of the Nicaraguan civil war, the rebel Contras would not have been able to stay in the field very long if they had not found a sanctuary in supposedly neutral Honduras. By June 1986, the Contras were said to occupy 450 square miles of Honduran territory along the Nicaraguan border, to have displaced 12,000 local peasants and coffee growers, and to have established a series of base camps housing an armed force larger than the Honduran Army. Honduras continued to claim neutral status.[26]

DUTIES OF NEUTRAL STATES    If a neutral state receives on its territory the troops of any belligerent, it is obliged to intern them as far as possible from the theater of war. At the end of the war, the various states that had members of their forces interned in neutral countries have to repay the latter for the expenses incurred in caring for the interned forces (V, Art. 12).[27]

RIGHT OF GRANTING TRANSIT    A neutral is free to authorize the passage across its territory of the sick and wounded belonging to belligerent forces, provided that their means of transport (trains, trucks, and so on) do not carry healthy personnel or war matériel.

After Russia attacked Finland on November 30, 1939, the British and French governments announced to the Norwegian and Swedish governments their intention of sending an expeditionary force to Finland. They requested transit privileges and, in return for this unneutral concession, promised to come to the aid of both countries if they were attacked by Russia in retaliation. The Swedish government refused the request at once, and the Norwegian government followed suit three days later.

---

[26] See, inter alia, Newsweek, June 30, 1986, 36, 41.
[27] The United States claimed to have a right to withhold full compliance with the 1954 Geneva Accord neutralizing Laos in view of violations of Laotian neutrality by a claimed force of 80,000 North Vietnamese in the country: International Herald Tribune (Paris), Aug. 10, 1971, 1.

Following their conquest of Norway in World War II, German forces stationed in that country encountered increasing difficulties in securing replacement personnel as well as supplies, owing to British naval supremacy in the North Sea. In consequence, Germany began to exert pressure on neutral Sweden to grant transit privileges to unarmed German troops and to military supplies so that a new route to Norway from the Baltic could be established. After much hesitation, Sweden acceded to this request, the alternative obviously being a German conquest of the country. The Western Allies appear to have been consulted by Sweden and to have agreed tacitly to the proposed transit agreement, which remained in effect from July 5, 1940, to August 20, 1943, when Sweden abrogated the agreement with German concurrence.

A more basic violation of Swedish neutral duties took place in the summer of 1941, after the outbreak of hostilities between Germany and the Soviet Union. Sweden succumbed to extraordinary German pressure and permitted the passage of a fully armed and equipped German division from Norway to Finland. This event led to formal British and Russian protests; the Swedish government replied that this was a concession *ad hoc*, granted for that one division and never to be repeated again.

## NEUTRAL RIGHTS AND DUTIES
## IN WARFARE AT SEA

DECLARATION OF PARIS (1856)    The Declaration of Paris (1856) contained certain provisions regarding warfare at sea: (1) it was established that a blockade had to be effective and not merely a "paper blockade" in order to be legally binding; (2) it was decided that a neutral flag covered an enemy's goods with the exception of contraband of war; and (3) it was asserted that neutral goods were immune from seizure on enemy ships.

### Convention XIII of the 1907 Hague Conference

The 1907 Hague Peace Conference produced a much more satisfactory document than did its predecessor, and a good deal of the modern law governing relations between belligerents and neutrals is based on Convention XIII Concerning the Rights and Duties of Neutral Powers in Naval War (hereafter cited as Convention XIII). This instrument, like the convention on land warfare, was largely declaratory of existing customary rules of law. It was signed but not ratified by Great Britain, then the greatest naval power; however, the inclusion of numerous customary rules made most of the instrument applicable to Great Britain.

INVIOLABILITY OF TERRITORIAL WATERS    Neutral territory, this time including neutral waters, was again declared to be inviolable (Art. 1). Accordingly, the commission of all hostile acts, including capture and the exercise of the right of search, undertaken by belligerent warships in neutral territorial waters was prohibited (Art. 2). If a vessel was captured in prohibited waters and was still within its jurisdiction, the neutral state had to employ all means at its disposal to release the prize and its crew and to intern the prize crew placed aboard the ship. If the captured vessel was no longer within neutral jurisdiction, the capture state had to release, on demand of the neutral in question, the prize and its crew (Art. 3).

VIOLATIONS OF NEUTRAL WATERS     The application of these principles, based on customary international law, may be illustrated through some well-known historical examples.

After a French privateer had captured the *Grange*, a British merchant vessel, in Delaware Bay in 1793, the prize was released to its owners at the request of the United States government. In 1864, the Union warship *Wachusett* captured the *Florida*, a Confederate vessel, in the harbor of Bahia, Brazil. The offended neutral government protested against the illegal invasion of its territorial jurisdiction, and the United States government ordered a court-martial of the captain of the *Wachusett* and set free the officers and crew of the *Florida*. The vessel itself could not be restored because it sank after a collision in Hampton Roads on its way to a Union port. The United States government then ordered an official salute to the Brazilian flag on the spot where the offense had originally taken place.

During the Russo-Japanese War in 1904–1905, Korea and Manchuria, although technically neutral territories, were regarded by both belligerents as being combat zones. Japanese destroyers entered the Chinese port of Chefoo and there captured a Russian destroyer, the *Peshitelni*. This action was so widely condemned as a violation of Chinese neutrality that the Japanese government felt compelled to issue an elaborate justification of its act, based primarily on an alleged Chinese incapacity to perform the duties of a neutral.[28]

In March 1915, when the German cruiser *Dresden* sought refuge in Cumberland Bay, located within Chile's territorial waters, the Chilean government ordered the vessel to leave within 24 hours. The captain of the *Dresden* refused to accede to this request. Five days later, a squadron of British warships entered the bay and ordered the German cruiser to surrender. The *Dresden* was thereupon scuttled by its crew. The British government offered an apology, but tempered it with observations that cast doubt on whether the *Dresden* had been interned properly as ordered by the government of Chile.

One of the most famous modern cases regarding an alleged violation of neutral waters was that of the *Altmark* during World War II. This celebrated incident revolved around the somewhat obvious rule that the immunity of neutral waters holds only as long as belligerent vessels enter such waters only for what is called *innocent passage*. The *Altmark* was an auxiliary vessel in the service of the German navy. It entered Norwegian neutral waters

[28]Takahashi, *International Law Applied to the Russo-Japanese War* (1908), 437–44; and also Tucker, *The Law of War and Neutrality at Sea* (1957), 221, n. 57.

on February 14, 1940, with 326 British seamen aboard. These men had been members of the crews of various British merchant vessels captured or sunk by the German battle cruiser *Admiral Graf Spee*. The British seamen were being taken to a German port. Norway, as a neutral, had the right to exclude the *Altmark* from its waters, but had chosen not to exercise this privilege. The German ship proceeded to sail along the coast of Norway, obviously attempting to evade capture by British warships. When news of this maneuver was received in Great Britain, the British destroyer *Cossack* drove the *Altmark* into Jössing Fjord and removed all of the British prisoners from the ship.

When the Norwegian government protested against this invasion of its territorial jurisdiction, Great Britain insisted that Norway had failed in its neutral duties as commonly understood in the meaning of Articles 1 and 2 of Convention XIII. The British notes emphasized that the Norwegian authorities had ignored a request by the commander of nearby British naval forces that the *Altmark* be searched to make certain that the ship carried no prisoners aboard. Article 5 of Convention XIII was also invoked; it states that "belligerents are forbidden to use neutral ports and waters as a base of naval operations against their adversaries."

The *Altmark* had passed through about 400 miles of Norwegian waters and had even been permitted to sail through the "Bergen Defended Area," forbidden to belligerent warships under the terms of the Norwegian neutrality legislation in force.[29]

RIGHT OF NEUTRAL STATES TO BAR BELLIGERENT WARSHIPS     Although Article 10 of Convention XIII specifically states that a state's neutrality is not violated (or compromised: *n'est pas compromise*) by the mere passage of a belligerent warship and its prizes, every neutral state does have an undoubted and generally acknowledged right to prohibit the passage of belligerent warships (and, by implication, naval auxiliaries) through its waters. Thus the Netherlands closed its waters to such ships in 1914, and Norway prohibited the passage of belligerent submarines in 1916. On the other hand, a neutral is not bound to issue such prohibitions, for either territorial waters or ports, as long as neutral jurisdiction is not used for the conduct of hostilities or as a basis of attack against enemies on the high seas. This last possibility was illustrated in the famous old case of the *Twee Gebroeders*.

---

[29] For further details, see Lauterpacht's *Oppenheim*, vol. 2, 693–96; Higgins-Colombos, 510–11. Consult, on the other hand, Borchard, "Was Norway Delinquent in the Case of the *Altmark?*" 34 *AJIL* 289 (1940), for a defense of the Norwegian position, based primarily on the "public vessel" character of the *Altmark*, which was held to have precluded visit, search, or even inspection by Norwegian authorities. The Norwegian government had adopted that attitude, stressing that the *Altmark* displayed the German government service flag, not a naval or merchant marine flag—hence was a "public" vessel and not a navy component in Norwegian eyes: see *Journal of Commerce*, Feb. 20, 1940, 3, 20; also Whiteman, vol. 11, 187–89, 193, 273–75, on the *Altmark* incident.

## THE TWEE GEBROEDERS
*British Prize Court, 1800,*
*3 C. Rob. 162*

FACTS    The *Twee Gebroeders* was a Dutch merchant vessel captured by the British man-of-war *L'Espiègle* outside the neutral territorial waters of Prussia during a war between Great Britain and the Netherlands. The British warship was lying inside those neutral waters but sent boats beyond the three-mile limit to capture the *Twee Gebroeders*, which was then sent to England under command of a prize crew. Prussia claimed in the British prize court that the vessel had been captured illegally and should be restored to its owners.

ISSUE    Was the *Twee Gebroeders* captured through a misuse of neutral territorial water for belligerent purposes?

DECISION    The court ruled in favor of Prussia and ordered restoration of the vessel but refused the costs and damages claimed because the violation of Prussian neutrality was asserted to have been unintentional and only by mistake.

REASONING    Sir William Scott, the judge, stated in part: "I cannot but think that such an act as this, that a ship should station herself on neutral territory, and send out her boats (as was done in this case) on hostile enterprises, is an act of hostility much too immediate to be permitted. For, suppose that even a direct hostile use should be required to bring it within the prohibition of the law of nations, nobody will say that the very act of sending out boats to effect a capture is not itself an act directly hostile, not complete, indeed, but inchoate, and clothed with all the characters of hostility. If this could be defended, it might as well be said that a ship lying in a neutral station might fire shot on a vessel lying out of the neutral territory; the injury in the case would not be consummated, nor received on neutral ground; but no one would say that such an act would not be a hostile act, immediately commenced within the neutral territory. And what does it signify to the nature of the act, considered for the present purpose, whether I send out a cannonshot which shall compel the submission of a vessel lying at two miles distance, or whether I send out a boat armed and manned, to effect the very same thing at the same distance? It is in both cases the direct act of the vessel lying in neutral ground. The act of hostility actually begins, in the latter case, with the launching and manning and arming the boat that is sent out on such an errand of force."

In a relevant case arising out of the World War I capture of the German merchant vessel *Düsseldorf* in Norwegian neutral waters, the British Privy Council decided that there had been a mistaken invasion of Norwegian waters. It ordered the return of the vessel to Norway, with suitable expression of regret, and it also ordered that the appellant, the Norwegian consul general in London, was entitled to be paid such expenses of removing the vessel from British waters to Norwegian or other foreign waters as would fall on the government of Norway.[30]

[30] The *Düsseldorf*, 1920, A.C. 1034–42.

PANAMA DECLARATION OF 1939    The controversies that had arisen during World War I about real or alleged misuses of Latin American territorial waters, together with the fear in 1939 that the new conflict would spread so close to the shores of Latin America as to represent a danger of involvement, caused the American republics to take swift action.

Acting in accordance with the provisions of the 1936 Buenos Aires Treaty and the 1938 Declaration of Lima, the foreign ministers of the republics met at the invitation of Panama in Panama City in September 1939 and approved a number of resolutions designed to preserve the neutral status of the participating countries.[31] The most important instruments were Resolutions V, VII, XIV, and XV. Of these, Resolution V was the General Declaration of Neutrality, establishing for the duration of the war an Inter-American Neutrality Committee . Resolution VII dealt with contraband of war, and Resolution XIV, termed the Declaration of Panama, asserted that

as a measure of continental self-protection, the American Republics, so long as they maintain their neutrality, are as of inherent right entitled to have those waters adjacent to the American continent, which they regard as of primary concern and direct utility in their relations, free from the commission of any hostile act by any non-American belligerent nation, whether such hostile act be attempted or made from land, sea or air.

A zone averaging 300 miles around the American continents, except Canada, then was defined, and the governments agreed to "endeavor, through joint representation" to the belligerents, to secure their compliance with the Declaration of Panama, "without prejudice to the exercise of the individual rights of each state inherent in their sovereignty"; to "consult together to determine upon the measures which they may individually or collectively undertake" to secure the observance of the declaration; and, to the best of their ability, to patrol their coastal waters within the area of the zone.

REACTION TO THE 300-MILE ZONE    These instruments were interesting for several reasons: some of the resolutions mentioned included provisions claimed to represent rules of international law, yet constituting principles not yet generally accepted by the community of nations, and the establishment of the 300-mile zone created, at the most, a new principle of regional international law and, at the least, represented an attempt by a group of states to legislate for the belligerent nations of Europe.

The second of these developments brought swift repercussions from countries at war: Great Britain, France, and Germany all refused to accept the validity of the Declaration of Panama. Legal opinion was also divided as to the merits of the 300-mile security zone established in Panama, and although many of the initial criticisms were based on rather obvious mis-

[31]Texts in 34 *AJIL* (1940), supp., pp. 1–17, see also Henkin, 359–60.

conceptions of the purposes of the declaration, other critical observations remained unanswered by the defenders of the new regional concept. [32]

NEUTRAL GRANT OF ASYLUM TO BELLIGERENT WARSHIPS    Just as a neutral may bar access to its waters to belligerent warships, so it may grant a temporary asylum to such vessels and their auxiliaries and to belligerent seaplanes, without being obliged to force them to disarm and to intern them. The reason for the grant of this privilege of asylum is that the ports of all states serve the interests of the traffic on the high seas, and the grant of hospitality is necessary under many conditions peculiar to this traffic. Naturally, a belligerent warship enjoying a stay in neutral waters is obligated not to misuse these waters as a base of hostile operations against the enemy. If a neutral admits the warships of one party in a conflict, then the warships of the opposing party must also be admitted on a basis of complete equality (Art. 9, Convention XIII).

PROBLEM OF BELLIGERENT SUBMARINES    A major problem with the neutral grant of asylum to belligerent warships arose during World War I in connection with submarines. The Allies had proposed to all neutrals in August 1916 that no asylum be granted to belligerent submarines of any sort. The neutrals could not agree on a joint course of action: the United States rejected the Allied proposal; Norway forbade its waters to all belligerent submarines except in the case of distress, a policy also followed by Sweden and the Netherlands; and Spain closed its waters to all belligerent submarines, regardless of prevailing circumstances.

Before entering World War II, the United States closed its waters to all belligerent submarines except in the case of *force majeure*, in which instance a submarine had to travel on the surface as soon as it entered American jurisdiction. Virtually all other neutral states during World War II followed the United States' example.

DETENTION OF WARSHIPS    If a belligerent warship is granted temporary admission to neutral waters and then refuses to leave after being requested to do so, the neutral host may take all measures necessary to make the vessel incapable of putting to sea as long as the war lasts.

One of the spectacular illustrations provided by World War II in connection with the asylum aspect of neutrality was the fate of the German pocket battleship *Admiral Graf Spee*. This ship, after a battle December 13, 1939, with three British cruisers in which it lost all of its firing-control system — among other damages sustained — found asylum in the harbor of Montevideo. The neutral Uruguayan government ordered the *Graf Spee* to leave when the 72 hours granted for its stay to make necessary repairs had expired. Be-

[32]See Fenwick, "The Declaration of Panama," 34 *AJIL* 116 (1940); Brown, "Protective Jurisdiction," *id.*, 112–16; Wild, "The 300-Mile Neutral Belt in International Law," 26 *American Bar Association Jl.* 237 (1940); and the "Recommendations" submitted by the Neutrality Committee to the participating governments on Apr. 27, 1940, in 35 *AJIL* 38 (1941 Supp.); as well as Whiteman, vol. 11, 451–61.

cause a British squadron had begun to assemble outside Uruguayan waters to await the emergence of the *Graf Spee*, the captain of the vessel ordered the bulk of his crew to transfer to the German merchant vessel *Tacoma*. He then took the *Graf Spee* with a skeleton complement to a point about six miles offshore, but within water claimed by Uruguay to be in its territorial limits. There the German warship was scuttled, and the captain committed suicide on the following day. The crew, on being landed, were interned by Uruguay, but managed to reach Argentina individually, so that by the end of the war hardly any of the crew remained under Uruguayan control. The *Tacoma* was interned by Uruguay for rendering unneutral services from neutral territory. The hulk of the *Graf Spee* was sold by the German government to a Montevideo contractor for removal.[33]

NEUTRAL ASYLUM    Abuse of neutral asylum by a visiting belligerent warship is not restricted to the commission of hostile acts in neutral water, but may occur through other acts entitling the neutral to end the asylum or to intern the vessel and its crew. Thus an abuse would take place if the vessel intentionally wintered in a neutral port to await reinforcements, if it undertook repairs calculated to increase its combat effectiveness (such as by repairing a damaged firing-control system), or if it stayed in its shelter for an undue time in order to escape from attack by an opposing naval force or unit.

An ancient rule, now embodied in Convention XIII, prohibits the establishment of prize courts by belligerents in neutral territory.[34] This practice was one of the offenses charged by the U.S. government against the French minister to the United States, Edmond C. Genêt, who, at the outbreak of the war between Great Britain and France in 1793, had attempted to set up in the U.S. prize courts connected with various French consulates.

## Regulations for Neutral Ports

RIGHT OF NEUTRAL STATES TO REGULATE THEIR PORTS    As mentioned earlier, any neutral state enjoys an absolute right to exclude all belligerent warships from its ports. This was done by several neutrals during the Russo-Japanese War, as well as during World War I. If such vessels are permitted to use neutral ports, the neutral government also has the right to issue regulations for such visits.

TIME LIMITS    If a neutral permits belligerent warships to enter its ports, the length of their stay must be limited. Under the provisions of Article 12 of Convention XIII, such vessels, in the absence of contrary domestic legislation of the neutral, are granted a maximum stay of 24 hours in neutral ports or waters. Article 14 exempts warships entering a neutral port in distress or because of adverse weather, as well as public vessels exclusively dedicated to religious, scientific, or philanthropic purposes.

[33]See Abranson, *Ships of the High Seas* (1976), 102–7, where earlier activities of the *Altmark* are mentioned. For the *Graf Spee*, see Pope, *The Battle of the River Plate* (1988).
[34]*The Betsey*, U.S. Supreme Court, 1794, 3 Dallas 6, 19.

If, at the outbreak of hostilities, a warship of one of the belligerents happens to be in a neutral port, it must be given notice to leave within 24 hours or within the limits prescribed by the neutral's domestic regulations (XIII, Art. 13). A well-known illustration of this situation was supplied by the Russian gunboat *Mandjur*, lying in the port of Shanghai at the outbreak of the Russo-Japanese War in 1904. The Chinese government ordered the vessel to leave within 24 hours, but the captain refused to carry out this lawful order because of the presence of a Japanese warship hovering outside the Chinese territorial waters. After some six weeks of discussion, the armament of the *Mandjur* was dismantled to the satisfaction of the Japanese authorities, and the ship was allowed to remain in the port until after the war had terminated.[35]

Should warships of opposing belligerents happen to be in the same neutral port, the provisions of Article 16 of Convention XIII apply: a period of not less than 24 hours must elapse between the departure of the ship of one belligerent and that belonging to the other. The order of departure is normally determined by the order of arrival in the port. If a merchant vessel of one belligerent and a warship of an opposing one happen to be in a neutral port, the warship is not permitted to leave until 24 hours have elapsed after the depature of the merchant vessel.

LIMIT ON NUMBER OF WARSHIPS IN PORT    Article 15 of Convention XIII limits the number of belligerent warships in a neutral port, at any given time, to three — in the absence of conflicting domestic regulations of the neutral state. Some neutrals have reduced this total to two, such as was done by the Netherlands for all ports in the then Netherlands East Indies during the Spanish-American War.

PERMISSIBLE REPAIRS    One of the problems posed by the visit of a belligerent warship to a neutral port is the permissible repairs to be undertaken on such a vessel. Article 17 of Convention XIII provides that only such repairs may be carried out as are absolutely necessary to render the vessel seaworthy; such repairs may not add in any manner whatever to the ship's fighting capacity. The local neutral authorities are to decide what repairs are necessary, and those must be carried out as speedily as possible.

Recent wars, especially the Russo-Japanese conflict and World War I, have provided numerous additional examples of the visits of belligerent warships to neutral ports and the resulting complications for the neutral. A problem arose in the case of the United States during World War I when a number of German warships (the *Prinz Eitel Friedrich*, the *Kronprinz Wilhelm*, and the *Geier*, together with the naval auxiliary *Locksun*) came to neutral American ports for repairs. Failing to achieve their avowed purpose in the relatively short time limit permitted them by the U.S. government, all the vessels

---

[35] Takahashi, *op. cit. supra* n. 28, 418–35; and see the case of the *Graf Spee*, above.

were interned, and on the entrance of the United States into the war as a belligerent, all the ships in question were seized as government property.[36]

REPROVISIONING AND REFUELING    In regard to reprovisioning and refueling belligerent warships in neutral ports and waters, the question of provisions is regulated by Article 19 of Convention XIII: reprovisioning is legal up to the peacetime standard of the vessel in question. The provisions of the same article (par. 2) dealing with refueling have, on the other hand, led to considerable controversy and caused Great Britain as well as Japan to reject them in 1907. The article stated that belligerent warships could take on only enough fuel to enable them to reach the nearest port of their own country. On the other hand, in neutral countries that had adopted the "bunker rule," a belligerent warship could take on enough fuel to fill its bunkers to capacity.[37]

Article 20 of Convention XIII states that belligerent warships that have refueled in a neutral port may not replenish their fuel supplies in a port belonging to the same neutral within a period of three months.

ARMED MERCHANT VESSELS    None of the foregoing rules governing belligerent warships in neutral waters has any application to defensively armed merchant vessels of belligerent registration. Such ships are properly regarded as falling into the category of private vessels, even if they are state property through some form of nationalization. However, many neutrals during both world wars laid down specific regulations as to what each considered to be purely defensive armament for merchant vessels. If a given ship exceeded the permitted maximum armament (caliber of guns, deck reinforcements, and so on), it was treated by the neutral in question as a warship and was subject to the rules applicable to that category.

SUPPLYING BELLIGERENT WARSHIPS AT SEA    What about supplying a belligerent warship at sea from neutral territory or waters? Thus far, there is no rule of international law governing this problem, although it appears obvious that a binding rule would be desirable. The British interpretation, dating back to 1870, is that as part of a neutral's duties of abstention, it must prevent vessels flying its flag from serving as suppliers of belligerent warships at sea. Other countries have not generally followed this concept, and thus it appeared lawful for German colliers to follow the Russian Baltic fleet on its epic and disastrous journey to the Far East during the Russo-Japanese War and to keep on supplying the Russians with food and especially fuel.

On a regional basis, the British view of the question was adopted in February 1940 by the Inter-American Neutrality Committee through a rec-

---

[36] Garner, *International Law and the World War* (1920), vol. 2, 423–25; and see, again, the *Graf Spee* example, above.
[37] See Higgins-Colombos, 525–28, for a British analysis of the controversy as well as of recent practice.

ommendation that a neutral state prevent merchant vessels in its waters from contacting belligerent warships for the purpose of supplying them with provisions and fuel. The recommendation was caused by the case of the *Tacoma*, a German merchant vessel in the service of the *Admiral Graf Spee* in 1939, while the *Tacoma* was in neutral waters and the German warship on the high seas.[38]

USE OF NEUTRAL PORTS FOR CAPTURED PRIZES    Articles 21–23 of Convention XIII regulate the use of neutral ports by prizes captured by belligerents. According to the definite terms of the instrument, prizes may be brought into neutral ports only because of lack of seaworthiness, unfavorable weather conditions, or a shortage of fuel or provisions. The prize must leave the neutral port as soon as the conditions causing its entry have ceased or have been removed. Should the vessel not leave then, the neutral is obligated to order an immediate departure and, failing to secure compliance, must employ all means available to free the vessel and crew and release them, while interning the prize crew (Art. 21).

If a prize crew brings a prize into a neutral port for any reason not mentioned in Article 21, the neutral government is obligated to release the prize and intern the prize crew (Art. 22). On the other hand, under the provisions of Article 23, the neutral may permit prizes to enter its ports if they are brought there for sequestration (or: seizure), pending a decision by the prize courts of the captor belligerent. The United States, Great Britain, and Japan all opposed this article at the 1907 Hague Conference and refused to accept it on signing Convention XIII. Despite the article's permissive wording, it obviously set aside, for practical purposes, the desirable prohibitions enshrined in Articles 21 and 22.

Articles 21 and 22 became well known through the case of the *Appam*.[39] This ship, a British passenger liner, had been captured by a German warship off Africa and had been brought across the Atlantic by a German prize crew. After the vessel arrived in the neutral American port of Newport News, Virginia, the United States government freed the ship's crew and passengers and interned the prize crew. The British owners then sued to obtain the release of the *Appam* itself. The U.S. District Court ruled that Articles 21 and 22 of Convention XIII, being declaratory of existing customary law, prohibited neutral ports from becoming places of asylum; that the *Appam* had been brought to the United States for reasons other than unseaworthiness, adverse weather, or lack of fuel or provisions; and that in accordance with international law, the vessel should be released to its owners. When the case came before the U.S. Supreme Court by appeal, the decision of the court of first instance was affirmed.

---

[38]See 34 *AJIL* 80 (1940 Supp.); and Whiteman, vol. 11, 256–61.
[39]U.S. Supreme Court, 1916, 243 U.S. 124; see also the comments of Scott in 10 *AJIL* 809 (1916).

## Transfer of Registry

TEST OF THE LAWFUL FLAG    It appears appropriate at this point to insert a brief comment on the rules governing transfers of state registry in time of war.

Even before World War I, a neutral state's flag was the decisive factor in determining a vessel's nationality only if the flag was used legitimately. If it was found that a given vessel had no right, under the law of a neutral state, to display the flag of that state, then further investigation had to determine the true nationality and hence the vessel's enemy or neutral character.

Article 57 of the Declaration of London made this test of the "lawful flag" conclusive except in the case of a transfer of registry. Both Great Britain and France initially adopted Article 57 as a guiding principle at the outbreak of World War I, but soon abandoned it again when it became evident that German interests were buying neutral vessels and sailing them under neutral flags in the interests of Germany. Both Great Britain and France then turned to the test of the owner's nationality vessel's as conclusive of the vessel's nationality.

THE PERSIAN GULF REFLAGGING OF 1987    Late in 1986, the government of the Persian Gulf state of Kuwait approached the Soviet Union and the United States to assist in protecting neutral Kuwaiti shipping in the Gulf against Iranian attacks. The United States agreed in 1987 to both reflag and protect 11 of 21 Kuwaiti oil tankers. The vessels then became American registered ships subject to American laws. None of them was allowed to carry contraband or to serve belligerent ports. The reflagged ships were owned by U.S. citizens or by corporations controlled by U.S. citizens. They had to have a U.S. master. When sailing in the Persian Gulf, the 11 reflagged tankers were escorted by U.S. Navy components, but the latter did not enter the territorial waters of Kuwait. Escort inside those waters was handled by Kuwaiti patrol vessels.

The first two reflagged tankers under U.S. escort moved into the Gulf on July 21, 1987. By November, already 13 convoys of this type had arrived safely in Kuwait. The last such convoy sailed on September 28, 1988. The naval convoy system was also used, but without the reflagging feature, for other vessels under the protection of Great Britain or France. The Soviet Union had leased three tankers to Kuwait, which then sailed under the protection of Soviet naval units.

Unrelated but of interest is the fact that the United States (May 1987) undertook for the first time the protective escort of a Kuwaiti merchant vessel carrying U.S. arms to Bahrain. The Department of Defense announced that it would approve, on a case-by-case basis, similar future protective escort services for shipments to friendly nonbelligerent countries. On April 22, 1988, the U.S. government announced that it would allow U.S. warships to aid all neutral merchant ships under attack in the Gulf.

TRANSFER OF AN ENEMY VESSEL TO A NEUTRAL FLAG    The transfer of a vessel's registry from belligerent to neutral flag posed a different problem.

This has been covered by Articles 55 and 56 of the Declaration of London, which provided that "the transfer of an enemy vessel to a neutral flag effected before the outbreak of hostilities is valid, unless it is proved that such transfer was made in order to evade the consequences to which an enemy vessel, as such, was exposed." There was, furthermore, a presumption that if the "bill of sale is not on board a vessel which has lost her belligerent nationality less than 60 days before the outbreak of hostilities, that the transfer is void. This presumption may be rebutted"; and "when the transfer was effected more than 30 days before the outbreak of hostilities, there is an absolute presumption that it is valid if it is unconditional, complete, and in conformity with the laws of the countries concerned, and if its effect is such that neither the control nor the profits earned by the vessel remain in the same hands as before the transfer."

In November 1939, it was reported that a number of German vessels, including the liner *Bremen*, had been sold to the Soviet Union against deliveries of war matériel and other products. The French government promptly announced that in accordance with French practice dating back to July 26, 1776, and with Article 56 of the 1909 Declaration of London, any such vessel would be treated as an enemy vessel and its sale to Russia would not be accepted as valid.

Generally, a prewar transfer of registry would also be regarded as void if the agreement provided for repurchase by the former owners as the termination of the war.

In all instances in which a transfer of registry is treated as void by a belligerent, the vessel is regarded as possessing enemy character. Its loss or seizure and confiscation does not result in a valid claim against the captor state.

TRANSFER OF TITLE TO A PUBLIC VESSEL   The title to a public vessel, particularly a warship of any kind, cannot be transferred from enemy to neutral hands after the outbreak of a war. The classic instance of such an attempt occurred in 1914, when the German government sold the cruisers *Breslau* and *Goeben* to the then still neutral government of Turkey. The two ships, caught in the Mediterranean at the outbreak of the conflict, found refuge at Constantinople. Past Anglo-American prize court decisions indicated clearly that such a transfer could not be accepted as valid by belligerents, and Great Britain was legally correct in holding, in 1914, that both cruisers were still enemy warships. The dispute became academic, of course, when Turkey entered the war as an ally of the Central Powers and the two cruisers, flying the Turkish flag, became a part of the fleets of Great Britain's enemies.[40]

It should be mentioned that once a neutral vessel has acquired enemy status, all enemy goods aboard may be confiscated or destroyed, and neutral goods aboard such vessels are presumed to be enemy goods unless and until the neutral owners can prove otherwise.

[40]See also the account, on a day-by-day basis, of the two vessels' trip to Turkey in Tuchman, *The Guns of August* (1962), 137–62.

## Contraband

Few areas in international law have caused as many disputes as has the problem of what goods are to be regarded as contraband of war and therefore subject to seizure by a belligerent.[41]

**○ CONCEPT ON CONTRABAND**    All authorities agree that the concept of contraband always involves two primary factors: the <u>nature</u> of the goods in question (their susceptibility to belligerent use) and an enemy <u>destination</u>. For several centuries, diplomats and jurists agreed that there were three categories: (1) absolute contraband, (2) conditional contraband, and (3) noncontraband—even though these terms were not always used in practice.

From the days of Hugo Grotius, a neutral supplying a belligerent with goods primarily useful for the prosecution of the war had to be regarded as being on that belligerent's side, and such goods could be captured and condemned by an opposing belligerent; such goods, traditionally including arms and other war matériel, were classified as *absolute contraband*. Goods useful in *both* peace and war and destined for a belligerent country were subject to seizure at an opposing belligerent's choice and could be included in the category of *conditional (occasional) contraband*. Goods obviously not contributing to a belligerent's war effort were considered *noncontraband* and could not be seized lawfully.

It became the practice of states to draw up lists of absolute and conditional contraband at the outbreak of hostilities. As war became more technological in character and as the "nation in arms" became more of a reality, more and more items were added to the list of conditional contraband goods, and at the same time, more and more items from that category were shifted to the absolute contraband lists. By the end of World War I, almost every item conceivably of use to the enemy was on the absolute contraband lists of both sides: even rubber dolls were included, as that material could be converted into war matériel. And World War II saw such an extension of the concept of absolute contraband that just about every commodity was subject to seizure and condemnation.

In the 1965 declared war between India and Pakistan, both states issued lists of contraband and applied them to neutral vessels in their respective territorial waters. A fairly recent case of a visit and search of a neutral vessel was the *Else Cat*, a small Danish vessel seized in the Strait of Hormuz by the Iranian navy after a visit and search (August 1981). The vessel was taken to the Iranian port of Bandar Abbas, and there part of its cargo, 177 tons of dynamite bound for Iraq, was taken off the ship before it was allowed to proceed on its voyage. Iran had categorized the dynamite as contraband and apparently left aboard a second consignment, this one of ammunition,

---

[41]Lauterpacht's *Oppenheim*, vol. 2, 798–830. See Higgins-Colombos, 541–63, for a brief but excellent discussion of the historical background, as well as Corbett, 243–47, for the modern period.

destined for the Emirate of Dubai. (See also Chapter 14 under "Straits" and Chapter 25 under "Locale of War at Sea" of additional details on war between Iraq and Iran.)

DOCTRINE OF CONTINUOUS VOYAGE    In determining the lawfulness of such a seizure, the doctrine of continuous voyage played a key role. This concept had its origin in the so-called Rule of the War of 1756. In that conflict between Great Britain and France, the latter, being cut off from direct trade with its colonies by British naval superiority, waived hitherto asserted monopolies and permitted neutral Dutch vessels to engage in trade between the colonies and the mother country, under special licenses. Other neutrals were, however, still barred from such trade. The British prize courts correctly assumed that the Dutch vessels engaged in this trade had identified with the French cause to an extent justifying the seizure and condemnation of both vessels and cargoes. When the French opened both colonial trade and coastal trade to all neutrals in 1793, Great Britain extended the Rule of 1756 to all such neutral commerce.[42] The United States accepted and followed this expanded doctrine and, during the American Civil War, extended the concept of continuous voyage to contraband. Repeated decisions of the U.S. Supreme Court affirmed that if contraband goods, ostensibly destined for a neutral country, were eventually to be carried on to a belligerent country, that ultimate destination became the governing factor, and thus the goods could be seized and condemned on their way to the neutral country.[43] Subsequent extensions of the doctrine applied it also to shipments that went from the ostensible neutral destination to their ultimate belligerent destination by way of land transport.[44]

Major maritime powers happily seized on this new doctrine, and it found general application in the Boer War as well as in both world wars. In all instances, however, the seizure of goods under the doctrine of continuous voyage had to be undertaken on the high seas and not in neutral waters, for that would have violated neutral territorial jurisdiction.

The Iraq–Iran conflict saw few neutral ships being stopped and searched under the theories of continuous voyage and contraband, such as the cases of the *President Taylor* (an American bulk carrier) on January 12, 1986, two Soviet vessels on September 2 and 3, 1986, and a Cypriot freighter on June 3, 1988. Normally freighters suspected of carrying cargo for Iraq were attacked without any check on the truth of the charge. The latter would probably have been true in most cases, for Kuwait was known to be a key transshipment point for supplies to Iraq. Iran also asserted repeatedly that

[42] See Baty, "The History of Continuous Voyage," 90 *University of Pennsa. Law Review* 127 (1941).
[43] See *The Peterhoff*, U.S. Supreme Court, 1866, 5 Wallace 28; *The Springbok*, 1866, 5 Wallace 1; *The Bermuda*, 1865, 3 Wallace 514.
[44] See Higgins-Colombos, 546, for the Italian prize court decision in the case of the *Doelwijk*. See also the illuminating decision in *In re part Cargo ex S.S. Monte Contes (Conservas Cerqueira Limitada)* v. *H.M. Procurator General*, Great Britain, Judicial Committee of the Privy Council, 1943, 60 *Times Law Reports* 57, in 38 *AJIL* 305 (1944).

attacks on Kuwaiti vessels were justified in retaliation for Kuwait's toleration of overflights by Iraqi military aircraft on their way to bomb Iranian facilities on Kharg, Larak, and other islands.

The burden of proof of the forbidden nature or destination of goods aboard neutral vessels used to be based on the papers aboard the ship. This old-fashioned reliance disappeared, for obvious reasons, when the doctrine of continuous voyage in its expanded form was applied to such shipments, because in every instance the papers in question gave an innocent, neutral destination. Hence one of the interesting aspects of the application of the doctrine during World War I pertained to the "rationing" of neutrals. The major belligerents in that conflict collected statistics on the average imports of certain commodities by selected neutral states over a period of years before 1914. When it could be shown that shipments of such goods greatly exceeded the average prewar imports, a presumption of ultimate enemy destination was asserted, and the goods were seized and condemned.

NAVICERT SYSTEM    In modern war, therefore, the burden of proof is shifted to the captor government, which has to prove to its own prize courts that the seized cargo was indeed destined for an opposing belligerent and consisted of prohibited goods.

In order to permit an unhindered flow of legitimate trade between neutrals themselves as well as between them and belligerents, a number of devices have been developed during recent wars. First, during World War I, came a series of agreements concluded between the British government and merchants' associations in various neutral countries. Those instruments provided for a guarantee by the merchants that the goods they imported would not reach the enemies of Great Britain, which, in turn, undertook not to interfere with shipments to the merchants' associations, subject to exceptional instances of suspected fraud. A little later the famous "navicert system" was devised. This consisted originally of the granting by the British government of "letters of assurance" to neutral shipping companies after the cargoes of particular shipments had been investigated and approved. Beginning in March 1916, American shippers began to use similar documents, called *navicerts*, issued to them by Allied diplomatic and consular agents in the United States. These documents allowed a vessel and its cargo to proceed without hindrance from the United States to its neutral destination—thus obviating the delay normally caused by enforced inspection in a British port. As the war went on, the navicert system was expanded and was applied also to shipments from Latin America. Navicerts were reintroduced at the outbreak of World War II and were expanded even beyond the scope that the system had attained in the earlier conflict. The system was expanded again in June 1941, when mailcerts began to be issued by the British Ministry of Economic Warfare in order to pass packages and letters containing merchandise.

DISPOSITION OF CAPTURED NEUTRAL VESSELS    A captured neutral vessel is not supposed to be sunk or otherwise destroyed but is to be taken to the nearest port of the captor for action by a prize court. This is an old principle of customary law, reinforced by Article 48 of the Declaration of London. However, Article 49 of the same instrument provides that if such transfer to a belligerent port entails great danger to the captor, the vessel may be destroyed, provided it is liable to condemnation by a prize court. During both world wars, the Allied Powers opposing Germany observed Article 47 fairly well, but German practice in World War I and Axis practice in World War II was more often the destruction of captured vessels than an attempt to bring them to a port of the captor state. In extenuation of these acts, particularly by Germany, British naval superiority made it exceedingly difficult and dangerous for German prize crews to try to bring captured Allied or neutral merchant vessels into German ports for judicial action.

Finally, a modern development full of perplexing questions to the jurist has been the emergence of neutral governments dealing in contraband goods. A lawful belligerent attempt to stop such traffic is bound to lead to an immediate dispute between two states. This vexatious kind of neutral activity had its origin early in World War II.[45] As yet, the legal conclusions to be drawn from such obvious unneutral services have not been delineated clearly.

## Unneutral Service

Neutral ships are subject to capture and condemnation if they engage in unneutral service or hostile assistance, in the terminology of the Declaration of London. This instrument asserted the existence of two categories of unneutral services (Arts. 45, 46), but this distinction was dropped in practice at about the middle of World War I. Henceforth the traditional rule prevailed again: a neutral ship performing services for an enemy belligerent is to be treated as an enemy ship.

What are unneutral services? The Declaration of London listed them, and the list is quite instructive.

PROSCRIBED PASSENGERS   A neutral ship may not not carry persons incorporated in the armed forces of a belligerent. If such individuals travel individually and not in uniform, then the direct knowledge of the ship's master or owner has to be proved before the vessel may be condemned. However, if such proscribed passengers are found aboard a neutral vessel, without the knowledge mentioned, they may be made prisoners of war and removed from the vessel even when the ship is not subject to capture.

PROSCRIBED SERVICES   A neutral vessel may not participate directly in hostilities; it may not be under the orders or control of an agent placed aboard by a belligerent government; it may not be in the exclusive service of such a government; it may not be exclusively engaged at the time in the transport of belligerent troops; and it may not be engaged at the time in the transmission of intelligence in the interests of a belligerent government.

[45] See Woolsey, "Government Traffic in Contraband," 34 AJIL 498 (1940)

A famous case involving the concept of unneutral service was that of the *Manouba*.[46] This vessel, a French mail steamer, was stopped during the Italo-Turkish War in 1912 by an Italian warship and taken to the Italian port of Cagliari. Aboard the *Manouba* were 29 Turkish citizens suspected of being in the Turkish armed forces. The Italian captain did not demand the surrender of these enemy citizens until they reached Cagliari. There the Turks were removed from the *Manouba*, and the vessel was released, having been in port one day. There was no evidence that the ship's owners and master had acted in bad faith. The French government protested against the taking of the *Manouba* to Italy, and the dispute was eventually submitted to the Permanent Court of Arbitration. The tribunal awarded damages to France because the arrest of the vessel should have been preceded by a demand for the Turks' surrender, but the court emphasized that such a demand would have been lawful on suspicion of the character of the passengers in question.

ENEMY MALE CITIZENS OF MILITARY AGE    Most recent decisions, particularly during World War II, have shown that a belligerent nowadays appears to have a right to remove male enemy citizens of military age and apparently good health from neutral vessels even if such individuals are not members of an enemy's armed forces.[47] The presumption justifying such capture is that the individuals in question, under generally prevailing conscription laws, will be recruited into the armed forces when they reach their own country and thus must be regarded as being on their way to swell the ranks of an enemy's military or naval forces.

COMMUNICATIONS    Other aspects of unneutral service, much emphasized in the days before radio communications, centered on the carrying of enemy dispatches, an act universally regarded as assisting an enemy, hence leading to confiscation of the vessel engaged in such carriage.

On the other hand, a neutral vessel may lawfully carry communications between a belligerent government and its accredited diplomatic and consular agents in neutral countries and may also carry these agents themselves without being guilty of an unneutral service. On rare occasions, the diplomatic agents of enemy belligerents have been removed from neutral vessels, but in every major case, following strong protests, they have been released again. Higgins and Colombos cited the case of the counselor at the British embassy in Moscow who was taken off an Estonian vessel by a German cruiser in December 1939, while he was on his way to a new post in neutral Bolivia. Following a strong protest by the Untied States (it was protecting British interests in Germany at the time), Germany released the British diplomat.

---

[46]*The Manouba*, Permanent Court of Arbitration, May 16, 1913; English text in Wilson, *Hague Arbitration Cases* (1915), 341–52.

[47]The traditional legal attitude was defended eloquently by Briggs, "Removal of Enemy Persons from Neutral Vessels on the High Seas," 34 *AJIL* 249 (1940), caused by the incident of the *Asama Maru* on Jan. 21, 1940; but see Lauterpacht's *Oppenheim*, vol. 2, 845–46, for additional modern examples of the practice.

It should be mentioned, before we close this subject, that if a neutral vessel is condemned for performing an unneutral service, its cargo, regardless of its ownership or nature, is normally condemned with the vessel.

## Neutral Rights and Duties in Air Warfare

The extensive use of aircraft for military purposes during World War I and the well-publicized failures of aircraft commanders to observe all regulations laid down at the 1907 Hague Conference led to a search for new rules applicable to the air age. The states participating in the 1922 Washington Conference on the Limitation of Armaments therefore appointed a commission of jurists to draft the Code of Air Warfare Rules, intended to supplement the Air Navigation Convention of 1919. The code was completed in 1923 but failed to be ratified. Nevertheless several governments announced on subsequent occasions that they would abide by the 1923 rules, which are generally termed the Hague Air Warfare Rules.

A number of articles of the Hague Air Warfare Rules referred to the position of neutrals in air warfare. Thus Article 30 specified the right of a belligerent to warn neutral aircraft off a particular area and to exclude them by force if need be. Article 35 dealt with the treatment of neutral aircraft over land and sea. Article 45 reaffirmed the then already-established rule that a neutral state was not obligated to prevent the (private) export of aircraft to belligerents, and Article 46 stated that a neutral state was bound to use the means at its disposal:

(1) to prevent the departure from its jurisdiction of any aircraft in a condition to make a hostile attack against a belligerent Power, or carrying or accompanied by appliances or materials the mounting or utilization of which would enable it to make a hostile attack, if there is reason to believe that such aircraft is destined for use against a belligerent Power; (2) to prevent the departure of any aircraft the personnel of which belongs to the combatant forces of a belligerent Power.

There is little doubt that today a few basic rules of customary law have been established with reference to aircraft: belligerent planes must not enter neutral airspace. If they do, then the neutral state is obligated to force them to land and, subsequently, to intern them and their crews for the duration of the conflict. In the case of aircraft carried aboard a warship, such craft may not leave their carriers as long as the latter are in neutral waters and the aircraft are treated as components of the vessel carrying them.[48]

In slight contrast with neutral practices during World War I, when personnel of belligerent aircraft rescued at sea by neutral merchant vessels were regarded as shipwrecked sailors and were not interned, Article 43 of the 1923 rules provided that such military personnel, if rescued by neutral military aircraft and brought to neutral jurisdiction, were to be interned.

[48]See Whiteman, vol. 11, 355–66.

In regard to blockades, legal authorities are virtually unanimous in agreeing that there can be no such thing as an aerial blockade. On the other hand, planes do play a vital part in modern blockades as auxiliaries to naval forces; in addition, planes may be used effectively in preventing the entry or departure of other planes from a blockaded area.

## Right of Angary and Doctrine of Necessity

EARLY CONCEPT OF THE RIGHT OF ANGARY    In the Middle Ages, a practice known as *jus angariae*, the law of angary, developed when belligerents lacked sufficient vessels for their purposes. They claimed, under these circumstances, a right to seize neutral merchant ships in their ports and to force them and their crews to carry troops, provisions, and matériel to certain places on payment of freight charges in advance. This practice spread widely until in the seventeenth century, various states concluded bilateral agreements under which their vessels were exempted from the application of the law of angary. The original concept thereupon lapsed from the practice of states until the twentieth century, when it reappeared in somewhat changed form.

MODERN CONCEPT OF THE RIGHT OF ANGARY    The modern right of angary is the right of belligerents to destroy, or use in case of need, neutral property on their own or on enemy territory and perhaps on the high seas. Unlike the original law, the modern concept applies only to property and does not permit the use of neutral crews of ships or trains seized under this right.

Every kind of neutral property is thus susceptible to belligerent seizure, provided it can be used for military purposes. However, in every case in which this right is applied, full compensation must be paid to the neutral owner. This rule is based on customary international law and should not be confused with the provisions for payment found in Article 53 of the Hague Regulations of 1907, which deals with compensation for means of transportation seized from the inhabitants of occupied enemy territory.[49] Examples of the exercise of the right of angary were not common until World War I. A celebrated example usually cited is the German sinking in 1871 of British coal carriers at Duclair in order to prevent French warships from severing German military communications by moving up the river Seine. When Great Britain protested the act, the Prussian government denied a responsibility to pay compensation to the vessels' owners, even though it had agreed to do so. Some writers have held that this case did not represent an exercise of the right of angary, claiming that it was an example of requisitioning.[50] The present writer cannot agree with this interpretation and believes the German act to have been based on the right of angary.[51]

[49]Lauterpacht, "Angary and Requisition of Neutral Property," 27 *BYIL* 455 (1950); Whiteman, vol. 11, 329–55; Jennings, "The Right of Angary," 3 *Cambridge Law Jl.* 49 (1927–1929).
[50]Higgins-Colombos, 445.
[51]See also a similar view in Lauterpacht's *Oppenheim*, vol. 2, 762, n. 5.

RIGHT OF ANGARY DURING WORLD WAR I    World War I witnessed the sudden rise to prominence of the doctrine underlying the right of angary. British prize courts frequently justified the seizure of neutral vessels and their cargoes under that right. In 1915, Italy, then at war with Austria-Hungary but not yet with Germany, seized 37 German ships in Italian ports, and Germany did not protest this action. In February 1916, Portugal seized 72 German vessels in Portuguese waters. In May 1917, Brazil took over 42 German ships that had found refuge in Brazilian ports. And in August 1918, Spain seized 90 German ships found in its ports. All the seizing states were neutrals at the time the events in question took place. Subsequent to, and in consequence of, the ship seizures, Germany declared war on Portugal and Brazil on Germany. On March 20, 1918, the United States seized 77 Dutch ships then in American ports, promising full compensation to the owners. Within a few days Great Britain, France, and Italy undertook similar steps, all claiming a right to do so under the concept of angary. The Dutch government protested vigorously but ineffectually against what it asserted to be "an ancient rule unearthed for the occasion and adapted to entirely new correlations in order to excuse seizure *en masse* by a belligerent of the merchant fleet of a neutral country." At the end of World War I, the United States paid in full for the use of the Dutch vessels and returned them reconditioned to their owners; two of the ships were sunk by German submarines, and the United States paid for those two vessels in full.

Ships under construction may also be seized by a belligerent under the right of angary: Great Britain was legally correct in confiscating four warships being built in English yards to the order of the Turkish government, at a time when Turkey was still a neutral in World War I. The United States also seized, in 1917, several incomplete Norwegian vessels and construction contracts. The compensation offered was rejected by Norway, and the issue was settled by arbitration, the United States being required to pay $12.239 million to Norway.

The action of Congress in passing on June 6, 1941, an act[52] enabling the president to purchase or seize, with just compensation, idle foreign ships in the waters under U.S. jurisdiction did not fall within the province of the normal right of angary, because this right is usually viewed as being reserved for belligerents, and at the time, the United States was theoretically neutral, though nonbelligerent. The action of the United States was followed, incidentally, by the other American republics in August and September 1941.

Much greater publicity than in the cases mentioned was given to the seizure of neutral vessels and cargoes by belligerents on the high seas. Most writers on the subject differ with Oppenheim in his assertion that belliger-

[52]Text in 35 *AJIL* 224 (1941 Supp.); see also Woolsey "The Taking of Foreign Ships in American Ports," 35 *AJIL* 497 (1941).

ent states have such a right under angary,[53] and instead they have asserted that the decision as to whether neutral property can be seized on the high seas is a matter for the courts, not for the executive branch, of a belligerent government.[54] The leading case on the subject, the well-known condemnation of the *Zamora*, illustrates this point clearly and points up the conditions under which the right of angary may be exercised on the high seas.

The *Zamora* was a Swedish vessel on its way from New York to Stockholm with a cargo of copper and grain. On April 8, 1915, the ship was stopped by British cruisers between the Shetland and Faeroe islands, was taken to Barrow-in-Furness, and was placed before a prize court. On condemnation of the cargo, the case came by appeal before the British Privy Council. In the absence of conclusive evidence that the cargo was urgently needed for the country's defense, the Privy Council disallowed the requisition authorized by the prize court. In reviewing the decision of the prize court in this case, the Judicial Committee of the Privy Council asserted that three conditions had to be met: (1) the neutral vessel or neutral goods had to be urgently required for the defense of the state, the prosecution of the war, or other matters of national security; (2) a real question had to be tried before the prize court so that it would be improper for the latter to order an immediate release of ship or goods; and (3) the applicability of the right of angary to the particular circumstances of each case had to be decided judicially by the prize court.[55]

Basically, seizure of neutral ships or cargoes on the high seas revolves around the concept of military necessity. In fact, whenever such a seizure is legitimized by a prize court, military necessity has triumphed over the undoubted legal rights of neutrals, despite the inevitable payment of compensation for seized property.

RIGHT OF ANGARY AND LAND WARFARE    One special aspect of the right of angary pertains to land warfare. Under the provisions of Article 19 of the Fifth Hague Convention of 1907, a belligerent may seize (or requisition) railroad material (regardless of ownership) coming into its territory from a neutral state, provided that it is absolutely necessary, that such seized properties (rolling stock and motive power) are returned to the country of origin as soon as possible, and that compensation is paid for the use of the properties. The article also provides that a neutral state whose railroad rolling stock has been seized by a belligerent is lawfully entitled to seize and retain, to a corresponding extent, rolling stock and motive power coming from the territory of that belligerent. It might be added that these rules have been extended in practice to cover neutral rolling stock and motive

[53]Lauterpacht's *Oppenheim*, vol. 2, 762; Sir Hersch Lauterpacht supported Oppenheim's view in every edition of Oppenheim's great work that he edited.
[54]Thus especially Higgins-Colombos, 446–48; see also Harley, "The Law of Angary," 13 *AJIL* 267 (1919).
[55]*The Zamora*, Great Britain, Judicial Committee of the Privy Council, 1916, 2 A.C. 77.

power found by a belligerent in occupied enemy territory or coming into such territory in the normal course of any traffic still permitted by the belligerent occupant.

## SUGGESTED READINGS

### Neutrality: General

The most comprehensive account of the history and practice of neutrality is in *Neutrality: Its History, Economics and Law*, 4 vols. 1: *The Origins*, Jessup and Deák (1935); 2: *The Napoleonic Period*, Phillips (1936); 3: *The World War Period*, Jessup (1936); 4: *Today and Tomorrow*, Jessup (1936); Lauterpacht's *Oppenheim*, vol. 2, 666–879.

CASES

*The Adula*, U.S. Supreme Court, 1900, 176 U.S. 361.
*The Kim*, Great Britain, High Court of Justice, Probate, Divorce and Admiralty Division, 1915, L.R. [1915] Probate 215.
*The Peterhoff*, U.S. Supreme Court, 1866, 5 Wallace 28.
*The Omaha*, U.S. Dist. Court, Puerto Rico, 71 F. Supp. 314, April 30, 1947, reported in 42 *AJIL* 223 (1948), appeal decision, Court of Appeals, 1st Cir., 168 F.2d 47, May 10, 1948, *id.*, 720. See also Woolsey, "Capture of the German Steamship 'Odenwald,' " 36 *AJIL* 96 (1942).
See also the incidents surrounding the *City of Flint*, in Hyde, "The City of Flint," 34 *AJIL* 89 (1940); Jessup, "The Reality of International Law," 51 *Current History* 13, 61 (Apr. 1940); and Taylor, "A Matter of Judgment," 84 *U.S. Naval Institute Proceedings* 70 (1958).

### Nonbelligerency

Eagleton, "The Duty of Impartiality on the Part of a Neutral," 34 *AJIL* 99 (1940); Borchard, "War, Neutrality and Non-Belligerency," 35 *AJIL* 618 (1941); Coudert, "Non-Belligerency in International Law," 29 *Virginia Law Rev.* 143 (1942).

### Destroyer-Bases Exchange

Greenberg, "U.S. Destroyers for British Bases—Fifty Old Ships Go to War," 88 *U.S. Naval Institute Proceedings* 70 (Nov. 1962); Wright, "The Transfer of Destroyers to Great Britain," 34 *AJIL* 680 (1940); Briggs, "Neglected Aspects of the Destroyer Deal," *id.*, 569–87; *NYT*, Aug. 18–Sept. 8, 1940, *passim*, Feb. 26, 1941, 1, 9.

### Lend Lease

USSR–United States, "Agreement Regarding Settlement of Lend-Lease, Reciprocal Aid and Claims (October 18, 1972)" in 11 *ILM* 1315 (1972); *NYT*, Sept. 27, 1970, 12.

# 27

# War Crimes

Any person, whether a civilian or a member of a state's armed forces, who commits an act that violates a rule of the international law governing armed conflicts is responsible for his act and is liable to punishment as a war criminal.

This statement, if written in 1914, would have represented merely a pious hope; in 1919, it would have caused derision; but now it represents general but not yet universal agreement on existing rules of international law governing armed conflicts.

A discussion of crimes under that law is greatly complicated by the fact that today three categories of such offenses are recognized, one of which is still a subject of much debate: (1) war crimes, (2) crimes against humanity, and (3) crimes against peace. The third of these centers, of course, on an interpretation of the Pact of Paris of 1928. (See Chapter 20).

## WAR CRIMES

Generally, a war crime is any act for which soldiers or other individuals may be punished by the enemy on capture of the offender. The category includes acts committed in violation of international law and the laws of the criminal's own country as well as acts in violation of the laws of war and undertaken by order and in the interest of the criminal's own state.

Current concepts regarding the nature of war crimes represent striking departures from traditional legal attitudes toward the subject. Thus it was assumed for many decades that offenses against the laws of war constituted crimes against the municipal law of belligerents.[1] The defenses of *act-of-state* and *superior orders* conditioned prosecution for war crimes. The asserted municipal character of penal offenses against the laws of war was based also on the orthodox belief that individuals were not subjects of international law. Again, none of the pre-1914 conventions dealing with war crimes designated the sanctions that would be applied to states or to individuals for violations of the rules governing warfare, with the exception of Article 3 of the Fourth

---

[1]Manner, "The Legal Nature and Punishment of Criminal Acts of Violence Contrary to the Laws of War," 37 *AJIL* 407, esp. 407, 414–15 (1943).

Hague Convention of 1907, which called for payment of compensation by the belligerent state guilty of violating the treaty. Lastly, the absence of an international authority made it the duty of states to incorporate the conventions' provisions in their national law and to enforce this law against their own nationals or subjects.[2]

All of these notions have been abandoned since the early days of World War II. Evidence for this change is available in abundance in national military manuals, in the four Geneva conventions of 1949, and in the decisions in the international and national war crimes trials. Today responsibility for war crimes can be placed on individuals, including heads of states; the defense of superior orders has been circumscribed drastically; international tribunals are possible for the trial of the offending individuals; and national judicial agencies (civil or military) may try alien war criminals. A revolution, mostly to the good, has thus taken place in this specialized aspect of international law, and at least in this sphere, the individual has at last become a subject of the law.

## Major Kinds of War Crimes

Most authorities concur that there are four kinds of war crimes: (1) violations of the rules governing warfare; (2) hostile armed acts committed by persons who are not members of recognized armed forces; (3) espionage, sabotage, and war treason, and (4) all marauding acts.

ACTS CONSTITUTING WAR CRIMES    The following list, although not complete, includes the major acts falling under the concept of violations of the laws of war: (1) using poisoned or otherwise forbidden arms or munitions, (2) treachery in asking for quarter or simulating sickness or wounds, (3) maltreating corpses, (4) firing on localities that are undefended and without military significance, (5) abusing or firing on a flag of truce, (6) misusing the Red Cross or similar emblems, (7) troops wearing civilian clothes to conceal their identity during the commission of combat acts, (8) improperly using privileged (exempt, immune) buildings for military purposes, (9) poisoning streams or wells, (10) pillaging, (11) committing purposeless destruction, (12) compelling prisoners of war to engage in prohibited types of labor, (13) forcing civilians to perform prohibited labor, (14) violating surrender terms, (15) killing or wounding military personnel who have laid down arms, surrendered, or are disabled by wounds or sickness,[3] (16) assassinating and hiring assassins, (17) ill-treating prisoners of war or the wounded and sick—including despoiling them of possessions not classifiable as public

---

[2]*Id.*, 408–9, citing Article 1 of the Hague Conventions on Land Warfare of 1899 and 1907; Articles 27–29 of the Red Cross Conventions of 1929; and Articles 82, 84, and 85 of the 1929 Convention Relating to the Treatment of Prisoners of War.

[3]Such as the massacre of more than 4,000 captive Polish army officers by the Russian secret police (NKVD) in the Katyn Forest in the spring of 1940: see *CSM*, March 22, 1989, 19 and April 11, 1989, 6; *Time*, Nov. 13, 1989, 57; and *infra*, n. 10.

property, (18) killing or attacking harmless civilians,[4] (19) compelling the inhabitants of occupied enemy territory to furnish information about the armed forces of the enemy or his means of defense, (20) appropriating or destroying the contents of privileged buildings, (21) bombarding from the air for the exclusive purpose of terrorizing or attacking civilian populations, (22) attacking enemy vessels that have indicated their surrender by lowering their flag, (23) attacking or seizing hospitals and all other violations of the Hague Convention for the Adaptation to Maritime Warfare of the Principles of the Geneva Convention, (24) committing unjustified destruction of enemy prizes, (25) using of enemy uniforms during combat and using the enemy flag during attack by a belligerent vessel, (26) attacking individuals supplied with safe-conducts, and other violations of special safeguards provided, (27) breaking parole, (28) grave breaches of Article 50 of the 1949 Geneva Convention for the Amelioration of the Condition of the Wounded and Sick in Armed Forces in the Field and of Article 51 of the 1949 Geneva Convention Applicable to Armed Forces at Sea: "wilful killing, torture or inhuman treatment, including biological experiments, wilfully causing great suffering or serious injury to body or health, and extensive destruction and appropriation of property not justified by military necessity and carried out unlawfully and wantonly," (29) grave breaches of the 1949 Geneva Convention Relative to the Treatment of Prisoners of War, as listed in Article 130: "wilful killing, torture or inhuman treatment, including biological experiments, wilfully causing great suffering or serious injury to body or health, compelling a prisoner of war to serve in the forces of the hostile Power, or wilfully depriving a prisoner of war of the rights of fair and regular trial prescribed" in the convention,[5] (30) grave breaches of the Fourth Geneva Convention of 1949, as detailed in Article 147: "wilful killing, torture or inhuman treatment, including biological experiments, wilfully causing great suffering or serious injury to body or health, unlawful deportation or transfer or unlawful confinement of a protected person, compelling a protected person to serve in the forces of a hostile Power, or wilfully depriving a protected person of the rights of fair and regular trial prescribed in the present Convention, taking of hostages and extensive destruction and appropriation of property, not justified by military necessity and carried out unlawfully and wantonly,"[6] (31) destroying civilian cultural objects and

---

[4]Such as the German massacre of 33,771 Jews at Babi Yar (Soviet Union) on September 29–30, 1941, and, in 1944, of all but one of the 644 inhabitants of the French village of Oradour-sur-Glane: see Korey, "What Monument to Babi Yar?" *Saturday Review*, Feb. 3, 1968, 18–19, 40; and "The Lammerding Affair," *Time*, Jan. 11, 1971, 22.

[5]Consult the fully documented study by Levie, "Penal Sanctions for Maltreatment of Prisoners of War," 56 *AJIL* 433 (1962), for a comprehensive analysis of all important issues in this area. See also Geneva Protocol-I of 1977, Arts. 43–45 [texts of PR-I and PR-II in 16 *ILM* 1391 (1977), and in 72 *AJIL* 457 (1978),]; as well as *NYT*, Dec. 10, 1973, 19; June 14, 1974, 10.

[6]Based on *Law of Land Warfare*, pars. 502–4; and on Lauterpacht's *Oppenheim*, vol. 2, 567–68, n. 2.

places of worship (unless, the present writer believes, true military necessity demands it),[7] (32) conspiring, directly inciting, and attempting to commit, as well as complicity in the commission of, crimes against laws of war, (33) taking hostages,[8] and (34) killing hostages.[9]

TREATMENT OF PRISONERS    Recent conflicts have witnessed widespread violations of the rules governing the treatment of prisoners of war. During World War II, several thousand Polish prisoners of war were executed by the Soviet Union, which was not a party to the 1929 Geneva Convention Relating to the Treatment of Prisoners of War but which was bound by customary law.[10] During the Korean War, numerous illegal executions of prisoners by the North Korean forces came to light. During the Vietnamese conflict, there were many authenticated instances of the maltreatment of prisoners by both sides.[11] In October 1965, the government of North Vietnam announced to the International Red Cross in Geneva that henceforth captured U.S. pilots would be tried as war criminals, a threat that was not carried out. North Vietnam had adhered to the Geneva Convention of 1949 in 1957, but had decided to ignore the prohibition on reprisals against prisoners of war. (See also the "Suggested Readings" at the end of this chapter.)

The crew of the U.S. surveillance ship USS *Pueblo*, captured in January 1968 by North Korea, were ill treated during most of their captivity, until released in December of the same year.[12]

DEFENSE OF SUPERIOR ORDERS    Violation of one of the laws of war on the order of a belligerent state or an individual commander of such a state does not remove the stigma of a war crime from the act. Hence the defense of superior orders no longer constitutes a valid defense for an individual accused of committing a war crime. Only if it can be shown that he did not know and could not reasonably have been expected to know that the

---

[7]PR-I of 1977, Art. 5.

[8]Geneva-IV of 1949, Art. 34; PR-I of 1977, Art. 75(2c); and PR-II, Art. 4(2c).

[9]Item 34 is now obsolete, in view of the prohibition against taking hostages. During World War II, the killing of hostages by belligerent occupants was permissible, provided the individuals bore some relation to the crime committed against the occupation forces. The American War Crimes Court (Nuremberg, 1948) held in the trial of Field Marshal Wilhelm List that the right to execute hostages had been recognized by many countries as the only way an occupying army could protect itself against partisan attacks.

[10]See *supra*, n. 3. Consult Zawodny, *Death in the Forest: The Story of the Katyn Forest Massacre* (1962); (London) *Daily Telegraph*, July 22, 1971, 4; *International Herald-Tribune* (Paris), July 22, 1971, 1; Jack Anderson's syndicated column, published in many U.S. newspapers on June 21, 1978. For a similar massacre of Russian prisoners by Germany in Poland, see *NYT*, Nov. 19, 1972, 3.

[11]Note the important qualification regarding such violations, by Falk: "In reading these materials, however, it is important to refrain from arriving at *legal* conclusions. These reports on battlefield operations are unverified newspaper accounts. Any particular report may be unreliable."—Falk, "International Law and the Conduct of the Vietnam War," 22–27, at 23, in Melman (director of research), *In the Name of America* (1968). See also "The Geneva Convention on Prisoners of War," *National Observer*, May 26, 1969, 7; and *U.S. News & World Report*, June 23, 1969, 47–49.

[12]For a summary, see *Time*, Jan. 3, 1969, 18–19.

act ordered was unlawful can such an accused person plead superior orders in his defense. However, most military manuals today hold that when the order is held not to constitute a defense, the fact that the accused acted in pursuance of orders may be considered a mitigating factor in the assessment of punishment (*Law of Land Warfare*, par. 509-a). [13]

The Charter of the International Military Tribunal (Nuremberg) created in 1945 expressly rejected the plea of superior orders as an absolute defense, but provided in Article 3 that superior orders might be considered in mitigation of punishment if the tribunal determined that justice required this to be done. The concept of superior orders as a defense has also been rejected by Article 8 of the London Charter (which established the Nuremberg Tribunal), the Charter of the International Military Tribunal for the Far East, by Control Council Law No. 10 (Allied Control Commission for Germany), and by most national courts trying war crimes. [14]

The question of acts done pursuant to orders issued by a superior poses, of course, serious problems to members of armed forces. It is their duty to obey all lawful orders; they cannot, under conditions of war discipline, be expected to weigh the legal merits of every order issued to them; they may realize that certain laws of war are worded somewhat ambiguously or are controversial and may not be able to determine, at the time, the status of the order received as it relates to the rule in question; and, very important from the point of view of violations of the rules, many acts normally classified as war crimes may be ordered as reprisals for prior acts committed by the enemy (*Land Warfare*, par. 509-b).

Even though the defense of superior orders, the "Nuremberg Defense," is no longer accepted as an absolute one, it is brought forward on occasion. It reappeared, for instance, in the trial (in an East Berlin court) for war crimes and crimes against humanity of a former SS officer, Heinz Barth. The defendant admitted shooting Czech civilians during World War II, but insisted that he "could not imagine" that carrying out orders for mass executions could be considered criminal. This defense also surfaced, although not in a war crimes trial, when the Supreme Court of Burma rejected (February 9, 1984) an appeal against death sentences imposed against two North Korean army officers for the Rangoon bombing of October 1983 that killed 21 people, including four South Korean cabinet ministers. The court ruled that the plea of superior orders was inadmissible.

RESPONSIBILITY OF MILITARY COMMANDERS    Military commanders may be responsible for war crimes committed by subordinates in their armed forces or by other persons under their control. This is always true of such acts as massacres and atrocities committed against enemy civilians or prisoners.

---

[13]Lewy, "Superior Orders, Nuclear Warfare, and the Dictates of Conscience: The Dilemma of Military Obedience in the Atomic Age," 55 *APSR* 3 (1961); *Time*, Jan. 25, 1971, 24; *U.S. News & World Report*, April 12, 1971, 24–25.

[14]Levie, "Some Comments on Professor D'Amato's 'Paradox,' " 80 *AJIL* 608, at 609 (1986); D'Amato, "Superior Orders vs. Command Responsibility," *id.*, 604.

Obviously, commanders have direct responsibility for war crimes committed under their orders. A commander is responsible if he has actual knowledge, or should have had knowledge through reports received by him or through other means, that troops or other persons subject to his control are planning to commit, or have committed, a war crime and if he fails to take the necessary and reasonable steps to ensure compliance with the laws of war or to punish the violators (*Land Warfare*, par. 501).

A commander's failure to take preventive steps or to punish acts already committed presumes approval of the act, or at least connivance. This was a major part of the reasoning that led to the 1946 death sentence imposed by a United States military commission in Manila on General Tomoyuki Yamashita.[15] There was persuasive evidence offered that General Yamashita was unable to control his disintegrating forces and that he did not order, permit voluntarily, or condone the conduct of which they were guilty in the Philippines. Similarly, Lieutenant General Shigenori Kuroda, charged with responsibility for crimes committed by his troops, was sentenced to life imprisonment at hard labor by a Philippine military commission. On the other hand, General Yasutsugu Okamura, similarly indicted, was tried and acquitted by a special military tribunal of the Republic of China.

RESPONSIBILITY OF HEADS OF STATE    If a war crime is committed or ordered by an individual who acted as head of a state or in the capacity of a responsible government official, he is not relieved of responsibility and is liable to punishment. And the fact that his own domestic law does not penalize an act that, under international law, is a war crime does not relieve the individual who committed or ordered the act of responsibility and punishment (*Law of Land Warfare*, pars. 510–11).

STATUS OF PRIVATE INDIVIDUALS WHO COMMITT HOSTILE ACTS    Private individuals who assert a right to take up arms and commit hostile acts against an enemy do not enjoy the rights and privileges of members of armed forces. They may therefore be treated as war criminals by the enemy, except in the case of a genuine *levée en masse*, as outlined in Chapter 21. When such individuals organize in accordance with the Hague Convention of 1907, they vacate private status and must be treated in accordance with the laws of war, provided they obey those laws. Thus the French Forces of the Interior were organized in June 1944 as a force under the command of a high French military officer. They were then recognized by the Supreme Commander of the Allied Expeditionary Force as a component part of that force, and when German units refused to honor that status, acts committed against the French Forces of the Interior were judged by the Allied command to be war crimes.

[15] *In re Yamashita*, U.S. Supreme Court, 1946, 327 U.S. 1, reprinted in 40 *AJIL* 432 (1946); Reel, *The Case of General Yamashita* (1949); Lael, *The Yamashita Precedent: War Crimes and Command Responsibility* (1982). See also Feldhaus, "The Trial of Yamashita," 13 *Current Legal Thought* 251 (1947); and especially Howard, "Command Responsibility for War Crimes," 12 *Jl. Public Law* 7 (1972). Consult Lauterpacht's *Oppenheim*, vol. 2, 573, n. 1, for similar cases cited there.

SABOTAGE    Individuals who, without meeting the conditions laid down in conventional law for recognition as lawful combatants, commit hostile acts behind the lines of the enemy are not treated as prisoners of war and may be sentenced to imprisonment or to execution. Such acts include sabotage and destruction of communications facilities. Actual commission of these acts is not necessary for imposition of punishment, for attempts as well as conspiracy to commit hostile acts are sufficient. Normally, states include in their military manuals acts of sabotage under the next topic, war treason.

WAR TREASON    Offenses included in the broad category of war treason include all acts committed *within the lines of a belligerent* and deemed injurious to him and intended to promote the cause of his enemy. Excluded from the concept of war treason are espionage and armed hostilities carried out by civilians in occupied enemy territory. A list of the major varieties of war treason includes the following acts:

1. Information of any kind given to the enemy.
2. The voluntary giving of supplies of any kind to the enemy.
3. Voluntary assistance given to military operations of the enemy.
4. Attempts to induce soldiers to desert, surrender, or spy.
5. Attempt to bribe officials or soliders in the interest of the enemy.
6. Liberation of enemy prisoners of war.
7. Entering into a conspiracy against the armed forces or against individual members of these forces.
8. Wrecking military trains or convoys, lines of communication, or communication media in the interests of the enemy, as well as the destruction of any war material for the same purpose.
9. Intentional misguiding of troops by hired or voluntary guides.
10. Acting as a courier for the enemy.
11. Harboring or protecting enemy personnel.[16]

The usual penalty for persons convicted of war treason is the death sentence, although imprisonment has been substituted at times. Enemy soldiers accused of war treason may be punished only if they have committed one of the acts in question during their stay in disguise within a belligerent's lines. Thus when two Japanese officers, dressed in Chinese civilian clothes, were caught behind the Russian lines (Russo-Japanese War of 1904) in an attempt to blow up a railroad bridge, they were properly sentenced to death. As in the case of espionage, acts labeled as war treason are permitted to a belligerent under the laws of war. But they have a twofold aspect, and a belligerent capturing enemy soldiers or enemy civilians guilty of committing these acts behind his lines has a perfect right to regard the acts as illegal warfare and to punish their perpetrators. Acts of war treason are not war crimes, however, in the strict meaning of that term.

[16]Based on Lauterpacht's *Oppenheim*, vol. 2, 575, n. 5; and on the *Law of Land Warfare*, par. 79 ("Aiding the Enemy"); see also *NYT*, May 31, 1964, 14; Aug. 15, 1965, 3; March 27, 1973, 11.

## The Punishment of War Crimes

Article III of the Hague Convention of 1907 on War on Land provided that "a belligerent party which violates the provisions of the said regulations shall, if the case demands, be liable to pay compensation. It shall be responsible for all acts committed by persons forming part of its armed forces." This wording implied that violations of the Hague Regulations would be satisfactorily remedied by a payment of money, but nothing was said about the trial and punishment of the offenders actually guilty of violating the laws of war.

## Pre-1945 Rules of Law

RULES OF LAND WARFARE (1940)    On the other hand, even under the pre-1945 rules of law, offending members of armed forces were held to be answerable, individually, to the wronged state. Many national military manuals stipulated that commanders ordering acts violating the laws of war were punishable by the injured belligerent once they fell into his hands. The revised version of the American manual (*Rules of Land Warfare*, 1940 edition) went even further and spelled out in detail the remedies of an injured belligerent (par. 346):

In the event of clearly established violation of the laws of war, the injured party may legally resort to such remedial action as may be deemed appropriate and necessary within the following classes, to wit: a. Publication of the facts, with a view to influencing public opinion against the offending belligerents. b. Protests and demand for punishment of individual offenders, sent to the offending belligerent through neutral diplomatic channels, or by parlementaire direct to the commander of the offending forces. c. Punishment of captured individual offenders. d. Reprisals.

It can thus be said that criminal punishment of individuals represented a sanction of the laws of war even before the post-World War II trials.[17]

TREATY OF VERSAILLES AND THE COMMISSION OF FIFTEEN    The first major attempt to punish offenders guilty of committing war crimes took place at the end of World War 1. On January 25, 1919, the Preliminary Peace Conference created the Commission of Fifteen to investigate and report on violations of international law that could be charged against Germany and its allies.[18] The commission, in its report, specifically denied immunity from responsibility to high officials of the Central Powers, including even chiefs of states. It recommended the establishment of the International High Tribunal, to apply "the principles of the law of nations as they result from the usages established among civilized peoples, from the laws of humanity, and from the dictates of public conscience" — words taken from the preamble

[17] See Wright, "War Criminals," 39 *AJIL* 257 (1945); note revision of quoted portion in *Land Warfare* (1956), pars. 496–97.
[18] The report of the "Commission on the Responsibility of the Authors of the War and on the Enforcement of Penalties," is in 14 *AJIL* 95 (1920 Supp.).

to the Hague conventions of 1899 and 1907. The American representatives on the commission differed with their Allied colleagues and wanted the law to be limited to the laws and customs of war only.

Over the dissenting views of the United States and Japanese members, the view of the majority was adopted, and Article 227 of the Treaty of Versailles provided for the creation of a tribunal of five judges to be appointed to try the ex-emperor of Germany, not for war crimes, but for "a supreme offense against international morality and the sanctity of treaties." Because the Kaiser had found asylum and the Netherlands refused to surrender him to the Allied and Associated Powers, the scheme came to naught.

The treaty contained, however, additional punitive provisions in the form of Articles 228–230. Under Article 228, the German government recognized "the right of the Allied and Associated Powers to bring before military tribunals persons accused of having committed acts in violation of the laws and customs of war. Such persons shall, if found guilty, be sentenced to punishments laid down by law." The German government was to hand over all such accused, who were to be specified, for trial. Article 229 provided meager details of the trial procedures, and Article 230 required Germany to supply all documents and information that might be considered necessary to ensure a "full knowledge of the incriminating acts, the discovery of offenders, and the just appreciation of responsibility."

WAR CRIMES TRIALS (POST–WORLD WAR I)    The Allied powers drew up a list of 896 names of persons accused of war crimes. Following strong German resistance to the surrender of those persons, a compromise was reached on German suggestions, and on May 7, 1920, a sample "abridged" list of 45 names was sent to the German government. These individuals were to be tried before the German Supreme Court at Leipzig. The trial began on May 23, 1921. Only 12 of the 45 persons named on the "test list" were actually tried, and only 6 of them were found guilty. The sentences imposed were nominal, ranging from six months' to a maximum of four years' imprisonment. The final bizarre touch of these regrettable proceedings was added by the escape from detention of Lieutenant Boldt, a former submarine commander, who had received a four-year sentence, and of another former submarine commander convicted of atrocities. The Allies then ceased all further attempts to continue the war crimes trials.[19]

---

[19]For a more detailed account, told more in sorrow than in anger, consult Glueck, *War Criminals, Their Prosecution & Punishment* (1944), 19–34; see also Garner, *Recent Developments in International Law* (1925), 455–63; Finch, "Retribution for War Crimes," 37 *AJIL* 81 (1943); Levy, "The Law and Procedure of War Crimes Trials," 37 *APSR* 1052, esp. 1056–63 (1943); and Schwarzenberger, *International Law and Totalitarian Lawlessness* (1943), 68–73, 113–47 for copious excerpts from the decisions at the Leipzig trials. The most recent account of the early trials is by Willis, *Prologue to Nuremberg: The Politics and Diplomacy of Punishing War Criminals of the First World War* (1982).

## International Military Tribunal (Nuremberg)

DEMANDS FOR POSTWAR PUNISHMENT OF WAR CRIMINALS    The almost un-believable violations of the laws of war at the hands of the Axis powers and their minor allies led early in World War II to demands for an effective post-war punishment of the guilty individuals.[20] The list of relevant statements and declarations is very long. The most important among them were the statements by President Roosevelt and Prime Minister Churchill of October 25, 1941, on Axis executions of hostages,[21] the resolutions adopted on Jan-uary 13, 1942, by representatives of nine European governments-in-exile at St. James's Palace in London, on postwar punishment of war criminals, particularly in regard to the shooting of hostages;[22] President Roosevelt's warning to war criminals on August 21 and October 7, 1942, regarding the trials of criminals in the national courts of the states in which their offenses had been committed; the announcement by the Lord Chancellor in the House of Commons on October 7, 1942, of the formation of the United Nations Commission for the Investigation of War Crimes, together with a warning that named offenders were to be surrendered at the time of any armistice and that their delivery would be requested from any neutral country to which they might have fled;[23] the Allied statement, delivered by the British Foreign Secretary on December 17, 1942, on retribution to be visited on war criminals; the Moscow Declaration of October 30, 1943;[24] statements by Roosevelt and Churchill of March 24, 1944; the proposal of a warning by the Provisional French Government on July 15, 1944, that Germany be told not to carry out any last-minute executions of French nationals; and the American–British–Russian Declaration of Potsdam, pub-lished on July 26, 1945, announcing (par. 10) that "stern justice shall be meted out to all war criminals, including those who have visited cruelties upon our prisoners,"[25] a sentiment reiterated in Articles III (A 5) and VII of the Report on the Tripartite Conference in Berlin (Potsdam).[26]

MOSCOW DECLARATION AND LONDON AGREEMENT    In implementing the Moscow Declaration, the governments of the United States, the United Kingdom, France, and the Soviet Union concluded on August 8, 1945, in London the Agreement for the Prosecution and Punishment of the Major War Criminals of the European Axis.[27] This instrument provided the details for

[20]Consult Whiteman, vol. 11, 874–80.

[21]Text in Schwarzenberger, *op. cit.*, n. 19, 147–48.

[22]*NYT*, Jan. 14, 1942. China and the Soviet Union had observers at the meeting. See also Bathurst, "The United Nations War Crimes Commission," 39 *AJIL* 565 (1945).

[23]See Neumann, "Neutral States and the Extradition of War Criminals," 45 *AJIL* 495 (1951), on the problems posed by the 1942 announcement.

[24]11 *Department of State Bulletin* 310–11 (1943).

[25]13 *Department of State Bulletin* 137–38 (1945).

[26]*Id.*, 155, 158.

[27]Consult *International Conference on Military Trials, London, 1945* (Department of State Pub-lication 3080), for the texts of all proposals at the meeting. The principles contained in the 1945 Agreement were recognized as binding in international law by UN General Assembly Resolution 95 (I) (Dec. 11, 1946).

the establishment of the International Military Tribunal. This body was to consist of four judges, each appointed by a party to the agreement, together with four alternates similarly chosen. Among other provisions, such as those dealing with the defense of superior orders, the individual's responsibility irrespective of official position, and the safeguarding of a fair trial, the key article of the charter of the tribunal was the sixth, which defined the jurisdiction of the court:

The following acts, or any of them, are crimes coming within the jurisdiction of the Tribunal for which there shall be individual responsibility:

(a) Crimes against Peace: Namely, planning, preparation, initiation or waging of a war of aggression, or a war in violation of international treaties, agreements or assurances, or participation in a common plan or conspiracy for the accomplishment of any of the foregoing;

(b) War Crimes: Namely, violations of the laws or customs of war. Such violations shall include, but not be limited to, murder, ill-treatment or deportation to slave labor or from any other purpose of civilian population of or in occupied territory, murder or ill-treatment of prisoners of war or persons on the seas, killing of hostages, plunder of public or private property, wanton destruction of cities, town or villages, or devastation not justified by military necessity;

(c) Crimes against Humanity: Namely, murder, extermination, enslavement, deportation, and other inhumane acts committed against any civilian population, before or during the war, or persecutions on political, racial or religious grounds in execution of or in connection with any crime within the jurisdiction of the Tribunal, whether or not in violation of the domestic law of the country where perpetrated.

Leaders, organizers, instigators, and accomplices participating in the formulation or execution of a common plan or conspiracy to commit any of the foregoing crimes are responsible for all acts performed by any persons in execution of such plan. . . .

In accordance with the provisions of the Moscow Declaration, the Nuremberg Tribunal was to deal with "German Criminals, whose offenses have no particular geographical localization" and who could be punished "by joint decision of the Allies."

The resulting trials conducted by the tribunal are too well known to discuss in detail, and the literature dealing with them has swollen to enormous proportions. Suffice it to state here that the trials began on November 20, 1945, and the hearing of evidence and the speeches of counsel ended on August 31, 1946. The tribunal gave its judgment on September 30, 1946,[28] and sentences were pronounced on October 1, 1946.

The London Agreement of 1945 was adhered to by 19 states (in addition to the original four signers) before the Nuremberg trial began.

---

[28] Text of judgment and the sentences reprinted in 41 *AJIL* 172–332 (1947); see also Whiteman, vol. 11, 880–934.

CRITICISMS OF THE NUREMBERG TRIALS    The trial itself has been the subject of much criticism, on a variety of grounds.[29] Leaving aside, for the time being, charges that *ex post facto* punishment was exacted for crimes against peace, there is no question that the convictions for traditional war crimes were legally correct, on the basis of customary and conventional international law.

More to the point was the criticism aimed at certain procedural details, notably the absence of neutral judges on the tribunal. This lack, in the opinion of several commentators, was a definite weakness in the court's constitution and, if it had been avoided, would have tended to remove charges that justice was really a form of revenge. But would the inclusion of neutral judges really have made any difference? The present writer cannot see that such judges would have supplied a truly impartial element to the tribunal's composition. The offenses of the accused were so horrifying, so lacking in the minimum of human decency and the aspects commonly associated with Judeo-Christian civilization, that neutral judges, listening to the evidence, could not have remained neutral. Furthermore, they would have had to consider whether their own state might be the victim of similar events if the offenders of World War II had not been punished, so that they might easily have been influenced in favor of punishment as a deterrent.

Some of the criticisms leveled at the tribunal were based on the absence of German judges on the court. Certainly the record of German justice at the Leipzig trials mentioned earlier could have cast doubts on the advisability of a second attempt to have nationals of a state help judge their own citizens accused of war crimes.[30]

One major criticism, voiced principally in German sources but echoed by individual Allied citizens, was the failure of the victors in World War II to investigate war crimes attributed to members of their own armed forces. The tribunal itself refused to undertake any such inquiry, and the terms of its charter justified this view. Thus the trials, conducted only against the losing party, were one-sided, to be sure. But leaving aside this factor, the introduction of an effective prosecution and punishment of war crimes may be regarded as a salutary object lesson for future prospective offenders against the laws of war. A procedural and legal set of precedents has been established and may well act as a deterrent in future wars. If the lessons of Nuremberg had been assimilated fully by the states of the world, a permanent structural unit, an international criminal court, might already have seen the light of day. This subject will be discussed later in this chapter.

---

[29]See Lord Hankey, *Politics, Trials and Errors* (1950); Veale, *Advance to Barbarism* (1953); Benton and Grimm, *Nuremberg: German Views of the War Trials* (1955); Ehard, "The Nuremberg Trial against the Major War Criminals and International Law," 43 *AJIL* 223 (1949); and Thorpe, "The Nuremberg Trials: Considerations and Suggestions," 13 *Intercom* (Jan.–Feb. 1971), 33–45.

[30]See Appleman, *Military Tribunals and International Crimes* (1954), 358–59, on the failure of numerous German denazification tribunals to pass adequate sentences on their fellow citizens.

### International Military Tribunal for the Far East (Tokyo)

Closely related to the Nuremberg trials was the establishment of the International Military Tribunal for the Far East. In this instance, too, the charter in question specified the categories of war crimes, crimes against peace, and crimes against humanity, together with a separate grouping of a crime of conspiracy to commit the foregoing crimes. The tribunal, in this case, consisted of 11 judges, representing the states at war against Japan.[31] The trials began on June 4, 1946, and the judgment was given on November 4, 1948. The initial proclamation setting up the tribunal was issued by General Douglas MacArthur as Supreme Commander for the Allied Powers in the Pacific. In 1948, in a significant decision, the Supreme Court of the United States ruled that the tribunal was not a court of the United States and that in consequence the Supreme Court had no jurisdiction to review or to set aside the tribunal's judgments.[32]

The major criticism of the Far East Tribunal centered on the inclusion of "crimes against peace" in its Charter. Numerous legal experts questioned whether "aggressive war" was in itself a crime different and apart from 'traditional' law of war violations occurring during hostilities. They agreed that the Kellogg-Briand Pact (Pact of Paris) *might* have rendered aggressive war illegal, but they doubted that such illegality could be transformed into a punishable offense as far as individuals were concerned.[33]

### Trials by "National" Tribunals

The publicity given to the proceedings of the two international military tribunals overshadowed the fact that most of the accused war criminals of World War II were dealt with, as prescribed in the Moscow Agreement, by military courts of individual occupants or were returned to the scenes of their offenses and there were tried and punished by local courts and under local laws.[34] In some countries, where domestic legislation required this, the accused offenders were tried in ordinary criminal courts for violating the local criminal laws. Most of them, however, were brought before military courts of particular states for violating the laws and customs of war.

By late November 1948, a total of 7,109 defendants had been arrested for war crimes, including the "major cases" at Nuremberg and Tokyo. The trials that took place resulted in 3,686 convictions and 924 acquittals. Of those convicted, 1,019 received death sentences, and 33 defendants committed

---

[31] Text of charter in 14 *Dept. of State Bulletin* 361 (1946).

[32] *Koki Hirota et al.* v. *Douglas MacArthur*, U.S. Supreme Court, 1948, 338 U.S. 197, digested in 43 *AJIL* 170 (1949); consult also Whiteman, vol. 11, 965–1009, 1017–19; and especially Piccigallo, *The Japanese on Trial: Allied War Crimes Operations in the East, 1945–1951* (1979), which covers the Tokyo trials as well as the thousands of national trials in the Pacific area.

[33] See Fenwick, 762–65. See also Wright, "The Law of the Nuremberg Trial," 41 *AJIL* 38 (1947), for the concept that war had become a crime.

[34] See Koessler, "American War Crimes Trials in Europe," 39 *Georgetown Law Jl.* 18 (1950); Cowles, "Trials of War Criminals (Non-Nuremberg)," 42 *AJIL* 299 (1948); Whiteman, vol. 11, 934–965.

suicide. Prison sentences were received by 2,667, and 2,499 cases were still pending.[35] By the end of 1958, the Western Allies had convicted 5,025 Germans of war crimes, 806 being sentenced to death (486 were actually executed), and the Soviet Union had convicted around 10,000, many of whom were sentenced to 25 years in jail, and others, to death. In the years since 1948, many other culprits have been discovered by their own governments (mostly in France and West Germany) and have been tried for war crimes. Thus by June 1973, 6,330 individuals had been convicted in West Germany, and as late as 1971–1972, 34 of its citizens were condemned to death for war crimes by the Soviet government, with 8 additional such convictions in 1973.

Unfortunately, the space available in a general text does not permit a detailed account of the thousands of national trials conducted (and continuing to be conducted at the time of this writing) in West Germany, France, and the Soviet Union and the hearings for deportation proceedings and/or for denaturalization purposes lately held in the United States.[36]

Many of these "national" trials were divorced from the Moscow Declaration and were based on violations of the laws of war as such. This, for instance, was true in the famous Belsen trial, dealing with the Auschwitz and Belsen camps, which was conducted by British authorities in their zone of occupation under the authority of a Royal Warrant.[37] The basis of such trials was international customary and conventional law as it existed at the time the alleged offense was committed.

A military tribunal trying an alien accused of war crimes is not bound by procedural safeguards established in that tribunal's own country, as was brought out clearly in the decision of the U.S. Supreme Court on an appeal by General Yamashita against his conviction by a U.S. military commission appointed for war crimes trials by General MacArthur in the Philippines.[38] The Supreme Court, in rejecting the appeal from the commander's conviction for failing to take appropriate measures to prevent violations of the laws of war by troops under his command, emphasized in a classic but much criticized opinion that military tribunals trying such cases are not bound by constitutional requirements for due process of law in the domestic sense.[39]

Conflicts after World War II have been replete with alleged or proven instances of war crimes. Thus the 1971 war in the Indian subcontinent resulted in Bangladesh's announced intention of placing 195 Pakistani pris-

[35]*Time*, November 29, 1948, 31.
[36]See, for illustrative purposes, Blum, *Wanted: The Search for Nazis in America* (1977); *NYT*, Jan. 20, 1975, 17; Aug. 29, 1975, 1, 4; Oct. 3, 1976, 1, 22; Oct. 18, 1976, 16; Nov. 28, 1976, E-5; and Nov. 10, 1978, A-3; *Time*, July 13, 1981, 43; and *Newsweek*, Nov. 26, 1979, 93–94; Feb. 25, 1980, 56. On deportation of war criminals from the United States, see *U.S. News & World Report*, June 30, 1980, 33; and Chapter 12.
[37]See *War Crimes Trials*, vol. 2, *The Belsen Trial* (1949).
[38]See *supra*, n. 15.
[39]See also Wright, "Due Process and International Law," 40 *AJIL* 398 (1946), on the Yamashita case.

oners of war on trial for war crimes (primarily murder and rape). However, in April 1974, Bangladesh agreed "as an act of clemency" to drop its plans for the trials. This concession appears to have been made in return for Pakistan's recognition of Bangladesh's independence. It was followed by apologies for the crimes committed by the Pakistan government and, subsequently, by Pakistan's Prime Minister Ali Bhutto personally.[40]

The Vietnam War brought with it a spate of claims of war crimes allegedly committed by both sides in the conflict. Regrettably, the charges appear to have been fully justified in many instances. No recorded instances of war crimes trials on the part of either the Vietnamese government or the Korean government (against members of its contingents in South Vietnam) are known to the writer (despite authenticated instances of the commission of such offenses by the military personnel of almost all parties to the conflict). On the other hand, the United States government has prosecuted (or at least filed charges against) a limited number of its military personnel, ranking in grade from privates to generals. Most publicized were the prosecutions of Captain Ernest L. Medina and of one of his platoon commanders, First Lieutenant William L. Calley, Jr. Both officers had been involved in what became known as the My Lai massacre of March 16, 1968.

Originally the U.S. Army had charged 25 officers and enlisted men with participating in the My Lai killings. Of this total, six were tried, and the charges against the rest were dismissed because of insufficient evidence. Of the six, all were acquitted except Lieutenant Calley, whose case became a true *cause célèbre*. He was convicted by a court-martial of the premeditated murder of 22 Vietnamese civilians. Originally given a life sentence, Calley, on appeal, had his conviction upheld, but had his sentence reduced to 20 years at hard labor, which was halved on April 16, 1974. On September 25, 1974, the U.S. District Court in Columbia, Georgia, overturned the My Lai murder conviction and ordered Calley freed on bond. The court ruled that Calley had been denied due process of law (massive adverse publicity, denial of his right to confront witnesses). On September 10, 1975, the U.S. Circuit Court in New Orleans reinstated Calley's court-martial conviction; the army then changed Calley's status to a federal parolee.

More recently, Sgt. Roberto Bryan, a U.S. Army paratrooper, was acquitted on August 31, 1990, by a U.S. Military jury of charges that he murdered an unarmed Panamanian civilian at a roadblock during the 1989 U.S. invasion of Panama.[41] Three days after his acquittal, Bryan was promoted to sergeant major, the Army's highest enlisted rank.

Pursuit of suspected war criminals has continued to the present time in or by a number of countries: France, the United States, Israel, Canada, Australia, the Soviet Union, and others. At the time of writing, the two Houses of the British Parliament were embroiled in controversy concerning

[40]See *NYT*, June 9, 1973, 9; April 11, 1974, 3; June 29, 1974, 1, 4.
[41]See *NYT*, Sept. 1, 1990, 7.

a bill enabling the prosecution of persons suspected of having committed "crimes against humanity" during World War II.[42]

## CRIMES AGAINST HUMANITY

The Charter of the International tribunal at Nuremberg listed in Article 6(a) a "new" category of crimes under international law, termed *crimes against humanity*.

This concept led to considerable criticism on the grounds that traditional international law had not recognized such an offense and that the trials of accused violators of such a new concept represented *ex post facto*, or retroactive, punishment.

OFFENSES CONSTITUTING CRIMES AGAINST HUMANITY    The wording of the section in question reveals a combination of two different sets of offenses. "Murder, extermination, enslavement, deportation, and other inhumane acts committed against any civilian population" represented, in time of war and applied to enemy citizens, crimes against the laws of war. The article went further, however, and specified not only the criminality of such acts in time of war but also "before" a war and then stipulated "or persecution on political, racial, or religious grounds in execution of or in connection with any crime within the jurisdiction of the Tribunal, whether or not in violation of the domestic law of the country where perpetrated."

The "before the war" part and the concluding portion of the quoted text must be taken to be a reiteration of the existence of fundamental human rights.[43] The tribunal itself decided that it could deal only with acts listed in Article 6(c) that had taken place after the beginning of the war and thus deliberately avoided the thorny issue of human rights.[44]

Only two of the accused were found guilty of crimes against humanity alone; all the other German leaders accused of such crimes and found guilty by the tribunal were also sentenced because of war crimes.

Basically, crimes against humanity, beyond the sphere of traditional war crimes, represented offenses committed against civilians, and not so much against individuals as against civilian populations. Obviously such a development meant an expansion in the scope of international law. The interesting and certainly debatable aspect centered on the fact that acts of Germans against their fellow citizens were deemed to fall within the purview of the Allies' authority, even though German law would have sanctioned a number of the acts in question. Such an unprecedented innovation in the law of nations must remain questionable,[45] particularly on the grounds that this

---

[42]See MacLeod, "Britain Debates Prosecution of War Crimes," *CSM*, June 22, 1990, 4.
[43]Schwelb, "Crimes against Humanity," 23 *BYIL* 178 (1946).
[44]Judgment, Oct. 1, 1946, in 41 *AJIL* 249 (1947).
[45]See Schick, "The Nuremberg Trial and the International Law of the Future," 41 *AJIL* 770, 785 (1947).

interpretation disregards a basic principle of the law: no state shall intervene in the territorial and personal sphere of validity of another national legal order.

## CRIMES AGAINST PEACE

The category of crimes against peace represented an even more debatable aspect of the Nuremberg and Tokyo trials. Today it can be asserted with some degree of validity, even though perhaps rather academically, that under the provisions of Article 39 of the Charter of the United Nations, the planning, preparation, and launching of a war not strictly in self-defense may be regarded as unlawful.

But it must be pointed out that at the time of German and Japanese defendants committed their alleged offenses, there was no rule of international law that forbade a sovereign state to plan or to carry out acts that could be termed afterward an aggressive war, despite the Covenant of the League of Nations and the Pact of Paris.

Many reasons could be cited to support the absence, then and now, of a crime against peace. The members of the community of nations, until recently unable to agree on a definition of aggression (see Chapter 20), made it logically difficult, to say the least, to determine whether a given act, when planned or carried out, would lead to an aggressive war, assuming that an accepted definition had been obtained. Peacetime national efforts to improve the military potential of a given state may represent a needed bolstering of defensive strength or preparation for an attack on a neighbor. Scientific research on new or more effective weapons may have both offensive and defensive aspects.

Looking back at the Nuremberg and Tokyo charges of crimes against peace, this writer sees them as having been based primarily on the body of post-1919 declarations, pacts, and resolutions asserting the illegality of aggression. Because this assortment of statements cannot be asserted to represent either customary law (for example, state practices) or conventional law and because no definition of aggression had been agreed on, it seems that the charges of crimes against peace were based on rather shaky foundations at best. In the opinion of this writer, the ancient principle of *nullum crimen sine lege* (no crime without a law) should not have been set aside in the case of the alleged crimes against peace, and the rather cavalier dismissal of the principle by the Nuremberg Tribunal deserves strong criticism.

## STATUTORY LIMITATIONS

Many countries have enacted a statute of limitations, that is, the preclusion of prosecution after the expiration of a specified period since a given crime was committed. The application of such statutes to war crimes (and crimes against humanity) would, after a passage of time, prevent the prosecution and punishment of persons allegedly responsible for the offenses. Logically, therefore, the UN General Assembly, on November 26, 1968, approved, by a vote of 58 to 7, the Convention on the Non-Applicability of Statutory Limitations to War Crimes and Crimes against Humanity.[46] The convention, opposed by both the United States and the United Kingdom, entered into force on November 11, 1970, after being ratified by all East European socialist countries, Mongolia, and Nigeria. The Soviet Union is the only major power that has ratified the treaty.

The Council of Europe also drafted its own European Convention on the Non-Applicability of Statutory Limitation to Crimes against Humanity and War Crimes (Strasbourg), opened for signature on January 25, 1974.[47] Most significant, however, was the action of the West German parliament when after long debate, it struck down on July 3, 1979, its 30-year statute of limitations. If this had not been done, Nazi-era criminals not yet apprehended would have been free from prosecution after December 31, 1979.[48]

### Draft Code of Crimes against the Peace and Security of Mankind

Did the Principles enunciated in the charters of the international tribunals and enforced in the decisions of both, as well as a multitude of national courts, greatly affect the body of international law? Did they create new rules of law, binding on the community of nations?

On December 11, 1946, the General Assembly of the United Nations unanimously adopted a resolution reaffirming the "principles of international law" recognized by the charter and the judgment of the Nuremberg Tribunal. Subsequently, by Resolution 177 (II) of November 21, 1947, the General Assembly directed the International Law Commission (ILC) to study the principles in question and to draft a "code of offenses against the peace and security of mankind," indicating clearly the place to be accorded in such a draft to the Nuremberg principles.

The commission began a preliminary study of this assignment at its first session in 1949 and at once encountered the question of the extent to which the principles embodied in the London charter and the judgments constituted principles of international law. The Nuremberg Tribunal, in its judgment, had asserted that its charter (including, of course, the principles found therein) was "the expression of international law existing at the time of its creation, and to that extent is itself a contribution to international law." The ILC, however, refused to express its opinion on this assertion and decided that its assigned task was merely one of formulation.[49]

---

[46]Text in 8 *ILM* 69 (1969); see also Miller, "The Convention on the Non-Applicability of Statutory Limitations to War Crimes and Crimes against Humanity," 65 *AJIL* 476 (1971).
[47]Text in 13 *ILM* 540 (1974).
[48]See *The Bulletin* (Bonn), Sept. 13, 1979 (entire issue devoted to the action on the statue of limitations).
[49]See United Nations, *Report of the I.L.C. Covering Its Second Session, June 5–July 29, 1950*, in 44 *AJIL* 105, esp. 125–26 (1950 Supp.).

The commission had already polled the members of the United Nations in order to obtain listings of additional offenses to be included in the draft code and had appointed a drafting committee. The resulting provisional text was referred to the special rapporteur, who submitted his second report on the code to the commission at its third session in 1951. At that time, the ILC adopted a draft code, which it submitted in its report to the General Assembly.

The General Assembly postponed the question of the draft code until its seventh session in 1952, but after comments on the draft had been solicited and received from only 14 members, discussion was again delayed, on the understanding that the matter would continue to be studied by the ILC. The ILC asked its rapporteur to prepare another draft of the code, and this was considered at length during the commission's sixth session in 1954. [50]

A major reason for the delay in taking action on the 1954 draft was the absence of a definition of aggression. Once a definition was adopted, as Resolution 3314 (XXIX) by the General Assembly on December 14, 1974 (see Chapter 20), interest in the draft code was stimulated, and the UN member states were invited to submit comments and observations. It appeared doubtful even then that much of a constructive nature would result. By 1989, the Commission had adopted only six articles of a new Draft Code. [51] The present writer's pessimism concerning the draft code is based on two considerations: the haziness of the United Nations' definition of aggression and an honest belief that not much genuine enthusiasm can be engendered among the nations of the world for the establishment of the proposed International Criminal Court. And above all, the problem of interference with national sovereignty and its prerogatives has not approached solution, nor does the 1954 draft code deal adequately with the question of penalties for violations.

## GENEVA CONVENTIONS OF 1949

The Geneva Diplomatic Conference of 1949 also was concerned with the subject of crimes under international law and, because its four conventions are in force, contributed to expanding the rules of law governing in this sphere. The participants in the conference carefully avoided the terms *war crimes* and *Nuremberg principles*, but wrote into the conventions much relevant material.

All four instruments include this common article:

The High Contracting Parties undertake to enact any legislation necessary to provide effective penal sanctions for persons committing, or ordering to be com-

---

[50] Text of the revised draft code with comments on the modifications made, in United Nations, *Report of the I.L.C. Covering the Work of Its Sixth Session, June 3–July 28, 1954*, in 49 *AJIL* 19 (1955 Supp.); see also Whiteman, vol. 11, 839–44.
[51] Text in 83 *AJIL* 153 (1989).

mitted, any of the grave breaches of the present Convention defined in the following Article.

Each High Contracting Party shall be under the obligation to search for persons alleged to have committed, or to have ordered to be committed, such grave breaches, and shall bring such persons, regardless of their nationality, before its own courts. It may also, if it prefers, and in accordance with the provisions of its own legislation, hand such persons over for trial to another High Contracting Party concerned, provided such High Contracting Party has made out a *prima facie* case.

Each High Contracting Party shall take measures necessary for the suppression of all acts contrary to the provisions of the present Convention other than the grave breaches defined in the following Article.

In all circumstances, the accused persons shall benefit by safeguards of proper trial and defense, which shall not be less favourable than those provided by Article 105 and those following of the Geneva Convention relative to the Treatment of Prisoners of War of August 12, 1949.[52]

Article 85 of the 1949 Prisoners of War Convention provided that "Prisoners of War prosecuted under the laws of the Detaining Power for acts committed prior to capture shall retain, even if convicted, the benefits of the present Convention." All the Soviet-bloc states made reservations to this article, under which individuals convicted of war crimes and crimes against humanity could be subjected "to the conditions obtaining in the country in question for those who undergo their punishment." Although the United States Senate, in approving ratification of the convention, rejected these reservations, it should be pointed out that the Soviet Union at least indicated clearly that its reservation was applicable only to conditions of punishment after a prisoner of war had been convicted and sentenced for a precapture act. Hence the Soviet Union appears to have accepted the Convention's provisions for the trial period of the prisoner in question, even though not for the punishment phase.[53]

In the fourth (Civilian) Convention of 1949, Article 148 asserts that no party to the Convention is permitted to absolve itself or any other contracting party of any liability incurred by itself or another party in respect to the grave breaches enumerated in Article 147 of the treaty—and the breaches parallel to a considerable extent the definitions laid down in Article 6(b and c) of the Charter of the Nuremberg Tribunal. The 1949 Convention Relative to the Treatment of Prisoners of War, on the other hand, appears to have created a limitation in regard to international trials of certain criminals.

---

[52] Article 49, Convention on Sick and Wounded; Article 50, Convention on Sick and Wounded at Sea; Article 129, Convention on Prisoners of War; Article 146, Civilian Convention. See also Levie, "Penal Sanctions for Maltreatment of Prisoners of War," 56 *AJIL* 433, 454–57 (1962), particularly with reference to possible extradition problems under the Geneva instrument of 1949.

[53] Levie, *op. cit. supra*, n. 52, 457, n. 98; see also Baxter, "The Geneva Conventions of 1949 before the United States Senate," 49 *AJIL* 550, 553 (1955).

The provisions of Articles 85, 99, and 102 of the Prisoner Convention require that prisoners of war accused of war crimes must be tried in the same courts and in accordance with the same law as would apply to the captor state's armed forces. Because the military law of few, if any, states permits, or is likely to permit, foreign officers to sit among the judges of military personnel, the countries may find it rather difficult to constitute tribunals of mixed-nationality composition. In the case of an international command, "national military tribunals . . . which try war criminals cannot be described as international tribunals if they operate only with the authorization of the supreme commander, and deserve that name only if they are convened at his direction."[54] This last principle was illustrated in *Flick* v. *Johnson*,[55] in which a U.S. court ruled that Military Tribunal IV, composed of U.S. military personnel and convened in Nuremberg by General Lucius Clay, the military governor and zone commander, under Control Council Law No. 10, was not a tribunal of the United States. Hence its judgments could not be reviewed by U.S. courts, even though the members of Tribunal IV all were U.S. citizens.

The tribunal, being convened under an inter-Allied law, was not a court of the United States, but if General Clay, in his capacity as zone commander, had authorized a military court to act, it might have been viewed as a court of the United States. Tribunal IV was operating under the authority of the "supreme commander," in this case the Quadripartite Control Council for Germany.

Last but not least, the provisions of the two 1977 Protocols Additional to the Geneva Conventions of 1949 (PR-I and PR-II) have contributed to the listing of acts that, if committed, would be war crimes—once the two protocols are in force. Although some might regard the subject matter of the two instruments as rating somewhat below the importance of the matters covered in the four Geneva conventions of 1949, it must be remembered that the 1977 protocols filled several gaps in the law relating to armed conflicts. Thus, if only on that account, they are important.

## EXTRADITION

It was pointed out in Chapter 12 that war crimes do not qualify as political offenses and hence cannot bar extradition to a seeking country. This doctrine is outlined in several UN General Assembly resolutions[56] and also in Article 7 of the UN Convention on Genocide, which reads, in part, "Genocide and the other acts enumerated in Article III shall not be considered as political

---

[54]Baxter, "Constitutional Forms and Some Legal Problems of International Military Command," 29 *BYIL* 325, at 354–55 (1952).
[55]U.S. Court of Appeals, Washington, D.C., 1949, 174 F. 2d 983, digested at length in 44 *AJIL* 187 (1950).
[56]Res. 3 (1946), UN Doc. A/50, and Res. 170 (1947), UN Doc. A/425.

crimes for the purpose of extradition." On the other hand, as Martin Gold pointed out,[57] numerous countries, including the Soviet Union, the United States, Great Britain, and Australia, have on occasion refused to surrender alleged war criminals to those countries seeking to prosecute them. The reasons for these refusals have varied greatly, with the common one being an expressed belief that the alleged war criminal would not receive a fair trial in the seeking country. On other occasions, refusal has been based on the real or alleged constitutional bar against extradition of one's own citizens to another country; in still other cases, the lack of reciprocity has been cited. As Gold observed, "The 1946 and 1947 UN resolutions did not have sufficient force of law to modify long standing judicial interpretation of what is a political offense." Happily, that judicial interpretation appears to be swinging gradually into line with the spirit and wording of the General Assembly resolutions.

## SUGGESTED READINGS

### War Crimes: General

Whiteman, vol. 11, 835–1021. See also the selections from three directives issued in 1967 and 1968 by the Headquarters, United States Military Assistance Command, Vietnam, dealing with war crimes, classification of detainees, and determination of eligibility to be treated as prisoners of war, in 62 *AJIL* 765 (1968); Rogat, *The Eichmann Trial and the Rule of Law* (1961), particularly 32–43; Baird, ed., *From Nuremberg to My Lai* (1972); Friedman, ed., *The Law of War: A Documentary History*. (2 vols., 1972), contains relevant rules and also a number of post–World War II decisions; de Zayas, *The Wehrmacht War Crimes Bureau 1939–1945* (1989); Chelminski, "Katyn: Anatomy of a Massacre," *Reader's Digest* (May 1990), 69–79.

CASES

*The Case of Abetz*, France, Cour de Cassation, 1950, Sirey, 1950, reported in 46 *AJIL* 161 (1952).
*The Peleus Trial* [War Crimes Trials, vol. 1] (1949).
Stig Jägerskiöld, "A Swedish Case on the Jurisdiction of States over Foreigners: *Crown* v. *von Herder* [Supreme Court of Sweden]," 41 *AJIL* 909 (1947).
*Case against Hermann Roechling and Others*, General Tribunal, Military Government of the French Zone of Occupation, Germany, June 30, 1948, digested in 43 *AJIL* 191 (1949).

### Defense of Superior Orders

Dinstein, *The Defense of "Obedience to Superior Orders" in International Law* (1965); *NYT*, Oct. 9, 1966, 24, regarding the new French Military Code of 1966 and its provisions relating to the problem of superior orders.

[57] Gold, "Non-extradition for Political Offenses: The Communist Perspective," 11 *Harvard Int'l Law Jl.* 191, 205–7 (1970).

## Nuremberg War Crimes Trials

The documentary material covering the trial is forbidding in scope: International Military Tribunal, Nuremberg, *Trial of the Major War Criminals before the International Military Tribunal, Nuremberg, 14 November 1945–1 October 1946* (42 vols., 1947–1949). Consult, *inter alia*, Jackson, *The Case against the Nazi War Criminals* (1946); Wright, "The Law of the Nuremberg Trial," 41 *AJIL* 38 (1947); Glueck, *The Nuremberg Trial and Aggressive War* (1946); Also see Woetzel, *The Nuremberg Trials in International Law* (1950); von Knieriem, *The Nuremberg Trials* (1959); Davidson, *The Trial of the Germans* (1967), and his *The Nuremberg Fallacy: Wars and War Crimes since World War II* (1973); Levy, "The Law and Procedure of War Crime Trials," 37 *ASPR* 1052 (1943); Borkin, *The Crime and Punishment of I. G. Farben* (1978); Smith, *Reaching Judgment at Nuremberg* (1979); and *The American Road to Nuremberg: The Documentary Record, 1944–1945* (1982).

## Vietnam War

(a) General:
Falk, Kolko, and Lifton, eds., *Crimes of War* (1971); Taylor, *Nuremberg and Vietnam: An American Tragedy* (1970).
(b) Korean Forces in Vietnam:
See *NYT*, Jan. 11, 1970, 5; Feb. 1, 1970, 2; Feb. 13, 1972, 4.
(c) War Crimes by Opposing Side:
*NYT*, Oct. 31, 1969, 32–33.
(d) U.S. Trials:
*Time*, Apr. 12, 1971, 13–21; June 14, 1971, 21; *Duluth* (Minn.) *Herald*, June 2, 1971, 1; *Duluth* (Minn.) *News-Tribune*, May 3, 1971, 2.
(d) Calley's Trial:
See, *inter alia*, Hammer, *The Court-Martial of Lt. Calley* (1971); Peers, *The My Lai Inquiry* (1979); Lesher, "The Calley Case Re-examined," *NYT* Magazine, July 11, 1971, 6–7, 14–26, *passim*; *NYT*, Nov. 30–Jan. 17, 1970, *passim*; Feb. 28–April 4, 1971, *passim*; June 4, 1972, 1, 58; April 17–May 5, 1974, *passim*; Sept. 11–Nov. 20, 1975, *passim*; *Time*, Nov. 28, 1969, 17–19; Dec. 5, 1969, 23–24, 75; Jan. 25, 1971, 24; April 19, 1971, 13–14; Nov. 25, 1974, 19–20; *U.S. News & World Report*, Dec. 22, 1969, 34–36; March 8, 1971, 29.

# Table of Cases,
# Arbitral Awards,
# and Advisory Opinions

*Italic indicates cases abstracted in the text; roman indicates cases, awards, or advisory opinions mentioned in the text or cited in footnotes*

# Index

903

Claims, international
bonded debts, 273
Calvo Clause, 272–73
Calvo Doctrine, 276
civil wars and, 274–78
compensation for, 278–80
contracts, 271–74
denial of justice, 253–54
diligence, lack of due, 258–63
Drago Doctrine, 274
expropriation, 157–58
local remedies, exhaustion of,
255–56
Codfish War, 497–99
Colombia, 116
Comity, 23
Commissioners, 531
Commissions. *See* Claims, inter-
national; Conciliation
commissions; Inquiry,
commissions of
Community of Nations, 53–73
Comoros Islands, 173
Compensation to aliens, 278–80
Conciliation commissions, 603–4
Conditions of admissions of states, 61
Condominiums, 67–68
Confederations, 57–58
Congo, 166, 373. *See also* Zaire
Connally Amendment, 192–95 *passim*,
615–17
Conquest, title by, 374–81
Consent, 6, 42, 46, 49
Conservation
treaties, 489
zones, 476–77
Consular agents, 539–50
classes of, 543–44
*exequatur*, 544–45
functions, 542–45
honorary, 544
privileges and immunities, 545–50
ranks and types, 543–44
relations, 540–42
Vienna Convention of, 55, 541–50
*passim*
Contadora Declaration, 599–600
Contiguous zones, 463–64
Convention on Territorial Seas and
the Contiguous Zone, 463

Continental shelf, 464–71
Convention on the ('58), 464–67
*passim*
Continuous voyage, 861–63
Contraband, 860–63
Contracts, breach of, 271–74
Contras (Nicaragua), 175–76, 191–99
*passim*
Conventions. *See* Treaties
Corfu
Incident (1923), 602–3
Strait of, 459–62
Costa Rica, 176, 247, 195–96
Council of Europe, 10, 628
Counterfeiting, 187
Covenant. *See* Human Rights; League
of Nations
Crimes against international law. *See
also* War crimes
genocide, 354–57
hijacking, 316–17, 320–22,
333–341
humanity, against, 885–86
peace, against, 886
piracy, 325–31
slavery, 323–25
terrorism, 299–302, 345–54
torture, 357–60
Cuba, 79, 80, 174–75, 176, 199,
304–5, 313, 335, 411, 412,
655–57
Customary law, 17–20, 37–43, 47,
697
Cyprus, 64–65
Czechoslovakia, 171, 235, 270–71

Dardanelles, 458
*Debellatio*, 723
Debts and state succession, 117–19
Declarations, 14, 560
Deportation, 782–84
Derecognition, 103
Destroyers for Naval Bases Agreement,
836–37
*Deutschland*, 643
Diligence, due, 258–63
Diplomatic agents, 503–39. *See also*
Tehran, U.S. Embassy and
hostages; Terrorism